THE GREAT PLAYWRIGHTS

THE
GREAT PLAYWRIGHTS

Twenty-five plays
with commentaries by critics and scholars
chosen and introduced by

ERIC BENTLEY

VOLUME TWO

1970
Doubleday & Company, Inc., Garden City, New York

Grateful acknowledgment is made for the use of the following copyrighted material:

Prometheus Bound by Aeschylus, translated by Charles R. Walker. Copyright © 1970 by Charles R. Walker. Used by permission of the translator.

"Prometheia" from *Aeschylus and Athens* by George Thomson. Reprinted by permission of Grosset & Dunlap, Inc. and Lawrence and Wishart Ltd.

King Oedipus by Sophocles, translated by William Butler Yeats, from *Collected Plays* by William Butler Yeats. Copyright 1934, 1952 by The Macmillan Company. Reprinted by permission of The Macmillan Company and A. P. Watt & Son.

"*Oedipus the King*: The Two Dramas, the Two Conflicts" by Simon O. Lesser, originally published in the December 1967 issue of College English. Copyright, 1967, by the National Council of Teachers of English. Copyright © 1970 by Simon O. Lesser. Reprinted by permission of the author and the National Council of Teachers of English.

The Antigone of Sophocles, an English version by Dudley Fitts and Robert Fitzgerald. Copyright, 1939, by Harcourt, Brace & World, Inc.; renewed 1967 by Dudley Fitts and Robert Fitzgerald. Reprinted by permission of Harcourt, Brace & World, Inc.

Essay on *Antigone* from *Form and Meaning in Drama* by H. D. F. Kitto. Reprinted by permission of Associated Book Publishers, Ltd.

The Bacchae by Euripides, an English version by Neil Curry. Copyright © 1970 by Neil Curry. Used by permission of LOM Associates, Limited.

"Euripides the Irrationalist" by E. R. Dodds, originally published in *Classical Review*, July 1929. Reprinted by permission of The Clarendon Press, Oxford.

"Human Relationships in Shakespeare" by V. G. Kiernan and "Troilus and Cressida and the Spirit of Capitalism" by Raymond Southall, from *Shakespeare in a Changing World* edited by Arnold Kettle. Copyright © 1964 by International Publishers Co., Inc. Reprinted by permission of the publisher.

Annotated versions of *Troilus and Cressida* and *King Lear* from *Shakespeare: The Complete Works*, edited by G. B. Harrison. Copyright 1948, 1952 by Harcourt, Brace & World, Inc. Reprinted by permission of the publisher.

"Lear and the Comedy of the Grotesque" from *The Wheel of Fire* by G. Wilson Knight. Reprinted by permission of Associated Book Publishers, Ltd.

Having in mind that in putting together this anthology I have sought out elements in the past that still have some future in them I wish to dedicate these volumes to my beloved sons, Eric and Philip.

—E. B.

CONTENTS

Contents

Contents

Volume II

WHAT IS MODERN?

Contents

What Is Modern?

HENRIK IBSEN

The Wild Duck
Rosmersholm

WHEN THE AUTHOR OF *The Great Society,* Graham Wallas, saw *The Wild Duck* by Henrik Ibsen (1828–1906), he felt that "the bottom dropped out of the universe." And even if it did not put an end to the universe, it was an epoch-making play. From it stems the work of Luigi Pirandello and Eugene O'Neill. Bernard Shaw's theory of Ibsenism derives in considerable part from a single character in *The Wild Duck:* Gregers Werle. The play also disabused many of the notion that Ibsen wrote little problem plays with a neat message. Seeing *The Wild Duck* on stage, the poet Rilke wrote: ". . . something very great, deep, essential. Doomsday and judgment. Something ultimate . . . A new poet . . . a man misunderstood in the midst of fame . . ." That there is something "deep," aboriginal, even Greek about Ibsen is still the first thing to say about him. The second is that he is still ultra-modern. He renewed the tragic spirit; yet his vision was not of heroes but of neurotics. He managed to avoid the trap that lies in wait for the average "Freudian" writer—that of handing ready-made neuroses to his characters, premeditated diagnoses. In Ibsen's plays, and outstandingly in *Rosmersholm,* we get the dynamics of neurosis, and indeed these become, one could almost say, the dynamics of his dramaturgy. It is fitting, then, to call upon Sigmund Freud himself to testify to the clinical authenticity of Ibsen. Such authenticity does not make a man a dramatist, but to the kind of drama Ibsen invented it is necessary; and profound psychological acumen is one quality we value him for. The subject of the dramatic art of Ibsen would take the reader beyond the bounds of this book—for example, to Hermann J. Weigand's *The Modern Ibsen* (1925), still the best guide to the middle and later plays.

THE WILD DUCK
[1884]

English Version by
MICHAEL MEYER

CHARACTERS

HAAKON WERLE	*a wholesale merchant*
GREGERS WERLE	*his son*
OLD EKDAL	
HJALMAR EKDAL	*his son, a photographer*
GINA EKDAL	HJALMAR'S *wife*
HEDVIG	*their daughter, aged 14*
MRS. SOERBY	*housekeeper to* HAAKON WERLE
RELLING	*a doctor*
MOLVIK	*sometime student of theology*
GRAABERG	*a clerk*
PETTERSEN	*servant to* HAAKON WERLE
JENSEN	*a hired waiter*
A PALE, FLABBY GENTLEMAN	
A BALDING GENTLEMAN	
A SHORT-SIGHTED GENTLEMAN	
SIX OTHER GENTLEMEN	*dinner guests of* HAAKON WERLE
SEVERAL HIRED WAITERS	

The first act takes place in HAAKON WERLE'S *house, the remaining acts in* HJALMAR EKDAL'S *studio.*

ACT ONE

The home of HAAKON WERLE, *a wholesale merchant. A study, expensively and comfortably furnished; bookcases, upholstered furniture. A desk, with papers and ledgers on it, stands in the middle of the room. Lighted lamps with green shades throw a soft light. In the rear wall folding doors stand open; the curtains across the entrance are drawn aside, and within can be seen a large and elegant room, brilliantly lit by lamps and candelabra. Downstage right in the study a small concealed door leads to the offices. Downstage left, a fireplace with coals glowing in it. Upstage of this a double door leads to the dining room.*

WERLE'S *servant,* PETTERSEN, *in livery, and a hired waiter,* JENSEN, *in black, are arranging the study. In the larger room two or three other hired waiters are moving around putting things in order and lighting more lamps. From the dining room can be heard the buzz of conversation and laughter. Someone taps a knife against a glass; silence; a toast is proposed; cries of "Bravo!"; then the buzz of conversation begins again.*

PETTERSEN [*lights a lamp on the mantelpiece above the fireplace, and puts a shade over it*] You hear that, Jensen? Now the old man's at it, proposing a toast to Mrs. Soerby.

JENSEN [*moves a chair forward*] Is it true what they say, that there's something between them?

PETTERSEN—I wouldn't know.

JENSEN—They say he's been a regular old billy goat in his time.

PETTERSEN—Could be.

JENSEN—Did you say he's giving this party for his son?

PETTERSEN—Yes. He came home yesterday.

JENSEN—I never knew old Werle had a son.

PETTERSEN—Oh yes, he's got a son. The boy spends all his time up at the sawmill, though, out at Hoydal. He's never set foot in town all the years I've worked in this house.

A HIRED WAITER [*in the doorway to the large room*] Pettersen, there's an old fellow here who wants to—

PETTERSEN [*beneath his breath*] What the devil—oh, not now!

OLD EKDAL *enters from the large room, right. He is wearing a threadbare coat with a high collar, and woollen gloves, and carries a stick and a fur hat in his hand and a brown paper parcel under his arm. He has a dirty, reddish-brown wig and small grey moustaches.*

[*Goes towards him.*]

Oh, Jesus! What do *you* want here?

E K D A L [*in the doorway*] Got to get into the office, Pettersen. It's very important.

P E T T E R S E N – The office has been shut for an hour—

E K D A L – They told me that downstairs, my boy. But Graaberg's still in there. Be a good lad, Pettersen, and let me nip in this way.

[*Points at the concealed door.*]

I've been this way before.

P E T T E R S E N – Oh, all right.

[*Opens the door.*]

But make sure you leave by the proper way. We've got company.

E K D A L – Yes, I know that—hm! Thanks, Pettersen, my boy. You're a good pal.

[*Mutters quietly.*]

Damn fool!

[*Goes into the office.* PETTERSEN *shuts the door after him.*]

J E N S E N – Does he work in the office, too?

P E T T E R S E N – No, he just takes stuff home to copy, when they've more than they can manage. Mind you, he's been quite a gentleman in his time, has old Ekdal.

J E N S E N – Yes, he looked as if he might have been around a bit.

P E T T E R S E N – Oh, yes. He was a lieutenant.

J E N S E N – What—him a lieutenant?

P E T T E R S E N – That's right. But then he went into timber or something of that sort. They say he did the dirty on old Werle once. The two of them used to work together at Hoydal. Oh, I know old Ekdal well. We often have a nip and a bottle of beer together down at Madame Eriksen's.

J E N S E N – But he can't have much to spend, surely?

P E T T E R S E N – I'm the one who does the spending. The way I look at it, it's only right to lend a helping hand to gentry who've come down in the world.

J E N S E N – What, did he go bankrupt?

P E T T E R S E N – Worse. He went to prison.

J E N S E N – Went to prison!

P E T T E R S E N – Ssh, they're getting up now.

The doors to the dining room are thrown open from inside by waiters.
MRS. SOERBY *comes out, engaged in conversation by two gentlemen. A few moments later, the rest of the company follow,* HAAKON WERLE *among them. Last come* HJALMAR EKDAL *and* GREGERS WERLE.

MRS. SOERBY [*as she goes through*] Pettersen, have the coffee served in the music room.
PETTERSEN — Very good, Mrs. Soerby.
[*She and the two gentlemen go into the large room and out towards the right.* PETTERSEN *and* JENSEN *follow them.*]
A PALE, FLABBY GENTLEMAN [*to one with little hair*] Whew —that dinner! Pretty exhausting work, eh?
BALDING GENTLEMAN — Ah, it's remarkable what one can get through in three hours, when one puts one's mind to it.
FLABBY GENTLEMAN — Yes, but afterwards, my dear sir! Afterwards!
A THIRD GENTLEMAN — I hear the—er—mocha and maraschino are to be served in the music room.
FLABBY GENTLEMAN — Capital! Then perhaps Mrs. Soerby will play something for us.
BALDING GENTLEMAN [*sotto voce*] Let's hope it isn't a marching song!
FLABBY GENTLEMAN — No fear of that. Berta won't give her old friends the shoulder.
[*They laugh and pass into the large room.*]
WERLE [*quietly, unhappily*] I don't think anyone noticed, Gregers.
GREGERS [*looks at him*] What?
WERLE — Didn't you notice, either?
GREGERS — Notice what?
WERLE — We were thirteen at table.
GREGERS — Thirteen? Oh, really?
WERLE [*glances at* HJALMAR EKDAL] We're usually twelve.
[*To the others.*]
Gentlemen—please!
[*He and the rest, except for* HJALMAR *and* GREGERS, *go out upstage right.*]
HJALMAR [*who has overheard their conversation*] You shouldn't have invited me, Gregers.
GREGERS — What! But this dinner is said to be in my honour. So why shouldn't I invite my one and only friend?
HJALMAR — I don't think your father approves. I mean, I never get invited to this house.
GREGERS — No, so I've heard. But I had to see you and speak with you; I'm not staying very long, you know. Yes, we've lost touch with each

other since we were at school, Hjalmar. We haven't seen each other for—why, it must be sixteen or seventeen years.

HJALMAR—Is it as long as that?

GREGERS—I'm afraid so. Well, how is everything with you? You look well. You've filled out a bit; you're quite stout now.

HJALMAR—Oh—I wouldn't say stout. I dare say I'm a bit broader across the shoulders than I used to be. After all, I'm a man now.

GREGERS—Oh, yes. You're as handsome as ever.

HJALMAR [*sadly*] But within, Gregers! There has been a change there. You must know how disastrously my world has crashed about me—and my family—since we last met.

GREGERS [*more quietly*] How is your father now?

HJALMAR—My dear friend, let us not talk about it. My poor unfortunate father lives with me, of course. He has no one else in the world to lean on. But all this is so distressing for me to talk about. Tell me now, how have things been for you up at the sawmill?

GREGERS—Oh, I've been wonderfully lonely. I've had plenty of time to brood over things. Come, let's make ourselves comfortable.

[*He sits in an armchair by the fire and motions* HJALMAR *into another beside him.*]

HJALMAR [*softly*] Thank you all the same, Gregers. I'm grateful to you for inviting me to your father's house. I know now that you no longer have anything against me.

GREGERS [*amazed*] What makes you think I have anything against you?

HJALMAR—You did at first.

GREGERS—At first?

HJALMAR—After the great disaster. Oh, it was only natural that you should. It was only by a hairsbreadth that your father himself escaped being dragged into all this—this dreadful business.

GREGERS—And I should hold that against you? Who gave you this idea?

HJALMAR—I know—I know you did, Gregers. Your father himself told me so.

GREGERS—Father! I see. Hm. Was that why you never wrote me a line?

HJALMAR—Yes.

GREGERS—Not even when you went and became a photographer?

HJALMAR—Your father said there would be no purpose in my writing to you about anything whatever.

GREGERS [*thoughtfully*] No, no; perhaps he was right. But, tell me, Hjalmar—are you quite satisfied the way things are now?

HJALMAR [*with a little sigh*] Oh yes, indeed I am. I can't complain.

At first, you know, I found it a little strange. It was such a different way of life from what I'd been used to. But everything had changed. The great disaster that ruined my father—the disgrace and the shame, Gregers—

GREGERS [*upset*] Yes, yes, of course, yes.

HJALMAR—Naturally, I had to give up any idea of continuing with my studies. We hadn't a shilling to spare—quite the reverse in fact. Debts. Mostly to your father, I believe—

GREGERS—Hm—

HJALMAR—Well, so I thought it'd be best, you see, to make a clean break. Cut myself off from everything that had to do with my old way of life. In fact, it was your father who advised me to do it—and as he was being so very helpful to me—

GREGERS—Father?

HJALMAR—Yes, surely you must know? How else could I have found the money to learn photography and equip a studio and set myself up? That costs a lot of money, you know.

GREGERS—And Father paid for all this?

HJALMAR—Yes, my dear fellow, didn't you know? I understood him to say he'd written to you.

GREGERS—He never said he was behind it. He must have forgotten. We never write to each other except on business. So it was Father—

HJALMAR—Why, yes. He's never wanted people to know about it; but it was he. And of course it was he who made it possible for me to get married. But—perhaps you don't know that either?

GREGERS—I had no idea.

[*Shakes him by the arm.*]

But, my dear Hjalmar, I can't tell you how happy I feel—and guilty. Perhaps I've been unjust to Father after all—in some respects. This proves that he has a heart, you see. A kind of conscience—

HJALMAR—Conscience?

GREGERS—Yes, or whatever you like to call it. No, I can't tell you how happy I am to hear this about Father. Well, and you're married, Hjalmar! That's more than I shall ever dare to do. Well, I trust you've found happiness in marriage.

HJALMAR—Oh, indeed I have. She's as capable and good a wife as any man could wish for. And she's not by any means uncultured.

GREGERS [*a little surprised*] I'm sure she isn't.

HJALMAR—Yes. Life is a great teacher. Being with me every day—and we have a couple of very gifted friends who visit us daily. I can assure you, you wouldn't recognise Gina.

GREGERS—Gina?

H J A L M A R —Yes, my dear fellow, don't you remember? Her name's Gina.

G R E G E R S —Whose name is Gina? I have no idea what you're—

H J A L M A R —But don't you remember? She used to work here once.

G R E G E R S [*looks at him*] You mean Gina Hansen?

H J A L M A R —Of course I mean Gina Hansen.

G R E G E R S —Who kept house for us when my mother was ill? The year before she died?

H J A L M A R —Yes, that's right. But, my dear fellow, I'm absolutely certain your father wrote and told you I'd got married.

G R E G E R S [*has got up*] Yes, he told me that. But what he didn't tell me was that—

[*Begins to pace up and down.*]

Ah, but wait a minute. Perhaps he did after all, now I think about it. But Father always writes such brief letters.

[*Half sits on the arm of his chair.*]

Look, tell me now, Hjalmar—this is very funny—how did you come to meet Gina—I mean, your wife?

H J A L M A R —Oh, it was quite straightforward. As you know, Gina didn't stay long with your father—everything was so upside down at that time —your mother's illness—it was all too much for Gina, so she gave notice and left. It was the year before your mother died. Or was it the same year?

G R E G E R S —The same year. And I was up at the sawmill. But then what happened?

H J A L M A R —Yes, well, then Gina went home to live with her mother, a Mrs. Hansen, a very excellent hard-working woman who ran a little café. Well, she had a room to let; a very nice, comfortable room.

G R E G E R S —And you were lucky enough to find out about it?

H J A L M A R —Yes—in fact, it was your father who suggested it. And it was there, you see, that I really got to know Gina.

G R E G E R S —And the engagement followed?

H J A L M A R —Yes. Well, you know how quickly young people become fond of each other—hm—

G R E G E R S [*gets up and walks up and down for a little*] Tell me—when you were engaged—was that when Father got you to—I mean, was that when you began to take up photography?

H J A L M A R —Yes, that's right. I was very keen to get married as soon as possible. And your father and I both came to the conclusion that photography would be the most convenient profession for me to take up. And Gina thought so too. Oh, and there was another thing. By a lucky chance, Gina had learned how to retouch photographs.

G R E G E R S —What a fortunate coincidence.

HJALMAR [*pleased, gets up*] Yes, wasn't it? Amazingly lucky, don't you think?

GREGERS—I certainly do. Father seems almost to have been a kind of fairy godfather to you.

HJALMAR [*emotionally*] He did not forget his old friend's son in his time of need. He's got a heart, you see, Gregers.

MRS. SOERBY [*enters with* HAAKON WERLE *on her arm*] Not another word, now, Mr. Werle. You mustn't walk around any longer in there with all those bright lights. It's not good for you.

WERLE [*lets go of her arm and passes his hand over his eyes*] Yes, I think you may be right.

[PETTERSEN *and* JENSEN *enter with trays.*]

MRS. SOERBY [*to the guests in the other room*] Gentlemen, please! If anyone wants a glass of punch, he must come in here.

FLABBY GENTLEMAN [*comes over to* MRS. SOERBY] Dammit, madame, is it true that you have deprived us of our sacred privilege, the cigar?

MRS. SOERBY—Yes. This is Mr. Werle's sanctum, sir, and here there is no smoking.

BALDING GENTLEMAN—When did you introduce this austere edict, Mrs. Soerby?

MRS. SOERBY—After our last dinner, sir; when certain persons permitted themselves to overstep the mark.

BALDING GENTLEMAN—And it is not permitted to overstep the mark a little, Madame Berta? Not even an inch or two?

MRS. SOERBY—No. Not in any direction, my dear Chamberlain.

[*Most of the guests have come into the study. The* SERVANTS *hand round glasses of punch.*]

HAAKON WERLE [*to* HJALMAR, *who is standing apart, by a table*] What's that you're looking at, Ekdal?

HJALMAR—It's only an album, sir.

BALDING GENTLEMAN [*who is wandering around*] Ah, photographs! Yes, that's rather down your street, isn't it?

FLABBY GENTLEMAN [*in an armchair*] Haven't you brought any of your own with you?

HJALMAR—No, I haven't.

FLABBY GENTLEMAN—You should have. It's so good for the digestion to sit and look at pictures.

BALDING GENTLEMAN—Adds to the fun. We've each got to contribute our mite, haven't we?

A SHORT-SIGHTED GENTLEMAN—All contributions will be gratefully received.

MRS. SOERBY—I think the gentlemen mean that if one is invited out one should work for one's dinner, Mr. Ekdal.

FLABBY GENTLEMAN—Where the table is so exquisite, that duty becomes a pleasure.

BALDING GENTLEMAN—Yes, by God! Particularly when it's a question of fighting for survival—

MRS. SOERBY—*Touché!*

[*They continue amid joking and laughter.*]

GREGERS [*quietly*] You must join in, Hjalmar.

HJALMAR [*twists uncomfortably*] What should I talk about?

FLABBY GENTLEMAN—Wouldn't you agree, Mr. Werle, that Tokay may be regarded as a comparatively safe drink for the stomach?

WERLE [*by the fireplace*] I'd guarantee the Tokay you drank tonight, anyway. It's an exceptional year, quite exceptional. But of course you would have noticed that.

FLABBY GENTLEMAN—Yes, it had a remarkably *soigné* bouquet.

HJALMAR [*uncertainly*] Is there some difference between the various years?

FLABBY GENTLEMAN [*laughs*] I say, that's good!

WERLE [*smiles*] It's a waste to offer you good wine.

BALDING GENTLEMAN—Tokay's like photography, Mr. Ekdal. It needs sunshine. Isn't that right?

HJALMAR—Oh yes, light is important, of course.

MRS. SOERBY—But that's like you, gentlemen. You're drawn towards the sun, too.

BALDING GENTLEMAN—For shame! That's not worthy of you.

SHORT-SIGHTED GENTLEMAN—Mrs. Soerby is displaying her wit.

FLABBY GENTLEMAN—At our expense.

[*Threateningly.*]

Oh, madame, madame!

MRS. SOERBY—But it's perfectly true. Vintages do differ greatly. The oldest are the best.

SHORT-SIGHTED GENTLEMAN—Do you count me among the old ones?

MRS. SOERBY—By no means.

BALDING GENTLEMAN—Indeed? And what about me, dear Mrs. Soerby?

FLABBY GENTLEMAN—Yes, and me. What vintage are we?

MRS. SOERBY—A sweet vintage, gentlemen!

[*She sips a glass of punch. The* GENTLEMEN *laugh and flirt with her.*]

WERLE—Mrs. Soerby always finds a way out—when she wants to. Fill your glasses, gentlemen! Pettersen, look after them. Gregers, let us take a glass together.

[GREGERS *does not move.*]

Won't you join us, Ekdal? I didn't get a chance to drink with you at dinner.

[GRAABERG, *the bookkeeper, looks in through the concealed door.*]

GRAABERG [*to* HAAKON WERLE] Excuse me, sir, but I can't get out.

WERLE—What, have you got locked in again?

GRAABERG—Yes. Flakstad's gone off with the keys.

WERLE—Well, you'd better come through here, then.

GRAABERG—But there's someone else—

WERLE—Well, let him come, too. Don't be frightened.

[GRAABERG *and* OLD EKDAL *come out of the office.*]
[*Involuntarily.*]

Oh, God!

The laughter and chatter of the GUESTS *dies away.* HJALMAR *shrinks at the sight of his father, puts down his glass and turns away towards the fireplace.*

EKDAL [*does not look up, but makes little bows to either side as he walks, mumbling*] Beg pardon. Come the wrong way. Door locked. Beg pardon.

[*He and* GRAABERG *go out upstage right.*]

WERLE [*between his teeth*] Damn that Graaberg!

GREGERS [*stares open-mouthed at* HJALMAR] Surely that wasn't—?

FLABBY GENTLEMAN—What's all this? Who was that?

GREGERS—Oh, no one. Just the bookkeeper and someone else.

SHORT-SIGHTED GENTLEMAN [*to* HJALMAR] Did you know that man?

HJALMAR—I don't know—I didn't notice—

FLABBY GENTLEMAN [*gets up*] What the devil's going on?

[*He goes over to some of the others, who are talking quietly amongst themselves.*]

MRS. SOERBY [*whispers to* PETTERSEN] Take something out to him. Something really nice.

PETTERSEN [*nods*] Very good, ma'am.

[*Goes out.*]

GREGERS [*quietly, emotionally, to* HJALMAR] Then it *was* he!

HJALMAR—Yes.

GREGERS—And you stood here and denied him!

HJALMAR [*whispers violently*] What could I do?

GREGERS—You denied your own father?

HJALMAR [*in pain*] Oh—if you were in my place, you'd—

1217

[*The talk among the* GUESTS, *which has been carried on in a low tone,
now switches over to a forced loudness.*]

BALDING GENTLEMAN [*goes amiably over to* HJALMAR *and* GRE-
GERS] Hullo, reviving old college memories, what? Don't you smoke,
Mr. Ekdal? Want a light? Oh, I'd forgotten—we mustn't—

HJALMAR—Thank you, I won't.

FLABBY GENTLEMAN—Haven't you some nice little poem you
could recite to us, Mr. Ekdal? You used to recite so beautifully.

HJALMAR—I'm afraid I can't remember one.

FLABBY GENTLEMAN—Pity. What else can we find to amuse ourselves with, Balle?

[*The* TWO GENTLEMEN *walk into the next room.*]

HJALMAR [*unhappily*] Gregers, I want to go. You know, when a man
has been as buffeted and tossed by the winds of Fate as I have— Say
good-bye to your father for me.

GREGERS—I will. Are you going straight home?

HJALMAR—Yes?

GREGERS—In that case I may drop in on you later.

HJALMAR—No, don't do that. You mustn't come to my home. It's a
miserable place, Gregers; especially after a brilliant gathering like this.
We can always meet somewhere in town.

MRS. SOERBY [*has come over to them, and says quietly*] Are you
leaving, Ekdal?

HJALMAR—Yes.

MRS. SOERBY—Give my regards to Gina.

HJALMAR—Thank you.

MRS. SOERBY—Tell her I'm coming out to see her one of these days.

HJALMAR—I will. Thank you.

[*To* GREGERS.]

Stay here. I don't want anyone to see me go.

[*Saunters into the other room and out to the right.*]

MRS. SOERBY [*to* PETTERSEN, *who has returned*] Well, did you give
the old man something?

PETTERSEN—Yes, I put a bottle of brandy into his pocket.

MRS. SOERBY—Oh, you might have found him something nicer than
that.

PETTERSEN—Why no, Mrs. Soerby. Brandy's what he likes best.

FLABBY GENTLEMAN [*in the doorway, with a sheet of music in
his hand*] Shall we play a duet together, Mrs. Soerby?

MRS. SOERBY—Yes, with pleasure.

GUESTS—Bravo, bravo!

She and all the GUESTS *go out to the right.* GREGERS *remains standing by
the fireplace.* HAAKON WERLE *starts looking for something on his desk,*

and seems to wish that GREGERS *would go. Seeing that* GREGERS *does not move, he goes towards the door.*

GREGERS – Father, would you mind waiting a moment?

WERLE [*stops*] What is it?

GREGERS – I've got to speak with you.

WERLE – Can't it wait till we're alone together?

GREGERS – No, it can't. We may never be alone together.

WERLE [*comes closer*] What does that mean?

[*During the following scene, piano music can be heard distantly from the music room.*]

GREGERS – How has that family been allowed to sink into this pitiable condition?

WERLE – You mean the Ekdals, I presume?

GREGERS – Yes, I mean the Ekdals. Lieutenant Ekdal and you used to be such close friends.

WERLE – Unfortunately, yes. Too close. All these years I've had to pay for it. It's him I have to thank for the stain I have suffered on my name and reputation.

GREGERS [*quietly*] Was he really the only one who was guilty?

WERLE – Who else?

GREGERS – You and he bought those forests together.

WERLE – But it was Ekdal who drew up that misleading map. It was he who had all that timber felled illegally on government property. He was in charge of everything up there. I was absolutely in the dark as to what Lieutenant Ekdal was doing.

GREGERS – Lieutenant Ekdal seems to have been pretty much in the dark himself.

WERLE – Quite possibly. But the fact remains that he was found guilty and I was acquitted.

GREGERS – Oh yes, I know nothing was proved against you.

WERLE – An acquittal means not guilty. Why do you rake up these old troubles, which turned me grey before my time? Is that what you've been brooding about all these years up there? I can assure you, Gregers, in this town the whole business has been forgotten long ago, as far as my reputation is concerned.

GREGERS – But what about those wretched Ekdals?

WERLE – What would you have had me do for them? When Ekdal was released he was a broken man, past help. There are some people in this world who sink to the bottom the moment they get a couple of pellets in their body, and never rise to the surface again. Upon my honour, Gregers, I did everything I could short of exposing myself to gossip and suspicion—

GREGERS – Suspicion? Oh, I see.

1219

W E R L E – I've arranged for Ekdal to do copying for the office, and I pay him a great deal more than the work's worth—

G R E G E R S [*without looking at him*] I don't doubt it.

W E R L E – You laugh? You don't think it's true? Oh, you won't find anything about it in the books. I don't keep account of that kind of payment.

G R E G E R S [*smiles coldly*] No, there are certain payments of which it's best to keep no account.

W E R L E – What do you mean by that?

G R E G E R S [*screwing up his courage*] Have you any account of what it cost you to have Hjalmar Ekdal taught photography?

W E R L E – Why should I have any account of that?

G R E G E R S – I know now that it was you who paid for it. And I also know that it was you who so generously enabled him to set himself up.

W E R L E – And still you say I've done nothing for the Ekdals? I can assure you, that family's cost me a pretty penny.

G R E G E R S – Have you accounted any of those pennies in your books?

W E R L E – Why do you ask that?

G R E G E R S – Oh, I have my reasons. Tell me—when you began to take such a warm interest in your old friend's son—wasn't that just about the time he was about to get married?

W E R L E – Yes, how the devil—how do you expect me to remember after all these years—?

G R E G E R S – You wrote me a letter at the time—a business letter, of course—and in a postscript you said—quite briefly—that Hjalmar Ekdal had married a Miss Hansen.

W E R L E – Yes, so he did. That was her name.

G R E G E R S – But what you didn't say was that this Miss Hansen was Gina Hansen—our former maid.

W E R L E [*laughs scornfully, but with an effort*] No. It didn't occur to me that you were particularly interested in our former maid.

G R E G E R S – I wasn't. But—

[*Lowers his voice.*]

—there was someone else in this house who was interested in her.

W E R L E – What do you mean?

[*Angrily.*]

You're not referring to me?

G R E G E R S [*quietly but firmly*] Yes, I am referring to you.

W E R L E – You dare to—you have the impertinence—! That ungrateful— that photographer—how dare he make such insinuations!

G R E G E R S – Hjalmar has never said a word about this. I don't think he suspects anything.

W E R L E – Where do you get it from, then? Who has said such a thing to you?

G R E G E R S – My unhappy mother told me. The last time I saw her.

W E R L E – Your mother! I might have known it. She and you always clung together. She turned you against me from the first.

G R E G E R S – No. It was all the suffering and humiliation she had to endure before she finally succumbed and came to such a pitiful end.

W E R L E – Oh, she didn't have to suffer. Not more than most people, anyway. But one can't do anything with people who are oversensitive and romantic. I've learned that much. And you nurse these suspicions and go around rooting up all kinds of old rumours and slanders about your own father! At your age, Gregers, it's time you found something more useful to do.

G R E G E R S – Yes, it's about time.

W E R L E – It might enable you to be a little more at peace with yourself than you seem to be now. What good can it do for you to stay up at the sawmill, year after year, drudging away like a common clerk and refusing to accept a penny more than the standard wage? It's absolutely idiotic.

G R E G E R S – I wish I was sure of that.

W E R L E – I understand how you feel. You want to be independent, you don't want to be in my debt. But now there is an opportunity for you to become independent, and be your own master in everything.

G R E G E R S – Oh? How?

W E R L E – When I wrote and told you it was necessary for you to travel here at once—hm—

G R E G E R S – Yes, what do you want me for? I've been waiting all day to find out.

W E R L E – I want to suggest that you become a partner in the firm.

G R E G E R S – I? Your partner?

W E R L E – Yes. It wouldn't mean we'd have to be together all the time. You could take over the business here, and I'd move up to the mill.

G R E G E R S – You?

W E R L E – Yes. You see, I'm not able to work as hard as I used to. I've got to take care of my eyes, Gregers. They've begun to grow a little weak.

G R E G E R S – They always were.

W E R L E – Not like now. Besides—circumstances might make it desirable for me to live up there. For a while, anyway.

G R E G E R S – I hadn't imagined anything like this.

W E R L E – Listen, Gregers. I know there are so many things that stand between us. But we're father and son. It seems to me we must be able to come to an understanding.

1221

GREGERS—You mean, we must appear to come to an understanding?

WERLE—Well, that is something. Think it over, Gregers. Don't you think it might be possible? Well?

GREGERS [*looks at him coldly*] What's behind all this?

WERLE—How do you mean?

GREGERS—You want to use me, don't you?

WERLE—In a relationship as close as ours, one can always be useful to the other.

GREGERS—That's what they say.

WERLE—I should like to have you living at home with me for a while. I'm a lonely man, Gregers. I've always felt lonely, all my life, but especially now that I'm growing old. I need to have someone near me—

GREGERS—You've got Mrs. Soerby.

WERLE—Yes, I have her. And she's become—well, almost indispensable to me. She's witty and good-humoured; she brightens the house for me. I need that—badly.

GREGERS—Well, then you have things the way you want them.

WERLE—Yes, but I'm afraid it can't continue like this. A woman in her situation may easily find herself compromised in the eyes of the world. Yes; and I dare say it's not very good for a man's reputation, either.

GREGERS—Oh, when a man gives dinners like this, he needn't worry about what people think.

WERLE—Yes, but what about her, Gregers? I'm afraid she won't want to put up with this for much longer. And even if she did—even if, for my sake, she were to set herself above the gossip and the slander— Don't you think then, Gregers—you with your stern sense of right and wrong—that—?

GREGERS [*interrupts*] Answer me one thing. Are you thinking of marrying her?

WERLE—Suppose I were? Would you be so insuperably opposed to that?

GREGERS—Not in the least.

WERLE—I didn't know if perhaps—out of respect to your late mother's memory—

GREGERS—I'm not a romantic.

WERLE—Well, whatever you are, you've taken a great weight from my mind. I'm delighted that I may count on your agreement to the action I propose to take.

GREGERS [*looks at him*] Now I see what you want to use me for.

WERLE—Use you? What kind of talk is that?

GREGERS—Oh, let's not be squeamish. Not when we're alone together.
[*Gives a short laugh.*]

I see. So that's why, at all costs, I had to come along and show myself here. So as to have a nice family reunion in Mrs. Soerby's honour. Father and son—*tableau!* That's something new, isn't it?

W E R L E — How dare you take that tone?

G R E G E R S — When has there been any family life here? Not for as long as I can remember. But now of course there's got to be a little. It'll look splendid if people can say that the son of the family has flown home on the wings of filial piety to attend his ageing father's wedding feast. What'll become then of all those dreadful rumours about the wrongs his poor dead mother had to put up with? They will vanish. Her son will dissipate them into thin air.

W E R L E — Gregers—I believe there's no one in the world you hate as much as you do me.

G R E G E R S [*quietly*] I've seen you at close quarters.

W E R L E — You have seen me with your mother's eyes.

[*Lowers his voice a little.*]

But you should remember that her vision was sometimes a little—blurred.

G R E G E R S [*trembling*] I know what you're trying to say. But who was to blame for that? You were! You and all those—! And the last of them you palmed off on to Hjalmar Ekdal, when you no longer—oh!

W E R L E [*shrugs his shoulders*] Word for word as though I were listening to your mother.

G R E G E R S [*not heeding him*] And there he sits, childlike and trusting, caught in this web of deceit—sharing his roof with a woman like that, never suspecting that what he calls his home is built upon a lie!

[*Comes a step closer.*]

When I look back on your career, I see a battlefield strewn with shattered lives.

W E R L E — It seems the gulf between us is too wide.

G R E G E R S [*bows coldly*] I agree. Therefore I take my hat and go.

W E R L E — Go? Leave the house?

G R E G E R S — Yes. Because now at last I see my vocation.

W E R L E — And what is that vocation?

G R E G E R S — You'd only laugh if I told you.

W E R L E — A lonely man does not laugh easily, Gregers.

G R E G E R S [*points upstage*] Look, Father. The gentlemen are playing blind man's buff with Mrs. Soerby. Good night, and good-bye.

[*He goes out upstage right. Sounds of laughter and merriment are heard from the* GUESTS, *as they come into sight in the other room.*]

W E R L E [*mutters scornfully after* GREGERS] Hm! Poor wretch! And he says he's not a romantic!

ACT TWO

HJALMAR EKDAL's *studio. It is quite a large room, and is evidently an attic. To the right is a sloping ceiling containing large panes of glass, which are half covered by a blue curtain. In the corner upstage right is the front door. Downstage of this is a door to the living room. In the left-hand wall are two more doors, with an iron stove between them. In the rear wall are broad double sliding doors. The studio is humbly but comfortably furnished. Between the doors on the right, a little away from the wall, stands a sofa, with a table and some chairs. On the table is a lighted lamp, with a shade. In the corner by the stove is an old armchair. Here and there, various pieces of photographic apparatus are set up. Against the rear wall, to the left of the sliding doors, is a bookcase, containing some books, boxes, bottles containing chemicals, various tools, instruments and other objects. Photographs and small articles such as brushes, sheets of paper and so forth, lie on the table.*

GINA EKDAL *is seated on a chair at the table, sewing.* HEDVIG *is seated on the sofa with her hands shading her eyes and her thumbs in her ears, reading a book.*

GINA [*glances at her a couple of times, as though with secret anxiety*] Hedvig!

[HEDVIG *does not hear.* GINA *repeats more loudly.*]
Hedvig!

HEDVIG [*drops her hands and looks up*] Yes, Mother?

GINA – Hedvig darling, don't read any more.

HEDVIG – Oh, but Mother, can't I go on a little longer? Just a little?

GINA – No, no; put the book away. Your father doesn't like it. He never reads in the evenings.

HEDVIG [*closes the book*] No, Father doesn't bother much about reading, does he?

GINA [*puts down her sewing and picks up a pencil and a small notebook from the table*] Can you remember how much we paid for that butter?

1224

HEDVIG – One crown sixty-five öre.

GINA – That's right.

[*Makes a note of it.*]

It's shocking how much butter gets eaten in this house. Then there was the sausages, and the cheese—let me see—

[*Writes.*]

And the ham—hm—

[*Adds it up.*]

Mm, that makes nearly—

HEDVIG – Don't forget the beer.

GINA – Oh yes, of course.

[*Writes.*]

It mounts up. But we've got to have it.

HEDVIG – But you and I didn't have to have a proper meal this evening, as Father was out.

GINA – Yes; that helped. Oh, and I got eight and a half crowns for those photographs.

HEDVIG – I say! As much as that?

GINA – Exactly eight and a half crowns.

[*Silence.* GINA *takes up her sewing again.* HEDVIG *picks up a pencil and paper and starts to draw, her left hand shading her eyes.*]

HEDVIG – Isn't it lovely to think of Father being invited by Mr. Werle to that big dinner?

GINA – He wasn't invited by Mr. Werle. It was his son who sent the invitation.

[*Short pause.*]

You know we've nothing to do with Mr. Werle.

HEDVIG – I'm so looking forward to Father coming home. He promised he'd ask Mrs. Soerby for something nice to bring me.

GINA – Yes, there's never any shortage of nice things in that house.

HEDVIG [*still drawing*] I think I'm beginning to get a bit hungry.

[OLD EKDAL, *his package of papers under his arm and another parcel in his coat pocket, comes in through the front door.*]

GINA – Hullo, Grandfather, you're very late tonight.

EKDAL – They'd shut the office. Graaberg kept me waiting. I had to go through the—hm.

HEDVIG – Did they give you anything new to copy, Grandfather?

EKDAL – All this. Look!

GINA – Well, that's good.

HEDVIG – And you've another parcel in your pocket.

EKDAL – Have I? Oh, nonsense—that's nothing.

[*Puts down his stick in a corner.*]

This'll keep me busy for a long time, this will, Gina.

[*Slides one of the doors in the rear wall a little to one side.*]
Ssh!

[*Looks inside for a moment, then closes the door again carefully.*]
He, he! They're all asleep. And she's lied down in her basket. He, he!

H E D V I G – Are you sure she won't be cold in that basket, Grandfather?

E K D A L – What an idea! Cold? With all that straw?

[*Goes towards the door upstage left.*]
Are there any matches?

G I N A – They're on the chest-of-drawers.

[EKDAL *goes into his room.*]

H E D V I G – Isn't it splendid Grandfather getting all that stuff to copy again, after so long?

G I N A – Yes, poor old Father. It'll mean a bit of pocket money for him.

H E D V I G – And he won't be able to spend all morning down at that horrid Mrs. Eriksen's restaurant, will he?

G I N A – Yes, there's that too.

[*Short silence.*]

H E D V I G – Do you think they're still sitting at table?

G I N A – God knows. It wouldn't surprise me.

H E D V I G – Think of all that lovely food Father's getting to eat! I'm sure he'll be in a good humour when he comes back. Don't you think, Mother?

G I N A – Oh, yes. But if only we were able to tell him we'd managed to let that room.

H E D V I G – But we don't have to worry about *that* tonight.

G I N A – It wouldn't do any harm. It's no use to us standing empty.

H E D V I G – No, I mean we don't have to worry about it because Father'll be jolly anyway. It'll be better if we can save the news about the room for another time.

G I N A [*glances across at her*] Does it make you happy to have good news to tell Father when he comes home in the evening?

H E D V I G – Yes, it makes things more cheerful here.

G I N A – Yes, there's something in that.

[OLD EKDAL *comes in again and goes towards the door downstage left.*]
[*Half turns in her chair.*]
Do you want something out of the kitchen, Grandfather?

E K D A L – Er—yes, yes. Don't get up.

[*Goes out.*]

G I N A – He's not messing about with the fire, is he?

[*Waits a moment.*]
Hedvig, go and see what he's up to.

[EKDAL *returns with a little jug of steaming water.*]

H E D V I G – Are you getting some hot water, Grandfather?

EKDAL—Yes, I am. Need it for something. Got some writing to do; and the ink's like porridge—hm!

GINA—But, Grandfather, you should eat your supper first. I've put it in there for you.

EKDAL—Can't be bothered with supper, Gina. I'm busy, I tell you. I don't want anyone to disturb me. Not anyone—hm!

[*He goes into his room.* GINA *and* HEDVIG *look at each other.*]

GINA [*quietly*] Where do you think he's got the money from?

HEDVIG—From Graaberg, I suppose.

GINA—No, he can't have. Graaberg always sends the money to me.

HEDVIG—He must have got a bottle on tick somewhere, then.

GINA—Poor Grandfather! No one'll give him anything on credit.

[HJALMAR EKDAL, *wearing an overcoat and a grey felt hat, enters right.*]

[GINA *drops her sewing and gets up.*]

Why, Hjalmar, are you here already?

HEDVIG [*simultaneously, jumping to her feet*] Oh Father, fancy your coming back so soon!

HJALMAR [*takes off his hat*] Yes, well, most of them had begun to leave.

HEDVIG—As early as this?

HJALMAR—Yes. It was a dinner party, you know.

[*Begins to take off his overcoat.*]

GINA—Let me help you.

HEDVIG—Me too.

[*They take off his coat.* GINA *hangs it up on the rear wall.*]

Were there many people there, Father?

HJALMAR—Oh no, not many. We were, oh, twelve or fourteen at table.

GINA—And you talked to them all?

HJALMAR—Oh yes, a little. But Gregers monopolised me most of the time.

GINA—Is he still as ugly as ever?

HJALMAR—Well, he's not very much to look at. Hasn't the old man come home?

HEDVIG—Yes, Grandfather's in his room, writing.

HJALMAR—Did he say anything?

GINA—No, what should he say?

HJALMAR—Didn't he mention anything about—? I thought I heard someone say he'd been up to see Graaberg. I'll go in and have a word with him.

GINA—No, no—don't.

HJALMAR—Why not? Did he say he didn't want to see me?

GINA—I don't think he wants to see anyone this evening.

[HEDVIG *makes signs to* HJALMAR. GINA *does not notice.*]
He's been out and fetched some hot water.

HJALMAR—Oh. He's—?

GINA—Yes.

HJALMAR—Dear God! Poor old Father! Bless his white hairs! Let him have his little pleasure.

[OLD EKDAL, *wearing a dressing gown and smoking a pipe, enters from his room.*]

EKDAL—So you're home? I thought I heard your voice.

HJALMAR—Yes, I've just got back.

EKDAL—You didn't see me, did you?

HJALMAR—No. But they said you'd been through, and so I thought I'd follow you.

EKDAL—Hm. Decent of you, Hjalmar. Who were all those people?

HJALMAR—Oh, all sorts. There was Mr. Flor—the Chamberlain—and Mr. Balle—he's one, too—and so's Mr. Kaspersen—and Mr.—what's his name, I don't remember what they were all called—

EKDAL [*nods*] You hear that, Gina? People from the palace—and Hjalmar!

GINA—Yes, they're very grand up there nowadays.

HEDVIG—Did the Chamberlains sing, Father? Or recite anything?

HJALMAR—No, they just chattered. They tried to get me to recite something. But I said: "No."

EKDAL—You said "No," did you?

GINA—Oh, you might have obliged them.

HJALMAR—No. One can't go round pandering to everyone.

[*Begins to walk up and down the room.*]
I won't, anyway.

EKDAL—No, no. You won't get round Hjalmar as easily as that.

HJALMAR—I don't see why I should have to provide the entertainment on the few occasions when I go out to enjoy myself. Let the others do some work for a change. Those fellows go from one dinner table to the next stuffing themselves every night. Let them work for their food and drink.

GINA—You didn't say all this?

HJALMAR [*hums to himself*] I gave them a piece of my mind.

EKDAL—You said this to their faces?

HJALMAR—Could be.

[*Nonchalantly.*]
Afterwards we had a little altercation about Tokay.

EKDAL—Tokay, did you say? That's a fine wine.

HJALMAR [*stops walking*] It *can* be a fine wine. But, let me tell you, all vintages are not equally fine. It depends on how much sunshine the grapes have had.

GINA – Oh, Hjalmar! You know about everything!

EKDAL – And they tried to argue about that?

HJALMAR – They tried. But they soon learned that it's the same as with Chamberlains. All vintages are not equally fine.

GINA – The things you think of!

EKDAL [*chuckles*] He, he! And they had to put that in their pipes and smoke it?

HJALMAR – Yes. It was said straight to their faces.

EKDAL – You hear that, Gina? He said it straight to the Chamberlains' faces.

GINA – Just fancy! Straight to their faces!

HJALMAR – Yes, but I don't want it talked about. One doesn't repeat such things. It was all very friendly, of course. They're decent, friendly people. Why should I hurt them?

EKDAL – But straight to their faces!

HEDVIG [*trying to please him*] What fun it is to see you in tails! You look splendid in tails, Father!

HJALMAR – Yes, I do, don't I? And it fits me perfectly; almost as though it had been made for me. Just a little tight under the arms, perhaps. Give me a hand, Hedvig.

[*Takes them off.*]

I think I'll put my jacket on. Where's my jacket, Gina?

GINA – Here it is.

[*Brings the jacket and helps him on with it.*]

HJALMAR – That's better! Don't forget to let Molvik have the tails back tomorrow morning.

GINA [*puts them away*] I'll see he gets them.

HJALMAR [*stretches*] Ah, now I feel more at home. Loose-fitting clothes suit my figure better. Don't you think, Hedvig?

HEDVIG – Yes, Father.

HJALMAR – When I loosen my tie so that the ends flow like this— Look! What do you think of that?

HEDVIG – Oh yes, that looks very good with your moustache and those big curls of yours.

HJALMAR – I wouldn't call them curls. Waves.

HEDVIG – Yes, they're such big curls.

HJALMAR – They are waves.

HEDVIG [*after a moment, tugs his jacket*] Father!

HJALMAR – Well, what is it?

HEDVIG – Oh, you know quite well what it is.

HJALMAR – No, I don't. Really.

1229

HEDVIG [*laughs and whimpers*] Oh yes, you do, Father. You mustn't tease me!

HJALMAR—But what *is* it?

HEDVIG—Oh, stop it! Give it to me, Father! You know! All those nice things you promised me!

HJALMAR—Oh, dear! Fancy my forgetting that!

HEDVIG—Oh, no, you're only teasing, Father! Oh, it's beastly of you! Where have you hidden it?

HJALMAR—No, honestly, I forgot. But wait a moment! I've something else for you, Hedvig.

[*Goes over to the tails and searches in the pockets.*]

HEDVIG [*jumps and claps her hands*] Oh, Mother, Mother!

GINA—There, you see. Just be patient, and—

HJALMAR [*holds out a card*] Look, here it is.

HEDVIG—That? That's only a piece of paper.

HJALMAR—It's the menu, Hedvig. The whole menu. Look here. It says *Déjeuner*. That means menu.

HEDVIG—Is that all?

HJALMAR—Well, I forgot the other things. But believe me, Hedvig, they're not much fun really, all those sickly sweet things. Sit over there at the table and read this menu, and then I'll describe to you how each dish tasted. Here you are, now, Hedvig.

HEDVIG [*swallows her tears*] Thank you.

[*She sits down but does not read.* GINA *makes a sign to her.* HJALMAR notices.*]

HJALMAR [*starts walking up and down*] Really, it's incredible the things a breadwinner's expected to remember. If one forgets the slightest little thing, there are sour faces all round one. Well, one gets used to it.

[*Stops by the stove, where* OLD EKDAL *is sitting.*]

Have you looked in there this evening, Father?

EKDAL—Yes, of course I have. She's gone into the basket.

HJALMAR—Gone into the basket, has she? She's beginning to get used to it, then.

EKDAL—What did I tell you? Well, now, you see, there are one or two little—

HJALMAR—Little improvements, yes.

EKDAL—We've got to have them, Hjalmar.

HJALMAR—Yes. Let's have a word about those improvements, Father. Come along, let's sit on the sofa.

EKDAL—Yes, let's. Er—I think I'll fill my pipe first. Oh, I'd better clean it, too. Hm.

[*Goes into his room.*]

GINA [*smiles at* HJALMAR] Clean his pipe!

HJALMAR—Oh, Gina, let him. Poor, shipwrecked old man! Yes, those improvements—I'd better get them done tomorrow.

GINA—But you won't have time tomorrow, Hjalmar.

HEDVIG [*interrupts*] Oh, yes, he will, Mother!

GINA—Don't forget those prints have to be retouched. They've sent for them so many times.

HJALMAR—Oh, are you on about those prints again? They'll be ready. Have there been any new orders at all?

GINA—No, I'm afraid not. I've nothing tomorrow but those two portraits I told you about.

HJALMAR—Is that all? Well, if one doesn't put one's mind to it—

GINA—But what can I do? I advertise as much as I can—

HJALMAR—Advertise, advertise! You see what good that does. I don't suppose anyone's come to look at the room either?

GINA—No, not yet.

HJALMAR—I might have known it. If one doesn't bother to keep one's eyes and ears open— One must try to make an effort, Gina.

HEDVIG [*goes towards him*] Can I bring your flute, Father?

HJALMAR—No. No flute. I don't need the pleasures of this world.

[*Starts walking again.*]

Yes, I'm going to work tomorrow. Don't you worry about that. I'll work as long as there's strength in these arms—

GINA—But my dear Hjalmar, I didn't mean it like that.

HEDVIG—Father, would you like a bottle of beer?

HJALMAR—Certainly not. I want nothing of anyone.

[*Stops.*]

Beer? Did you say beer?

HEDVIG [*alive*] Yes, Father. Lovely, cool beer.

HJALMAR—Well—if you want to, bring in a bottle.

GINA—Yes, do. That's a nice idea.

[HEDVIG *runs towards the kitchen door.*]

HJALMAR [*by the stove, stops her, looks at her, takes her head in his hands and presses her to him*] Hedvig! Hedvig!

HEDVIG [*happy, crying*] Oh, dear, kind, Father!

HJALMAR—No, don't call me that. I have been eating at the rich man's table. Gorging my belly at the groaning board. And yet I could—

GINA [*sitting at the table*] Oh, nonsense, nonsense, Hjalmar.

HJALMAR—It's true. But you mustn't judge me too harshly. You know I love you both. In spite of everything—

HEDVIG [*throws her arms round him*] And we love you very, very much, Father.

HJALMAR—And if I should, once in a while, be unreasonable—dear

God!—remember that I am a man besieged by a host of sorrows. Oh, well.

[*Dries her eyes.*]

This is not the moment for beer. Give me my flute.

[HEDVIG *runs to the bookcase and fetches it.*]

Thank you. Ah, this is better. With my flute in my hand, and you two by my side—ah!

HEDVIG *sits at the table by* GINA. HJALMAR *walks up and down, then begins to play a Bohemian folk dance, with spirit, in a slow and mournful tempo, and sensitively. Stops playing, stretches out his left hand to* GINA *and says emotionally.*

Life may be poor and humble under our roof. But it is home. And I tell you, Gina—it is good to be here.

[*He begins to play again.*]

[*After a few moments, there is a knock on the front door.*]

GINA [*gets up*] Hush, Hjalmar. I think there's someone at the door.

HJALMAR [*puts the flute away in the bookcase*] Oh, here we go again.

GREGERS WERLE [*outside on the landing*] Excuse me, but—

GINA [*starts back slightly*] Oh!

GREGERS—Doesn't Mr. Ekdal live here? The photographer.

GINA—Yes, he does.

HJALMAR [*goes over to the door*] Gregers! Are you here? Well, you'd better come in.

GREGERS [*enters*] But I told you I'd visit you.

HJALMAR—But—tonight? Have you left the party?

GREGERS—Yes. I have left the party. And my home, too. Good evening, Mrs. Ekdal. I don't suppose you recognise me?

GINA—Why, yes, Mr. Gregers. I recognise you.

GREGERS—Yes. I'm like my mother. And I've no doubt you remember her.

HJALMAR—Did you say you had left your father's house?

GREGERS—Yes. I've moved to a hotel.

HJALMAR—Oh, I see. Well, since you've come, take off your coat and sit down.

GREGERS—Thank you.

[*He takes off his coat. He has changed into a simple grey suit of a provincial cut.*]

HJALMAR—Here, on the sofa. Make yourself comfortable.

[GREGERS *sits on the sofa,* HJALMAR *on a chair by the table.*]

GREGERS [*looks around*] So this is it, Hjalmar. This is where you live.

HJALMAR—This room is my studio, as you see.

GINA—We usually sit here, because there's more space.

HJALMAR—We had a nicer place before, but this apartment has one great advantage. The bedrooms—

GINA—And we've a spare room on the other side of the passage that we can let.

GREGERS [*to* HJALMAR] Oh, I see. You take lodgers as well?

HJALMAR—No, not yet. It takes time, you know. One's got to keep one's eyes and ears open.

> [*To* HEDVIG.]

Let's have that beer now.

> [HEDVIG *nods and goes out into the kitchen.*]

GREGERS—So that's your daughter?

HJALMAR—Yes, that is Hedvig.

GREGERS—Your only child?

HJALMAR—Yes, she is the only one. Our greatest joy.

> [*Drops his voice.*]

And also our greatest sorrow, Gregers.

GREGERS—What do you mean?

HJALMAR—There is a grave risk that she may lose her eyesight.

GREGERS—Go blind?

HJALMAR—Yes. As yet there are only the first symptoms, and she may be all right for some while. But the doctor has warned us. It will happen in the end.

GREGERS—What a terrible tragedy. What's the cause?

HJALMAR [*sighs*] It's probably hereditary.

GREGERS [*starts*] Hereditary?

GINA—Hjalmar's mother had weak eyes, too.

HJALMAR—So my father says. Of course, I can't remember.

GREGERS—Poor child. And how does she take it?

HJALMAR—Oh, you don't imagine we have the heart to tell her? She suspects nothing. Carefree and gay, singing like a little bird, she will fly into the night.

> [*Overcome.*]

Oh, it will be the death of me, Gregers.

[HEDVIG *brings a tray with beer and glasses, and sets it on the table.*
> HJALMAR *strokes her head.*]

Thank you, Hedvig.

> [*She puts her arm round his neck and whispers in his ear.*]

No, no sandwiches now.

> [*Glances at* GREGERS.]

Unless you'd like some, Gregers?

GREGERS—No, no, thank you.

HJALMAR [*still melancholy*] Well, you might bring a few in, anyway. A crust will be enough for me. Put plenty of butter on it, mind.

> [HEDVIG *nods happily and goes back into the kitchen.*]

GREGERS [*follows her with his eyes*] She looks quite strong and healthy, apart from that, I think.

GINA – Yes, there's nothing else the matter with her, thank God.

GREGERS – She's going to look very like you, Mrs. Ekdal. How old would she be now?

GINA – Almost exactly fourteen. It's her birthday the day after to-morrow.

GREGERS – Quite big for her age.

GINA – Yes, she's certainly shot up this last year.

GREGERS – Seeing these young people grow up makes one realise how old one's getting oneself. How long have you two been married now?

GINA – We've been married—er—yes, nearly fifteen years.

GREGERS – Good Lord, is it as long as that?

GINA [*suddenly alert; looks at him*] Yes, that's right.

HJALMAR – It certainly is. Fifteen years, all but a few months.

> [*Changes his tone.*]

They must have seemed long to you, those years up at the mill, Gregers.

GREGERS – They seemed long at the time. Looking back on them, I hardly know where they went.

[OLD EKDAL *enters from his room, without his pipe but wearing his old army helmet. He walks a little unsteadily.*]

EKDAL – Well, Hjalmar, now we can sit down and talk about that—er—. What was it we were going to talk about?

HJALMAR [*goes over to him*] Father, we have a guest. Gregers Werle. I don't know if you remember him.

EKDAL [*looks at* GREGERS, *who has got up*] Werle? The son? What does he want with me?

HJALMAR – Nothing. He's come to see me.

EKDAL – Oh. Nothing's wrong, then?

HJALMAR – No, of course not. Nothing at all.

EKDAL [*waves an arm*] Mind you, I'm not afraid. It's just that—

GREGERS [*goes over to him*] I only wanted to bring you a greeting from your old hunting grounds, Lieutenant Ekdal.

EKDAL – Hunting grounds?

GREGERS – Yes—up around Hoydal.

EKDAL – Oh, up there. Yes, I used to know that part well, in the old days.

GREGERS – You were a famous hunter then.

EKDAL – Oh, well. Maybe I was. I won't deny it. You're looking at my uniform. I don't ask anyone's permission to wear it in here. As long as I don't go out into the street in it—

[HEDVIG *brings a plate of sandwiches and puts it on the table.*]

HJALMAR—Sit down now, Father, and have a glass of beer. Gregers, please.

EKDAL *mumbles to himself and stumbles over to the sofa.* GREGERS *sits in the chair nearest to him,* HJALMAR *on the other side of* GREGERS. GINA *sits a little away from the table, sewing.* HEDVIG *stands beside her father.*

GREGERS—Do you remember, Lieutenant Ekdal, how Hjalmar and I used to come up and visit you during the summer, and at Christmas?

EKDAL—Did you? No, no, no, I don't remember it. But though I say it myself, I was a first-rate shot. I've killed bears too, you know. Nine of them.

GREGERS [*looks at him sympathetically*] And now your hunting days are over?

EKDAL—Oh, I wouldn't say that, my boy. Do a bit of hunting now and again. Not quite the way I used to. You see, the forest—the forest, you see, the forest—

[*Drinks.*]

How does the forest look up there now? Still good, eh?

GREGERS—Not as good as in your day. It's been thinned out a lot.

EKDAL—Thinned out? Chopped down?

[*More quietly, as though in fear.*]

That's dangerous. Bad things'll come of that. The forest'll have its revenge.

HJALMAR [*fills his glass*] Have a little more, Father.

GREGERS—How can a man like you, a man who loves the open air as you do, bear to live in the middle of a stuffy town, boxed between four walls?

EKDAL [*gives a short laugh and glances at* HJALMAR] Oh, it's not too bad here. Not bad at all.

GREGERS—But what about the cool, sweeping breezes, the free life in the forest, and up on the wide, open spaces among animals and birds? These things which had become part of you?

EKDAL [*smiles*] Hjalmar, shall we show it to him?

HJALMAR [*quickly, a little embarrassed*] Oh, no, Father, no. Not tonight.

GREGERS—What does he want to show me?

HJALMAR—It's only something that—. You can see it another time.

GREGERS [*continues speaking to* EKDAL] What I was going to suggest, Lieutenant Ekdal, was that you should come with me back to the mill.

I shall be returning there soon. I'm sure we could find you some copying to do up there, too. And there's nothing here to keep you cheerful and interested.

EKDAL [*stares at him, amazed*] Nothing here—?

GREGERS—Of course you have Hjalmar; but then he has his own family. And a man like you, who has always been drawn to a life that is wild and free—

EKDAL [*strikes the table*] Hjalmar, he *shall* see it!

HJALMAR—But, Father, what's the point of showing it to him now? It's dark.

EKDAL—Nonsense, there's the moonlight.

[*Gets up.*]

He shall see it, I tell you. Let me come through. Come and help me, Hjalmar.

HEDVIG—Oh, yes, do, Father!

HJALMAR [*gets up*] Oh, very well.

GREGERS [*to* GINA] What are they talking about?

GINA—Oh, don't take any notice. It's nothing very much.

EKDAL *and* HJALMAR *go to the rear wall, and each of them pushes back one of the sliding doors.* HEDVIG *helps the old man.* GREGERS *remains standing by the sofa.* GINA *continues calmly with her sewing. Through the open doors can be seen a long and irregularly shaped loft, full of dark nooks and crannies, with a couple of brick chimney-pipes coming through the floor. Through small skylights bright moonlight shines on to various parts of the loft, while the rest lies in shadow.*

EKDAL [*to* GREGERS] You can come right in, if you like.

GREGERS [*goes over to them*] What is it, exactly?

EKDAL—Have a look. Hm.

HJALMAR [*somewhat embarrassed*] This belongs to my father, you understand.

GREGERS [*in the doorway, peers into the loft*] Why, you keep chickens, Lieutenant Ekdal.

EKDAL—I should think we do keep chickens! They've gone to roost now. But you should just see them by daylight!

HEDVIG—And then there's the—!

EKDAL—Ssh! Don't say anything yet.

GREGERS—And you've pigeons, too, I see.

EKDAL—Why, yes! Of course we've pigeons. They've got their roosting-boxes up there under the roof. Pigeons like to nest high, you know.

HJALMAR—They're not all ordinary pigeons.

EKDAL—Ordinary! No, I should say not! We've tumblers. And a pair of pouters, too. But come over here! Do you see that hutch over there against the wall?

GREGERS—Yes. What do you use that for?

EKDAL—The rabbits go there at night.

GREGERS—Oh, you have rabbits, too?

EKDAL—You're damn right we've got rabbits. You hear that, Hjalmar? He asks if we've got rabbits! Hm! But now I'll show you! This is really something. Move over, Hedvig. Stand here. That's right. Now look down there. Can you see a basket with straw in it?

GREGERS—Yes. And there's a bird lying in the straw.

EKDAL—Hm! A bird!

GREGERS—Isn't it a duck?

EKDAL [*hurt*] Of course it's a duck.

HJALMAR—Ah, but what *kind* of a duck?

HEDVIG—It's not just an ordinary duck—

EKDAL—Ssh!

GREGERS—It's not one of those Muscovy ducks, is it?

EKDAL—No, Mr. Werle, it's not a Muscovy duck. It's a wild duck.

GREGERS—Oh, is it really? A wild duck?

EKDAL—Yes, that's what it is. That "bird," as you called it—that's a wild duck, that is. That's our wild duck, my boy.

HEDVIG—My wild duck. I own it.

GREGERS—But can it live up here in this loft? Is it happy here?

EKDAL—Well, naturally she has a trough of water to splash about in.

HJALMAR—Fresh water every other day.

GINA [*turns towards* HJALMAR] Hjalmar dear, it's getting icy cold up here.

EKDAL—Mm. Well, let's shut up, then. It's best not to disturb them when they're sleeping, anyway. Give me a hand, Hedvig.

[HJALMAR *and* HEDVIG *slide the doors together.*]

Some other time you must have a proper look at her.

[*Sits in the armchair by the stove.*]

Ah, they're strange creatures, you know, these wild ducks.

GREGERS—But how did you manage to catch it, Lieutenant Ekdal?

EKDAL—I didn't catch it. There's a certain gentleman in this town whom we have to thank for that.

GREGERS [*starts slightly*] You don't mean my father, surely?

EKDAL—Indeed I do. Your father. Hm.

HJALMAR—How odd that you should guess that, Gregers.

GREGERS—You told me earlier that you were indebted to my father for so many things, so I thought perhaps—

GINA—Oh, we didn't get it from Mr. Werle himself—

E K D A L – All the same, it's Haakon Werle we have to thank for her, Gina.

[*To* GREGERS.]

He was out in his boat, you see, and he shot her. But his eyesight isn't very good. Hm. So he only winged her.

G R E G E R S – Oh, I see. She got a couple of pellets in her.

H J A L M A R – Yes, two or three.

H E D V I G – She got them under her wing, so that she couldn't fly.

G R E G E R S – Oh, and so she dived to the bottom, I suppose?

E K D A L [*sleepily, in a thick voice*] Of course. Wild ducks always do that. Dive down to the bottom, as deep as they can go, and hold on with their beaks to the seaweed or whatever they can find down there. And they never come up again.

G R E G E R S – But your wild duck did come up again, Lieutenant Ekdal.

E K D A L – He had such a damned clever dog, your father. And that dog— he dived down after the duck, and brought her to the surface.

G R E G E R S [*turns to* HJALMAR] And then you took her in here?

H J A L M A R – Not at once. To begin with, they took her home to your father's house. But she didn't seem to thrive there. So Pettersen was told to wring her neck.

E K D A L [*half asleep*] Hm. Yes. Pettersen. Damn fool—

H J A L M A R [*speaks more softly*] That was how we got her, you see. Father knows Pettersen, and when he heard all this about the wild duck he got him to give it to us.

G R E G E R S – And now she's thriving in your loft.

H J A L M A R – Yes, she's doing extraordinarily well. She's got fat. Well, she's been in there so long now that she's forgotten what it's like to live the life she was born for; that's the whole trick.

G R E G E R S – Yes, you're right there, Hjalmar. Just make sure she never gets a glimpse of the sky or the sea. But I mustn't stay longer. I think your father's fallen asleep.

H J A L M A R – Oh, never mind about that.

G R E G E R S – By the bye, you said you had a room to let.

H J A L M A R – Yes, why? Do you know anyone who—?

G R E G E R S – Could I have it?

H J A L M A R – You?

G I N A – No, but Mr. Werle, it isn't—

G R E G E R S – Can I have that room? I'd like to move in right away. Tomorrow morning.

H J A L M A R – Why, yes, with the greatest pleasure—

G I N A – Oh no, Mr. Werle, it's not at all the kind of room for you.

H J A L M A R – Why, Gina, how can you say that?

G I N A – Well, it's dark and poky.

GREGERS — That won't bother me, Mrs. Ekdal.

HJALMAR — Personally I think it's quite a nice room. Not too badly furnished, either.

GINA — Don't forget those two who live down below.

GREGERS — Who are they?

GINA — Oh, one of them used to be a tutor—

HJALMAR — A Mr. Molvik.

GINA — And the other's a doctor called Relling.

GREGERS — Relling? I know him slightly. He had a practice up at Hoydal once.

GINA — They're a real couple of good-for-nothings. They often go out on the spree and come home very late at night, and aren't always—

GREGERS — One soon gets accustomed to that sort of thing. I hope I shall manage to acclimatise myself like the wild duck.

GINA — Well, I think you ought to sleep on it first, all the same.

GREGERS — You evidently don't want to have me living here, Mrs. Ekdal.

GINA — For heaven's sake! How can you think that?

HJALMAR — You're really behaving very strangely, Gina.

[*To* GREGERS.]

But tell me, are you thinking of staying in town for a while?

GREGERS [*puts on his overcoat*] Yes, now I'm staying.

HJALMAR — But not at home with your father? What do you intend to do?

GREGERS — Ah, if only I knew that, Hjalmar, it wouldn't be so bad. But when one has the misfortune to be called Gregers—with Werle on top of it—Hjalmar, have you ever heard anything so awful?

HJALMAR — Oh, I don't think it's awful at all.

GREGERS — Oh, nonsense. Ugh! I'd want to spit on anyone who had a name like that.

HJALMAR [*laughs*] If you weren't Gregers Werle, what would you like to be?

GREGERS — If I could choose, I think most of all I'd like to be a clever dog.

GINA — A dog?

HEDVIG [*involuntarily*] Oh, no!

GREGERS — Oh, yes. A tremendously clever dog. The sort that dives down after wild ducks when they have plunged to the bottom and gripped themselves fast in the seaweed and the mud.

HJALMAR — Honestly, Gregers, I don't understand a word of all this.

GREGERS — Oh, well, it doesn't mean much really. I'll move in to-morrow morning, then.

[*To* GINA.]

I shan't cause you any trouble. I do everything for myself.

[*To* HJALMAR.]

We'll talk about everything else tomorrow. Good night, Mrs. Ekdal.

[*Nods to* HEDVIG.]

Good night.

GINA – Good night, Mr. Werle.

HEDVIG – Good night.

HJALMAR [*who has lit a candle*] Wait a moment. I'll have to light you down. It's very dark on the stairs.

[GREGERS *and* HJALMAR *go out through the front door.*]

GINA [*thoughtfully, her sewing in her lap*] Wasn't that a funny thing, saying he'd like to be a dog?

HEDVIG – You know, Mother—I think when he said that he meant something else.

GINA – What could he mean?

HEDVIG – I don't know. But I felt as though he meant something different from what he was saying all the time.

GINA – You think so? Yes, it certainly was strange.

HJALMAR [*comes back*] The light was still on.

[*Snuffs the candle and puts it down.*]

Ah, now I can get a little food inside me at last.

[*Begins eating the sandwiches.*]

Well, there you are, Gina. If one only keeps one's eyes and ears open—

GINA – How do you mean?

HJALMAR – Well, it's jolly lucky we've managed to let that room at last, isn't it? And, what's more, to a man like Gregers. A dear old friend.

GINA – Well, I don't know what to say about it.

HEDVIG – Oh, Mother! You'll see—it'll be such fun!

HJALMAR – You're very awkward. You were aching to let the room, and now we've done it you're not happy.

GINA – Oh, yes I am, Hjalmar. I only wish it had been to someone else. But what do you suppose the old man will say?

HJALMAR – Old Werle? It's none of his business.

GINA – Can't you see? They must have quarrelled again if his son's walked out of the house. You know how things are between those two.

HJALMAR – That may well be, but—

GINA – Now perhaps Mr. Werle'll think you're behind it all.

HJALMAR – All right, let him think so, if he wants to! Old Werle's done a great deal for me, I admit it. But that doesn't make me his vassal for life.

GINA – But, dear Hjalmar, he might take it out of Grandfather. Maybe now he'll lose the little bit of money he gets through Graaberg.

HJALMAR – Good riddance—I've half a mind to say. Don't you think it's a little humiliating for a man like me to see his grey old father treated like a leper? But I've a feeling the time is getting ripe.

[*Takes another sandwich.*]

As sure as I have a mission in life, it shall be fulfilled.

HEDVIG—Oh, Father, yes! It must, it must!

GINA—Ssh! For heaven's sake, don't wake him.

HJALMAR [*more quietly*] It shall be accomplished. The day will come, I tell you—and that's why it's good we've let that room—it makes me more independent.

[*Over by the armchair, emotionally.*]

My poor old father! Bless his white hairs! Put your trust in your son. He has broad shoulders—well, strong shoulders, anyway. One fine day you will wake up—

[*To* GINA.]

Don't you believe it?

GINA [*gets up*] Of course I believe it. But let's get him to bed first.

HJALMAR—Yes, let's.

[*They take hold of the old man gently.*]

ACT THREE

HJALMAR EKDAL's *studio. It is morning. The daylight is shining in through the large window in the sloping ceiling, from which the curtain is drawn back.*

HJALMAR *is seated at the table re-touching a photograph. Several others lie in front of him. After a few moments,* GINA *enters through the front door wearing a hat and coat. She has a lidded basket on her arm.*

H J A L M A R – Back already, Gina?

G I N A – Yes, I've no time to waste.

> [*Puts the basket down on a chair and takes off her coat.*]

H J A L M A R – Did you look in on Gregers?

G I N A – I'll say I did. Lovely it looks. He's made it really nice and cosy for himself right from the start.

H J A L M A R – Oh, how?

G I N A – Manage for himself, he said he would. So he starts lighting the stove. Well, he shoved that damper in so far the whole room got full of smoke. Ugh! It stank like a—

H J A L M A R – Oh dear, oh dear!

G I N A – That's not all. Then he wants to put out the fire, so he throws all his washing water into the stove. That floor's swimming like a pigsty.

H J A L M A R – Oh, I'm sorry about that.

G I N A – I've got the caretaker's wife to clean up after him, the pig. But that room won't be fit to live in till this afternoon.

H J A L M A R – What's he doing with himself meanwhile?

G I N A – He said he'd go out for a bit.

H J A L M A R – I went in there too for a moment. After you'd gone.

G I N A – So I gathered. I hear you've invited him for lunch.

H J A L M A R – Just a little snack, I thought. After all, it's his first day here—we can't very well not. You've got something, I suppose?

G I N A – I'll have to find something, won't I?

H J A L M A R – Don't skimp it too much. Relling and Molvik may be looking in, too, I think. I ran into Relling on the stairs just now, you see, so I couldn't very well—

1242

G I N A – Oh, we're having those two as well, are we?

H J A L M A R – Good God, a couple more or less, what difference does that make?

O L D   E K D A L [*opens his door and looks out*] I say, Hjalmar—

[*Notices* GINA.]

Oh.

G I N A – Do you want something, Grandfather?

O L D   E K D A L – Oh, no. It doesn't matter. Hm!

[*Goes inside again.*]

G I N A [*picks up the basket*] Watch him. See he doesn't go out.

H J A L M A R – All right, all right. I say, Gina, a little of that herring salad of yours mightn't be a bad idea. I think Relling and Molvik were out on the tiles again last night.

G I N A – Well, as long as they don't come too soon—

H J A L M A R – Of course, of course. You take your time.

G I N A – Yes, well; and you can get a little work done in the meantime.

H J A L M A R – I *am* working! I'm working as hard as I can!

G I N A – I only meant, then you'll have it out of the way.

[*She goes out with her basket to the kitchen.* HJALMAR *sits working at the photograph with a brush, slowly and listlessly.*]

E K D A L [*pokes his head in, looks around the room and says in a whisper*] Are you working?

H J A L M A R – Yes, can't you see I'm struggling away at these pictures?

E K D A L – Oh. Well, never mind. If you're working so hard, I—Hm.

[*Goes out again. His door remains open.*]

H J A L M A R [*continues silently for a few moments, then puts down his brush and goes across to the door*] Are *you* working, Father?

E K D A L [*grumblingly, from the other room*] If you're working, I'm working, too. Hm!

H J A L M A R – Yes, yes, of course.

[*Goes back to his work.*]

E K D A L [*after a moment, reappears in the doorway*] You know—I'm not working as hard as all that, Hjalmar.

H J A L M A R – I thought you were writing.

E K D A L – Damn it, that Graaberg can wait a day or two. It's not a matter of life and death, is it?

H J A L M A R – No. Anyway, you're not a slave, are you?

E K D A L – And then there's that thing in there—

H J A L M A R – I was just thinking of that. Did you want to go in? Shall I open the door for you?

E K D A L – That's not a bad idea.

H J A L M A R [*gets up*] Then we'd have it out of the way.

EKDAL—That's what I was thinking. We've got to have it ready by tomorrow morning. It is tomorrow, isn't it? Eh?

HJALMAR—Yes, of course it's tomorrow.

HJALMAR *and* EKDAL *each slide back one of the doors. Within, the morning sun is shining in through the skylights. Some pigeons are flying back and forth, while others perch, cooing, on the rafters. Now and then the hens cackle further back in the loft.*

Well now. Get on with it, Father.

EKDAL [*goes inside*] Aren't you going to help?

HJALMAR—You know, I think I—

[*Sees* GINA *in the kitchen doorway.*]

Me? No, I've no time. I've got to work. Oh—my contraption—

He pulls a cord. A curtain falls in the attic; the lower section of this consists of a strip of old sailcloth, the upper of a piece of fishing net, stretched taut. The floor of the attic is thus no longer visible.

[*Goes over to the table.*]

Good. Now perhaps I can be allowed to work in peace for a few minutes.

GINA—Is he messing around in there again?

HJALMAR—Would you rather he sneaked off down to Madame Eriksen's?

[*Sits.*]

Did you want something? You were saying—

GINA—I only wanted to ask whether you think it'd be all right if we eat in here.

HJALMAR—Yes, we haven't any early sittings today, have we?

GINA—Only those two young lovers who want to be taken together.

HJALMAR—Why the devil can't they be taken together some other day?

GINA—It's all right, dear. I've fixed for them to come after lunch, when you'll be having your nap.

HJALMAR—Oh, good. Very well, then, let's eat in here.

GINA—All right. But there's no hurry about laying the table just yet. You can go on using it for a bit longer.

HJALMAR—Surely you can see I'm working as hard as I can!

GINA—I only meant, then you'll be free later.

[*She goes back into the kitchen. Short pause.*]

EKDAL [*peers through the net in the loft*] Hjalmar!

HJALMAR—What is it?

EKDAL—Afraid we'll have to move that water trough after all.

HJALMAR—That's what I've said all along.

EKDAL—Hm—hm—hm.

[*Goes away from the door again.*]

[HJALMAR *works for a few moments, then glances towards the attic and half rises.* HEDVIG *comes in from the kitchen.*]

HJALMAR [*sits quickly down*] What do you want?

HEDVIG—I only wanted to be with you, Father.

HJALMAR [*after a moment*] What are you nosing around for? Have you been told to keep an eye on me?

HEDVIG—No, of course not.

HJALMAR—What's your mother up to now?

HEDVIG—Oh, she's in the middle of the herring salad.

[*Goes over to the table.*]

Isn't there some little thing I could help you with, Father?

HJALMAR—Oh, no. I'd better cope with it alone. While I still can. All will be well, Hedvig. As long as your father's strength holds out—

HEDVIG—Oh, no, Father, you mustn't say such dreadful things.

[*She wanders around for a little, then stops by the open doorway and looks into the loft.*]

HJALMAR—What's he up to, Hedvig?

HEDVIG—I think he's making a new path up to the water trough.

HJALMAR—He'll never manage that by himself! And I'm forced to sit here—

HEDVIG [*comes over to him*] Let me take the brush, Father. I know how to do it.

HJALMAR—Oh, no, you'll only ruin your eyes.

HEDVIG—Nonsense. Come on, give me the brush.

HJALMAR [*gets up*] Yes, well, it won't take more than a minute or two.

HEDVIG—Oh, what does it matter?

[*Takes the brush.*]

There, now.

[*Sits.*]

Here's one I can start on.

HJALMAR—But listen—if you ruin your eyes, I won't take the responsibility. On your own head be it. You hear?

HEDVIG [*busy on the photograph*] Yes, yes, I know.

HJALMAR—You're a clever girl, Hedvig. It'll only take a couple of minutes—

[*He squeezes into the loft past the edge of the curtain.* HEDVIG *sits working.* HJALMAR *and* EKDAL *can be heard arguing in the loft.*]

HJALMAR [*comes back through the curtain*] Hedvig, get me those pliers from that shelf. And the chisel.

[*Turns round towards the loft.*]

Now you'll see, Father. Just let me show you.

[HEDVIG *gets the tools from the bookcase and hands them to him.*]

HJALMAR–Ah, thanks. Good thing I came, Hedvig.

He goes away from the doorway. They can be heard working and chatting inside. HEDVIG *stands watching them. After a moment, there is a knock on the front door. She does not hear it.*

GREGERS [*enters bareheaded and without an overcoat. He pauses in the doorway*] Hm—

HEDVIG [*turns and goes towards him*] Good morning. Please come in.

GREGERS–Thank you.

[*Looks towards the attic.*]

Have you got workmen in the house?

HEDVIG–No, that's only Father and Grandfather. I'll tell them you're here.

GREGERS–No, no, don't do that. I'd rather wait.

[*Sits on the sofa.*]

HEDVIG–It's so untidy in here.

[*Begins to clear away the photographs.*]

GREGERS–Oh, never mind that. Are those photographs that have to be—er—finished off?

HEDVIG–Yes, just a few I'm helping Father with.

GREGERS–Please don't let me disturb you.

HEDVIG–All right.

[*Arranges the things again and sits down to work.* GREGERS *watches her in silence.*]

GREGERS–Did the wild duck sleep well last night?

HEDVIG–Yes, thank you, I think so.

GREGERS [*turns towards the loft*] It looks quite different in there by daylight.

HEDVIG–Oh, yes. It varies a lot. In the morning it looks quite different from what it does in the afternoon. And when it's raining it looks different from when it's fine.

GREGERS–You've noticed that, have you?

HEDVIG–Yes, you can't help seeing it.

GREGERS–Do you like being in there with the wild duck, too?

HEDVIG–Yes, when I'm able to—

GREGERS–But you haven't so much spare time, I dare say. You go to school, of course?

HEDVIG–No, not any longer. Father's afraid I shall ruin my eyes.

GREGERS–Oh. So he reads with you himself?

HEDVIG–Father's promised to read with me, but he hasn't found time for it yet.

GREGERS–But isn't there someone else who could help you a little?

HEDVIG–Yes, there's Mr. Molvik–he's a student who lives downstairs –but he isn't always–er–altogether quite–

GREGERS–Does he drink?

HEDVIG–I think he does.

GREGERS–Oh. Then you've time for all sorts of things. In there, it's like a different world, I suppose?

HEDVIG–Quite, quite different. And there are so many strange things in there.

GREGERS–Oh?

HEDVIG–Yes. There are big cupboards with books in them. And a lot of the books have got pictures.

GREGERS–Ah.

HEDVIG–And there's an old bureau with drawers and bits that slide out, and a big clock with figures that are meant to pop out. But the clock doesn't work any more.

GREGERS–So time has stopped in there with the wild duck.

HEDVIG–Yes. And there are old paintboxes and things like that. And all the books.

GREGERS–And you read books, I suppose?

HEDVIG–Oh yes, when I can get the chance. But most of them are in English, and I can't understand that. But I look at the pictures. There's a great big book called *Harrison's History of London*–I should think it must be a hundred years old–and that's got heaps and heaps of pictures in it. On the front there's a picture of death with an hourglass, and a girl. That's horrid, I think. But then there are lots of other pictures of churches and castles and streets and great ships sailing on the sea.

GREGERS–But tell me, where have all these wonderful things come from?

HEDVIG–Oh, there was an old sea captain who used to live here once, and he brought them home. They called him The Flying Dutchman. It's funny, because he wasn't a Dutchman.

GREGERS–Wasn't he?

HEDVIG–No. But in the end he got lost at sea and left all these things behind.

GREGERS–Tell me–as you sit in there and look at the pictures, don't you feel you want to get out and see the world as it really is?

HEDVIG–Oh, no! I want to stay at home always, and help Father and Mother.

GREGERS—Help them retouch photographs?

HEDVIG—No, not only that. Most of all I'd like to learn to engrave pictures like the ones in the English books.

GREGERS—Hm. What does your father say to that?

HEDVIG—I don't think Father likes the idea. He's so strange about anything like that. Imagine, he talks about my learning how to plait straw and make baskets! I don't think there can be any future in that.

GREGERS—No, neither do I.

HEDVIG—But Father's right when he says that if I'd learned basket-making I could have made the new basket for the wild duck.

GREGERS—Yes, so you could. It was your job really, wasn't it?

HEDVIG—Yes, because it's my wild duck.

GREGERS—Of course it is.

HEDVIG—Oh, yes. I own it. But Father and Grandfather are allowed to borrow it whenever they want.

GREGERS—Oh, and what do they do with it?

HEDVIG—Oh, they look after it and build things for it, and that kind of thing.

GREGERS—I should think so. The wild duck's the most important thing in there, isn't it?

HEDVIG—Oh, yes. She's a real wild bird, you see. That's why I feel so sorry for her. She's got no one to care for, poor thing.

GREGERS—No family like the rabbits.

HEDVIG—No. The hens have got friends they used to be chicks with; but she's been separated from all her family. And there's so much that's strange about the wild duck. No one knows her. And no one knows where she came from.

GREGERS—And she's been down to the bottom of the deep blue sea.

HEDVIG [*glances quickly at him and represses a smile*] Why do you say "the deep blue sea"?

GREGERS—What should I have said?

HEDVIG—You could have said the "sea bed," or just the "bottom of the sea."

GREGERS—Oh, why can't I say "the deep blue sea"?

HEDVIG—Yes, but it always sounds so odd to me when other people talk about "the deep blue sea."

GREGERS—Why? Tell me.

HEDVIG—No, I won't. It's silly.

GREGERS—Not at all. Tell me now, why did you smile?

HEDVIG—It's because if I suddenly—without thinking—remember what's in there, I always think of it all as being "the deep blue sea." But that's just silly.

GREGERS—No, you mustn't say that.

HEDVIG—Well, it's only a loft.

GREGERS [*looks hard at her*] Are you so sure?

HEDVIG [*astonished*] That it's only a loft?

GREGERS—Yes. You are quite certain about that?

[HEDVIG *stares silently at him, open-mouthed.* GINA *comes from the kitchen with cutlery and tablecloth.*]

[GREGERS *gets up.*]

I'm afraid I've come too early.

GINA—Oh, you've got to sit somewhere. Anyway, I'll be ready in a minute. Clear the table, Hedvig.

[HEDVIG *clears the table. She and* GINA *lay the cloth, etc., during the following scene.* GREGERS *sits in an armchair and turns the pages of an album.*]

GREGERS—I hear you know how to retouch photographs, Mrs. Ekdal.

GINA [*gives him a quick glance*] Why—yes, I know how.

GREGERS—That was a lucky chance, wasn't it?

GINA—Why lucky?

GREGERS—Since Hjalmar was to become a photographer, I mean.

HEDVIG—Mother can take photographs, too.

GINA—Oh, yes, I've had to teach myself that.

GREGERS—Then it's really you who run the business?

GINA—Yes, when Hjalmar hasn't time himself, I—

GREGERS—His old father takes up a lot of his time, I dare say.

GINA—Yes. And anyway it's no real job for a man like Hjalmar to have to take the portraits of just anyone.

GREGERS—I quite agree. But after all, he has chosen this profession—

GINA—Hjalmar isn't just an ordinary photographer, you know, Mr. Werle.

GREGERS—I'm sure he isn't. But—

[*A shot is fired inside the loft.*]

GREGERS [*jumps up*] What's that?

GINA—Ugh, they're shooting again.

GREGERS—Do they shoot too?

HEDVIG—They go hunting.

GREGERS—What!

[*By the door of the loft.*]

Are you hunting, Hjalmar?

HJALMAR [*from beyond the curtain*] Are you here? Oh, I didn't know. I was so busy with—

[*To* HEDVIG.]

Why didn't you tell us?

[*Comes into the studio.*]

GREGERS—Do you go shooting in the loft?

H J A L M A R [*shows him a double-barrelled pistol*] Oh, only with this.

G I N A – You and Grandfather'll do yourselves an injury one of these fine days with that popgun.

H J A L M A R [*irritated*] This is a pistol, as I think I've told you before.

G I N A – I don't see that that improves matters.

G R E G E R S – So you've turned hunter, too, Hjalmar?

H J A L M A R – Oh, I just go out after rabbits now and then. Mostly for the old man's sake, you know.

G I N A – Men are funny creatures. Always got to have something to diverge themselves with.

H J A L M A R [*bad-temperedly*] Quite so. As Gina says, we've always got to have something to divert ourselves with.

G I N A – Isn't that what I said?

H J A L M A R – Hm. Well–.

[*To* GREGERS.]

Yes, you see, as luck would have it the loft's placed in such a way that no one can hear us when we shoot.

[*Puts down the pistol on the top shelf of the bookcase.*]

Don't touch that pistol, Hedvig. One of the barrels is loaded. Now don't forget.

G R E G E R S [*peers in through the net*] You've a shotgun too, I see.

H J A L M A R – That's Father's old gun. It's no use any longer, something's gone wrong with the lock. But it's quite fun to have it around. We can take it to pieces now and then and clean it and grease it and put it together again. Of course it's mostly Father who fiddles around like that.

H E D V I G [*to* GREGERS] Now you can see the wild duck properly.

G R E G E R S – Yes, I was just looking at her. She droops a little on one wing, doesn't she?

H J A L M A R – No wonder. That's where she was shot.

G R E G E R S – And she trails one foot a little. Am I right?

H J A L M A R – Perhaps just a little.

H E D V I G – Yes, that's where the dog bit her.

H J A L M A R – But otherwise there's nothing wrong with her. It's really marvellous when you think she's had a charge of shot in her and has been between the teeth of a dog–

G R E G E R S [*glances at* HEDVIG] And has been on the bottom of the deep blue sea for so long.

H E D V I G [*smiles*] Yes.

G I N A [*laying the table*] Oh, that blessed wild duck. You make too much of a song and dance about her.

H J A L M A R – Hm. Are you nearly ready with that?

G I N A – Yes, I shan't be a minute. Hedvig, come and give me a hand.

[GINA *and* HEDVIG *go out into the kitchen.*]

HJALMAR [*in a low voice*] I think you'd better not stand there watching Father. He doesn't like it.

[GREGERS *comes away from the loft door.*]

HJALMAR – I'd better close up before the others arrive.

[*Claps his hands to frighten the birds.*]

Shoo, shoo! Get away with you!

[*Pulls up the curtain and closes the doors as he speaks.*]

I invented these gadgets myself. It's really rather fun to have something like this to fiddle with, and fix when it goes wrong. We've got to have it, because Gina doesn't like rabbits and hens in here.

GREGERS – No, no. It's your wife who runs the studio, I suppose?

HJALMAR – I generally leave the details of the business to her. Then I can lock myself away in the parlour and think about more important things.

GREGERS – What kind of things, Hjalmar?

HJALMAR – I wonder you haven't asked me that before. But perhaps you haven't heard about my invention?

GREGERS – Your invention? No.

HJALMAR – Really? Haven't you? Oh no, I suppose being cut off up there in those forests–

GREGERS – So you've invented something?

HJALMAR – It's not quite finished yet. But I'm working on it. As you can imagine, when I decided to give up my life to the service of photography it wasn't because I wanted to take portraits of the *bourgeoisie*.

GREGERS – No, that's what your wife said just now.

HJALMAR – I made a vow that if I was going to dedicate my powers to this craft, I would exalt it to the level of both an art and a science. And so I decided to make this astonishing invention.

GREGERS – But what *is* this invention? What's the idea behind it?

HJALMAR – Oh, my dear fellow, you mustn't ask me about details yet. It takes time, you know. And you mustn't think it's vanity that's inspiring me to do this. It isn't for myself that I'm doing it. Oh, no. I have a mission in life that I can never forget.

GREGERS – What kind of mission?

HJALMAR – Have you forgotten that old man with the silver hair?

GREGERS – Your poor father. Yes, but there isn't very much you can do for him, is there?

HJALMAR – I can rekindle his self-respect by restoring to the name of Ekdal the honour and dignity which it once had.

GREGERS – And that's your mission?

HJALMAR – I want to save that shipwrecked soul, yes. Right from the moment the storm broke over him, he was a wreck. And during those terrible investigations he was no longer himself. That pistol over there,

Gregers—the one we use for shooting rabbits—has played its part in the tragedy of the House of Ekdal.

G R E G E R S – Really? That pistol?

H J A L M A R – When sentence had been pronounced and he was about to be taken to prison—he had the pistol in his hand—

G R E G E R S – You mean—?

H J A L M A R – Yes. But he didn't dare. He was a coward. His spirit had been broken. Can you understand it? He, a soldier, who had killed nine bears, and was descended from two lieutenant colonels—one after the other, of course— Can you understand it, Gregers?

G R E G E R S – Yes, I understand it very well.

H J A L M A R – I can't. But that wasn't the last time that pistol played a part in the history of our family. When he was in his grey garb, under lock and key—oh, it was a terrible time for me, believe me. I kept the blinds drawn over both my windows. When I peeped out I saw that the sun still shone. I couldn't understand it. I saw people in the street, laughing and chatting, about trivial things. I couldn't understand it. I thought the whole world ought to stand still, as though in eclipse.

G R E G E R S – That is how I felt when my mother died.

H J A L M A R – At such a moment, Hjalmar Ekdal held the pistol pointed at his own breast.

G R E G E R S – You mean you, too, thought of—?

H J A L M A R – Yes.

G R E G E R S – But you didn't fire?

H J A L M A R – No. At the critical moment, I triumphed over myself. I decided to remain alive. But I can tell you, Gregers, it takes courage under such circumstances to choose life.

G R E G E R S – Yes, well—that depends on how one—

H J A L M A R – Believe me, Gregers, I am right. Anyway, it was better so. Now I shall make my invention; and then, Dr. Relling agrees with me, Father may be allowed to wear his uniform again. I shall demand it as my sole reward.

G R E G E R S – So it's the uniform he—?

H J A L M A R – Yes, that's what he longs for most. You can't imagine how my heart bleeds for him. Every time we have any little family celebration—for example, Gina's and my wedding anniversary, or whatever it may be—the old man appears as the lieutenant he used to be in happier days. But if there's a knock on the door he scampers back to his room as fast as his old legs will carry him, because he daren't show himself to strangers. Oh, it's heart-rending for a son to have to witness such things, Gregers.

G R E G E R S – How soon do you expect this invention to be ready?

H J A L M A R – Good heavens, you can't expect me to work to a schedule.

An invention is something that even the inventor himself isn't completely master of. It depends largely on intuition—on inspiration—and it's almost impossible to predict when that's going to come.

GREGERS—But you're making progress?

HJALMAR—Of course I am. I think about it every day. It's always with me. Every afternoon, after I've eaten, I shut myself up in the parlour where I can meditate in peace. But I mustn't be rushed. That won't help at all. Relling says so too.

GREGERS—And you don't think that all that business in the loft distracts you too much, and dissipates your energies?

HJALMAR—No, no, no—quite the contrary. I can't spend all my time brooding over the same exhausting problem. I must have some distraction while I wait for the inspiration to come. Inspiration, you see, comes when it comes.

GREGERS—My dear Hjalmar, I really believe there is something of the wild duck in you.

HJALMAR—The wild duck? How do you mean?

GREGERS—You've plunged to the bottom and are holding on to the seaweed.

HJALMAR—Are you referring to that stroke of fate which crippled Father—and me as well?

GREGERS—Not that so much. I wouldn't say you've been crippled. You've wandered into a poisonous swamp, Hjalmar. You've got a creeping disease in your body, and you've sunk to the bottom to die in the dark.

HJALMAR—Me? Die in the dark? Now really, Gregers, you must stop that talk.

GREGERS—Don't worry. I shall get you up again. I've found a mission in life, too, you see. I found it yesterday.

HJALMAR—I dare say, but please leave me out of it. I can assure you that—apart from a certain melancholy, which is easily explained—I'm as contented with life as anyone could wish to be.

GREGERS—That's another effect of the poison.

HJALMAR—Oh, my dear Gregers, do stop talking about diseases and poisons. I'm not used to this kind of conversation. In my house we don't talk about disagreeable matters.

GREGERS—No, I can well believe that.

HJALMAR—Yes—it's not good for me, you see. And you won't find any poisonous fumes here, as you insinuate. In the poor photographer's home the roof is low, I know that well. And the circumstances are narrow. But I am an inventor, Gregers—the breadwinner for my family—and that lifts me above the poverty of my surroundings. Ah, lunch!

GINA *and* HEDVIG *bring in bottles of beer, a decanter of aquavit, glasses, etc. . . . . At the same time* RELLING *and* MOLVIK *enter from the passage. Neither has a hat or overcoat.* MOLVIK *is dressed in black.*

GINA [*putting the things on the table*] Trust those two to come on time!

RELLING–Molvik thought he could smell herring salad, so there was no holding him. Good morning again, Ekdal.

HJALMAR–Gregers, may I present Mr. Molvik? Dr.–but of course you know Relling.

GREGERS–Yes, we have met.

RELLING–Oh, it's Mr. Werle Junior. Yes, we two have clashed before, up at Hoydal. You moved in here?

GREGERS–I moved in this morning.

RELLING–Molvik and I live underneath, so you haven't far to go for a doctor or a priest, if you should ever need either of them.

GREGERS–Thank you, I well may. Yesterday we were thirteen at table.

HJALMAR–Oh, don't start that awful business again.

RELLING–Take it easy, Ekdal. You were one of the twelve.

HJALMAR–I hope so, for my family's sake. But now let's sit down, and eat and drink and be merry.

GREGERS–Oughtn't we to wait for your father?

HJALMAR–No, he wants his taken in to him later. Come along now, everybody!

[*The men sit down at the table, and start eating and drinking.* GINA *and* HEDVIG *come and go, waiting on them.*]

RELLING–Molvik was as tight as a drum again last night, Mrs. Ekdal.

GINA–Oh? Last night again?

RELLING–Didn't you hear him when I brought him home?

GINA–No, I can't say I did.

RELLING–That's as well. Molvik was *awful* last night.

GINA–Is this true, Molvik?

MOLVIK–Let us draw a veil over the events of last night. It was not a manifestation of my better self.

RELLING [*to* GREGERS] It comes on him like an inspiration. And then I have to go out and paint the town with him. Molvik's daemonic, you see.

GREGERS–Daemonic?

RELLING–Yes, daemonic.

GREGERS–Hm.

RELLING–And people who are born daemonic can't keep a straight course through life. They have to go off the rails now and then. Well, so you're still sticking it out at that ugly black mill, are you?

GREGERS – I have stuck it out until now.

RELLING – And did you manage to enforce that claim you went round pestering everyone with?

GREGERS – Claim?

[*Understands him.*]

I see.

HJALMAR – Have you been acting as a debt collector, Gregers?

GREGERS – Oh, nonsense.

RELLING – Oh yes, he has. He went round all the workmen's cottages, shoving something in their faces which he called the "claim of the ideal."

GREGERS – I was young then.

RELLING – You're right there. You were very young. And as for that claim of the ideal—you never got anyone to honour it before I left.

GREGERS – Nor since, either.

RELLING – Then I hope you've grown wise enough to reduce your demands a little.

GREGERS – Not when I stand face to face with a man.

HJALMAR – Well, that sounds reasonable enough. A little butter, Gina.

RELLING – And a slice of pork for Molvik.

MOLVIK – Oh no, not pork!

[*There is a knock on the door of the loft.*]

HJALMAR – Open the door, Hedvig. Father wants to come out.

[HEDVIG *goes across and opens the door a little.* OLD EKDAL *comes out with a fresh rabbit skin. She closes the door behind him.*]

EKDAL – Morning, gentlemen. Good hunting today. I've shot a big one.

HJALMAR – Why did you have to skin it before I came?

EKDAL – Salted it, too. It's good, tender meat, rabbit meat. Sweet, too. Tastes like sugar. Enjoy your dinner, gentlemen!

[*Goes into his room.*]

MOLVIK [*gets up*] Excuse me—I can't—I must—quickly—

RELLING – Drink some soda water, man!

MOLVIK [*hurries out*] Ah—ah!

[*Goes out through the front door.*]

RELLING [*to* HJALMAR] Let's drink to the old huntsman.

HJALMAR [*clinks glasses with him*] A great sportsman at the end of the road.

RELLING – His hair tempered with grey—

[*Drinks.*]

By the way, tell me, is his hair grey or white?

HJALMAR – Oh—somewhere between the two. Actually, he hasn't very many hairs left on his head.

RELLING – Well, one can get through the world with a wig, as one can with a mask. You're a lucky man, Ekdal. A beautiful mission to fight for—

HJALMAR – And I do fight for it, believe me.

RELLING – And a clever wife, jogging quietly in and out in her felt slippers, rocking her hips and making everything nice and comfortable for you.

HJALMAR – Yes, Gina.

[*Nods to her.*]

You are a good companion to have on life's journey.

GINA – Oh, get along with you!

RELLING – And then you have your little Hedvig.

HJALMAR [*moved*] My child, yes. Above all, my child. Hedvig, come to me.

[*Strokes her hair.*]

What day is it tomorrow, Hedvig?

HEDVIG [*shakes him*] Oh no, Father, you mustn't tell them!

HJALMAR – It wounds me like a knife through the heart when I think how poor it must be. Just a little party in the attic—

HEDVIG – But Father, that's just what's so wonderful!

RELLING – And just you wait till your father's ready with his great invention, Hedvig.

HJALMAR – Yes, then you'll see! Hedvig, I have resolved to secure your future. You shall never want. I shall make it a condition that you get—er—something or other. That shall be the poor inventor's sole reward.

HEDVIG [*whispers, her arm round his neck*] Oh, dear, kind Father!

RELLING [*to* GREGERS] Well, don't you find it pleasant for a change to sit down to a good meal surrounded by a happy family?

HJALMAR – Yes, I think I appreciate these hours at the table more than anything.

GREGERS – Personally I don't like poisonous fumes.

RELLING – Poisonous fumes!

HJALMAR – Oh, for heaven's sake, don't start that again.

GINA – By God, you'll find no fumes in here, Mr. Werle. I give the whole place a good airing every day.

GREGERS [*leaving the table*] You can't drive out the stench I mean by opening the windows.

HJALMAR – Stench!

GINA – How do you like that, Hjalmar!

RELLING – I beg your pardon—you couldn't possibly have brought the stench in yourself from those pits up there?

GREGERS – Yes, it's like you to call what I bring with me a stench.

RELLING [*goes over to him*] Listen, Mr. Werle Junior. I've a strong suspicion you're still carrying that "claim of the ideal" unabridged in your back pocket.

GREGERS—I carry it in my heart.

RELLING—Well, wherever you have the bloody thing I'm damned if I'll let you blackmail anyone with it as long as I'm in this house.

GREGERS—And if I choose to ignore your warning?

RELLING—Then you'll go headfirst down those stairs. Now you know.

HJALMAR [*gets up*] But—but, Relling—

GREGERS—All right, throw me out.

GINA [*goes between them*] Relling, you can't do that. But I must say, Mr. Werle, after the mess you made with your stove you're in no position to come and complain to me about fumes.

[*There is a knock on the front door.*]

HEDVIG—Mother, someone's knocking.

HJALMAR—Oh, now that's going to start.

GINA—Let me take care of it.

[*Goes over, opens the door and steps back in surprise.*]
Oh! Oh, no!

[HAAKON WERLE, *in a fur-lined coat with a fur collar, takes a step into the room.*]

WERLE—I beg your pardon, but I believe my son is living in this house.

GINA [*swallows*] Yes.

HJALMAR [*goes towards him*] Wouldn't you do us the honour, sir, to—?

WERLE—Thank you, I only want to speak to my son.

GREGERS—Well? I'm here. What is it?

WERLE—I want to speak to you in your room.

GREGERS—Oh? In my room?

[*Moves towards the door.*]

GINA—No, for heaven's sake, that's in no state—

WERLE—Out in the passage, then. I want to speak with you alone.

HJALMAR—You can do that here, sir. Relling, come into the parlour.
[HJALMAR *and* RELLING *go out to the right.* GINA *takes* HEDVIG *into the kitchen.*]

GREGERS [*after a short pause*] Well. Now we're alone.

WERLE—You let drop a few remarks last night about— And since you've now come to lodge with the Ekdals I can only assume that you intend some action directed against me.

GREGERS—I intend to open the eyes of Hjalmar Ekdal. He must see his situation as it really is. That is all.

WERLE—And that is the mission in life you spoke of yesterday?

GREGERS – Yes. It's the only one you have left me.

WERLE – So it's I who have soured your mind, Gregers?

GREGERS – You have soured my whole life. Oh, I'm not just thinking of what happened to my mother. But it's you I have to thank for the fact that I'm continually haunted by a guilty conscience.

WERLE – Oh, so it's your conscience that's queasy, is it?

GREGERS – I ought to have stood up to you when those traps were laid for Lieutenant Ekdal. I ought to have warned him. I knew in my mind what was going on.

WERLE – Then you ought to have spoken out.

GREGERS – I was frightened. I was a coward. I was so miserably afraid of you then. And long afterwards.

WERLE – You seem to have got over that very well now.

GREGERS – Yes, thank God, I have. The crimes that have been committed against old Ekdal, by me and by–others–can never be undone. But at least I can free Hjalmar from the conspiracy of silence and deceit which is killing him here.

WERLE – And you think that'd be doing him a service?

GREGERS – I have no doubt of it.

WERLE – You think this photographer is the kind of man who would thank you for such a proof of friendship?

GREGERS – Yes. He is that kind of man.

WERLE – Well. We shall see.

GREGERS – And besides–if I am to go on living, I must try to find some cure for my sick conscience.

WERLE – Your conscience has been sickly ever since you were a child. There's no cure for it. That's an heirloom from your mother, Gregers. The only thing she left you.

GREGERS [*with a scornful smile*] Haven't you got over your disappointment yet? You miscalculated badly, didn't you, when you thought you'd get rich through her.

WERLE – Don't try to distract me with irrelevancies. Are you still resolved to carry out your intention of guiding Ekdal on to what you suppose to be the right path?

GREGERS – Yes. I am resolved.

WERLE – In that case I might have saved myself the trouble of climbing the stairs. I don't suppose it's any use now asking if you'll come back home?

GREGERS – No.

WERLE – And you won't enter the firm either, I suppose?

GREGERS – No.

WERLE – Very good. But since I am intending to enter into a new marriage, I will arrange for the estate to be divided between us.

GREGERS [*quickly*] No, I don't want that.

WERLE—You don't want it?

GREGERS—No. My conscience won't allow me.

WERLE [*after a moment*] Are you going back to the mill?

GREGERS—No. I have left your service.

WERLE—But what will you do?

GREGERS—I shall simply fulfil my mission. That is all.

WERLE—But afterwards? How will you live?

GREGERS—I have saved a little out of my salary.

WERLE—Yes, but how long will that last?

GREGERS—I think it will see me through.

WERLE—What does that mean?

GREGERS—I think you've asked me enough questions.

WERLE—Good-bye, then, Gregers.

GREGERS—Good-bye.

[HAAKON WERLE *goes out.*]

HJALMAR [*looks in*] Has he gone?

GREGERS—Yes.

[HJALMAR *and* RELLING *come in.* GINA *and* HEDVIG *enter from the kitchen.*]

RELLING—Well, that's the end of our lunch.

GREGERS—Get your coat, Hjalmar. You and I must take a long walk together.

HJALMAR—Yes, let's. What did your father want? Was it anything to do with me?

GREGERS—Come along. We must have a little talk. I'll go and fetch my coat.

[*Goes out through the front door.*]

GINA—I don't like you going out with him, Hjalmar.

RELLING—She's right. Stay here with us.

HJALMAR [*takes his hat and overcoat*] What! When an old school-fellow feels the need to pour out his heart to me—?

RELLING—But, for Christ's sake—don't you see the fellow's mad, twisted, out of his mind?

GINA—There you are! Well, what do you expect? His mother had weird fits like that too, sometimes.

HJALMAR—All the more need for someone to keep a friendly eye on him, then.

[*To* GINA.]

Make sure dinner's ready in good time. Good-bye for now.

[*Goes out through the front door.*]

RELLING—What a pity that fellow didn't fall into one of his own mines and drop right down to Hell!

GINA—Mercy on us! Why do you say that?

RELLING [*mutters*] Oh, I have my reasons.

GINA—Do you think young Mr. Werle's really mad?

RELLING—No, worse luck. He's no madder than most people. He's sick all right, though.

GINA—What do you think's wrong with him?

RELLING—I'll tell you, Mrs. Ekdal. He's suffering from a surfeit of self-righteousness.

GINA—Surfeit of self-righteousness?

HEDVIG—Is that a disease?

RELLING—Yes. It's a national disease. But it only very seldom becomes acute.

[*Nods to* GINA.]

Thanks for the lunch.

[*Goes out through the front door.*]

GINA [*walks round uneasily*] Ugh! That Gregers Werle. He always was a queer fish.

HEDVIG [*stands by the table and looks searchingly at her*] I think this is all very strange.

ACT FOUR

HJALMAR EKDAL'S *studio. A photograph has just been taken; a camera with a cloth over it, a stand, two or three chairs, a folding table, etc., stand round the room. Afternoon light; the sun is just going down; a little later it begins to grow dark.* GINA *is standing in the open doorway with a small box and a wet glass plate in her hand, talking to someone outside.*

GINA – Yes, definitely. When I make a promise I always keep it. I'll have the first dozen ready by Monday. Good-bye, good-bye.

[*The other person goes downstairs.* GINA *closes the door, puts the glass plate in the box and places the latter in the covered camera.*]

HEDVIG [*comes in from the kitchen*] Have they gone?

GINA [*tidying up*] Yes, thank God, I got rid of them at last.

HEDVIG – Why do you suppose Father hasn't come home yet?

GINA – Are you sure he's not down with Relling?

HEDVIG – No, he's not there. I've just run down the back stairs to ask.

GINA – And his dinner's getting cold too, I suppose?

HEDVIG – It's funny—Father's always on time for dinner.

GINA – Oh, he'll be here soon. You'll see.

HEDVIG – I wish he'd come. Everything seems so strange suddenly.

GINA [*cries out*] Here he is!

[HJALMAR EKDAL *comes in through the front door.*]

HEDVIG [*runs towards him*] Oh, Father! Oh, we've waited and waited for you!

GINA [*gives him a glance*] You've been a long time, Hjalmar.

HJALMAR [*without looking at her*] Yes, I have rather, haven't I?

[*He takes off his overcoat.* GINA *and* HEDVIG *try to help him, but he gestures them away.*]

GINA – Have you eaten with Werle?

HJALMAR [*hangs up his coat*] No.

GINA [*goes towards the kitchen door*] I'll bring in your food, then.

HJALMAR – No, never mind the food. I don't want any.

HEDVIG [*goes closer*] Aren't you well, Father?

1261

H J A L M A R – Well? Oh yes, tolerably. We had rather a tiring walk, Gregers and I.

G I N A – You shouldn't do that, Hjalmar. You're not used to it.

H J A L M A R – But there are a lot of things in life a man's got to get used to.

[*Wanders round a little.*]

Anyone been here while I was out?

G I N A – Only those two sweethearts.

H J A L M A R – No new orders?

G I N A – No, not today.

H E D V I G – There'll be some tomorrow, Father. You'll see.

H J A L M A R – Let's hope so. Because tomorrow I intend to start working in real earnest.

H E D V I G – Tomorrow? But don't you remember what day it is tomorrow?

H J A L M A R – Ah, that's true. Well, the day after tomorrow, then. From now on I'm going to do everything myself. I'm going to manage the whole business on my own.

G I N A – But why should you do that, Hjalmar? It'll only make you miserable. No, I'll take care of the photography, and you can go on puzzling with your invention.

H E D V I G – And think of the wild duck, Father. And all the hens and rabbits, and—

H J A L M A R – Don't talk to me about all that nonsense. From now on I shall never set foot in that loft again.

H E D V I G – But Father, you promised tomorrow we'd have a party—

H J A L M A R – Hm, that's true. Well, from the day after tomorrow, then. I'd like to wring the neck of that damned wild duck.

H E D V I G [*screams*] The wild duck!

G I N A – I never heard such nonsense!

H E D V I G [*shaking him*] But Father! It's my wild duck!

H J A L M A R – That's why I won't do it. I haven't the heart to—I haven't the heart—because of you, Hedvig. But I know in my heart that I ought to do it. I ought not to allow any creature to live under my roof which has been in *his* hands.

G I N A – For heaven's sake! Just because Grandfather got it from that wretched Pettersen—

H J A L M A R [*wandering around*] There are certain demands—demands a man makes of himself—how shall I put it?—a striving for perfection —one might say the demands of an ideal—which a man may not ignore without danger to his soul.

H E D V I G [*goes after him*] But Father, the wild duck! The poor wild duck!

HJALMAR [*stops*] I've told you I shall spare it. For your sake. I shall not touch a hair of its—well, as I told you, I shall spare it. I have more important tasks than that to get down to. But you'd better go and take your walk now, Hedvig. It's getting dark—the light won't hurt your eyes now.

HEDVIG—No, I won't bother to go out today.

HJALMAR—Yes, you must. You screw up your eyes so; all these fumes in here are bad for you. The air under this roof is unclean.

HEDVIG—All right, all right. I'll run down the back stairs and go for a little walk. My coat and hat? Oh, they're in my room. Father, you won't hurt the wild duck while I'm out?

HJALMAR—Not a feather of its head shall be touched.

[*Presses her to him.*]

You and I, Hedvig—we two—! Well, run along.

[HEDVIG *nods to her parents and goes out through the kitchen.*]

HJALMAR [*walks around without looking up*] Gina.

GINA—Yes?

HJALMAR—From tomorrow—or let's say the day after tomorrow—I'd like to keep the household accounts myself.

GINA—You want to look after the household accounts too now?

HJALMAR—Yes. I want to find out where the money comes from.

GINA—Well, heaven knows that won't take you long.

HJALMAR—One would imagine it would. You seem to make it go a remarkably long way.

[*Stops and looks at her.*]

How do you do it?

GINA—It's because Hedvig and I need so little.

HJALMAR—Is it true that Father gets paid very generously for the copying he does for Mr. Werle?

GINA—I don't know if it's so very generous. But then I don't know what that kind of work is worth.

HJALMAR—Well, roughly how much does he get? Come on, tell me!

GINA—It varies. On an average about what it costs us to keep him, and a bit of pocket money over.

HJALMAR—What it costs us to keep him! And you never told me!

GINA—How could I? You were so happy because you thought he got everything from you.

HJALMAR—And all the time he gets it from Mr. Werle!

GINA—Oh, there's more where that comes from.

HJALMAR—I suppose we'd better light that lamp.

GINA [*lights it*] Of course, we don't know if it's the old man himself. It might easily be Graaberg—

HJALMAR—Why drag in Graaberg?

GINA—No, I don't know. I just thought—

HJALMAR—Hm!

GINA—I didn't get this work for Grandfather. It was Berta—when she came to live there.

HJALMAR—Your voice has gone funny.

GINA [*puts the shade on the lamp*] My voice?

HJALMAR—And your hands are trembling. Do you deny it?

GINA [*firmly*] Don't beat about the bush, Hjalmar. What's he been telling you about me?

HJALMAR—Is it true—can it be true—that there was a kind of relationship between you and Mr. Werle when you were in his service?

GINA—No, it's not true. Not at that time. Oh, he was after me, all right. And Mrs. Werle thought there was something doing; she created a great hullaballoo, and pulled my hair, she did, so I gave my notice and went.

HJALMAR—But it happened afterwards!

GINA—Yes, well I went home. And Mother—she wasn't such a simple soul as you thought, Hjalmar. She kept talking to me about one thing and another. Well, the old man was a widower by then, you see—

HJALMAR—Go on!

GINA—Well, I suppose you'd better know. He wouldn't give in till he'd had his way.

HJALMAR—And this is the mother of my child! How could you keep such a thing from me?

GINA—Yes, it was very wrong. I ought to have told you about it long ago.

HJALMAR—You ought to have told me at once. Then I'd have known what kind of woman you were.

GINA—If I had, would you have married me?

HJALMAR—What do you think?

GINA—Yes, well, that's why I didn't dare to say anything to you at the time. You know how fond I'd grown of you. How could I throw away my whole life?

HJALMAR [*walking about*] And this is the mother of my Hedvig! And to know that everything I see around me—

[*Kicks a chair.*]

—my entire home—I owe to a predecessor in your favours! Oh, that seductive old Werle!

GINA—Do you regret the fifteen years we have lived together?

HJALMAR [*stops in front of her*] Have you not every day, every moment, regretted the web of concealment and deceit that you've spun around me like a spider? Answer me that! Do you mean to tell me that all this time you haven't been living in anguish and remorse?

GINA – Oh, my dear Hjalmar, I've had enough to think about trying to run the house without—

HJALMAR – Then you never probe your past with a questioning eye?

GINA – You know, I'd almost forgotten the whole dirty business.

HJALMAR – Oh, this soulless, unfeeling complacency! It always fills me with moral indignation. And what is more, you don't even regret it!

GINA – Yes, but tell me, Hjalmar. What would have become of you if you hadn't had a wife like me?

HJALMAR – Like you?

GINA – Yes; I've always been a little more down-to-earth and practical than you. Well, it's natural, I suppose, I'm just that much older.

HJALMAR – What would have become of me!

GINA – Yes. You'd gone a bit off the rails when you met me. You surely won't deny that.

HJALMAR – You call that going off the rails? Oh, you don't understand what it's like when a man is full of sorrow and despair. Particularly a man of my fiery temperament.

GINA – No, no. Perhaps I don't. Anyway, I'm not complaining; you became such a good man once you'd got a house and home of your own. And now it was getting to be so homely and nice here; and Hedvig and I were just thinking we might be able to spend a little on food and clothes.

HJALMAR – Yes, in this swamp of deceit.

GINA – Oh, why did that repulsive little man have to come to our house?

HJALMAR – I too used to think this was a good home. It was a delusion. Where shall I now find the strength I need to transfer my invention into terms of reality? Perhaps it will die with me. And it will be your past, Gina, which will have killed it.

GINA [*on the verge of tears*] No, you mustn't say things like that, Hjalmar. All our married life I've never thought of anyone but you.

HJALMAR – I ask you—what will become of the breadwinner's dream now? As I lay in there on the sofa brooding over the invention I had a feeling that it would devour my energies to the last drop. I sensed that the day on which I held the patent in my hands—that day would spell my release. And it was my dream that you should live on as the late inventor's prosperous widow.

GINA [*drying her tears*] Now you mustn't talk like that, Hjalmar. May the good Lord never let me live to see myself a widow.

HJALMAR – Oh, what does it matter? It's all finished now. Everything!

[GREGERS WERLE *cautiously opens the front door and looks in.*]

GREGERS – May one come in?

HJALMAR – Yes, come in.

GREGERS [*comes forward with a radiant, gratified expression and holds out his hands to them*] Well, my dear friends!

> [*Looks from one to the other and whispers to* HJALMAR.]

Hasn't it happened yet?

HJALMAR–Oh, it has happened.

GREGERS–It has!

HJALMAR–I have just lived through the bitterest moment of my life.

GREGERS–But also, surely, the most sublime.

HJALMAR–Well, we've put that behind us. For the time being, anyway.

GINA–May God forgive you, Mr. Werle.

GREGERS [*greatly amazed*] But what I don't see is—

HJALMAR–What don't you see?

GREGERS–From such a crisis there must spring a mutual understanding on which a whole new life can be founded—a partnership built on truth, without concealment.

HJALMAR–Yes, I know, Gregers. I know.

GREGERS–I felt so sure, that when I walked through that door you would be standing there transfigured, and that my eyes would be dazzled by the light. And instead I see nothing but this dull heaviness and misery—

GINA–Oh, I see.

> [*Takes the shade off the lamp.*]

GREGERS–You don't want to understand me, Mrs. Ekdal. Ah, well. I suppose you need a bit more time. But you, Hjalmar, you? Surely you must have gained a higher understanding now that the crisis is over?

HJALMAR–Yes, of course I have. That is—in a kind of way.

GREGERS–For there is nothing in the world that can compare with the joy of forgiving someone who has sinned, and raising her to one's heart in love.

HJALMAR–Do you think that a man can so easily digest the bitter draught that I have just drained?

GREGERS–Not an ordinary man, perhaps. But a man like you—

HJALMAR–Oh yes, I know, I know. But you mustn't rush me, Gregers. It takes time, you see.

GREGERS–There's a lot of the wild duck in you, Hjalmar.

> [RELLING *has entered through the front door.*]

RELLING–So the wild duck's in the air again?

HJALMAR–Yes. Mr. Werle's winged victim.

RELLING–Mr. Werle? Are you talking about him?

HJALMAR–About him and—the rest of us.

RELLING [*aside, to* GREGERS] You bloody fool, why don't you go to Hell?

HJALMAR – What did you say?

RELLING – I was expressing my heartfelt desire to see this quack doctor back where he belongs. If he stays here he's quite capable of messing up both your lives.

GREGERS – You needn't fear for these two, Dr. Relling. I shan't speak about Hjalmar. We both know him. But in her too, deep in her heart, there is something of honesty and truthfulness.

GINA [*near to tears*] Then you ought to have let me stay as I was.

RELLING – Would it be impertinent to ask exactly what it is you're trying to do in this house?

GREGERS – I want to lay the foundations of a true marriage.

RELLING – Then you don't think their marriage is good enough as it stands?

GREGERS – It's probably as good a marriage as most others, I'm afraid. But it is not yet a true marriage.

HJALMAR – You've never had much faith in ideals, Dr. Relling.

RELLING – Rubbish, my boy! May I ask, Mr. Werle—how many true marriages have you seen in your life? Just roughly.

GREGERS – I hardly think I've seen a single one.

RELLING – Neither have I.

GREGERS – But I've seen so many, many marriages of the opposite kind. And I've had the opportunity to study one at sufficiently close quarters to realise how it can demoralise two human beings.

HJALMAR – The whole moral foundation of a man's life can crumble under his feet. That's the terrible thing.

RELLING – Yes, well, I've never been what you'd call married, so I wouldn't presume to judge. But I do know this, that children are as much a part of any marriage as their parents. So you leave that child alone.

HJALMAR – Ah! Hedvig! My poor Hedvig!

RELLING – Yes, I'll thank you to keep Hedvig out of this. You two are adults; muck about with your own lives if you enjoy it. But I'm warning you, be gentle with Hedvig, or you may do her irreparable harm.

HJALMAR – Harm?

RELLING – Yes, or she may come to do herself harm—and perhaps others too.

GINA – What would you know about that, Relling?

HJALMAR – There isn't any immediate danger to her eyes, is there?

RELLING – This has nothing to do with her eyes. Hedvig's at a difficult age just now. She's capable of getting up to anything.

GINA – Yes, that's true—I've noticed it already. She's started fooling around with the kitchen stove. She calls it playing with fire. I'm often afraid she'll burn down the house.

RELLING – There you are. You see. I thought as much.

GREGERS [*to* RELLING] But how would you explain that kind of behaviour?

RELLING [*quietly*] My boy. Her voice is breaking.

HJALMAR – As long as the child has me— As long as my head is above the ground—

[*There is a knock on the door.*]

GINA – Quiet, Hjalmar. There's someone on the landing.

[*Calls.*]

Come in.

[MRS. SOERBY *enters, in an overcoat.*]

MRS. SOERBY – Good evening.

GINA [*goes to greet her*] Berta, is it you?

MRS. SOERBY – Yes, it's me. But perhaps I've come at an inconvenient moment?

HJALMAR – Of course not. Any messenger from that house is always—

MRS. SOERBY [*to* GINA] To be honest, I hoped I might find you alone at this hour of the evening, so I looked in to have a chat and to say good-bye.

GINA – Oh? Are you going away?

MRS. SOERBY – Yes. Tomorrow morning. Up to Hoydal. Mr. Werle left this afternoon.

[*Casually, to* GREGERS.]

He asked to be remembered to you.

GINA – Well, fancy that!

HJALMAR – So Mr. Werle has gone away. And you're going after him?

MRS. SOERBY – Yes. What have you got to say about that, Ekdal?

HJALMAR – I say: take care!

GREGERS – I'd better explain. My father is marrying Mrs. Soerby.

HJALMAR – Going to *marry* her?

GINA – Berta! So it's happened at last!

RELLING [*with a slight tremor in his voice*] This isn't true, surely?

MRS. SOERBY – Yes, dear Relling, it's perfectly true.

RELLING – You want to get married again?

MRS. SOERBY – Yes, I've decided I do. Mr. Werle has obtained a special licence, and we're going to get married quite quietly up at Hoydal.

GREGERS – Well, in that case nothing remains but to wish you happiness, as a dutiful stepson.

MRS. SOERBY—Thank you; if you really mean it. I certainly hope it will bring happiness to Mr. Werle and to me.

RELLING—Oh, I'm sure it will. Mr. Werle never gets drunk—as far as I know—and I don't think he's in the habit of beating up his wives, as the late lamented horse-doctor used to.

MRS. SOERBY—Oh, let Soerby rest in peace. He had his good points.

RELLING—But Mr. Werle, we gather, has better ones.

MRS. SOERBY—At least he hasn't wasted all that was best in him. Men who do that must accept the consequences.

RELLING—I'm going out with Molvik tonight.

MRS. SOERBY—Don't do that, Relling. Please, for my sake.

RELLING—What else do you suggest?

[*To* HJALMAR.]

Care to join us?

GINA—No, thank you. Hjalmar doesn't go on that kind of spree.

HJALMAR [*aside, irritated*] Oh, be quiet.

RELLING—Good-bye, Mrs.—Werle.

[*Goes out through front door.*]

GREGERS [*to* MRS. SOERBY] It seems that you and Dr. Relling know each other pretty well.

MRS. SOERBY—Yes, we've known each other for many years. At one time it even seemed as though our friendship might lead to something more permanent.

GREGERS—Lucky for you it didn't.

MRS. SOERBY—I know. But I've always been wary of acting on impulse. A woman can't just throw herself away, can she?

GREGERS—Aren't you afraid I might tell my father about this old friendship?

MRS. SOERBY—You don't imagine I haven't told him myself?

GREGERS—Oh?

MRS. SOERBY—Anything anyone could truthfully say about me I have already told him. It was the first thing I did when I gathered his intentions.

GREGERS—In that case you've been uncommonly frank.

MRS. SOERBY—I've always been frank. It's by far the best policy for a woman.

HJALMAR—What do you say to that, Gina?

GINA—Oh, we women are so different. We can't all be like Berta.

MRS. SOERBY—Well, Gina, I really believe I did the only sensible thing. Mr. Werle hasn't hidden anything from me, either. And perhaps that's what binds us so closely. Now he can talk to me as freely as a child. He's never been able to do that with anyone before. Fancy a strong and vigorous man like him having to spend all his youth and the best years of his life listening to sermons—very often occasioned by quite imaginary offences, from what I've heard.

GINA – Yes, that's true enough.

GREGERS – If you ladies are going to discuss that subject, I had better go.

MRS. SOERBY – Don't bother. I've had my say. I haven't lied to him or kept anything from him. I dare say you think I've done very well for myself. Well, perhaps I have. But I don't think I'm taking more than I shall be able to give him. I shall never fail him. I shall serve him and look after him better than anyone, now that he's growing helpless.

HJALMAR – He? Growing helpless?

GREGERS [*to* MRS. SOERBY] Look, I'd rather we didn't discuss that.

MRS. SOERBY – It's no use trying to hide it any longer, though I know he wants to. He's going blind.

HJALMAR [*starts*] Going blind? That's strange. Is he going blind, too?

GINA – It happens to lots of people.

MRS. SOERBY – It's not hard to imagine what that must mean to a man like him. Well, I shall try to make my eyes serve for the two of us as best I can. But I mustn't stay any longer, I've so much to do just now. Oh, what I wanted to tell you, Ekdal, was that if there's anything Mr. Werle can ever do for you, just go and speak to Graaberg.

GREGERS – I hardly think Hjalmar Ekdal will want to accept that offer.

MRS. SOERBY – Oh? I haven't noticed in the past that he—

GINA – Yes, Berta. Hjalmar doesn't need to take anything from Mr. Werle any longer.

HJALMAR [*slowly and emphatically*] Will you present my compliments to your future husband and tell him that I intend at the earliest opportunity to visit Mr. Graaberg—

GREGERS – Hjalmar!

HJALMAR – I repeat, to visit Mr. Graaberg and demand from him an account of the sum I owe his employer. I shall repay this debt of honour—

[*Laughs.*]

—debt of honour! But enough of that. I shall repay it to the last penny, with five per cent interest.

GINA – But my dear Hjalmar, we haven't the money to do that.

HJALMAR – Will you please tell your fiancé that I am working indefatigably at my invention. Will you tell him that my spirit is sustained throughout this exhausting struggle by the desire to be rid of the embarrassing burden of this debt. That is why I have become an inventor.

The entire profits shall be used to free me from the money of which your prospective husband has seen fit to disgorge himself.

M R S . S O E R B Y – What's been going on in this house?

H J A L M A R – Never mind.

M R S . S O E R B Y – Well, good-bye. There was something else I wanted to talk to you about, Gina; but it'll have to wait till another time. Good-bye.

[H JALMAR *and* GREGERS *bow silently.* GINA *accompanies* MRS. SOERBY *to the door.*]

H J A L M A R – Not beyond the threshold, Gina.

[MRS. SOERBY *goes.* GINA *closes the door behind her.*]

There, Gregers. Thank God I've managed to get that debt off my conscience.

G R E G E R S – Well, you will soon, anyway.

H J A L M A R – I think I can claim I behaved correctly.

G R E G E R S – You behaved exactly as I always knew you would.

H J A L M A R – A time comes when a man can no longer ignore the command of his ideals. As the family breadwinner I am continually tormented by this command. I tell you, Gregers, it isn't easy for a man of small means to repay an old debt on which, as one might say, there has settled the dust of oblivion. But there's no other way. I must do what is right.

G R E G E R S [*puts his hand on* H JALMAR'S *shoulders*] My dear Hjalmar. Aren't you glad I came?

H J A L M A R – Yes.

G R E G E R S – Aren't you glad to see yourself as you really are?

H J A L M A R [*a little impatiently*] Of course I'm glad. But there's one thing which troubles my sense of justice. Well, but I don't know whether I should speak so bluntly about your father.

G R E G E R S – Say what you like. I don't mind.

H J A L M A R – Well, then—it offends me to think that it is he, and not I, who is going to make a true marriage.

G R E G E R S – What are you saying!

H J A L M A R – But it's true. Your father and Mrs. Soerby are entering upon a marriage founded on absolute trust, with complete frankness on both sides. They are keeping nothing from each other. They have confessed their sins, if I may so put it, and have forgiven each other.

G R E G E R S – Well, what of it?

H J A L M A R – But that's the whole point. You just said yourself that it's only by overcoming all that that you can found a true marriage.

G R E G E R S – But that's quite different, Hjalmar. You surely don't compare yourself or her with these two—? Well, you know what I mean.

H J A L M A R – I can't get away from the fact that there's something here

1271

which wounds and offends my sense of justice. Well, it looks as though there's no just power ruling this world.

GINA–Oh, Hjalmar, really! You mustn't speak like that!

GREGERS–Hm—let's not get on to that subject!

HJALMAR–But on the other hand I seem to see the finger of fate at work restoring the balance. He is going blind.

GINA–Oh, we don't know for sure about that.

HJALMAR–Can we doubt it? At least, we ought not to; for there lie justice and retribution. He has blinded a loyal and trusting friend—

GREGERS–I'm afraid he has blinded many.

HJALMAR–And now comes the inexorable, the unfathomable, and demands his own eyes.

GINA–Oh, how can you say such a horrible thing? You make me feel quite frightened.

HJALMAR–It is useful to face up to the darker aspects of existence now and then.

[HEDVIG, *in her hat and coat, enters happy and breathless through the front door.*]

GINA–Are you back already?

HEDVIG–Yes, I didn't want to walk any more. And a good thing too, for I met someone coming out of the front door.

HJALMAR–That Mrs. Soerby, I suppose.

HEDVIG–Yes.

HJALMAR [*walking up and down*] I hope you have seen her for the last time.

[*Silence.* HEDVIG *looks timidly from one to the other as though to find out what is the matter.*]

HEDVIG [*goes nearer him; wooingly*] Father.

HJALMAR–Well, what is it, Hedvig?

HEDVIG–Mrs. Soerby brought something for me.

HJALMAR [*stops*] For you?

HEDVIG–Yes. Something for tomorrow.

GINA–Berta always brings something for your birthday.

HJALMAR–What is it?

HEDVIG–No, you mustn't know yet. Mother's going to bring it to me in bed tomorrow morning.

HJALMAR–Oh, this conspiracy to keep me out of everything!

HEDVIG [*quickly*] No, of course you can see it. It's a big letter.
[*Takes the letter from her coat pocket.*]

HJALMAR–A letter too?

HEDVIG–Only a letter. The present'll come later, I suppose. But fancy —a letter! I've never had a letter before. And there's "Miss" written on the outside!

[*Reads.*]
"Miss Hedvig Ekdal." That's me!

HJALMAR – Let me see that letter.

HEDVIG [*holds it out to him*] Here—look!

HJALMAR – This is Mr. Werle's writing.

GINA – Are you sure, Hjalmar?

HJALMAR – Look for yourself.

GINA – How should I know?

HJALMAR – Hedvig, may I open this letter and read it?

HEDVIG – Yes, certainly, if you want to.

GINA – No, Hjalmar, not tonight. It's for tomorrow.

HEDVIG [*quietly*] Oh, do let him read it, please! It's sure to be something nice, and then Father'll be happy, and it'll be nice here again.

HJALMAR – I may open it, then?

HEDVIG – Yes, do, Father. It'll be fun to know what's in it.

HJALMAR – Right.

[*Opens the letter, takes out a sheet of paper, reads it and looks bewildered.*]
What on earth—?

GINA – What does it say?

HEDVIG – Oh yes, Father! Do tell us!

HJALMAR – Be quiet!

[*Reads it through again. Then, pale but controlled, he says.*]
It's a deed of gift, Hedvig.

HEDVIG – I say! What do I get?

HJALMAR – See for yourself.

[HEDVIG *goes over to the lamp and reads the letter under it.* HJALMAR *softly, clenching his fists.*]
The eyes! The eyes! And this letter!

HEDVIG [*looks up from her reading*] But I think Grandfather ought to have it.

HJALMAR [*takes the letter from her*] Gina, can you make any sense of this?

GINA – You know I don't understand anything. Tell me what it's about.

HJALMAR – Mr. Werle writes to Hedvig that her old grandfather need no longer trouble to copy letters but that he can henceforth draw from the office the sum of one hundred crowns per month—

GINA – Really?

HEDVIG – A hundred crowns, Mother! That's what it says!

GINA – Well, that'll be nice for Grandfather.

HJALMAR – One hundred crowns, for as long as he needs it. That means, of course, for as long as he lives.

GINA – Well, at least he's provided for then, poor old man.

H J A L M A R – But there's something else. You didn't read this part, Hedvig. Afterwards, this money is to be paid to you.

H E D V I G – To me? All of it?

H J A L M A R – "You are assured of this sum for the rest of your life," he writes. Did you hear that, Gina?

G I N A – Yes, I heard.

H E D V I G – Imagine all the money I'm going to have!

[*Shakes him.*]

Oh, Father, Father, aren't you happy–?

H J A L M A R [*avoids her*] Happy!

[*Walks about.*]

Oh, what vistas, what perspectives begin to unroll before my eyes! It's Hedvig! She's the one he remembers so generously!

G I N A – Yes–well, it's Hedvig's birthday.

H E D V I G – But you shall have it all, Father! I want to give all the money to you and Mother!

H J A L M A R – Yes, to Mother! There we have it!

G R E G E R S – Hjalmar, this is a trap which has been laid for you.

H J A L M A R – You think this is another trap?

G R E G E R S – When he was here this morning, he said to me: "Hjalmar Ekdal is not the man you think he is."

H J A L M A R – Not the man–!

G R E G E R S – "You'll see," he said.

H J A L M A R – Meaning that I would let myself be fobbed off with money!

H E D V I G – Mother, what are they talking about?

G I N A – Go in there and take your coat off.

[HEDVIG *goes out through the kitchen door, almost in tears.*]

G R E G E R S – Well, Hjalmar, now we shall see which of us is right. He or I.

H J A L M A R [*slowly tears the letter in two and puts the pieces on the table*] There is my reply.

G R E G E R S – I knew it would be.

H J A L M A R [*goes over to* GINA *who is standing by the stove and says in a low voice*] And now let's have the truth. If it was all over between you and him when you–began to grow fond of me, as you put it–why did he make it possible for us to get married?

G I N A – I suppose he thought he could have a key.

H J A L M A R – Was that all? Wasn't he afraid of a certain possibility?

G I N A – I don't know what you mean.

H J A L M A R – I want to know if–your child has the right to live beneath my roof.

G I N A [*draws herself up; her eyes flash*] You ask me that?

H J A L M A R – Answer me! Is Hedvig mine or–? Well?

GINA [*looks at him in cold defiance*] I don't know.

HJALMAR [*trembles slightly*] You don't know!

GINA – How could I? You know yourself what I'm like.

HJALMAR [*quietly, turning away from her*] Then I have no further business in this house.

GREGERS – Consider, Hjalmar!

HJALMAR [*puts on his overcoat*] There's nothing for a man like me to consider.

GREGERS – You're wrong. There's a great deal to consider. You three must stay together if you are to win the forgiveness that comes with self-sacrifice.

HJALMAR – I don't want to win it! Never, never! My hat!

[*Takes his hat.*]

My home has crashed in ruins about me!

[*Bursts into tears.*]

Gregers, I have no child!

HEDVIG [*who has opened the kitchen door*] What are you saying!

[*Runs over to him.*]

Daddy, daddy!

GINA – There, you see!

HJALMAR – Don't come near me, Hedvig! Go–go far away! I can't bear to look at you! Ah–those eyes! Good-bye!

[*Goes towards the door.*]

HEDVIG [*clings tightly to him and screams*] No! No! Don't leave me!

GINA [*cries*] Look at the child, Hjalmar! Look at the child!

HJALMAR – I won't! I can't! I must get away! Away from all this!

[*Tears himself free from* HEDVIG *and goes out through the front door.*]

HEDVIG [*with despair in her eyes*] He's leaving us, Mother! He's leaving us! He'll never come back again!

GINA – Don't cry, Hedvig. Daddy will come back.

HEDVIG [*throws herself sobbing on the sofa*] No, no. He'll never come back to us again.

GREGERS – Will you believe that I meant it all for your good, Mrs. Ekdal?

GINA – Yes, I believe it. But God forgive you.

HEDVIG [*lying on the sofa*] Oh, I shall die, I shall die! What have I done to him? Mother, you must make him come back home!

GINA – Yes, yes, yes, all right. Calm yourself, and I'll go out and look for him.

[*Puts on her overcoat.*]

Perhaps he's just gone down to Relling. But you mustn't lie there and cry. Promise me?

HEDVIG [*sobbing convulsively*] Yes, I'll stop. When Father comes back.

GREGERS [*to* GINA, *as she is about to go*] Wouldn't it be better to let him fight his bitter battle to the end?

GINA – Oh, that'll have to wait. Now we must think of the child.

[*Goes out through the front door.*]

HEDVIG [*sits up and dries her tears*] I want to know what all this means. Why won't Father look at me any more?

GREGERS – You mustn't ask that till you're grown up.

HEDVIG [*catches her breath*] But I can't go on being unhappy like this all the time till I'm grown up. I know what it is. I'm not really Daddy's child.

GREGERS [*uneasily*] How on earth could that be?

HEDVIG – Mummy might have found me. And perhaps Father's got to know about it. I've read of things like that.

GREGERS – Well, but even if it were true—

HEDVIG – Yes, I think he should love me just the same. Or even more. After all, we got the wild duck sent to us as a present, but I love it very much.

GREGERS [*changing the conversation*] Yes, that's true. Let's talk for a moment about the wild duck, Hedvig.

HEDVIG – The poor wild duck. He can't bear to look at her any longer, either. Do you know, he wants to wring her neck!

GREGERS – Oh, I'm sure he won't do that.

HEDVIG – No, but he said it. And I think it was such a horrid thing for Father to say. I say a prayer for the wild duck every evening. I pray that she may be delivered from death and from all evil.

GREGERS [*looks at her*] Do you always say your prayers at night?

HEDVIG – Oh, yes.

GREGERS – Who taught you to do that?

HEDVIG – I taught myself. Once when Father was very ill, and had leeches on his neck. He said death was staring him in the face.

GREGERS – Yes?

HEDVIG – So I said a prayer for him after I'd gone to bed. And since then I've kept it up.

GREGERS – And now you pray for the wild duck, too?

HEDVIG – I thought I'd better include her, because she was so ill when she first came to us.

GREGERS – Do you say your prayers in the morning, too?

HEDVIG – Oh, no. Of course not.

GREGERS – Well, why not in the morning?

HEDVIG – In the morning it's light, and then there's nothing to be afraid of any more.

GREGERS – And your father wanted to wring the neck of the wild duck, which you love so much?

HEDVIG – No, he said he ought to, but he'd spare her for my sake. That was kind of him, wasn't it?

GREGERS [*a little closer*] Yes, but what if you now gave up the wild duck for his sake?

HEDVIG [*rises*] The wild duck?

GREGERS – Yes. Suppose you sacrificed for him the most precious of your possessions—the thing you love most dearly?

HEDVIG – Do you think that would help?

GREGERS – Try it, Hedvig.

HEDVIG [*quietly, her eyes aglow*] Yes, I will try it.

GREGERS – Do you think you have the strength to do it?

HEDVIG – I'll ask Grandfather to shoot the wild duck for me.

GREGERS – Yes, do that. But not a word to your mother about this!

HEDVIG – Why not?

GREGERS – She doesn't understand us.

HEDVIG – The wild duck! I'll do it tomorrow morning.

[GINA *comes in through the front door.*]

[HEDVIG *goes to meet her.*]

Did you find him, Mother?

GINA – No. But I heard he'd called in to see Relling and they'd gone off together.

GREGERS – Are you sure?

GINA – Yes, the caretaker told me. Molvik went with them too, she said.

GREGERS – Now, when he needs to wrestle with his soul alone!

GINA [*takes off her coat*] Well, men are difficult creatures. God knows where Relling's dragged him off to. I ran over to Mrs. Eriksen's, but they weren't there.

HEDVIG [*trying not to cry*] Oh, suppose he never comes back!

GREGERS – He'll come back. I shall tell him the news tomorrow, and then you'll see how quickly he will come. Don't worry, Hedvig. You can sleep in peace. Good night.

[*Goes out through the front door.*]

HEDVIG [*throws her arms, sobbing, round* GINA's *neck*] Mummy, mummy!

GINA [*pats her on the back and sighs*] Oh, yes, Relling was right. This is what happens when people go round preaching about the commands of the ideal.

ACT FIVE

HJALMAR EKDAL's *studio. A cold, grey morning light. Wet snow lies on the large panes of glass in the roof.* GINA, *wearing an apron, enters from the kitchen with a brush and duster and goes towards the parlour door. At the same moment,* HEDVIG *runs in from the passage.*

GINA [*stops*] Well?

HEDVIG – Yes, Mother, I think he's down with Relling–

GINA – There you are!

HEDVIG – The caretaker said Relling had two people with him when he came back last night.

GINA – I thought as much.

HEDVIG – But that's no good, if he won't come up and see us.

GINA – You leave it to me. I'll go down and have a word with him.

[OLD EKDAL, *in a dressing gown and slippers and with a lighted pipe, appears in the doorway of his room.*]

EKDAL – Hjalmar, I! Isn't Hjalmar at home?

GINA – No, he seems to have gone out.

EKDAL – What, already? And in this blizzard? Oh, well. Let him. I can go for a walk by myself.

[*He pushes aside the door of the loft.* HEDVIG *helps him. He goes in, and she closes the door behind him.*]

HEDVIG [*softly*] Poor Grandfather! What will he say when he hears Father's leaving us?

GINA – Don't be silly, Grandfather mustn't be told about that. Thank God he wasn't here yesterday when all the hullaballoo was going on.

HEDVIG – Yes, but–

[GREGERS *enters through the front door.*]

GREGERS – Well? Have you found where he is?

GINA – They say he's downstairs with Relling.

GREGERS – With Relling! Has he really been out with those people?

GINA – So it seems.

GREGERS – But he needed so much to be alone, and to collect his thoughts–

GINA – Yes, you may well say that.

1278

[RELLING *enters from the passage.*]

HEDVIG [*goes towards him*] Is Father with you?

GINA [*simultaneously*] Is he there?

RELLING—He certainly is.

HEDVIG—And you didn't tell us!

RELLING—Yes, I'm a beast. But I had to put the other beast to bed first—I refer of course to our daemonic friend—and then I fell asleep—

GINA—What has Hjalmar got to say today?

RELLING—Nothing.

HEDVIG—Doesn't he say anything?

RELLING—Not a damn thing.

GREGERS—No, no. I can understand that so well.

GINA—But what's he doing, then?

RELLING—He's on the sofa, snoring.

GINA—Is he? Yes, Hjalmar's a terrible snorer.

HEDVIG—You mean he's asleep?

RELLING—It certainly sounds like it.

GREGERS—It's quite understandable. After the spiritual conflict that's been rending him—

GINA—And he's not used to wandering around outside at night.

HEDVIG—Perhaps it's a good thing he's getting some sleep, Mother.

GINA—Yes, I was just thinking that. We'd better not wake him up too soon. Thanks, Relling. I must just clean the place up a bit, and then I'll— Come and give me a hand, Hedvig.

[GINA *and* HEDVIG *go into the parlour.*]

GREGERS [*turns to* RELLING] Can you explain this spiritual turmoil in Hjalmar Ekdal?

RELLING—Can't say I've ever noticed any spiritual turmoil in him.

GREGERS—What! At such a crisis, when his whole life has been given a new moral foundation—! How do you suppose a man of Hjalmar's personality—?

RELLING—Personality—*him?* If he ever had any tendency to the kind of abnormalities you call personality, they were nipped out of him, root and branch, before his voice broke. You take my word for it.

GREGERS—That's surprising, considering the love and care with which he was brought up.

RELLING—By those two twisted, hysterical maiden aunts, you mean?

GREGERS—At least they were idealists—but I suppose you'll laugh at me again for saying that.

RELLING—No, I'm not in the mood for that. I know all about it. I've had to endure vomits of rhetoric about his "two spiritual mothers." But I don't think he's got much to be grateful to them for. Hjalmar's tragedy is that all his life he's been regarded by everyone around him as a genius—

GREGERS—Well, isn't he? Deep down inside?

RELLING—I've never noticed any evidence of it. Oh, his father thought so, but—well, *he's* been a bloody fool all his life.

GREGERS—No, he has kept the innocence of a child all his life. That's something you can't understand.

RELLING—All right, have it your way. But when dear little Hjalmar somehow got to university, he was at once hailed as the great white hope there too. Well, he was handsome of course—that helps—you know, peaches and cream, the shopgirl's dream—and with his romantic temperament and throbbing voice and talent for declaiming other people's poetry and ideas—

GREGERS [*indignantly*] Are you talking about Hjalmar Ekdal?

RELLING—Yes. With your permission, that's what this idol you grovel to really looks like when you take him apart.

GREGERS—Well, I don't think I'm completely blind.

RELLING—You're not far off. You're a sick man too, you know.

GREGERS—Yes, you're right there.

RELLING—Oh, yes. Yours is a complicated case. To begin with, you've this tiresome rash of righteousness; and what's worse, you live in a perpetual delirium of hero-worship. You've always got to have something outside yourself that you can idolise.

GREGERS—That's true. I have to seek it outside myself.

RELLING—It's pathetic the way you make a fool of yourself over these supermen you imagine you see all around you. This is just another of those workmen's cottages where you started hawking your ideals. We're all insolvent here.

GREGERS—If that's your opinion of Hjalmar Ekdal, how can you spend so much time with him?

RELLING—I'm meant to be a doctor of sorts, God forgive me. I've got to do something for these wretched cripples I share a roof with.

GREGERS—I see. So Hjalmar Ekdal is sick too?

RELLING—Well, who isn't?

GREGERS—And what medicine are you giving him?

RELLING—My usual one. I feed the life-lie in him.

GREGERS—Life-*lie*, did you say?

RELLING—Yes, that's right. The universal stimulant.

GREGERS—And what is the life-lie with which Hjalmar Ekdal is infected, if I may ask?

RELLING—You may not. I don't betray professional secrets to quacks. I wouldn't put it past you to make an even worse mess of him. But my remedy's infallible. I've used it on Molvik for years. I've made him daemonic. That's the serum I've injected into his skull.

G R E G E R S – Isn't he daemonic, then?

R E L L I N G – What the hell does it mean, daemonic? It's just a bit of claptrap I thought up to keep him alive. If I hadn't done it the poor swine would have succumbed to self-contempt and despair years ago. And what about the old lieutenant? Well, he found the cure himself.

G R E G E R S – Lieutenant Ekdal? How do you mean?

R E L L I N G – What about that? The great bear hunter going into that musty old loft to chase rabbits? There isn't a happier sportsman in the world than that old man when they let him potter around in there among all that junk. Those four or five withered Christmas trees smell the same to him as the great forests of Hoydal; the chickens are the wild game in the pine tops; and the rabbits that flop across the floor are bears to challenge the strength and skill of the mighty hunter.

G R E G E R S – Poor Lieutenant Ekdal! Yes, he's had to abandon his youthful ideals.

R E L L I N G – While I remember it, Mr. Werle Junior, forget that foreign word "ideals." Why not use that good old Norwegian word: "lies"?

G R E G E R S – Do you suggest the two are related?

R E L L I N G – About as closely as typhus and putrid fever.

G R E G E R S – Dr. Relling, I will not give up until I have rescued Hjalmar Ekdal from your clutches.

R E L L I N G – So much the worse for him. Deprive the average human being of his life-lie, and you rob him of his happiness.

[*To* HEDVIG, *as she enters from the parlour.*]
Well, little wild-duck-mother, I'm off downstairs to see if your father's still pondering his great invention on my sofa.

[*Goes out through front door.*]

G R E G E R S [*goes closer to* HEDVIG] I can see it, Hedvig. You haven't done it.

H E D V I G – What? Oh, that thing about the wild duck. No.

G R E G E R S – Your strength of purpose failed you when the moment for action came, I suppose.

H E D V I G – No, it wasn't that. It was just that when I woke this morning and remembered what we'd been talking about, I thought it all seemed so strange.

G R E G E R S – Strange?

H E D V I G – I don't know. Yesterday evening, when you first mentioned it, I thought there was something so beautiful in the idea; but when I'd slept on it and thought about it again, it didn't seem so good.

GREGERS—Oh, no. Of course you can't have grown up in this house without some rot setting in.

HEDVIG—I don't care about that. If only Father would come back, I'd—

GREGERS—Oh, if only your eyes could be opened to what really matters in life! If only you had the courage to make your sacrifice truly and joyfully, you'd see—he'd come back to you! But I still believe in you, Hedvig. I believe in you.

[*He goes out through the front door.*]

HEDVIG *walks around for a little; then she is about to go into the kitchen when there is a knock on the door of the loft.* HEDVIG *goes over and opens it slightly.* OLD EKDAL *comes out. She closes the door again.*

EKDAL—Hm! It's not much fun having to take my exercise alone.

HEDVIG—Didn't you feel like hunting today, Grandfather?

EKDAL—It's bad weather for hunting today. Dark. You can hardly see your hand in front of your face.

HEDVIG—Don't you ever feel you'd like to shoot something else besides rabbits?

EKDAL—What's wrong with rabbits? Aren't they good enough?

HEDVIG—Yes, but what about—well, the wild duck?

EKDAL [*laughs*] Oh, so you're afraid I'll shoot your wild duck, are you? Don't you worry, my child. I'd never do that.

HEDVIG—No, of course, you couldn't. I've heard it's very difficult to shoot wild ducks.

EKDAL—Couldn't? What do you mean? Of course I could.

HEDVIG—How would you go about it, Grandfather? I don't mean with my wild duck, but with other ones?

EKDAL—I'd shoot them under the breast, Hedvig. That's the safest place. And you've got to shoot against the feathers, mind, not with them.

HEDVIG—Do they die then, Grandfather?

EKDAL—You bet they die, if you shoot them properly. Well, I must go in and—hm—clean myself up. You understand—hm?

He goes into his room. HEDVIG *waits a few moments, glances towards the door of the parlour, goes over to the bookcase, reaches up on tiptoe, takes down the double-barrelled pistol from the shelf and looks at it.* GINA *enters from the parlour with her duster and brush.* HEDVIG *quickly puts down the pistol, unnoticed.*

GINA—Don't stand there messing about with your father's things, Hedvig.

HEDVIG [*leaves the bookcase*] I only wanted to tidy up a little.

GINA – Go into the kitchen and see if the coffee's still hot. I'll take the tray when I go down.

HEDVIG *goes out.* GINA *begins to sweep and clean the studio. After a few moments, the front door is cautiously opened and* HJALMAR *looks in. He is wearing his overcoat but is hatless and unwashed. His hair is tousled and his eyes are dull and tired.*

GINA [*stands with the brush in her hand and looks at him*] Oh. Hullo, Hjalmar. You've come.

HJALMAR [*walks in and answers in a flat voice*] I've come—but only to go at once.

GINA – Yes, yes, of course. But, my goodness, look at you!

HJALMAR – At me?

GINA – And your nice winter coat! Well, that's done for.

HEDVIG [*in the kitchen doorway*] Mother, hadn't I better—?

[*Sees* HJALMAR, *gives a cry of joy and runs towards him.*] Oh, Father, Father!

HJALMAR [*turns away with a gesture of rejection*] Get away, get away, get away!

[*To* GINA.]

Get her away from me!

GINA [*softly*] Go into the parlour, Hedvig.

[HEDVIG *goes silently out.*]

HJALMAR [*feverishly pulls out the drawer of the table*] I must take my books with me. Where are my books?

GINA – What books?

HJALMAR – My scientific books, of course. The technical magazines I need for my invention.

GINA [*looks in the bookcase*] Are these the ones, without any covers?

HJALMAR – Of course they are.

GINA [*puts a heap of magazines on the table*] Shall I get Hedvig to cut the pages for you?

HJALMAR – I don't want them cut.

[*Short silence.*]

GINA – So you're really leaving us, Hjalmar?

HJALMAR [*rummaging among the books*] Have I any choice?

GINA – No, no.

HJALMAR [*vehemently*] I can't go on being pierced to the heart every hour of every day!

GINA – May God forgive you for thinking so vilely of me!

HJALMAR – Give me proof—!

GINA—I think you're the one who needs to do the proving.

HJALMAR—With your past! There are certain things a man has a right to demand—one might be tempted to call them demands of the ideal—

GINA—What about Grandfather? What's going to become of him, poor old man?

HJALMAR—I know my duty. That helpless old man leaves with me. I shall go into town and make arrangements. Hm—

[*Unwillingly.*]

Has anyone seen my hat on the stairs?

GINA—No. Have you lost your hat?

HJALMAR—I had it on when I came back last night. Naturally. There can be no doubt about that. But I haven't been able to find it today.

GINA—For mercy's sake, where on earth did you get to with those two scallywags?

HJALMAR—Don't bother me with trivialities. Do you suppose I'm in a mood to recall details?

GINA—Well, I only hope you haven't caught cold, Hjalmar.

[*Goes out into the kitchen.*]

HJALMAR [*mutters to himself, half audibly and furiously as he empties the drawer beneath the table*] You're a scoundrel, Relling! A cad, that's what you are! Oh, you vile seducer! I wish I could hire someone to stick a knife in your back!

He puts some old letters on one side, finds the letter he tore up yesterday, picks it up and looks at the pieces, then puts it quickly down again as GINA *returns.*

GINA [*puts a tray with coffee, etc., on the table*] I've brought you a cup of something warm, in case you feel inclined. And some bread and butter and a bit of cold fish.

HJALMAR [*glances at the tray*] Cold fish? Under this roof? Never! I've had no solid food for nearly twenty-four hours, but no matter. My notes! The first chapter of my memoirs! Where's my diary? Where are all my important papers?

[*Opens the parlour door, but shrinks back.*]

There she is again!

GINA—But for heaven's sake, the child's got to be somewhere.

HJALMAR—Come out.

[*He moves aside to make way for her.* HEDVIG *enters, frightened.*]

HJALMAR [*with his hand on the door handle, says to* GINA] During my last minutes in what *was* my home, I wish to be spared the presence of outsiders.

[*Goes out into the parlour.*]

1284

HEDVIG [*runs to her mother and asks softly, trembling*] Does he mean me?

GINA – Stay in the kitchen, Hedvig. No, you'd better go to your room.
[*To* HJALMAR, *as she goes in to him.*]
Stop rummaging in those drawers. I know where everything is.

HEDVIG [*stands motionless for a moment, anguished and bewildered, biting her lips to keep back her tears. Then she clenches her fists convulsively and says quietly*] The wild duck!

She steals over and takes the pistol from the shelf, opens the loft door a few inches, creeps in and pulls it shut behind her. In the parlour offstage, HJALMAR *and* GINA *begin to argue.*

HJALMAR [*comes out with some notebooks and old loose papers, which he puts down on the table*] Oh, that old bag's no use. There are hundreds of things I've got to lug away.

GINA [*comes after him with the bag*] Well, just take a shirt and a pair of pants with you. You can come back for the rest later.

HJALMAR – Phew! It's so exhausting, all this packing!
[*Tears off his overcoat and throws it on the sofa.*]

GINA – And now your coffee's getting cold, too.

HJALMAR – Hm.
[*Automatically takes a mouthful; then another.*]

GINA [*dusting the backs of the chairs*] The big difficulty'll be to find another big loft like this for the rabbits.

HJALMAR – What! Do you expect me to drag all those rabbits along too?

GINA – Well, you know Grandfather can't live without his rabbits.

HJALMAR – Well, he'll have to learn. I'm giving up more important things than rabbits.

GINA [*dusting the bookshelves*] Shall I pack the flute?

HJALMAR – No. No flute for me. Give me the pistol, though.

GINA – Are you going to take the pistol?

HJALMAR – Yes. My loaded pistol.

GINA [*looks for it*] It's gone. He must have taken it with him.

HJALMAR – Is he in the loft?

GINA – Yes, of course he's in the loft.

HJALMAR – Hm. The lonely old man!
[*Takes a piece of bread and butter, eats it and empties his cup.*]

GINA – If only we hadn't let that room, you could have moved in there.

HJALMAR – What! Live under the same roof as—? Never! Never!

GINA – Couldn't you manage in the parlour for a day or two? You'd be alone there.

H J A L M A R – Within these walls? Never!

G I N A – Well, how about downstairs with Relling and Molvik?

H J A L M A R – Don't mention their names to me! The mere thought of them makes me lose my appetite. No, I must go out into the wind and snow, wandering from door to door seeking shelter for myself and my old father.

G I N A – But you've no hat, Hjalmar. You've lost your hat.

H J A L M A R – Scum! Vice-ridden scum, that's what they are! We must find a hat.

> [*Takes another piece of bread and butter.*]

Something must be done. I don't intend to die of exposure.

G I N A – What are you looking for?

H J A L M A R – Butter.

G I N A – Coming up right away.

> [*Goes out into the kitchen.*]

H J A L M A R [*shouts after her*] Oh, it doesn't matter. I can eat dry bread.

G I N A [*comes back with a butter-dish*] Here, this is meant to be fresh.

[*She pours him another cup of coffee. He sits on the sofa, spreads more butter on his bread, and eats and drinks for a few moments in silence.*]

H J A L M A R – Would I really not be bothered by anyone if I stayed a couple of days in that room? Anyone at all?

G I N A – No, of course not. Why don't you?

H J A L M A R – I can't see any hope of getting all Father's things moved out all at once.

G I N A – And don't forget you've got to break the news to him about your not wanting to live with us any longer.

H J A L M A R [*pushes away his coffee cup*] Yes, there's that too. I've got to dig up all those complications again. I must think things over. I must give myself breathing-space. I can't cope with so many different burdens in one day.

G I N A – No, of course not. Especially with the weather what it is.

H J A L M A R [*touches* WERLE's *letter*] I see that letter's still lying around.

G I N A – Yes, I haven't touched it.

H J A L M A R – Of course, it's nothing to do with me—

G I N A – Well, I certainly don't want to make anything out of it.

H J A L M A R – Still, there's no point in letting it get lost. In the confusion of my moving, it might easily—

G I N A – I'll see it doesn't.

H J A L M A R – Of course, this deed of gift really belongs to Father. It's up to him to decide whether it's to be used or not.

G I N A [*sighs*] Yes, poor old Father!

H J A L M A R – Perhaps for safety's sake—where can I find some glue?

G I N A [*goes over to the bookcase*] The pot's here.

H J A L M A R – And a brush.

G I N A – The brush is here, too.

> [*Brings them to him.*]

H J A L M A R [*takes a pair of scissors*] Just a strip of paper along the back—

> [*Cuts and glues.*]

Far be it from me to deprive other people of what belongs to them. Least of all a destitute old man. Or—any other person. There, now! Let that stand for a few minutes. And when it's dry, take it away. I never want to see the thing again. Never!

> [GREGERS WERLE *enters from the passage.*]

G R E G E R S [*a little surprised*] Oh! Are you here, Hjalmar?

H J A L M A R [*gets up quickly*] I was overcome by fatigue.

G R E G E R S – I see you've had breakfast, however.

H J A L M A R – The body makes its demands too, you know.

G R E G E R S – Well, what have you decided?

H J A L M A R – For a man like me, there is no choice. I'm just getting my most important belongings together. But that takes time, you know.

G I N A [*a little impatiently*] Well, shall I make the room ready or shall I pack your bag?

H J A L M A R [*gives an annoyed glance at* GREGERS] Pack. *And* make it ready.

G I N A [*takes the bag*] Well, well. I'll put in a shirt and p—and the other thing.

> [*Goes into the parlour and closes the door behind her.*]

G R E G E R S [*after a short silence*] I'd never envisaged it ending like this. Must you really leave your home?

H J A L M A R [*wanders around restlessly*] Well, what do you want me to do? I wasn't cut out to suffer, Gregers. I must have peace and calm and comfort around me.

G R E G E R S – Well, why not? Try! It seems to me that now you have firm ground to build on. Start afresh! And remember, you have your invention to live for too.

H J A L M A R – Oh, don't talk about the invention. That may be further off than you think.

G R E G E R S – Oh?

H J A L M A R – Well, dammit, what *is* there for me to invent? Other people have invented almost everything already. It's becoming more and more difficult every day—

G R E G E R S – But you've put so much work into it.

H J A L M A R – It was that drunkard Relling who started me off on it.

GREGERS—Relling?

HJALMAR—Yes. It was he who first made me conscious that I had the talent to make some invention that would revolutionise photography.

GREGERS—I see. So it was Relling.

HJALMAR—Oh, it's made me so happy thinking about it! Not so much for the sake of the invention itself, but because Hedvig believed in it —believed in it as passionately and trustingly as only a child can believe in a thing. What I mean to say is—I was fool enough to delude myself into thinking she believed in it.

GREGERS—Do you seriously believe that Hedvig hasn't been sincere?

HJALMAR—I can believe anything now. Hedvig's the one who stands in my way. Her shadow is going to shut the sunlight out of my life.

GREGERS—Hedvig? Are you talking about Hedvig?

HJALMAR—I loved that child beyond words. I felt so incredibly happy every time I came back to this humble home and she ran to greet me with those sweet eyes peering at me. Oh, what a credulous fool I was! I loved her so, I loved her so. And I dreamed, I deluded myself into believing that she loved me too.

GREGERS—You call that a delusion?

HJALMAR—How can I know? I can't get anything out of Gina—and anyway, she's so totally insensitive to the idealistic aspect of all these complicated— But to you, Gregers, I feel impelled to open my heart. There's this dreadful doubt in my mind that perhaps Hedvig has never really and truly loved me.

GREGERS—Perhaps you may be given proof that she does.

[*Listens.*]

What was that? I think I can hear the wild duck crying.

HJALMAR—Yes, that's her quacking. Father's there in the loft.

GREGERS—Is he?

[*His eyes shine with joy.*]

I tell you, you may perhaps be given proof that your poor, misjudged Hedvig does love you.

HJALMAR—Oh, what proof can she give me? I couldn't believe anything from those lips.

GREGERS—Hedvig is incapable of deceit.

HJALMAR—Oh, Gregers, that's just what I can't be sure of. Who knows what Gina and that Mrs. Soerby may not have said when they were gossiping up here? And that child keeps her ears open. That deed of gift may not have come as such a surprise to her as she made out. I thought I noticed something odd in her manner.

GREGERS—What on earth has come over you?

HJALMAR—I've had my eyes opened. Just you wait—you'll see. That deed of gift is only the beginning. Mrs. Soerby's always had a soft spot for Hedvig, and now she's in a position to do anything she likes for the child. They can take her from me any moment they want.

GREGERS—Hedvig will never leave you.

HJALMAR—I wouldn't be too sure of that. If they stand there beckoning to her with their hands full of—and I, who loved her so much, so much! I couldn't imagine any greater happiness than to take her gently by the hand and lead her as a man leads a child who is afraid of the dark through a large, empty room. I can see it now so clearly—the poor photographer in his attic has never really meant very much to her. She was just cunning enough to keep on good terms with him until the time was ripe.

GREGERS—Oh, Hjalmar, you don't believe that.

HJALMAR—The tragedy is that I don't know what to believe—and that I never will know. Oh, you're too much of an idealist, my dear Gregers. If they came to her with their hands full of gold and cried to the child: "Leave him! We can offer you life!"—

GREGERS [*swiftly*] Yes? What do you think she would reply?

HJALMAR—If I were to ask her: "Hedvig, will you sacrifice your life for me?"—

[*He laughs scornfully.*]

Oh, yes! You'd hear what answer she'd give me!

[*A pistol shot is heard from the loft.*]

GREGERS [*cries joyfully*] Hjalmar!

HJALMAR [*enviously*] Oh, now he's started hunting.

GINA [*enters, worried*] Oh, Hjalmar, Grandfather's banging away in there on his own.

HJALMAR—I'll go and have a look.

GREGERS [*alive, excited*] Wait! Do you know what that was?

HJALMAR—Of course I do.

GREGERS—No, you don't. But I know. It was the proof you wanted.

HJALMAR—What proof?

GREGERS—A child's sacrifice. She has got your father to shoot the wild duck.

HJALMAR—Shoot the wild duck?

GINA—What an idea!

HJALMAR—But why?

GREGERS—She wanted to sacrifice for you the most precious of her possessions, because she thought that then you would have to love her again.

HJALMAR [*gently, emotionally*] Oh, child, child!

GINA—The things she gets up to!

GREGERS—She only wanted you to love her again, Hjalmar. She couldn't live without it.

GINA [*almost in tears*] There, Hjalmar, you see.

HJALMAR–Where is she, Gina?

GINA [*sniffs*] Sitting outside in the kitchen, I suppose, poor child.

HJALMAR [*walks across and flings open the kitchen door*] Hedvig, come here. Come and talk to me.

[*Looks round.*]

No, she isn't here.

GINA–She must be in her room, then.

HJALMAR [*outside*] No, she isn't there, either.

[*Comes back.*]

She must have gone out.

GINA–Well, you didn't want to have her in the house.

HJALMAR–Oh, I wish she'd come home again soon, so that I can tell her! Now everything will be all right, Gregers. Now I think we can start life afresh.

GREGERS [*quietly*] I knew it. Through the child will come resurrection.

[OLD EKDAL *appears in the doorway of his room. He is in full uniform, and is busy buckling on his sword.*]

HJALMAR [*amazed*] Father! Have you been in there?

GINA–Have you been shooting in your room?

EKDAL [*indignantly, comes closer*] So you go hunting alone now, do you, Hjalmar?

HJALMAR [*confused*] Then it wasn't you who fired that shot in the loft?

EKDAL–Wasn't me? Hm!

GREGERS [*cries to* HJALMAR] Hjalmar! She has shot the wild duck herself!

HJALMAR–What's going on round here?

[*Runs over to the door of the loft, pulls it open, looks in and cries.*] Hedvig!

GINA [*runs over to the door*] Oh, God! What is it?

HJALMAR [*goes inside*] She's lying on the floor.

GREGERS–Lying on the floor? Hedvig?

[*Joins* HJALMAR *inside.*]

GINA [*simultaneously*] Hedvig!

[*Goes into the loft.*]

Oh, no, no, no!

EKDAL [*laughs*] Now she's started hunting too!

[HJALMAR, GINA *and* GREGERS *drag* HEDVIG *into the studio. Her right hand is hanging down with the pistol tightly clasped between her fingers.*]

HJALMAR [*distraught*] The pistol's gone off! She's shot herself! Call for help! Help!

GINA [*runs out into the passage and calls down*] Relling! Relling! Dr. Relling! Come upstairs! As quick as you can!

[HJALMAR *and* GREGERS *lay* HEDVIG *on the sofa.*]

EKDAL [*quietly*] The forest has taken its revenge.

HJALMAR [*on his knees beside her*] She's coming round now! She'll be all right!

GINA [*comes back*] Where's the wound? I can't see anything—

[RELLING *hurries in.* MOLVIK *follows, with no waistcoat or tie, and with his coat hanging open.*]

RELLING—What's happened?

GINA—They say Hedvig's shot herself.

HJALMAR—Come here and help us.

RELLING—Shot herself!

[*Pushes the table aside and begins to examine her.*]

HJALMAR [*lying on the floor, gazes up at him in anguish*] It can't be dangerous? Can it, Relling? She's hardly bleeding at all. It can't be dangerous, can it?

RELLING—How did it happen?

HJALMAR—Oh, how do I know?

GINA—She was going to shoot the wild duck.

RELLING—The wild duck?

HJALMAR—The pistol must have gone off.

RELLING—Hm. I see.

EKDAL—The forest has taken its revenge. But I'm not afraid of it.

[*Goes into the loft and closes the door behind him.*]

HJALMAR—Well, Relling, why don't you say something?

RELLING—The bullet has entered her breast.

HJALMAR—But she'll be all right?

RELLING—Surely you can see that Hedvig is dead.

GINA [*bursts into tears*] Oh, my child, my child!

GREGERS [*hoarsely*] The deep blue sea—!

HJALMAR [*jumps up*] Yes, yes, she must live! Oh, God bless you, Relling, only for a moment! Only long enough for me to tell her how much I loved her—always—always!

RELLING—The bullet entered her heart. Internal haemorrhage. She died instantaneously.

HJALMAR—And I drove her from me like an animal! And she crept into the loft in terror, and died there—because she loved me!

[*Sobs.*]

I can never atone for this—never tell her—!

[*Clasps his hands and cries upwards.*]

Oh—You up there—if You exist! Why have You done this to me?

G I N A – Hush, hush, don't carry on like that. We had no right to keep her—I suppose—

M O L V I K – The child is not dead, but sleepeth.

R E L L I N G – Rubbish!

H J A L M A R [*becomes calm, goes across to the sofa and looks down at* HEDVIG, *with folded hands*] How stiff and still she lies!

R E L L I N G [*tries to free the pistol from her fingers*] She's holding on to it so tightly. So tightly.

G I N A – No, no, Relling, don't break her fingers. Let the pistol stay there.

H J A L M A R – Let her keep it.

G I N A – Yes, let her. But the child mustn't lie here like a show. We'll take her into her own room. Help me, Hjalmar.

[H J A L M A R *and* G I N A *pick* HEDVIG *up.*]

H J A L M A R [*as they carry her out*] Oh, Gina, Gina! How shall we live after this?

G I N A – We must help each other. Now she belongs to both of us, you know.

M O L V I K [*stretches out his arms and mumbles*] Praised be the Lord! To dust thou shalt return! To dust thou shalt return!

R E L L I N G [*whispers*] Shut up, man. You're drunk.

[H J A L M A R *and* G I N A *carry the body out through the kitchen door.* REL-LING *shuts it behind them.* MOLVIK *slinks out into the passage.*]

R E L L I N G [*goes over to* GREGERS *and says*] No one's ever going to make me believe that this was an accident.

G R E G E R S [*who has stood overcome by horror, shaking convulsively*] No one will ever know how this dreadful thing happened.

R E L L I N G – The powder had burned her dress. She must have pressed the pistol against her breast before she fired.

G R E G E R S – Hedvig has not died in vain. Did you see how grief set free all that is most noble in him?

R E L L I N G – Most men are noble when they stand by a death-bed. But how long do you think this nobility will last?

G R E G E R S – For as long as he lives. And it will grow, and grow.

R E L L I N G – In nine months, little Hedvig will be nothing more to him than a theme for a recitation.

G R E G E R S – You dare to say that about Hjalmar Ekdal!

R E L L I N G – Let's talk about it again when the first grasses have with-ered on her grave. Then you'll hear him gulping about "the child un-timely ripped from her father's bosom." You'll see him stewing in emotion and self-admiration and self-pity. Just you wait.

G R E G E R S – If you are right and I am wrong, life is not worth living.

R E L L I N G – Oh, life would be all right if we didn't have to put up with these damned creditors who keep pestering us with the demands of their ideals.

GREGERS [*stares ahead of him*] In that case, I am glad that my destiny is what it is.

RELLING—And what, if I may ask, is your destiny?

GREGERS [*as he goes towards the door*] To be the thirteenth at table.

[RELLING *laughs and spits.*]

IDEALS AND IDEALISTS

By Bernard Shaw

WE HAVE SEEN that as Man grows through the ages, he finds himself bolder by the growth of his courage: that is, of his spirit (for so the common people name it), and dares more and more to love and trust instead of to fear and fight. But his courage has other effects: he also raises himself from mere consciousness to knowledge by daring more and more to face facts and tell himself the truth. For in his infancy of helplessness and terror he could not face the inexorable; and facts being of all things the most inexorable, he masked all the threatening ones as fast as he discovered them; so that now every mask requires a hero to tear it off. The king of terrors, Death, was the Arch-Inexorable: Man could not bear the dread of that. He must persuade himself that Death can be propitiated, circumvented, abolished. How he fixed the mask of personal immortality on the face of Death for this purpose we all know. And he did the like with all disagreeables as long as they remained inevitable. Otherwise he must have gone mad with terror of the grim shapes around him, headed by the skeleton with the scythe and hourglass. The masks were his ideals, as he called them; and what, he would ask, would life be without ideals? Thus he became an idealist, and remained so until he dared to begin pulling the masks off and looking the spectres in the face— dared, that is, to be more and more a realist. But all men are not equally brave; and the greatest terror prevailed whenever some realist bolder

From *The Quintessence of Ibsenism* by Bernard Shaw, 3rd edition. New York: Hill & Wang, Inc., 1957. Reprinted by permission of The Public Trustee, London, and the Society of Authors, London.

than the rest laid hands on a mask which they did not yet dare to do without.

We have plenty of these masks around us still: some of them more fantastic than any of the Sandwich islanders' masks in the British Museum. In our novels and romances especially we see the most beautiful of all the masks: those devised to disguise the brutalities of the sexual instinct in the earlier stages of its development, and to soften the rigorous aspect of the iron laws by which Society regulates its gratification. When the social organism becomes bent on civilization, it has to force marriage and family life on the individual, because it can perpetuate itself in no other way whilst love is still known only by fitful glimpses, the basis of sexual relationship being in the main mere physical appetite. Under these circumstances men try to graft pleasure on necessity by desperately pretending that the institution forced upon them is a congenial one, making it a point of public decency to assume always that men spontaneously love their kindred better than their chance acquaintances, and that the woman once desired is always desired: also that the family is woman's proper sphere, and that no really womanly woman ever forms an attachment, or even knows what it means, until she is requested to do so by a man. Now if anyone's childhood has been embittered by the dislike of his mother and the ill-temper of his father; if his wife has ceased to care for him and he is heartily tired of his wife; if his brother is going to law with him over the division of the family property, and his son acting in studied defiance of his plans and wishes, it is hard for him to persuade himself that passion is eternal and that blood is thicker than water. Yet if he tells himself the truth, all his life seems a waste and a failure by the light of it. It comes then to this, that his neighbors must either agree with him that the whole system is a mistake, and discard it for a new one, which cannot possibly happen until social organization so far outgrows the institution that Society can perpetuate itself without it; or else they must keep him in countenance by resolutely making believe that all the illusions with which it has been masked are realities.

For the sake of precision, let us imagine a community of a thousand persons, organized for the perpetuation of the species on the basis of the British family as we know it at present. Seven hundred of them, we will suppose, find the British family arrangement quite good enough for them. Two hundred and ninety-nine find it a failure, but must put up with it since they are in a minority. The remaining person occupies a position to be explained presently. The 299 failures will not have the courage to face the fact that they are irremediable failures, since they cannot prevent the 700 satisfied ones from coercing them into conformity with the marriage law. They will accordingly try to persuade themselves that,

1295

whatever their own particular domestic arrangements may be, the family is a beautiful and holy natural institution. For the fox not only declares that the grapes he cannot get are sour: he also insists that the sloes he *can* get are sweet. Now observe what has happened. The family as it really is is a conventional arrangement, legally enforced, which the majority, because it happens to suit them, think good enough for the minority, whom it happens not to suit at all. The family as a beautiful and holy natural institution is only a fancy picture of what every family would have to be if everybody was to be suited, invented by the minority as a mask for the reality, which in its nakedness is intolerable to them. We call this sort of fancy picture an Ideal; and the policy of forcing individuals to act on the assumption that all ideals are real, and to recognize and accept such action as standard moral conduct, absolutely valid under all circumstances, contrary conduct or any advocacy of it being discountenanced and punished as immoral, may therefore be described as the policy of Idealism. Our 299 domestic failures are therefore become idealists as to marriage; and in proclaiming the ideal in fiction, poetry, pulpit and platform oratory, and serious private conversation, they will far outdo the 700 who comfortably accept marriage as a matter of course, never dreaming of calling it an "institution," much less a holy and beautiful one, and being pretty plainly of opinion that Idealism is a crackbrained fuss about nothing. The idealists, hurt by this, will retort by calling them Philistines. We then have our society classified as 700 Philistines and 299 idealists, leaving one man unclassified: the man strong enough to face the truth the idealists are shirking.

Such a man says of marriage, "This thing is a failure for many of us. It is insufferable that two human beings, having entered into relations which only warm affection can render tolerable, should be forced to maintain them after such affections have ceased to exist, or in spite of the fact that they have never arisen. The alleged natural attractions and repulsions upon which the family ideal is based do not exist; and it is historically false that the family was founded for the purpose of satisfying them. Let us provide otherwise for the social ends which the family subserves, and then abolish its compulsory character altogether." What will be the attitude of the rest to this outspoken man? The Philistines will simply think him mad. But the idealists will be terrified beyond measure at the proclamation of their hidden thought—at the presence of the traitor among the conspirators of silence—at the rending of the beautiful veil they and their poets have woven to hide the unbearable face of the truth. They will crucify him, burn him, violate their own ideals of family affection by taking his children away from him, ostracize him, brand him as immoral, profligate, filthy, and appeal against him to the despised Philistines, specially idealized for the occasion as Society. How far they will proceed against him depends on how far his courage exceeds theirs. At his worst, they call him cynic and paradoxer: at his best they do their utmost to ruin him if not to take his life. Thus, purblindly courageous moralists like Mandeville and Larochefoucauld, who merely state unpleasant facts without denying the validity of current ideals, and who indeed depend on those ideals to make their statements piquant, get off with nothing worse than this name of cynic, the free use of which is a familiar mark of the zealous idealist. But take the case of the man who has already served us an an example: Shelley. The idealists did not call Shelley a cynic: they called him a fiend until they invented a new illusion to enable them to enjoy the beauty of his lyrics, this illusion being nothing less than the pretence that since he was at bottom an idealist himself, his ideals must be identical with those of Tennyson and Longfellow, neither of whom ever wrote a line in which some highly respectable ideal was not implicit.[1]

Here the admission that Shelley, the realist, was an idealist too, seems to spoil the whole argument. And it certainly spoils its verbal consistency. For we unfortunately use this word ideal indifferently to denote both the institution which the ideal masks and the mask itself, thereby producing desperate confusion of thought, since the institution may be an effete and poisonous one, whilst the mask may be, and indeed generally is, an image of what we would fain have in its place. If the existing facts, with their masks on, are to be called ideals, and the future possibilities which the masks depict are also to be called ideals—if, again, the man who is defending existing institutions by maintaining their identity with their masks is to be confounded under one name with the man who is striving to realize the future possibilities by tearing the mask and the thing masked asunder, then the position cannot be intelligibly described by mortal pen: you and I, reader, will be at cross purposes at every sen-

---

[1] The following are examples of the two stages of Shelley criticism:

"We feel as if one of the darkest of the fiends had been clothed with a human body to enable him to gratify his enmity against the human race, and as if the supernatural atrocity of his hate were only heightened by his power to do injury. So strongly has this impression dwelt upon our minds that we absolutely asked a friend, who had seen this individual, to describe him to us—as if a cloven hoof, or horn, or flames from the mouth, must have marked the external appearance of so bitter an enemy of mankind." (Literary Gazette, 19th May 1821.)

"A beautiful and ineffectual angel, beating in the void his luminous wings in vain." (MATTHEW ARNOLD, in the preface to his selection of poems by Byron, dated 1881.)

The 1881 opinion is much sillier than the 1821 opinion. Further samples will be found in the articles of Henry Salt, one of the few writers on Shelley who understand his true position as a social pioneer.

tence unless you allow me to distinguish pioneers like Shelley and Ibsen as realists from the idealists of my imaginary community of one thousand. If you ask why I have not allotted the terms the other way, and called Shelley and Ibsen idealists and the conventionalists realists, I reply that Ibsen himself, though he has not formally made the distinction, has so repeatedly harped on conventions and conventionalists as ideals and idealists that if I were now perversely to call them realities and realists, I should confuse readers of *The Wild Duck* and *Rosmersholm* more than I should help them. Doubtless I shall be reproached for puzzling people by thus limiting the meaning of the term ideal. But what, I ask, is that inevitable passing perplexity compared to the inextricable tangle I must produce if I follow the custom, and use the word indiscriminately in its two violently incompatible senses? If the term realist is objected to on account of some of its modern associations, I can only recommend you, if you must associate it with something else than my own description of its meaning (I do not deal in definitions), to associate it, not with Zola and Maupassant, but with Plato.

Now let us return to our community of 700 Philistines, 299 idealists, and 1 realist. The mere verbal ambiguity against which I have just provided is as nothing beside that which comes of any attempt to express the relations of these three sections, simple as they are, in terms of the ordinary systems of reason and duty. The idealist, higher in the ascent of evolution than the Philistine, yet hates the highest and strikes at him with a dread and rancor of which the easy-going Philistine is guiltless. The man who has risen above the danger and the fear that his acquisitiveness will lead him to theft, his temper to murder, and his affections to debauchery: this is he who is denounced as an arch-scoundrel and libertine, and thus confounded with the lowest because he is the highest. And it is not the ignorant and stupid who maintain this error, but the literate and the cultured. When the true prophet speaks, he is proved to be both rascal and idiot, not by those who have never read of how foolishly such learned demonstrations have come off in the past, but by those who have themselves written volumes on the crucifixions, the burnings, the stonings, the headings and hangings, the Siberia transportations, the calumny and ostracism which have been the lot of the pioneer as well as of the camp follower. It is from men of established literary reputation that we learn that William Blake was mad, that Shelley was spoiled by living in a low set, that Robert Owen was a man who did not know the world, that Ruskin was incapable of comprehending political economy, that Zola was a mere blackguard, and that Ibsen was "a Zola with a wooden leg." The great musician, accepted by the unskilled listener, is vilified by his fellow-musicians: it was the musical culture of Europe that pronounced Wagner the inferior of Mendelssohn and Meyerbeer. The great artist finds his foes among the painters, and not among the men in the street: it was the Royal Academy which placed forgotten nobodies above Burne-Jones. It is not rational that it should be so; but it is so, for all that.

The realist at last loses patience with ideals altogether, and sees in them only something to blind us, something to numb us, something to murder self in us, something whereby, instead of resisting death, we can disarm it by committing suicide. The idealist, who has taken refuge with the ideals because he hates himself and is ashamed of himself, thinks that all this is so much the better. The realist, who has come to have a deep respect for himself and faith in the validity of his own will, thinks it so much the worse. To the one, human nature, naturally corrupt, is held back from ruinous excesses only by self-denying conformity to the ideals. To the other these ideals are only swaddling clothes which man has outgrown, and which insufferably impede his movements. No wonder the two cannot agree. The idealist says, "Realism means egotism; and egotism means depravity." The realist declares that when a man abnegates the will to live and be free in a world of the living and free, seeking only to conform to ideals for the sake of being, not himself, but "a good man," then he is morally dead and rotten, and must be left unheeded to abide his resurrection, if that by good luck arrive before his bodily death.[2] Unfortunately, this is the sort of speech that nobody but a realist understands. It will be more amusing as well as more convincing to take an actual example of an idealist criticizing a realist.

"THE WILD DUCK," 1884

After *An Enemy of the People*, Ibsen, as I have said, left the vulgar ideals for dead, and set about the exposure of those of the choicer spirits, beginning with the incorrigible idealists who had idealized his very self, and were becoming known as Ibsenites. His first move in this direction was such a tragi-comic slaughtering of sham Ibsenism that his astonished victims plaintively declared that *The Wild Duck*, as the new play was called, was a satire on his former works; whilst the pious, whom he had disappointed so severely by his interpretation of Brand, began to hope that he was coming back repentant to the fold. The household to which

---

[2] The above was written in 1890, ten years before Ibsen, in *When We Dead Awaken*, fully adopted its metaphor without, as far as I know, having any knowledge of my essay. Such an anticipation is a better proof than any mere argument that I found the right track of Ibsen's thought. (1912.)

we are introduced in *The Wild Duck* is not, like Mrs. Alving's, a handsome one made miserable by superstitious illusions, but a shabby one made happy by romantic illusions. The only member of it who sees it as it really is is the wife, a good-natured Philistine who desires nothing better. The husband, a vain, petted, spoilt dawdler, believes that he is a delicate and high-souled man, devoting his life to redeeming his old father's name from the disgrace brought on it by imprisonment for breach of the forest laws. This redemption he proposes to effect by making himself famous as a great inventor some day when he has the necessary inspiration. Their daughter, a girl in her teens, believes intensely in her father and in the promised invention. The disgraced grandfather cheers himself by drink whenever he can get it; but his chief resource is a wonderful garret full of rabbits and pigeons. The old man has procured a number of second-hand Christmas trees; and with these he has turned the garret into a sort of toy forest, in which he can play at bear hunting, which was one of the sports of his youth and prosperity. The weapons employed in the hunting expeditions are a gun which will not go off, and a pistol which occasionally brings down a rabbit or a pigeon. A crowning touch is given to the illusion by a wild duck, which, however, must not be shot, as it is the special property of the girl, who reads and dreams whilst her mother cooks, washes, sweeps and carries on the photographic work which is supposed to be the business of her husband. Mrs. Ekdal does not appreciate Hjalmar's highly strung sensitiveness of character, which is constantly suffering agonizing jars from her vulgarity; but then she does not appreciate that other fact that he is a lazy and idle impostor. Downstairs there is a disgraceful clergyman named Molvik, a hopeless drunkard; but even he respects himself and is tolerated because of a special illusion invented for him by another lodger, Dr. Relling, upon whom the lesson of the household above has not been thrown away. Molvik, says the doctor, must break out into drinking fits because he is daimonic, an imposing explanation which completely relieves the reverend gentleman from the imputation of vulgar tippling.

Into this domestic circle there comes a new lodger, an idealist of the most advanced type. He greedily swallows the daimonic theory of the clergyman's drunkenness, and enthusiastically accepts the photographer as the high-souled hero he supposes himself to be; but he is troubled because the relations of the man and his wife do not constitute an ideal marriage. He happens to know that the woman, before her marriage, was the cast-off mistress of his own father; and because she has not told her husband this, he conceives her life as founded on a lie, like that of Bernick in *Pillars of Society*. He accordingly sets himself to work out the woman's salvation for her, and establish ideally frank relations between the pair, by simply blurting out the truth, and then asking them, with fatuous self-satisfaction, whether they do not feel much the better for it. This wanton piece of mischief has more serious results than a mere domestic scene. The husband is too weak to act on his bluster about outraged honor and the impossibility of his ever living with his wife again; and the woman is merely annoyed with the idealist for telling on her; but the girl takes the matter to heart and shoots herself. The doubt cast on her parentage, with her father's theatrical repudiation of her, destroy her ideal place in the home, and make her a source of discord there; so she sacrifices herself, thereby carrying out the teaching of the idealist mischief-maker, who has talked a good deal to her about the duty and beauty of self-sacrifice, without foreseeing that he might be taken in mortal earnest. The busybody thus finds that people cannot be freed from their failings from without. They must free themselves. When Nora is strong enough to live out of the doll's house, she will go out of it of her own accord if the door stands open; but if before that period you take her by the scruff of the neck and thrust her out, she will only take refuge in the next establishment of the kind that offers to receive her. Woman has thus two enemies to deal with: the old-fashioned one who wants to keep the door locked, and the new-fashioned one who wants to thrust her into the street before she is ready to go. In the cognate case of a hypocrite and liar like Bernick, exposing him is a mere police measure: he is none the less a liar and hypocrite when you have exposed him. If you want to make a sincere and truthful man of him, all you can wisely do is to remove what you can of the external obstacles to his exposing himself, and then wait for the operation of his internal impulse to confess. If he has no such impulse, then you must put up with him as he is. It is useless to make claims on him which he is not yet prepared to meet. Whether, like Brand, we make such claims because to refrain would be to compromise with evil, or, like Gregers Werle, because we think their moral beauty must recommend them at sight to every one, we shall alike incur Relling's impatient assurance that "life would be quite tolerable if we could only get rid of the confounded duns that keep on pestering us in our poverty with the claims of the ideal."

"ROSMERSHOLM," 1886

Ibsen did not in *The Wild Duck* exhaust the subject of the danger of forming ideals for other people, and interfering in their lives with a view to enabling them to realize those ideals. Cases far more typical than that of the meddlesome lodger are those of the priest who regards the ennobling of mankind as a sort of trade process of which his cloth gives him a monopoly, and the clever woman who pictures a noble career for the man she loves, and devotes herself to helping him to achieve it. In *Rosmersholm*, the play with which Ibsen followed up *The Wild Duck*, there is an unpractical country parson, a gentleman of ancient stock, whose family has been for many years a centre of social influence. The tradition of that influence reinforces his priestly tendency to regard the ennoblement of the world as an external operation to be performed by himself; and the need of such ennoblement is very evident to him; for his nature is a fine one: he looks at the world with some dim prevision of "the third empire." He is married to a woman of passionately affectionate nature, who is very fond of him, but does not regard him as a regenerator of the human race. Indeed she does not share any of his dreams, and only acts as an extinguisher on the sacred fire of his idealism. He, she, her brother Kroll the headmaster, Kroll's wife, and their set, form a select circle of the best people in the place, comfortably orbited in our social system, and quite planetary in ascertained position and unimpeachable respectability. Into the orbit comes presently a wandering star, one Rebecca Gamvik, an unpropertied orphan, who has been allowed to read advanced books, and is a Freethinker and a Radical: things that disqualify a poor woman for admission to the Rosmer world. However, one must live somewhere; and as the Rosmer world is the only one in which an ambitious and cultivated woman can find powerful allies and educated companions, Rebecca, being both ambitious and cultivated, makes herself agreeable to the Rosmer circle with such success that the affectionate and impulsive but unintelligent Mrs. Rosmer becomes wildly fond of her, and is not content until she has persuaded her to come and live with them. Rebecca, then a mere adventuress fighting for a foothold in polite society (which has hitherto shewn itself highly indignant at her thrusting herself in where nobody has thought of providing room for her), accepts the offer all the more readily because she has taken the measure of Parson Rosmer, and formed the idea of playing upon his aspirations, and making herself a leader in politics and society by using him as a figurehead.

But now two difficulties arise. First, there is Mrs. Rosmer's extinguishing effect on her husband: an effect which convinces Rebecca that nothing can be done with him whilst his wife is in the way. Second—a contingency quite unallowed for in her provident calculations—she finds herself passionately enamored of him. The poor parson, too, falls in love with her; but he does not know it. He turns to the woman who understands him like a sunflower to the sun, and makes her his real friend and companion. The wife feels this soon enough; and he, quite unconscious of it, begins to think that her mind must be affected, since she has become so intensely miserable and hysterical about nothing—nothing that he can see. The truth is that she has come under the curse of Rebecca's ideal: she sees herself standing, a useless obstacle, between her husband and the woman he really loves, the woman who can help him to a glorious career. She cannot even be the mother in the household; for she is childless. Then comes Rebecca, fortified with a finely reasoned theory that Rosmer's future is staked against his wife's life, and says that it is better for all their sakes that she should quit Rosmersholm. She even hints that she must go at once if a grave scandal is to be avoided. Mrs. Rosmer, regarding a scandal in Rosmersholm as the most terrible thing that can happen, and seeing that it could be averted by the marriage of Rebecca and Rosmer if she were out of the way, writes a letter secretly to Rosmer's bitterest enemy, the editor of the local Radical paper, a man who has forfeited his moral reputation by an intrigue which Rosmer has pitilessly denounced. In this letter she implores him not to believe or publish any stories that he may hear about Rosmer, to the effect that he is in any way to blame for any thing that may happen to her. Then she sets Rosmer free to marry Rebecca, and to realize his ideals, by going out into the garden and throwing herself into the millstream that runs there.

Now follows a period of quiet mourning at Rosmersholm. Everybody except Rosmer suspects that Mrs. Rosmer was not mad, and guesses why she committed suicide. Only it would not do to compromise the aristocratic party by treating Rosmer as the Radical editor was treated. So the neighbors shut their eyes and condole with the bereaved clergyman; and the Radical editor holds his tongue because Radicalism is growing respectable, and he hopes, with Rebecca's help, to get Rosmer over to his side presently. Meanwhile the unexpected has again happened to Rebecca. Her passion is worn out; but in the long days of mourning she has found the higher love; and it is now for Rosmer's own sake that she urges him to become a man of action, and brood no more over the dead. When his friends start a Conservative paper and ask him to become editor, she induces him to reply by declaring himself a Radical and Freethinker. To his utter amazement, the result is, not an animated discussion of his views, but just such an attack on his home life and private conduct as he had formerly made on those of the Radical editor. His friends tell him plainly that the compact of silence is broken by his defection, and that there will be no mercy for the traitor to the party. Even the Radical editor not only refuses to publish the fact that his new ally is a Freethinker (which would destroy all his social weight as a Radical recruit), but brings up the dead woman's letter as a proof that the attack is sufficiently well-founded to make it unwise to go too far. Rosmer, who at first had been simply shocked that men whom he had always honored as gentlemen should descend to such hideous calumny, now sees that he really did love Rebecca, and is indeed guilty of his wife's death. His first impulse is to shake off the spectre of the dead woman by marrying Rebecca; but she, knowing that the guilt is hers, puts that temptation behind her and refuses. Then, as he thinks it all over, his dream of ennobling the world slips away from him: such work can only be done by a man conscious of his own innocence. To save him from despair, Rebecca makes a great sacrifice. She "gives him back his innocence" by confessing how she drove his wife to kill herself; and, as the confession is made in the presence of Kroll, she ascribes the whole plot to her ambition, and says not a word of her passion. Rosmer, confounded as he realizes what helpless puppets they have all been in the hands of this clever woman, for the moment misses the point that unscrupulous ambition, though it explains her crime, does not account for her confession. He turns his back on her and leaves the house with Kroll. She quietly packs up her trunk, and is about to vanish from Rosmersholm without another word when he comes back alone to ask why she confessed. She tells him why, offering him her self-sacrifice as a proof that his power of ennobling others was no vain dream, since it is his companionship that has changed her from the selfish adventuress she was to the devoted woman she has just proved herself to be. But he has lost his faith in himself, and cannot believe her. The proof seems to him subtle, artful: he cannot forget that she duped him by flattering this very weakness of his before. Besides, he knows now that it is not true: people are not ennobled from without. She has no more to say; for she can think of no further proof. But he has thought of an unanswerable one. Dare she make all doubt impossible by sacrificing her share in his future in the only absolutely final way: that is, by doing for his sake what his wife did? She asks what would happen if she had the heart and the will to do it. "Then," he replies, "I should have to believe in you. I should recover my faith in my mission. Faith in my power to ennoble human souls. Faith in the human soul's power to attain nobility." "You shall have your faith again," she answers. At this pass the inner truth of the situation comes out; and the thin veil of a demand for proof, with its monstrous sequel of asking the woman to kill herself in order to restore the man's good opinion of himself, falls away. What is really driving Rosmer is the superstition of expiation by sacrifice. He sees that when Rebecca goes into the millstream he must go too. And he speaks his real mind in the words, "There is no judge over us: therefore we must do justice upon ourselves." But the woman's soul is free of this to the end; for when she says, "I am under the power of the Rosmersholm view of life *now*. What I have sinned it is fit I should expiate," we feel in that speech a protest against the Rosmersholm view of life: the view that denied her right to live and be happy from the first, and now at the end, even in denying its God, exacts her life as a vain blood-offering for its own blindness. The woman has the higher light: she goes to her death out of fellowship with the man who is driven thither by the superstition which has destroyed his will. The story ends with his taking her solemnly as his wife, and casting himself with her into the millstream.

It is unnecessary to repeat here what is said on page 1294 as to the vital part played in this drama by the evolution of the lower into the higher love. Peer Gynt, during the prophetic episode in his career, shocks the dancing girl Anitra into a remonstrance by comparing himself to a cat. He replies, with his wisest air, that from the standpoint of love there is perhaps not so much difference between a tomcat and a prophet as she may imagine. The number of critics who have entirely missed the point of Rebecca's transfiguration seems to indicate that the majority of men, even among critics of dramatic poetry, have not got beyond Peer Gynt's opinion in this matter. No doubt they would not endorse it as a definitely stated proposition, aware, as they are, that there is a poetic convention to the contrary. But if they fail to recognize the only possible alternative proposition when it is not only stated in so many words by Rebecca West, but when without it her conduct dramatically contradicts her character—when they even complain of the contradiction as a blemish on the play, I am afraid there can be no further doubt that the extreme perplexity into which the first performance of *Rosmersholm* in England plunged the Press was due entirely to the prevalence of Peer Gynt's view of love among the dramatic critics.

ROSMERSHOLM
[1886]

English Version by
MICHAEL MEYER

CHARACTERS

JOHN ROSMER   *owner of Rosmersholm, a former parish priest*
REBECCA WEST   *living at Rosmersholm*
DR. KROLL   *a headmaster, brother-in-law to* ROSMER
ULRIK BRENDEL
PETER MORTENSGAARD
MRS. HELSETH   *housekeeper at Rosmersholm*

The action takes place at Rosmersholm, an old country seat in the neighbourhood of a small town by a fjord in western Norway.

ACT ONE

The morning-room at Rosmersholm; spacious, old-fashioned and comfortable. Downstage on the right-hand wall is a tiled stove decorated with fresh birch branches and wild flowers. Upstage of this, a door. In the rear wall, folding doors to the hall. In the left-hand wall, a window. Downstage of this, a stand with flowers and plants. By the stove, a table with a sofa and easy chairs. Around the walls hang portraits, some old, some comparatively new, of priests, officers, and court officials in uniform. The window is open, as are the door to the hall and the front door beyond. Outside, an avenue of old trees is visible, leading to the estate. A summer evening. The sun has set.

REBECCA WEST *is seated in an armchair by the window, crocheting a large white woollen shawl, which is almost completed. Now and then she glances enquiringly out from behind the flowers. After a few moments* MRS. HELSETH *enters right.*

MRS. HELSETH—I'd better start laying the table soon, hadn't I, miss?

REBECCA—Yes, would you? I'm sure the Pastor will be back soon.

MRS. HELSETH—Isn't it draughty there, miss?

REBECCA—A little. Would you close it, please?

[MRS. HELSETH *goes over and shuts the door leading to the hall. Then she crosses to the window.*]

MRS. HELSETH [*about to close it, looks out*] Why, isn't that the Pastor coming now?

REBECCA [*quickly*] Where? [*Gets up.*] Yes, that's him. [*Behind the curtain.*] Get back. Don't let him see us.

MRS. HELSETH [*moves back into the room*] Oh, look, miss! Fancy that! He's beginning to use the mill-path again.

REBECCA—He did the day before yesterday, too. [*Peers out between the curtain and the window-frame.*] But now we'll see whether—

MRS. HELSETH—Will he dare take the footbridge?

REBECCA—That's what I want to find out. [*After a pause.*] No. He's turning. He's going round the top today, too. [*Leaves the window.*] The long way round.

MRS. HELSETH – Ah well, miss. It must be hard for the Pastor to cross that bridge. After what happened there—

REBECCA [*gathers her crocheting*] They cling to their dead here at Rosmersholm.

MRS. HELSETH – If you want my opinion, miss, it's the dead who cling to Rosmersholm.

REBECCA [*looks at her*] The dead?

MRS. HELSETH – Yes. It's almost as though they couldn't free themselves from the ones they left behind.

REBECCA – What makes you say that?

MRS. HELSETH – Well, otherwise this white horse wouldn't keep on appearing.

REBECCA – Mrs. Helseth, what exactly is all this about this white horse?

MRS. HELSETH – Oh, it's nothing. You wouldn't believe such things, anyway.

REBECCA – Do you believe in it, then?

MRS. HELSETH [*goes across and shuts the window*] Ah, you'd only laugh at me, miss. [*Looks out.*] Why—isn't that the Pastor on the mill-path again—?

REBECCA [*looks out*] That? [*Goes to the window.*] No, that's—why, that's Dr. Kroll!

MRS. HELSETH – Yes, so it is!

REBECCA – Well, that's a pleasant surprise. He must be coming to call on us.

MRS. HELSETH – He walks straight over the bridge, he does. Though she was his sister, and his own flesh and blood. Well, I'll go in and lay then, miss.

She goes out right. REBECCA *stands for a moment at the window; then she waves, smiles and nods towards the new visitor. Dusk is beginning to fall.*

REBECCA [*walks over and speaks through the door, right*] Mrs. Helseth, do you think you could give us something a little extra tonight? I expect you know what the headmaster likes best.

MRS. HELSETH [*offstage*] Very good, miss. You leave it to me.

REBECCA [*opens the door to the hall*] Well, at last—! Dear Dr. Kroll, how good to see you!

DR. KROLL [*in the hall, puts down his stick*] Thank you. I trust I don't call at an inconvenient moment?

1310

REBECCA—You? Don't be absurd.

KROLL [*enters*] Enchanting as ever! [*Looks around.*] Is Rosmer up in his study?

REBECCA—No, he's taking a walk. He's been a little longer than usual. But he'll be back any minute now. [*Indicates the sofa.*] Do please sit down until he comes.

KROLL [*puts down his hat*] Thank you, thank you. [*Sits and looks around.*] Well, how very attractive you've made this old room look! Flowers everywhere.

REBECCA—Mr. Rosmer loves to have fresh flowers around.

KROLL—So do you, I imagine.

REBECCA—Yes. I find them so beautifully soothing. In the old days we had to deny ourselves that pleasure.

KROLL [*nods sadly*] Poor Beata couldn't stand their perfume.

REBECCA—Nor their colours. They—confused her.

KROLL—Yes. I remember. [*More lightly.*] Well, how are things out here?

REBECCA—Oh, life goes on. Quiet and peaceful. One day very like another. And how are things with you? Your wife—?

KROLL—Ah, my dear Miss West, let's not talk about me. Every family has its troubles. Especially in such times as we live in now.

REBECCA [*after a moment, sits in an armchair by the sofa*] Why haven't you come out to see us? You haven't been once these holidays.

KROLL—Well, one doesn't like to bother people—

REBECCA—If you knew how we've missed you—

KROLL——and anyway, I've been away—

REBECCA—So I've heard. I gather you've been addressing public meetings.

KROLL [*nods*] Yes, what do you say to that? Never thought I'd turn political agitator in my old age, did you?

REBECCA [*smiles*] You've always been a bit of an agitator, Dr. Kroll.

KROLL—For my own amusement, yes. But now I'm taking it seriously. Do you ever see these radical newspapers?

REBECCA—Well, yes, I can't deny—

KROLL—My dear Miss West, there's no earthly reason why you shouldn't. A person such as yourself—

REBECCA—That's what I think. I have to keep up with things. Keep informed about what's going on—

KROLL—Of course I suppose one can't expect you as a woman to take active sides in this civil dispute—I nearly said civil war—that's raging here. But then, you must have read all this mud that's been thrown at me by these so-called representatives of the people? It's really infamous the crudities that they indulge in.

1311

REBECCA—I thought you gave them a pretty good nip or two.

KROLL—I did! I say it myself. Yes, I've tasted blood now! They'll learn I'm not the cheek-turning kind—! [*Breaks off.*] But let's not discuss this distressing subject this evening.

REBECCA—No, dear Dr. Kroll, I'd rather not.

KROLL—Tell me, how are you finding life at Rosmersholm now that you're alone here? Since our poor Beata—?

REBECCA—Oh, thank you, I'm quite happy. Of course it seems very empty without her. And sad—I miss her terribly. But apart from that—

KROLL—Do you plan to stay? Permanently, I mean?

REBECCA—Dear Dr. Kroll, I don't really think about it one way or the other. I've grown so used to the place now, I almost feel I belong here.

KROLL—But of course. So I should hope.

REBECCA—And as long as Mr. Rosmer feels I can be of any use and comfort to him—well, I think I'll stay.

KROLL [*looks at her, moved*] You know, it's a pretty noble thing for a woman to sacrifice her youth for other people.

REBECCA—What else would I have had to live for?

KROLL—First you had that foster-father of yours to look after—I know how unreasonable he was, once he got paralysed, and what a strain that must have been—

REBECCA—Oh, he wasn't so—unreasonable in the old days, when we were living up in the north. It was those dreadful sea voyages that broke him. But once we'd moved down here—yes, we did have one or two difficult years before his troubles ended.

KROLL—Weren't the years that followed even more difficult for you?

REBECCA—No, how can you say such a thing! I loved Beata—and she so needed care and affection, the poor darling.

KROLL—Bless you for remembering her so charitably.

REBECCA [*moves a little closer to him*] Dear Dr. Kroll, you say that so kindly and sincerely—I'm sure you have no bad feeling about this.

KROLL—Bad feeling? What do you mean?

REBECCA—Well, it wouldn't be so strange if you found it rather painful to see a stranger like me running Rosmersholm.

KROLL—Great heavens alive, how—?

REBECCA—But you don't. [*Gives him her hand.*] Thank you, dear Dr. Kroll! Thank you, thank you!

KROLL—But how in heaven's name could such an idea enter your head?

REBECCA—I began to worry a little because you so seldom visited us.

KROLL—Then you've been barking up the wrong tree, Miss West. And besides—nothing has really changed here. I mean, it was you, and you alone, who ran Rosmersholm during those last unhappy months of poor Beata's life.

R E B E C C A – I was only a substitute for Mrs. Rosmer.

K R O L L – Yes, well– You know what, Miss West? For my own part, I shouldn't be at all sorry to see you–but one mustn't speak of such things yet.

R E B E C C A – What do you mean?

K R O L L – If things should so turn out that you should fill the place left by–

R E B E C C A – I have the place I want, Dr. Kroll.

K R O L L – Materially, perhaps; but not–

R E B E C C A [*interrupts earnestly*] Shame on you, Dr. Kroll! How can you sit here joking about such a subject?

K R O L L – Ah well, our good John Rosmer probably feels he's had his share of matrimony. All the same–

R E B E C C A – No, please, this is really too ridiculous.

K R O L L – All the same–! Tell me, Miss West–if it isn't an impertinent question–how old are you?

R E B E C C A – I'm ashamed to admit I am already twenty-nine, Dr. Kroll. Coming up to thirty.

K R O L L – Really. And Rosmer–how old is he? Let me see. He's five years younger than I am–well then, he must be around forty-three. I think that would be highly suitable.

R E B E C C A [*rises*] Indeed, yes. Most suitable. Will you take tea with us this evening?

K R O L L – Thank you–yes, I had thought of staying. There's something I want to discuss with our friend. And, by the way, Miss West–just in case you should start having any further foolish thoughts, I intend to visit you both regularly–just like in the old days.

R E B E C C A – Oh yes, please do! [*Presses his hands.*] Thank you, thank you! You're so good and kind!

K R O L L [*a little growlishly*] Am I? That's more than I ever hear at home.

[JOHN ROSMER *enters right.*]

R E B E C C A – Mr. Rosmer–do you see who's sitting here?

R O S M E R – Mrs. Helseth told me.

[DR. KROLL *has got up.*]

R O S M E R [*softly, emotionally, clasps* KROLL'S *hands*] Welcome back to Rosmersholm, my dear Kroll! [*Puts his hands on* KROLL'S *shoulders and looks him in the eyes.*] My dear old friend! I knew everything would be all right between us again.

K R O L L – But, my dear fellow–have you too had this idiotic delusion that there was something wrong?

R E B E C C A [*to* ROSMER] What a blessing it was only an idiotic delusion!

1313

ROSMER—Was it really, Kroll? But then, why did you never come to see us?

KROLL [*earnestly, softly*] Because I didn't want to be a living reminder of your years of unhappiness—and of—of her who ended in the mill-race.

ROSMER—That was very kind of you. You're always so considerate. But I promise you it was quite unnecessary. Come, Kroll—let's sit down on the sofa. [*They sit.*] No, I don't find it painful to be reminded of Beata. We speak about her every day.

KROLL—Do you really?

REBECCA [*lights the lamp*] Indeed we do.

ROSMER—But it stands to reason. We both loved her so dearly. And Rebec—Miss West and I both know we did all we could to help the poor darling. We have nothing with which to reproach ourselves. Our memory of Beata is purely a happy one.

KROLL—You dear, good people! From now on I shall come and visit you every day.

REBECCA [*sits in an armchair*] Well, let's see if you keep your word.

ROSMER [*somewhat hesitantly*] Kroll—I'm deeply grieved that our friendship was ever interrupted. I've always greatly valued your advice, all the years we've known each other. Ever since I left school.

KROLL—Well, yes, and I'm proud of it. Is there something particular at the moment that—?

ROSMER—There's a lot I want to discuss with you. I'd very much welcome a heart-to-heart talk.

REBECCA—Yes, do. I think it must be such a comfort to have an old friend one can—

KROLL—Oh, believe me, there's even more that I want to discuss with you. I suppose you know I've now become an active politician?

ROSMER—Yes, so you have. How did that happen?

KROLL—I had to, Rosmer. Couldn't help it—though I put on a pretty stiff fight against it! One can't just go on being an idle observer. Now that these dreadful radicals have come to power, I feel the moment has come. So I've persuaded our little circle of friends in town to close their ranks. The moment has come, I tell you!

REBECCA [*with a gentle smile*] Isn't it a little late, now?

KROLL—Well, I won't deny it would have been better if we could have stemmed the tide earlier. But who could have foreseen what was going to happen? Not I, at any rate. [*Gets up and walks round the room.*] But now my eyes have been opened. Would you believe it, the spirit of anarchy has forced its way into the school itself!

ROSMER—The school? Surely not your school?

KROLL—Indeed it has. My own school. What do you think of that! I

have discovered that for over six months the boys in the Sixth Form—
some of them, anyway—have been running a secret society! And they've
taken out a subscription to that damned paper of Mortensgaard's!

R E B E C C A – The *Morning Star?*

K R O L L – Yes—fine mental sustenance for the future leaders of our country, eh? But the worst of the matter is that it's all my best pupils who
have banded together in this conspiracy against me. It's only the dunces
and the idlers who've kept aloof.

R E B E C C A – Does this worry you so much, Dr. Kroll?

K R O L L – Worry me! To see my whole life's work obstructed and threatened! But that's not the worst. There's something else. [*Looks round.*]
There isn't anyone listening?

R E B E C C A – No, of course not.

K R O L L – Well, then—you will hardly credit it, but this discord and
subversion has penetrated into my own house—into the calm and peace
of my very home! It has destroyed the tenor of my family life.

R O S M E R [*rises*] What! Your own home—!

R E B E C C A [*goes over to* KROLL] But, my dear Dr. Kroll, what on
earth has happened?

K R O L L – Would you believe it—my own children—! Well, to cut a long
story short, Lauritz is the ringleader of the conspiracy. And Hilda has
embroidered a red cover to hide the *Morning Star* in.

R O S M E R – That I'd never have imagined! In your own home—!

K R O L L – Who'd have dreamed it was possible! In my home, where
obedience and order have always reigned—where until now all voices
have spoken as one—!

R E B E C C A – How does your wife take all this?

K R O L L – That's the most incredible thing of all. All her life, in great
things and small, she's shared my opinions and supported everything
I've said—and now even she's started taking the children's side. And
she blames *me* for what has happened. Says I've repressed them. As
though it weren't necessary to give them an occasional—! Well, so I've
had trouble at home, too. But of course I don't talk about it. Such
things are best kept quiet. [*Walks across the room.*] Oh dear, oh dear,
oh dear! [*Stops by the window with his hands behind his back and
looks out.*]

R E B E C C A [*has gone over to* ROSMER *and, unnoticed by* KROLL, *whispers quickly*] Tell him!

R O S M E R [*similarly*] Not tonight.

R E B E C C A [*as before*] Yes, now.

[*She goes over and attends to the lamp.*]

K R O L L [*comes across the room*] Well, my dear Rosmer, so now you
know how the spirit of the age has cast its shadow over my domestic

as well as my official life. These decadent, cankerous, demoralizing heresies—must I not fight them with all the weapons I can muster? Yes, Rosmer, that is what I intend to do! Not only with my tongue, but with my pen!

ROSMER—Do you think you'll be able to achieve anything?

KROLL—I shall at any rate have performed my duty as a citizen. And I regard it as the duty of every right-minded and patriotic Norwegian to do the same. Actually, that's the chief reason I came out to see you this evening.

ROSMER—But, my dear fellow, what could I—?

KROLL—You must rally to our cause. Help your old friends, lend us all your strength.

REBECCA—But, Dr. Kroll, you know how Mr. Rosmer hates that kind of public activity.

KROLL—He must overcome his hatred. You're too passive, Rosmer. You sit here walled in by your books—oh, heaven knows I've every respect for research and scholarship. But this is no time for such indulgences, more's the pity. You don't seem to realize what the situation in our country is. Practically every single accepted idea has been turned topsy-turvy. It's going to be a battle to get these vicious heresies rooted out.

ROSMER—I agree. But that kind of work is hardly in my line.

REBECCA—And I think Mr. Rosmer has come to look at life from a more liberal viewpoint than before.

KROLL [*starts*] More liberal—!

REBECCA—More open-minded. Less prejudiced.

KROLL—What on earth do you mean? Rosmer—surely you couldn't be so feeble as to imagine that these demagogues have won anything more than a temporary victory?

ROSMER—My dear Kroll, you know how little I understand politics. But I believe that in recent years people have perhaps begun to think more independently.

KROLL—And you regard that as a good thing? Anyway, you're quite wrong, my friend. Just you find out for yourself the opinions that these radicals are propagating! It's hardly any different from the rubbish that's preached in the pages of the *Morning Star*.

REBECCA—Yes, Mortensgaard has a lot of influence over people around here.

KROLL—Isn't it incredible! A man with a past like that! Thrown out of his teaching job for an immoral relationship! A man like that setting himself up as a leader of the people! And he's succeeding! He's actually succeeding! I hear he's now planning to expand his newspaper. I'm told on good authority that he's looking for a partner.

REBECCA–Why don't you and your friends start a rival newspaper?

KROLL–That's exactly what we're doing. This very day we have bought the *County Telegraph*. The financial question presented no difficulties. But–[*Turns to* ROSMER.] Well, this is really what I came to speak to you about. It's the running of the paper–the editorial side–that is our problem, you see. Tell me, Rosmer–remembering the issues at stake, couldn't you see your way to helping us out?

ROSMER   [*almost as though frightened*] I?

REBECCA–How could you imagine such a thing?

KROLL–I know you hate public meetings and don't want to expose yourself to the kind of rough stuff that goes on there. But the more secluded work of an editor, or what I might rather call the–

ROSMER–No, no, my dear chap, you mustn't ask me to do this.

KROLL–I'd gladly have a shot at it myself. But I couldn't possibly manage it. I'm already so overburdened with obligations. You, on the other hand, no longer have any professional commitments. Of course the rest of us will give you all the help we can–

ROSMER–I can't, Kroll. I'm not the right man for it.

KROLL–Not the right man? That's what you said when your father procured this living for you–

ROSMER–I was right. That was why I went my own way.

KROLL–Oh, if you're only as good an editor as you were a man of God, we shan't complain.

ROSMER–Look, Kroll, I'm telling you once and for all. I won't do it.

KROLL–Well, at least you'll let us use your name.

ROSMER–My name?

KROLL–Yes, the mere name of John Rosmer will be a great asset to our paper. The rest of us are known to be politically committed. I gather that I myself am already branded as a furious fanatic. So our names aren't likely to make any converts among the misguided masses. But you–you've always stood outside the battle. Your goodness and incorruptibility, your sensitivity and intellect, your unimpeachable integrity, are known and prized by everyone throughout the county. To say nothing of the honour and respect which you command as a former man of God! And, last but by no means least, there's the name of your family.

ROSMER–Oh, the name of my family–

KROLL   [*points to the portraits*] The Rosmers of Rosmersholm. Men of God and men of war. Respected servants of their country. Every one of them a man of honour who knew his duty. A family that for nigh on two hundred years has been venerated and looked up to as the first in the county. [*Puts a hand on* ROSMER's *shoulder.*] Rosmer–you owe it to yourself and to the traditions of your family to defend and protect everything that has hitherto been held sacred in our society. [*Turns.*] Well, what do you say, Miss West?

REBECCA [*with a soft, quiet laugh*] Dear Dr. Kroll! I find all this unspeakably ludicrous.

KROLL – What! Ludicrous!

REBECCA – Yes. You might as well know—

ROSMER [*quickly*] No, no—please! Not now!

KROLL [*looks from one to the other*] My dear friends, what on earth—? [*Breaks off.*] Hm!

[MRS. HELSETH *enters through the door right.*]

MRS. HELSETH [*to* ROSMER] There's a man at the servants' entrance. He says he wants to speak with you, sir.

ROSMER [*relieved*] Is there? Well, tell him to come in.

MRS. HELSETH – Here? Into the drawing room?

ROSMER – Of course.

MRS. HELSETH – But he doesn't look the type to bring in here.

REBECCA – How does he look, Mrs. Helseth?

MRS. HELSETH – Oh, not at all respectable, miss.

ROSMER – Didn't he say who he was?

MRS. HELSETH – Yes, I think he said he was called Hekman or something.

ROSMER – I don't know anyone of that name.

MRS. HELSETH – He said something about being called Ulrik, too.

ROSMER [*starts*] Ulrik Hetman! Was that it?

MRS. HELSETH – Hetman—yes, that was it.

KROLL – I'm sure I've heard that name before—

REBECCA – Wasn't that the name he used to write under—you remember, that strange old—?

ROSMER [*to* KROLL] It is Ulrik Brendel's pen-name, Kroll.

KROLL – Ulrik Brendel! That charlatan. Yes, I remember him.

REBECCA – So he's still alive.

ROSMER – The last I heard of him, he'd joined up with a troupe of strolling players.

KROLL – The last *I* heard of him, he was in the workhouse.

ROSMER – Please ask him to come in, Mrs. Helseth.

MRS. HELSETH – As you say, sir. [*She goes.*]

KROLL – Are you really going to allow that man into your drawing room?

ROSMER – Surely you remember? He used to be my tutor.

KROLL – I remember he used to come here and stuff your head full of radical nonsense, until your father chased him out of the door with a horsewhip.

ROSMER   [*a little bitterly*] Father always acted the Major, even in his own house.

KROLL – Thank him in his grave for it, my dear Rosmer. Ha!

MRS. HELSETH *opens the door on the right for* ULRIK BRENDEL, *exits and closes it behind him. He is a handsome figure, somewhat emaciated, but brisk and lively, with grey hair and beard. He is dressed like a common tramp, in a worn frock coat and bad shoes; no shirt is visible. Old black gloves; a soft, dirty hat beneath his arm; and a walking stick in his hand.*

ULRIK BRENDEL   [*hesitates at first, then walks briskly over to* KROLL *and holds out his hands*] Good evening, John!

KROLL – I beg your pardon—

BRENDEL – Didst think to see my face again Within these hated walls?

KROLL – I beg your pardon. [*Points.*] *That is—*

BRENDEL   [*turns*] But of course! *Le voilà!* John—*mon garçon—ah, mon petit chéri—!*

ROSMER   [*shakes his hand*] My dear old tutor!

BRENDEL – Certain memories notwithstanding, I was loth to pass this ancient seat without a fleeting visit.

ROSMER – You are most heartily welcome here. Never fear that.

BRENDEL – And this charming lady—? [*Bows.*] Your wife, of course.

ROSMER – Miss West.

BRENDEL – A close relative, no doubt. And yon stranger—? A brother of the cloth, I see.

KROLL – My name is Kroll, sir. I am the local headmaster.

BRENDEL – Kroll? Kroll? *Momento!* Had you, sir, in your salad days, pretensions towards philology?

KROLL – Naturally I read the subject.

BRENDEL – Why, *Donnerwetter*, then I used to know you!

KROLL   [*deprecatingly*] Please!

BRENDEL – Weren't you—?

KROLL   [*as before*] Please!

BRENDEL – —one of those crusading moralisers who got me expelled from the University Debating Society?

KROLL – Very possibly. But I must disclaim any closer relationship.

BRENDEL – Ah, well. *Nach Belieben*, Herr Doctor! What boots it? Ulrik Brendel remains the man he is.

REBECCA – Are you making for town, Mr. Brendel?

BRENDEL – A hit, madam—a palpable hit! At intervals in life I find myself impelled to strike a blow for existence. Against the grain; but, *enfin!—la necessité—!*

1319

R O S M E R – But, my dear Mr. Brendel, won't you let me help you? Somehow or other–?

B R E N D E L – Ha? What a suggestion! Wouldst thou profane the bond that binds us? Never, John–never!

R O S M E R – But what are you planning to do in town? Believe me, you won't find it easy to–

B R E N D E L – Leave that to me, my boy. The die is cast. You see me at the outset of a great campaign, that dwarfs my previous reconnoitrings. [*To* KROLL.] Dare I ask the Herr Professor if–*unter uns*–there chances to be a reasonably respectable and capacious lecture hall in your esteemed town?

K R O L L – I suppose the largest is the Workers' Union–

B R E N D E L – And has Your Honour any influence in this doubtless august body?

K R O L L – I have nothing whatever to do with them.

R E B E C C A   [*to* BRENDEL] You ought to get in touch with Peter Mortensgaard.

B R E N D E L – *Pardon, madame!* What kind of a *fou* is that?

R O S M E R – What makes you think he's a fool?

B R E N D E L – The very name tells me that the bearer is a plebeian.

K R O L L – I hadn't expected that answer.

B R E N D E L – But I will conquer my nausea. I have no choice. When a man such as myself stands at a crossroads in his life–*enfin!* It is ordained. I shall contact this individual–enter into negotiations–

R O S M E R – Are you seriously at a crossroads?

B R E N D E L – My dear boy, don't you know that Ulrik Brendel is always serious? Yes, John! I intend to become a new man. To abandon the role of modest onlooker.

R O S M E R – But how do you–?

B R E N D E L – I now descend into the arena of life! We live in a storm-wracked and ecliptical age. I shall step forth to lay my humble mite upon the altar of emancipation!

K R O L L – You too–?

B R E N D E L   [*to them all*] Is the company acquainted with my *obiter scripta?*

K R O L L – No, to be frank, I–

R E B E C C A – I've read several. My guardian used to have them.

B R E N D E L – Then, fair lady, you have wasted your time. It is all bunk. Take my word for it.

R E B E C C A – Oh?

B R E N D E L – What you have read. My major works remain unknown. Save to myself.

R E B E C C A – Why is that?

BRENDEL – Because they are not yet written.

ROSMER – But, my dear Mr. Brendel–

BRENDEL – As you remember, *cher Jean,* I'm a bit of a sybarite. A gourmet. Always have been. I like to savour things in solitude. Then I enjoy them doubly–nay, tenfold! When golden dreams descended on me, enveloping me in mist–when new and dazzling ideas were born in me, and wafted me heavenwards on their swift pinions–I fashioned them into poems, visions, images! In draft, you understand–

ROSMER – Yes, yes.

BRENDEL – Ah, John! I have drunk deep of pleasure! The riddling mystery of creation–in draft, as I said–the applause, the eulogies, the fame, the laurels–I have garnered them all with hands that shook with joy. I have sated myself in secret dreams with a rapture–ah!–that drugged my senses–

KROLL – Hm!

ROSMER – But you never wrote any of it down?

BRENDEL – Not a word. The dull toil of the scribe has always repelled me. And why should I profane my own ideals when I can enjoy them undisturbed in their virgin purity? But now I offer them up. I feel like a mother about to deliver her unspotted daughters into the rough arms of their husbands. But I offer them, notwithstanding–a sacrifice upon the altar of emancipation. A sequence of inspiring lectures– throughout the country–!

REBECCA [*animatedly*] This is a noble gesture, Mr. Brendel! You are sacrificing the dearest thing you possess.

ROSMER – The only thing.

REBECCA [*looks meaningly at* ROSMER] How many other men would do this? Would have the courage to do it?

ROSMER [*returns her glance*] Who knows?

BRENDEL – My audience is moved. That quickens my heart–and strengthens my will. I shall proceed to action. One thing, though– [*To* KROLL.] Can Your Reverence tell me–is there a Temperance Association in this town? A Society of Total Abstinence? Doubtless there is.

KROLL – Indeed, yes. I myself am its president, at your service.

BRENDEL – I knew it by your face! Well, then, it is not impossible that I may look in on you and enrol for a week.

KROLL – I beg your pardon. We do not enrol members by the week.

BRENDEL – *À la bonheur,* Herr Pedagogue. Ulrik Brendel has never forced his presence on such institutions. [*Turns.*] But I must not tarry longer in this house, so rich in memories. I must press on to town, and select a suitable abode. There is, I trust, a respectable hotel?

REBECCA – Won't you have a drink to warm you before you go?

BRENDEL – In what way "warm" me, gracious lady?

REBECCA – A cup of tea, or—

BRENDEL – Thanks, bountiful hostess. I never presume on private hospitality. [*Makes a farewell gesture to them all with his hand.*] *Auf Wiedersehen, mein Herrschaft!* [*Goes towards the door, but turns.*] Ah, true, I had forgotten. John—Pastor Rosmer—will you, for auld lang syne, do your old tutor a small service?

ROSMER – With all my heart.

BRENDEL – *Bien!* Then lend me—just for a day or two—a well-ironed evening shirt.

ROSMER – Is that all?

BRENDEL – For once I march on foot. My luggage is being sent after me.

ROSMER – Of course. But isn't there anything else—?

BRENDEL – Well—since you mention it—could you conceivably spare an old, used, summer overcoat?

ROSMER – Yes, yes, of course.

BRENDEL – And if you should chance to have a decent pair of boots to match the coat—

ROSMER – I'm sure that can be arranged. As soon as we know your address I'll have them all sent on.

BRENDEL – Under no circumstances! I wish no inconvenience to be caused. I'll take these trifles with me.

ROSMER – Very well. Come upstairs with me, then.

REBECCA – No, let me. Mrs. Helseth and I can see to it.

BRENDEL – Never could I permit this *belle madame*—

REBECCA – Oh, nonsense. Now just you come with me, Mr. Brendel. [*Goes out right.*]

ROSMER [*detains him*] Tell me—isn't there anything else I can do to help you?

BRENDEL – Other way? I really can't imagine—*oui, parbleu,* now I think of it—! John—you haven't by any chance five shillings on you?

ROSMER – We'll see. [*Opens his purse.*] I've a couple of ten shilling notes—

BRENDEL – Don't bother. I can always get them changed in town. You shall have the change shortly. Don't forget—two ten shilling notes. *Guten nacht,* my own, dear boy! Worshipful sir, good night. [*He goes right, where* ROSMER *takes leave of him and closes the door behind him.*]

KROLL – Merciful heaven! So that was the Ulrik Brendel who people once believed would reshape the world!

ROSMER [*quietly*] At least he has had the courage to live life the way he thought it should be lived. I don't think that's so small an achievement.

KROLL – What! A life like his! Don't tell me he's turning your head again.

ROSMER – Oh, no, Kroll. Now I see my way clearly.

KROLL – Let us hope so, my dear Rosmer. You're so impressionable.

ROSMER – Come and sit down. I want to talk to you.

KROLL – By all means. [*They sit on the sofa.*]

ROSMER [*after a few moments*] We've made it pleasant and comfortable here, don't you think?

KROLL – Yes. It is very pleasant and comfortable here now. And peaceful. Yes, you've found yourself a home, Rosmer. And I have lost mine.

ROSMER – Don't say that, Kroll. Things will come right.

KROLL – Never. Never. The memory will always rankle. Things will never be as they were.

ROSMER – Now listen, Kroll. We two have been very close for so many years. Do you think anything could happen that could ever make us cease to be friends?

KROLL – I can't imagine anything that could make us enemies. Why do you ask?

ROSMER – You mind so violently if people don't share your opinions.

KROLL – Well, possibly—but you and I agree on pretty well everything. In essentials, anyway.

ROSMER [*quietly*] No. Not any longer.

KROLL [*tries to jump up*] What do you mean?

ROSMER [*puts a hand to restrain him*] No, you must sit still. Please, Kroll. I beg you.

KROLL – What is this? I don't understand you.

ROSMER – A new spring has dawned in my mind. A new youth, a new way of thought. So that—now I stand—

KROLL – Where? Where do you stand?

ROSMER – Where your children stand.

KROLL – You? You! But that's impossible! Where do you say you stand?

ROSMER – On the same side as Lauritz and Hilda.

KROLL [*bows his head*] An apostate! John Rosmer an apostate!

ROSMER – I ought to have felt a sense of joy at what you call my apostasy. But it grieved me. Because I knew it would grieve you deeply.

KROLL – Rosmer—Rosmer! I shall never recover from this. [*Looks sadly at him.*] To think that you can ally yourself with the forces of evil that are seeking to destroy our unhappy country.

ROSMER – I want to ally myself with the forces of emancipation.

KROLL – Yes, I know. That is the name given to it by the seducers, and by the victims they lead astray. But do you really believe that there is any emancipation to be hoped for from this spirit that is doing its best to poison our whole communal life?

ROSMER – I am not identifying myself with that spirit. Nor with either of the contending parties. I want to bring together men from all sides in a spirit of unity. As many as possible, and as urgently as possible. I want to devote my life and all my strength to this one end, of creating a responsible public opinion in our country.

KROLL – Don't you think we've had enough of public opinions? Personally, I think we're all well on the way to being dragged down into the gutter where only the common people can thrive.

ROSMER – That is exactly where I feel the task of public opinion lies.

KROLL – Task? What task?

ROSMER – To make all the people in this country noblemen.

KROLL – All the people–?

ROSMER – As many as possible, anyway.

KROLL – How?

ROSMER – By emancipating their minds and purifying their wills.

KROLL – You're a dreamer, Rosmer. Will *you* emancipate them? Will *you* purify them?

ROSMER – No, my dear friend. I can only try to open their eyes to the need for it. They must do it themselves.

KROLL – And you think they can?

ROSMER – Yes.

KROLL – By their own strength?

ROSMER – Yes, by their own strength. There is no other.

KROLL [*gets up*] Is this proper language from a man of God?

ROSMER – I am no longer a man of God.

KROLL – Yes, but–the faith you were brought up in–?

ROSMER – I no longer have it.

KROLL – No longer–!

ROSMER [*gets up*] I have given it up. I *had* to give it up, Kroll.

KROLL [*controls his emotion*] I see. Yes, yes, yes. The one follows the other. Was that why you left the Church?

ROSMER – Yes. When I saw things clearly–when I knew for sure that it was not a passing temptation, but something that I never could nor would escape from–then I left.

KROLL – So it has been fermenting inside you all this time. And we– your friends–were told nothing about it. Rosmer, Rosmer–how could you hide this dreadful truth from us?

ROSMER – Because I thought it was something that concerned only myself. Besides, I didn't want to cause you and my other friends unnecessary distress. I thought I could go on living here as before, quiet and peaceful and happy. I wanted to read, to bury myself in those fields of thought that had hitherto been closed to me. To find my way into the great world of truth and freedom to which my eyes have now been opened.

KROLL – Apostate! Every word proves it. But why are you confessing all this? And why just now?

ROSMER – You have forced me to, Kroll.

KROLL – I? I forced you–!

ROSMER – When I heard about your violent conduct at those meetings–when I read about all the cruel speeches you made there–those hateful outbursts against your opponents–your scornful condemnation of everything they stood for–! Oh, Kroll! That you, you, could become like that! Then I saw my duty plainly. This strife that is being waged makes people evil. Their hearts must be filled with peace and joy and understanding. That is why I now stand forth to declare myself openly. I, too, want to test my strength. Couldn't you–from your side–help me, Kroll?

KROLL – Never while I draw breath shall I compromise with the forces that are seeking to destroy our society.

ROSMER – Then if we must fight, at least let us fight with honourable weapons.

KROLL – Whoever is not with me in such issues, him I no longer know. And I owe him no consideration.

ROSMER – Does that apply to me too?

KROLL – It's you who have broken with me, Rosmer.

ROSMER – Is this a breach, then?

KROLL – Yes! It is a breach with all those who have hitherto been your friends. Now you must face the consequences.

[REBECCA WEST *enters right, and throws the door wide open.*]

REBECCA – There! Now he's off to his sacrificial orgy. And now we can go and eat. Dr. Kroll!

KROLL [*takes his hat*] Good night, Miss West. I have no further business in this house.

REBECCA [*tensely*] What is it? [*Shuts the door and comes closer.*] Have you told him–?

ROSMER – Yes, he knows now.

KROLL – We won't let you go, Rosmer. We'll force you to come back to us.

ROSMER – I shall never do that.

KROLL – We'll see. You are not the kind of man who can stand alone.

ROSMER – I shall not be alone. There are two of us to bear the solitude together.

KROLL – Ah–! [*A suspicion crosses his mind.*] That too! Beata's words–!

ROSMER—Beata—?

KROLL [*dismisses the thought*] No, no. That was vile. Forgive me.

ROSMER—What? What do you mean?

KROLL—Please forget it. No, it's unthinkable! Forgive me. Goodbye. [*Goes towards the door leading to the hall.*]

ROSMER [*goes after him*] Kroll! We can't part like this. I'll come and see you tomorrow.

KROLL [*in the hall, turns*] You shall not set foot in my house! [*Takes his stick and goes.*]

[ROSMER *stands for a second in the open doorway. Then he closes the door and walks across to the table.*]

ROSMER—It doesn't matter, Rebecca. We shall manage. We two loyal friends. You and I.

REBECCA—What do you think he meant when he said: "It's unthinkable"?

ROSMER—Oh, don't bother about that, my dear. Whatever it was, he didn't believe it. Tomorrow I'll go in and see him. Good night.

REBECCA—Are you going to bed so early again tonight? After this?

ROSMER—Tonight as always. I feel so at peace now that it's over. You see—I am quite calm, Rebecca. You must take it calmly too, my dear. Good night.

REBECCA—Good night, dear friend. And sleep well.

ROSMER *goes out through the hall door. We hear him mount the stairs.* REBECCA *walks over and pulls a bellrope by the stove. After a few moments* MRS. HELSETH *enters right.*

REBECCA—You can clear the table again, Mrs. Helseth. The Pastor doesn't want anything. And the Doctor has gone home.

MRS. HELSETH—The Doctor gone? What's wrong with him?

REBECCA [*takes her crochet-work*] He thought a storm was blowing up—

MRS. HELSETH—That's strange. There isn't a cloud in the sky this evening.

REBECCA—As long as he doesn't see the white horse. I'm afraid we may soon be hearing from one of these ghosts of yours.

MRS. HELSETH—God forgive you, Miss West! Don't say such wicked things!

REBECCA—All right, all right—

MRS. HELSETH [*lowers her voice*] Do you really think someone's going to go soon, miss?

REBECCA—No, of course not. But there are so many kinds of white horses in this world, Mrs. Helseth. Well, good night. I'm going to my room.

MRS. HELSETH—Good night, miss.

[REBECCA *goes out right with her crochet-work.*]

MRS. HELSETH [*turns down the lamp, shakes her head and mumbles to herself*] Blessed Jesus! That Miss West. The way she talks sometimes.

ACT TWO

JOHN ROSMER'S *study. In the left-hand wall is the entrance door. In the rear wall, a doorway with a curtain drawn aside from it, leading into his bedroom. Right, a window. In front of it, a desk, covered with books and papers. Bookshelves and bookcases around the walls. Frugally furnished. Downstage left, an old-fashioned couch with a table by it.*

JOHN ROSMER, *wearing a smoking jacket, is seated in a high-backed chair at the desk. He is cutting a pamphlet and glancing through it, pausing now and then to dwell.*

[*There is a knock on the door left.*]

ROSMER [*without turning*] Come in.

[REBECCA WEST *enters in a dressing gown.*]

REBECCA – Good morning.

ROSMER [*turning the pages*] Good morning, my dear. Is there something you want?

REBECCA – I only wanted to ask if you've slept well.

ROSMER – Oh, yes. So deeply and peacefully. No dreams– [*Turns.*] And you?

REBECCA – Oh–yes, thank you. Towards morning.

ROSMER – I don't know when I last felt as easy in my heart as I do now. Oh, I'm so thankful I got that off my chest.

REBECCA – Yes, you shouldn't have kept it to yourself for so long, John.

ROSMER – I can't understand how I could have been such a coward.

REBECCA – Oh, it isn't a question of cowardice–

ROSMER – Oh, yes it was. When I think about it honestly, there was a good deal of cowardice in it.

REBECCA – All the more credit to you, then, for managing to overcome it. [*Sits down beside him on a chair by the desk.*] But now I want to tell you about something I've done–you mustn't be angry with me–

ROSMER – Angry? My dear, how could you imagine–?

REBECCA – Well, it was perhaps a little high-handed of me, but–

1328

ROSMER—Well, tell me what it was.

REBECCA—Last night, when that Ulrik Brendel was leaving, —I wrote him a few lines to take to Mortensgaard.

ROSMER [*a little doubtfully*] But, my dear Rebecca—! Well, what did you write?

REBECCA—I said he'd be doing you a service if he took care of that unfortunate man and gave him all the help he could.

ROSMER—My dear, you shouldn't have done that. That'll only have done Brendel harm. Besides, I'd much rather not have anything to do with Mortensgaard. You know the trouble I had with him once.

REBECCA—Don't you think it might be a good idea if you made things up with him?

ROSMER—I? With Mortensgaard? Why do you say that?

REBECCA—Well, you can't really feel safe now—now that you've quarrelled with your friends.

ROSMER [*looks at her and shakes his head*] Surely you don't imagine that Kroll or any of the others would want to be vindictive? That they might be thinking of—?

REBECCA—First reactions, you know—one can't be sure. I think possibly—after the way he took it—

ROSMER—Oh, you ought to know him better than that. Kroll's nothing if not a gentleman. I'll go along this evening and have a word with him. I'll talk to all of them. You'll see, everything'll be all right—

[MRS. HELSETH *enters through the door left.*]

REBECCA [*rises*] What is it, Mrs. Helseth?

MRS. HELSETH—Dr. Kroll's downstairs in the hall.

ROSMER [*gets up quickly*] Kroll!

REBECCA—Do you think he—?

MRS. HELSETH—He asks if he can come up and speak with you, sir.

ROSMER [*to* REBECCA] What did I tell you! Yes, of course he can. [*Goes to the door and calls down the stairs.*] Come up, my dear fellow. I'm delighted to see you.

ROSMER *stands holding the door open.* MRS. HELSETH *goes.* REBECCA *draws the curtain across the open doorway. Then she begins tidying here and there.* DR. KROLL *enters, hat in hand.*

ROSMER [*quiet, moved*] I knew it couldn't be the last time we'd—

KROLL —Today I see things in a different light from yesterday.

ROSMER—I knew you would. Now you've had time to think the matter over—

KROLL—You completely misunderstand me. [*Puts his hat on the table by the couch.*] It is imperative that I speak with you privately.

ROSMER—Surely Miss West—?

REBECCA—No, no, Mr. Rosmer. I'll go.

KROLL [*looks her up and down*] I must ask you to excuse me, Miss West, for calling so early, and catching you before you have had time to—

REBECCA [*surprised*] What do you mean? Do you find it improper that I should walk around at home in a dressing gown?

KROLL—Heaven forbid. I don't pretend to know what is regarded as proper nowadays at Rosmersholm.

ROSMER—Kroll—what on earth's come over you today?

REBECCA—Good morning, Dr. Kroll. [*She goes out left.*]

KROLL—By your leave— [*Sits on the couch.*]

ROSMER—Yes, my dear fellow, let's sit down and have a frank talk about this. [*Sits on a chair opposite* KROLL.]

KROLL—I haven't closed my eyes since I left this house. I lay awake all night, thinking and thinking.

ROSMER—And what have you come to tell me?

KROLL—It'll take a long time, Rosmer. Let me begin with a kind of— prologue. I can tell you a little about Ulrik Brendel.

ROSMER—Has he been to see you?

KROLL—No. He got himself settled in some low tavern. In the lowest possible company, naturally. He drank and stood drinks as long as his pockets were full. Then he started abusing them, called them scum and riff-raff. Which of course they were. Then they beat him up and threw him in the gutter.

ROSMER—I'm afraid he's quite incorrigible.

KROLL—He'd pawned your coat, too. But it seems he's managed to get that redeemed. Can you guess by whom?

ROSMER—You?

KROLL—No. The gallant Mr. Mortensgaard.

ROSMER—I see.

KROLL—I gather the first call Mr. Brendel made was upon that "idiot" and "plebeian."

ROSMER—It seems to have turned out well for him—

KROLL—Very. [*Leans over the table, a little closer to* ROSMER.] But that brings me to something about which—for the sake of our old—our former friendship—I feel it my duty to warn you.

ROSMER—What on earth do you mean, Kroll?

KROLL—I mean that there's some game being played in this house behind your back.

ROSMER—How can you say that? Are you referring to Reb—to Miss West?

KROLL – I am. I can well understand her point of view. She's been accustomed for so long to having her own way here. None the less—

ROSMER – My dear chap, you're completely mistaken. She and I have no secrets from each other. On any subject.

KROLL – Do her confessions to you include the fact that she's been corresponding with the editor of the *Morning Star?*

ROSMER – Oh, you mean that note she gave Ulrik Brendel.

KROLL – You know about it, then. And do you approve of her opening up a relationship with this scandalmonger who seeks every week to make a laughing-stock of me, both professionally and in my public life?

ROSMER – My dear Kroll, I'm sure that aspect of the matter hasn't even occurred to her. In any case, she is perfectly free to act as she chooses, just as I am.

KROLL – Indeed? Yes, I suppose that's all part of this new philosophy you've become so enamoured of. I assume Miss West shares your standpoint?

ROSMER – She does. The two of us have worked towards it together.

KROLL [*looks at him and slowly shakes his head*] Oh, you poor, blind dupe!

ROSMER – I? What makes you say that?

KROLL – Because I dare not—*will* not think the worst. No, no! Let me finish! You do value my friendship, Rosmer? And my respect? Or perhaps you don't?

ROSMER – I surely don't need to answer that question.

KROLL – Very well. But there are other questions that do demand an answer—a full explanation on your part. Will you allow me to submit you to a kind of—cross-examination?

ROSMER – Cross-examination?

KROLL – Yes. I want to question you on certain matters which you may find it painful to be reminded of. You see—this business of your apostasy—your emancipation, as you call it—ties up with much else about which, for your own sake, I want you to speak frankly to me.

ROSMER – My dear fellow, ask anything you like. I've nothing to hide.

KROLL – Tell me, then. What do you really think was the main reason Beata killed herself?

ROSMER – Have you any doubts? Or rather—can anyone ever hope to know why a poor, irresponsible mental invalid decides to end her misery?

KROLL – Are you so sure that Beata was insane? The doctors were by no means certain.

ROSMER – If the doctors had seen her as I so often saw her, they would have had no doubts.

KROLL – I had none—at the time.

1331

R O S M E R – How could one? Those uncontrollable, sick fits of sensuality —and the way she expected me to reciprocate them. She—frightened me. And then that illogical and remorseless way she reproached herself during those last years.

K R O L L – Yes, when she learned she'd never be able to have any children.

R O S M E R – Yes, well, I mean—! To feel such appalling and inescapable anguish about something that was in no way her fault! Is that sanity?

K R O L L – Hm—! Do you happen to recall whether you had any books in the house that dealt with the—purpose of marriage—from the so-called "progressive," modern viewpoint?

R O S M E R – I remember Miss West lent me a book about that. She'd inherited her guardian's library, as you know. But, my dear Kroll, you surely don't imagine we were so careless as to mention anything like that to poor Beata? I assure you on my honour, we are completely innocent in this matter. It was her own deranged imagination that gave her these wild ideas.

K R O L L – I can tell you one thing, anyway. That poor, tormented, overstrung woman ended her life in order that you might be happy—and free to live—the life you wanted to.

R O S M E R [*half rises from his chair*] What do you mean by that?

K R O L L – You must listen calmly to me now, Rosmer, because now at last I can tell you this. During the year before she died, Beata twice visited me to tell me how desperate and frightened she was.

R O S M E R – About this?

K R O L L – No. The first time she came and said she feared you were in danger of becoming an apostate. That you were thinking of abandoning your ancestral faith.

R O S M E R [*eagerly*] That's impossible, Kroll! Quite impossible! You must be mistaken about this.

K R O L L – Why?

R O S M E R – Because as long as Beata was alive, I was still in doubt—still battling with myself. And I fought that battle alone. I didn't speak of it to a soul. I don't think even Rebecca—

K R O L L – Rebecca?

R O S M E R – I mean—Miss West. I call her Rebecca for convenience.

K R O L L – So I have noticed.

R O S M E R – So I can't imagine how Beata could ever have got that idea. And why didn't she talk to me about it? She never did. She never said a word.

K R O L L – Poor creature. She begged and prayed *me* to speak to you.

R O S M E R – Then why didn't you?

K R O L L – I naturally assumed she was distraught. Making an accusation

1332

like that against a man like you! Well, then she came again—about a
month later. She seemed calmer then. But as she was leaving, she said:
"Soon now they can expect to see the white horse at Rosmersholm."

ROSMER—Yes, yes. The white horse. She spoke so often about that.

KROLL—And when I tried to persuade her to stop having such morbid
ideas, she simply replied: "I haven't much time left. John must marry
Rebecca now—at once."

ROSMER [*almost speechless*] What did you say? *I* marry—?

KROLL—It was a Thursday afternoon. On the Saturday evening, she
threw herself off the bridge into the mill-race.

ROSMER—And you never warned us—!

KROLL—You know yourself how often she used to say she hadn't long
to live.

ROSMER—Yes, I know. All the same—you should have warned us!

KROLL—I thought of it. But by then it was too late.

ROSMER—But why haven't you mentioned it since? Why have you
kept quiet about all this?

KROLL—What good would it have done to come here and cause you
still further suffering? I naturally supposed it was just some crazy delusion. Until last night.

ROSMER—And now you don't?

KROLL—Was Beata deluded when she said you were going to abandon
your childhood faith?

ROSMER [*stares unseeingly*] Yes. That I can't understand. That's the
most incredible thing—

KROLL—Incredible or not, she proved right. And now I ask you, Rosmer—how much truth is there in her other accusation? Her final one,
I mean?

ROSMER—Accusation? How was that an accusation?

KROLL—You don't seem to have noticed the way she phrased it. She
had to go, she said. Why? Well?

ROSMER—So that I could marry Rebecca—

KROLL—Those weren't quite her words. Beata used a different expression. She said: "I haven't much time left. John *must* marry Rebecca
now—at once."

ROSMER [*looks at him for a moment, then rises*] Now I understand
you, Kroll.

KROLL—Well? What is your answer?

ROSMER [*quite calm and controlled the whole time*] To such a question—? The only proper answer would be to show you the door.

KROLL [*gets up*] As you wish.

ROSMER [*moves in front of him*] Now you listen to me. For over a
year—ever since Beata died—Rebecca West and I have lived alone to-

gether here at Rosmersholm. All that time you have known of Beata's accusation against us. But never for a single moment have I noticed that you objected to Rebecca and me living here together.

KROLL – I didn't know until last night that this was an association between an apostate and a—an emancipated woman.

ROSMER – Ah—! Then you think there is no purity of spirit to be found in apostates and emancipated people? You don't believe they can have any sense of morality?

KROLL – I have little faith in any morality that is not rooted in Christian faith.

ROSMER – And you assume that this applies to Rebecca and me too? To our relationship—!

KROLL – With all deference to both of you, I cannot shrug off the opinion that there is no great gulf between free thought and—hm!

ROSMER – And what?

KROLL – And free love—since you force me to use the words.

ROSMER [*quietly*] And you aren't ashamed to say that to me! You, who have known me ever since I was a child.

KROLL – That is precisely the reason. I know how easily you let yourself be influenced by the people you associate with. And this Rebecca of yours—well, this Miss West—we don't know so very much about her. In short, Rosmer—I am not giving you up. And you—for God's sake try to save yourself while there's still time.

ROSMER – Save myself? How—?

[MRS. HELSETH *looks in through the door left.*]

ROSMER – What is it?

MRS. HELSETH – I wanted to ask Miss West if she could come down.

ROSMER – Miss West is not up here.

MRS. HELSETH – Oh? [*Looks round.*] That's strange. [*Goes.*]

ROSMER – You were saying—?

KROLL – Now listen. I'm not going to ask what went on here in secret while Beata was alive—or what may still be going on here now. I know you were deeply unhappy in your marriage. And that must to some degree excuse your conduct.

ROSMER – Oh, how little you really know me—!

KROLL – Don't interrupt me. What I wish to say is—that if this association with Miss West is to continue, it is absolutely essential that this change of heart, this dreadful apostasy into which she has lured you, be hushed up. Let me speak! Let me speak! I say that if you must be mad, then in God's name think and believe anything you wish—one way or the other. But keep your opinions to yourself. This is after all a purely personal matter. You don't have to shout these things from every street corner.

ROSMER—I do have to abandon a position which is both false and ambiguous.

KROLL—But you have a duty to your family traditions, Rosmer. Remember that! Since time immemorial Rosmersholm has been a stronghold of order and morality—of respect and reverence for everything that is accepted and upheld by the best elements in our society. The whole county has always taken its tone from Rosmersholm. Should the rumour become current that you yourself have broken with what I may call the Rosmer tradition, it will cause the most fatal and irreparable confusion.

ROSMER—My dear Kroll, I can't see it like that. I feel I have a bounden duty to create a little light and happiness in those places where for so many years the Rosmer family has created nothing but darkness and misery.

KROLL [*looks sternly at him*] A worthy ambition for a man who is to be the last of his line! Let sleeping dogs lie, Rosmer. That is no task for you. You were born to live peacefully among your books.

ROSMER—Possibly. But now I want to take part in the battle of life, at least once. I too!

KROLL—The battle of life! Do you know what that will mean for you? It will mean a battle to the death with all your friends.

ROSMER [*quietly*] They are not all as fanatical as you.

KROLL—You're an ingenuous fool, Rosmer. You've no experience of life. You don't realize what a storm is about to break over you.

[MRS. HELSETH *peers in through the door.*]

MRS. HELSETH—Miss West asked me to say—

ROSMER—What is it?

MRS. HELSETH—There's a man downstairs who wants a word with you, sir.

ROSMER—Is it the one who was here last night?

MRS. HELSETH—No, it's that Mortensgaard.

ROSMER—Mortensgaard!

KROLL—Aha! So it's come to that, has it? It's come to that already!

ROSMER—What does he want with me? Why didn't you tell him to go away?

MRS. HELSETH—Miss West said I was to ask if he might come up.

ROSMER—Tell him I'm engaged—

KROLL [*to* MRS. HELSETH] Ask him to come up, Mrs. Helseth.

[MRS. HELSETH *goes.*]

KROLL [*takes his hat*] I quit the field—for the moment. But the main battle has still to be fought.

ROSMER—As truly as I live, Kroll—I have nothing whatever to do with Mortensgaard.

KROLL – I no longer believe you. In anything. From now on I can never believe you. Now it is war to the knife. We'll see if we can't clip your wings.

ROSMER – Oh, Kroll! How can you sink so low?

KROLL – That comes well from you. Have you forgotten Beata?

ROSMER – Are you going to start all that again?

KROLL – No. The riddle of the mill-race I leave to you, and to your conscience. If you still have any.

[PETER MORTENSGAARD *softly and quietly enters the room left. He is a slightly-built little man with thinning reddish hair and beard.*]

KROLL [*throws a look of hatred at him*] So! The *Morning Star!* Standing sentinel over Rosmersholm! [*Buttons his coat.*] Well, that leaves me in no doubt which course I must steer.

MORTENSGAARD [*quietly, to* KROLL] The *Morning Star* will always shine to guide you on your path.

KROLL – Yes, you've long shown your goodwill towards me. I seem to remember a Commandment which says: "Thou shalt not bear false witness against thy neighbour."

MORTENSGAARD – You don't need to school me in the Commandments, Dr. Kroll.

KROLL – Not the Seventh?

ROSMER – Kroll–!

MORTENSGAARD – If I should need instruction, the Pastor is surely the most appropriate person.

KROLL [*with suppressed scorn*] The Pastor? Yes–Pastor Rosmer is unquestionably the best-informed authority on that subject. Well, gentlemen–I wish you a fruitful conversation. [*Goes, banging the door behind him.*]

ROSMER [*stands staring at the door, and says to himself*] Well, well –so be it, then. [*Turns.*] Tell me, Mr. Mortensgaard, what brings you out here to visit me?

MORTENSGAARD – It was actually Miss West I came to see. I felt I had to thank her for the kind letter she sent me yesterday.

ROSMER – I know she wrote to you. Have you spoken with her?

MORTENSGAARD – For a moment. [*With a slight smile.*] I hear there has been a change of heart regarding certain matters here at Rosmersholm.

ROSMER – My attitude has changed towards many things. I might almost say–everything.

MORTENSGAARD – So Miss West gave me to understand. She thought it might be a good idea if I came up and had a little chat with you about this.

ROSMER – About what, Mr. Mortensgaard?

MORTENSGAARD—May I have your permission to announce in the *Morning Star* that you have changed your views—and that you are devoting yourself to the cause of liberalism and progress?

ROSMER—Certainly you may. Indeed, I beg you to.

MORTENSGAARD—Then I shall publish it tomorrow morning. This will be a sensational item of news, that Pastor Rosmer of Rosmersholm now feels he can fight the good fight under our banner too.

ROSMER—I don't quite follow you.

MORTENSGAARD—Well, I mean, it gives our party a strong moral boost every time we win a devout Christian to our cause.

ROSMER [*somewhat surprised*] Then you don't know—? Didn't Miss West tell you about that too?

MORTENSGAARD—What, Pastor? Miss West seemed in rather a hurry. She said I should come upstairs and hear the rest from you.

ROSMER—Well then, I must tell you that I have emancipated myself in more senses than one. In every direction. I have completely renounced the teaching of the Church.

MORTENSGAARD [*looks at him amazed*] Well, strike me dumb! *You* renounce the—!

ROSMER—Yes, I now stand where you yourself have stood for so long. You can publish that in the *Morning Star* tomorrow too.

MORTENSGAARD—Publish that? No, my dear Pastor. I'm sorry, but I think we'd best turn a blind eye to that.

ROSMER—Turn a blind eye—?

MORTENSGAARD—To begin with, I mean.

ROSMER—But I don't understand—

MORTENSGAARD—Well, you see, Pastor—you probably don't know the ins and outs of things the way I do. But since you've come over to the liberal way of thinking—and since, as Miss West said, you want to lend a hand in the movement—then I take it you want to help us in every way you possibly can.

ROSMER—Indeed I do.

MORTENSGAARD—Well, I only want to let you know, Pastor, that if you come into the daylight about this business of your leaving the Church, you tie your hands from the start.

ROSMER—You think so?

MORTENSGAARD—Yes, don't you deceive yourself. There won't be much you'll be able to achieve then, not in this part of the country. Besides—we've enough freethinkers in the movement already, Pastor. I had it on the tip of my tongue to say "too many"! What the party needs is good Christians—that's something everyone has to respect. And that's what we're so short of. So it'd be best if you could keep mum about everything that the public don't need to know. That's only my opinion.

ROSMER–I see. In other words, you daren't associate yourself with me if I openly declare my apostasy?

MORTENSGAARD [*shakes his head*] I couldn't risk it, Pastor. I've made it a rule of late never to support anyone or anything that's anti-Church.

ROSMER–Have you, of late, yourself rejoined the Church?

MORTENSGAARD–That's another matter.

ROSMER–I see. Yes, I follow you.

MORTENSGAARD–Pastor—you must remember that my hands, more than most people's, aren't completely free.

ROSMER–What binds them?

MORTENSGAARD–The fact that I am a marked man.

ROSMER–Ah—I see.

MORTENSGAARD–A marked man, Pastor. You of all people ought to remember that. It was you who put the mark on me.

ROSMER–If I had felt then as I do now, I would have dealt less harshly with your misdemeanour.

MORTENSGAARD–I don't doubt it. But now it's too late. You've branded me once and for all. Branded me for my whole life. I don't suppose you fully realize what a thing like that means. But now you may soon be feeling the pinch yourself, Pastor.

ROSMER–I?

MORTENSGAARD–Yes. Surely you don't suppose Dr. Kroll and his cronies are going to forgive you for what you've done to them? And the *County Telegraph* is going to be pretty rough from now on, I hear. You may find yourself a marked man too.

ROSMER–I don't think they'll be able to hurt me. My conscience is clean.

MORTENSGAARD [*with a quiet smile*] That's a bold claim to make, Pastor.

ROSMER–Maybe. But I have the right to make it.

MORTENSGAARD–Even if you examine your own conduct as closely as you once examined mine?

ROSMER–You say that very strangely. What are you driving at? Have you something special in mind?

MORTENSGAARD–Yes, there is one thing. Only one. But it'd be enough, if any nasty-minded enemy of yours happened to hear about it.

ROSMER–Will you be good enough to let me know what this might be?

MORTENSGAARD–Can't you guess, Pastor?

ROSMER – No, I can't. I haven't the faintest idea.

MORTENSGAARD – Well, then, I'd better tell you. I have in my possession an odd letter that was once written here at Rosmersholm.

ROSMER – Miss West's letter, you mean? Is there anything odd about that?

MORTENSGAARD – No, not about that. But I did once get another letter from this house.

ROSMER – Also from Miss West?

MORTENSGAARD – No, Pastor.

ROSMER – Well, from whom, then? From whom?

MORTENSGAARD – From the late Mrs. Rosmer.

ROSMER – From my wife? *You* received a letter from my wife?

MORTENSGAARD – I did.

ROSMER – When?

MORTENSGAARD – Shortly before the poor lady's death. It'd be about eighteen months ago now. And it struck me as very odd.

ROSMER – You know that my wife was mentally ill at that time.

MORTENSGAARD – I know many people thought that. But I don't think you'd notice it from this letter. When I say it was odd, I mean in another way.

ROSMER – What in heaven's name did my poor wife find to write to you about?

MORTENSGAARD – I have the letter at home. She starts by saying that she is living in great fear and trembling. There are so many wicked people around here, she writes. And these people only think of causing you mischief and injury.

ROSMER – Me?

MORTENSGAARD – So she says. And then there comes the really odd thing. Shall I tell you, Pastor?

ROSMER – Yes! Tell me everything! Everything!

MORTENSGAARD – The poor lady begs and beseeches me to be magnanimous. She says she knows it was the Pastor that got me sacked from my school. But she begs me with all her heart not to take my revenge.

ROSMER – How did she think you could take revenge?

MORTENSGAARD – She says in the letter that if I should happen to hear any rumours about sinful goings-on at Rosmersholm, I mustn't pay any attention to them, because it was only bad people spreading such things around to make you unhappy.

ROSMER – Does it say that in the letter?

MORTENSGAARD – You can read it yourself, Pastor, any time that's convenient.

ROSMER – But I don't understand–! What did she think these wicked rumours referred to?

MORTENSGAARD – Firstly, that you'd abandoned the faith you'd been brought up in. Mrs. Rosmer said that was quite untrue. Secondly –hm–

ROSMER – Secondly?

MORTENSGAARD – Well, secondly she writes–it's a bit confused, this part–that she knows nothing whatever of any immoral relationship at Rosmersholm. That no wrong has ever been done to her as a wife–and if such rumours should come to my ears, she begs me not to mention them in the *Morning Star*.

ROSMER – Did she name anyone?

MORTENSGAARD – No.

ROSMER – Who brought you this letter?

MORTENSGAARD – I've promised not to tell. It was brought to me one evening, after dark.

ROSMER – If you had bothered to enquire, you would have learned that my poor unhappy wife was not completely in her right mind.

MORTENSGAARD – I did enquire, Pastor. But I must say that wasn't exactly the impression I received.

ROSMER – No? But why do you choose to warn me now about this old and confused letter?

MORTENSGAARD – To warn you to be very careful, Pastor Rosmer.

ROSMER – Personally, you mean?

MORTENSGAARD – Yes. You must remember that, from now on, you are no longer sacrosanct.

ROSMER – You seem convinced I have something I ought to hide.

MORTENSGAARD – I can't see myself why a man who's found emancipation shouldn't be allowed to live his life to the full. But, as I said, from now on you'd best be careful. If any rumour should get about that might offend people's sense of right and wrong, you can be sure the whole of our progressive movement will suffer for it. Goodbye, Pastor Rosmer.

ROSMER – Goodbye.

MORTENSGAARD – And I'll go straight down to the press and print the great news in the *Morning Star*.

ROSMER – Print everything.

MORTENSGAARD – I'll print everything that our good readers need to know.

[*He bows and leaves.* ROSMER *remains standing in the doorway while* MORTENSGAARD *goes down the stairs. The front door is heard to close.*]

ROSMER [*in the doorway, calls softly*] Rebecca! Reb–! Hm. [*Louder.*] Mrs. Helseth–isn't Miss West down there?

MRS. HELSETH [*from the hall*] No, Pastor. She's not here.

[*The curtain backstage is drawn aside, and* REBECCA *is revealed in the doorway.*]

REBECCA—John!

ROSMER [*turns*] What! Were you in my bedroom! My dear, what were you doing there?

REBECCA [*goes over to him*] I was listening.

ROSMER—But Rebecca—how could you do such a thing?

REBECCA—Yes, I could. He said it so horribly, that thing about the dressing gown—

ROSMER—Ah, so you were there already when Kroll—?

REBECCA—Yes. I wanted to know what he was up to.

ROSMER—I would have told you.

REBECCA—You wouldn't have told me everything. And certainly not in his words.

ROSMER—Did you hear everything, then?

REBECCA—Most of it. I had to go downstairs for a moment when Mortensgaard came.

ROSMER—And then you came back—

REBECCA—Please don't be angry with me, my dear.

ROSMER—You must do whatever you think right. You are a free woman. But what do you think about all this, Rebecca? I've never felt I needed you as I do now.

REBECCA—We both knew this would happen sometime.

ROSMER—No, no. Not this.

REBECCA—Not this?

ROSMER—I always feared that sooner or later our pure and beautiful friendship might be misinterpreted and reviled. Not by Kroll. I'd never imagined anything like this of him. But by all those others, with their foul minds and their ignoble eyes. Oh yes, Rebecca—I was right to keep our relationship so jealously to ourselves. It was a dangerous secret.

REBECCA—Oh, what does it matter what other people think? *We* know that we are guiltless.

ROSMER—I? Guiltless? Yes, I used to think that—until today. But now —now, Rebecca—

REBECCA—Well, now what?

ROSMER—How am I to explain that terrible accusation of Beata's?

REBECCA [*vehemently*] Oh, don't talk about Beata! Don't think about Beata any more! You've managed to free yourself from her at last. She's dead.

ROSMER—Since I learned this, she has become hideously alive again.

REBECCA—No, no! You mustn't, John! You mustn't!

ROSMER–Yes, I tell you. We must try to get to the bottom of this. How can she have got this mad idea into her head?

REBECCA–Surely you aren't beginning to doubt that she was—mad?

ROSMER–Yes, Rebecca—that's just what I can't be so sure of any longer. And besides—even if she was—

REBECCA–If she was—? Yes, what then?

ROSMER–I mean—what was it that drove her sick mind over the edge into madness?

REBECCA–Oh, what good can it do to go around brooding about it?

ROSMER–I can't help it, Rebecca. I can't stop these doubts nagging at me, even if I wanted to.

REBECCA–But it can be dangerous—to circle continuously around one morbid thought.

ROSMER [*paces around restlessly, pondering*] I must have betrayed my feelings somehow. She must have noticed how happy I began to feel after *you* came here.

REBECCA–But, my dear, even if this is true—

ROSMER–Think. . . . She must have noticed that we read the same books. That we loved to be together, and to talk about all these new ideas. But—I don't understand! I was so careful not to let her suspect anything. When I think back, why, it was almost as though my life depended on it, the way I kept her apart from us, and from everything that concerned us. Didn't I, Rebecca?

REBECCA–Yes, yes, of course you did.

ROSMER–And you did too. And yet—! Oh, it's too dreadful to think of! So she was going round here, in her sick love for me—always silent, silent—watching us—noting everything—and misinterpreting everything.

REBECCA [*clasps her hands*] Oh, I should never have come to Rosmersholm!

ROSMER–To think what she must have suffered in silence! All the dreadful fantasies her sick brain must have built up around us! Did she never say anything to you that led you to suspect anything?

REBECCA [*seems startled*] To me! Do you suppose I'd have stayed here a day longer?

ROSMER–No, no, of course not. Oh, what a struggle it must have been for her! And she fought it alone, Rebecca. In despair, and quite alone. And then, in the end, that terrible accusing victory—in the millrace.

[*He throws himself down in the chair at the desk, puts his elbows on it and covers his face with his hands.*]

REBECCA [*approaches him cautiously from behind*] Now, listen, John. If it lay in your power to call Beata back—to you—to Rosmersholm —would you do it?

ROSMER – Oh, how can I tell what I would or wouldn't do? I can think of nothing but this one thing–that can never be undone.

REBECCA – You were just beginning to live, John. You *had* already begun. You had made yourself free–free in every way. You felt so relieved and happy–

ROSMER – Oh, yes, Rebecca. I did, I did. And now this dreadful discovery–

REBECCA [*behind him, her arms on the back of his chair*] How beautiful it was when we used to sit downstairs in the drawing-room in the dusk. Helping each other to plan our lives anew. You were going to lay hold of life–the living life of today, you called it! You wanted to go like a liberating angel from home to home, winning people's hearts and souls. Creating nobility all around you–in wider and ever wider circles.

ROSMER – Happy, noble men.

REBECCA – Yes–happy.

ROSMER – Because it is happiness that makes men noble, Rebecca.

REBECCA – Don't you think–suffering too? Deep suffering?

ROSMER – Yes–if one manages to survive it. Overcome it. Conquer it.

REBECCA – That is what you must do.

ROSMER [*shakes his head sadly*] I shall never conquer this–not completely. There will always remain a doubt. A question. I shall never again be able to enjoy the one thing that makes life so wonderful to live.

REBECCA [*over the back of the chair, more quietly*] What is that, John?

ROSMER [*looks up at her*] The sense of calm and happy innocence.

REBECCA [*takes a step back*] Yes. Innocence.

[*Short pause.*]

ROSMER [*with his elbow on the desk, leans his head on his hand and looks straight ahead of him*] And the way she managed to work it all out. How systematically she must have pieced it all together! First she begins to doubt my faith. How could she have suspected that? But she did. And then her suspicion increased to certainty. And then–yes, of course, then it was easy for her to imagine all the rest. [*Sits up in his chair and runs his hands through his hair.*] Oh, all these dreadful speculations! I shall never be free from them. I feel it. I know it. They will always haunt me, and remind me of the dead.

REBECCA – Like the white horse of Rosmersholm.

ROSMER – Yes. Rushing out from the darkness. From the silence.

REBECCA – And for the sake of this accursed chimaera you are prepared to turn your back upon life–that burning life, which you had begun to awake to?

ROSMER–Yes, it is hard. Hard, Rebecca. But I have no choice. How could I possibly forget all this?

REBECCA [*behind the chair*] By creating a new relationship.

ROSMER [*starts and looks up*] A new relationship?

REBECCA–Yes. A new relationship to the world outside. Live, work, act. Don't sit here brooding over insoluble riddles.

ROSMER [*gets up*] A new relationship? [*Walks across the room, stops by the door, then comes back.*] One question occurs to me. Haven't you too asked yourself that question, Rebecca?

REBECCA [*catches her breath*] I don't–know–what you mean.

ROSMER–How do you suppose our relationship is going to shape itself after today?

REBECCA–I think our friendship will continue–whatever happens.

ROSMER–That's not quite what I meant. What first brought us together–and binds us so closely–our belief that man and woman can live together in pure comradeship–

REBECCA–Yes, yes–well?

ROSMER–I mean, such a relationship–like ours–doesn't it demand a life led in serenity and peace?

REBECCA–Go on.

ROSMER–But what I see lying ahead of me is a life of strife and unrest, and emotional disturbance. I want to live, Rebecca! I'm not going to let myself be beaten by fear. I'm not going to let my life be dictated, either by the living or by–anyone else.

REBECCA–No, no, you mustn't. Be free, John! You must be free!

ROSMER–Then can't you guess what I'm thinking? Don't you know? Can't you see that the only way I can free myself from all these nagging memories–from the horror of the past–?

REBECCA–Yes?

ROSMER––is to confront it with something new, and living, and real?

REBECCA [*catches at the back of the chair*] What do you mean?

ROSMER [*comes closer*] Rebecca–if I were now to ask you–will you be my second wife?

REBECCA [*is speechless for a moment, then cries in joy*] Your wife! Your–! I!

ROSMER–Yes. Let us try. We two shall be one. The place left here by the dead must not stand empty.

REBECCA–I–take Beata's place–?

ROSMER–Then her part in the saga of Rosmersholm will be finished. Completely finished. For ever and ever.

REBECCA [*quietly, trembling*] Do you believe that, John?

ROSMER–It must be so. It must! I can't–I will not go through life with a corpse on my back. Help me to throw it off, Rebecca. And then let us lay all memories to rest in freedom, and joy, and love. You shall be my wife—the only wife I have ever had.

REBECCA [*controlled*] Don't ever speak of this again. I shall never be your wife.

ROSMER—What! Never? But—don't you think you could come to love me? Isn't there already—something of love—in our friendship?

REBECCA [*puts her hands to her ears as though in terror*] Don't talk like that, John! Don't say such things!

ROSMER [*grasps her arm*] Yes, yes. It could happen. I can see from your face, you feel it too. Don't you, Rebecca?

REBECCA [*again calm and composed*] Listen, now. I tell you—if ever you speak of this again, I shall leave Rosmersholm.

ROSMER—Leave! You? You couldn't. It's impossible.

REBECCA—It is even more impossible that I should become your wife. That I can never be. Never in this world.

ROSMER [*looks surprised at her*] "Can't," you said? And you said it so strangely. Why can't you?

REBECCA [*clasps both his hands*] My dear—for both our sakes—don't ask me why. [*Lets go of him.*] No, John. [*She goes towards the door, left.*]

ROSMER—From now on, I can ask no other question but "Why?"

REBECCA [*turns and looks at him*] Then it is finished.

ROSMER—Between you and me?

REBECCA—Yes.

ROSMER—It will never be finished between us. You will never leave Rosmersholm.

REBECCA [*her hand on the door-knob*] No, perhaps I won't. But if you ever ask me that again—it will be finished none the less, John.

ROSMER—Finished none the less? How?

REBECCA—Because then I shall go the way Beata went. Now you know, John.

ROSMER—Rebecca!

REBECCA [*in the doorway, nods slowly*] Now you know. [*Goes.*]

ROSMER [*stares as though lost at the closed door*] Rebecca!

ACT THREE

The living room at Rosmersholm. The window and the hall door stand open. Morning sunshine outside.

REBECCA WEST, *dressed as in Act One, is standing at the window, watering and arranging the flowers. Her crochet-work is lying in the armchair.* MRS. HELSETH *is going around with a feather mop, dusting the furniture.*

R E B E C C A [*after a brief silence*] The Pastor's very late down this morning.

M R S . H E L S E T H – Oh, he's often like that. He'll be here soon.

R E B E C C A – Have you seen him at all?

M R S . H E L S E T H – Only for a moment. When I came up with the coffee, he went into his bedroom and started dressing.

R E B E C C A – I ask because yesterday he wasn't very well.

M R S . H E L S E T H – Yes, he looked poorly. I wonder if there isn't something the matter between him and his brother-in-law.

R E B E C C A – What could that be?

M R S . H E L S E T H – I wouldn't know. Perhaps that Mortensgaard's set them against each other.

R E B E C C A – That's quite possible. Do you know this Peter Mortensgaard?

M R S . H E L S E T H – I do not. The idea, miss! A man like that!

R E B E C C A – You mean, because he edits that nasty paper?

M R S . H E L S E T H – Oh, it isn't just that. Surely you heard, miss. He had a child with some married woman whose husband had left her.

R E B E C C A – Yes, I did hear that. But that must have been long before I came here.

M R S . H E L S E T H – Oh goodness, yes, miss. He was quite a young man. I reckon she ought to have known better. He wanted to marry her. But they put a stop to that. And they made him suffer for it, all right. But since then, my word, he's done all right for himself. There's plenty of people as aren't ashamed to run after him now.

R E B E C C A – Yes, most of the poorer people turn to him when they need help.

MRS. HELSETH—Oh, it isn't only the poor ones—

REBECCA [*gives her a furtive glance*] Oh?

MRS. HELSETH [*by the sofa, dusting busily*] The kind of people you'd least expect, so I've heard say, miss.

REBECCA [*arranging the flowers*] That's just an idea you've got, Mrs. Helseth. You couldn't know about a thing like that.

MRS. HELSETH—You think I couldn't know, miss? Oh yes, I know all right. If you want the truth, I once took a letter to Mortensgaard myself.

REBECCA [*turns*] No—did you?

MRS. HELSETH—Indeed I did. And that letter was written here at Rosmersholm.

REBECCA—Really, Mrs. Helseth?

MRS. HELSETH—As I stand here. And written on fine paper it was, too. With fine red wax on the envelope.

REBECCA—And it was entrusted to you? Well then, Mrs. Helseth, it isn't difficult to guess who sent it.

MRS. HELSETH—Oh?

REBECCA—Obviously poor Mrs. Rosmer, when she was ill—

MRS. HELSETH—It's you that say so, miss, not me.

REBECCA—But what was in the letter? No, of course—you can't know.

MRS. HELSETH—Hm—maybe I do, for all that.

REBECCA—Did she tell you what she'd written?

MRS. HELSETH—No, she didn't do that. But when he, that Mortensgaard, had read it, he started asking me all kinds of questions, sly-like, so that I soon knew what was in it.

REBECCA—What do you think she said? Oh, dear Mrs. Helseth, do please tell me!

MRS. HELSETH—No, I won't, miss. Not for all the money in the world.

REBECCA—Oh, you can tell me. You and I are such good friends.

MRS. HELSETH—God forbid I should ever let on to you about that, miss. I can't say more than that it was some awful thing they'd gone and put into that poor woman's sick mind.

REBECCA—Who had?

MRS. HELSETH—Wicked people, Miss West. Wicked people.

REBECCA—Wicked—?

MRS. HELSETH—That's the word I used. Really wicked people, they must have been.

REBECCA—Who do you think it could have been?

MRS. HELSETH—Oh, I know what I think. But heaven forbid I should open *my* mouth. There's a certain lady in town—hm—!

REBECCA—I can see you mean Mrs. Kroll.

MRS. HELSETH—Yes, she's a fine one. Always been snooty to me, she has. And she's never had any liking for you.

REBECCA—Do you think Mrs. Rosmer was in her right mind when she wrote that letter to Mortensgaard?

MRS. HELSETH—Depends what you mean by right mind, miss. I wouldn't say she was out of it.

REBECCA—But she became so distressed when she learned she could never have any children. That was when the madness started.

MRS. HELSETH—Yes, she took that badly, poor woman.

REBECCA [*takes her crochet-work and sits in the chair by the window*] Actually—don't you think that was a good thing for the Pastor, Mrs. Helseth?

MRS. HELSETH—What, miss?

REBECCA—That there weren't any children. Hm?

MRS. HELSETH—Well, I don't know what I ought to answer to that.

REBECCA—Yes, believe you me. It was the best thing for him. Pastor Rosmer wasn't made to sit here listening to little children crying.

MRS. HELSETH—Little children don't cry at Rosmersholm, miss.

REBECCA [*looks at her*] Don't cry?

MRS. HELSETH—No. Little children have never cried in this house, not as long as anyone can remember.

REBECCA—That's strange.

MRS. HELSETH—Yes, isn't it, miss? But it's part of the Rosmers. And there's another strange thing. When they grow up, they never laugh. Never laugh until the day they die.

REBECCA—That's most extraordinary—

MRS. HELSETH—Have you ever heard or seen the Pastor laugh?

REBECCA—No—now I think of it, I almost believe you're right. But people in general don't laugh much around here, I think.

MRS. HELSETH—That they don't. It started at Rosmersholm, people say. And then it spread around like a kind of plague, I shouldn't be surprised.

REBECCA—You're a deep woman, Mrs. Helseth.

MRS. HELSETH—Ah, you mustn't sit there making fun of me, miss— [*Listens.*] Ssh, ssh! Here's the Pastor coming down. He doesn't like seeing dusters about.

[*She goes out through the door right.* JOHN ROSMER, *stick and hat in hand, enters from the hall.*]

ROSMER—Good morning, Rebecca.

REBECCA—Good morning, my dear. [*After a moment, crocheting.*] Are you going out?

ROSMER – Yes.

REBECCA – It's a lovely day.

ROSMER – You didn't come up to see me this morning.

REBECCA – No—I didn't. Not today.

ROSMER – Aren't you going to from now on?

REBECCA – Oh, I don't know yet.

ROSMER – Is there anything for me?

REBECCA – The *County Telegraph* has come.

ROSMER – The *County Telegraph*—!

REBECCA – It's lying there on the table.

ROSMER [*puts down his hat and stick*] Is there anything in it about—?

REBECCA – Yes.

ROSMER – And you didn't send it up—?

REBECCA – You'll read it soon enough.

ROSMER – I see. [*Takes the paper and reads it standing at the table.*] What! ". . . cannot warn our readers sufficiently against irresponsible renegades . . ." [*Looks at her.*] They call me a renegade, Rebecca.

REBECCA – They mention no names.

ROSMER – What difference does that make? [*Reads on.*] "Secret traitors against justice and morality"—Judases who have the impertinence to blazon their apostasy as soon as they think that the most appropriate —and most profitable—moment has come." "Outrageous attacks on the posthumous reputations of our ancestors"—"in the hope that those temporarily in power will not omit suitably to reward. . . ." [*Puts the paper down on the table.*] And they write this about me. These people who have known me so long and so well. They don't believe it, they know there isn't a word of truth in it, but they write it, all the same.

REBECCA – There's more to come.

ROSMER [*takes up the paper again*] "Immaturity of judgment the only possible excuse . . . corrupting influence—possibly extending also to fields of personal conduct which we do not at present wish to make the subject of public discussion or complaint. . . ." [*Looks at her.*] What does that mean?

REBECCA – That's a reference to me.

ROSMER [*puts down the paper*] Rebecca—this is the action of dishonourable men.

REBECCA – Yes, I hardly think they're the ones to complain about Mortensgaard.

ROSMER [*walks up and down*] Something must be done. Everything that is good in men will be destroyed if this kind of thing is allowed to continue. But it shall not! Oh, how happy—how happy I would feel if I could bring a little light into all this gloom and ugliness!

REBECCA [*rises*] Yes, John, yes! That would be something great and noble to live for!

ROSMER—If only I could awake them to self-knowledge. Bring them to a feeling of shame and repentance. Teach them to approach one another in tolerance and love, Rebecca.

REBECCA—Yes! Only put all your energies into that, and you'll see. You will win!

ROSMER—I think it could be done. If I could succeed, what a joy it would be to be alive! No more hateful strife. Only emulation. Every eye directed towards the same goal. Every will, every mind, striving forwards—upwards—each by its own natural and predestined path. Happiness for all—created by all. [*Chances to look out through the window, starts and says sadly.*] Ah! Not through me.

REBECCA—Not—? Not through you?

ROSMER—And not *for* me, either.

REBECCA—Oh, John, you mustn't let such doubts get the better of you.

ROSMER—Happiness—my dear Rebecca—happiness consists above all else in a calm and happy sense of innocence. Freedom from guilt—

REBECCA [*stares straight ahead*] Oh, can't you ever stop thinking about guilt?

ROSMER—You don't know how it feels. But I—

REBECCA—You least of all.

ROSMER [*points out through the window*] The mill-race—

REBECCA—Oh, John—!

[MRS. HELSETH *looks in through the door right.*]

MRS. HELSETH—Miss!

REBECCA—Later, later. Not now.

MRS. HELSETH—Just a word, miss.

[REBECCA *goes over to the door.* MRS. HELSETH *tells her something. They whisper together for a moment.* MRS. HELSETH *nods and goes.*]

ROSMER [*uneasily*] Was it for me?

REBECCA—No, only something about the housekeeping. You ought to go out and get some fresh air, John. Take a good long walk.

ROSMER [*takes his hat*] Yes, come along. We'll go together.

REBECCA—No, my dear, I can't just now. You go on your own. But stop brooding about these things. Promise me that.

ROSMER—I'm afraid I shall never be able to forget them.

REBECCA—But how can you let anything so groundless have such power over you—?

ROSMER—Is it so groundless, Rebecca? I've been lying awake all night thinking about it. Wasn't Beata perhaps right after all?

REBECCA—What do you mean?

ROSMER—In believing that I was in love with you, Rebecca.

REBECCA—Wasn't—she—right?

ROSMER   [*puts his hat on the table*] This is the question I keep asking myself. Have we two been deceiving ourselves in calling our relationship a friendship?

REBECCA—You mean we ought to have called it—?

ROSMER—Love. Yes, Rebecca, I mean that. Even when Beata was alive, I thought only of you. You were the one I yearned for. With you I found a happiness that was calm and joyful and not merely based on sensuality. When you really think about it, Rebecca—we were like two children falling sweetly and secretly in love. We made no demands, we dreamed no dreams. Wasn't that how you felt too? Tell me.

REBECCA   [*torn within herself*] Oh—I don't know what to reply to that.

ROSMER—And this life we lived so passionately—with each other and for each other—we mistook for friendship. No, Rebecca—our relationship has been a spiritual marriage—perhaps from the first moment we knew each other. So that I am guilty. I had no right to do this—no right, for Beata's sake.

REBECCA—No right to live in happiness? Do you believe that, John?

ROSMER—She saw our relationship through the eyes of *her* love. Condemned it by the measure of *her* love. She had to. Beata couldn't have judged us in any other way than she did.

REBECCA—But then how can you blame yourself for what finally happened?

ROSMER—It was her love for me that threw her into the mill-race. That fact remains inescapable, Rebecca. And it is useless for me to try to escape from it.

REBECCA—Don't think about it! Think only of the great and noble task to which you have dedicated your life!

ROSMER   [*shakes his head*] That can never be accomplished, Rebecca. Not by me. Not after what I know now.

REBECCA—Why not by you?

ROSMER—Because there can never be victory for a cause that is rooted in guilt.

REBECCA   [*bursts out*] Oh, these doubts, these fears, these scruples—are all inherited! They talk at Rosmersholm about the dead haunting the living in the shape of white horses. I think this is just one of them.

ROSMER—Perhaps it is. But what help is that if I cannot escape from it? You must believe me, Rebecca. What I say is true. For a cause to win a lasting victory, it must be led by a man whose soul is joyful and free from guilt.

REBECCA – Is joy something that means so much to you, John?

ROSMER – Joy? Yes, Rebecca. It is.

REBECCA – You, who can never laugh?

ROSMER – Yes, in spite of that. Oh, Rebecca—believe me—I could be the most joyful man on earth.

REBECCA – You must go for your walk now, my dear. Take a good, long one. You hear? Look, here's your hat. And your stick.

ROSMER [*takes them*] Thank you. You won't come with me?

REBECCA – No, no, I can't just now.

ROSMER – Very well. I shall feel you're with me, though. As I always do.

[*He goes out through the hall. After a few moments* REBECCA *glances out after him through the open door. Then she walks towards the door right.*]

REBECCA [*opens it and calls softly*] All right, Mrs. Helseth. You can let him in now.

[*She goes over towards the window. Shortly afterwards* DR. KROLL *enters right. He bows silently and formally, and keeps his hat in his hand.*]

KROLL – Has he gone?

REBECCA – Yes.

KROLL – Does he usually stay out long?

REBECCA – Usually, yes. But today I wouldn't be sure. So if you don't want to meet him—

KROLL – No, no. I want to talk to you. Alone.

REBECCA – Then we'd better start. Please sit down.

[*She sits in an armchair by the window.* DR. KROLL *sits in a chair beside her.*]

KROLL – Miss West—you can hardly imagine how deeply this hurts me —this change that has taken place in John Rosmer.

REBECCA – We expected it would—at first.

KROLL – Only at first?

REBECCA – Mr. Rosmer was sure that sooner or later you would come to feel as he does.

KROLL – I?

REBECCA – You and all his friends.

KROLL – Well, there you see what poor judgment he has where life and human nature are concerned.

REBECCA – In any case—since he now feels bound to free himself from all former ties—

KROLL – Ah but, you see, that's exactly what I don't believe.

REBECCA – What do you believe, then?

KROLL – I think you're the one who's behind all this.

REBECCA – Your wife gave you that idea, Dr. Kroll.

KROLL – Never mind where I got it from. The point is that I feel strong

1352

doubts—overwhelmingly strong doubts—when I consider the sum of your conduct since first you came here.

REBECCA [*looks at him*] I seem to remember there was a time when you felt an overwhelmingly strong belief in me, dear Dr. Kroll. A passionate belief in me, I might almost have said.

KROLL [*lowers his voice*] Whom could you not bewitch—if you put your mind to it?

REBECCA—Are you suggesting that—?

KROLL—Yes, you did. I'm not any longer so foolish as to suppose that you felt anything for me. You merely wanted to gain admittance to Rosmersholm. Get a footing here. And you wanted me to help you. Yes, I see it all now.

REBECCA—You seem to have forgotten that it was Beata herself who begged and prayed me to come here.

KROLL—Yes, after you'd bewitched her too. Or would you call that friendship, what she came to feel for you? She began to worship you, to idolize you, and in the end it developed into a—what shall I call it? —into a kind of desperate infatuation. Yes, that's the word for it.

REBECCA—You must please remember your sister's state of mind. I don't really think *I* can be described as emotionally unstable.

KROLL—No, indeed you are not. But that makes you all the more dangerous to people you want to get into your clutches. You find it so easy to act remorselessly and ruthlessly, simply because you are so cold-blooded.

REBECCA—Cold-blooded? Are you so sure of that?

KROLL—Quite sure, now. Otherwise you couldn't have gone on here year after year pursuing your end so calculatedly. Yes, yes—you've got what you wanted. You have him in your power—and Rosmersholm too. But to achieve all this, you didn't shrink from sacrificing his personal happiness.

REBECCA—That's not true! It isn't I, it's you who have made him unhappy.

KROLL—I?

REBECCA—Yes, when you led him to believe that he was to blame for the dreadful thing that happened to Beata.

KROLL—So he feels deeply about that?

REBECCA—Of course he does. You know how sensitive he is—

KROLL—I thought these so-called emancipated men were able to set themselves above such scruples. But that's how it is, eh? Ah well— I knew it really. The descendant of these men who look down on us here can't find it so easy to tear himself free from something that's been handed down in his family from generation to generation.

REBECCA [*drops her eyes thoughtfully*] John Rosmer is deeply rooted in the traditions of his family. That is certainly true.

KROLL—Yes, and you ought to have remembered it if you'd had any real feeling for him. But of course you couldn't have that kind of feeling. Your background is so vastly different from his.

REBECCA—What do you mean, my background?

KROLL—I mean your family background. Your—origins, Miss West.

REBECCA—I see. Yes, that's quite true. My background is very humble. All the same—

KROLL—I don't mean socially. I was thinking of your moral background.

REBECCA—I don't understand.

KROLL—The circumstances of your birth.

REBECCA—I beg your pardon?

KROLL—I say this merely because it explains your whole conduct.

REBECCA—I don't follow you. Kindly explain what you mean.

KROLL—I assumed you knew. Otherwise one would hardly see why you were adopted by Dr. West—

REBECCA [*rises*] Ah. Now I understand.

KROLL—And took his name. Your mother's name was Gamvik.

REBECCA [*walks across the room*] My father's name was Gamvik, Dr. Kroll.

KROLL—Your mother's occupation must of course have brought her into frequent contact with the district physician.

REBECCA—It did.

KROLL—And as soon as your mother dies, he takes you into his own home. He treats you harshly. Yet you stay with him. You know he won't leave you a penny—all you got was a case of books. Yet you stay with him. Put up with his tantrums—look after him until the day he dies.

REBECCA [*over by the table, looks scornfully at him*] And all this you can only explain by the suggestion that there was something immoral—something criminal—about my birth?

KROLL—What you did for him I attribute to an unconscious filial instinct. Your whole conduct seems to me irrefutable evidence of your birth.

REBECCA [*vehemently*] There isn't a word of truth in anything you say! Dr. West hadn't even arrived in the district when I was born.

KROLL—I beg your pardon, Miss West. He came there the previous year. I have done a little research into the matter.

REBECCA—You're wrong, I tell you! Completely wrong!

KROLL—You said the day before yesterday that you were twenty-nine. Coming up to thirty.

R E B E C C A – Oh? Did I say that?

K R O L L – You did. From which I calculate–

R E B E C C A – Stop. There's no need to calculate anything. I may as well tell you at once: I am a year older than I admitted.

K R O L L [*smiles disbelievingly*] This is something new. What is the explanation?

R E B E C C A – When I reached twenty-five I thought I was a little old to be unmarried. So I subtracted a year.

K R O L L – You? An emancipated woman? Do you have old-fashioned prejudices regarding the right age for marriage?

R E B E C C A – Yes. It was silly of me–laughable, even. But one always has some little prejudice clinging to one that one can't shake off. That's human nature.

K R O L L – Possibly. But my calculation may be correct all the same. Because Dr. West paid your district a brief visit the year before he became employed there.

R E B E C C A [*cries*] That's a lie!

K R O L L – Is it?

R E B E C C A – Yes. My mother never mentioned that.

K R O L L – Didn't she?

R E B E C C A – No. Never. Nor Dr. West. Not a word.

K R O L L – Might that not have been because they both had reason to forget a year? Just as you have done, Miss West. Perhaps it's a family trait.

R E B E C C A [*walks around, twisting and untwisting her hands*] It isn't possible. It's only something you're trying to make me imagine. It can't be true. It can't! Not possibly–!

K R O L L [*gets up*] But my dear–why in heaven's name are you taking it so to heart? You quite frighten me. What am I to imagine–?

R E B E C C A – Nothing. You are to imagine nothing.

K R O L L – Then you really must explain to me why this fact–this possibility, if you like–so alarms you?

R E B E C C A [*composes herself*] It's quite simple, Dr. Kroll. I just don't want people to think of me as illegitimate.

K R O L L – I see. Well, let's settle for that explanation–for the moment. So you have retained a certain–prejudice on that issue too?

R E B E C C A – Yes, I have.

K R O L L – Well, I suppose it's the same with most of this so-called emancipation of yours. You've read books that have given you a whole lot of new ideas and opinions. You've picked up a smattering of newfangled theories about this and that–theories that seem to upset much of what has hitherto been regarded as gospel and unchallengeable. But you've only accepted all this intellectually, Miss West. You don't really feel it in your blood.

REBECCA [*thoughtfully*] You may be right about that.

KROLL—Yes, just ask yourself honestly, and you'll see! And if it's like that with you, then it's easy to guess how John Rosmer must feel about it. It's pure and absolute madness—it's—why, it's suicide for him even to think of standing forth publicly and claiming to be an apostate! We know what a shy and reticent man he is. Imagine him being repudiated and persecuted by his old associates! Exposed to the contempt and ridicule of all the best people in society! He's never the kind of man to endure that.

REBECCA—He must. It's too late for him to draw back now.

KROLL—It is certainly not too late. By no means. The whole matter can be hushed up—or at least explained away as a temporary, if regrettable, aberration. But—one condition is absolutely imperative.

REBECCA—And what is that?

KROLL—You must get him to legalise the relationship, Miss West.

REBECCA—His relationship with me?

KROLL—Yes. You must make him do that.

REBECCA—You can't rid yourself of the conviction that our relationship is of the kind that requires to be—legalised, as you put it?

KROLL—I have no wish to get involved in the matter personally. But I have observed in the past that the prejudices, as you would call them, which people find it easiest to overcome—hm—!

REBECCA—Concern the relationship between man and woman?

KROLL—Yes—to speak frankly—that is my experience.

REBECCA [*wanders across the room and looks out through the window*] It was on the tip of my tongue to say—I hope you are right, Dr. Kroll.

KROLL—What do you mean by that? You said it so strangely.

REBECCA—Oh, nothing. Let's not talk any more about it. Ah—here he is.

KROLL—Already! Then I'll be off.

REBECCA [*goes over to him*] No—wait. There's something I'd like you to hear.

KROLL—Not now. I don't think I could bear to see him.

REBECCA—Please stay, I beg you. Do. Or you'll regret it later. This is the last time I shall beg anything of you.

KROLL [*looks at her amazed, and puts down his hat*] Very well, Miss West. So be it.

[*A moment's silence. Then* JOHN ROSMER *enters from the hall.*]

ROSMER [*sees* KROLL *and stops in the doorway*] What! You here?

REBECCA—He didn't want to meet you, John.

KROLL [*involuntarily*] John!

REBECCA – Yes, Dr. Kroll. Mr. Rosmer and I call each other by our Christian names. Our relationship has led to that excess.

KROLL – Was that what you wanted me to hear?

REBECCA – That—and other things too.

ROSMER [*comes closer*] Why have you come here?

KROLL – I wanted to make one last effort to stop you, and to win you back.

ROSMER [*points to the newspaper*] After what I have read here?

KROLL – I did not write that.

ROSMER – Did you do anything to stop it?

KROLL – That would have been a betrayal of the cause I stand for. And anyway, it did not lie within my power.

REBECCA [*tears the newspaper into pieces, crumples them and throws them behind the stove*] There. Now they're out of sight. Let them be out of mind, too. There's going to be nothing more like that, John.

KROLL – Yes, if you can persuade him to see sense—

REBECCA – Come, my dear, let's sit down—all three of us. I want to tell you everything.

ROSMER [*sits unwillingly*] What's come over you, Rebecca? You're so —dreadfully calm. What is it?

REBECCA – The calmness of decision. [*Sits.*] You sit down too, Dr. Kroll.

[KROLL *sits on the sofa.*]

ROSMER – Of decision, you say. What decision?

REBECCA – I want to give you back what you need to be able to live. You shall have your joyful innocence returned to you, my dear.

ROSMER – What on earth is all this?

REBECCA – I just want to tell you something. That's all that's necessary.

ROSMER – Well, tell me.

REBECCA – When I came down here from the north—with Dr. West— I felt that a great new world was opening up for me. The Doctor had taught me so many things. Everything I knew about life—then. [*With difficulty, and scarcely audibly.*] But then—

KROLL – Yes?

ROSMER – But, Rebecca—I know all this.

REBECCA [*composes herself*] Yes, yes—you're right really. I suppose you do know all this.

KROLL [*looks closely at her*] I think perhaps I should go.

REBECCA – No, stay where you are, Dr. Kroll. [*To* ROSMER.] Yes, that was it, you see—I wanted to be part of this new age that was dawning. To share in all these new discoveries—! Dr. Kroll told me one day that

1357

Ulrik Brendel had had a great influence over you when you were young. I thought it must surely be possible for me to carry on what he had begun.

ROSMER – Did you come here with that purpose–?

REBECCA – I wanted us two to go forward together into freedom. Onward–always onward. But between you and full freedom there was always this dreadful and insuperable barrier.

ROSMER – What barrier?

REBECCA – I mean, John, that you could only blossom into freedom outside in the bright sunshine. But you stayed here, ailing and sickening in the darkness of that dreadful marriage.

ROSMER – You never spoke of my marriage like that before.

REBECCA – No, I didn't dare. I was afraid you might hate me for it.

KROLL [*nods to* ROSMER] You hear that!

REBECCA [*continues*] But I knew well where your salvation lay. Your only hope of salvation. So I took action.

ROSMER – What do you mean, took action?

KROLL – Are you saying that you–!

REBECCA – Yes, John. [*Rises.*] Please don't move. Nor you, Dr. Kroll. It wasn't you, John. You are innocent. It was I who lured–who ended by luring Beata into the labyrinth.

ROSMER [*jumps up*] Rebecca!

KROLL [*rises from the sofa*] The labyrinth!

REBECCA – The labyrinth–that led to the mill-race. Now you know, both of you.

ROSMER [*stunned*] But I don't understand–! What is she saying? I don't understand a word–!

KROLL – Oh, yes, Rosmer. I am beginning to understand.

ROSMER – But what did you do? What could you have said to her? There was nothing. Absolutely nothing.

REBECCA – She learned that you were emancipating yourself from your old-fashioned prejudices.

ROSMER – But I wasn't, not then.

REBECCA – I knew you soon would.

KROLL [*nods to* ROSMER] Aha!

ROSMER – Go on. What else? I want to know the rest, too.

REBECCA – Not long afterwards–I begged and prayed her to let me leave Rosmersholm.

ROSMER – Why did you want to leave then?

REBECCA – I didn't want to leave. I wanted to stay here. But I told her I felt it would be best for us all–if I went away for a while. I let her understand that if I stayed any longer–something might–something might happen–

ROSMER—You said that? You did that?

REBECCA—Yes, John.

ROSMER—And—that is what you meant when you said you "took action"?

REBECCA [*in a broken voice*] Yes.

ROSMER [*after a moment*] Have you confessed everything now, Rebecca?

REBECCA—Yes.

KROLL—Not everything.

REBECCA [*looks at him, frightened*] What else could there be?

KROLL—Didn't you, in the end, make Beata understand that it was necessary—not merely that it was best, but that it was necessary—for your sake and for Rosmer's—that you should go away somewhere—as quickly as possible? Well?

REBECCA [*softly and barely audibly*] I may perhaps have said something like that.

ROSMER [*sinks into the armchair by the window*] And she—the poor, sick creature—went around here believing in this web of lies and treachery! Believing in it implicitly! Unquestioningly! [*Looks up at* REBECCA.] And she never turned to me. Never said a word— Oh, Rebecca. I see it now. *You* dissuaded her!

REBECCA—She had got it into her head that because she was a barren wife she had no right to be here. And then she got it into her head that it was her duty to you to make room for someone else.

ROSMER—And you—you did nothing to put this idea out of her head?

REBECCA—No.

KROLL—Perhaps you even encouraged it? Answer! Did you?

REBECCA—She may have understood me so.

ROSMER—Yes, yes! She always bowed to you in everything. And so she made room. [*Jumps up.*] How could you—how could you play this ghastly game?

REBECCA—I thought it was a choice between two lives, John.

KROLL [*sternly and magisterially*] You had no right to make such a choice.

REBECCA [*vehemently*] But do you think I did all this calculatedly and in cold blood? No, I was different then from what I am now—standing here and talking about it. And besides—I think a person can have two wills. I wanted to be rid of Beata. Somehow or other. But I never thought it would happen. Every step that I ventured forward, I felt as though a voice cried within me: "No further! Not an inch further!" But I *couldn't* stop! I had to venture another inch. Just one. And then another—just one more. And then it happened. That's how such things do happen.

[*Short silence.*]

R O S M E R [*to* REBECCA] And what do you suppose will happen to you now? When this becomes known?

R E B E C C A – I don't care what happens to me. It doesn't much matter.

K R O L L – No word of remorse. Perhaps you feel none?

R E B E C C A [*coldly aloof*] I'm sorry, Dr. Kroll, but that is something which concerns no one but myself. I shall settle that matter alone.

K R O L L [*to* ROSMER] And this is the woman with whom you share your roof. In an intimate relationship! [*Looks around at the portraits.*] Oh, if those who are gone had eyes to see you now!

R O S M E R – Are you going back to town?

K R O L L [*takes his hat*] Yes. As quickly as possible.

R O S M E R [*takes his hat likewise*] Then I shall accompany you.

K R O L L – You will! Yes, I knew we hadn't lost you for good.

R O S M E R – Come then, Kroll. Come!

They go out through the hall without looking at REBECCA. *After a few moments, she goes cautiously over to the window and peers out through the flowers.*

R E B E C C A [*speaks half-aloud to herself*] Not over the bridge today, either. Round. Never past the mill-race. Never. [*Leaves the window.*] Ah, well. [*Goes over and pulls the bellrope. After a few seconds* MRS. HELSETH *enters right.*]

M R S . H E L S E T H – What is it, miss?

R E B E C C A – Mrs. Helseth, will you be so kind as to have my trunk brought down from the attic?

M R S . H E L S E T H – Trunk?

R E B E C C A – Yes, the brown sealskin trunk. You know.

M R S . H E L S E T H – Yes, I know. But good heavens, miss—surely you're not going on a journey?

R E B E C C A – Yes, Mrs. Helseth. I am going on a journey.

M R S . H E L S E T H – Not at once?

R E B E C C A – As soon as I've packed.

M R S . H E L S E T H – Well, I never heard the like! But you'll soon be back, of course, miss?

R E B E C C A – No, I shall never come back here again.

M R S . H E L S E T H – Never! But, blessed Jesus, what's to become of Rosmersholm once you've left? Just when the poor Pastor was beginning to be so happy and comfortable.

R E B E C C A – Yes. But today something frightened me, Mrs. Helseth.

M R S . H E L S E T H – Frightened you? Mercy on us, what?

R E B E C C A – I thought I caught a glimpse of white horses.

MRS. HELSETH—White horses! In broad daylight?

REBECCA—Oh, they never sleep, the white horses of Rosmersholm.
[*Changes her tone.*] Well—my trunk then, please, Mrs. Helseth.

MRS. HELSETH—Very good, Miss West. Your trunk.

[*They both go out right.*]

ACT FOUR

The living room at Rosmersholm. It is late evening. The lamp, beneath its shade, is burning on the table. REBECCA WEST *is standing by the table packing some small belongings in a valise. Her cloak, hat, and the white crocheted shawl are hanging over the back of the sofa.*

[MRS. HELSETH *enters right.*]

MRS. HELSETH [*speaks softly and seems uneasy*] All your things are down now, miss. They're inside the back door.

REBECCA – Good. You've ordered the coachman?

MRS. HELSETH – Yes. He asks what time you'll be requiring him.

REBECCA – I should think about eleven. The steamer leaves at midnight.

MRS. HELSETH [*hesitates a little*] But the Pastor? Suppose he isn't back by then.

REBECCA – I shall leave in any case. If I don't see him, you can tell him I'll write. A long letter. Tell him that.

MRS. HELSETH – Well, that's all very well, writing. But—poor Miss West—I think you ought to try and speak with him once more.

REBECCA – Perhaps. And perhaps not.

MRS. HELSETH – Dear oh dear, that I should live to see this day! I'd never have believed it.

REBECCA – Wouldn't have believed what, Mrs. Helseth?

MRS. HELSETH – Well, I really thought Pastor Rosmer had more in him than this.

REBECCA – More in him?

MRS. HELSETH – Indeed yes, miss.

REBECCA – But, my dear Mrs. Helseth, what do you mean by that?

MRS. HELSETH – I mean what's right and proper, miss. He oughtn't to run away from things like that.

REBECCA [*looks at her*] Now listen, Mrs. Helseth. Tell me honestly. Why do you think I'm going away?

MRS. HELSETH – Bless you, miss, you've no choice! Oh dear, oh dear, oh dear. But I don't think the Pastor's acted rightly. That Mortens-

1362

gaard had some excuse—*she* still had her husband alive. So they couldn't have married, however much they wanted. But the Pastor—well!

REBECCA [*with a faint smile*] Could you have imagined anything like that between me and Pastor Rosmer?

MRS. HELSETH—Never. I mean—not until today.

REBECCA—But today—?

MRS. HELSETH—Well—after all those terrible things people say they've written about the Pastor in the newspapers—

REBECCA—Aha.

MRS. HELSETH—A man as can go over to Mortensgaard's way of thinking—well, he's capable of anything. That's my opinion.

REBECCA—Perhaps. But what about me, then? What do you say about me?

MRS. HELSETH—God bless you, miss—I don't see as how anyone can blame you. It isn't so easy for a single woman to hold out on her own. I mean, we're all human, Miss West.

REBECCA—That's very true, Mrs. Helseth. We are all human. What are you listening for?

MRS. HELSETH [*quietly*] Blessed Jesus, miss, I do believe that's him.

REBECCA [*starts*] Then he's—! [*Resolutely.*] Very well. So be it.

[JOHN ROSMER *enters from the hall.*]

ROSMER [*sees her clothes and valise, turns to* REBECCA *and asks*] What does this mean?

REBECCA—I am leaving.

ROSMER—Now?

REBECCA—Yes. [*To* MRS. HELSETH.] Eleven o'clock, then.

MRS. HELSETH—Very good, miss. [*Goes out right.*]

ROSMER [*after a short pause*] Where are you going, Rebecca?

REBECCA—North with the steamer.

ROSMER—North? Why there?

REBECCA—That's where I came from.

ROSMER—But you have nothing to do up there now.

REBECCA—I've nothing here either.

ROSMER—What do you intend to do?

REBECCA—I don't know. I just want to be finished with it all.

ROSMER—Be finished with it?

REBECCA—Rosmersholm has broken me.

ROSMER [*suddenly alert*] What?

REBECCA—Broken me completely. When I first came here, I was so alive and fearless. Now I am a slave to a strange and foreign law. After today I don't think I shall ever dare attempt anything again.

R O S M E R – Why not? What is this law you say you–?

R E B E C C A – Oh, my dear, let's not talk about that now. What happened between you and Dr. Kroll?

R O S M E R – We have settled our differences.

R E B E C C A – I see. So that's how it ended.

R O S M E R – He gathered all our old friends together at his house. They made me realize that the task of making the world noble is not for me. And anyway, it's such a hopeless idea, Rebecca. I shall forget about it.

R E B E C C A – Ah, well. Perhaps it's best that way.

R O S M E R – You say that now? Do you believe that?

R E B E C C A – I have come to believe it. During the past few days.

R O S M E R – You are lying, Rebecca.

R E B E C C A – Lying–?

R O S M E R – Yes, you are lying. You have never believed in me. You have never believed that I was the man to carry that cause to victory.

R E B E C C A – I believed we two might do it together.

R O S M E R – That isn't true. You believed that *you* might be able to achieve something in life. And that you could use me to that end. That I could serve your purpose. That's what you believed.

R E B E C C A – Now listen, John–

R O S M E R [*sits sadly on the sofa*] Oh, never mind. I see the whole thing clearly now. You've used me like a kind of glove.

R E B E C C A – Now listen, John. Let's talk about this. It will be for the last time. [*Sits in a chair by the sofa.*] I was going to write to you about it, when I had got back to the north. But perhaps you'd better hear it now.

R O S M E R – Have you something more to confess?

R E B E C C A – Yes. The most important thing of all.

R O S M E R – The most important thing?

R E B E C C A – The thing you've never guessed. The thing that both excuses and condemns all the rest.

R O S M E R [*shakes his head*] I don't understand any of this.

R E B E C C A – It's quite true that I once intrigued to gain admittance to Rosmersholm. I thought I might manage to find success and happiness here. One way or another–you understand.

R O S M E R – Then you achieved what you wanted.

R E B E C C A – I think I could have achieved anything–then. Because I feared nothing. I still had a free will. I had no inhibitions. I wasn't afraid of human relationships. But then there came–the thing that broke my will–and frightened me for ever.

R O S M E R – What happened? Speak so that I can understand you.

R E B E C C A – It came over me–this blinding, uncontrollable passion–! Oh, John–!

ROSMER—Passion? You—! For what?

REBECCA—For you.

ROSMER [*tries to spring up*] What!

REBECCA [*restrains him*] Sit still, my dear. There's something else you have to hear.

ROSMER—Are you trying to say—that you've loved me—in that way!

REBECCA—I thought it was love—then. Yes, I thought it was love. But it wasn't. It was what I tell you. A blinding, uncontrollable passion.

ROSMER [*with difficulty*] Rebecca—is it really *you—you*—that you're talking about?

REBECCA—Yes, John. Whom else?

ROSMER—Then it was this that—it was this that made you "take action," as you call it.

REBECCA—It swept over me like a storm at sea. Like one of those storms we sometimes get in the winter, far up in the north. It seizes you—and carries you with it, John—whithersoever it will. It's useless even to try to resist it.

ROSMER—And it swept poor Beata into the mill-race.

REBECCA—Yes. It was a fight for survival. Between Beata and me.

ROSMER—You were always the strongest at Rosmersholm. Stronger than Beata and me together.

REBECCA—I knew you so well, John. I knew I could never reach you until you'd been set free. Physically and mentally.

ROSMER—But I don't understand you, Rebecca. You—you and everything you've done—it's all an insoluble riddle to me. Now I am free—physically and mentally. Now you stand at the goal you set yourself from the beginning. And yet—

REBECCA—I have never been further from my goal than now.

ROSMER—And yet—when I asked you yesterday—when I begged you: "Be my wife!"—you cried out in terror that it could never happen.

REBECCA—I was crying in despair, John.

ROSMER—Why?

REBECCA—Because Rosmersholm has drained my strength. It has broken my courage and paralysed my will. The time is past when I was afraid of nothing. I have lost the power to take action, John.

ROSMER—Tell me how this has happened.

REBECCA—It has happened through living with you.

ROSMER—But how? How?

REBECCA—When I found myself alone here with you—and you had found yourself—

ROSMER—Yes, yes?

REBECCA——because you were never really yourself, as long as Beata was alive—

1365

R O S M E R – I'm afraid you're right there—

R E B E C C A – But then, when I began living here with you—alone in peace, just the two of us—when you shared all your thoughts with me, unreservedly—every mood and feeling, just as it came to you—then the great change happened. To me, I mean. Gradually, you understand. Almost imperceptibly—but irresistibly. To the very depths of my soul.

R O S M E R – Rebecca!

R E B E C C A – All the rest—that blinding, sickening passion—faded away from me. All my tormenting furies fell silent and still. A calm came over me—the kind of calm you find on a bird-cliff up in the far north, under the midnight sun.

R O S M E R – Go on. Tell me all you can.

R E B E C C A – There isn't much else, John. Only that—it was then that I began to love. The great and selfless love that asks for nothing more than companionship. The way it's been between us.

R O S M E R – Oh, if only I'd had any inkling of all this—!

R E B E C C A – It's best the way it is. Yesterday—when you asked me if I would be your wife—my heart cried aloud with joy—

R O S M E R – Yes, Rebecca. I sensed it.

R E B E C C A – Just for a moment, I was able to forget myself. My old spirit and will were crying out for their freedom. But now they no longer have any power or strength.

R O S M E R – How do you explain what has happened to you?

R E B E C C A – It's the Rosmer view of life—or yours, anyway. It has infected my will.

R O S M E R – Infected—?

R E B E C C A – And poisoned it. Enslaved it to a law which I had not previously recognized. You—being with you—has ennobled my soul—

R O S M E R – Oh, if I could only believe that!

R E B E C C A – You can believe it all right. The Rosmer view of life ennobles. But—[*shakes her head*]—but—but—

R O S M E R – But—? Well?

R E B E C C A – But it kills happiness, John.

R O S M E R – How can you say that, Rebecca?

R E B E C C A – For me, anyway.

R O S M E R – Can you be so sure of that? If I were to ask you again now— if I were to go on my knees and beg you—?

R E B E C C A – Oh, my dearest—please don't ever speak of that again. It's impossible—! You'd better know, John. Before I came to Rosmersholm —something happened to me—

R O S M E R – More than you've told me?

R E B E C C A – Yes. Something else. Something more terrible—

ROSMER [*with a faint smile*] Isn't it strange, Rebecca? Do you know, once or twice I'd wondered about that.

REBECCA – Did you? And yet–? In spite of that–?

ROSMER – I never believed it. I just–played with the thought, you know.

REBECCA – If you want me to, I'll tell you about that too.

ROSMER – No, no! I don't want to hear a word about it. Whatever it may be–I can forget it.

REBECCA – But I can't.

ROSMER – Oh, Rebecca–

REBECCA – Yes, John. That's what's so dreadful–that now, when all life's happiness is offered to me with open hands–now I've become the kind of person whose conscience about the past makes it impossible for me to accept it.

ROSMER – Your past is dead, Rebecca. It no longer has any hold on you. It has nothing to do with you. All that happened to someone else.

REBECCA – Oh, my dearest, those are just words. What about that sense of innocence you spoke about? Where shall I find that?

ROSMER [*sadly*] Yes, yes. Innocence.

REBECCA – Yes, innocence. The secret of joy and happiness. Wasn't that the lesson you wanted to teach your new generation of happy, noble men?

ROSMER – Oh, don't remind me of that. That was only a hopeless dream, Rebecca. A wild delusion that I no longer believe in. People cannot be ennobled from without, Rebecca.

REBECCA [*quietly*] Not even by love, don't you think?

ROSMER [*thoughtfully*] Ah, that would be the thing! The greatest thing that life could have to offer. If it were true. [*Writhes in distress.*] But how can I find the answer to that question? The real answer?

REBECCA – Don't you believe me, John?

ROSMER – Oh, Rebecca–how can I believe you in anything now? You've hidden so much from me. Now you come forward with this new idea. If you've some hidden purpose behind all this, for God's sake tell me straight out what it is! If there's anything you want, I'll willingly do anything I can for you.

REBECCA [*twists her hands*] Oh, this killing doubt–! John, John!

ROSMER – Yes, isn't it terrible, Rebecca? But I can't help it. I shall never be able to free myself from this doubt. Never be sure that you really love me, purely and with all your heart.

REBECCA – But doesn't something deep inside you tell you that a change has taken place in me? And that this change has been caused by you, and by you alone?

1367

ROSMER—Oh, Rebecca—I no longer believe in my ability to change people. I no longer have any faith in myself. Neither in myself nor in you.

REBECCA [*looks sadly at him*] How will you be able to live then, John?

ROSMER—I don't know. I don't know at all. I don't think I can live. In any case, I don't know anything worth living for.

REBECCA—Oh, life—life is its own renewer. Let us hold fast to it, John. We leave it soon enough.

ROSMER [*jumps up restlessly*] Then give me back my faith! My faith in you, Rebecca! My faith in your love! I want proof! Proof!

REBECCA—Proof? But how can I give you proof—?

ROSMER—You must. [*Walks across the room.*] I can't stand this desolation—this emptiness—this—this—

[*There is a loud knock on the door leading from the hall.*]

REBECCA [*jumps up from her chair*] Ah—did you hear that?

The door opens. ULRIK BRENDEL *enters. He is wearing a stiff shirt, a black coat, and good boots outside his trousers. Otherwise he is dressed as before. He looks confused.*

ROSMER—Oh, is it you, Mr. Brendel?

BRENDEL—John, my boy! *Ave—atque vale!*

ROSMER—Where are you going so late?

BRENDEL—Downhill.

ROSMER—What do you—?

BRENDEL—I am homeward bound, *mon cher élève!* My heart is homesick for the great void.

ROSMER—Something has happened to you, Mr. Brendel. What is it?

BRENDEL—You perceive the transformation? Ah—well you may. When I last set foot in this room, I stood before you as a man of substance, slapping my breast pocket.

ROSMER—Oh? I don't quite understand—

BRENDEL—But tonight you see a dethroned monarch kneeling on the ashes of his incinerated palace.

ROSMER—If there's any way I can help you—

BRENDEL—You have retained the heart of a child, my dear John. Can you spare me a loan?

ROSMER—Yes, yes, of course.

BRENDEL—Could you possibly stretch to an ideal or two?

ROSMER—What did you say?

BRENDEL—A few cast-off ideals. You'd be doing a good deed. I'm cleaned out, dear boy. Absolutely stripped.

R E B E C C A – Didn't you give your lecture?

B R E N D E L – No, seductive lady. Would you believe it! As I raised my hand to empty the cornucopia of plenty, I made the distressing discovery that I was bankrupt.

R E B E C C A – But all those unwritten works you spoke about?

B R E N D E L – For five and twenty years I have squatted like a miser on his padlocked money-bags. And then yesterday, when I opened them to bring my riches forth—there was nothing! The mills of time had ground everything into dust. *Nichts*—nothing!

R O S M E R – But are you sure of this?

B R E N D E L – No room for doubt, my duck. The President convinced me of that.

R O S M E R – The President?

B R E N D E L – His Excellency, if you prefer. *Ganz nach belieben.*

R O S M E R – Whom do you mean?

B R E N D E L – Peter Mortensgaard, of course.

R O S M E R – What!

B R E N D E L   [*confidentially*] Ssh, ssh, ssh! Peter Mortensgaard is the lord and master of the future! Never have I encountered so sublime a presence. Peter Mortensgaard possesses the secret of omnipotence. He can do anything he sets his mind to.

R O S M E R – Don't you believe that.

B R E N D E L – Yes, my boy! Because Peter Mortensgaard never wants to do more than lies within his power. Peter Mortensgaard knows how to live life without ideals. And *that*, you see—*that* is precisely the secret of action and of victory. It is the sum of all the world's wisdom. *Basta!*

R O S M E R   [*softly*] Now I understand. Yes, you are leaving here poorer than you came.

B R E N D E L – *Bien!* And now take a *Beispiel* of your old tutor. Blot out everything he ever imprinted on your mind. Build not thy citadel on shifting sand. And take care—proceed warily—before you build on this charming creature who now sweetens your existence.

R E B E C C A – Do you mean me?

B R E N D E L – I do, bewitching lady from the sea.

R E B E C C A – Why should I be nothing for a man to build his life on?

B R E N D E L   [*takes a step closer*] I gather that my former pupil has a cause which he wishes to carry to victory.

R E B E C C A – Well?

B R E N D E L – His victory is assured. But—mark this well—on one inescapable condition.

R E B E C C A – What is that?

B R E N D E L   [*takes her gently by the wrist*] That the woman who loves him shall, with a glad heart, go out into the kitchen and chop off her

1369

delicate rosy-white finger—*here*—just *here* at the middle joint. *Item,* that the aforesaid adoring woman—equally gladly—shall snip off her incomparably formed left ear. [*Lets go of her and turns to* ROSMER.] Farewell, Johannes! Forward to victory!

ROSMER—Are you going now? It's a dark night.

BRENDEL—Night and darkness are best. Peace be with you.

[*He goes.*]
[*There is a moment's silence in the room.*]

REBECCA [*takes a deep breath*] Oh, how close and suffocating it is in here!

[*She goes to the window, opens it, and remains standing there.*]

ROSMER [*sits in the armchair by the stove*] There's no other way, Rebecca. I see it now. You *must* leave.

REBECCA—Yes. I see no choice.

ROSMER—Let us make the most of these last moments. Come over here and sit beside me.

REBECCA [*goes over and sits on the sofa*] What is it, John?

ROSMER—First I want to tell you that you have no need to worry about your future.

REBECCA [*smiles*] Hm. *My* future.

ROSMER—I prepared for all contingencies a long time ago. Whatever may happen, you are provided for.

REBECCA—That too, my dear?

ROSMER—Surely you must have known—?

REBECCA—It's a long time since I thought of anything like that.

ROSMER—Yes, yes—you must have imagined things could never be different between us from the way they were.

REBECCA—Yes, I did feel that.

ROSMER—So did I. But if I were to go—

REBECCA—Oh, John. You will live longer than I.

ROSMER—This wretched life is my own to do what I wish with.

REBECCA—What do you mean? You aren't thinking of—?

ROSMER—Would it be so strange? After the humiliating defeat I have suffered? I, who was to carry my cause to victory—! And now I have fled the field—before the battle has even begun!

REBECCA—Take up the fight again, John! Only try, and you'll see! You will win! You will ennoble hundreds of souls—thousands! Only try!

ROSMER—Oh, Rebecca! I no longer have any faith in that cause.

REBECCA—But it has already stood the test. You have ennobled one human being at least. Me, for as long as I live.

ROSMER—If only I could believe you.

REBECCA [*clasps her hands*] Oh, John! Is there nothing—nothing that could make you believe it?

ROSMER [*starts as though in fear*] Don't say that, Rebecca! Please! Don't ever talk about that!

REBECCA—Yes, we must talk about it. Do you know of anything that could dispel your doubt? I can't think of a way.

ROSMER—Thank God that you can't. Thank God for us both.

REBECCA—No, no, no—I can't rest satisfied with that! If you know of anything that can acquit me in your eyes, I demand it as my right that you name it.

ROSMER [*as though forced to speak against his will*] Let's see, then. You say you have discovered the true meaning of love. That through me your soul has been ennobled. Is this true? Have you calculated correctly, Rebecca? Shall we check your calculation?

REBECCA—I am ready.

ROSMER—When?

REBECCA—Anytime. The sooner the better.

ROSMER—Then show me, Rebecca—if you—for my sake—this very night—! [*Breaks off.*] Oh, no, no, no!

REBECCA—Yes, John! Yes, yes! Tell me, and you'll see!

ROSMER—Have you the courage—and the will—with a glad heart, as Ulrik Brendel said—for my sake, now, tonight—freely and willingly—to go the way that Beata went?

REBECCA [*draws herself up from the sofa and says almost speechlessly*] John!

ROSMER—Yes, Rebecca. This is the question I shall never be able to escape from—after you are gone. Every hour of the day it will haunt me. Oh—I seem to see you there before my eyes. You are standing on the bridge. In the middle of it. Now you are leaning out over the parapet. You sway as the rushing water draws you down. No. Then you shrink back. You have not the courage to do as she did.

REBECCA—But if I had the courage? And the will, to do it gladly? What then?

ROSMER—Then I would have to believe you. I would regain my faith in my life's work. Faith in my ability to ennoble humanity. Faith in the capacity of man to be ennobled.

REBECCA [*slowly takes her shawl, throws it over her head and says calmly*] You shall have your faith back.

ROSMER—Have you the courage—and the will—to do this, Rebecca?

REBECCA—That you will be able to judge tomorrow—or later—when they fish me up.

ROSMER [*clutches at his forehead*] There's a—demonic fascination—in this—!

REBECCA—I don't want to stay lying down there. Longer than necessary. You must see that they find me.

ROSMER [*jumps up*] But all this—is madness! Go—or stay. I will believe you—I will take your word for it. This time too.

REBECCA—Words, John! Let's have no more cowardice and running away. How can you take my word for anything after today?

ROSMER—But I don't want to see you defeated, Rebecca.

REBECCA—There will be no defeat.

ROSMER—There will be. You will never have the courage to go Beata's way.

REBECCA—You think not?

ROSMER—Never. You are not like Beata. You don't see life through distorted eyes.

REBECCA—But I see it through Rosmer eyes. The crime that I have committed—demands atonement.

ROSMER [*looks fixedly at her*] Is that what you believe in your heart?

REBECCA—Yes.

ROSMER [*with decision*] Very well. Then I kneel to our emancipated view of life, Rebecca. We acknowledge no judge over us. Therefore we must pass judgment upon ourselves.

REBECCA [*misunderstands him*] Yes, John, yes. If I go, it will save what is best in you.

ROSMER—There is nothing left in me to save.

REBECCA—There is. But I—after today I would be like a sea-troll, hanging on to the ship that is to carry you forward and holding it back. I must be cast overboard. Would you have me linger on up here in the world, dragging my life along like a cripple? I must retire from the game, John.

ROSMER—If you go—then I shall go with you.

REBECCA [*smiles almost imperceptibly, looks at him and says more quietly*] Yes, John. Come with me—and witness—

ROSMER—I shall go with you, I said.

REBECCA—To the bridge, yes. You will never dare to walk on it.

ROSMER—You have noticed that?

REBECCA [*sadly, broken*] Yes. That was what made my love hopeless.

ROSMER—Rebecca, now I place my hand on your head. [*He does as he says.*] And take you in marriage as my lawful wife.

REBECCA [*clasps both his hands and bows her head against his breast*] Thank you, John. [*Lets go of him.*] And now I go—gladly.

ROSMER—Man and wife should go together.

REBECCA—Only as far as the bridge, John.

ROSMER—And on to it. As far as you go, I shall go with you. Now I am no longer afraid.

REBECCA – Are you so completely sure—that this way is the best one for you?

ROSMER – I know that it is the only one.

REBECCA – Suppose you are wrong? Suppose it is only an illusion? One of those white horses of Rosmersholm?

ROSMER – That may be. We shall never escape them—we who live in this house.

REBECCA – Then stay, John!

ROSMER – Man and wife should go together.

REBECCA – But first tell me this. Is it you who are going with me? Or I with you?

ROSMER – That we shall never know.

REBECCA – I should like to know.

ROSMER – We go together, Rebecca. I with you, and you with me.

REBECCA – Yes. I think you are right.

ROSMER – For now we two are one.

REBECCA – Yes. Now we are one. Come! Let us go gladly!

They go out hand in hand through the hall, and turn to the left. The door remains open behind them. For a few moments the room is empty. Then MRS. HELSETH *opens the door right.*

MRS. HELSETH – Miss—the carriage is—! [*Looks round.*] Not here? Out together at this hour? Well, I must say! Hm! [*Goes out into the hall, looks round and comes back again.*] They're not on the seat. Well, well. [*Goes to the window and looks out.*] Blessed Jesus! What's that white thing over there—? Upon my soul, if they're not both standing on the bridge! God forgive the sinful creatures! If they're not putting their arms round each other—! [*Screams aloud.*] Ah! They've fallen—both of them! Into the mill-race! Help! Help! [*Her knees tremble; she holds on, shaking, to the back of the chair, hardly able to speak.*] No. No help. The dead mistress has taken them.

THOSE WRECKED BY SUCCESS
[Authorized Translation]

By Sigmund Freud

Psycho-analytic work has furnished us with the rule that people fall ill of a neurosis as a result of *frustration*. The frustration meant is that of satisfaction for their libidinal desires and a long circumlocution is necessary before the law becomes comprehensible. That is to say, for a neurosis to break out there must be a conflict between the libidinal desires of a person and that part of his being which we call his ego, the expression of his instinct of self-preservation, which also contains his ideals of his own character. A pathogenic conflict of this kind takes place only when the libido is desirous of pursuing paths and aims which the ego has long overcome and despised, and has therefore henceforth proscribed; and this the libido never does until it is deprived of the possibility of an ideal satisfaction consistent with the ego. Hence privation, frustration of a real satisfaction, is the first condition for the outbreak of a neurosis, although, indeed, it is far from being the only one.

So much the more surprising, indeed bewildering, must it appear when as a physician one makes the discovery that people occasionally fall ill precisely because a deeply-rooted and long-cherished wish has come to fulfilment. It seems then as though they could not endure their bliss, for of the causative connection between this fulfilment and the falling-ill there can be no question. I had an opportunity in this way of obtaining

From "Some Character-Types Met With in Psycho-Analytic Work" in *The Collected Papers of Sigmund Freud* (Chapter XVIII, Volume 4), edited by Ernest Jones. New York: Basic Books, Inc., 1959. Reprinted by permission of Basic Books, Inc. and the Hogarth Press.

insight into a woman's story, which I propose to describe as typical of these tragic occurrences.

Well-born and well-brought-up, as a quite young girl she could not restrain her zest for life; she ran away from home and roved adventurously till she made the acquaintance of an artist who could appreciate her feminine charms but could also divine, despite her degradation, the finer qualities she possessed. He took her to live with him, and she proved a faithful and devoted companion, apparently needing only social rehabilitation for complete happiness. After many years of life together, he succeeded in getting his family to recognize her, and was then prepared to make her his legal wife. At this critical moment she began to go to pieces. She neglected the house whose rightful mistress she was now about to become, imagined herself persecuted by his relatives, who wanted to take her into the family, debarred her lover, through senseless jealousy, from all social intercourse, hindered him in his artistic work, and soon fell into incurable mental illness.

On another occasion I observed a most respectable man who, himself professor at a university, had for many years cherished the natural wish to succeed the master who had initiated him into the life of learning. When this elder man retired, and the other's colleagues intimated that it was he whom they desired as successor, he began to hesitate, depreciated his own merits, declared himself unworthy to fill the position designed for him, and fell into a state of melancholy which unfitted him for all activity for some years after.

Different as these two cases are, they yet coincide on this one point— that illness followed close upon the wish-fulfilment, and annihilated all enjoyment of it.

The contradiction between such experiences and the rule that frustration induces illness is not insoluble. The distinction between an *internal* and an *external* frustration dispels it. When in actuality the object in which the libido can find its satisfaction is withheld, this is an external frustration. In itself it is inoperative, not pathogenic, until an internal frustration has joined hands with it. This must proceed from the ego, and must dispute the right of the libido to the other objects that it then desires to possess. Only then does a conflict arise, and the possibility of neurotic illness, *i.e.* of a substitutive gratification proceeding circuitously by way of the repressed unconscious. The internal frustration is present, therefore, in every case, only it does not come into operation until the external, actual frustration has prepared the ground for it. In those exceptional cases where illness ensues on success, the internal frustration has operated alone—has indeed only made its appearance when an external frustration has been replaced by fulfilment of the wish. At first sight

there remains something astonishing about this; but on closer consideration we shall reflect that it is not so very unusual for the ego to tolerate a
wish as harmless so long as this exists in phantasy alone and seems remote from fulfilment, while it will defend itself hotly against such a
wish as soon as it approaches fulfilment and threatens to become an
actuality. The distinction between this and familiar situations in neurosis-
formation is merely that usually it is internal intensifications of the
libidinal cathexis which turn the phantasy, that has hitherto been thought
little of and tolerated, into a dreaded opponent; while in these cases of
ours the signal for the outbreak of conflict is given by an actual external
alteration in circumstances.

Analytic work soon shows us that it is forces of conscience which forbid
the person to gain the long-hoped-for enjoyment from the fortunate
change in reality. It is a difficult task, however, to discover the essence
and origin of these censuring and punishing tendencies, which so often
surprise us by their presence where we do not expect to find them. What
we know or conjecture on the point I shall discuss, for the usual reasons,
in relation not to cases of clinical observation, but to figures which great
writers have created from the wealth of their knowledge of the soul.

A person who collapses on attaining her aim, after striving for it with
single-minded energy, is Shakespeare's Lady Macbeth. In the beginning
there is no hesitation, no sign of any inner conflict in her, no endeavour
but that of overcoming the scruples of her ambitious and yet gentle-
hearted husband. She is ready to sacrifice even her womanliness to her
murderous intention, without reflecting on the decisive part which this
womanliness must play when the question arises of preserving the aim
of her ambition, which has been attained through a crime.

> Come, you spirits
> That tend on mortal thoughts, unsex me here
> . . . Come to my woman's breasts,
> And take my milk for gall, you murdering ministers!
> (Act 1. Scene 5.)

> . . . I have given suck, and know
> How tender 'tis to love the babe that milks me:
> I would, while it was smiling in my face,
> Have pluck'd my nipple from his boneless gums,
> And dashed the brains out, had I so sworn as you
> Have done to this.   (Act 1. Scene 7.)

One solitary stirring of unwillingness comes over her before the deed:

> . . . Had he not resembled
> My father as he slept, I had done it. . . .

Then, when she has become Queen by the murder of Duncan, she betrays for a moment something like disillusion, like satiety. We know not why.

> . . . Nought's had, all's spent,
> Where our desire is got without content:
> 'Tis safer to be that which we destroy,
> Than by destruction dwell in doubtful joy.   (Act III. Scene 2.)

Nevertheless, she holds out. In the banquet-scene which follows on these words, she alone keeps her head, cloaks her husband's distraction, and finds a pretext for dismissing the guests. And then we see her no more; until (in the first scene of the fifth act) we again behold her as a sleep-walker, with the impressions of that night of murder fixed on her mind. Again, as then, she seeks to put heart into her husband:

> 'Fie, my lord, fie! a soldier, and afeard? What need we fear who knows it, when none can call our power to account?'

She hears the knocking at the door, which terrified her husband after the deed. Next, she strives to 'undo the deed which cannot be undone'. She washes her hands, which are blood-stained and smell of blood, and is conscious of the futility of the attempt. Remorse seems to have borne her down—she who had seemed so remorseless. When she dies, Macbeth, who meanwhile has become as inexorable as she had been in the beginning, can find only a brief epitaph for her:

> She should have died hereafter;
> There would have been a time for such a word.   (Act v. Scene 5.)

And now we ask ourselves what it was that broke this character which had seemed forged from the most perdurable metal? Is it only disillusion, the different aspect shown by the accomplished deed, and are we to infer that even in Lady Macbeth an originally gentle and womanly nature had been worked up to a concentration and high tension which could not long endure, or ought we to seek for such signs of a deeper motivation as will make this collapse more humanly intelligible to us?

It seems to me impossible to come to any decision. Shakespeare's *Macbeth* is a *pièce d'occasion*, written for the accession of James, who had hitherto been King of Scotland. The plot was ready-made, and had been handled by other contemporary writers, whose work Shakespeare probably made use of in his customary manner. It offered remarkable analogies to the actual situation. The 'virginal' Elizabeth, of whom it was rumoured that she had never been capable of childbearing and who had once described herself as 'a barren stock',[1] in an anguished outcry at the news of James's birth, was obliged by this very childlessness of hers to let the Scottish king become her successor. And he was the son of that Mary Stuart whose execution she, though reluctantly, had decreed, and who, despite the clouding of their relations by political concerns, was yet of her blood and might be called her guest.

The accession of James I. was like a demonstration of the curse of unfruitfulness and the blessings reserved for those who carry on the race. And Shakespeare's *Macbeth* develops on the theme of this same contrast. The three Fates, the 'weird sisters', have assured him that he shall indeed be king, but to Banquo they promise that *his* children shall obtain possession of the crown. Macbeth is incensed by this decree of destiny; he is not content with the satisfaction of his own ambition, he desires to found a dynasty and not to have murdered for the benefit of strangers. This point is overlooked when Shakespeare's play is regarded only as a tragedy of ambition. It is clear that Macbeth cannot live for ever, and thus there is but one way for him to disprove that part of the prophecy which opposes his wishes—namely, to have children himself, children who can succeed him. And he seems to expect them from his vigorous wife:

> Bring forth men-children only!
> For thy undaunted mettle should compose
> Nothing but males. . . .   (Act i. Scene 7.)

And equally it is clear that if he is deceived in this expectation he must submit to destiny; otherwise his actions lose all purpose and are transformed into the blind fury of one doomed to destruction, who is resolved to destroy beforehand all that he can reach. We watch Macbeth undergo this development, and at the height of the tragedy we hear that shattering cry from Macduff, which has often ere now been recognized to have many meanings and possibly to contain the key to the change in Macbeth:

> He has no children!   (Act iv. Scene 3.)

[1] Cf. *Macbeth*, Act iii. Scene 1:

> Upon my head they placed a fruitless crown,
> And put a barren sceptre in my gripe,
> Thence to be wrenched with an unlineal hand,
> No son of mine succeeding. . . .

Undoubtedly that signifies 'Only because he is himself childless could he murder my children'; but more may be implied in it, and above all it might be said to lay bare the essential motive which not only forces Macbeth to go far beyond his own true nature, but also assails the hard character of his wife at its only weak place. If one looks back upon *Macbeth* from the culmination reached in these words of Macduff's, one sees that the whole play is sown with references to the father-and-children relation. The murder of the kindly Duncan is little else than parricide; in Banquo's case, Macbeth kills the father while the son escapes him; and he kills Macduff's children because the father has fled from him. A bloody child, and then a crowned one, are shown him by the witches in the conjuration-scene; the armed head seen previously is doubtless Macbeth's own. But in the background arises the sinister form of the avenger, Macduff, who is himself an exception to the laws of generation, since he was not born of his mother but ripp'd from her womb.

It would be a perfect example of poetic justice in the manner of the talion if the childlessness of Macbeth and the barrenness of his Lady were the punishment for their crimes against the sanctity of geniture—if Macbeth could not become a father because he had robbed children of their father and a father of his children, and if Lady Macbeth had suffered the unsexing she had demanded of the spirits of murder. I believe one could without more ado explain the illness of Lady Macbeth, the transformation of her callousness into penitence, as a reaction to her childlessness, by which she is convinced of her impotence against the decrees of nature, and at the same time admonished that she has only herself to blame if her crime has been barren of the better part of its desired results.

In the *Chronicle* of Holinshed (1577), whence Shakespeare took the plot of *Macbeth*, Lady Macbeth is only once mentioned as the ambitious wife who instigates her husband to murder that she may herself be queen. Of her subsequent fate and of the development of her character there is no word at all. On the other hand, it would seem that there the change in Macbeth to a sanguinary tyrant is motivated just in the way we have suggested. For in Holinshed ten years pass between the murder of Duncan, whereby Macbeth becomes king, and his further misdeeds; and in these ten years he is shown as a stern but righteous ruler. It is not until after this period that the change begins in him, under the influence of the tormenting apprehension that the prophecy to Banquo will be fulfilled as was that of his own destiny. Then only does he contrive the murder of Banquo, and, as in Shakespeare, is driven from one crime to another. Holinshed does not expressly say that it was his childlessness which urged him to these courses, but there is warrant enough—both time and occasion—for this probable motivation. Not so in Shakespeare. Events crowd breathlessly on one another in the tragedy, so that to judge by the statements made by the persons in the play about one week represents the duration of time assigned to it.[2] This acceleration takes the ground from under our attempts at reconstructing the motives for the change in the characters of Macbeth and his wife. There is no time for a long-drawn disappointment of their hopes of offspring to enervate the woman and drive the man to an insane defiance; and it remains impossible to resolve the contradiction that so many subtle inter-relations in the plot, and between it and its occasion, point to a common origin of them in the motive of childlessness, and that yet the period of time in the tragedy expressly precludes a development of character from any but a motive contained in the play.

What, however, these motives can have been which in so short a space of time could turn the hesitating, ambitious man into an unbridled tyrant, and his steely-hearted instigator into a sick woman gnawed by remorse, it is, in my view, impossible to divine. I think we must renounce the hope of penetrating the triple obscurity of the bad preservation of the text, the unknown intention of the dramatist, and the hidden purport of the legend. But I should not admit that such investigations are idle in view of the powerful effect which the tragedy has upon the spectator. The dramatist can indeed, during the representation, overwhelm us by his art and paralyse our powers of reflection; but he cannot prevent us from subsequently attempting to grasp the psychological mechanism of that effect. And the contention that the dramatist is at liberty to shorten at will the natural time and duration of the events he brings before us, if by the sacrifice of common probability he can enhance the dramatic effect, seems to me irrelevant in this instance. For such a sacrifice is justified only when it merely affronts probability,[3] and not when it breaks the causal connection; besides, the dramatic effect would hardly have suffered if the time-duration had been left in uncertainty, instead of being expressly limited to some few days.

One is so unwilling to dismiss a problem like that of *Macbeth* as insoluble that I will still make another attempt, by introducing another comment which points towards a new issue. Ludwig Jekels, in a recent Shakespearean study,[4] thinks he has divined a technical trick of the poet, which might have to be reckoned with in *Macbeth*, too. He is of opinion that Shakespeare frequently splits up a character into two personages, each of whom then appears not altogether comprehensible until once more conjoined with the other. It might be thus with Macbeth and the Lady; and then it would of course be futile to regard her as an independ-

---

[2] J. Darmstetter, *Macbeth*, Édition classique, p. lxxv., Paris, 1887.
[3] As in Richard III.'s wooing of Anne beside the bier of the King whom he has murdered.
[4] See *Selected Papers*. New York, 1952.

ent personage and seek to discover her motivation without considering the Macbeth who completes her. I shall not follow this hint any further, but I would add, nevertheless, a remark which strikingly confirms the idea—namely, that the stirrings of fear which arise in Macbeth on the night of the murder, do not develop further in him, but in the Lady.[5] It is he who has the hallucination of the dagger before the deed, but it is she who later succumbs to mental disorder; he, after the murder, hears the cry from the house: 'Sleep no more! Macbeth does murder sleep . . .', and so 'Macbeth shall sleep no more', but we never hear that King Macbeth could not sleep, while we see that the Queen rises from her bed and betrays her guilt in somnambulistic wanderings. He stands helpless with bloody hands, lamenting that not great Neptune's ocean can wash them clean again, while she comforts him: 'A little water clears us of this deed'; but later it is she who washes her hands for a quarter of an hour and cannot get rid of the bloodstains. 'All the perfumes of Arabia will not sweeten this little hand.' Thus is fulfilled in her what his pangs of conscience had apprehended; she is incarnate remorse after the deed, he incarnate defiance—together they exhaust the possibilities of reaction to the crime, like two disunited parts of the mind of a single individuality, and perhaps they are the divided images of a single prototype.

If we have been unable to give any answer to the question why Lady Macbeth should collapse after her success, we may perhaps have a better chance with the creation of another great dramatist, who loves to pursue with unrelenting rigour the task of the psychological reckoning.

Rebecca Gamvik, the daughter of a midwife, has become, under the influence of her adoptive father, Dr. West, a freethinker and a contemner of all those restrictions upon desires in life which are imposed by morality founded on religious belief. After the doctor's death she obtains a footing at Rosmersholm, the ancestral seat of an old family whose members are unacquainted with laughter and have sacrificed joy to stern fulfilment of duty. At Rosmersholm dwell Pastor Johannes Rosmer and his invalid wife, the childless Beata. Overcome by 'a wild, uncontrollable passion' for the love of the aristocratic Rosmer, Rebecca resolves to remove the wife who stands in her way, and to this end is served by her 'fearless, freeborn' will, which is restrained by no ethical considerations. She contrives that Beata shall read a medical book in which the begetting of offspring is represented as the sole aim of marriage, so that the poor woman begins to doubt whether her own union is an honourable one. Rebecca then hints that Rosmer, whose studies and ideas she shares, is about to abandon the old faith and join the party of enlightenment; and

---

[5] Cf. Darmstetter, *loc. cit.*

after she has thus shaken the wife's confidence in the moral uprightness of her husband, gives her finally to understand that she, Rebecca, must soon leave the house in order to conceal the consequences of illicit intercourse with Rosmer. The criminal scheme succeeds. The poor wife, who has passed for melancholic and crazy, throws herself from the path beside the mill into the mill-race, possessed by the sense of her own worthlessness and desirous of standing no longer between her beloved husband and his bliss.

For more than a year Rebecca and Rosmer have been living alone at Rosmersholm in a relationship which he wishes to regard as a purely intellectual and ideal friendship. But when from outside the first shadow of evil gossip falls upon this relationship, and at the same time there arise tormenting doubts in Rosmer in regard to the motives for which his wife had put an end to herself, he begs Rebecca to become his second wife, so that they may oppose to the unhappy past a new living reality (Act ii.). For one instant she cries out with joy at this proposal, but immediately afterwards declares that it can never be, and that if he urges her further she will 'go the way Beata went'. Rosmer cannot at all understand this rejection; and still less can we, who know more of Rebecca's actions and designs. All we can be certain of is that her 'No' is meant in good earnest.

How has it come about that the adventuress with the fearless, freeborn will, which forged its way relentlessly to its desired goal, should now refuse to pluck the fruit which is offered her? She herself gives us the explanation in the fourth Act: '*This* is the terrible part of it: that now when all life's happiness is within my grasp—my heart is changed, and my own past bars my way to happiness'. That is, she has become a different being, her conscience has awakened, she has a conviction of guilt which denies her happiness.

And how has her conscience been awakened? Let us listen to her, and consider whether we can accord her our full credence: 'It is the Rosmer view of life—or your view, at any rate—that has infected my will. . . . And made it sick. Enslaved it to laws that had no power over me before. You—life with you—has ennobled my mind.'

This influence, we are further to understand, has only become effective since she has been living alone with Rosmer: 'In quiet—in solitude—when you showed me all your thoughts without reserve—every tender and delicate feeling, just as it came to you—then the great change came over me'.

Shortly before this she has lamented the other aspect of the change: 'Because Rosmersholm has sapped my strength, my old fearless will has had its wings clipped here. It is paralysed! The time is past when I had courage for anything in the world. I have lost the power of action, Rosmer.'

Rebecca makes this declaration after she has revealed herself a wrong-doer in a voluntary confession to Rosmer and Rector Kroll, the brother of the dead wife. Ibsen has made it clear by many little touches, worked in with masterly subtlety, that this Rebecca does not actually lie, but is never entirely straightforward. Just as, in spite of all her freedom from prejudice, she understated her age by a year, so is her confession to the two men not entirely complete, and through the persistence of Kroll it is supplemented on some important points. Hence it is open to us, too, to conjecture that the explanation of her refusal only exposes one motive in order to conceal another.

Assuredly we have no reason to disbelieve her when she declares that the atmosphere of Rosmersholm and her intercourse with the high-souled Rosmer have ennobled and—paralysed her. She expresses there what she knows and has felt. But this is not necessarily all that has happened to her, nor is she necessarily competent to explain to herself that all. The influence of Rosmer might even only be a cloak which conceals another influence that was operative, and a notable indication points in this new direction.

Even after her confession, in their last interview which brings the play to an end, Rosmer again beseeches her to be his wife. He forgives her the crime committed for love of him. And now she does not answer, as she might, that no forgiveness can rid her of the consciousness of guilt incurred by her malignant deception of poor Beata; but charges herself with another reproach which affects us as coming strangely from this freethinking woman, and in no wise corresponds to the importance which Rebecca attaches to it: 'Dear—never speak of this again! It is impossible—. For you must know, Rosmer, I have—a past behind me.' She means, of course, that she has had sexual relations with another man; and we do not fail to observe that these relations, which occurred at a time when she was free and accountable to nobody, seem to her a greater hindrance to the union with Rosmer than her truly criminal action against his wife.

Rosmer refuses to hear anything about this past. We can divine what it was, though everything that refers to it in the play is, so to speak, sub-terranean and has to be pieced together from hints. But it is true they are hints inserted with such art that it is impossible to misunderstand them.

Between Rebecca's first refusal and her confession something occurs which has a decisive influence on her future destiny. Rector Kroll arrives one day at the house on purpose to humiliate Rebecca by telling her that he knows she is an illegitimate child, the daughter of that very Dr. West who had adopted her after her mother's death. Hate has sharpened his perceptions, yet he does not suppose that this is any news to her. 'I really did not suppose you were ignorant of this, otherwise it would have been very odd that you should have let Dr. West adopt you——' 'And then he takes you into his house—as soon as your mother dies. He treats you harshly. And yet you stay with him. You know that he won't leave you a halfpenny—as a matter of fact you got only a case of books—and yet you stay on; you bear with him; your nurse him to the last.' 'I attribute your care for him to the natural filial instinct of a daughter. Indeed, I believe your whole conduct is a natural result of your origin.'

But Kroll was mistaken. Rebecca had no idea at all that she could be West's daughter. When Kroll began with dark hints at her past, she could not but think he was referring to something else. After she knew what he did mean, she could still retain her composure awhile, for she was able to suppose that her enemy was basing his calculations on her age, which she had given falsely on an earlier visit of his. But when Kroll demolished this objection by saying: 'Well, so be it, but my calculation may be right, none the less; for Dr. West was up there on a short visit the year before he got the appointment' . . . after this new information, she loses all control. 'It is not true!' She walks about wringing her hands. 'It is impossible. You want to cheat me into believing it. This can never, never be true. It cannot be true. Never in this world!——' Her agitation is so extreme that Kroll cannot attribute it to his information alone.

KROLL – But, my dear Miss West—why in Heaven's name are you so terribly excited? You quite frighten me. What am I to think—to believe——?
REBECCA – Nothing! You are not to think anything or believe anything.
KROLL – Then you must really tell me how you can take this affair—this possibility—so terribly to heart.
REBECCA [*controlling herself*] It is perfectly simple, Rector Kroll. I have no wish to be taken for an illegitimate child.

The enigma of Rebecca's behaviour is susceptible of only one solution. The news that Dr. West was her father is the heaviest blow that can befall her, for she was not only the adopted daughter, but she had been the mistress of this man. When Kroll began to speak, she thought that he was hinting at these relations, the truth about which she would probably have admitted and justified by her emancipated ideas. But this was far from the Rector's intention; he knew nothing of the love-affair with Dr. West, as she knew nothing of West being her father. She *cannot* have had anything else in her mind when she accounted for her final rejection of Rosmer on the ground that she had a past which made her unworthy to be his wife. Probably, if Rosmer had consented to hear of this past, she would have made only a half-confession and have kept silence on the more serious part of it.

But now we do indeed understand that this past must seem to her the more serious obstacle to their union—the more serious . . . crime.

After she has learnt that she has been the mistress of her own father, she surrenders herself wholly to her now overmastering sense of guilt. She confesses to Rosmer and Kroll that she was a murderess; she rejects for ever the happiness to which she has paved the way by crime; and prepares for departure. But the true origin of her sense of guilt, which wrecks her at the moment of attainment, remains a secret. We have seen that it is something quite other than the atmosphere of Rosmersholm and the refining influence of Rosmer.

No one who has followed us so far will neglect to bring forward an objection which may justify some doubts. The first refusal of Rosmer by Rebecca occurs before the second visit of Kroll, and therefore before his exposure of her illicit origin and at a time when she as yet knows nothing of her incest—if we have rightly understood the dramatist. Yet her first refusal is given in very serious earnest. The sense of guilt which bids her renounce the fruit of her actions is thus effective before she knows anything of her cardinal crime; and if we grant so much it is perhaps incumbent on us to ignore the incest as the source of that sense of guilt.

Hitherto, we have treated Rebecca West as if she were a living person and not a creation of Ibsen's phantasy, one which is always subject to the most critical tests of reason. We shall attempt to meet the objection aforesaid on this same ground. It is a just objection that, before the knowledge of her incest, conscience was in some sort awakened in Rebecca. There is nothing to prevent our making the influence which is acknowledged and accused by Rebecca herself responsible for this change. But we shall not thus escape recognition of the second motive. The behaviour of Rebecca on hearing what Kroll has to tell her, the confession which is her immediate reaction, leave no doubt that now only does the stronger and more decisive motive for renunciation begin to take effect. It is in fact a case of manifold motivation, in which a deeper motive comes to the surface from beneath the superficial one. Laws of poetical economy necessitate this way of presenting the situation, for this deeper motive could not be explicitly set forth, it had to be dissimulated, kept from the direct perception of the spectator or the reader; otherwise such serious resistances, based on most painful emotions, would have arisen that the effect of the tragedy might have been imperilled.

We have, however, a right to demand that the ostensible motive shall not be without an inherent relation to the dissimulated one, but shall appear as a mitigation of, and a derivation from, the latter. And relying on the dramatist to have arranged his conscious dramatic combination in logical accordance with unconscious possibilities, we can now try to show that he has fulfilled this demand. Rebecca's feeling of guilt finds its source in the shame of incest, even before Kroll with his analytic insight has made her aware of it. When we fully reconstruct and supplement the past indicated by the author, we shall feel sure that she cannot have been without an inkling of the intimate relation between her mother and Dr. West. It must have made a strong impression on her when she became her mother's successor with this man; and she thus stood under the domination of the Oedipus-complex, even though she did not know that this universal phantasy had been a reality in her case. When she came to Rosmersholm, the inward force of this first experience drove her to bring about, by definite action, the same situation which had been realized in the original instance, though not by her doing—to get rid of the wife and mother, that she might take her place with the husband and father. She describes with a convincing insistence how against her will she was obliged to proceed, step by step, to the removal of Beata.

'You think then that I was cool and calculating and self-possessed all the time! I was not the same woman then that I am now, as I stand here telling it all. Besides, there are two sorts of will in us, I believe. I wanted Beata away by one means or another, but I never really believed that it would come to pass. As I felt my way forward, at each step I ventured, I seemed to hear something within me cry out: No farther! Not a step farther!—And yet I could not stop. I *had* to venture the least little bit farther. And only one hair's-breadth more. And then one more—and always one more. . . . And so it happened. That is the way such things come about.'

That is no plea for extenuation, but an authentic description. Everything that befell her at Rosmersholm, the passion for Rosmer and the enmity towards his wife, was from the first a consequence of the Oedipus-complex—a compulsive replica of her relations with her mother and Dr. West.

And so the sense of guilt which first causes her to reject Rosmer's proposal is at bottom indistinguishable from the deeper one which drives her to confession after Kroll has opened her eyes. But just as under the influence of Dr. West she had become a freethinker and contemner of religious morality, so she is transformed by her love for Rosmer into a being with a conscience and an ideal. This much of the mental processes within her she does herself understand, and so she is justified in describing Rosmer's influence as the motive of the change in her—the only one of which she could be aware.

The practising psycho-analytic physician knows how frequently, or how invariably, the girl who enters a household as servant, companion or governess, will consciously or unconsciously weave a day-dream, which derives from the Oedipus-complex, about the disappearance of the mistress of the house and the master taking the newcomer to wife in her stead. *Rosmersholm* is the greatest work of art among those which treat of this common girlish phantasy. What makes it a tragedy is the circumstance that the early history of the heroine in actual fact had completely anticipated her day-dream.[6]

After long lingering in the sphere of literature, we now return to clinical experience. But only to establish in a few words the complete agreement between them. Psycho-analytic work teaches that the forces of conscience which induce illness on attainment of success, as in other cases on a frustration, are closely connected with the Oedipus-complex, the relation to father and mother, as perhaps, indeed, is all our sense of guilt in general.

---

[6] An exposition of the incest-theme in *Rosmersholm* has already been made, by similar methods to my own, in the extremely comprehensive work by Otto Rank, *Das Inzest-Motiv in Dichtung und Sage*.

AUGUST STRINDBERG

Miss Julie

THE PHENOMENON AUGUST STRINDBERG (1849–1912) might well be regarded as a watershed between two centuries, our own and the previous
one. Commonly, too, his plays are seen in two groups—the Naturalistic
and the Expressionistic—one of which is typically of the nineteenth, the
other of the early twentieth, century. Latterly, however, critics have been
able to show that the two groups of plays are not as different as had been
thought. The Naturalistic plays have Expressionistic elements, and vice
versa. *Miss Julie* is a Naturalistic tragedy, yet it contains non-Naturalistic
elements of mime, ballet, and music which the author makes much of in
his preface. Of that preface, it has been said that not everything in it
corresponds to what we actually find in the play. Even so, no better
commentary on the play has been written in all the eighty years that
have passed . . . The present Editor's reasoning has been that if Strindberg could not be represented here by at least five hundred pages, which
was out of the question, his power and even his "two-sidedness" can best
be suggested by *Miss Julie*, which can also best be explicated by himself.
From there, the reader could later go to the ample collections of Strindberg in Anchor Books and elsewhere. The best general account of his
work is probably *Strindberg: An Introduction* by B. M. E. Mortensen
and Brian W. Downs (1949).

MISS JULIE

[1888]

English Version by
ELIZABETH SPRIGGE

CHARACTERS

MISS JULIE   *aged 25*
JEAN   *the valet, aged 30*
KRISTIN   *the cook, aged 35*

Scene: *The large kitchen of a Swedish manor house in a country district in the eighties.*

Midsummer eve.

The kitchen has three doors, two small ones into Jean's and Kristin's bedrooms, and a large, glass-fronted double one, opening on to a court-yard. This is the only way to the rest of the house. Through these glass doors can be seen part of a fountain with a cupid, lilac bushes in flower and the tops of some Lombardy poplars. On one wall are shelves edged with scalloped paper on which are kitchen utensils of copper, iron and tin. To the left is the corner of a large tiled range and part of its chimney-hood, to the right the end of the servants' dinner table with chairs beside it. The stove is decorated with birch boughs, the floor strewn with twigs of juniper. On the end of the table is a large Japanese spice jar full of lilac. There are also an ice-box, a scullery table and a sink. Above the double door hangs a big old-fashioned bell; near it is a speaking-tube. A fiddle can be heard from the dance in the barn near-by. Kristin is standing at the stove, frying something in a pan. She wears a light-coloured cotton dress and a big apron.

[*Jean enters, wearing livery and carrying a pair of large riding-boots with spurs, which he puts in a conspicuous place.*]

J E A N — Miss Julie's crazy again to-night, absolutely crazy.

K R I S T I N — Oh, so you're back, are you?

J E A N — When I'd taken the Count to the station, I came back and dropped in at the Barn for a dance. And who did I see there but our young lady leading off with the gamekeeper. But the moment she sets eyes on me, up she rushes and invites me to waltz with her. And how she waltzed—I've never seen anything like it! She's crazy.

K R I S T I N — Always has been, but never so bad as this last fortnight since the engagement was broken off.

J E A N — Yes, that was a pretty business, to be sure. He's a decent enough chap, too, even if he isn't rich. Oh, but they're choosy! [*Sits down at the end of the table.*] In any case, it's a bit odd that our young—er—lady would rather stay at home with the yokels than go with her father to visit her relations.

K R I S T I N — Perhaps she feels a bit awkward, after that bust-up with her fiancé.

JEAN—Maybe. That chap had some guts, though. Do you know the sort of thing that was going on, Kristin? I saw it with my own eyes, though I didn't let on I had.

KRISTIN—You saw them . . . ?

JEAN—Didn't I just! Came across the pair of them one evening in the stable-yard. Miss Julie was doing what she called "training" him. Know what that was? Making him jump over her riding-whip—the way you teach a dog. He did it twice and got a cut each time for his pains, but when it came to the third go, he snatched the whip out of her hand and broke it into smithereens. And then he cleared off.

KRISTIN—What goings on! I never did!

JEAN—Well, that's how it was with that little affair . . . Now, what have you got for me, Kristin? Something tasty?

KRISTIN [serving from the pan to his plate] Well, it's just a little bit of kidney I cut off their joint.

JEAN [smelling it] Fine! That's my special delice. [Feels the plate.] But you might have warmed the plate.

KRISTIN—When you choose to be finicky you're worse than the Count himself.

[Pulls his hair affectionately.]

JEAN [crossly] Stop pulling my hair. You know how sensitive I am.

KRISTIN—There, there! It's only love, you know.

[JEAN eats. KRISTIN brings a bottle of beer.]

JEAN—Beer on Midsummer Eve? No thanks! I've got something better than that. [From a drawer in the table brings out a bottle of red wine with a yellow seal.] Yellow seal, see! Now get me a glass. You use a glass with a stem of course when you're drinking it straight.

KRISTIN [giving him a wine-glass] Lord help the woman who gets you for a husband, you old fusser!

[She puts the beer in the ice-box and sets a small saucepan on the stove.]

JEAN—Nonsense! You'll be glad enough to get a fellow as smart as me. And I don't think it's done you any harm people calling me your fiancé. [Tastes the wine.] Good. Very good indeed. But not quite warmed enough. [Warms the glass in his hand.] We bought this in Dijon. Four francs the litre without the bottle, and duty on top of that. What are you cooking now? It stinks.

KRISTIN—Some bloody muck Miss Julie wants for Diana.

JEAN—You should be more refined in your speech, Kristin. But why should you spend a holiday cooking for that bitch? Is she sick or what?

KRISTIN—Yes, she's sick. She sneaked out with the pug at the lodge and got in the usual mess. And that, you know, Miss Julie won't have.

JEAN—Miss Julie's too high-and-mighty in some respects, and not enough in others, just like her mother before her. The Countess was more at home in the kitchen and cowsheds than anywhere else, but would she ever go driving with only one horse? She went round with her cuffs filthy, but she had to have the coronet on the cuff-links. Our young lady—to come back to her—hasn't any proper respect for herself or her position. I mean she isn't refined. In the Barn just now she dragged the gamekeeper away from Anna and made him dance with her—no waiting to be asked. We wouldn't do a thing like that. But that's what happens when the gentry try to behave like the common people—they become common . . . Still she's a fine girl. Smashing! What shoulders! And what—er—etcetera!

KRISTIN – Oh come off it! I know what Clara says, and she dresses her.

JEAN – Clara? Pooh, you're all jealous! But I've been out riding with her . . . and as for her dancing!

KRISTIN – Listen, Jean. You will dance with me, won't you, as soon as I'm through.

JEAN – Of course I will.

KRISTIN – Promise?

JEAN – Promise? When I say I'll do a thing I do it. Well, thanks for the supper. It was a real treat. [*Corks the bottle.*]

[JULIE *appears in the doorway, speaking to someone outside.*]

JULIE – I'll be back in a moment. Don't wait.

[JEAN *slips the bottle into the drawer and rises respectfully.* JULIE *enters and joins* KRISTIN *at the stove.*]

Well, have you made it?

[KRISTIN *signs that* JEAN *is near them.*]

JEAN [*gallantly*] Have you ladies got some secret?

JULIE [*flipping his face with her handkerchief*] You're very inquisitive.

JEAN – What a delicious smell! Violets.

JULIE [*coquettishly*] Impertinence! Are you an expert of scent too? I must say you know how to dance. Now don't look. Go away.

[*The music of a schottische begins.*]

JEAN [*with impudent politeness*] Is it some witches' brew you're cooking on Midsummer Eve? Something to tell your stars by, so you can see your future?

JULIE [*sharply*] If you could see that you'd have good eyes. [*To* KRISTIN.] Put it in a bottle and cork it tight. Come and dance this schottische with me, Jean.

JEAN [*hesitating*] I don't want to be rude, but I've promised to dance this one with Kristin.

JULIE – Well, she can have another, can't you, Kristin? You'll lend me Jean, won't you?

KRISTIN [*bottling*] It's nothing to do with me. When you're so condescending, Miss, it's not his place to say no. Go on, Jean, and thank Miss Julie for the honour.

JEAN – Frankly speaking, Miss, and no offence meant, I wonder if it's wise for you to dance twice running with the same partner, specially as those people are so ready to jump to conclusions.

JULIE [*flaring up*] What did you say? What sort of conclusions? What do you mean?

JEAN [*meekly*] As you choose not to understand, Miss Julie, I'll have to speak more plainly. It looks bad to show a preference for one of your retainers when they're all hoping for the same unusual favour.

JULIE – Show a preference! The very idea! I'm surprised at you. I'm doing the people an honour by attending their ball when I'm mistress of the house, but if I'm really going to dance, I mean to have a partner who can lead and doesn't make me look ridiculous.

JEAN – If those are your orders, Miss, I'm at your service.

JULIE [*gently*] Don't take it as an order. To-night we're all just people enjoying a party. There's no question of class. So now give me your arm. Don't worry, Kristin. I shan't steal your sweetheart.

[JEAN *gives* JULIE *his arm and leads her out.*]

Left alone, KRISTIN *plays her scene in an unhurried, natural way, humming to the tune of the schottische, played on a distant violin. She clears* JEAN's *place, washes up and puts things away, then takes off her apron, brings out a small mirror from a drawer, props it against the jar of lilac, lights a candle, warms a small pair of tongs and curls her fringe. She goes to the door and listens, then turning back to the table finds* MISS JULIE's *forgotten handkerchief. She smells it, then meditatively smooths it out and folds it.*

[*Enter* JEAN.]

JEAN – She really *is* crazy. What a way to dance! With people standing grinning at her too from behind the doors. What's got into her, Kristin?

KRISTIN – Oh, it's just her time coming on. She's always queer then. Are you going to dance with me now?

JEAN – Then you're not wild with me for cutting that one.

KRISTIN – You know I'm not – for a little thing like that. Besides, I know my place.

JEAN [*putting his arm round her waist*] You're a sensible girl, Kristin, and you'll make a very good wife . . .

[*Enter* JULIE, *unpleasantly surprised.*]

JULIE [*with forced gaiety*] You're a fine beau – running away from your partner.

JEAN – Not away, Miss Julie, but as you see back to the one I deserted.

JULIE [*changing her tone*] You really can dance, you know. But why are you wearing your livery on a holiday. Take it off at once.

JEAN – Then I must ask you to go away for a moment, Miss. My black coat's here.

[*Indicates it hanging on the door to his room.*]

JULIE – Are you so shy of me—just over changing a coat? Go into your room then—or stay here and I'll turn my back.

JEAN – Excuse me then, Miss.

[*He goes to his room and is partly visible as he changes his coat.*]

JULIE – Tell me, Kristin, is Jean your fiancé? You seem very intimate.

KRISTIN – My fiancé? Yes, if you like. We call it that.

JULIE – Call it?

KRISTIN – Well, you've had a fiancé yourself, Miss, and . . .

JULIE – But we really were engaged.

KRISTIN – All the same it didn't come to anything.

[JEAN *returns in his black coat.*]

JULIE – Très gentil, Monsieur Jean. Très gentil.

JEAN – Vous voulez plaisanter, Madame.

JULIE – Et vous voulez parler français. Where did you learn it?

JEAN – In Switzerland, when I was sommelier at one of the biggest hotels in Lucerne.

JULIE – You look quite the gentleman in that get-up. Charming.

[*Sits at the table.*]

JEAN – Oh, you're just flattering me!

JULIE [*annoyed*] Flattering you?

JEAN – I'm too modest to believe you would pay real compliments to a man like me, so I must take it you are exaggerating—that this is what's known as flattery.

JULIE – Where on earth did you learn to make speeches like that? Perhaps you've been to the theatre a lot.

JEAN – That's right. And travelled a lot too.

JULIE – But you come from this neighbourhood, don't you?

JEAN – Yes, my father was a labourer on the next estate—the District Attorney's place. I often used to see you, Miss Julie, when you were little, though you never noticed me.

JULIE – Did you really?

JEAN – Yes. One time specially I remember . . . but I can't tell you about that.

JULIE – Oh do! Why not? This is just the time.

JEAN – No, I really can't now. Another time perhaps.

JULIE – Another time means never. What harm in now?

JEAN—No harm, but I'd rather not. [*Points to* KRISTIN, *now fast asleep.*] Look at her.

JULIE—She'll make a charming wife, won't she? I wonder if she snores.

JEAN—No, she doesn't, but she talks in her sleep.

JULIE [*cynically*] How do you know she talks in her sleep?

JEAN [*brazenly*] I've heard her.

[*Pause. They look at one another.*]

JULIE—Why don't you sit down?

JEAN—I can't take such a liberty in your presence.

JULIE—Supposing I order you to.

JEAN—I'll obey.

JULIE—Then sit down. No, wait a minute. Will you get me a drink first?

JEAN—I don't know what's in the ice-box. Only beer, I expect.

JULIE—There's no only about it. My taste is so simple I prefer it to wine.

[JEAN *takes a bottle from the ice-box, fetches a glass and plate and serves the beer.*]

JEAN—At your service.

JULIE—Thank you. Won't you have some yourself?

JEAN—I'm not really a beer-drinker, but if it's an order . . .

JULIE—Order? I should have thought it was ordinary manners to keep your partner company.

JEAN—That's a good way of putting it.

[*He opens another bottle and fetches a glass.*]

JULIE—Now drink my health. [*He hesitates.*] I believe the man really is shy.

[JEAN *kneels and raises his glass with mock ceremony.*]

JEAN—To the health of my lady!

JULIE—Bravo! Now kiss my shoe and everything will be perfect. [*He hesitates, then boldly takes hold of her foot and lightly kisses it.*] Splendid. You ought to have been an actor.

JEAN [*rising*] We can't go on like this, Miss Julie. Someone might come in and see us.

JULIE—Why would that matter?

JEAN—For the simple reason that they'd talk. And if you knew the way their tongues were wagging out there just now, you . . .

JULIE—What were they saying? Tell me. Sit down.

JEAN [*sitting*] No offence meant, Miss, but . . . well, their language wasn't nice, and they were hinting . . . oh, you know quite well what. You're not a child, and if a lady's seen drinking alone at night with a man—and a servant at that—then . . .

J U L I E – Then what? Besides, we're not alone. Kristin's here.

J E A N – Yes, asleep.

J U L I E – I'll wake her up. [*Rises.*] Kristin, are you asleep? [KRISTIN *mumbles in her sleep.*] Kristin! Goodness, how she sleeps!

K R I S T I N [*in her sleep*] The Count's boots are cleaned—put the coffee on—yes, yes, at once . . . [*Mumbles incoherently.*]

J U L I E [*tweaking her nose*] Wake up, can't you!

J E A N [*sharply*] Let her sleep.

J U L I E – What?

J E A N – When you've been standing at the stove all day you're likely to be tired at night. And sleep should be respected.

J U L I E [*changing her tone*] What a nice idea. It does you credit. Thank you for it. [*Holds out her hand to him.*] Now come out and pick some lilac for me.

   [*During the following* KRISTIN *goes sleepily in to her bedroom.*]

J E A N – Out with you, Miss Julie?

J U L I E – Yes.

J E A N – It wouldn't do. It really wouldn't.

J U L I E – I don't know what you mean. You can't possibly imagine that . . .

J E A N – I don't, but others do.

J U L I E – What? That I'm in love with the valet?

J E A N – I'm not a conceited man, but such a thing's been known to happen, and to these rustics nothing's sacred.

J U L I E – You, I take it, are an aristocrat.

J E A N – Yes, I am.

J U L I E – And I am coming down in the world.

J E A N – Don't come down, Miss Julie. Take my advice. No one will believe you came down of your own accord. They'll all say you fell.

J U L I E – I have a higher opinion of our people than you. Come and put it to the test. Come on.

[*Gazes into his eyes.*]

J E A N – You're very strange, you know.

J U L I E – Perhaps I am, but so are you. For that matter everything is strange. Life, human beings, everything, just scum drifting about on the water until it sinks—down and down. That reminds me of a dream I sometimes have, in which I'm on top of a pillar and can't see any way of getting down. When I look down I'm dizzy; I have to get down but I haven't the courage to jump. I can't stay there and I long to fall, but I don't fall. There's no respite. There can't be any peace at all for me until I'm down, right down on the ground. And if I did get to the ground I'd want to be under the ground . . . Have you ever felt like that?

J E A N – No. In my dream I'm lying under a great tree in a dark wood. I want to get up, up to the top of it, and look out over the bright landscape where the sun is shining and rob that high nest of its golden eggs. And I climb and climb, but the trunk is so thick and smooth and it's so far to the first branch. But I know if I can once reach that first branch I'll go to the top just as if I'm on a ladder. I haven't reached it yet, but I shall get there, even if only in my dreams.

J U L I E – Here I am chattering about dreams with you. Come on. Only into the park.

[*She takes his arm and they go towards the door.*]

J E A N – We must sleep on nine midsummer flowers tonight; then our dreams will come true, Miss Julie.

[*They turn at the door. He has a hand to his eye.*]

J U L I E – Have you got something in your eye? Let me see.

J E A N – Oh, it's nothing. Just a speck of dust. It'll be gone in a minute.

J U L I E – My sleeve must have rubbed against you. Sit down and let me see to it. [*Takes him by the arm and makes him sit down, bends his head back and tries to get the speck out with the corner of her handkerchief.*] Keep still now, quite still. [*Slaps his hand.*] Do as I tell you. Why, I believe you're trembling, big, strong man though you are! [*Feels his biceps.*] What muscles!

J E A N [*warning*] Miss Julie!

J U L I E – Yes, Monsieur Jean?

J E A N – Attention. Je ne suis qu'un homme.

J U L I E – Will you stay still! There now. It's out. Kiss my hand and say thank you.

J E A N [*rising*] Miss Julie, listen. Kristin's gone to bed now. Will you listen?

J U L I E – Kiss my hand first.

J E A N – Very well, but you'll have only yourself to blame.

J U L I E – For what?

J E A N – For what! Are you still a child at twenty-five? Don't you know it's dangerous to play with fire?

J U L I E – Not for me. I'm insured.

J E A N [*bluntly*] No, you're not. And even if you are, there's still stuff here to kindle a flame.

J U L I E – Meaning yourself?

J E A N – Yes. Not because I'm me, but because I'm a man and young and . . .

J U L I E – And good-looking? What incredible conceit! A Don Juan perhaps? Or a Joseph? Good Lord, I do believe you are a Joseph!

J E A N – Do you?

J U L I E – I'm rather afraid so.

1400

[JEAN *goes boldly up and tries to put his arms round her and kiss her.*
She boxes his ears.]

How dare you!

J E A N – Was that in earnest or a joke?

J U L I E – In earnest.

J E A N – Then what went before was in earnest too. You take your games too seriously and that's dangerous. Anyhow I'm tired of playing now and beg leave to return to my work. The Count will want his boots first thing and it's past midnight now.

J U L I E – Put those boots down.

J E A N – No. This is my work, which it's my duty to do. But I never undertook to be your playfellow and I never will be. I consider myself too good for that.

J U L I E – You're proud.

J E A N – In some ways—not all.

J U L I E – Have you even been in love?

J E A N – We don't put it that way, but I've been gone on quite a few girls. And once I went sick because I couldn't have the one I wanted. Sick, I mean, like those princes in the Arabian Nights who couldn't eat or drink for love.

J U L I E – Who was she? [*No answer.*] Who was she?

J E A N – You can't force me to tell you that.

J U L I E – If I ask as an equal, ask as a—friend? Who was she?

J E A N – You.

J U L I E [*sitting*] How absurd!

J E A N – Yes, ludicrous if you like. That's the story I wouldn't tell you before, see, but now I will . . . Do you know what the world looks like from below? No, you don't. No more than the hawks and falcons do whose backs one hardly ever sees because they're always soaring up aloft. I lived in a labourer's hovel with seven other children and a pig, out in the grey fields where there isn't a single tree. But from the window I could see the wall round the Count's park with apple-trees above it. That was the Garden of Eden, guarded by many terrible angels with flaming swords. All the same I and the other boys managed to get to the tree of life. Does all this make you despise me?

J U L I E – Goodness, all boys steal apples!

J E A N – You say that now, but all the same you do despise me. However, one time I went into the Garden of Eden with my mother to weed the onion beds. Close to the kitchen garden there was a Turkish pavilion hung all over with jasmine and honeysuckle. I hadn't any idea what it was used for, but I'd never seen such a beautiful building. People used to go in and then come out again, and one day the door was left open. I crept up and saw the walls covered with pictures of

1401

kings and emperors, and the windows had red curtains with fringes—
you know now what the place was, don't you? I . . . [*Breaks off a
piece of lilac and holds it for* JULIE *to smell. As he talks, she takes it
from him.*] I had never been inside the manor, never seen anything
but the church, and this was more beautiful. No matter where my
thoughts went, they always came back—to that place. The longing
went on growing in me to enjoy it fully, just once. Enfin, I sneaked in,
gazed and admired. Then I heard someone coming. There was only
one way out for the gentry, but for me there was another and I had no
choice but to take it. [JULIE *drops the lilac on the table.*] Then I took
to my heels, plunged through the raspberry canes, dashed across the
strawberry beds and found myself on the rose terrace. There I saw a
pink dress and a pair of white stockings—it was you. I crawled into a
weed pile and lay there right under it among prickly thistles and
damp rank earth. I watched you walking among the roses and said to
myself: "If it's true that a thief can get to heaven and be with the
angels, it's pretty strange that a labourer's child here on God's earth
mayn't come in the park and play with the Count's daughter."

JULIE [*sentimentally*] Do you think all poor children feel the way
you did?

JEAN [*taken aback, then rallying*] All poor children? . . . Yes, of
course they do. Of course.

JULIE—It must be terrible to be poor.

JEAN [*with exaggerated distress*] Oh yes, Miss Julie, yes. A dog may
lie on the Countess's sofa, a horse may have his nose stroked by a
young lady, but a servant . . . [*change of tone*] well, yes, now and then
you meet one with guts enough to rise in the world, but how often?
Anyhow, do you know what I did? Jumped in the millstream with my
clothes on, was pulled out and got a hiding. But the next Sunday,
when Father and all the rest went to Granny's, I managed to get left
behind. Then I washed with soap and hot water, put my best clothes
on and went to church so as to see you. I did see you and went home
determined to die. But I wanted to die beautifully and peacefully,
without any pain. Then I remembered it was dangerous to sleep under
an elder bush. We had a big one in full bloom, so I stripped it and
climbed into the oats-bin with the flowers. Have you ever noticed how
smooth oats are? Soft to touch as human skin . . . Well, I closed the
lid and shut my eyes, fell asleep, and when they woke me I was very
ill. But I didn't die, as you see. What I meant by all that I don't know.
There was no hope of winning you—you were simply a symbol of the
hopelessness of ever getting out of the class I was born in.

JULIE—You put things very well, you know. Did you go to school?

JEAN—For a while. But I've read a lot of novels and been to the theatre.

Besides, I've heard educated folk talking—that's what's taught me most.

J U L I E – Do you stand round listening to what we're saying?

J E A N – Yes, of course. And I've heard quite a bit too! On the carriage box or rowing the boat. Once I heard you, Miss Julie, and one of your young lady friends . . .

J U L I E – Oh! Whatever did you hear?

J E A N – Well, it wouldn't be nice to repeat it. And I must say I was pretty startled. I couldn't think where you had learnt such words. Perhaps, at bottom, there isn't as much difference between people as one's led to believe.

J U L I E – How dare you! We don't behave as you do when we're engaged.

J E A N [*looking hard at her*] Are you sure? It's no use making out so innocent to me.

J U L I E – The man I gave my love to was a rotter.

J E A N – That's what you always say—afterwards.

J U L I E – Always?

J E A N – I think it must be always. I've heard the expression several times in similar circumstances.

J U L I E – What circumstances?

J E A N – Like those in question. The last time . . .

J U L I E [*rising*] Stop. I don't want to hear any more.

J E A N – Nor did *she*—curiously enough. May I go to bed now please?

J U L I E [*gently*] Go to bed on Midsummer Eve?

J E A N – Yes. Dancing with that crowd doesn't really amuse me.

J U L I E – Get the key of the boathouse and row me out on the lake. I want to see the sun rise.

J E A N – Would that be wise?

J U L I E – You sound as though you're frightened for your reputation.

J E A N – Why not? I don't want to be made a fool of, nor to be sent packing without a character when I'm trying to better myself. Besides, I have Kristin to consider.

J U L I E – So now it's Kristin.

J E A N – Yes, but it's you I'm thinking about too. Take my advice and go to bed.

J U L I E – Am I to take orders from you?

J E A N – Just this once, for your own sake. Please. It's very late and sleepiness goes to one's head and makes one rash. Go to bed. What's more, if my ears don't deceive me, I hear people coming this way. They'll be looking for me, and if they find us here, you're done for.

[*The* CHORUS *approaches, singing. During the following dialogue the song is heard in snatches, and in full when the peasants enter.*]

> Out of the wood two women came,
> Tridiri-ralla, tridiri-ra.
> The feet of one were bare and cold,
> Tridiri-ralla-la.

> The other talked of bags of gold,
> Tridiri-ralla, tridiri-ra.
> But neither had a sou to her name,
> Tridiri-ralla-la.

> The bridal wreath I give to you,
> Tridiri-ralla, tridiri-ra.
> But to another I'll be true,
> Tridiri-ralla-la.

JULIE – I know our people and I love them, just as they do me. Let them come. You'll see.

JEAN – No, Miss Julie, they don't love you. They take your food, then spit at it. You must believe me. Listen to them, just listen to what they're singing . . . No, don't listen.

JULIE [*listening*] What are they singing?

JEAN – They're mocking—you and me.

JULIE – Oh no! How horrible! What cowards!

JEAN – A pack like that's always cowardly. But against such odds there's nothing we can do but run away.

JULIE – Run away? Where to? We can't get out and we can't go into Kristin's room.

JEAN – Into mine then. Necessity knows no rules. And you can trust me. I really am your true and devoted friend.

JULIE – But supposing . . . supposing they were to look for you in there?

JEAN – I'll bolt the door, and if they try to break in I'll shoot. Come on. [*Pleading.*] Please come.

JULIE [*tensely*] Do you promise . . . ?

JEAN – I swear!

[JULIE *goes quickly into his room and he excitedly follows her.*]

Led by the fiddler, the peasants enter in festive attire with flowers in their hats. They put a barrel of beer and a keg of spirits, garlanded with leaves, on the table, fetch glasses and begin to carouse. The scene becomes a ballet. They form a ring and dance and sing and mime: "Out of the wood two women came." Finally they go out, still singing.

JULIE *comes in alone. She looks at the havoc in the kitchen, wrings her hands, then takes out her powder puff and powders her face.*

[JEAN *enters in high spirits.*]

JEAN – Now you see! And you heard, didn't you? Do you still think it's possible for us to stay here?

JULIE – No, I don't. But what can we do?

JEAN – Run away. Far away. Take a journey.

JULIE – Journey? But where to?

JEAN – Switzerland. The Italian lakes. Ever been there?

JULIE – No. Is it nice?

JEAN – Ah! Eternal summer, oranges, evergreens . . . ah!

JULIE – But what would we do there?

JEAN – I'll start a hotel. First-class accommodation and first-class customers.

JULIE – Hotel?

JEAN – There's life for you. New faces all the time, new languages— no time for nerves or worries, no need to look for something to do— work rolling up of its own accord. Bells ringing night and day, trains whistling, buses coming and going, and all the time gold pieces rolling on to the counter. There's life for you!

JULIE – For *you*. And I?

JEAN – Mistress of the house, ornament of the firm. With your looks, and your style . . . oh, it's bound to be a success! Terrific! You'll sit like a queen in the office and set your slaves in motion by pressing an electric button. The guests will file past your throne and nervously lay their treasure on your table. You've no idea the way people tremble when they get their bills. I'll salt the bills and you'll sugar them with your sweetest smiles. Ah, let's get away from here! [*Produces a timetable.*] At once, by the next train. We shall be at Malmö at six-thirty, Hamburg eight-forty next morning, Frankfurt-Basle the following day, and Como by the St. Gothard pass in—let's see—three days. Three days!

JULIE – That's all very well. But Jean, you must give me courage. Tell me you love me. Come and take me in your arms.

JEAN [*reluctantly*] I'd like to, but I daren't. Not again in this house. I love you—that goes without saying. You can't doubt that, Miss Julie, can you?

JULIE [*shyly, very feminine*] Miss? Call me Julie. There aren't any barriers between us now. Call me Julie.

JEAN [*uneasily*] I can't. As long as we're in this house, there *are* barriers between us. There's the past and there's the Count. I've never been so servile to anyone as I am to him. I've only got to see his gloves on a chair to feel small. I've only to hear his bell and I shy like a horse.

Even now, when I look at his boots, standing there so proud and stiff, I feel my back beginning to bend. [*Kicks the boots.*] It's those old, narrow-minded notions drummed into us as children . . . but they can soon be forgotten. You've only got to get to another country, a republic, and people will bend themselves double before my porter's livery. Yes, double they'll bend themselves, but I shan't. I wasn't born to bend. I've got guts, I've got character, and once I reach that first branch, you'll watch me climb. Today I'm valet, next year I'll be proprietor, in ten years I'll have made a fortune, and then I'll go to Roumania, get myself decorated and I may, I only say *may*, mind you, end up as a Count.

JULIE [*sadly*] That would be very nice.

JEAN – You see in Roumania one can buy a title, and then you'll be a Countess after all. My Countess.

JULIE – What do I care about all that? I'm putting those things behind me. Tell me you love me, because if you don't . . . if you don't, what am I?

JEAN – I'll tell you a thousand times over—later. But not here. No sentimentality now or everything will be lost. We must consider this thing calmly like reasonable people. [*Takes a cigar, cuts and lights it.*] You sit down there and I'll sit here and we'll talk as if nothing has happened.

JULIE – My God, have you no feelings at all?

JEAN – Nobody has more. But I know how to control them.

JULIE – A short time ago you were kissing my shoe. And now . . .

JEAN [*harshly*] Yes, that was then. Now we have something else to think about.

JULIE – Don't speak to me so brutally.

JEAN – I'm not. Just sensibly. One folly's been committed, don't let's have more. The Count will be back at any moment and we've got to settle our future before that. Now, what do you think of my plans? Do you approve?

JULIE – It seems a very good idea—but just one thing. Such a big undertaking would need a lot of capital. Have you got any?

JEAN [*chewing his cigar*] I certainly have. I've got my professional skill, my wide experience and my knowledge of foreign languages. That's capital worth having, it seems to me.

JULIE – But it won't buy even one railway ticket.

JEAN – Quite true. That's why I need a backer to advance some ready cash.

JULIE – How could you get that at a moment's notice?

JEAN – You must get it, if you want to be my partner.

JULIE – I can't. I haven't any money of my own.

[*Pause.*]

J E A N – Then the whole thing's off.

J U L I E – And . . . ?

J E A N – We go on as we are.

J U L I E – Do you think I'm going to stay under this roof as your mistress? With everyone pointing at me. Do you think I can face my father after this? No. Take me away from here, away from this shame, this humiliation. Oh my God, what have I done? My God, my God!

[*Weeps.*]

J E A N – So that's the tune now, is it? What have you done? Same as many before you.

J U L I E   [*hysterically*] And now you despise me. I'm falling, I'm falling.

J E A N – Fall as far as me and I'll lift you up again.

J U L I E – Why was I so terribly attracted to you? The weak to the strong, the falling to the rising? Or was it love? Is that love? Do you know what love is?

J E A N – Do I? You bet I do. Do you think I never had a girl before?

J U L I E – The things you say, the things you think!

J E A N – That's what life's taught me, and that's what I am. It's no good getting hysterical or giving yourself airs. We're both in the same boat now. Here, my dear girl, let me give you a glass of something special.

[*Opens the drawer, takes out the bottle of wine and fills two used glasses.*]

J U L I E – Where did you get that wine?

J E A N – From the cellar.

J U L I E – My father's burgundy.

J E A N – Why not, for his son-in-law?

J U L I E – And I drink beer.

J E A N – That only shows your taste's not so good as mine.

J U L I E – Thief!

J E A N – Are you going to tell on me?

J U L I E – Oh God! The accomplice of a petty thief! Was I blind drunk? Have I dreamt this whole night? Midsummer Eve, the night for innocent merrymaking.

J E A N – Innocent, eh?

J U L I E – Is anyone on earth as wretched as I am now?

J E A N – Why should *you* be? After such a conquest. What about Kristin in there? Don't you think she has any feelings?

J U L I E – I did think so, but I don't any longer. No. A menial is a menial . . .

J E A N – And a whore is a whore.

J U L I E   [*falling to her knees, her hands clasped*] O God in heaven, put

1407

an end to my miserable life! Lift me out of this filth in which I'm sinking. Save me! Save me!

JEAN – I must admit I'm sorry for you. When I was in the onion bed and saw you up there among the roses, I . . . yes, I'll tell you now . . . I had the same dirty thoughts as all boys.

JULIE – You, who wanted to die because of me?

JEAN – In the oats-bin? That was just talk.

JULIE – Lies, you mean.

JEAN [*getting sleepy*] More or less. I think I read a story in some paper about a chimney-sweep who shut himself up in a chest full of lilac because he'd been summonsed for not supporting some brat . . .

JULIE – So this is what you're like.

JEAN – I had to think up something. It's always the fancy stuff that catches the women.

JULIE – Beast!

JEAN – Merde!

JULIE – Now you have seen the falcon's back.

JEAN – Not exactly its *back*.

JULIE – I was to be the first branch.

JEAN – But the branch was rotten.

JULIE – I was to be a hotel sign.

JEAN – And I the hotel.

JULIE – Sit at your counter, attract your clients and cook their accounts.

JEAN – I'd have done that myself.

JULIE – That any human being can be so steeped in filth!

JEAN – Clean it up then.

JULIE – Menial! Lackey! Stand up when I speak to you.

JEAN – Menial's whore, lackey's harlot, shut your mouth and get out of here! Are you the one to lecture me for being coarse? Nobody of my kind would ever be as coarse as you were tonight. Do you think any servant girl would throw herself at a man that way? Have you ever seen a girl of my class asking for it like that? I haven't. Only animals and prostitutes.

JULIE [*broken*] Go on. Hit me, trample on me—it's all I deserve. I'm rotten. But help me! If there's any way out at all, help me.

JEAN [*more gently*] I'm not denying myself a share in the honour of seducing you, but do you think anybody in my place would have dared look in your direction if you yourself hadn't asked for it? I'm still amazed . . .

JULIE – And proud.

JEAN – Why not? Though I must admit the victory was too easy to make me lose my head.

JULIE – Go on hitting me.

JEAN [*rising*] No. On the contrary I apologise for what I've said. I don't hit a person who's down—least of all a woman. I can't deny there's a certain satisfaction in finding that what dazzled one below was just moonshine, that that falcon's back is grey after all, that there's powder on the lovely cheek, that polished nails can have black tips, that the handkerchief is dirty although it smells of scent. On the other hand it hurts to find that what I was struggling to reach wasn't high and isn't real. It hurts to see you fallen so low you're far lower than your own cook. Hurts like when you see the last flowers of summer lashed to pieces by rain and turned to mud.

JULIE – You're talking as if you're already my superior.

JEAN – I am. I might make you a Countess, but you could never make me a Count, you know.

JULIE – But I am the child of a Count, and you could never be that.

JEAN – True, but I might be the father of Counts if . . .

JULIE – You're a thief. I'm not.

JEAN – There are worse things than being a thief—much lower. Besides, when I'm in a place I regard myself as a member of the family to some extent, as one of the children. You don't call it stealing when children pinch a berry from overladen bushes. [*His passion is roused again.*] Miss Julie, you're a glorious woman, far too good for a man like me. You were carried away by some kind of madness, and now you're trying to cover up your mistake by persuading yourself you're in love with me. You're not, although you may find me physically attractive, which means your love's no better than mine. But I wouldn't be satisfied with being nothing but an animal for you, and I could never make you love me.

JULIE – Are you sure?

JEAN – You think there's a chance? Of my loving you, yes, of course. You're beautiful, refined—[*takes her hand*]—educated, and you can be nice when you want to be. The fire you kindle in a man isn't likely to go out. [*Puts his arm round her.*] You're like mulled wine, full of spices, and your kisses . . .

[*He tries to pull her to him, but she breaks away.*]

JULIE – Let go of me! You won't win me that way.

JEAN – Not that way, how then? Not by kisses and fine speeches, not by planning the future and saving you from shame? How then?

JULIE – How? How? I don't know. There isn't any way. I loathe you—loathe you as I loathe rats, but I can't escape from you.

JEAN – Escape with me.

JULIE [*pulling herself together*] Escape? Yes, we must escape. But I'm so tired. Give me a glass of wine. [*He pours it out. She looks at her watch.*] First we must talk. We still have a little time.

[*Empties the glass and holds it out for more.*]

J E A N – Don't drink like that. You'll get tipsy.

J U L I E – What's that matter?

J E A N – What's it matter? It's vulgar to get drunk. Well, what have you got to say?

J U L I E – We've got to run away, but we must talk first—or rather, I must, for so far you've done all the talking. You've told me about your life, now I want to tell you about mine, so that we really know each other before we begin this journey together.

J E A N – Wait. Excuse my saying so, but don't you think you may be sorry afterwards if you give away your secrets to me?

J U L I E – Aren't you my friend?

J E A N – On the whole. But don't rely on me.

J U L I E – You can't mean that. But anyway everyone knows my secrets. Listen. My mother wasn't well-born; she came of quite humble people, and was brought up with all those new ideas of sex-equality and women's rights and so on. She thought marriage was quite wrong. So when my father proposed to her, she said she would never become his *wife* . . . but in the end she did. I came into the world, as far as I can make out, against my mother's will, and I was left to run wild, but I had to do all the things a boy does—to prove women are as good as men. I had to wear boys' clothes; I was taught to handle horses—and I wasn't allowed in the dairy. She made me groom and harness and go out hunting; I even had to try to plough. All the men on the estate were given the women's jobs, and the women the men's, until the whole place went to rack and ruin and we were the laughing-stock of the neighbourhood. At last my father seems to have come to his senses and rebelled. He changed everything and ran the place his own way. My mother got ill—I don't know what was the matter with her, but she used to have strange attacks and hide herself in the attic or the garden. Sometimes she stayed out all night. Then came the great fire which you have heard people talking about. The house and the stables and the barns—the whole place burnt to the ground. In very suspicious circumstances. Because the accident happened the very day the insurance had to be renewed, and my father had sent the new premium, but through some carelessness of the messenger it arrived too late.

[*Refills her glass and drinks.*]

J E A N – Don't drink any more.

J U L I E – Oh, what does it matter? We were destitute and had to sleep in the carriages. My father didn't know how to get money to rebuild, and then my mother suggested he should borrow from an old friend of hers, a local brick manufacturer. My father got the loan and, to his surprise, without having to pay interest. So the place was rebuilt. [*Drinks.*] Do you know who set fire to it?

JEAN – Your lady mother.

JULIE – Do you know who the brick manufacturer was?

JEAN – Your mother's lover?

JULIE – Do you know whose the money was?

JEAN – Wait . . . no, I don't know that.

JULIE – It was my mother's.

JEAN – In other words the Count's, unless there was a settlement.

JULIE – There wasn't any settlement. My mother had a little money of her own which she didn't want my father to control, so she invested it with her—friend.

JEAN – Who grabbed it.

JULIE – Exactly. He appropriated it. My father came to know all this. He couldn't bring an action, couldn't pay his wife's lover, nor prove it was his wife's money. That was my mother's revenge because he made himself master in his own house. He nearly shot himself then—at least there's a rumour he tried and didn't bring it off. So he went on living, and my mother had to pay dearly for what she'd done. Imagine what those five years were like for me. My natural sympathies were with my father, yet I took my mother's side, because I didn't know the facts. I'd learnt from her to hate and distrust men—you know how she loathed the whole male sex. And I swore to her I'd never become the slave of any man.

JEAN – And so you got engaged to that attorney.

JULIE – So that he should be my slave.

JEAN – But he wouldn't be.

JULIE – Oh yes, he wanted to be, but he didn't have the chance. I got bored with him.

JEAN – Is that what I saw—in the stable-yard?

JULIE – What did you see?

JEAN – What I saw was him breaking off the engagement.

JULIE – That's a lie. It was I who broke it off. Did he say it was him? The cad.

JEAN – He's not a cad. Do you hate men, Miss Julie?

JULIE – Yes . . . most of the time. But when that weakness comes, oh . . . the shame!

JEAN – Then do you hate me?

JULIE – Beyond words. I'd gladly have you killed like an animal.

JEAN – Quick as you'd shoot a mad dog, eh?

JULIE – Yes.

JEAN – But there's nothing here to shoot with—and there isn't a dog. So what do we do now?

J U L I E – Go abroad.

J E A N – To make each other miserable for the rest of our lives?

J U L I E – No, to enjoy ourselves for a day or two, for a week, for as long as enjoyment lasts, and then–to die . . .

J E A N – Die? How silly! I think it would be far better to start a hotel.

J U L I E   [*without listening*] . . . die on the shores of Lake Como, where the sun always shines and at Christmas time there are green trees and glowing oranges.

J E A N – Lake Como's a rainy hole and I didn't see any oranges outside the shops. But it's a good place for tourists. Plenty of villas to be rented by–er–honeymoon couples. Profitable business that. Know why? Because they all sign a lease for six months and all leave after three weeks.

J U L I E   [*naïvely*] After three weeks? Why?

J E A N – They quarrel, of course. But the rent has to be paid just the same. And then it's let again. So it goes on and on, for there's plenty of love although it doesn't last long.

J U L I E – You don't want to die with me?

J E A N – I don't want to die at all. For one thing I like living and for another I consider suicide's a sin against the Creator who gave us life.

J U L I E – You believe in God–*you*?

J E A N – Yes, of course. And I go to church every Sunday. Look here, I'm tired of all this. I'm going to bed.

J U L I E – Indeed! And do you think I'm going to leave things like this? Don't you know what you owe the woman you've ruined?

J E A N   [*taking out his purse and throwing a silver coin on the table*] There you are. I don't want to be in anybody's debt.

J U L I E   [*pretending not to notice the insult*] Don't you know what the law is?

J E A N – There's no law unfortunately that punishes a woman for seducing a man.

J U L I E – But can you see anything for it but to go abroad, get married and then divorce?

J E A N – What if I refuse this mésalliance?

J U L I E – Mésalliance?

J E A N – Yes, for me. I'm better bred than you, see! Nobody in my family committed arson.

J U L I E – How do you know?

J E A N – Well, you can't prove otherwise, because we haven't any family records outside the Registrar's office. But I've seen your family tree in that book on the drawing-room table. Do you know who the founder of your family was? A miller who let his wife sleep with the King one

1412

night during the Danish war. I haven't any ancestors like that. I haven't any ancestors at all, but I might become one.

J U L I E – This is what I get for confiding in someone so low, for sacrificing my family honour . . .

J E A N – Dishonour! Well, I told you so. One shouldn't drink, because then one talks. And one shouldn't talk.

J U L I E – Oh, how ashamed I am, how bitterly ashamed! If at least you loved me!

J E A N – Look here—for the last time—what do you want? Am I to burst into tears? Am I to jump over your riding whip? Shall I kiss you and carry you off to Lake Como for three weeks, after which . . . What am I to do? What do you want? This is getting unbearable, but that's what comes of playing around with women. Miss Julie, I can see how miserable you are; I know you're going through hell, but I don't understand you. We don't have scenes like this; we don't go in for hating each other. We make love for fun in our spare time, but we haven't all day and all night for it like you. I think you must be ill. I'm sure you're ill.

J U L I E – Then you must be kind to me. You sound almost human now.

J E A N – Well, be human yourself. You spit at me, then won't let me wipe it off—on you.

J U L I E – Help me, help me! Tell me what to do, where to go.

J E A N – Jesus, as if I knew!

J U L I E – I've been mad, raving mad, but there must be a way out.

J E A N – Stay here and keep quiet. Nobody knows anything.

J U L I E – I can't. People do know. Kristin knows.

J E A N – They don't know and they wouldn't believe such a thing.

J U L I E [*hesitating*] But—it might happen again.

J E A N – That's true.

J U L I E – And there might be—consequences.

J E A N [*in panic*] Consequences! Fool that I am I never thought of that. Yes, there's nothing for it but to go. At once. I can't come with you. That would be a complete giveaway. You must go alone—abroad—anywhere.

J U L I E – Alone? Where to? I can't.

J E A N – You must. And before the Count gets back. If you stay, we know what will happen. Once you've sinned you feel you might as well go on, as the harm's done. Then you get more and more reckless and in the end you're found out. No. You must go abroad. Then write to the Count and tell him everything, except that it was me. He'll never guess that—and I don't think he'll want to.

J U L I E – I'll go if you come with me.

J E A N – Are you crazy, woman? "Miss Julie elopes with valet." Next day it would be in the headlines, and the Count would never live it down.

JULIE – I can't go. I can't stay. I'm so tired, so completely worn out. Give me orders. Set me going. I can't think any more, can't act . . .

JEAN – You see what weaklings you are. Why do you give yourselves airs and turn up your noses as if you're the lords of creation? Very well, I'll give you your orders. Go upstairs and dress. Get money for the journey and come down here again.

JULIE [*softly*] Come up with me.

JEAN – To your room? Now you've gone crazy again. [*Hesitates a moment.*] No! Go along at once.

[*Takes her hand and pulls her to the door.*]

JULIE [*as she goes*] Speak kindly to me, Jean.

JEAN – Orders always sound unkind. Now you know. Now you know.

Left alone, JEAN *sighs with relief, sits down at the table, takes out a note-book and pencil and adds up figures, now and then aloud. Dawn begins to break.* KRISTIN *enters dressed for church, carrying his white dickey and tie.*

KRISTIN – Lord Jesus, look at the state the place is in! What have you been up to?

[*Turns out the lamp.*]

JEAN – Oh, Miss Julie invited the crowd in. Did you sleep through it? Didn't you hear anything?

KRISTIN – I slept like a log.

JEAN – And dressed for church already.

KRISTIN – Yes, you promised to come to Communion with me today.

JEAN – Why, so I did. And you've got my bib and tucker, I see. Come on then. [*Sits.* KRISTIN *begins to put his things on. Pause. Sleepily.*] What's the lesson today?

KRISTIN – It's about the beheading of John the Baptist, I think.

JEAN – That's sure to be horribly long. Hi, you're choking me! Oh Lord, I'm so sleepy, so sleepy!

KRISTIN – Yes, what have you been doing up all night? You look absolutely green.

JEAN – Just sitting here talking with Miss Julie.

KRISTIN – She doesn't know what's proper, that one.

[*Pause.*]

JEAN – I say, Kristin.

KRISTIN – What?

JEAN – It's queer really, isn't it, when you come to think of it? Her.

KRISTIN – What's queer?

1414

J E A N – The whole thing.

[*Pause.*]

K R I S T I N [*looking at the half-filled glasses on the table*] Have you been drinking together too?

J E A N – Yes.

K R I S T I N – More shame you. Look me straight in the face.

J E A N – Yes.

K R I S T I N – Is it possible? Is it possible?

J E A N [*after a moment*] Yes, it is.

K R I S T I N – Oh! This I would never have believed. How low!

J E A N – You're not jealous of her, surely?

K R I S T I N – No, I'm not. If it had been Clara or Sophie I'd have scratched your eyes out. But not of her. I don't know why; that's how it is though. But it's disgusting.

J E A N – You're angry with her then.

K R I S T I N – No. With you. It was wicked of you, very very wicked. Poor girl. And, mark my words, I won't stay here any longer now—in a place where one can't respect one's employers.

J E A N – Why should one respect them?

K R I S T I N – You should know since you're so smart. But you don't want to stay in the service of people who aren't respectable, do you? I wouldn't demean myself.

J E A N – But it's rather a comfort to find out they're no better than us.

K R I S T I N – I don't think so. If they're no better there's nothing for us to live up to. Oh and think of the Count! Think of him. He's been through so much already. No, I won't stay in the place any longer. A fellow like you too! If it had been that attorney now or somebody of her own class . . .

J E A N – Why, what's wrong with . . .

K R I S T I N – Oh, you're all right in your own way, but when all's said and done there is a difference between one class and another. No, this is something I'll never be able to stomach. That our young lady who was so proud and so down on men you'd never believe she'd let one come near her should go and give herself to one like you. She who wanted to have poor Diana shot for running after the lodge-keeper's pug. No, I must say . . . ! Well, I won't stay here any longer. On the twenty-fourth of October I quit.

J E A N – And then?

K R I S T I N – Well, since you mention it, it's about time you began to look around, if we're ever going to get married.

J E A N – But what am I to look for? I shan't get a place like this when I'm married.

K R I S T I N – I know you won't. But you might get a job as porter or

1415

caretaker in some public institution. Government rations are small but sure, and there's a pension for the widow and children.

JEAN – That's all very fine, but it's not in my line to start thinking at once about dying for my wife and children. I must say I had rather bigger ideas.

KRISTIN – You and your ideas! You've got obligations too, and you'd better start thinking about them.

JEAN – Don't *you* start pestering me about obligations. I've had enough of that. [*Listens to a sound upstairs.*] Anyway we've plenty of time to work things out. Go and get ready now and we'll be off to church.

KRISTIN – Who's that walking about upstairs?

JEAN – Don't know—unless it's Clara.

KRISTIN [*going*] You don't think the Count could have come back without our hearing him?

JEAN [*scared*] The Count? No, he can't have. He'd have rung for me.

KRISTIN – God help us! I've never known such goings on.

[*Exit.*]

The sun has now risen and is shining on the treetops. The light gradually changes until it slants in through the windows. JEAN *goes to the door and beckons.* JULIE *enters in travelling clothes, carrying a small bird-cage covered with a cloth which she puts on a chair.*

JULIE – I'm ready.

JEAN – Hush! Kristin's up.

JULIE [*in a very nervous state*] Does she suspect anything?

JEAN – Not a thing. But, my God, what a sight you are!

JULIE – Sight? What do you mean?

JEAN – You're white as a corpse and—pardon me—your face is dirty.

JULIE – Let me wash then. [*Goes to the sink and washes her face and hands.*] There. Give me a towel. Oh! The sun is rising!

JEAN – And that breaks the spell.

JULIE – Yes. The spell of Midsummer Eve . . . But listen, Jean. Come with me. I've got the money.

JEAN [*sceptically*] Enough?

JULIE – Enough to start with. Come with me. I can't travel alone to-day. It's Midsummer Day, remember. I'd be packed into a suffocating train among crowds of people who'd all stare at me. And it would stop at every station while I yearned for wings. No, I can't do that, I simply can't. There will be memories too; memories of Midsummer Days when I was little. The leafy church—birch and lilac—the gaily spread dinner table, relatives, friends—evening in the park—dancing and music and

1416

flowers and fun. Oh, however far you run away—there'll always be memories in the baggage car—and remorse and guilt.

J E A N — I will come with you, but quickly now then, before it's too late.
At once.

J U L I E — Put on your things.

[*Picks up the cage.*]

J E A N — No luggage mind. That would give us away.

J U L I E — No, only what we can take with us in the carriage.

J E A N [*fetching his hat*] What on earth have you got there? What is it?

J U L I E — Only my greenfinch. I don't want to leave it behind.

J E A N — Well, I'll be damned! We're to take a bird-cage along, are we?
You're crazy. Put that cage down.

J U L I E — It's the only thing I'm taking from my home. The only living
creature who cares for me since Diana went off like that. Don't be
cruel. Let me take it.

J E A N — Put that cage down, I tell you—and don't talk so loud. Kristin
will hear.

J U L I E — No, I won't leave it in strange hands. I'd rather you killed it.

J E A N — Give the little beast here then and I'll wring its neck.

J U L I E — But don't hurt it, don't . . . no, I can't.

J E A N — Give it here. I *can*.

J U L I E [*taking the bird out of the cage and kissing it*] Dear little
Serena, must you die and leave your mistress?

J E A N — Please don't make a scene. It's *your* life and future we're worrying about. Come on, quick now!

[*He snatches the bird from her, puts it on a board and picks up a chopper.
JULIE turns away.*]

You should have learnt how to kill chickens instead of target-shooting.
Then you wouldn't faint at a drop of blood.

J U L I E [*screaming*] Kill me too! Kill me! You who can butcher an
innocent creature without a quiver. Oh, how I hate you, how I loathe
you! There is blood between us now. I curse the hour I first saw you.
I curse the hour I was conceived in my mother's womb.

J E A N — What's the use of cursing. Let's go.

J U L I E [*going to the chopping-block as if drawn against her will*] No,
I won't go yet. I can't . . . I must look. Listen! There's a carriage.
[*Listens without taking her eyes off the board and chopper.*] You don't
think I can bear the sight of blood. You think I'm so weak. Oh, how
I should like to see your blood and your brains on a chopping-block!
I'd like to see the whole of your sex swimming like that in a sea of
blood. I think I could drink out of your skull, bathe my feet in your
broken breast and eat your heart roasted whole. You think I'm weak.
You think I love you, that my womb yearned for your seed and I want

1417

to carry your offspring under my heart and nourish it with my blood. You think I want to bear your child and take your name. By the way, what is your name? I've never heard your surname. I don't suppose you've got one. I should be "Mrs. Hovel" or "Madam Dunghill." You dog wearing my collar, you lackey with my crest on your buttons! I share you with my cook; I'm my own servant's rival! Oh! Oh! Oh! . . . You think I'm a coward and will run away. No, now I'm going to stay —and let the storm break. My father will come back . . . find his desk broken open . . . his money gone. Then he'll ring that bell—twice for the valet—and then he'll send for the police . . . and I shall tell everything. Everything. Oh how wonderful to make an end of it all—a real end! He has a stroke and dies and that's the end of all of us. Just peace and quietness . . . eternal rest. The coat of arms broken on the coffin and the Count's line extinct . . . But the valet's line goes on in an orphanage, wins laurels in the gutter and ends in jail.

JEAN—There speaks the noble blood! Bravo, Miss Julie. But now, don't let the cat out of the bag.

[KRISTIN *enters dressed for church, carrying a prayer-book.* JULIE *rushes to her and flings herself into her arms for protection.*]

JULIE—Help me, Kristin! Protect me from this man!

KRISTIN [*unmoved and cold*] What goings-on for a feast day morning! [*Sees the board.*] And what a filthy mess. What's it all about? Why are you screaming and carrying on so?

JULIE—Kristin, you're a woman and my friend. Beware of that scoundrel!

JEAN [*embarrassed*] While you ladies are talking things over, I'll go and shave.

[*Slips into his room.*]

JULIE—You must understand. You must listen to me.

KRISTIN—I certainly don't understand such loose ways. Where are you off to in those travelling clothes? And he had his hat on, didn't he, eh?

JULIE—Listen, Kristin. Listen, I'll tell you everything.

KRISTIN—I don't want to know anything.

JULIE—You must listen.

KRISTIN—What to? Your nonsense with Jean? I don't care a rap about that; it's nothing to do with me. But if you're thinking of getting him to run off with you, we'll soon put a stop to that.

JULIE [*very nervously*] Please try to be calm, Kristin, and listen. I can't stay here, nor can Jean—so we must go abroad.

KRISTIN—Hm, hm!

JULIE [*brightening*] But you see, I've had an idea. Supposing we all three go—abroad—to Switzerland and start a hotel together . . . I've got some money, you see . . . and Jean and I could run the whole thing—and I thought you would take charge of the kitchen. Wouldn't that be splendid? Say yes, do. If you come with us everything will be fine. Oh do say yes!

[*Puts her arms round* KRISTIN.]

KRISTIN [*coolly thinking*] Hm, hm.

JULIE [*presto tempo*] You've never travelled, Kristin. You should go abroad and see the world. You've no idea how nice it is travelling by train—new faces all the time and new countries. On our way through Hamburg we'll go to the zoo—you'll love that—and we'll go to the theatre and the opera too . . . and when we get to Munich there'll be the museums, dear, and pictures by Rubens and Raphael—the great painters, you know . . . You've heard of Munich, haven't you? Where King Ludwig lived—you know, the king who went mad. . . . We'll see his castles—some of his castles are still just like in fairy-tales . . . and from there it's not far to Switzerland—and the Alps. Think of the Alps, Kristin dear, covered with snow in the middle of summer . . . and there are oranges there and trees that are green the whole year round . . .

JEAN *is seen in the door of his room, sharpening his razor on a strop which he holds with his teeth and his left hand. He listens to the talk with satisfaction and now and then nods approval.* JULIE *continues, tempo prestissimo.*

And then we'll get a hotel . . . and I'll sit at the desk, while Jean receives the guests and goes out marketing and writes letters . . . There's life for you! Trains whistling, buses driving up, bells ringing upstairs and downstairs . . . and I shall make out the bills—and I shall cook them too . . . you've no idea how nervous travellers are when it comes to paying their bills. And you—you'll sit like a queen in the kitchen . . . of course there won't be any standing at the stove for you. You'll always have to be nicely dressed and ready to be seen, and with your looks—no, I'm not flattering you—one fine day you'll catch yourself a husband . . . some rich Englishman, I shouldn't wonder—they're the ones who are easy—[*slowing down*]—to catch . . . and then we'll get rich and build ourselves a villa on Lake Como . . . of course it rains there a little now and then—but—[*dully*]—the sun must shine there too sometimes—even though it seems gloomy—and if not—then we can come home again—come back—[*pause*]—here—or somewhere else . . .

KRISTIN—Look here, Miss Julie, do you believe all that yourself?

JULIE [*exhausted*] Do I believe it?

KRISTIN—Yes.

JULIE [*wearily*] I don't know. I don't believe anything any more. [*Sinks down on the bench; her head in her arms on the table.*] Nothing. Nothing at all.

KRISTIN [*turning to* JEAN] So you meant to beat it, did you?

JEAN [*disconcerted, putting the razor on the table*] Beat it? What are you talking about? You've heard Miss Julie's plan, and though she's tired now with being up all night, it's a perfectly sound plan.

KRISTIN—Oh, is it? If you thought I'd work for that . . .

JEAN [*interrupting*] Kindly use decent language in front of your mistress. Do you hear?

KRISTIN—Mistress?

JEAN—Yes.

KRISTIN—Well, well, just listen to that!

JEAN—Yes, it would be a good thing if you did listen and talked less. Miss Julie is your mistress and what's made you lose your respect for her now ought to make you feel the same about yourself.

KRISTIN—I've always had enough self-respect——

JEAN—To despise other people.

KRISTIN——not to go below my own station. Has the Count's cook ever gone with the groom or the swineherd? Tell me that.

JEAN—No, you were lucky enough to have a high-class chap for your beau.

KRISTIN—High-class all right—selling the oats out of the Count's stable.

JEAN—You're a fine one to talk—taking a commission on the groceries and bribes from the butcher.

KRISTIN—What the devil . . . ?

JEAN—And now you can't feel any respect for your employers. You, you!

KRISTIN—Are you coming to church with me? I should think you need a good sermon after your fine deeds.

JEAN—No, I'm not going to church today. You can go alone and confess your own sins.

KRISTIN—Yes, I'll do that and bring back enough forgiveness to cover yours too. The Saviour suffered and died on the cross for all our sins, and if we go to Him with faith and a penitent heart, He takes all our sins upon Himself.

JEAN—Even grocery thefts?

JULIE—Do you believe that, Kristin?

KRISTIN—That is my living faith, as sure as I stand here. The faith I learnt as a child and have kept ever since, Miss Julie. "But where sin abounded, grace did much more abound."

JULIE—Oh, if I had your faith! Oh, if . . .

1420

KRISTIN – But you see you can't have it without God's special grace, and it's not given to all to have that.

JULIE – Who is it given to then?

KRISTIN – That's the great secret of the workings of grace, Miss Julie. God is no respecter of persons, and with Him the last shall be first . . .

JULIE – Then I suppose He does respect the last.

KRISTIN [*continuing*] . . . and it is easier for a camel to go through the eye of a needle than for a rich man to enter into the kingdom of God. That's how it is, Miss Julie. Now I'm going—alone, and on my way I shall tell the groom not to let any of the horses out, in case anyone should want to leave before the Count gets back. Goodbye.

[*Exit.*]

JEAN – What a devil! And all on account of a greenfinch.

JULIE [*wearily*] Never mind the greenfinch. Do you see any way out of this, any end to it?

JEAN [*pondering*] No.

JULIE – If you were in my place, what would you do?

JEAN – In your place? Wait a bit. If I was a woman—a lady of rank who had—fallen. I don't know. Yes, I do know now.

JULIE [*picking up the razor and making a gesture*] This?

JEAN – Yes. But I wouldn't do it, you know. There's a difference between us.

JULIE – Because you're a man and I'm a woman? What is the difference?

JEAN – The usual difference—between man and woman.

JULIE [*holding the razor*] I'd like to. But I can't. My father couldn't either, that time he wanted to.

JEAN – No, he didn't want to. He had to be revenged first.

JULIE – And now my mother is revenged again, through me.

JEAN – Didn't you ever love your father, Miss Julie?

JULIE – Deeply, but I must have hated him too—unconsciously. And he let me be brought up to despise my own sex, to be half woman, half man. Whose fault is what's happened? My father's, my mother's or my own? My own? I haven't anything that's my own. I haven't one single thought that I didn't get from my father, one emotion that didn't come from my mother, and as for this last idea—about all people being equal—I got that from him, my fiancé—that's why I call him a cad. How can it be my fault? Push the responsibility on to Jesus, like Kristin does? No, I'm too proud and—thanks to my father's teaching —too intelligent. As for all that about a rich person not being able to get into heaven, it's just a lie, but Kristin, who has money in the savings-bank, will certainly not get in. Whose fault is it? What does it matter whose fault it is? In any case I must take the blame and bear the consequences.

JEAN—Yes, but . . .

[*There are two sharp rings on the bell.* JULIE *jumps to her feet.* JEAN *changes into his livery.*]

The Count is back. Supposing Kristin . . .

[*Goes to the speaking-tube, presses it and listens.*]

JULIE—Has he been to his desk yet?

JEAN—This is Jean, sir. [*Listens.*] Yes, sir. [*Listens.*] Yes, sir, very good, sir. [*Listens.*] At once, sir? [*Listens.*] Very good, sir. In half an hour.

JULIE [*in panic*] What did he say? My God, what did he say?

JEAN—He ordered his boots and his coffee in half an hour.

JULIE—Then there's half an hour . . . Oh, I'm so tired! I can't do anything. Can't be sorry, can't run away, can't stay, can't live—can't die. Help me. Order me, and I'll obey like a dog. Do me this last service—save my honour, save his name. You know what I ought to do, but haven't the strength to do. Use your strength and order me to do it.

JEAN—I don't know why—I can't now—I don't understand . . . It's just as if this coat made me—I can't give you orders—and now that the Count has spoken to me—I can't quite explain, but . . . well, that devil of a lackey is bending my back again. I believe if the Count came down now and ordered me to cut my throat, I'd do it on the spot.

JULIE—Then pretend you're him and I'm you. You did some fine acting before, when you knelt to me and played the aristocrat. Or . . . Have you ever seen a hypnotist at the theatre? [*He nods.*] He says to the person "Take the broom," and he takes it. He says "Sweep," and he sweeps . . .

JEAN—But the person has to be asleep.

JULIE [*as if in a trance*] I am asleep already . . . the whole room has turned to smoke—and you look like a stove—a stove like a man in black with a tall hat—your eyes are glowing like coals when the fire is low—and your face is a white patch like ashes. [*The sunlight has now reached the floor and lights up* JEAN.] How nice and warm it is! [*She holds out her hands as though warming them at a fire.*] And so light—and so peaceful.

JEAN [*putting the razor in her hand*] Here is the broom. Go now while it's light—out to the barn—and . . .

[*Whispers in her ear.*]

JULIE [*waking*] Thank you. I am going now—to rest. But just tell me that even the first can receive the gift of grace.

JEAN—The first? No, I can't tell you that. But wait . . . Miss Julie, I've got it! You aren't one of the first any longer. You're one of the last.

JULIE – That's true. I'm one of the very last. I *am* the last. Oh! . . .
But now I can't go. Tell me again to go.

JEAN – No, I can't now either. I can't.

JULIE – And the first shall be last.

JEAN – Don't think, don't think. You're taking my strength away too
and making me a coward. What's that? I thought I saw the bell move
. . . To be so frightened of a bell! Yes, but it's not just a bell. There's
somebody behind it—a hand moving it—and something else moving
the hand—and if you stop your ears—if you stop your ears—yes, then it
rings louder than ever. Rings and rings until you answer—and then it's
too late. Then the police come and . . . and . . . [*The bell rings
twice loudly.* JEAN *flinches, then straightens himself up.*] It's horrible.
But there's no other way to end it . . . Go!

[JULIE *walks firmly out through the door.*]

"MISS JULIE," A FOREWORD

By August Strindberg
Translated by Elizabeth Sprigge

THEATRE has long seemed to me—in common with much other art—a *Biblia Pauperum,* a Bible in pictures for those who cannot read what is written or printed; and I see the playwright as a lay preacher peddling the ideas of his time in popular form, popular enough for the middle-classes, mainstay of theatre audiences, to grasp the gist of the matter without troubling their brains too much. For this reason theatre has always been an elementary school for the young, the semi-educated and for women who still have a primitive capacity for deceiving themselves and letting themselves be deceived—who, that is to say, are susceptible to illusion and to suggestion from the author. I have therefore thought it not unlikely that in these days, when that rudimentary and immature thought-process operating through fantasy appears to be developing into reflection, research and analysis, that theatre, like religion, might be discarded as an outworn form for whose appreciation we lack the necessary conditions. This opinion is confirmed by the major crisis still prevailing in the theatres of Europe, and still more by the fact that in those countries of culture, producing the greatest thinkers of the age, namely England and Germany, drama—like other fine arts—is dead.

Some countries, it is true, have attempted to create a new drama by using the old forms with up-to-date contents, but not only has there been insufficient time for these new ideas to be popularized, so that the

From *Six Plays of Strindberg,* translated by Elizabeth Sprigge. New York: Doubleday Anchor Books, 1955. Copyright © 1955 by Elizabeth Sprigge. Reprinted by permission of Collins-Knowlton-Wing, Inc.

audience can grasp them, but also people have been so wrought up by the taking of sides that pure, disinterested appreciation has become impossible. One's deepest impressions are upset when an applauding or a hissing majority dominates as forcefully and openly as it can in the theatre. Moreover, as no new form has been devised for these new contents, the new wine has burst the old bottles.

In this play I have not tried to do anything new, for this cannot be done, but only to modernize the form to meet the demands which may, I think, be made on this art today. To this end I chose—or surrendered myself to—a theme which claims to be outside the controversial issues of today, since questions of social climbing or falling, of higher or lower, better or worse, of man and woman, are, have been and will be of lasting interest. When I took this theme from a true story told me some years ago, which made a deep impression, I saw it as a subject for tragedy, for as yet it is tragic to see one favoured by fortune go under, and still more to see a family heritage die out, although a time may come when we have grown so developed and enlightened that we shall view with indifference life's spectacle, now seeming so brutal, cynical and heartless. Then we shall have dispensed with those inferior, unreliable instruments of thought called feelings, which become harmful and superfluous as reasoning develops.

The fact that my heroine rouses pity is solely due to weakness; we cannot resist fear of the same fate overtaking us. The hyper-sensitive spectator may, it is true, go beyond this kind of pity, while the man with belief in the future may actually demand some suggestion for remedying the evil—in other words some kind of policy. But, to begin with, there is no such thing as absolute evil; the downfall of one family is the good fortune of another, which thereby gets a chance to rise, and, fortune being only comparative, the alternation of rising and falling is one of life's principal charms. Also, to the man of policy, who wants to remedy the painful fact that the bird of prey devours the dove, and lice the bird of prey, I should like to put the question: why should it be remedied? Life is not so mathematically idiotic as only to permit the big to eat the small; it happens just as often that the bee kills the lion or at least drives it mad.

That my tragedy depresses many people is their own fault. When we have grown strong as the pioneers of the French revolution, we shall be happy and relieved to see the national parks cleared of ancient rotting trees which have stood too long in the way of others equally entitled to a period of growth—as relieved as we are when an incurable invalid dies.

My tragedy "The Father" was recently criticised for being too sad—as if one wants cheerful tragedies! Everybody is clamouring for this supposed "joy of life," and theatre managers demand farces, as if the joy of life consisted in being ridiculous and portraying all human beings as suffering from St. Vitus's dance or total idiocy. I myself find the joy of life in its strong and cruel struggles, and my pleasure in learning, in adding to my knowledge. For this reason I have chosen for this play an unusual situation, but an instructive one—an exception, that is to say, but a great exception, one proving the rule, which will no doubt annoy all lovers of the commonplace. What will offend simple minds is that my plot is not simple, nor its point of view single. In real life an action—this, by the way, is a somewhat new discovery—is generally caused by a whole series of motives, more or less fundamental, but as a rule the spectator chooses just one of these—the one which his mind can most easily grasp or that does most credit to his intelligence. A suicide is committed. Business troubles, says the man of affairs. Unrequited love, say the women. Sickness, says the invalid. Despair, says the down-and-out. But it is possible that the motive lay in all or none of these directions, or that the dead man concealed his actual motive by revealing quite another, likely to reflect more to his glory.

I see Miss Julie's tragic fate to be the result of many circumstances: the mother's character, the father's mistaken upbringing of the girl, her own nature, and the influence of her fiancé on a weak, degenerate mind. Also, more directly, the festive mood of Midsummer Eve, her father's absence, her monthly indisposition, her pre-occupation with animals, the excitement of dancing, the magic of dusk, the strongly aphrodisiac influence of flowers, and finally the chance that drives the couple into a room alone—to which must be added the urgency of the excited man.

My treatment of the theme, moreover, is neither exclusively physiological nor psychological. I have not put the blame wholly on the inheritance from her mother, nor on her physical condition at the time, nor on immorality. I have not even preached a moral sermon; in the absence of a priest I leave this to the cook.

I congratulate myself on this multiplicity of motives as being up-to-date, and if others have done the same thing before me, then I congratulate myself on not being alone in my "paradoxes," as all innovations are called.

In regard to the drawing of the characters, I have made my people somewhat "characterless" for the following reasons. In the course of time the word character has assumed manifold meanings. It must have originally signified the dominating trait of the soul-complex, and this was confused with temperament. Later it became the middle-class term for the automaton, one whose nature had become fixed or who had adapted himself to a particular rôle in life. In fact a person who had ceased to grow was called a character, while one continuing to develop—the skilful navigator of life's river, sailing not with sheets set fast, but veering before the wind to luff again—was called characterless, in a derogatory sense, of course, because he was so hard to catch, classify and keep track of. This middle-class conception of the immobility of the soul was transferred to the stage where the middle-class has always ruled. A character came to signify a man fixed and finished: one who invariably appeared either drunk or jocular or melancholy, and characterization required nothing more than a physical defect such as a club-foot, a wooden leg, a red nose; or the fellow might be made to repeat some such phrase as: "That's capital!" or: "Barkis is willin'!" This simple way of regarding human beings still survives in the great Molière. Harpagon is nothing but a miser, although Harpagon might have been not only a miser, but also a first-rate financier, an excellent father and a good citizen. Worse still, his "failing" is a distinct advantage to his son-in-law and his daughter, who are his heirs, and who therefore cannot criticise him, even if they have to wait a while to get to bed. I do not believe, therefore, in simple stage characters; and the summary judgments of authors—this man is stupid, that one brutal, this jealous, that stingy, and so forth—should be challenged by the Naturalists who know the richness of the soul-complex and realise that vice has a reverse side very much like virtue.

Because they are modern characters, living in a period of transition more feverishly hysterical than its predecessor at least, I have drawn my figures vacillating, disintegrated, a blend of old and new. Nor does it seem to me unlikely that, through newspapers and conversations, modern ideas may have filtered down to the level of the domestic servant.

My souls (characters) are conglomerations of past and present stages of civilization, bits from books and newspapers, scraps of humanity, rags and tatters of fine clothing, patched together as is the human soul. And I have added a little evolutionary history by making the weaker steal and repeat the words of the stronger, and by making the characters borrow ideas or "suggestions" from one another.

Miss Julie is a modern character, not that the half-woman, the man-hater, has not existed always, but because now that she has been discovered she has stepped to the front and begun to make a noise. The half-woman is a type who thrusts herself forward, selling herself nowadays for power, decorations, distinctions, diplomas, as formerly for money. The type implies degeneration; it is not a good type and it does not endure; but it can unfortunately transmit its misery, and degenerate men seem instinctively to choose their mates from among such women, and so they breed, producing offspring of indeterminate sex to whom life is torture. But fortunately they perish, either because they cannot come to terms with reality, or because their repressed instincts break out uncontrollably, or again because their hopes of catching up with men are shattered. The type is tragic, revealing a desperate fight against nature, tragic too in its Romantic inheritance now dissipated by Naturalism, which wants nothing but happiness—and for happiness strong and sound species are required.

But Miss Julie is also a relic of the old warrior nobility now giving way to the new nobility of nerve and brain. She is a victim of the discord which a mother's "crime" has produced in a family, a victim too of the day's complaisance, of circumstances, of her own defective constitution, all of which are equivalent to the Fate or Universal Law of former days. The Naturalist has abolished guilt with God, but the consequences of the action—punishment, imprisonment or the fear of it—he cannot abolish, for the simple reason that they remain whether he is acquitted or not. An injured fellow-being is not so complacent as outsiders, who have not been injured, can afford to be. Even if the father had felt impelled to take no vengeance, the daughter would have taken vengeance on herself, as she does here, from that innate or acquired sense of honour which the upper-classes inherit—whether from Barbarism or Aryan forebears, or from the chivalry of the Middle Ages, who knows? It is a very beautiful thing, but it has become a danger nowadays to the preservation of the race. It is the nobleman's *hara-kiri*, the Japanese law of inner conscience which compels him to cut his own stomach open at the insult of another, and which survives in modified form in the duel, a privilege of the nobility. And so the valet Jean lives on, but Miss Julie cannot live without honour. This is the thrall's advantage over the nobleman, that he lacks this fatal preoccupation with honour. And in all of us Aryans there is something of the nobleman, or the Don Quixote, which makes us sympathize with the man who commits suicide because he has done something ignoble and lost his honour. And we are noblemen enough to suffer at the sight of fallen greatness littering the earth like a corpse— yes, even if the fallen rise again and make restitution by honourable deeds. Jean, the valet, is a race-builder, a man of marked characteristics. He was a labourer's son who has educated himself towards becoming a gentleman. He has learnt easily, through his well-developed senses (smell, taste, vision)—and he also has a sense of beauty. He has already bettered himself, and is thick-skinned enough to have no scruples about using other people's services. He is already foreign to his associates, despising them as part of the life he has turned his back on, yet also fearing and fleeing from them because they know his secrets, pry into his plans, watch his rise with envy, and look forward with pleasure to his fall. Hence his dual, indeterminate character, vacillating between love of the heights and hatred of those who have already achieved them. He is, he says himself, an aristocrat; he has learned the secrets of good society. He is polished, but vulgar within; he already wears his tails with taste, but there is no guarantee of his personal cleanliness.

He has some respect for his young lady, but he is frightened of Kristin, who knows his dangerous secrets, and he is sufficiently callous not to allow the night's events to wreck his plans for the future. Having both the slave's brutality and the master's lack of squeamishness, he can see blood without fainting and take disaster by the horns. Consequently he emerges from the battle unscathed, and probably ends his days as a hotel-keeper. And even if *he* does not become a Roumanian Count, his son will doubtless go to the university and perhaps become a county attorney.

The light which Jean sheds on a lower-class conception of life, life seen from below, is on the whole illuminating—when he speaks the truth, which is not often, for he says what is favourable to himself rather than what is true. When Miss Julie suggests that the lower-classes must be oppressed by the attitude of their superiors, Jean naturally agrees, as his object is to gain her sympathy; but when he perceives the advantage of separating himself from the common herd, he at once takes back his words.

It is not because Jean is now rising that he has the upper hand of Miss Julie, but because he is a man. Sexually he is the aristocrat because of his virility, his keener senses and his capacity for taking the initiative. His inferiority is mainly due to the social environment in which he lives, and he can probably shed it with his valet's livery.

The slave mentality expresses itself in his worship of the Count (the boots), and his religious superstition; but he worships the Count chiefly because he holds that higher position for which Jean himself is striving. And this worship remains even when he has won the daughter of the house and seen how empty is that lovely shell.

I do not believe that a love relationship in the "higher" sense could exist between two individuals of such different quality, but I have made Miss Julie imagine that she is in love, so as to lessen her sense of guilt, and I let Jean suppose that if his social position were altered he would truly love her. I think love is like the hyacinth which has to strike roots in darkness *before* it can produce a vigorous flower. In this case it shoots up quickly, blossoms and goes to seed all at the same time, which is why the plant dies so soon.

As for Kristin, she is a female slave, full of servility and sluggishness acquired in front of the kitchen fire, and stuffed full of morality and religion, which are her cloak and scape-goat. She goes to church as a quick and easy way of unloading her household thefts on to Jesus and taking on a fresh cargo of guiltlessness. For the rest she is a minor character, and I have therefore sketched her in the same manner as the Pastor and the Doctor in "The Father," where I wanted ordinary human beings, as are most country pastors and provincial doctors. If these minor characters seem abstract to some people this is due to the fact that ordinary people are to a certain extent abstract in pursuit of their work; that is to say, they are without individuality, showing, while working, only one side of themselves. And as long as the spectator does not feel a need to see them from other sides, there is nothing wrong with my abstract presentation.

In regard to the dialogue, I have departed somewhat from tradition by not making my characters catechists who ask stupid questions in order to elicit a smart reply. I have avoided the symmetrical, mathematical construction of French dialogue, and let people's minds work irregularly, as they do in real life where, during a conversation, no topic is drained to the dregs, and one mind finds in another a chance cog to engage in. So too the dialogue wanders, gathering in the opening scenes material which is later picked up, worked over, repeated, expounded and developed like the theme in a musical composition.

The plot speaks for itself, and as it really only concerns two people, I have concentrated on these, introducing only one minor character, the cook, and keeping the unhappy spirit of the father above and behind the action. I have done this because it seems to me that the psychological process is what interests people most today. Our inquisitive souls are no longer satisfied with seeing a thing happen; we must also know how it happens. We want to see the wires themselves, to watch the machinery, to examine the box with the false bottom, to take hold of the magic ring in order to find the join, and look at the cards to see how they are marked.

In this connection I have had in view the documentary novels of the brothers de Goncourt, which appeal to me more than any other modern literature.

As far as the technical side of the work is concerned I have made the experiment of abolishing the division into acts. This is because I have come to the conclusion that our capacity for illusion is disturbed by the intervals, during which the audience has time to reflect and escape from the suggestive influence of the author-hypnotist. My play will probably take an hour and a half, and as one can listen to a lecture, a sermon or a parliamentary debate for as long as that or longer, I do not think a theatrical performance will be fatiguing in the same length of time. As early as 1872, in one of my first dramatic attempts, "The Outlaw," I tried this concentrated form, although with scant success. The play was written in five acts, and only when finished did I become aware of the restless, disjointed effect that it produced. The script was burnt and from the ashes rose a single well-knit act—fifty pages of print, playable in one hour. The form of the present play is, therefore, not new, but it appears to be my own, and changing tastes may make it timely. My hope is one day to have an audience educated enough to sit through a whole evening's entertainment in one act, but one would have to try this out to see. Meanwhile, in order to provide respite for the audience and the players, without allowing the audience to escape from the illusion, I have introduced three art forms: monologue, mime and ballet. These are all part of drama, having their origins in classic tragedy, monody having become monologue and the chorus, ballet.

Monologue is now condemned by our realists as unnatural, but if one provides motives for it one makes it natural, and then can use it to advantage. It is, surely, natural for a public speaker to walk up and down the room practicing his speech, natural for an actor to read his part aloud, for a servant girl to talk to her cat, a mother to prattle to her child, an old maid to chatter to her parrot, and a sleeper to talk in his sleep. And in order that the actor may have a chance, for once, of working independently, free from the author's direction, it is better that the monologue should not be written, but only indicated. For since it is of small importance what is said in one's sleep or to the parrot or to the cat—none of it influences the action—a talented actor, identifying himself with the atmosphere and the situation, may improvise better than the author, who cannot calculate ahead how much may be said or how long taken without waking the audience from the illusion.

Some Italian theatres have, as we know, returned to improvisation, thereby producing actors who are creative, although within the bounds set by the author. This may well be a step forward, or even the beginning of a new art-form worthy to be called *productive*.

In places where monologue would be unnatural I have used mime, leaving here an even wider scope for the actor's imagination, and more chance for him to win independent laurels. But so as not to try the audience beyond endurance, I have introduced music—fully justified by the Midsummer Eve dance—to exercise its powers of persuasion during the dumb show. But I beg the musical director to consider carefully his choice of compositions, so that conflicting moods are not induced by selections from the current operetta or dance show, or by folk-tunes of too local a character.

The ballet I have introduced cannot be replaced by the usual kind of "crowd-scene," for such scenes are too badly played—a lot of grinning idiots seizing the opportunity to show off and thus destroying the illusion. And as peasants cannot improvise their taunts, but use ready-made phrases with a double meaning, I have not composed their lampoon, but taken a little-known song and dance which I myself noted down in the Stockholm district. The words are not quite to the point, but this too is intentional, for the cunning, i.e. weakness, of the slave prevents him from direct attack. Nor can there be clowning in a serious action, or coarse joking in a situation which nails the lid on a family coffin.

As regards the scenery, I have borrowed from impressionist painting its asymmetry and its economy; thus, I think, strengthening the illusion. For the fact that one does not see the whole room and all the furniture leaves scope for conjecture—that is to say imagination is roused and complements what is seen. I have succeeded too in getting rid of those tiresome exits through doors, since scenery doors are made of canvas, and rock at the slightest touch. They cannot even express the wrath of an irate head of the family who, after a bad dinner, goes out slamming the door behind him, "so that the whole house shakes." On the stage it rocks. I have also kept to a single set, both in order to let the characters develop in their métier and to break away from over-decoration. When one has only one set, one may expect it to be realistic; but as a matter of fact nothing is harder than to get a stage room that looks something like a room, however easily the scene painter can produce flaming volcanoes and waterfalls. Presumably the walls must be of canvas; but it seems about time to dispense with painted shelves and cooking utensils. We are asked to accept so many stage conventions that we might at least be spared the pain of painted pots and pans.

I have set the back wall and the table diagonally so that the actors may play full-face and in half-profile when they are sitting opposite one another at the table. In the opera AÏDA I saw a diagonal background, which led the eye to unfamiliar perspectives and did not look like mere reaction against boring straight lines.

Another much needed innovation is the abolition of foot-lights. This lighting from below is said to have the purpose of making the actors' faces fatter. But why, I ask, should all actors have fat faces? Does not this underlighting flatten out all the subtlety of the lower part of the face, specially the jaw, falsify the shape of the nose and throw shadows up over the eyes? Even if this were not so, one thing is certain: that the lights hurt the performers' eyes, so that the full play of their expression is lost. The foot-lights strike part of the retina usually protected—except in sailors who have to watch sunlight on water—and therefore one seldom sees anything other than a crude rolling of the eyes, either sideways or up towards the gallery, showing their whites. Perhaps this too causes that tiresome blinking of the eyelashes, especially by actresses. And when anyone on the stage wants to speak with his eyes, the only thing he can do is to look straight at the audience, with whom he or she then gets into direct communication, outside the framework of the set—a habit called, rightly or wrongly, "greeting one's friends."

Would not sufficiently strong side-lighting, with some kind of reflectors, add to the actor's powers of expression by allowing him to use the face's greatest asset:—the play of the eyes?

I have few illusions about getting the actors to play *to* the audience instead of *with* it, although this is what I want. That I shall see an actor's back throughout a critical scene is beyond my dreams, but I do wish crucial scenes could be played, not in front of the prompter's box, like duets expecting applause, but in the place required by the action. So, no revolutions, but just some small modifications, for to make the stage into a real room with the fourth wall missing would be too upsetting altogether.

I dare not hope that the actresses will listen to what I have to say about make-up, for they would rather be beautiful than life-like, but the actor might consider whether it is to his advantage to create an abstract character with grease-paints, and cover his face with it like a mask. Take the case of a man who draws a choleric charcoal line between his eyes and then, in this fixed state of wrath, has to smile at some repartee. What a frightful grimace the result is! And equally, how is that false forehead, smooth as a billiard ball, to wrinkle when the old man loses his temper?

In a modern psychological drama, where the subtlest reactions of a character need to be mirrored in the face rather than expressed by sound and gesture, it would be worth while experimenting with powerful side-lighting on a small stage and a cast without make-up, or at least with the minimum.

If, in addition, we could abolish the visible orchestra, with its distracting lamps and its faces turned toward the audience; if we could have the stalls raised so that the spectators' eyes were higher than the players' knees; if we could get rid of the boxes (the centre of my target), with their tittering diners and supper-parties, and have total darkness in the auditorium during the performance; and if, first and foremost, we could have a *small* stage and a *small* house, then perhaps a new dramatic art might arise, and theatre once more become a place of entertainment for educated people. While waiting for such a theatre it is as well for us to go on writing so as to stock that repertory of the future.

I have made an attempt. If it has failed, there is time enough to try again.

OSCAR WILDE

The Importance of Being Earnest

THE ANTHOLOGIST has no problem choosing a play by Oscar Wilde (1854–1900): only one of them is a masterpiece. But how great a masterpiece it is has hardly even yet been recognized. Is it not called "trivial" by the author himself? Have not even the critics who praised it done so in such a manner as to turn the attention away from what it is saying? Here is William Archer:

> . . . this play which imitates nothing, represents nothing, is nothing, except a sort of *rondo capriccioso*, in which the artist's fingers run with crisp irresponsibility up and down the keyboard of life. Why attempt to analyse and class such a play?

And yet . . . and yet . . . the play is as tightly packed with observations about the world we live in as any play one could mention, even a Shaw play. How is it these comments can seem to add up to "nothing"? Ah, because the author's attitude is "irresponsible" (*crisply* so, according to Archer, a rather baffling modifier). But should the "irresponsibility" prove to be a paradox, even a deliberate, ironical pose? The critical comments of Otto Reinert and Arthur Ganz will carry this speculation further.

The play appears here in its original form, as submitted by Oscar Wilde to the actor-manager George Alexander. Later, at Alexander's request, Wilde made a shorter, three-act version, which, indeed, has been the version printed and reprinted over the years. The original text was unpublished until 1956, and then published only in a very small printing of a very expensive edition. The present anthology marks its first "popular" appearance in print, though Methuen's have put out a sort of compromise text—midway between the revised and the original versions. (It should be added that the revised text was not simply an abridgement. New lines were written and names of some characters were changed. The reader will have no trouble finding copies of the revised text should he wish to make a fuller comparison.)

THE IMPORTANCE OF BEING EARNEST,

A Trivial Comedy for Serious People,
In Four Acts as Originally Written

[1894]

DRAMATIS PERSONAE

JOHN WORTHING, J. P.	*of the Manor House. Wilton, Hereford-shire*
ALGERNON MONTFORD	*his friend*
REV. CANON CHASUBLE, D.D.	*Rector of Wilton*
THOMAS R. HUBBARD	*of the firm of Hubbard and Harrow. Solicitors, London*[1]
MATHEWS	*butler to Mr. Worthing*[2]
LANE	*Mr. Montford's manservant*
LADY BRANCASTER	
HON. GWENDOLEN FAIRFAX	*her daughter*
CECILY CARDEW	*John Worthing's ward*
MISS PRISM	*her governess*

THE SCENES OF THE PLAY

ACT I *Algernon Montford's rooms in Half-Moon Street, W.*
ACT II *The Garden at the Manor House, Wilton.*[3]
ACT III *Drawing-Room at the Manor House, Wilton.*[4]
ACT IV *Same as Act III.*

Time: The Present.

[1] The name of this character is changed to Gribsby and the firm's name is Parker and Gribsby in the second act where he appears.

[2] When this character appears in the second act and throughout the rest of the play he is called Merriman. These two names persisted in the *Dramatis Personae* until the second typescript of October, 1894. (For further details on the different typescripts, etc., see the Introduction to the two-volume edition of the play as published by The New York Public Library in 1956.)

[3] This name is changed in the text to Woolton.

[4] See note 3.

FIRST ACT

Scene: ALGERNON's *room in Half Moon Street. Door r.u. and door l.c. Fireplace r.c. The room is luxuriously and artistically furnished.*

> [BUTLER *is arranging afternoon tea on table.*
> ALGERNON *is standing close by.*]

A L G E R N O N – Have you got the cucumber sandwiches cut for Lady Brancaster?

L A N E – Yes, sir.

A L G E R N O N – Ahem! where are they?

L A N E – Here, sir.

> [*Shows plate.*]

A L G E R N O N [*takes one and eats it*] Oh! . . . by the way, Lane, I see from your book that on Thursday night, when Lord Shoreham and Mr. Worthing were dining with me, eight bottles of champagne are entered.

L A N E – Yes, sir. Eight bottles and a pint.

A L G E R N O N – Why is it that at a bachelor's establishment the servants invariably drink the champagne?

L A N E – I attribute it to the superior quality of the wine, sir. I have often observed that in married households the champagne is rarely of a first-rate brand.

A L G E R N O N – Good heavens! Is marriage so demoralizing as that?

L A N E [*gravely*] I believe it *is* a very pleasant state, sir. I have had very little experience of it myself up to the present. I have only been married once. That was in consequence of a misunderstanding between myself and a young person.

A L G E R N O N – I don't know that I am much interested in your family life, Lane.

L A N E – No, sir; it is not a very interesting subject. I never think of it myself.

A L G E R N O N – Very natural, I am sure. Ah! . . . Just let me look at those cucumber sandwiches again. [LANE *hands the sandwiches.*] Any brute try to see me this morning?

LANE – The wine merchant waited in the hall, sir, from ten to a quarter to one.

ALGERNON – I hope you gave him an uncomfortable chair.

LANE – Yes, sir. I took one from your own room. A chippendale. . . . Your tailor also called.

ALGERNON – Oh! that is all right. Tailors are gentlemen. . . . Wish to goodness some ass would leave me a large fortune. Can't go on as I am going on now. It is ridiculous.

LANE [*arranging tea-cups*] It is very unpleasant waiting for a better place, sir. I know the feeling myself.

ALGERNON [*looking at him with an amused smile*] That will do, Lane, thank you.

LANE – Thank you, sir.

[*False exit.*]

ALGERNON – Ah! . . . Just give me another cucumber sandwich.

LANE – Yes, sir.

[*Returns and hands plate.*]
[*Enter footman.*]

GEORGE[5] – Mr. Worthing.

[*Enter* JACK.]

ALGERNON – How are you, my dear Ernest? What brings you up to town?

JACK – Oh, pleasure, pleasure! What else would bring one up?

[*Putting his hand on* ALGERNON'S *shoulder.*]

Eating as usual, I see, dear Algy!

ALGERNON [*stiffly*] I believe it is usual to take some slight refreshment at five o'clock. Where exactly have you been since last Thursday?

JACK [*sitting down*] Oh! in the country.

ALGERNON – You are always in the country. It is most mysterious.

JACK – You are invariably in town. It is excessively suspicious.

ALGERNON – What on earth do you do in the country, Ernest?

JACK [*pulling off his gloves*] Oh! when one is in town one amuses oneself. When one is in the country one amuses other people. It is excessively boring.

ALGERNON – And who are the people you amuse?

JACK [*airily*] Oh, neighbours, neighbours.

ALGERNON – Got nice neighbours in your part of Shropshire?

JACK – Perfectly horrid. Never speak to one of them.

ALGERNON – How immensely you must amuse them! Shropshire is your county, isn't it?

[*Goes over and takes sandwich.*]

[5] The name of this character does not appear again.

JACK – Ah? . . . yes.

ALGERNON – How extraordinary! It was Wiltshire the last time you were here.

JACK – What do you say?

ALGERNON – My dear Ernest, the last time you did me the honour of dining with me you told me your family place was in Wiltshire.

JACK – Oh! it is just on the borders, you know. The stables are in Wiltshire, I believe.

ALGERNON – A hundred and fifty miles from the house! Don't you find that rather inconvenient? . . . Ernest, where is your country place?

JACK [getting up] My dear fellow! Surely you don't expect me to be accurate about geography? No gentleman is accurate about geography. Why, I got a prize for geography when I was at school. . . . I can't be expected to know anything about it now. [Turning.] You don't seem to realize, Algy, that when one is young one gets prizes for what one knows, and that when one grows up one gets prizes for what one doesn't know. A much better system. You must find it most convenient.

[Goes over to tea-table.]

ALGERNON – I do, dear boy.

JACK – Hallo! Why all these cups? Who is coming to tea?

ALGERNON – Oh! Aunt Augusta and Gwendolen. That is all.

JACK – How perfectly delightful! I mean how perfectly delightful that Gwendolen is coming. I am fearfully afraid of Lady Brancaster.

ALGERNON – Aunt Augusta is rather a typical woman, when one comes to think of it.

JACK – The most typical woman I know. She freezes me.

ALGERNON – I'm afraid she won't quite approve of your being here, Ernest.

JACK – Why?

ALGERNON – My dear fellow, the way you flirt with Gwendolen is perfectly disgraceful. In fact it is almost as bad as the way Gwendolen flirts with you.

JACK – I am in love with Gwendolen.

ALGERNON – I know. You have been telling me that for the last three months.

JACK – Well, I have come up to town to propose to her.

ALGERNON – I thought you had come up to town for pleasure? . . . I call that business.

JACK – How utterly unromantic you are!

ALGERNON – I really don't see anything romantic in proposing to be married. It is very romantic to be in love. But there is nothing romantic about a definite proposal. Why, one may be accepted. One usually is,

I believe. Then the excitement is all over. The very essence of romance is uncertainty. Even if I was married, I'd always try and forget the fact.

J A C K – I have no doubt about that, dear Algy. The Divorce Court was specially invented for people whose memories are so peculiar.

A L G E R N O N – My dear boy, there is no use speculating on that subject. It is merely waste of time. Divorces are made in Heaven. My dear fellow, please don't touch the cucumber sandwiches. They are specially meant for Aunt Augusta.

[*Takes one and eats it.*]

J A C K – Well, you have been eating them all the time.

A L G E R N O N – That is quite a different affair. She is my aunt. Have some tea-cake. It is ordered specially for Gwendolen. She is devoted to tea-cake.

J A C K [*eating tea-cake*] And very good tea-cake it is too.

A L G E R N O N – Well, my dear fellow, you need not eat it all. You behave as if you were married to her already. You are not married to her already and I don't think you ever will.

J A C K – Why on earth do you say that?

A L G E R N O N – Well, in the first place girls never marry the men they flirt with. Girls don't think it right.

J A C K – Oh, that is nonsense!

A L G E R N O N – It isn't. It is a great truth. It accounts for the quite extraordinary number of bachelors that one sees all over the shop. In the second place, I don't give my consent.

J A C K – Your consent! What utter nonsense you talk!

A L G E R N O N – My dear fellow, Gwendolen is my first cousin. And she is extremely fond of riding. And if your country house is in Shropshire, and the stables a hundred and fifty miles off in Wiltshire, she is not likely to have a very happy married life. That is all.

J A C K – I really don't see what on earth it matters to you where my country house is.

A L G E R N O N – It matters a great deal to me. We want another country house in the family very much. And of course if you and Gwendolen get married I should naturally stay the greater part of the year with you.

J A C K – You certainly won't do anything of the kind, if I have anything to say in the matter.

A L G E R N O N [*carelessly, while taking another sandwich*] You won't, dear boy. Gwendolen has one of those soft yielding natures that always have their own way. Besides, there is the question of Cecily. That requires clearing up.

J A C K – Cecily! What on earth do you mean? [A L G E R N O N *goes to bell and rings it. Then returns to tea-table and eats another sandwich.*] What do you mean, Algy, by Cecily? I don't know anyone of the name of Cecily . . . as far as I remember.

[*Enter* LANE.]

ALGERNON–Bring me that cigarette case Mr. Worthing left in the hall the last time he dined here.

LANE–Yes, sir.

[*Exit.*]

JACK–Do you mean to say you have had my cigarette case all this time? I wish to goodness you had let me know. I have been writing frantic letters to Scotland Yard about it. I was very nearly offering a reward.

ALGERNON–Well, I wish you would offer one. I happen to be more than usually hard up.

JACK–There is no good offering a reward now that the thing is found.

[*Enter* LANE *with the cigarette case on a salver.* ALGERNON *takes it.*]

ALGERNON–I think that is rather mean of you, Ernest, I must say. [*Opens case and examines it.*] However, it makes no matter, for, now that I look at the inscription again I find that the thing isn't yours after all.

JACK–Of course it is mine. You have seen me with it a hundred times. And you have no right whatsoever to look at what is written inside. It is a very ungentlemanly thing to read a private cigarette case.

ALGERNON–Oh! that is ridiculous. It is absurd to have a hard-and-fast rule about what one should read and what one shouldn't. One should read everything. That is the true basis of modern culture. More than half of modern culture depends on the unreadable.

JACK–I am not arguing on that point. I simply want my cigarette case back.

ALGERNON–Yes; but this isn't your cigarette case. This cigarette case is a present from someone of the name of Cecily, and you said you didn't know anyone of that name.

JACK–I said I didn't remember knowing anyone of that name. I do remember now. She is my aunt.

ALGERNON–Your aunt!

JACK–Yes. Charming old lady she is, too. Just give it back to me, Algy.

[*Goes across stage to take it.*]

ALGERNON [*retreating*] But why does she call herself little Cecily, if she is your aunt? [*Reading.*] "From little Cecily with her fondest love."

JACK–My dear fellow, what on earth is there in that? Some aunts are tall, some aunts are not tall. That is a matter that surely an aunt may be allowed to decide for herself. You seem to think that every aunt should be exactly like your aunt! That is absurd! There is a great variety in aunts. You can have aunts of any shape or size you like. My aunt is a small aunt. For Heaven's sake give me back my cigarette case.

[*Advances.*]

A L G E R N O N [*sheltering himself behind a table*] Yes, my dear fellow. But why does your aunt call you her uncle? "From little Cecily, with her fondest love, to her dear Uncle Jack." There is no objection, I admit, to an aunt being a small aunt, but why an aunt, no matter what her size may be, should call her own nephew her dear uncle, I can't make out. Besides, your name isn't Jack at all; it is Ernest.

J A C K – It isn't Ernest; it's Jack.

A L G E R N O N – You have always told me it was Ernest. I have introduced you to everyone as Ernest. You answer to the name of Ernest. You look as if your name was Ernest. It is perfectly absurd your saying your name isn't Ernest.

J A C K – Well, my name is Ernest in town but Jack in the country, and the cigarette case was given to me in the country.

A L G E R N O N – Yes, but that does not account for the fact that your Aunt Cecily calls you her uncle. Come, my dear fellow, you had better have the thing out.

J A C K – My dear Algy, you talk exactly as if you were a dentist. It is very vulgar to talk like a dentist when one isn't a dentist. It produces a false impression.

A L G E R N O N – Well, that is what dentists usually do.[6] Now go on! Tell me the whole thing. I may mention that I have always suspected you of being a confirmed and secret Bunburyist; and I am quite sure of it now.

J A C K – What on earth do you mean by a Bunburyist?

A L G E R N O N – I'll reveal to you the meaning of that incomparable expression as soon as you are kind enough to inform me why you are Ernest in town and Jack in the country.

J A C K – Well, produce my cigarette case first.

A L G E R N O N – Here it is. [*Hands cigarette case.*] Now produce your explanation, and pray make it remarkable. The bore about most explanations is that they are never half so remarkable as the things they try to explain. That is why modern science is so absolutely tedious.

J A C K – My dear fellow, there is nothing remarkable about this explanation at all. In fact it is perfectly ordinary. Old Mr. Cardew, who adopted me when I was a little boy, made me in his will guardian to his grand-daughter, Miss Cecily Cardew. Cecily, who addresses me as

6 Insertion from typescript of first act giving omitted portion of text.

her uncle from motives of respect, resides at my place in the country under the charge of her admirable governess, Miss Prism.

A L G E R N O N – Where is that place in the country, by the way?

J A C K – That is nothing to you, dear boy. You are not going to be invited. . . . I may tell you candidly that the place is not in Shropshire.

A L G E R N O N – I suspected that, my dear fellow! I have Bunburyed all over Shropshire on two separate occasions. Now, go on. Why are you Jack in the country and Ernest in town?

J A C K – My dear Algy, I don't know whether you will be able to understand my real motives. You are hardly serious enough. When one is placed in the position of a guardian, one has to adopt a very high moral tone on all subjects. It is one's duty to do so. And as a high moral tone can hardly be said to conduce very much to either one's health or happiness if carried to excess, in order to get up to town I have always pretended I have a younger brother of the name of Ernest, who lives in the Albany, and gets into most dreadful scrapes. That, my dear Algy, is the whole truth pure and simple.[7]

A L G E R N O N – The truth is rarely pure and never simple. Modern life would be very tedious if it were either, and modern literature a complete impossibility!

J A C K – That wouldn't be at all a bad thing.

A L G E R N O N – Literary criticism is not your forte, my dear fellow. You shouldn't try it. What you really are is a Bunburyist. I was quite right in saying you were a Bunburyist. You are one of the best Bunburyists I know.

J A C K – What on earth do you mean?

A L G E R N O N – You have invented a very useful younger brother called Ernest, in order that you may be able to come up to town as often as you like. I have invented an invaluable permanent invalid called Bunbury, in order that I may go down into the country whenever I choose.

J A C K – What nonsense!

A L G E R N O N – It isn't nonsense. Bunbury is perfectly invaluable. If it wasn't for Bunbury's extraordinary bad health, for instance, I wouldn't be able to dine with you at Willis's to-night, for I have been really engaged to Aunt Augusta for more than a week.

J A C K – I haven't asked you to dine with me anywhere to-night.

A L G E R N O N – I know. You are absurdly careless about sending out invitations. It is very foolish of you. Nothing annoys people so much as not receiving invitations. The last five times I have dined with you I have had to ask myself. It gets a bore at the end. The next time I shall certainly not ask myself at all. I'll simply come.

[7] End of insertion.

JACK – You had much better dine with your Aunt Augusta.

ALGERNON – I haven't the smallest intention of doing anything of the kind. To begin with, I dined there on Monday, and once a week is quite enough. In the second place, whenever I do dine together I am always treated as a near relation, and sent down with either no woman at all, or two. In the third place, I know perfectly well whom she will place me next to-night. She will place me next Mary Farquhar, who always flirts with her own husband across the dinner-table. That is not very pleasant. Indeed, it is not even decent . . . and that sort of thing is enormously on the increase. The amount of women in London who flirt with their own husbands is perfectly scandalous. It looks so bad. It is like washing one's clean linen in public.

JACK – Well, if Gwendolen accepts me I shall naturally kill my brother. And I strongly advise you to do the same with your friend Bunbury. Inventions of that kind are all very well in their way, but they are invariably found out at the end.

ALGERNON – I don't at all agree with you. My experience of life is that whenever one tells a lie one is corroborated on every side. When one tells the truth one is left in a very lonely and painful position, and no one believes a word one says. As for killing Bunbury, that would be worse than heartless; it would be very foolish. I assure you I haven't the smallest intention of doing anything of the kind. And if you ever get married, which seems to me extremely problematic, you will be very glad to know Bunbury. A man who marries without knowing a Bunbury has a very tedious time of it.

JACK – That is nonsense. If I marry a charming girl like Gwendolen, and she is the only girl I ever saw in my life that I would marry, I certainly won't want to know Bunbury.

ALGERNON – Then your wife will. You don't seem to realize, my dear fellow, that in married life three is company and two is none.

JACK [*sententiously*] That, my dear Algy, is the theory that the corrupt French Drama has been propounding for the last fifty years.

ALGERNON – Yes; and that the happy English home has proved in half the time. That is the worst of the English. They are always degrading truths into facts. And when truths become facts they lose all their intellectual value.

JACK – Do you always really understand what you say, Algy?

ALGERNON [*after consideration*] Yes . . . if I listen attentively.

JACK – Then you have certainly more brains than I have given you credit for.

ALGERNON – My dear fellow, until you believe that I have got absolute genius there will always be a slight coldness between us. [*A ring.*] Ah! there is Aunt Augusta, at last. Now, if I get her out of the way for ten minutes, so that you can have an opportunity for proposing to Gwendolen, may I dine with you to-night at Willis's?

J A C K – Certainly; provided of course that Gwendolen accepts me.

A L G E R N O N – My dear fellow, that is not my business.

J A C K – Well, if she won't have me, I shan't have much appetite for dinner.

A L G E R N O N – Oh! I don't mind that. There will be all the more for me. However, if you won't agree to have me to dine in any case, I'll take Gwendolen off into the music-room, and leave you alone with Aunt Augusta.

J A C K – Good heavens, my dear fellow, don't do that. I'll agree to anything.

A L G E R N O N – Yes, but you must be serious about it. I hate people who are not serious about meals.

[*Enter* SERVANT.]

L A N E – Lady Brancaster and Miss Fairfax.

[*Enter* LADY BRANCASTER *and* GWENDOLEN.]

A L G E R N O N [*going to meet them*] Good day, Aunt Augusta. [*To* GWENDOLEN.] Dear me, you are smart this afternoon.

G W E N D O L E N – I am always smart.

A L G E R N O N – I know; that is why I said it. If a woman isn't always smart she is never smart.

G W E N D O L E N – Now don't try to be clever, Algy. It doesn't become you at all.

A L G E R N O N – It is not becoming to anybody.

G W E N D O L E N – On the contrary. It is excessively becoming to me.

L A D Y B R A N C A S T E R – Now, children, don't quarrel. So sorry, Algernon, if we are a little late. But I was obliged to call on dear Lady Harbury. I hadn't been there since her poor husband's death. I never saw a woman so altered; she looks quite twenty years younger. [*Sees* JACK *and bows coldly to him.*] Good afternoon, Mr. Worthing.

A L G E R N O N – I am afraid, Aunt Augusta, I have rather bad news in a way to tell you.

L A D Y B R A N C A S T E R – Now I hope no new debts, Algernon. Of course I never mention anything about them to your uncle. Indeed, as you know, I never mention anything to him at all.

A L G E R N O N – Oh! my debts are all right.

L A D Y B R A N C A S T E R – I am delighted to hear it.

A L G E R N O N – I mean they are just the same as they used to be. It is merely that I shall have to give up dining with you to-night. It is a great bore, but the fact is I have just had a telegram to say that poor Bunbury is very ill again. They seem to think I should be with him. I have promised to go down by the 6.40 from King's Cross.

1447

LADY BRANCASTER – It is very strange. This Mr. Bunbury seems to suffer from curiously bad health.

ALGERNON – Yes; poor Bunbury is a sad invalid.

LADY BRANCASTER – I must say, Algernon, that I think it is high time that this Mr. Bunbury made up his mind whether he was going to live or not. This shilly-shallying with the question is absurd. It shows a very ill-balanced intellect and a lack of decision that is quite lamentable. I should like to see him and speak to him on the subject.

ALGERNON – Oh! Bunbury doesn't come to town. He lives quite the life of a recluse.

LADY BRANCASTER – Well, considering his state of health I am not surprised. But someone should speak to him.

GWENDOLEN – Dear mamma, I must say that I think it is very nice of Algy to show such sympathy for his friend Mr. Bunbury.

LADY BRANCASTER – I do not at all approve of this modern sympathy with invalids. I consider it quite morbid. Illness of any kind is hardly a thing to be encouraged in others. Health is the primary duty of life. I am always telling that to your poor father. But he never seems to take any notice . . . as far as any improvement in his state of health goes. Well, Algernon, of course, if you are obliged to be by the bedside of Mr. Bunbury I have nothing more to say. It is extremely inconvenient as it will put my table out. Your uncle will have to dine upstairs, that is all. Fortunately he is accustomed to that. . . . I hope, Algernon, I may rely on you for next Saturday evening without fail. It is, as you know, my last reception this season and I count on you to arrange my music for me as usual. I would be much obliged if you would ask Mr. Bunbury, from me, to be kind enough not to have a relapse on Saturday morning.

ALGERNON – I'll certainly give him your message and I think you can rely on his being all right on Saturday. By the way, I am very glad you mentioned next Saturday, because I want to talk to you about the music.

LADY BRANCASTER – Ah! yes. That is very important. One wants something that will encourage conversation, particularly at the end of the season when everyone has practically said whatever they had to say.

ALGERNON – Ah! that is the difficulty, Aunt Augusta. You see, if one plays good music, they don't listen, and if one plays bad music they don't talk. But I'll tell you my ideas on the subject. I don't care to talk to Gwendolen about music any longer. She has grown far too intellectual during the three months. She seems to think that music does not contain enough useful information.

GWENDOLEN – Algy!! How dare you be so impertinent? And you don't know anything about the University Extension Scheme at all; I never return from any one of those lectures without having been excessively admired.

LADY BRANCASTER—Well, I can't say that I think music contains too much useful information. My objection to modern music is that it seems to discuss every possible topic far too openly, especially orchestral music which is so popular at present. A little more reticence would be an advantage.

ALGERNON—Well, will you come into the next room, Aunt Augusta? And I'll show the programme I have arranged.

LADY BRANCASTER—Thank you, Algernon. It is very kind of you to have thought of it. One can't be too carefull now-a-days. There are so many young girls in society and they know so much more than they should. I regret anything that tampers with the ignorance of a young girl. Ignorance is like a beautiful exotic fruit. Touch it and the bloom is gone. . . . But I don't think, Algernon, I could possibly leave Gwendolen and Mr. Worthing alone. . . . You see, like most people whom one meets everywhere, one doesn't know anything about him. And he seems to be paying considerable attentions to Gwendolen, who I regret to say does not treat him with the marked coldness that—

ALGERNON—Oh! that is all right, Aunt Augusta. He is not at all in love with her. He was just telling me so when you came in. The fact simply is that they are both very much interested in questions like the "Better housing of the upper classes," [and] "The bringing of Culture within the easy reach of the rich."

LADY BRANCASTER—Ah! those are subjects that I do not consider at all dangerous. . . . They are not in any way practical. Gwendolen, I am going with Algernon into the music-room for a moment to expurgate the programme for Saturday night. I should like your father to be able to be present. . . . I will see you again, no doubt, Mr. Worthing.

[JACK *bows. Exit* LADY BRANCASTER *with* ALGERNON.]

JACK—I would like, Miss Fairfax, to take advantage of Lady Brancaster's temporary absence.

GWENDOLEN—Yes, Mr. Worthing, I would certainly advise you to do so.

JACK [*a little taken aback*] Ahem! . . . I hope that what I am going to say to you will not be in any way a shock to you.

GWENDOLEN—Oh! I am sure it won't. I have never been shocked in my life. I think to be shocked by anything shows a very low ethical standard. Nobody is ever shocked now-a-days except the clergy and the middle classes. It is the profession of the one and the punishment of the other.

JACK—Ever since I met you I have admired you more than any girl I have ever met, since I met you.

GWENDOLEN—Yes, I know. And I often wish that in public, at any rate, you had been more demonstrative. For me you have always had an irresistible fascination. Even before I met you. [JACK *looks at her in amazement.*] We live, as you know, Mr. Worthing, in an age of ideals. And my ideal has always been to love some one of the name of Ernest. There is something in that name that inspires absolute confidence. The moment Algernon first mentioned to me that he had a friend called Ernest I adored you. None of his other friends had been called Ernest, nor indeed anyone I had ever met. The name, fortunately for my peace of mind, is, as far as my own experience goes, extremely rare.

JACK—Then you love me, Gwendolen?

GWENDOLEN—Passionately.

JACK—Darling Gwendolen!

GWENDOLEN—My own Ernest!

[*They embrace.*]

JACK—Of course, you don't really mean to say that you couldn't love me if my name wasn't Ernest?

GWENDOLEN—But your name is Ernest.

JACK—Yes, I know it is. But supposing it wasn't? Supposing it was something else? Do you mean to say you couldn't love me then?

GWENDOLEN—Ah! that is clearly a metaphysical speculation, and like all metaphysical speculations has very little reference at all to the actual facts of real life, as we know them.

JACK—Personally, darling, to speak quite candidly, I don't care much about the name of Ernest. . . . I don't think the name suits me at all.

GWENDOLEN—It suits you perfectly. It is a divine name. It has a music of its own. It produces vibrations.

JACK—Well, really, Gwendolen, I must say that I think there are lots of other much nicer names. I think Jack, for instance, a charming name.

GWENDOLEN—Jack? . . . No, there is very little music in the name Jack, if any at all, indeed. It does not thrill. It produces absolutely no vibrations. . . . I have known several Jacks, and they all, without exception, were more than usually plain. Besides, Jack is a domesticity for John, is it not?

JACK—Yes, a diminutive.

GWENDOLEN—It is the same thing. I pity any woman who is married to a man called John. She would probably have a very tedious life. She would probably never be allowed to know the pleasure of a moment's solitude.

JACK—Gwendolen, we must get married at once. There is no time to be lost.

GWENDOLEN [*surprised*] Married, Mr. Worthing?

J A C K [*astounded*] Well . . . surely. You know I love you and you led me to believe, Miss Fairfax, that you loved me, too.

G W E N D O L E N – I adore you. But you haven't proposed to me yet. Nothing has been said at all about marriage. The subject has not even been touched on. We were discussing love. That is a different thing, surely?

J A C K – Well . . . may I propose to you now?

G W E N D O L E N – I think it would be an admirable opportunity. To spare you any possible disappointment, Mr. Worthing, I think it only fair to tell you quite frankly beforehand that I am fully determined to accept you.

J A C K [*going down on his knees*] Gwendolen!

G W E N D O L E N – Yes, Mr. Worthing, what have you got to say to me?

J A C K – You know what I have got to say to you.

G W E N D O L E N – Yes, but you don't say it.

J A C K – Gwendolen! will you marry me?

G W E N D O L E N – Of course I will, darling. How long you have been about it! I am afraid you have had very little experience in how to propose.

J A C K – My own one, I have never loved anyone but you.

G W E N D O L E N – I know that. But men often propose for practice. I know Algy does. He tells me so. What sweet eyes you have, Ernest! They are quite, quite blue. I hope you will always look at me just like that, especially when there are other people present.

[*Enter* LADY BRANCASTER.]

L A D Y B R A N C A S T E R – Mr. Worthing! Rise, sir, from this semi-recumbent posture. It is most indecorous.

[JACK *rises.*]

G W E N D O L E N – Mamma! I must beg you to retire. This is no place for you. Besides, Mr. Worthing has not quite finished yet.

L A D Y B R A N C A S T E R – Finished what, may I ask?

G W E N D O L E N – I am engaged to Mr. Worthing, mamma. He was proposing to me when you interrupted us. I am sure he has a great deal more to say. I know I have.

L A D Y B R A N C A S T E R – Is the modern idea that the engagement should come first, and the proposal afterwards?

G W E N D O L E N – Yes, mamma.

L A D Y B R A N C A S T E R – I cannot say that I approve of so strange an inversion of the more customary procedure in such matters. But, as I am told, you are fond of useful information, Gwendolen,—a taste of which I cannot say that I approve in one of your years—you will be interested to learn that you are not engaged at all. When you do become engaged to anyone, I, or your father, should his health permit him, will inform you of the fact. An engagement should come on a

1451

young girl as a surprise, pleasant or unpleasant, as the case may be. It is hardly a matter that she could be allowed to arrange for herself. . . . And now I have a few questions to put to you, Mr. Worthing.

J A C K – I shall be charmed to reply to any questions, Lady Brancaster.

G W E N D O L E N – You mean, if you know the answers to them.

L A D Y   B R A N C A S T E R   [*continuing*] While I am putting the questions, you, Gwendolen, will wait for me in the carriage.

G W E N D O L E N   [*reproachfully*] Mamma!

L A D Y   B R A N C A S T E R   [*severely*] In the carriage, Gwendolen! [G W E N-D O L E N *and* J A C K *blow kisses to each other behind* L A D Y   B R A N C A S T E R'S *back.* L A D Y   B R A N C A S T E R *looks vaguely about as if she could not understand what the noise was. Finally turns round.*] Gwendolen, the carriage! And at once.

G W E N D O L E N – Yes, mamma.

[*Exit.*]

L A D Y   B R A N C A S T E R   [*sitting down*] You can take a chair.

[*Looks in her pocket for notebook and pencil.*]

J A C K – Thank you, Lady Brancaster, I prefer standing up.

[*Pulls out cigarette case from his pocket and opens it.* L A D Y   B R A N C A S T E R *glares at him. He looks ashamed and replaces it quietly in his pocket.*]

L A D Y   B R A N C A S T E R   [*pencil and notebook in hand*] You are not down on my list of eligible young men, Mr. Worthing, although I have the same list as the dear Duchess of Bolton has. We work together, in fact. However, I am quite ready to enter your name as a possible candidate, should your answers be what a really affectionate mother requires.

J A C K – Thank you, Lady Brancaster.

L A D Y   B R A N C A S T E R – How old are you?

J A C K – I was twenty-five my last birthday. My birthday is in the month of May.

L A D Y   B R A N C A S T E R – A very good age to be married at. I have always been of opinion that a man who desires to get married should either know everything or nothing. You, I presume, know nothing.

J A C K – Nothing at all, Lady Brancaster.

L A D Y   B R A N C A S T E R – I am very pleased to hear it. I do not approve of anything that tampers with a young man's natural ignorance. Ignorance is like a delicate exotic fruit. Touch it and the bloom is gone.[8] What is your income?

J A C K – Between seven and eight thousand a year.

---

[8] This is a repetition of her speech on p. 1449 where Lady Brancaster uses the same simile. The earlier passage was taken out before the November typescript and does not of course appear in the first edition.

LADY BRANCASTER [*makes note in her book*] In land, or in investments?

JACK—In investments, Lady Brancaster.

LADY BRANCASTER—That is satisfactory. Land, now-a-days, is simply a question of life-duties and death-duties. Both of them intolerable.

JACK—I have a country house, with some land of course attached, but I don't depend on that for my income.

LADY BRANCASTER—A country house! How many bedrooms?

JACK—I really don't know, Lady Brancaster; I would have to ask the housekeeper.

LADY BRANCASTER—Well, that point can be cleared up afterwards. [*Makes note.*] You have a town house, I hope? A girl with a simple, unspoiled nature, like Gwendolen, could hardly be expected to reside in the country.

JACK—Well, I own a house in Belgrave Square, but it is let. I have never lived in it. Of course, I can get it back whenever I like.

LADY BRANCASTER—What number, in Belgrave Square?

JACK—149.

LADY BRANCASTER [*examines a Red Book*] That is the unfashionable side. But I do not wish to seem in any way to speak slightingly of Belgrave Square—There is far too little reverence shown, now-a-days, as it is, for the few places left to us in England that are of any social importance. I merely mentioned that the side was not the fashionable side. But that could be altered.

JACK—Do you mean the fashion, or the side, Lady Brancaster?

LADY BRANCASTER—Both, if necessary, I suppose. And now I have got your age, income, and address. What are your politics?

JACK—Well, I am afraid I really have none, Lady Brancaster. I am a Liberal Unionist, I suppose.

LADY BRANCASTER—Oh, they count as Tories. They dine with us. Or come in the evening, at any rate. You have, of course, no sympathy of any kind with the Radical Party?

JACK—Oh, I don't want to pit the asses against the classes, if that is what you mean, Lady Brancaster.

LADY BRANCASTER—That is exactly what I mean. . . . Ahem . . . you have had, I suppose, the ordinary maladies of childhood? You are not likely to develop measles or the whooping cough? You will not bring an epidemic into the family?

JACK—My health is—

LADY BRANCASTER—And now about your family. . . . Christian name, Ernest?

JACK—Yes.

LADY BRANCASTER—Surname, Worthing?

Oscar Wilde

J A C K – Yes.

L A D Y   B R A N C A S T E R – I think that Worthing-Worthing with a hyphen would be better. I have known a hyphen produce a wonderful social effect, when judiciously used. However, that point can stand over for the present. . . . Are your parents living?

J A C K – I have lost both my parents.

L A D Y   B R A N C A S T E R – Both? . . . To lose one parent may be regarded as a misfortune. To lose both seems like carelessness. Who was your father? A country gentleman?

takes it literally

J A C K – I am afraid I don't really know, Lady Brancaster.

L A D Y   B R A N C A S T E R – May I ask what you mean, Mr. Worthing?

J A C K – Well, the fact is, Lady Brancaster, I said I had lost my parents. The truth is that my parents seem to have lost me. . . . I don't actually know who I am. I was . . . well, I was found.

actually is true

L A D Y   B R A N C A S T E R – Found, sir!

J A C K   [*defiantly*] Yes, Lady Brancaster, the late Mr. Thomas Cardew, an old gentleman of a very charitable and kindly nature, found me, and gave me the name of Worthing because he happened to have a ticket for Worthing in his pocket at the time. Worthing is a place in Sussex.

L A D Y   B R A N C A S T E R – Where did this charitable gentleman find you?

J A C K   [*gravely*] In a hand-bag.

L A D Y   B R A N C A S T E R – A hand-bag?

J A C K   [*very seriously*] Yes, Lady Brancaster, I was in a hand-bag—a somewhat large leather hand-bag, with handles to it—an ordinary hand-bag in fact.

L A D Y   B R A N C A S T E R – Where did Mr. Cardew come across this ordinary hand-bag?

J A C K – In the cloak-room at Victoria Station. It was given to him in mistake for his own. He did not discover the error till he arrived at his own house. All subsequent efforts to ascertain who I was were unavailing.

L A D Y   B R A N C A S T E R – The cloak-room at Victoria Station, I think you said?

J A C K – Yes. The cloak-room at Victoria Station, Brighton line.

L A D Y   B R A N C A S T E R – The line is immaterial. Mr. Worthing, I confess I feel somewhat bewildered by what you have just told me. To be born, or at any rate bred, in a hand-bag, whether it had handles or not, seems to me to display a contempt for family life that reminds one of the worst excesses of the French Revolution. And I presume you know what that unfortunate movement led to? As for the locality in which the hand-bag was found, a cloak-room at a railway station might serve

1454

to conceal a social indiscretion—has probably, indeed, been used for that purpose before now—but it could hardly be regarded as an assured basis for a recognized position in good society. Indeed, I do not think that under any circumstances the "Morning Post" could possibly notice you, although that paper has become sadly democratic lately; which is strange, as it is only a few years since it lowered its price in order to suit the diminished incomes of the aristocracy.

JACK—My dear Lady Brancaster, to speak to you candidly, I don't care twopence whether the "Morning Post" notices me or not. Who on earth would care?

LADY BRANCASTER—The price of the paper is, I am glad to say, merely one penny. And, if you will allow me to say so, I am sorry, for your own sake, to hear you speak in slighting terms of that admirable journal. It is the only document of our time from which the history of the English people in the XIXth century could be written with any regard to decorum or even decency.

[*Rises to go.*]

JACK—May I ask you then what you would advise me to do? I need not say I would do anything in the world to ensure Gwendolen's happiness.

LADY BRANCASTER—I would strongly advise you, Mr. Worthing, to try and acquire some relations as soon as possible, and to make a definite effort to produce at any rate one parent, of either sex, before the season is quite over.

JACK—Well, I don't see how I could possibly manage to do that. I can produce the hand-bag at any moment. It is in my bedroom at home. I really think that should satisfy you, Lady Brancaster.

LADY BRANCASTER [*indignantly*] Me, sir! What has it to do with me? You do not, I sincerely trust, suppose for an instant that I would tolerate as a son-in-law a gentleman who by his own admission is closely connected with unclaimed luggage.

JACK—Do you mean to say, Lady Brancaster, you won't allow my engagement to Gwendolen?

LADY BRANCASTER [*rising*] You can hardly imagine, sir, that I and Lord Brancaster would dream of allowing our only daughter—a girl brought up with the utmost care—to marry into a cloak-room and form an alliance with a parcel? [JACK *starts indignantly.*] Kindly open the door for me, sir. You will, of course, understand that for the future there is to be no communication of any kind between you and Miss Fairfax.

[*Exit.*]

[ALGERNON *inside strikes up the Wedding March.*
JACK *looks perfectly furious.*]

JACK [*going to door of room*] For God's sake, don't play that ghastly tune, Algy! How idiotic you are!

[*Enter* ALGERNON *cheerily.*]

ALGERNON – Well? How did it all go off? Did you get a chance of speaking to Gwendolen? I did my best for you. I got my dear aunt out of the way for a whole quarter of an hour, didn't I? Bunbury is quite invaluable. Everybody should have a Bunbury.

JACK – I had a long, rather serious talk with Gwendolen.

ALGERNON – Well?

JACK – Oh, she is as right as a trivet. We are engaged.

ALGERNON – My dear old boy, I am delighted to hear it. There is no chap in the world I would sooner see Gwendolen married to than yourself.

JACK – For heaven's sake, Algy, stop. I know perfectly well you are going on to tell me that you are quite sure I'll make your cousin a good husband, or some . . . nonsense of that kind.

ALGERNON – Oh, no good chap makes a good husband. If a chap makes a good husband there must have been something rather peculiar about him when he was a bachelor. To be a good husband requires considerable practice.

JACK – I think your views quite idiotic, absurd, and ridiculous. You'll find that out for yourself, too, some day, if you can get a charming good nice sweet girl to accept you. But I don't suppose you ever will be able to do that. I don't suppose you would take the trouble. No, all I said was that no one likes to be formally told, in a serious voice, that it is confidently expected that he will make a good husband. It sounds so tedious and second-rate.

ALGERNON – But, I didn't tell it to you.

JACK – Well, I never said you did. I was talking quite generally.

[*A pause.*]

ALGERNON – Are the cigarettes there?

JACK – I don't know.

ALGERNON – Oh, I see them. They are just on the mantelpiece behind you, old boy.

JACK – Oh! . . . [*Hands them and takes one himself.*] You smoke far too much, Algy. You are always smoking.

[ALGERNON *lights a cigarette. So does* JACK.]

JACK – I love Gwendolen; Gwendolen is the most perfect darling in the whole world: there is not a girl in England fit to hold a candle to her. She is far too good for me, I know.

ALGERNON – My dear fellow, all women are far too good for the men they marry. That is why men tire of their wives so quickly.

JACK – I don't care much about discussing that question. It is rather too abstract a question for 6.30 p.m. [*Pulling out watch.*] All I said was that Gwendolen was the smartest girl in London and she is. Her mother is perfectly unbearable. Never met such a Gorgon. . . . I don't really know what a Gorgon is like, but I am quite sure that Lady Brancaster is one. She is a monster, without being a myth, which is rather unfair of her. . . . I beg your pardon, Algy, I suppose I shouldn't talk about your own aunt in that way before you.

A L G E R N O N – My dear boy, I love hearing my relations abused. It is the only thing that makes me put up with them at all. I hate the whole set myself, except Gwendolen, who is a darling; and Mary Farquhar perhaps when she isn't chattering about her husband; and Gladys when she isn't chattering about someone else's husband; and dear old Uncle Geoffrey who isn't half a bad sort in his silly way, considering what a thoroughly typical woman Aunt Augusta is. But as a broad general rule, relations are simply a tedious pack of people, who haven't got the remotest knowledge of how to live, nor the smallest instinct about when to die.

J A C K – Ah! I haven't got any relations. Don't know anything about relations.

A L G E R N O N – You are a lucky fellow. Relations never lend one any money, and won't give one credit, even for genius. They are a sort of aggravated form of the public.

J A C K – Your aunt is strongly of opinion I should have relations. She [*Lights a cigarette.*] talks of them as if they were things one could buy in a shop.

A L G E R N O N – Oh, I should think one could get them at sales, at the end of the season. One can always pick up unfashionable things at sales. One gets them [at] great bargains, I am told. So Aunt Augusta has been worrying you about your family, has she?

J A C K [*slowly*] Yes . . . about my want of it. [*Throws cigarette away.*]

A L G E R N O N – And what did Aunt Augusta say?

J A C K – Oh, she was positively violent. I never heard such language in the whole course of my life from anyone. She might just as well have been in a pulpit. I shouldn't be at all surprised if she took to philanthropy or something of the kind and abused her fellow creatures for the rest of her life.

A L G E R N O N – Good heavens! do tell me what she said.

J A C K – Oh, everything she shouldn't have said. She said amongst other things that she couldn't possibly be expected to allow a girl like Gwendolen to "marry into a cloak-room and form an alliance with a parcel."

A L G E R N O N [*laughing*] I am bound to say I should rather like to have heard Aunt Augusta say that.

JACK—I didn't like it. I am afraid we hold different views about what polite conversation should be. Besides, it is absurd her saying that I was a parcel. I wasn't. A parcel is a thing done up in brown paper with string round it. I was in a carpet-bag. That is quite a different thing. There is no reason why one shouldn't be in a carpet-bag if one chooses. I know lots of fellows who have been in very much worse places, when they were old enough to know better. I believe I was only about twelve months old, myself, at the time. I think a baby of that age should always be in a carpet-bag. Much safer than a perambulator and not nearly so annoying to other people. I think I set a very good example to other babies. [*Lights a cigarette.*] And after all what does it matter whether a man has ever had a father and mother or not? Mothers, of course, are all right. They pay a chap's bills and don't bother him. But fathers bother a chap and never pay his bills. I don't know a single chap at the club who speaks to his father.

ALGERNON—Yes. Fathers are certainly not popular just at present.

JACK—Popular! I bet you anything you like that there is not a single chap, of all the chaps that you and I know, who would be seen walking down St. James's Street with his own father.

[*Throws cigarette away.*]

ALGERNON [*taking up evening newspaper*] Oh, there are ups and downs in everything. At present fathers are at a terrible discount. They are like these chaps, the minor poets. They are never even quoted.

JACK—Very good thing, too . . . in both cases, I should think. [*A pause.*] Anything in the papers?

ALGERNON [*still reading*] Nothing.

JACK—What a comfort!

ALGERNON—There never is anything in the papers, as far as I can see.

JACK—I think there is usually a great deal too much in them. They are always bothering one about people one doesn't know, one has never met, and one doesn't care twopence about. Brutes!

ALGERNON—I think people one hasn't met are charming. I'm very much interested at present in a girl I have never met; very much interested indeed.

JACK—Oh, that is nonsense!

ALGERNON—It isn't.

JACK—Well, I won't argue about the matter. You always want to argue about things.

ALGERNON—That is exactly what things were originally made for.

JACK—Upon my word, if I thought that, I'd shoot myself. . . . [*A pause.*] You don't think there is any chance of Gwendolen becoming like her mother in about a hundred and fifty years, do you, Algy?

ALGERNON [*drawlingly and sententiously*] All women become like their mothers. That is their tragedy. No man does. That is his.

JACK—Is that clever?

ALGERNON—It is perfectly phrased! and quite as true as anything in modern life should be.

JACK—I am sick to death of cleverness. Everybody is clever now-a-days. You can't go anywhere without meeting clever people. The thing has become an absolute public nuisance. I wish to goodness we had a few fools left.

ALGERNON—We have.

JACK—I should extremely like to meet them. What do they talk about?

ALGERNON—The fools? Oh! about the clever people, of course.

JACK—What fools! . . . [*Throws cigarette away.*] Don't think much of these cigarettes of yours, Algy.

ALGERNON—Yes, I see you throw them away almost as soon as you have lit them.

JACK—I am tired of gold-tipped cigarettes. You can get them quite cheap now. No particular advantage in smoking them any longer.

ALGERNON—Ah! those cigarettes are rather smart. They have got my monogram on each of them.

JACK [*sneeringly*] I don't quite see how that can make the tobacco any better.

ALGERNON—It does, to me.

JACK—Oh! you are an egotist, Algy.

ALGERNON [*imperturbable*] I am, dear boy. That is why my temper is so astoundingly good.

JACK—Did I tell you that Gwendolen said to me that she wouldn't have loved me if my name hadn't been Ernest?

ALGERNON—No.

JACK—She did say it. She said she couldn't love me under any other name. Gwendolen is, of course, the most beautiful girl in the whole world, and quite the dearest. But I must say that I think that was rather silly of her. The fact is women aren't nearly so clever as we men say they are.

ALGERNON—No; but they are much cleverer than we men think they are.

JACK—Oh, that is cynical. I hate cynical things. It is so perfectly easy to be cynical.

ALGERNON—It isn't easy to be anything now-a-days. Such a lot of damned competition about the place.

[*A pause.*]

JACK—What are you doing to-morrow?

A L G E R N O N [*pleasantly and buoyantly*] To-morrow, my dear fellow? To-morrow I go to the country, Bunburying.[9]

J A C K – Nonsense.

A L G E R N O N – I do really. I start in the morning. It will probably be a capital day for Bunburying.

J A C K – Where are you going to Bunbury at?

A L G E R N O N – I'll tell you when I come back. Come and sup at the Club to-morrow night at twelve, and I'll possibly let you know whether I have had a successful Bunbury or not.

J A C K – Oh, I don't want to know anything about it. All I say is that you'll get yourself into a serious scrape some day.

A L G E R N O N – I like scrapes. They are the only things that are never serious.

J A C K – I have made up my mind to kill that brother of mine.

A L G E R N O N – It is rather heartless of you. He has been a very good brother to you, and very useful.

J A C K – My dear fellow, you have never had a brother. I have had a brother for the last eight months. Quite long enough for anyone to have a brother, I should fancy.

A L G E R N O N – Well, Bunbury is no relation of mine, but I wouldn't kill him for anything. I couldn't live without Bunbury.

J A C K – Ah! I am engaged you see, and I think it is high time to give up all that sort of nonsense.

A L G E R N O N – Then I suppose you are going to tell Gwendolen the truth?

J A C K [*in a very patronising manner*] My dear fellow, the truth isn't quite the sort of thing one tells to a nice sweet refined girl. What extraordinary ideas you have about the way to behave to women!

A L G E R N O N – The only way to behave to women is to make love to them.

J A C K – Oh, that is nonsense.

A L G E R N O N – What about the young lady whose guardian you are! Miss Cardew?

J A C K – Oh! Cecily is all right. Before the end of the week I shall have got rid of my brother. . . . I think I'll probably kill him in Paris.

A L G E R N O N – Why Paris?

---

[9] In the original manuscript of this act the second entrance of Gwendolen and her conversation with Jack, in which she asks for the address of his country house, are omitted. Since Algernon does not know where it is, this scene is essential to the action, as otherwise he would not know how to find Cecily. The passage, in the author's hand on three pages, was sent to the typewriting agency; it is marked: "page 38 of Act I," and was apparently inserted in the first or September typescript. It appears in the November typescript, in somewhat shortened form.

JACK – Oh! less trouble—no nonsense about a funeral and that sort of thing—Yes, I'll kill him in Paris. . . . Apoplexy will do perfectly well. Lots of people die of apoplexy, quite suddenly, don't they?

ALGERNON – Yes, but it's hereditary, my dear fellow. It's a sort of thing that runs in families.

JACK – Good heavens, then I certainly won't choose that. What can I say?

ALGERNON – Oh, say the influenza.

JACK – Oh, no! That wouldn't sound probable at all. Far too many people have had it. The thing is quite played out.

ALGERNON – Oh well, say anything you like. Say a severe chill. That's all right.

JACK – You are sure a severe chill isn't hereditary or anything dreadful of that kind?

ALGERNON – Of course it isn't.

JACK – Very well then. That is settled. Ernest is carried off by a severe chill in Paris. I'll wear mourning for him of course; that would be only decent. I don't at all mind wearing mourning. I think that all black, with a good pearl pin, rather smart. Then I'll go down home and break the news to my household. Of course, I know they will insist on being awfully sympathetic about it. But I don't mind that. The thing will be forgotten in a week.

ALGERNON – But I thought you said that . . . Miss Cardew was a little too much interested in your brother Ernest?

JACK – Oh, that is all right. Cecily is not a romantic girl at all. She has got a capital appetite, and goes [on] long walks, and everything of that kind.

ALGERNON – I should rather like to see Cecily.

JACK – I will take very good care you never do. And you are not to speak of her as Cecily.

ALGERNON – Ah! I believe she is plain. Yes, I know perfectly well what she is like. She is one of those dull, intellectual girls one meets all over the place. Girls who have got large minds and large feet. I am sure she is more than usually plain, and I suspect she is about 39 and looks it.

JACK – She happens to be excessively pretty, and she is only just eighteen.

ALGERNON – Have you told Gwendolen that you have an excessively pretty young ward who is only just eighteen?

JACK – Oh! one doesn't blurt these things out to people. Life is a question of tact. One leads up to the thing gradually. Probably half an hour after they have met, they will be calling each other sister.

1461

ALGERNON – Women only do that when they have had a fearful quarrel, and called each other a lot of other things first.

JACK – What nonsense you talk! What on earth should Gwendolen and Cecily quarrel about?

ALGERNON – You and I quarrel, my dear fellow.

JACK – Oh! I quarrel with you because you never lose your temper. You are perfectly maddening sometimes, in that way.

ALGERNON – I think it is very nice of me not to lose my temper.

JACK – It is nothing of the kind. A quarrel is a sort of thing like a . . . oh! like a duet in music, I should think. If the other person does not do exactly the same thing as one does oneself, the whole business is a failure.

ALGERNON – My dear boy, if we want to get a good table at the Savoy, we really must go and dress. Do you know it is nearly seven?

JACK – Oh! it is always nearly seven.

ALGERNON – Well, I'm hungry.

JACK – I never knew you not to be hungry. However, all right, I'll go round to the Albany and meet you at the Savoy, at eight. You can call for me on your way, if you like.

ALGERNON – All right. What shall we do after dinner? Go to the theatre?

JACK – Oh no! I loathe listening.

ALGERNON – Well, let us go to the Club?

JACK – No. I hate talking.

ALGERNON – Well, we might trot round to the Empire at ten?

JACK – Oh no! I can't bear looking at things. It is so silly.

ALGERNON – Well, what shall we do?

JACK – Oh! nothing. What else is there to do?

ALGERNON – It is awfully hard work doing nothing.

JACK – I don't mind hard work where there is nothing to be gained, and no definite object of any kind. . . . May I ring your bell?

ALGERNON – Oh! ring for anything you like, old boy.

[JACK *rings bell*.]

JACK – What do you seem so amused at, Algy? Why are you laughing?

ALGERNON – Oh! I am a little anxious about poor Bunbury. That is all.

[*Enter* MARKBY.][10]

JACK – If you take my advice you'll drop Bunbury.

[*A pause.*]

[10] This is apparently an error for Lane, the name of Algernon's manservant. It will be noticed that this name is given to Cecily's firm of solicitors, later in the play.

ALGERNON – I hope to goodness to-morrow will be a fine day.

JACK – It never is. A brandy and soda, please.

MARKBY – Yes, sir.

[*False exit.*]

ALGERNON – Two, Markby.

MARKBY – Yes, sir.

[*Exit.*]

ALGERNON – My dear boy, if Bunburying turns out well to-morrow, I shall Bunbury for the rest of my life. If it doesn't I shall give him up. But I have got a feeling that Bunbury is going to be an immense success.

JACK – Oh, what nonsense you talk!

ALGERNON – I love nonsense.[11]

[*Enter* MARKBY *with brandy and sodas.* JACK *and* ALGERNON *drain theirs, and look severely at each other.*]

[*Enter* LANE.]

LANE – Miss Fairfax.

[*Enter* GWENDOLEN. *Exit* LANE.]

ALGERNON – Gwendolen!

GWENDOLEN – Algy, kindly turn your back. I have something very particular to say to Mr. Worthing. As it is of a private character, you will of course listen.

ALGERNON – Really, Gwendolen, I don't think I can allow this at all.

GWENDOLEN – Algy, you always adopt an immoral attitude towards life. You are not quite old [enough] to do that. Pray oblige me by looking out of the window. [ALGERNON *turns away.*] . . . Ernest!

JACK – My own darling!

GWENDOLEN – Ernest, we may never be married. From the expression on mamma's face I fear we never shall. Few parents now-a-days pay any regard to what their children say to them. The old-fashioned respect for the young is rapidly dying out. Whatever influence I ever had over mamma I lost at the age of two. But though she may prevent us from becoming man and wife, and I may marry someone else, and marry often, nothing that she can do can alter my eternal devotion to you.

JACK – Darling!

GWENDOLEN – The story of your romantic origin, as related to me with unpleasing comments by mamma, has naturally stirred the deeper fibres of my nature. Your name is an irresistible fascination. The simplicity of your nature makes you exquisitely incomprehensible to me.

[11] The next passage, up to the end of the act, is transcribed from the manuscript mentioned in note 9. Several lines are repeated, as can be seen. Before it was printed, the closing scene was to undergo considerable further revision.

Your town address at the Albany I have. What is your address in the country?

JACK—The Manor House, Woolton, Herefordshire.

[ALGERNON *writes the address on his cuff.*]

GWENDOLEN—There is a good postal service, I suppose? It may be necessary to do something desperate. That of course will require serious consideration. I will communicate with you daily.

JACK—My own one!

GWENDOLEN—Algy, you may turn round. Good-bye.

[*Exit.*]

JACK—What a splendid creature. Only girl I have ever loved in my life. Let us go off and dine. I'll give you the best dinner in London. What on earth are you laughing at?

ALGERNON—I hope to goodness to-morrow will be a fine day.

JACK—It never is . . . but what are you going to do to-morrow?

ALGERNON—To-morrow, my dear boy, I am going Bunburying.

JACK—What nonsense.

ALGERNON—I love nonsense.

SECOND ACT

Scene: Garden at the Manor House. Door leading into house r. The garden an old-fashioned one full of roses, yew hedges. Time of year, July. Basket chairs, and table covered with books.[12]

[MISS PRISM *discovered seated at table.*]

MISS PRISM [*calling into the garden*] Cecily, Cecily! Surely it is more Moulton's duty than yours to water the roses! Your German lesson has been waiting for you now for nearly twenty minutes.

[*Enter* CECILY *with watering-pot.*]

CECILY – Oh, I wish you would give Moulton the German lesson instead of me. It must be quite cold by this time, Moulton!

MOULTON [*looking out from behind a hedge, with a broad grin on his face*] Eh, Miss Cecily?

CECILY – Wouldn't you like to know German, Moulton? German is the language talked by the people who live in Germany.

MOULTON [*shaking his head*] I don't hold with them furrin tongues, Miss. [*Bowing to* MISS PRISM.] No offence to you, ma'am.

[*Disappears behind hedge.*]

CECILY – Dear Moulton! I quite agree with everything that Moulton said. I always agree with what Moulton says.

MISS PRISM – Cecily, this will never do. Pray open your Schiller at once.

CECILY – But I don't like German.

MISS PRISM – You should not talk flippantly of a language whose grammar displays such interesting varieties of syntax, gender, and expression.

CECILY – Yes . . . but it isn't at all a becoming language, at any rate for a young girl. I know perfectly well that I always look quite plain after my German lesson, if I have given it any attention at all. But I don't often do that, do I?

[12] As shown in the facsimile of the second act in volume two, opposite the first page there is an unused epigram, reading: "Not to waste one's time is to misuse it."

MISS PRISM – Child, you know how anxious your guardian is that you should improve yourself in every way. He laid particular stress on your German, as he was leaving for town yesterday. Indeed, he remarked to me privately in the hall when you had gone upstairs for your hat, that he had always been of opinion that true femininity could not be attained without a thorough knowledge of foreign languages, mathematics, and the ascertained principles of Political Economy.

CECILY – Dear Uncle Jack is so very serious! Sometimes he is so serious that I think he cannot be quite well.

MISS PRISM – Your guardian enjoys the best of health, and his gravity of demeanour is specially to be commended in one so comparatively young as he is. I know no one who has a higher sense of duty and responsibility. And, above all, he has truthfulness. He means whatever he says. He never deviates from facts. He would consider it dishonourable to do so.

CECILY – I suppose that is why he often looks a little bored when we three dine together.

MISS PRISM – Cecily! I am surprised at you. Mr. Worthing has many troubles in his life. Idle merriment and triviality would be out of place in his conversation. You must remember his constant anxiety about that unfortunate young man his brother.

CECILY – You really think that Mr. Ernest is a very bad young man?

MISS PRISM – I should fancy that he was as bad as any young man who has chambers in the Albany, or indeed even in the vicinity of Picadilly, can possibly be. And that is saying a good deal now-a-days, when sin, I am told, has reached the suburbs.

CECILY – I wish Uncle Jack would allow him to come here sometimes. I have often asked him to do so. But he has always refused, and in quite a stern voice too. I think he is a little hard on poor Mr. Ernest. Ernest is such a very beautiful name.

MISS PRISM – I trust that unhappy young profligate will never desecrate with his presence the quiet precincts of this refined home. I would not feel safe.

CECILY – But, if we didn't leave each other unprotected, we might have such a good influence over him, Miss Prism. I am sure you certainly would. You know German, and geology, and things of that kind, that influence a man very much. Men have always despised women for their ignorance, and nothing so impresses a man as when he finds out that a woman knows half as much as he does. He thinks so much more of the other half.

MISS PRISM [*shaking her head*] I do not think that even I would produce any effect on a character that according to his own brother's admission is irretrievably weak and vacillating. Indeed I am not sure that I would desire to reclaim him. The opportunities of moral reformation should be rare. They should not be given to everyone. I [am] not in favour of this modern mania for turning bad people into good people at a moment's notice. It is interfering with Providence. As a man sows so let him reap.

CECILY – But men don't sew, Miss Prism . . . and if they did, I don't see why they should be punished for it. There is a great deal too much punishment in the world. German is a punishment, certainly. And there is far too much German. You told me yourself yesterday that Germany was over-populated.

MISS PRISM – That is no reason why you should be writing your diary instead of translating "William Tell." You must put away your diary, Cecily.

CECILY – Dear Miss Prism, nothing at all has happened this morning, so I was just making a note of the fact. It is a thing that one might very easily have forgotten, especially as it occurs so often, in the country.

MISS PRISM – I really don't see why you should keep a diary at all.

CECILY – I keep a diary in order to enter the wonderful secrets of my life. If I didn't write them down I should probably forget all about them.

MISS PRISM – Memory, my dear Cecily, is the diary we all carry about with us.

CECILY – Yes, but it usually chronicles the things that have never happened, and couldn't possibly have happened. I believe that Memory is responsible for nearly all the three-volume novels that every cultivated woman writes now-a-days, and that no cultivated man ever reads.

MISS PRISM – Do not speak slightingly of the three-volume novel, Cecily. I wrote one myself in earlier days. It is connected with the one great tragedy of my life.

CECILY – How very strange! I knew that three-volume novels often saddened the lives of other people. But I had no idea that to write one was a tragedy. Though now that I think of it I feel it must be true. Was your novel ever published?

MISS PRISM – No, it was abandoned. I use the word in the sense of lost or mislaid. To your work, child; these speculations are profitless.

CECILY – Certainly, Miss Prism, but I see dear Dr. Chasuble coming up through the garden.

MISS PRISM – Dr. Chasuble! This is indeed a pleasure.

[*Enter* CANON CHASUBLE *through the garden.*]

CHASUBLE – And how are we this morning? Miss Prism, you are, I trust, well?

CECILY – Miss Prism has just been complaining of a bad headache. I think it would do her so much good to have a short stroll with you in the Park.

MISS PRISM — Cecily, I have not mentioned anything about a headache.

CECILY — No, dear Miss Prism. You are a little thoughtless sometimes, if I may say so. You don't talk enough about yourself. It is a very bad habit. It is what makes people so morbid.

MISS PRISM — Cecily, what do you mean?

CECILY — Merely that you had a slight headache and should take a long walk in the Park with Doctor Chasuble. I had an instinct about it. [*To* DR. CHASUBLE.] I'm afraid I never have an instinct about my lessons. I always have an instinct about other things.

CHASUBLE — I hope, Miss Cecily, you are not inattentive.

CECILY — Oh, I am a terribly inattentive pupil. I have given myself a certificate for being inattentive.

CHASUBLE — That is strange. Were I Miss Prism's pupil, I would hang upon her lips. [MISS PRISM *glares.*] I spoke metaphorically . . . metaphorically. [*Walks across stage.*] Ahem! Mr. Worthing has, I suppose, not returned from town yet?

MISS PRISM — We do not expect Mr. Worthing till Monday.

CHASUBLE — Ah yes, he usually likes to pass his Sunday in London. He is not one of those who live for pleasure, as that unfortunate young man his brother seems, from all accounts, to be. . . . By the way, I met Mr. Worthing yesterday as he was driving to the station, and from the few remarks he made I saw that he was more than usually distressed about his brother. Indeed he said he thought that emigration was the only thing. He spoke of Australia.

MISS PRISM — I urged it strongly upon him.

CECILY — I hope he will come down here before he goes. I should like to see him once.

MISS PRISM — The sight would probably shock you, Cecily.

CECILY — I could read between the lines.

CHASUBLE — I must not disturb Egeria and her pupil any longer.

MISS PRISM — Egeria? My name is Laetitia, Doctor.

CHASUBLE — A classical allusion merely—

MISS PRISM — I think, dear Doctor, I will have a short stroll with you. It might do my headache good.

CHASUBLE — With pleasure, Miss Prism, with pleasure.

MISS PRISM — Cecily, you will read your Political Economy in my absence. The chapter on the Fall of the Rupee you may omit. It is somewhat too exciting for a young girl.

CHASUBLE — Reading Political Economy, Cecily? It is wonderful how girls are educated now-a-days. I suppose you know all about the rela-

tions between Capital and Labour. I wish I did. I am compelled, like
most of my brother clergy, to treat scientific subjects from the point of
view of sentiment. But that is more impressive I think. Accurate knowledge is out of place in a pulpit. It is secular.

CECILY—I am afraid I'm not learned at all. All I know is about the
relations between Capital and Idleness—and that is merely from observation, so I don't suppose it is true.

MISS PRISM—Cecily, that sounds like Socialism. And I suppose you
know where Socialism leads to?

CECILY—Oh yes, that leads to Rational Dress, Miss Prism. And I suppose that when a woman is dressed rationally, she is treated rationally
—She certainly deserves to be.

CHASUBLE—A willful lamb! Dear child!

MISS PRISM [*smilingly*] A sad trouble sometimes.

CHASUBLE—I envy you such tribulation.

[*Exit.*]

CECILY [*throws all the books on the ground*] Horrid Political Economy! Horrid Geography! Horrid, horrid German! . . . Moulton!

MOULTON—Yes, Miss Cecily.

CECILY—Give me the watering-pot. I haven't finished the roses.

MOULTON—Them is all watered now, Miss Cecily.

CECILY—Moulton, you are very unkind. You might have left some of
the watering for me. I have left you all my German lesson. I haven't
even touched it. Sit down and learn your German.

MOULTON [*grinning*] I am afeared of Miss Prasm.

CECILY—So am I. But I take care to show it. You don't. It's cowardly
of you, Moulton.

[*Enter* BUTLER.]

MERRIMAN [*presents card on salver*] Mr. Ernest Worthing has
just driven over from the station. He has brought his luggage with him.

CECILY [*takes card*] "Mr. Ernest Worthing, B.4, The Albany, W."
Uncle Jack's brother! Did you tell him Mr. Worthing was in town?

MERRIMAN—Yes, Miss. He seemed very much disappointed. I told
him that you and Miss Prism were in the garden. He said he was anxious to speak to you both for a moment.

CECILY [*to herself*] I don't think Miss Prism would like my being
alone with him. So I had better send for him at once before she comes
in. [*To butler.*] Ask Mr. Ernest Worthing to come out here. I suppose
you had better speak to the housekeeper about a room for him.

MERRIMAN—I have already sent his luggage up to the Blue Room,
Miss, next Mr. Worthing's own room.

CECILY—Oh! that is all right.

[*Exit* MERRIMAN.]

C E C I L Y – I have never met any really wicked person before. I feel rather frightened. I am afraid he will look just like everyone else. He does!

[*Enter* ALGERNON, *very gay and debonnair.*]

A L G E R N O N [*raising his hat*] You are little Miss Cecily, I am sure.

C E C I L Y – You are under some strange mistake. I am not little. In fact, I believe I am more than usually tall for my age. [ALGERNON *is rather taken aback.*] You, I see from your card, are Uncle Jack's wicked brother.

A L G E R N O N – I am not really wicked at all, Miss Cecily. You mustn't think that I am wicked.

C E C I L Y – If you are not, then you have certainly been deceiving us all in a very inexcusable manner. You have made Uncle Jack believe that you are very bad. I hope you have not been leading a double life, pretending to be wicked, and being really good. That would be hypocrisy.

A L G E R N O N [*looks at her in amazement*] Oh! Of course I have been rather reckless.

C E C I L Y – I am glad to hear it.

A L G E R N O N – In fact, I have been very wicked, in my own small way.

C E C I L Y – I don't think you should look so pleased, though I am sure it must have been very pleasant.

A L G E R N O N – It is much pleasanter being here with you.

C E C I L Y – I can't understand how you are here at all. Uncle Jack telegraphed to you yesterday at the Albany to say that he would see you for the last time at six o'clock. He lets me read all the telegrams he sends you. I know some of them by heart.

A L G E R N O N – The fact is I didn't get the telegram till it was too late. Then I missed him at the Club, and the hall porter said he thought he had come down here. So, of course, I followed as I knew he wanted to see me.

C E C I L Y – He won't be back till Monday afternoon.

A L G E R N O N – That is a great disappointment, as I am obliged to go up by the first train on Monday morning.

C E C I L Y – I think you had better wait over Monday. I know he wants to speak to you about your emigrating.

A L G E R N O N – About my what, Miss Cecily?

C E C I L Y – About your emigrating. He has gone up to buy your outfit.

A L G E R N O N – I certainly wouldn't let Jack buy my outfit. He has no taste in neckties at all.

C E C I L Y – I don't think you will require neckties. Uncle Jack is sending you to Australia.

A L G E R N O N – Australia? I'd sooner shoot myself.

CECILY – Well, he said you would have to choose between this world, the next world, and Australia.

ALGERNON – Oh, well! The accounts I have received of Australia and the next world are not encouraging. This world is good enough for me, cousin Cecily.

CECILY – Yes, but are you good enough for it? How do you propose to spend your life?

ALGERNON – In your company, if you don't mind.

CECILY – Well, I should like a holiday now and then.

ALGERNON – Yes, we might spend our holidays together.

CECILY – I would, if you were not so bad.

ALGERNON – I wish you would reform me. You might make that your mission.

CECILY – How dare you suggest that I have a mission.

ALGERNON – I beg your pardon; but I thought that every woman had a mission of some kind, now-a-days.

CECILY – Every female has! No woman—

ALGERNON – Well, would you mind taking it up as a luxury? I should like to be good again.

CECILY – Were you ever good?

ALGERNON – Oh, everyone is good till they learn how to talk.

CECILY – Then the world must be very moral. Very few people know how to talk now-a-days. There is far more culture than conversation. That is why society is so dull.

ALGERNON – Well, would you mind my reforming myself?

CECILY – It is rather Quixotic of you. But I think you should try.

ALGERNON – I feel better already.

CECILY – You are looking a little worse.

ALGERNON – That is because I am hungry.

CECILY – How thoughtless of me. I should have remembered that when one is going to lead an entirely new life one requires regular and wholesome meals. Miss Prism and I lunch at 2 off some roast mutton.

ALGERNON – I fear that would be too rich for me.

CECILY – Uncle Jack, whose health has been sadly undermined by the late hours you keep in town, has been ordered by his London doctor to have *pâté-de-foie-gras* sandwiches and 1874 champagne at 12. I don't know if such invalid's fare would suit you.

ALGERNON – You are sure the champagne is '74?

CECILY – Poor Uncle Jack has not been allowed to drink anything else for the last two years. Even the cheaper clarets are, he tells us, strictly forbidden to him.

ALGERNON – Oh! I will be quite content with '74 champagne.

CECILY—I am glad to see you have such simple tastes. This is the dining-room.

ALGERNON—Thank you. Might I have a button-hole before I lunch? I never have an appetite for lunch unless I have a button-hole.

CECILY—A red rose.

ALGERNON—No, a pink one.

CECILY—Why?

ALGERNON—Because you are just like a pink rose, Cecily.

CECILY—I don't think it can be right for you to talk to me like that. Miss Prism never says such things to me.

ALGERNON—Then Miss Prism is a short-sighted old lady. You are the prettiest girl I ever saw.

CECILY—Miss Prism says that all good looks are a snare. I am sure I hope they are.

ALGERNON—They are a snare that every sensible man would like to be caught in.

CECILY—Oh! I don't think I would care to catch a sensible man. I wouldn't know what to talk to him about.[13] Perhaps you would like your sandwiches now?

ALGERNON—Yes, I would like some champagne. I am afraid you are very clever, Cecily.

CECILY—Women are not so clever as men say they are, but they are much cleverer than men think they are.

[*Exit into dining-room.*]

[*Enter* DR. CHASUBLE *and* MISS PRISM.]

CHASUBLE [*looking round*] I thought I heard voices as we approached.

MISS PRISM—Impossible. There is no one at home but Cecily, and she, I am glad to say, has not the bad habit of talking to herself, as far at least as I know.

CHASUBLE—I question whether that really is a bad habit. I find my own conversation very improving at times, and commune often with myself.

MISS PRISM—You are too much alone, dear Dr. Chasuble. What you require is to have someone always to listen to. You should get married. A misanthrope I can understand—a womanthrope, never!

CHASUBLE—I fear I do not deserve so harsh an epithet. Your sex fills me with wonder and admiration. I speak broadly . . . generally. . . . But the precept as well as the practice of the Primitive Church was distinctly against matrimony.

[13] The next sentence and the following two speeches are lined through by the author.

MISS PRISM—That is obviously the reason why the Primitive Church has not lasted up to the present day. And you do not seem to realize, dear Doctor, that by persistently remaining single a man converts himself into a permanent public temptation. You should be more careful; you may lead weaker vessels astray.

CHASUBLE—But is a man not equally attractive if married?

MISS PRISM—No married man is ever attractive except to his wife.

CHASUBLE—And often, I have been told, not even to her.

MISS PRISM—That depends on the intellectual sympathies of the woman. Maturity can always be depended on. Ripeness can be trusted. Young women are green. [DR. CHASUBLE *starts.*] I spoke horticulturally. My metaphor was drawn from fruits.

CHASUBLE—Fruits grown in the pleasant garden of memory, I doubt not. [*Aside.*] An admirable woman, though somewhat slow of wit.

MISS PRISM—A sluggish intellect, though a good man. More violent measures are necessary. Dr. Chasuble, we have had quite a long walk. May I offer you a glass of sherry?

CHASUBLE—Thank you, thank you. A glass of sherry would not be unacceptable to the inner man.

MISS PRISM—And yet I fear it was not known to the Primitive Church.

CHASUBLE—Sherry, under its modern name, undoubtedly was not known at the time. But they had wines. Tertullian mentions instances of intoxication. [MISS PRISM *starts.* DR. CHASUBLE *waves his hand in a deprecatory way.*] They are in Latin, in Latin. Such details are perhaps better referred to in a dead language.

MISS PRISM—I am decidedly of your opinion. That I conceive to be the use of Greek and Latin. And now, if you will excuse me, I will go into the dining-room for a moment and tell Merriman to bring the sherry out. [*Turns round to go to the door. Enter* JACK *from back of garden.*] Mr. Worthing! This is indeed a surprise. We did not look for you till Monday afternoon.

JACK [*shakes* MISS PRISM'S *hand in a tragic manner*] I have returned sooner than I expected. [*To* DR. CHASUBLE *who has risen.*] Doctor Chasuble, I hope you are well.

CHASUBLE—Dear Mr. Worthing, I trust this garb of woe does not betoken some terrible calamity?

JACK [*sitting down*] My brother!

MISS PRISM—More shameful debts and extravagances?

CHASUBLE—Still leading his life of pleasure?

JACK [*shaking his head*] Dead!

CHASUBLE—Your brother Ernest dead?

JACK—Quite dead.

MISS PRISM—How terribly sudden! What a lesson for him! I trust he will profit by it.

CHASUBLE—Death is the inheritance of us all, Miss Prism. Nor should we look on it as a special judgment, but rather as a general providence. Life were incomplete without it. . . . Mr. Worthing, I offer you my sincere condolences. You have at least the consolation of knowing you were always the most generous and forgiving of brothers.

JACK—Poor Ernest! He had many faults, but it is a sad blow.

CHASUBLE—Very sad indeed. Were you with him at the end?

JACK—No. He died abroad; in Paris. I had a telegram last night from the manager of the hotel.

CHASUBLE—Was the cause of death mentioned?

JACK—A severe chill, it seems.

MISS PRISM—As a man sows, so shall he reap.

CHASUBLE [*raising his hand*] Charity, dear Miss Prism, charity! None of us are perfect. I myself am peculiarly susceptible to draughts. Will the . . . interment take place here?

JACK—No. He seemed to have expressed a desire to be buried in Paris.

CHASUBLE—In Paris? [*Shakes his head.*] I fear that hardly points to any very serious state of mind at the last.]You would, no doubt, wish me to make some slight allusion to this unhappy calamity at morning service next Sunday. [JACK *presses his hand convulsively*.] My sermon on the meaning of the manna in the wilderness can be adapted to almost any occasion, joyful, or, as in the present case, distressing. I have preached it at harvest celebrations, christenings, confirmations, on days of humiliation, and festal days. The last time I delivered it was in the Cathedral, as a charity sermon on behalf of the Society for the Prevention of Cruelty to Children. The Bishop, who was present, was much struck by some of the analogies I drew.

JACK—Ah! that reminds me, you mentioned christenings I think, Dr. Chasuble? I suppose you know how to christen all right? [DR. CHASUBLE *looks astounded*.] I mean, of course, you are continually christening, aren't you?

MISS PRISM—It is, I regret to say, one of the Rector's most constant duties in this parish. The amount of christenings that seem necessary every year point clearly to a certain recklessness of living, and a sad lack of thrift. I have often spoken to the poorer classes about it.

CHASUBLE—The Church rejects no babe, Miss Prism. In every child, even in those belonging to the poorer classes, there is the making of a saint. But is there any particular infant in whom you are interested? Any infant of either sex you would wish me to baptise? Your brother was, I believe, unmarried, was he not?

J A C K [*mournfully*] Oh yes.

M I S S P R I S M [*bitterly*] People who live entirely for pleasure usually are.

J A C K — Oh, it is not for any child, dear Doctor. I am very fond of children. No! the fact is, I would like to be baptised myself, this afternoon, if you have nothing better to do.

C H A S U B L E — But surely, Mr. Worthing, you have been baptised already?

J A C K — I don't remember anything about it.

C H A S U B L E — But have you any grave doubts on the subject?

J A C K — I have the very gravest doubts. There are circumstances, unnecessary to mention at present, connected with my birth and early life that make me think I was a good deal neglected. I certainly wasn't properly looked after, at any rate. Of course I don't know if the thing would bother you in any way, or if you think I am a little too old now.

C H A S U B L E — Oh, I am not by any means a bigoted Paedobaptist. The sprinkling, and, indeed, the immersion of adults was a common practice of the Primitive Church.

J A C K — Immersion! You don't mean to say that. . . .

C H A S U B L E — Oh no. You need have no apprehensions. That form of ritual, strangely enough, is now confined to certain religious bodies not in direct communion with us. Sprinkling is all that is necessary, or indeed, I think, advisable. Our weather is so changeable there is great mortality amongst the Baptists. At what hour would you wish the ceremony performed?

J A C K — Oh, I might trot round after lunch, about three, if that would suit you.

C H A S U B L E — Oh, perfectly! In fact I have two similar ceremonies to perform at that time. A case of twins that occurred recently in one of the outlying cottages on your own estate. Poor Jenkins, the carter, a most hard-working man. I do not know, however, if you would care to join them at the Font. Personally I do not approve myself of the obliteration of class-distinctions. I think they were ordered for our profit and instruction.

J A C K — Oh! I don't see much fun in being christened along with other babies. It would be childish. Besides, I don't want the thing talked about at all. Things like that are best hushed up, I think. Would half-past five do?

C H A S U B L E — I have a churching at four. Jenkins's wife in fact desires to return thanks. But it is not a popular ceremony. Indeed I am told that Jenkins himself declines to be present. I am going to speak to him in the vestry on the subject. All calamities should be welcomed in a cheerful spirit.

JACK – Oh, I'll come round at half-past five.

CHASUBLE [*enters note*] 5.30. Very well. And now, dear Mr. Worthing, I will not intrude any longer into a house of sorrow. I would merely beg you not to be too much bowed down by grief. What seems to us bitter trials are often blessings in disguise.

MISS PRISM – This seems to me a blessing of an extremely obvious kind.

CHASUBLE – Your turning to the Church and its holy ceremonies for consolation seems to me to show that it has left a deep impression—I trust before long to prepare you for confirmation.

[*Enter* CECILY.]

CECILY – Uncle Jack! Oh, I am pleased to see you back. [*Goes towards him. He kisses her brow in a melancholy manner.*] What horrid clothes you have got on! Do go and change them.

MISS PRISM – Cecily!

CECILY – What is the matter? Uncle Jack, do look happy! I have got a surprise for you! Who do you think is in the dining-room?

JACK – My dear child, I really don't know, and under the present circumstances I cannot take any form of interest in the arrival of visitors, whoever they may be. For the next few months we must live in comparative retirement.

CECILY – But your brother is in the dining-room.

JACK – Who?

CECILY – Your brother Ernest. He arrived about half an hour ago.

JACK – What nonsense! I haven't got a brother.

CECILY – Oh, don't say that. However badly he may have behaved to you in the past he is still your brother. You couldn't be so heartless as to disown him. I'll tell him to come out. And you will shake hands with him, won't you, Uncle Jack?

[*Exit.*]

CHASUBLE – These are very joyful tidings. That telegram from Paris seems to have been a somewhat heartless jest by one who wished to play upon your feelings.

MISS PRISM – After being resigned to his loss, his sudden return seems to me peculiarly distressing.

JACK – My brother in the dining-room? I don't know what it all means. I think it is perfectly absurd.

[*Enter* ALGERNON *and* CECILY.]

ALGERNON [*going right over to* JACK *and holding out his hand*] Brother John, I have come down from town to tell you that I am very sorry for all the trouble I have given you, and I intend to lead a better life in the future.

[JACK *glares at him, and does not take his hand.*]

CHASUBLE [*to* MISS PRISM] There is good in that young man. He seems to me sincerely repentant.

MISS PRISM—These sudden conversions do not please me. They belong to dissent. They savour of the laxity of the Nonconformist.

CECILY—Uncle Jack, you are not going to refuse your own brother's hand?

JACK—Nothing will induce me to take his hand. I think his coming down here disgraceful. He knows perfectly well why.

CHASUBLE—Young man, you have had a very narrow escape of your life. I hope it will be a warning to you. We were mourning your demise, when you entered.

ALGERNON—Yes. I see Jack has got a new suit of clothes. They don't fit him properly. His necktie is wrong.

CECILY—Uncle Jack, do be nice. Why, there is some good in everyone, even the most wicked. And Ernest has been just telling me about his poor invalid friend, Mr. Bunbury, whom he goes to see so often. If a young man leaves London to go and see a sick friend there must be some good in him.

CHASUBLE—Mr. Worthing, your brother has been unexpectedly restored to you, by the mysterious dispensation of Providence, who seems to desire your reconciliation. And indeed it is good for brothers to dwell together in amity.

ALGERNON—Of course I admit that the faults were all on my side. But I must say I think that Brother John's coldness to me is peculiarly painful. I expected a warmer welcome, especially considering it is the first time I have come here.

CECILY—Uncle Jack, do shake hands with Ernest! I will never forgive you if you don't.

JACK—I suppose I must then. [*Shakes hands.*] You young scoundrel! You must get out of this place as soon as possible. I don't allow any Bunburying here.

[*Enter* MERRIMAN.]

MERRIMAN—I have put Mr. Ernest's things in the room next to yours, sir. I suppose that is all right?

JACK—What?

MERRIMAN—Mr. Ernest's luggage, sir. I have unpacked it and I have put it in the room next to your own.

ALGERNON—I am afraid I can't stay more than a week, Jack, this time.

CECILY—A week? Will you really be able to stay over Monday?

ALGERNON—I think I can manage to stop over Monday, now.

CECILY—I am so glad.

MERRIMAN [*to* ERNEST] I beg your pardon, sir, there is an elderly gentleman wishes to see you. He has just come in a cab from the station.

[*Hands card on salver.*]

ALGERNON – To see me?

MERRIMAN – Yes, sir.

ALGERNON [*reads card*] "Parker and Gribsby, Solicitors."[14] I don't know anything about them. Who are they?

JACK [*takes card*] Parker and Gribsby. I wonder who they can be. I expect, Ernest, they have come about some business for your friend Bunbury. Perhaps Bunbury wants to make his will, and wishes you to be executor. [*To* MERRIMAN.] Show Messrs. Parker and Gribsby in at once.

MERRIMAN – There is only one gentleman in the hall, sir.

JACK – Show either Mr. Parker or Mr. Gribsby in.

MERRIMAN – Yes, sir.

[*Exit.*]

JACK – I hope, Ernest, that I may rely on the statement you made to me last week when I finally settled all your bills for you. I hope you have no outstanding accounts of any kind.

ALGERNON – I haven't any debts at all, dear Jack. Thanks to your generosity I don't owe a penny, except for a few neckties I believe.

JACK – I am sincerely glad to hear it.

MERRIMAN – Mr. Gribsby.

[*Enter* GRIBSBY.]

GRIBSBY [*to* CANON CHASUBLE] Mr. Ernest Worthing?

MISS PRISM – This is Mr. Ernest Worthing.

GRIBSBY – Mr. Ernest Worthing?

ALGERNON – Yes.

GRIBSBY – Of B.4, the Albany–?

ALGERNON – Yes, that is my address.

GRIBSBY – I am very sorry, Mr. Worthing, but we have a writ of attachment for 20 days against you at the suit of the Savoy Hotel Co. Limited for £762.14.2.

ALGERNON – What perfect nonsense! I never dine at the Savoy at my own expense. I always dine at Willis's. It is far more expensive. I don't owe a penny to the Savoy.

GRIBSBY – The writ is marked as having been on you personally at the Albany on May the 27th. Judgment was given in default against you on the fifth of June. Since then we have written to you no less than thirteen times, without receiving any reply. In the interest of our clients we

---

[14] This name differs from the one given for the solicitors in the *Dramatis Personae*, as indicated in note 1.

had no option but to obtain an order for committal of your person. But, no doubt, Mr. Worthing, you will be able to settle the account without any further unpleasantness. Seven and six should be added to the bill of costs for expense of the cab which was hired for your convenience in case of any necessity of removal, but that, I am sure, is a contingency that is not likely to occur.

A L G E R N O N – Removal! What on earth do you mean by removal? I haven't the smallest intention of going away. I am staying here for a week. I am staying with my brother.

[*Points to* JACK.]

G R I B S B Y [*to* JACK] Pleased to meet you, sir.

A L G E R N O N [*to* GRIBSBY] If you imagine I am going up to town the moment I arrive you are extremely mistaken.

G R I B S B Y – I am merely a solicitor myself. I do not employ personal violence of any kind. The officer of the court whose function it is to seize the person of the debtor is waiting in the fly outside. He has considerable experience in these matters. In the point of fact he has arrested in the course of his duties nearly all the younger sons of the aristocracy, as well as several eldest sons, besides of course a good many members of the House of Lords. His style and manner are considered extremely good. Indeed, he looks more like a betting man than a court-official. That is why we always employ him. But no doubt you will prefer to pay the bill.

A L G E R N O N – Pay it? How on earth am I going to do that? You don't suppose I have got any money? How perfectly silly you are. No gentleman ever has any money.

G R I B S B Y – My experience is that it is usually relatives who pay.

J A C K – Kindly allow me to see this bill, Mr. Gribsby . . . [*Turns over immense folio.*] . . . £762.14.2 since last October. . . . I am bound to say I never saw such reckless extravagance in all my life.

[*Hands it to* DR. CHASUBLE.]

M I S S P R I S M – 762 pounds for eating! How grossly materialistic! There can be little good in any young man who eats so much, and so often.

C H A S U B L E – It certainly is a painful proof of the disgraceful luxury of the age. We are far away from Wordsworth's plain living and high thinking.

J A C K – Now, Dr. Chasuble, do you consider that I am in any way called upon to pay this monstrous account for my brother?

C H A S U B L E – I am bound to say that I do not think so. It would be encouraging his profligacy.

M I S S P R I S M – As a man sows, so let him reap. This proposed incarceration might be most salutary. It is to be regretted that [it] is only for 20 days.

JACK—I am quite of your opinion.

ALGERNON—My dear fellow, how ridiculous you are! You know perfectly well that the bill is really yours.

JACK—Mine?

ALGERNON—Yes, you know it is.

CHASUBLE—Mr. Worthing, if this is a jest, it is out of place.

MISS PRISM—It is gross effrontery. Just what I expected from him.

CECILY—It is ingratitude. I didn't expect that.

JACK—Never mind what he says. This is the way he always goes on. You mean now to say that you are not Ernest Worthing, residing at B.4, The Albany? I wonder, as you are at it, that you don't deny being my brother at all. Why don't you?

ALGERNON—Oh! I am not going to do that, my dear fellow; it would be absurd. Of course, I'm your brother. And that is why you should pay this bill for me. What is the use of having a brother, if he doesn't pay one's bills for one?

JACK—Personally, if you ask me, I don't see any use in having a brother. As for paying your bill, I have not the smallest intention of doing anything of the kind. Dr. Chasuble, the worthy Rector of this parish, and Miss Prism, in whose admirable and sound judgment I place great reliance, are both of opinion that incarceration would do you a great deal of good. And I think so, too.

GRIBSBY [*pulls out watch*] I am sorry to disturb this pleasant family meeting, but time presses. We have to be at Holloway not later than four o'clock; otherwise it is difficult to obtain admission. The rules are very strict.

ALGERNON—Holloway!

GRIBSBY—It is at Holloway that detentions of this character take place always.

ALGERNON—Well, I really am not going to be imprisoned in the suburbs for having dined in the West End. It is perfectly ridiculous.

GRIBSBY—The bill is for suppers, not for dinners.

ALGERNON—I really don't care. All I say is that I am not going to be imprisoned in the suburbs.

GRIBSBY—The surroundings, I admit, are middle class; but the gaol itself is fashionable and well-aired, and there are ample opportunities of taking exercise at certain stated hours of the day. In the case of a medical certificate, which is always easy to obtain, the hours can be extended.

ALGERNON—Exercise! Good God! No gentleman ever takes exercise. You don't seem to understand what a gentleman is.

GRIBSBY—I have met so many of them, sir, that I am afraid I don't. There are the most curious varieties of them. The result of cultivation, no doubt. Will you kindly come now, sir, if it will not be inconvenient to you.

ALGERNON [*appealingly*] Jack!

MISS PRISM—Pray be firm, Mr. Worthing.

CHASUBLE—This is an occasion on which any weakness would be out of place. It would be a form of self-deception.

JACK—I am quite firm; and I don't know what weakness or deception of any kind is.

CECILY—Uncle Jack! I think you have a little money of mine haven't you? Let me pay this bill. I wouldn't like your own brother to be in prison.

JACK—Oh, you can't pay it, Cecily, that is nonsense.

CECILY—Then you will, won't you? I think you would be sorry if you thought your own brother was shut up. Of course, I am quite disappointed with him.

JACK—You won't speak to him again, Cecily, will you?

CECILY—Certainly not, unless, of course, he speaks to me first; it would be very rude not to answer him.

JACK—Well, I'll take care he doesn't speak to you. I'll take care he doesn't speak to anybody in this house. The man should be cut, Mr. Gribsby—

GRIBSBY—Yes, sir.

JACK—I'll pay this bill for my brother. It is the last bill I shall ever pay for him, too. How much is it?

GRIBSBY—£762.14.2. May I ask your full name, sir?

JACK—Mr. John Worthing J.P., The Manor House, Woolton. Does that satisfy you?

GRIBSBY—Oh, certainly, sir, certainly! It was a mere formality. [*To* MISS PRISM.] Handsome place. Ah! the cab will be 5/9 extra—hired for the convenience of the client.

JACK—All right.

MISS PRISM—I must say that I think such generosity quite foolish. Especially paying the cab.

CHASUBLE [*with a wave of the hand*] The heart has its wisdom as well as the head, Miss Prism.

JACK—Payable to Gribsby and Parker, I suppose.

GRIBSBY—Yes, sir. Kindly don't cross the cheque. Thank you.

JACK—You are Gribsby, aren't you? What is Parker like?

GRIBSBY—I am both, sir. Gribsby when I am on unpleasant business, Parker on occasions of a less serious kind.

JACK—The next time I see you I hope you will be Parker.

GRIBSBY—I hope so, sir. [*To* DR. CHASUBLE.] Good day. [DR. CHASUBLE *bows coldly.*] Good day. [MISS PRISM *bows coldly.*] Hope I shall have the pleasure of meeting you again.

[*To* ALGERNON.]

ALGERNON—I sincerely hope not. What ideas you have of the sort of society a gentleman wants to mix in. No gentleman ever wants to know a solicitor who wants to imprison one in the suburbs.

GRIBSBY—Quite so, quite so.

ALGERNON—By the way, Gribsby. Gribsby, you are not to go back to the station in that cab. That is my cab. It was taken for my convenience. You and the gentleman who looks like the betting-man have got to walk to the station. And a very good thing, too. Solicitors don't walk nearly enough. They bolt. But then don't walk. I don't know any solicitor who takes sufficient exercise. As a rule they sit in stuffy offices all day long neglecting their business.

JACK—You can take the cab, Mr. Gribsby.

GRIBSBY—Thank you, sir.

[*Exit.*]

ALGERNON—Well, I must say that I think you might have let me play my joke on Gribsby. It was rather a good joke in its way. And of course I wasn't serious about it.

CECILY—The day is getting very sultry, isn't it, Dr. Chasuble?

CHASUBLE—There is thunder in the air.

MISS PRISM—The atmosphere requires to be cleared.

CHASUBLE—Have you read the "Times" this morning, Mr. Worthing? There is a very interesting article on the growth of religious feeling among the laity.

JACK—I am keeping it for after dinner.

MERRIMAN—Luncheon is on the table, sir.

ALGERNON—Ah, that is good news. I am excessively hungry.[15]

JACK [*to* DR. CHASUBLE] You will stop to luncheon, Dr. Chasuble, of course.

CHASUBLE—Thank you, thank you.

CECILY [*interposing*] But you have lunched already.

JACK—Lunched already?

CECILY—Yes, Uncle Jack. He had a large number of *pâté-de-foie-gras* sandwiches, and a small bottle of that champagne that your doctor ordered for you.

JACK—My '74 champagne!

CECILY—Yes, I thought you'd like him to have the same wine as yourself.

[15] The next two speeches are lined through by the author.

JACK – Oh well, if he has lunched once, he can't be expected to lunch twice. It would be absurd.

MISS PRISM – To partake of two luncheons in one day would not be liberty. It would be licence.

CHASUBLE – Even the pagan philosophers condemned excess in eating. Aristotle speaks of it with severity. He uses the [same] terms about it as he does about usury.

ALGERNON – But I have an extremely good appetite. Country air gives me almost as good an appetite as town air does. I've not been so hungry since yesterday.

MISS PRISM – The appetites were given us to be checked, not to be gratified. Cecily, luncheon is waiting. Let us set an example of punctuality.

CECILY – Certainly, Miss Prism. Two luncheons would not be really good for your brother Ernest. He might lose his figure.

JACK – Cecily, I am delighted to see you are so reasonable. Doctor, will you escort the ladies in to lunch?

CHASUBLE – With pleasure. [*To* MISS PRISM.] What we have seen this morning has been an interesting object lesson, Miss Prism; better than many sermons.

MISS PRISM – Not better than yours, dear Doctor; though shorter.

[DR. CHASUBLE *bridles a little and goes into house with* MISS PRISM *and* CECILY.]

JACK – Your Bunburying has not been a great success after all, Algy. I don't think it is a good day for Bunburying, myself.

ALGERNON – Oh, there are ups and downs in Bunburying, just as there are in everything else. I'd be all right if you would let me have some lunch. I have seen Cecily; she is a darling.

JACK – You are not to talk of Miss Cardew like that. You are not going to have any lunch. You have lunched already.

ALGERNON – I only had some champagne and a sandwich, or two.

JACK – Yes, my champagne and my sandwich or two.

ALGERNON – Well, I don't like your clothes at all. You look perfectly ridiculous in them. There is no use in being in mourning for me any longer. I have never been in better health than I am at the present moment. Why on earth don't you go up and change? It is perfectly ridiculous to be in deep mourning for a man who happens to be staying for a week with you in your own house as a guest.

JACK – You are certainly not staying with me for a week, as a guest or anything else. You have got to leave. I want you to go.

ALGERNON – I certainly won't leave you as long as you are in mourning. It would be most unfriendly. If I was in mourning you would stay with me, I suppose.

J A C K – Well, will you go if I change my clothes?

A L G E R N O N – Yes, if you are not too long. I never saw anybody take so long to dress and with such little result.

J A C K – I shan't take long this time, my dear boy, you may be quite sure.

A L G E R N O N – It is all very well, but one can't Bunbury when one is hungry. I think I'll join them at lunch.

[*Goes towards door.*]

C E C I L Y – I promised Uncle Jack I wouldn't speak to you again, unless you asked me a question. I can't understand why you don't ask me a question of some kind. I am afraid you are not quite so intellectual as I thought you were at first.

A L G E R N O N – Cecily, am I forgiven? If you forgive me I don't care twopence about anyone else.

C E C I L Y – I wonder you can look me in the face after your conduct.

A L G E R N O N – I love looking you in the face.

C E C I L Y – Well, of course, I can understand that. . . . But why did you try to put your horrid bill on poor Uncle Jack? I think that was inexcusable of you.

A L G E R N O N – I know it was; but the fact is I have a most wretched memory. I quite forgot I owed the Savoy £762.15.4.[16]

C E C I L Y – Well, I admit that I am glad to hear you have a bad memory. Good memories are not a quality that women admire much in men.

A L G E R N O N – Cecily, brother Jack is upstairs. Mayn't I come in to lunch?

C E C I L Y – I can't quite understand your being so hungry, considering all you have had to eat since last October.

A L G E R N O N – Oh, those suppers were for poor Bunbury. Late suppers are the only things his doctor allows him to eat.

C E C I L Y – Well, I don't wonder then Mr. Bunbury is always so ill, if he eats supper for six or eight people every night of the week.

A L G E R N O N – That is what I always tell him. But he seems to think his doctors know best. He's perfectly silly about doctors.

C E C I L Y – Of course I don't want you to starve, so I have told the butler to send you out some lunch.

A L G E R N O N – Cecily, what a perfect angel you are!

C E C I L Y – I think you had better call me Miss Cardew.

A L G E R N O N – What a perfect angel you are, Miss Cardew.

[*Enter footman with lunch.*]

C E C I L Y – Here is your lunch. As you said you thought roast mutton too rich for you I told the butler to bring you lobsters.

A L G E R N O N – Lobsters!

---

[16] The amount was previously given as £762.14.2.

CECILY – Yes, six lobsters. Those are all the lobsters we seem to have in the house, I am sorry to say. Of course if we had known you were coming we would have asked the housekeeper to order twelve.

ALGERNON – I assure you six is quite enough. I never eat more than six lobsters for lunch.

CECILY – I am glad to hear you are not so greedy as Miss Prism and dear Doctor Chasuble seem to think you.

ALGERNON – Oh! they don't understand me at all. They are quite mistaken about me. Quite mistaken, I assure you.

CECILY – I hope so.

ALGERNON – May I not see you before I go, Cecily? I mean Miss Cardew?

CECILY – Miss Prism and I will be here after lunch, Mr. Worthing, I mean Ernest. I always have my afternoon lessons under the yew tree.

ALGERNON – Will Miss Prism be with you?

CECILY – Certainly, she rarely leaves my side.

ALGERNON – Oh, bother Miss Prism!

CECILY – I am afraid I do.

ALGERNON – Can't you invent something to get her out of the way?

CECILY – Do you mean invent a falsehood?

ALGERNON – Oh, not a falsehood of course. Simply something that is not quite true, but should be.

CECILY – I am afraid I couldn't possibly do that. I shouldn't know how. People never think of cultivating a young girl's imagination. It is the great defect of modern education. Of course if you happened to mention that dear Doctor Chasuble was waiting somewhere to see Miss Prism, she would certainly go to meet him. She never likes to keep him waiting. And has so few opportunities of doing so.

ALGERNON – What a capital suggestion!

CECILY – I didn't suggest anything, Mr. Worthing, I mean Ernest. Nothing would induce me to deceive Miss Prism in the smallest detail. I merely pointed out that if you adopted a certain line of conduct a certain result would follow.

ALGERNON – Of course; I beg your pardon, Miss Cardew. Then I shall come here at half past three. I have something very serious to say to you.[17]

CECILY – Serious?

ALGERNON – Yes, very serious.

CECILY – In that case I think we had better meet in the house drawing-room. I don't like talking seriously in the open air. It looks so artificial.

[17] This passage is much confused in the manuscript. We are here using the text of the German translation of the second act which was made from a type-script before the play was condensed.

A L G E R N O N – Then where shall we meet?

[*Enter* JACK.]

J A C K – The dog-cart is at the door. You have got to go. Your place is by Bunbury. [*Sees* CECILY.] Cecily. . . . Don't you think, Cecily, you had better return to Miss Prism and Dr. Chasuble?

C E C I L Y – Yes, Uncle Jack.

J A C K – What is behind you, Cecily? What are you trying to conceal?

C E C I L Y – Nothing, Uncle Jack. I have no past of any kind. That is the great drawback of living in the country. It puts one at such a disadvantage with other girls.

J A C K [*getting round*] What on earth are all those lobsters doing here?

C E C I L Y – Cousin Ernest said that he was afraid that roast mutton would be too rich for him. So I ordered lobsters for his second lunch. I thought he should have some light refreshment before he went.

J A C K – I will join you, Cecily, in the dining-room.

C E C I L Y – Thank you, Uncle Jack. Good-bye, Cousin Ernest. I am afraid I shan't see you again as I shall be doing my lessons with Miss Prism in the drawing-room at half-past three.

A L G E R N O N – Good-bye, Cecily. You have been very kind to me.

[*Exit* CECILY.]

J A C K – Now, look here, Algy, you have got to go. And the sooner you go the better. Bunbury is extremely ill, and your place is by his side.

A L G E R N O N – I can't go at the present moment. I have only just begun my second lunch. And you will be pleased to hear Bunbury is very much better.

J A C K – You said you would go if I changed my clothes, and I have.

A L G E R N O N – I said I'd go if you weren't too long; and you have been too long.

J A C K – Well, you will have to go at 3.50 at any rate. I ordered your things to be packed, and the dog-cart to come round.

THIRD ACT

Scene: Sitting-room at the Manor House

[CECILY *and* MISS PRISM *discovered; each writing at a separate table.*]

MISS PRISM – Cecily! [CECILY *makes no answer.*] Cecily!

CECILY – Did you speak, Miss Prism? I am merely occupied in trying to improve my handwriting.

MISS PRISM – Cecily, you cannot deceive me. You are again making entries in your diary. I think I have had occasion more than once to speak to you about that morbid habit of yours.

CECILY – I am merely, as I always do, taking you for my example, Miss Prism. Your own diary is, I observe, lying in front of you, and, for some reason or other, your entries have been more than usually copious, this afternoon.

MISS PRISM – When one has thoroughly mastered the principles of Bimetallism one has a right to lead an introspective life. Hardly before. I must beg you to return to your Political Economy. The chapter on the Fall of the Rupee you may omit. It is somewhat too exciting for a young girl.

CECILY – In one moment, Miss Prism. The fact is, I have only chronicled the events of to-day up till 2.15, and it was at 2.30 that the fearful catastrophe occurred.

MISS PRISM – Pardon me, Cecily, it was exactly at 1.45 that Dr. Chasuble mentioned the very painful views held by the Primitive Church on marriage.

CECILY – I was not referring to Dr. Chasuble at all. And the views of the Primitive Church on marriage, however painful they may be, seem to me to be hardly a suitable subject for a young girl. They would probably be too exciting. I was alluding to poor Mr. Ernest Worthing's terrible debts, to the tragic exposé of his reckless and wicked character, and to his coming expulsion from his own brother's house.

MISS PRISM – I highly disapprove of Mr. Ernest Worthing. I have always highly disapproved of him.

CECILY – I suppose that he really is what is generally termed a thoroughly bad young man?

1487

MISS PRISM—I think there can be no possible doubt now about that matter.

CECILY—I myself am certainly inclined to think so. It is the only explanation I can find of his strange attractiveness.

MISS PRISM [*rising*] Cecily, let me entreat of you not to be led away by whatever superficial qualities this unfortunate young man may possess.

CECILY—Ah! Believe me, dear Miss Prism, it is only the superficial qualities that last. Man's deeper nature is soon found out.

MISS PRISM—Cecily! I do not know where you get such ideas. They are certainly not to be found in any of the educational books that I have procured for you.

CECILY—Are there ever any ideas in educational books, dear [Miss] Prism? I fear not. I get my ideas in the garden.

MISS PRISM—Then you should certainly not be there so much. The fact is you have fallen lately, Cecily, into a bad habit of thinking for yourself. You should give it up. It is not quite womanly. . . . Mr. Worthing! I thought, I may say I was in hopes, that you had already returned to town.

[*Enter* ALGERNON, *r.c.*]

ALGERNON—My departure will not long be delayed. I have come to bid you good-bye, Miss Cardew. My brother is, I regret to say, quite relentless. He insists on my leaving the house at 3.45. [*Pulls out watch, and looks at it.*] A simple and quite natural request of mine to be allowed to stay to afternoon tea he rejected with violence and jests that, considering everything, seemed to me somewhat out of place. I am informed that a dog-cart has been already ordered for me. I have no option but to go back again into the cold world.

CECILY—I hardly know, Mr. Worthing, what you can mean by using such an expression. The day, especially for the month of June, is unusually warm. Even in the house I find it almost oppressive. Miss Prism, I feel sure you should take the air. You work too much. Incessant Bimetallic studies cannot be good for anyone, and on a sultry afternoon like this even the dead languages can hardly be refreshing.

MISS PRISM—Much as I might like the balmy air of the garden, Cecily, I fear that it would not be right of me to leave you alone with this young gentleman. I do not wish to seem more than necessarily harsh to him, but I feel sure that your guardian would not approve of his conversing further with you. For the last three years he has suffered much through the conduct of his brother. We have already to-day had a sad but vivid object-lesson of the inevitable results of profligacy and extravagance.

A L G E R N O N – Far be it from me, Miss Prism, to make any attempt to justify my brother's past. . . . I mean my own past. Indeed, I may say candidly, that I had no idea in the world that my past was so bad as it now turns out to be. Those unhappy bills, to which you have alluded, were a terrible shock to me, a most painful surprise. Such is the carelessness of my nature that I confess I had completely forgotten all about them. Even now they bring back to me no recollections of any kind.

M I S S P R I S M – Profligacy is apt to dull the senses, Mr. Worthing.

A L G E R N O N – No doubt. I am far from defending myself. I think, however, that without dwelling further on this distressing subject, it is only my duty to mention to you, Miss Prism, that Dr. Chasuble is expecting you in the vestry.

M I S S P R I S M – In the vestry! That sounds serious. It can hardly be for any trivial purpose that the Rector selects for an interview a place of such peculiarly solemn associations. I hardly think that it would be right to keep him waiting, Cecily?

C E C I L Y – It would be very, very wrong. The vestry is, I am told, excessively damp.

M I S S P R I S M – True! I had not thought of that, and Dr. Chasuble is sadly rheumatic. In spite of all that I can say he absolutely declines to wear flannels next the skin. I had better go at once. During my absence I trust you will proceed with your studies. The standard works on Political Economy are all here. If you wish for lighter reading you will find under my work-basket on that table a treatise on Physical Geography. It contains most interesting diagrams of the mountainous elevations of the world, drawn to scale and executed on copper plate.

C E C I L Y – Thank you so much, dear [Miss] Prism. By the time that you return I feel sure that I shall know very much more than I do at present.

M I S S P R I S M [*to* ALGERNON] Mr. Worthing, we shall probably not meet again. You will allow me, I trust, to express a sincere hope that you will now turn over a new leaf in life.

A L G E R N O N – I have already begun an entire volume, Miss Prism.

M I S S P R I S M – That is indeed good news. If you would only take your brother as your example all would be well.

A L G E R N O N – Believe me, that is exactly what I intend to do.

M I S S P R I S M – I am delighted to hear it. [*Puts on large unbecoming hat.*] And do not forget that there is always hope even for the most depraved. Cecily, is this hat becoming? For the last three years and a half I have had grave doubts as to whether it really becomes me or not. I really did not much like changing it. I feared that might have looked as if I studied the trivial levities of London and Paris fashions, and thought merely of hollow appearances.

C E C I L Y—You are a great dear in the hat. Perhaps the strings might be tied on the side. Yes, they are much better on the side.

[*Ties the strings.*]

M I S S   P R I S M—My sweet child! Good-bye, Mr. Worthing. Ah! If you had only remembered that as a man sows so shall he reap you would not find yourself now in such a painful and humiliating position. [*To* CECILY.] You really think the strings are better tied at the side?

C E C I L Y—I am sure of it. The moral qualities of others often escape my notice, but in questions concerned with personal appearance I am rarely wrong.

M I S S   P R I S M—The Physical Geography is there. Cecily; pray study it. It is a subject that grows on one.

Exit through door at back. A pause. CECILY *and* ALGERNON *look at each other. She cannot help smiling. He looks excessively serious. Enter* MISS PRISM.

M I S S   P R I S M—I had forgotten my sunshade. Ah! Here it is. [*Takes up sunshade.*] Do not be idle, Cecily.

C E C I L Y—I have no intention of being idle, Miss Prism. I realize only too strongly that I have a great deal of serious work before me.

M I S S   P R I S M—Ah! That is quite as it should be, dear.

[*Exit* MISS PRISM.]

A L G E R N O N   [*after a pause*] This parting, Miss Cardew, is very painful.

C E C I L Y—It is always peculiarly painful to part from people whom one has known for a very brief space of time. The absence of old friends one can endure with perfect equanimity. But even a momentary separation from anyone to whom one has just been introduced is almost unbearable.

A L G E R N O N—Thank you. I hope you will not forget me entirely, Miss Cardew, when I am in exile.

C E C I L Y—I am afraid I could hardly promise to write to you more than once a day. Miss Prism might not like it. She is, as you know, excessively severe. Of course, if you thought it would do you any good, I could write twice on Sundays.

A L G E R N O N—If you would do that, Miss Cardew, I could begin a completely new life every Monday morning, after the second post had arrived.

C E C I L Y—I am not sure that that would be good for you, Mr. Worthing. It might prove too exciting. It seems to me that what you require at present is absolute rest, and never to be by yourself. You should be removed from all bad influences.

[*Enter* MERRIMAN.]

MERRIMAN – The dog-cart is at the door, sir.

[ALGERNON *looks at* CECILY *appealingly.*]

CECILY – It can wait, Merriman. For five minutes.

MERRIMAN – Yes, Miss.

[*Exit.*]

ALGERNON [*pulls out his watch*] I have still five minutes, Miss Cardew, I hope I shall not offend you if I state quite frankly and openly that ever since I met you I have adored you, and that you seem to me to be in every way the visible personification of absolute perfection.

CECILY – Believe me, I am not at all offended by what you have just said, Mr. Worthing. Indeed I think your frankness does you great credit. If you will allow me, I will copy your remark into my diary.

[*Goes over to table and begins writing in diary.*]

ALGERNON [*following over*] Do you really keep a diary?

CECILY – Of course. I am very fond of History. The improbable is always a pleasant distraction.

ALGERNON – But what do you write in your diary?

CECILY – Oh! As you have seen for yourself, all the little trivial incidents of a quiet country life, as they occur, day by day.

ALGERNON – I'd give anything to look at it. May I look at it?

CECILY – I am afraid I could hardly allow you to do that. You see, it is simply a very young girl's diary of her own thoughts and impressions, and consequently meant for publication. But pray, Mr. Worthing, don't stop your wonderful flow of language. I delight in taking down from dictation. It is the only one of my lessons I am really fond of. I have arrived as far as "absolute perfection." You can go on. I am quite ready.

ALGERNON [*somewhat taken aback*] Ahem! Ahem!

CECILY – Oh, don't cough, Mr. Worthing. When one is dictating one should speak fluently, and not cough. Besides, I don't know how to spell a cough. I know it is done by realistic novelists who write in horrid dialect, but I don't think it ever looks quite nice on a page.

ALGERNON [*speaking very rapidly*] Miss Cardew, ever since half-past twelve this afternoon, when I first looked upon your wonderful and incomparable beauty, I have not merely been your abject slave and servant but, soaring upon the pinions of a possibly monstrous ambition, I have dared to love you wildly, passionately, devotedly, hopelessly.

1491

CECILY [*laying down her pen*] Oh! please say that all over again. You speak far too fast and far too indistinctly. Kindly say it all over again.

ALGERNON—Miss Cardew, ever since you were half-past twelve. . . . I mean ever since it was half-past twelve this afternoon, when I first looked upon your wonderful and incomparable beauty. . . .

CECILY—Yes, I have got that, all right.

ALGERNON [*stammering*] I . . . I. . . .

CECILY [*laying down her pen*] Now you are hesitating again. It really is not brilliant of you. I know that ultimately excessive youth makes the memory fail, but still you might be as clever as writers of modern memoirs and invent your reminiscences.

ALGERNON [*desperately*] I have not merely been your abject slave and servant, but, soaring on the pinions of a possibly monstrous ambition, I have dared to love you wildly, passionately, devotedly, hopelessly.

CECILY [*after writing for some time looks up*] I have not taken down "hopelessly." It doesn't seem to make much sense, does it?

[*A slight pause.*]

ALGERNON [*starting back*] Cecily!

CECILY—Is that the beginning of an entirely new paragraph? Or should it be followed by a note of admiration?

ALGERNON [*rapidly and romantically*] It is the beginning of an entirely new existence for me, and it shall be followed by such notes of admiration that my whole life shall be a subtle and sustained symphony of Love, Praise, and Adoration combined.

CECILY—Oh! I don't think that makes any sense at all. The fact is that men should never try to dictate to women. They never know how to do it, and when they do do it, they always say something particularly foolish.

ALGERNON—I don't care whether what I say is foolish or not. All that I know is that I love you, Cecily. I love you. I want you. I can't live without you. Cecily! You know I love you. Will you marry me? Will you be my wife?

[*Rushes over to her and puts his hand on hers.*]

CECILY [*rising*] Oh! You have made me make a blot! And yours is the only actual proposal I have ever had in all my little life. I should like to have entered it neatly.

[*Enter* MERRIMAN.]

MERRIMAN—The dog-cart is waiting, sir.

ALGERNON—Tell it to come round to-morrow at the same hour.

MERRIMAN [*looks at* CECILY, *who makes no sign*] Yes, sir.

[*Exit.*]

CECILY—Uncle Jack would be very much annoyed if he knew you were staying till to-morrow.

ALGERNON—Oh! I don't care about Uncle Jack.

CECILY—Your own brother!

ALGERNON—He is not my brother. I mean I cannot regard him as a brother; I cannot respect him as a brother. I do not approve of him as a brother.

CECILY—Oh! I don't like you when you talk like that. It is so ungrateful, after all he has done for you.

ALGERNON—Yes, that is perfectly true, of course. And I am quite ready to acknowledge that no one ever had such a brother as I have. But at the present moment I don't like anybody in the world but you. I don't care for anybody in the world but you. Cecily! You will marry me, won't you?

CECILY—You silly boy! Of course. Why, we have been engaged for the last eight months.[18]

ALGERNON—Darling!

[*Kisses her.*]

CECILY—Darling!

[*A pause.* ALGERNON *heaves a sigh of deep satisfaction.*]

ALGERNON—Darling. . . . . . [*Kisses her again.*] Cecily?

CECILY—Yes, Ernest.

ALGERNON—It is rather a surprise for you, isn't it?

CECILY—What?

ALGERNON—Well, everything. Your finding yourself here with your little head resting on my shoulder.

CECILY—Oh! that does not surprise me at all, Ernest. Why should it? For the last eight months I have regarded myself as practically engaged to you, and have consequently made myself as charming as possible to other people, as engaged girls always do.

[*Goes to table and opens drawer.*]

ALGERNON—For the last eight months?

CECILY—Eight months all but a few days. [*Looks at diary, turns over page.*] Yes, it will be exactly eight months on Thursday. You see, it is nearly a year ago since dear Uncle Jack first confessed to us, with much humiliation and distress, that he had a younger brother who was very wicked, and told us what a sad trouble and expense you were to him. Since then you, naturally, have formed the chief topic of conversation between myself and Miss Prism. We have been left so much to ourselves in the long winter evenings. Poor Uncle Jack, as no one knows better than you do, has been obliged to go up to town al-

[18] The next eight speeches are lined through by the author.

most every Saturday to Monday, to save you from the sad consequences of your innumerable follies, and pay your extravagant bills.

ALGERNON—I didn't know. Very few people now-a-days ever realize the position in which they are placed. The age is a thoughtless one.

CECILY—It is no wonder that my thoughts were always fixed on you. Indeed it was to distract my mind from a subject that she always spoke of as demoralizing that Miss Prism tried to make me interested in the burning questions of Political Economy. You see what I have had to go through already on your account.

ALGERNON—My poor darling! But when did we become engaged?

CECILY—On the 14th of February last. Worn out by your entire ignorance of my existence, I determined to end the matter one way or the other, and after a long struggle with myself I accepted you one evening in the garden. The next day I bought this little ring in your name; and put it down to an account I have opened for you at a very artistic jeweller's who has such a nice shop in our little county town. You see I always wear it, Ernest, and though it shows that you are sadly extravagant, still I have long ago forgiven you for that. Here in this drawer are all the little presents I have given you from time to time, neatly numbered and labelled. This is the pearl necklace you gave me on my birthday. And this is the box in which I keep all your dear letters.

[*Opens box and produces letters tied up with blue ribbons.*]

ALGERNON—My letters! But my own sweet Cecily, I have never written you any letters.

CECILY—You need hardly remind me of that, Ernest. I remember it all too well. I grew tired of asking the postman every morning if he had a London letter for me. My health began to give way under the strain and anxiety. Indeed I grew so ill that all my girl-friends told me I was looking very interesting. So I wrote your letters for you, and had them posted to me in the village, by my maid. I wrote always three times a week, and sometimes oftener. Indeed, but for your letters I would not have been able to endure the fact of my never having met you at all.

ALGERNON—Oh, do let me read my letters, Cecily.

CECILY—Oh, no! I couldn't possibly. They would make you far too conceited. Why, they are perfect masterpieces of literary style. The three despairing letters you wrote me after I had broken off the engagement are so beautiful and so pathetic that I can never read them without crying bitterly.

ALGERNON—But was our engagement ever broken off?

CECILY—Of course it was. On the 22nd of last March. You can see the entry if you like. [*Shows diary.*] "To-day I broke off my engagement with Ernest. I feel it is better to do so. The weather still continues charming."

ALGERNON—But why on earth did you break it off? What had I done? I had done nothing at all. Cecily, I am very much hurt, indeed, to hear you broke it off.

CECILY—Men seem to forget very easily. I should have thought you would have remembered the violent letter you wrote to me because that silly scatter-brained young Duchess of Bolton had told you that I had danced three times running with Lord Kelso at the county ball. Of course it wasn't true at all. And even if it had been, Lord Kelso is unmarried. And it was not likely I should have taken any interest in an unmarried man. It is so easy to take an unmarried man at an unfair advantage. But you chose to believe it, and I of course was far too proud to deny it for a moment. I merely pointed out to you that if you tried to control my conduct before we were actually married it was more than likely you would try to do the same after we became man and wife; and that marriage as an institution was quite impossible unless the husband gave up to the wife in every single thing.

ALGERNON—A most sensible view, Cecily. The most sensible view I ever heard.

CECILY—Yes, that is what you said in the letter in which you took it all back, and begged for my forgiveness. Only you said it there far more eloquently.

ALGERNON—But I did say it, Cecily, didn't I?

CECILY—Of course you said it. Otherwise I wouldn't have forgiven you, or accepted this little gold bangle with the turquoise and diamond heart, that you sent me the next day.

[*Shows bangle.*]

ALGERNON—It's very pretty, Cecily, isn't it?

CECILY—Yes, you have wonderfully good taste, Ernest. I have always said that of you.

ALGERNON—My own one! So we have been engaged for five months, Cecily.

CECILY—Yes, how the time has flown, hasn't it?

ALGERNON—I don't think so. I have found the days very long and very dreary without you.

CECILY—That means, I suppose, that you want us to get married at once, you silly impetuous boy! Why there are a heap of things to be done before that happens. We have got to get Uncle Jack's consent first.

ALGERNON—You'll never break it off again, Cecily?

CECILY—I don't think I could break it off now. Besides, of course, there is the question of your name. I don't know any other—

ALGERNON–How do you mean?

CECILY–You must not laugh at me darling, but from the first time I ever heard of you there was a particular reason, besides your bad conduct, why I felt so strangely drawn towards you.

ALGERNON–What was that, darling?

CECILY–Well, it had always been a girlish dream of mine to love someone whose name was Ernest, to be loved by someone whose name was Ernest. There is something in the name of Ernest that seems to inspire absolute confidence. I pity any married woman whose husband is not called Ernest.

ALGERNON–But, my dear child, do you mean to say you could not love me if I had some other name?

CECILY–But you have no other name. I made special enquiries of Uncle Jack, the first evening that he broke to us the painful news of his not being alone in the world, and he told me you had only one Christian name.

ALGERNON–That is quite true. Of course I have only one Christian name. But supposing that my godfathers and godmother had given me some other name, do you mean to say then, Cecily, that you could not have loved me?

CECILY–Ah! that, dear Ernest, is clearly a metaphysical speculation, and like most metaphysical speculations quite profitless as far as any actual relation to practical life is concerned.

ALGERNON–No, but Cecily, supposing I had been called–oh! any name you like–Algernon–for instance. . . .

CECILY–But I don't like the name of Algernon.

ALGERNON–Well, my own sweet darling, I really can't see why you should object to the name of Algernon. It is not at all a bad name. In fact, it is rather an aristocratic name.

CECILY–I fear it must be. I have often come across it in the newspapers in connection with rather painful cases.

ALGERNON–Oh! Of course there are Algies and Algies: but I know lots of Algies who are very respectable Algies.

CECILY–Oh! I don't think I would like those Algies at all.

ALGERNON–But seriously, Cecily, if my name was Algy couldn't you love me?

CECILY–I might respect you, Ernest. I might admire your character. But I fear that I would not be able to give you my undivided attention.

ALGERNON–How perfectly terrible!

CECILY–Why, Ernest?

ALGERNON–Oh! nothing, darling . . . ahem! Cecily! Your Rector here is, I suppose, thoroughly experienced in the practice of all the rites and ceremonies of the Church?

CECILY—Oh yes. Dr. Chasuble is a most learned man. He has never written a single book, so you can imagine how much he knows.

ALGERNON—I must see him on important business at once.

CECILY—You foolish, impetuous, absurd boy! Why, one can't get married at once. Marriage is a very serious thing. One has to order a lot of dresses when one's going to get married. And besides, we have got to get Uncle Jack's consent first, and that I am afraid will take at least a quarter of an hour or twenty minutes. Uncle Jack is very stern as you know. He has got such strict principles about everything. He is not like you.

ALGERNON—Oh! I am bound to say that I think Jack and I are very like each other. I really don't see much difference between us.

CECILY—How conceited of you to say such a thing! Why, he is a very, very good man, and you are a very very . . . very bad boy.

ALGERNON—Darling! [A *pause*.] I must leave you, and go and see Dr. Chasuble immediately.

CECILY [*pained*] Oh!

ALGERNON—I shan't be away more than half an hour, darling.

CECILY—Considering that we have been engaged since February the 14th, and that I only met you to-day for the first time, I think it is rather hard that you should leave me for so long a period as half an hour.

ALGERNON—Dear pretty flowerlike thing! With your tossed gold hair! And your eyes like violets! Believe me, it is absolutely necessary that I should see Dr. Chasuble immediately. Once the christening, I mean the interview, takes place, I will return to you your own true, loyal, devoted Ernest.

CECILY—You have always been that. I have never doubted you.

ALGERNON—Sweet!

CECILY—Own one!

ALGERNON—I will be back in no time.

CECILY—You will give orders for the church to be exquisitely decorated for the ceremony, won't you?

ALGERNON—Do you really think that necessary?

CECILY—Of course it is. And there must be horrid school-children to scatter flowers, and all that kind of thing. We must be married in proper style, mustn't we?

ALGERNON—Oh, of course, yes. I'll settle all about that. That is what I am going about.

CECILY—You silly boy! As if I didn't know that! What else should you go about?

ALGERNON—Nothing else of course. How clever of you to guess it!

CECILY—Women are not so clever as men say they are. But they are much cleverer than men think they are.[19]

ALGERNON—Ah! You are pretty, and that is a great deal better than being anything else, is it not?

CECILY—I have always thought so, but Miss Prism says that beauty of any kind is a snare. I am sure I hope it is.

ALGERNON—It is a snare that every sensible man would like to be caught in.

CECILY—I don't think I would care to catch sensible men.

ALGERNON—Why not, darling?

CECILY—Miss Prism says that men are so selfish that they always want to get out of entanglements.

ALGERNON—Oh, bother Miss Prism!

CECILY—I am afraid I do.

ALGERNON—Good-bye, sweetest.

CECILY—Good-bye, darling.

[Exit ALGERNON.]

CECILY—Dear sweet boy he is! I like his hair so much. I must enter his proposal in my diary. [Goes over to table and sits down.] How did he propose? He wasn't eloquent, I know. But that makes me feel that he must have been quite sincere. Style and sincerity never go together. That is why literature is so important, as a record of its age. . . . [Bites her pen meditatively.] Oh! I remember now. He said to me, "Cecily, will you marry me?" It is curious how simplicity touches one! It must be a very complex thing.

[Makes entry in her diary.]
[Enter MERRIMAN.]

MERRIMAN—Miss Gwendolen Fairfax has just called to see Mr. Worthing. On important business, Miss Fairfax states.

CECILY—Is Mr. Worthing not in his library?

MERRIMAN—Mr. Worthing went over in the direction of the Rector's some time ago. He has not returned yet.

CECILY—Oh! . . . Pray show Miss Fairfax in; Mr. Worthing is sure to be back soon. And you can bring tea.

MERRIMAN—Yes, Miss.

[Exit.]

CECILY—Miss Fairfax! Who can she be? I suppose one of the good ladies who is associated with Uncle Jack in some of his philanthropic work in London. I don't quite like ladies who are interested in philanthropic work. I think it is so forward of them.

---

[19] It will be observed that this speech is the same as the passage lined through by the author, indicated in note 13.

[*Enter* MERRIMAN.]

MERRIMAN—Miss Fairfax.

[*Enter* GWENDOLEN.]

[*Exit* MERRIMAN.]

CECILY [*advancing to meet her*] Pray let me introduce myself to you, Miss Fairfax. My name is Cecily Cardew. You must take me as your hostess, for the moment, until Mr. Worthing comes in. He has just gone down to the Rectory.

GWENDOLEN—Cecily Cardew? What a very sweet name! Something tells me that we are going to be great friends. I like you already more than I can say. My first impressions of people are never wrong.

CECILY—How nice of you to like me so much after we have known each other such a short time. Pray sit down.

GWENDOLEN [*still standing up*] I may call you Cecily, may I not?

CECILY—With pleasure!

GWENDOLEN—And you will always call me Gwendolen, won't you?

CECILY—If you wish.

GWENDOLEN [*sitting down*] Then that is all quite settled, is it not?

CECILY—I hope so.

[*A pause.*]

GWENDOLEN [*after examining* CECILY *carefully through a lorgnette*] You are here on a short visit, I suppose, dear Cecily?

CECILY—Oh no, Gwendolen! I live here.

GWENDOLEN [*slightly frowning*] Really?

CECILY—Yes, I have lived here for the last four years.

GWENDOLEN [*severely*] Indeed? Your mother, no doubt, or some female relative of advanced years, resides here also?

CECILY—Oh no! I have no mother, nor, indeed relatives of any sex; my guardian, aided by Miss Prism, has the painful duty of looking after me.

GWENDOLEN—Your guardian?

CECILY—Yes, I am Mr. Worthing's ward.

GWENDOLEN—Oh! It is strange he never mentioned to me that he had a ward. How secretive of him! He grows more interesting hourly. I am not sure, however, that the news inspires me with feelings of unmixed delight. I am very fond of you, Cecily; I have liked you ever since I met you! But I am bound to state that now that I know that you are Mr. Worthing's ward, I cannot help expressing the wish you were—well, just a little older than you seem to be—and not quite so very attractive. In fact, if I may speak candidly—

CECILY—Oh, pray do! I think that whenever one has anything unpleasant to say, one should always be quite candid.

GWENDOLEN—Well, to speak candidly, Cecily, I wish that you

were fully thirty-five and more than usually plain for your age. Mr. Worthing has a strong upright nature. He is the very soul of truth and honour. But even men of the noblest possible moral character are extremely susceptible to the influence of the physical charms of others. The prominent facts of both English and French history, ancient and modern, seem to me to point clearly to that conclusion—and, high-principled though Ernest is, and I know no one whose principles are so remarkably high and varied, I see no reason why he should be an exception to what my researches have taught me is undoubtedly the general rule.

CECILY—I beg your pardon, Gwendolen. Did you say Ernest?

GWENDOLEN—Yes.

CECILY—Oh, but it is not Ernest who is my guardian. It is his brother —his elder brother.

GWENDOLEN—It is curious; he never mentioned to me that he had a brother.

CECILY—I am sorry to say they have not been on good terms for a long time.

GWENDOLEN—Ah! that accounts for it. And now that I think of it, I have never heard any man mention his brother. The subject seems distasteful to men. Dearest Cecily, you have lifted a load from my mind. I was growing quite anxious. It would have been terrible if any cloud had come across a friendship like ours, would it not? Of course you are quite, quite sure that it is not Mr. Ernest Worthing who is your guardian.

CECILY—Quite sure. [*A pause.*] In fact, I am going to be his.

GWENDOLEN [*enquiringly*] I beg your pardon?

CECILY [*rather shyly and confidingly*] Dearest Gwendolen, there is no reason why I should make any secret of it to you. Our little county newspaper is sure to chronicle the fact next week. Mr. Ernest Worthing and I are engaged to be married.

GWENDOLEN [*quite politely*] My darling Cecily, I think there must be some slight error. Mr. Ernest Worthing is engaged to me. The announcement, in spite of my mother's opposition to the match, will appear in the "Morning Post" on Saturday at the latest.

CECILY [*very politely*] I am afraid you must be under some misconception. Ernest proposed to me exactly ten minutes ago. I had just made a note of the fact in my diary, when you were kind enough to call.
[*Shows diary.*]

GWENDOLEN [*examines diary through her lorgnette carefully*] It is very strange, for he asked me to be his wife yesterday afternoon at 5.30. If you would care to verify the incident, pray do so. [*Produces diary of her own.*] I never travel without my diary. One should always have something exciting to read in a train. I am so sorry, dear Cecily, if it is any disappointment to you, but I fear *I* have the prior claim.

C E C I L Y – It would distress me more than I can tell you, dear Gwendolen, if it caused you any mental or physical anguish, but I feel bound to point out that since Ernest proposed to you he has clearly changed his mind.

G W E N D O L E N – It would not be right for me to release him. It might not be for his good.

C E C I L Y – It would be very wrong of me to give him up. It might ruin his young life.

G W E N D O L E N [*with some irritation*] You hardly understand, dearest, that I have worshipped this man for six weeks. No brief period in the existence of one who lives in a whirl of fashionable life.

C E C I L Y – You don't quite seem to realize, Gwendolen, that I have adored him since morning. A long time in the life of a young girl who lives in the country.

G W E N D O L E N [*hotly*] The first moment I saw him I said to myself, Ernest shall be mine. And my first impressions of people are invariably right.

C E C I L Y [*hotly*] I got engaged to him months before I saw him. The moment I heard of his existence I felt instinctively that he belonged to me.

G W E N D O L E N [*meditatively*] If the poor fellow has been entrapped into any foolish promise, I will consider it my duty to rescue him at once, and with a firm hand.

C E C I L Y [*thoughtfully and sadly*] Whatever unfortunate entanglement the dear boy may have got into I will never reproach him with it.

G W E N D O L E N [*rising*] Do you allude to me, Miss Cardew, as an entanglement? You are presumptuous. On an occasion of this kind it becomes more than a moral duty to speak one's mind. It becomes a pleasure.

C E C I L Y [*rising*] Do you suggest, Miss Fairfax, that I entrapped Ernest into an engagement? How dare you? This is no time for wearing the shallow mask of manners. When I see a spade I call it a spade.

G W E N D O L E N [*satirically*] I am glad to say that I have never seen a spade. It is obvious that our social spheres have been widely different.

CECILY *is about to make a retort when* MERRIMAN *enters, followed by a footman, with tea-tray, etc. The presence of the servants exercises a restraining influence under which both girls chafe.*

M E R R I M A N – Shall I lay tea here as usual, Miss?
C E C I L Y [*sternly, in a clear voice*] Yes.

[MERRIMAN *lays tea on table close to* CECILY. *A long pause.* CECILY *and*
GWENDOLEN *glare at each other.*]
GWENDOLEN [*looking round*] Charming room this is, of yours, Miss
Cardew.
CECILY – I am so glad you like it, Miss Fairfax.
GWENDOLEN – I had no idea there was anything approaching good
taste in the more remote country districts. It is quite a surprise to me.
CECILY – Ah! I am afraid you judge of the country from what one sees
in the large towns, Miss Fairfax. I know most London houses are extremely vulgar.
GWENDOLEN – Oh! I don't judge of the country from anything. I
merely detest the country. I cannot understand how anybody manages
to exist in the country, if anybody does. I know the country always
bores me to death.
CECILY – Ah, yes; I have often heard of that curious effect that the
country has on some people. It is called I think agricultural depression, is it not? I know the aristocracy are suffering very much from it
just at present. It is almost an epidemic amongst them, I am told. May
I offer you some tea, Miss Fairfax?
GWENDOLEN [*with elaborate politeness*] Thank you. [*Aside.*] De-
testable girl! But I require tea!
CECILY [*sweetly*] Sugar?
[*Holds up tongs.*]
GWENDOLEN [*superciliously*] No, thank you. [CECILY *puts down
tongs.*] Sugar is not fashionable.
[CECILY *looks angrily at her, takes up tongs again and puts four lumps of
sugar into the cup.*]
CECILY [*severely*] Cake or bread and butter?
GWENDOLEN [*in a bored manner*] Bread and butter, please. [CECILY
puts bread and butter on tray.] Cake is rarely seen at the best houses
now-a-days.
[CECILY *cuts a very large slice of cake, removes the bread and butter and
puts the slice of cake on the tray.*]
CECILY [*to* MERRIMAN *who is waiting with a small salver on which
the cup of tea stands*] Hand that to Miss Fairfax. [MERRIMAN *hands
the salver.*] That will do, Merriman.
[*Exit* MERRIMAN.]
GWENDOLEN [*drinks the tea, and makes a grimace and puts the cup
down at once. Reaches out her hand to the bread and butter, looks at
it and finds it is cake. Rises in indignation*] You have filled my tea
with lumps of sugar, and though I asked most distinctly for bread and
butter you have given me cake. I am known for the gentleness of my

disposition, and the extraordinary sweetness of my nature, but I warn you, Miss Cardew, you may go too far.

CECILY [*rising*] To save my poor innocent trusting boy from the machinations of any other girl there are no lengths to which I would not go.

GWENDOLEN [*haughtily*] You don't quite seem to realize to whom you are talking.

CECILY [*coldly*] I am afraid you are forgetting yourself, Miss Fairfax. You are not in your own house.

GWENDOLEN – From the moment I saw you I distrusted you. I felt that you were false and deceitful. I am never deceived in such matters. My first impressions of people are invariably right.

CECILY – It seems to me, Miss Fairfax, that I am trespassing on your valuable time. No doubt you have many other calls of a similar kind to make in the neighbourhood.

GWENDOLEN – Am I to understand that you are asking me to go? If I thought that I would stay here for ever.

CECILY – Oh no! How could you imagine such a thing? Though, of course, should you wish to go, do not let me detain you. The station is merely a short walk of some six or seven miles, along a very nice straight road, and there is a most reliable slow train to London that starts at a quarter to eight. I am told that the waiting-room is considered quite comfortable.

GWENDOLEN [*sitting down*] I will certainly not leave the house till I have had a private interview with Ernest. It would not be just to him.

CECILY – I admit you have a right to ask for it. I will certainly make a point of being present. My absence would hardly be fair to him.

GWENDOLEN – Perhaps we had better talk of some other subject. Is your part of the country healthy, Miss Cardew?

CECILY – The air is considered by physicians more than usually salubrious.

GWENDOLEN – The neighbourhood possesses no doubt many pleasant walks, drives and views.

CECILY – Its walks and drives are regarded by many to constitute its chief attractions. And from the top of a well-wooded hill, in the vicinity, one can see, I believe, no less than six counties.

GWENDOLEN [*with a satirical smile*] Six counties; I don't think that I should much care for that. I hate crowds. I think they are so very vulgar, Miss Cardew.

CECILY – I suppose that is why you like living in London so much, Miss Fairfax.

[*Enter* JACK *behind.*]

GWENDOLEN [*rising*] Miss Cardew! . . . Ernest! Ernest! my own Ernest!

JACK [*advancing*] Gwendolen! What on earth are you doing down here? I mean, how delighted I am to see you, darling!

[*Offers to kiss her.*]

GWENDOLEN [*drawing back*] A moment, Ernest. My mother has informed me of the painful facts concerned with your birth, and I have come down in consequence to assure you of my unalterable devotion; but first may I ask, are you engaged to be married to this young lady?

[*Points to* CECILY.]

JACK [*laughing*] To dear little Cecily! Of course not! What could have put such an idea into your head?

GWENDOLEN – Thank you. You may. [*Offers her cheek.*] It is true that we had been separated for nearly twenty-four hours, but I felt that even that long lapse of time could not make you untrue to me. To one whose name is Ernest deception of any kind would be quite impossible.

JACK [*rather confused and looking anxiously at* CECILY] Of course, dear, of course.

CECILY [*very sweetly*] I think it only just to both of us, Miss Fairfax, that I should mention that the gentleman whose arm is at present round your waist is my dear guardian, Uncle Jack.

GWENDOLEN – I beg your pardon?

CECILY – I knew there must be some misunderstanding. This is Uncle Jack.

GWENDOLEN [*receding*] Jack! Oh!

[*Enter* ALGERNON.]

CECILY – Here is Ernest.

ALGERNON [*goes straight over to* CECILY *without noticing anyone else*] My own love! you see I have come back to you earlier than I expected. [*Offers to kiss her.*] The appointment has had to be put off for half an hour, darling!

CECILY [*drawing back*] A moment! Ernest! May I ask if you are engaged to be married to this young lady?

ALGERNON [*looking round*] To what young lady? Good heavens! Gwendolen!

CECILY – Yes! to good heavens, Gwendolen, I mean to Gwendolen.

ALGERNON [*laughing*] Of course not! What could have put such an idea into your pretty little head?

CECILY – Thank you. [*Presenting her cheek to be kissed.*] You may. [ALGERNON *kisses her.*] It is true that we had been engaged for nearly five months. I knew that no one of the name of Ernest could be untrue.

ALGERNON [*looking anxiously at* GWENDOLEN] Of course not, my own one.

GWENDOLEN—I think it only fair to both of us, Miss Cardew, that I should mention that the gentleman who is now embracing you is my cousin, Algy Montford.

CECILY [*breaking away from* ALGERNON] Algernon! Oh!

[*The two girls come towards each other and put their arms round each other's waists as if for protection.*]

CECILY [*to* ALGERNON] Are you called Algernon?

ALGERNON [*flinging himself in despair on the sofa*] I cannot deny it.

CECILY—Oh!

GWENDOLEN—Is your name really John?

JACK [*standing rather proudly*] I could deny it if I liked. I could deny anything if I liked. But my name certainly is John. It has been John for years. Now you know everything. I am sorry you have forced me to speak the thing right out. I would have wished personally, Gwendolen, for your sake as well as for my own, to have broken the thing gently to you. It had always been my intention to do so.

GWENDOLEN—Broken it gently to me! As if John was a name that could be broken gently to anyone. I had no idea you were so cynical.

ALGERNON—I would like to be allowed to say, Miss Cardew, that I regret you insisted on a frank answer to your question. I had hoped to have found an opportunity of gradually leading up to the name of Algernon.

CECILY—As if one could gradually lead up to Algernon. I am afraid, Mr. Montford, you are little more than a mere sentimentalist. A type I have but little respect for, common though it is at the end of this, as of every century.

GWENDOLEN [*to* CECILY] It is evident that we have been shamefully deceived.

CECILY [*to* GWENDOLEN] A gross deception has been practiced on both of us.

GWENDOLEN—My poor wounded Cecily!

CECILY—My sweet wronged Gwendolen!

GWENDOLEN [*slowly and seriously*] You will call me sister, will you not?

CECILY [*after a pause*] Thank you for those words.

[*They kiss.*]

CECILY [*rather brightly*] There is just one question I would like to be allowed to ask my guardian.

GWENDOLEN—An admirable idea! Mr. Worthing, there is just one question I would like to be permitted to put to you. Where is your brother Ernest? We are both engaged to be married to Ernest, so it is a matter of some importance to us to know where Ernest is at present.

C E C I L Y – We would naturally like to learn something about Ernest's personal appearance.

G W E N D O L E N – Any information regarding Ernest's income would be eagerly welcomed.

C E C I L Y – Would the excitements of a country life be too much for Ernest?

G W E N D O L E N – Could Ernest stand the quiet of a London season?

C E C I L Y – Is Ernest physically repulsive? Let us know the worst.

G W E N D O L E N – Is Ernest socially possible? Let us face facts.

J A C K   [*slowly and hesitatingly*] Gwendolen–Cecily–it is very painful for me to be forced to speak the truth. It is the first time in my life that I have ever been reduced to such a painful position, and I am really quite inexperienced in doing anything of the kind, so you must excuse me if I stammer in my tale. . . .

G W E N D O L E N – I must beg you to do nothing of the kind, Mr. Worthing. Stammering always gets upon my nerves. Pray say what you have to say without the smallest hesitation in your speech.

J A C K – In that case I will tell you quite frankly that I have no brother Ernest. I have no brother at all. I never had a brother in my life, and I certainly have not the smallest intention of ever having one in the future.

C E C I L Y   [*going towards him*] No brother at all?

J A C K   [*cheerily*] None!

G W E N D O L E N   [*severely*] Had you never a brother of any kind?

J A C K   [*pleasantly*] Never. Not even of any kind.

G W E N D O L E N – Then it is quite clear, Cecily, that neither of us is engaged to be married to anyone.

C E C I L Y – It is only too obvious that we are both quite free.

G W E N D O L E N – It is not a very pleasant position for a young girl to suddenly find herself in. Is it?

C E C I L Y – I had no idea that it was so . . . so very, very depressing.[20]

G W E N D O L E N – There is no one in the world to whom I can go now for sympathy, but you, Cecily.

C E C I L Y – You are the only friend I have left to whom I can confide my troubles, Gwendolen.

G W E N D O L E N – We are terribly alone.

C E C I L Y – We are quite isolated.

J A C K   [*with a pleasant smile*] Gwendolen!

[20] The next four speeches are lined through by the author.

GWENDOLEN [*with a stony glare*] Mr. John Worthing, I . . . I really think you are making some mistake.

[JACK *retreats.*]

ALGERNON [*pleadingly*] Cecily!

CECILY [*with a look of surprise*] Mr. Algernon Montford, I can't remember your ever having been introduced to me.

[ALGERNON *retreats.*]

GWENDOLEN – Let us go out into the garden, Cecily. They will hardly dare to come after us.

CECILY – Men are so cowardly, aren't they?

Exeunt into garden, with scornful looks. CECILY *takes a hat from the table as she passes. Each stops in front of a glass for a moment, and arranges her hair.* JACK *and* ALGERNON *look at each other for a short time. Then they turn away from each other.* JACK, *who looks very angry, walks up and down the room. Kicks footstool aside in a very irritated way.* ALGERNON *goes over to tea-table and eats some muffins after lifting up the covers of several dishes.*

JACK – Pretty mess you have got us into. [ALGERNON *sits down at tea-table and pours out some tea. He seems quite unconcerned.*] What on earth did you mean by coming down here and pretending to be my brother? Perfectly monstrous of you!

ALGERNON [*eating muffins*] What on earth did you mean by pretending to have a brother? It was absolutely disgraceful!

[*Eats muffins.*]

JACK – This ghastly state of things is what you call Bunburying, I suppose?

ALGERNON – Yes, and a perfectly wonderful Bunbury it is. The most wonderful Bunbury I have ever had in my life.

JACK – Well, you've no right whatsoever to Bunbury in my house.

ALGERNON – That is absurd. One has a right to Bunbury anywhere one chooses. That is the great advantage of Bunburying.

JACK – I wish to goodness you wouldn't talk about this idiotic Bunburying. It drives me perfectly frantic.

ALGERNON – I didn't introduce the subject of Bunburying. It was you. I always keep the thing quite secret. Every serious Bunburyist does.

JACK – I told you to go away by the 3.50. I ordered the dog-cart for you. Why on earth didn't you take it?

ALGERNON – I hadn't had my tea.

JACK – And as for your conduct towards Miss Cardew, I must say, Algy, that your taking in a sweet simple innocent girl like that, is quite inexcusable. To say nothing of the fact that she is my ward.

A L G E R N O N – I can see no possible defence at all for your deceiving a brilliant, clever, thoroughly experienced girl like Miss Fairfax. To say nothing of the fact that she is my cousin.

J A C K – I wanted to be engaged to Gwendolen, that is all. I love her.

A L G E R N O N – Well, I simply wanted to be engaged to Cecily. I adore her.

J A C K – There is certainly no chance of your marrying Miss Cardew.

A L G E R N O N – I don't think there is much likelihood, Jack, of you and Miss Fairfax being united.

J A C K – Well, that is no business of yours.

A L G E R N O N – If it was my business, I wouldn't talk about it. It is very vulgar to talk about one's business. Only people like stockbrokers do that, and then only at dinner parties.

J A C K – How can you sit there, calmly eating muffins when we are in this horrible trouble, I can't make out. You seem to me to be perfectly heartless.

A L G E R N O N – Well, I can't eat muffins in an agitated manner. The butter might soil one's clothes. One should always eat muffins quite calmly. It is the only way to eat them.

J A C K – I say it is perfectly heartless your eating muffins at all, under the circumstances.

A L G E R N O N – When I am in trouble, eating is the only thing that consoles me. Indeed, when I am in really great trouble, I refuse everything except food and drink. At the present moment I am eating muffins because I am unhappy. Besides, I am particularly fond of muffins.

J A C K [*going over to tea-table and sitting down*] Well, that is no reason why you should eat them all in that greedy way.

[*Helps himself to muffins.*]

A L G E R N O N [*offering tea-cake*] I wish you would have tea-cake instead. I don't like tea-cake.

J A C K – Good heavens! I suppose a man may eat his own muffins in his own house.

A L G E R N O N – But you have just said it was perfectly heartless to eat muffins.

J A C K – I said it was perfectly heartless of you, under the circumstances. That is a very different thing.

A L G E R N O N – That may be. But the muffins are the same.

[*Removes muffin-plate.*]

J A C K – Algy, I wish to goodness you would leave my house—I don't want you here. I insist on your going. What on earth are you staying for?

A L G E R N O N – I have not finished my tea yet. And after that, I have got to be baptised. I have a heap of things to get through before dinner. What time, by the way, do you dine, Jack? Eight?

J A C K – I have not invited you to dinner. I won't let you stay to dinner. You have got to go.

A L G E R N O N – You can't possibly ask me to go without having some dinner. It is absurd. I never go without my dinner. No one ever does, except vegetarians and people who have got fads.

J A C K – What do you mean by talking about being baptised, after tea?

A L G E R N O N – I have just made arrangements with Dr. Chasuble to be baptised at a quarter to six, under the name of Ernest. I don't like being called Ernest at all, but it is only the gentlemanly thing to be called, under the circumstances. Jack, you are eating the muffins again! I wish you wouldn't. There are only two left. [*Removes plate again.*] I told you I was particularly fond of muffins.

J A C K – But I hate tea-cake.

A L G E R N O N – Why on earth do you have it for your guests then? What an idea you have of hospitality!

J A C K – As for the nonsense you talk about being baptised the sooner you give that up, the better. I made arrangements this morning with Dr. Chasuble to be baptised myself at 5.30. I naturally will take the name of Ernest. Gwendolen would wish it. We can't both be christened Ernest. It would be absurd. Besides, I have a perfect right to be baptised, if I like. There is no evidence at all that I ever have been baptised by any body. I should think it extremely probable I never was, and so does Dr. Chasuble. It is entirely different in your case. You have been baptised already.

A L G E R N O N – Yes, but I have not been baptised for years.

J A C K – Yes, but you have been baptised. That is the important thing.

A L G E R N O N – Quite so. So I know my constitution can stand it. If you are not quite sure about your ever having been baptised, I must say I think it rather dangerous your venturing on it now. It might make you very unwell. You can hardly have forgotten that your own brother was carried off this week in Paris by a severe chill.

J A C K – Yes, but you said yourself it was not hereditary, or anything of that kind.

A L G E R N O N – It usen't to be, I know—but I daresay it is, now. Science is always making wonderful improvements in things.

J A C K – May I ask, Algy, what on earth you propose to do?

A L G E R N O N – Nothing. That is what I have been trying to do for the last ten minutes, and you have kept on doing everything in your power to distract my attention from my work.

J A C K – Well, I shall go out in the garden and see Gwendolen. I feel quite sure she expects me.

A L G E R N O N – I know from her extremely cold manner that Cecily expects me, so I certainly shan't go out into the garden. When a man does exactly what a woman expects him to do, she doesn't think much of him. One should always do what a woman doesn't expect, just as one should always say what she doesn't understand. The result is invariably perfect sympathy, on both sides.

JACK—Oh, that is nonsense; you are always talking nonsense.

ALGERNON—It is much cleverer to talk nonsense than to listen to it, my dear fellow. And a much rarer thing, too, in spite of all the public may say.

JACK—I don't listen to you. I can't listen to you.

ALGERNON—Oh! That is merely false modesty. You know perfectly well you could listen to me if you tried. You always underrate yourself; an absurd thing to do now-a-days, when there are such a lot of people about.

FOURTH ACT

The same

[*Enter behind* GWENDOLEN *and* CECILY.]

G W E N D O L E N – The fact that they did not follow us at once into the garden, as anyone else would have done, seems to me to show that they have some sense of shame left.

C E C I L Y – They have been eating muffins. That looks like repentance.

G W E N D O L E N – Nothing of course can undo the past. But simply as a matter of curiosity I would like to know if Mr. Worthing has any explanation to offer to me.

C E C I L Y – Everything is over between myself and Algernon, but I would be sorry not to hear what he has to say. When one is in trouble the only thing that can distract one's mind from grief is some form of light fiction.

A L G E R N O N [*sees the girls and rises*] I don't care what you say, Jack. I will go out and see Cecily. . . . I beg your pardon, Miss Cardew. I didn't see you.

C E C I L Y – That is not a very polite thing to say, Mr. Montford, when you have been looking at me for nearly half a minute.

G W E N D O L E N – I have something very particular to ask you, Mr. Worthing. Much depends on your reply.

C E C I L Y – Gwendolen, your common sense is invaluable. Mr. Montford, kindly answer me the following question. Why did you pretend to be my guardian's brother?

A L G E R N O N – In order that I might have an opportunity of meeting you, Miss Cardew.

C E C I L Y [*to* GWENDOLEN] That certainly seems a satisfactory explanation, does it not?

G W E N D O L E N – Yes, if you can believe him.

C E C I L Y – I don't. But that does not affect the wonderful beauty of his answer.

G W E N D O L E N –⌈True. In matters of grave importance, style, not sincerity is the vital thing.⌋ [*To* JACK.] Mr. Worthing, what explanation

1511

can you offer to me for pretending to have a brother? Was it in order
that you might have an opportunity of coming up to town to see me as
often as possible?

J A C K – Can you doubt it, Gwendolen?

G W E N D O L E N – I have the gravest doubts upon the subject. But I intend to crush them. This is no time for scepticism. There is too much
scepticism in the age as it is. [*To* CECILY.] Their explanations appear
to be quite satisfactory, especially the one I was generous enough to
suggest to Mr. Worthing. That seems to me to have the stamp of truth
on it.

C E C I L Y – I am more than content with what Mr. Montford said. His
voice alone inspires one with absolute credulity.

G W E N D O L E N – Then you think we should forgive them?

C E C I L Y – I am sure it is our duty to do so.

G W E N D O L E N – No! I had forgotten. Forgiveness of any kind is obviously out of the question.

C E C I L Y – True! how the thing slipped my memory I cannot understand.

G W E N D O L E N – There is clearly nothing to be done.

C E C I L Y – Personally, I see no way out of it.

G W E N D O L E N – There are principles at stake that one cannot surrender.

C E C I L Y – To give up one's ideals would be a fatal weakness.

J A C K – But what is the matter? I distinctly understood that I had been
forgiven for a harmless deception.

A L G E R N O N – You certainly led me to believe, Miss Cardew, that you
had pardoned me for what was after all but a slight lapse of memory.

G W E N D O L E N [*to* CECILY] This is either effrontery, or innocence.

C E C I L Y – It seems to be like innocence.

G W E N D O L E N – I fear so. We will have to break it to them, gently.

C E C I L Y – We will be obliged to gradually lead up to it.

G W E N D O L E N – Which of us should tell them? The task is not a pleasant one.

C E C I L Y – You are older than I am, dear Gwendolen. Perhaps it would
produce more effect if you did it.

G W E N D O L E N [*somewhat wounded*] It seems to me, dearest Cecily,
that the truth would sound better from the lips of a mere child like
yourself.

C E C I L Y – Could we not both speak at the same time?

G W E N D O L E N – An excellent idea! I often speak at the same time as
other people. Let us begin at once. Will you take the time from me?

C E C I L Y – With pleasure.

1512

GWENDOLEN and CECILY [*speaking together*] Your Christian names are what we object to. That is all.

JACK and ERNEST[21] [*speaking together*] Our Christian names! Is that all?

CECILY [*looking at* ALGERNON] Well, I feel bound to admit that if you were called Ernest I wouldn't mind so much. I like to think of Uncle Jack as being Uncle Jack still.

GWENDOLEN [*to* JACK] I don't mind acknowledging that, if Ernest was your name, I think I would be able to bear the fact of cousin Algy being still cousin Algy.

CECILY – But as it is. . . .

GWENDOLEN – We see no possible hope

CECILY – of reconciliation

GWENDOLEN – of any kind.

JACK – But dearest Gwendolen, if I may be once more allowed to call you so, I was trying to break the news gently to you when you turned from me. The plain fact is that at 5.30 this afternoon, in our simple little village church, Dr. Chasuble is going to baptise me by the name of Ernest.

GWENDOLEN – How noble you are!

ALGERNON – My own Cecily, if I may address you in such terms for the last time, I was trying to lead up gradually to what I have to tell you, when you shrunk from all converse with me. The simple truth is that I have a baptismal appointment with the Rector of this parish at a quarter to six. Ernest is the name I am to receive at the font.

CECILY – How brave you are!

GWENDOLEN [*to* JACK] For my sake you are prepared to do this terrible thing?

JACK – Certainly.

CECILY [*to* ALGERNON] To please me you are ready to face this fearful ordeal?

ALGERNON – I am!

GWENDOLEN [*to* CECILY] How absurd to talk of the equality of the sexes! Where questions of self-sacrifice are concerned, men are infinitely beyond us.

CECILY [*to* GWENDOLEN] They have moments of physical courage of which we women know absolutely nothing.

JACK [*to* GWENDOLEN] Darling!

ALGERNON [*to* CECILY] Darling!

[*They fall into each other's arms.*]

[21] Ernest in error for Algernon.

[*Enter* MERRIMAN. *When he enters he coughs loudly, seeing the situation.*]

MERRIMAN—Ahem! Ahem! Lady Brancaster!

JACK—Good heavens! The Gorgon!

GWENDOLEN—My mother!

ALGERNON—My aunt!

GWENDOLEN *clings to* JACK. ALGERNON *disappears with* CECILY *behind a screen l.c. and remains in full sight of the audience.* ALGERNON *makes signs to* CECILY *to keep quite still, and from time to time says "Hush"!*

[*Enter* LADY BRANCASTER. *General consternation, and scuffle. Exit* MERRIMAN.]

LADY BRANCASTER—Gwendolen! What does this mean?

GWENDOLEN—It merely means that I am engaged to Mr. Worthing, mamma.

LADY BRANCASTER—You are sadly mistaken, Gwendolen. Such an engagement is quite impossible. It would be, in fact, revolting. A cloak-room at a railway station might conceal a social indiscretion. It could hardly create a social existence of any kind, even in the suburbs where birth is practically unknown. Come over here, Gwendolen, at once.

GWENDOLEN—Certainly, mamma. [*Goes over.*] But I am engaged to be married to Mr. Worthing.

LADY BRANCASTER—Silence, child. When you do become engaged to be married to anyone, I, or your father, if his health allows him, will inform you of the fact. It is not a thing that a well brought-up girl should ever know anything about, herself. An engagement should come on a girl as a pleasant, or unpleasant surprise, arranged for her beforehand by her parents. But I will talk to you more fully about this subject at home. [*Turns to* JACK.] Mr. Worthing, apprised of my daughter's sudden flight by her French maid whose confidence I purchased by means of a small coin, I followed her at once, by a luggage train.

ALGERNON [*behind the screen to* CECILY *who is laughing*] Hush!

LADY BRANCASTER [*looks vaguely about and then proceeds*] Her unhappy father is, I am glad to say, still in ignorance of her disgraceful conduct. He is under the impression that she is attending a more than usually lengthy lecture at the University Extension Scheme. I do not propose to undeceive Lord Brancaster. During the whole course of my married life I have never undeceived Lord Brancaster about anything. As a natural consequence, he has the most perfect trust in whatever I tell him. But of course, you will clearly understand that all communication between yourself and my daughter must cease immediately. On this point, as indeed on all points, I am firm.

A L G E R N O N   [*to* CECILY *behind screen*] Hush!

L A D Y   B R A N C A S T E R   [*looks round again at* GWENDOLEN *and* JACK *with troubled expression, then proceeds*] The painful circumstances of your origin, Mr. Worthing, make you, as I am sure you will frankly admit yourself, quite impossible as a suitor for the hand of Lord Brancaster's only child, and mine.

J A C K — I am engaged to be married to Gwendolen, Lady Brancaster!

L A D Y   B R A N C A S T E R — You are nothing of the kind, sir. Nor have you any right to make such a statement in the presence of her mother, whose decision in this matter, as in all matters indeed, is final. Gwendolen, we will return to town at once. To-morrow I will make arrangements for taking you abroad. I am going to order your father to Carlsbad; and a course of those saline waters would I think have a chastening effect on your foolish attempts at independence. In your father's case, at any rate, I have never found them fail. And your conduct to-day reminds me somewhat of his own behaviour in the early days of our happy married life.

A L G E R N O N   [*behind screen to* CECILY *who is whispering and laughing*] Hush!

L A D Y   B R A N C A S T E R — Mr. Worthing, is it you who keeps on saying "Hush" whenever I am talking?

J A C K — No, Lady Brancaster. I have been listening with the deepest interest to everything you say.

L A D Y   B R A N C A S T E R — It is clear then that there is someone who says "Hush" concealed in this apartment. The ejaculation has reached my ears more than once. It is not at any time a very refined expression, and its use, when I am talking, is extremely vulgar, and indeed insolent. I suspect it to have proceeded from the lips of someone who is of more than usually low origin.

J A C K — I really think you must be mistaken about it, Lady Brancaster. There is a sort of echo I believe in this room. I have no doubt it is that.

L A D Y   B R A N C A S T E R   [*with a bitter smile*] In the course of my travels I have visited many of the localities most remarkable for their echoes, both at home and abroad. I am ready to admit that the accuracy of their powers of repetition has been grossly overestimated, no doubt for the sake of gain, but in no instance have I ever found an echo to say "Hush" in answer to an observation. Such an occurrence would be most improper. It would be a kind of miracle. It would tend to superstition. My hearing, I may mention, is unusually acute, as indeed are all my senses: my sight, my touch, my capacity for discerning odours. [*Looks about room carefully with her lorgnette. Finally, catch-*

ing sight of a glance between JACK *and* GWENDOLEN, *she turns her attention to the screen. She glares at it for a short time.*] Mr. Worthing, might I ask you to be kind enough to move aside that screen?

JACK [*cheerily*] What screen, Lady Brancaster?

LADY BRANCASTER [*stonily*] That screen, if you please. I see no other in the room.

[JACK *is obliged to move back the screen.* ALGERNON *and* CECILY *are discovered; they are holding each other's hands.*]

Algernon! You here?

ALGERNON—Yes, Aunt Augusta.

LADY BRANCASTER—May I ask if it is in this house that your invalid friend Mr. Bunbury resides?

ALGERNON—No, Aunt Augusta. Bunbury doesn't live here. Bunbury is somewhere else at present.

LADY BRANCASTER—I suppose he has quite recovered from his indisposition, then, as you seem to have been able to leave his bedside so soon, and to come on a visit to your friend Mr. Worthing.

[ALGERNON—Oh! Bunbury is dead, Aunt Augusta. That is all right.

LADY BRANCASTER—Dead?

ALGERNON—Yes, quite dead.

LADY BRANCASTER—But when did Mr. Bunbury die? His death must have been very sudden.

ALGERNON—I killed him this afternoon. I mean he died this afternoon.

LADY BRANCASTER—What did he die of?

ALGERNON—Bunbury? Oh, he was exploded.

LADY BRANCASTER—Exploded! I did not [know] he was a sufficiently eminent politician to be entitled to be in any way the object of revolutionary outrages.

ALGERNON—Oh, [I] mean he was found out! The doctors found out that he could not live, that is what I mean—so he died.

LADY BRANCASTER—He seems to have had great confidence in the opinion of his physicians. Were you with him at the end?

ALGERNON [*cheerily*] Oh, yes! I saw the last of Bunbury. Poor old chap.]

LADY BRANCASTER—You will miss him, no doubt, very much.

ALGERNON—Bunbury! Certainly not. He was very useful in his way, of course, but he is not necessary any more.

LADY BRANCASTER—Well, you bear his loss with wonderful equanimity, considering the devotion you displayed to him during his lifetime. I am glad to have the opportunity of noting that in that respect you take after my side of the family. I never indulge in useless regrets of any kind. They seem to me morbid. . . . I did not know the late

Mr. Bunbury personally, nor I believe did Gwendolen. Did you ever meet the late Mr. Bunbury, Gwendolen?

GWENDOLEN—No, mamma. From what I have heard of him I think he must have led somewhat of the life of a recluse.

LADY BRANCASTER—Considering his state of health I am not at all surprised. And now that we have comfortably buried Mr. Bunbury at last, may I ask, Mr. Worthing, who is that young lady whose hand my nephew Algernon is now holding in what seems to me a peculiarly marked manner, not to say affectionate?

JACK—This, Lady Brancaster, is Miss Cardew, my ward.

[LADY BRANCASTER *bows coldly to* CECILY.]

ALGERNON—I am engaged to be married to Cecily, Aunt Augusta.

LADY BRANCASTER—I beg your pardon?

CECILY—Mr. Montford and I are engaged to be married, Lady Brancaster.

LADY BRANCASTER [*with a shiver*] I do not know whether there is anything peculiarly exciting in the air of this part of Herefordshire, but the amount of engagements that go on seems to me considerably above the proper average that statistics have laid down for our guidance. I think, Algernon, some preliminary enquiries on my part would not be out of place. Mr. Worthing, is Miss Cardew at all connected with any of the larger railway stations in London? I ask merely for information. Until yesterday I had no idea that there were any families or persons whose origin was a Terminus.

[JACK *looks perfectly furious, but restrains himself.*]

JACK [*in a clear, cold voice*] Miss Cardew is the grand-daughter of the late Sir Thomas Cardew of 149, Belgrave Square, S.W.; Gervase Park, Dorking, Surrey; and the Glen, Fifeshire, N.B.

LADY BRANCASTER—That sounds not unsatisfactory. Three addresses always inspire confidence. But what proof have I of their authenticity?

JACK [*indignantly*] Proof, Lady Brancaster?

LADY BRANCASTER—The word I believe is not an uncommon one in the English language. A dictionary that did not contain it would be sadly incomplete. It would probably be of American origin.

[JACK *gets very angry.* GWENDOLEN *makes signs to him to keep quiet.* ALGERNON *plucks at his coat-tails.* CECILY *puts her hand on his arm.*]

JACK [*with an elaborate bow*] I have carefully preserved the Court Guides of the period. They are open to your inspection, Lady Brancaster.

LADY BRANCASTER [*grimly*] I have known strange errors in that publication.

JACK—Miss Cardew's family solicitors are Messrs. Markby, Markby, and Markby of 149a Lincoln Inn's Fields, Western Central District, London. I have no doubt they will be happy to supply you with any further information.

LADY BRANCASTER [*bowing*] Markby, Markby, and Markby? A firm of the very highest position in their profession. Indeed I am told that one of the Mr. Markbys is occasionally to be met, if not at dinner parties, at any rate at evening receptions. So far I am satisfied.

JACK [*very irritably*] How extremely kind of you, Lady Brancaster! I have also in my possession, you will be pleased to hear, certificates of Miss Cardew's birth, registration, baptism, whooping cough, vaccination, confirmation and the measles; both the German and the English variety.

[CECILY *looks reproachfully at* JACK.]

LADY BRANCASTER [*calmly*] Ah! A life crowded with incident, I see; though perhaps somewhat too exciting for a young girl. I am not myself in favour of premature experiences. In the life of a well-ordered and well-balanced young woman marriage should be the first event of any importance, and the last. But the modern girl, as I am now only too well aware, has a mania for collecting experiences. A somewhat expensive hobby. The experiences of the modern girl fetch little, when they come to be valued. . . . One more question, Mr. Worthing, and I have done. Has Miss Cardew any little fortune? I am naturally anxious to know all about her character, tastes, and disposition.

JACK – Well, it would be rather difficult to state exactly the amount of Miss Cardew's little fortune.

LADY BRANCASTER [*satirically*] I feared so, from the first. [*Looks at her watch.*] Gwendolen! the time approaches for our departure. We have not a moment to lose. Where is my parasol?

GWENDOLEN – Here, mamma, and your smelling-salts.

LADY BRANCASTER – Thank you. Algernon! You will, of course, escort us to town?

ALGERNON – I should be charmed, Aunt Augusta, but Mr. Worthing expects me to stay to dinner.

LADY BRANCASTER – I am sure he will excuse you on this occasion.

JACK – With the greatest pleasure! I am sorry, Lady Brancaster, that I have not been able to give you the exact information you required, but property in London and Surrey is so increasing in value every year, that it is really difficult to state within ten or twenty thousand pounds what Miss Cardew's little fortune exactly is.

LADY BRANCASTER [*stopping short*] Within ten or twenty thousand pounds! [*Looks at her watch.*] I see that we have more time for catching our train than I had at first supposed. [*Sits down.*] Speaking broadly, Mr. Worthing, what estimate would [you] give of Miss Cardew's fortune?

J A C K – Oh! at present about a hundred and thirty or a hundred and forty thousand pounds. That is all. But the property is sure to increase largely in value in the course of the next six or seven years.

L A D Y   B R A N C A S T E R – Miss Cardew seems to me a most attractive young lady. Few girls now-a-days have any really solid qualities, any of the qualities that last, and improve with time. We live, I regret to say, in an age of surfaces. [*To* CECILY.] Come over here, dear. [CECILY *goes across*.] Pretty child! Your dress is sadly simple, and your hair seems almost as Nature might have left it. But we can soon alter all that. A thoroughly experienced French maid produces a really marvellous result in a very brief space of time. I remember once recommending a French maid to young Lady Lancing,[22] Lord Shoreham's daughter, and after three months her own husband did not know her.

J A C K – And after six months nobody knew her.

L A D Y   B R A N C A S T E R   [*looks angrily at* JACK *but controls herself*] Kindly turn round, sweet child. [CECILY *turns completely round*.] No, the side view is what I want. [CECILY *turns her profile*.] Yes, quite as I expected. There are distinct social possibilities in your profile.

C E C I L Y – Really, Lady Brancaster? How very gratifying!

L A D Y   B R A N C A S T E R – Child! never fall into the habit, so unfortunately common now-a-days, of talking trivially about serious things. The two weak points that one observes in people are their want of principle and their want of profile. The chin, a little higher, please. Style largely depends on the way the chin is worn. They are worn very high, just at present. Gwendolen. . . . [*Sees* GWENDOLEN *in private conversation with* JACK, *and repeats the name with emphasis*.] Gwendolen!

G W E N D O L E N   [*coming over*] What, dear mamma?

L A D Y   B R A N C A S T E R – Don't you agree with me, my love, that there are distinct social possibilities in Miss Cardew's profile?

G W E N D O L E N   [*kissing* CECILY *and releasing her from the painful position of posing in front of* LADY BRANCASTER] Cecily is a perfect darling! The moment I met her I said to myself: "There is the wife of my cousin Algernon." My first impressions of people are never wrong.

A L G E R N O N   [*coming over and taking* CECILY *by the two hands*] Cecily is the prettiest girl in the whole world.

G W E N D O L E N   [*in indignant surprise*] Algy!

A L G E R N O N – The prettiest girl in the whole world, for me.

G W E N D O L E N   [*relieved and going back to* JACK] Oh! That is another

[22] This is the only time the name is mentioned in the play. [Wilde had pretended for a while that the play was entitled *Lady Lancing*.–E.B.]

point. I don't a bit mind your saying that. Only painfully plain girls are ever admired by their own relations.

ALGERNON [*still holding* CECILY's *hands*] And the dearest girl in the whole world for me, and the sweetest, for everyone.

CECILY [*after a pause*] Don't stop, Algy. I could listen to you for ever when you talk to me about myself. It is only when you change the subject that I become at all inattentive.

ALGERNON — I will never change the subject.

CECILY — I certainly think it is better to concentrate oneself entirely on one subject. I do not care for versatility, however fashionable it may be.

ALGERNON — Darling!

[*Kisses her.*]

LADY BRANCASTER [*first glares at them kissing; then puts on a forced smile and taps* ALGERNON *with her fan*] You pair of headstrong lovers! It is quite charming to see such sweet natural romance. [*To* JACK.] I think you said a hundred and thirty thousand pounds, Mr. Worthing?

JACK — Yes. A hundred and thirty or a hundred and forty thousand at present, Lady Brancaster.

LADY BRANCASTER [*to* CECILY] Dear child, the longer I know you the more I like you. You seem to grow on one. . . . Of course you know that my dear nephew Algernon has nothing but his debts to depend on. But I do not approve of mercenary marriages. When I married Lord Brancaster, who was then one of the richest commoners in England, I had no fortune of any kind. But I never dreamed of letting that stand in my way. Well, I suppose I must give my consent.

ALGERNON — Thank you, Aunt Augusta.

LADY BRANCASTER — Cecily, you may kiss me!

CECILY [*kisses her*] Thank you, Lady Brancaster.

LADY BRANCASTER — You may also address me as Aunt Augusta for the future.

CECILY — Thank you, Aunt Augusta.

JACK [*coming over*] I beg your pardon, Lady Brancaster. I didn't quite catch what you said a few moments ago.

LADY BRANCASTER — That is strange, for I believe my enunciation is more than usually clear. The fact, however, is that I have yielded at last to the persistent entreaties of these young people, and given my consent to their engagement. Of course I must consult Lord Brancaster on the subject as soon as I return to town, which I see must be in a few minutes. [*Pulls out watch.*] But Lord Brancaster is in the habit of agreeing with me on all points. It is the keynote to his character.

J A C K [*smiling*] Oh! I don't think I would bother Lord Brancaster about it. I know he has a great many worries in his life, already.

L A D Y B R A N C A S T E R [*looks angrily at him; then smiles*] Oh! consulting Lord Brancaster is a mere formality. It is a kind of formality, however, that is always observed in families of high birth. I can guarantee to you, Mr. Worthing, that his answer will be favourable. Believe me, you have no cause for anxiety on that point. It is true that he has not seen Cecily yet, but I feel confident that what I can tell him about the solid qualities she possesses will more than satisfy him.

J A C K [*still smiling and genial*] I am afraid you don't quite understand me, Lady Brancaster. This engagement is quite out of the question. Nothing could induce me to give my consent. In this matter I am firm, as indeed in all matters I am firm. I do not allow Miss Cardew to become engaged to your nephew. I forbid it absolutely.

C E C I L Y – Uncle Jack!

A L G E R N O N – My dear fellow! Not allow me to marry Cecily. I never heard anything so monstrous in the whole course of my life.

J A C K – Then you can have listened but carelessly to the conversation of other people.

L A D Y B R A N C A S T E R – Sir, I do not understand by what right you take upon yourself to forbid an engagement that I myself have sanctioned, and of which Lord Brancaster will highly approve.

J A C K – You seem to forget, Madam, that I am Miss Cardew's guardian. She cannot marry without my consent until she comes of age. That consent I absolutely decline to give.

L A D Y B R A N C A S T E R – Upon what grounds may I ask? My nephew Algernon is entitled by birth, position, and social standing, to form an alliance with anyone. He is an extremely, I may almost say an ostentatiously, eligible young man. To my own knowledge he is on the list of nearly all the mothers in London.

J A C K – It pains me very much to have to speak frankly to you, Lady Brancaster, about your nephew, but the fact is that I do not approve at all of his moral character. In fact, I suspect him of being untruthful.

[ALGERNON *and* CECILY *look at him in amazement.*]

L A D Y B R A N C A S T E R – Untruthful! My nephew Algernon? Impossible!

J A C K – He obtained admission into my house, into my home-circle indeed, under the false pretence of being my brother. Under an assumed name he drank an entire bottle of my '74 champagne, a wine I was specially reserving for myself. Continuing his disgraceful deception, he succeeded in the course of the afternoon in alienating the affections of my only ward. He subsequently stayed to tea. And what makes his conduct all the more heartless is, that he was perfectly well aware from

1521

the first that I have no brother, and that I never had a brother, not even of any kind. I distinctly told him so myself in Half Moon Street, yesterday.

C E C I L Y – But, dear Uncle Jack, you informed us all that you had a brother. You dwelt continually on the subject. Algy merely corroborated your statement. It was noble of him.

J A C K – Pardon me, Cecily, you are a little too young to understand these matters. To invent anything at all is an act of sheer genius, and, in a commercial age like ours, shows considerable physical courage— Few of our modern novelists ever dare to invent a single thing. It is an open secret that they don't know how to do it. Upon the other hand, to corroborate a lie is a distinctly cowardly action. I know it is a thing that the newspapers do one for the other, every day. But it is not the act of a gentleman. No gentleman ever corroborates a thing that he knows to be untrue.

A L G E R N O N [*furiously*] Jack! I never heard such a thing in my life. I really won't stand it.

J A C K [*with a pained look*] A moment, Algernon. Nor is this all, Lady Brancaster, worse remains behind.

L A D Y B R A N C A S T E R – My experience of life is that it usually does. . . . But proceed, Mr. Worthing, in your story. I need not tell you how much it distresses me. I shall certainly consider it my painful duty to conceal all the facts from Lord Brancaster. Fortunately, it has been my habit to do that for years. Indeed I may say that he never knows about anything that occurs to any single member of his family. Proceed, Mr. Worthing. I am listening with all an aunt's natural anxiety.

J A C K – At two o'clock this afternoon, Lady Brancaster, in order to save your nephew from immediate imprisonment, I paid for him out of my own pocket bills amounting to £376.14.2.[23] I think it right to add that these bills showed on the surface that they were contracted by one whose life was more than usually reckless and extravagant. The two chief creditors were the Willis Restaurant, and Mr. Arundel, the jeweller of Bond Street.[24] We all know what that ends in. . . . I think, Lady Brancaster, that now that you see that but for my intervention your nephew would at this moment be leading the luxurious and indolent existence of a first-class misdemeanant, you will realize how impossible I find it to entrust to so weak and foolish a character the care of the future happiness of my dear ward. [*Rings bell. Enter* MERRIMAN.] Some sherry, please.

[23] This differs considerably from amounts given previously, as shown in note 16.
[24] In the second act it was stated that the suit against Ernest Worthing was brought by the Savoy Hotel.

MERRIMAN—Yes, sir.
[*Exit.*]
LADY BRANCASTER—I can only promise you, Mr. Worthing, that these unfortunate incidents will be carefully kept from Lord Brancaster.
ALGERNON [*after a whisper with* CECILY] My dear fellow, you are playing it a little too high, aren't you? I don't think I can quite pass that. Aunt Augusta, it is only fair to myself to tell you that the bills weren't mine at all, they were his. I had nothing whatsoever to do with them.
[*Enter* MERRIMAN *with sherry.* JACK *takes a glass.*]
JACK—I had hoped, Algernon, to have spared you the necessity of making that painful confession. In the eyes of any sensible person, it puts your conduct in a light that is, if possible, still more disgraceful. As, however, you have chosen yourself to make the matter public, you must bear the necessary consequences. [ALGERNON *approaches table where the sherry is.* JACK *removes the decanter to a table just behind him. r.f.*] Your nephew, Lady Brancaster, as he has just admitted himself, compelled me at 2 o'clock this afternoon to pay my own bills, a thing I have not done for years, a thing that is strictly against my principles, a thing that I in every way disapprove of. In taking that attitude, I am not merely speaking for myself, but for others. More young men are ruined now-a-days by paying their bills than by anything else. I know many fashionable young men in London, young men of rank and position, whose rooms are absolutely littered with receipts, and who, with a callousness that seems to me absolutely cynical, have no hesitation in paying ready money for the mere luxuries of life. Such conduct seems to me to strike at the very foundation of things. The only basis for good Society is unlimited credit. Without that, Society, as we know it, crumbles. Why is it that we all despise the middle classes? Simply because they invariably pay what they owe. . . . You are now in full possession of the sad details about your nephew's conduct, Lady Brancaster. I hope you will lay them before Lord Brancaster on your return to town, and ask his opinion about them.
[*Drinks sherry.*]
LADY BRANCASTER—I think I shall. It might be too great a shock to Lord Brancaster to be asked his opinion about anything. . . . Ahem! Ahem. . . . Algernon, pray be more reposeful. [*To* ALGERNON *who is consoling* CECILY.] You are much too demonstrative, and demonstrations of any kind are extremely vulgar and democratic. We have far too many of them, now-a-days, as it is. I am told that Hyde Park, on the one day of the week on which one doesn't want to use it, is

quite unbearable. . . . Ahem! Mr. Worthing, after careful consideration I have decided to overlook my nephew's conduct—painful to you though it undoubtedly has been. Cecily, I still consent to your engagement with Algernon. Indeed, I may say that I insist upon it. When my heart is touched, I become like granite. Nothing can move me.

C E C I L Y – Thank you, Aunt Augusta.

J A C K – Cecily, your addressing Lady Brancaster as your Aunt Augusta is not merely historically inaccurate, but expresses a disregard of your kind guardian's wise decision about your future life which both surprises and wounds me.

C E C I L Y – Uncle Jack! An expression that I may mention is historically inaccurate. I think you are perfectly horrid! I can't understand you.

J A C K – Young girls are not expected to understand very abstruse problems.

C E C I L Y – I don't think you are an abstruse problem at all. I simply think you are very cruel, and so unreasonable that I suspect you of being a fallacy of some kind.

J A C K – Believe me, dear Cecily, I am acting for the best.

C E C I L Y – People always say that when they do their worst.

J A C K – Child! Who taught you such a pessimistic idea?

C E C I L Y – No one; if I had been taught it, I wouldn't believe it.

J A C K – I will not argue with you, Cecily. Guardians, like judges, curates, and people in high authority never argue. It is safer, and more impressive. I forbid your engagement with Mr. Algernon Montford.

L A D Y   B R A N C A S T E R – I was prepared for that, Mr. Worthing. Indeed I am always prepared for everything. It is one of the characteristics of my nature. . . . Lord Brancaster and my family are quite familiar with it. . . . I don't think that your consent to this alliance is, after all, a matter of much, if any, importance. . . . It seems to me that we can afford to do without it. [*To* CECILY.] Come here, sweet child. [CECILY *goes over*.] How old are you, dear?

C E C I L Y – Well, I am really only eighteen, but I always admit to twenty when I go to evening parties.

L A D Y   B R A N C A S T E R – You are perfectly right in making some slight alteration, dear. Indeed, nowhere should a woman ever be quite accurate about her age. It looks so calculating. . . . [*In meditative manner.*] Eighteen, but admitting to twenty at evening parties. Well, whichever date you choose, dear, it will not be very long before you are of age, and free from the restraints of tutelage. And to speak frankly, I am personally strongly in favour of somewhat lengthy engagements. People have time to get rid of that demonstrative period of affection which in married people is always out of place, and indeed, I am glad to say, practically unknown now-a-days in good society at any rate. There is no reason for impatience of any kind. A few more roses in the garden, and in your pretty cheeks, and you will be twenty-one, Cecily. At that period Mr. Worthing will cease to have the right to exercise any tyrannical supervision over you, and your little fortune.

J A C K – Pray excuse me, Lady Brancaster, for interrupting you, but it is only fair to tell you that according to the terms of her grandfather's will Miss Cardew does not come legally of age till she is thirty-five. Should she marry without my consent before then, it becomes my duty to transfer her property to some charitable institution. The choice, and indeed, foundation of the institution, if I so desire it, are left entirely to my judgment.

L A D Y   B R A N C A S T E R   [*severely*] I should like to inspect that will.

J A C K – It can be seen any day, Lady Brancaster, between the hours of three and five at the offices of Miss Cardew's solicitors, Messrs. Markby, Markby, and Markby, of 149a–

L A D Y   B R A N C A S T E R   [*waving her hand*] You have already mentioned the address, Mr. Worthing, and even the most interesting pieces of useful information pall a little on repetition. I accept your statement about the will, and I do not see that the proviso you mention need cause us any anxiety. Thirty-five is a very attractive age. London society is full of women of the very highest birth who have, of their own free choice, remained thirty-five for years. Lady Dumbleton is an instance in point. To my own knowledge she has been thirty-five ever since she arrived at the age of forty, which was many years ago now. And Lady Dumbleton is very much admired, in the evening. I see no reason why our dear Cecily should not be even still more attractive at the age you mention than she is now. There will be large accumulations of property.

C E C I L Y   [*to* J A C K] You are quite sure that I can't marry without your consent until I am thirty-five?

J A C K – That is the wise provision of your grandfather's will, Cecily. He undoubtedly forsaw the sort of difficulty that would be likely to occur.

C E C I L Y – Then grandpapa must have had a very extraordinary imagination. I am sure that nothing has ever occurred in history at all resembling the present state of things. But I don't want to talk to you at all, Uncle Jack. As far as I can make out at present I don't like you. Algy, could you wait for me till I was thirty-five? Don't speak hastily. It is a very serious question. And much of my future happiness depends upon your answer.

A L G E R N O N – Of course I could, Cecily. How can you ask me such a question? I could wait forever for you. You know I could.

C E C I L Y – Yes, I felt it instinctively. And I am so sorry for you, Algy. Because I couldn't wait all that time. I hate waiting even five minutes

for anybody. It always makes me rather cross. I am not punctual myself, I know, but I do like punctuality in others, and waiting, even to
be married, is quite out of the question. I am afraid you don't know
that I have a very impatient nature, and that the very smallest delay
often makes me a little irritable.

ALGERNON—Then what is to be done, Cecily?

CECILY—I don't know. Uncle Jack is so unkind and unreasonable. And
he doesn't seem to have any better nature, so perhaps if Aunt Augusta
would appeal to it something might be done.

ALGERNON [*to* LADY BRANCASTER] I wish, Aunt Augusta, you would
appeal to Cecily's guardian. It would be difficult for me to do so, as I
am not on speaking terms with him at present. But I am sure you
would produce a wonderful effect. You always do.

LADY BRANCASTER—I am not in the habit, as you are well aware,
Algernon, of making appeals of any kind, charitable or otherwise.
However, in the present case I shall make an exception. It would be
an act of criminal folly to allow a girl so richly endowed as Miss Car-
dew to pass entirely out of our family. . . . My dear Mr. Worthing,
I would beg of you to reconsider your decision.

JACK—But, my dear Lady Brancaster, the matter is entirely in your
own hands. The moment you consent to my marriage with Gwendolen,
I will most gladly allow your nephew to form an alliance with my
ward. It is true that I am not on speaking terms with Algy. But where
the happiness of Miss Cardew is concerned, vague questions of possible conversation with a third party in the future are of but little
importance.

LADY BRANCASTER [*drawing herself up*] Mr. Worthing, you must
be quite aware that what you propose is out of the question. Nothing
would induce me to allow Gwendolen to marry a person who cannot
point to a single parent, of either sex, and the fact of whose very birth
seems extremely problematic.

JACK—That is your final decision, Lady Brancaster?

LADY BRANCASTER—My final decision.

JACK—Then this interview had better close at once.

Turns round to look for sherry. Finds that ALGERNON *has removed it to
another table and is drinking some. Goes over with a pained serious face
and brings the sherry back.*

LADY BRANCASTER—I am quite of your opinion. [*Pulls out her
watch.*] Gwendolen! We have already missed five, if not six, trains.
To miss any more might expose us to comment on the platform. Come,
my love.

GWENDOLEN—But, mamma. . . .

CECILY [*to* LADY BRANCASTER] Oh! do stop a few moments. I would like to make one last appeal to my guardian.

LADY BRANCASTER—I hardly fancy that where I have failed, you will succeed. However, [*looks at watch*] I can give you three minutes and a half.

CECILY [*to* JACK] Uncle Jack! I had no idea that you were so selfish. It is a most painful surprise to me. Why even the copybooks know that selfishness is wrong. And they are not very advanced.

JACK—Child! You seem to me to use words without understanding their proper meaning. I am afraid your good governess has sadly neglected her duties. What is a selfish person? A selfish person is surely one who seeks to keep his joys and sorrows to himself. I am not like that. When I am unhappy, as I am now, I desire everyone else to share in my unhappiness. I give freely of my misfortunes. I do not treat my misery as a miser treats his gold. On the contrary, I scatter it abroad with a lavish hand. If I am blighted there is a general blight, and no one can complain that they are left out or overlooked.

CECILY—Gwendolen, will you appeal to him.

GWENDOLEN—I will be very glad indeed to tell him what I think of his conduct. [*Goes over to* JACK.] . . . Up to the present moment I frankly admit that I have always admired you. Now I simply adore you. It requires merely physical courage to sacrifice oneself. To sacrifice others moral courage is necessary.

[*Enter* DR. CHASUBLE *from the garden.*]

CHASUBLE—Everything is quite ready for the christenings. I have been waiting in the church porch for now nearly half an hour.

LADY BRANCASTER—The christenings, sir! Is not that somewhat premature? The marriages have not taken place yet.

[DR. CHASUBLE *looks enquiringly at* JACK, *who introduces him at once to* LADY BRANCASTER.]

JACK—Lady Brancaster, allow me to introduce to you Canon Chasuble, the worthy Rector of our parish.

[LADY BRANCASTER *bows coldly.*]

LADY BRANCASTER—May I ask you, Canon Chasuble, to what christenings you refer?

CHASUBLE [*looking rather puzzled, and pointing to* JACK *and* ALGERNON] These gentlemen have expressed the desire for immediate baptism.

LADY BRANCASTER—At their age! The idea is grotesque and irreligious!

CHASUBLE—I would be prepared to argue that point, Lady Brancaster.

LADY BRANCASTER [*severely*] I think not, sir.

CHASUBLE—The sprinkling, and indeed immersion, of adults was a common practice of the Primitive Church.

LADY BRANCASTER [*bridling*] That may be, sir. But it is hardly in accordance with our modern ideas of decorum— [*To* ALGERNON.] Algernon, I forbid you to be baptised. I will not hear of such excesses. Lord Brancaster would be highly displeased if he learned that that was the way in which you wasted your time.

CECILY [*to* ALGERNON] There is not much use now in your being baptised at all, is there?

ALGERNON—None, I am afraid.

GWENDOLEN—I think, that under the circumstances, I had better retain Ernest as a girlish dream. There is nothing to be gained by this proposed ceremony. Your facing the font would be merely foolhardy.

JACK—I fear so.

CHASUBLE—Am I to understand then that there are to be no baptisms at all this afternoon?

JACK—I don't think that, as things now stand, it would be of any practical value to either of us, Dr. Chasuble.

CHASUBLE—I am grieved to hear such sentiments from you, Mr. Worthing. Baptismal regeneration is not to be lightly spoken of. Indeed, by the unanimous opinion of the Fathers baptism is a form of new birth. . . . However, in the case of adults compulsory christening is uncanonical, so I shall return to the church at once. Indeed, I have just been informed by the pew-opener that Miss Prism has been waiting for me in the vestry for the last hour and a half.

LADY BRANCASTER [*starting*] Miss Prism! Did I hear you mention a Miss Prism?

CHASUBLE—Yes, Lady Brancaster; she is at present in the vestry. I am on my way to join her.

LADY BRANCASTER [*anxiously*] Pray allow me to detain you for a moment. This matter may prove to be of vital importance to Lord Brancaster and myself. A few enquiries will not be out of place. Is this Miss Prism a female of repellent aspect, remotely connected with education?

CHASUBLE [*somewhat indignant*] She is the most cultivated of ladies, and the very picture of respectability.

LADY BRANCASTER [*thoughtfully*] It is obviously the same person. May I ask what position she holds in your household?

CHASUBLE [*severely*] I am a celibate, Lady Brancaster.

JACK [*interposing*] Miss Prism, Lady Brancaster, has been for the last three years Miss Cardew's esteemed governess and companion.

LADY BRANCASTER—Then let me strongly advise you, Mr. Worthing, should she turn out to be the person I suspect her of being, never to allow her, under any circumstances, to take Miss Cardew out in a perambulator. The result might be lamentable. I must see this Miss Prism at once. Let her be sent for.

CHASUBLE   [*looking off*] She approaches; she is here.

[*Enter* MISS PRISM *hurriedly.*]

MISS PRISM – I was told you expected me in the vestry, dear Canon. I have been waiting for you there for an hour and three quarters.

Catches sight of LADY BRANCASTER *who has fixed her with a stony glare.* MISS PRISM *grows pale and quails. She looks anxiously round as if desirous to escape.*

LADY BRANCASTER   [*in a severe, judicial voice*] Prism! [MISS PRISM *bows her head in shame.*] Come here, Prism! [MISS PRISM *approaches in a humble manner.*] Prism! Where is the baby? [*General consternation. The* CANON *starts back in horror.* ALGERNON *and* JACK *pretend to be anxious to shield* CECILY *and* GWENDOLEN *from hearing a terrible scandal.* PRISM *makes no answer.*] Twenty-five years ago, Prism, on the ninth of October, 1869, you left Lord Brancaster's house, then Number 104, Upper Grosvenor Street, in charge of a perambulator that contained a baby, of the male sex. You never returned. A few weeks later, through the elaborate investigations of the metropolitan police, the perambulator was discovered at midnight, standing by itself in a remote corner of Hyde Park. It contained the manuscript of a three-volume novel of more than usually revolting sentimentality. [MISS PRISM *starts in involuntary indignation.*] But the baby was not there! [*Everyone looks at* MISS PRISM.] Prism! Where is that baby?

[*A pause.*]

MISS PRISM – Lady Brancaster, I admit with shame that I do not know. I only wish I did. The plain facts of the case are these. On the morning of the day you mention, a day that is for ever branded on my memory, I prepared as usual to take the baby out in its perambulator. I had also with me a somewhat old, but capacious hand-bag in which I intended to place the manuscript of a three-volume novel that I had written in my unoccupied moments. In a moment of mental abstraction, for which I never can forgive myself, I deposited the manuscript in the bassinette, and placed the baby in my hand-bag.

JACK   [*who has been listening attentively*] But where did you deposit the hand-bag that contained the baby?

LADY BRANCASTER – I do not see how that can matter now. It was, I suppose, left at the offices of one of those publishers who do not return rejected contributions unless accompanied by stamps. With your usual carelessness, Prism, I suppose you never dreamed of putting stamps with the baby. That unfortunate child is probably at the present moment lying in the waste-paper basket of some large commercial house.

J A C K – Lady Brancaster, this is a matter of no small importance to me. Miss Prism, I insist on knowing where you deposited the hand-bag that contained the infant.

M I S S   P R I S M – I left it, Mr. Worthing, in the cloak-room of one of the large railway stations in London. As soon as, alarmed by the unwonted silence that proceeded from the perambulator, I had examined it and discovered my fatal mistake, I hurried back to the station and presented the ticket. But the bag was gone.

J A C K – What was the railway station, Miss Prism?

M I S S   P R I S M   [*quite crushed*] Victoria. The Brighton line.

L A D Y   B R A N C A S T E R   [*looking at* JACK] A mere coincidence. I sincerely hope nothing improbable is going to happen. The improbable is always in bad, or at any rate, questionable taste.

J A C K – A wild hope dawns across my life. . . . Miss Prism . . . one word more. . . . Could you recognize the hand-bag?

M I S S   P R I S M – I think so. I had had it for many years. My mother had had it before me. It was almost an heirloom.

J A C K – I must retire for a moment to my bedroom.

C H A S U B L E – This news seems to have upset you, Mr. Worthing. I trust your indisposition is merely temporary.

J A C K – I will be back in a few moments, dear Canon. [*To* LADY BRANCASTER.] You said, I think, that if I was able to produce even one parent it would be enough.

L A D Y   B R A N C A S T E R – To ask for more would, I fear, be exorbitant. However, should this be more than a mere coincidence, which I strongly doubt, I am afraid you will still be unable to produce any. But, you can try. The motive of the search is laudable.

J A C K – Gwendolen! Can you trust me?

G W E N D O L E N – No, dear. If I could do that, I fear I would find you tedious. But I am watching your movements with interest.

J A C K – I will return shortly. Wait for me.

G W E N D O L E N – I will wait for you all my life.

[*Exit* JACK.]

C H A S U B L E – What do you think this means, Lady Brancaster?

L A D Y   B R A N C A S T E R – I dare not even suspect, Dr. Chasuble. I need hardly tell you in families of high position strange coincidences are not supposed to occur. They are hardly considered the thing.

[*Noises heard overhead as if someone was throwing trunks about. Everyone looks up.*]

1530

CECILY [*looking up*] Uncle Jack seems strangely agitated.

MISS PRISM—He has a very emotional nature.

LADY BRANCASTER—The noise is extremely unpleasant. It sounds as if he was having an argument with the furniture. I dislike arguments of any kind. They are excessively vulgar.

CHASUBLE [*looking up*] It has stopped now.

[*Loud bang overhead.*]

CECILY—No, it has begun again.

GWENDOLEN—This suspense is terrible. I hope it will last.

[*Enter* JACK *with a hand-bag of black leather in his hand.*]

JACK [*rushing over to* MISS PRISM] Is this the hand-bag, Miss Prism? [*Hands it to her.*] Examine it carefully before you speak. The happiness of more than one life depends on your answer.

MISS PRISM [*puts on her spectacles*] Yes, it seems to be mine. Here is the injury it received through the upsetting of a Gower Street omnibus in my younger and happier days. [*Opens bag.*] Here is the indelible stain left on the lining by the accidental explosion of a lemonade bottle, an event that occurred during the terribly hot summer of '62. [*In a more confident and joyful voice.*] Yes, and here, on the lock, are my initials. I had forgotten that I had had them placed there. The bag is undoubtedly mine. I am delighted to have it so unexpectedly restored to me. It has been a great inconvenience being without it.

JACK [*in a pathetic voice*] More is restored to you than the hand-bag. I was the baby you placed in it.

MISS PRISM [*amazed*] You! Mr. Worthing!

JACK [*embracing her*] Yes . . . mother!

MISS PRISM [*recoiling in indignant astonishment*] Mr. Worthing! I am unmarried!

JACK—Unmarried! I do not deny that that is a serious blow. But after all, who has the right to throw a stone against one who has suffered? Cannot repentance wipe out an act of folly? Why should there be one law for men, and another for women? Mother, I forgive you.

[*Tries to embrace her again.*]

MISS PRISM [*still more indignant*] But, Mr. Worthing, there is some error. I have never had a child in my life. The suggestion, if it were not made before such a large number of people, would be almost indelicate. [*Pointing to* LADY BRANCASTER.] There stands the lady who can tell you who you really are.

[*Retires to back of stage.*]

JACK [*after a pause*] Lady Brancaster, I hate to seem inquisitive, but would you kindly inform me who I am? It is a matter about which I can hardly help feeling some slight interest as I have known myself now for many years. I hope you will not consider my desire in any way morbid?

LADY BRANCASTER—I am afraid that the news I have to give you will not altogether please you. You are the son of my poor sister, Mrs. Montford, and consequently Algernon's elder brother.

JACK—Algy's elder brother! Then I have a brother after all. I knew I had a brother! I always said I had a brother! . . . [*To* ALGERNON.] Algy, you young scoundrel, you will have to treat me with more respect in the future. You have never behaved to me like a brother in your life.

ALGERNON—Not till to-day, old boy, I admit.

[*Shakes hands.*]

JACK—Cecily . . . Gwendolen . . . how could you have ever doubted that I had a brother?

GWENDOLEN—We were wrong.

CECILY—Very wrong indeed.

GWENDOLEN [*to* JACK] Darling! . . . You can call mamma Aunt Augusta now, can't you?

JACK—Yes, what a pleasure that will be!

LADY BRANCASTER—Under these strange and unforseen circumstances you can kiss your Aunt Augusta.

JACK [*staying where he is*] I am dazed with happiness.

[*Kisses* GWENDOLEN. ALGERNON *takes opportunity to kiss* CECILY.]

MISS PRISM [*advancing, after coughing slightly*] Mr. Worthing . . . Mr. Montford as I should call you now . . . after what has just occurred I feel it my duty to resign my position in this household. Any inconvenience I may have caused you in your infancy through placing you inadvertently in this hand-bag I sincerely apologize for. We all have our moments of forgetfulness. And I may mention that I was only thirty-four at the time, an age when one is still sadly thoughtless and frivolous.

JACK—Don't mention it, dear Miss Prism. Don't mention anything. I am sure I had a very pleasant time in your nice hand-bag, in spite of the slight damage it received through the overturning of an omnibus in your happier days. As for leaving us, the suggestion is absurd. You are quite invaluable here. But for you and me, Miss Prism, the high moral tone of this house could hardly be sustained. The truth, the naked truth, has always been our motto, whatever others may have done, in the way of cheap clothing.

MISS PRISM [*who has shuddered visibly at the expression: the naked truth*] I have to thank you for so flattering a testimonial, Mr. Montford. Should you find time to commit it to writing the document will remain the sole consolation of a life that I fear will be extremely solitary. For it is my duty to leave. It had never occurred to me before that as a woman sows, so shall she reap. I had thought that that aphorism only applied to the male sex. I was in error. And besides I have really nothing more to teach dear Cecily. In the very difficult accomplishment of getting married, I fear my sweet and clever pupil has far outstripped her teacher.

CHASUBLE—A moment . . . Laetitia!

MISS PRISM—Dr. Chasuble!

CHASUBLE—Laetitia, when I entered this room a short time ago I found it a scene of painful discord. It is to you, and to you alone, that the present harmony is due. It is to you also that our esteemed and honoured host owes the fact that we can still look up to him as a man of the very strictest veracity even in details about his family life, a point in which most men as a rule go sadly astray. . . . I have also come to the conclusion that the Primitive Church was in error on certain points. Corrupt readings seem to have crept into the text. . . . Laetitia, I beg to solicit the honour of your hand.

MISS PRISM—Frederick, at the present moment words fail me to express my feelings. But I will forward you this evening the three last volumes of my diary; in these you will be able to peruse a full account of the sentiments that I have entertained towards you for the last eighteen months.

[*Enter* MERRIMAN.]

MERRIMAN—Lady Brancaster's flyman says he cannot wait any longer.

LADY BRANCASTER [*rising*] True; I must return to town at once. [*Pulls out watch.*] I see I have now missed no less than nine trains. . . . [*Exit* MERRIMAN. LADY BRANCASTER *moves towards the door.*] Prism, from your last observation to Dr. Chasuble I learn with regret that you have not yet given up your ridiculous passion for sentimental fiction in three volumes. And, if you really are going to enter into the state of matrimony, which at your age seems to me, I feel bound to say, rather like flying in the face of providence, I trust you will be more careful of your husband than you were of your charge, and not leave poor Dr. Chasuble lying about at railway stations in hand-bags or receptacles of any kind. [MISS PRISM *bows her head meekly.*] . . . Dr. Chasuble, you have my sincere good wishes, and if baptism be, as you say it is, a form of new birth, I would strongly advise you to have Miss Prism baptised without delay. To be born again would be of considerable advantage to her. Whether such a procedure be in accordance with the practice of the Primitive Church I do not know. But it is hardly probable, I should fancy, that they had to grapple with such extremely advanced problems. [*Turning sweetly to* CECILY, *and patting her cheek.*] Sweet child! We will expect you to come and stay with us at Park Lane in a few days.

CECILY – Thank you, Aunt Augusta.

LADY BRANCASTER [*smiling*] Your severe guardian will hardly decline now to give his consent to your marriage with his own brother.

JACK – Dear Aunt Augusta, that marriage has been the dream of my life, for the last ten minutes. Of course you could not refuse me cousin Gwendolen's hand after what has occurred.

LADY BRANCASTER – Well, I am bound to state quite candidly that you have both compromised each other in such a grave and public manner that I feel sure Lord Brancaster will insist upon your union in the interests of the higher morality. Wickedness may go unpunished; usually does indeed—but a social indiscretion never. . . . Come, Gwendolen!

GWENDOLEN [*to* JACK] My own! . . . But what own are you? What is your Christian name, now that you have become someone else?

JACK – Good heavens! . . . I had forgotten that point. Your decision on the subject of my name is irrevocable, I suppose?

GWENDOLEN – I never change, except in my affections.

JACK – Then the point had better be cleared up at once. . . . Aunt Augusta, a moment. . . . How old was I when Miss Prism deposited me in the hand-bag?

LADY BRANCASTER – I cannot speak quite accurately on the subject. But you were certainly within a few weeks of ten months.

JACK – Had I been christened already? Pray be calm, Aunt Augusta. This is a terrible crisis, and much depends on your answer.

LADY BRANCASTER [*quite calmly*] Every luxury that money could buy, including christening, had been lavished on you by your fond and doting parents.

JACK – Then I was christened! That is settled. Now, what name was I given? Let me know the worst.

LADY BRANCASTER [*after a pause*] Being the eldest son you were naturally christened after your father. I distinctly remember your being christened after your father.

JACK [*irritably*] Yes, but what was my father's Christian name? Pray don't be so calm, Aunt Augusta. This is a terrible crisis, and everything hangs on the nature of your reply. What was my father's Christian name?

LADY BRANCASTER [*meditatively*] I cannot at the present moment recall what the General's Christian name was. Your poor dear mother always addressed him as "General." That I remember perfectly. Indeed, I don't think she would have dared to have called him by his Christian name. But I have no doubt he had one. He was violent in his manner, but there was nothing eccentric about him in any way. In fact, he was rather a martinet about the little details of daily life. Too much so, I used to tell my dear sister.

JACK [*agitated and impressive*] His name would appear in the Army Lists of the period, I suppose, Aunt Augusta?

LADY BRANCASTER—Oh! in many lists of different kinds. Towards the end of his life he was most unfortunate in his speculations. Indeed, I believe that what he paid in the pound is still a painful memory amongst the commercial classes.

JACK—The Army Lists of the last forty years are here. [*Pointing to bookcase.*] I see now how foolish I have been to neglect them for more trivial works like books on agriculture and novels with a purpose. These delightful records should have been my constant study. But it is not too late to take up the subject now. [*Rushes to bookcase and tears the books out. Distributes them rapidly.*] Here, Dr. Chasuble. Miss Prism, two for you. Cecily . . . Cecily, an Army List. Make a précis of it at once. Algernon . . . pray search English history for our father's Christian name, if you have the smallest filial affection left. Gwendolen . . . no; it would agitate you too much. Leave these researches to calmer natures like ours.

GWENDOLEN [*heroically*] Give me six copies of any period. This century or the last. I do not care which.

JACK—Noble girl! Here are a dozen! More might be an inconvenience to you. [*Brings her a pile of Army Lists. Rushes through them himself, taking each one from her hands as she tries to examine it.*] No, just let me look. No, allow me, dear. Darling, I think I can find it out sooner. Just allow me, my love.

CHASUBLE—What station, Mr. Montford, did you say you wished to go to?

JACK [*pausing in despair*] Station! Who on earth is talking about a station? I merely want to find out my father's Christian name. After I have found that out, I may take a train anywhere and end my life as I began it, in a lonely cloak-room.

CHASUBLE—But you have handed me a Bradshaw. [*Looks at it.*] Of 1869, I observe. A book of considerable antiquarian interest, but not in any way bearing on the question of the names usually conferred on generals at baptism.

CECILY—I am so sorry, Uncle Jack. But generals don't seem to be even alluded to in the "History of our own Times," although it is the cheap edition.

MISS PRISM—To me, Mr. Montford, you have given two copies of the Price Lists of the Civil Service Stores. I do not find generals marked anywhere. There seems to be either no demand, or no supply.

JACK [*very irritable indeed; to* ALGERNON] Good heavens! And what

1535

nonsense are you reading, Algy? [*Takes book from him.*] The Army List! Well, I don't suppose you knew it was the Army List. And you've got it open at the wrong page! Besides, there is the thing staring you in the face. M. Generals. . . . Mallam, what ghastly names they have —Markby, Migsby, Mobbs, Montford . . . Montford . . . Lieutenant 1840, Captain, Lieutenant-Colonel, Colonel, General 1860. . . . Christian names, Ernest John. [*Puts book very quietly down and speaks quite calmly.*] I always told you, Gwendolen, my name was Ernest, didn't I? Well, it is Ernest after all. I mean it naturally is Ernest.

LADY BRANCASTER—Yes, I remember now that the General was called Ernest. I knew I had some particular reason for disliking the name. Come, Gwendolen!

[*Exit.*]

GWENDOLEN—Ernest! My own Ernest! I felt from the first that you could have had no other name! Even all man's useless information, wonderful though it is, is nothing compared to the instinct of a good woman.

JACK—Gwendolen, it is a terrible thing for a man to find out suddenly that all his life he has been speaking nothing but the truth. Can you forgive me?

GWENDOLEN—I can. For I feel that you are sure to change. There is always hope even for those who are most accurate in their statements.

JACK—My own one!

CHASUBLE—Laetitia!

[*Embraces her.*]

ALGERNON—Cecily!

[*Embraces her.*]

JACK—Gwendolen!

[*Embraces her.*]

[*Enter* LADY BRANCASTER.]

LADY BRANCASTER—I have missed the eleventh train! Oh!

SATIRIC STRATEGY IN "THE IMPORTANCE OF BEING EARNEST"

By Otto Reinert

ALMOST EVERYONE agrees that *The Importance of Being Earnest* is good fun, but few have tried to show that it is also a good play. To say that Wilde has written a brilliant farce is not to say why it seems both funnier and more significant than other superior farces, and to say that the farce satirizes Victorianism is not, at this late date, to tell us why it amuses at all. From some of the incidental comments one gets the impression that the play is untouchable, so exquisite that criticism would be fatal—stupid abuse of something bright and fragile. A few critics, who take their business more seriously, refuse even to be charmed. The play "never transcends . . . the incomplete or the trivial," Edouard Roditi writes in his generally perceptive book on Wilde (1947). "Its tone is that of satire, but of a satire which, for lack of a moral point of view, has lost its sting and degenerated into the almost approving banter of a P. G. Wodehouse."

But only a curious form of critical blindness can dismiss *Earnest* as a trifle of dialogues. It merits attention both as satire and as drama. The farce is meaningful. Tone and plot have been successfully integrated, and the whole is more truly comic—because normative—than a well-made play to end all well-made plays, a vehicle for the utterance of witty nonsense. Awareness of its satirical strategy precludes the criticism that it is elusive of reasoned analysis for lack of any kind of rationale.

From *College English*, Vol. 18, No. 1, October 1956. Copyright, 1956, by The National Council of Teachers of English. Reprinted by permission of the author and The National Council of Teachers of English.

Wilde first employed a pattern of ironic inversion in *An Ideal Husband*, the play immediately preceding *Earnest*. Its hero, Lord Goring, is not the irresponsible dandy he seems to be, the surface frivolity is not the real man, and his flippant paradoxes emphasize the irony of his moral position relative to that of Lord Chiltern, the pretended pillar of society. For the first time in his plays Wilde puts the fine art of epigram to serious purposes: it participates in the total meaning of the play.

Lord Goring's wit expresses that ironic attitude to life that guarantees moral salvation in Wilde's world. But though the brand of wit is similar in *Earnest*, such an attitude cannot be attributed to any one or several of the characters in the later play, simply because it has no hero (or heroine) in the sense in which Lord Goring is the hero of *An Ideal Husband*. The characters in *Earnest* never stop being flippant; their flippancy is their whole nature and not, like Lord Goring's, the mocking mask of enlightened irony in a pompous society. The only ironist in *Earnest* is Wilde himself, who not only has abandoned the simple ethics of thesis melodrama but also has deliberately sacrificed the illusionistic conventions of naturalism in order to gain what Francis Fergusson calls (in *The Idea of a Theater*, 1949) a "limited perspective, shared with the audience, as the basis of the fun," showing "human life *as* comic . . . because . . . consistent according to some narrowly defined, and hence unreal, basis."

That is why there is no reason to be embarrassed by the farce label. The play's merit is that it is *all* farce, capable of serving as a lucid image of the non-farcical reality that is kept strictly outside the play. Wilde has respected his paradoxes. He is no longer putting them to menial service as bright spots in sentimental thesis plays or as devices of crude melodramatic irony. *The Importance of Being Earnest* is one sustained metaphor, and esthetic detachment is the only mood in which it can be intelligently enjoyed. It insists on being acted straight, for if we should feel, even for a moment, that the characters are aware of what absurdities they are saying, the whole thing vanishes. Once object and image are confused there is a blurring of vision. No one in his right mind gets emotionally involved with the destinies of Algernon and Cecily, Gwendolen and Jack. But it is precisely their emotive neutrality as figures of farce that allows Wilde's characters to establish his "limited perspective": Wilde's basic formula for satire is their assumption of a code of behavior that represents the reality that Victorian convention pretends to ignore.

Algernon is explaining his reluctance to attend Lady Bracknell's[1] dinner party: "She will place me next Mary Farquhar, who always flirts

[1] Lady Brancaster in the version printed above.—E.B.

with her own husband across the dinner table. That is not very pleasant. Indeed, it is not even decent . . . and that sort of thing is enormously on the increase. The amount of women in London who flirt with their own husbands is perfectly scandalous. It looks so bad. It is simply washing one's clean linen in public." To say that Algernon's tone here is consciously flippant is to miss the joke altogether. The quip is not a quip; it means what it says. Algernon is indignant with a woman who spoils his fun by parading her romance with her husband. He is shocked at convention. And his tone implies that he is elevating break of convention into a moral norm. He is not the first figure in English satire to do so; among his ancestors are Martin Scriblerus, other assumed identities in Pope and Swift (including Gulliver), and the apologist for Jonathan Wild. What they all have in common is that they derive their ideals for conduct from the actual practice of their societies, their standards are the standards of common corruption, they are literal-minded victims of their environments, realists with a vengeance.

Here is Algernon on conventional love institutions: "I really don't see anything romantic in proposing. It is very romantic to be in love. But there is nothing romantic about a definite proposal. Why, one may be accepted. One usually is, I believe. Then the excitement is all over." And here is his vision of the post honeymoon tea table:

ALGERNON – Have some bread and butter. The bread and butter is for Gwendolen. Gwendolen is devoted to bread and butter.

JACK – And very good bread and butter it is too.

ALGERNON – Well, my dear fellow, you need not eat as if you were going to eat it all. You behave as if you were married to her already. . . .

The girls, too, implicitly accept this inverted code. In the proposal scene between Jack and Gwendolen the latter acts out reality: girls about to be proposed to quite realize the situation and are annoyed by their suitors' conventionally bungling approach. In the second act Gwendolen explains to Cecily that she always travels with her diary in order to "have something sensational to read in the train." One of Cecily's first speeches expresses her concern for "dear Uncle Jack" who is so "very serious" that "I think he cannot be quite well." When Algernon, at their first meeting, begs her not to think him wicked, she sternly replies: "If you are not, then you have certainly been deceiving us all in a very inexcusable manner. I hope you have not been leading a double life, pretending to be wicked and being really good all the time. That would be hypocrisy." Paradoxical morality cannot be argued much further than this, and the speech upsets even Algernon. In context it cuts down to the

very core of the problem of manners with which Wilde is concerned. It
epitomizes the central irony of the play, for the Bunburying Algernon,
in escaping the hypocrisy of convention, becomes a hypocrite himself by
pretending to be somebody he is not. (Even Miss Prism participates. She
is telling Cecily about her youthful novel: "The good ended happily,
and the bad unhappily. That is what Fiction means.")

Only Jack and Lady Bracknell seem at first glance to be outside the
pattern of inversion, expressing shock when confronted with the code of
cynical realism. But their conventionality is not genuine. Jack is a confirmed Bunburyist long before Algernon explains the term to him, and
Bunburyism is most simply defined as a means of escape from convention. He occasionally acts the role of naive elicitor of Algernon's dis-
courses on Bunburyism and is not such a consistent theorist of the realist
code, but his behavior is certainly not conventional.

One of Lady Bracknell's main plot functions is to be an obstacle to
Jack's romance with Gwendolen, but a systematic analysis of her speeches
will show, I think, that she has no illusions about the reality her professed convention is supposed to conceal: ". . . I do not approve of
mercenary marriages. When I married Lord Bracknell I had no fortune of
any kind." To her the speech is neither cynical nor funny. It represents
that compromise between practical hardheadedness and conventional morality that she has worked out to her own satisfaction and behind which
she has retired in dignified immunity. In other speeches she advocates
Algernon's code with as much sanctimoniousness as he: "Well, I must
say, Algernon, that I think it is high time that Mr. Bunbury made up his
mind whether he was going to live or to die. This shilly-shallying with
the question is absurd. Nor do I in any way approve of the modern sympathy with invalids. I consider it morbid." She moralizes on behalf of
people who take it for granted that illness in others is always faked and
that consequently sympathy with invalids is faked also, a concession to
an artificial and—literally—morbid code. The frivolous banter accom-
plishes something serious. It exposes the polite cynicism that negates all
values save personal convenience and salon decorum. Life and death have
become matters of *savoir-vivre*.

The following speech presents a somewhat more complex case, because
Lady Bracknell is here simultaneously deferring to convention and exposing its sham: "French songs I cannot possibly allow. People always
seem to think that they are improper, and either look shocked, which is
vulgar, or laugh, which is worse. But German sounds a thoroughly respectable language, and indeed, I believe is so." To laugh at presumably
improper songs is to fly in the face of convention and break the delicate
fabric of social decorum. But the opposite reaction is hardly less repre-
hensible. To register shock at indecency is indecently to call attention to

something people realize the existence of but refuse to recognize. In her last sentence she quietly gives away the polite fiction that people in society know foreign languages.

When the pattern of inversion operates the characters either express or assume a morality that is deduced from the actual behavior of high society, though the existence of conventional morality is sometimes recognized as a fact to come to terms with. What the accumulation of paradox adds up to is an exposure both of hypocrisy and of the unnatural convention that necessitates hypocrisy. In elegant accents of pompous bigotry Wilde's puppets turn moral values upside down. "Good heavens," Algernon exclaims when Lane tells him that married households rarely serve first-rate champagne. "Is marriage so demoralizing as that?" We are made to share Wilde's view of the ludicrous and sinister realities behind the fashionable façade of an over-civilized society where nothing serious is considered serious and nothing trivial trivial.

But *Earnest* is, before anything else, a play, an imitation of *action*, and no discussion of tone apart from its dramatic setting can account for the extraordinary impact of the play as play. It is rather odd, therefore, to notice that even critics who have been aware of serious satiric implications in the dialogue have been prone to dismiss the plot as negligible, as, at best, "inspired nonsense." "The plot," writes Eric Bentley, in *The Playwright as Thinker* (1946), "is one of those Gilbertian absurdities of lost infants and recovered brothers which can only be thought of to be laughed at," and he defines the function of "the ridiculous action" as constantly preventing the play from "breaking into bitter criticism." There is truth in that, but the action has another and far more important function as well: it informs the satiric dialogue with coherent meaning.

The action of *The Importance of Being Earnest* is about just that—the importance of being earnest. The title is as straightforward a statement of theme as any literalist could ask for. Specifically, the play deals with the consequences of that way of not being earnest that Algernon calls Bunburying, and it is Bunburying that gives the plot moral significance. The key speech in the play is Algernon's little lecture to Jack: "Well, one must be serious about something, if one wants to have any amusement in life. I happen to be serious about Bunburying. What on earth you are serious about I haven't got the remotest idea. About everything, I should fancy. You have an absolutely trivial nature." Bunburying means to invent a fictitious character, who can serve as a pretext for escaping a frustrating social routine, regulated by a repressive convention. The pretended reason for getting away is perfectly respectable, even commendable, according to convention: to comfort a dying friend, to rescue a fallen brother. Thus defined, Bunburying is simply the mechanism that sets in motion the preposterously elaborate plot of mistaken identities. But the word has also a wider meaning. Significantly, Algernon *happens* to be serious about Bunburying—that is, it is not the subterfuge itself that is important, but the commitment to a course of action that will provide fun. The Bunburyist in the wider sense is serious about not being serious, and Bunburyism is the alternative to a convention that fails to reckon with the facts of human nature. It stands for behavior that will give experience the shading and perspective that convention denies it. To be serious about everything is to be serious about nothing; that is, to trifle. Algernon charges Jack (unfairly, as it happens) with a failure to discriminate among life values, to see that monotone of attitude blunts the spirit and deadens joy. And this is precisely Wilde's charge against Victorianism.

The Bunburyist lives in a world of irresponsibility, freed from the enslavement of a hypocritical convention. He enjoys himself. But life beyond hypocrisy is life in a dangerous climate of moral anarchy, and, like most states of revolt, Bunburyism is not ideal. The escape from convention is itself a flagrant instance of hypocrisy: pretense is the price the Bunburyist pays for freedom from the pretense of convention. In his title pun Wilde catches the moral failure of dandyism. Just as the conformist pretends to be, but is not, earnest, so Algernon and Jack pretend to be, but are not, Ernest.

What Wilde is saying, then, is that all normal Victorians who want to retain the respect of their conventional society are, perforce, Bunburyists, leading double lives, one respectable, one frivolous, neither earnest. Bunburyism, as Algernon confesses in the opening of the play, is the application of science to life, to the exclusion of sentiment. Sentiment properly belongs to art. The science is the science of having a good time. These are obviously false distinctions, and all that can be said for Bunburyism as a way of life is that it offers relief from a social round where, in Lady Bracknell's words, good behavior and well being "rarely go together," and where, according to Jack, "a high moral tone can hardly be said to conduce very much to either one's health or one's happiness." Bunburyism marks one of the extreme points in the swing of the pendulum, Victorianism the other.

Neither of the two Bunburyists is either earnest or Ernest—before the very end.[2] It is only then that they become, and in more than a single

[2] It is the one flaw in a superbly constructed play that Algernon remains Algernon at the end and thus ineligible as a husband for Cecily. To say that she does not seem to mind at that point or that Dr. Chasuble is quite ready for the christening cannot conceal the flaw. It staggers the imagination to try to think of any way in which Wilde could have turned Algernon into a second Ernest, but, given the plot, he ought to have done so.

sense, themselves. When the action begins they have already escaped the mortifying seriousness of convention, but it takes them three acts and the movement from town to country—the movement has symbolic relevance as a return to "naturalness"—to regain their balance and become earnest, that is, neither conventionally nor frivolously hypocritical. At the end of the play the respectable (though amorous) Miss Prism (her name suggests "prim prison") has been unmasked, the four young people are romantically engaged, Jack has discovered his Bunburying identity to be his true self, and Lady Bracknell must recognize the contemptible orphan of Act I, "born, or at any rate, bred in a handbag," as her own sister's son. The plot, as it were, makes a fool of respectability and proves the two Bunburyists "right" in their escapade. But it also repudiates Bunburyism. Algernon, who as a Bunburyist spoke cynically about proposals and matrimony in Act I, is happily proposing marriage to Cecily in Act II, and at the end his initial false dichotomies between life and art, science and sentiment, have been resolved in romance. The radical remedy of Bunburying has effected a cure, the pendulum rests in the perpendicular, and we share Jack's final conviction of "the vital Importance of Being Earnest." The two adjectives have not been chosen lightly.

THE MEANING OF THE
IMPORTANCE OF BEING EARNEST

By Arthur Ganz

IN ACT II OF *The Importance of Being Earnest* Jack returns to his country house and announces the death of his supposed brother, the profligate Ernest.

DR. CHASUBLE – Was the cause of death mentioned?
JACK – A severe chill, it seems.
MISS PRISM – As a man sows, so shall he reap.
DR. CHASUBLE [*raising his hand*] Charity, dear Miss Prism, charity! None of us is perfect. I myself am peculiarly susceptible to draughts.

This sequence is more than a delightful joke. It is symptomatic of the emotional and intellectual attitudes that underlie the play and, in fact, Wilde's work. What we laugh at, perhaps a little uneasily, is Chasuble's inability to distinguish between a moral and a physical quality. When the rector cautions Miss Prism about the inevitable imperfections of man and goes on to name one of his own, we naturally expect a moral failing, but we get instead a susceptibility to draughts. If we are uneasy, it is because in the world in which Dr. Chasuble exists, the world of perfect Wildean dandyism, the rector's attitude is entirely reasonable. This is a world of pure form, and the distinction between a moral and a physical failing, between external and internal, does not exist. Chasuble is right and we are wrong.

From *Modern Drama*, May 1963. Reprinted by permission of the author and *Modern Drama*.

Even such a brief analysis of one line suggests that the conventional description of *The Importance* as, in the words of Arthur Symons, "a sort of sublime farce, meaningless and delightful," is inadequate. William Archer was so puzzled by the play that he asked, "What can a poor critic do with a play which raises no principle, whether of art or morals . . . and is nothing but an absolutely wilful expression of an irrepressibly witty personality?" With the advantage of distance, we can see now that art and morals are precisely the subjects of *The Importance of Being Earnest* and that the world of dandyism, though delightful, is far from meaningless.

For Wilde, dandyism was a philosophy and an attitude toward life. Embodied in his plays, it functions as a rationale for the actions and attitudes of his characters, as a coherent system which forms the basis for their thoughts and their conduct. In the great tradition of the Romantic exile artist, Wilde rejected the middle-class, Philistine society of his day. Its coarseness, its pitiless morality, and its incomprehension of beauty were all alien to him. Searching for a new basis for life, Wilde, the most extreme of esthetic critics, turned to the only part of experience in which he had faith, to art—whose secret for him lay always in the achievement of perfect form. He took form, the basis of art, turned it into a philosophy of life in which esthetics replaces ethics and, as we shall see, introduced it into his plays cloaked with the elegance and wit of nineteenth-century dandyism.

This dandyism, from which Wilde drew so many elements sympathetic to him, had existed long before he made use of it. The nineteenth century produced many dandies, and Wilde must have seen himself as a follower of such men as Brummell, Byron, d'Orsay, and, probably above all others, Benjamin Disraeli. In Disraeli, Wilde saw an artist like himself, a man apart from the crass bourgeoisie, whose wit and extraordinary dress were instruments with which he had achieved a position of power. With Disraeli in mind, a remark by Lord Illingworth in *A Woman of No Importance*, "a man who can dominate a London dinner table can dominate the world," is a little less bizarre than it at first seems.

Disraeli, however, was only an example. The theorists of dandyism as a philosophy of life and art were Jules Barbey d'Aurevilly and Charles Baudelaire. Barbey d'Aurevilly, still a figure of some note when Wilde frequented Parisian literary circles, had produced *Du Dandysme et de Georges Brummell*, the most elaborate nineteenth-century disquisition on dandyism. Barbey never saw dandyism as a mere matter of elegance in dress, but as a philosophy, as a "manner of living composed entirely of nuance, as always happens in societies at once very ancient and very civilized." His insistence on dandyism as a rule of conduct for a society past its prime must have impressed the decadents of the nineties, but the element which would most have appealed to Wilde was Barbey's view of the dandy as individualist, as "the element of caprice in a stratified and symmetrical society." The dandy demonstrates his individualism and superiority with his wit, by shocking without being shocked. He is one of those "who wish to produce surprise while remaining impassive." If Wilde did not learn the theory of dandyism from Barbey, he undoubtedly learned, or at any rate reinforced, it through the essay "Le Dandy" in *Le peintre de la vie moderne* by Charles Baudelaire. Wilde admired Baudelaire and could not have been unfamiliar with an essay by him on a subject so important in Wilde's own work. Like Barbey, Baudelaire insisted that "dandyism is not, as many unreflecting persons seem to think, an immoderate taste for dress and material elegance. These things are for the perfect dandy only a symbol of the aristocratic superiority of his spirit." Dandyism is individualism, "the ardent need to produce something original . . . it is a kind of cult of the self . . . it is the pleasure of astonishing and the proud satisfaction of never being astonished." The dandy is hostile to his society, for only in an effete and unworthy age would he feel this compulsion to distinguish himself from the ordinary. "Dandyism," wrote Baudelaire, "is the last burst of heroism in a decadent age." Wilde called dandyism a philosophy; Baudelaire went even further: "in fact," he wrote, "I would not be entirely wrong in considering dandyism as a sort of religion."

Now we can turn to Wilde's plays and see what led him to make the religion of dandyism his personal code, what he took from his sources, and what he added to them. To Wilde, as to Barbey d'Aurevilly and Baudelaire, dandyism was not an affectation of dress but an attitude toward the world, and specifically toward the world of Victorian Philistinism with its coarseness, its materialism, and its code of Puritanical morality. The French theorists reinforced in Wilde the idea of the dandy as a heroic individualist who, like Disraeli as Wilde saw him, used his grace and wit to oppose and dominate the crass world about him. It is of the essence of *The Importance of Being Earnest*, however, that this Philistine world, though often spoken of, is never present. If it were, the play as we know it could not exist. Wilde's society comedies, in which the Philistine world has equal status with the dandiacal, are disfigured by the conflict between them. In each play a similar pattern of melodramatic action is centered around a character with a secret sin in his past: Mrs. Erlynne, Mrs. Arbuthnot, Sir Robert Chiltern. Each is opposed by a strict Puritan—Lady Windermere, Hester Worsley, Lady Chiltern—who at first allows of no compromise between good and bad and demands that sin be punished. In each case, however, the sinner is shown to have remained pure at heart and to desire forgiveness while the Puritan is educated to grant it and even to come to love him. Like the dandy, the sinner is an exile, but one who cannot bear his solitude and begs to be forgiven and accepted by the ordinary Philistine world. The dandy, however, glories in his alienation. It is the uncomfortable yoking of these antithetical attitudes that finally destroys the society comedies. To write his masterpiece, Wilde had to reject the passionate sinner with his admission of guilt and speak only in the critical voice of the dandy.

But dandiacal criticism should be distinguished from satire, for when the dandy is satirical at all, he is so only incidentally. Wilde can satirize such things as the methodical husband hunting of fashionable society, as when Lady Bracknell tells Jack that he is not down on her list of eligible young men, "although," she says, "I have the same list as the dear Duchess of Bolton has. We work together, in fact." In this case, Wilde agrees with the ostensible opinion of society, that arranged, mercenary marriages are evil. This agreement, rare in Wilde, is essential to the satirist who accepts a social norm and criticizes deviations from it, but the dandy is himself a deviation and criticizes the social norm. Dandyism, as Baudelaire and Barbey maintained, is hostile to ordinary society. The dandy is not a reformer but a subversive.

To call such a dandy as the charming and witty Algernon a subversive may seem at first unduly harsh. Algernon, one might say, is only trivial. But triviality is the dandy's disguise. It is, in fact, the traditional clown's mask, from the concealment of which he can say what he wishes without fear of retaliation. In Wilde's other plays the dandies are often openly villainous, but here, through the unreality of the situations and the delicacy of the language, Wilde has thrown a cloak of seeming innocence over a very sinister personage. Algernon's statements, then, may be flippant in tone, but they are not innocuous in content. Where the satirist makes fun of the abuses of marriage, the dandy criticizes the institution itself. When the manservant Lane observes that in married households the champagne is rarely of a first-rate brand, Algernon exclaims, "Good Heavens! Is marriage so demoralizing as that?" He tries to avoid Lady Bracknell's dinner party because he knows he will be placed "next Mary Farquhar, who always flirts with her own husband across the dinner table. That is not very pleasant. Indeed, it is not even decent." Lady Bracknell herself, though she is an arch-Philistine, often assumes the dandiacal voice and shares Algernon's point of view. "I'm sorry if we are a little late, Algernon," she says upon entering, "but I was obliged to call upon dear Lady Harbury. I hadn't seen her since her poor husband's death. I never saw a woman so altered; she looks quite twenty years younger." In the third act she makes herself even clearer. Commenting on Jack's father, she remarks that he was eccentric, "but only in later years. And that was the result of the Indian climate, and marriage, and indigestion, and other things of that kind." Like Dr. Chasuble, she cannot distinguish between the physical and the spiritual, between indigestion and a sacrament of the church.

Lady Bracknell and Dr. Chasuble are dandies by indirection; just as they conceal their dandyism beneath a Philistine exterior, so Jack, seemingly virtuous and respectable, is as belligerent as they are. Several times during the play he refers to truth, a quality admired by all righteous men, but when Algernon asks him if he intends to tell Gwendolen the truth about being Ernest in town and Jack in the country, Jack replies patronizingly, "My dear fellow, the truth isn't quite the sort of thing one tells to a nice, sweet, refined girl." Later, when forced to admit his deception, he says, "Gwendolen—Cecily—it is very painful for me to be forced to speak the truth. It is the first time in my life that I have ever been reduced to such a painful position, and I am really quite inexperienced in doing anything of the kind." When it is finally revealed that Jack's name really is Ernest, he can only exclaim, "Gwendolen, it is a terrible thing for a man to find out suddenly that all his life he has been speaking nothing but the truth. Can you forgive me?"

Even the ingenuous Cecily turns out to be a foe of rectitude and morality. "Dear Uncle Jack is so very serious," she remarks. "Sometimes he is so serious that I think he cannot be quite well." When Gwendolen is announced, Cecily at first supposes her to be an elderly lady interested in philanthropic work. "I don't quite like women who are interested in philanthropic work," she says to herself. "I think it so forward of them." Cecily shares this distaste with Lady Bracknell who, misunderstanding Algernon's statement that Bunbury had been quite exploded, cries, "Exploded! Was he the victim of a revolutionary outrage? I was not aware that Mr. Bunbury was interested in social legislation. If so, he is well punished for his morbidity."

It is, in fact, the arch-Philistine Lady Bracknell who, when speaking in her dandiacal voice, most openly defies the Philistine standards:

LADY BRACKNELL—Is this Miss Prism a female of repellent aspect, remotely connected with education?

CHASUBLE [*somewhat indignantly*] She is the most cultivated of ladies, and the very picture of respectability.

LADY BRACKNELL—It is obviously the same person.

It is unnecessary to continue adding examples. Whenever ordinary morality appears, it is made to seem ridiculous. Even Miss Prism becomes an unintentional exponent of the dandiacal attitude. When it is announced that the carefree Ernest is dead, she exclaims, "What a lesson for him! I trust he will profit by it." When we laugh at her obtuseness, we are forced to laugh at even the possibility of moral reform.

Miss Prism also illustrates another significant element in the play, the intense individualism that was one of Wilde's major preoccupations. Absorbed in the contemplation of his own feelings, the dandiacal individualist seems reluctant to admit the existence of others, or at least to react to their emotions. When, for example, Jack rushes in with the crucial handbag and begs Miss Prism to identify it and thus establish his parentage, she examines it carefully and at considerable length:

> MISS PRISM — . . . And here on the lock are my initials. I had forgotten that in an extravagant mood I had had them placed there. The bag is undoubtedly mine. I am delighted to have it so unexpectedly restored to me. It has been a great inconvenience being without it all these years.

At this climactic moment of the play when the secret of Jack's birth is about to be penetrated, Miss Prism's mind is centered on a minor personal acquisition.

Although our laughter at the incongruousness of her remark conceals its inhumanity, there is in Miss Prism's foolish preoccupation with her handbag something similar to the icy self-sufficiency of Gwendolen and Cecily, both of whom happily center their affections on the name Ernest before they come to know its possessor. Cecily, in fact, manages to conduct an elaborate courtship in the absence of her beloved. Lady Bracknell is not only an individualist in her self-sufficiency but in what she implies about keeping the personality inviolate. When Jack hurries upstairs to hunt frantically for the handbag, she remarks, "This noise is extremely unpleasant. It sounds as if he was having an argument. I dislike arguments of any kind. They are always vulgar and often convincing." Beneath this joke is Wilde's reluctance to let any exterior force affect his personality. He was engrossed in what Baudelaire called "the cult of the self." Even in prison Wilde wrote, "I am far more of an individualist than I ever was. Nothing seems to me of the smallest value except what one gets out of oneself. My nature is seeking a fresh mode of self-realization. That is all I am concerned with."

The dandy's individualism is closely connected with his social belligerence. By taking the limits of his own personality as the boundaries of admissible reality, he can protect himself against the claims of society. If all values come from the self, then the moral standards of others are irrelevant to him; he may abuse or disregard them as he pleases. For him other persons have little real existence; they are only one of the mediums through which sensations, pleasant or otherwise, are conveyed to him. But the sensations themselves are important, for it is through them that the dandy creates the self. The theory of sensation came to Wilde from Walter Pater, his master at Oxford, whose famous conclusion to *The Renaissance* emphasized "not the fruit of experience, but experience itself." To the dandy, remote from society and centered on himself, his own feelings are matters of extraordinary interest. The more exquisite sensations he can experience, the richer will be the self which he is trying to realize.

It is this desire to savor a novel experience that makes Algernon, when returning Jack's cigarette case and asking his friend to explain why he is Ernest in town and Jack in the country, say, as he hands Jack the case, "Here it is. Now produce your explanation, and pray make it improbable." However, the characters most given to relishing new sensations are Cecily and Gwendolen. While awaiting the entrance of the reprobate Ernest, impersonated by Algernon, Cecily remarks, "I have never met any really wicked person before. I feel rather frightened. I am so afraid he will look just like everyone else." And when Algernon enters, "very gay and debonair," she sighs in disappointment, "he does!" Cecily does not fear Ernest's wickedness; she fears that if he does not *seem* wicked, he will fail to give her the *nouveau frisson* that she seeks. Later, when Algernon-Ernest says that their parting will be very painful, Cecily replies, "It is always painful to part from people whom one has known for a very brief space of time. The absence of old friends one can endure with equanimity. But even a momentary separation from anyone to whom one has just been introduced is almost unbearable." A new acquaintance is a "new thrill." It is the loss of the sensation, not the friend, that Cecily fears. Perhaps the clearest illustration of the dandy's self-centered relishing of sensation is the line Gwendolen speaks while Jack is upstairs frantically hunting for the handbag that will reveal his identity. "This suspense is terrible," she exclaims; "I hope it will last." The continuation of Gwendolen's pleasurable sensation is dependent upon the continuation of Jack's distress, but such a consideration cannot affect her. Locked within the confines of the individual self, the dandy must feed upon a succession of novelties or starve to death.

Although the stress on sensation was added by Wilde to the belligerence and individualism inherited from Barbey and Baudelaire, it is not the Wildean dandy's most distinctive element. This is his faith in the superiority of esthetic form. "In matters of grave importance," says Gwendolen, "style not sincerity is the vital thing." Baudelaire also stressed the superiority of the artificial to the natural and admired the conscious artifice of the dandy's toilette, but he emphasized the dandy's revulsion from the moral standards of his age and only by implication connected him with esthetics. For Wilde, the dandy embodied, above all, his theories of art. When Wilde wrote that Phipps, the dandiacal butler of *An Ideal Husband*, "represents the dominance of form," he made the dandy the incarnation of esthetic form; and for Wilde form, as he explained in "The Critic as Artist," was the basis of all art:

> For the real artist is he who proceeds, not from feeling to form, but from form to thought and passion . . . realizing the beauty of the sonnet-scheme, he conceives certain modes of music and methods of rhyme, and the mere form suggests what is to fill it and make it intellectually and emotionally complete. . . . He gains his inspiration from form, and from form purely, as an artist should. . . . In every sphere of life Form is the beginning of things. The rhythmic harmonious gestures of dancing convey, Plato tells us, both rhythm and harmony into the mind. . . . Yes, Form is everything. It is the secret of life.

It is this element, this absolute faith in pure esthetic form, that makes the Wildean dandy unique, and because it is dominated by him *The Importance of Being Earnest* is a unique play. It stands alone among English comedies, not only because of the quality of its wit, but because it is an expression of Wilde's theories and attitudes, and no other writer has approached the theater with a comparable point of view. It stands alone among Wilde's plays because the dandiacal element in *The Importance*, unlike that in the society comedies, is not in open conflict with a Philistine element and limited to its own sections of the play but appears everywhere and makes of the entire work a kind of dandiacal Utopia, a world of perfect form. "For the canons of good society," Wilde wrote in *Dorian Gray*, "are, or should be, the same as the canons of art. Form is absolutely essential to it."

Form for Wilde is found only in art, never in nature. It is in speaking of nature that the dandy's preference for the artificial is most clearly revealed. During the interview scene in Act I, Lady Bracknell expresses her disapproval of Jack's house in the country. "A country house!" she exclaims, ". . . You have a town house, I hope? A girl with a simple, unspoiled nature, like Gwendolen, could hardly be expected to reside in the country." The opening pages of "The Decay of Lying" offer a particularly clear gloss on this speech. "My own experience," says Vivian, the elegant purveyor of dandiacal opinions, "is that the more we study Art, the less we care for Nature. What Art really reveals to us is Nature's lack of design, her curious crudities . . . her absolutely unfinished condition. . . . Art is our spirited protest, our gallant attempt to teach Nature her proper place." Lady Bracknell takes the same attitude toward Cecily's lack of artificial elegance:

LADY BRACKNELL —. . . . Pretty child! Your dress is sadly simple, and your hair seems almost as nature might have left it. But we can soon alter all that. A thoroughly experienced French maid produces a really marvelous effect in a very brief space of time.

It is always perfection of form that the dandy seeks; content is irrelevant to him. After one of Algernon's more outrageous sallies, Jack exclaims in exasperation, "Is that clever?" Algernon replies, "It is perfectly phrased! and quite as true as any observation in civilized life should be." Even Algernon's servant, Lane, is revealed as a dandy. When Algernon remarks, "Lane, you're a perfect pessimist," the manservant replies, "I do my best to give satisfaction, sir." For the dandy, to be recognized as having achieved perfection in anything is the highest accolade.

This insistence on perfect esthetic form has many disguises, as, for example, when Gwendolen asks, "Cecily, mamma, whose views on education are remarkably strict, has brought me up to be extremely short-sighted; it is part of her system; so do you mind my looking at you through my glasses?" The fact that Gwendolen may have twenty-twenty vision is irrelevant if propriety demands that she be short-sighted. She is a conscious, artistic creation and must obey the rules of form.

Often, however, the dandy speaks without any disguise, and no one is more open than the seemingly innocent Cecily. When Algernon says that he has pretended to be Ernest in order to meet her, she asks Gwendolen's opinion of this excuse:

CECILY [*to* GWENDOLEN] That certainly seems a satisfactory explanation, does it not?

GWENDOLEN — Yes, dear, if you can believe him.

CECILY — I don't. But that does not affect the wonderful beauty of his answer.

The dandy, with his code of artistic form, is indifferent to both Philistine truth and Philistine morality. When Algernon admires a trinket which Cecily has given herself on his behalf, she remarks, "Yes, you've wonderfully good taste, Ernest. It's the excuse I've always given for your leading such a bad life." This obliteration of conventional morality is nowhere so apparent as in Cecily's first words to the disguised Algernon:

CECILY — You, I see from your card, are Uncle Jack's brother, my cousin Ernest, my wicked cousin Ernest.

ALGERNON — Oh! I am not really wicked at all, cousin Cecily. You mustn't think that I am wicked.

CECILY – If you are not, then you have certainly been deceiving us all in a very inexcusable manner. I hope you have not been leading a double life, pretending to be wicked and being really good all the time. That would be hypocrisy.

In the dandiacal system moral standards do not exist, although the terminology of morality is sometimes used. The dandy is concerned only with propriety; for him the proper course of conduct for a wicked brother is to be wicked. Goodness would be indecorous and the pretense of wickedness hypocritical. But since dandiacal wickedness is only a particular mode of achieving beauty, evil cannot exist in the dandy's world, and Cecily has no more sense of it than Dr. Chasuble, who cannot distinguish between a moral flaw and a susceptibility to draughts.

In one form or another dandyism dominates *The Importance of Being Earnest*. Even the pun in its title conceals a dandiacal meaning. As the various couples embrace at the end of the play, Lady Bracknell rebukes her new-found nephew:

LADY BRACKNELL – My nephew, you seem to be displaying signs of triviality.
JACK – On the contrary, Aunt Augusta, I've now realized for the first time in my life the vital Importance of Being Earnest.

When Lady Bracknell accuses Jack of being trivial, he replies that he realizes the importance of being earnest, or sincere and moral, but lurking beneath the reassuring, Philistine earnest is the dandiacal Ernest, for the name Ernest is a beautiful form which the self-centered, dandiacal heroines love while remaining indifferent to its content, the character of its bearer. To realize the importance of being Ernest is to understand the dominance of form; it is to be a Wildean dandy. The graceful pun that seems to set a tone of careless humor epitomizes in itself the meaning that can be found on almost every page of Wilde's masterpiece.

In discussing *The Importance of Being Earnest* and the dandiacal code which it embodies, I have run the risk of making the play sound like a piece of disguised art criticism. Yet such an evaluation would not be entirely untrue for, from one point of view, almost everything Wilde wrote was disguised art criticism. Art was the center of Wilde's life; it was his religion, however inadequate as such, or as near as he ever came to having one. Wilde was the product of an age in which old religions seemed to be lost and men struggled to produce new ones. The religion of art was not peculiar to Wilde, but in him it achieves its extreme expression. If one of the functions of religion is to provide a rule of conduct for life, then in the religion of art esthetics must logically take the place of ethics. Wilde accepted this position and produced the code of dandyism. The dandy's judgments are artistic rather than moral; he uses beautiful sensations to perfect his unique personality and disdains all that is crass and Philistine.

Such ideas could only alienate Wilde from the society around him and, like many artists of his time, Wilde was an exile and one whose position was made even more remote by his sexual habits. But in art Wilde seemed to find a point of stability. In art he found the real subject matter of his work. For him there was no distinction between criticism and creation. He was the supreme example of the critic as artist.

ANTON CHEKHOV

The Three Sisters

IN THE LAST YEARS of a short life Anton Chekhov (1860–1904) wrote four dramatic masterpieces: *The Seagull, Uncle Vanya, The Three Sisters,* and *The Cherry Orchard.* Of these *The Three Sisters* is certainly the most subtle and elaborate, and probably the finest: which is the reason for reprinting it here. Rather than print a second Chekhov play— and with the inclusion of a second the temptation to include a third would have arisen—the Editor has chosen to print David Magarshack's lengthy exegesis of *The Three Sisters.* Chekhov's art is elusive. The reader may want to check his own responses to it with those of other critics, such as Stark Young (in his Modern Library edition of Chekhov and elsewhere), Francis Fergusson (in *The Idea of a Theatre,* 1949), Robert Brustein (in *The Theatre of Revolt,* 1964), Maurice Valency (in *The Breaking String,* 1966), and the present Editor himself in *In Search of Theatre* (1953) and *What Is Theatre? and Other Reviews* (1968). A paragraph from a review of a *Three Sisters* production in the last-named book will perhaps suffice to set the stage: "There is no more beautiful modern play than *The Three Sisters.* It is curious that this should be so. The subject matter suggests neither celestial loveliness nor infernal grandeur, nothing that might make up a Shakespearean drama, comic or tragic. Middle-class life is boring, and traditionally it entered the drama only to be made fun of. Ibsen took a different tack. His idea was that suburbia only *seemed* boring; the house behind the façade was haunted; the man behind the stolid brow was neurotic. Ibsen's is a dramatic idea, while Chekhov's seems not to be so: it is to place the very

1555

boresomeness of lower middle-class culture on the stage. Not content with being a great playwright, Chekhov wished, it would seem, to give himself the greatest possible handicap—to fight, as it were, with his right hand tied behind his back. But this is only a manner of speaking. Great artists like being trussed up. *"In der Beschränkung zeigt sich erst der Meister,"* says Goethe ("The first way the master shows mastery is in limiting himself"). It is the Chekhov characters not their author who are inhibited and constricted. It may be said of Chekhov as of Shakespeare that he was "of an open and free nature," a phrase no one would apply to our minor playwrights, nor yet to Ibsen and Strindberg. Chekhov seems to me the only democrat among the major modern dramatists, or perhaps I mean the only Christian: the only one who can depict the "little" people around him with a deeply romantic and passionate love . . . This may be the fundamental reason why his plays are beautiful. It is not an intended beauty. It is a beauty that radiates from a beautiful spirit, and its radiance is an irreducibly real love of his fellow men."

THE THREE SISTERS
[*1901*]

English Version by
DAVID MAGARSHACK

CHARACTERS

ANDREY PROZOROV	
NATASHA	*his fiancée, afterwards his wife*
OLGA	*his sisters*
MASHA (MARIA)	
IRINA	
FYODOR KULYGIN	*secondary school teacher, Masha's husband*
ALEXANDER VERSHININ	*Lieutenant Colonel, battery commander*
NICHOLAS TUSENBACH	*Baron, lieutenant*
VASILY SOLYONY	*subaltern*
IVAN CHEBUTYKIN	*army doctor*
ALEXEY FEDOTIK	*second lieutenant*
VLADIMIR RODÉ	*second lieutenant*
FERAPONT	*an old District Council porter*
ANFISA	*a nurse, an old woman of eighty*

The action takes place in a county town.

ACT ONE

A drawing room in the Prozorovs' house separated from a large ballroom by a row of columns. Noon; it is a bright, sunny day. In the ballroom the table is being laid for lunch.

OLGA, wearing the dark blue regulation dress of a secondary school mistress is correcting her pupils' exercise books, standing or walking about the room; MASHA, in a black dress, is sitting reading a book, her hat on her lap; IRINA, in white, stands lost in thought.

OLGA—It is just a year since Father died—on this very day, the fifth of May—your birthday, Irina. It was dreadfully cold, it was snowing then. I felt as though I'd never be able to live through it, and you were lying in a dead faint. But now a whole year has gone by and the thought of it no longer troubles us. You're wearing a white dress again, you look so radiant. [*The clock strikes twelve.*] Then, too, the clock struck twelve. [*Pause.*] I remember the military band playing at Father's funeral, and they fired a salute at the cemetery. Though Father was a general and a brigade commander, there were not many people at his funeral. It is true, it was raining then. Pouring with rain, and snowing.

IRINA—Why must you talk about it?

[*In the dining room behind the columns, Baron* TUSENBACH, CHEBUTYKIN, *and* SOLYONY *appear near the table.*]

OLGA—It is warm today, the windows can be opened wide, but the birch trees have not opened up yet. It is eleven years since Father was given his brigade and left Moscow with us, and, I distinctly remember it, the flowers were in bloom in Moscow just at this time—the beginning of May. Oh, it was so warm then, and everything was drenched in sunlight. Eleven years have passed, but I can remember everything just as if we had left Moscow only yesterday. My goodness! When I woke up this morning and saw the bright sunshine, saw the spring, my heart leapt for joy and I felt such a passionate longing to be back home!

1559

CHEBUTYKIN—The devil you did!

TUSENBACH—It's all nonsense, of course!

[MASHA, *daydreaming over her book, whistles a tune softly.*]

OLGA—Don't whistle, Masha. How can you? [*Pause.*] I suppose it's because I'm at school all day and giving private lessons in the evenings that I'm getting these constant headaches and these thoughts, just as if I were old already. And, really, all these four years, while I've been working at school, I've felt as though my strength and my youth were draining out of me drop by drop. And one longing only grows stronger and stronger—

IRINA——to go to Moscow. Sell the house, finish with everything here, and leave for Moscow.

OLGA—Yes! To Moscow, as soon as possible.

[CHEBUTYKIN *and* TUSENBACH *laugh.*]

IRINA—I expect Andrey will get a professorship soon, and, anyway, he's not going to live here much longer. The only difficulty is poor old Masha.

OLGA—Masha could come to Moscow every year and stay with us the whole summer.

[MASHA *continues whistling her tune softly.*]

IRINA—Let's hope everything will turn out all right. [*Looking through the window.*] Oh, what a beautiful day! I don't know why I'm feeling so calm and serene. This morning I remembered that it was my birthday and, suddenly, I felt so happy. I remembered our childhood when Mother was still alive and such wonderful, exciting thoughts kept flashing through my mind—oh, what wonderful thoughts!

OLGA—You look so radiant today, more beautiful than ever. Masha, too, is beautiful. Andrey would have been quite goodlooking if he had not put on so much weight. It doesn't suit him at all. As for me, I've grown old and a lot thinner. I suppose it must be because I get so irritable with the girls at school. Today, I'm free, I'm at home, I haven't got a headache and I feel much younger than I did yesterday. After all, I'm only twenty-eight, except that . . . Everything's all right, everything's as God wills, but I can't help thinking that if I'd got married and stayed at home all day, things would be much better. [*Pause.*] I'd have loved my husband.

TUSENBACH [*to* SOLYONY] What nonsense you talk—I'm sick of listening to you. [*Going into the drawing room.*] I forgot to tell you: Vershinin, our new battery commander, will be calling on you today.

[*Sits down at the piano.*]

OLGA—Will he? He'll be very welcome.

IRINA—Is he old?

TUSENBACH—No, not really. Forty—forty-five at most. [*Plays quietly.*]

An excellent fellow by all accounts. Not a fool by any means—that's certain. He talks too much, though.

IRINA—Is he an interesting man?

TUSENBACH—Yes, I should say so, only, you see, he's got a wife, a mother-in-law, and two little girls. It's his second wife. He calls on people and tells everybody that he has a wife and two little girls. He's sure to tell you all about it. His second wife, I'm sorry to say, seems to be not altogether in her right mind. She wears a long plait like a girl, uses very grandiloquent language, philosophises, and, every now and again, tries to commit suicide. Apparently, to annoy her husband. I'd have left a woman like that long ago, but he puts up with it. Just keeps on complaining.

SOLYONY [*enters the drawing room with* CHEBUTYKIN] I can only lift half a hundredweight with one hand, but with two I can lift a hundredweight and more. From which I infer that two men are not only twice but three or even more times as strong as one.

CHEBUTYKIN [*reads a newspaper while he comes in*] For falling hair—one hundred and thirty grains of naphthaline in half a bottle of spirits—dissolve and apply daily. [*Writes it down in his notebook.*] Let's make a note of it. [*To* SOLYONY.] Well, as I was saying, you put a cork into the bottle and pass a glass tube through the cork . . . Then you take a pinch of ordinary powdered alum . . .

IRINA—I say, Doctor, dear Doctor—

CHEBUTYKIN—What is it, child? What is it, my sweet?

IRINA—Tell me, why am I so happy today? I feel as if I were sailing under a wide blue sky and great white birds were flying above me. Why is it? Why?

CHEBUTYKIN [*kissing both her hands, tenderly*] My lovely white bird . . .

IRINA—When I woke this morning, got up and washed, I suddenly felt as if everything in the world had become clear to me and I knew how one ought to live. Dear Doctor, I do know everything. Man must work, work by the sweat of his brow, whoever he might be. That alone gives a meaning and a purpose to his life, his happiness, his success. Oh, how wonderful it must be to be a laborer, who gets up with the sun and breaks stones by the roadside, or a shepherd, or a schoolmaster teaching children, or a driver of a railway engine. Why, dear Lord, better be an ox or a horse and go on working than a young woman who wakes up at twelve, drinks her coffee in bed, then takes two hours dressing . . . Oh, how dreadful! Just as one is sometimes dying for a drink of water on a hot day, so I'm dying to do some work. Why, if I don't get up early and do some real work, don't count me among your friends any more, Doctor.

Anton Chekhov

CHEBUTYKIN [*tenderly*] I won't . . . I won't . . .

OLGA—Father trained us to get up at seven o'clock. That is why Irina always wakes up at seven and lies in bed at least till nine thinking about all sorts of things. How serious she looks!

[*Laughs.*]

IRINA—You're so used to looking on me as a little girl that it seems strange to you when I look serious.

TUSENBACH—Dear Lord, how well I understand this craving for work. I've never done a stroke of work in my life. I was born in Petersburg, a cold and idle city. My family never knew what work or worry meant. I remember when I came home from the military academy, a valet would pull off my boots while I swore at him. My mother looked at me with adoring eyes and was genuinely surprised when people looked differently at me. I was carefully guarded against work. But they did not succeed in shielding me from it. Not now, at any rate. The time is coming when something huge is about to overwhelm us—a mighty hurricane is on the way, it is quite near already and soon, very soon, it will sweep away from our society idleness, complacency, prejudice against work and effete boredom. I shall work and in another twenty-five or thirty years everyone will work—everyone.

CHEBUTYKIN—I won't work.

TUSENBACH—You don't count.

SOLYONY—In twenty-five years you won't be alive, thank goodness. In a couple of years you will die of a stroke or I'll lose my temper and put a bullet through your head, dear fellow.

[*Takes a scent bottle from his pocket and sprinkles the scent over his chest and hands.*]

CHEBUTYKIN [*laughs*] It's quite true, I have never done a stroke of work in my life. As soon as I left the university, I never lifted a finger or opened a book. I only read newspapers . . . [*Takes another newspaper out of his pocket.*] Here . . . I know from the papers that we had—er—a critic by the name of Dobrolyubov, but I'm hanged if I know what he wrote about . . . [*Somebody is heard knocking on the floor from downstairs.*] There . . . Somebody wants to see me downstairs. They're calling me to come down. I'll be back in a moment. I won't be long.

[*Goes out hurriedly, stroking his beard.*]

IRINA—He's up to something.

TUSENBACH—I think so too. He's gone out looking very solemn. I expect he's gone to fetch your present.

IRINA—Oh, how I hate it!

OLGA—Yes, it is dreadful. He's always doing something silly.

1562

MASHA – "And he on honey-dew hath fed, and drunk the milk of paradise . . . and drunk the milk of paradise"[1] . . .

[*Gets up, humming quietly.*]

OLGA – You're not very cheerful today, Masha.

[MASHA *puts on her hat, humming.*]

OLGA – Where are you off to?

MASHA – Home.

IRINA – Strange!

TUSENBACH – Leave a birthday party!

MASHA – What does it matter? I'll be back this evening. Goodbye, darling . . . [*Kisses* IRINA.] Let me wish you again—good health and happiness. In the old days, when father was alive, we always used to have thirty or forty army officers at our birthday parties—such noisy parties—but today we've only got a man and a half and it's quiet as a desert. I'm going home. I'm in a terribly merlerncholy mood today. I'm not feeling particularly cheerful, so you'd better not listen to me. [*Laughing, through tears.*] We'll have a good talk later, goodbye for now, my darling. I'll just go somewhere, anywhere.

IRINA [*displeased*] Really, Masha . . .

OLGA [*tearfully*] I understand you, Masha.

SOLYONY – If a man philosophises it is philosophistry or, if you like, sophistry, but if a woman or a couple of women start philosophising, it's a lot of nonsense.

MASHA – What do you mean by that, you frightfully terrible man?

SOLYONY – Nothing. He had barely time to catch his breath before the bear was hugging him to death.

MASHA [*to* OLGA, *crossly*] Don't howl.

[*Enter* ANFISA *and* FERAPONT *with a cake.*]

ANFISA – This way, my good man. Come in, your boots are clean. [*To* IRINA.] From the District Council, my dear, from Mr. Protopopov, Mikhail Ivanovitch—a cake.

IRINA – Thank you. Please give my thanks to Mr. Protopopov.

---

[1] The first two lines from Pushkin's epilogue to *Ruslan and Lyudmila* which Masha repeats twice in Act I and twice in Act IV are full of magic and mystery. But this is only apparent in the original and can only be perceived by a Russian audience familiar with those lines from childhood. When translated—"A green oaktree grows at the bay/A golden chain is on that oaktree."—they are meaningless. To convey this feeling, I have chosen two lines from Coleridge's *Kubla Khan*, which are not only similar, but which also help to understand Masha's sudden attraction to the idealist Vershinin, the man who fits most closely the two lines of Coleridge's poem. It must be remembered that Masha knew English and would most certainly have read *Kubla Khan* in the original—not that it matters, since the important thing is to convey Masha's feeling and mood to an English speaking audience. [D.M.]

[*Accepts the cake.*]

FERAPONT—Beg pardon, Miss?

IRINA [*louder*] Thank Mr. Protopopov.

OLGA—Nanny, let him have some pie. Go to the kitchen Ferapont. They'll give you some pie there.

FERAPONT—Beg pardon, Miss?

ANFISA—Come along, my dear, come along.

[*Goes out with* FERAPONT.]

MASHA—I don't like this Protopopov, this Mikhail Potapych or Ivanych.[2] I don't think we ought to invite him.

IRINA—I didn't invite him.

MASHA—Good!

[*Enter* CHEBUTYKIN, *followed by a soldier carrying a silver samovar; murmurs of astonishment and displeasure.* OLGA *covers her face.*]

OLGA—A samovar! This is awful.

[*Goes through to the ballroom and stands by the table.*]

IRINA—Oh, dear Doctor, what are you doing?

TUSENBACH [*laughs*] I told you so.

MASHA—Really, Doctor, you ought to be ashamed of yourself!

CHEBUTYKIN—My dear, sweet darlings, you're all I have, you're all I hold most dear in the world. I shall soon be sixty. I'm an old man, a lonely, worthless old man. There's nothing good about me except my love for you. But for you I'd have been dead long ago. [*To* IRINA.] My darling, my dear child, I've known you ever since you were born—I used to carry you about in my arms—I loved your mother—

IRINA—But why such expensive presents?

CHEBUTYKIN [*through tears, crossly*] Expensive presents! Don't talk such nonsense. [*To his orderly.*] Take the samovar to the other room. [*In a mocking voice.*] Expensive presents!

[*The orderly carries off the samovar to the ballroom.*]

ANFISA [*crossing the drawing room*] My dears, a strange colonel's just arrived. He's taken off his coat and he's coming here now. Irina, darling, be nice and polite to him. [*Going out.*] Lunch should have been served long ago . . . Dear, oh dear.

[*Goes out.*]

TUSENBACH—I expect it must be Vershinin.

[*Enter* VERSHININ.]

---

[2] The Russian folk name for a bear is Mishka, a pet name for Mikhail. Sometimes the patronymic Potapych is added. Protopopov's name is also Mikhail, but his patronymic is Ivanovych or Ivanych. Coming so quickly after Solyony's quotation from Krylov's fable *The Peasant and the Bear*, the indirect implication is that the bear Protopopov will, in the end, bring about the ruin of the three sisters. [D.M.]

TUSENBACH – Lieutenant Colonel Vershinin!

VERSHININ [*to* MASHA *and* IRINA] Allow me to introduce myself: Vershinin. I'm very glad, very glad indeed, that I'm here at last. Good heavens, how you've grown!

IRINA – Please, be seated. We're very pleased to meet you, Colonel.

VERSHININ [*gaily*] I'm so glad, so glad! But, surely, there are three of you, three sisters. I remember three little girls. I don't remember their faces, but I do remember that your father, Colonel Prozorov, had three little girls. I remember it very well. I saw them myself. How time flies! Dear me, how time flies!

TUSENBACH – The colonel comes from Moscow.

IRINA – Moscow? Are you from Moscow?

VERSHININ – Yes, I'm from Moscow. Your father was a battery commander there and I served in the same brigade. [*To* MASHA.] I seem to remember your face a little.

MASHA – I'm afraid I don't remember you.

IRINA – Olga! Olga! [*Shouts into the dining room.*] Olga! Do come! [OLGA *comes in from the ballroom.*] Lieutenant Colonel Vershinin, it seems, comes from Moscow.

VERSHININ – So you're Olga, the eldest sister. And you are Maria. And you are Irina, the youngest.

OLGA – You are from Moscow?

VERSHININ – Yes, I went to school in Moscow, and began my service in Moscow. I served there a long time and, at last, was put in command of the battery here. Moved over here, as you see. I do not really remember you. All I remember is that there were three sisters. I remember your father very well. I have only to shut my eyes to see him just as if he were alive. I used to visit you in Moscow.

OLGA – I thought I remembered everybody, and suddenly . . .

VERSHININ – My christian name is Alexander.

IRINA – Alexander Vershinin, and you are from Moscow. What a surprise!

OLGA – You see, we're going to live there.

IRINA – Yes, we hope to be there by the autumn. It's our home town. We were born there, in old Basmanny Street.

[*Both laugh happily.*]

MASHA – Meeting a fellow townsman so unexpectedly . . . [*With animation.*] Now I remember! Do you remember, Olga, there was someone we used to call "the lovesick Major." You were only a lieutenant then and you were in love with some girl and, for some reason, we all nicknamed you, teasingly, the major.

VERSHININ [*laughs*] That's it! That's it! The lovesick major. Yes, that's true.

MASHA – In those days you only had a moustache. Oh, you look so much older! [*Through tears.*] So much older!

VERSHININ – Yes, when I was known as the lovesick major I was still a young man. I was in love then. It's different now.

OLGA – But you haven't got a single grey hair. You've grown older, but you're not an old man.

VERSHININ – I shall soon be forty-three all the same. How long have you been away from Moscow?

IRINA – Eleven years. What are you crying for, Masha? You funny girl! [*Through tears.*] You're making me cry, too.

MASHA – I'm all right. And where did you live?

VERSHININ – In Old Basmanny Street.

OLGA – We lived there, too.

VERSHININ – At one time I lived in German Street. I used to walk from there to the barracks. I had to cross a gloomy bridge on the way, the water rushed so noisily under it. It made me feel so sad when walking over it by myself. [*Pause.*] But here you have such a fine river, such a wonderful river!

OLGA – Yes, only it's very cold. It's very cold here and lots of mosquitoes.

VERSHININ – You can't mean it! Here you have such a good, healthy climate, a real Russian climate. Forest, river . . . and also birch trees. Dear, modest birch trees. I love them more than any other trees. It's nice living here. The only trouble is that the railway is fifteen miles from the town. Nobody seems to know why.

SOLYONY – I know why. [*Everyone looks at him.*] Because, you see, if the railway station had been near, it wouldn't have been far, and if it's far, it's because it is not near.

[*An awkward silence.*]

TUSENBACH – He likes his little joke, our subaltern does.

OLGA – Now I've remembered you, too. Yes, I remember you.

VERSHININ – I knew your mother.

CHEBUTYKIN – She was a good woman, God rest her soul.

IRINA – Mother was buried in Moscow.

OLGA – At the Novo-Devichy Monastery.

MASHA – I'm afraid I'm already beginning to forget what she looked like. I suppose people will forget us, too, in the same way. They'll forget us.

VERSHININ – Yes, they'll forget us. Such is our fate. There's nothing we can do about it. The things which seem great, significant and very important to us now will no more seem to be important with time. [*Pause.*] It's certainly an interesting fact that we cannot possibly know today what will be considered great and important or just pitiful and ridiculous in the future. Did not the discoveries of Copernicus or, let's say, Columbus, appear to be useless and ridiculous at the time, while some utter drivel, written by some crank, seemed to be a great truth? It is quite likely that our present life, to which we are so reconciled, will in time appear to be odd, uncomfortable, stupid, not particularly clean and, perhaps, even immoral.

TUSENBACH – Who knows? Perhaps our life will be considered to have been noble and will be remembered with respect. We have no longer tortures, public executions, or invasions, and yet there's still so much suffering.

SOLYONY [*in a high-pitched voice*] Cluck, cluck, cluck . . . No need to scatter corn for the Baron, just give him a chance to philosophise.

TUSENBACH – Leave me alone, will you? [*Changes his place.*] It's getting rather boring.

SOLYONY [*in a high-pitched voice*] Cluck, cluck, cluck . . .

TUSENBACH [*to* VERSHININ] The suffering that we can observe today—and there's so much of it—still shows a certain degree of moral uplift already achieved by our society.

VERSHININ – Yes, yes, of course.

CHEBUTYKIN – You've said just now, Baron, that our present life may be called great, but people are rather small all the same. [*Gets up.*] Look, how small I am. It's solely to console me that one has to say that my life is noble. That, I think, is clear enough.

[*A violin is played off stage.*]

MASHA – It's our brother, Andrey, playing the violin.

IRINA – He's our scholar. We hope he's going to be a professor one day. Father was a soldier, but his son has chosen an academic career.

MASHA – It was Father's wish.

OLGA – We've been teasing him today. We think he's a little in love.

IRINA – With a local girl. She'll be calling on us today, most probably.

MASHA – Heavens, how she dresses! It isn't that her clothes are not pretty or fashionable—they are just pathetic. Some sort of bright yellow frock with a cheap-looking fringe and a red blouse. Her cheeks, too, are so thoroughly scrubbed! Andrey's not in love with her—I just can't believe it, for, after all, he has got some taste. I think he's simply doing it to tease us. It's his way of playing the fool. I was told yesterday that she was going to marry Protopopov, the chairman of our District Council. And an excellent thing, too! [*Calls through the side door.*] Andrey, come here! Just for a moment, dear!

[*Enter* ANDREY.]

OLGA – This is my brother, Andrey.

VERSHININ – Vershinin.

A N D R E Y – Prozorov. [*Wipes the perspiration from his face.*] Are you our new battery commander?

O L G A – Just imagine! Colonel Vershinin comes from Moscow.

A N D R E Y – Oh? Well, I congratulate you. Now my sisters won't give you any peace.

V E R S H I N I N – I'm afraid your sisters must be getting bored with me already.

I R I N A – Look what a lovely picture frame Andrey gave me today for a present. [*Shows him the frame.*] Andrey made it himself.

V E R S H I N I N [*looks at the picture frame and is at a loss for what to say*] Well, yes, er–it's–er–very nice.

I R I N A – And the little frame over the piano, he made that too.

[ANDREY *waves his hand deprecatingly and walks off.*]

O L G A – He's our scholar, he plays the violin and he's very clever with a fretsaw. In fact, he can turn his hand to anything. Andrey, don't go. He has a habit of always walking away. Come here!

[MASHA *and* IRINA *take* ANDREY *by the arms and lead him back, laughing.*]

M A S H A – Come on, come on!

A N D R E Y – Leave me alone, please.

M A S H A – You are funny! We used to call Colonel Vershinin the lovesick major and he was never cross.

V E R S H I N I N – Not a bit!

M A S H A – I'd like to call you the lovesick fiddler!

I R I N A – Or the lovesick professor.

O L G A – He's fallen in love. Our little Andrey has fallen in love. [*Clapping her hands.*] Bravo, bravo! Encore! Our little brother is in love!

C H E B U T Y K I N [*walks up behind* ANDREY *and puts his arms round his waist.*] It's for love alone that nature has created us.

[*Bursts out laughing, still holding his newspaper in his hand.*]

A N D R E Y – All right, that'll do, that'll do . . . [*Wipes his face.*] I didn't sleep a wink last night and I'm not in top form now, as they say. I read till four o'clock and then went to bed. But it was no use. I kept thinking of one thing and another and before I knew it was dawn and the sun was simply pouring into the bedroom. I'd like to translate a book from the English during the summer while I'm here.

V E R S H I N I N – Do you read English?

A N D R E Y – Yes. Father, may he rest in peace, inflicted education upon us. This may sound silly and ridiculous, but I must confess, all the same, that since he died I've been putting on weight. Indeed, in one year I've put on so much weight that it is as if my body had burst its bonds. But thanks to Father, my sisters and I know French, German and English, and Irina knows Italian too. But at what a cost!

M A S H A – To speak three languages in this town is an unnecessary luxury. Why, it isn't even a luxury, just a sort of useless appendage, like a sixth finger. We know a lot that is of no use to us.

V E R S H I N I N – Good heavens! [*Laughs.*] You know a lot that is of no use to you. Well, I can't help thinking there's no town so dull and depressing that an intelligent, educated man would be superfluous in it. Let's assume that among the hundred thousand people in this town, who, I admit, are rather backward and coarse, there are only three people like you. It stands to reason that you won't be able to convert the uneducated mass of people around you. But in the course of your life you will have to make some concessions till, little by little, you'll get lost among these hundred thousand people. Life will stifle you but, nevertheless, you'll not be lost entirely. Neither will you be gone without having exerted some influence. Six people like you will perhaps emerge after you, then twelve, and so on, until the majority of people will have become like you. In two or three hundred years life on earth will become incredibly beautiful and marvellous. Man must have a life like that. If it isn't here yet, he must be able to anticipate it, to wait for it, to dream about it and to prepare himself for it. To make sure of it, he must be able to see and know more than his father and grandfather did. [*Laughs.*] And you're complaining that you know a lot that's of no use to you.

M A S H A [*takes off her hat*] I'm staying to lunch.

I R I N A [*with a sigh*] Really, someone should have written it all down.

[ANDREY *has left the room unnoticed.*]

T U S E N B A C H – You say that many years later life on earth will be beautiful, marvellous. That's true. But to take part in it now, even at a distance, one has to prepare for it, one has to work for it.

V E R S H I N I N [*gets up*] Yes, indeed. What a lot of flowers you have here! [*Looks round.*] And what a wonderful place you have here! I envy you. All my life I've lived in lodgings with two chairs, a sofa and a stove which invariably smoked. What I missed most in my life were just such flowers . . . [*Rubs his hands.*] Oh, well, what's the use . . .

T U S E N B A C H – Yes, we must work. I expect you must be thinking: that German has grown sentimental all of a sudden. But I assure you, I'm a Russian. I don't speak a word of German. My father was Greek Orthodox.

[*Pause.*]

V E R S H I N I N [*walks up and down the stage*] I often wonder what it would be like if we were to start our life all over again. Consciously, I mean. If our first life had been, as it were, only a rough copy and our second a fair one. In that case, I believe, every one of us would first of all do his utmost not to repeat himself. At least he would create a dif-

1569

ferent environment for himself. He would, for instance, get himself a place like this, with flowers and full of light. I have a wife and two little girls. My wife, I'm sorry to say, always complains of being poorly, and so on and so forth. Well, if I had to start my life all over again, I wouldn't get married . . . No, certainly not.

[*Enter* KULYGIN, *wearing his schoolmaster's uniform.*]

KULYGIN [*walks up to* IRINA] Congratulations, dear sister. Many happy returns. I wish you good health and everything a girl of your age ought to have. Let me, finally, present you with this book. [*Hands her a book.*] It's the history of our school for the last fifty years. I wrote it myself. Not a very important book, I admit. I wrote it in my spare time, having nothing better to do, but you should read it all the same. Good morning, ladies and gentlemen. [*To* VERSHININ.] Let me introduce myself: Kulygin, a master at the secondary school here, civil servant of the seventh rank. [*To* IRINA.] In this book you'll find a list of all the pupils who've completed their course of studies at our school during the last fifty years. *Feci, quod potui, faciant meliora potentes.*

[*Kisses* MASHA.]

IRINA – But you gave me this book as a present last Easter!

KULYGIN [*laughs*] Impossible! In that case, you'd better give it back to me, or, no, better give it to the colonel. Please take it, Colonel. You may read it one day when you've nothing better to do.

VERSHININ – Thank you. [*Is about to leave.*] I'm very glad to have made your acquaintance.

OLGA – You're not going, are you? Please, don't.

IRINA – You must stay and have lunch with us. Please!

OLGA – Please, do.

VERSHININ [*bows*] I seem to have dropped in on your birthday party. I'm sorry, I didn't know. I didn't offer you my congratulations.

[*Goes into the ballroom with* OLGA.]

KULYGIN – Today, ladies and gentlemen, is Sunday, a day of rest. Let us, therefore, rest. Let us make merry, each in accordance with his age and position in life. The carpets will have to be taken up for the summer and put away till the winter. Must sprinkle them first with Persian powder or naphthaline. The Romans were healthy because they knew how to work and how to rest. They had *mens sana in corpore sano.* Their life ran according to well established forms. Our headmaster says: the main thing in life is form. Anything that loses its form is finished. It's the same in our everyday life. [*Takes* MASHA *by the waist, laughing.*] Masha loves me. My wife loves me. The curtains, too, will have to be put away with the carpets . . . Today, I'm happy. I'm in excellent spirits. [*To* MASHA.] At four o'clock, my dear, we have to be at the headmaster's. An outing has been arranged for the teachers and their families.

MASHA – Sorry, I'm not going.

KULYGIN [*chagrined*] My dear Masha, why not?

MASHA – We'll talk about it later . . . [*Crossly.*] Oh, very well, I'll come. Only leave me alone, please.

[*Walks away.*]

KULYGIN – Afterwards, we'll spend the evening at the headmaster's. Though in bad health, that man is doing his best to be sociable above all. A fine man, a man of irreproachable conduct. A most excellent man! After the staff meeting yesterday he said to me: I'm tired, my dear fellow, I'm tired! [*Looks at the clock, then at his watch.*] Your clock is seven minutes fast. Yes, he said, I'm tired.

[*Someone is playing a violin offstage.*]

OLGA – Please, gentlemen, lunch is served. We're having a pie!

KULYGIN – My dear, dear Olga, yesterday I began work in the morning and I went on working till eleven o'clock at night. I felt tired, but now I feel happy. [*Goes into the ballroom to the table.*] Dear Olga!

CHEBUTYKIN [*puts the newspaper in his pocket and combs his beard*] A pie! Excellent!

MASHA [*to* CHEBUTYKIN, *sternly*] Mind, no drinking today. Do you hear? It's bad for you.

CHEBUTYKIN – Don't worry. That's all in the past. Haven't had a real drinking bout for two years. [*Impatiently.*] Good Lord, my dear woman, does it really matter so much?

MASHA – All the same, don't you dare to drink. Don't you dare! [*Crossly, but trying not to be overheard by her husband.*] Damnation, another boring evening at the headmaster's.

TUSENBACH – If I were you, I wouldn't go. Very simple.

CHEBUTYKIN – Don't go, my dear.

MASHA – Don't go, indeed! A damnable, unbearable life!

[*Goes into the ballroom.*]

CHEBUTYKIN [*goes after her*] Oh, well!

SOLYONY [*crossing into the ballroom*] Cluck, cluck, cluck . . .

TUSENBACH – Chuck it, my dear sir, chuck it!

SOLYONY – Cluck, cluck, cluck . . .

KULYGIN [*gaily*] Your health, Colonel. I'm a schoolmaster and quite at home here. I'm Masha's husband. She's a good woman, a very good woman.

VERSHININ – I'll have some of that dark brandy . . . [*Drinks.*] Your health! [*To* OLGA.] I feel so happy here.

[*Only* IRINA *and* TUSENBACH *remain in the drawing room.*]

IRINA – Masha's in a bad mood today. She got married when she was

1571

eighteen. At the time, her husband seemed the most intelligent man in the world to her. It's quite different now. He's the most good-natured but not the most intelligent of men.

OLGA [*impatiently*] Andrey, are you coming?

ANDREY [*offstage*] One moment.

[*Comes in and goes to the table.*]

TUSENBACH — What are you thinking of?

IRINA — Oh, I don't know. I don't like that Solyony of yours. I'm afraid of him. He says such stupid things.

TUSENBACH — He's a strange fellow. I'm both sorry for him and annoyed by him. Mostly sorry, though. I think he's shy. When I'm alone with him, he's very intelligent and friendly, but, in company, he's coarse, a bully. Don't go in there yet. Not before they've taken their places at the table. Stay with me a little longer. What are you thinking of? [*Pause.*] You're twenty, and I'm not yet thirty. Think of the years we still have ahead of us. A long succession of days, each one full of my love for you.

IRINA — Please, don't talk to me about love.

TUSENBACH [*not listening*] I've such a passionate yearning for life, for work, to strive for a better life. This yearning has, somehow, become mingled with my love for you, Irina. And, as luck would have it, you are beautiful and life also seems to be so beautiful to me. What are you thinking of?

IRINA — You say life is beautiful. Yes, but what if it only seems so. Our life, I mean the lives of us three sisters, has not been particularly beautiful so far. Life has stifled us like a weed. I'm sorry, I'm crying. I mustn't. [*Quickly dries her eyes and smiles.*] We must work, work! We are so unhappy and we have so gloomy a view of life because we don't know the meaning of work. We're the children of people who despised work . . .

[NATASHA *enters, wearing a pink dress with a green belt.*]

NATASHA — Good heavens, they've gone in to lunch already . . . I'm late . . . [*Throws a quick glance at herself in the mirror and tidies herself up.*] My hair's all right, I think. [*Catches sight of* IRINA.] Dear Irina, congratulations. [*Gives her a hearty and drawn-out kiss.*] You've got such a lot of visitors . . . I feel quite shy . . . Good morning, Baron.

OLGA [*enters the drawing room*] Ah, here you are Natasha. How are you, my dear?

[*They kiss.*]

NATASHA — Congratulations. You've such a lot of people. I'm so shy.

OLGA — It's all right, they're all old friends. [*Lowering her voice, frightened.*] My dear, you're wearing a green belt. That's not nice.

NATASHA — Is it unlucky?

OLGA – No, it simply doesn't suit you and—er—it looks a little out of place.

NATASHA [*in a tearful voice*] Does it? It isn't really green, you know. It's not shiny.

[*Follows* OLGA *into the dining room.*]
[*They are all seated at the table now. The drawing room is empty.*]

KULYGIN – I wish you a good husband, Irina. It's time you got married.

CHEBUTYKIN – I wish you a nice fiancé too, Natasha.

KULYGIN – Natasha has one already, I believe.

MASHA [*strikes her plate with a fork*] Let's have a glass of vodka! Oh, life is sweet! What the hell—

KULYGIN – Four marks out of ten for conduct.

VERSHININ – The brandy's excellent. What is it made of?

SOLYONY – Cockroaches!

IRINA [*tearfully*] Ugh! How disgusting!

OLGA – We're having roast turkey for dinner tonight and an apple turnover for dessert. Thank goodness I'm at home all day today. At home this evening, too. Please, you must all come this evening.

VERSHININ – I'd like to come this evening, if you don't mind.

IRINA – Please do.

NATASHA – They don't stand on ceremony here.

CHEBUTYKIN – It's for love alone that nature has created us.

[*Laughs.*]

ANDREY [*crossly*] Do stop it, please. Haven't you had enough?

[FEDOTIK *and* RODÉ *come in with a large basket of flowers.*]

FEDOTIK – We're late. They're having lunch.

RODÉ [*in a loud voice and mispronouncing his r's*] Are they? Good Lord, yes, so they are!

FEDOTIK – One moment, please. [*Takes a snapshot.*] One! One moment. [*Takes another snapshot.*] Two! That's all!

[*They pick up the basket and go into the ballroom, where they get a noisy reception.*]

RODÉ [*in a loud voice*] Congratulations! I wish you all the best. Gorgeous weather today. Simply marvellous! I spent the morning with some schoolboys. I'm a games master, you see.

FEDOTIK – You can move now, Irina, if you want to. [*Taking a snapshot.*] You look lovely today. [*Takes a humming top out of his pocket.*] Here, by the way, is a top. It's got a marvellous hum.

IRINA – It's lovely!

MASHA – "For he on honey-dew hath fed and drunk the milk of paradise . . . and drunk the milk of paradise." [*Tearfully.*] Why do I go on saying this? Can't get these lines out of my head since morning.

KULYGIN – Thirteen at table!

RODÉ [*in a loud voice*] Surely you're not superstitious, are you?

[*Laughter.*]

KULYGIN – When there are thirteen at table it means that some of them are in love. It isn't you Doctor, by any chance?

[*Laughter.*]

CHEBUTYKIN – I'm an old sinner, but why Natasha should look so embarrassed I simply fail to understand.

[*Loud laughter;* NATASHA *runs out of the ballroom into the drawing room.* ANDREY *follows her.*]

ANDREY – Please don't pay any attention to them. Don't go, I beg you.

NATASHA – I feel so ashamed. I don't know what I've done wrong and they're just laughing at me. I know it wasn't nice to leave the table like that, but I couldn't help it.

[*Covers her face with her hands.*]

ANDREY – Oh, my dear, I beg you, I implore you, do not be upset. I assure you, they're only joking. They don't mean to be unkind. My dear, my dear, my beautiful one! They're all nice, kindly people and they're fond of us both. Come over to the window. They won't be able to see us there.

[*Looks round.*]

NATASHA – I'm so unaccustomed to being with people!

ANDREY – Oh, you're so young, so beautifully, so splendidly young. My dear, my darling, do not be upset. Do believe me. Believe me. I'm so happy, my heart is so full of love, of ecstasy . . . No, they can't see us from here, they can't! Why, why did I fall in love with you, when did I fall in love with you– Oh, I don't understand anything. My darling, my beautiful darling, my pure one, be my wife! I love you, I love you, as I've never loved anyone before.

[*A kiss.*]

[*Two army officers come in and, seeing the kissing couple, stop dead in amazement.*]

ACT TWO

The scene is the same as in Act I

It is eight o'clock in the evening. Off stage, in the street, the sound of an accordion can be heard faintly. The stage is dark. Enter NATASHA in a dressing gown, carrying a candle; she walks across the stage and stops at the door leading to ANDREY's room.

N A T A S H A – What are you doing, Andrey dear? Reading? Never mind, I just . . . [Goes to another door, opens it, looks into the room, and shuts it again.] Must make sure there's no light left burning . . .

A N D R E Y [comes in with a book in his hand] What's the matter, Natasha?

N A T A S H A – I'm just making sure no one's left a light burning. It's Shrovetide—carnival time. The servants are all excited and you have to make sure that nothing goes wrong. About twelve o'clock last night I walked through the dining room and there was a candle alight on the table. I just couldn't find out who lit it. [Puts the candle down.] What's the time?

A N D R E Y [glancing at the clock] A quarter past eight.

N A T A S H A – Olga and Irina are out. Not back yet. Still hard at work, poor darlings. Olga at her staff meeting and Irina at the telegraph office . . . [Sighs.] Only this morning, I said to your sister: you must take more care of yourself, Irina darling. But she won't listen to me. A quarter past eight, did you say? I'm afraid our Bobby isn't at all well. Why is he so cold? Yesterday he had a temperature. But today he's quite cold. I'm so worried.

A N D R E Y – Don't worry, Natasha. The boy's well enough.

N A T A S H A – All the same I think we ought to be more careful about his diet. I'm worried. I'm told, dear, that after nine o'clock some carnival dancers are expected to come. I wish they weren't coming, Andrey dear.

A N D R E Y – Well, I don't know. They've been invited, you see.

N A T A S H A – This morning our little darling woke up, looked at me and suddenly smiled. He must have recognised me. Good morning Bobby,

1575

I said, good morning, darling. He laughed. Little children understand, oh, they understand everything. You don't mind, Andrey dear, if I tell the servants not to let the dancers in, do you?

A N D R E Y [*hesitatingly*] But, you see, it depends on my sisters. It's their house.

N A T A S H A — Yes, it's their house, too, I suppose. I'll tell them. They're so kind. [*Going.*] I've ordered sour milk for supper. The doctor says you ought to eat nothing but sour milk. Otherwise you won't lose weight. [*Stops.*] Bobby is so cold. I'm afraid his room is too cold. We'll have to find him another room. At least till the warm weather. Now, Irina's room is just right for a baby. It's dry and it gets the sun all day long. I must tell her. She could share Olga's room for the time being. She isn't at home during the day, anyway. She only sleeps here. [*Pause.*] Darling, why don't you say anything?

A N D R E Y — Oh, I was thinking . . . There's nothing really I can say, is there?

N A T A S H A — Now, what is it I wanted to tell you? Oh, yes. Ferapont from the District Council is here. He wants to see you about something.

A N D R E Y [*yawns*] Tell him to come in.

NATASHA *goes out.* ANDREY, *bending over the candle she has left behind, is reading his book. Enter* FERAPONT. *He wears a shabby old overcoat with a turned-up collar. His ears are muffled.*

A N D R E Y — Hello, old man. What have you got to tell me?

F E R A P O N T — The chairman, sir, sent you this register and a document. Here . . .

[*Hands him the book and the document.*]

A N D R E Y — Thanks. That's all right. But why are you so late? It's past eight o'clock.

F E R A P O N T — Beg pardon, sir?

A N D R E Y [*louder*] I said you've come too late. It's gone eight.

F E R A P O N T — That's right, sir. When I came here it was still daylight, but they wouldn't let me in. The master's busy, they said. Well, I thought to myself, if he's busy, he's busy. I'm in no hurry. [*Thinking that* ANDREY *has asked him about something.*] Beg pardon, sir?

A N D R E Y — Nothing. [*Turning over the pages of the book.*] Tomorrow's Friday. There's no council meeting, but I'll go to the office just the same. Do some work. It's boring at home. [*Pause.*] My dear old fellow, how strangely everything changes, how life deceives us! Today I picked up this book—I was bored, you see, had nothing else to do—my old university lectures, and I couldn't help laughing. Good Lord, I am the secretary of the District Council, the Council of which Protopopov is chairman. I am a secretary, and the most I can hope for is to become a member of the Council. A member of a District Council! I—who used to dream every night that I was a professor of Moscow University, a famous scholar of whom the whole of Russia is proud.

FERAPONT—Afraid I don't know, sir. Don't hear very well.

ANDREY—If you could hear properly, I might not be talking to you like this. I must talk to someone. My wife does not understand me and for some reason I'm afraid of my sisters. I'm afraid they will ridicule me, make me feel ashamed of myself . . . I don't drink and I don't like going to pubs, but, my dear fellow, you can't imagine how I'd love to spend some time in Moscow at Testov's or at the Great Moscow Restaurant.

FERAPONT—Did you say Moscow, sir? A contractor was telling us at the office the other day about some businessmen who was eating pancakes in Moscow. One of them who ate forty pancakes apparently died. Was it forty or fifty? Don't remember.

ANDREY—You sit in a big dining room of a restaurant in Moscow: you know no one, no one knows you, but you don't feel you're a stranger. Here, you know everyone and everyone knows you, but you're a stranger, a stranger . . . A stranger and all alone.

FERAPONT—Beg pardon, sir? [*Pause.*] The same contractor said—he may be lying for all I know—that a rope is stretched right across the whole of Moscow.

ANDREY—Whatever for?

FERAPONT—Don't know, sir. The contractor said so.

ANDREY—Nonsense! [*Reads his book.*] Have you ever been to Moscow?

FERAPONT [*after a pause*] No, sir. It wasn't God's will that I should go there, I suppose. [*Pause.*] Can I go now, sir?

ANDREY—You can go. Goodbye. [FERAPONT *goes out.*] Goodbye. [*Reads.*] Come and take the papers tomorrow morning. You can go now. [*Pause.*] He's gone. [*A bell rings.*] Yes, that's how it is . . .
[*Stretches himself and goes back to his room unhurriedly.*]

Off stage nurse is heard singing while rocking the baby to sleep. Enter MASHA *and* VERSHININ. *While they talk, a maid lights a lamp and candles.*

MASHA—I don't know. [*Pause.*] I don't know. Habit's very important, of course. For instance, after Father died it took us a long time to get accustomed to the idea that we no longer had any orderlies. But quite apart from habit, it seems to me that what I said was only fair. It may be different somewhere else, but in our town the military are the most well-bred and well-educated people.

VERSHININ—I'm thirsty. I'd love some tea.

MASHA [*glancing at the clock*] They'll bring it in presently. I was married off when I was eighteen. I was afraid of my husband because he was a schoolmaster and I had only just left school. He seemed to me frightfully learned, clever and distinguished. Now, I'm sorry to say, it's quite different.

VERSHININ—Yes, I see.

MASHA—But I'm not discussing my husband. I've got used to him. You see, there are so many coarse, ill-bred, uneducated people among the civilians. Coarseness upsets and offends me. I suffer physically in the presence of a man who is not sufficiently well-bred, not sufficiently delicate or courteous. I suffer agonies in the company of schoolmasters, my husband's colleagues.

VERSHININ—Well, yes, but I should have thought that in a town like this there was nothing to choose between a civilian and an army officer. It really makes no difference. Listen to any educated person here, civilian or army officer, and he'll tell you that he's sick and tired of his wife, or his family, or his estate or his horses. A Russian is particularly susceptible to high thinking but, tell me, why does he aim so low in life? Why?

MASHA—Why?

VERSHININ—Why is he sick and tired of his children, sick and tired of his wife, and why are his wife and children sick and tired of him?

MASHA—You're not in a very good mood today, are you?

VERSHININ—Perhaps not. I haven't had any lunch today. I haven't had anything to eat since morning. One of my daughters is not very well, and when my little girls are not well, I'm worried. You see, I can't help thinking that it's my fault they have such a mother. Oh, if you'd seen her today—what a nonentity! We started quarrelling at seven o'clock and at nine I walked out, slamming the door behind me. [*Pause.*] I never talk about it to anyone and, curiously enough, it's to you alone that I complain. [*Kisses her hand.*] Don't be angry with me. I've no one but you. No one.

MASHA—Listen to that noise in the chimney! Before Father died the wind howled in the chimney just like that. Exactly like that.

VERSHININ—You're not superstitious, are you?

MASHA—Yes, I am.

VERSHININ—That's strange. [*Kisses her hand.*] You're a magnificent, wonderful woman. Magnificent, wonderful! It's dark here, but I can see your eyes gleaming.

MASHA [*sits down on another chair*] There's more light here . . .

VERSHININ—I love you, I love you, I love you! I love your eyes, your movements. I dream about them. Magnificent, wonderful woman!

M A S H A [*laughing softly*] When you talk to me like that I somehow cannot help laughing, though I'm terrified. Don't say it again, I beg you. [*In an undertone.*] Yes, yes, do go on. [*Covers her face with her hands.*] I don't mind. Someone's coming. Talk about something else.

[IRINA *and* TUSENBACH *come in through the ballroom.*]

T U S E N B A C H – I have a triple-barrelled name: Baron Tusenbach-Krone-Altschauer, but I'm a Russian, a Greek Orthodox like you. There's little of the German left in me, except perhaps patience and the obstinacy with which I'm boring you. I see you home every night.

I R I N A – I'm so tired!

T U S E N B A C H – And I'll go on coming to the telegraph office and seeing you off home every day for ten or twenty years, if necessary, until you drive me away. [*Catching sight of* MASHA *and* VERSHININ, *joyfully.*] Is it you? Good evening.

I R I N A – At home at last. [*To* MASHA.] A woman came to the telegraph office an hour or so ago. She wanted to send a telegram to her brother in Saratov to tell him that her son had died today, but she just couldn't remember the address. So I sent on the telegram without an address. Simply to Saratov. She was crying. I was rude to her. I don't know why. I'm sorry, I said, I'm in a hurry. It was so stupid. We are having the carnival dancers in today, aren't we?

M A S H A – Yes.

I R I N A [*sits down in an armchair*] Must rest. Awfully tired.

T U S E N B A C H [*with a smile*] Every time you come back from the office you look so young, so unhappy.

[*Pause.*]

I R I N A – I'm tired. I'm afraid I don't like the telegraph office. Don't like it at all.

M A S H A – You've grown thinner. [*Whistles.*] And you look younger. You look like a boy.

T U S E N B A C H – That's because of the way she does her hair.

I R I N A – I'll have to find another job. This one doesn't suit me. It isn't what I was looking for, what I was dreaming of. Work without poetry, without thought. [*A knock on the floor from below.*] The doctor's knocking. [*To* TUSENBACH.] Please, be an angel and answer him. I can't. I'm tired.

[TUSENBACH *knocks on the floor.*]

I R I N A – He'll be here in a moment. We must do something. Yesterday the doctor and Andrey went to the club and lost at cards again. Apparently, Andrey lost two hundred roubles.

M A S H A [*with indifference*] It's a little late to do anything about it.

I R I N A – Two weeks ago he lost, in December he lost. I wish he'd hurry up and lose everything he's got. Perhaps we'd leave for Moscow then.

Dear Lord, every night I dream of Moscow. I'm going quite off my head. [*Laughs.*] We shall be going there in June, but before June there's still—February, March, April, May—nearly half a year!

MASHA—We must make sure Natasha doesn't find out about his losses.

IRINA—I don't think she cares.

CHEBUTYKIN, *who has only just got out of bed—he had a nap after dinner—enters the ballroom combing his beard. He sits down at the table and takes a newspaper out of his pocket.*

MASHA—Just look at him! Has he paid his rent?

IRINA [*laughs*] Good Lord, no. Not a penny for the last eight months. Forgotten all about it, I dare say.

MASHA [*laughs*] How importantly he sits!

[*They all laugh; pause.*]

IRINA—Why so silent, Colonel?

VERSHININ—Don't know. I'm dying for a cup of tea. Half a life for a cup of tea! Haven't had a bite since morning.

CHEBUTYKIN—Irina, my dear.

IRINA—What is it?

CHEBUTYKIN—Please, come here. *Venez ici.* [IRINA *goes over and sits at the table.*] You must help me.

[IRINA *lays out the cards for a game of patience.*]

VERSHININ—Well, if we can't have any tea, let's at least have a talk.

TUSENBACH—Let's. What about?

VERSHININ—What about? Let's just—er—imagine what life will be like after we're gone—er—say, in two or three hundred years.

TUSENBACH—Well, I suppose after us people will fly about in balloons, wear a different cut of coat, perhaps discover and develop a sixth sense, but life will still remain the same as ever: a hard life, a life full of all sorts of mysteries and—a happy life. A thousand years hence, man will still be sighing: "Oh, life is hard!" At the same time, he'll be just as afraid of death, just as unwilling to die as he is now.

VERSHININ [*thinking it over*] Now, how shall I put it? I can't help thinking that everything on earth must change little by little. Indeed, it is already changing before our very eyes. In two hundred, three hundred, or even a thousand years—the actual time doesn't matter—a new and happy life will begin. We shan't take part in it, of course, but we're living for it now—working and—well—suffering for it, creating it . . . This alone is the goal of our existence and, if you like, our happiness.

[MASHA *laughs quietly.*]

TUSENBACH—What's the matter?

MASHA—Don't know. I've been laughing all day today. Ever since morning.

VERSHININ—I went to the same school as you. I did not go to the Military Academy. I read a lot, but I don't know what books to choose. I shouldn't be at all surprised if I read all the wrong books. Yet, the longer I live, the more I want to know. My hair's turning grey, I'm almost an old man, but I know little—oh, how little! Nevertheless, I think I know what matters most now. I'm certain of that. What I'd most like to prove to you is that there is no such thing as happiness, that there must not be, and that it will not be for us. All we must do is work, work and work. Happiness is for our distant descendants. [*Pause.*] If not for me, then at least for the descendants of my descendants.

[FEDOTIK *and* RODÉ *come into the ballroom; they sit down and sing softly, strumming a guitar.*]

TUSENBACH—According to you, one oughtn't even to dream of happiness. But what if I am happy!

VERSHININ—You're not.

TUSENBACH [*flinging up his hands and laughing*] I'm afraid we don't understand one another. How am I to convince you?

[MASHA *laughs quietly.*]

TUSENBACH [*pointing a finger at her*] Laugh! [*To* VERSHININ.] Life will be the same, not only in two or three hundred years, but in a million years. It never changes, it remains constant, it follows its own laws regardless of us. At least, those laws will always remain a mystery to you. Migrant birds, cranes for instance, fly and fly, and whatever thoughts—great or little—might be drifting through their heads, they will go on flying without knowing where or why. They'll fly and go on flying, however many philosophers may be born among them. Indeed, let them philosophise as much as they like so long as they go on flying.

MASHA—But there must be some meaning, mustn't there?

TUSENBACH—A meaning . . . Look, it's snowing. What meaning is there in that?

[*Pause.*]

MASHA—It seems to me that a man must either be religious or be seeking some religion. Otherwise, his life is empty, empty. To live and not to know why cranes fly, why children are born, why there are stars in the sky . . . You must either know what you live for or else nothing matters any more. It's all nonsense.

[*Pause.*]

VERSHININ—All the same, it is a pity that I'm no longer young.

MASHA—Gogol says: It's a boring world, my friends.

TUSENBACH—And I say: It's difficult to argue with you, my friends. Let's drop the subject . . .

CHEBUTYKIN [*reading his paper*] Balzac was married in Berdichev.
[IRINA *hums softly.*]
CHEBUTYKIN – In a hole like Berdichev! I think I'll make a note of that. [*Writes down in his notebook.*] Balzac was married in Berdichev.
[*Reads his paper.*]
IRINA [*laying out patience, reflectively*] Balzac was married in Berdichev.
TUSENBACH – The die is cast. I've sent in my resignation. Did you know that, Masha?
MASHA – Yes, I did. I must say, I can't see anything good about it. I don't like civilians.
TUSENBACH – Makes no difference. [*Gets up.*] I'm not handsome—what sort of a soldier am I? Well, anyway, it makes no difference. I'll work . . . Spend at least one day of my life working so hard that when I come home in the evening I'll fall on my bed dead tired and go to sleep at once. [*Going into the dining room.*] I expect workers sleep soundly.
FEDOTIK [*to* IRINA] I've just bought some coloured pencils for you at Pyzhikov's in the Moscow Road. And this penknife.
IRINA – You still go on treating me like a child. You forget I'm a grown-up woman. [*Accepts pencils and penknife, joyfully.*] They're lovely!
FEDOTIK – I bought a knife for myself. Have a look: one blade, another blade, a third for scooping out your ears, a fourth for cleaning your nails . . .
RODÉ [*aloud*] Doctor, how old are you?
CHEBUTYKIN – Me? Thirty-two.
[*Laughter.*]
FEDOTIK – Let me show you another game of patience.
[*Lays out the cards.*]

A samovar is put on the table. ANFISA *is busy at the samovar. A little later,* NATASHA *comes in and also busies herself at the table; enter* SOLYONY *who, after greeting everybody, sits down at the table.*

VERSHININ – What a wind, though!
MASHA – Yes. I'm tired of winter. I've already forgotten what summer's like.
IRINA – I can see it's working out. We shall be in Moscow.
FEDOTIK – It's not working out. See! The eight has to cover the two of spades. [*Laughs.*] Which means, you won't be in Moscow.
CHEBUTYKIN [*reads his paper*] Tsitsihar. Smallpox is raging here.

ANFISA [*going up to* MASHA] Masha, tea, darling. [*To* VERSHININ.] Please, sir. I'm sorry I've forgotten your name.

MASHA – Bring it here, Nanny. I'm not going over there.

IRINA – Nanny!

ANFISA – Coming, dear.

NATASHA [*to* SOLYONY] Little babies understand very well. Good morning, Bobby, I said. Good morning, darling! He gave me a knowing look. You think it's the mother in me speaking, don't you? It isn't. Believe me, it isn't! It's quite an extraordinary child.

SOLYONY – If it was my child, I'd roast him in a frying pan and eat him.

[*Goes into the drawing room with his glass of tea and sits down in a corner.*]

NATASHA [*covering her face with her hands*] What a coarse, ill-bred fellow!

MASHA – Anyone who doesn't notice whether it's summer or winter now is a happy man. I can't help thinking that if I were in Moscow I'd be indifferent to the weather.

VERSHININ – The other day I read the diary of a French Cabinet Minister. He wrote it in prison. He'd been sentenced for the Panama affair. With what rapturous delight does he mention the birds he sees through the prison window, the birds he never noticed before when he was a minister. Of course, now that he's been released, he doesn't notice the birds any more. Neither will you notice Moscow when living there. Happiness doesn't exist. It cannot exist. We merely desire it.

TUSENBACH [*takes a chocolate box from the table*] Where are the chocolates?

IRINA – Solyony's eaten them.

TUSENBACH – All of them?

ANFISA [*serving tea*] Here's a letter for you, sir.

VERSHININ – For me? [*Takes the letter.*] From my daughter. [*Reads.*] Yes, of course . . . Excuse me, Masha, I'll slip out quietly. I won't have any tea. [*Gets up, excitedly.*] Always the same thing . . .

MASHA – What is it? It's not a secret, is it?

VERSHININ [*in a low voice*] My wife's taken poison again. I must go. I'll go out unobserved. Terribly unpleasant—all this. [*Kisses* MASHA's *hand.*] My dear one—you're so good, so sweet . . . I'll go this way—quietly . . .

[*Goes out.*]

ANFISA – Where is he off to? I've just given him tea. Well, I must say . . .

MASHA [*angrily*] Leave me alone! Pestering me! Not a moment's peace! [*Goes to the table with her cup of tea.*] I'm tired of you, old woman!

ANFISA—Why are you so cross, my dear?

ANDREY [*off stage*] Anfisa!

ANFISA [*mimicking*] Anfisa! Sitting there . . .

[*Goes out.*]

MASHA [*in the ballroom, crossly*] Let me sit down, will you? [*Mixing up the cards on the table.*] Sprawling all over the place with your cards. Why don't you drink your tea?

IRINA—You've got a foul temper, Masha!

MASHA—Don't talk to me if I've a foul temper. Leave me alone!

CHEBUTYKIN [*laughing*] Leave her alone, leave her alone . . .

MASHA—You're sixty, but you're always talking some damned nonsense as if you were a silly little boy.

NATASHA [*sighs*] My dear Masha, why must you use such language? I assure you that with your attractive appearance you'd be simply bewitching in any refined society, if it were not for your language. *Je vous prie, pardonnez moi, Marie, mais vous avez des mannières un peu grossières.*

TUSENBACH [*restraining his laughter*] Please . . . please . . . pass me . . . There's some brandy, I think.

NATASHA—*Il parait, que mon Bobby déjà ne dort pas—*he's awake. I'm afraid he isn't well today. I'd better go and see. Excuse me . . .

[*Goes out.*]

IRINA—And where has the colonel gone?

MASHA—Home. He's having some trouble with his wife again.

TUSENBACH [*goes up to* SOLYONY *with a decanter of brandy*] You always sit alone thinking, goodness knows what about. Come, let's make it up. Let's have some brandy. [*They drink.*] I expect I'll have to play the piano all night—all sort of rubbish . . . Oh, well!

SOLYONY—Why make it up? We haven't quarrelled, have we?

TUSENBACH—You always make me feel as if something's happened between us. You've a strange character, I must say.

SOLYONY [*declaiming*] I am strange. Who isn't? Do not be angry, Aleko!

TUSENBACH—What's Aleko got to do with it?

[*Pause.*]

SOLYONY—When I'm alone with someone, I'm all right. I'm just like the rest. But in company I feel depressed, I'm shy and—and I talk a lot of nonsense. But all the same I'm a damn sight better and more honest than a lot of other people. And I can prove it.

TUSENBACH—I'm often angry with you, you continually pick on me when we're in company, but I like you for all that. I don't know why. Anyway, I'm going to get drunk tonight. Let's have another drink!

S O L Y O N Y – Let's. [*They drink.*] I've never had anything against you, Baron. But my character is like Lermontov's. [*In a low voice.*] I even look a little like Lermontov. So I'm told.

[*Takes a scent bottle from his pocket and sprinkles his hands.*]

T U S E N B A C H – I've sent in my resignation. I've had enough. I've been thinking about it for five years and I've made up my mind at last. I shall work.

S O L Y O N Y [*declaiming*] Do not be angry, Aleko . . . Forget, forget your dreams . . .

[*While they are talking,* ANDREY *enters quietly with a book and sits down by the candle.*]

T U S E N B A C H – I shall work.

C H E B U T Y K I N [*going into the drawing room with* IRINA] And the food was genuinely Caucasian: onion soup and for a roast—mutton, chekhartma.

S O L Y O N Y – Cheremsha isn't meat at all, it's a plant, something like our onion.

C H E B U T Y K I N – No, sir. No, my angel. Chekhartma isn't an onion, it's roast mutton.

S O L Y O N Y – And I'm telling you cheremsha is an onion.

C H E B U T Y K I N – And I'm telling you chekhartma is mutton.

S O L Y O N Y – And I'm telling you cheremsha is an onion.

C H E B U T Y K I N – What's the use of arguing with you? You've never been to the Caucasus and you've never eaten chekhartma.

S O L Y O N Y – Haven't eaten it because I can't stand it. Cheremsha reeks like garlic.

A N D R E Y [*imploringly*] Enough, gentlemen. Please!

T U S E N B A C H – When will the carnival dancers come along?

I R I N A – They promised to be here by nine—which means any moment now.

T U S E N B A C H [*embraces* ANDREY] Oh, my bright, my beautiful hall-way, my beautiful new hallway . . .[3]

A N D R E Y [*dances and sings*] My maple-wood hall . . .

C H E B U T Y K I N [*dances*] My latticed hall . . .

[*Laughter.*]

T U S E N B A C H [*kisses* ANDREY] Hang it all, let's drink! Andrey, my dear fellow, let's drink to our friendship. I'll come to Moscow with you, to the university.

S O L Y O N Y – Which one? There are two universities in Moscow.

---

[3] A traditional Russian folk song and dance.

ANDREY–There's only one university in Moscow.

SOLYONY–And I tell you there are two.

ANDREY–Three, if you like. So much the better.

SOLYONY–There are two universities in Moscow. [*Murmurs of protest and booing.*] There are two universities in Moscow: the old and the new. But, if you don't want to listen to me, if my words annoy you, I'll shut up. I can even go to another room.

[*Goes out through one of the doors.*]

TUSENBACH–Bravo, bravo! [*Laughs.*] Let's start, ladies and gentlemen. I'm sitting down at the piano. Funny fellow—that Solyony.

[*Sits down at the piano and plays a waltz.*]

MASHA [*dances by herself*] The Baron's drunk, the Baron's drunk, the Baron's drunk . . .

[*Enter* NATASHA.]

NATASHA [*to* CHEBUTYKIN] Doctor . . .

[*Speaks to* CHEBUTYKIN, *then goes out quietly.* CHEBUTYKIN *touches* TUSENBACH *on the shoulder and whispers something to him.*]

IRINA–What is it?

CHEBUTYKIN–Time we were going. Goodbye.

TUSENBACH–Goodnight. It's time we were off.

IRINA–Wait a minute. What about the carnival dancers?

ANDREY [*greatly embarrassed*] There won't be any. You see, my dear, Natasha says that Bobby isn't very well and that's why . . . Anyway, I don't know . . . I don't care a damn . . .

IRINA [*shrugging*] Bobby isn't well!

MASHA–Oh, all right! If they're kicking us out, we'd better go. [*To* IRINA.] It isn't Bobby who's ill, it's she herself . . . Here! [*Taps her forehead.*] The stupid, selfish, trivial creature!

[ANDREY *goes to his room through the righthand door.* CHEBUTYKIN *follows him. In the ballroom they are saying goodbye.*]

FEDOTIK–What a shame! I counted on spending the evening here, but, of course, if the baby's ill . . . I'll bring him some toys tomorrow.

RODÉ [*in a loud voice*] I had a good sleep after lunch because I thought I was going to dance all night. Why, it's only nine o'clock!

MASHA–Let's go outside. We can talk there. We'll decide what to do.

Voices saying "Goodbye" and "Goodnight" can be heard. TUSENBACH *is heard laughing gaily. All go out.* ANFISA *and a maid clear the table, put out the lights. The nurse is heard singing a lullaby.* ANDREY, *wearing an overcoat and a hat, and* CHEBUTYKIN *enter quietly.*

CHEBUTYKIN–I never managed to get married because my life flashed by like a streak of lightning. Also because I was madly in love with your mother, a married woman.

ANDREY – One shouldn't marry. One shouldn't because it's so boring.

CHEBUTYKIN – That may be so, but what about the loneliness? Say what you like, but loneliness, my dear fellow, is a terrible thing. Although, as a matter of fact—I mean, it makes absolutely no difference, does it?

ANDREY – Let's get out quickly.

CHEBUTYKIN – What's the hurry? Plenty of time.

ANDREY – I'm afraid my wife may stop me.

CHEBUTYKIN – Oh!

ANDREY – I won't gamble today. I'll just sit and watch. Don't feel too well . . . What am I to do for my asthma, Doctor?

CHEBUTYKIN – Why ask me? I can't remember, dear boy. Don't know.

ANDREY – Let's go through the kitchen. [*They go out.*]

[*The doorbell rings twice; voices and laughter are heard.*]

IRINA [*comes in*] What's that?

ANFISA [*in a whisper*] The mummers!

[*The doorbell rings.*]

IRINA – Tell them, Nanny, there's no one at home. Say we're sorry.

[ANFISA *goes out.* IRINA *paces the room pensively: she's upset. Enter*
SOLYONY.]

SOLYONY [*bewildered*] No one here. Where's everybody?

IRINA – Gone home.

SOLYONY – Strange. Are you alone here?

IRINA – Yes. [*Pause.*] Goodbye.

SOLYONY – I'm sorry I behaved rather tactlessly a short while ago . . . forgot myself. But you're not like the rest. You're high-minded and pure. You see the truth . . . You alone can understand me. I love you, I love you deeply, passionately . . .

IRINA – Goodbye. Please, go away.

SOLYONY – I can't live without you. [*Going after her.*] Oh, my joy! [*Through tears.*] Oh, my happiness! Lovely, exquisite, wonderful eyes, eyes unlike those of any other woman I've ever known.

IRINA [*coldly*] Don't, please.

SOLYONY – It's the first time I've spoken to you of my love and I feel as though I'm not on earth but on another planet. [*Rubs his forehead.*] Oh, never mind. I can't force you to love me, of course. But I shall not put up with any successful rivals. I shan't. I swear to you by all that I hold sacred that I shall kill my rival. Oh, my wonderful one!

[NATASHA *enters carrying a candle.*]

NATASHA [*glances into one room, then into another, and passes the door leading into her husband's room*] Andrey's there. Let him read. [*To* SOLYONY.] I'm sorry. I didn't know you were here. Excuse my dressing gown.

Anton Chekhov

s o l y o n y – Don't mind me. Goodbye.

[*Goes out.*]

n a t a s h a – You look tired, darling. Oh, you poor child! [*Kisses* irina.] You ought to go to bed earlier.

i r i n a – Is Bobby asleep?

n a t a s h a – Yes, he is. But he's very restless. By the way, my dear, I've been wanting to say something to you, but either you've been out or I've been too busy. I can't help thinking that the nursery is too cold and damp for Bobby. Your room is just what a baby wants. Darling, don't you think you could move into Olga's room? Just for a short time.

i r i n a [*not understanding*] Where?

[*The harness bells of a troika can be heard as it drives up to the house.*]

n a t a s h a – You and Olga will share one room, for the time being, I mean, and Bobby will have your room. He's such a darling! Today I said to him: Bobby, you're mine! Mine! And he looked at me with his sweet little eyes. [*The doorbell rings.*] Must be Olga. She *is* late! [*The maid goes up to* natasha *and whispers in her ear.*] Protopopov? What a funny man! Protopopov asked me to go for a drive with him in his troika. [*Laughs.*] These men are strange, aren't they? [*The doorbell rings.*] Somebody's come. I suppose I could go for a drive for a quarter of an hour. [*To the maid.*] Tell him I shan't be long. [*The doorbell rings.*] The doorbell again. That must be Olga.

[*Goes out.*]

[*The maid runs off;* irina *sits lost in thought; enter* kulygin *and* olga, *followed by* vershinin.]

k u l y g i n – How do you like that? I was told they'd be having a party.

v e r s h i n i n – I must be off. I left not so long ago, half an hour ago to be precise, and they were expecting carnival dancers.

i r i n a – They've all gone.

k u l y g i n – Masha gone too? What's Protopopov waiting for outside in a troika? Who is he waiting for?

i r i n a – Don't ask me. I'm tired.

k u l y g i n – Oh, you naughty child!

o l g a – The staff meeting has only just ended. I'm dead tired. Our headmistress is ill and I'm deputising for her. Oh, my head! My head's aching . . . [*Sits down.*] Andrey lost two hundred roubles at cards yesterday. The whole town is talking about it.

k u l y g i n – Yes, our staff meeting has made me tired too.

[*Sits down.*]

v e r s h i n i n – My wife's taken it into her head to frighten me. She nearly poisoned herself. Everything's all right, I'm glad to say. I'm no longer worried, thank goodness. I suppose we must go, mustn't we?

Well, in that case, I wish you all the best. What about coming with me, Kulygin? I can't stay at home, I simply can't. Come on!

KULYGIN – Too tired. Sorry, I can't go with you. [*Gets up.*] Too tired. Has my wife gone home?

IRINA – I suppose so.

KULYGIN [*kisses* IRINA'S *hand*] Goodbye. I shall take it easy all day tomorrow and the day after tomorrow. All the best. [*Going.*] I'd love a cup of tea. Counted on spending the evening in pleasant company and—O, *fallacem hominum spem!* The accusative case in exclamations!

VERSHININ – Oh, well, I'll be going somewhere by myself.

[*Goes out with* KULYGIN, *whistling.*]

OLGA – My head, my head aches . . . Andrey lost . . . The whole town's talking. I'll go and lie down. [*Going.*] Tomorrow I'm free. Goodness, that really is lovely! Free tomorrow, free the day after tomorrow. My head aches—my head . . .

[*Goes out.*]

IRINA [*alone*] All gone. No one's left.

[*The sound of an accordion from the street; the nurse sings a lullaby.*]

NATASHA [*walks across the ballroom in a fur coat, followed by the maid*] I'll be back in half an hour. Just going out for a little drive.

[*Goes out.*]

IRINA [*alone, longingly*] To Moscow! To Moscow! To Moscow!

ACT THREE

OLGA's *and* IRINA's *room. Screened off beds on the right and the left. It is past two o'clock in the morning. Off stage a fire alarm bell is ringing on account of a fire which has started a long time before. It is clear that no one in the house has yet gone to bed.* MASHA *is lying on a sofa, dressed, as usual, in black.* OLGA *and* ANFISA *come in.*

ANFISA – They're downstairs, sitting under the staircase. Please, I says to them, come upstairs. You can't carry on like that. But they go on crying. We don't know where Daddy is, they says. He's probably been burnt in the fire. The things they think of! In the yard, too, there are some people . . . also in their night clothes.

OLGA [*takes dresses out of the wardrobe*] Take this grey one . . . this one too . . . also this blouse. And this frock, too, Nanny. Goodness me, how awful! The entire Kirsanov Lane seems to have burnt down . . . Take this too . . . And this. [*Throws clothes into her hands.*] The poor Vershinins! They were terrified. Their house nearly burnt down. Let them spend the night here. They mustn't be allowed to go home. Poor old Fedotik lost everything in the fire. Nothing left.

ANFISA – I think I'd better call Ferapont, dear. I can't carry it all.

OLGA [*rings*] They never answer. [*Calls through the door.*] Anyone there? Come here, please. [*Through the open door, a window, red with the glow of the fire, can be seen; a fire engine can be heard passing the house.*] Oh, the horror of it! And what a mess it is! [*Enter* FERAPONT.] Take all this downstairs. You'll find the Kolotilin girls under the staircase—give it to them. And this . . .

FERAPONT – Yes'm. In 1812 Moscow was also burnt down. Dear, oh dear, weren't the French surprised!

OLGA – Go on. Hurry up.

FERAPONT – Yes'm.

[*Goes out.*]

OLGA – Nanny dear, give everything away. We don't want anything. Give it all away. I'm dead tired. Can hardly stand on my feet. We mustn't let the Vershinins go back home. The girls can sleep in the drawing room, and the colonel downstairs with the Baron. Fedotik

1590

can also stay with the Baron or else in the ballroom. The doctor would get drunk, dead drunk, just now, and we can't let anyone go into his room. Vershinin's wife, too, in the drawing room.

A N F I S A [*in a tired voice*] Don't turn me out of the house, Olga dear. Please don't turn me out.

O L G A – Don't talk nonsense, Nanny. No one is turning you out.

A N F I S A [*puts her head on* OLGA's *bosom*] My darling child, my precious, you know I work as hard as I can. But as soon as I grows too weak for work, they're all sure to say: out with her! Where could I go? Where? I'm eighty. Nearly eighty-two.

O L G A – You'd better sit down, Nanny. You're tired, poor dear. [*Makes her sit down.*] Rest a while, dear. You're so pale.

[NATASHA *enters.*]

N A T A S H A – They're saying we ought to form a committee as soon as possible to raise funds for the people made homeless by the fire. Well, why not? It's an excellent idea. Anyway, it's the duty of the rich to help the poor. Bobby and little Sophie are peacefully asleep. The little darlings are asleep as if nothing had happened. There are people everywhere, the house is full of them whichever way you turn. There's a flu epidemic in town. I'm afraid the children might catch it.

O L G A [*not listening to her*] We can't see the fire in this room. It's quiet here.

N A T A S H A – Yes . . . I must be an awful sight. [*Stands in front of the mirror.*] People say I've got fat—it just isn't true! I'm no fatter. Masha's asleep. She's tired out, poor girl. [*To* ANFISA, *coldly.*] Don't you dare sit down in my presence! Get up! Get out of here! [ANFISA *goes out; pause.*] I simply can't understand why you keep the old woman!

O L G A [*taken aback*] I'm sorry, but I don't understand . . .

N A T A S H A – She's quite useless in the house. She's a peasant and she ought to live in the country. Spoiling her, aren't you? I like order in the house. There should be no superfluous people in the house. [*Strokes* OLGA's *cheek.*] Oh, you poor thing! You're tired. Our headmistress is tired. When my little Sophie grows up and goes to school, I'll be afraid of you.

O L G A – I shan't be a headmistress.

N A T A S H A – They're going to appoint you, dearest. It's settled.

O L G A – I'll refuse. I couldn't . . . It's beyond me. [*Drinks water.*] You treated Nanny so abominably just now. I'm sorry, but I can't bear it. It made me feel quite faint.

N A T A S H A [*excitedly*] I'm sorry, Olga, I'm sorry. I didn't want to upset you.

[MASHA *gets up, picks up a pillow and walks out angrily.*]

O L G A – Please understand, my dear. We may have been brought up in a rather peculiar way, but I can't bear this sort of thing. Such an attitude cuts me to the quick. It makes me ill . . . I simply lose heart.

NATASHA–I'm sorry, I'm sorry . . .

[*Kisses her.*]

OLGA–Any rudeness, however slight, any harsh word, upsets me.

NATASHA–I admit I often say things I shouldn't, but, my dear, you must agree that there's no reason why she shouldn't live in the country.

OLGA–She's been with us for thirty years.

NATASHA–But she can't do any work now! Either I don't understand or you don't want to understand me. She's incapable of doing any work. All she does is sleep or sit about.

OLGA–Well, let her sit about.

NATASHA [*in surprise*] Let her sit about? But she's a servant, isn't she? [*Through tears.*] I don't understand you, Olga. I have a nanny, I have a wet nurse, we have a maid, a cook,–whatever do we want this old woman for? What for?

[*Fire alarm off stage.*]

OLGA–I've aged ten years tonight.

NATASHA–We must come to an understanding, Olga. You're at school, I'm at home. You've got your teaching, I've got to run the house. And if I talk about it, I know what I'm talking about. I know what I'm talk-ing a-bout! By tomorrow I want that old thief, that old hag out of my house. [*Stamps her foot.*] The old witch! Don't you dare exasperate me! Don't you dare! [*Recollecting herself.*] Really, Olga, if you don't move downstairs we'll always be quarreling. This is dreadful!

[*Enter* KULYGIN.]

KULYGIN–Where's Masha? Time we went home. They say the fire is subsiding. [*Stretching himself.*] Only one block has burnt down. There was a strong wind, though, and it did seem at first that the whole town was on fire. [*Sits down.*] Oh, I'm tired, dear Olga. I often think that if it hadn't been for Masha, I'd have married you, dear. You're so good . . . Oh, I'm exhausted.

[*Listens.*]

OLGA–What is it?

KULYGIN–The doctor is on one of his drinking sprees. It would happen just now. Terribly drunk. [*Gets up.*] I believe he's coming here. Listen! Yes, he's coming here. [*Laughs.*] What a man! Really! I'd better hide myself. [*Goes towards the wardrobe and stands in the corner.*] What a bandit!

OLGA–He hasn't been drinking for two years and now, all of a sudden, he goes and gets drunk.

[*Retires, with* NATASHA, *to the back of the room.*]

Enter CHEBUTYKIN, *walks across the room without swaying, just as if he were sober, looks round, goes up to the washstand and starts washing his hands.*

CHEBUTYKIN [*morosely*] To hell with all of them—to blazes with them! They think I'm a doctor, that I can treat any illness. The truth is I know absolutely nothing, forgotten everything I ever knew, remember nothing, absolutely nothing. [OLGA *and* NATASHA *go out, unnoticed by him.*] To hell with it! Last Wednesday I attended a woman in Zasyp. She died, and it was my fault that she died. Yes . . . Twenty-five years ago I knew something or other, but I don't remember a damn thing now. Not a damn thing. Perhaps I'm not a human being at all, but merely imagine that I have hands and feet and a head; perhaps I don't exist at all, but merely imagine that I walk, eat and sleep. [*Weeps.*] Oh, if only I did not exist! [*Stops weeping, morosely.*] Oh, hell! Day before yesterday they were talking at the club—heard them say: Shakespeare, Voltaire . . . Never read them, not a single word, but I did my best to look as if I had. The others did the same. The vulgarity of it! The baseness! But then I remembered the woman I killed on Wednesday—remembered everything and I felt dirty, nasty, loathesome . . . I went and got drunk.

[*Enter* IRINA, VERSHININ *and* TUSENBACH. TUSENBACH *is wearing a new, fashionable suit.*]

IRINA—Let's sit down. No one will come in here.

VERSHININ—If it weren't for the soldiers, the whole town would have burnt down. Stout fellows! [*Rubs his hands with pleasure.*] What a splendid people! Fine men, every one of them!

KULYGIN [*going up to them*] What's the time?

TUSENBACH—Gone three. It's getting light.

IRINA—Everyone's sitting in the ballroom. No one thinks of going home. Your Solyony's there too. [*To* CHEBUTYKIN.] You'd better go to bed, Doctor.

CHEBUTYKIN—Never mind me, thank you.

[*Combs his beard.*]

KULYGIN [*laughs*] Sozzled, eh, Doctor? [*Slaps him on the shoulder.*] Good lad! *In vino veritas*, the ancients used to say.

TUSENBACH—Everyone's asking me to organise a concert in aid of the homeless.

IRINA—But who—

TUSENBACH—It could be arranged if we tried. If you ask me, Masha plays the piano beautifully.

KULYGIN—She plays wonderfully.

1593

IRINA—She's forgotten how to. She hasn't played for three years . . . or four.

TUSENBACH—There's absolutely no one in this town who appreciates music, not a soul, but I do, and I assure you that Masha plays wonderfully, almost like a concert pianist.

KULYGIN—You're quite right, Baron. I love Masha very much. She's a dear.

TUSENBACH—To be able to play so splendidly and to know all the time that there's no one to appreciate you—no one!

KULYGIN [sighs] Yes—but do you think it would be correct for her to take part in a concert? [Pause.] I know nothing about such matters, of course. It may be all right. I must say our head is a decent fellow, a very decent fellow indeed, and very intelligent too, but he has—er—well, views . . . Of course, it's not his business, but, all the same, I might perhaps have a talk to him.

[CHEBUTYKIN picks up a porcelain clock and examines it.]

VERSHININ—I got so filthy at the fire, I look like nothing on earth. [Pause.] I heard a rumour yesterday that our brigade is to be transferred somewhere very far away. Some say to Poland, others to Chita.

TUSENBACH—I heard it too. Yes, well, I suppose the town will be quite deserted then.

IRINA—We shall be gone, too!

CHEBUTYKIN [drops the clock, which breaks] Smashed to bits!

[Pause; everyone looks upset and embarrassed.]

KULYGIN [picking up the pieces] Break an expensive thing like that! Oh, Doctor, Doctor, zero minus for conduct!

IRINA—That was Mother's clock.

CHEBUTYKIN—Possibly. So it was your mother's clock. Perhaps I didn't smash it, but it just seems as though I did. Perhaps we only imagine that we exist, but we don't really exist at all. I don't know anything. Nobody knows anything. [Stops at the door.] What are you staring at? Natasha is having a disgusting affair with Protopopov and you don't see it. You're just sitting about here and don't see anything while Natasha is having her disgusting affair with Protopopov. [Sings.] Won't you accept this little present from me?

[Goes out.]

VERSHININ—Well, well . . . [Laughs.] As a matter of fact, the whole thing is rather odd. [Pause.] When the fire broke out, I hurried off home. I got there—our house wasn't damaged and wasn't in danger, but my two little girls were standing at the front door in their night clothes; their mother wasn't there, people were rushing about, horses galloping past, dogs—and the girls looked upset, frightened, appealing, I don't know what else. My heart sank when I saw their faces. Good Lord, I thought, what else will these girls have to experience during a long life? I snatched them up, started running, and all the time kept thinking one and the same thing: what else would they have to experience in this world? [*Fire alarm; pause.*] I come here, their mother's here . . . angry, shouting.

> [MASHA *enters with a pillow and sits down on the sofa.*]

VERSHININ–When my little girls were standing at the front door in their night clothes and the street was red with the glow of the fire and the noise around was terrifying, the thought occurred to me that something like it must have happened many years ago when an enemy made a sudden raid, looted, burned . . . And yet, what a difference between what was happening now and what had happened before. When a little more time has passed, say, in two or three hundred years, people will look upon our present life, too, with horror and contempt. Everything we accept now will seem to them clumsy and dreadful, extremely uncomfortable and strange. I'm sure of it! Oh, what a wonderful life it will be, what a life! [*Laughs.*] I'm sorry, I'm off again! Please, let me continue. I'd awfully like to go on airing my views. I'm in the mood for it now. [*Pause.*] They all seem to be asleep. So, as I was saying, what a wonderful life it will be. You can just imagine it . . . There are only three like you in the town now, but in the generations to come there will be more, and more, and more, and the time will come when everything will change as you would have it, people will live as you do now, and then you, too, will become antiquated. People will be born who will be better than you . . . [*Laughs.*] I'm in a curious kind of mood. Damn it, I want to live and live!

[*Sings.*]

"To love all ages are in thrall,
  Her impulses are good for all".[4]

[*Laughs.*]

MASHA – Tram-tum-tum.
VERSHININ – Tam-tam.
MASHA – Tra-ra-ra
VERSHININ – Tra-ta-ta . . .

[*Laughs.*]
[*Enter* FEDOTIK.]

FEDOTIK [*dances*] Burnt down! Burnt down! To the last cinder!
IRINA – You're joking! Everything burned?

---

[4] The old general's aria from *Eugèn Onegin*.

FEDOTIK [*laughs*] Everything to the last cinder. Nothing left. My guitar, my camera, and all my letters.

[*Enter* SOLYONY.]

IRINA [*to* SOLYONY] Please go away. You can't come in here.

SOLYONY – Why can the Baron and I can't?

VERSHININ – We really ought to go. How's the fire?

SOLYONY – Dying down, I'm told. But I really can't see why the Baron can and I can't.

[*Takes out a scent bottle and sprinkles himself.*]

VERSHININ – Tram-tam-tam.

MASHA – Tam-tam.

VERSHININ [*laughs, to* SOLYONY] Let's go to the ballroom.

SOLYONY – Very well. We'll make a note of that, "I could make my tale much more clear, but that may irritate the geese, I fear".[5] [*Looking at* TUSENBACH.] Cluck-cluck-cluck.

[*Goes out with* VERSHININ *and* FEDOTIK.]

IRINA – What a stink Solyony's left behind him. [*Bewildered.*] The Baron's asleep! Baron! Baron!

TUSENBACH [*waking*] Sorry, I'm terribly tired . . . The brick works . . . I'm not talking in my sleep. I really will start work at a brick works soon. Start work . . . I've discussed it already. [*Tenderly, to* IRINA.] You are so pale, so beautiful, so fascinating. Your pallor, it seems to me, irradiates the dark air like a shaft of light. You're sad, you're dissatisfied with life. Oh, come away with me! Come away and let's work together.

MASHA – Go away, Baron.

TUSENBACH [*laughing*] You here? I can't see. [*Kisses* IRINA's *hand.*] Goodbye, I'm going. I look at you now and it comes back to me how a long time ago, on your birthday, you were so bright and cheerful and talked of the joys of life. At the time I, too, looked forward to a happy life. Where is it? [*Kisses her hand.*] There are tears in your eyes. You ought to go to bed. It's getting light, the day's dawning. Oh, if only I was allowed to give my life for you!

MASHA – Go away! Well, really! . . .

TUSENBACH – I'm going . . .

[*Goes out.*]

MASHA [*lying down*] Are you asleep, Fyodor?

KULYGIN – Eh?

MASHA – Why don't you go home?

KULYGIN – My dear Masha, my darling Masha . . .

IRINA – She's tired. Let her have a rest.

[5] A quotation from Krylov's fable *Geese*.

K U L Y G I N – I'll go in a minute. My wife's a good, nice woman. I love you, my only one.

M A S H A   [*angrily*] *Amo, amas, amat, amamus, amatis, amant* . . .

K U L Y G I N   [*laughs*] Isn't she wonderful? I've been married to you for seven years, but it seems as if we only left the church yesterday. On my word of honour! You really are a wonderful woman. I'm content, content, content.

M A S H A – I'm bored, bored, bored. [*Sits up.*] I can't get it out of my head. It's simply disgraceful. It preys on my mind. I can't keep silent. I mean about Andrey. He's mortgaged the house to a bank and his wife's grabbed all the money, but the house doesn't belong to him alone, does it? It belongs to all four of us. He should have known that, if he's an honest man.

K U L Y G I N – Why should you worry, Masha? What do you care? Andrey's up to his neck in debt. Well, let him do what he likes.

M A S H A – It's disgraceful, however you look at it.

[*Sits down.*]

K U L Y G I N – You and I aren't poor. I work, I teach at the high school, I give private lessons, I'm an honest man. A plain man. *Omnia mea mecum porto*, as they say.

M A S H A – I don't want anything, but I can't bear injustice. [*Pause.*] Go home, Fyodor.

K U L Y G I N   [*kisses her*] You're tired. Rest for half an hour. I'll sit and wait for you downstairs. Try to sleep. [*Going.*] I'm content, content, content.

[*Goes out.*]

I R I N A – Our Andrey really has degenerated, gone to seed and grown old beside that woman. Once upon a time he was thinking of becoming a professor; yesterday he was boasting of having at last been made a member of the local council. He's a member of the council, while Protopopov is chairman. The whole town's talking and laughing about it. He alone doesn't see or know anything. Here's everyone rushing off to the fire, but he sits in his room as if nothing were happening. Just plays his fiddle. [*Distractedly.*] Oh, it's awful, awful, awful! [*Weeps.*] I can't, I can't bear it any longer. I can't, I can't.

[OLGA *comes in and starts tidying up things on her bedside table.*]

I R I N A   [*sobs loudly*] Throw me out, throw me out. I can't bear it any longer!

O L G A   [*frightened*] What's the matter? What is it, darling?

I R I N A   [*sobbing*] Where, where has it all gone to? Where is it? Oh God, oh God! I've forgotten everything, forgotten . . . It's got all mixed up in my head. I can't remember the Italian for window or for ceiling. I'm forgetting everything, every day I'm forgetting, and life's passing and will never return, never! We'll never go to Moscow. I can see that we'll never go.

OLGA – Darling, darling . . .

IRINA [*controlling herself*] I'm so unhappy. I can't work. I won't work. I've had enough, thank you. I worked as a telegraphist, now I've got a job at the town council, and I hate and despise everything I have to do there. I'm twenty-three. I've worked for a long time and my brain's dried up. I'm growing thin, I'm losing my looks, I'm getting old, and there's nothing, nothing, I can look forward to, no satisfaction out of life I can hope for. Time's flying past, and I seem to be getting further and further away from real life, from a life that is beautiful, and heading for some horrible disaster. I'm in despair and I simply can't understand how I go on living, how I haven't killed myself before now.

OLGA – Don't cry, darling. I can't bear to see you cry.

IRINA – I'm not crying – I'm not crying. I've stopped now. See? I'm not crying any more. I've stopped. I've stopped.

OLGA – Darling, I'm talking to you as your sister, as your friend, if you take my advice, you'll marry the Baron!

[IRINA *cries softly*.]

OLGA – You do respect him, don't you? You think highly of him. It's true he's not handsome, but he's such an honest, decent man. After all, people don't marry for love, but to do their duty. At least, I think so. I wouldn't hesitate to marry a man I didn't love. I would marry anyone who asked me, provided he was a decent man. I'd even marry an old man.

IRINA – I was always waiting until we moved to Moscow, where I hoped to meet the right man for me, the man I've dreamed of, the man I'd love . . . But, as it turned out, it was all nonsense . . . all nonsense.

OLGA [*embraces her sister*] My dear, my sweet sister, I understand, I understand everything. When the Baron left the army and came to see us in civilian clothes, I thought he looked so unprepossessing that I even started crying. He asked me why I was crying, but I couldn't tell him that, could I? But I'd be very happy if he married you. That's quite a different matter, quite different.

[NATASHA, *carrying a lighted candle, walks across the stage in silence from the door on the right to the door on the left.*]

MASHA – She walks as if she had set the town on fire herself.

OLGA – You're silly, Masha. You're the silliest in our family. I'm sorry.

MASHA – I'd like to confess to you, dear sisters. My heart is heavy. Let me confess to you and never to anyone again, never again. I'll tell you now. [*Softly.*] It's my secret, but you must know everything. I can't be silent any more . . . [*Pause.*] I love him, I love him, I love that man. You've just seen him. Well, why conceal it? I love Vershinin.

OLGA [*goes behind the screen*] Don't. I'm not listening anyway.

MASHA – What am I to do? [*Clutches at her head.*] At first I thought him rather strange, then I began to pity him, and then I fell in love with him . . . I fell in love with his voice, his talk, his misfortunes, his two little daughters.

OLGA [*behind the screen*] I'm telling you I'm not listening. You can say any stupid thing you like, I'm not listening.

MASHA – Oh, you are stupid, Olga. I love him—well, you can't do anything about it, can you? It's happened. It's fate. He loves me, too. It's terrible, is it? It's not nice, is it? [*Draws* IRINA *to her by her hand.*] Oh, my dear, what's to become of us? What's our life going to be like? When you read some love story, it all seems so old and so obvious, but when you fall in love yourself, you realise that no one knows anything and that everyone has to decide for himself. My dear, dear sisters . . . I've told you everything and now I shall be silent. I shall be like Gogol's madman—silence . . . silence . . .

[*Enter* ANDREY, *followed by* FERAPONT.]

ANDREY [*crossly*] What do you want? I don't understand.

FERAPONT [*in the doorway, impatiently*] I've told you a dozen times already.

ANDREY – . . . Sir! . . .

FERAPONT – . . . sir. The firemen, sir, are asking for permission to drive down to the river through your garden. Otherwise they has to drive all the way round, which, they says, sir, is a terrible nuisance.

ANDREY – Oh, all right. Tell them it's all right. [FERAPONT *goes out.*] Fed up! Where's Olga? [OLGA *comes out from behind the screen.*] I've come to ask you for the key of the cupboard. I've lost mine. You've got it. The little key.

[OLGA *gives him the key in silence.* IRINA *goes behind the screen in her part of the room. Pause.*]

ANDREY – What a terrific fire! It's dying down now. Damn that Ferapont! He made me furious and made me say something silly. Sir . . . [*Pause.*] Why are you so silent, Olga? [*Pause.*] It's time you dropped this nonsense and stopped sulking like this without rhyme or reason. You're here, Masha, and so are you, Irina. Excellent! Let's have a frank talk—once and for all. What have you got against me? What?

OLGA – Leave it, Andrey dear. We'll have our talk tomorrow. [*Agitatedly.*] What an awful night!

ANDREY [*looking very embarrassed*] Don't get excited. I'm perfectly calm and I'm asking you what you've got against me. Tell me straight.

VERSHININ [*off stage*] Tram-tam-tam.

M A S H A [*gets up, aloud*] Tra-ta-ta! [*To* OLGA.] Goodbye, Olga. God bless. [*Goes behind the screen and kisses* IRINA.] Sleep well. Goodbye, Andrey. Go away now. They're tired. Talk it over tomorrow.

[*Goes out.*]

O L G A – Really, Andrey dear, why not put it off till tomorrow? [*Goes behind the screen to her part of the room.*] Time to go to bed.

A N D R E Y – Let me say what's on my mind and I'll go at once. To begin with, you've got something against Natasha, my wife. I've noticed it ever since the first day of our marriage. Natasha's a fine and honest person, straightforward and honourable—that's my opinion. I love and respect my wife—understand?—respect, and I demand that others should also respect her. I repeat, she's an honest and decent person, and, I'm sorry to say, the reason why you resent her so much is because you're so eager to find fault with her. [*Pause.*] Secondly, you seem to be angry with me because I'm not a professor and because I've given up my studies. But I work at the district council and I'm a member of its board. I regard my service there as honourable and as important as service to science. I'm a member of the board of the district council and I'm proud of it, if you want to know. [*Pause.*] Thirdly . . . there's one thing more I'd like to say—I've mortgaged the house without your consent. It was wrong of me—yes. I'm sorry, I was driven to it by my debts . . . thirty-five thousand. I've given up gambling for some time now, but the chief thing I have to say to justify myself is that you girls, you get Father's pension, while I—haven't anything—I mean, any income . . .

[*Pause.*]

K U L Y G I N [*at the door*] Isn't Masha here? [*Anxiously.*] Where is she? That's funny . . .

[*Goes out.*]

A N D R E Y – They're not listening. Natasha's an excellent, honest person. [*Paces the stage in silence and then stops dead.*] When I got married, I thought we'd be happy, all of us happy. But, my God . . . [*Weeps.*] My dear sisters, my darling sisters, don't believe me, don't believe . . .

[*Goes out.*]

K U L Y G I N [*at the door, anxiously*] Where's Masha? Isn't Masha here? Extraordinary business!

[*Goes out.*]

[*Fire alarm; the stage is empty.*]

I R I N A [*behind the screen*] Olga, who's knocking on the floor?

O L G A – It's the doctor. He's drunk.

I R I N A – What a restless night! [*Pause.*] Olga! [*Looks out from behind the screen.*] Have you heard? The brigade's been ordered to leave. It's being transferred somewhere far away.

OLGA – It's only a rumour.

IRINA – We shall be left all alone then . . . Olga!

OLGA – Well?

IRINA – Oh, my dear, my darling, I respect the Baron. I think a lot of him. He's a fine man. I will marry him. I agree. Only, let's go to Moscow. Please, please let's go. There's no place like Moscow in the whole world. Let's go, Olga. Let's go!

ACT FOUR

The old garden of the Prozorovs' house. A long avenue of firs, with a river at the end of it. On the other side of the river—a forest. On the right—a verandah: empty bottles and glasses on a table make it obvious that champagne has just been drunk. It is midday. Passers-by occasionally walk through the garden on their way to the river from the street; five soldiers march past rapidly.

CHEBUTYKIN, *in a goodhumoured frame of mind which doesn't desert him throughout the whole of the act, is sitting in an easy chair in the garden waiting to be called; he is wearing his army cap and holding a walking stick.* IRINA, KULYGIN, *with a decoration round his neck and with his moustache shaved off, and* TUSENBACH, *standing on the verandah, are seeing off* FEDOTIK *and* RODÉ, *who are coming down the steps: both officers are in field dress.*

TUSENBACH [*exchanging kisses with* FEDOTIK] You're a good fellow. We got on well together. [*Exchanging kisses with* RODÉ] Again . . . Goodbye, dear friend.

IRINA—Au revoir.

FEDOTIK—Not au revoir, but goodbye. We shall never meet again.

KULYGIN—Who knows? [*Wipes his eyes, smiles.*] Look at me—crying!

IRINA—We shall meet one day.

FEDOTIK—In ten or fifteen years? But we'll hardly know each other then. Exchange cold greetings. [*Takes a snapshot.*] Stand still, please . . . For the last time.

RODÉ [*embraces* TUSENBACH] We shan't meet again. [*Kisses* IRINA's *hand.*] Thanks for everything, for everything!

FEDOTIK [*annoyed*] Wait!

TUSENBACH—Let's hope we shall meet. Write to us. Be sure to write.

RODÉ [*glancing round the garden*] Goodbye, trees! [*Shouts.*] Ho-ho! [*Pause.*] Goodbye, echo!

KULYGIN—For all we know you may get married there—in Poland. Your Polish wife will throw her arms round you and say: *Kochane!* [*Laughs.*]

1602

FEDOTIK [*glancing at his watch*] There's less than an hour left. Solyony is the only one from our battery who's going on the barge. The rest of us are marching with the troops. Three batteries are leaving today, another three tomorrow—the town will be quiet and peaceful at last.

TUSENBACH – And terribly boring.

RODÉ – Where's Masha?

KULYGIN – In the garden.

FEDOTIK – Must say goodbye to her.

RODÉ – Goodbye. We must go or I'll burst into tears. [*Embraces quickly* TUSENBACH *and* KULYGIN *and kisses* IRINA's *hand.*] We've had a lovely time here.

FEDOTIK [*to* KULYGIN] Here's something to remember me by—a notebook with a pencil. We'll go down to the river from here.

[*They go away, both looking round several times.*]

RODÉ [*shouts*] Ho-ho!

KULYGIN [*shouts*] Goodbye!

[*At the back of the stage* FEDOTIK *and* RODÉ *meet* MASHA *and take leave of her;* MASHA *goes off with them.*]

IRINA – They've gone.

[*Sits down on the bottom step of the verandah.*]

CHEBUTYKIN – They forgot to say goodbye to me.

IRINA – What about you?

CHEBUTYKIN – Well, yes, I, too, forgot, somehow. Still, I shall be seeing them soon. I'm leaving tomorrow. Yes . . . one more day. In another year I shall be put on the retired list, I shall come back here and spend the rest of my life near you. There's only one more year left before I qualify for a pension. [*Puts a newspaper in his pocket and takes out another.*] I'll come back to you here and change my way of life drastically. I shall become a very quiet, well-behaved, decent little man.

IRINA – You jolly well have to change your way of life, dear Doctor. You really must.

CHEBUTYKIN – Yes, I feel it. [*Sings softly.*] Tara-ra-boom-di-ay . . . I'm sitting in a room-di-ay . . .

KULYGIN – The doctor's incorrigible. Incorrigible!

CHEBUTYKIN – Why don't you give me a few lessons? I'd become a reformed character then.

IRINA – Fyodor's shaved off his moustache. I can't bear to look at him.

KULYGIN – Why not?

CHEBUTYKIN – I could tell you what your face looks like, only I wouldn't like to.

KULYGIN—Ah well! I'm afraid it's the accepted thing, the *modus vivendi*. Our headmaster has shaved off his moustache and so have I now that I have become second master. No one likes it, but I don't care. I'm content. Whether with or without a moustache—I'm content.

[*Sits down.*]

[*At the back of the stage* ANDREY *is wheeling a pram with a sleeping baby.*]

IRINA—Dear Doctor, I'm terribly worried. You were out on the boulevard yesterday. Be a darling and tell me what happened there.

CHEBUTYKIN—What happened? Nothing. Nothing at all. [*Reads his newspaper.*] It's of no importance.

KULYGIN—I'm told Solyony and the Baron met yesterday on the boulevard near the theatre . . .

TUSENBACH—Do shut up! Really! . . . [*Waves his hand and goes into the house.*]

KULYGIN—. . . near the theatre. Solyony began picking a quarrel with the Baron, and the latter lost his temper and said something offensive.

CHEBUTYKIN—Don't know. It's all nonsense.

KULYGIN—In some seminary a teacher wrote "nonsense" in Russian on an essay and the pupil thought it was written in Latin, but couldn't find the word in a dictionary. [*Laughs.*] Terribly funny. They say that Solyony's in love with Irina and that he's grown to hate the Baron. Well, that's understandable. Irina's a very nice girl. She's very like Masha, just as given to daydreaming. Except that your character, Irina, is more gentle. Though I must say, Masha, too, has a very good character. I love her. I love my Masha.

[*At the back of the stage someone shouts: "Coo-ee!" "Hey!"*]

IRINA [*shudders*] Everything seems to startle me today for some reason. [*Pause.*] I've got everything packed. I'm sending my things off after lunch. The Baron and I are getting married tomorrow. We're leaving for the brickworks tomorrow, and the day after I shall be at the school. A new life will begin. May God help me! When I was sitting for my teacher's diploma I cried for joy, so conscious was I of the importance of the career I was about to embark on. [*Pause.*] The cart will be here in a moment for my things.

KULYGIN—Yes, that's how it is. And yet, it doesn't seem to be serious. All this, I mean. It's all just fine ideas, nothing very serious. Still, I wish you every success with all my heart.

CHEBUTYKIN [*deeply moved*] My sweet child, my good, my precious girl . . . You've gone so far ahead of me that I shall never catch up with you. I've been left behind, an old migrant bird which can't fly. Fly, my dear ones, fly and God bless you. [*Pause.*] You shouldn't have shaved off your moustache, Kulygin.

KULYGIN—Drop it for goodness sake. [*Sighs.*] The soldiers will be gone today, and everything will go on as before. Whatever people may say, Masha's a good, honest woman. I love her very much and I thank my fate. Everyone's fate is different. A certain Kozyryov, an excise officer, was at school with me. He was expelled from the fifth class because he seemed quite unable to understand *ut consecutivum*. He's terribly hard up now and in bad health too. Every time I meet him I say to him: "How d'you do, *ut consecutivum!*" "Yes, indeed, that's just it: *consecutivum*," he replies, and starts coughing. But I've been lucky all my life, I'm happy, have even been awarded the order of Stanislav, second class, and am now myself teaching others the *ut consecutivum*. Of course, I'm a clever man, much cleverer than most people, but that's no guarantee of happiness.

[The Maiden's Prayer *is being played on the piano in the house.*]

IRINA—Tomorrow night, thank goodness, I shan't have to listen to the Maiden's Prayer, shan't have to meet Protopopov . . . [*Pause.*] Protopopov's sitting there in the drawing room. He's here today, too . . .

KULYGIN—The headmistress hasn't arrived yet, has she?

IRINA—No. We've sent for her. Oh, if only you knew how difficult it is for me to live here by myself, without Olga. She lives at the school; she's the headmistress, she's busy all day, while I'm alone here. I'm bored, I have nothing to do and I hate the room I live in. So what I've decided is that if I'm not going to live in Moscow, then I must make the best of it. I suppose it's fate and there's nothing to be done about it. It's all the will of God—that's clear. The Baron proposed to me. Well, I thought it over and decided to accept. He's a good man, it's really quite extraordinary how good he is. It was then that my soul, as it were, suddenly grew a pair of wings. I felt cheerful again, light-hearted, and, once more, I wanted to work, work. Only something happened yesterday, and some kind of awful uncertainty seems to hang over me.

CHEBUTYKIN—Nonsense!

NATASHA [*through the window*] The headmistress!

KULYGIN—The headmistress has arrived. Let's go.

[*Goes with* IRINA *into the house.*]

CHEBUTYKIN [*reads his papers, humming a tune*] Tara-ra-boom-di-ay—I'm sitting in a room-di-ay . . .

[MASHA *walks up; at the back of the stage* ANDREY *is wheeling the pram.*]

MASHA—There he sits, enjoying himself.

CHEBUTYKIN—And why not?

MASHA [*sits down*] Oh, nothing. [*Pause.*] Were you in love with my mother?

CHEBUTYKIN – Yes, very much.

MASHA – Was she in love with you?

CHEBUTYKIN [*after a pause*] That, I'm afraid, I don't remember.

MASHA – Is my man here? That's what our cook Marfa used to call her policeman: "my man". Is he here?

CHEBUTYKIN – No, not yet.

MASHA – When you have to snatch your happiness piecemeal, in little bits, and then lose it as I've lost it, you gradually become coarse and bitter. [*Pointing to her breast.*] I feel it seething here. [*Looking at her brother* ANDREY *who is wheeling the pram.*] There's old Andrey, our darling brother. All our hopes have perished. Thousands of people were raising a bell, much money and labour was spent on it, and then it suddenly fell and got smashed to bits. That is Andrey!

ANDREY – When are they going to be quiet in the house? Such a noise!

CHEBUTYKIN – Soon. [*Looks at his watch.*] This is a very old watch. It chimes. [*Winds his watch, which chimes.*] The first, second and fifth battery will be leaving at exactly one o'clock. [*Pause.*] I'm leaving tomorrow.

ANDREY – For good?

CHEBUTYKIN – Don't know. I may return in about a year. Damned if I know . . . It makes no difference . . .
[*Somewhere far away a harp and a violin can be heard being played.*]

ANDREY – The town will be deserted. Just as if a bell-glass had been put over it. [*Pause.*] Something happened outside the theatre yesterday. Everyone's talking about it, but I don't know anything.

CHEBUTYKIN – Nothing much. Solyony began picking a quarrel with the Baron, who lost his temper and insulted him. In the end, of course, Solyony was obliged to challenge him to a duel. [*Looks at his watch.*] I think it's time . . . At half past twelve, in the forest there, on the other side of the river. You can see it from here. Bang-bang! [*Laughs.*] Solyony imagines he's a second Lermontov. He even writes poetry. Joking apart, though, it's his third duel.

MASHA – Whose third duel?

CHEBUTYKIN – Solyony's.

MASHA – And the Baron's?

CHEBUTYKIN – What about the Baron?

MASHA – I'm all confused. Anyway, they shouldn't be allowed to fight. He might wound the Baron, or even kill him.

CHEBUTYKIN – The Baron is an excellent fellow, but one Baron more or less—what difference does it make? Let them! It makes no difference. [*Beyond the garden somebody shouts: "Coo-ee! Ho-ho!"*] That's

Skvortsov shouting, one of the seconds. He's waiting in the boat. Let him wait.

[*Pause.*]

A N D R E Y – If you ask me, it's simply immoral to fight a duel or to be present at one as a doctor.

C H E B U T Y K I N – It only seems so. We don't exist, nothing exists in the world. It only seems that we exist. Besides, what difference does it make?

M A S H A – They just talk, talk all day long. [*Going.*] You live in a climate where it may start snowing any moment, and here they go on talking. [*Stopping.*] I won't go into the house. I can't go there. Please, tell me when Vershinin comes. [*Walks off along the avenue.*] The birds are already flying away. [*Looks upwards.*] Swans or geese. Oh, my dear, my happy birds! . . .

[*Goes out.*]

A N D R E Y – There'll be no one left in the house. The army officers will go, you will go, my sister will get married, and I'll be left alone.

C H E B U T Y K I N – What about your wife?

[FERAPONT *comes in with papers.*]

A N D R E Y – A wife's a wife. My wife's an honest, decent woman and— well, yes!—a kind woman, but for all that there's something in her that brings her down to the level of a mean, blind animal, a sort of horrible, rough-skinned animal. In any case, she's not a human being. I'm telling you this as a friend for you're the only person to whom I can open up my heart. I love Natasha, that's quite true. But sometimes she strikes me as extraordinarily vulgar and then I feel completely lost, I don't understand why—for what reason—I love her so much, or, anyway, did love her.

C H E B U T Y K I N [*gets up*] Well, my dear fellow, I'm going away to-morrow, and we may never meet again, so here's my advice to you: put on your hat, take your walking stick in your hand, and go away—go away and go on walking without looking back. The further you go the better.

[SOLYONY *walks across the back of the stage with two army officers; see-ing* CHEBUTYKIN, *he turns toward him; the officers go on.*]

S O L Y O N Y – It's time, Doctor. Half past twelve already.

[*Exchanges greetings with* ANDREY.]

C H E B U T Y K I N – One moment, please. Oh, I'm sick of the lot of you. [*To* ANDREY.] I say, my dear fellow, if anyone should ask for me, tell him I'll be back presently. [*Sighs.*] Dear, oh dear!

S O L Y O N Y – He had barely time to catch his breath before the bear was hugging him to death. [*Goes with him.*] What are you groaning about, old man?

CHEBUTYKIN—Well!

SOLYONY—How do you feel?

CHEBUTYKIN [angrily] Fit as a fiddle.

SOLYONY—There's nothing to be upset about, old man. I shan't go too far. I'll only wing him like a woodcock. [Takes out a scent bottle and sprinkles his hands.] I've emptied a whole bottle on my hands today and still they smell—smell like a corpse. [Pause.] Yes, sir . . . Remember Lermontov's lines? And he, the rebel, the raging tempest seeks, as though peace in tempests could be found.

CHEBUTYKIN—Yes. He had barely time to catch his breath before the bear was hugging him to death.

[They go out.]
[Shouts of "Coo-ee! Ho-ho!" are heard.
ANDREY and FERAPONT come in.]

FERAPONT—Papers to sign, sir.

ANDREY [nervously] Leave me alone, will you? Leave me alone. Please!

[Goes off with the pram.]

FERAPONT—What's papers for if not to be signed?

[Goes off to the back of the stage.]
[Enter IRINA and TUSENBACH in a straw hat. KULYGIN walks across the stage shouting: "Coo-ee, Masha, coo-ee!"]

TUSENBACH—He seems to be the only person in town who's glad the soldiers are going away.

IRINA—That's understandable. [Pause.] Our town will be deserted.

TUSENBACH—Darling, I'll be back presently.

IRINA—Where are you going?

TUSENBACH—I've something to see to in town. Then I must—see off all my colleagues.

IRINA—It's not true. Nicholas, why are you so preoccupied today? [Pause.] What happened outside the theatre yesterday?

TUSENBACH [making an impatient movement] I'll be back in an hour and I'll be with you again. [Kisses her hand.] My dearest darling . . . [Gazes into her eyes.] It's five years since I fell in love with you and I still can't get used to it. You seem more and more beautiful to me. What lovely, wonderful hair! What lovely eyes! I'm going to take you away tomorrow. We shall work. We shall be rich. My dreams will come true. You will be happy, darling. Only one thing—one thing only worries me: you don't love me!

IRINA—I can't help that. I shall be your wife, your true and faithful wife, but I don't love you. We can't do anything about it. [Weeps.] I've never been in love, and, oh, how I dreamed of love, dreamed of it for years and years, night and day, but my heart is like an expensive

1608

grand-piano that is locked and the key is lost. [*Pause.*] You look troubled.

TUSENBACH – I didn't sleep last night. There's nothing in my life I'm afraid of, it's only the lost key I'm worried about. Say something to me. [*Pause.*] Say something to me.

IRINA – What? What do you want me to say? What?

TUSENBACH – Just something.

IRINA – Don't fret, dear. Don't please. [*Pause.*]

TUSENBACH – It is strange how sometimes little things, mere stupid trifles, suddenly, without rhyme or reason, become important in our life. One laughs at them, as one always does, one considers them of no importance, but one goes on all the same and one hasn't got the strength to stop. Oh, don't let's talk about it! I feel fine! I feel as though I were seeing those firs, maples and birch trees for the first time in my life, as though they were all looking curiously at me and— waiting. How beautiful these trees are and how beautiful life ought really to be near them. [*There is a shout: "Coo-ee! Ho-ho!"*] I must go. It's time. This tree here is dead but it goes on swaying in the wind with the others. So I, too, can't help feeling that if I should die, I'd go on taking part in life one way or another. Goodbye, darling. [*Kisses her hands.*] The papers which you gave me are on my desk under the calendar.

IRINA – I'm coming with you.

TUSENBACH [*uneasily*] No, no! [*Walks away quickly but stops in the avenue.*] Irina!

IRINA – What?

TUSENBACH [*not knowing what to say*] I haven't had my coffee today. Please tell them to get it ready for me.

[*Goes off quickly.*]

IRINA *stands, lost in thought, then walks off to the back of the stage and sits down on a swing. Enter* ANDREY *with the pram:* FERAPONT *appears.*

FERAPONT – The papers, sir, belong to the office. They're not mine, sir. I didn't make 'em.

ANDREY – Oh, where's my past? Where's it gone to? Where's the time when I was young, gay, clever, when my dreams and thoughts were so exquisite? When the present and the future were so bright with hope? Why is it that before we even begin to live, we become dull, drab, uninteresting, lazy, indifferent, useless, unhappy? Our town's been in existence for two hundred years, it has a hundred thousand inhabitants, and yet not one of them is different from the others. Not one saint— now or in the past, not one scholar, not one artist. Not one fairly outstanding man who could arouse envy or a passionate desire to emulate him. They just eat, drink, sleep, then die—others are born and they, too, eat, drink, sleep or, to avoid lapsing into complete idiocy out of sheer boredom, try to introduce some variety into their lives by nasty gossip, drink, cards, or malicious litigation. The wives deceive their husbands, the husbands tell lies, pretend not to see anything, not to hear anything, and their profoundly vulgar influence has so crushing an effect on their children that the divine spark in them is extinguished and they become just as pitiable corpses, and as like to one another, as their fathers and mothers . . . [*To* FERAPONT, *crossly.*] What do you want?

FERAPONT—Beg pardon, sir. The papers to sign, sir.

ANDREY—I'm sick and tired of you.

FERAPONT [*handing him the papers*] The porter of the Tax Collector's Office was telling me just now, sir, that there was two hundred degrees of frost in Petersburg this winter.

ANDREY—The present is hateful, but whenever I think of the future everything becomes so wonderful! I feel so lighthearted, so unconfined. In the distance I can discern a glimmer of light, I can see freedom, I can see my children becoming free from idleness, from kvas, from geese with cabbage stuffing, from after-dinner naps, from a life of mean sponging.

FERAPONT—He was saying, sir, that two thousand people was frozen to death. Frightened to death, they was. In Petersburg or Moscow—can't remember rightly.

ANDREY [*in an access of tenderness*] My dear, dear sisters! My wonderful sisters! [*Through tears.*] Masha, my sister . . .

NATASHA [*at the window*] Who's talking so loudly out there? Is that you, Andrey dear? You'll wake little Sophie. *Il ne faut pas faire du bruit, la Sophie est dormée déjà. Vous êtes un ours.* [*Getting angry.*] If you must talk, give the pram with the child to someone else. Ferapont, take the pram from the master.

FERAPONT—Yes'm.

[*Takes the pram.*]

ANDREY [*embarrassed*] I was talking quietly.

NATASHA [*behind the window, caressing her little boy*] Bobby darling! Naughty Bobby! Bad Bobby!

ANDREY [*glancing through the papers*] All right, I'll go through them, sign if necessary, and you can take them back to the office.

[*Goes into the house, reading the papers;* FERAPONT *is pushing the pram at the back of the stage.*]

NATASHA [*behind the window*] Darling Bobby, what's your Mummy's name? You sweet little darling! And who's this? It's Auntie Olga. Say to your auntie: good morning, Olga.

Two street musicians, a man and a girl, play on a violin and a harp; VERSHININ, OLGA *and* ANFISA *come out of the house and stand listening for a moment in silence;* IRINA *comes up to them.*

OLGA – Our garden's like a public thoroughfare. Everyone walks and drives through it. Give something to the musicians, Nanny.

ANFISA [*Gives some money to the musicians*] Get along with you, my dears. [*The musicians bow and go out.*] Poor wretches! You don't play music in the street on a full stomach. [*To* IRINA.] How are you, my darling? [*Kisses her.*] Well, my little one, I'm having a lovely time now. A lovely time! Living with dear Olga in her flat at school. The Lord has been good to me, dear, in my old age. I've never lived so comfortably before, sinner that I am. It's a large apartment, no rent to pay, and I've got a room to myself and a lovely bed. Nothing to pay. I wakes up at night and—oh, dear God, holy Mother of God, there's no one happier than me.

VERSHININ [*glancing at his watch*] We shall be leaving soon, Olga. It's time I went. [*Pause.*] I wish you all the best—all the best. Where's Masha?

IRINA – She's somewhere in the garden. I'll go and look for her.

VERSHININ – Thank you. I *am* in a hurry.

ANFISA – I'll go and look for her, too. [*Shouts.*] Masha, coo-ee! [*They go together to the back of the garden.*] Coo-ee! Coo-ee!

VERSHININ – Everything comes to an end. We, too, must part. [*Looks at his watch.*] The town gave us a sort of farewell lunch, we drank champagne, the mayor made a speech, I ate and listened, but in spirit I was here with you. [*Looking round the garden.*] I've got used to you.

OLGA – Shall we ever meet again?

VERSHININ – I don't suppose we shall. [*Pause.*] My wife and my two little girls will be staying here for another two months. Please, if anything happens, if they should need anything . . .

OLGA – Of course, of course. You needn't worry. [*Pause.*] There won't be a single soldier left in the town tomorrow, it will be all a memory and, of course, a new life will begin for us. [*Pause.*] Nothing happens as we want it to. I didn't want to be a headmistress and yet I'm one now. So we shan't be in Moscow . . .

VERSHININ – Oh, well, thank you for everything. Forgive me if things haven't turned out exactly as—er . . . I'm afraid I've been talking a lot. Too much, indeed. Please forgive me for that too. Don't think too badly of me.

OLGA [*wipes her tears*] Why isn't Masha coming?

VERSHININ—What else can I tell you before leaving? Any more views to air? [*Laughs.*] Life is hard. To many of us it seems dull and hopeless, but we must admit nevertheless that it is getting brighter and easier and I should say that the time is not far off when it will be quite bright. [*Looks at his watch.*] It's time, high time, I went. Before, mankind was busy making war, its whole existence was taken up with campaigns, invasions and victories, but now all that is out of date. It's left a huge vacuum behind it, which we don't seem to know how to fill: mankind is passionately looking for something to fill it with and will, I have no doubt, find it one day. Oh, if only we hadn't to wait too long! [*Pause.*] You know, if only we could add education to diligence and diligence to education . . . [*Looks at his watch.*] I'm afraid I simply must go . . .

OLGA—Here she comes!

[*Enter* MASHA.]

VERSHININ—I've come to say goodbye.

[OLGA *walks away a little so as not to interfere with them.*]

MASHA [*gazes at his face*] Goodbye.

[*A prolonged kiss.*]

OLGA—There . . . There . . .

[MASHA *sobs bitterly.*]

VERSHININ—Write to me. Don't forget me. Let me go now—it's time. Olga, please take her. I have to go . . . I'm late as it is.

[*Deeply moved, he kisses* OLGA's *hands, then embraces* MASHA *again, and goes out quickly.*]

OLGA—There, there, darling. Don't, don't . . .

[*Enter* KULYGIN.]

KULYGIN [*embarassed*] Never mind, let her cry, let her. My good Masha, my sweet Masha . . . You're my wife and I'm happy, whatever may have happened. I'm not complaining, I don't reproach you . . . I don't. Olga's my witness. Let's live again as we used to. You won't hear a word from me, not a hint.

MASHA [*suppressing her sobs*] For he on honey-dew hath fed and drunk the milk of paradise . . . and drunk the milk of paradise . . . I'm going mad . . . on honey-dew hath fed . . .

OLGA—Take a hold of yourself, Masha. Take a hold of yourself . . . Give her some water.

MASHA—I'm not crying any more.

KULYGIN—She's not crying . . . She's good . . .

[*A dull report of a distant shot is heard.*]

MASHA—For he on honey-dew hath fed and drunk the milk of paradise . . . singing of Mount Abora . . . I'm getting all mixed up. [*Drinks*

water.] My life's a failure. . . . I don't want anything any more now
. . . I'll be all right in a moment . . . It doesn't matter . . . Honey-
dew—what's honey-dew? Why can't I get this word out of my head?
My thoughts are all in a muddle.

[IRINA *comes in.*]

OLGA—Compose yourself, Masha. That's right . . . Clever girl . . .
Let's go indoors.

MASHA [*angrily*] I'm not going into that house. [*Sobs but stops immediately.*] I won't go into that house again—never again!

IRINA—Let's sit down together and, please, don't let's talk. I'm going
away tomorrow.

[*Pause.*]

KULYGIN—Yesterday I took this false beard and moustache away from
a boy in the third class. [*Puts on the false beard and moustache.*] I
look like our German master, don't I? [*Laughs.*] Those boys are funny
beggars.

MASHA—You do look like your German.

OLGA [*laughs*] Yes.

[MASHA *cries.*]

IRINA—Stop it, Masha.

KULYGIN—I certainly look like him.

[*Enter* NATASHA.]

NATASHA [*to the maid*] What? Mr. Protopopov will sit with little
Sophie and let your master take out Bobby in the pram. Children are
such a bother! [*To* IRINA.] You're leaving tomorrow, aren't you Irina?
What a pity! Why don't you stay here another week? [*Gives a little
scream on catching sight of* KULYGIN *who laughs and takes off the beard
and moustache.*] Good heavens, you frightened me to death! [*To*
IRINA.] I've got so used to you that it won't be so easy for me to part
from you. I'll tell Andrey to move into your room with his fiddle—let
him saw away there, and I'll put darling Sophie in his room. Oh, she's
such a lovely child! Such a darling little girl! Today she looked at me
with such big eyes and said—Mummy!

KULYGIN—A lovely child—that's true!

NATASHA—So it seems I shall be alone here tomorrow. [*Sighs.*] First
of all, I shall have this avenue of trees cut down, then that maple—it's
so unsightly in the evening. [*To* IRINA.] My dear, that belt doesn't
suit you at all. It's such bad taste. You ought to get something bright
and shiny. And here I shall have flowers, flowers, flowers everywhere
and there'll be such a lovely smell . . . [*Severely.*] Why's this fork
left lying about on the seat? [*On the way back to the house, to the
maid.*] Why's this fork left lying about on the seat, I asked you.
[*Screams.*] Don't answer me back!

KULYGIN—There she goes again!
[A *march is played off stage; they all listen.*]
OLGA—They're going away.
[CHEBUTYKIN *comes in.*]
MASHA—Our friends are going away. Well . . . happy journey to them. [*To her husband.*] We must go home. Where's my hat and cape?
KULYGIN—I left them indoors. I'll fetch them at once.
CHEBUTYKIN—I say, Olga . . .
OLGA—What is it. [*Pause.*] What?
CHEBUTYKIN—Oh, nothing. I don't know how to tell you . . .
[*Whispers in her ear.*]
OLGA [*aghast*] It can't be!
CHEBUTYKIN—Yes. Too bad . . . I'm awfully tired—exhausted. I'm not going to say another word. [*Vexed.*] Still, it makes no difference!
MASHA—What's happened?
OLGA [*embraces* IRINA] What a dreadful day! I don't know how to tell you, my dear.
IRINA—What is it? Tell me quickly: what? For God's sake!
[*Bursts into tears.*]
CHEBUTYKIN—The Baron has just been killed in a duel.
IRINA [*cries quietly*] I knew . . . I knew . . .
CHEBUTYKIN [*sits down on a garden seat at the back of the stage*] Tired out . . . [*Takes a newspaper out of his pocket.*] Let her have a good cry. [*Sings softly.*] Tara-ra-boom-di-ay . . . I'm sitting in a room-di-ay . . . What difference does it make?
[*The three sisters are standing, clinging to each other.*]
MASHA—Oh, how gay the music sounds! They're going away from us, —one has already gone, gone for ever—and we shall be left alone to start our life anew. We must live . . . We must live.
IRINA [*lays her head on* OLGA's *breast*] The time will come when there will be no more secrets, when all that is now hidden will be made plain, and when all will know what these sufferings are for. Till then we must live—we must work, just work! Tomorrow I shall go away alone, I shall teach in a school, and I shall give my life to those who may need it . . . It is autumn now, it will be winter soon, and everything will be covered with snow. But I shall be working—I shall be working . . .
OLGA [*embraces her two sisters*] The music is so cheerful and gay and I want to live. Dear God! Time will pass and we shall be gone for ever. We shall be forgotten, and people will no longer remember our voices or our faces or how many of us there were. But our sufferings will pass into joy for those who live after us—peace and happiness will reign on earth, and we who live now will be remembered with gratitude and will

1614

be blessed. Oh, my dear, dear sisters, our lives are not finished yet. Let us live! The music is so gay, so joyful, and it almost seems that in a little while we shall know why we live and why we suffer. Oh, if only we knew—if only we knew!

The music is growing fainter and fainter; KULYGIN, *looking happy and smiling, comes in carrying the hat and cape.* ANDREY *is wheeling the pram in which Bobby is sitting.*

C H E B U T Y K I N [*sings softly*] Tara-ra-boom-di-ay . . . I'm sitting in a room-di-ay . . . [*Reads his newspaper.*] It makes no difference! It makes no difference!

O L G A — If only we knew—if only we knew!

PLAYS OF INDIRECT ACTION

By David Magarshack

THE PREDOMINANCE of the chorus element in *The Three Sisters* creates a new kind of relationship between the auditorium and the stage, the spectator's perception of the dramatic action being, as a rule, much more complex than that of the characters. This becomes clear at once from Chekhov's use of the messenger element in this play as an inseparable part of the chorus element. For instance, Olga's part in the opening chorus of the three sisters is mainly narrative in character so far as the audience is concerned. But the sisters themselves as well as Tusenbach and Chebutykin know the facts mentioned by Olga, such as the General's death, his funeral, his arrival with his family from Moscow eleven years earlier, and so on. The only thing about these facts which is of importance to them is Olga's reaction to them; it is the way in which she narrates them and not the narration itself that evokes their comments. But this dual method of treatment of the audience and the characters occasionally provides the spectator with a glimpse into the future which is completely hidden from the characters and in this way helps to intensify the play's suspense. Such an instance occurs at the very opening of the play. The fine spring morning which filled Olga with such a passionate yearning for home and made Irina feel that the whole meaning of life lay in hard work, brought nothing but unhappiness to Mary, the second sister, who is married to a dull-witted schoolmaster and who could hope for no change in her life from the projected return to Moscow. She de-

Reprinted from *Chekhov the Dramatist*, by David Magarshack. New York: Hill and Wang, Inc., 1960. Reprinted by permission of the publisher.

cides suddenly to go home. Olga sympathises with her. "I understand you, Mary," she says, "with tears." It is at this point that Solyony makes one of his usual rude remarks about the difference between men's and women's intellects. Mary turns on him at once and asks him what he meant by his remark adding mockingly, "you frightfully terrible man!" Solyony resents this characterisation of him just because it describes too well the affected ferocity of his manner with which he hopes to disguise his natural "shyness" and emptiness of soul. He replies quickly, "Nothing," but, to get his own back on Mary, quotes two very familiar lines from Krylov's fable *The Peasant and the Farm Labourer*: "He had hardly time to catch his breath before the bear was hugging him to death." Now, the relevance of the quotation is obvious: Solyony is referring to the swift way Mary has pounced on him. But this quotation has a much deeper meaning, as appears immediately from the following dialogue.

[*Enter* ANFISA *and* FERAPONT *with a cake.*]
ANFISA – Come in, my good man, come in. Your boots are clean. [*To* IRINA.] From the district council, my dear, from Mr. Proto-popov, Mikhail Ivanych—a cake.
IRINA – Thank you. Please give my thanks to Mr. Protopopov.
[*Accepts the cake.*]
FERAPONT – Beg pardon, Miss?
IRINA   [*louder*] Thank Mr. Protopopov!
OLGA – Nanny, please give him some pie. Ferapont, go to the kitchen, they'll give you some pie there.
FERAPONT – Beg pardon, Miss?
ANFISA – Come along, my dear, come along.
[*Goes out with* FERAPONT.]
MARY – I don't like this Protopopov, this Mikhail Potapych or Ivanych. You shouldn't have invited him.
IRINA – I didn't invite him.
MARY – Excellent.

This is the first mention of Protopopov in the play, the same Proto-popov who, though he never appears on the stage, will be responsible for the eviction of the three sisters from their house and the installation of Natasha and himself in it. From the very beginning, then, Protopopov makes his presence felt through his unwanted birthday cake. But it is the sensitive Mary, the only true artist in the family, who perceives some-thing ominous about him. She cannot help disliking him. And here Chekhov adds an unexpected touch, connecting Protopopov with the bear in Krylov's fable. Mary seems uncertain about Protopopov's patronymic and, as though still remembering Solyony's quotation, calls him Mikhail

1617

Potapych, the humorous name given by Russian peasants to a bear. (The familiar name for a bear in Russian is "Mishka", the diminutive of Mikhail–Michael.) Not one of the characters of course suspects that Protopopov will actually play the part of the bear in the two lines from the fable, but a Russian audience seeing the play for the first time could not help but associate, however vaguely, the very familiar two lines from Krylov's fable with Mary's "Mikhail Potapych". Indeed, Chekhov has here summarised in a symbolic form the whole peripetia element of the play: in the first act the three sisters are the owners of the beautiful house and the considerable fortune their father had left them, but in the last act the situation is completely reversed, for Natasha with the help of Protopopov (she is too stupid and too cowardly a creature to have schemed it all by herself) has evicted the three sisters from their house and grabbed their money. That Chekhov used the Krylov quotation deliberately (another instance, incidentally, of his effective use of literary echoes) because he wanted it to be associated with Protopopov is proved by the fact that he repeats it twice at the end of the play. It is again Solyony who quotes the two lines first. Solyony comes to hurry up Chebutykin, as he wants his duel with Tusenbach to be over as soon as possible. He means to kill Irina's fiancé and he means to do it before Irina leaves the house: his revenge will be more complete that way.

SOLYONY – It's time, doctor. Half past twelve already.

[*Exchanges greetings with* ANDREY.]

CHEBUTYKIN – One moment, please. I'm sick of the lot of you. [*To* ANDREY.] I say, my dear fellow, if anyone should ask for me, tell him that I shall be back presently. [*Sighs.*] Dear Lord!

SOLYONY – He had hardly time to catch his breath before the bear was hugging him to death. [*Going with him.*] What are you groaning about, old man?

CHEBUTYKIN – Well!

SOLYONY – How do you feel?

CHEBUTYKIN [*angrily*] Fit as a fiddle.

SOLYONY – There's nothing to be so upset about, old chap. I shan't go too far, I shall only wing him like a woodcock. [*Takes out his bottle of scent and sprinkles his hands.*] I've emptied a whole bottle on my hands today and still they smell—smell like a corpse. [*Pause.*] Yes, sir. Remember Lermontov's lines—and he, the rebel, the raging tempest seeks, as though peace in the tempest can be found.

CHEBUTYKIN – Yes. He had hardly time to catch his breath before the bear was hugging him to death.

[*They go out.*]

There is a double meaning in this repeated quotation of Krylov's lines: they refer not only to Tusenbach's coming death, but also—by a previous association of ideas—to Protopopov's triumph over the three sisters: a double triumph of evil over good synthesised with the help of two lines from a fable.

In a play where the chorus element predominates to such an extent that the whole inner movement of the action is subordinated to it, as is the case with *The Three Sisters*, the contrast between the realistic and symbolic planes of perception assumes quite exceptional importance. That is why almost every character in the play has a number of symbols attached to him or her in order to emphasise the fact that they belong to a world of art rather than to ordinary life. Solyony is one of them, and it is his hands—the hands of a destroyer of life—on which Chekhov concentrates the attention of the audience. The very first words Solyony utters as he comes into the drawing room with Chebutykin are about hands. "With one hand," Solyony says, "I can only lift half a hundredweight, but with two I can lift a hundredweight or more. From that I infer that two men are not only twice as strong as one, but three times or even more." And a little later Chekhov makes him produce his bottle of scent and sprinkle his chest and hands. Towards the end of the second act after Solyony's words, "I even look a bit like Lermontov—so I'm told," Chekhov makes him again take out his bottle of scent and, this time, sprinkle only his hands. These two stage directions Chekhov only added to the text of the play published in 1902, which shows how much importance he ascribed to this attempt of Solyony's to deaden the smell of decay which his hands seemed to exude. In the middle of Act III and at the end of Act IV, Chekhov gives Solyony the same stage direction, but it is only in Act IV that he supplies the reason for Solyony's sprinkling his hands with scent.

Solyony, as has been suggested earlier, is a direct descendant of Fyodor in *The Wood Demon*, a villain with a literary background, but while Fyodor is a purely melodramatic villain, Solyony is a villain with a soul, and it is the utter emptiness of his soul that provides the key to his character and his actions. He cannot abide Tusenbach just because the baron has an aim to which he is ready to devote his whole life. Solyony has no aim except the satisfaction of his own selfish desires. When Irina tells Tusenbach that she is afraid of Solyony and that he talks nothing but rubbish, Tusenbach agrees that he is a queer fish, but he finds that it is his "shyness" that is to blame for his rudeness. "When we're alone together," he says, "he is very intelligent and friendly, but in company he is rude and a bully." Solyony himself confirms Tusenbach's analysis of his character. In Act II he tells Tusenbach immediately after uttering his veiled threat ("I'm queer, but who is not queer? Do not be angry,

Aleko!"—Aleko being the character in Pushkin's poem *The Gipsies* who in a fit of jealousy kills his wife and her lover): "When I am alone with someone, I'm all right—I'm just like the rest, but in company I feel depressed, I am shy and—I just talk a lot of nonsense. But all the same," he adds characteristically, "I'm a damned sight better and more honest than a lot of other people. And I can prove it, too." He always gets involved in all sorts of absurd arguments, such as whether there is one or two universities in Moscow. (Chekhov was referring to the New and the Old University, the names the Moscow University students of his day gave to two different buildings of one and the same university.) These arguments prove both Solyony's utter ignorance and his resentment of the way people, whom he knows to be better educated than he, react to it. He does not care a rap whether he is educated or not, or whether he is right or not; what matters to him is his own opinion. If he says something, however absurd, it is right and he is "ready to prove it" by forcing people to accept it whether they agree with him or not. He is the typical fascist: he exalts his own neurosis to an article of faith. He is sincere in his love for Irina. "I'm sorry I behaved so indiscreetly and tactlessly a moment ago," he tells Irina at the end of Act II, "but you're not like the others— you're high-minded and pure—you can see the truth." This leads him quite logically to the conclusion that she alone could understand him, and having raised her to so high a pinnacle as to be the only person in the world to be able to understand him, it naturally follows that he expects her to reciprocate his love. Irina's blunt refusal to have anything to do with him (IRINA. Goodnight! Please, go away!) makes no impression on him whatever.

> SOLYONY – I can't live without you. [*Going after her.*] Oh, my joy! [*Through tears.*] Oh, my happiness! Lovely, exquisite, wonderful eyes, the most beautiful eyes in all the world——
> IRINA [*coldly*] Don't please!
> SOLYONY – It's the first time I've spoken of my love to you and I feel as though I am not on earth but on another planet. [*Passes his hand feverishly a few times across his forehead.*] Never mind. I can't force you to love me, of course. But I shall tolerate no successful rivals. I swear to you by all the saints that I shall kill my rival. Oh, my wonderful one!

It is in these last few words that the true Solyony is revealed. The idea that Irina might prefer someone else to him is something that he is incapable of accepting. If there should be such a man, he must be destroyed. And he does destroy him. It is the only way by which he can re-establish himself in his own estimation. No one seems to take him seriously otherwise. It is only with Natasha that he succeeds in getting his own back without having to resort to extreme measures. For in Natasha he meets his match in stupidity and selfishness. In the second act Natasha is just beginning to feel her way as the future mistress of the house. Her chief weapon is her little boy. To make the life of the three sisters as humiliating as possible, she invents an illness of Bobby, since that would put an end to the Shrovetide festivities the sisters were planning for the evening. She overcomes her husband's objections by simply ignoring them. Then, flushed with her success, she comes into the drawing-room eager to pounce on anyone who would be willing to listen to her stories about what a wonderful child her Bobby was. But the only person she can get to listen to her is the always silent and morose Solyony. He listens to her prattle with feigned attention, waiting patiently for the right moment to crush her. Then he begins quietly, "If this child had been mine——" Natasha beams at him in expectation of some really nice compliment— "I'd fry him in a pan——" Solyony goes on slowly, enjoying the sudden startled expression in Natasha's eyes—"and eat him," he finishes with relish, and then walks quietly off into the drawing-room with his glass of tea and sits down in a corner, leaving the horrified Natasha to express her disgust with him as best she can. This is the only time Solyony can expect the audience to sympathise with him, for Natasha can make even an innocent child into a horror.

Chekhov was anxious that Solyony should not be acted as a melodramatic villain. In a letter to Olga Knipper, he insisted that the actor taking his part should not make him "too coarse".

Chebutykin is the constant butt of Solyony. He is the fourth and last doctor in Chekhov's plays, but he derives from the improvident Triletsky in *Platonov* rather than from the wise and humane Dorn or the idealist Astrov. It is characteristic of Chebutykin and Solyony that, though they always argue, they are so preoccupied with themselves, that they never seem to listen to each other. For instance, in their furious quarrel in Act II about the meaning of "cheremsha", a wild onion, and "chekhartma", mutton roasted in the Caucasian manner, Chekhov has chosen two unusual words that would sound alike to people who are not so much concerned with convincing each other as with proving that their opponent is wrong. And in contrast to the great issues discussed by Vershinin and Tusenbach, the subject of their disputes is always trifling. All this is brought out immediately on their first appearance in Act I. Solyony is preoccupied with his hands. He is trying to convince Chebutykin that with two hands he can lift a weight three times as heavy as with one hand (an absurdly futile argument considering that he wants only one hand to kill a man). But Chebutykin is not listening to him. He is reading his newspaper, which is treated by Chekhov as the symbol of Chebutykin's crass ignorance. He never reads serious books, or indeed any books. He has forgotten all he has ever known about medicine. His mind has been frittered away. His soul, too, is empty. The popular newspaper (in the earlier versions of the play Chekhov actually mentioned the two popular newspapers Chebutykin is reading) is the only source from which he can fill his vacant mind, since a vacant mind has to be filled with something. (It is very likely that the idea of using the newspaper as one of the visual symbols of Chebutykin's character was indirectly suggested to Chekhov by Nemirovich-Danchenko, who in one of his letters urging Chekhov to get on with the writing of *The Three Sisters* warned him against reading newspapers as they tended to distract the mind from serious work.) But Chebutykin not only reads his newspaper, he also puts down everything that strikes him as important into his note-book, a pathetic reminder of his university days when he used to take down his lectures in the same way:

> CHEBUTYKIN [*reads a newspaper while he walks in*] For falling hair— 130 grains of naphthaline in half a bottle of spirit—dissolve and apply daily. [*Writes it down in his notebook.*] Let me make a note of it.

His very first words, then, give the audience a clear idea of this old doctor whose medical knowledge has been reduced to taking down some absurd prescription from a popular newspaper. But while in the stage directions the newspaper appears many times, it is only on three occasions that Chekhov actually makes Chebutykin read out an item of news from it. The second time it supplies Chebutykin with one of his most famous lines: "Balzac was married in Berdichev." This line comes after the argument between Vershinin and Tusenbach about happiness. Vershinin argues that happiness does not exist, or, at any rate, that it cannot and must not exist for them. "We must only work and work, but happiness—that's for our remote descendants. [*Pause.*] If not for me, then at least let it be for the descendants of my descendants." Tusenbach does not agree, for he, poor man, is happy! And he goes on to argue that life will always be the same, for it follows certain laws which man will never know. And when Mary asks him whether he really thinks that life has no meaning at all, he replies: "A meaning? Look, it's snowing. What meaning is there in that?" Mary, however, refuses to accept such a complete dissociation of man from his fate, and she insists that man must have faith, or must seek some kind of faith, for otherwise his life is empty. Man, she demands, must know what he is living for, or else (and here she would have been justified in pointing to Chebutykin who was immersed in reading his paper) nothing in life matters any more. Vershinin, looking at Mary, with whom he could have been happy, bursts out: "All the same it is a pity that I'm no longer young." Mary, catching the hidden meaning of his words, quotes the last line from Gogol's famous story of the quarrel between Ivan Ivanovich and Ivan Nikiforovich (another literary echo!): "It's a boring world, my friends!"

TUSENBACH – But I say it's difficult to argue with you, my friends. Oh, let's drop the subject——
CHEBUTYKIN [*reading his paper*] Balzac was married in Berdichev.
[*Irina hums softly.*]
CHEBUTYKIN – I think I'll make a note of that. [*Writes it down in his notebook.*] Balzac was married in Berdichev.
[*Reads his paper.*]
IRINA [*laying out patience, reflectively*] Balzac was married in Berdichev.

What is the meaning of this thrice repeated phrase? Berdichev, the Wigan of Russia, is the last place one would expect one of the greatest of French writers to be married in, or, to go back to the rather inconclusive ending of the argument about happiness, to find happiness in. And it is Irina who has been counting the days (there were seemingly only a few of them left) before her return to Moscow, where alone she believed she could find happiness, who repeats the line reflectively: happiness (and this is emphasised again and again by Chekhov whenever the Moscow theme is brought up) is not only to be found in Moscow, where people are also searching in vain for happiness, but even in such a proverbially dull town as Berdichev, and not only ordinary people can find happiness there, but even a great genius like Balzac. It is in this way that Chekhov uses the chorus element both to provide an answer to an inconclusive argument and a comment on one of the main themes of the play. (The association of marriage with happiness is here purely subjective: Irina's dreams of Moscow revolve round her illusion that it is only there that she would meet the man with whom she would fall in love; Tusenbach is happy because, having sent in his resignation from his regiment, he is now more than ever convinced that Irina will accept his proposal of marriage; and Vershinin's as well as Mary's thoughts of happiness also revolve round their own intimate feelings for one another.)

The other two symbols associated with Chebutykin are the silver samovar and the porcelain clock. To present a young girl of twenty with a tea-urn for her birthday could have occurred only to a man who had lost all touch with life. He wanted to get a really expensive present for Irina, the daughter of the only woman he ever loved, and a silver samovar (usually given as a silver-wedding present in middle-class families) was the only thing he could think of. He is therefore quite incapable of understanding the gasp of horror his present has produced.

OLGA [*covers her eyes*] A samovar! That's awful! [*Goes out.*]
IRINA – Oh, you poor darling, what are you doing?
TUSENBACH [*laughs*] I told you.
MARY – Really, doctor, you ought to be ashamed of yourself!
CHEBUTYKIN – My dear, sweet darlings, you are all I have. You're all I hold most dear in the world. I shall soon be sixty. I'm an old man, a lonely, insignificant old man. There's nothing good about me except my love for you, and, but for you, I should have been dead long ago. [*To* IRINA.] My darling, I've known you ever since you were born— I used to carry you about in my arms—I loved your mother——
IRINA – But why such expensive presents?
CHEBUTYKIN [*through tears, angrily*] Expensive presents! Don't talk such nonsense! [*To his orderly.*] Take the samovar to the other room. [*In a mocking voice.*] Expensive presents!
    [*The orderly carries off the samovar to the dining room.*]

This complete divorce from life and living people is of course characteristic of the old doctor. His callousness towards his patients is only another side of it. Life, in fact, no longer exists for him. It is all a delusion. "Perhaps," he mumbles drunkenly in his soliloquy in Act III, "I am not a human being at all, but merely imagine that I have hands and feet and a head; perhaps I don't exist at all, but just imagine that I walk, eat and sleep. [*Weeps.*] Oh, if only I did not exist!"

Chebutykin is "not a human being at all" and in this phrase Chekhov has stripped him of all the finer attributes of man, but, unlike Natasha, whom her husband also describes as "not a human being", he had been a human being once when he was capable of devoted and selfless love for a woman, and his final degradation, his final dehumanisation, is symbolically represented in his smashing of the porcelain clock which had been one of the treasured possessions of the woman he loved. It happens shortly after his soliloquy in Act III. Vershinin announces that the brigade of which he is in command is to leave the town soon for some distant destination. Irina declares emphatically that they, too, will leave the town.

IRINA – And we are going too.
CHEBUTYKIN [*drops the clock which breaks*] Smashed to bits!
    [*Pause; everyone is upset and embarrassed.*]
KULYGIN [*picking up the pieces*] To smash an expensive thing like that! Oh, doctor, doctor, zero minus for conduct!
IRINA – That was mother's clock.

CHEBUTYKIN – Possibly. So it was your mother's clock. Perhaps I didn't smash it, but it just seems as though I did. Perhaps we only imagine that we exist, but we don't really exist at all. I don't know anything. Nobody knows anything.

But somewhere deep inside him the smashing of the clock has aroused bitter memories of his own wasted life, for as he is about to leave the room, he suddenly stops and shouts at them furiously. "What are you looking at? Natasha is having a disgusting affair with Protopopov and you don't see it. You're just sitting about here while Natasha is having her disgusting affair with Protopopov and you don't see it. [*Sings.*] Won't you accept this little present from me? [*Goes out.*]"

Chebutykin's degradation is completed in Act III. In Act IV he is no longer a human being. Nothing makes any impression on him any more. The officers forget to take leave of him, but he just dismisses it with a shrug. Throughout the whole of the act he is, according to the stage direction, "in a good humoured mood," sitting in a chair in the garden and waiting to be called to the duel between Solyony and Tusenbach. He could have stopped the duel by telling Irina about it, but as he says to Mary: "One baron more or less in the world—what difference does it make?" It does not occur to him that Tusenbach's death will also affect Irina. When Irina tries to find out from him about the quarrel between Solyony and Tusenbach the day before, he refuses to tell her anything. "What's happened?" he says. "Nothing. Rubbish. [*Reads his newspaper.*] It makes no difference." Kulygin has also heard rumours of the impending duel, but Chebutykin refuses to enlighten him. "I don't know," he says. "It's all nonsense." It is then that Kulygin tells his funny story about the divinity student whose essay his professor marked with the word "nonsense", which the student, thinking it was written in Roman and not in Russian characters, read as "renyxa". (The Russian word for nonsense —*chepukha*—when written out can be mistaken for a "Latin" word since all its letters are identical with the letters of the Roman alphabet.) The nonsense word "renyxa", which strikes Chebutykin as the very quintessence of nonsense and which he repeats with such relish, epitomises his own attitude towards life. And when he returns from the duel, he just announces the news of Tusenbach's death and sits down, still in his goodhumoured mood, reading his paper and humming "Tararaboomdeay". He has been reduced to the state of an idiot to whom nothing matters and who keeps his good humour irrespective of what calamities may be happening around him.

Protopopov, of course, never appears, but his cake (the personification of middle-class propriety) is there in Act I and his carriage (the emblem of his good social position) can be heard as it draws up before the house in Act II, and it is standing in front of the house in Act IV, while its owner is listening to his mistress's playing "The Maiden's Prayer" on the piano. A cake and a carriage—what better symbols of middle-class respectability does one want?

Kulygin, the classics master and Mary's husband, is only given one symbol—his own magnum opus, his book describing the history of the school, where he is soon to become second master, for the past fifty years. He presents it to Irina as a birthday present in Act I, having forgotten that he already gave her the same book as an Easter present. Still, that does not dismay him: he presents it to Colonel Vershinin instead—to read when he feels bored!

Andrey, poor Andrey, who is the unwitting instrument of the undoing of his sisters, has quite a number of symbols. There is his fiddle, which, escapist that he is, he plays to drown the realisation of his failure in his chosen career of a university teacher. "He is our scholar," Irina tells Vershinin proudly in Act I. "He will probably be a professor. Father was a soldier, but his son has chosen an academic career." And Mary adds, significantly: "At Father's wish." Then there are the picture frames he makes.

> IRINA – Look what a lovely picture frame Andrey gave me as a birthday present! [*Shows the picture frame.*] He made it himself.
> VERSHININ   [*looks at the picture frame and does not know what to say*] Yes—it's something——
> IRINA – And that picture frame over the piano he made, too.
>   [ANDREY *waves his hand and walks away.*]
> OLGA – He is a scholar, he plays the violin and he is very clever with a fretsaw—in a word, he can turn his hand to anything. Don't go, Andrey. He has a habit of always walking away. Come here!
> [MARY *and* IRINA *take him by the arms and bring him laughing back.*]

Then there is his book. He had been reading it till four o'clock in the morning, he tells Vershinin, then he went to bed, still reading it presumably, but "nothing came of it". It must have been the English book he was proposing to translate during the summer, but nothing comes of it, either. Andrey uses an illuminating phrase about his learning. "Father," he tells Vershinin, "inflicted education upon us." And that, no doubt, explains his failure as a budding university professor. "Today," he tells Ferapont at the beginning of Act II (the old fellow is very deaf and Andrey finds it very convenient to have someone to unburden his soul to, someone, that is, who would not ask awkward questions), "today . . . I picked up this book—my old university lectures, and I could not help laughing. Good Lord, I am the secretary of the district council, the same council of which Protopopov is chairman, I am a secretary, and the most I can hope for is to become a member of the district council! I—a member of the district council, I—who dream every night that I am a professor of Moscow University, a famous scholar of whom the whole of Russia is proud!" His violin playing and his fretwork are merely outward manifestations of his utter loneliness. He is a stranger even in his own house. And what could be more pathetic than the way he walks quietly in towards the end of Act II and sits down near the candle with his book— the symbol of his shattered academic career.

Then there is the key from the cupboard he has lost—at least so he says when he comes in to ask Olga for it in Act III; but what he really has lost is the key to his sisters' hearts. And, finally, there is the bell. It is Mary, the most poetic and sensitive of the three sisters, who in Act IV applies this symbol to Andrey as she sees him wheeling the pram with his little son, while Protopopov is dandling his own daughter in the house. "There is Andrey, our darling brother," she says. "All our hopes have perished. Thousands of people were raising a bell, much money and labour was spent on it, and then suddenly it fell and got smashed to bits. Suddenly, for no reason at all. That is Andrey."

Andrey's tragedy is that he realises very well how low he has fallen but cannot do anything about it. A little later in the fourth act he has again a talk with the deaf Ferapont during which he lays bare his soul to the audience. According to Luzhsky, Chekhov demanded that in this last monologue Andrey should be very excited. "He must almost threaten the audience with his fists," Chekhov said.

Andrey's wife, Natasha, has several symbols, too. There is, above all, her green belt. She is the personification of the *petite bourgeoise* in mind, manners, morals, and outward appearance. "Heavens, how she dresses!" Mary exclaims in Act I. "It isn't that her clothes are not pretty or fashionable—they are just pitiful! A queer sort of bright yellowish frock with a cheap-looking fringe and a red blouse." But when Natasha appears at the end of Act I, she wears a green belt on her pink dress. Olga gasps with horror at the sight of it. "My dear," she says in a frightened voice, "you're wearing a green belt! That's not nice!" But Natasha misunderstands her. Very typically, she thinks that a green belt must be unlucky. "No," Olga explains, "it simply doesn't suit you and—and it looks a little strange." Natasha is dismayed. She has come dressed for the kill, and now it seems that she has done something awful. Will Andrey notice it, too? But Andrey does not notice anything. Earlier Mary remarked that she did not believe Andrey was in love with Natasha, for "after all, he has taste!" And, besides, she was told that Natasha was going to marry Protopopov. But if Andrey had taste, his infatuation for Natasha had killed it, and as for Natasha and Protopopov, they have other plans.

It is characteristic of Natasha that she never forgets Olga's remark about her green belt which she took as a personal snub. At the end of the last act, three and a half years later, when she appears for the last time in the garden of the house which now belongs to her, she turns to Irina with the words: "My dear, that belt doesn't suit you at all. It's such bad taste. You ought to get something bright and shiny."

But the most important symbol associated with Natasha is the lighted candle. There is an interval of about a year between the first and second act. Chekhov's stage directions for the second act are most precise: "It is eight o'clock in the evening. From behind the scenes, from the street, come the faint strains of an accordion. There are no lights in the house. Enter Natasha in her dressing-gown with a lighted candle." What is Natasha doing? She is putting out the lights in the house. The drawing room with the columns which was so bright with sunshine in Act I is dark now. Only Natasha's candle throws a trembling light on the changed scene. It is Natasha, now sure of herself, who plunges the house into darkness. It is she who now gives the orders. Her very first words, addressed to Andrey, so solicitous for the welfare of his sisters, are full of venom and hypocrisy. "And Olga and Irina aren't back yet. Still hard at work, poor things. Olga at her staff meeting, Irina at the telegraph office. Only this morning I said to your sister, 'You must take more care of yourself, Irina, darling.' But she won't listen to me." The sisters won't listen to her: that's what makes her so furious. And almost in the same breath she goes on hatching her plot to show the sisters that it is she who is now the real mistress in the house. But—and this is the characteristic touch— while so anxious to put out all the candles for fear of a fire, Natasha leaves her own lighted candle behind her. At the end of Act II after Solyony's threat to kill his rival, Natasha again appears with a lighted candle in her hand. It is in Act III that her lighted candle assumes a sinister significance. At the end of the act (by that time Natasha has already succeeded in throwing Irina out of her room and making her share Olga's bedroom), when the fire in the town has almost been put out, Natasha enters Olga's bedroom with a lighted candle. Chekhov gives her nothing to say. There is only the stage direction: "Natasha with a candle passes across the stage in silence from the door on the right through the door on the left." It is Mary who remarks, as she sits down: "She walks as if she had set the town on fire herself." But Natasha had not set the town on fire: she had set the house of the three sisters on fire. The house might as well have been burnt down to the ground, for it no longer belonged to them. They had given shelter to the people who had been rendered homeless, but they were as homeless as the people whose houses had burnt down. Here again we get the synthesis of two symbols: the fire in the town and Natasha's candle in the house.

Finally, in the last act, Chekhov again uses several objects as symbols to add the last few touches to Natasha's character: the fir-tree avenue, the beautiful maple tree, the flowers and, last but not least, the fork on the garden seat. (There is nothing superfluous on Chekhov's stage!) Natasha appears at the end of the act accompanied by her maid. In a few lines of dialogue Chekhov lays bare with superb skill the really devilish nature of Natasha, using his symbols only to deepen the stark horror such a character must evoke. Protopopov and Andrey are to take charge of their respective children, the first nursing his little girl in the house and the second wheeling his little boy in the garden. "Children are such a bother!" Still, with two fathers to look after them things are not too bad. Then she turns to Irina to commiserate hypocritically with her for having to leave the house and to tell her that Andrey is to be thrown out of his room as she was before him. Little Sophie, Protopopov's child, is to have her husband's room. "What a lovely child! Such a darling! Today she looked at me with such big eyes and said—Mummy!" She ignores Kulygin's compliment to her "lovely child", and sums up the position in one short sentence: "So I shall be alone here tomorrow," following up her triumphant remark with a hypocritical sigh. It is then that she turns to her future plans: "First of all I shall have this avenue of firs cut down, then that maple—it is so unsightly in the evenings." Full mistress of the house and garden at last, she is destroying beauty everywhere (a little earlier Tusenbach was praising the beauty of the trees Natasha is now going to cut down), and even the flowers, which Vershinin admired so much in the drawing-room in Act I, become an abomination in her mouth: "I shall have flowers, flowers, flowers everywhere and there'll be such a lovely scent!" Her wonderful plans, however, are met with icy silence, and that infuriates her. It is then that she notices the fork on the garden seat and asks "severely": "Why is the fork left lying about on the seat?" But her question is completely ignored, and as she walks off into the house, she vents her spite on the maid: "Why is the fork left lying about on the seat, I ask you? [*Screams.*] Don't answer me back!" The only comment comes from Kulygin: "There she goes again!" Deep down she feels her inferiority to the three sisters, and her last scream of rage is her acknowledgement of the fact that, though she had driven them out of their house, they are still her superiors.

Chekhov's use of symbols with the positive characters of the play, that is, with the three sisters, Tusenbach and Vershinin, is much more subtle. There are, for instance, the images of the grand-piano, the lost key and the dead tree which deepen the poignancy of the farewell scene between Irina and Tusenbach in Act IV. The scene is so poignant because neither of them realises that it is the last time they will see one another, but the symbols help to cast a shadow over a relationship that is none too happy as it is. One cannot help feeling that it is just because Irina does not love Tusenbach that a deeper note of tragedy is added to their last meeting.

> TUSENBACH — . . . I'm going to take you away tomorrow. We shall work. We shall be rich. And my dreams will come true. You will be happy, darling. Only one thing—one thing only worries me: you don't love me!
>
> IRINA — I can't help that! I shall be your wife, your true and faithful wife, but I don't love you. We can't do anything about it! [*Cries.*] I've never been in love. Oh, how I dreamed of love, dreamed of it for years and years, night and day, but my heart is like an expensive grand-piano that is locked and the key is lost. [*Pause.*] You look troubled.
>
> TUSENBACH — I didn't sleep last night. There's nothing in my own life I'm afraid of, and it is only the lost key I'm worried about. That's what destroys my sleep. Say something to me. [*Pause.*] Say something to me.
>
> IRINA — What? What do you want me to say? What?
>
> TUSENBACH — Just something.
>
> IRINA — Don't fret, dear. Don't, please!
>
> TUSENBACH — It is strange how little things, mere stupid trifles, sometimes become important in our lives without rhyme or reason, and so suddenly, too. You laugh at them, as you always do, but you go on all the same and you haven't got the strength to stop. Oh, don't let's talk about it! I feel fine. I feel as though I'm seeing these firs, maples and birches for the first time in my life, and that all of them are looking curiously at me and—waiting. How beautiful these trees are and how beautiful life ought really to be near them! [*There is a shout from his seconds who are waiting to take him to his duel with Solyony.*] I must go. It's time. This tree here is dead but it goes on swaying in the wind with the others. So I too, I can't help feeling, if I should die, will go on taking part in life one way or another.

The grand-piano in a more material sense is used by Chekhov at the beginning of Act III to describe in a few sentences the tragedy of Mary's life. Mary is an accomplished pianist, but for the last three or four years she has not gone near her piano, and her art withers because there is no one to appreciate it. Far from encouraging her, all that Kulygin, her husband, thinks about is that the head of his school might disapprove of her taking part in a public concert.

TUSENBACH – I'm being asked to organise a concert in aid of the homeless.

IRINA – But who——

TUSENBACH – It could be arranged if we tried. Mary plays the piano beautifully, in my opinion.

KULYGIN – She plays wonderfully.

IRINA – She's forgotten how. She hasn't played for three or four years.

TUSENBACH – There's absolutely no one in this town who appreciates music, not a soul, but I do and I assure you that Mary plays wonderfully, almost like a concert pianist.

KULYGIN – You're quite right, baron. I love Mary very much. She's a dear.

TUSENBACH – To be able to play so well and to know all the time that there is no one to appreciate it—no one!

KULYGIN [*sighs*] Yes—but do you think it would be correct for her to take part in a concert? [*Pause.*] I know nothing about such matters, of course. It may be all right. I must say our head is a decent fellow, a very decent fellow, indeed, and very intelligent, too, but he has such views——Of course, it's not his business, but all the same I might perhaps have a talk to him.

Kulygin loves his wife very much, but it never occurs to him that it is he who is destroying her soul. How full of action Chekhov's pauses are can be plainly seen from the one pause in this little scene. Chekhov does not describe the reaction of the other characters to Kulygin's extraordinary statement that Mary's appearance at a public concert may not be correct, but the way Kulygin squirms at their disapproval, which each of them expresses in his or her own way (what latitude Chekhov gives to his producers!) shows clearly how truly dramatic the action of this scene is.

The idea that the yearning of the sisters for Moscow is the main theme of the play and expresses, as a modern Russian critic put it,[1] "a kind of poetic symbol which introduces a certain unreality in the delineation of everyday facts," is far from true. The producers of *The Three Sisters* make too much of this all too obvious theme in conformity with the popular notion that the chief characters of the play are "Chekhovian" ineffectual characters, whereas the truth is that they are far from ineffectual. The important fact that the play does not end on a note of resignation but on a note of triumph is somehow completely ignored by them. It must be remembered that the Moscow theme is to a large extent autobiographical, expressing, as it does, Chekhov's own yearning to re-

[1] A. Roskin. *The Three Sisters* on the Moscow Art Theatre Stage. Leningrad, 1946.

turn to Moscow from the Crimea where his illness kept him confined for the last five years of his life. In his play Chekhov uses it to point a moral rather than to wallow in one of those moods which critics are so fond of ascribing to him, but which in fact he detested. It is significant that every time Moscow is mentioned in the play, Chekhov immediately underlines the absurdity of such a purely romantic craving for the unattainable. He does so at the very opening of the play in the chorus scene of the three sisters. Then, in the middle of Act I, Vershinin, in reply to the ecstatic cries of Olga and Irina when they find out that he, too, had been in Moscow, tells them of the "gloomy bridge" which made him feel so depressed every time he had to cross it, and—immediately after Irina's remark that her mother was buried in the cemetery attached to the Novo-Devichy Monastery, one of the oldest monasteries in Moscow (Chekhov was buried there), Vershinin says that with time "what seems so very important to us now, will be forgotten and will seem trivial". In Act II, in the scene between Andrey and Ferapont, Andrey's wish to sit in a large restaurant in Moscow where he would not feel as lonely as he does at home, is countered with Ferapont's story of the merchant who choked himself to death with a pancake in a Moscow restaurant, the whole point of the story being that Moscow can be as coarse and as uncivilised as the least cultured provincial town. A little later in the same act the whole unreality of Irina's dream about Moscow is emphasised twice. First, in her unconscious failure to realise that Andrey's losses at cards would prevent her from going to Moscow.

> IRINA – A fortnight ago he lost, and in December he lost. I wish he'd hurry up and lose everything he's got—perhaps we'd leave for Moscow then. Oh dear, I dream of Moscow every night. I'm going quite off my head. [*Laughs.*] We move there in June, and before June there is still—February, March, April, May—nearly half a year!

And later in the same act when Irina is laying out the cards in a game of patience—

> IRINA – It's coming out—I can see. We shall go to Moscow.
> FEDOTIK – No, it won't come out. See? The eight of spades is on top of the two. [*Laughs.*] That means that you won't go to Moscow.
> CHEBUTYKIN [*reads the paper*] Tsitsihar. Smallpox is raging here.

Here again, as in the case of Berdichev, Chekhov introduces an apparently irrelevant statement, but what he really does is to use the chorus element as a detached comment on the dialogue, in this instance Irina's remark about Moscow. Tsitsihar—what an exotic place, even more desirable and unattainable than Moscow, and yet in reality it is nothing but a pest hole. (An English spectator would see the point of Chebutykin's line more clearly if Chekhov had used Samarkand instead of Tsitsihar.) And a little later after Mary's remark that if she had been in Moscow she would not notice the bad weather, Vershinin tells them the parable of the imprisoned French Cabinet Minister who for the first time in his life found real delight in watching the birds from his prison window, but who did not notice them any more after his release from prison. "So," Vershinin goes on, "you won't notice Moscow when you live there."

Chekhov ends Act II and Act III with the Moscow theme, but in both these curtains it is used merely to emphasise the delusive nature of Irina's dream. In Act II it follows close upon Natasha's departure for her sleigh ride with Protopopov, the two persons who will rob the sisters of their fortune and will make it impossible for them to go to Moscow; and in Act III it follows Irina's decision to marry Tusenbach, who has got himself a job far away from Moscow. Indeed, a little earlier in the same act Irina herself realises at last that she would never go to Moscow.

In Act IV comes Irina's final reconciliation with the idea that she would never see Moscow again. She says: "What I have decided is that if I am not going to live in Moscow, then it just can't be helped. I suppose it's fate, and there's nothing to be done about it." And the same note of reconciliation rather than resignation is sounded by Olga at the end of Act IV: "There won't be a single soldier left in town tomorrow, everything will become just a memory, and for us of course a new life will begin. Nothing has turned out as we expected. I did not want to be a headmistress, but I've become one. Which means that I shall never go to Moscow. . . ."

The whole thing, in fact, is nothing but a delusion, and the time has now come for the sisters to face reality, and they do it with courage and hope, as the final chorus of the three sisters shows—and it is this and not Moscow that is the leitmotif of the play.

The love theme forms almost as complex a profusion of triangles in *The Three Sisters* as in *The Seagull* and in *Uncle Vanya*. There is the Irina-Tusenbach-Solyony triangle, the Mary-Kulygin-Vershinin triangle, and the Natasha-Andrey-Protopopov triangle. And again as in the two previous plays the love affairs end unhappily: Tusenbach is killed, Vershinin has to leave with his regiment, and Andrey becomes a stranger in his own house in more senses than one. But of all these love affairs the only real one is between Mary and Vershinin. Irina does not love Tusenbach and their proposed marriage is just an arrangement which she accepts because there seems nothing better she can hope for. And even then she is practically pushed into it by her elder sister.

IRINA – . . . I'm twenty-three now, I've worked for a long time, and my brain has dried up, I'm growing thin, I'm losing my looks, I'm getting old, and there's nothing, nothing I can look forward to, no satisfaction out of life I can hope for. Time is flying past, and I seem to be getting further and further away from real life, from a life that is beautiful, and heading for some horrible disaster. I'm in despair and I simply can't understand how I go on living, how I haven't killed myself before now.

OLGA – Don't cry, darling. I can't bear to see you cry.

IRINA – I'm not crying–I'm not crying. I've stopped now. See? I'm not crying any more. I've stopped–I've stopped!

OLGA – Darling, I'm telling you this as your sister, as your friend–if you take my advice, you'll marry the baron.

[IRINA *cries softly.*]

OLGA – You do respect him, don't you? You think highly of him. It's true he's not handsome, but he's such an honest and decent man. People don't marry for love but to fulfil their duty. At least, I think so, and I wouldn't hesitate to marry a man I didn't love. I would marry anyone who asked me, if he was a decent man. I would even marry an old man.

Olga with her deep sense of duty and Irina with her deep sense of the sanctity of labour–how carefully drawn their characters are and how absurd it is to regard either of them as ineffectual! But it was on Mary that Chekhov lavished all the rare gifts of his genius. Mary with her sensitive soul of an artist, with her superstitions and her bluntness of speech and manner. "Remember, no drinking today," she tells Chebutykin in Act I shortly after being told by her husband that he expected her to spend the evening with him at the headmaster's. "Do you hear? It's bad for you!" And in reply to Chebutykin's assurance that he had not been really drunk for the past two years, and what did it matter, anyway, Mary says: "All the same, don't you dare to drink! Don't you dare! [*Gruffly, but not so loud as to be overheard by her husband.*] Damn, I shall have to spend another boring evening at the headmaster's, it seems!" And later at the dining-room table it is she who offends against all middle-class proprieties by banging her fork against her plate and exclaiming: "Let's have a glass of vodka! Oh, life is sweet–what the hell––" Which at once brings down the rebuke of her husband on her:

KULYGIN – Four marks out of ten for conduct.

But it is Natasha, that typical *petite bourgeoise*, who is really shocked by Mary's language. When in Act II Mary, worried by Vershinin's wife's latest attempt to poison herself, shouts at the old nurse, mixes up Irina's cards, and tells Chebutykin that at his age he should not be talking such damned nonsense, Natasha gives her a lecture on how a lady ought to behave in society.

> NATASHA [*sighs*] My dear Mary, why must you use such expressions? I assure you that with your attractive appearance you'd be simply bewitching in any refined society if it were not for your language. *Je vous prie, pardonnez moi, Marie, mais vous avez des manières un peu grossières.*

How revealing Natasha's hypocritical sigh is and the French sentence with which she shows off her own refined education and which make Mary's *manières un peu grossières* more attractive. No wonder Tusenbach can hardly restrain himself from laughing at Natasha's lady-like pretensions. Natasha, indeed, uses the most vulgar expressions when in a temper, while Mary is never vulgar. "Coarseness," she tells Vershinin in Act II, "hurts and upsets me. I can't bear it when a man is not sufficiently sensitive or sufficiently gentle and courteous."

But it is in the unfolding of Mary's love for Vershinin that Chekhov reveals her truly poetic nature. He achieves it by the use of a literary echo, the two first lines from Pushkin's fairy-tale poem of *Ruslan and Lyudmila*, twice in Act I and twice in Act IV, and by the exchange of a snatch of a tune between Mary and Vershinin in Act III. Ever since she had got up on the morning of Irina's birthday, Mary had felt a strange uneasiness, a vague premonition that something important was going to happen that day, and at the beginning of Act I she just sits quietly over her book, lost in thought and whistling some tune. The very first words she utters are the two lines from *Ruslan and Lyudmila*, lines that are full of magic and mystery and that evoke a mood full of wonder and expectation. She then gets up, humming a tune quietly, and is about to leave.

> OLGA – You're not very cheerful today.
>
> [MARY *puts on her hat, still humming the tune softly.*]
>
> OLGA – Where are you off to?
>
> MARY – Home.
>
> IRINA – Strange—
>
> TUSENBACH – Leaving a birthday party!

But Mary will not be persuaded to stay. She tries to rationalise her feeling of uneasiness by putting it down to the few people who turned up at the birthday party as compared with the thirty or forty officers who used to come to it when her father was still alive. Olga sympathises with her: it is only a year since their father died and the contrast between the past and the present can still be felt acutely, but that is not what makes Mary feel so sad. "Don't howl!" she tells Olga gruffly. Then, after the short episode with Chebutykin's silver samovar, Vershinin comes in. What were Mary's feelings during their first meeting? She tells her sisters about it in Act III: "At first I thought him queer, then I felt sorry for him and—and then I fell in love with him." Her first words to Vershinin, after he told her that her face was familiar, are: "I don't remember you!" But in another minute she does remember him:

MARY—. . . Now I've remembered! [*To* OLGA.] Don't you remember we used to talk of the lovesick Major? You were only a Lieutenant then and you were in love with someone, and for some reason everyone used to tease you by calling you a Major.
VERSHININ [*laughs*] Yes, yes—the lovesick Major—that's right.

Then quite unaccountably Mary bursts into tears. "You had only a moustache then," she says to Vershinin. "Oh, how old you've grown! How old you've grown!" A wave of pity for the prematurely old colonel, who can still talk with such boyish enthusiasm, passes over her, and after his first long speech of the wonderful world there will be in two or three hundred years time she forgets all about her depression and her wish to leave the party.

MARY [*takes off her hat*] I'm staying for lunch.

At the end of Act I, those two magic lines of poetry came spontaneously to her lips again, but this time she already perceives the stirrings of a great passion in her and she is annoyed with herself for mumbling words the full significance of which she is as yet unable to grasp:

MARY—. . . [*tearfully*] Now why do I keep on saying that? I just haven't been able to get it out of my head all day.

It was indeed a fateful day for Mary, and an ominous one, too, for no sooner did she become aware of her feelings for Vershinin than her husband announced: "There are thirteen at the table." And she was so superstitious!

Act II begins about nine months after the end of Act I. The time element in the play is curiously relative. The whole action lasts about three and a half years, for Chekhov gives us the most precise information about the beginning and the end of the play. It opens on May 5th, Irina's twentieth birthday, and Act IV takes place in the autumn when Irina is in her twenty-fourth year. Between Act I and Act II Andrey and Natasha get married and have a child. Act II takes place in February—Shrovetide. (Irina, counting the months before their proposed moving to Moscow, starts with February.) Act III quite likely follows almost immediately after Act II, that is to say, the fire in the town must have occurred only a few months after the end of the second act. That seems to agree with the small lapse of time that is implicit in the lighted candle symbol and Irina's expulsion from her room. But if that is so, then two and a half years must have passed between Act III and Act IV, which is most improbable since in Act III Vershinin announces that his regiment is leaving town, while in Act IV we are actually present at its departure. And yet Natasha bears Protopopov a child between Act III and Act IV! There is therefore an artistic compression of time in the whole play, and this relativity of time is particularly noticeable in the case of Mary and Vershinin. For while the other characters in the play clearly reveal the lapse of time at the beginning of Act II, the first scene between Mary and Vershinin in that act seems to follow immediately after the end of Act I. It is almost as if it is their second meeting. Indeed, if, as it seems likely, they had met several times before, there is no indication of any such meeting. And yet it is in this scene that Vershinin declares his love for Mary and that we hear for the first time Mary's soft, happy laughter. Their love, then, has something of a fairy-tale in it: time means nothing to two truly loving hearts. But their real understanding comes only in Act III. By that time, however, their spiritual intimacy has become so close that all they need is to exchange a few snatches of a tune—the most original love declaration in the whole literature of the stage!

MARY — Trum-tum-tum—
VERSHININ — Tum-tum—
MARY — Tra-ra-ra—
VERSHININ — Tra-ta-ta—

[*Laughs.*]

A few minutes later a shorter exchange of the same snatch of a tune takes place, but this time, according to Chekhov, "Vershinin says 'trum-tum-tum' in the form of a question and Mary in the form of an answer. Mary thinks it such an original joke that she pronounces her 'trum-tum' with a grin and, having uttered it, bursts out laughing, but not loudly, just a little laugh, barely audible." What happens, then, is that at first this exchange is just a declaration of love, a confirmation that they belong to each other; the second time, Vershinin asks Mary whether she will be his and she replies in the affirmative; the third time, Vershinin sings the tune behind the stage, that is to say, he uses it as a signal to tell Mary that he is waiting for her. Mary gets up and replies in a loud voice: "Tra-ta-ta!" to tell him that she is coming. She then takes leave of her sisters and her brother: "Goodbye, Olga. Bless you, my dear. [*Goes behind the screen and kisses* IRINA.] Sleep well. Goodbye, Andrey. Go away now, they're tired. You'll talk to them tomorrow. [*Goes out.*]"

But immediately before this last exchange with Vershinin, Mary tells her sisters of her love, beginning with the words: "I should like to confess to you, my dears." Chekhov was very anxious to make it absolutely clear that "Mary's confession in Act III is not a confession at all but merely a frank conversation. Mary," Chekhov went on, "must act this scene nervously, but not hysterically. She must not raise her voice; she must smile occasionally; above all, her acting must convey the fact that it is very late and that she is very tired. She should also make the audience feel that she considers herself much more intelligent than her sisters."

The whole action of Act III, Chekhov insisted in his instructions to the actors, must be conducted quietly "so that the audience should feel that the people on the stage are tired and want to go to sleep. . . . The noise of the fire should come from a distance, from behind the scenes, and it should be subdued and indistinct."

In Act IV the parting scene between Mary and Vershinin is very brief. Before that Mary appears for only a short time to exchange a few words with Chebutykin. "When you have to snatch your happiness piecemeal, in little bits," she tells him, "and then lose it, you gradually become coarse and bitter. [*Pointing to her breast.*] I feel it seething here." That is all we know of her feelings, except for her last words, expressing her longing to go away with Vershinin, as she walks away along the avenue of trees: "And the birds are already flying away. [*Looks upwards.*] Geese or swans. Oh, my dear ones, my happy ones! [*Goes out.*]" Brief though it is, the parting scene is charged with emotion.

VERSHININ – I've come to say goodbye.

> [OLGA *walks away a little so as not to interfere with them.*]

MARY [*gazes at his face*] Goodbye!

> > [*A long kiss.*]

OLGA – There, there, Mary, be brave.

> > [MARY *sobs bitterly.*]

VERSHININ – Write to me. Don't forget me. Let me go now—it's time. Olga, please take her. I have to go. I'm late as it is.

> > [*Deeply moved he kisses* OLGA'S *hands, then embraces* MARY *again and goes out quickly.*]

Kulygin comes in and, as usual, says the wrong things. It is then that Mary again repeats the two lines from Pushkin's poem, but this time they have lost their magic and the words convey nothing to her. "I'm going mad," she murmurs desperately. Olga tries to calm her, but she has already stopped crying. A distant shot is heard: Tusenbach is killed. Then again the words of Pushkin's poem burst confusedly from her lips. One word sticks in her mind, but she doesn't know even what it means any more. Irina comes in. Mary refuses to go inside the house. "I'm not going into that house again," she declares firmly, "and I shan't go in there ever!" Irina reminds her that she is going away next day and proposes that they should spend a few minutes quietly together. Kulygin, the pathetic idiot, tries to amuse his wife by putting on a false beard he has confiscated from one of his schoolboys. (Chekhov made him shave off his beard specially for this scene.)

> KULYGIN – I look like our German master, don't I? [*Laughs.*] Those
>   boys are funny beggars.
> MARY – You do look like your German.
> OLGA   [*laughs*] Yes.
>
> > [MARY *cries.*]
>
> IRINA – Stop it, Mary.
> KULYGIN – Yes, I certainly look very like him.

Nothing in this scene is irrelevant; everything in it has been nicely calculated to evoke the right kind of response from the audience; everything shows the touch of a master of stage technique. And it would be the greatest mistake to interpret this scene as an instance of what is so generally assumed to be the expression of "Chekhovian" frustration and gloom. Mary, indeed, says in the bitterness of her heart that her life is a failure and that there is nothing more she wants, but as her little speech in the chorus of the three sisters shows, she soon recovers from her feeling of desolation. Parting is such sweet sorrow—and Chekhov makes it quite clear that it is not by any means the end.

The other great themes of the play—the theme of the illusion of happiness, the theme of mankind's future, and, above all, the theme of the regenerative powers of work—are all carefully interwoven with the action and find a *gay* affirmation of life in the final chorus of the three sisters to the accompaniment of an invigorating march by the band of the departing regiment.

> MARY – Oh, how gay the music sounds! They are going away from us
>   —one has already gone, gone for ever—and we shall be left alone to
>   start our life anew. We must live. We must live. . . .

IRINA [*lays her head on* OLGA's *breast*] The time will come when there will be no more secrets, when all that is now hidden will be made plain, and when all will know what these sufferings are for. Till then we must live—we must work, just work! Tomorrow I shall go away alone, I shall teach in a school, and I shall give my life to those who may need it. It is autumn now; it will be winter soon and everything will be covered with snow. But I shall be working—I shall be working.

OLGA [*embraces the two sisters*] The music is so cheerful and gay and I want to live! Dear God! Time will pass and we shall be gone for ever. We shall be forgotten, and people will no longer remember our voices, or our faces, or how many of us there were. But our sufferings will pass into joy for those who live after us—peace and happiness will reign on earth, and we who live now will be remembered with gratitude and will be blessed. Oh, my dear, dear sisters, our lives are not finished yet. Let us live! The music is so gay, so joyful, and it almost seems that in a little while we shall know why we live and why we suffer. Oh, if only we knew—if only we knew!

BERNARD SHAW

Major Barbara
Saint Joan

THERE IS NO WORK which is obviously *the* masterpiece of Bernard Shaw (1856–1950), nor would it be shrewd for an anthologist to follow the author in his predilection for the works which carry the largest load of teaching, such as *Back to Methuselah*. There would be a strong case for just the opposite, since it is arguable that Shaw came nearest to artistic perfection in plays that carry the lightest didactic load, such as *Pygmalion*. At this point the present Editor must admit to having departed from exclusively aesthetic criteria. Shaw is read, and legitimately so, not only for his "merit" but for his "interest." *Major Barbara*, if less perfect than *Pygmalion*, is likely to interest the reader more. Some of the reasons for this are given in Professor Crompton's commentary. Then again, since two Shaw plays are reprinted here, there is an interesting continuity as between *Major Barbara* and *Saint Joan*. It is interesting to the biographer who lurks in each of us that the ageing male playwright should twice identify himself with the aspiration and heartbreak of a young girl. It is interesting to the psychologist in us that both plays are, in a sense, studies of father and daughter. At the center of *Major Barbara* is the moment when, disenchanted by what her father has shown her, Barbara cries: "My God, my God, why hast Thou forsaken me?" At the center of *Saint Joan* is the moment when Joan, abandoned by her King and the others, asks: "What is my loneliness before the loneliness of my country and my God?" God is, of course, Joan's Father, and she is still talking to him at the end . . . *Major Barbara* and *Saint Joan* have proved among Shaw's most influential plays. Bertolt Brecht even tried to combine them in a single drama, his *Saint Joan of the Stockyards*. None of which is to concede that, on purely aesthetic grounds, either play would have to be excluded from the present book.

MAJOR BARBARA

[1905]

CHARACTERS

LADY BRITOMART UNDERSHAFT

STEPHEN UNDERSHAFT

MORRISON

BARBARA UNDERSHAFT

SARAH UNDERSHAFT

CHARLES LOMAX

ADOLPHUS CUSINS

ANDREW UNDERSHAFT

RUMMY MITCHENS

SNOBBY PRICE

JENNY HILL

PETER SHIRLEY

BILL WALKER

MRS. BAINES

BILTON

ACT ONE

It is after dinner in January 1906, in the library in LADY BRITOMART
UNDERSHAFT'S *house in Wilton Crescent. A large and comfortable settee
is in the middle of the room, upholstered in dark leather. A person sitting
on it (it is vacant at present) would have, on his right,* LADY BRITO-
MART'S *writing table, with the lady herself busy at it; a smaller writing
table behind him on his left; the door behind him on* LADY BRITOMART'S
*side; and a window with a window seat directly on his left. Near the win-
dow is an armchair.*

LADY BRITOMART *is a woman of fifty or thereabouts, well dressed and
yet careless of her dress, well bred and quite reckless of her breeding,
well mannered and yet appallingly outspoken and indifferent to the
opinion of her interlocutors, amiable and yet peremptory, arbitrary, and
high-tempered to the last bearable degree, and withal a very typical
managing matron of the upper class, treated as a naughty child until she
grew into a scolding mother, and finally settling down with plenty of
practical ability and worldly experience, limited in the oddest way with
domestic and class limitations, conceiving the universe exactly as if it
were a large house in Wilton Crescent, though handling her corner of it
very effectively on that assumption, and being quite enlightened and
liberal as to the books in the library, the pictures on the walls, the music
in the portfolios, and the articles in the papers.*

Her son, STEPHEN, *comes in. He is a gravely correct young man under
25, taking himself very seriously, but still in some awe of his mother,
from childish habit and bachelor shyness rather than from any weakness
of character.*

STEPHEN – Whats the matter?

LADY BRITOMART – Presently, Stephen.

[STEPHEN *submissively walks to the settee and sits down. He takes up a
Liberal weekly called The Speaker.*]

LADY BRITOMART – Dont begin to read, Stephen. I shall require all
your attention.

STEPHEN – It was only while I was waiting—

1645

LADY BRITOMART – Dont make excuses, Stephen. [*He puts down The Speaker.*] Now! [*She finishes her writing; rises; and comes to the settee.*] I have not kept you waiting very long, I think.

STEPHEN – Not at all, mother.

LADY BRITOMART – Bring me my cushion. [*He takes the cushion from the chair at the desk and arranges it for her as she sits down on the settee.*] Sit down. [*He sits down and fingers his tie nervously.*] Dont fiddle with your tie, Stephen: there is nothing the matter with it.

STEPHEN – I beg your pardon.

[*He fiddles with his watch chain instead.*]

LADY BRITOMART – Now are you attending to me, Stephen?

STEPHEN – Of course, mother.

LADY BRITOMART – No: it's not of course. I want something much more than your everyday matter-of-course attention. I am going to speak to you very seriously, Stephen. I wish you would let that chain alone.

STEPHEN [*hastily relinquishing the chain*] Have I done anything to annoy you, mother? If so, it was quite unintentional.

LADY BRITOMART [*astonished*] Nonsense! [*With some remorse.*] My poor boy, did you think I was angry with you?

STEPHEN – What is it, then, mother? You are making me very uneasy.

LADY BRITOMART [*squaring herself at him rather aggressively*] Stephen: may I ask how soon you intend to realize that you are a grown-up man, and that I am only a woman?

STEPHEN [*amazed*] Only a—

LADY BRITOMART – Dont repeat my words, please: it is a most aggravating habit. You must learn to face life seriously, Stephen. I really cannot bear the whole burden of our family affairs any longer. You must advise me: you must assume the responsibility.

STEPHEN – I!

LADY BRITOMART – Yes, you, of course. You were 24 last June. Youve been at Harrow and Cambridge. Youve been to India and Japan. You must know a lot of things, now; unless you have wasted your time most scandalously. Well, advise me.

STEPHEN [*much perplexed*] You know I have never interfered in the household—

LADY BRITOMART – No: I should think not. I dont want you to order the dinner.

STEPHEN – I mean in our family affairs.

LADY BRITOMART – Well, you must interfere now; for they are getting quite beyond me.

STEPHEN [*troubled*] I have thought sometimes that perhaps I ought;

1646

but really, mother, I know so little about them; and what I do know is so painful! it is so impossible to mention some things to you—

[*He stops, ashamed.*]

LADY BRITOMART—I suppose you mean your father.

STEPHEN [*almost inaudibly*] Yes.

LADY BRITOMART—My dear: we cant go on all our lives not mentioning him. Of course you were quite right not to open the subject until I asked you to; but you are old enough now to be taken into my confidence, and to help me to deal with him about the girls.

STEPHEN—But the girls are all right. They are engaged.

LADY BRITOMART [*complacently*] Yes: I have made a very good match for Sarah. Charles Lomax will be a millionaire at 35. But that is ten years ahead; and in the meantime his trustees cannot under the terms of his father's will allow him more than £800 a year.

STEPHEN—But the will says also that if he increases his income by his own exertions, they may double the increase.

LADY BRITOMART—Charles Lomax's exertions are much more likely to decrease his income than to increase it. Sarah will have to find at least another £800 a year for the next ten years; and even then they will be as poor as church mice. And what about Barbara? I thought Barbara was going to make the most brilliant career of all of you. And what does she do? Joins the Salvation Army; discharges her maid; lives on a pound a week; and walks in one evening with a professor of Greek whom she has picked up in the street, and who pretends to be a Salvationist, and actually plays the big drum for her in public because he has fallen head over ears in love with her.

STEPHEN—I was certainly rather taken aback when I heard they were engaged. Cusins is a very nice fellow, certainly: nobody would ever guess that he was born in Australia; but—

LADY BRITOMART—Oh, Adolphus Cusins will make a very good husband. After all, nobody can say a word against Greek: it stamps a man at once as an educated gentleman. And my family, thank Heaven, is not a pig-headed Tory one. We are Whigs, and believe in liberty. Let snobbish people say what they please: Barbara shall marry, not the man they like, but the man I like.

STEPHEN—Of course I was thinking only of his income. However, he is not likely to be extravagant.

LADY BRITOMART—Dont be too sure of that, Stephen. I know your quiet, simple, refined, poetic people like Adolphus: quite content with the best of everything! They cost more than your extravagant people, who are always as mean as they are second rate. No: Barbara will need at least £2000 a year. You see it means two additional households. Besides, my dear, you must marry soon. I dont approve of the present fashion of philandering bachelors and late marriages; and I am trying to arrange something for you.

STEPHEN—It's very good of you, mother; but perhaps I had better arrange that for myself.

LADY BRITOMART—Nonsense! you are much too young to begin matchmaking: you would be taken in by some pretty little nobody. Of course I dont mean that you are not to be consulted: you know that as well as I do. [STEPHEN *closes his lips and is silent.*] Now dont sulk, Stephen.

STEPHEN—I am not sulking, mother. What has all this got to do with —with—with my father?

LADY BRITOMART—My dear Stephen: where is the money to come from? It is easy enough for you and the other children to live on my income as long as we are in the same house; but I cant keep four families in four separate houses. You know how poor my father is: he has barely seven thousand a year now; and really, if he were not the Earl of Stevenage, he would have to give up society. He can do nothing for us. He says, naturally enough, that it is absurd that he should be asked to provide for the children of a man who is rolling in money. You see, Stephen, your father must be fabulously wealthy, because there is always a war going on somewhere.

STEPHEN—You need not remind me of that, mother. I have hardly ever opened a newspaper in my life without seeing our name in it. The Undershaft torpedo! The Undershaft quick firers! The Undershaft ten inch! the Undershaft disappearing rampart gun! the Undershaft submarine! and now the Undershaft aerial battleship! At Harrow they called me the Woolwich Infant. At Cambridge it was the same. A little brute at King's who was always trying to get up revivals, spoilt my Bible—your first birthday present to me—by writing under my name, 'Son and heir to Undershaft and Lazarus, Death and Destruction Dealers: address Christendom and Judea.' But that was not so bad as the way I was kowtowed to everywhere because my father was making millions by selling cannons.

LADY BRITOMART—It is not only the cannons, but the war loans that Lazarus arranges under cover of giving credit for the cannons. You know, Stephen, it's perfectly scandalous. Those two men, Andrew Undershaft and Lazarus, positively have Europe under their thumbs. That is why your father is able to behave as he does. He is above the law. Do you think Bismarck or Gladstone or Disraeli could have openly defied every social and moral obligation all their lives as your father has? They simply wouldnt have dared. I asked Gladstone to take it up. I asked The Times to take it up. I asked the Lord Chamberlain to take it up. But it was just like asking them to declare war on the Sultan.

They wouldn't. They said they couldnt touch him. I believe they were afraid.

STEPHEN—What could they do? He does not actually break the law.

LADY BRITOMART—Not break the law! He is always breaking the law. He broke the law when he was born: his parents were not married.

STEPHEN—Mother! Is that true?

LADY BRITOMART—Of course it's true: that was why we separated.

STEPHEN—He married without letting you know this!

LADY BRITOMART [*rather taken aback by this inference*] Oh no. To do Andrew justice, that was not the sort of thing he did. Besides, you know the Undershaft motto: Unashamed. Everybody knew.

STEPHEN—But you said that was why you separated.

LADY BRITOMART—Yes, because he was not content with being a foundling himself: he wanted to disinherit you for another foundling. That was what I couldnt stand.

STEPHEN [*ashamed*] Do you mean for—for—for—

LADY BRITOMART—Dont stammer, Stephen. Speak distinctly.

STEPHEN—But this is so frightful to me, mother. To have to speak to you about such things!

LADY BRITOMART—It's not pleasant for me, either, especially if you are still so childish that you must make it worse by a display of embarrassment. It is only in the middle classes, Stephen, that people get into a state of dumb helpless horror when they find that there are wicked people in the world. In our class, we have to decide what is to be done with wicked people; and nothing should disturb our self-possession. Now ask your question properly.

STEPHEN—Mother: have you no consideration for me? For Heaven's sake either treat me as a child, as you always do, and tell me nothing at all; or tell me everything and let me take it as best I can.

LADY BRITOMART—Treat you as a chid! What do you mean? It is most unkind and ungrateful of you to say such a thing. You know I have never treated any of you as children. I have always made you my companions and friends, and allowed you perfect freedom to do and say whatever you liked, so long as you liked what I could approve of.

STEPHEN [*desperately*] I daresay we have been the very imperfect children of a very perfect mother; but I do beg you to let me alone for once, and tell me about this horrible business of my father wanting to set me aside for another son.

LADY BRITOMART [*amazed*] Another son! I never said anything of the kind. I never dreamt of such a thing. This is what comes of interrupting me.

STEPHEN—But you said—

LADY BRITOMART [*cutting him short*] Now be a good boy,

Stephen, and listen to me patiently. The Undershafts are descended from a foundling in the parish of St Andrew Undershaft in the city. That was long ago, in the reign of James the First. Well, this foundling was adopted by an armorer and gun-maker. In the course of time the foundling succeeded to the business; and from some notion of gratitude, or some vow or something, he adopted another foundling, and left the business to him. And that foundling did the same. Ever since that, the cannon business has always been left to an adopted foundling named Andrew Undershaft.

STEPHEN—But did they never marry? Were there no legitimate sons?

LADY BRITOMART—Oh yes: they married just as your father did; and they were rich enough to buy land for their own children and leave them well provided for. But they always adopted and trained some foundling to succeed them in the business; and of course they always quarrelled with their wives furiously over it. Your father was adopted in that way; and he pretends to consider himself bound to keep up the tradition and adopt somebody to leave the business to. Of course I was not going to stand that. There may have been some reason for it when the Undershafts could only marry women in their own class, whose sons were not fit to govern great estates. But there could be no excuse for passing over my son.

STEPHEN [*dubiously*] I am afraid I should make a poor hand of managing a cannon foundry.

LADY BRITOMART—Nonsense! you could easily get a manager and pay him a salary.

STEPHEN—My father evidently had no great opinion of my capacity.

LADY BRITOMART—Stuff, child! you were only a baby: it had nothing to do with your capacity. Andrew did it on principle, just as he did every perverse and wicked thing on principle. When my father remonstrated, Andrew actually told him to his face that history tells us of only two successful institutions: one the Undershaft firm, and the other the Roman Empire under the Antonines. That was because the Antonine emperors all adopted their successors. Such rubbish! The Stevenages are as good as the Antonines, I hope; and you are a Stevenage. But that was Andrew all over. There you have the man! Always clever and unanswerable when he was defending nonsense and wickedness: always awkward and sullen when he had to behave sensibly and decently!

STEPHEN—Then it was on my account that your home life was broken up, mother. I am sorry.

LADY BRITOMART—Well, dear, there were other differences. I really cannot bear an immoral man. I am not a Pharisee, I hope; and I should not have minded his merely doing wrong things: we are none

of us perfect. But your father didnt exactly do wrong things: he said
them and thought them: that was what was so dreadful. He really had
a sort of religion of wrongness. Just as one doesnt mind men practising
immorality so long as they own that they are in the wrong by preaching morality; so I couldnt forgive Andrew for preaching immorality
while he practised morality. You would all have grown up without
principles, without any knowledge of right and wrong, if he had been
in the house. You know, my dear, your father was a very attractive
man in some ways. Children did not dislike him; and he took advantage of it to put the wickedest ideas into their heads, and make them
quite unmanageable. I did not dislike him myself: very far from it;
but nothing can bridge over moral disagreement.

STEPHEN – All this simply bewilders me, mother. People may differ
about matters of opinion, or even about religion; but how can they
differ about right and wrong? Right is right; and wrong is wrong; and
if a man cannot distinguish them properly, he is either a fool or a
rascal: thats all.

LADY BRITOMART [*touched*] Thats my own boy! [*She pats his
cheek.*] Your father never could answer that: he used to laugh and
get out of it under cover of some affectionate nonsense. And now that
you understand the situation, what do you advise me to do?

STEPHEN – Well, what can you do?

LADY BRITOMART – I must get the money somehow.

STEPHEN – We cannot take money from him. I had rather go and live
in some cheap place like Bedford Square or even Hampstead than
take a farthing of his money.

LADY BRITOMART – But after all, Stephen, our present income
comes from Andrew.

STEPHEN [*shocked*] I never knew that.

LADY BRITOMART – Well, you surely didnt suppose your grandfather had anything to give me. The Stevenages could not do everything for you. We gave you social position. Andrew had to contribute
something. He had a very good bargain, I think.

STEPHEN [*bitterly*] We are utterly dependent on him and his cannons, then?

LADY BRITOMART – Certainly not: the money is settled. But he
provided it. So you see it is not a question of taking money from him
or not: it is simply a question of how much. I dont want any more for
myself.

STEPHEN – Nor do I.

LADY BRITOMART – But Sarah does; and Barbara does. That is,
Charles Lomax and Adolphus Cusins will cost them more. So I must

1651

put my pride in my pocket and ask for it, I suppose. That is your advice, Stephen, is it not?

STEPHEN – No.

LADY BRITOMART [*sharply*] Stephen!

STEPHEN – Of course if you are determined—

LADY BRITOMART – I am not determined: I ask your advice; and I am waiting for it. I will not have all the responsibility thrown on my shoulders.

STEPHEN [*obstinately*] I would die sooner than ask him for another penny.

LADY BRITOMART [*resignedly*] You mean that I must ask him. Very well, Stephen: it shall be as you wish. You will be glad to know that your grandfather concurs. But he thinks I ought to ask Andrew to come here and see the girls. After all, he must have some natural affection for them.

STEPHEN – Ask him here!!!

LADY BRITOMART – Do not repeat my words, Stephen. Where else can I ask him?

STEPHEN – I never expected you to ask him at all.

LADY BRITOMART – Now dont tease, Stephen. Come! you see that it is necessary that he should pay us a visit, dont you?

STEPHEN [*reluctantly*] I suppose so, if the girls cannot do without his money.

LADY BRITOMART – Thank you, Stephen: I knew you would give me the right advice when it was properly explained to you. I have asked your father to come this evening. [STEPHEN *bounds from his seat.*] Dont jump, Stephen: it fidgets me.

STEPHEN [*in utter consternation*] Do you mean to say that my father is coming here tonight—that he may be here at any moment?

LADY BRITOMART [*looking at her watch*] I said nine. [*He gasps. She rises.*] Ring the bell, please. [STEPHEN *goes to the smaller writing table; presses a button on it; and sits at it with his elbows on the table and his head in his hands, outwitted and overwhelmed.*] It is ten minutes to nine yet; and I have to prepare the girls. I asked Charles Lomax and Adolphus to dinner on purpose that they might be here. Andrew had better see them in case he should cherish any delusions as to their being capable of supporting their wives. [*The butler enters:* LADY BRITOMART *goes behind the settee to speak to him.*] Morrison: go up to the drawing room and tell everybody to come down here at once. [MORRISON *withdraws.* LADY BRITOMART *turns to* STEPHEN.] Now remember, Stephen: I shall need all your countenance and authority. [*He rises and tries to recover some vestige of these attributes.*] Give me a chair, dear. [*He pushes a chair forward from the wall to where she stands, near the smaller writing table. She sits down; and he goes to the armchair, into which he throws himself.*] I dont know how Barbara will take it. Ever since they made her a major in the Salvation Army she has developed a propensity to have her own way and order people about which quite cows me sometimes. It's not ladylike: I'm sure I dont know where she picked it up. Anyhow, Barbara shant bully me; but still it's just as well that your father should be here before she has time to refuse to meet him or make a fuss. Dont look nervous, Stephen: it will only encourage Barbara to make difficulties. *I* am nervous enough, goodness knows; but I dont shew it.

SARAH *and* BARBARA *come in with their respective young men,* CHARLES LOMAX *and* ADOLPHUS CUSINS. SARAH *is slender, bored, and mundane.* BARBARA *is robuster, jollier, much more energetic.* SARAH *is fashionably dressed:* BARBARA *is in Salvation Army uniform.* LOMAX, *a young man about town, is like many other young men about town. He is afflicted with a frivolous sense of humor which plunges him at the most inopportune moments into paroxysms of imperfectly suppressed laughter.* CUSINS *is a spectacled student, slight, thin haired, and sweet voiced, with a more complex form of* LOMAX's *complaint. His sense of humor is intellectual and subtle, and is complicated by an appalling temper. The lifelong struggle of a benevolent temperament and a high conscience against impulses of inhuman ridicule and fierce impatience has set up a chronic strain which has visibly wrecked his constitution. He is a most implacable, determined, tenacious, intolerant person who by mere force of character presents himself as—and indeed actually is—considerate, gentle, explanatory, even mild and apologetic, capable possibly of murder, but not of cruelty or coarseness. By the operation of some instinct which is not merciful enough to blind him with the illusions of love, he is obstinately bent on marrying* BARBARA. LOMAX *likes* SARAH *and thinks it will be rather a lark to marry her. Consequently he has not attempted to resist* LADY BRITOMART's *arrangements to that end.*

All four look as if they had been having a good deal of fun in the drawing room. The girls enter first, leaving the swains outside. SARAH *comes to the settee.* BARBARA *comes in after her and stops at the door.*

BARBARA—Are Cholly and Dolly to come in?

LADY BRITOMART [*forcibly*] Barbara: I will not have Charles called Cholly: the vulgarity of it positively makes me ill.

BARBARA—It's all right, mother: Cholly is quite correct nowadays. Are they to come in?

LADY BRITOMART—Yes, if they will behave themselves.

BARBARA [*through the door*] Come in, Dolly; and behave yourself.

[BARBARA *comes to her mother's writing table.* CUSINS *enters smiling, and wanders towards* LADY BRITOMART.]

SARAH [*calling*] Come in, Cholly.

[LOMAX *enters, controlling his features very imperfectly, and places himself vaguely between* SARAH *and* BARBARA.]

LADY BRITOMART [*peremptorily*] Sit down, all of you. [*They sit.* CUSINS *crosses to the window and seats himself there.* LOMAX *takes a chair.* BARBARA *sits at the writing table and* SARAH *on the settee.*] I dont in the least know what you are laughing at, Adolphus. I am surprised at you, though I expected nothing better from Charles Lomax.

CUSINS [*in a remarkably gentle voice*] Barbara has been trying to teach me the West Ham Salvation March.

LADY BRITOMART—I see nothing to laugh at in that; nor should you if you are really converted.

CUSINS [*sweetly*] You were not present. It was really funny, I believe.

LOMAX—Ripping.

LADY BRITOMART—Be quiet, Charles. Now listen to me, children. Your father is coming here this evening.

[*General stupefaction.* LOMAX, SARAH, *and* BARBARA *rise:* SARAH *scared, and* BARBARA *amused and expectant.*]

LOMAX [*remonstrating*] Oh I say!

LADY BRITOMART—You are not called on to say anything, Charles.

SARAH—Are you serious, mother?

LADY BRITOMART—Of course I am serious. It is on your account, Sarah, and also on Charles's. [*Silence.* SARAH *sits, with a shrug.* CHARLES *looks painfully unworthy.*] I hope you are not going to object, Barbara.

BARBARA—I! why should I? My father has a soul to be saved like anybody else. He's quite welcome as far as I am concerned.

[*She sits on the table, and softly whistles 'Onward, Christian Soldiers'.*]

LOMAX [*still remonstrant*] But really, dont you know! Oh I say!

LADY BRITOMART [*frigidly*] What do you wish to convey, Charles?

LOMAX—Well, you must admit that this is a bit thick.

LADY BRITOMART [*turning with ominous suavity to* CUSINS] Adolphus: you are a professor of Greek. Can you translate Charles Lomax's remarks into reputable English for us?

CUSINS [*cautiously*] If I may say so, Lady Brit, I think Charles has rather happily expressed what we all feel. Homer, speaking of Autolycus, uses the same phrase. Pukinòn dómon elthein means a bit thick.

LOMAX [*handsomely*] Not that I mind, you know, if Sarah dont.

[*He sits.*]

LADY BRITOMART [*crushingly*] Thank you. Have I your permission, Adolphus, to invite my own husband to my own house?

1654

CUSINS [*gallantly*] You have my unhesitating support in everything you do.

LADY BRITOMART – Tush! Sarah: have you nothing to say?

SARAH – Do you mean that he is coming regularly to live here?

LADY BRITOMART – Certainly not. The spare room is ready for him if he likes to stay for a day or two and see a little more of you; but there are limits.

SARAH – Well, he cant eat us, I suppose. *I* dont mind.

LOMAX [*chuckling*] I wonder how the old man will take it.

LADY BRITOMART – Much as the old woman will, no doubt, Charles.

LOMAX [*abashed*] I didnt mean—at least—

LADY BRITOMART – You didnt think, Charles. You never do; and the result is, you never mean anything. And now please attend to me, children. Your father will be quite a stranger to us.

LOMAX – I suppose he hasnt seen Sarah since she was a little kid.

LADY BRITOMART – Not since she was a little kid, Charles, as you express it with that elegance of diction and refinement of thought that seem never to desert you. Accordingly—er—[*Impatiently.*] Now I have forgotten what I was going to say. That comes of your provoking me to be sarcastic, Charles. Adolphus: will you kindly tell me where I was.

CUSINS [*sweetly*] You were saying that as Mr Undershaft has not seen his children since they were babies, he will form his opinion of the way you have brought them up from their behavior tonight, and that therefore you wish us all to be particularly careful to conduct ourselves well, especially Charles.

LADY BRITOMART [*with emphatic approval*] Precisely.

LOMAX – Look here, Dolly: Lady Brit didnt say that.

LADY BRITOMART [*vehemently*] I did, Charles. Adolphus's recollection is perfectly correct. It is most important that you should be good; and I do beg you for once not to pair off into opposite corners and giggle and whisper while I am speaking to your father.

BARBARA – All right, mother. We'll do you credit.

[*She comes off the table, and sits in her chair with ladylike elegance.*]

LADY BRITOMART – Remember, Charles, that Sarah will want to feel proud of you instead of ashamed of you.

LOMAX – Oh I say! theres nothing to be exactly proud of, dont you know.

LADY BRITOMART – Well, try and look as if there was.

[MORRISON, *pale and dismayed, breaks
into the room in unconcealed disorder.*]

MORRISON – Might I speak a word to you, my lady?

LADY BRITOMART – Nonsense! Shew him up.

MORRISON – Yes, my lady.

[*He goes.*]

L O M A X – Does Morrison know who it is?

L A D Y   B R I T O M A R T – Of course. Morrison has always been with us.

L O M A X – It must be a regular corker for him, dont you know.

L A D Y   B R I T O M A R T – Is this a moment to get on my nerves, Charles, with your outrageous expressions?

L O M A X – But this is something out of the ordinary, really—

M O R R I S O N   [*at the door*] The—er—Mr Undershaft.

[*He retreats in confusion.*]

[ANDREW UNDERSHAFT *comes in. All rise.* LADY BRITOMART *meets him in the middle of the room behind the settee.*]

ANDREW *is, on the surface, a stoutish, easygoing elderly man, with kindly patient manners, and an engaging simplicity of character. But he has a watchful, deliberate, waiting, listening face, and formidable reserves of power, both bodily and mental, in his capacious chest and long head. His gentleness is partly that of a strong man who has learnt by experience that his natural grip hurts ordinary people unless he handles them very carefully, and partly the mellowness of age and success. He is also a little shy in his present very delicate situation.*

L A D Y   B R I T O M A R T – Good evening, Andrew.

U N D E R S H A F T – How d'ye do, my dear.

L A D Y   B R I T O M A R T – You look a good deal older.

U N D E R S H A F T   [*apologetically*] I am somewhat older. [*Taking her hand with a touch of courtship.*] Time has stood still with you.

L A D Y   B R I T O M A R T   [*throwing away his hand*] Rubbish! This is your family.

U N D E R S H A F T   [*surprised*] Is it so large? I am sorry to say my memory is failing very badly in some things.

[*He offers his hand with paternal kindness to* LOMAX.]

L O M A X   [*jerkily shaking his hand*] Ahdedoo.

U N D E R S H A F T – I can see you are my eldest. I am very glad to meet you again, my boy.

L O M A X   [*remonstrating*] No, but look here dont you know—[*Overcome.*] Oh I say!

L A D Y   B R I T O M A R T   [*recovering from momentary speechlessness*] Andrew: do you mean to say that you dont remember how many children you have?

U N D E R S H A F T – Well, I am afraid I–. They have grown so much—er. Am I making any ridiculous mistake? I may as well confess: I recollect only one son. But so many things have happened since, of course—er—

LADY BRITOMART [*decisively*] Andrew: you are talking nonsense. Of course you have only one son.

UNDERSHAFT – Perhaps you will be good enough to introduce me, my dear.

LADY BRITOMART – That is Charles Lomax, who is engaged to Sarah.

UNDERSHAFT – My dear sir, I beg your pardon.

LOMAX – Notatall. Delighted, I assure you.

LADY BRITOMART – This is Stephen.

UNDERSHAFT [*bowing*] Happy to make your acquaintance, Mr Stephen. Then [*Going to* CUSINS.] you must be my son. [*Taking* CUSINS' *hands in his.*] How are you, my young friend? [*To* LADY BRITOMART.] He is very like you, my love.

CUSINS – You flatter me, Mr Undershaft. My name is Cusins: engaged to Barbara. [*Very explicitly.*] That is Major Barbara Undershaft, of the Salvation Army. That is Sarah, your second daughter. This is Stephen Undershaft, your son.

UNDERSHAFT – My dear Stephen, I beg your pardon.

STEPHEN – Not at all.

UNDERSHAFT – Mr Cusins: I am much indebted to you for explaining so precisely. [*Turning to* SARAH.] Barbara, my dear—

SARAH [*prompting him*] Sarah.

UNDERSHAFT – Sarah, of course. [*They shake hands. He goes over to* BARBARA.] Barbara—I am right this time, I hope?

BARBARA – Quite right.

[*They shake hands.*]

LADY BRITOMART [*resuming command*] Sit down, all of you. Sit down, Andrew.

She comes forward and sits on the settee. CUSINS *also brings his chair forward on her left.* BARBARA *and* STEPHEN *resume their seats.* LOMAX *gives his chair to* SARAH *and goes for another.*

UNDERSHAFT – Thank you, my love.

LOMAX [*conversationally, as he brings a chair forward between the writing table and the settee, and offers it to* UNDERSHAFT] Takes you some time to find out exactly where you are, dont it?

UNDERSHAFT [*accepting the chair, but remaining standing*] That is not what embarrasses me, Mr Lomax. My difficulty is that if I play the part of a father, I shall produce the effect of an intrusive stranger; and if I play the part of a discreet stranger, I may appear a callous father.

1657

LADY BRITOMART – There is no need for you to play any part at all, Andrew. You had much better be sincere and natural.

UNDERSHAFT [*submissively*] Yes, my dear: I daresay that will be best. [*He sits down comfortably.*] Well, here I am. Now what can I do for you all?

LADY BRITOMART – You need not do anything, Andrew. You are one of the family. You can sit with us and enjoy yourself.

[*A painfully conscious pause.* BARBARA *makes a face at* LOMAX, *whose too long suppressed mirth immediately explodes in agonized neighings.*]

LADY BRITOMART [*outraged*] Charles Lomax: if you can behave yourself, behave yourself. If not, leave the room.

LOMAX – I'm awfully sorry, Lady Brit; but really you know, upon my soul!

> [*He sits on the settee between* LADY BRITOMART
> *and* UNDERSHAFT, *quite overcome.*]

BARBARA – Why dont you laugh if you want to, Cholly? It's good for your inside.

LADY BRITOMART – Barbara: you have had the education of a lady. Please let your father see that; and dont talk like a street girl.

UNDERSHAFT – Never mind me, my dear. As you know, I am not a gentleman; and I was never educated.

LOMAX [*encouragingly*] Nobody'd know it, I assure you. You look all right, you know.

CUSINS – Let me advise you to study Greek, Mr Undershaft. Greek scholars are privileged men. Few of them know Greek; and none of them know anything else; but their position is unchallengeable. Other languages are the qualifications of waiters and commercial travellers: Greek is to a man of position what the hallmark is to silver.

BARBARA – Dolly: dont be insincere. Cholly: fetch your concertina and play something for us.

LOMAX [*jumps up eagerly, but checks himself to remark doubtfully to* UNDERSHAFT] Perhaps that sort of thing isnt in your line, eh?

UNDERSHAFT – I am particularly fond of music.

LOMAX [*delighted*] Are you? Then I'll get it.

> [*He goes upstairs for the instrument.*]

UNDERSHAFT – Do you play, Barbara?

BARBARA – Only the tambourine. But Cholly's teaching me the concertina.

UNDERSHAFT – Is Cholly also a member of the Salvation Army?

BARBARA – No: he says it's bad form to be a dissenter. But I dont despair of Cholly. I made him come yesterday to a meeting at the dock gates, and take the collection in his hat.

UNDERSHAFT [*looks whimsically at his wife*]!!

LADY BRITOMART – It is not my doing, Andrew. Barbara is old enough to take her own way. She has no father to advise her.

BARBARA – Oh yes she has. There are no orphans in the Salvation Army.

UNDERSHAFT – Your father there has a great many children and plenty of experience, eh?

BARBARA [*looking at him with quick interest and nodding*] Just so. How did you come to understand that?

[LOMAX *is heard at the door trying the concertina.*]

LADY BRITOMART – Come in, Charles. Play us something at once.

LOMAX – Righto!

[*He sits down in his former place, and preludes.*]

UNDERSHAFT – One moment, Mr Lomax. I am rather interested in the Salvation Army. Its motto might be my own: Blood and Fire.

LOMAX [*shocked*] But not your sort of blood and fire, you know.

UNDERSHAFT – My sort of blood cleanses: my sort of fire purifies.

BARBARA – So do ours. Come down tomorrow to my shelter—the West Ham shelter—and see what we're doing. We're going to march to a great meeting in the Assembly Hall at Mile End. Come and see the shelter and then march with us: it will do you a lot of good. Can you play anything?

UNDERSHAFT – In my youth I earned pennies, and even shillings occasionally, in the streets and in public house parlors by my natural talent for stepdancing. Later on, I became a member of the Undershaft orchestral society, and performed passably on the tenor trombone.

LOMAX [*scandalized—putting down the concertina*] Oh I say!

BARBARA – Many a sinner has played himself into heaven on the trombone, thanks to the Army.

LOMAX [*to* BARBARA, *still rather shocked*] Yes; but what about the cannon business, dont you know? [*To* UNDERSHAFT.] Getting into heaven is not exactly in your line, is it?

LADY BRITOMART – Charles!!!

LOMAX – Well; but it stands to reason, dont it? The cannon business may be necessary and all that: we cant get on without cannons; but it isnt right, you know. On the other hand, there may be a certain amount of tosh about the Salvation Army—I belong to the Established Church myself—but still you cant deny that it's religion; and you cant go against religion, can you? At least unless youre downright immoral, dont you know.

UNDERSHAFT – You hardly appreciate my position, Mr Lomax—

LOMAX [*hastily*] I'm not saying anything against you personally—

UNDERSHAFT – Quite so, quite so. But consider for a moment. Here I am, a profiteer in mutilation and murder. I find myself in a specially amiable humor just now because, this morning, down at the foundry, we blew twenty-seven dummy soldiers into fragments with a gun which formerly destroyed only thirteen.

L O M A X [*leniently*] Well, the more destructive war becomes, the sooner it will be abolished, eh?

U N D E R S H A F T – Not at all. The more destructive war becomes the more fascinating we find it. No, Mr Lomax: I am obliged to you for making the usual excuse for my trade; but I am not ashamed of it. I am not one of those men who keep their morals and their business in water-tight compartments. All the spare money my trade rivals spend on hospitals, cathedrals, and other receptacles for conscience money, I devote to experiments and researches in improved methods of destroying life and property. I have always done so; and I always shall. Therefore your Christmas card moralities of peace on earth and goodwill among men are of no use to me. Your Christianity, which enjoins you to resist not evil, and to turn the other cheek, would make me a bankrupt. My morality—my religion—must have a place for cannons and torpedoes in it.

S T E P H E N [*coldly—almost sullenly*] You speak as if there were half a dozen moralities and religions to choose from, instead of one true morality and one true religion.

U N D E R S H A F T – For me there is only one true morality; but it might not fit you, as you do not manufacture aerial battleships. There is only one true morality for every man; but every man has not the same true morality.

L O M A X [*overtaxed*] Would you mind saying that again? I didnt quite follow it.

C U S I N S – It's quite simple. As Euripides says, one man's meat is another man's poison morally as well as physically.

U N D E R S H A F T – Precisely.

L O M A X – Oh, that! Yes, yes, yes. True. True.

S T E P H E N – In other words, some men are honest and some are scoundrels.

B A R B A R A – Bosh! There are no scoundrels.

U N D E R S H A F T – Indeed? Are there any good men?

B A R B A R A – No. Not one. There are neither good men nor scoundrels: there are just children of one Father; and the sooner they stop calling one another names the better. You neednt talk to me: I know them. Ive had scores of them through my hands: scoundrels, criminals, infidels, philanthropists, missionaries, county councillors, all sorts. Theyre all just the same sort of sinner; and theres the same salvation ready for them all.

U N D E R S H A F T – May I ask have you ever saved a maker of cannons?

BARBARA—No. Will you let me try?

UNDERSHAFT—Well, I will make a bargain with you. If I go to see you tomorrow in your Salvation Shelter, will you come the day after to see me in my cannon works?

BARBARA—Take care. It may end in your giving up the cannons for the sake of the Salvation Army.

UNDERSHAFT—Are you sure it will not end in your giving up the Salvation Army for the sake of the cannons?

BARBARA—I will take my chance of that.

UNDERSHAFT—And I will take my chance of the other. [*They shake hands on it.*] Where is your shelter?

BARBARA—In West Ham. At the sign of the cross. Ask anybody in Canning Town. Where are your works?

UNDERSHAFT—In Perivale St Andrews. At the sign of the sword. Ask anybody in Europe.

LOMAX—Hadnt I better play something?

BARBARA—Yes. Give us Onward, Christian Soldiers.

LOMAX—Well, thats rather a strong order to begin with, dont you know. Suppose I sing Thourt passing hence, my brother. It's much the same tune.

BARBARA—It's too melancholy. You get saved, Cholly; and youll pass hence, my brother, without making such a fuss about it.

LADY BRITOMART—Really, Barbara, you go on as if religion were a pleasant subject. Do have some sense of propriety.

UNDERSHAFT—I do not find it an unpleasant subject, my dear. It is the only one that capable people really care for.

LADY BRITOMART [*looking at her watch*] Well, if you are determined to have it, I insist on having it in a proper and respectable way. Charles: ring for prayers.

[*General amazement. STEPHEN rises in dismay.*]

LOMAX [*rising*] Oh I say!

UNDERSHAFT [*rising*] I am afraid I must be going.

LADY BRITOMART—You cannot go now, Andrew: it would be most improper. Sit down. What will the servants think?

UNDERSHAFT—My dear: I have conscientious scruples. May I suggest a compromise? If Barbara will conduct a little service in the drawing room, with Mr Lomax as organist, I will attend it willingly. I will even take part, if a trombone can be procured.

LADY BRITOMART—Dont mock, Andrew.

UNDERSHAFT [*shocked—to* BARBARA] You dont think I am mocking, my love, I hope.

BARBARA—No, of course not; and it wouldnt matter if you were: half the Army came to their first meeting for a lark. [*Rising.*] Come along.

[*She throws her arm round her father and sweeps him out, calling to the others from the threshold.*] Come, Dolly. Come, Cholly.

[CUSINS *rises.*]

LADY BRITOMART—I will not be disobeyed by everybody. Adolphus: sit down. [*He does not.*] Charles: you may go. You are not fit for prayers: you cannot keep your countenance.

LOMAX—Oh I say!

[*He goes out.*]

LADY BRITOMART [*continuing*] But you, Adolphus, can behave yourself if you choose to. I insist on your staying.

CUSINS—My dear Lady Brit: there are things in the family prayer book that I couldnt bear to hear you say.

LADY BRITOMART—What things, pray?

CUSINS—Well, you would have to say before all the servants that we have done things we ought not to have done, and left undone things we ought to have done, and that there is no health in us. I cannot bear to hear you doing yourself such an injustice, and Barbara such an injustice. As for myself, I flatly deny it: I have done my best. I shouldnt dare to marry Barbara—I couldnt look you in the face—if it were true. So I must go to the drawing room.

LADY BRITOMART [*offended*] Well, go. [*He starts for the door.*] And remember this, Adolphus [*he turns to listen*]: I have a very strong suspicion that you went to the Salvation Army to worship Barbara and nothing else. And I quite appreciate the very clever way in which you systematically humbug me. I have found you out. Take care Barbara doesnt. Thats all.

CUSINS [*with unruffled sweetness*] Dont tell on me.

[*He steals out.*]

LADY BRITOMART—Sarah: if you want to go, go. Anything's better than to sit there as if you wished you were a thousand miles away.

SARAH [*languidly*] Very well, mamma.

[*She goes.*]

[LADY BRITOMART, *with a sudden flounce, gives way to a little gust of tears.*]

STEPHEN [*going to her*] Mother: whats the matter?

LADY BRITOMART [*swishing away her tears with her handkerchief*] Nothing. Foolishness. You can go with him, too, if you like, and leave me with the servants.

STEPHEN—Oh, you mustnt think that, mother. I—I dont like him.

LADY BRITOMART—The others do. That is the injustice of a woman's lot. A woman has to bring up her children; and that means to restrain them, to deny them things they want, to set them tasks, to punish them when they do wrong, to do all the unpleasant things. And then the father, who has nothing to do but pet them and spoil them, comes in when all her work is done and steals their affection from her.

STEPHEN – He has not stolen our affection from you. It is only curiosity.

LADY BRITOMART [*violently*] I wont be consoled, Stephen. There is nothing the matter with me.

> [*She rises and goes towards the door.*]

STEPHEN – Where are you going, mother?

LADY BRITOMART – To the drawing room, of course. [*She goes out. "Onward, Christian Soldiers," on the concertina, with tambourine accompaniment, is heard when the door opens.*] Are you coming, Stephen?

STEPHEN – No. Certainly not.

> [*She goes. He sits down on the settee, with compressed lips and an expression of strong dislike.*]

ACT TWO

The yard of the West Ham shelter of the Salvation Army is a cold place on a January morning. The building itself, an old warehouse, is newly whitewashed. It's gabled and projects into the yard in the middle, with a door on the ground floor, and another in the left above it without any balcony or ladder, but with a pulley rigged over it for hoisting sacks. Those who come from this central gable end into the yard have the gateway leading to the street on their left, with a stone horse-trough just beyond it, and, on the right, a penthouse shielding a table from the weather. There are forms at the table; and on them are seated a man and a woman, both much down on their luck, finishing a meal of bread (one thick slice each, with margarine and golden syrup) and diluted milk.

The man, a workman out of employment, is young, agile, a talker, a poser, sharp enough to be capable of anything in reason except honesty or altruistic considerations of any kind. The woman is a commonplace old bundle of poverty and hard-worn humanity. She looks sixty and probably is forty-five. If they were rich people, gloved and muffed and well wrapped up in furs and overcoats, they would be numbed and miserable; for it is a grindingly cold raw January day; and a glance at the background of grimy warehouses and leaden sky visible over the whitewashed walls of the yard would drive any idle rich person straight to the Mediterranean. But these two, being no more troubled with visions of the Mediterranean than of the moon, and being compelled to keep more of their clothes in the pawnshop, and less on their persons, in winter than in summer, are not depressed by the cold: rather are they stung into vivacity, to which their meal has just now given an almost jolly turn. The man takes a pull at his mug, and then gets up and moves about the yard with his hands deep in his pockets, occasionally breaking into a stepdance.

THE WOMAN—Feel better arter your meal, sir?

THE MAN—No. Call that a meal! Good enough for you, praps; but wot is it to me, an intelligent workin man.

THE WOMAN—Workin man! Wot are you?

1664

T H E   M A N – Painter.

T H E   W O M A N   [*sceptically*] Yus, I dessay.

T H E   M A N – Yus, you dessay! I know. Every loafer that cant do nothink calls isself a painter. Well, I'm a real painter: grainer, finisher, thirty-eight bob a week when I can get it.

T H E   W O M A N – Then why dont you go and get it?

T H E   M A N – I'll tell you why. Fust: I'm intelligent—fffff! it's rotten cold here [*he dances a step or two*]—yes: intelligent beyond the station o life into which it has pleased the capitalists to call me; and they dont like a man that sees through em. Second, an intelligent bein needs a doo share of appiness; so I drink somethink cruel when I get the chawnce. Third, I stand by my class and do as little as I can so's to leave arf the job for me fellow workers. Fourth, I'm fly enough to know wots inside the law and wots outside it; and inside it I do as the capitalists do: pinch wot I can lay me ands on. In a proper state of society I am sober, industrious and honest: in Rome, so to speak, I do as the Romans do. Wots the consequence? When trade is bad—and it's rotten bad just now—and the employers az to sack arf their men, they generally start on me.

T H E   W O M A N – Whats your name?

T H E   M A N – Price. Bronterre O'Brien Price. Usually called Snobby Price, for short.

T H E   W O M A N – Snobby's a carpenter, aint it? You said you was a painter.

P R I C E – Not that kind of snob, but the genteel sort. I'm too uppish, owing to my intelligence, and my father being a Chartist and a reading, thinking man: a stationer, too. I'm none of your common hewers of wood and drawers of water; and dont you forget it. [*He returns to his seat at the table, and takes up his mug.*] Wots your name?

T H E   W O M A N – Rummy Mitchens, sir.

P R I C E   [*quaffing the remains of his milk to her*] Your elth, Miss Mitchens.

R U M M Y   [*correcting him*] Missis Mitchens.

P R I C E – Wot! Oh Rummy, Rummy! Respectable married woman, Rummy, gittin rescued by the Salvation Army by pretendin to be a bad un. Same old game!

R U M M Y – What am I to do? I cant starve. Them Salvation lasses is dear good girls; but the better you are, the worse they likes to think you were before they rescued you. Why shouldnt they av a bit o credit, poor loves? theyre worn to rags by their work. And where would they get the money to rescue us if we was to let on we're no worse than other people? You know what ladies and gentlemen are.

PRICE—Thievin swine! Wish I ad their job, Rummy, all the same. Wot does Rummy stand for? Pet name praps?

RUMMY—Short for Romola.

PRICE—For wot!?

RUMMY—Romola. It was out of a new book. Somebody me mother wanted me to grow up like.

PRICE—We're companions in misfortune, Rummy. Both on us got names that nobody cawnt pronounce. Consequently I'm Snobby and youre Rummy because Bill and Sally wasnt good enough for our parents. Such is life!

RUMMY—Who saved you, Mr Price? Was it Major Barbara?

PRICE—No: I come here on my own. I'm going to be Bronterre O'Brien Price, the converted painter. I know wot they like. I'll tell em how I blasphemed and gambled and wopped my poor old mother—

RUMMY [*shocked*] Used you to beat your mother?

PRICE—Not likely. She used to beat me. No matter: you come and listen to the converted painter, and youll hear how she was a pious woman that taught me me prayers at er knee, an how I used to come home drunk and drag her out o bed be er snow white airs, an lam into er with the poker.

RUMMY—Thats whats so unfair to us women. Your confessions is just as big lies as ours: you dont tell what you really done no more than us; but you men can tell your lies right out at the meetins and be made much of for it; while the sort o confessions we az to make az to be wispered to one lady at a time. It aint right, spite of all their piety.

PRICE—Right! Do you spose the Army'd be allowed if it went and did right? Not much. It combs our air and makes us good little blokes to be robbed and put upon. But I'll play the game as good as any of em. I'll see somebody struck by lightnin, or hear a voice sayin 'Snobby Price: where will you spend eternity?' I'll av a time of it, I tell you.

RUMMY—You wont be let drink, though.

PRICE—I'll take it out in gorspellin, then. I dont want to drink if I can get fun enough any other way.

JENNY HILL, *a pale, overwrought, pretty Salvation lass of 18, comes in through the yard gate, leading* PETER SHIRLEY, *a half hardened, half worn-out elderly man, weak with hunger.*

JENNY [*supporting him*] Come! pluck up. I'll get you something to eat. Youll be all right then.

PRICE [*rising and hurrying officiously to take the old man off* JENNY'S *hands*] Poor old man! Cheer up, brother: youll find rest and peace and appiness ere. Hurry up with the food, miss: e's fair done. [JENNY *hurries into the shelter.*] Ere, buck up, daddy! she's fetchin y'a thick slice o breadn treacle, an a mug o skyblue.

[*He seats him at the corner of the table.*]

R U M M Y   [*gaily*] Keep up your old art! Never say die!

S H I R L E Y – I'm not an old man. I'm ony 46. I'm as good as ever I was. The grey patch come in my hair before I was thirty. All it wants is three pennorth o hair dye: am I to be turned on the streets to starve for it? Holy God! Ive worked ten to twelve hours a day since I was thirteen, and paid my way all through; and now am I to be thrown into the gutter and my job given to a young man that can do it no better than me because Ive black hair that goes white at the first change?

P R I C E   [*cheerfully*] No good jawrin about it. Youre ony a jumped-up, jerked-off, orspittle-turned-out incurable of an ole workin man: who cares about you? Eh? Make the thievin swine give you a meal: theyve stole many a one from you. Get a bit o your own back. [JENNY *returns with the usual meal.*] There you are, brother. Awsk a blessin an tuck that into you.

S H I R L E Y   [*looking at it ravenously but not touching it, and crying like a child*] I never took anything before.

J E N N Y   [*petting him*] Come, come! the Lord sends it to you: he wasnt above taking bread from his friends; and why should you be? Besides, when we find you a job you can pay us for it if you like.

S H I R L E Y   [*eagerly*] Yes, yes: thats true. I can pay you back: it's only a loan. [*Shivering.*] Oh Lord! oh Lord!

[*He turns to the table and attacks the meal ravenously.*]

J E N N Y – Well, Rummy, are you more comfortable now?

R U M M Y – God bless you, lovey! youve fed my body and saved my soul, havnt you? [JENNY, *touched, kisses her.*] Sit down and rest a bit: you must be ready to drop.

J E N N Y – Ive been going hard since morning. But theres more work than we can do. I mustnt stop.

R U M M Y – Try a prayer for just two minutes. Youll work all the better after.

J E N N Y   [*her eyes lighting up*] Oh isnt it wonderful how a few minutes prayer revives you! I was quite lightheaded at twelve o'clock, I was so tired; but Major Barbara just sent me to pray for five minutes; and I was able to go on as if I had only just begun. [*To* PRICE.] Did you have a piece of bread?

P R I C E   [*with unction*] Yes, miss; but Ive got the piece that I value more; and thats the peace that passeth hall hannerstennin.

R U M M Y   [*fervently*] Glory Hallelujah!

[BILL WALKER, *a rough customer of about 25, appears at the yard gate and looks malevolently at* JENNY.]

J E N N Y – That makes me so happy. When you say that, I feel wicked for loitering here. I must get to work again.

She is hurrying to the shelter, when the new-comer moves quickly up to the door and intercepts her. His manner is so threatening that she retreats as he comes at her truculently, driving her down the yard.

B I L L – Aw knaow you. Youre the one that took awy maw girl. Youre the one that set er agen me. Well, I'm gowin to ev er aht. Not that Aw care a carse for er or you: see? Bat Aw'll let er knaow; and Aw'll let you knaow. Aw'm gowing to give her a doin thatll teach er to cat away from me. Nah in wiv you and tell er to cam aht afore Aw came in and kick er aht. Tell er Bill Walker wants er. She'll knaow wot thet means; and if she keeps me witin itll be worse. You stop to jawr beck at me; and Aw'll stawt on you: d'ye eah? Theres your wy. In you gow. [*He takes her by the arm and slings her towards the door of the shelter. She falls on her hand and knee.* RUMMY *helps her up again.*]
P R I C E [*rising, and venturing irresolutely towards* BILL] Easy there, mate. She aint doin you no arm.
B I L L – Oo are you callin mite? [*Standing over him threateningly.*] Youre gowin to stend ap for er, aw yer? Put ap your ends.
R U M M Y [*running indignantly to him to scold him*] Oh, you great brute—

He instantly swings his left hand back against her face. She screams and reels back to the trough, where she sits down, covering her bruised face with her hands and rocking herself and moaning with pain.

J E N N Y [*going to her*] Oh, God forgive you! How could you strike an old woman like that?
B I L L [*seizing her by the hair so violently that she also screams, and tearing her away from the old woman*] You Gawd forgimme again an Aw'll Gawk forgive you one on the jawr thetll stop you pryin for a week. [*Holding her and turning fiercely on* PRICE.] Ev you ennything to sy agen it?
P R I C E [*intimidated*] No, matey: she aint anything to do with me.
B I L L – Good job for you! Aw'd pat two meals into you and fawt you with one finger arter, you stawved cur. [*To* JENNY.] Nah are you gowin to fetch aht Mog Ebbijem; or em Aw to knock your fice off you and fetch her meself?
J E N N Y [*writhing in his grasp*] Oh please someone go in and tell Major Barbara—

[*She screams again as he wrenches her head down;
and* PRICE *and* RUMMY *flee into the shelter.*]

BILL—You want to gow in and tell your Mijor of me, do you?

JENNY—Oh please dont drag my hair. Let me go.

BILL—Do you or downt you? [*She stifles a scream.*] Yus or nao?

JENNY—God give me strength—

BILL [*striking her with his fist in the face*] Gow an shaow her thet, and tell her if she wants one lawk it to cam and interfere with me. [JENNY, *crying with pain, goes into the shed. He goes to the form and addresses the old man.*] Eah: finish your mess; an git aht o maw wy.

SHIRLEY [*springing up and facing him fiercely, with the mug in his hand*] You take a liberty with me, and I'll smash you over the face with the mug and cut your eye out. Aint you satisfied—young whelps like you—with takin the bread out o the mouths of your elders that have brought you up and slaved for you, but you must come shovin and cheekin and bullyin in here, where the bread o charity is sickenin in our stummicks?

BILL [*contemptuously, but backing a little*] Wot good are you, you aold palsy mag? Wot good are you?

SHIRLEY—As good as you and better. I'll do a day's work agen you or any fat young soaker of your age. Go and take my job at Horrockses, where I worked for ten year. They want young men there: they cant afford to keep men over forty-five. Theyre very sorry—give you a character and happy to help you to get anything suited to your years—sure a steady man wont be long out of a job. Well, let em try you. Theyll find the differ. What do you know? Not as much as how to beeyave yourself—layin your dirty fist across the mouth of a respectable woman!

BILL—Downt provowk me to ly it acrost yours: d'ye eah?

SHIRLEY [*with blighting contempt*] Yes: you like an old man to hit, dont you, when youve finished with the women. I aint seen you hit a young one yet.

BILL [*stung*] You loy, you aold soupkitchener, you. There was a yang menn eah. Did Aw offer to itt him or did Aw not?

SHIRLEY—Was he starvin or was he not? Was he a man or only a crosseyed thief an a loafer? Would you hit my son-in-law's brother?

BILL—Oo's ee?

SHIRLEY—Todger Fairmile o Balls Pond. Him that won £20 off the Japanese wrastler at the music hall by standin out 17 minutes 4 seconds agen him.

BILL [*sullenly*] Aw'm nao music awl wrastler. Ken he box?

SHIRLEY—Yes: an you cant.

BILL—Wot! Aw cawnt, cawnt Aw? Wots thet you sy? [*Threatening him.*]

SHIRLEY [*not budging an inch*] Will you box Todger Fairmile if I put him on to you? Say the word.

BILL [*subsiding with a slouch*] Aw'll stend ap to enny menn alawv, if he was ten Todger Fairmawls. But Aw dont set ap to be a perfeshnal.

SHIRLEY [*looking down on him with unfathomable disdain*] You box! Slap an old woman with the back o your hand! You hadnt even the sense to hit her where a magistrate couldnt see the mark of it, you silly young lump of conceit and ignorance. Hit a girl in the jaw and ony make her cry! If Todger Fairmile'd done it, she wouldnt a got up inside o ten minutes, no more than you would if he got on to you. Yah! I'd set about you myself if I had a week's feedin in me instead o two months' starvation.

[*He turns his back on him and sits down moodily at the table.*]

BILL [*following him and stooping over him to drive the taunt in*] You loy! youve the bread and treacle in you that you cam eah to beg.

SHIRLEY [*bursting into tears*] Oh God! it's true: I'm only an old pauper on the scrap heap. [*Furiously.*] But youll come to it yourself; and then youll know. Youll come to it sooner than a teetotaller like me, fillin yourself with gin at this hour o the mornin!

BILL — Aw'm nao gin drinker, you oald lawr; bat wen Aw want to give my girl a bloomin good awdin Aw lawk to ev a bit o devil in me: see? An eah Aw emm, talkin to a rotten aold blawter like you sted o givin her wot for. [*Working himself into a rage.*] Aw'm gowin in there to fetch her aht.

[*He makes vengefully for the shelter door.*]

SHIRLEY — Youre going to the station on a stretcher, more likely; and theyll take the gin and the devil out of you there when they get you inside. You mind what youre about: the major here is the Earl o Stevenage's granddaughter.

BILL [*checked*] Garn!

SHIRLEY — Youll see.

BILL [*his resolution oozing*] Well, Aw aint dan nathin to er.

SHIRLEY — Spose she said you did! who'd believe you?

BILL [*very uneasy, skulking back to the corner of the penthouse*] Gawd! theres no jastice in this cantry. To think wot them people can do! Aw'm as good as er.

SHIRLEY — Tell her so. It's just what a fool like you would do.

BARBARA, *brisk and businesslike, comes from the shelter with a note book, and addresses herself to* SHIRLEY. BILL, *cowed, sits down in the corner on a form, and turns his back on them.*

1670

BARBARA—Good morning.

SHIRLEY [*standing up and taking off his hat*] Good morning, miss.

BARBARA—Sit down: make yourself at home. [*He hesitates; but she puts a friendly hand on his shoulder and makes him obey.*] Now then! since youve made friends with us, we want to know all about you. Names and addresses and trades.

SHIRLEY—Peter Shirley. Fitter. Chucked out two months ago because I was too old.

BARBARA [*not at all surprised*] Youd pass still. Why didnt you dye your hair?

SHIRLEY—I did. Me age come out at a coroner's inquest on me daughter.

BARBARA—Steady?

SHIRLEY—Teetotaller. Never out of a job before. Good worker. And sent to the knackers like an old horse!

BARBARA—No matter: if you did your part God will do his.

SHIRLEY [*suddenly stubborn*] My religion's no concern of anybody but myself.

BARBARA [*guessing*] I know. Secularist?

SHIRLEY [*hotly*] Did I offer to deny it?

BARBARA—Why should you? My own father's a Secularist, I think. Our Father—yours and mine—fulfils himself in many ways; and I daresay he knew what he was about when he made a Secularist of you. So buck up, Peter! we can always find a job for a steady man like you. [SHIRLEY, *disarmed and a little bewildered, touches his hat. She turns from him to* BILL.] Whats your name?

BILL [*insolently*] Wots thet to you?

BARBARA [*calmly making a note*] Afraid to give his name. Any trade?

BILL—Oo's afride to give is nime? [*Doggedly, with a sense of heroically defying the House of Lords in the person of Lord Stevenage.*] If you want to bring a chawge agen me, bring it. [*She waits, unruffled.*] Moy nime's Bill Walker.

BARBARA [*as if the name were familiar: trying to remember how*] Bill Walker? [*Recollecting.*] Oh, I know: youre the man that Jenny Hill was praying for inside just now.

[*She enters his name in her note book.*]

BILL—Oo's Jenny Ill? And wot call as she to pry for me?

BARBARA—I dont know. Perhaps it was you that cut her lip.

BILL [*defiantly*] Yus, it was me that cat her lip. Aw aint afride o you.

BARBARA—How could you be, since youre not afraid of God? Youre a brave man, Mr Walker. It takes some pluck to do our work here; but none of us dare lift our hand against a girl like that, for fear of her father in heaven.

BILL [*sullenly*] I want nan o your kentin jawr. I spowse you think Aw cam eah to beg from you, like this demmiged lot eah. Not me. Aw downt want your bread and scripe and ketlep. Aw dont blieve in your Gawd, no more than you do yourself.

BARBARA [*sunnily apologetic and ladylike, as on a new footing with him*] Oh, I beg your pardon for putting your name down, Mr Walker. I didnt understand. I'll strike it out.

BILL [*taking this as a slight, and deeply wounded by it*] Eah! you let maw nime alown. Aint it good enaff to be in your book?

BARBARA [*considering*] Well, you see, theres no use putting down your name unless I can do something for you, is there? Whats your trade?

BILL [*still smarting*] Thets nao concern o yours.

BARBARA – Just so. [*Very businesslike.*] I'll put you down as [*writing*] the man who—struck—poor little Jenny Hill—in the mouth.

BILL [*rising threateningly*] See eah. Awve ed enaff o this.

BARBARA [*quite sunny and fearless*] What did you come to us for?

BILL – Aw cam for maw gel, see? Aw cam to tike her aht o this and to brike er jawr for er.

BARBARA [*complacently*] You see I was right about your trade. [BILL, *on the point of retorting furiously, finds himself, to his great shame and terror, in danger of crying instead. He sits down again suddenly.*] Whats her name?

BILL [*dogged*] Er nime's Mog Ebbijem: thets wot her nime is.

BARBARA – Mog Habbijam! Oh, she's gone to Canning Town, to our barracks there.

BILL [*fortified by his resentment of* MOG'S *perfidy*] Is she? [*Vindictively.*] Then Aw'm gowin to Kennintahn arter her. [*He crosses to the gate; hesitates; finally comes back at* BARBARA.] Are you loyin to me to git shat o me?

BARBARA – I dont want to get shut of you. I want to keep you here and save your soul. Youd better stay: youre going to have a bad time today, Bill.

BILL – Oo's gowin to give it to me? You, preps?

BARBARA – Someone you dont believe in. But youll be glad afterwards.

BILL [*slinking off*] Aw'll gow to Kennintahn to be aht o reach o your tangue. [*Suddenly turning on her with intense malice.*] And if Aw downt fawnd Mog there, Aw'll cam beck and do two years for you, selp me Gawd if Aw downt!

BARBARA [*a shade kindlier, if possible*] It's no use, Bill. She's got another bloke.

BILL – Wot!

BARBARA – One of her own converts. He fell in love with her when he saw her with her soul saved, and her face clean, and her hair washed.

1672

BILL [*surprised*] Wottud she wash it for, the carroty slat? It's red.

BARBARA—It's quite lovely now, because she wears a new look in her eyes with it. It's a pity youre too late. The new bloke has put your nose out of joint, Bill.

BILL—Aw'll put his nowse aht o joint for him. Not that Aw care a carse for er, mawnd thet. But Aw'll teach her to drop me as if Aw was dirt. And Aw'll teach him to meddle with maw judy. Wots iz bleedin nime?

BARBARA—Sergeant Todger Fairmile.

SHIRLEY [*rising with grim joy*] I'll go with him, miss. I want to see them two meet. I'll take him to the infirmary when it's over.

BILL [*to* SHIRLEY, *with undissembled misgiving*] Is thet im you was speakin on?

SHIRLEY—Thats him.

BILL—Im that wrastled in the music awl?

SHIRLEY—The competitions at the National Sportin Club was worth nigh a hundred a year to him. He's gev em up now for religion; so he's a bit fresh for want of the exercise he was accustomed to. He'll be glad to see you. Come along.

BILL—Wots is wight?

SHIRLEY—Thirteen four.

[BILL's *last hope expires.*]

BARBARA—Go and talk to him, Bill. He'll convert you.

SHIRLEY—He'll convert your head into a mashed potato.

BILL [*sullenly*] Aw aint afride of im. Aw aint afride of ennybody. Bat e can lick me. She's dan me.

[*He sits down moodily on the edge of the horse trough.*]

SHIRLEY—You aint going. I thought not.

[*He resumes his seat.*]

BARBARA [*calling*] Jenny!

JENNY [*appearing at the shelter door with a plaster on the corner of her mouth*] Yes, Major.

BARBARA—Send Rummy Mitchens out to clear away here.

JENNY—I think she's afraid.

BARBARA [*her resemblance to her mother flashing out for a moment*] Nonsense! she must do as she's told.

JENNY [*calling into the shelter*] Rummy: the Major says you must come.

[JENNY *comes to* BARBARA, *purposely keeping on the side next* BILL, *lest he should suppose that she shrank from him or bore malice.*]

BARBARA—Poor little Jenny! Are you tired? [*Looking at the wounded cheek.*] Does it hurt?

JENNY—No: it's all right now. It was nothing.

BARBARA [*critically*] It was as hard as he could hit, I expect. Poor Bill! You dont feel angry with him, do you?

JENNY – Oh no, no, no: indeed I dont, Major, bless his poor heart!

BARBARA *kisses her; and she runs away merrily into the shelter.* BILL *writhes with an agonizing return of his new and alarming symptoms, but says nothing.* RUMMY MITCHENS *comes from the shelter.*

BARBARA [*going to meet* RUMMY] Now Rummy, bustle. Take in those mugs and plates to be washed; and throw the crumbs about for the birds.

[RUMMY *takes the three plates and mugs; but* SHIRLEY *takes back his mug from her, as there is still some milk left in it.*]

RUMMY – There aint any crumbs. This aint a time to waste good bread on birds.

PRICE [*appearing at the shelter door*] Gentleman come to see the shelter, Major. Says he's your father.

BARBARA – All right. Coming.

[SNOBBY *goes back into the shelter, followed by* BARBARA.]

RUMMY [*stealing across to* BILL *and addressing him in a subdued voice, but with intense conviction*] I'd av the lor of you, you flat eared pignosed potwalloper, if she'd let me. Youre no gentleman, to hit a lady in the face.

[BILL, *with greater things moving in him, takes no notice.*]

SHIRLEY [*following her*] Here! in with you and dont get yourself into more trouble by talking.

RUMMY [*with hauteur*] I aint ad the pleasure o being hintroduced to you, as I can remember.

[*She goes into the shelter with the plates.*]

SHIRLEY – Thats the—

BILL [*savagely*] Downt you talk to me, d'ye eah? You lea me alown, or Aw'll do you a mischief. Aw'm not dirt under your feet, ennywy.

SHIRLEY [*calmly*] Dont you be afeerd. You aint such prime company that you need expect to be sought after.

[*He is about to go into the shelter when* BARBARA *comes out, with* UNDERSHAFT *on her right.*]

BARBARA – Oh, there you are, Mr Shirley! [*Between them.*] This is my father: I told you he was a Secularist, didnt I? Perhaps youll be able to comfort one another.

UNDERSHAFT [*startled*] A Secularist! Not the least in the world: on the contrary, a confirmed mystic.

BARBARA – Sorry, I'm sure. By the way, papa, what is your religion? in case I have to introduce you again.

UNDERSHAFT – My religion? Well, my dear, I am a Millionaire. That is my religion.

BARBARA – Then I'm afraid you and Mr Shirley wont be able to comfort one another after all. Youre not a Millionaire, are you, Peter?

SHIRLEY – No; and proud of it.

UNDERSHAFT [*gravely*] Poverty, my friend, is not a thing to be proud of.

SHIRLEY [*angrily*] Who made your millions for you? Me and my like. Whats kep us poor? Keepin you rich. I wouldnt have your conscience, not for all your income.

UNDERSHAFT – I wouldnt have your income, not for all your conscience, Mr Shirley.

[*He goes to the penthouse and sits down on a form.*]

BARBARA [*stopping* SHIRLEY *adroitly as he is about to retort*] You wouldnt think he was my father, would you, Peter? Will you go into the shelter and lend the lasses a hand for a while: we're worked off our feet.

SHIRLEY [*bitterly*] Yes: I'm in their debt for a meal, aint I?

BARBARA – Oh, not because youre in their debt, but for love of them, Peter, for love of them. [*He cannot understand, and is rather scandalized.*] There! dont stare at me. In with you; and give that conscience of yours a holiday.

[*Bustling him into the shelter.*]

SHIRLEY [*as he goes in*] Ah! it's a pity you never was trained to use your reason, miss. Youd have been a very taking lecturer on Secularism.

[BARBARA *turns to her father.*]

UNDERSHAFT – Never mind me, my dear. Go about your work; and let me watch it for a while.

BARBARA – All right.

UNDERSHAFT – For instance, whats the matter with that outpatient over there?

BARBARA [*looking at* BILL, *whose attitude has never changed, and whose expression of brooding wrath has deepened*] Oh, we shall cure him in no time. Just watch. [*She goes over to* BILL *and waits. He glances up at her and casts his eyes down again, uneasy, but grimmer than ever.*] It would be nice to just stamp on Mog Habbijam's face, wouldn't it, Bill?

BILL [*starting up from the trough in consternation*] It's a loy: Aw never said so. [*She shakes her head.*] Oo taold you wot was in moy mawnd?

BARBARA – Only your new friend.

BILL – Wot new friend?

BARBARA — The devil, Bill. When he gets round people they get miserable, just like you.

BILL [*with a heartbreaking attempt at devil-may-care cheerfulness*] Aw aint miserable.

> [*He sits down again, and stretches his legs in an attempt to seem indifferent.*]

BARBARA — Well, if youre happy, why dont you look happy, as we do?

BILL [*his legs curling back in spite of him*] Aw'm eppy enaff, Aw tell you. Woy cawnt you lea me alown? Wot ev I dan to you? Aw aint smashed your fice, ev Aw?

BARBARA [*softly: wooing his soul*] It's not me thats getting at you, Bill.

BILL — Oo else is it?

BARBARA — Somebody that doesnt intend you to smash women's faces, I suppose. Somebody or something that wants to make a man of you.

BILL [*blustering*] Mike a menn o me! Aint Aw a menn? eh? Oo sez Aw'm not a menn?

BARBARA — Theres a man in you somewhere, I suppose. But why did he let you hit poor little Jenny Hill? That wasnt very manly of him, was it?

BILL [*tormented*] Ev dan wiv it, Aw tell you. Chack it. Aw'm sick o your Jenny Ill and er silly little fice.

BARBARA — Then why do you keep thinking about it? Why does it keep coming up against you in your mind? Youre not getting converted, are you?

BILL [*with conviction*] Not ME. Not lawkly.

BARBARA — Thats right, Bill. Hold out against it. Put out your strength. Dont lets get you cheap. Todger Fairmile said he wrestled for three nights against his salvation harder than he ever wrestled with the Jap at the music hall. He gave in to the Jap when his arm was going to break. But he didnt give in to his salvation until his heart was going to break. Perhaps youll escape that. You havnt any heart, have you?

BILL — Wot d'ye mean? Woy aint Aw got a awt the sime as ennybody else?

BARBARA — A man with a heart wouldnt have bashed poor little Jenny's face, would he?

BILL [*almost crying*] Ow, will you lea me alown? Ev Aw ever offered to meddle with you, that you cam neggin and provowkin me lawk this?

> [*He writhes convulsively from his eyes to his toes.*]

BARBARA [*with a steady soothing hand on his arm and a gentle voice that never lets him go*] It's your soul thats hurting you, Bill, and not me. Weve been through it all ourselves. Come with us, Bill. [*He looks wildly round.*] To brave manhood on earth and eternal glory in heaven. [*He is on the point of breaking down.*] Come. [*A drum is heard in the shelter; and* BILL, *with a gasp, escapes from the spell as* BARBARA *turns quickly.* ADOLPHUS *enters from the shelter with a big drum.*] Oh! there you are, Dolly. Let me introduce a new friend of mine, Mr Bill Walker. This is my bloke, Bill: Mr Cusins.

[CUSINS *salutes with his drumstick.*]

BILL – Gowin to merry im?

BARBARA – Yes.

BILL [*fervently*] Gawd elp im! Gaw-aw-aw-awd elp im!

BARBARA – Why? Do you think he wont be happy with me?

BILL – Awve aony ed to stend it for a mawnin: e'll ev to stend it for a lawftawm.

CUSINS – That is a frightful reflection, Mr Walker. But I cant tear myself away from her.

BILL – Well, Aw ken. [*To* BARBARA.] Eah! do you knaow where Aw'm gowin to, and wot Aw'm gowin to do?

BARBARA – Yes: youre going to heaven; and youre coming back here before the week's out to tell me so.

BILL – You loy. Aw'm gowin to Kennintahn, to spit in Todger Fairmawl's eye. Aw beshed Jenny Ill's fice; an nar Aw'll git me aown fice beshed and cam beck and shaow it to er. Ee'll itt me ardern Aw itt her. Thatll mike us square. [*To* ADOLPHUS.] Is thet fair or is it not? Youre a genlmn: you oughter knaow.

BARBARA – Two black eyes wont make one white one, Bill.

BILL – Aw didnt awst you. Cawnt you never keep your mahth shat? Oy awst the genlmn.

CUSINS [*reflectively*] Yes: I think youre right, Mr Walker. Yes: I should do it. It's curious: it's exactly what an ancient Greek would have done.

BARBARA – But what good will it do?

CUSINS – Well, it will give Mr Fairmile some exercise; and it will satisfy Mr Walker's soul.

BILL – Rot! there aint nao sach a thing as a saoul. Ah kin you tell wevver Awve a saoul or not? You never seen it.

BARBARA – Ive seen it hurting you when you went against it.

BILL [*with compressed aggravation*] If you was maw gel and took the word aht o me mahth lawk thet, Aw'd give you sathink youd feel urtin, Aw would. [*To* ADOLPHUS.] You tike maw tip, mite. Stop er jawr; or youll doy afoah your tawm. [*With intense expression.*] Wore aht: thets wot youll be: wore aht.

[*He goes away through the gate.*]

CUSINS [*looking after him*] I wonder!

BARBARA – Dolly!

Bernard Shaw

[*Indignant, in her mother's manner.*]
CUSINS–Yes, my dear, it's very wearing to be in love with you. If it lasts, I quite think I shall die young.
BARBARA–Should you mind?
CUSINS–Not at all.

He is suddenly softened, and kisses her over the drum, evidently not for the first time, as people cannot kiss over a big drum without practice. UNDERSHAFT *coughs.*

BARBARA–It's all right, papa, weve not forgotten you. Dolly: explain the place to papa: I havnt time.
[*She goes busily into the shelter.*]

UNDERSHAFT *and* ADOLPHUS *now have the yard to themselves.* UNDERSHAFT, *seated on a form, and still keenly attentive, looks hard at* ADOLPHUS. ADOLPHUS *looks hard at him.*

UNDERSHAFT–I fancy you guess something of what is in my mind, Mr Cusins. [CUSINS *flourishes his drumsticks as if in the act of beating a lively rataplan, but makes no sound.*] Exactly so. But suppose Barbara finds you out!
CUSINS–You know, I do not admit that I am imposing on Barbara. I am quite genuinely interested in the views of the Salvation Army. The fact is, I am a sort of collector of religions; and the curious thing is that I find I can believe them all. By the way, have you any religion?
UNDERSHAFT–Yes.
CUSINS–Anything out of the common?
UNDERSHAFT–Only that there are two things necessary to Salvation.
CUSINS [*disappointed, but polite*] Ah, the Church Catechism. Charles Lomax also belongs to the Established Church.
UNDERSHAFT–The two things are—
CUSINS–Baptism and—
UNDERSHAFT–No. Money and gunpowder.
CUSINS [*surprised, but interested*] That is the general opinion of our governing classes. The novelty is in hearing any man confess it.
UNDERSHAFT–Just so.
CUSINS–Excuse me: is there any place in your religion for honor, justice, truth, love, mercy and so forth?
UNDERSHAFT–Yes: they are the graces and luxuries of a rich, strong, and safe life.
CUSINS–Suppose one is forced to choose between them and money or gunpowder?

UNDERSHAFT – Choose money and gunpowder; for without enough of both you cannot afford the others.
CUSINS – That is your religion?
UNDERSHAFT – Yes.

The cadence of this reply makes a full close in the conversation, CUSINS *twists his face dubiously and contemplates* UNDERSHAFT. UNDERSHAFT *contemplates him.*

CUSINS – Barbara wont stand that. You will have to choose between your religion and Barbara.
UNDERSHAFT – So will you, my friend. She will find out that that drum of yours is hollow.
CUSINS – Father Undershaft: you are mistaken: I am a sincere Salvationist. You do not understand the Salvation Army. It is the army of joy, of love, of courage: it has banished the fear and remorse and despair of the old hell-ridden evangelical sects: it marches to fight the devil with trumpet and drum, with music and dancing, with banner and palm, as becomes a sally from heaven by its happy garrison. It picks the waster out of the public house and makes a man of him: it finds a worm wriggling in a back kitchen, and lo! a woman! Men and women of rank too, sons and daughters of the Highest. It takes the poor professor of Greek, the most artificial and self-suppressed of human creatures, from his meal of roots, and lets loose the rhapsodist in him; reveals the true worship of Dionysos to him; sends him down the public street drumming dithyrambs.
[*He plays a thundering flourish on the drum.*]
UNDERSHAFT – You will alarm the shelter.
CUSINS – Oh, they are accustomed to these sudden ecstasies. However, if the drum worries you—
[*He pockets the drumsticks; unhooks the drum; and stands it on the ground opposite the gateway.*]
UNDERSHAFT – Thank you.
CUSINS – You remember what Euripides says about your money and gunpowder?
UNDERSHAFT – No.
CUSINS [*declaiming*]
One and another
In money and guns may outpass his brother;
And men in their millions float and flow
And seethe with a million hopes as leaven;
And they win their will; or they miss their will;
And their hopes are dead or are pined for still;

But who'er can know
As the long days go
That to live is happy, has found his heaven.

My translation: what do you think of it?

UNDERSHAFT—I think, my friend, that if you wish to know, as the long days go, that to live is happy, you must first acquire money enough for a decent life, and power enough to be your own master.

CUSINS—You are damnably discouraging.

[*He resumes his declamation.*]

Is it so hard a thing to see
That the spirit of God—whate'er it be—
The law that abides and changes not, ages long,
The Eternal and Nature-born: these things be strong?
What else is Wisdom? What of Man's endeavor,
Or God's high grace so lovely and so great?
To stand from fear set free? to breathe and wait?
To hold a hand uplifted over Fate?
And shall not Barbara be loved for ever?

UNDERSHAFT—Euripides mentions Barbara, does he?

CUSINS—It is a fair translation. The word means Loveliness.

UNDERSHAFT—May I ask—as Barbara's father—how much a year she is to be loved for ever on?

CUSINS—As for Barbara's father, that is more your affair than mine. I can feed her by teaching Greek: that is about all.

UNDERSHAFT—Do you consider it a good match for her?

CUSINS [*with polite obstinacy*] Mr Undershaft: I am in many ways a weak, timid, ineffectual person; and my health is far from satisfactory. But whenever I feel that I must have anything, I get it, sooner or later. I feel that way about Barbara. I dont like marriage: I feel intensely afraid of it; and I dont know what I shall do with Barbara or what she will do with me. But I feel that I and nobody else must marry her. Please regard that as settled.—Not that I wish to be arbitrary; but why should I waste your time in discussing what is inevitable?

UNDERSHAFT—You mean that you will stick at nothing: not even the conversion of the Salvation Army to the worship of Dionysos.

CUSINS—The business of the Salvation Army is to save, not to wrangle about the name of the pathfinder. Dionysos or another: what does it matter?

UNDERSHAFT [*rising and approaching him*] Professor Cusins: you are a young man after my own heart.

CUSINS—Mr Undershaft: you are, as far as I am able to gather, a most infernal old rascal; but you appeal very strongly to my sense of ironic humor.

[UNDERSHAFT *mutely offers his hand. They shake.*]

UNDERSHAFT [*suddenly concentrating himself*] And now to business.

CUSINS – Pardon me. We are discussing religion. Why go back to such an uninteresting and unimportant subject as business?

UNDERSHAFT – Religion is our business at present, because it is through religion alone that we can win Barbara.

CUSINS – Have you, too, fallen in love with Barbara?

UNDERSHAFT – Yes, with a father's love.

CUSINS – A father's love for a grown-up daughter is the most dangerous of all infatuations. I apologize for mentioning my own pale, coy, mistrustful fancy in the same breath with it.

UNDERSHAFT – Keep to the point. We have to win her; and we are neither of us Methodists.

CUSINS – That doesnt matter. The power Barbara wields here—the power that wields Barbara herself—is not Calvinism, not Presbyterianism, not Methodism—

UNDERSHAFT – Not Greek Paganism either, eh?

CUSINS – I admit that. Barbara is quite original in her religion.

UNDERSHAFT [*triumphantly*] Aha! Barbara Undershaft would be. Her inspiration comes from within herself.

CUSINS – How do you suppose it got there?

UNDERSHAFT [*in towering excitement*] It is the Undershaft inheritance. I shall hand on my torch to my daughter. She shall make my converts and preach my gospel—

CUSINS – What! Money and gunpowder!

UNDERSHAFT – Yes, money and gunpowder. Freedom and power. Command of life and command of death.

CUSINS [*urbanely: trying to bring him down to earth*] This is extremely interesting, Mr Undershaft. Of course you know that you are mad.

UNDERSHAFT [*with redoubled force*] And you?

CUSINS – Oh, mad as a hatter. You are welcome to my secret since I have discovered yours. But I am astonished. Can a madman make cannons?

UNDERSHAFT – Would anyone else than a madman make them? And now [*with surging energy*] question for question. Can a sane man translate Euripides?

CUSINS – No.

UNDERSHAFT [*seizing him by the shoulder*] Can a sane woman make a man of a waster or a woman of a worm?

CUSINS [*reeling before the storm*] Father Colossus—Mammoth Millionaire—

UNDERSHAFT [*pressing him*] Are there two mad people or three in this Salvation shelter today?

CUSINS—You mean Barbara is as mad as we are?

UNDERSHAFT [*pushing him lightly off and resuming his equanimity suddenly and completely*] Pooh, Professor! let us call things by their proper names. I am a millionaire; you are a poet; Barbara is a savior of souls. What have we three to do with the common mob of slaves and idolators?

[*He sits down again with a shrug of contempt for the mob.*]

CUSINS—Take care! Barbara is in love with the common people. So am I. Have you never felt the romance of that love?

UNDERSHAFT [*cold and sardonic*] Have you ever been in love with Poverty, like St Francis? Have you ever been in love with Dirt, like St Simeon? Have you ever been in love with disease and suffering, like our nurses and philanthropists? Such passions are not virtues, but the most unnatural of all the vices. This love of the common people may please an earl's granddaughter and a university professor; but I have been a common man and a poor man; and it has no romance for me. Leave it to the poor to pretend that poverty is a blessing: leave it to the coward to make a religion of his cowardice by preaching humility: we know better than that. We three must stand together above the common people: how else can we help their children to climb up beside us? Barbara must belong to us, not to the Salvation Army.

CUSINS—Well, I can only say that if you think you will get her away from the Salvation Army by talking to her as you have been talking to me, you dont know Barbara.

UNDERSHAFT—My friend: I never ask for what I can buy.

CUSINS [*in a white fury*] Do I understand you to imply that you can buy Barbara?

UNDERSHAFT—No; but I can buy the Salvation Army.

CUSINS—Quite impossible.

UNDERSHAFT—You shall see. All religious organizations exist by selling themselves to the rich.

CUSINS—Not the Army. That is the Church of the poor.

UNDERSHAFT—All the more reason for buying it.

CUSINS—I dont think you quite know what the Army does for the poor.

UNDERSHAFT—Oh yes I do. It draws their teeth: that is enough for me as a man of business.

CUSINS—Nonsense! It makes them sober—

UNDERSHAFT—I prefer sober workmen. The profits are larger.

CUSINS — —honest—

UNDERSHAFT — Honest workmen are the most economical.

CUSINS — —attached to their homes—

UNDERSHAFT — So much the better: they will put up with anything sooner than change their shop.

CUSINS — —happy—

UNDERSHAFT — An invaluable safeguard against revolution.

CUSINS — —unselfish—

UNDERSHAFT — Indifferent to their own interests, which suits me exactly.

CUSINS — —with their thoughts on heavenly things—

UNDERSHAFT [*rising*] And not on Trade Unionism nor Socialism. Excellent.

CUSINS [*revolted*] You really are an infernal old rascal.

UNDERSHAFT [*indicating* PETER SHIRLEY, *who has just come from the shelter and strolled dejectedly down the yard between them*] And this is an honest man!

SHIRLEY — Yes; and what av I got by it?

[*He passes on bitterly and sits on the form, in the corner of the penthouse.*]

SNOBBY PRICE, *beaming sanctimoniously, and* JENNY HILL., *with a tambourine full of coppers, come from the shelter and go to the drum, on which* JENNY *begins to count the money.*

UNDERSHAFT [*replying to* SHIRLEY] Oh, your employers must have got a good deal by it from first to last.

He sits on the table, with one foot on the side form, CUSINS, *overwhelmed, sits down on the same form nearer the shelter.* BARBARA *comes from the shelter to the middle of the yard. She is excited and a little overwrought.*

BARBARA — Weve just had a splendid experience meeting at the other gate in Cripps's lane. Ive hardly ever seen them so much moved as they were by your confession, Mr Price.

PRICE — I could almost be glad of my past wickedness if I could believe that it would elp to keep hathers stright.

BARBARA — So it will, Snobby. How much, Jenny?

JENNY — Four and tenpence, Major.

BARBARA — Oh Snobby, if you had given your poor mother just one more kick, we should have got the whole five shillings!

PRICE – If she heard you say that, miss, she'd be sorry I didnt. But I'm glad. Oh what a joy it will be to her when she hears I'm saved!

UNDERSHAFT – Shall I contribute the odd twopence, Barbara? The millionaire's mite, eh?

[*He takes a couple of pennies from his pocket.*]

BARBARA – How did you make that twopence?

UNDERSHAFT – As usual. By selling cannons, torpedoes, submarines, and my new patent Grand Duke hand grenade.

BARBARA – Put it back in your pocket. You cant buy your salvation here for twopence: you must work it out.

UNDERSHAFT – Is twopence not enough? I can afford a little more, if you press me.

BARBARA – Two million millions would not be enough. There is bad blood on your hands; and nothing but good blood can cleanse them. Money is no use. Take it away. [*She turns to* CUSINS.] Dolly: you must write another letter for me to the papers. [*He makes a wry face.*] Yes: I know you dont like it; but it must be done. The starvation this winter is beating us: everybody is unemployed. The General says we must close this shelter if we cant get more money. I force the collections at the meetings until I am ashamed: dont I, Snobby?

PRICE – It's a fair treat to see you work it, miss. The way you got them up from three-and-six to four-and-ten with that hymn, penny by penny and verse by verse, was a caution. Not a Cheap Jack on Mile End Waste could touch you at it.

BARBARA – Yes; but I wish we could do without it. I am getting at last to think more of the collection than of the people's souls. And what are those hatfuls of pence and halfpence? We want thousands! tens of thousands! hundreds of thousands! I want to convert people, not to be always begging for the Army in a way I'd die sooner than beg for myself.

UNDERSHAFT [*in profound irony*] Genuine unselfishness is capable of anything, my dear.

BARBARA [*unsuspectingly, as she turns away to take the money from the drum and put it in a cash bag she carries*] Yes, isnt it?

[UNDERSHAFT *looks sardonically at* CUSINS.]

CUSINS [*aside to* UNDERSHAFT] Mephistopheles! Machiavelli!

BARBARA [*tears coming into her eyes as she ties the bag and pockets it*] How are we to feed them? I cant talk religion to a man with bodily hunger in his eyes. [*Almost breaking down.*] It's frightful.

JENNY [*running to her*] Major, dear—

BARBARA [*rebounding*] No: dont comfort me. It will be all right. We shall get the money.

UNDERSHAFT – How?

J E N N Y – By praying for it, of course. Mrs Baines says she prayed for it last night; and she has never prayed for it in vain: never once.

[*She goes to the gate and looks out into the street.*]

B A R B A R A [*who has dried her eyes and regained her composure*] By the way, dad, Mrs Baines has come to march with us to our big meeting this afternoon; and she is very anxious to meet you, for some reason or other. Perhaps she'll convert you.

U N D E R S H A F T – I shall be delighted, my dear.

J E N N Y [*at the gate: excitedly*] Major! Major! heres that man back again.

B A R B A R A – What man?

J E N N Y – The man that hit me. Oh, I hope he's coming back to join us.

BILL WALKER, *with frost on his jacket, comes through the gate, his hands deep in his pockets and his chin sunk between his shoulders, like a cleaned-out gambler. He halts between* BARBARA *and the drum.*

B A R B A R A – Hullo, Bill! Back already!

B I L L [*nagging at her*] Bin talkin ever sence, ev you?

B A R B A R A – Pretty nearly. Well, has Todger paid you out for poor Jenny's jaw?

B I L L – Nao e aint.

B A R B A R A – I thought your jacket looked a bit snowy.

B I L L – Sao it is snaowy. You want to knaow where the snaow cam from, downt you?

B A R B A R A – Yes.

B I L L – Well, it cam from orf the grahnd in Pawkinses Corner in Kennintahn. It got rabbed orf be maw shaoulders: see?

B A R B A R A – Pity you didnt rub some off with your knees, Bill! That would have done you a lot of good.

B I L L [*with sour mirthless humor*] Aw was sivin anather menn's knees at the tawm. E was kneelin on moy ed, e was.

J E N N Y – Who was kneeling on your head?

B I L L – Todger was. E was pryin for me: pryin camfortable wiv me as a cawpet. Sow was Mog. Sao was the aol bloomin meetin. Mog she sez 'Ow Lawd brike is stabborn sperrit; bat downt urt is dear art.' Thet was wot she said. 'Downt urt is dear art'! An er blowk—thirteen stun four!—kneelin wiv all is wight on me. Fanny, aint it?

J E N N Y – Oh no. We're so sorry, Mr Walker.

B A R B A R A [*enjoying it frankly*] Nonsense! of course it's funny. Served you right, Bill! You must have done something to him first.

B I L L [*doggedly*] Aw did wot Aw said Aw'd do. Aw spit in is eye. E looks ap at the skoy and sez, 'Ow that Aw should be fahnd worthy to

1685

be spit upon for the gospel's sike!' e sez; an Mog sez 'Glaory Allelloo-lier!'; an then e called me Braddher, an dahned me as if Aw was a kid and e was me mather worshin me a Setterda nawt. Aw ednt jast nao shaow wiv im at all. Arf the street pryed; an the tather arf larfed fit to split theirselves. [*To* BARBARA.] There! are you settisfawd nah?

BARBARA [*her eyes dancing*] Wish I'd been there, Bill.

BILL – Yus: youd a got in a hextra bit o talk on me, wouldnt you?

JENNY – I'm so sorry, Mr Walker.

BILL [*fiercely*] Downt you gow being sorry for me: youve no call. Listen eah. Aw browk your jawr.

JENNY – No, it didnt hurt me: indeed it didnt, except for a moment. It was only that I was frightened.

BILL – Aw downt want to be forgive be you, or be ennybody. Wot Aw did Aw'll py for. Aw trawd to gat me aown jawr browk to settisfaw you—

JENNY [*distressed*] Oh no—

BILL [*impatiently*] Tell y' Aw did: cawnt you listen to wots bein taold you? All Aw got be it was bein mide a sawt of in the pablic street for me pines. Well, if Aw cawnt settisfaw you one wy, Aw ken anather. Listen eah! Aw ed two quid sived agen the frost; an Awve a pahnd of it left. A mite o mawn last week ed words with the judy e's gowing to merry. E give er wot-for; an e's bin fawnd fifteen bob. E ed a rawt to itt er cause they was gowin to be merrid; but Aw ednt nao rawt to itt you; sao put anather fawv bob on an call it a pahnd's worth. [*He pro-duces a sovereign.*] Eahs the manney. Tike it; and lets ev no more o your forgivin an prying and your Mijor jawrin me. Let wot Aw dan be dan an pide for; and let there be a end of it.

JENNY – Oh, I couldnt take it, Mr Walker. But if you would give a shilling or two to poor Rummy Mitchens! you really did hurt her; and she's old.

BILL [*contemptuously*] Not lawkly. Aw'd give her anather as soon as look at er. Let her ev the lawr o me as she threatened! She aint for-given me: not mach. Wot Aw dan to er is not on me mawnd—wot she [*indicating* BARBARA] mawt call on me conscience—no more than stickin a pig. It's this Christian gime o yours that Aw wownt ev plyed agen me: this bloomin forgivin an neggin an jawrin that mikes a menn thet sore that iz lawf's a burdn to im. Aw wownt ev it, Aw tell you; sao tike your manney and stop thraowin your silly beshed fice hap agen me.

JENNY – Major: may I take a little of it for the Army?

BARBARA – No: the Army is not to be bought. We want your soul, Bill; and we'll take nothing less.

BILL [*bitterly*] Aw knaow. Me an maw few shillins is not good enaff

for you. Youre a earl's grendorter, you are. Nathink less than a andered
pahnd for you.

UNDERSHAFT – Come, Barbara! you could do a great deal of good with
a hundred pounds. If you will set this gentleman's mind at ease by
taking his pound, I will give the other ninety-nine.

[BILL, *dazed by such opulence, instinctively touches his cap.*]

BARBARA – Oh, youre too extravagant, papa. Bill offers twenty pieces
of silver. All you need offer is the other ten. That will make the standard price to buy anybody who's for sale. I'm not; and the Army's not.
[*To* BILL.] Youll never have another quiet moment, Bill, until you
come round to us. You cant stand out against your salvation.

BILL [*sullenly*] Aw cawnt stend aht agen music awl wrastlers and
awtful tangued women. Awve offered to py. Aw can do no more. Tike it
or leave it. There it is.

He throws the sovereign on the drum, and sits down on the horse-trough.
The coin fascinates SNOBBY PRICE, *who takes an early opportunity of drop-*
ping his cap on it.

MRS BAINES *comes from the shelter. She is dressed as a Salvation Army*
Commissioner. She is an earnest looking woman of about 40, with a
caressing, urgent voice, and an appealing manner.

BARBARA – This is my father, Mrs Baines. [UNDERSHAFT *comes from*
the table, taking his hat off with marked civility.] Try what you can
do with him. He wont listen to me, because he remembers what a fool
I was when I was a baby.

[*She leaves them together and chats with* JENNY.]

MRS BAINES – Have you been shewn over the shelter, Mr Undershaft?
You know the work we're doing, of course.

UNDERSHAFT [*very civilly*] The whole nation knows it, Mrs Baines.

MRS BAINES – No, sir: the whole nation does not know it, or we
should not be crippled as we are for want of money to carry our work
through the length and breadth of the land. Let me tell you that there
would have been rioting this winter in London but for us.

UNDERSHAFT – You really think so?

MRS BAINES – I know it. I remember 1886, when you rich gentlemen hardened your hearts against the cry of the poor. They broke the
windows of your clubs in Pall Mall.

UNDERSHAFT [*gleaming with approval of their method*] And the
Mansion House Fund went up next day from thirty thousand pounds
to seventy-nine thousand! I remember quite well.

MRS BAINES – Well, wont you help me to get at the people? They
wont break windows then. Come here, Price. Let me shew you to this

gentleman. [PRICE *comes to be inspected.*] Do you remember the window breaking?

PRICE — My ole father thought it was the revolution, maam.

MRS BAINES — Would you break windows now?

PRICE — Oh no, maam. The windows of eaven av bin opened to me. I know now that the rich man is a sinner like myself.

RUMMY [*appearing above at the loft door*] Snobby Price!

SNOBBY — Wot is it?

RUMMY — Your mother's askin for you at the other gate in Cripps's Lane. She's heard about your confession. [PRICE *turns pale.*]

MRS BAINES — Go, Mr Price; and pray with her.

JENNY — You can go through the shelter, Snobby.

PRICE [*to* MRS BAINES] I couldnt face her now, maam, with all the weight of my sins fresh on me. Tell her she'll find her son at ome, waitin for her in prayer.

[*He skulks off through the gate, incidentally stealing the sovereign on his way out by picking up his cap from the drum.*]

MRS BAINES [*with swimming eyes*] You see how we take the anger and the bitterness against you out of their hearts, Mr Undershaft.

UNDERSHAFT — It is certainly most convenient and gratifying to all large employers of labor, Mrs Baines.

MRS BAINES — Barbara: Jenny: I have good news: most wonderful news. [JENNY *runs to her.*] My prayers have been answered. I told you they would, Jenny, didnt I?

JENNY — Yes, yes.

BARBARA [*moving nearer to the drum*] Have we got money enough to keep the shelter open?

MRS BAINES — I hope we shall have enough to keep all the shelters open. Lord Saxmundham has promised us five thousand pounds—

BARBARA — Hooray!

JENNY — Glory!

MRS BAINES — —if—

BARBARA — 'If!' If what?

MRS BAINES — —if five other gentlemen will give a thousand each to make it up to ten thousand.

BARBARA — Who is Lord Saxmundham? I never heard of him.

UNDERSHAFT [*who has pricked up his ears at the peer's name, and is now watching* BARBARA *curiously*] A new creation, my dear. You have heard of Sir Horace Bodger?

BARBARA — Bodger! Do you mean the distiller? Bodger's whisky!

UNDERSHAFT — That is the man. He is one of the greatest of our public benefactors. He restored the cathedral at Hakington. They made him a baronet for that. He gave half a million to the funds of his party: they made him a baron for that.

SHIRLEY – What will they give him for the five thousand?

UNDERSHAFT – There is nothing left to give him. So the five thousand, I should think, is to save his soul.

MRS BAINES – Heaven grant it may! Oh Mr Undershaft, you have some very rich friends. Cant you help us towards the other five thousand? We are going to hold a great meeting this afternoon at the Assembly Hall in the Mile End Road. If I could only announce that one gentleman had come forward to support Lord Saxmundham, others would follow. Dont you know somebody? couldnt you? wouldnt you? [*Her eyes fill with tears.*] Oh, think of those poor people, Mr Undershaft: think of how much it means to them, and how little to a great man like you.

UNDERSHAFT [*sardonically gallant*] Mrs Baines: you are irresistible. I cant disappoint you; and I cant deny myself the satisfaction of making Bodger pay up. You shall have your five thousand pounds.

MRS BAINES – Thank God!

UNDERSHAFT – You dont thank me?

MRS BAINES – Oh sir, dont try to be cynical: dont be ashamed of being a good man. The Lord will bless you abundantly; and our prayers will be like a strong fortification round you all the days of your life. [*With a touch of caution.*] You will let me have the cheque to shew at the meeting, wont you? Jenny: go in and fetch a pen and ink.

[JENNY *runs to the shelter door.*]

UNDERSHAFT – Do not disturb Miss Hill: I have a fountain pen.

[JENNY *halts. He sits at the table and writes the cheque.* CUSINS *rises to make room for him. They all watch him silently.*]

BILL [*cynically, aside to* BARBARA, *his voice and accent horribly debased*] Wot prawce selvytion nah?

BARBARA – Stop. [UNDERSHAFT *stops writing: they all turn to her in surprise.*] Mrs Baines: are you really going to take this money?

MRS BAINES [*astonished*] Why not, dear?

BARBARA – Why not! Do you know what my father is? Have you forgotten that Lord Saxmundham is Bodger the whisky man? Do you remember how we implored the County Council to stop him from writing Bodger's Whisky in letters of fire against the sky; so that the poor drink-ruined creatures on the Embankment could not wake up from their snatches of sleep without being reminded of their deadly thirst by that wicked sky sign? Do you know that the worst thing I have had to fight here is not the devil, but Bodger, Bodger, Bodger, with his whisky, his distilleries, and his tied houses? Are you going to make our shelter another tied house for him, and ask me to keep it?

BILL – Rotten dranken whisky it is too.

MRS BAINES – Dear Barbara: Lord Saxmundham has a soul to be saved like any of us. If heaven has found the way to make a good use of his money, are we to set ourselves up against the answer to our prayers?

BARBARA – I know he has a soul to be saved. Let him come down here; and I'll do my best to help him to his salvation. But he wants to send his cheque down to buy us, and go on being as wicked as ever.

UNDERSHAFT [*with a reasonableness which* CUSINS *alone perceives to be ironical*] My dear Barbara: alcohol is a very necessary article. It heals the sick—

BARBARA – It does nothing of the sort.

UNDERSHAFT – Well, it assists the doctor: that is perhaps a less questionable way of putting it. It makes life bearable to millions of people who could not endure their existence if they were quite sober. It enables Parliament to do things at eleven at night that no sane person would do at eleven in the morning. Is it Bodger's fault that this inestimable gift is deplorably abused by less than one per cent of the poor?

[*He turns again to the table; signs the cheque; and crosses it.*]

MRS BAINES – Barbara: will there be less drinking or more if all those poor souls we are saving come tomorrow and find the doors of our shelters shut in their faces? Lord Saxmundham gives us the money to stop drinking—to take his own business from him.

CUSINS [*impishly*] Pure self-sacrifice on Bodger's part, clearly! Bless dear Bodger!

[BARBARA *almost breaks down as* ADOLPHUS, *too, fails her.*]

UNDERSHAFT [*tearing out the cheque and pocketing the book as he rises and goes past* CUSINS *to* MRS BAINES] I also, Mrs Baines, may claim a little disinterestedness. Think of my business! think of the widows and orphans! the men and lads torn to pieces with shrapnel and poisoned with lyddite! [MRS BAINES *shrinks; but he goes on remorselessly.*] the oceans of blood, not one drop of which is shed in a really just cause! the ravaged crops! the peaceful peasants forced, women and men, to till their fields under the fire of opposing armies on pain of starvation! the bad blood of the fierce little cowards at home who egg on others to fight for the gratification of their national vanity! All this makes money for me: I am never richer, never busier than when the papers are full of it. Well, it is your work to preach peace on earth and good will to men. [MRS BAINES'S *face lights up again.*] Every convert you make is a vote against war. [*Her lips move in prayer.*] Yet I give you this money to help you to hasten my own commercial ruin.

[*He gives her the cheque.*]

CUSINS [*mounting the form in an ecstasy of mischief*] The millennium will be inaugurated by the unselfishness of Undershaft and Bodger. Oh be joyful!

[*He takes the drum-sticks from his pocket and flourishes them.*]

MRS BAINES [*taking the cheque*] The longer I live the more proof I see that there is an Infinite Goodness that turns everything to the work of salvation sooner or later. Who would have thought that any good could have come out of war and drink? And yet their profits are brought today to the feet of salvation to do its blessed work.

[*She is affected to tears.*]

JENNY [*running to* MRS BAINES *and throwing her arms round her*] Oh dear! how blessed, how glorious it all is!

CUSINS [*in a convulsion of irony*] Let us seize this unspeakable moment. Let us march to the great meeting at once. Excuse me just an instant.

[*He rushes into the shelter.* JENNY *takes her tambourine from the drum head.*]

MRS BAINES – Mr Undershaft: have you ever seen a thousand people fall on their knees with one impulse and pray? Come with us to the meeting. Barbara shall tell them that the Army is saved, and saved through you.

CUSINS [*returning impetuously from the shelter with a flag and a trombone, and coming between* MRS BAINES *and* UNDERSHAFT] You shall carry the flag down the first street, Mrs Baines. [*He gives her the flag.*] Mr Undershaft is a gifted trombonist: he shall intone an Olympian diapason to the West Ham Salvation March. [*Aside to* UNDERSHAFT, *as he forces the trombone on him.*] Blow, Machiavelli, blow.

UNDERSHAFT [*aside to him, as he takes the trombone*] The trumpet in Zion! [CUSINS *rushes to the drum, which he takes up and puts on.* UNDERSHAFT *continues, aloud.*] I will do my best. I could vamp a bass if I knew the tune.

CUSINS – It is a wedding chorus from one of Donizetti's operas; but we have converted it. We convert everything to good here, including Bodger. You remember the chorus. 'For thee immense rejoicing—immenso giubilo—immenso giubilo.' [*With drum obbligato.*] Rum tum ti tum tum, tum tum ti ta—

BARBARA – Dolly: you are breaking my heart.

CUSINS – What is a broken heart more or less here? Dionysos Undershaft has descended. I am possessed.

MRS BAINES – Come, Barbara: I must have my dear Major to carry the flag with me.

JENNY – Yes, yes, Major darling.

CUSINS [*snatches the tambourine out of* JENNY's *hand and mutely offers it to* BARBARA]

BARBARA [*coming forward a little as she puts the offer behind her with a shudder, whilst* CUSINS *recklessly tosses the tambourine back to* JENNY *and goes to the gate*] I cant come.

JENNY – Not come!

MRS BAINES [*with tears in her eyes*] Barbara: do you think I am wrong to take the money?

BARBARA [*impulsively going to her and kissing her*] No, no: God help you, dear, you must: you are saving the Army. Go; and may you have a great meeting!

JENNY – But arnt you coming?

BARBARA – No.

[*She begins taking off the silver S brooch from her collar.*]

MRS BAINES – Barbara: what are you doing?

JENNY – Why are you taking your badge off? You cant be going to leave us, Major.

BARBARA [*quietly*] Father: come here.

UNDERSHAFT [*coming to her*] My dear!

[*Seeing that she is going to pin the badge on his collar, he retreats to the penthouse in some alarm.*]

BARBARA [*following him*] Dont be frightened. [*She pins the badge on and steps back towards the table, shewing him to the others.*] There! It's not much for £5000, is it?

MRS BAINES – Barbara: if you wont come and pray with us, promise me you will pray for us.

BARBARA – I cant pray now. Perhaps I shall never pray again.

MRS BAINES – Barbara!

JENNY – Major!

BARBARA [*almost delirious*] I cant bear any more. Quick march!

CUSINS [*calling to the procession in the street outside*] Off we go. Play up, there! Immenso giubilo.

He gives the time with his drum; and the band strikes up the march, which rapidly becomes more distant as the procession moves briskly away.

MRS BAINES – I must go, dear. Youre overworked: you will be all right tomorrow. We'll never lose you. Now Jenny: step out with the old flag. Blood and Fire!

[*She marches out through the gate with her flag.*]

JENNY – Glory Hallelujah!

[*Flourishing her tambourine and marching.*]

UNDERSHAFT [*to* CUSINS, *as he marches out past him easing the slide of his trombone*] 'My ducats and my daughter'!

CUSINS [*following him out*] Money and gunpowder!

BARBARA – Drunkenness and Murder! My God: why hast thou forsaken me?

[*She sinks on the form with her face buried in her hands. The march passes away into silence.* BILL WALKER *steals across to her.*]

BILL [*taunting*] Wot prawce selvytion nah?

SHIRLEY – Dont you hit her when she's down.

BILL – She itt me wen aw wiz dahn. Waw shouldnt Aw git a bit o me aown beck?

BARBARA [*raising her head*] I didnt take your money, Bill.

[*She crosses the yard to the gate and turns her back on the two men to hide her face from them.*]

BILL [*sneering after her*] Naow, it warnt enaff for you. [*Turning to the drum, he misses the money.*] Ellow! If you aint took it sammun else ez. Weres it gorn? Bly me if Jenny Ill didnt tike it arter all!

RUMMY [*screaming at him from the loft*] You lie, you dirty blackguard! Snobby Price pinched it off the drum when he took up his cap. I was up here all the time an see im do it.

BILL – Wot! Stowl maw manney! Waw didnt you call thief on him, you silly aold macker you?

RUMMY – To serve you aht for ittin me acrost the fice. It's cost y'pahnd, that az. [*Raising a pœan of squalid triumph.*] I done you. I'm even with you. Uve ad it aht o y—

BILL *snatches up* SHIRLEY'S *mug and hurls it at her. She slams the loft door and vanishes. The mug smashes against the door and falls in fragments.*

BILL [*beginning to chuckle*] Tell us, aol menn, wot o'clock this mawnin was it wen im as they call Snobby Prawce was sived?

BARBARA [*turning to him more composedly, and with unspoiled sweetness*] About half past twelve, Bill. And he pinched your pound at a quarter to two. *I* know. Well, you cant afford to lose it. I'll send it to you.

BILL [*his voice and accent suddenly improving*] Not if Aw wiz to stawve for it. Aw aint to be bought.

SHIRLEY – Aint you? Youd sell yourself to the devil for a pint o beer; only there aint no devil to make the offer.

BILL [*unashamed*] Sao Aw would, mite, and often ev, cheerful. But she cawnt baw me. [*Approaching* BARBARA.] You wanted maw saoul, did you? Well, you aint got it.

B A R B A R A — I nearly got it, Bill. But weve sold it back to you for ten thousand pounds.

S H I R L E Y — And dear at the money!

B A R B A R A — No, Peter: it was worth more than money.

B I L L [*salvationproof*] It's nao good: you cawnt get rahnd me nah. Aw downt blieve in it; and Awve seen tody that Aw was rawt. [*Going.*] Sao long, aol soupkitchener! Ta, ta, Mijor Earl's Grendorter! [*Turning at the gate.*] Wot prawce selvytion nah? Snobby Prawce! Ha! ha!

B A R B A R A [*offering her hand*] Goodbye, Bill.

B I L L [*taken aback, half plucks his cap off; then shoves it on again defiantly*] Git aht. [B A R B A R A *drops her hand, discouraged. He has a twinge of remorse.*] But thets aw rawt, you knaow. Nathink pasnl. Naow mellice. Sao long, Judy.

[*He goes.*]

B A R B A R A — No malice. So long, Bill.

S H I R L E Y [*shaking his head*] You make too much of him, miss, in your innocence.

B A R B A R A [*going to him*] Peter: I'm like you now. Cleaned out, and lost my job.

S H I R L E Y — Youve youth an hope. Thats two better than me.

B A R B A R A — I'll get you a job, Peter. Thats hope for you: the youth will have to be enough for me. [*She counts her money.*] I have just enough left for two teas at Lockharts, a Rowton doss for you, and my tram and bus home. [*He frowns and rises with offended pride. She takes his arm.*] Dont be proud, Peter: it's sharing between friends. And promise me youll talk to me and not let me cry.

[*She draws him towards the gate.*]

S H I R L E Y — Well, I'm not accustomed to talk to the like of you—

B A R B A R A [*urgently*] Yes, yes: you must talk to me. Tell me about Tom Paine's books and Bradlaugh's lectures. Come along.

S H I R L E Y — Ah, if you would only read Tom Paine in the proper spirit, miss!

[*They go out through the gate together.*]

ACT THREE

Next day after lunch LADY BRITOMART *is writing in the library in Wilton Crescent.* SARAH *is reading in the armchair near the window.* BARBARA, *in ordinary fashionable dress, pale and brooding, is on the settee.* CHARLES LOMAX *enters. He starts on seeing* BARBARA *fashionably attired and in low spirits.*

LOMAX—Youve left off your uniform!

[BARBARA *says nothing; but an expression of pain passes over her face.*]

LADY BRITOMART [*warning him in low tones to be careful*] Charles!

LOMAX [*much concerned, coming behind the settee and bending sympathetically over* BARBARA] I'm awfully sorry, Barbara. You know I helped you all I could with the concertina and so forth. [*Momentously.*] Still, I have never shut my eyes to the fact that there is a certain amount of tosh about the Salvation Army. Now the claims of the Church of England—

LADY BRITOMART—Thats enough, Charles. Speak of something suited to your mental capacity.

LOMAX—But surely the Church of England is suited to all our capacities.

BARBARA [*pressing his hand*] Thank you for your sympathy, Cholly. Now go and spoon with Sarah.

LOMAX [*dragging a chair from the writing table and seating himself affectionately by* SARAH's *side*] How is my ownest today?

SARAH—I wish you wouldnt tell Cholly to do things, Barbara. He always comes straight and does them. Cholly: we're going to the works this afternoon.

LOMAX—What works?

SARAH—The cannon works.

LOMAX—What? your governor's shop!

SARAH—Yes.

LOMAX—Oh I say!

[CUSINS *enters in poor condition. He also starts visibly when he sees* BARBARA *without her uniform.*]

1695

BARBARA – I expected you this morning, Dolly. Didnt you guess that?

CUSINS [*sitting down beside her*] I'm sorry. I have only just break-fasted.

SARAH – But weve just finished lunch.

BARBARA – Have you had one of your bad nights?

CUSINS – No: I had rather a good night: in fact, one of the most re-markable nights I have ever passed.

BARBARA – The meeting?

CUSINS – No: after the meeting.

LADY BRITOMART – You should have gone to bed after the meeting. What were you doing?

CUSINS – Drinking.

LADY BRITOMART –	Adolphus!
SARAH –	Dolly!
BARBARA –	Dolly!
LOMAX –	Oh I say!

LADY BRITOMART – What were you drinking, may I ask?

CUSINS – A most devilish kind of Spanish burgundy, warranted free from added alcohol: a Temperance burgundy in fact. Its richness in natural alcohol made any addition superfluous.

BARBARA – Are you joking, Dolly?

CUSINS [*patiently*] No. I have been making a night of it with the nominal head of this household: that is all.

LADY BRITOMART – Andrew made you drunk!

CUSINS – No: he only provided the wine. I think it was Dionysos who made me drunk. [*To* BARBARA.] I told you I was possessed.

LADY BRITOMART – Youre not sober yet. Go home to bed at once.

CUSINS – I have never before ventured to reproach you, Lady Brit; but how could you marry the Prince of Darkness?

LADY BRITOMART – It was much more excusable to marry him than to get drunk with him. That is a new accomplishment of Andrew's, by the way. He usent to drink.

CUSINS – He doesnt now. He only sat there and completed the wreck of my moral basis, the rout of my convictions, the purchase of my soul. He cares for you, Barbara. That is what makes him so dangerous to me.

BARBARA – That has nothing to do with it, Dolly. There are larger loves and diviner dreams than the fireside ones. You know that, dont you?

CUSINS – Yes: that is our understanding. I know it. I hold to it. Unless he can win me on that holier ground he may amuse me for a while; but he can get no deeper hold, strong as he is.

BARBARA – Keep to that; and the end will be right. Now tell me what happened at the meeting?

CUSINS – It was an amazing meeting. Mrs Baines almost died of emotion. Jenny Hill simply gibbered with hysteria. The Prince of Darkness played his trombone like a madman: its brazen roarings were like the laughter of the damned. 117 conversions took place then and there. They prayed with the most touching sincerity and gratitude for Bodger, and for the anonymous donor of the £5000. Your father would not let his name be given.

LOMAX – That was rather fine of the old man, you know. Most chaps would have wanted the advertisement.

CUSINS – He said all the charitable institutions would be down on him like kites on a battle-field if he gave his name.

LADY BRITOMART – Thats Andrew all over. He never does a proper thing without giving an improper reason for it.

CUSINS – He convinced me that I have all my life been doing improper things for proper reasons.

LADY BRITOMART – Adolphus: now that Barbara has left the Salvation Army, you had better leave it too. I will not have you playing that drum in the streets.

CUSINS – Your orders are already obeyed, Lady Brit.

BARBARA – Dolly: were you ever really in earnest about it? Would you have joined if you had never seen me?

CUSINS [*disingenuously*] Well—er—well, possibly, as a collector of religions—

LOMAX [*cunningly*] Not as a drummer, though, you know. You are a very clearheaded brainy chap, Dolly; and it must have been apparent to you that there is a certain amount of tosh about—

LADY BRITOMART – Charles: if you must drivel, drivel like a grown-up man and not like a schoolboy.

LOMAX [*out of countenance*] Well, drivel is drivel, dont you know, whatever a man's age.

LADY BRITOMART – In good society in England, Charles, men drivel at all ages by repeating silly formulas with an air of wisdom. Schoolboys make their own formulas out of slang, like you. When they reach your age, and get political private secretaryships and things of that sort, they drop slang and get their formulas out of the Spectator or The Times. You had better confine yourself to The Times. You will find that there is a certain amount of tosh about The Times; but at least its language is reputable.

LOMAX [*overwhelmed*] You are so awfully strong-minded, Lady Brit—

LADY BRITOMART – Rubbish! [MORRISON *comes in.*] What is it?

MORRISON – If you please, my lady, Mr Undershaft has just drove up to the door.

LADY BRITOMART – Well, let him in. [MORRISON *hesitates.*] Whats the matter with you?

MORRISON – Shall I announce him, my lady; or is he at home here, so to speak, my lady?

LADY BRITOMART – Announce him.

MORRISON – Thank you, my lady. You wont mind my asking, I hope. The occasion is in a manner of speaking new to me.

LADY BRITOMART – Quite right. Go and let him in.

MORRISON – Thank you, my lady.

[*He withdraws.*]

LADY BRITOMART – Children: go and get ready. [SARAH *and* BARBARA *go upstairs for their out-of-door wraps.*] Charles: go and tell Stephen to come down here in five minutes: you will find him in the drawing room. [CHARLES *goes.*] Adolphus: tell them to send round the carriage in about fifteen minutes.

[ADOLPHUS *goes.*]

MORRISON [*at the door*] Mr Undershaft.

[UNDERSHAFT *comes in.* MORRISON *goes out.*]

UNDERSHAFT – Alone! How fortunate!

LADY BRITOMART [*rising*] Dont be sentimental, Andrew. Sit down. [*She sits on the settee: he sits beside her, on her left. She comes to the point before he has time to breathe.*] Sarah must have £800 a year until Charles Lomax comes into his property. Barbara will need more, and need it permanently, because Adolphus hasnt any property.

UNDERSHAFT [*resignedly*] Yes, my dear: I will see to it. Anything else? for yourself, for instance?

LADY BRITOMART – I want to talk to you about Stephen.

UNDERSHAFT [*rather wearily*] Dont, my dear. Stephen doesnt interest me.

LADY BRITOMART – He does interest me. He is our son.

UNDERSHAFT – Do you really think so? He has induced us to bring him into the world; but he chose his parents very incongruously, I think. I see nothing of myself in him, and less of you.

LADY BRITOMART – Andrew: Stephen is an excellent son, and a most steady, capable, highminded young man. You are simply trying to find an excuse for disinheriting him.

UNDERSHAFT – My dear Biddy: the Undershaft tradition disinherits him. It would be dishonest of me to leave the cannon foundry to my son.

LADY BRITOMART – It would be most unnatural and improper of you to leave it to anyone else, Andrew. Do you suppose this wicked

1698

and immoral tradition can be kept up for ever? Do you pretend that Stephen could not carry on the foundry just as well as all the other sons of the big business houses?

UNDERSHAFT—Yes: he could learn the office routine without understanding the business, like all the other sons; and the firm would go on by its own momentum until the real Undershaft—probably an Italian or a German—would invent a new method and cut him out.

LADY BRITOMART—There is nothing that any Italian or German could do that Stephen could not do. And Stephen at least has breeding.

UNDERSHAFT—The son of a foundling! Nonsense!

LADY BRITOMART—My son, Andrew! And even you may have good blood in your veins for all you know.

UNDERSHAFT—True. Probably I have. That is another argument in favour of a foundling.

LADY BRITOMART—Andrew: dont be aggravating. And dont be wicked. At present you are both.

UNDERSHAFT—This conversation is part of the Undershaft tradition, Biddy. Every Undershaft's wife has treated him to it ever since the house was founded. It is mere waste of breath. If the tradition be ever broken it will be for an abler man than Stephen.

LADY BRITOMART [*pouting*] Then go away.

UNDERSHAFT [*deprecatory*] Go away!

LADY BRITOMART—Yes: go away. If you will do nothing for Stephen, you are not wanted here. Go to your foundling, whoever he is; and look after him.

UNDERSHAFT—The fact is, Biddy—

LADY BRITOMART—Dont call me Biddy. I dont call you Andy.

UNDERSHAFT—I will not call my wife Britomart: it is not good sense. Seriously, my love, the Undershaft tradition has landed me in a difficulty. I am getting on in years; and my partner Lazarus has at last made a stand and insisted that the succession must be settled one way or the other; and of course he is quite right. You see, I havent found a fit successor yet.

LADY BRITOMART [*obstinately*] There is Stephen.

UNDERSHAFT—Thats just it: all the foundlings I can find are exactly like Stephen.

LADY BRITOMART—Andrew!!

UNDERSHAFT—I want a man with no relations and no schooling: that is, a man who would be out of the running altogether if he were not a strong man. And I cant find him. Every blessed foundling nowadays is snapped up in his infancy by Barnardo homes, or School Board officers, or Boards of Guardians; and if he shews the least ability he is fastened on by schoolmasters; trained to win scholarships like a racehorse; crammed with secondhand ideas; drilled and disciplined in docility and what they call good taste; and lamed for life so that he is fit for nothing but teaching. If you want to keep the foundry in the family, you had better find an eligible foundling and marry him to Barbara.

LADY BRITOMART – Ah! Barbara! Your pet! You would sacrifice Stephen to Barbara.

UNDERSHAFT – Cheerfully. And you, my dear, would boil Barbara to make soup for Stephen.

LADY BRITOMART – Andrew: this is not a question of our likings and dislikings: it is a question of duty. It is your duty to make Stephen your successor.

UNDERSHAFT – Just as much as it is your duty to submit to your husband. Come, Biddy! these tricks of the governing class are of no use with me. I am one of the governing class myself; and it is waste of time giving tracts to a missionary. I have the power in this matter; and I am not to be humbugged into using it for your purposes.

LADY BRITOMART – Andrew: you can talk my head off; but you cant change wrong into right. And your tie is all on one side. Put it straight.

UNDERSHAFT [*disconcerted*] It wont stay unless it's pinned.
[*He fumbles at it with childish grimaces.*]
[STEPHEN *comes in.*]

STEPHEN [*at the door*] I beg your pardon. [*About to retire.*]

LADY BRITOMART – No: come in, Stephen.
[STEPHEN *comes forward to his mother's writing table.*]

UNDERSHAFT [*not very cordially*] Good afternoon.

STEPHEN [*coldly*] Good afternoon.

UNDERSHAFT [*to* LADY BRITOMART] He knows all about the tradition, I suppose?

LADY BRITOMART – Yes. [*To* STEPHEN.] It is what I told you last night, Stephen.

UNDERSHAFT [*sulkily*] I understand you want to come into the cannon business.

STEPHEN – I go into trade! Certainly not.

UNDERSHAFT [*opening his eyes, greatly eased in mind and manner*] Oh! in that case—

LADY BRITOMART – Cannons are not trade, Stephen. They are enterprise.

STEPHEN – I have no intention of becoming a man of business in any sense. I have no capacity for business and no taste for it. I intend to devote myself to politics.

UNDERSHAFT [*rising*] My dear boy: this is an immense relief to me.

1700

And I trust it may prove an equally good thing for the country. I was afraid you would consider yourself disparaged and slighted.

[*He moves towards* STEPHEN *as if to shake hands with him.*]

LADY BRITOMART [*rising and interposing*] Stephen: I cannot allow you to throw away an enormous property like this.

STEPHEN [*stiffly*] Mother: there must be an end of treating me as a child, if you please. [LADY BRITOMART *recoils, deeply wounded by his tone.*] Until last night I did not take your attitude seriously, because I did not think you meant it seriously. But I find now that you left me in the dark as to matters which you should have explained to me years ago. I am extremely hurt and offended. Any further discussion of my intentions had better take place with my father, as between one man and another.

LADY BRITOMART—Stephen!

[*She sits down again, her eyes filling with tears.*]

UNDERSHAFT [*with grave compassion*] You see, my dear, it is only the big men who can be treated as children.

STEPHEN—I am sorry, mother, that you have forced me—

UNDERSHAFT [*stopping him*] Yes, yes, yes, yes: thats all right, Stephen. She wont interfere with you any more: your independence is achieved: you have won your latchkey. Don't rub it in; and above all, don't apologize. [*He resumes his seat.*] Now what about your future, as between one man and another—I beg your pardon, Biddy: as between two men and a woman.

LADY BRITOMART [*who has pulled herself together strongly*] I quite understand, Stephen. By all means go your own way if you feel strong enough.

[STEPHEN *sits down magisterially in the chair at the writing table with an air of affirming his majority.*]

UNDERSHAFT—It is settled that you do not ask for the succession to the cannon business.

STEPHEN—I hope it is settled that I repudiate the cannon business.

UNDERSHAFT—Come, come! dont be so devilishly sulky: it's boyish. Freedom should be generous. Besides, I owe you a fair start in life in exchange for disinheriting you. You cant become prime minister all at once. Havnt you a turn for something? What about literature, art, and so forth?

STEPHEN—I have nothing of the artist about me, either in faculty or character, thank Heaven!

UNDERSHAFT—A philosopher, perhaps? Eh?

STEPHEN—I make no such ridiculous pretension.

UNDERSHAFT—Just so. Well, there is the army, the navy, the Church, the Bar. The Bar requires some ability. What about the Bar?

STEPHEN—I have not studied law. And I am afraid I have not the necessary push—I believe that is the name barristers give to their vulgarity—for success in pleading.

UNDERSHAFT—Rather a difficult case, Stephen. Hardly anything left but the stage, is there? [STEPHEN *makes an impatient movement.*] Well, come! is there anything you know or care for?

STEPHEN [*rising and looking at him steadily*] I know the difference between right and wrong.

UNDERSHAFT [*Hugely tickled*] You dont say so! What! no capacity for business, no knowledge of law, no sympathy with art, no pretension to philosophy; only a simple knowledge of the secret that has puzzled all the philosophers, baffled all the lawyers, muddled all the men of business, and ruined most of the artists: the secret of right and wrong. Why, man, youre a genius, a master of masters, a god! At twentyfour, too!

STEPHEN [*keeping his temper with difficulty*] You are pleased to be facetious. I pretend to nothing more than any honorable English gentleman claims as his birthright.

[*He sits down angrily.*]

UNDERSHAFT—Oh, thats everybody's birthright. Look at poor little Jenny Hill, the Salvation lassie! she would think you were laughing at her if you asked her to stand up in the street and teach grammar or geography or mathematics or even drawing room dancing; but it never occurs to her to doubt that she can teach morals and religion. You are all alike, you respectable people. You cant tell me the bursting strain of a ten-inch gun, which is a very simple matter; but you all think you can tell me the bursting strain of a man under temptation. You darent handle high explosives; but youre all ready to handle honesty and truth and justice and the whole duty of man, and kill one another at that game. What a country! What a world!

LADY BRITOMART [*uneasily*] What do you think he had better do, Andrew?

UNDERSHAFT—Oh, just what he wants to do. He knows nothing and he thinks he knows everything. That points clearly to a political career. Get him a private secretaryship to someone who can get him an Under Secretaryship; and then leave him alone. He will find his natural and proper place in the end on the Treasury Bench.

STEPHEN [*springing up again*] I am sorry, sir, that you force me to forget the respect due to you as my father. I am an Englishman and I will not hear the Government of my country insulted.

[*He thrusts his hands in his pockets, and walks angrily across to the window.*]

UNDERSHAFT [*with a touch of brutality*] The government of your country! *I* am the government of your country: I, and Lazarus. Do you suppose that you and half a dozen amateurs like you, sitting in a row in that foolish gabble shop, can govern Undershaft and Lazarus? No, my friend: you will do what pays us. You will make war when it suits us, and keep peace when it doesnt. You will find out that trade requires certain measures when we have decided on those measures. When I want anything to keep my dividends up, you will discover that my want is a national need. When other people want something to keep my dividends down, you will call out the police and military. And in return you shall have the support and applause of my newspapers, and the delight of imagining that you are a great statesman. Government of your country! Be off with you, my boy, and play with your caucuses and leading articles and historic parties and great leaders and burning questions and the rest of your toys. *I* am going back to my counting-house to pay the piper and call the tune.

STEPHEN [*actually smiling, and putting his hand on his father's shoulder with indulgent patronage*] Really, my dear father, it is impossible to be angry with you. You dont know how absurd all this sounds to me. You are very properly proud of having been industrious enough to make money; and it is greatly to your credit that you have made so much of it. But it has kept you in circles where you are valued for your money and deferred to for it, instead of in the doubtless very old-fashioned and behind-the-times public school and university where I formed my habits of mind. It is natural for you to think that money governs England; but you must allow me to think I know better.

UNDERSHAFT—And what does govern England, pray?

STEPHEN—Character, father, character.

UNDERSHAFT—Whose character? Yours or mine?

STEPHEN—Neither yours nor mine, father, but the best elements in the English national character.

UNDERSHAFT—Stephen: Ive found your profession for you. Youre a born journalist. I'll start you with a high-toned weekly review. There!

Before STEPHEN *can reply* SARAH, BARBARA, LOMAX, *and* CUSINS *come in ready for walking.* BARBARA *crosses the room to the window and looks out.* CUSINS *drifts amiably to the armchair.* LOMAX *remains near the door, whilst* SARAH *comes to her mother.*

STEPHEN *goes to the smaller writing table and busies himself with his letters.*

SARAH—Go and get ready, mamma: the carriage is waiting.

[LADY BRITOMART *leaves the room.*]

1703

UNDERSHAFT [*to* SARAH] Good day, my dear. Good afternoon, Mr Lomax.

LOMAX [*vaguely*] Ahdedoo.

UNDERSHAFT [*to* CUSINS] Quite well after last night, Euripides, eh?

CUSINS – As well as can be expected.

UNDERSHAFT – Thats right. [*To* BARBARA.] So you are coming to see my death and devastation factory, Barbara?

BARBARA [*at the window*] You came yesterday to see my salvation factory. I promised you a return visit.

LOMAX [*coming forward between* SARAH *and* UNDERSHAFT] Youll find it awfully interesting. Ive been through the Woolwich Arsenal; and it gives you a ripping feeling of security, you know, to think of the lot of beggars we could kill if it came to fighting. [*To* UNDERSHAFT, *with sudden solemnity*.] Still, it must be rather an awful reflection for you, from the religious point of view as it were. Youre getting on, you know, and all that.

SARAH – You dont mind Cholly's imbecility, papa, do you?

LOMAX [*much taken aback*] Oh I say!

UNDERSHAFT – Mr Lomax looks at the matter in a very proper spirit, my dear.

LOMAX – Just so. Thats all I meant, I assure you.

SARAH – Are you coming, Stephen?

STEPHEN – Well, I am rather busy—er— [*Magnanimously*] Oh well, yes: I'll come. That is, if there is room for me.

UNDERSHAFT – I can take two with me in a little motor I am experimenting with for field use. You wont mind its being rather unfashionable. It's not painted yet; but it's bullet proof.

LOMAX [*appalled at the prospect of confronting* Wilton Crescent *in an unpainted motor*] Oh I say!

SARAH – The carriage for me, thank you. Barbara doesnt mind what she's seen in.

LOMAX – I say, Dolly, old chap: do you really mind the car being a guy? Because of course if you do I'll go in it. Still—

CUSINS – I prefer it.

LOMAX – Thanks awfully, old man. Come, my ownest.

[*He hurries out to secure his seat in the carriage.* SARAH *follows him.*]

CUSINS [*moodily walking across to* LADY BRITOMART's *writing table*] Why are we two coming to this Works Department of Hell? that is what I ask myself.

BARBARA – I have always thought of it as a sort of pit where lost creatures with blackened faces stirred up smoky fires and were driven and tormented by my father? Is it like that, dad?

1704

UNDERSHAFT [*scandalized*] My dear! It is a spotlessly clean and beautiful hillside town.

CUSINS–With a Methodist chapel? Oh do say theres a Methodist chapel.

UNDERSHAFT–There are two: a Primitive one and a sophisticated one. There is even an Ethical Society; but it is not much patronized, as my men are all strongly religious. In the High Explosives Sheds they object to the presence of Agnostics as unsafe.

CUSINS–And yet they dont object to you!

BARBARA–Do they obey all your orders?

UNDERSHAFT–I never give them any orders. When I speak to one of them it is 'Well, Jones, is the baby doing well? and has Mrs Jones made a good recovery?' 'Nicely, thank you, sir.' And thats all.

CUSINS–But Jones has to be kept in order. How do you maintain discipline among your men?

UNDERSHAFT–I dont. They do. You see, the one thing Jones wont stand is any rebellion from the man under him, or any assertion of social equality between the wife of the man with 4 shillings a week less than himself, and Mrs Jones! Of course they all rebel against me, theoretically. Practically, every man of them keeps the man just below him in his place. I never meddle with them. I never bully them. I dont even bully Lazarus. I say that certain things are to be done; but I dont order anybody to do them. I dont say, mind you, that there is no ordering about and snubbing and even bullying. The men snub the boys and order them about; the carmen snub the sweepers; the artisans snub the unskilled laborers; the foremen drive and bully both the laborers and artisans; the assistant engineers find fault with the foremen; the chief engineers drop on the assistants; the departmental managers worry the chiefs; and the clerks have tall hats and hymnbooks and keep up the social tone by refusing to associate on equal terms with anybody. The result is a colossal profit, which comes to me.

CUSINS [*revolted*] You really are a—well, what I was saying yesterday.

BARBARA–What was he saying yesterday?

UNDERSHAFT–Never mind, my dear. He thinks I have made you unhappy. Have I?

BARBARA–Do you think I can be happy in this vulgar silly dress? I! who have worn the uniform. Do you understand what you have done to me? Yesterday I had a man's soul in my hand. I set him in the way of life with his face to salvation. But when we took your money he turned back to drunkenness and derision. [*With intense conviction.*] I will never forgive you that. If I had a child, and you destroyed its body with your explosives—if you murdered Dolly with your horrible guns— I could forgive you if my forgiveness would open the gates of heaven to

1705

you. But to take a human soul from me, and turn it into the soul of a wolf! that is worse than any murder.

UNDERSHAFT – Does my daughter despair so easily? Can you strike a man to the heart and leave no mark on him?

BARBARA [*her face lighting up*] Oh, you are right: he can never be lost now: where was my faith?

CUSINS – Oh, clever clever devil!

BARBARA – You may be a devil; but God speaks through you sometimes. [*She takes her father's hands and kisses them.*] You have given me back my happiness: I feel it deep down now, though my spirit is troubled.

UNDERSHAFT – You have learnt something. That always feels at first as if you had lost something.

BARBARA – Well, take me to the factory of death; and let me learn something more. There must be some truth or other behind all this frightful irony. Come, Dolly. [*She goes out.*]

CUSINS – My guardian angel! [*To* UNDERSHAFT] Avaunt!

[*He follows* BARBARA.]

STEPHEN [*quietly, at the writing table*] You must not mind Cusins, father. He is a very amiable good fellow; but he is a Greek scholar and naturally a little eccentric.

UNDERSHAFT – Ah, quite so. Thank you, Stephen. Thank you.

[*He goes out.*]

STEPHEN *smiles patronizingly; buttons his coat responsibly; and crosses the room to the door.* LADY BRITOMART, *dressed for out-of-doors, opens it before he reaches it. She looks round for others; looks at* STEPHEN; *and turns to go without a word.*

STEPHEN [*embarrassed*] Mother—

LADY BRITOMART – Dont be apologetic, Stephen. And dont forget that you have outgrown your mother.

[*She goes out.*]

Perivale St Andrews lies between two Middlesex hills, half climbing the northern one. It is an almost smokeless town of white walls, roofs of narrow green slates or red tiles, tall trees, domes, campaniles, and slender chimney shafts, beautifully situated and beautiful in itself. The best view of it is obtained from the crest of a slope about half a mile to the east, where the high explosives are dealt with. The foundry lies hidden in the depths between, the tops of its chimneys sprouting like huge skittles into the middle distance. Across the crest runs an emplacement of concrete, with a firestep, and a parapet which suggests a fortification, because there is a huge cannon of the obsolete Woolwich Infant pattern peering across it at the town. The cannon is mounted on an experimental gun carriage: possibly the original model of the Undershaft disappearing rampart gun alluded to by STEPHEN. *The firestep, being a convenient place to sit, is furnished here and there with straw disc cushions; and at one place there is the additional luxury of a fur rug.*

BARBARA *is standing on the firestep, looking over the parapet towards the town. On her right is the cannon; on her left the end of a shed raised on piles, with a ladder of three or four steps up to the door, which opens outwards and has a little wooden landing at the threshold, with a fire bucket in the corner of the landing. Several dummy soldiers more or less mutilated, with straw protruding from their gashes, have been shoved out of the way under the landing. A few others are nearly upright against the shed; and one has fallen forward and lies, like a grotesque corpse, on the emplacement. The parapet stops short of the shed, leaving a gap which is the beginning of the path down the hill through the foundry to the town. The rug is on the firestep near this gap. Down on the emplacement behind the cannon is a trolley carrying a huge conical bombshell with a red band painted on it. Further to the right is the door of an office, which, like the sheds, is of the lightest possible construction.*

CUSINS *arrives by the path from the town.*

BARBARA – Well?

CUSINS – Not a ray of hope. Everything perfect! wonderful! real! It only needs a cathedral to be a heavenly city instead of a hellish one.

BARBARA – Have you found out whether they have done anything for old Peter Shirley?

CUSINS – They have found him a job as gatekeeper and timekeeper. He's frightfully miserable. He calls the time-keeping brainwork, and says he isnt used to it; and his gate lodge is so splendid that he's ashamed to use the rooms, and skulks in the scullery.

BARBARA – Poor Peter!

[STEPHEN *arrives from the town. He carries a fieldglass.*]

STEPHEN [*enthusiastically*] Have you two seen the place? Why did you leave us?

CUSINS – I wanted to see everything I was not intended to see; and Barbara wanted to make the men talk.

STEPHEN – Have you found anything discreditable?

CUSINS – No. They call him Dandy Andy and are proud of his being a cunning old rascal; but it's all horribly, frightfully, immorally, unanswerably perfect.

[SARAH *arrives.*]

S A R A H – Heavens! what a place! [*She crosses to the trolley.*] Did you see the nursing home!?

[*She sits down on the shell.*]

S T E P H E N – Did you see the libraries and schools!?

S A R A H – Did you see the ball room and the banqueting chamber in the Town Hall!?

S T E P H E N – Have you gone into the insurance fund, the pension fund, the building society, the various applications of cooperation!?

[UNDERSHAFT *comes from the office, with a sheaf of telegrams in his hand.*]

U N D E R S H A F T – Well, have you seen everything? I'm sorry I was called away. [*Indicating the telegrams.*] Good news from Manchuria.

S T E P H E N – Another Japanese victory?

U N D E R S H A F T – Oh, I dont know. Which side wins does not concern us here. No: the good news is that the aerial battleship is a tremendous success. At the first trial it has wiped out a fort with three hundred soldiers in it.

C U S I N S [*from the platform*] Dummy soldiers?

U N D E R S H A F T [*striding across to* STEPHEN *and kicking the prostrate dummy brutally out of his way*] No: the real thing.

CUSINS *and* BARBARA *exchange glances. Then* CUSINS *sits on the step and buries his face in his hands.* BARBARA *gravely lays her hand on his shoulder. He looks up at her in whimsical desperation.*

U N D E R S H A F T – Well, Stephen, what do you think of the place?

S T E P H E N – Oh, magnificent. A perfect triumph of modern industry. Frankly, my dear father, I have been a fool: I had no idea of what it all meant: of the wonderful forethought, the power of organization, the administrative capacity, the financial genius, the colossal capital it represents. I have been repeating to myself as I came through your streets 'Peace hath her victories no less renowned than War.' I have only one misgiving about it all.

U N D E R S H A F T – Out with it.

S T E P H E N – Well, I cannot help thinking that all this provision for every want of your workmen may sap their independence and weaken their sense of responsibility. And greatly as we enjoyed our tea at that splendid restaurant—how they gave us all that luxury and cake and jam and cream for threepence I really cannot imagine!—still you must remember that restaurants break up home life. Look at the continent, for instance! Are you sure so much pampering is really good for the men's characters?

U N D E R S H A F T – Well you see, my dear boy, when you are organizing

1708

civilization you have to make up your mind whether trouble and anxiety are good things or not. If you decide that they are, then, I take it, you simply dont organize civilization; and there you are, with trouble and anxiety enough to make us all angels! But if you decide the other way, you may as well go through with it. However, Stephen, our characters are safe here. A sufficient dose of anxiety is always provided by the fact that we may be blown to smithereens at any moment.

SARAH – By the way, papa, where do you make the explosives?

UNDERSHAFT – In separate little sheds, like that one. When one of them blows up, it costs very little; and only the people quite close to it are killed.

STEPHEN, *who is quite close to it, looks at it rather scaredly, and moves away quickly to the cannon. At the same moment the door of the shed is thrown abruptly open; and a foreman in overalls and list slippers comes out on the little landing and holds the door for* LOMAX, *who appears in the doorway.*

LOMAX [*with studied coolness*] My good fellow: you neednt get into a state of nerves. Nothing's going to happen to you; and I suppose it wouldnt be the end of the world if anything did. A little bit of British pluck is what you want, old chap.

[*He descends and strolls across to* SARAH.]

UNDERSHAFT [*to the foreman*] Anything wrong, Bilton?

BILTON [*with ironic calm*] Gentleman walked into the high explosives shed and lit a cigaret, sir: thats all.

UNDERSHAFT – Ah, quite so. [*Going over to* LOMAX.] Do you happen to remember what you did with the match?

LOMAX – Oh come! I'm not a fool. I took jolly good care to blow it out before I chucked it away.

BILTON – The top of it was red hot inside, sir.

LOMAX – Well, suppose it was! I didnt chuck it into any of your messes.

UNDERSHAFT – Think no more of it, Mr Lomax. By the way, would you mind lending me your matches.

LOMAX [*offering his box*] Certainly.

UNDERSHAFT – Thanks.

[*He pockets the matches.*]

LOMAX [*lecturing to the company generally*] You know, these high explosives dont go off like gunpowder, except when theyre in a gun. When theyre spread loose, you can put a match to them without the least risk: they just burn quietly like a bit of paper. [*Warming to the scientific interest of the subject*] Did you know that, Undershaft? Have you ever tried?

UNDERSHAFT – Not on a large scale, Mr Lomax. Bilton will give you a sample of gun cotton when you are leaving if you ask him. You can experiment with it at home.

[BILTON *looks puzzled.*]

SARAH – Bilton will do nothing of the sort, papa. I suppose it's your business to blow up the Russians and Japs; but you might really stop short of blowing up poor Cholly. [BILTON *gives it up and retires into the shed.*]

LOMAX – My ownest, there is no danger.

[*He sits beside her on the shell.*]

[LADY BRITOMART *arrives from the town with a bouquet.*]

LADY BRITOMART [*impetuously*] Andrew: you shouldnt have let me see this place.

UNDERSHAFT – Why, my dear?

LADY BRITOMART – Never mind why: you shouldnt have: thats all. To think of all that [*indicating the town*] being yours! and that you have kept it to yourself all these years!

UNDERSHAFT – It does not belong to me. I belong to it. It is the Undershaft inheritance.

LADY BRITOMART – It is not. Your ridiculous cannons and that noisy banging foundry may be the Undershaft inheritance; but all that plate and linen, all that furniture and those houses and orchards and gardens belong to us. They belong to me: they are not a man's business. I wont give them up. You must be out of your senses to throw them all away; and if you persist in such folly, I will call in a doctor.

UNDERSHAFT [*stooping to smell the bouquet*] Where did you get the flowers, my dear?

LADY BRITOMART – Your men presented them to me in your William Morris Labor Church.

CUSINS – Oh! It needed only that. A Labor Church!

[*He mounts the firestep distractedly, and leans with his elbows on the parapet, turning his back to them.*]

LADY BRITOMART – Yes, with Morris's words in mosaic letters ten feet high round the dome. No MAN IS GOOD ENOUGH TO BE ANOTHER'S MASTER. The cynicism of it!

UNDERSHAFT – It shocked the men at first, I am afraid. But now they take no more notice of it than of the ten commandments in church.

LADY BRITOMART – Andrew: you are trying to put me off the subject of the inheritance by profane jokes. Well, you shant. I dont ask it any longer for Stephen: he has inherited far too much of your perversity to be fit for it. But Barbara has rights as well as Stephen. Why should not Adolphus succeed to the inheritance? I could manage the town for him; and he can look after the cannons, if they are really necessary.

UNDERSHAFT—I should ask nothing better if Adolphus were a foundling. He is exactly the sort of new blood that is wanted in English business. But he's not a foundling; and theres an end of it.

[*He makes for the office door.*]

CUSINS [*turning to them*] Not quite. [*They all turn and stare at him.*] I think—Mind! I am not committing myself in any way as to my future course—but I think the foundling difficulty can be got over.

[*He jumps down to the emplacement.*]

UNDERSHAFT [*coming back to him*] What do you mean?

CUSINS—Well, I have something to say which is in the nature of a confession.

SARAH—
LADY BRITOMART— } Confession!
BARBARA—
STEPHEN—

LOMAX—Oh I say!

CUSINS—Yes, a confession. Listen, all. Until I met Barbara I thought myself in the main an honorable, truthful man, because I wanted the approval of my conscience more than I wanted anything else. But the moment I saw Barbara, I wanted her far more than the approval of my conscience.

LADY BRITOMART—Adolphus!

CUSINS—It is true. You accused me yourself, Lady Brit, of joining the Army to worship Barbara; and so I did. She bought my soul like a flower at a street corner; but she bought it for herself.

UNDERSHAFT—What! Not for Dionysos or another?

CUSINS—Dionysos and all the others are in herself. I adored what was divine in her, and was therefore a true worshipper. But I was romantic about her too. I thought she was a woman of the people, and that a marriage with a professor of Greek would be far beyond the wildest social ambitions of her rank.

LADY BRITOMART—Adolphus!!

LOMAX—Oh I say!!!

CUSINS—When I learnt the horrible truth—

LADY BRITOMART—What do you mean by the horrible truth, pray?

CUSINS—That she was enormously rich; that her grandfather was an earl; that her father was the Prince of Darkness—

UNDERSHAFT—Chut!

CUSINS——and that I was only an adventurer trying to catch a rich wife, then I stooped to deceive her about my birth.

BARBARA [*rising*] Dolly!

LADY BRITOMART—Your birth! Now Adolphus, dont dare to make up a wicked story for the sake of these wretched cannons. Remember: I have seen photographs of your parents; and the Agent General for South Western Australia knows them personally and has assured me that they are most respectable married people.

CUSINS—So they are in Australia; but here they are outcasts. Their marriage is legal in Australia, but not in England. My mother is my father's deceased wife's sister; and in this island I am consequently a foundling.

[*Sensation.*]

BARBARA—Silly!

[*She climbs to the cannon, and leans, listening, in the angle it makes with the parapet.*]

CUSINS—Is the subterfuge good enough, Machiavelli?

UNDERSHAFT [*thoughtfully*] Biddy: this may be a way out of the difficulty.

LADY BRITOMART—Stuff! A man cant make cannons any the better for being his own cousin instead of his proper self.

[*She sits down on the rug with a bounce that expresses her downright contempt for their casuistry.*]

UNDERSHAFT [*to* CUSINS] You are an educated man. That is against the tradition.

CUSINS—Once in ten thousand times it happens that the schoolboy is a born master of what they try to teach him. Greek has not destroyed my mind: it has nourished it. Besides, I did not learn it at an English public school.

UNDERSHAFT—Hm! Well, I cannot afford to be too particular: you have cornered the foundling market. Let it pass. You are eligible, Euripides: you are eligible.

BARBARA—Dolly: yesterday morning, when Stephen told us all about the tradition, you became very silent; and you have been strange and excited ever since. Were you thinking of your birth then?

CUSINS—When the finger of Destiny suddenly points at a man in the middle of his breakfast, it makes him thoughtful.

UNDERSHAFT—Aha! You have had your eye on the business, my young friend, have you?

CUSINS—Take care! There is an abyss of moral horror between me and your accursed aerial battleships.

UNDERSHAFT—Never mind the abyss for the present. Let us settle the practical details and leave your final decision open. You know that you will have to change your name. Do you object to that?

CUSINS—Would any man named Adolphus—any man called Dolly!—object to be called something else?

UNDERSHAFT—Good. Now, as to money! I propose to treat you handsomely from the beginning. You shall start at a thousand a year.

CUSINS [*with sudden heat, his spectacles twinkling with mischief*] A thousand! You dare offer a miserable thousand to the son-in-law of a millionaire! No, by Heavens, Machiavelli! you shall not cheat me. You cannot do without me; and I can do without you. I must have two thousand five hundred a year for two years. At the end of that time, if I am a failure, I go. But if I am a success, and stay on, you must give me the other five thousand.

UNDERSHAFT—What other five thousand?

CUSINS—To make the two years up to five thousand a year. The two thousand five hundred is only half pay in case I should turn out a failure. The third year I must have ten per cent on the profits.

UNDERSHAFT [*taken aback*] Ten per cent! Why, man, do you know what my profits are?

CUSINS—Enormous, I hope: otherwise I shall require twenty-five per cent.

UNDERSHAFT—But, Mr Cusins, this is a serious matter of business. You are not bringing any capital into the concern.

CUSINS—What! no capital! Is my mastery of Greek no capital? Is my access to the subtlest thought, the loftiest poetry yet attained by humanity, no capital? My character! my intellect! my life! my career! what Barbara calls my soul! are these no capital? Say another word; and I double my salary.

UNDERSHAFT—Be reasonable—

CUSINS [*peremptorily*] Mr Undershaft: you have my terms. Take them or leave them.

UNDERSHAFT [*recovering himself*] Very well. I note your terms; and I offer you half.

CUSINS [*disgusted*] Half!

UNDERSHAFT [*firmly*] Half.

CUSINS—You call yourself a gentleman; and you offer me half!!

UNDERSHAFT—I do not call myself a gentleman; but I offer you half.

CUSINS—This to your future partner! your successor! your son-in-law!

BARBARA—You are selling your own soul, Dolly, not mine. Leave me out of the bargain, please.

UNDERSHAFT—Come! I will go a step further for Barbara's sake. I will give you three fifths; but that is my last word.

CUSINS—Done!

LOMAX—Done in the eye! Why, *I* get only eight hundred, you know.

CUSINS—By the way, Mac, I am a classical scholar, not an arithmetical one. Is three fifths more than half or less?

UNDERSHAFT—More, of course.

CUSINS—I would have taken two hundred and fifty. How you can succeed in business when you are willing to pay all that money to a University don who is obviously not worth a junior clerk's wages!—well! What will Lazarus say?

UNDERSHAFT—Lazarus is a gentle romantic Jew who cares for nothing but string quartets and stalls at fashionable theatres. He will be blamed for your rapacity in money matters, poor fellow! as he has hitherto been blamed for mine. You are a shark of the first order, Euripides. So much the better for the firm!

BARBARA—Is the bargain closed, Dolly? Does your soul belong to him now?

CUSINS—No: the price is settled: that is all. The real tug of war is still to come. What about the moral question?

LADY BRITOMART—There is no moral question in the matter at all, Adolphus. You must simply sell cannons and weapons to people whose cause is right and just, and refuse them to foreigners and criminals.

UNDERSHAFT [*determinedly*] No: none of that. You must keep the true faith of an Armorer, or you dont come in here.

CUSINS—What on earth is the true faith of an Armorer?

UNDERSHAFT—To give arms to all men who offer an honest price for them, without respect of persons or principles: to aristocrat and republican, to Nihilist and Tsar, to Capitalist and Socialist, to Protestant and Catholic, to burglar and policeman, to black man, white man and yellow man, to all sorts and conditions, all nationalities, all faiths, all follies, all causes and all crimes. The first Undershaft wrote up in his shop IF GOD GAVE THE HAND, LET NOT MAN WITHHOLD THE SWORD. The second wrote up ALL HAVE THE RIGHT TO FIGHT: NONE HAVE THE RIGHT TO JUDGE. The third wrote up TO MAN THE WEAPON: TO HEAVEN THE VICTORY. The fourth had no literary turn; so he did not write up anything; but he sold cannons to Napoleon under the nose of George the Third. The fifth wrote up PEACE SHALL NOT PREVAIL SAVE WITH A SWORD IN HER HAND. The sixth, my master, was the best of all. He wrote up NOTHING IS EVER DONE IN THIS WORLD UNTIL MEN ARE PREPARED TO KILL ONE ANOTHER IF IT IS NOT DONE. After that, there was nothing left for the seventh to say. So he wrote up, simply, UNASHAMED.

CUSINS—My good Machiavelli, I shall certainly write something up on the wall; only, as I shall write it in Greek, you wont be able to read it. But as to your Armorer's faith, if I take my neck out of the noose of my own morality I am not going to put it into the noose of yours. I shall sell cannons to whom I please and refuse them to whom I please. So there!

UNDERSHAFT – From the moment when you become Andrew Undershaft, you will never do as you please again. Dont come here lusting for power, young man.

CUSINS – If power were my aim I should not come here for it. You have no power.

UNDERSHAFT – None of my own, certainly.

CUSINS – I have more power than you, more will. You do not drive this place: it drives you. And what drives the place?

UNDERSHAFT [*enigmatically*] A will of which I am a part.

BARBARA [*startled*] Father! Do you know what you are saying; or are you laying a snare for my soul?

CUSINS – Dont listen to his metaphysics, Barbara. The place is driven by the most rascally part of society, the money hunters, the pleasure hunters, the military promotion hunters; and he is their slave.

UNDERSHAFT – Not necessarily. Remember the Armorer's Faith. I will take an order from a good man as cheerfully as from a bad one. If you good people prefer preaching and shirking to buying my weapons and fighting the rascals, dont blame me. I can make cannons: I cannot make courage and conviction. Bah! you tire me, Euripides, with your morality mongering. Ask Barbara: she understands. [*He suddenly reaches up and takes* BARBARA's *hands, looking powerfully into her eyes.*] Tell him, my love, what power really means.

BARBARA [*hypnotized*] Before I joined the Salvation Army, I was in my own power; and the consequence was that I never knew what to do with myself. When I joined it, I had not time enough for all the things I had to do.

UNDERSHAFT [*approvingly*] Just so. And why was that, do you suppose?

BARBARA – Yesterday I should have said, because I was in the power of God. [*She resumes her self-possession, withdrawing her hands from his with a power equal to his own.*] But you came and shewed me that I was in the power of Bodger and Undershaft. Today I feel—oh! how can I put it into words? Sarah: do you remember the earthquake at Cannes, when we were little children?—how little the surprise of the first shock mattered compared to the dread and horror of waiting for the second? That is how I feel in this place today. I stood on the rock I thought eternal; and without a word of warning it reeled and crumbled under me. I was safe with an infinite wisdom watching me, an army marching to Salvation with me; and in a moment, at a stroke of your pen in a cheque book, I stood alone; and the heavens were empty. That was the first shock of the earthquake: I am waiting for the second.

1715

UNDERSHAFT—Come, come, my daughter! dont make too much of your little tinpot tragedy. What do we do here when we spend years of work and thought and thousands of pounds of solid cash on a new gun or an aerial battleship that turns out just a hairsbreadth wrong after all? Scrap it. Scrap it without wasting another hour or another pound on it. Well, you have made for yourself something that you call a morality or a religion or what not. It doesnt fit the facts. Well, scrap it. Scrap it and get one that does fit. That is what is wrong with the world at present. It scraps its obsolete steam engines and dynamos; but it wont scrap its old prejudices and its old moralities and its old religions and its old political constitutions. Whats the result? In machinery it does very well; but in morals and religion and politics it is working at a loss that brings it nearer bankruptcy every year. Dont persist in that folly. If your old religion broke down yesterday, get a newer and a better one for tomorrow.

BARBARA—Oh how gladly I would take a better one to my soul! But you offer me a worse one. [*Turning on him with sudden vehemence.*] Justify yourself: shew me some light through the darkness of this dreadful place, with its beautifully clean workshops, and respectable workmen, and model homes.

UNDERSHAFT—Cleanliness and respectability do not need justification, Barbara: they justify themselves. I see no darkness here, no dreadfulness. In your Salvation shelter I saw poverty, misery, cold and hunger. You gave them bread and treacle and dreams of heaven. I give from thirty shillings a week to twelve thousand a year. They find their own dreams; but I look after the drainage.

BARBARA—And their souls?

UNDERSHAFT—I save their souls just as I saved yours.

BARBARA [*revolted*] You saved my soul! What do you mean?

UNDERSHAFT—I fed you and clothed you and housed you. I took care that you should have money enough to live handsomely—more than enough; so that you could be wasteful, careless, generous. That saved your soul from the seven deadly sins.

BARBARA [*bewildered*] The seven deadly sins!

UNDERSHAFT—Yes, the deadly seven. [*Counting on his fingers.*] Food, clothing, firing, rent, taxes, respectability and children. Nothing can lift those seven millstones from Man's neck but money; and the spirit cannot soar until the millstones are lifted. I lifted them from your spirit. I enabled Barbara to become Major Barbara; and I saved her from the crime of poverty.

CUSINS—Do you call poverty a crime?

UNDERSHAFT—The worst of crimes. All the other crimes are virtues beside it: all the other dishonors are chivalry itself by comparison.

Poverty blights whole cities; spreads horrible pestilences; strikes dead the very souls of all who come within sight, sound, or smell of it. What you call crime is nothing: a murder here and a theft there, a blow now and a curse then: what do they matter? they are only the accidents and illnesses of life: there are not fifty genuine professional criminals in London. But there are millions of poor people, abject people, dirty people, ill fed, ill clothed people. They poison us morally and physically: they kill the happiness of society: they force us to do away with our own liberties and to oganize unnatural cruelties for fear they should rise against us and drag us down into their abyss. Only fools fear crime: we all fear poverty. Pah! [*Turning on* BARBARA.] you talk of your half-saved ruffian in West Ham: you accuse me of dragging his soul back to perdition. Well, bring him to me here; and I will drag his soul back again to salvation for you. Not by words and dreams; but by thirtyeight shillings a week, a sound house in a handsome street, and a permanent job. In three weeks he will have a fancy waistcoat; in three months a tall hat and a chapel sitting; before the end of the year he will shake hands with a duchess at a Primrose League meeting, and join the Conservative Party.

BARBARA – And will he be the better for that?

UNDERSHAFT – You know he will. Dont be a hypocrite, Barbara. He will be better fed, better housed, better clothed, better behaved; and his children will be pounds heavier and bigger. That will be better than an American cloth mattress in a shelter, chopping firewood, eating bread and treacle, and being forced to kneel down from time to time to thank heaven for it: knee drill, I think you call it. It is cheap work converting starving men with a Bible in one hand and a slice of bread in the other. I will undertake to convert West Ham to Mahometanism on the same terms. Try your hand on my men: their souls are hungry because their bodies are full.

BARBARA – And leave the east end to starve?

UNDERSHAFT [*his energetic tone dropping into one of bitter and brooding remembrance*] I was an east ender. I moralized and starved until one day I swore that I would be a full-fed free man at all costs; that nothing should stop me except a bullet, neither reason nor morals nor the lives of other men. I said 'Thou shalt starve ere I starve'; and with that word I became free and great. I was a dangerous man until I had my will: now I am a useful, beneficent, kindly person. That is the history of most self-made millionaires, I fancy. When it is the history of every Englishman we shall have an England worth living in.

LADY BRITOMART – Stop making speeches, Andrew. This is not the place for them.

UNDERSHAFT [*punctured*] My dear: I have no other means of conveying my ideas.

LADY BRITOMART—Your ideas are nonsense. You got on because you were selfish and unscrupulous.

UNDERSHAFT—Not at all. I had the strongest scruples about poverty and starvation. Your moralists are quite unscrupulous about both: they make virtues of them. I had rather be a thief than a pauper. I had rather be a murderer than a slave. I dont want to be either; but if you force the alternative on me, then, by Heaven, I'll choose the braver and more moral one. I hate poverty and slavery worse than any other crimes whatsoever. And let me tell you this. Poverty and slavery have stood up for centuries to your sermons and leading articles: they will not stand up to my machine guns. Dont preach at them: dont reason with them. Kill them.

BARBARA—Killing. Is that your remedy for everything?

UNDERSHAFT—It is the final test of conviction, the only lever strong enough to overturn a social system, the only way of saying Must. Let six hundred and seventy fools loose in the streets; and three policemen can scatter them. But huddle them together in a certain house in Westminster; and let them go through certain ceremonies and call themselves certain names until at last they get the courage to kill; and your six hundred and seventy fools become a government. Your pious mob fills up ballot papers and imagines it is governing its masters; but the ballot paper that really governs is the paper that has a bullet wrapped up in it.

CUSINS—That is perhaps why, like most intelligent people, I never vote.

UNDERSHAFT—Vote! Bah! When you vote, you only change the names of the cabinet. When you shoot, you pull down governments, inaugurate new epochs, abolish old orders and set up new. Is that historically true, Mr Learned Man, or is it not?

CUSINS—It is historically true. I loathe having to admit it. I repudiate your sentiments. I abhor your nature. I defy you in every possible way. Still, it is true. But it ought not to be true.

UNDERSHAFT—Ought! ought! ought! ought! ought! Are you going to spend your life saying ought, like the rest of our moralists? Turn your oughts into shalls, man. Come and make explosives with me. Whatever can blow men up can blow society up. The history of the world is the history of those who had courage enough to embrace this truth. Have you the courage to embrace it, Barbara?

LADY BRITOMART—Barbara: I positively forbid you to listen to your father's abominable wickedness. And you, Adolphus, ought to know better than to go about saying that wrong things are true. What does it matter whether they are true if they are wrong?

UNDERSHAFT — What does it matter whether they are wrong if they are true?

LADY BRITOMART [*rising*] Children: come home instantly. Andrew: I am exceedingly sorry I allowed you to call on us. You are wickeder than ever. Come at once.

BARBARA [*shaking her head*] It's no use running away from wicked people, mamma.

LADY BRITOMART — It is every use. It shews your disapprobation of them.

BARBARA — It does not save them.

LADY BRITOMART — I can see that you are going to disobey me. Sarah: are you coming home or are you not?

SARAH — I daresay it's very wicked of papa to make cannons; but I dont think I shall cut him on that account.

LOMAX [*pouring oil on the troubled waters*] The fact is, you know, there is a certain amount of tosh about this notion of wickedness. It doesnt work. You must look at facts. Not that I would say a word in favor of anything wrong; but then, you see, all sorts of chaps are always doing all sorts of things; and we have to fit them in somehow, dont you know. What I mean is that you cant go cutting everybody; and thats about what it comes to. [*Their rapt attention to his eloquence makes him nervous.*] Perhaps I dont make myself clear.

LADY BRITOMART — You are lucidity itself, Charles. Because Andrew is successful and has plenty of money to give to Sarah, you will flatter him and encourage him in his wickedness.

LOMAX [*unruffled*] Well, where the carcase is, there will the eagles be gathered, dont you know. [*To* UNDERSHAFT.] Eh? What?

UNDERSHAFT — Precisely. By the way, may I call you Charles?

LOMAX — Delighted. Cholly is the usual ticket.

UNDERSHAFT [*to* LADY BRITOMART] Biddy—

LADY BRITOMART [*violently*] Dont dare call me Biddy. Charles Lomax: you are a fool. Adolphus Cusins: you are a Jesuit. Stephen: you are a prig. Barbara: you are a lunatic. Andrew: you are a vulgar tradesman. Now you all know my opinion; and my conscience is clear, at all events.

[*She sits down with a vehemence that the rug fortunately softens.*]

UNDERSHAFT — My dear: you are the incarnation of morality. [*She snorts.*] Your conscience is clear and your duty done when you have called everybody names. Come, Euripides! it is getting late; and we all want to go home. Make up your mind.

CUSINS — Understand this, you old demon—

LADY BRITOMART – Adolphus!

UNDERSHAFT – Let him alone, Biddy. Proceed, Euripides.

CUSINS – You have me in a horrible dilemma. I want Barbara.

UNDERSHAFT – Like all young men, you greatly exaggerate the difference between one young woman and another.

BARBARA – Quite true, Dolly.

CUSINS – I also want to avoid being a rascal.

UNDERSHAFT [*with biting contempt*] You lust for personal righteousness, for self-approval, for what you call a good conscience, for what Barbara calls salvation, for what I call patronizing people who are not so lucky as yourself.

CUSINS – I do not: all the poet in me recoils from being a good man. But there are things in me that I must reckon with. Pity—

UNDERSHAFT – Pity! The scavenger of misery.

CUSINS – Well, love.

UNDERSHAFT – I know. You love the needy and the outcast: you love the oppressed races, the negro, the Indian ryot, the underdog everywhere. Do you love the Japanese? Do you love the French? Do you love the English?

CUSINS – No. Every true Englishman detests the English. We are the wickedest nation on earth; and our success is a moral horror.

UNDERSHAFT – That is what comes of your gospel of love, is it?

CUSINS – May I not love even my father-in-law?

UNDERSHAFT – Who wants your love, man? By what right do you take the liberty of offering it to me? I will have your due heed and respect, or I will kill you. But your love! Damn your impertinence!

CUSINS [*grinning*] I may not be able to control my affections, Mac.

UNDERSHAFT – You are fencing, Euripides. You are weakening: your grip is slipping. Come! try your last weapon. Pity and love have broken in your hand: forgiveness is still left.

CUSINS – No: forgiveness is a beggar's refuge. I am with you there: we must pay our debts.

UNDERSHAFT – Well said. Come! you will suit me. Remember the words of Plato.

CUSINS [*starting*] Plato! You dare quote Plato to me!

UNDERSHAFT – Plato says, my friend, that society cannot be saved until either the Professors of Greek take to making gunpowder, or else the makers of gunpowder become Professors of Greek.

CUSINS – Oh, tempter, cunning tempter!

UNDERSHAFT – Come! choose, man, choose.

CUSINS – But perhaps Barbara will not marry me if I make the wrong choice.

BARBARA – Perhaps not.

CUSINS [*desperately perplexed*] You hear!

BARBARA – Father: do you love nobody?

UNDERSHAFT – I love my best friend.

LADY BRITOMART – And who is that, pray?

UNDERSHAFT – My bravest enemy. That is the man who keeps me up to the mark.

CUSINS – You know, the creature is really a sort of poet in his way. Suppose he is a great man, after all!

UNDERSHAFT – Suppose you stop talking and make up your mind, my young friend.

CUSINS – But you are driving me against my nature. I hate war.

UNDERSHAFT – Hatred is the coward's revenge for being intimidated. Dare you make war on war? Here are the means: my friend Mr Lomax is sitting on them.

LOMAX [*springing up*] Oh I say! You dont mean that this thing is loaded, do you? My ownest: come off it.

SARAH [*sitting placidly on the shell*] If I am to be blown up, the more thoroughly it is done the better. Dont fuss, Cholly.

LOMAX [*to* UNDERSHAFT, *strongly remonstrant*] Your own daughter, you know!

UNDERSHAFT – So I see. [*To* CUSINS.] Well, my friend, may we expect you here at six tomorrow morning?

CUSINS [*firmly*] Not on any account. I will see the whole establishment blown up with its own dynamite before I will get up at five. My hours are healthy, rational hours: eleven to five.

UNDERSHAFT – Come when you please: before a week you will come at six and stay until I turn you out for the sake of your health. [*Calling.*] Bilton! [*He turns to* LADY BRITOMART, *who rises.*] My dear: let us leave these two young people to themselves for a moment. [BILTON *comes from the shed.*] I am going to take you through the gun cotton shed.

BILTON [*barring the way*] You cant take anything explosive in here, sir.

LADY BRITOMART – What do you mean? Are you alluding to me?

BILTON [*unmoved*] No, maam. Mr Undershaft has the other gentleman's matches in his pocket.

LADY BRITOMART [*abruptly*] Oh! I beg your pardon. [*She goes into the shed.*]

UNDERSHAFT – Quite right, Bilton, quite right: here you are. [*He gives* BILTON *the box of matches.*] Come, Stephen. Come, Charles. Bring Sarah.

[*He passes into the shed.*]
[BILTON *opens the box and deliberately drops
the matches into the fire-bucket.*]
LOMAX–Oh! I say [BILTON *stolidly hands him the empty box.*] Infernal nonsense! Pure scientific ignorance!

[*He goes in.*]
SARAH–Am I all right, Bilton?
BILTON–Youll have to put on list slippers, miss: thats all. Weve got em inside.

[*She goes in.*]
STEPHEN [*very seriously to* CUSINS] Dolly, old fellow, think. Think before you decide. Do you feel that you are a sufficiently practical man? It is a huge undertaking, an enormous responsibility. All this mass of business will be Greek to you.
CUSINS–Oh, I think it will be much less difficult than Greek.
STEPHEN–Well, I just want to say this before I leave you to yourselves. Dont let anything I have said about right and wrong prejudice you against this great chance in life. I have satisfied myself that the business is one of the highest character and a credit to our country. [*Emotionally.*] I am very proud of my father. I–

[*Unable to proceed, he presses* CUSINS'
hand and goes hastily into the shed, followed by BILTON.]
[BARBARA *and* CUSINS, *left alone together, look at one another silently.*]
CUSINS–Barbara: I am going to accept this offer.
BARBARA–I thought you would.
CUSINS–You understand, dont you, that I had to decide without consulting you. If I had thrown the burden of the choice on you, you would sooner or later have despised me for it.
BARBARA–Yes: I did not want you to sell your soul for me any more than for this inheritance.
CUSINS–It is not the sale of my soul that troubles me: I have sold it too often to care about that. I have sold it for a professorship. I have sold it for an income. I have sold it to escape being imprisoned for refusing to pay taxes for hangmen's ropes and unjust wars and things that I abhor. What is all human conduct but the daily and hourly sale of our souls for trifles? What I am now selling it for is neither money nor position nor comfort, but for reality and for power.
BARBARA–You know that you will have no power, and that he has none.
CUSINS–I know. It is not for myself alone. I want to make power for the world.
BARBARA–I want to make power for the world too; but it must be spiritual power.

CUSINS—I think all power is spiritual: these cannons will not go off by themselves. I have tried to make spiritual power by teaching Greek. But the world can never be really touched by a dead language and a dead civilization. The people must have power; and the people cannot have Greek. Now the power that is made here can be wielded by all men.

BARBARA—Power to burn women's houses down and kill their sons and tear their husbands to pieces.

CUSINS—You cannot have power for good without having power for evil too. Even mother's milk nourishes murderers as well as heroes. This power which only tears men's bodies to pieces has never been so horribly abused as the intellectual power, the imaginative power, the poetic, religious power that can enslave men's souls. As a teacher of Greek I gave the intellectual man weapons against the common man. I now want to give the common man weapons against the intellectual man. I love the common people. I want to arm them against the lawyers, the doctors, the priests, the literary men, the professors, the artists, and the politicians, who, once in authority, are more disastrous and tyrannical than all the fools, rascals, and impostors. I want a power simple enough for common men to use, yet strong enough to force the intellectual oligarchy to use its genius for the general good.

BARBARA—Is there no higher power than that? [*Pointing to the shell.*]

CUSINS—Yes; but that power can destroy the higher powers just as a tiger can destroy a man: therefore Man must master that power first. I admitted this when the Turks and Greeks were last at war. My best pupil went out to fight for Hellas. My parting gift to him was not a copy of Plato's Republic, but a revolver and a hundred Undershaft cartridges. The blood of every Turk he shot—if he shot any—is on my head as well as on Undershaft's. That act committed me to this place for ever. Your father's challenge has beaten me. Dare I make war on war? I must. I will. And now, is it all over between us?

BARBARA [*touched by his evident dread of her answer*] Silly baby Dolly! How could it be!

CUSINS [*overjoyed*] Then you—you—you—Oh for my drum!

[*He flourishes imaginary drumsticks.*]

BARBARA [*angered by his levity*] Take care, Dolly, take care. Oh, if only I could get away from you and from father and from it all! if I could have the wings of a dove and fly away to heaven!

CUSINS—And leave me!

BARBARA—Yes, you, and all the other naughty mischievous children of men. But I cant. I was happy in the Salvation Army for a moment. I escaped from the world into a paradise of enthusiasm and prayer and soul saving; but the moment our money ran short, it all came back to Bodger: it was he who saved our people: he, and the Prince of Darkness, my papa. Undershaft and Bodger: their hands stretch everywhere: when we feed a starving fellow creature, it is with their bread, because there is no other bread; when we tend the sick, it is in the hospitals they endow; if we turn from the churches they build, we must kneel on the stones of the streets they pave. As long as that lasts, there is no getting away from them. Turning our backs on Bodger and Undershaft is turning our backs on life.

CUSINS—I thought you were determined to turn your back on the wicked side of life.

BARBARA—There is no wicked side: life is all one. And I never wanted to shirk my share in whatever evil must be endured, whether it be sin or suffering. I wish I could cure you of middle-class ideas, Dolly.

CUSINS [*gasping*] Middle cl—! A snub! A social snub to me! from the daughter of a foundling!

BARBARA—That is why I have no class, Dolly: I come straight out of the heart of the whole people. If I were middle-class I should turn my back on my father's business; and we should both live in an artistic drawing room, with you reading the reviews in one corner, and I in the other at the piano, playing Schumann: both very superior persons, and neither of us a bit of use. Sooner than that, I would sweep out the guncotton shed, or be one of Bodger's barmaids. Do you know what would have happened if you had refused papa's offer?

CUSINS—I wonder!

BARBARA—I should have given you up and married the man who accepted it. After all, my dear old mother has more sense than any of you. I felt like her when I saw this place—felt that I must have it—that never, never, never could I let it go; only she thought it was the houses and the kitchen ranges and the linen and china, when it was really all the human souls to be saved: not weak souls in starved bodies, sobbing with gratitude for a scrap of bread and treacle, but fullfed, quarrelsome, snobbish, uppish creatures, all standing on their little rights and dignities, and thinking that my father ought to be greatly obliged to them for making so much money for him—and so he ought. That is where salvation is really wanted. My father shall never throw it in my teeth again that my converts were bribed with bread. [*She is transfigured.*] I have got rid of the bribe of bread. I have got rid of the bribe of heaven. Let God's work be done for its own sake: the work he had to create us to do because it cannot be done except by living men and women. When I die, let him be in my debt, not I in his; and let me forgive him as becomes a woman of my rank.

CUSINS—Then the way of life lies through the factory of death?

BARBARA—Yes, through the raising of hell to heaven and of man to

God, through the unveiling of an eternal light in the Valley of The Shadow. [*Seizing him with both hands.*] Oh, did you think my courage would never come back? did you believe that I was a deserter? that I, who have stood in the streets, and taken my people to my heart, and talked of the holiest and greatest things with them, could ever turn back and chatter foolishly to fashionable people about nothing in a drawing room? Never, never, never, never: Major Barbara will die with the colors. Oh! and I have my dear little Dolly boy still; and he has found me my place and my work. Glory Hallelujah!

[*She kisses him.*]

CUSINS – My dearest: consider my delicate health. I cannot stand as much happiness as you can.

BARBARA – Yes: it is not easy work being in love with me, is it? But it's good for you. [*She runs to the shed, and calls, childlike.*] Mamma! Mamma! [BILTON *comes out of the shed, followed by* UNDERSHAFT.] I want Mamma.

UNDERSHAFT – She is taking off her list slippers, dear. [*He passes on to* CUSINS.] Well? What does she say?

CUSINS – She has gone right up into the skies.

LADY BRITOMART [*coming from the shed and stopping on the steps, obstructing* SARAH, *who follows with* LOMAX. BARBARA *clutches like a baby at her mother's skirt.*] Barbara: when will you learn to be independent and to act and think for yourself? I know as well as possible what that cry of 'Mamma, Mamma,' means. Always running to me!

SARAH [*touching* LADY BRITOMART'S *ribs with her finger tips and imitating a bicycle horn*] Pip! pip!

LADY BRITOMART [*highly indignant*] How dare you say Pip! pip! to me, Sarah? You are both very naughty children. What do you want, Barbara?

BARBARA – I want a house in the village to live in with Dolly. [*Dragging at the skirt.*] Come and tell me which one to take.

UNDERSHAFT [*to* CUSINS] Six o'clock tomorrow morning, Euripides.

FROM: *THE BACCHAE* IN RELATION TO CERTAIN CURRENTS OF THOUGHT IN THE FIFTH CENTURY

By Gilbert Murray

THE OLD POET chose a curiously simple and even barbaric subject. It is much what we should call a Mystery Play. Dionysus, the young god born of Zeus and the Theban princess, Semelê, travelling through the world to announce his godhead, comes to his own people of Thebes, and—his own receive him not. They will not worship him simply and willingly; he constrains them to worship him with the enthusiasm of madness. The King, Pentheus, insults and imprisons the god, spies on his mystic worship, is discovered by the frenzied saints and torn limb from limb; his own mother, Agâvê, being the first to rend him.

Now it is no use pretending that this is a moral and sympathetic tale, or that Euripides palliates the atrocity of it, and tries to justify Dionysus. Euripides never palliates things. He leaves this savage story as savage as he found it. The sympathy of the audience is with Dionysus while he is persecuted; doubtful while he is just taking his vengeance; utterly against him at the end of the play. Note how Agâvê, when restored to her right mind, refuses even to think of him and his miserable injured pride:—

AGAVE – 'Tis Dionyse hath done it. Now I see.
CADMUS – Ye wronged him! Ye denied his deity.
AGAVE – Show me the body of the son I love!

Note how Dionysus is left answerless when Agâvê rebukes him:—

From *Euripides*, translated into English rhyming verse by Gilbert Murray. London: George Allen & Unwin Ltd., 1904. Reprinted by permission of the publisher.

1726

DIONYSUS – Ye mocked me being God. This is your wage.
AGAVE – Should God be like a proud man in his rage?
DIONYSUS – 'Tis as my sire, Zeus, willed it long ago.

A helpless, fatalistic answer, abandoning the moral standpoint.

But the most significant point against Dionysus is the change of tone
—the conversion, one might almost call it—of his own inspired 'Wild
Beasts,' the Chorus of Asiatic Bacchanals, after the return of Agâvê with
her son's severed head. The change is clearly visible in that marvellous
scene itself. It is emphasized in the sequel. Those wild singers, who raged
so loudly in praises of the god's vengeance before they saw what it was,
fall, when once they have seen it, into dead silence. True, there is a
lacuna in the MS. at one point, so it is possible that they may have
spoken; but as the play stands, their Leader speaks only one couplet addressed to Cadmus, whom the god has wronged:—

> Lo, I weep with thee. 'Twas but due reward
> God sent on Pentheus; but for thee . . . 'tis hard!

And they go off at the end with no remark, good or evil, about their triumphant and hateful Dionysus, uttering only those lines of brooding
resignation with which Euripides closed so many of his tragedies.

Such silence in such a situation is significant. Euripides is, as usual,
critical or even hostile towards the moral tone of the myth that he celebrates. There is nothing in that to surprise us.

Some critics have even tried to imagine that Pentheus is a 'sympathetic' hero; that he is right in his crusade against this bad god, as much
as Hippolytus was right. But the case will not bear examination. Euripides
might easily have made Pentheus 'sympathetic' if he had chosen. And
he certainly has not chosen. No. As regards the conflict between Dionysus and Pentheus, Euripides has merely followed a method very usual
with him, the method, for instance, of the *Electra*. He has given a careful
objective representation of the facts as alleged in the myth: "If the story
is true," he says, "then it must have been like this." We have the ordinary hot-tempered and narrowly practical tyrant—not very carefully studied, by the way, and apparently not very interesting to the poet; we have
a well-attested god and suitable miracles; we have a most poignant and
unshrinking picture of the possibilities of religious madness. That may
be taken as the groundwork of the play. It is quite probable that Euripides had seen some glimpses of Dionysus-worship on the Macedonian
mountains which gave a fresh reality in his mind to the legends of raven-
ing and wonder-working Maenads.

But when all this is admitted, there remains a fact of cardinal importance, which was seen by the older critics, and misled them so greatly that modern writers are often tempted to deny its existence. There is in *The Bacchae* real and heartfelt glorification of Dionysus.

The 'objectivity' is not kept up. Again and again in the lyrics you feel that the Maenads are no longer merely observed and analysed. The poet has entered into them, and they into him. Again and again the words that fall from the lips of the Chorus or its Leader are not the words of a raving Bacchante, but of a gentle and deeply musing philosopher.

Probably all dramatists who possess strong personal beliefs, yield at times to the temptation of using one of their characters as a mouthpiece for their own feelings. And the Greek Chorus, a half-dramatic, half-lyrical creation, both was and was felt to be particularly suitable for such use. Of course a writer does not—or at least should not—use the drama to express his mere 'views' on ordinary and commonplace questions, to announce his side in politics or his sect in religion. But it is a method wonderfully contrived for expressing those vaguer faiths and aspirations which a man feels haunting him and calling to him, but which he cannot state in plain language or uphold with a full acceptance of responsibility. You can say the thing that wishes to be said; you 'give it its chance'; you relieve your mind of it. And if it proves to be all nonsense, well, it is not you that said it. It is only a character in one of your plays!

The religion of Dionysus as Euripides found it, already mysticised and made spiritual, half-reformed and half-petrified in sacerdotalism, by the Orphic movement, was exactly that kind of mingled mass which lends itself to dramatic and indirect expression. It was gross as it stood; yet it could be so easily and so wonderfully idealised! Euripides seems to have felt a peculiar and almost enthusiastic interest in a further sublimation of its doctrines, a philosophic or prophet-like interpretation of the spirit that a man might see in it if he would. And meantime he did not bind himself. He let his Bacchanals rave from time to time, as they were bound to rave. He had said his say, and he was not responsible for the whole of Dionysus-worship nor yet of Orphism.

Dionysus, as Euripides takes him from the current conceptions of his day, is the God of all high emotion, inspiration, intoxication. He is the patron of poetry, especially of dramatic poetry. He has given man Wine, which is his Blood and a religious symbol. He purifies from Sin. It is unmeaning, surely, to talk of a 'merely ritual' purification as opposed to something real. Ritual, as long as it fully lives, is charged with spiritual meaning, and can often express just those transcendent things which words fail to utter—much as a look or the clasp of a hand can at times express more than a verbal greeting. Dionysus purified as spiritually as the worshipper's mind required. And he gave to the Purified a mystic

Joy, surpassing in intensity that of man, the Joy of a god or a free wild animal. The Bacchanals in this play worshipped him by his many names:

> 'Iacchos, Bromios, Lord,
> God of God born;' and all the mountain felt
> And worshipped with them, and the wild things knelt,
> And ramped and gloried, and the wilderness
> Was filled with moving voices and dim stress.   (vv. 725 ff.)

That is the kind of god he celebrates.

Euripides had lived most of his life in a great town, among highly educated people; amid restless ambitions and fierce rivalries; amid general scepticism, originally caused, no doubt, in most cases, by higher religious aspirations than those of the common man, but ending largely in arid irreligion; in an ultra political community, led of late years by the kind of men of whom Plato said that if you looked into the soul of one of them you could see "its bad little eye glittering with sharpness"; in a community now hardened to the condition described in the long passage quoted above from Thucydides. Euripides had lived all his life in this society; for many years he had led it, at least in matters of art and intellect; for many years he had fought with it. And now he was free from it!

He felt like a hunted animal escaped from its pursuers; like a fawn fled to the forest, says one lyric, in which the personal note is surely audible as a ringing undertone:

> Oh, feet of a fawn to the greenwood fled
> Alone in the grass and the loveliness,
> Leap of the Hunted, no more in dread . . .   (vv. 862 ff.)

But there is still a terror in the distance behind him; he must go onward yet, to lonely regions where no voice of either man or hound may reach. "What else is wisdom?" he asks, in a marvellous passage:—

> What else is wisdom? What of man's endeavour
> Or God's high grace so lovely and so great?
> To stand from fear set free, to breathe and wait;
> To hold a hand uplifted over Hate;
>   And shall not loveliness be loved for ever?

He was escaped and happy; he was beyond the reach of Hate. Nay, he was safe, and those who hated him were suffering. A judgment seemed to be upon them, these men who had resolved to have no dealings with "the three deadly enemies of Empire, Pity and Eloquent Sentiments and

1729

the Generosity of Strength"; who lived, as Thucydides says in another passage (VI. 90), in dreams of wider and wider conquest, the conquest of Sicily, of South Italy, of Carthage and all her empire, of every country that touched the sea. They had forgotten the essence of religion, forgotten the eternal laws, and the judgment in wait for those who "worship the Ruthless Will"; who dream—

> Dreams of the proud man, making great
>   And greater ever
> Things that are not of God.—   (vv. 885 ff.)

It is against the essential irreligion implied in these dreams that he appeals in the same song:—

> And is thy faith so much to give?
> Is it so hard a thing to see,
> That the Spirit of God, whate'er it be,
> The Law that abides and falters not, ages long,
> The Eternal and Nature-born—these things be strong?

In the epode of the same chorus, taking the ritual words of certain old Bacchic hymns and slightly changing them, he expresses his own positive doctrine more clearly:—

> Happy he, On the weary sea,
>   Who hath fled the tempest and won the haven;
> Happy, whoso hath risen, free,
>   Above his strivings!

Men strive with many ambitions, seethe with divers hopes, mostly conflicting, mostly of inherent worthlessness; even if they are achieved, no one is a whit the better.

> But whoe'er can know, As the long days go,
>   That *to live is happy*, hath found his Heaven!

Could not the wise men of Athens understand what a child feels, what a wild beast feels, what a poet feels, that to live—to live in the presence of Nature, of Dawn and Sunset, of eternal mysteries and discoveries and wonders—is in itself a joyous thing?

"Love thou the day and the night," he says in another place. It is only so that Life can be made what it really is, a Joy: by loving not only your neighbour—he is so vivid an element in life that, unless you do love him, he will spoil all the rest!—but the actual details and processes of living. Life becomes like the voyage of Dionysus himself over magic seas, or rather, perhaps, like the more chequered voyage of Shelley's lovers:—

> While Night
> And Day, and Storm and Calm pursue their flight,
> Our ministers across the boundless sea,
> Treading each other's heels unheededly—

the alternations and pains being only "ministers" to the great composite joy.

It seemed to Euripides, in that favourite metaphor of his, which was always a little more than a metaphor, that a God had been rejected by the world that he came from. Those haggard, striving, suspicious men, full of ambition and the pride of intellect, almost destitute of emotion, unless political hatreds can be called emotion, were hurrying through Life in the presence of august things which they never recognised, of joy and beauty which they never dreamed of. Thus it is that "the world's wise are not wise" (v. 395). The poet may have his special paradise, away from the chosen places of ordinary men, better than the sweetness of Cyprus or Paphos:—

> The high still dell Where the Muses dwell,
> Fairest of all things fair—

it is there that he will find the things truly desired of his heart, and the power to worship in peace his guiding Fire of inspiration. But Dionysus gives his Wine to all men, not to poets alone. Only by "spurning joy" can men harden his heart against them. For the rest—

> The simple nameless herd of Humanity
> Hath deeds and faith that are truth enough for me!

It is a mysticism which includes democracy as it includes the love of your neighbour. They are both necessary details in the inclusive end. It implies that trust in the 'simple man' which is so characteristic of most idealists and most reformers. It implies the doctrine of Equality—a doctrine essentially religious and mystical, continually disproved in every fresh sense in which it can be formulated, and yet remaining one of the living faiths of men.

It is at first sight strange, this belittling of 'the Wise' and all their learning. Euripides had been all his life the poet militant of knowledge, the apostle of progress and enlightenment. Yet there is no real contradiction. It is only that the Wise are not wise enough, that the Knowledge which a man has attained is such a poor and narrow thing compared with the Knowledge that he dreamed of. In one difficult and beautiful passage Euripides seems to give us his own apology:

> Knowledge, we are not foes!
>   I seek thee diligently;
> But the world with a great wind blows,
>   Shining, and not from thee;
> Blowing to beautiful things,
>   On amid dark and light,
> Till Life through the trammellings
>   Of Laws that are not the Right,
> Breaks, clean and pure, and sings
>   Glorying to God in the height! (vv. 1005 ff.)

One feels grateful for that voice from the old Euripides amid the strange new tones of *The Bacchae*.

SHAW'S CHALLENGE TO LIBERALISM

By Louis Crompton

MAJOR BARBARA, together with *Man and Superman* and *John Bull's Other Island*, forms part of a trilogy of philosophical comedies, all of which deal with the bankruptcy of nineteenth-century liberalism in the face of the brute facts of sex, nationalism, and poverty. This propagandistic purpose has been from the start a bone of contention. It is not by chance that critics holding a formalist position, from Shaw's friend A. B. Walkley down to Francis Fergusson[1] in our own day, have denounced the play as a kind of literary monster, while philosopher-critics[2] have regarded it as one of the few dramas with anything serious to say on the subject of politics. Indeed, *Major Barbara* raises the central issue of modern aesthetics as squarely as any piece of writing can. This question—putting it in the simplest possible terms—I take to be whether art is to be regarded as autonomous and *sui generis* or whether it is to be judged in relation to some ulterior standard of reality, that is, as a form of science or knowledge. But even if you accept this second view of the nature of art—which is certainly Shaw's view—you will still have to ask yourself whether your conception of this ulterior reality corresponds to Shaw's.

"Shaw's Challenge to Liberalism" by Louis Crompton. From *Prairie Schooner*, XXXVII, No. 3 (Fall 1963), 229–44. Copyright © 1963 by the University of Nebraska Press. Reprinted by permission of *Prairie Schooner* and the author.

[1] See Walkley, *Drama and Life* (1907); Fergusson, *The Idea of a Theater* (1949).

[2] Charles Frankel, "Efficient Power and Inefficient Virtue" in *Great Moral Dilemmas in Literature*, ed. R. M. MacIver (1956).

Thus the play presents a double challenge—first to the dominant literary theory of our day, and second to our political and social ideals.

Only the inordinate length of *Man and Superman* kept Shaw from publishing his three philosophical comedies together in a set, as he did the *Plays Pleasant and Unpleasant* and the *Three Plays for Puritans*. For his German edition, Shaw suggested that they be grouped and given the title *Comedies of Science and Religion*. Like the grouped plays of the other cycles, these plays share, besides their common theme, a common mood and a common dramatic structure.

It is this latter feature—their unique dramatic form—which has first of all confused, puzzled, and exasperated critics. What Shaw does is to mix together a Molièresque comedy and a Socratic dialogue. Each play begins by presenting us with a high-minded idealist, who takes himself with earnest seriousness and looks upon himself as an enlightened reformer. He is then made the subject of a comedy in the style of Molière, not with the idea of unmasking his hypocrisy, but of exposing the comic contradictions within his ideals and temperament. The problems raised by this character, which appear originally in a farcical-satirical light, are treated more and more seriously until they are shown to be bound up with what Shaw calls "the destiny of nations," and the audience which has settled down for a night of fun finds it must either transform itself from an audience of pleasure-seekers into a "pit of philosophers" or founder hopelessly in the dream sequence of *Man and Superman* or the last acts of *John Bull's Other Island* and *Major Barbara*. An impossible procedure you will complain. But not, Shaw would answer, to someone who believed that "Every joke is an earnest in the womb of time," and that the prophet who did not make his audience laugh would suffer, at worst, the fate of Socrates and Christ, and at best that of Rousseau and Tom Paine.

The idealistic liberals who are the butts of the satire are Roebuck Ramsden in *Man and Superman*, Tom Broadbent in *John Bull's Other Island*, and Lady Britomart Undershaft in *Major Barbara*, but since our subject is the latter play let us look at Lady Britomart as a representative of her species. The character of Lady Britomart, like most of those in *Major Barbara*, was drawn from a real person. It is a well-known fact that Shaw based Adolphus Cusins, his professor of Greek, on Gilbert Murray, but it is less well-known that he based Lady Britomart on Murray's real-life mother-in-law, Lady Rosalind Frances, Countess of Carlisle. (Indeed, Shaw jokingly told Murray in a letter that he was at work on a play to be called "Murray's Mother-in-Law".) The Countess of Carlisle was, like Lady Britomart, a Whig peeress; her father was the Liberal whip in parliament, and she was herself a crusading temperance reformer and the leader for eighteen years of the national Woman's Liberal Federation. Since her husband was more interested in art than in estate management, she ran the extensive family estates like a personal fiefdom, attending in minute detail to the farmers' personal welfare— and to their moral characters. Castle Howard and her house in Kensington were salons for the Liberal intelligentsia. Murray himself has paid tribute to her crusading enthusiasm and to the heartening quality of her formidable benevolence.

The clue to Shaw's treatment of the comic contradictions in Lady Britomart's character may be found in a remark by James Froude, Carlyle's biographer, on the subject of Lady Rosalind. Froude, who disapproved of her politics but admired her character, said that though she professed to be a Liberal, she was by temperament better fitted to be an "empress." Hence if Shaw had chosen to make her the central figure of the play he might have imitated Molière's "Bourgeois Gentleman" to the extent of calling it "The Imperious Liberal." By family tradition and personal conviction Lady Britomart is an avowed believer in free speech and a democratic franchise, but every speech that she utters shows her native aristocratic spirit and natural masterfulness at odds with these ideals. Where Lady Britomart's moralism is not an aristocratic Mrs. Grundyism, a Queen Victoria-ism so to speak, it is merely a rationalization of her class prejudices and privileges, "right" and "propriety" being whatever furthers the Stevenage family interests and "wrong" or "impropriety" being whatever conflicts with them. For the central issue of the first act, and indeed of the play as a whole, is who will inherit the armament factory owned by Lady Britomart's husband, Andrew Undershaft.

The question of the Undershaft inheritance has caused a rift between the husband and wife: according to the tradition of the firm, the inheritance must go not to a son of the owner but to some promising adopted heir. This condition, utterly at odds with aristocratic belief in birth and blood, so offends Lady Britomart that it is useless for Andrew to argue that the Roman Empire was run successfully on this scheme and that it brought to the throne Marcus Aurelius. She is so used to thinking of the Stevenages as governors by natural right that when Andrew had refused to break the firm's law of succession in favor of his son Stephen the resulting quarrel led to a legal separation. Lady Britomart's way of putting this is to declare that nothing can bridge fundamental "moral" disagreement.

We have only to spend two minutes in Stephen's presence to realize the soundness of his father's decision, for Stephen is a conscientious, thoroughly well-intentioned prig and moral pedant, tediously prating about "right" being "right" and "wrong" being "wrong." His sister Sarah lacks his pretentiousness, but also his starchy character, and is, in fact, no more than a fashionable nonentity. Only in their third child, Barbara, has the Undershaft-Stevenage marriage justified itself as an evolutionary experiment in the crossing of types and classes, for Barbara has Lady Britomart's genius for leadership and mothering, with none of her class limitations. So little is she concerned with mere propriety and decorum and so intensely does she identify herself with the religious spirit of the race that she has joined the least snobbish of the reforming religious sects of the day, the Salvation Army.

As the play opens we learn that Sarah and Barbara have both become engaged, Sarah to Charles Lomax, an amiable aristocratic noodle as empty-headed as herself, and Barbara to a man as complex and subtle in his moral and intellectual perceptions as Lomax is silly. Shaw shows us in Cusins a representative of the humane conscience in its most tender and perceptive form. In writing to Gilbert Murray, Shaw pointed out that he had taken pains to make his professor "the reverse in every point of the theatrical strong man":

> I want him to go on his quality wholly, and not to make the smallest show of physical robustness or brute determination. His selection by Undershaft should be a standing puzzle to the people who believe in the strong-silent still-waters-run-deep hero of melodrama. The very name Adolphus Cusins is selected to that end.[3]

In choosing Murray as his model, Shaw had in mind a type of liberal in strong contrast to the active, bustling Lady Britomart. Cusins is the academic, cloistered, sympathetic, skeptical, ironic, supercivilized liberal who shrinks instinctively from what E. M. Forster has called the world of "telegrams and anger."

Murray's liberalism sprang from several sources—from the radicalism of Castle Howard, from his Irish rebel background, and from a strain of Shelleyan humanitarianism that made him, like Shaw, a vegetarian and a hater of all forms of cruelty. The other side of the picture was his Hellenism. For Murray, Greek literature was a living force having direct bearing on modern politics, morals, and culture. Here is how he writes of Euripides, the Greek playwright to whom he felt especially drawn:

> His contemporary public denounced him as dull, because he tortured them with personal problems; as malignant, because he made them see truths they wished not to see; as blasphemous and foul-

---

[3] October 7, 1905; printed in Murray, *An Unfinished Autobiography* (1960), pp. 155–56. This whole letter is of great interest for the play.

minded, because he made demands on their spiritual and religious natures which they could neither satisfy nor overlook.[4]

In short, Murray regarded Euripides as standing in relation to the golden age of Athens as the "New Drama" of Ibsen and Shaw stood in relation to the age of Victoria and Edward VII. (Shaw returned the compliment by hailing Murray's translations of Euripides as modern masterpieces that had earned their place on the contemporary stage in their own right.) In *Major Barbara* Shaw makes Undershaft give Cusins the nickname "Euripides," thus implying that he looks on human affairs with the same mixture of ironic pessimism and pity as his Greek predecessor.

Lady Britomart has invited her estranged husband to her West End mansion with the eminently practical intention of extracting dowries from him for the two brides-to-be, her estimate of the earning power of a feckless man-about-town and a classics professor being realistically small. But her attempt to bring up once more the matter of the inheritance meets flinty resistance from Undershaft. Indeed, only the unexpected interest Undershaft shows in Barbara's novel religious aspirations saves the family reunion from shipwreck. It is an immense puzzle to both the naïve and the sophisticated members of the family group that Undershaft should show such a concern with her new faith, particularly since he is resolutely unashamed of his destructive trade and even seems to glory in it, declaring, "Your Christianity, which enjoins you to resist not evil, and to turn the other cheek, would make me a bankrupt. My morality— my religion—must have a place for cannons and torpedoes in it." Barbara challenges him to maintain this faith after visiting her East End Salvation Army shelter. Her father accepts the invitation, and issues a counterchallenge: she shall in return pay a visit to his arms factory and face the temptation offered by a religion of "money and gunpowder."

The scene at the Salvation Army shelter is a remarkable piece of lowlife melodrama, equalled in English only by the works of O'Casey. The refugees at the barracks include a cynically smart young man and an old crone, both posing as redeemed sinners, and Peter Shirley, who is brought in in a state of semi-starvation. Turned out of his job as overage, Shirley finds the necessity of accepting charity all the more bitter because he holds the faith of a secularist, in contrast to the others who believe in nothing but their right to bilk and exploit capitalist society as it has bilked and exploited them. Finally, Bill Walker enters, a half-drunk, blustering bully in a very mean mood, who bawls angrily for his girl, and curses the Army for taking her from him.

[4] *A History of Ancient Greek Literature* (1897), p. 250. See also *Euripides and His Age* (1913).

This scene ends with Barbara's struggle for Bill's soul. This is a fight which comes very near to success and only fails through a stroke of diablerie on the part of her father. The latter frustrates her simply by demonstrating that although the Salvation Army can afford to refuse to sell the blackguard his salvation for twenty shillings, it cannot, no matter how scrupulous it affects to be, refuse to sell the millionaire his for, say, five thousand pounds. Barbara had refused to accept her father's tuppence in the collection plate because the money was earned through the creation of destructive forces far more brutal in their effect than anything the slum ruffian might aspire to. But when the Army commissioner comes to plead for money to carry on the Army's work in a hard winter, she is forced to accept Undershaft's proffer of the aforementioned thousands despite his sardonic emphasis on the terrifying nature of his enterprises. The ruffian, when he sees the rich man's gift accepted where his own conscience money was rejected, turns on Barbara with cynical scorn, and Barbara, facing at once the failure of her attempt at salvation and a realization that the Salvation Army, if it is to exist at all, can only exist as the pensioner of the distillery and cannon industries, utters her bitter and heart-rending cry of despair, "My God: why hast thou forsaken me?"

It is at this point that the play takes the most surprising of its many surprising turns. For at the moment that Barbara's God, the God of Evangelical Christianity, appears to have failed her, the professor of Greek hails as a new deity the very man Barbara now fears as anti-Christ, her diabolical-seeming father. Cusins, in a transport of ecstasy, declares himself to be possessed by the spirit of Undershaft, whom he addresses as the new "Dionysos." Barbara in the pain and confusion of her loss can, of course, see nothing in this behavior but a piece of perverse irony.

It may be well at this point to ask what Shaw means by his idea of a "new" Dionysos. What has the ancient Greek god to do with modern society? The answer is to be found in the meaning Dionysiac religion had in the Greek world. Historians and philosophers, of whom Nietzsche is the most famous, have repeatedly emphasized the strange disparity between the serene rationalism of Greek society as we usually conceive it and the wild barbarity of the Bacchic cult which entered Greece from Thrace and Macedonia in the tenth century before Christ. Nietzsche traces the birth of dramatic tragedy itself to this irruption of frenzied rites and ecstatic orgies into the calm order and moral rationalism of Greek life, which the new religion challenged with its worship of supernormal psychic energy and its identification of the worshipper both with the new God and with the life processes of the animal and vegetative world. Cusins had earlier praised the services of the Salvation Army as the "true worship of Dionysos," finding in the Army's ecstasy and enthusiasm (literally, a standing outside oneself and possession by the divine will) an analogue of the uncouth religion that shocked the cultivated Greeks as the Army shocked the conventional Anglicanism of the West End. In its stirring religious music he had seen the primitive dithyramb reborn, its trombones, timbrels, and drums being the antithesis both of tepid hymns sung in fashionable churches and of the salon music of the fashionable drawing room. Even its symbols, Blood and Fire, Cusins points out, are Dionysiac symbols. Its joy and happiness are those of the God-possessed, as Barbara's later grief is that of the God-forsaken.

Thus Dionysianism is what Bergson calls a "dynamic religion,"[5] with its basis not in conventional morality or institutionalism but in a mystical union with the divine will. It breaks down social barriers, taking the intellectual into University Settlements in the slums, and pitting him actively against evil. It carries its devotees beyond the bounds of logic and reason. Aroused and lacking rational direction, it finds its expression in the frenzy of the revolutionary mob. Cusins is a sophisticated intellectual who has joined the Army, as Lady Britomart puts it, to worship Barbara. (No bad object of worship, Shaw would insist.) As a student of comparative religion and a disciple of Sir James Frazer, his view of the Army is, to say the least, not that of a fundamentalist. But Barbara's obvious religious genius attracts him strongly, and her evangelicalism, on its practical side, is not at all incompatible with his own religion of love, pity, and forgiveness. Indeed, for all his sardonic irony, he faces a crisis of his own beliefs at the same moment Barbara faces hers. As we have already seen, Cusins, in his skepticism and humanitarianism, is akin to the young Euripides who casts doubts on the traditional Greek attitudes towards patriotism, religion, women, and slaves.

But the Greek playwright's later development has a strange and unforeseen twist to it. For Euripides, who first turned the Greek drama away from its roots in Dionysiac religion toward a critical and skeptical direction, does return to Dionysos at the end of his career. In what is generally regarded as the last work of his old age, *The Bacchae*, the humanistic and humanitarian playwright does come face to face with the religion in which the drama had its origin. It is probably no exaggeration to say that *The Bacchae* is, by a good margin, the most terrifying, unedifying, and enigmatic of all Greek tragedies. You will recall that in this play Dionysos visits in disguise the city of Thebes where his rites have been forbidden by the moralistic King Pentheus and works a horrifying revenge. The problem Euripides' drama poses, put in the briefest terms, is this: what attitude are we to adopt to this new force in society, at once so terrible and so fascinating? Does Dionysos' ghastly triumph

[5] *The Two Sources of Morality and Religion* (1935).

over Pentheus signify the rebirth of vital religion or does he symbolize some dark, demonic power from which we are to recoil in dread?

Now, like the Greeks of Euripides' day, Cusins has also been brought face to face with a brutal, primitive force of life and death which the cultivated, sensitive side of him recoils from, but which the clear-headed student of society is forced to take into account. And Shaw, to emphasize the fact that he has had the parallel with Euripides' drama in mind all along, has Cusins quote some twenty or thirty lines from the play in the Salvation Army scene, in what Cusins identifies as his "own" (that is, Murray's) new translation.[6]

It is no exaggeration to say that Shaw's Undershaft has created the same bafflement in critics as Euripides' Dionysos, whether the critic be as naïve as the *Time* reviewer who accused Shaw of making a "complete about-face" and firing on his own socialist ranks, or as sophisticated as Mr. Francis Fergusson who for all his learning and intelligence, denounces *Major Barbara* as a tissue of "unresolved paradoxes."

What then *are* we to make of this man who has so puzzled Shaw's commentators? It may perhaps be best to turn first to the living models from whom Shaw may have obtained hints for his millionaire munitions maker. One was a neighbor at Ayot Saint Lawrence, Charles McEvoy, a quiet and gentle man, who had manufactured torpedoes for the North during the American Civil War. But I should like to suggest that Shaw, in drawing the sardonic side of Undershaft's character, seems to have had in mind the Swedish arms maker Alfred Nobel, the inventor of nitroglycerine. During the closing decades of the nineteenth century, Nobel's success in creating more and more powerful explosives had sent a wave of panic around the world. A leading figure in European business and international finance, Nobel was also a man of an intellectual and literary cast; like Undershaft, he belonged to a munitions dynasty. In thought and sentiment, he was a Shelleyan radical and humanitarian, but this did not limit his hardheadedness in business, and he sold his patents indiscriminately to autocratic and liberal states alike. (In a manuscript draft of *Major Barbara* Shaw makes Undershaft boast that he has sold a new rifle to the Swedish, Italian, and German governments without any compunctions on the score of politics.[7]) Nobel's motto, "My home is where my work is, and my work is everywhere" might well have been Undershaft's. And, of course, one of the last deeds of this complex and enigmatic man was his endowment of the Nobel Peace Prize, which challenged the humanitarian liberals among his personal friends to solve the problem his

[6] The lines are quoted from Murray's *Euripides*, see above, pages 1679–80. —E.B.

[7] British Museum additional MS 50616B, folio 53. The passage is cancelled. This draft of act one is dated "Sandgate 4/4/05."

discoveries had created. The Peace Prize was first awarded in 1901, four years before Shaw began his play.

This will perhaps explain, in part, one of the paradoxes of *Major Barbara*—that it is a dealer in lethal weapons who plays the role of Socrates in this socialist drama. But what of Undershaft's peculiar commercial ruthlessness, that specifically cold-blooded side of his personality that has so shocked and baffled critics and audiences? To unravel this puzzle we must begin by considering his background. Undershaft is a slum boy, reared in that wilderness of desolation that was East London in the middle of the nineteenth century. He has, like all the members of his dynasty, assumed the name of the firm's founder, an abandoned orphan reared in the parish of St. Andrew Undershaft in the city.[8] Determined to escape from the indignities of poverty, he has taken for his own the stern old Scots slogan: "Thou shalt starve ere I starve."

Here the second paradox appears, for as a socialist we expect Shaw especially to condemn this spirit. But he condones it and even insists that for a poor person it is indeed the only possible "manly" attitude. (Undershaft's Christian name, "Andrew," means "manly.") For Shaw, the great cardinal virtues are courage and self-respect, and he believed that if the poor in a democracy let themselves be exploited, starved, and snubbed, it is only because of their own inveterate abjectness. Hence the cutting remarks which Undershaft, the ex-slum boy, addresses to Peter Shirley, the down-trodden, long-suffering worker, in the Salvation Army shelter:

> SHIRLEY [*angrily*] – Who made your millions for you? Me and my like. Whats kep us poor? keepin you rich. I wouldn't have your conscience, not for all your income.
> UNDERSHAFT – I wouldn't have your income, not for all your conscience, Mr. Shirley.

Undershaft is driving home the point that the play makes over and over again, that a mere conviction of moral superiority is in itself the hollowest of consolations, the last resource of the weak and cowardly, and the treacherous quagmire in which true worth and manhood are lost.

Honor, justice, and truth are indeed part of Undershaft's religion, but he stresses that these can be had only as the "graces and luxuries of a rich, strong, and safe life." Any liberal like Cusins who preaches these virtues to the poor without taking into account economic realities is a fool. Undershaft can even declare that his determinedly ruthless conduct

[8] The odd epithet "Undershaft" was applied to the church because of the custom of setting up a maypole outside its doors.

satisfies the Kantian test, since the world would be an immeasurably better place if all the poor behaved exactly as he has. But first we must rid ourselves of the liberal belief that moral virtue by itself is ever capable of becoming a significant force in the world. Shaw made this point abundantly clear in a speech of Undershaft's in the unpublished Derry manuscript of the play:

> Come, come, my young friends; let us live in the real world. Your moral world is a vacuum; nothing is done there, though a good deal is eaten and drunk by the moralists at the expense of the real world. It is nice to live in a vacuum and repeat the fine phrases and edifying sentiments a few literary people have manufactured for you: but you know as well as I do that your morality is tolerated only on the assumption that nothing is to come of it. Your Christmas carols about peace and goodwill to men are very pretty; but you order cannons from me just the same. You ring out the old, ring in the new: that is, you discard muzzleloaders and introduce breechloaders. Barbara converts laborers whose conversion dont matter, because they have no responsibility and no power; but she does not convert the Secretary of State for war. Euripides abhors war, he says; but he will not stop it by Greek verses. It can be stopped only by a mighty power which is not in his class room.[9]

Undershaft soon indicates that this power is the power of bombs.

Liberal intellectuals frequently distrust power and decry the use of force. In so doing, they overlook the fact that the authority of governments in liberal democracies rests on the police and army as surely as in any authoritarian state. Shaw, speaking through Undershaft, defines a government as a body of men with the courage to kill. Stephen, the conventionally-minded parliamentarian, must himself be as ready to kill his political opponents as Caesar, Cromwell, Washington, Lincoln, and Stalin were to kill theirs. Being a totally conventional young man with his head stuffed full of moral clichés and a conviction of the divinely righteous nature of upper-class British interests, he will kill stupidly and senselessly. How little his high-mindedness represents anything in the way of real scruples we see when the Undershaft party arrives at the factory. Stephen, who has earlier expressed priggish horror at his father's business, is now all admiration for this triumph of industry.

But for the intellectual humanitarian and the former Salvationist the reconciliation to the factory of death is not so easy. The last scene of the

[9] British Museum MS 50616D, folios 35–36. This first "Irish" version is dated "Derry 8/9/1905."

play is at once an intellectual argument and a religious wooing of the souls of Cusins and Barbara by Mephistopheles-Dionysos-Undershaft. Cusins may admit that force is the basis of present-day society and that a capitalist state exists for the sake of protecting the rich man's dividends, just as the Salvation Army inadvertently plays into the hands of the rich by diverting the attention of the poor from revolution. But perhaps the answer is not to use force against force but to abandon force completely and to appeal for social justice on the grounds of Christianity, love, and mercy. No: Undershaft inexorably insists, government and rule mean killing: all political progress (not to mention political conservatism) rests ultimately on the willingness to kill.

Let us see if we can determine exactly what Undershaft means before we raise the cry of "unresolved paradox." I think that Shaw's intention is clear enough if we give full weight to what Undershaft says in the final scene, but since these relatively straightforward statements have been for most people as music to the deaf and sunsets to the blind, we may profitably take another look at the unpublished manuscript version of the play in the possession of the British Museum. Here Undershaft does not, I think, depart from any of the positions he maintains in the final version of the play, but he is perhaps more explicit:

UNDERSHAFT [*grimly*] —Why do [the poor] starve? Because they have been taught that it is their duty to starve. "Blessed are the poor in spirit"—eh? But now mark my highest claim, my proudest boast. To those who are worth their salt as slaves I give the means of life. But to those who will not or cannot sell their manhood—to those who will not stand tamely by and suffer their country to be ravaged by poverty and preyed upon by skulkers and idlers—I give the means of death. Poverty and slavery have stood up for centuries to sermons and Bibles and leading articles and pious platitudes: they will not stand up to my machine guns. Let every English citizen resolve to kill or be killed sooner than tolerate the existence of one poor person or one idler on the English soil; and poverty and slavery will vanish tomorrow.

BARBARA – Killing! Is that your remedy?

UNDERSHAFT – It is the final test of conviction, the sole lever strong enough to lift a whole people. It is the right of every man who will stake his own life on his faith. It is the only way of saying Must.[10]

Here it is perhaps natural to ask whether Shaw, in giving Undershaft these speeches, was expressing his own political philosophy or merely

[10] British Museum MS 50616D, folio 18.

presenting an idea, so to speak, dramatically. Any doubts on this subject may be resolved by consideration of another British Museum manuscript, that which contains Shaw's notes for a lecture on Darwin delivered to the Fabian Society in 1906, the year after the production of *Major Barbara*:

> Revolutions, remember, can only be made by men and women with courage enough to meet the ferocity and pugnacity of the common soldier and vanquish it. Do not delude ourselves with any dream of a peaceful evolution of Capitalism into Socialism, of automatic Liberal Progress, of the conciliation of our American bosses, and South African Randlords and British county society and Pall Mall military caste by the Fabian Society. The man who is not a Socialist is quite prepared to fight for his private property, or at least pay someone else to fight for him. He has no doubt whatever of the necessity and morality of such warfare. . . .
>
> We must clear our minds from cant and cowardice on this subject. It is true that the old barricade revolutionists were childishly and romantically wrong in their methods; and the Fabians were right in making an end of them and formulating constitutional Socialism. But nothing is as constitutional as fighting. Rents cannot be collected now without force, nor are they socialized—to the small extent to which they are already socialized—without force.[11]

Shaw is here appealing to history to verify Undershaft's statement that "the ballot paper that really governs us is the paper that has a bullet wrapped up in it." The Commune of 1871 had demonstrated the willingness of the proprietorial class to fight for their property rights. Later in this same Fabian lecture Shaw argues that the classic instance of non-violent change, the passage of the Reform Bill of 1832, is really an instance in favor of his view; for the Reform Bill passed only when the temper of the English nation reached the point where it was clearly a choice between passing the bill and facing a revolution.

I have called the last act a religious wooing of souls. Undershaft, seeing in Cusins the brains and sensitivity he thinks necessary in anyone who is to run a factory of death (or let us say, a democratic, or any other kind of state) offers him the management of the munitions work. The intelligentsia is to undertake the responsibilities of political power, that is, the power of life and death over millions. Cusins finds himself in the position of a famous predecessor of academic fame; Mephistopheles has once again put in a bid for a professor's soul, and though Cusins,

[11] British Museum, MS 50661, folios 81–82.

wiser than Faust, realizes that he has already sold his soul for his professorship, this does not make his dilemma less cruel.

For Barbara's engagement to Cusins is both a love match and something more again. Their marriage is to be a religious marriage in a sense of devoting them to something beyond themselves, to "larger loves and diviner dreams than the fireside ones." Their understanding is that unless their marriage can foster this religious side of themselves they are to part and seek other mates, or join the legion of the world's celibate saints and philosophers. If Cusins elects to sell his soul to Undershaft he thus jeopardizes his relation with Barbara, who is first of all a "salvationist" (in an unsectarian sense) and only secondly a fiancée.

At this point Shaw turns to an episode from real life to solve the dilemma. When an idealistic student[12] of Murray's set out for the Greco-Turkish War in 1897, Murray had given the young man, not a copy of Plato's *Republic*, but a revolver. Shaw ascribes this incident to Cusins, and makes Undershaft seize upon it to demonstrate to the professor that he is, for all his hatred of war, committed to the side of the industrialist. Cusins is forced to concur, and declares that he will choose the "reality and power" of the factory of death, even if it means losing Barbara.

But Barbara, for all her talk about turning her back on wickedness, can no more turn away from life than can Cusins. Now she will be able to preach to the well-fed, self-respecting men and women in Undershaft's model factory-town and know that, when they abandon their snobbishness and selfishness for higher ends, they are not simply being tempted by the bribe of bread. She has regained her faith and courage: the enthusiasm of the new Dionysianism possesses her and she goes "right up into the skies," saved forever from the fate she has most dreaded, the boredom and triviality of the genteel drawing room.

[12] The young man was H. N. Brailsford; see *An Unfinished Autobiography*, p. 97.

SAINT JOAN

[1923]

CHARACTERS

ROBERT DE BAUDRICOURT	
STEWARD	
JOAN	
BERTRAND DE POULENGEY	
THE ARCHBISHOP OF RHEIMS	
LA TRÉMOUILLE	*Constable of France*
COURT PAGE	
GILLES DE RAIS	*Bluebeard*
CAPTAIN LA HIRE	
THE DAUPHIN	(later *Charles* VII)
THE DUCHESSE DE LA TRÉMOUILLE	
DUNOIS	*Bastard of Orleans*
DUNOIS' PAGE	
RICHARD DE BEAUCHAMP	*Earl of Warwick*
CHAPLAIN DE STOGUMBER	
PETER CAUCHON	*Bishop of Beauvais*
WARWICK'S PAGE	
THE INQUISITOR	
D'ESTIVET	*Canon of Bayeux*
DE COURCELLES	*Canon of Paris*
BROTHER MARTIN LADVENU	
THE EXECUTIONER	
AN ENGLISH SOLDIER	
A GENTLEMAN	

SCENE ONE

A fine spring morning on the river Meuse, between Lorraine and Champagne, in the year 1429 A.D., in the castle of Vaucouleurs.

CAPTAIN ROBERT DE BAUDRICOURT, *a military squire, handsome and physically energetic, but with no will of his own, is disguising that defect in his usual fashion by storming terribly at his steward, a trodden worm, scanty of flesh, scanty of hair, who might be any age from 18 to 55, being the sort of man whom age cannot wither because he has never bloomed.*

The two are in a sunny stone chamber on the first floor of the castle. At a plain strong oak table, seated in chair to match, the captain presents his left profile. The STEWARD stands facing him at the other side of the table, if so deprecatory a stance as his can be called standing. The mullioned thirteenth-century window is open behind him. Near it in the corner is a turret with a narrow arched doorway leading to a winding stair which descends to the courtyard. There is a stout fourlegged stool under the table, and a wooden chest under the window.

ROBERT – No eggs! No eggs!! Thousand thunders, man, what do you mean by no eggs?

STEWARD – Sir: it is not my fault. It is the act of God.

ROBERT – Blasphemy. You tell me there are no eggs; and you blame your Maker for it.

STEWARD – Sir: what can I do? I cannot lay eggs.

ROBERT [*sarcastic*] Ha! You jest about it.

STEWARD – No, sir, God knows. We all have to go without eggs just as you have, sir. The hens will not lay.

ROBERT – Indeed! [*Rising.*] Now listen to me, you.

STEWARD [*humbly*] Yes, sir.

ROBERT – What am I?

STEWARD – What are you, sir?

ROBERT [*coming at him*] Yes: what am I? Am I Robert, squire of Baudricourt and captain of this castle of Vaucouleurs; or am I a cowboy?

STEWARD – Oh, sir, you know you are a greater man here than the king himself.

ROBERT – Precisely. And now, do you know what you are?

STEWARD – I am nobody, sir, except that I have the honor to be your steward.

ROBERT [*driving him to the wall, adjective by adjective*] You have not only the honor of being my steward, but the privilege of being the worst, most incompetent, drivelling snivelling jibbering jabbering idiot of a steward in France.

[*He strides back to the table.*]

STEWARD [*cowering on the chest*] Yes, sir: to a great man like you I must seem like that.

ROBERT [*turning*] My fault, I suppose. Eh?

STEWARD [*coming to him deprecatingly*] Oh, sir: you always give my most innocent words such a turn!

ROBERT – I will give your neck a turn if you dare tell me when I ask you how many eggs there are that you cannot lay any.

STEWARD [*protesting*] Oh sir, oh sir—

ROBERT – No: not oh sir, oh sir, but no sir, no sir. My three Barbary hens and the black are the best layers in Champagne. And you come and tell me that there are no eggs! Who stole them? Tell me that, before I kick you out through the castle gate for a liar and a seller of my goods to thieves. The milk was short yesterday, too: do not forget that.

STEWARD [*desperate*] I know, sir. I know only too well. There is no milk: there are no eggs: tomorrow there will be nothing.

ROBERT – Nothing! You will steal the lot: eh?

STEWARD – No, sir: nobody will steal anything. But there is a spell on us: we are bewitched.

ROBERT – That story is not good enough for me. Robert de Baudricourt burns witches and hangs thieves. Go. Bring me four dozen eggs and two gallons of milk here in this room before noon, or Heaven have mercy on your bones! I will teach you to make a fool of me.

[*He resumes his seat with an air of finality.*]

STEWARD – Sir: I tell you there are no eggs. There will be none—not if you were to kill me for it—as long as The Maid is at the door.

ROBERT – The Maid! What maid? What are you talking about?

STEWARD – The girl from Lorraine, sir. From Domrémy.

ROBERT [*rising in fearful wrath*] Thirty thousand thunders! Fifty thousand devils! Do you mean to say that that girl, who had the impudence to ask to see me two days ago, and whom I told you to send back to her father with my orders that he was to give her a good hiding, is here still?

STEWARD – I have told her to go, sir. She wont.

ROBERT – I did not tell you to tell her to go: I told you to throw her out. You have fifty men-at-arms and a dozen lumps of able-bodied servants to carry out my orders. Are they afraid of her?

STEWARD – She is so positive, sir.

ROBERT [*seizing him by the scruff of the neck*] Positive! Now see here. I am going to throw you downstairs.

STEWARD – No, sir. Please.

ROBERT – Well, stop me by being positive. It's quite easy: any slut of a girl can do it.

STEWARD [*hanging limp in his hands*] Sir, sir: you cannot get rid of her by throwing me out. [ROBERT *has to let him drop. He squats on his knees on the floor, contemplating his master resignedly.*] You see, sir, you are much more positive than I am. But so is she.

ROBERT – I am stronger than you are, you fool.

STEWARD – No, sir: it isnt that: it's your strong character, sir. She is weaker than we are: she is only a slip of a girl; but we cannot make her go.

ROBERT – You parcel of curs: you are afraid of her.

STEWARD [*rising cautiously*] No sir: we are afraid of you; but she puts courage into us. She really doesnt seem to be afraid of anything. Perhaps you could frighten her, sir.

ROBERT [*grimly*] Perhaps. Where is she now?

STEWARD – Down in the courtyard, sir, talking to the soldiers as usual. She is always talking to the soldiers except when she is praying.

ROBERT – Praying! Ha! You believe she prays, you idiot. I know the sort of girl that is always talking to soldiers. She shall talk to me a bit. [*He goes to the window and shouts fiercely through it.*] Hallo, you there!

A GIRL'S VOICE [*bright, strong and rough*] Is it me, sir?

ROBERT – Yes, you.

THE VOICE – Be you captain?

ROBERT – Yes, damn your impudence, I be captain. Come up here. [*To the soldiers in the yard.*] Shew her the way, you. And shove her along quick.

> [*He leaves the window, and returns to his place at the table, where he sits magisterially.*]

STEWARD [*whispering*] She wants to go and be a soldier herself. She wants you to give her soldier's clothes. Armor, sir! And a sword! Actually!

> [*He steals behind* ROBERT.]

JOAN *appears in the turret doorway. She is an ablebodied country girl of 17 or 18, respectably dressed in red, with an uncommon face; eyes very wide apart and bulging as they often do in very imaginative people, a long well-shaped nose with wide nostrils, a short upper lip, resolute but full-lipped mouth, and handsome fighting chin. She comes eagerly to the table, delighted at having penetrated to* BAUDRICOURT's *presence at last, and full of hope as to the results. His scowl does not check or frighten her in the least. Her voice is normally a hearty coaxing voice, very confident, very appealing, very hard to resist.*

J O A N [*bobbing a curtsey*] Good morning, captain squire. Captain: you are to give me a horse and armor and some soldiers, and send me to the Dauphin. Those are your orders from my Lord.

R O B E R T [*outraged*] Orders from your lord! And who the devil may your lord be? Go back to him, and tell him that I am neither duke nor peer at his orders: I am squire of Baudricourt; and I take no orders except from the king.

J O A N [*reassuringly*] Yes, squire: that is all right. My Lord is the King of Heaven.

R O B E R T — Why, the girl's mad. [*To the* STEWARD.] Why didnt you tell me so, you blockhead?

S T E W A R D — Sir: do not anger her: give her what she wants.

J O A N [*impatient, but friendly*] They all say I am mad until I talk to them, squire. But you see that it is the will of God that you are to do what He has put into my mind.

R O B E R T — It is the will of God that I shall send you back to your father with orders to put you under lock and key and thrash the madness out of you. What have you to say to that?

J O A N — You think you will, squire; but you will find it all coming quite different. You said you would not see me; but here I am.

S T E W A R D [*appealing*] Yes, sir. You see, sir.

R O B E R T — Hold your tongue, you.

S T E W A R D [*abjectly*] Yes, sir.

R O B E R T [*to* JOAN, *with a sour loss of confidence*] So you are presuming on my seeing you, are you?

J O A N [*sweetly*] Yes, squire.

R O B E R T [*feeling that he has lost ground, brings down his two fists squarely on the table, and inflates his chest imposingly to cure the unwelcome and only too familiar sensation*] Now listen to me. I am going to assert myself.

J O A N [*busily*] Please do, squire. The horse will cost sixteen francs. It is a good deal of money: but I can save it on the armor. I can find a soldier's armor that will fit me well enough: I am very hardy; and I do not need beautiful armor made to my measure like you wear. I shall not want many soldiers: the Dauphin will give me all I need to raise the siege of Orleans.

ROBERT [*flabbergasted*] To raise the siege of Orleans!

JOAN [*simply*] Yes, squire: that is what God is sending me to do. Three men will be enough for you to send with me if they are good men and gentle to me. They have promised to come with me. Polly and Jack and—

ROBERT—Polly!! You impudent baggage, do you dare call squire Bertrand de Poulengey Polly to my face?

JOAN—His friends call him so, squire: I did not know he had any other name. Jack—

ROBERT—That is Monsieur John of Metz, I suppose?

JOAN—Yes, squire. Jack will come willingly: he is a very kind gentleman, and gives me money to give to the poor. I think John Godsave will come, and Dick the Archer, and their servants John of Honecourt and Julian. There will be no trouble for you, squire: I have arranged it all: you have only to give the order.

ROBERT [*contemplating her in a stupor of amazement*] Well, I am damned!

JOAN [*with unruffled sweetness*] No, squire: God is very merciful; and the blessed saints Catherine and Margaret, who speak to me every day [*he gapes*], will intercede for you. You will go to paradise; and your name will be remembered for ever as my first helper.

ROBERT [*to the* STEWARD, *still much bothered, but changing his tone as he pursues a new clue*] Is this true about Monsieur de Poulengey?

STEWARD [*eagerly*] Yes, sir, and about Monsieur de Metz too. They both want to go with her.

ROBERT [*thoughtful*] Mf! [*He goes to the window, and shouts into the courtyard.*] Hallo! You there: send Monsieur de Poulengey to me, will you? [*He turns to* JOAN.] Get out; and wait in the yard.

JOAN [*smiling brightly at him*] Right, squire.

[*She goes out.*]

ROBERT [*to the* STEWARD] Go with her, you, you dithering imbecile. Stay within call; and keep your eye on her. I shall have her up here again.

STEWARD—Do so in God's name, sir. Think of those hens, the best layers in Champagne; and—

ROBERT—Think of my boot; and take your backside out of reach of it.

The STEWARD *retreats hastily and finds himself confronted in the doorway by* BERTRAND DE POULENGEY, *a lymphatic French gentleman-at-arms, aged 36 or thereabout, employed in the department of the provost-marshal,*

dreamily absent-minded, seldom speaking unless spoken to, and then slow and obstinate in reply; altogether in contrast to the self-assertive, loud-mouthed, superficially energetic, fundamentally will-less ROBERT. *The* STEWARD *makes way for him, and vanishes.*
POULENGEY *salutes, and stands awaiting orders.*

ROBERT [*genially*] It isnt service, Polly. A friendly talk. Sit down. [*He hooks the stool from under the table with his instep.*]

POULENGEY, *relaxing, comes into the room: places the stool between the table and the window: and sits down ruminatively.* ROBERT, *half sitting on the end of the table, begins the friendly talk.*

ROBERT – Now listen to me, Polly. I must talk to you like a father. [POULENGEY *looks up at him gravely for a moment, but says nothing.*]
ROBERT – It's about this girl you are interested in. Now, I have seen her. I have talked to her. First, she's mad. That doesnt matter. Second, she's not a farm wench. She's a bourgeoise. That matters a good deal. I know her class exactly. Her father came here last year to represent his village in a lawsuit: he is one of their notables. A farmer. Not a gentleman farmer: he makes money by it, and lives by it. Still, not a laborer. Not a mechanic. He might have a cousin a lawyer, or in the Church. People of this sort may be of no account socially; but they can give a lot of bother to the authorities. That is to say, to me. Now no doubt it seems to you a very simple thing to take this girl away, humbugging her into the belief that you are taking her to the Dauphin. But if you get her into trouble, you may get me into no end of a mess, as I am her father's lord, and responsible for her protection. So friends or no friends, Polly, hands off her.
POULENGEY [*with deliberate impressiveness*] I should as soon think of the Blessed Virgin herself in that way, as of this girl.
ROBERT [*coming off the table*] But she says you and Jack and Dick have offered to go with her. What for? You are not going to tell me that you take her crazy notion of going to the Dauphin seriously, are you?
POULENGEY [*slowly*] There is something about her. They are pretty foulmouthed and foulminded down there in the guardroom, some of them. But there hasnt been a word that has anything to do with her being a woman. They have stopped swearing before her. There is something. Something. It may be worth trying.
ROBERT – Oh, come, Polly! pull yourself together. Commonsense was never your strong point; but this is a little too much.
[*He retreats disgustedly.*]

POULENGEY [*unmoved*] What is the good of commonsense? If we had any commonsense we should join the Duke of Burgundy and the English king. They hold half the country, right down to the Loire. They have Paris. They have this castle: you know very well that we had to surrender it to the Duke of Bedford, and that you are only holding it on parole. The Dauphin is in Chinon, like a rat in a corner, except that he wont fight. We dont even know that he is the Dauphin: his mother says he isnt; and she ought to know. Think of that! the queen denying the legitimacy of her own son!

ROBERT – Well, she married her daughter to the English king. Can you blame the woman?

POULENGEY – I blame nobody. But thanks to her, the Dauphin is down and out; and we may as well face it. The English will take Orleans: the Bastard will not be able to stop them.

ROBERT – He beat the English the year before last at Montargis. I was with him.

POULENGEY – No matter: his men are cowed now; and he cant work miracles. And I tell you that nothing can save our side now but a miracle.

ROBERT – Miracles are all right, Polly. The only difficulty about them is that they dont happen nowadays.

POULENGEY – I used to think so. I am not so sure now. [*Rising, and moving ruminatively towards the window.*] At all events this is not a time to leave any stone unturned. There is something about the girl.

ROBERT – Oh! You think the girl can work miracles, do you?

POULENGEY – I think the girl herself is a bit of a miracle. Anyhow, she is the last card left in our hand. Better play her than throw up the game.

[*He wanders to the turret.*]

ROBERT [*wavering*] You really think that?

POULENGEY [*turning*] Is there anything else left for us to think?

ROBERT [*going to him*] Look here, Polly. If you were in my place would you let a girl like that do you out of sixteen francs for a horse?

POULENGEY – I will pay for the horse.

ROBERT – You will!

POULENGEY – Yes: I will back my opinion.

ROBERT – You will really gamble on a forlorn hope to the tune of sixteen francs?

POULENGEY – It is not a gamble.

ROBERT – What else is it?

POULENGEY – It is a certainty. Her words and her ardent faith in God have put fire into me.

ROBERT [*giving him up*] Whew! You are as mad as she is.

POULENGEY [*obstinately*] We want a few mad people now. See where the sane ones have landed us!

ROBERT [*his irresoluteness now openly swamping his affected decisiveness*] I shall feel like a precious fool. Still, if you feel sure—?

POULENGEY—I feel sure enough to take her to Chinon—unless you stop me.

ROBERT—This is not fair. You are putting the responsibility on me.

POULENGEY—It is on you whichever way you decide.

ROBERT—Yes: thats just it. Which way am I to decide? You dont see how awkward this is for me. [*Snatching at a dilatory step with an unconscious hope that* JOAN *will make up his mind for him.*] Do you think I ought to have another talk to her?

POULENGEY [*rising*] Yes. [*He goes to the window and calls.*] Joan!

JOAN'S VOICE—Will he let us go, Polly?

POULENGEY—Come up. Come in. [*Turning to* ROBERT.] Shall I leave you with her?

ROBERT—No: stay here; and back me up.

POULENGEY *sits down on the chest.* ROBERT *goes back to his magisterial chair, but remains standing to inflate himself more imposingly.* JOAN *comes in, full of good news.*

JOAN—Jack will go halves for the horse.

ROBERT—Well!!

[*He sits, deflated.*]

POULENGEY [*gravely*] Sit down, Joan.

JOAN [*checked a little, and looking to* ROBERT] May I?

ROBERT—Do what you are told.

[JOAN *curtsies and sits down on the stool between them.* ROBERT *outfaces his perplexity with his most peremptory air.*]

ROBERT—What is your name?

JOAN [*chattily*] They always call me Jenny in Lorraine. Here in France I am Joan. The soldiers call me The Maid.

ROBERT—What is your surname?

JOAN—Surname? What is that? My father sometimes calls himself d'Arc; but I know nothing about it. You met my father. He—

ROBERT—Yes, yes; I remember. You come from Domrémy in Lorraine, I think.

JOAN—Yes; but what does it matter? we all speak French.

ROBERT—Dont ask questions: answer them. How old are you?

JOAN—Seventeen: so they tell me. It might be nineteen. I dont remember.

ROBERT—What did you mean when you said that St Catherine and St Margaret talked to you every day?

JOAN – They do.

ROBERT – What are they like?

JOAN [*suddenly obstinate*] I will tell you nothing about that: they have not given me leave.

ROBERT – But you actually see them; and they talk to you just as I am talking to you?

JOAN – No: it is quite different. I cannot tell you: you must not talk to me about my voices.

ROBERT – How do you mean? voices?

JOAN – I hear voices telling me what to do. They come from God.

ROBERT – They come from your imagination.

JOAN – Of course. That is how the messages of God come to us.

POULENGEY – Checkmate.

ROBERT – No fear! [*To* JOAN.] So God says you are to raise the siege of Orleans?

JOAN – And to crown the Dauphin in Rheims Cathedral.

ROBERT [*gasping*] Crown the D—! Gosh!

JOAN – And to make the English leave France.

ROBERT [*sarcastic*] Anything else?

JOAN [*charming*] Not just at present, thank you, squire.

ROBERT – I suppose you think raising a siege is as easy as chasing a cow out of a meadow. You think soldiering is anybody's job?

JOAN – I do not think it can be very difficult if God is on your side, and you are willing to put your life in His hand. But many soldiers are very simple.

ROBERT [*grimly*] Simple! Did you ever see English soldiers fighting?

JOAN – They are only men. God made them just like us; but He gave them their own country and their own language; and it is not His will that they should come into our country and try to speak our language.

ROBERT – Who has been putting such nonsense into your head? Dont you know that soldiers are subject to their feudal lord, and that it is nothing to them or to you whether he is the duke of Burgundy or the king of England or the king of France? What has their language to do with it?

JOAN – I do not understand that a bit. We are all subject to the King of Heaven; and He gave us our countries and our languages, and meant us to keep to them. If it were not so it would be murder to kill an Englishman in battle; and you, squire, would be in great danger of hell fire. You must not think about your duty to your feudal lord, but about your duty to God.

POULENGEY – It's no use, Robert: she can choke you like that every time.

ROBERT – Can she, by Saint Dennis! We shall see. [*To* JOAN.] We are not talking about God: we are talking about practical affairs. I ask you

1757

again, girl, have you ever seen English soldiers fighting? Have you ever seen them plundering, burning, turning the countryside into a desert? Have you heard no tales of their Black Prince who was blacker than the devil himself, or of the English king's father?

J O A N – You must not be afraid, Robert—

R O B E R T – Damn you, I am not afraid. And who gave you leave to call me Robert?

J O A N – You were called so in church in the name of our Lord. All the other names are your father's or your brother's or anybody's.

R O B E R T – Tcha!

J O A N – Listen to me, squire. At Domrémy we had to fly to the next village to escape from the English soldiers. Three of them were left behind, wounded. I came to know these three poor goddams quite well. They had not half my strength.

R O B E R T – Do you know why they are called goddams?

J O A N – No. Everyone calls them goddams.

R O B E R T – It is because they are always calling on their God to condemn their souls to perdition. That is what goddam means in their language. How do you like it?

J O A N – God will be merciful to them; and they will act like His good children when they go back to the country He made for them, and made them for. I have heard the tales of the Black Prince. The moment he touched the soil of our country the devil entered into him, and made him a black fiend. But at home, in the place made for him by God, he was good. It is always so. If I went into England against the will of God to conquer England, and tried to live there and speak its language, the devil would enter into me; and when I was old I should shudder to remember the wickedness I did.

R O B E R T – Perhaps. But the more devil you were the better you might fight. That is why the goddams will take Orleans. And you cannot stop them, nor ten thousand like you.

J O A N – One thousand like me can stop them. Ten like me can stop them with God on our side. [*She rises impetuously, and goes at him, unable to sit quiet any longer.*] You do not understand, squire. Our soldiers are always beaten because they are fighting only to save their skins; and the shortest way to save your skin is to run away. Our knights are thinking only of the money they will make in ransoms: it is not kill or be killed with them, but pay or be paid. But I will teach them all to fight that the will of God may be done in France; and then they will drive the poor goddams before them like sheep. You and Polly will live to see the day when there will not be an English soldier on the soil of France; and there will be but one king there: not the feudal English king, but God's French one.

ROBERT [*to* POULENGEY] This may be all rot, Polly; but the troops might swallow it, though nothing that we can say seems able to put any fight into them. Even the Dauphin might swallow it. And if she can put fight into him, she can put it into anybody.

POULENGEY—I can see no harm in trying. Can you? And there is something about the girl—

ROBERT [*turning to* JOAN] Now listen you to me; and [*desperately*] dont cut in before I have time to think.

JOAN [*plumping down on the stool again, like an obedient schoolgirl*] Yes, squire.

ROBERT—Your orders are, that you are to go to Chinon under the escort of this gentleman and three of his friends.

JOAN [*radiant, clasping her hands*] Oh, squire! Your head is all circled with light, like a saint's.

POULENGEY—How is she to get into the royal presence?

ROBERT [*who has looked up for his halo rather apprehensively*] I dont know: how did she get into my presence? If the Dauphin can keep her out he is a better man than I take him for. [*Rising.*] I will send her to Chinon; and she can say I sent her. Then let come what may: I can do no more.

JOAN—And the dress? I may have a soldier's dress, maynt I, squire?

ROBERT—Have what you please. I wash my hands of it.

JOAN [*wildly excited by her success*] Come, Polly. [*She dashes out.*]

ROBERT [*shaking* POULENGEY's *hand*] Goodbye, old man, I am taking a big chance. Few other men would have done it. But as you say, there is something about her.

POULENGEY—Yes: there is something about her. Goodbye.

[*He goes out.*]

ROBERT, *still very doubtful whether he has not been made a fool of by a crazy female, and a social inferior to boot, scratches his head and slowly comes back from the door.*

The STEWARD *runs in with a basket.*

STEWARD—Sir, sir—

ROBERT—What now?

STEWARD—The hens are laying like mad, sir. Five dozen eggs!

ROBERT [*stiffens convulsively: crosses himself: and forms with his pale lips the words*] Christ in heaven! [*Aloud but breathless.*] She did come from God.

SCENE TWO

Chinon, in Touraine. An end of the throne room in the castle, curtained off to make an antechamber. The ARCHBISHOP OF RHEIMS, *close on 50, a full-fed prelate with nothing of the ecclesiastic about him except his imposing bearing, and the* LORD CHAMBERLAIN, *Monseigneur de la Trémouille, a monstrous arrogant wineskin of a man, are waiting for the* DAUPHIN. *There is a door in the wall to the right of the two men. It is late in the afternoon on the 8th of March, 1429. The* ARCHBISHOP *stands with dignity whilst the* CHAMBERLAIN, *on his left, fumes about in the worst of tempers.*

LA TRÉMOUILLE–What the devil does the Dauphin mean by keeping us waiting like this? I dont know how you have the patience to stand there like a stone idol.

THE ARCHBISHOP–You see, I am an archbishop; and an archbishop is a sort of idol. At any rate he has to learn to keep still and suffer fools patiently. Besides, my dear Lord Chamberlain, it is the Dauphin's royal privilege to keep you waiting, is it not?

LA TRÉMOUILLE–Dauphin be damned! saving your reverence. Do you know how much money he owes me?

THE ARCHBISHOP–Much more than he owes me, I have no doubt, because you are a much richer man. But I take it he owes you all you could afford to lend him. That is what he owes me.

LA TRÉMOUILLE–Twenty-seven thousand: that was his last haul. A cool twenty-seven thousand!

THE ARCHBISHOP–What becomes of it all? He never has a suit of clothes that I would throw to a curate.

LA TRÉMOUILLE–He dines on a chicken or a scrap of mutton. He borrows my last penny; and there is nothing to shew for it. [*A page appears in the doorway.*] At last!

THE PAGE–No, my lord: it is not His Majesty. Monsieur de Rais is approaching.

LA TRÉMOUILLE–Young Bluebeard! Why announce him?

THE PAGE–Captain La Hire is with him. Something has happened, I think.

GILLES DE RAIS, *a young man of 25, very smart and self-possessed, and sporting the extravagance of a little curled beard dyed blue at a clean-shaven court, comes in. He is determined to make himself agreeable, but lacks natural joyousness, and is not really pleasant. In fact when he defies the Church some eleven years later he is accused of trying to extract pleasure from horrible cruelties, and hanged. So far, however, there is no shadow of the gallows on him. He advances gaily to the* ARCHBISHOP. *The page withdraws.*

BLUEBEARD—Your faithful lamb, Archbishop. Good day, my lord. Do you know what has happened to La Hire?

LA TRÉMOUILLE—He has sworn himself into a fit, perhaps.

BLUEBEARD—No: just the opposite. Foul Mouthed Frank, the only man in Touraine who could beat him at swearing, was told by a soldier that he shouldnt use such language when he was at the point of death.

THE ARCHBISHOP—Nor at any other point. But was Foul Mouthed Frank on the point of death?

BLUEBEARD—Yes: he has just fallen into a well and been drowned. La Hire is frightened out of his wits.

[CAPTAIN LA HIRE *comes in: a war dog with no court manners and pronounced camp ones.*]

BLUEBEARD—I have just been telling the Chamberlain and the Archbishop. The Archbishop says you are a lost man.

LA HIRE [*striding past* BLUEBEARD, *and planting himself between the* ARCHBISHOP *and* LA TRÉMOUILLE] This is nothing to joke about. It is worse than we thought. It was not a soldier, but an angel dressed as a soldier.

THE ARCHBISHOP
THE CHAMBERLAIN } [*exclaiming all together*] An angel!
BLUEBEARD

LA HIRE—Yes, an angel. She has made her way from Champagne with half a dozen men through the thick of everything: Burgundians, God-dams, deserters, robbers, and Lord knows who; and they never met a soul except the country folk. I know one of them: de Poulengey. He says she's an angel. If ever I utter an oath again may my soul be blasted to eternal damnation!

THE ARCHBISHOP—A very pious beginning, Captain.

[BLUEBEARD *and* LA TRÉMOUILLE *laugh at him. The page returns.*]

THE PAGE—His Majesty.

They stand perfunctorily at court attention. The DAUPHIN, *aged 26, really* KING CHARLES THE SEVENTH *since the death of his father, but as yet uncrowned, comes in through the curtains with a paper in his hands. He is a poor creature physically; and the current fashion of shaving closely, and hiding every scrap of hair under the headcovering or head-dress, both by women and men, makes the worst of his appearance. He has little narrow eyes, near together, a long pendulous nose that droops over his thick short upper lip, and the expression of a young dog accustomed to be kicked, yet incorrigible and irrepressible. But he is neither vulgar nor stupid; and he has a cheeky humor which enables him to hold his own in conversation. Just at present he is excited, like a child with a new toy. He comes to the* ARCHBISHOP'S *left hand.* BLUEBEARD *and* LA HIRE *retire towards the curtains.*

CHARLES – Oh, Archbishop, do you know what Robert de Baudricourt is sending me from Vaucouleurs?

THE ARCHBISHOP [*contemptuously*] I am not interested in the newest toys.

CHARLES [*indignantly*] It isnt a toy. [*Sulkily.*] However, I can get on very well without your interest.

THE ARCHBISHOP – Your Highness is taking offence very unnecessarily.

CHARLES – Thank you. You are always ready with a lecture, arnt you?

LA TRÉMOUILLE [*roughly*] Enough grumbling. What have you got there?

CHARLES – What is that to you?

LA TRÉMOUILLE – It is my business to know what is passing between you and the garrison at Vaucouleurs.

He snatches the paper from the DAUPHIN'S *hand, and begins reading it with some difficulty, following the words with his finger and spelling them out syllable by syllable.*

CHARLES [*mortified*] You all think you can treat me as you please because I owe you money, and because I am no good at fighting. But I have the blood royal in my veins.

THE ARCHBISHOP – Even that has been questioned, your Highness. One hardly recognizes in you the grandson of Charles the Wise.

CHARLES – I want to hear no more of my grandfather. He was so wise that he used up the whole family stock of wisdom for five generations, and left me the poor fool I am, bullied and insulted by all of you.

THE ARCHBISHOP – Control yourself, sir. These outbursts of petulance are not seemly.

CHARLES – Another lecture! Thank you. What a pity it is that though you are an archbishop saints and angels dont come to see you!

THE ARCHBISHOP – What do you mean?

CHARLES – Aha! Ask that bully there.

[*Pointing to* LA TRÉMOUILLE.]

LA TRÉMOUILLE [*furious*] Hold your tongue. Do you hear?

CHARLES – Oh, I hear. You neednt shout. The whole castle can hear. Why dont you go and shout at the English, and beat them for me?

LA TRÉMOUILLE [*raising his fist*] You young—

CHARLES [*running behind the* ARCHBISHOP] Dont you raise your hand to me. It's high treason.

LA HIRE – Steady, Duke! Steady!

THE ARCHBISHOP [*resolutely*] Come, come! this will not do. My Lord Chamberlain: please! please! we must keep some sort of order. [*To the* DAUPHIN.] And you, sir: if you cannot rule your kingdom, at least try to rule yourself.

CHARLES – Another lecture! Thank you.

LA TRÉMOUILLE [*handing over the paper to the* ARCHBISHOP] Here: read the accursed thing for me. He has sent the blood boiling into my head: I cant distinguish the letters.

CHARLES [*coming back and peering round* LA TRÉMOUILLE's *left shoulder*] I will read it for you if you like. I can read, you know.

LA TRÉMOUILLE [*with intense contempt, not at all stung by the taunt*] Yes: reading is about all you are fit for. Can you make it out, Archbishop?

THE ARCHBISHOP – I should have expected more commonsense from De Baudricourt. He is sending some cracked country lass here—

CHARLES [*interrupting*] No: he is sending a saint: an angel. And she is coming to me: to me, the king, and not to you, Archbishop, holy as you are. She knows the blood royal if you dont.

[*He struts up to the curtains between* BLUEBEARD *and* LA HIRE.]

THE ARCHBISHOP – You cannot be allowed to see this crazy wench.

CHARLES [*turning*] But I am the king; and I will.

LA TRÉMOUILLE [*brutally*] Then she cannot be allowed to see you. Now!

CHARLES – I tell you I will. I am going to put my foot down—

BLUEBEARD [*laughing at him*] Naughty! What would your wise grandfather say?

CHARLES – That just shews your ignorance, Bluebeard. My grandfather had a saint who used to float in the air when she was praying, and told him everything he wanted to know. My poor father had two saints, Marie de Maillé and the Gasque of Avignon. It is in our family; and I dont care what you say: I will have my saint too.

THE ARCHBISHOP – This creature is not a saint. She is not even a respectable woman. She does not wear women's clothes. She is dressed like a soldier, and rides round the country with soldiers. Do you suppose such a person can be admitted to your Highness's court?

LA HIRE—Stop. [*Going to the* ARCHBISHOP.] Did you say a girl in armor, like a soldier?

THE ARCHBISHOP—So De Baudricourt describes her.

LA HIRE—But by all the devils in hell—Oh, God forgive me, what am I saying?—by Our Lady and all the saints, this must be the angel that struck Foul Mouthed Frank dead for swearing.

CHARLES [*triumphant*] You see! A miracle!

LA HIRE—She may strike the lot of us dead if we cross her. For Heaven's sake, Archbishop, be careful what you are doing.

THE ARCHBISHOP [*severely*] Rubbish! Nobody has been struck dead. A drunken blackguard who has been rebuked a hundred times for swearing has fallen into a well, and been drowned. A mere coincidence.

LA HIRE—I do not know what a coincidence is. I do know that the man is dead, and that she told him he was going to die.

THE ARCHBISHOP—We are all going to die, Captain.

LA HIRE [*crossing himself*] I hope not.

[*He backs out of the conversation.*]

BLUEBEARD—We can easily find out whether she is an angel or not. Let us arrange when she comes that I shall be the Dauphin, and see whether she will find me out.

CHARLES—Yes: I agree to that. If she cannot find the blood royal I will have nothing to do with her.

THE ARCHBISHOP—It is for the Church to make saints: let De Baudricourt mind his own business, and not dare usurp the function of his priest. I say the girl shall not be admitted.

BLUEBEARD—But, Archbishop—

THE ARCHBISHOP [*sternly*] I speak in the Church's name. [*To the* DAUPHIN.] Do you dare say she shall?

CHARLES [*intimidated but sulky*] Oh, if you make it an excommunication matter, I have nothing more to say, of course. But you havnt read the end of the letter. De Baudricourt says she will raise the siege of Orleans, and beat the English for us.

LA TRÉMOUILLE—Rot!

CHARLES—Well, will you save Orleans for us, with all your bullying?

LA TRÉMOUILLE [*savagely*] Do not throw that in my face again: do you hear? I have done more fighting than you ever did or ever will. But I cannot be everywhere.

THE DAUPHIN—Well, thats something.

BLUEBEARD [*coming between the* ARCHBISHOP *and* CHARLES] You have Jack Dunois at the head of your troops in Orleans: the brave

Dunois, the handsome Dunois, the wonderful invincible Dunois, the darling of all the ladies, the beautiful bastard. Is it likely that the country lass can do what he cannot do?

CHARLES—Why doesnt he raise the siege, then?

LA HIRE—The wind is against him.

BLUEBEARD—How can the wind hurt him at Orleans? It is not on the Channel.

LA HIRE—It is on the river Loire; and the English hold the bridgehead. He must ship his men across the river and upstream, if he is to take them in the rear. Well, he cannot, because there is a devil of a wind blowing the other way. He is tired of paying the priests to pray for a west wind. What he needs is a miracle. You tell me that what the girl did to Foul Mouthed Frank was no miracle. No matter: it finished Frank. If she changes the wind for Dunois, that may not be a miracle either; but it may finish the English. What harm is there in trying?

THE ARCHBISHOP [*who has read the end of the letter and become more thoughtful*] It is true that De Baudricourt seems extraordinarily impressed.

LA HIRE—De Baudricourt is a blazing ass; but he is a soldier; and if he thinks she can beat the English, all the rest of the army will think so too.

LA TRÉMOUILLE [*to the* ARCHBISHOP, *who is hesitating*] Oh, let them have their way. Dunois' men will give up the town in spite of him if somebody does not put some fresh spunk into them.

THE ARCHBISHOP—The Church must examine the girl before anything decisive is done about her. However, since his Highness desires it, let her attend the Court.

LA HIRE—I will find her and tell her.

[*He goes out.*]

CHARLES—Come with me, Bluebeard; and let us arrange so that she will not know who I am. You will pretend to be me.

[*He goes out through the curtains.*]

BLUEBEARD—Pretend to be that thing! Holy Michael!

[*He follows the* DAUPHIN.]

LA TRÉMOUILLE—I wonder will she pick him out!

THE ARCHBISHOP—Of course she will.

LA TRÉMOUILLE—Why? How is she to know?

THE ARCHBISHOP—She will know what everybody in Chinon knows: that the Dauphin is the meanest-looking and worst-dressed figure in the Court, and that the man with the blue beard is Gilles de Rais.

LA TRÉMOUILLE—I never thought of that.

THE ARCHBISHOP—You are not so accustomed to miracles as I am. It is part of my profession.

LA TRÉMOUILLE [*puzzled and a little scandalized*] But that would not be a miracle at all.

THE ARCHBISHOP [*calmly*] Why not?

LA TRÉMOUILLE—Well, come! what is a miracle?

THE ARCHBISHOP—A miracle, my friend, is an event which creates faith. That is the purpose and nature of miracles. They may seem very wonderful to the people who witness them, and very simple to those who perform them. That does not matter: if they confirm or create faith they are true miracles.

LA TRÉMOUILLE—Even when they are frauds, do you mean?

THE ARCHBISHOP—Frauds deceive. An event which creates faith does not deceive: therefore it is not a fraud, but a miracle.

LA TRÉMOUILLE [*scratching his neck in his perplexity*] Well, I suppose as you are an archbishop you must be right. It seems a bit fishy to me. But I am no churchman, and dont understand these matters.

THE ARCHBISHOP—You are not a churchman; but you are a diplomatist and a soldier. Could you make our citizens pay war taxes, or our soldiers sacrifice their lives, if they knew what is really happening instead of what seems to them to be happening?

LA TRÉMOUILLE—No, by Saint Dennis: the fat would be in the fire before sundown.

THE ARCHBISHOP—Would it not be quite easy to tell them the truth?

LA TRÉMOUILLE—Man alive, they wouldnt believe it.

THE ARCHBISHOP—Just so. Well, the Church has to rule men for the good of their souls as you have to rule them for the good of their bodies. To do that, the Church must do as you do: nourish their faith by poetry.

LA TRÉMOUILLE—Poetry! I should call it humbug.

THE ARCHBISHOP—You would be wrong, my friend. Parables are not lies because they describe events that have never happened. Miracles are not frauds because they are often—I do not say always—very simple and innocent contrivances by which the priest fortifies the faith of his flock. When this girl picks out the Dauphin among his courtiers, it will not be a miracle for me, because I shall know how it has been done, and my faith will not be increased. But as for the others, if they feel the thrill of the supernatural, and forget their sinful clay in a sudden sense of the glory of God, it will be a miracle and a blessed one. And you will find that the girl herself will be more affected than anyone else. She will forget how she really picked him out. So, perhaps, will you.

LA TRÉMOUILLE—Well, I wish I were clever enough to know how

much of you is God's archbishop and how much the most artful fox in Touraine. Come on, or we shall be late for the fun; and I want to see it, miracle or no miracle.

THE ARCHBISHOP [*detaining him a moment*] Do not think that I am a lover of crooked ways. There is a new spirit rising in men: we are at the dawning of a wider epoch. If I were a simple monk, and had not to rule men, I should seek peace for my spirit with Aristotle and Pythagoras rather than with the saints and their miracles.

LA TRÉMOUILLE – And who the deuce was Pythagoras?

THE ARCHBISHOP – A sage who held that the earth is round, and that it moves round the sun.

LA TRÉMOUILLE – What an utter fool! Couldnt he use his eyes?

They go out together through the curtains, which are presently withdrawn, revealing the full depth of the throne room with the Court assembled. On the right are two Chairs of State on a dais. BLUEBEARD *is standing theatrically on the dais, playing the king, and, like the courtiers, enjoying the joke rather obviously. There is a curtained arch in the wall behind the dais; but the main door, guarded by men-at-arms, is at the other side of the room; and a clear path across is kept and lined by the courtiers.* CHARLES *is in this path in the middle of the room.* LA HIRE *is on his right. The* ARCHBISHOP, *on his left, has taken his place by the dais:* LA TRÉMOUILLE *at the other side of it. The* DUCHESS DE LA TRÉMOUILLE, *pretending to be the queen, sits in the consort's chair, with a group of ladies in waiting close by, behind the* ARCHBISHOP.*

The chatter of the courtiers makes such a noise that nobody notices the appearance of the page at the door.

THE PAGE – The Duke of–[*Nobody listens.*] The Duke of–[*The chatter continues. Indignant at his failure to command a hearing, he snatches the halberd of the nearest man-at-arms, and thumps the floor with it. The chatter ceases; and everybody looks at him in silence.*] Attention! [*He restores the halberd to the man-at-arms.*] The Duke of Vendôme presents Joan the Maid to his Majesty.

CHARLES [*putting his finger on his lip*] Ssh!
<blockquote>[*He hides behind the nearest courtier, peering out to see what happens.*]</blockquote>

BLUEBEARD [*majestically*] Let her approach the throne.

JOAN, *dressed as a soldier, with her hair bobbed and hanging thickly round her face, is led in by a bashful and speechless nobleman, from whom she detaches herself to stop and look round eagerly for the* DAUPHIN.

Bernard Shaw

THE DUCHESS [*to the nearest lady in waiting*] My dear! Her hair!
[*All the ladies explode in uncontrollable laughter.*]
BLUEBEARD [*trying not to laugh, and waving his hand in depreca-
tion of their merriment*] Ssh—ssh! Ladies! Ladies!!
JOAN [*not at all embarrassed*] I wear it like this because I am a soldier.
Where be Dauphin?
[*A titter runs through the Court as she walks to the dais.*]
BLUEBEARD [*condescendingly*] You are in the presence of the
Dauphin.

JOAN *looks at him sceptically for a moment, scanning him hard up and
down to make sure. Dead silence, all watching her. Fun dawns in her
face.*

JOAN—Coom, Bluebeard! Thou canst not fool me. Where be Dauphin?

A roar of laughter breaks out as GILLES, *with a gesture of surrender, joins
in the laugh, and jumps down from the dais beside* LA TRÉMOUILLE.
JOAN, *also on the broad grin, turns back, searching along the row of
courtiers, and presently makes a dive, and drags out* CHARLES *by the arm.*

JOAN [*releasing him and bobbing him a little curtsey*] Gentle little
Dauphin, I am sent to you to drive the English away from Orleans
and from France, and to crown you king in the cathedral at Rheims,
where all true kings of France are crowned.
CHARLES [*triumphant, to the Court*] You see, all of you: she knew
the blood royal. Who dare say now that I am not my father's son?
[*To* JOAN.] But if you want me to be crowned at Rheims you must
talk to the Archbishop, not to me. There he is! [*He is standing behind
her.*]
JOAN [*turning quickly, overwhelmed with emotion*] Oh, my lord!
[*She falls on both knees before him, with bowed head, not daring to
look up.*] My lord: I am only a poor country girl; and you are filled
with the blessedness and glory of God Himself; but you will touch
me with your hands, and give me your blessing, wont you?
BLUEBEARD [*whispering to* LA TRÉMOUILLE] The old fox blushes.
LA TRÉMOUILLE—Another miracle!
THE ARCHBISHOP [*touched, putting his hand on her head*] Child:
you are in love with religion.
JOAN [*startled; looking up at him*] Am I? I never thought of that. Is
there any harm in it?
THE ARCHBISHOP—There is no harm in it, my child. But there is
danger.

1768

J O A N [*rising, with a sunflush of reckless happiness irradiating her face*] There is always danger, except in heaven. Oh, my lord, you have given me such strength, such courage. It must be a most wonderful thing to be Archbishop.

[*The Court smiles broadly: even titters a little.*]

T H E   A R C H B I S H O P [*drawing himself up sensitively*] Gentlemen: your levity is rebuked by this maid's faith. I am, God help me, all unworthy; but your mirth is a deadly sin.

[*Their faces fall. Dead silence.*]

B L U E B E A R D – My lord: we were laughing at her, not at you.

T H E   A R C H B I S H O P – What? Not at my unworthiness but at her faith! Gilles de Rais: this maid prophesied that the blasphemer should be drowned in his sin—

J O A N [*distressed*] No!

T H E   A R C H B I S H O P [*silencing her by a gesture*] I prophesy now that you will be hanged in yours if you do not learn when to laugh and when to pray.

B L U E B E A R D – My lord: I stand rebuked. I am sorry: I can say no more. But if you prophesy that I shall be hanged, I shall never be able to resist temptation, because I shall always be telling myself that I may as well be hanged for a sheep as a lamb.

[*The courtiers take heart at this. There is more tittering.*]

J O A N [*scandalized*] You are an idle fellow, Bluebeard; and you have great impudence to answer the Archbishop.

L A   H I R E [*with a huge chuckle*] Well said, lass! Well said!

J O A N [*impatiently to the* ARCHBISHOP] Oh, my lord, will you send all these silly folks away so that I may speak to the Dauphin alone?

L A   H I R E [*goodhumoredly*] I can take a hint.

[*He salutes; turns on his heel; and goes out.*]

T H E   A R C H B I S H O P – Come, gentlemen. The Maid comes with God's blessing, and must be obeyed.

The courtiers withdraw, some through the arch, others at the opposite side. The ARCHBISHOP *marches across to the door, followed by the* DUCHESS *and* LA TRÉMOUILLE. *As the* ARCHBISHOP *passes* JOAN, *she falls on her knees, and kisses the hem of his robe fervently. He shakes his head in instinctive remonstrance; gathers the robe from her; and goes out. She is left kneeling directly in the* DUCHESS'S *way.*

T H E   D U C H E S S [*coldly*] Will you allow me to pass, please?

J O A N [*hastily rising, and standing back*] Beg pardon, maam, I am sure.

[*The* DUCHESS *passes on.* JOAN *stares after her; then whispers to the*
                                                                    DAUPHIN.]

JOAN – Be that Queen?

CHARLES – No. She thinks she is.

JOAN [*again staring after the* DUCHESS] Oo-oo-ooh!

                    [*Her awe-struck amazement at the figure cut by*
               the magnificently dressed lady is not wholly complimentary.]

LA TRÉMOUILLE [*very surly*] I'll trouble your Highness not to
gibe at my wife.

                    [*He goes out. The others have already gone.*]

JOAN [*to the* DAUPHIN] Who be old Gruff-and-Grum?

CHARLES – He is the Duke de la Trémouille.

JOAN – What be his job?

CHARLES – He pretends to command the army. And whenever I find
a friend I can care for, he kills him.

JOAN – Why dost let him?

CHARLES [*petulantly moving to the throne side of the room to escape
from her magnetic field*] How can I prevent him? He bullies me. They
all bully me.

JOAN – Art afraid?

CHARLES – Yes: I am afraid. It's no use preaching to me about it. It's
all very well for these big men with their armor that is too heavy for
me, and their swords that I can hardly lift, and their muscle and their
shouting and their bad tempers. They like fighting: most of them are
making fools of themselves all the time they are not fighting; but I am
quiet and sensible; and I dont want to kill people: I only want to be
left alone to enjoy myself in my own way. I never asked to be a king:
it was pushed on me. So if you are going to say 'Son of St Louis: gird
on the sword of your ancestors, and lead us to victory' you may spare
your breath to cool your porridge; for I cannot do it. I am not built
that way; and there is an end of it.

JOAN [*trenchant and masterful*] Blethers! We are all like that to begin
with. I shall put courage into thee.

CHARLES – But I dont want to have courage put into me. I want to
sleep in a comfortable bed, and not live in continual terror of being
killed or wounded. Put courage into the others, and let them have
their bellyful of fighting; but let me alone.

JOAN – It's no use, Charlie: thou must face what God puts on thee.
If thou fail to make thyself king, thoult be a beggar: what else art fit
for? Come! Let me see thee sitting on the throne. I have looked forward to that.

CHARLES – What is the good of sitting on the throne when the other fellows give all the orders? However! [*He sits enthroned, a piteous figure.*] here is the king for you! Look your fill at the poor devil.

JOAN – Thourt not king yet, lad: thourt but Dauphin. Be not led away by them around thee. Dressing up dont fill empty noddle. I know the people: the real people that make thy bread for thee; and I tell thee they count no man king of France until the holy oil has been poured on his hair, and himself consecrated and crowned in Rheims Cathedral. And thou needs new clothes, Charlie. Why does not Queen look after thee properly?

CHARLES – We're too poor. She wants all the money we can spare to put on her own back. Besides, I like to see her beautifully dressed; and I dont care what I wear myself: I should look ugly anyhow.

JOAN – There is some good in thee, Charlie; but it is not yet a king's good.

CHARLES – We shall see. I am not such a fool as I look. I have my eyes open; and I can tell you that one good treaty is worth ten good fights. These fighting fellows lose all on the treaties that they gain on the fights. If we can only have a treaty, the English are sure to have the worst of it, because they are better at fighting than at thinking.

JOAN – If the English win, it is they that will make the treaty: and then God help poor France! Thou must fight, Charlie, whether thou will or no. I will go first to hearten thee. We must take our courage in both hands: aye, and pray for it with both hands too.

CHARLES [*descending from his throne and again crossing the room to escape from her dominating urgency*] Oh do stop talking about God and praying. I cant bear people who are always praying. Isnt it bad enough to have to do it at the proper times?

JOAN [*pitying him*] Thou poor child, thou hast never prayed in thy life. I must teach thee from the beginning.

CHARLES – I am not a child: I am a grown man and a father; and I will not be taught any more.

JOAN – Aye, you have a little son. He that will be Louis the Eleventh when you die. Would you not fight for him?

CHARLES – No: a horrid boy. He hates me. He hates everybody, selfish little beast! I dont want to be bothered with children. I dont want to be a father; and I dont want to be a son: especially a son of St Louis. I dont want to be any of these fine things you all have your heads full of: I want to be just what I am. Why cant you mind your own business, and let me mind mine?

JOAN [*again contemptuous*] Minding your own business is like minding your own body: it's the shortest way to make yourself sick. What is my business? Helping mother at home. What is thine? Petting lapdogs and sucking sugarsticks. I call that muck. I tell thee it is God's business we are here to do: not our own. I have a message to thee from God; and thou must listen to it, though thy heart break with the terror of it.

CHARLES—I dont want a message; but can you tell me any secrets? Can you do any cures? Can you turn lead into gold, or anything of that sort?

JOAN—I can turn thee into a king, in Rheims Cathedral; and that is a miracle that will take some doing, it seems.

CHARLES—If we go to Rheims, and have a coronation, Anne will want new dresses. We cant afford them. I am all right as I am.

JOAN—As you are! And what is that? Less than my father's poorest shepherd. Thourt not lawful owner of thy own land of France till thou be consecrated.

CHARLES—But I shall not be lawful owner of my own land anyhow. Will the consecration pay off my mortgages? I have pledged my last acre to the Archbishop and that fat bully. I owe money even to Bluebeard.

JOAN [*earnestly*] Charlie: I come from the land, and have gotten my strength working on the land; and I tell thee that the land is thine to rule righteously and keep God's peace in, and not to pledge at the pawnshop as a drunken woman pledges her children's clothes. And I come from God to tell thee to kneel in the cathedral and solemnly give thy kingdom to Him for ever and ever, and become the greatest king in the world as His steward and His bailiff, His soldier and His servant. The very clay of France will become holy: her soldiers will be the soldiers of God: the rebel dukes will be rebels against God: the English will fall on their knees and beg thee let them return to their lawful homes in peace. Wilt be a poor little Judas, and betray me and Him that sent me?

CHARLES [*tempted at last*] Oh, if I only dare!

JOAN—I shall dare, dare, and dare again, in God's name! Art for or against me?

CHARLES [*excited*] I'll risk it, I warn you I shant be able to keep it up; but I'll risk it. You shall see. [*Running to the main door and shouting.*] Hallo! Come back, everybody. [*To* JOAN, *as he runs back to the arch opposite.*] Mind you stand by and dont let me be bullied. [*Through the arch.*] Come along, will you: the whole Court. [*He sits down in the royal chair as they all hurry in to their former places, chattering and wondering.*] Now I'm in for it; but no matter: here goes! [*To the page.*] Call for silence, you little beast, will you?

THE PAGE [*snatching a halberd as before and thumping with it repeatedly*] Silence for His Majesty the King. The King speaks. [*Peremptorily.*] Will you be silent there?

[*Silence.*]

CHARLES [*rising*] I have given the command of the army to The Maid. The Maid is to do as she likes with it.

[*He descends from the dais.*]

[*General amazement.* LA HIRE, *delighted, slaps his steel thighpiece with his gauntlet.*]

LA TRÉMOUILLE [*turning threateningly towards* CHARLES] What is this? I command the army.

JOAN *quickly puts her hand on* CHARLES's *shoulder as he instinctively recoils.* CHARLES, *with a grotesque effort culminating in an extravagant gesture, snaps his fingers in the* CHAMBERLAIN's *face.*

JOAN – Thourt answered, old Gruff-and-Grum. [*Suddenly flashing out her sword as she divines that her moment has come.*] Who is for God and His Maid? Who is for Orleans with me?

LA HIRE [*carried away, drawing also*] For God and His Maid! To Orleans!

ALL THE KNIGHTS [*following his lead with enthusiasm*] To Orleans!

JOAN, *radiant, falls on her knees in thanksgiving to God. They all kneel, except the* ARCHBISHOP, *who gives his benediction with a sigh, and* LA TRÉMOUILLE, *who collapses, cursing.*

SCENE THREE

Orleans, April 29th, 1429. DUNOIS, *aged 26, is pacing up and down a patch of ground on the south bank of the silver Loire, commanding a long view of the river in both directions. He has had his lance stuck up with a pennon, which streams in a strong east wind. His shield with its bend sinister lies beside it. He has his commander's baton in his hand. He is well built, carrying his armor easily. His broad brow and pointed chin give him an equilaterally triangular face, already marked by active service and responsibility, with the expression of a good-natured and capable man who has no affectations and no foolish illusions. His page is sitting on the ground, elbows on knees, cheeks on fists, idly watching the water. It is evening; and both man and boy are affected by the loveliness of the Loire.*

DUNOIS [*halting for a moment to glance up at the streaming pennon and shake his head wearily before he resumes his pacing*] West wind, west wind, west wind. Strumpet: steadfast when you should be wanton, wanton when you should be steadfast. West wind on the silver Loire: what rhymes to Loire? [*He looks again at the pennon, and shakes his fist at it.*] Change, curse you, change, English harlot of a wind, change. West, west, I tell you. [*With a growl he resumes his march in silence, but soon begins again.*] West wind, wanton wind, wilful wind, womanish wind, false wind from over the water, will you never blow again?

THE PAGE [*bounding to his feet*] See! There! There she goes!

DUNOIS [*startled from his reverie: eagerly*] Where? Who? The Maid?

THE PAGE — No: the kingfisher. Like blue lightning. She went into that bush.

DUNOIS [*furiously disappointed*] Is that all? You infernal young idiot: I have a mind to pitch you into the river.

THE PAGE [*not afraid, knowing his man*] It looked frightfully jolly, that flash of blue. Look! There goes the other!

DUNOIS [*running eagerly to the river brim*] Where? Where?

THE PAGE [*pointing*] Passing the reeds.

DUNOIS [*delighted*] I see.

[*They follow the flight till the bird takes cover.*]

1774

THE PAGE—You blew me up because you were not in time to see them yesterday.

DUNOIS—You knew I was expecting The Maid when you set up your yelping. I will give you something to yelp for next time.

THE PAGE—Arnt they lovely? I wish I could catch them.

DUNOIS—Let me catch you trying to trap them, and I will put you in the iron cage for a month to teach you what a cage feels like. You are an abominable boy.

THE PAGE [*laughs, and squats down as before*]!

DUNOIS [*pacing*] Blue bird, blue bird, since I am friend to thee, change thou the wind for me. No: it does not rhyme. He who has sinned for thee: thats better. No sense in it, though. [*He finds himself close to the page.*] You abominable boy! [*He turns away from him.*] Mary in the blue snood, kingfisher color: will you grudge me a west wind?

A SENTRY'S VOICE WESTWARD—Halt! Who goes there?

JOAN'S VOICE—The Maid.

DUNOIS—Let her pass. Hither, Maid! To me!

JOAN, *in splendid armor, rushes in in a blazing rage. The wind drops; and the pennon flaps idly down the lance; but* DUNOIS *is too much occupied with* JOAN *to notice it.*

JOAN [*bluntly*] Be you Bastard of Orleans?

DUNOIS [*cool and stern, pointing to his shield*] You see the bend sinister. Are you Joan the Maid?

JOAN—Sure.

DUNOIS—Where are your troops?

JOAN—Miles behind. They have cheated me. They have brought me to the wrong side of the river.

DUNOIS—I told them to.

JOAN—Why did you? The English are on the other side!

DUNOIS—The English are on both sides.

JOAN—But Orleans is on the other side. We must fight the English there. How can we cross the river?

DUNOIS [*grimly*] There is a bridge.

JOAN—In God's name, then, let us cross the bridge, and fall on them.

DUNOIS—It seems simple; but it cannot be done.

JOAN—Who says so?

DUNOIS—I say so; and older and wiser heads than mine are of the same opinion.

JOAN [*roundly*] Then your older and wiser heads are fatheads: they have made a fool of you; and now they want to make a fool of me too, bringing me to the wrong side of the river. Do you not know that I bring you better help than ever came to any general or any town?

DUNOIS [*smiling patiently*] Your own?

JOAN—No: the help and counsel of the King of Heaven. Which is the way to the bridge?

DUNOIS—You are impatient, Maid.

JOAN—Is this a time for patience? Our enemy is at our gates; and here we stand doing nothing. Oh, why are you not fighting? Listen to me: I will deliver you from fear. I—

DUNOIS [*laughing heartily, and waving her off*] No, no, my girl: if you delivered me from fear I should be a good knight for a story book, but a very bad commander of the army. Come! let me begin to make a soldier of you. [*He takes her to the water's edge.*] Do you see those two forts at this end of the bridge? the big ones?

JOAN—Yes. Are they ours or the goddams'?

DUNOIS—Be quiet, and listen to me. If I were in either of those forts with only ten men I could hold it against an army. The English have more than ten times ten goddams in those forts to hold them against us.

JOAN—They cannot hold them against God. God did not give them the land under those forts: they stole it from Him. He gave it to us. I will take those forts.

DUNOIS—Single-handed?

JOAN—Our men will take them. I will lead them.

DUNOIS—Not a man will follow you.

JOAN—I will not look back to see whether anyone is following me.

DUNOIS [*recognizing her mettle, and clapping her heartily on the shoulder*] Good. You have the makings of a soldier in you. You are in love with war.

JOAN [*startled*] Oh! And the Archbishop said I was in love with religion.

DUNOIS—I, God forgive me, am a little in love with war myself, the ugly devil! I am like a man with two wives. Do you want to be like a woman with two husbands?

JOAN [*matter-of-fact*] I will never take a husband. A man in Toul took an action against me for breach of promise; but I never promised him. I am a soldier: I do not want to be thought of as a woman. I will not dress as a woman. I do not care for the things women care for. They dream of lovers, and of money. I dream of leading a charge, and of placing the big guns. You soldiers do not know how to use the big guns: you think you can win battles with a great noise and smoke.

DUNOIS [*with a shrug*] True. Half the time the artillery is more trouble than it is worth.

J O A N – Aye, lad; but you cannot fight stone walls with horses: you must
have guns, and much bigger guns too.

D U N O I S [*grinning at her familiarity, and echoing it*] Aye, lass; but a
good heart and a stout ladder will get over the stoniest wall.

J O A N – I will be first up the ladder when we reach the fort, Bastard. I
dare you to follow me.

D U N O I S – You must not dare a staff officer, Joan: only company officers
are allowed to indulge in displays of personal courage. Besides, you
must know that I welcome you as a saint, not as a soldier. I have dare-
devils enough at my call, if they could help me.

J O A N – I am not a daredevil: I am a servant of God. My sword is sacred:
I found it behind the altar in the church of St Catherine, where God
hid it for me; and I may not strike a blow with it. My heart is full of
courage, not of anger. I will lead; and your men will follow: that is all
I can do. But I must do it: you shall not stop me.

D U N O I S – All in good time. Our men cannot take those forts by a sally
across the bridge. They must come by water, and take the English in
the rear on this side.

J O A N [*her military sense asserting itself*] Then make rafts and put
big guns on them; and let your men cross to us.

D U N O I S – The rafts are ready; and the men are embarked. But they
must wait for God.

J O A N – What do you mean? God is waiting for them.

D U N O I S – Let Him send us a wind then. My boats are downstream:
they cannot come up against both wind and current. We must wait
until God changes the wind. Come: let me take you to the church.

J O A N – No. I love church; but the English will not yield to prayers:
they understand nothing but hard knocks and slashes. I will not go to
church until we have beaten them.

D U N O I S – You must: I have business for you there.

J O A N – What business?

D U N O I S – To pray for a west wind. I have prayed; and I have given
two silver candlesticks; but my prayers are not answered. Yours may
be: you are young and innocent.

J O A N – Oh yes: you are right. I will pray: I will tell St Catherine:
she will make God give me a west wind. Quick: shew me the way to
the church.

T H E P A G E [*sneezes violently*] At-cha!!!

J O A N – God bless you, child! Coom, Bastard.

*They go out. The page rises to follow. He picks up the shield, and is
taking the spear as well when he notices the pennon, which is now streaming eastward.*

THE PAGE [*dropping the shield and calling excitedly after them*] Seigneur! Seigneur! Mademoiselle!

DUNOIS [*running back*] What is it? The kingfisher?

[*He looks eagerly for it up the river.*]

JOAN [*joining them*] Oh, a kingfisher! Where?

THE PAGE—No: the wind, the wind, the wind [*pointing to the pennon*]: that is what made me sneeze.

DUNOIS [*looking at the pennon*] The wind has changed. [*He crosses himself.*] God has spoken. [*Kneeling and handing his baton to JOAN.*] You command the king's army. I am your soldier.

THE PAGE [*looking down the river*] The boats have put off. They are ripping upstream like anything.

DUNOIS [*rising*] Now for the forts. You dared me to follow. Dare you lead?

JOAN [*bursting into tears and flinging her arms round DUNOIS, kissing him on both cheeks*] Dunois, dear comrade in arms, help me. My eyes are blinded with tears. Set my foot on the ladder, and say 'Up, Joan.'

DUNOIS [*dragging her out*] Never mind the tears: make for the flash of the guns.

JOAN [*in a blaze of courage*] Ah!

DUNOIS [*dragging her along with him*] For God and Saint Dennis!

THE PAGE [*shrilly*] The Maid! The Maid! God and The Maid! Hurray-ay-ay!

[*He snatches up the shield and lance, and capers out after them, mad with excitement.*]

SCENE FOUR

A tent in the English camp. A bullnecked English CHAPLAIN *of 50 is sitting on a stool at a table, hard at work writing. At the other side of the table an imposing* NOBLEMAN, *aged 46, is seated in a handsome chair turning over the leaves of an illuminated Book of Hours. The* NOBLEMAN *is enjoying himself: the* CHAPLAIN *is struggling with suppressed wrath. There is an unoccupied leather stool on the* NOBLEMAN's *left. The table is on his right.*

THE NOBLEMAN—Now this is what I call workmanship. There is nothing on earth more exquisite than a bonny book, with well-placed columns of rich black writing in beautiful borders, and illuminated pictures cunningly inset. But nowadays, instead of looking at books, people read them. A book might as well be one of those orders for bacon and bran that you are scribbling.

THE CHAPLAIN—I must say, my lord, you take our situation very coolly. Very coolly indeed.

THE NOBLEMAN [*supercilious*] What is the matter?

THE CHAPLAIN—The matter, my lord, is that we English have been defeated.

THE NOBLEMAN—That happens, you know. It is only in history books and ballads that the enemy is always defeated.

THE CHAPLAIN—But we are being defeated over and over again. First, Orleans—

THE NOBLEMAN [*poohpoohing*] Oh, Orleans!

THE CHAPLAIN—I know what you are going to say, my lord: that was a clear case of witchcraft and sorcery. But we are still being defeated. Jargeau, Meung, Beaugency, just like Orleans. And now we have been butchered at Patay, and Sir John Talbot taken prisoner. [*He throws down his pen, almost in tears.*] I feel it, my lord: I feel it very deeply. I cannot bear to see my countrymen defeated by a parcel of foreigners.

THE NOBLEMAN—Oh! you are an Englishman, are you?

THE CHAPLAIN—Certainly not, my lord: I am a gentleman. Still, like your lordship, I was born in England; and it makes a difference.

1779

THE NOBLEMAN—You are attached to the soil, eh?

THE CHAPLAIN—It pleases your lordship to be satirical at my expense: your greatness privileges you to be so with impunity. But your lordship knows very well that I am not attached to the soil in a vulgar manner, like a serf. Still, I have a feeling about it; [*with growing agitation*] and I am not ashamed of it; and [*rising wildly*] by God, if this goes on any longer I will fling my cassock to the devil, and take arms myself, and strangle the accursed witch with my own hands.

THE NOBLEMAN [*laughing at him goodnaturedly*] So you shall, chaplain: so you shall, if we can do nothing better. But not yet, not quite yet.

[*The* CHAPLAIN *resumes his seat very sulkily.*]

THE NOBLEMAN [*airily*] I should not care very much about the witch—you see, I have made my pilgrimage to the Holy Land; and the Heavenly Powers, for their own credit, can hardly allow me to be worsted by a village sorceress—but the Bastard of Orleans is a harder nut to crack; and as he has been to the Holy Land too, honors are easy between us as far as that goes.

THE CHAPLAIN—He is only a Frenchman, my lord.

THE NOBLEMAN—A Frenchman! Where did you pick up that expression? Are these Burgundians and Bretons and Picards and Gascons beginning to call themselves Frenchmen, just as our fellows are beginning to call themselves Englishmen? They actually talk of France and England as their countries. Theirs, if you please! What is to become of me and you if that way of thinking comes into fashion?

THE CHAPLAIN—Why, my lord? Can it hurt us?

THE NOBLEMAN—Men cannot serve two masters. If this cant of serving their country once takes hold of them, goodbye to the authority of their feudal lords, and goodbye to the authority of the Church. That is, goodbye to you and me.

THE CHAPLAIN—I hope I am a faithful servant of the Church; and there are only six cousins between me and the barony of Stogumber, which was created by the Conqueror. But is that any reason why I should stand by and see Englishmen beaten by a French bastard and a witch from Lousy Champagne?

THE NOBLEMAN—Easy, man, easy: we shall burn the witch and beat the bastard all in good time. Indeed I am waiting at present for the Bishop of Beauvais, to arrange the burning with him. He has been turned out of his diocese by her faction.

THE CHAPLAIN—You have first to catch her, my lord.

THE NOBLEMAN—Or buy her. I will offer a king's ransom.

THE CHAPLAIN—A king's ransom! For that slut!

THE NOBLEMAN—One has to leave a margin. Some of Charles's people will sell her to the Burgundians; the Burgundians will sell her to us; and there will probably be three or four middlemen who will expect their little commissions.

THE CHAPLAIN—Monstrous. It is all those scoundrels of Jews: they get in every time money changes hands. I would not leave a Jew alive in Christendom if I had my way.

THE NOBLEMAN—Why not? The Jews generally give value. They make you pay; but they deliver the goods. In my experience the men who want something for nothing are invariably Christians.

[*A page appears.*]

THE PAGE—The Right Reverend the Bishop of Beauvais: Monseigneur Cauchon.

[CAUCHON, *aged about 60, comes in. The page withdraws. The two Englishmen rise.*]

THE NOBLEMAN [*with effusive courtesy*] My dear Bishop, how good of you to come! Allow me to introduce myself: Richard de Beauchamp, Earl of Warwick, at your service.

CAUCHON—Your lordship's fame is well known to me.

WARWICK—This reverend cleric is Master John de Stogumber.

THE CHAPLAIN [*glibly*] John Bowyer Spenser Neville de Stogumber, at your service, my lord: Bachelor of Theology, and Keeper of the Private Seal to His Eminence the Cardinal of Winchester.

WARWICK [*to* CAUCHON] You call him the Cardinal of England, I believe. Our king's uncle.

CAUCHON—Messire John de Stogumber: I am always the very good friend of His Eminence.

[*He extends his hand to the* CHAPLAIN, *who kisses his ring.*]

WARWICK—Do me the honor to be seated.

[*He gives* CAUCHON *his chair, placing it at the head of the table.*]

CAUCHON *accepts the place of honor with a grave inclination.* WARWICK *fetches the leather stool carelessly, and sits in his former place. The* CHAPLAIN *goes back to his chair.*

Though WARWICK *has taken second place in calculated deference to the* BISHOP, *he assumes the lead in opening the proceedings as a matter of course. He is still cordial and expansive; but there is a new note in his voice which means that he is coming to business.*

WARWICK—Well, my Lord Bishop, you find us in one of our unlucky moments. Charles is to be crowned at Rheims, practically by the young woman from Lorraine; and—I must not deceive you, nor flatter your hopes—we cannot prevent it. I suppose it will make a great difference to Charles's position.

CAUCHON—Undoubtedly. It is a masterstroke of The Maid's.

THE CHAPLAIN [*again agitated*] We were not fairly beaten, my lord. No Englishman is ever fairly beaten.

[CAUCHON *raises his eyebrow slightly, then quickly composes his face.*]

WARWICK—Our friend here takes the view that the young woman is a sorceress. It would, I presume, be the duty of your reverend lordship to denounce her to the Inquisition, and have her burnt for that offence.

CAUCHON—If she were captured in my diocese: yes.

WARWICK [*feeling that they are getting on capitally*] Just so. Now I suppose there can be no reasonable doubt that she is a sorceress.

THE CHAPLAIN—Not the least. An arrant witch.

WARWICK [*gently reproving the interruption*] We are asking for the Bishop's opinion, Messire John.

CAUCHON—We shall have to consider not merely our own opinions here, but the opinions—the prejudices, if you like—of a French court.

WARWICK [*correcting*] A Catholic court, my lord.

CAUCHON—Catholic courts are composed of mortal men, like other courts, however sacred their function and inspiration may be. And if the men are Frenchmen, as the modern fashion calls them, I am afraid the bare fact that an English army has been defeated by a French one will not convince them that there is any sorcery in the matter.

THE CHAPLAIN—What! Not when the famous Sir Talbot himself has been defeated and actually taken prisoner by a drab from the ditches of Lorraine!

CAUCHON—Sir John Talbot, we all know, is a fierce and formidable soldier, Messire; but I have yet to learn that he is an able general. And though it pleases you to say that he has been defeated by this girl, some of us may be disposed to give a little of the credit to Dunois.

THE CHAPLAIN [*contemptuously*] The Bastard of Orleans!

CAUCHON—Let me remind—

WARWICK [*interposing*] I know what you are going to say, my lord. Dunois defeated me at Montargis.

CAUCHON [*bowing*] I take that as evidence that the Seigneur Dunois is a very able commander indeed.

WARWICK—Your lordship is the flower of courtesy. I admit, on our side, that Talbot is a mere fighting animal, and that it probably served him right to be taken at Patay.

THE CHAPLAIN [*chafing*] My lord: at Orleans this woman had her throat pierced by an English arrow, and was seen to cry like a child from the pain of it. It was a death wound; yet she fought all day; and when our men had repulsed all her attacks like true Englishmen, she walked alone to the wall of our fort with a white banner in her hand; and our men were paralyzed, and could neither shoot nor strike whilst the French fell on them and drove them on to the bridge, which immediately burst into flames and crumbled under them, letting them down into the river, where they were drowned in heaps. Was this your bastard's generalship? or were those flames the flames of hell, conjured up by witchcraft?

W A R W I C K – You will forgive Messire John's vehemence, my lord; but he has put our case. Dunois is a great captain, we admit; but why could he do nothing until the witch came?

C A U C H O N – I do not say that there were no supernatural powers on her side. But the names on that white banner were not the names of Satan and Beelzebub, but the blessed names of our Lord and His holy mother. And your commander who was drowned—Clahz-da I think you call him—

W A R W I C K – Glasdale. Sir William Glasdale.

C A U C H O N – Glass-dell, thank you. He was no saint; and many of our people think that he was drowned for his blasphemies against The Maid.

W A R W I C K [*beginning to look very dubious*] Well, what are we to infer from all this, my lord? Has The Maid converted you?

C A U C H O N – If she had, my lord, I should have known better than to have trusted myself here within your grasp.

W A R W I C K [*blandly deprecating*] Oh! oh! My lord!

C A U C H O N – If the devil is making use of this girl—and I believe he is—

W A R W I C K [*reassured*] Ah! You hear, Messire John? I knew your lordship would not fail us. Pardon my interruption. Proceed.

C A U C H O N – If it be so, the devil has longer views than you give him credit for.

W A R W I C K – Indeed? In what way? Listen to this, Messire John.

C A U C H O N – If the devil wanted to damn a country girl, do you think so easy a task would cost him the winning of half a dozen battles? No, my lord: any trumpery imp could do that much if the girl could be damned at all. The Prince of Darkness does not condescend to such cheap drudgery. When he strikes, he strikes at the Catholic Church, whose realm is the whole spiritual world. When he damns, he damns the souls of the entire human race. Against that dreadful design The Church stands ever on guard. And it is as one of the instruments of that design that I see this girl. She is inspired, but diabolically inspired.

T H E C H A P L A I N – I told you she was a witch.

C A U C H O N [*fiercely*] She is not a witch. She is a heretic.

T H E C H A P L A I N – What difference does that make?

C A U C H O N – You, a priest, ask me that! You English are strangely blunt in the mind. All these things that you call witchcraft are capable of a natural explanation. The woman's miracles would not impose on a rabbit: she does not claim them as miracles herself. What do her victories prove but that she has a better head on her shoulders than your swearing Glass-dells and mad bull Talbots, and that the courage of faith, even though it be a false faith, will always outstay the courage of wrath?

THE CHAPLAIN [*hardly able to believe his ears*] Does your lordship compare Sir John Talbot, three times Governor of Ireland, to a mad bull?!!!

WARWICK—It would not be seemly for you to do so, Messire John, as you are still six removes from a barony. But as I am an earl, and Talbot is only a knight, I may make bold to accept the comparison. [*To the* BISHOP.] My lord: I wipe the slate as far as the witchcraft goes. None the less, we must burn the woman.

CAUCHON—I cannot burn her. The Church cannot take life. And my first duty is to seek this girl's salvation.

WARWICK—No doubt. But you do burn people occasionally.

CAUCHON—No. When The Church cuts off an obstinate heretic as a dead branch from the tree of life, the heretic is handed over to the secular arm. The Church has no part in which the secular arm may see fit to do.

WARWICK—Precisely. And I shall be the secular arm in this case. Well, my lord, hand over your dead branch; and I will see that the fire is ready for it. If you will answer for The Church's part, I will answer for the secular part.

CAUCHON [*with smouldering anger*] I can answer for nothing. You great lords are too prone to treat The Church as a mere political convenience.

WARWICK [*smiling and propitiatory*] Not in England, I assure you.

CAUCHON—In England more than anywhere else. No, my lord: the soul of this village girl is of equal value with yours or your king's before the throne of God; and my first duty is to save it. I will not suffer your lordship to smile at me as if I were repeating a meaningless form of words, and it were well understood between us that I should betray the girl to you. I am no mere political bishop: my faith is to me what your honor is to you; and if there be a loophole through which this baptized child of God can creep to her salvation, I shall guide her to it.

THE CHAPLAIN [*rising in a fury*] You are a traitor.

CAUCHON [*springing up*] You lie, priest. [*Trembling with rage.*] If you dare do what this woman has done—set your country above the holy Catholic Church—you shall go to the fire with her.

THE CHAPLAIN—My lord: I—I went too far. I—

[*He sits down with a submissive gesture.*]

WARWICK [*who has risen apprehensively*] My lord: I apologize to you for the word used by Messire John de Stogumber. It does not mean in England what it does in France. In your language traitor means betrayer: one who is perfidious, treacherous, unfaithful, disloyal. In our country it means simply one who is not wholly devoted to our English interests.

CAUCHON—I am sorry: I did not understand.

[*He subsides into his chair with dignity.*]

WARWICK [*resuming his seat, much relieved*] I must apologize on my own account if I have seemed to take the burning of this poor girl too lightly. When one has seen whole countrysides burnt over and over again as mere items in military routine, one has to grow a very thick skin. Otherwise one might go mad: at all events, I should. May I venture to assume that your lordship also, having to see so many heretics burned from time to time, is compelled to take—shall I say a professional view of what would otherwise be a very horrible incident?

CAUCHON—Yes: it is a painful duty: even, as you say, a horrible one. But in comparison with the horror of heresy it is less than nothing. I am not thinking of this girl's body, which will suffer for a few moments only, and which must in any event die in some more or less painful manner, but of her soul, which may suffer to all eternity.

WARWICK—Just so; and God grant that her soul may be saved! But the practical problem would seem to be how to save her soul without saving her body. For we must face it, my lord: if this cult of The Maid goes on, our cause is lost.

THE CHAPLAIN [*his voice broken like that of a man who has been crying*] May I speak, my lord?

WARWICK—Really, Messire John, I had rather you did not, unless you can keep your temper.

THE CHAPLAIN—It is only this. I speak under correction; but The Maid is full of deceit: she pretends to be devout. Her prayers and confessions are endless. How can she be accused of heresy when she neglects no observance of a faithful daughter of The Church?

CAUCHON [*flaming up*] A faithful daughter of The Church! The Pope himself at his proudest dare not presume as this woman presumes. She acts as if she herself were The Church. She brings the message of God to Charles; and The Church must stand aside. She will crown him in the cathedral of Rheims: she, not The Church! She sends letters to the king of England giving him God's command through her to return to his island on pain of God's vengeance, which she will execute. Let me tell you that the writing of such letters was the practice of the accursed Mahomet, the anti-Christ. Has she ever in all her utterances said one word of The Church? Never. It is always God and herself.

WARWICK – What can you expect? A beggar on horseback! Her head is turned.

CAUCHON – Who has turned it? The devil. And for a mighty purpose. He is spreading this heresy everywhere. The man Hus, burnt only thirteen years ago at Constance, infected all Bohemia with it. A man named WcLeef, himself an anointed priest, spread the pestilence in England; and to your shame you let him die in his bed. We have such people here in France too: I know the breed. It is cancerous: if it be not cut out, stamped out, burnt out, it will not stop until it has brought the whole body of human society into sin and corruption, into waste and ruin. By it an Arab camel driver drove Christ and His Church out of Jerusalem, and ravaged his way west like a wild beast until at last there stood only the Pyrenees and God's mercy between France and damnation. Yet what did the camel driver do at the beginning more than this shepherd girl is doing? He had his voices from the angel Gabriel: she has her voices from St Catherine and St Margaret and the Blessed Michael. He declared himself the messenger of God, and wrote in God's name to the kings of the earth. Her letters to them are going forth daily. It is not the Mother of God now to whom we must look for intercession, but to Joan the Maid. What will the world be like when The Church's accumulated wisdom and knowledge and experience, its councils of learned, venerable pious men, are thrust into the kennel by every ignorant laborer or dairymaid whom the devil can puff up with the monstrous self-conceit of being directly inspired from heaven? It will be a world of blood, of fury, of devastation, of each man striving for his own hand: in the end a world wrecked back into barbarism. For now you have only Mahomet and his dupes, and the Maid and her dupes; but what will it be when every girl thinks herself a Joan and every man a Mahomet? I shudder to the very marrow of my bones when I think of it. I have fought it all my life; and I will fight it to the end. Let all this woman's sins be forgiven her except only this sin; for it is the sin against the Holy Ghost; and if she does not recant in the dust before the world, and submit herself to the last inch of her soul to her Church, to the fire she shall go if she once falls into my hand.

WARWICK [*unimpressed*] You feel strongly about it, naturally.

CAUCHON – Do not you?

WARWICK – I am a soldier, not a churchman. As a pilgrim I saw something of the Mahometans. They were not so ill-bred as I had been led to believe. In some respects their conduct compared favorably with ours.

C A U C H O N [*displeased*] I have noticed this before. Men go to the East to convert the infidels. And the infidels pervert them. The Crusader comes back more than half a Saracen. Not to mention that all Englishmen are born heretics.

T H E C H A P L A I N – Englishmen heretics!!! [*Appealing to* WARWICK.] My lord: must we endure this? His lordship is beside himself. How can what an Englishman believes be heresy? It is a contradiction in terms.

C A U C H O N – I absolve you, Messire de Stogumber, on the ground of invincible ignorance. The thick air of your country does not breed theologians.

W A R W I C K – You would not say so if you heard us quarrelling about religion, my lord! I am sorry you think I must be either a heretic or a blockhead because, as a travelled man, I know that the followers of Mahomet profess great respect for our Lord, and are more ready to forgive St Peter for being a fisherman than your lordship is to forgive Mahomet for being a camel driver. But at least we can proceed in this matter without bigotry.

C A U C H O N – When men call the zeal of the Christian Church bigotry I know what to think.

W A R W I C K – They are only east and west views of the same thing.

C A U C H O N [*bitterly ironical*] Only east and west! Only!!

W A R W I C K – Oh, my Lord Bishop, I am not gainsaying you. You will carry The Church with you; but you have to carry the nobles also. To my mind there is a stronger case against The Maid than the one you have so forcibly put. Frankly, I am not afraid of this girl becoming another Mahomet, and superseding The Church by a great heresy. I think you exaggerate that risk. But have you noticed that in these letters of hers, she proposes to all the kings of Europe, as she has already pressed on Charles, a transaction which would wreck the whole social structure of Christendom?

C A U C H O N – Wreck The Church. I tell you so.

W A R W I C K [*whose patience is wearing out*] My lord: pray get The Church out of your head for a moment; and remember that there are temporal institutions in the world as well as spiritual ones. I and my peers represent the feudal aristocracy as you represent The Church. We are the temporal power. Well, do you not see how this girl's idea strikes at us?

C A U C H O N – How does her idea strike at you, except as it strikes at all of us, through The Church?

W A R W I C K – Her idea is that the kings should give their realms to God, and then reign as God's bailiffs.

C A U C H O N [*not interested*] Quite sound theologically, my lord. But the king will hardly care, provided he reign. It is an abstract idea: a mere form of words.

WARWICK—By no means. It is a cunning device to supersede the aristocracy, and make the king sole and absolute autocrat. Instead of the king being merely the first among his peers, he becomes their master. That we cannot suffer: we call no man master. Nominally we hold our lands and dignities from the king, because there must be a keystone to the arch of human society; but we hold our lands in our own hands, and defend them with our own swords and those of our own tenants. Now by The Maid's doctrine the king will take our lands—our lands!—and make them a present to God; and God will then vest them wholly in the king.

CAUCHON—Need you fear that? You are the makers of kings after all. York or Lancaster in England, Lancaster or Valois in France: they reign according to your pleasure.

WARWICK—Yes; but only as long as the people follow their feudal lords, and know the king only as a travelling show, owning nothing but the highway that belongs to everybody. If the people's thoughts and hearts were turned to the king, and their lords became only the king's servants in their eyes, the king could break us across his knee one by one; and then what should we be but liveried courtiers in his halls?

CAUCHON—Still you need not fear, my lord. Some men are born kings; and some are born statesmen. The two are seldom the same. Where would the king find counsellors to plan and carry out such a policy for him?

WARWICK [*with a not too friendly smile*] Perhaps in the Church, my lord.

[CAUCHON, *with an equally sour smile, shrugs his shoulders, and does not contradict him.*]

WARWICK—Strike down the barons; and the cardinals will have it all their own way.

CAUCHON [*conciliatory, dropping his polemical tone*] My lord: we shall not defeat The Maid if we strive against one another. I know well that there is a Will to Power in the world. I know that while it lasts there will be a struggle between the Emperor and the Pope, between the dukes and the political cardinals, between the barons and the kings. The devil divides us and governs. I see you are no friend to The Church: you are an earl first and last, as I am a churchman first and last. But can we not sink our differences in the face of a common enemy? I see now that what is in your mind is not that this girl has never once mentioned The Church, and thinks only of God and herself, but that she has never once mentioned the peerage, and thinks only of the king and herself.

W A R W I C K – Quite so. These two ideas of hers are the same idea at bottom. It goes deep, my lord. It is the protest of the individual soul against the interference of priest or peer between the private man and his God. I should call it Protestantism if I had to find a name for it.

C A U C H O N [*looking hard at him*] You understand it wonderfully well, my lord. Scratch an Englishman, and find a Protestant.

W A R W I C K [*playing the pink of courtesy*] I think you are not entirely void of sympathy with The Maid's secular heresy, my lord. I leave you to find a name for it.

C A U C H O N – You mistake me, my lord. I have no sympathy with her political presumptions. But as a priest I have gained a knowledge of the minds of the common people; and there you will find yet another most dangerous idea. I can express it only by such phrases as France for the French, England for the English, Italy for the Italians, Spain for the Spanish, and so forth. It is sometimes so narrow and bitter in country folk that it surprises me that this country girl can rise above the idea of her village for its villagers. But she can. She does. When she threatens to drive the English from the soil of France she is undoubtedly thinking of the whole extent of country in which French is spoken. To her the French-speaking people are what the Holy Scriptures describe as a nation. Call this side of her heresy Nationalism if you will: I can find you no better name for it. I can only tell you that it is essentially anti-Catholic and anti-Christian; for the Catholic Church knows only one realm, and that is the realm of Christ's kingdom. Divide that kingdom into nations, and you dethrone Christ. Dethrone Christ, and who will stand between our throats and the sword? The world will perish in a welter of war.

W A R W I C K – Well, if you will burn the Protestant, I will burn the Nationalist, though perhaps I shall not carry Messire John with me there. England for the English will appeal to him.

T H E C H A P L A I N – Certainly England for the English goes without saying: it is the simple law of nature. But this woman denies to England her legitimate conquests, given her by God because of her peculiar fitness to rule over less civilized races for their own good. I do not understand what your lordships mean by Protestant and Nationalist: you are too learned and subtle for a poor clerk like myself. But I know as a matter of plain commonsense that the woman is a rebel; and that is enough for me. She rebels against Nature by wearing man's clothes, and fighting. She rebels against The Church by usurping the divine authority of the Pope. She rebels against God by her damnable league with Satan and his evil spirits against our army. And all these rebellions are only excuses for her great rebellion against England. That is not to be endured. Let her perish. Let her burn. Let her not infect the whole flock. It is expedient that one woman die for the people.

WARWICK [*rising*] My lord: we seem to be agreed.

CAUCHON [*rising also, but in protest*] I will not imperil my soul. I will uphold the justice of the Church. I will strive to the utmost for this woman's salvation.

WARWICK—I am sorry for the poor girl. I hate these severities. I will spare her if I can.

THE CHAPLAIN [*implacably*] I would burn her with my own hands.

CAUCHON [*blessing him*] Sancta simplicitas!

SCENE FIVE

The ambulatory in the cathedral of Rheims, near the door of the vestry.
A pillar bears one of the stations of the cross. The organ is playing the
people out of the nave after the coronation. JOAN *is kneeling in prayer*
before the station. She is beautifully dressed, but still in male attire.
The organ ceases as DUNOIS, *also splendidly arrayed, comes into the am-*
bulatory from the vestry.

DUNOIS – Come, Joan! you have had enough praying. After that fit of
crying you will catch a chill if you stay here any longer. It is all over:
the cathedral is empty; and the streets are full. They are calling for
The Maid. We have told them you are staying here alone to pray; but
they want to see you again.

JOAN – No: let the king have all the glory.

DUNOIS – He only spoils the show, poor devil. No, Joan: you have
crowned him; and you must go through with it.

JOAN [*shakes her head reluctantly*].

DUNOIS [*raising her*] Come come! it will be over in a couple of
hours. It's better than the bridge at Orleans: eh?

JOAN – Oh, dear Dunois, how I wish it were the bridge at Orleans
again! We lived at that bridge.

DUNOIS – Yes, faith, and died too: some of us.

JOAN – Isnt it strange, Jack? I am such a coward: I am frightened beyond words before a battle; but it is so dull afterwards when there is
no danger: oh, so dull! dull! dull!

DUNOIS – You must learn to be abstemious in war, just as you are in
your food and drink, my little saint.

JOAN – Dear Jack: I think you like me as a soldier likes his comrade.

DUNOIS – You need it, poor innocent child of God. You have not many
friends at court.

JOAN – Why do all these courtiers and knights and churchmen hate
me? What have I done to them? I have asked nothing for myself except that my village shall not be taxed; for we cannot afford war taxes.
I have brought them luck and victory: I have set them right when they

1791

were doing all sorts of stupid things: I have crowned Charles and made him a real king; and all the honors he is handing out have gone to them. Then why do they not love me?

DUNOIS [*rallying her*] Sim-ple-ton! Do you expect stupid people to love you for shewing them up? Do blundering old military dug-outs love the successful young captains who supersede them? Do ambitious politicians love the climbers who take the front seats from them? Do archbishops enjoy being played off their own altars, even by saints? Why, I should be jealous of you myself if I were ambitious enough.

JOAN – You are the pick of the basket here, Jack: the only friend I have among all these nobles. I'll wager your mother was from the country. I will go back to the farm when I have taken Paris.

DUNOIS – I am not so sure that they will let you take Paris.

JOAN [*startled*] What!

DUNOIS – I should have taken it myself before this if they had all been sound about it. Some of them would rather Paris took you, I think. So take care.

JOAN – Jack: the world is too wicked for me. If the goddams and the Burgundians do not make an end of me, the French will. Only for my voices I should lose all heart. That is why I had to steal away to pray here alone after the coronation. I'll tell you something, Jack. It is in the bells I hear my voices. Not to-day, when they all rang: that was nothing but jangling. But here in this corner, where the bells come down from heaven, and the echoes linger, or in the fields, where they come from a distance through the quiet of the countryside, my voices are in them. [*The cathedral clock chimes the quarter.*] Hark! [*She becomes rapt.*] Do you hear? Dear-child-of-God': just what you said. At the half-hour they will say 'Be-brave-go-on'. At the three-quarters they will say 'I-am-thy-Help'. But it is at the hour, when the great bell goes after 'God-will-save-France': it is then that St Margaret and St Catherine and sometimes even the blessed Michael will say things that I cannot tell beforehand. Then, oh then—

DUNOIS [*interrupting her kindly but not sympathetically*] Then, Joan, we shall hear whatever we fancy in the booming of the bell. You make me uneasy when you talk about your voices: I should think you were a bit cracked if I hadnt noticed that you give me very sensible reasons for what you do, though I hear you telling others you are only obeying Madame Saint Catherine.

JOAN [*crossly*] Well, I have to find reasons for you, because you do not believe in my voices. But the voices come first; and I find the reasons after: whatever you may choose to believe.

DUNOIS – Are you angry, Joan?

JOAN—Yes. [*Smiling.*] No: not with you. I wish you were one of the village babies.

DUNOIS—Why?

JOAN—I could nurse you for awhile.

DUNOIS—You are a bit of a woman after all.

JOAN—No: not a bit: I am a soldier and nothing else. Soldiers always nurse children when they get a chance.

DUNOIS—That is true. [*He laughs.*]

KING CHARLES, *with* BLUEBEARD *on his left and* LA HIRE *on his right, comes from the vestry, where he has been disrobing.* JOAN *shrinks away behind the pillar.* DUNOIS *is left between* CHARLES *and* LA HIRE.

DUNOIS—Well, your Majesty is an anointed king at last. How do you like it?

CHARLES—I would not go through it again to be emperor of the sun and moon. The weight of those robes! I thought I should have dropped when they loaded that crown on to me. And the famous holy oil they talked so much about was rancid: phew! The Archbishop must be nearly dead: his robes must have weighed a ton: they are stripping him still in the vestry.

DUNOIS [*drily*] Your majesty should wear armor oftener. That would accustom you to heavy dressing.

CHARLES—Yes: the old jibe! Well, I am not going to wear armor: fighting is not my job. Where is The Maid?

JOAN [*coming forward between* CHARLES *and* BLUEBEARD, *and falling on her knee*] Sire: I have made you king: my work is done. I am going back to my father's farm.

CHARLES [*surprised, but relieved*] Oh, are you? Well, that will be very nice.

[JOAN *rises, deeply discouraged.*]

CHARLES [*continuing heedlessly*] A healthy life, you know.

DUNOIS—But a dull one.

BLUEBEARD—You will find the petticoats tripping you up after leaving them off for so long.

LA HIRE—You will miss the fighting. It's a bad habit, but a grand one, and the hardest of all to break yourself of.

CHARLES [*anxiously*] Still, we dont want you to stay if you would really rather go home.

JOAN [*bitterly*] I know well that none of you will be sorry to see me go. [*She turns her shoulder to* CHARLES *and walks past him to the more congenial neighborhood of* DUNOIS *and* LA HIRE.]

1793

LA HIRE – Well, I shall be able to swear when I want to. But I shall miss you at times.

JOAN – La Hire: in spite of all your sins and swears we shall meet in heaven; for I love you as I love Pitou, my old sheep dog. Pitou could kill a wolf. You will kill the English wolves until they go back to their country and become good dogs of God, will you not?

LA HIRE – You and I together: yes.

JOAN – No: I shall last only a year from the beginning.

ALL THE OTHERS – What!

JOAN – I know it somehow.

DUNOIS – Nonsense!

JOAN – Jack: do you think you will be able to drive them out?

DUNOIS [*with quiet conviction*] Yes: I shall drive them out. They beat us because we thought battles were tournaments and ransom markets. We played the fool while the goddams took war seriously. But I have learnt my lesson, and taken their measure. They have no roots here. I have beaten them before; and I shall beat them again.

JOAN – You will not be cruel to them, Jack?

DUNOIS – The goddams will not yield to tender handling. We did not begin it.

JOAN [*suddenly*] Jack: before I go home, let us take Paris.

CHARLES [*terrified*] Oh no no. We shall lose everything we have gained. Oh dont let us have any more fighting. We can make a very good treaty with the Duke of Burgundy.

JOAN – Treaty!

[*She stamps with impatience.*]

CHARLES – Well, why not, now that I am crowned and anointed? Oh, that oil!

[*The* ARCHBISHOP *comes from the vestry, and joins the group between* CHARLES *and* BLUEBEARD.]

CHARLES – Archbishop: The Maid wants to start fighting again.

THE ARCHBISHOP – Have we ceased fighting, then? Are we at peace?

CHARLES – No: I suppose not; but let us be content with what we have done. Let us make a treaty. Our luck is too good to last; and now is our chance to stop before it turns.

JOAN – Luck! God has fought for us; and you call it luck! And you would stop while there are still Englishmen on this holy earth of dear France!

THE ARCHBISHOP [*sternly*] Maid: the king addressed himself to me, not to you. You forget yourself. You very often forget yourself.

JOAN [*unabashed, and rather roughly*] Then speak, you; and tell him that it is not God's will that he should take his hand from the plough.

THE ARCHBISHOP – If I am not so glib with the name of God as you are, it is because I interpret His will with the authority of the Church and of my sacred office. When you first came you respected it, and would not have dared to speak as you are now speaking. You came clothed with the virtue of humility; and because God blessed your enterprises accordingly, you have stained yourself with the sin of pride. The old Greek tragedy is rising among us. It is the chastisement of hubris.

C H A R L E S – Yes: she thinks she knows better than everyone else.

J O A N [*distressed, but naïvely incapable of seeing the effect she is producing*] But I do know better than any of you seem to. And I am not proud: I never speak unless I know I am right.

B L U E B E A R D ⎫ Ha ha!
C H A R L E S   ⎭ Just so.

T H E A R C H B I S H O P – How do you know you are right?

J O A N – I always know. My voices—

C H A R L E S – Oh, your voices, your voices. Why dont the voices come to me? I am king, not you.

J O A N – They do come to you; but you do not hear them. You have not sat in the field in the evening listening for them. When the angelus rings you cross yourself and have done with it; but if you prayed from your heart, and listened to the thrilling of the bells in the air after they stop ringing, you would hear the voices as well as I do. [*Turning brusquely from him.*] But what voices do you need to tell you what the blacksmith can tell you: that you must strike while the iron is hot? I tell you we must make a dash at Compiègne and relieve it as we relieved Orleans. Then Paris will open its gates; or if not, we will break through them. What is your crown worth without your capital?

L A H I R E – That is what I say too. We shall go through them like a red hot shot through a pound of butter. What do you say, Bastard?

D U N O I S – If our cannon balls were all as hot as your head, and we had enough of them, we should conquer the earth, no doubt. Pluck and impetuosity are good servants in war, but bad masters: they have delivered us into the hands of the English every time we have trusted to them. We never know when we are beaten: that is our great fault.

J O A N – You never know when you are victorious: that is a worse fault. I shall have to make you carry looking-glasses in battle to convince you that the English have not cut off all your noses. You would have been besieged in Orleans still, you and your councils of war, if I had not made you attack. You should always attack; and if you only hold on long enough the enemy will stop first. You dont know how to begin a battle; and you dont know how to use your cannons. And I do.

[*She squats down on the flags with crossed ankles, pouting.*]

D U N O I S – I know what you think of us, General Joan.

J O A N – Never mind that, Jack. Tell them what you think of me.

D U N O I S – I think that God was on your side; for I have not forgotten how the wind changed, and how our hearts changed when you came; and by my faith I shall never deny that it was in your sign that we conquered. But I tell you as a soldier that God is no man's daily drudge, and no maid's either. If you are worthy of it He will sometimes snatch you out of the jaws of death and set you on your feet again; but that is all: once on your feet you must fight with all your might and all your craft. For He has to be fair to your enemy too: dont forget that. Well, He set us on our feet through you at Orleans; and the glory of it has carried us through a few good battles here to the coronation. But if we presume on it further, and trust to God to do the work we should do ourselves, we shall be defeated; and serve us right!

J O A N – But—

D U N O I S – Sh! I have not finished. Do not think, any of you, that these victories of ours were won without generalship. King Charles: you have said no word in your proclamations of my part in this campaign; and I make no complaint of that; for the people will run after The Maid and her miracles and not after the Bastard's hard work finding troops for her and feeding them. But I know exactly how much God did for us through The Maid, and how much He left me to do by my own wits; and I tell you that your little hour of miracles is over, and that from this time on he who plays the war game best will win—if the luck is on his side.

J O A N – Ah! if, if, if, if! If ifs and ans were pots and pans there'd be no need of tinkers. [*Rising impetuously.*] I tell you, Bastard, your art of war is no use, because your knights are no good for real fighting. War is only a game to them, like tennis and all their other games: they make rules as to what is fair and what is not fair, and heap armor on themselves and on their poor horses to keep out the arrows; and when they fall they cant get up, and have to wait for their squires to come and lift them to arrange about the ransom with the man that has poked them off their horse. Cant you see that all the like of that is gone by and done with? What use is armor against gunpowder? And if it was, do you think men that are fighting for France and for God will stop to bargain about ransoms, as half your knights live by doing? No: they will fight to win; and they will give up their lives out of their own hand into the hand of God when they go into battle, as I do. Common folks understand this. They cannot afford armor and cannot pay ransoms; but they followed me half naked into the moat and up the ladder and over the wall. With them it is my life or thine, and God defend the right! You may shake your head, Jack; and Bluebeard may twirl his billygoat's beard and cock his nose at me; but remember the day your knights and captains refused to follow me to attack the English at Orleans! You locked the gates to keep me in; and it was the townsfolk and the common people that followed me, and forced the gate, and shewed you the way to fight in earnest.

BLUEBEARD [*offended*] Not content with being Pope Joan, you must be Caesar and Alexander as well.

THE ARCHBISHOP – Pride will have a fall, Joan.

JOAN – Oh, never mind whether it is pride or not: is it true? is it commonsense?

LA HIRE – It is true. Half of us are afraid of having our handsome noses broken; and the other half are out for paying off their mortgages. Let her have her way, Dunois: she does not know everything; but she has got hold of the right end of the stick. Fighting is not what it was; and those who know least about it often make the best job of it.

DUNOIS – I know all that. I do not fight in the old way: I have learnt the lesson of Agincourt, of Poitiers and Crecy. I know how many lives any move of mine will cost; and if the move is worth the cost I make it and pay the cost. But Joan never counts the cost at all: she goes ahead and trusts to God: she thinks she has God in her pocket. Up to now she has had the numbers on her side; and she has won. But I know Joan; and I see that some day she will go ahead when she has only ten men to do the work of a hundred. And then she will find that God is on the side of the big battalions. She will be taken by the enemy. And the lucky man that makes the capture will receive sixteen thousand pounds from the Earl of Ouareek.

JOAN [*flattered*] Sixteen thousand pounds! Eh, laddie, have they offered that for me? There cannot be so much money in the world.

DUNOIS – There is, in England. And now tell me, all of you, which of you will lift a finger to save Joan once the English have got her? I speak first, for the army. The day after she has been dragged from her horse by a goddam or a Burgundian, and he is not struck dead: the day after she is locked in a dungeon, and the bars and bolts do not fly open at the touch of St Peter's angel: the day when the enemy finds out that she is as vulnerable as I am and not a bit more invincible, she will not be worth the life of a single soldier to us; and I will not risk that life, much as I cherish her as a companion-in-arms.

JOAN – I dont blame you, Jack: you are right. I am not worth one soldier's life if God lets me be beaten; but France may think me worth my ransom after what God has done for her through me.

CHARLES – I tell you I have no money; and this coronation, which is all your fault, has cost me the last farthing I can borrow.

JOAN – The Church is richer than you. I put my trust in the Church.

THE ARCHBISHOP – Woman: they will drag you through the streets, and burn you as a witch.

JOAN [*running to him*] Oh, my lord, do not say that. It is impossible. I a witch!

THE ARCHBISHOP – Peter Cauchon knows his business. The University of Paris has burnt a woman for saying that what you have done was well done, and according to God.

JOAN [*bewildered*] But why? What sense is there in it? What I have done is according to God. They could not burn a woman for speaking the truth.

THE ARCHBISHOP – They did.

JOAN – But you know that she was speaking the truth. You would not let them burn me.

THE ARCHBISHOP – How could I prevent them?

JOAN – You would speak in the name of the Church. You are a great prince of the Church. I would go anywhere with your blessing to protect me.

THE ARCHBISHOP – I have no blessing for you while you are proud and disobedient.

JOAN – Oh, why will you go on saying things like that? I am not proud and disobedient. I am a poor girl, and so ignorant that I do not know A from B. How could I be proud? And how can you say that I am disobedient when I always obey my voices, because they come from God.

THE ARCHBISHOP – The voice of God on earth is the voice of the Church Militant; and all the voices that come to you are the echoes of your own wilfulness.

JOAN – It is not true.

THE ARCHBISHOP [*flushing angrily*] You tell the Archbishop in his cathedral that he lies; and yet you say you are not proud and disobedient.

JOAN – I never said you lied. It was you that as good as said my voices lied. When have they ever lied? If you will not believe in them: even if they are only the echoes of my own commonsense, are they not always right? and are not your earthly counsels always wrong?

THE ARCHBISHOP [*indignantly*] It is waste of time admonishing you.

CHARLES – It always comes back to the same thing. She is right; and everyone else is wrong.

THE ARCHBISHOP – Take this as your last warning. If you perish through setting your private judgment above the instructions of your spiritual directors, the Church disowns you, and leaves you to whatever fate your presumption may bring upon you. The Bastard has told you that if you persist in setting up your military conceit above the counsels of your commanders—

DUNOIS [*interposing*] To put it quite exactly, if you attempt to relieve the garrison in Compiègne without the same superiority in numbers you had at Orleans—

THE ARCHBISHOP—The army will disown you, and will not rescue you. And His Majesty the King has told you that the throne has not the means of ransoming you.

CHARLES—Not a penny.

THE ARCHBISHOP—You stand alone: absolutely alone, trusting to your own conceit, your own ignorance, your own headstrong presumption, your own impiety in hiding all these sins under the cloak of a trust in God. When you pass through these doors into the sunlight, the crowd will cheer you. They will bring you their little children and their invalids to heal: they will kiss your hands and feet, and do what they can, poor simple souls, to turn your head, and madden you with the self-confidence that is leading you to your destruction. But you will be none the less alone: they cannot save you. We and we only can stand between you and the stake at which our enemies have burnt that wretched woman in Paris.

JOAN [*her eyes skyward*] I have better friends and better counsel than yours.

THE ARCHBISHOP—I see that I am speaking in vain to a hardened heart. You reject our protection, and are determined to turn us all against you. In future, then, fend for yourself; and if you fail, God have mercy on your soul.

DUNOIS—That is the truth, Joan. Heed it.

JOAN—Where would you all have been now if I had heeded that sort of truth? There is no help, no counsel, in any of you. Yes: I am alone on earth: I have always been alone. My father told my brothers to drown me if I would not stay to mind his sheep while France was bleeding to death: France might perish if only our lambs were safe. I thought France would have friends at the court of the king of France; and I find only wolves fighting for pieces of her poor torn body. I thought God would have friends everywhere, because He is the friend of everyone; and in my innocence I believed that you who now cast me out would be like strong towers to keep harm from me. But I am wiser now; and nobody is any the worse for being wiser. Do not think you can frighten me by telling me that I am alone. France is alone; and God is alone; and what is my loneliness before the loneliness of my country and my God? I see now that the loneliness of God is His strength: what would He be if He listened to your jealous little counsels? Well, my loneliness shall be my strength too; it is better to be alone with God; His friendship will not fail me, nor His counsel, nor His love. In His strength I will dare, and dare, and dare, until I die. I will go out now to the common people, and let the love in their eyes comfort me for the hate in yours. You will all be glad to see me burnt; but if I go through the fire I shall go through it to their hearts for ever and ever. And so, God be with me!

> [*She goes from them. They stare after her in glum silence
> for a moment. Then* GILLES DE RAIS *twirls his beard.*]

BLUEBEARD—You know, the woman is quite impossible. I dont dislike her, really; but what are you to do with such a character?

DUNOIS—As God is my judge, if she fell into the Loire I would jump in in full armor to fish her out. But if she plays the fool at Compiègne, and gets caught, I must leave her to her doom.

LA HIRE—Then you had better chain me up; for I could follow her to hell when the spirit rises in her like that.

THE ARCHBISHOP—She disturbs my judgment too: there is a dangerous power in her outbursts. But the pit is open at her feet; and for good or evil we cannot turn her from it.

CHARLES—If only she would keep quiet, or go home!

> [*They follow her dispiritedly.*]

SCENE SIX

Rouen, 30th May 1431. A great stone hall in the castle, arranged for a trial-at-law, but not a trial-by-jury, the court being the Bishop's court with the Inquisition participating: hence there are two raised chairs side by side for the BISHOP *and the* INQUISITOR *as judges. Rows of chairs radiating from them at an obtuse angle are for the canons, the doctors of law and theology, and the Dominican monks, who act as assessors. In the angle is a table for the scribes, with stools. There is also a heavy rough wooden stool for the prisoner. All these are at the inner end of the hall. The further end is open to the courtyard through a row of arches. The court is shielded from the weather by screens and curtains.*

Looking down the great hall from the middle of the inner end, the judicial chairs and scribes' table are to the right. The prisoner's stool is to the left. There are arched doors right and left. It is a fine sunshiny May morning.

WARWICK *comes in through the arched doorway on the judges' side, followed by his page.*

THE PAGE [*pertly*] I suppose your lordship is aware that we have no business here. This is an ecclesiastical court; and we are only the secular arm.

WARWICK—I am aware of that fact. Will it please your impudence to find the Bishop of Beauvais for me, and give him a hint that he can have a word with me here before the trial, if he wishes?

THE PAGE [*going*] Yes, my lord.

WARWICK—And mind you behave yourself. Do not address him as Pious Peter.

THE PAGE—No, my lord. I shall be kind to him, because, when The Maid is brought in, Pious Peter will have to pick a peck of pickled pepper.

[CAUCHON *enters through the same door with a Dominican monk and a canon, the latter carrying a brief.*]

THE PAGE—The Right Reverend his lordship the Bishop of Beauvais. And two other reverend gentlemen.

WARWICK – Get out; and see that we are not interrupted.

THE PAGE – Right, my lord. [*He vanishes airily.*]

CAUCHON – I wish your lordship good-morrow.

WARWICK – Good-morrow to your lordship. Have I had the pleasure of meeting your friends before? I think not.

CAUCHON [*introducing the monk, who is on his right*] This, my lord, is Brother John Lemaître, of the order of St Dominic. He is acting as deputy for the Chief Inquisitor into the evil of heresy in France. Brother John: the Earl of Warwick.

WARWICK – Your Reverence is most welcome. We have no Inquisitor in England, unfortunately; though we miss him greatly, especially on occasions like the present.

[*The* INQUISITOR *smiles patiently, and bows. He is a mild elderly gentleman, but has evident reserves of authority and firmness.*]

CAUCHON [*introducing the Canon, who is on his left*] This gentleman is Canon John D'Estivet, of the Chapter of Bayeux. He is acting as Promoter.

WARWICK – Promoter?

CAUCHON – Prosecutor, you would call him in civil law.

WARWICK – Ah! prosecutor. Quite, quite. I am very glad to make your acquaintance, Canon D'Estivet.

[D'ESTIVET *bows. He is on the young side of middle age, well mannered, but vulpine beneath his veneer.*]

WARWICK – May I ask what stage the proceedings have reached? It is now more than nine months since The Maid was captured at Compiègne by the Burgundians. It is fully four months since I bought her from the Burgundians for a very handsome sum, solely that she might be brought to justice. It is very nearly three months since I delivered her up to you, my Lord Bishop, as a person suspected of heresy. May I suggest that you are taking a rather unconscionable time to make up your minds about a very plain case? Is this trial never going to end?

THE INQUISITOR [*smiling*] It has not yet begun, my lord.

WARWICK – Not yet begun! Why, you have been at it eleven weeks!

CAUCHON – We have not been idle, my lord. We have held fifteen examinations of The Maid: six public and nine private.

THE INQUISITOR [*always patiently smiling*] You see, my lord, I have been present at only two of these examinations. They were proceedings of the Bishop's court solely, and not of the Holy Office. I have only just decided to associate myself—that is, to associate the Holy Inquisition—with the Bishop's court. I did not at first think that this was a case of heresy at all. I regarded it as a political case, and The Maid as a prisoner of war. But having now been present at two of the examinations, I must admit that this seems to be one of the gravest cases of heresy within my experience. Therefore everything is now in order, and we proceed to trial this morning.

[*He moves towards the judicial chairs.*]

CAUCHON – This moment, if your lordship's convenience allows.

WARWICK [*graciously*] Well, that is good news, gentlemen. I will not attempt to conceal from you that our patience was becoming strained.

CAUCHON – So I gathered from the threats of your soldiers to drown those of our people who favor The Maid.

WARWICK – Dear me! At all events their intentions were friendly to you, my lord.

CAUCHON [*sternly*] I hope not. I am determined that the woman shall have a fair hearing. The justice of the Church is not a mockery, my lord.

THE INQUISITOR [*returning*] Never has there been a fairer examination within my experience, my lord. The Maid needs no lawyers to take her part: she will be tried by her most faithful friends, all ardently desirous to save her soul from perdition.

D'ESTIVET – Sir: I am the Promoter; and it has been my painful duty to present the case against the girl; but believe me, I would throw up my case today and hasten to her defence if I did not know that men far my superiors in learning and piety, in eloquence and persuasiveness, have been sent to reason with her, to explain to her the danger she is running, and the ease with which she may avoid it. [*Suddenly bursting into forensic eloquence, to the disgust of* CAUCHON *and the* INQUISITOR, *who have listened to him so far with patronizing approval.*] Men have dared to say that we are acting from hate; but God is our witness that they lie. Have we tortured her? No. Have we ceased to exhort her; to implore her to have pity on herself; to come to the bosom of her Church as an erring but beloved child? Have we—

CAUCHON [*interrupting drily*] Take care, Canon. All that you say is true; but if you make his lordship believe it I will not answer for your life, and hardly for my own.

WARWICK [*deprecating, but by no means denying*] Oh, my lord, you are very hard on us poor English. But we certainly do not share your pious desire to save The Maid: in fact I tell you now plainly that her death is a political necessity which I regret but cannot help. If the Church lets her go—

CAUCHON [*with fierce and menacing pride*] If the Church lets her go, woe to the man, were he the Emperor himself, who dares lay a finger on her! The Church is not subject to political necessity, my lord.

THE INQUISITOR [*interposing smoothly*] You need have no anxiety about the result, my lord. You have an invincible ally in the matter: one who is far more determined than you that she shall burn.

1803

WARWICK–And who is this very convenient partisan, may I ask?

THE INQUISITOR–The Maid herself. Unless you put a gag in her mouth you cannot prevent her from convicting herself ten times over every time she opens it.

D'ESTIVET–That is perfectly true, my lord. My hair bristles on my head when I hear so young a creature utter such blasphemies.

WARWICK–Well, by all means do your best for her if you are quite sure it will be of no avail. [*Looking hard at* CAUCHON.] I should be sorry to have to act without the blessing of the Church.

CAUCHON [*with a mixture of cynical admiration and contempt*] And yet they say Englishmen are hypocrites! You play for your side, my lord, even at the peril of your soul. I cannot but admire such devotion; but I dare not go so far myself. I fear damnation.

WARWICK–If we feared anything we could never govern England, my lord. Shall I send your people in to you?

CAUCHON–Yes: it will be very good of your lordship to withdraw and allow the court to assemble.

WARWICK *turns on his heel, and goes out through the courtyard.* CAUCHON *takes one of the judicial seats; and* D'ESTIVET *sits at the scribes' table, studying his brief.*

CAUCHON [*casually, as he makes himself comfortable*] What scoundrels these English nobles are!

THE INQUISITOR [*taking the other judicial chair on* CAUCHON'S *left*] All secular power makes men scoundrels. They are not trained for the work; and they have not the Apostolic Succession. Our own nobles are just as bad.

The BISHOP'S *assessors hurry into the hall, headed by* CHAPLAIN DE STOGUMBER *and* CANON DE COURCELLES, *a young priest of 30. The scribes sit at the table, leaving a chair vacant opposite* D'ESTIVET. *Some of the assessors take their seats: others stand chatting, waiting for the proceedings to begin formally.* DE STOGUMBER, *aggrieved and obstinate, will not take his seat: neither will the* CANON, *who stands on his right.*

CAUCHON–Good morning, Master de Stogumber. [*To the* INQUISITOR.] Chaplain to the Cardinal of England.

THE CHAPLAIN [*correcting him*] Of Winchester, my lord. I have to make a protest, my lord.

CAUCHON–You make a great many.

THE CHAPLAIN–I am not without support, my lord. Here is Master de Courcelles, Canon of Paris, who associates himself with me in my protest.

CAUCHON — Well, what is the matter?

THE CHAPLAIN [*sulkily*] Speak you, Master de Courcelles, since I do not seem to enjoy his lordship's confidence.

[*He sits down in dudgeon next to* CAUCHON, *on his right.*]

COURCELLES — My lord: we have been at great pains to draw up an indictment of The Maid on sixty-four counts. We are now told that they have been reduced, without consulting us.

THE INQUISITOR — Master de Courcelles: I am the culprit. I am overwhelmed with admiration for the zeal displayed in your sixty-four counts; but in accusing a heretic, as in other things, enough is enough. Also you must remember that all the members of the court are not so subtle and profound as you, and that some of your very great learning might appear to them to be very great nonsense. Therefore I have thought it well to have your sixty-four articles cut down to twelve—

COURCELLES [*thunderstruck*] Twelve!!!

THE INQUISITOR — Twelve will, believe me, be quite enough for your purpose.

THE CHAPLAIN — But some of the most important points have been reduced almost to nothing. For instance, The Maid has actually declared that the blessed saints Margaret and Catherine, and the holy Archangel Michael, spoke to her in French. That is a vital point.

THE INQUISITOR — You think, doubtless, that they should have spoken in Latin?

CAUCHON — No: he thinks they should have spoken in English.

THE CHAPLAIN — Naturally, my lord.

THE INQUISITOR — Well, as we are all here agreed, I think, that these voices of The Maid are the voices of evil spirits tempting her to her damnation, it would not be very courteous to you, Master de Stogumber, or to the King of England, to assume that English is the devil's native language. So let it pass. The matter is not wholly omitted from the twelve articles. Pray take your places, gentlemen; and let us proceed to business.

[*All who have not taken their seats, do so.*]

THE CHAPLAIN — Well, I protest. That is all.

COURCELLES — I think it hard that all our work should go for nothing. It is only another example of the diabolical influence which this woman exercises over the court.

[*He takes his chair, which is on the* CHAPLAIN's *right.*]

CAUCHON — Do you suggest that I am under diabolical influence?

COURCELLES — I suggest nothing, my lord. But it seems to me that there is a conspiracy here to hush up the fact that The Maid stole the Bishop of Senlis's horse.

CAUCHON [*keeping his temper with difficulty*] This is not a police court. Are we to waste our time on such rubbish?

COURCELLES [*rising, shocked*] My lord: do you call the Bishop's horse rubbish?

THE INQUISITOR [*blandly*] Master de Courcelles: The Maid alleges that she paid handsomely for the Bishop's horse, and that if he did not get the money the fault was not hers. As that may be true, the point is one on which The Maid may well be acquitted.

COURCELLES — Yes, if it were an ordinary horse. But the Bishop's horse! how can she be acquitted for that?

[*He sits down again, bewildered and discouraged.*]

THE INQUISITOR — I submit to you, with great respect, that if we persist in trying The Maid on trumpery issues on which we may have to declare her innocent, she may escape us on the great main issue of heresy, on which she seems so far to insist on her own guilt. I will ask you, therefore, to say nothing, when The Maid is brought before us, of these stealings of horses, and dancings round fairy trees with the village children, and prayings at haunted wells, and a dozen other things which you were diligently inquiring into until my arrival. There is not a village girl in France against whom you could not prove such things: they all dance round haunted trees, and pray at magic wells. Some of them would steal the Pope's horse if they got the chance. Heresy, gentlemen, heresy is the charge we have to try. The detection and suppression of heresy is my peculiar business: I am here as an inquisitor, not as an ordinary magistrate. Stick to the heresy, gentlemen; and leave the other matters alone.

CAUCHON — I may say that we have sent to the girl's village to make inquiries about her, and there is practically nothing serious against her.

THE CHAPLAIN [*rising and clamoring together*] Nothing serious, my lord—
COURCELLES What! The fairy tree not—

CAUCHON [*out of patience*] Be silent, gentlemen; or speak one at a time.

[COURCELLES *collapses into his chair, intimidated.*]

THE CHAPLAIN [*sulkily resuming his seat*] That is what The Maid said to us last Friday.

CAUCHON — I wish you had followed her counsel, sir. When I say nothing serious, I mean nothing that men of sufficiently large mind to conduct an inquiry like this would consider serious. I agree with my colleague the Inquisitor that it is on the count of heresy that we must proceed.

L A D V E N U [*a young but ascetically fine-drawn Dominican who is sitting next* COURCELLES, *on his right*] But is there any great harm in the girl's heresy? Is it not merely her simplicity? Many saints have said as much as Joan.

T H E I N Q U I S I T O R [*dropping his blandness and speaking very gravely*] Brother Martin: if you had seen what I have seen of heresy, you would not think it a light thing even in its most apparently harmless and even lovable and pious origins. Heresy begins with people who are to all appearance better than their neighbors. A gentle and pious girl, or a young man who has obeyed the command of our Lord by giving all his riches to the poor, and putting on the garb of poverty, the life of austerity, and the rule of humility and charity, may be the founder of a heresy that will wreck both Church and Empire if not ruthlessly stamped out in time. The records of the Holy Inquisition are full of histories we dare not give to the world, because they are beyond the belief of honest men and innocent women; yet they all began with saintly simpletons. I have seen this again and again. Mark what I say: the woman who quarrels with her clothes, and puts on the dress of a man, is like the man who throws off his fur gown and dresses like John the Baptist: they are followed, as surely as the night follows the day, by bands of wild women and men who refuse to wear any clothes at all. When maids will neither marry nor take regular vows, and men reject marriage and exalt their lusts into divine inspirations, then, as surely as the summer follows the spring, they begin with polygamy, and end by incest. Heresy at first seems innocent and even laudable; but it ends in such a monstrous horror of unnatural wickedness that the most tender-hearted among you, if you saw it at work as I have seen it, would clamor against the mercy of the Church in dealing with it. For two hundred years the Holy Office has striven with these diabolical madnesses; and it knows that they begin always by vain and ignorant persons setting up their own judgment against the Church, and taking it upon themselves to be the interpreters of God's will. You must not fall into the common error of mistaking these simpletons for liars and hypocrites. They believe honestly and sincerely that their diabolical inspiration is divine. Therefore you must be on your guard against your natural compassion. You are all, I hope, merciful men: how else could you have devoted your lives to the service of our gentle Savior? You are going to see before you a young girl, pious and chaste; for I must tell you, gentlemen, that the things said of her by our English friends are supported by no evidence, whilst there is abundant testimony that her excesses have been excesses of religion and charity and not of worldliness and wantonness. This girl is not one of those whose hard features are the sign of hard hearts, and whose brazen looks and lewd demeanor condemn them before they are accused. The devilish pride that has led her into her present peril has left no mark on her countenance. Strange as it may seem to you, it has even left no mark on her character outside those special matters in which she is proud; so that you will see a diabolical pride and a natural humility seated side by side in the selfsame soul. Therefore be on your guard. God forbid that I should tell you to harden your hearts; for her punishment if we condemn her will be so cruel that we should forfeit our own hope of divine mercy were there one grain of malice against her in our hearts. But if you hate cruelty—and if any man here does not hate it I command him on his soul's salvation to quit this holy court—I say, if you hate cruelty, remember that nothing is so cruel in its consequences as the toleration of heresy. Remember also that no court of law can be so cruel as the common people are to those whom they suspect of heresy. The heretic in the hands of the Holy Office is safe from violence, is assured of a fair trial, and cannot suffer death, even when guilty, if repentance follows sin. Innumerable lives of heretics have been saved because the Holy Office has taken them out of the hands of the people, and because the people have yielded them up, knowing that the Holy Office would deal with them. Before the Holy Inquisition existed, and even now when its officers are not within reach, the unfortunate wretch suspected of heresy, perhaps quite ignorantly and unjustly, is stoned, torn in pieces, drowned, burned in his house with all his innocent children, without a trial, unshriven, unburied save as a dog is buried: all of them deeds hateful to God and most cruel to man. Gentlemen: I am compassionate by nature as well as by my profession; and though the work I have to do may seem cruel to those who do not know how much more cruel it would be to leave it undone, I would go to the stake myself sooner than do it if I did not know its righteousness, its necessity, its essential mercy. I ask you to address yourself to this trial in that conviction. Anger is a bad counsellor: cast out anger. Pity is sometimes worse: cast out pity. But do not cast out mercy. Remember only that justice comes first. Have you anything to say, my lord, before we proceed to trial?

CAUCHON—You have spoken for me, and spoken better than I could. I do not see how any sane man could disagree with a word that has fallen from you. But this I will add. The crude heresies of which you have told us are horrible; but their horror is like that of the black death: they rage for a while and then die out, because sound and sensible men will not under any incitement be reconciled to nakedness and incest and polygamy and the like. But we are confronted today throughout Europe with a heresy that is spreading among men not weak in mind nor diseased in brain: nay, the stronger the mind, the more obstinate the heretic. It is neither discredited by fantastic extremes nor corrupted by the common lusts of the flesh; but it, too, sets up the private judgment of the single erring mortal against the considered wisdom and experience of the Church. The mighty structure of Catholic Christendom will never be shaken by naked madmen or by the sins of Moab and Ammon. But it may be betrayed from within, and brought to barbarous ruin and desolation, by this arch heresy which the English Commander calls Protestantism.

THE ASSESSORS [*whispering*] Protestantism! What was that? What does the Bishop mean? Is it a new heresy? The English Commander, he said. Did you ever hear of Protestantism? etc., etc.

CAUCHON [*continuing*] And that reminds me. What provision has the Earl of Warwick made for the defence of the secular arm should The Maid prove obdurate, and the people be moved to pity her?

THE CHAPLAIN – Have no fear on that score, my lord. The noble earl has eight hundred men-at-arms at the gates. She will not slip through our English fingers even if the whole city be on her side.

CAUCHON [*revolted*] Will you not add, God grant that she repent and purge her sin?

THE CHAPLAIN – That does not seem to me to be consistent; but of course I agree with your lordship.

CAUCHON [*giving him up with a shrug of contempt*] The court sits.

THE INQUISITOR – Let the accused be brought in.

LADVENU [*calling*] The accused. Let her be brought in.

JOAN, *chained by the ankles, is brought in through the arched door behind the prisoner's stool by a guard of English soldiers. With them is the* EXECUTIONER *and his assistants. They lead her to the prisoner's stool, and place themselves behind it after taking off her chain. She wears a page's black suit. Her long imprisonment and the strain of the examinations which have preceded the trial have left their mark on her; but her vitality still holds; she confronts the court unabashed, without a trace of the awe which their formal solemnity seems to require for the complete success of its impressiveness.*

THE INQUISITOR [*kindly*] Sit down, Joan. [*She sits on the prisoner's stool*]. You look very pale today. Are you not well?

JOAN – Thank you kindly: I am well enough. But the Bishop sent me some carp; and it made me ill.

CAUCHON – I am sorry. I told them to see that it was fresh.

JOAN – You meant to be good to me, I know; but it is a fish that does not agree with me. The English thought you were trying to poison me—

CAUCHON
THE CHAPLAIN } [*together*] { What!
No, my lord.

JOAN [*continuing*] They are determined that I shall be burnt as a witch; and they sent their doctor to cure me; but he was forbidden to bleed me because the silly people believe that a witch's witchery leaves her if she is bled; so he only called me filthy names. Why do you leave me in the hands of the English? I should be in the hands of the Church. And why must I be chained by the feet to a log of wood? Are you afraid I will fly away?

D'ESTIVET [*harshly*] Woman: it is not for you to question the court: it is for us to question you.

COURCELLES—When you were left unchained, did you not try to escape by jumping from a tower sixty feet high? If you cannot fly like a witch, how is it that you are still alive?

JOAN—I suppose because the tower was not so high then. It has grown higher every day since you began asking me questions about it.

D'ESTIVET—Why did you jump from the tower?

JOAN—How do you know that I jumped?

D'ESTIVET—You were found lying in the moat. Why did you leave the tower?

JOAN—Why would anybody leave a prison if they could get out?

D'ESTIVET—You tried to escape?

JOAN—Of course I did; and not for the first time either. If you leave the door of the cage open the bird will fly out.

D'ESTIVET [*rising*] That is a confession of heresy. I call the attention of the court to it.

JOAN—Heresy, he calls it! Am I a heretic because I try to escape from prison?

D'ESTIVET—Assuredly, if you are in the hands of the Church, and you wilfully take yourself out of its hands, you are deserting the Church; and that is heresy.

JOAN—It is great nonsense. Nobody could be such a fool as to think that.

D'ESTIVET—You hear, my lord, how I am reviled in the execution of my duty by this woman.

[*He sits down indignantly.*]

CAUCHON—I have warned you before, Joan, that you are doing yourself no good by these pert answers.

JOAN—But you will not talk sense to me. I am reasonable if you will be reasonable.

THE INQUISITOR [*interposing*] This is not yet in order. You forget, Master Promoter, that the proceedings have not been formally opened. The time for questions is after she has sworn on the Gospels to tell us the whole truth.

JOAN – You say this to me every time. I have said again and again that I will tell you all that concerns this trial. But I cannot tell you the whole truth: God does not allow the whole truth to be told. You do not understand it when I tell it. It is an old saying that he who tells too much truth is sure to be hanged. I am weary of this argument: we have been over it nine times already. I have sworn as much as I will swear; and I will swear no more.

COURCELLES – My lord: she should be put to the torture.

THE INQUISITOR – You hear, Joan? That is what happens to the obdurate. Think before you answer. Has she been shewn the instruments?

THE EXECUTIONER – They are ready, my lord. She has seen them.

JOAN – If you tear me limb from limb until you separate my soul from my body you will get nothing out of me beyond what I have told you. What more is there to tell that you could understand? Besides, I cannot bear to be hurt; and if you hurt me I will say anything you like to stop the pain. But I will take it all back afterwards; so what is the use of it?

LADVENU – There is much in that. We should proceed mercifully.

COURCELLES – But the torture is customary.

THE INQUISITOR – It must not be applied wantonly. If the accused will confess voluntarily, then its use cannot be justified.

COURCELLES – But this is unusual and irregular. She refuses to take the oath.

LADVENU [*disgusted*] Do you want to torture the girl for the mere pleasure of it?

COURCELLES [*bewildered*] But it is not a pleasure. It is the law. It is customary. It is always done.

THE INQUISITOR – That is not so, Master, except when the inquiries are carried on by people who do not know their legal business.

COURCELLES – But the woman is a heretic. I assure you it is always done.

CAUCHON [*decisively*] It will not be done today if it is not necessary. Let there be an end of this. I will not have it said that we proceeded on forced confessions. We have sent our best preachers and doctors to this woman to exhort and implore her to save her soul and body from the fire: we shall not now send the executioner to thrust her into it.

COURCELLES – Your lordship is merciful, of course. But it is a great responsibility to depart from the usual practice.

JOAN – Thou art a rare noodle, Master. Do what was done last time is thy rule, eh?

COURCELLES [*rising*] Thou wanton: dost thou dare call me noodle?

THE INQUISITOR—Patience, Master, patience: I fear you will soon be only too terribly avenged.

COURCELLES [*mutters*] Noodle indeed!

[*He sits down, much discontented.*]

THE INQUISITOR—Meanwhile, let us not be moved by the rough side of a shepherd lass's tongue.

JOAN—Nay: I am no shepherd lass, though I have helped with the sheep like anyone else. I will do a lady's work in the house—spin or weave—against any woman in Rouen.

THE INQUISITOR—This is not a time for vanity, Joan. You stand in great peril.

JOAN—I know it: have I not been punished for my vanity? If I had not worn my cloth of gold surcoat in battle like a fool, that Burgundian soldier would never have pulled me backwards off my horse; and I should not have been here.

THE CHAPLAIN—If you are so clever at woman's work why do you not stay at home and do it?

JOAN—There are plenty of other women to do it; but there is nobody to do my work.

CAUCHON—Come! we are wasting time on trifles. Joan: I am going to put a most solemn question to you. Take care how you answer; for your life and salvation are at stake on it. Will you for all you have said and done, be it good or bad, accept the judgment of God's Church on earth? More especially as to the acts and words that are imputed to you in this trial by the Promoter here, will you submit your case to the inspired interpretation of the Church Militant?

JOAN—I am a faithful child of the Church. I will obey the Church—

CAUCHON [*hopefully leaning forward*] You will?

JOAN——provided it does not command anything impossible.

[CAUCHON *sinks back in his chair with a heavy sigh. The* INQUISITOR *purses his lips and frowns.* LADVENU *shakes his head pitifully.*]

D'ESTIVET—She imputes to the Church the error and folly of commanding the impossible.

JOAN—If you command me to declare that all that I have done and said, and all the visions and revelations I have had, were not from God, then that is impossible: I will not declare it for anything in the world. What God made me do I will never go back on; and what He has commanded or shall command I will not fail to do in spite of any man alive. That is what I mean by impossible. And in case the Church should bid me do anything contrary to the command I have from God, I will not consent to it, no matter what it may be.

THE ASSESSORS [*shocked and indignant*] Oh! The Church contrary to God! What do you say now? Flat heresy. This is beyond everything, etc., etc.

D'ESTIVET [*throwing down his brief*] My lord: do you need anything more than this?

CAUCHON—Woman: you have said enough to burn ten heretics. Will you not be warned? Will you not understand?

THE INQUISITOR—If the Church Militant tells you that your revelations and visions are sent by the devil to tempt you to your damnation, will you not believe that the Church is wiser than you?

JOAN—I believe that God is wiser than I; and it is His commands that I will do. All the things that you call my crimes have come to me by the command of God. I say that I have done them by the order of God: it is impossible for me to say anything else. If any Churchman says the contrary I shall not mind him: I shall mind God alone, whose command I always follow.

LADVENU [*pleading with her urgently*] You do not know what you are saying, child. Do you want to kill yourself? Listen. Do you not believe that you are subject to the Church of God on earth?

JOAN—Yes. When have I ever denied it?

LADVENU—Good. That means, does it not, that you are subject to our Lord the Pope, to the cardinals, the archbishops, and the bishops for whom his lordship stands here today?

JOAN—God must be served first.

D'ESTIVET—Then your voices command you not to submit yourself to the Church Militant?

JOAN—My voices do not tell me to disobey the Church; but God must be served first.

CAUCHON—And you, and not the Church, are to be the judge?

JOAN—What other judgment can I judge by but my own?

THE ASSESSORS [*scandalized*] Oh!

[*They cannot find words.*]

CAUCHON—Out of your own mouth you have condemned yourself. We have striven for your salvation to the verge of sinning ourselves: we have opened the door to you again and again; and you have shut it in our faces and in the face of God. Dare you pretend, after what you have said, that you are in a state of grace?

JOAN—If I am not, may God bring me to it: if I am, may God keep me in it!

LADVENU—That is a very good reply, my lord.

COURCELLES—Were you in a state of grace when you stole the Bishop's horse?

CAUCHON [*rising in a fury*] Oh, devil take the Bishop's horse and you too! We are here to try a case of heresy; and no sooner do we come

1813

to the root of the matter than we are thrown back by idiots who understand nothing but horses.

[*Trembling with rage, he forces himself to sit down.*]

THE INQUISITOR – Gentlemen, gentlemen: in clinging to these small issues you are The Maid's best advocates. I am not surprised that his lordship has lost patience with you. What does the Promoter say? Does he press these trumpery matters?

D'ESTIVET – I am bound by my office to press everything; but when the woman confesses a heresy that must bring upon her the doom of excommunication, of what consequence is it that she has been guilty also of offences which expose her to minor penances? I share the impatience of his lordship as to these minor charges. Only, with great respect, I must emphasize the gravity of two very horrible and blasphemous crimes which she does not deny. First, she has intercourse with evil spirits, and is therefore a sorceress. Second, she wears men's clothes, which is indecent, unnatural, and abominable; and in spite of our most earnest remonstrances and entreaties, she will not change them even to receive the sacrament.

JOAN – Is the blessed St Catherine an evil spirit? Is St Margaret? Is Michael the Archangel?

COURCELLES – How do you know that the spirit which appears to you is an archangel? Does he not appear to you as a naked man?

JOAN – Do you think God cannot afford clothes for him?

[*The assessors cannot help smiling, especially as the joke is against* COURCELLES.]

LADVENU – Well answered, Joan.

THE INQUISITOR – It is, in effect, well answered. But no evil spirit would be so simple as to appear to a young girl in a guise that would scandalize her when he meant her to take him for a messenger from the Most High. Joan: the Church instructs you that these apparitions are demons seeking your soul's perdition. Do you accept the instruction of the Church?

JOAN – I accept the messenger of God. How could any faithful believer in the Church refuse him?

CAUCHON – Wretched woman: again I ask you, do you know what you are saying?

THE INQUISITOR – You wrestle in vain with the devil for her soul, my lord: she will not be saved. Now as to this matter of the man's dress. For the last time, will you put off that impudent attire, and dress as becomes your sex?

JOAN – I will not.

D'ESTIVET [*pouncing*] The sin of disobedience, my lord.

JOAN [*distressed*] But my voices tell me I must dress as a soldier.

1814

LADVENU–Joan, Joan: does not that prove to you that the voices are the voices of evil spirits? Can you suggest to us one good reason why an angel of God should give you such shameless advice?

JOAN–Why, yes: what can be plainer commonsense? I was a soldier living among soldiers. I am a prisoner guarded by soldiers. If I were to dress as a woman they would think of me as a woman; and then what would become of me? If I dress as a soldier they think of me as a soldier, and I can live with them as I do at home with my brothers. That is why St Catherine tells me I must not dress as a woman until she gives me leave.

COURCELLES–When will she give you leave?

JOAN–When you take me out of the hands of the English soldiers. I have told you that I should be in the hands of the Church, and not left night and day with four soldiers of the Earl of Warwick. Do you want me to live with them in petticoats?

LADVENU–My lord: what she says is, God knows, very wrong and shocking; but there is a grain of worldly sense in it such as might impose on a simple village maiden.

JOAN–If we were as simple in the village as you are in your courts and palaces, there would soon be no wheat to make bread for you.

CAUCHON–That is the thanks you get for trying to save her, Brother Martin.

LADVENU–Joan: we are all trying to save you. His lordship is trying to save you. The Inquisitor could not be more just to you if you were his own daughter. But you are blinded by a terrible pride and self-sufficiency.

JOAN–Why do you say that? I have said nothing wrong. I cannot understand.

THE INQUISITOR–The blessed St Athanasius has laid it down in his creed that those who cannot understand are damned. It is not enough to be simple. It is not enough even to be what simple people call good. The simplicity of a darkened mind is no better than the simplicity of a beast.

JOAN–There is great wisdom in the simplicity of a beast, let me tell you; and sometimes great foolishness in the wisdom of scholars.

LADVENU–We know that, Joan: we are not so foolish as you think us. Try to resist the temptation to make pert replies to us. Do you see that man who stands behind you? [*He indicates the* EXECUTIONER.]

JOAN [*turning and looking at the man*] Your torturer? But the Bishop said I was not to be tortured.

LADVENU–You are not to be tortured because you have confessed everything that is necessary to your condemnation. That man is not only the torturer: he is also the Executioner. Executioner: let The

Maid hear your answers to my questions. Are you prepared for the burning of a heretic this day?

THE EXECUTIONER—Yes, Master.

LADVENU—Is the stake ready?

THE EXECUTIONER—It is. In the market-place. The English have built it too high for me to get near her and make the death easier. It will be a cruel death.

JOAN [*horrified*] But you are not going to burn me now?

THE INQUISITOR—You realize it at last.

LADVENU—There are eight hundred English soldiers waiting to take you to the market-place the moment the sentence of excommunication has passed the lips of your judges. You are within a few short moments of that doom.

JOAN [*looking round desperately for rescue*] Oh God!

LADVENU—Do not despair, Joan. The Church is merciful. You can save yourself.

JOAN [*hopefully*] Yes: my voices promised me I should not be burnt. St Catherine bade me be bold.

CAUCHON—Woman: are you quite mad? Do you not yet see that your voices have deceived you?

JOAN—Oh no: that is impossible.

CAUCHON—Impossible! They have led you straight to your excommunication, and to the stake which is there waiting for you.

LADVENU [*pressing the point hard*] Have they kept a single promise to you since you were taken at Compiègne? The devil has betrayed you. The Church holds out its arms to you.

JOAN [*despairing*] Oh, it is true: it is true: my voices have deceived me. I have been mocked by devils: my faith is broken. I have dared and dared; but only a fool will walk into a fire: God, who gave me my commonsense, cannot will me to do that.

LADVENU—Now God be praised that He has saved you at the eleventh hour!

[*He hurries to the vacant seat at the scribes' table, and snatches a sheet of paper, on which he sets to work writing eagerly.*]

CAUCHON—Amen!

JOAN—What must I do?

CAUCHON—You must sign a solemn recantation of your heresy.

JOAN—Sign? That means to write my name. I cannot write.

CAUCHON—You have signed many letters before.

JOAN—Yes; but someone held my hand and guided the pen. I can make my mark.

THE CHAPLAIN [*who has been listening with growing alarm and indignation*] My lord: do you mean that you are going to allow this woman to escape us?

THE INQUISITOR—The law must take its course, Master de Stogumber. And you know the law.

THE CHAPLAIN [*rising, purple with fury*] I know that there is no faith in a Frenchman. [*Tumult, which he shouts down.*] I know what my lord the Cardinal of Winchester will say when he hears of this. I know what the Earl of Warwick will do when he learns that you intend to betray him. There are eight hundred men at the gate who will see that this abominable witch is burnt in spite of your teeth.

THE ASSESSORS [*meanwhile*] What is this? What did he say? He accuses us of treachery! This is past bearing. No faith in a Frenchman! Did you hear that? This is an intolerable fellow. Who is he? Is this what English Churchmen are like? He must be mad or drunk, etc., etc.

THE INQUISITOR [*rising*] Silence, pray! Gentlemen: pray silence! Master Chaplain: bethink you a moment of your holy office: of what you are, and where you are. I direct you to sit down.

THE CHAPLAIN [*folding his arms doggedly, his face working convulsively*] I will NOT sit down.

CAUCHON—Master Inquisitor: this man has called me a traitor to my face before now.

THE CHAPLAIN—So you are a traitor. You are all traitors. You have been doing nothing but begging this damnable witch on your knees to recant all through this trial.

THE INQUISITOR [*placidly resuming his seat*] If you will not sit, you must stand: that is all.

THE CHAPLAIN—I will NOT stand.

[*He flings himself back into his chair.*]

LADVENU [*rising with the paper in his hand*] My lord: here is the form of recantation for The Maid to sign.

CAUCHON—Read it to her.

JOAN—Do not trouble. I will sign it.

THE INQUISITOR—Woman: you must know what you are putting your hand to. Read it to her, Brother Martin. And let all be silent.

LADVENU [*reading quietly*] 'I, Joan, commonly called The Maid, a miserable sinner, do confess that I have most grievously sinned in the following articles. I have pretended to have revelations from God and the angels and the blessed saints, and perversely rejected the Church's warnings that these were temptations by demons. I have blasphemed abominably by wearing an immodest dress, contrary to the Holy Scripture and the canons of the Church. Also I have clipped my hair in the style of a man, and, against all the duties which have made my sex specially acceptable in heaven, have taken up the sword, even to the shedding of human blood, inciting men to slay each other, invoking evil spirits to delude them, and stubbornly and most blasphemously imputing these sins to Almighty God. I confess to the sin of sedition, to the sin of idolatry, to the sin of disobedience, to the sin of pride, and to the sin of heresy. All of which sins I now renounce and abjure and depart from, humbly thanking you Doctors and Masters who have brought me back to the truth and into the grace of our Lord. And I will never return to my errors, but will remain in communion with our Holy Church and in obedience to our Holy Father the Pope of Rome. All this I swear by God Almighty and the Holy Gospels, in witness whereto I sign my name to this recantation.'

THE INQUISITOR—You understand this, Joan?

JOAN [*listless*] It is plain enough, sir.

THE INQUISITOR—And it is true?

JOAN—It may be true. If it were not true, the fire would not be ready for me in the market-place.

LADVENU [*taking up his pen and a book, and going to her quickly lest she should compromise herself again*] Come, child: let me guide your hand. Take the pen. [*She does so; and they begin to write, using the book as a desk.*] J.E.H.A.N.E. So. Now make your mark by yourself.

JOAN [*makes her mark, and gives him back the pen, tormented by the rebellion of her soul against her mind and body*] There!

LADVENU [*replacing the pen on the table, and handing the recantation to* CAUCHON *with a reverence*] Praise be to God, my brothers, the lamb has returned to the flock; and the shepherd rejoices in her more than in ninety and nine just persons. [*He returns to his seat.*]

THE INQUISITOR [*taking the paper from* CAUCHON] We declare thee by this act set free from the danger of excommunication in which thou stoodest.

> [*He throws the paper down to the table.*]

JOAN—I thank you.

THE INQUISITOR—But because thou has sinned most presumptuously against God and the Holy Church, and that thou mayst repent thy errors in solitary contemplation, and be shielded from all temptation to return to them, we, for the good of thy soul, and for a penance that may wipe out thy sins and bring thee finally unspotted to the throne of grace, do condemn thee to eat the bread of sorrow and drink the water of affliction to the end of thy earthly days in perpetual imprisonment.

JOAN [*rising in consternation and terrible anger*] Perpetual imprisonment! Am I not then to be set free?

LADVENU [*mildly shocked*] Set free, child, after such wickedness as yours! What are you dreaming of?

J O A N – Give me that writing. [*She rushes to the table; snatches up the paper; and tears it into fragments.*] Light your fire: do you think I dread it as much as the life of a rat in a hole? My voices were right.

L A D V E N U – Joan! Joan!

J O A N – Yes: they told me you were fools [*the word gives great offence*], and that I was not to listen to your fine words nor trust to your charity. You promised me my life; but you lied. [*Indignant exclamations.*] You think that life is nothing but not being stone dead. It is not the bread and water I fear: I can live on bread: when have I asked for more? It is no hardship to drink water if the water be clean. Bread has no sorrow for me, and water no affliction. But to shut me from the light of the sky and the sight of the fields and flowers; to chain my feet so that I can never again ride with the soldiers nor climb the hills; to make me breathe foul damp darkness, and keep from me everything that brings me back to the love of God when your wickedness and foolishness tempt me to hate Him: all this is worse than the furnace in the Bible that was heated seven times. I could do without my warhorse; I could drag about in a skirt; I could let the banners and the trumpets and the knights and soldiers pass me and leave me behind as they leave the other women, if only I could still hear the wind in the trees, the larks in the sunshine, the young lambs crying through the healthy frost, and the blessed blessed church bells that send my angel voices floating to me on the wind. But without these things I cannot live; and by your wanting to take them away from me, or from any human creature, I know that your counsel is of the devil, and that mine is of God.

T H E   A S S E S S O R S   [*in great commotion*] Blasphemy! blasphemy! She is possessed. She said our counsel was of the devil. And hers of God. Monstrous! The devil is in our midst, etc., etc.

D ' E S T I V E T   [*shouting above the din*] She is a relapsed heretic, obstinate, incorrigible, and altogether unworthy of the mercy we have shewn her. I call for her excommunication.

T H E   C H A P L A I N   [*to the* EXECUTIONER] Light your fire, man. To the stake with her.

[*The* EXECUTIONER *and his assistants hurry out through the courtyard.*]

L A D V E N U – You wicked girl: if your counsel were of God would He not deliver you?

J O A N – His ways are not your ways. He wills that I go through the fire to His bosom; for I am His child, and you are not fit that I should live among you. That is my last word to you.

[*The soldiers seize her.*]

C A U C H O N   [*rising*] Not yet.

They wait. There is a dead silence. CAUCHON *turns to the* INQUISITOR *with an inquiring look. The* INQUISITOR *nods affirmatively. They rise solemnly, and intone the sentence antiphonally.*

C A U C H O N – We decree that thou art a relapsed heretic.

T H E   I N Q U I S I T O R – Cast out from the unity of the Church.

C A U C H O N – Sundered from her body.

T H E   I N Q U I S I T O R – Infected with the leprosy of heresy.

C A U C H O N – A member of Satan.

T H E   I N Q U I S I T O R – We declare that thou must be excommunicate.

C A U C H O N – And now we do cast thee out, segregate thee, and abandon thee to the secular power.

T H E   I N Q U I S I T O R – Admonishing the same secular power that it moderate its judgment of thee in respect of death and division of the limbs.

[*He resumes his seat.*]

C A U C H O N – And if any true sign of penitence appear in thee, to permit our Brother Martin to administer to thee the sacrament of penance.

T H E   C H A P L A I N – Into the fire with the witch. [*He rushes at her, and helps the soldiers to push her out.*]

JOAN *is taken away through the courtyard. The assessors rise in disorder, and follow the soldiers, except* LADVENU, *who has hidden his face in his hands.*

C A U C H O N   [*rising again in the act of sitting down*] No, no: this is irregular. The representative of the secular arm should be here to receive her from us.

T H E   I N Q U I S I T O R   [*also on his feet again*] That man is an incorrigible fool.

C A U C H O N – Brother Martin: see that everything is done in order.

L A D V E N U – My place is at her side, my lord. You must exercise your own authority. [*He hurries out.*]

C A U C H O N – These English are impossible: they will thrust her straight into the fire. Look!

He points to the courtyard, in which the glow and flicker of fire can now be seen reddening the May daylight. Only the BISHOP *and the* INQUISITOR *are left in the court.*

C A U C H O N   [*turning to go*] We must stop that.

T H E   I N Q U I S I T O R   [*calmly*] Yes; but not too fast, my lord.

C A U C H O N   [*halting*] But there is not a moment to lose.

THE INQUISITOR—We have proceeded in perfect order. If the English choose to put themselves in the wrong, it is not our business to put them in the right. A flaw in the procedure may be useful later on: one never knows. And the sooner it is over, the better for that poor girl.

CAUCHON [*relaxing*] That is true. But I suppose we must see this dreadful thing through.

THE INQUISITOR—One gets used to it. Habit is everything. I am accustomed to the fire: it is soon over. But it is a terrible thing to see a young and innocent creature crushed between these mighty forces, the Church and the Law.

CAUCHON—You call her innocent!

THE INQUISITOR—Oh, quite innocent. What does she know of the Church and the Law? She did not understand a word we were saying. It is the ignorant who suffer. Come, or we shall be late for the end.

CAUCHON [*going with him*] I shall not be sorry if we are: I am not so accustomed as you.

[*They are going out when* WARWICK *comes in, meeting them.*]

WARWICK—Oh, I am intruding. I thought it was all over.

[*He makes a feint of retiring.*]

CAUCHON—Do not go, my lord. It is all over.

THE INQUISITOR—The execution is not in our hands, my lord; but it is desirable that we should witness the end. So by your leave—

[*He bows, and goes out through the courtyard.*]

CAUCHON—There is some doubt whether your people have observed the forms of law, my lord.

WARWICK—I am told that there is some doubt whether your authority runs in this city, my lord. It is not in your diocese. However, if you will answer for that I will answer for the rest.

CAUCHON—It is to God that we both must answer. Good morning, my lord.

WARWICK—My lord: good morning.

They look at one another for a moment with unconcealed hostility. Then CAUCHON *follows the* INQUISITOR *out.* WARWICK *looks round. Finding himself alone, he calls for attendance.*

WARWICK—Hallo: some attendance here! [*Silence.*] Hallo, there! [*Silence.*] Hallo! Brian, you young blackguard, where are you? [*Silence.*] Guard! [*Silence.*] They have all gone to see the burning: even that child.

[*The silence is broken by someone frantically howling and sobbing.*]

WARWICK—What in the devil's name—?

The CHAPLAIN *staggers in from the courtyard like a demented creature, his face streaming with tears, making the piteous sounds that* WARWICK *has heard. He stumbles to the prisoner's stool, and throws himself upon it with heartrending sobs.*

WARWICK [*going to him and patting him on the shoulder*] What is it, Master John? What is the matter?

THE CHAPLAIN [*clutching at his hand*] My lord, my lord: for Christ's sake pray for my wretched guilty soul.

WARWICK [*soothing him*] Yes, yes: of course I will. Calmly, gently—

THE CHAPLAIN [*blubbering miserably*] I am not a bad man, my lord.

WARWICK—No, no: not at all.

THE CHAPLAIN—I meant no harm. I did not know what it would be like.

WARWICK [*hardening*] Oh! You saw it, then?

THE CHAPLAIN—I did not know what I was doing. I am a hot-headed fool; and I shall be damned to all eternity for it.

WARWICK—Nonsense! Very distressing, no doubt; but it was not your doing.

THE CHAPLAIN [*lamentably*] I let them do it. If I had known, I would have torn her from their hands. You dont know: you havnt seen: it is so easy to talk when you dont know. You madden yourself with words: you damn yourself because it feels grand to throw oil on the flaming hell of your own temper. But when it is brought home to you; when you see the thing you have done; when it is blinding your eyes, stifling your nostrils, tearing your heart, then—then—[*Falling on his knees.*] O God, take away this sight from me! O Christ, deliver me from this fire that is consuming me! She cried to Thee in the midst of it: Jesus! Jesus! Jesus! She is in Thy bosom; and I am in hell for evermore.

WARWICK [*summarily hauling him to his feet*] Come come, man! you must pull yourself together. We shall have the whole town talking of this. [*He throws him not too gently into a chair at the table.*] If you have not the nerve to see these things, why do you not do as I do, and stay away?

THE CHAPLAIN [*bewildered and submissive*] She asked for a cross. A soldier gave her two sticks tied together. Thank God he was an Englishman! I might have done it; but I did not: I am a coward, a mad dog, a fool. But he was an Englishman too.

WARWICK—The fool! they will burn him too if the priests get hold of him.

THE CHAPLAIN [*shaken with a convulsion*] Some of the people laughed at her. They would have laughed at Christ. They were French people, my lord: I know they were French.

WARWICK – Hush! someone is coming. Control yourself.

LADVENU *comes back through the courtyard to* WARWICK'S *right hand, carrying a bishop's cross which he has taken from a church. He is very grave and composed.*

WARWICK – I am informed that it is all over, Brother Martin.

LADVENU [*enigmatically*] We do not know, my lord. It may have only just begun.

WARWICK – What does that mean, exactly?

LADVENU – I took this cross from the church for her that she might see it to the last: she had only two sticks that she put into her bosom. When the fire crept round us, and she saw that if I held the cross before her I should be burnt myself, she warned me to get down and save myself. My lord: a girl who could think of another's danger in such a moment was not inspired by the devil. When I had to snatch the cross from her sight, she looked up to heaven. And I do not believe that the heavens were empty. I firmly believe that her Savior appeared to her then in His tenderest glory. She called to Him and died. This is not the end for her, but the beginning.

WARWICK – I am afraid it will have a bad effect on the people.

LADVENU – It had, my lord, on some of them. I heard laughter. Forgive me for saying that I hope and believe it was English laughter.

THE CHAPLAIN [*rising frantically*] No: it was not. There was only one Englishman there that disgraced his country; and that was the mad dog, de Stogumber. [*He rushes wildly out, shrieking.*] Let them torture him. Let them burn him. I will go pray among her ashes. I am no better than Judas: I will hang myself.

WARWICK – Quick, Brother Martin: follow him: he will do himself some mischief. After him, quick.

LADVENU *hurries out,* WARWICK *urging him. The* EXECUTIONER *comes in by the door behind the judges' chairs; and* WARWICK, *returning, finds himself face to face with him.*

WARWICK – Well, fellow: who are you?

THE EXECUTIONER [*with dignity*] I am not addressed as fellow, my lord. I am the Master Executioner of Rouen: it is a highly skilled mystery. I am come to tell your lordship that your orders have been obeyed.

WARWICK – I crave your pardon, Master Executioner; and I will see that you lose nothing by having no relics to sell. I have your word, have I, that nothing remains, not a bone, not a nail, not a hair?

THE EXECUTIONER — Her heart would not burn, my lord; but everything that was left is at the bottom of the river. You have heard the last of her.

WARWICK [*with a wry smile, thinking of what* LADVENU *said*] The last of her? Hm! I wonder!

EPILOGUE

A *restless fitfully windy night in June 1456, full of summer lightning
after many days of heat.* KING CHARLES THE SEVENTH OF FRANCE, *formerly*
JOAN'S DAUPHIN, *now* CHARLES THE VICTORIOUS, *aged 51, is in bed in one
of his royal chateaux. The bed, raised on a dais of two steps, is towards
the side of the room so as to avoid blocking a tall lancet window in the
middle. Its canopy bears the royal arms in embroidery. Except for the
canopy and the huge down pillows there is nothing to distinguish it from
a broad settee with bed-clothes and a valance. Thus its occupant is in
full view from the foot.*

CHARLES *is not asleep: he is reading in bed, or rather looking at the
pictures in Fouquet's Boccaccio with his knees doubled up to make a
reading-desk. Beside the bed on his left is a little table with a picture
of the Virgin, lighted by candles of painted wax. The walls are hung
from ceiling to floor with painted curtains which stir at times in the
draughts. At first glance the prevailing yellow and red in these hanging
pictures is somewhat flamelike when the folds breathe in the wind.*

The door is on CHARLES'S *left, but in front of him close to the corner
farthest from him. A large watchman's rattle, handsomely designed and
gaily painted, is in the bed under his hand.*

CHARLES *turns a leaf. A distant clock strikes the half-hour softly.*
CHARLES *shuts the book with a clap; throws it aside; snatches up the rattle;
and whirls it energetically, making a deafening clatter.* LADVENU *enters,
25 years older, strange and stark in bearing, and still carrying the cross
from Rouen.* CHARLES *evidently does not expect him; for he springs out
of bed on the farther side from the door.*

C H A R L E S — Who are you? Where is my gentleman of the bedchamber?
What do you want?

L A D V E N U [*solemnly*] I bring you glad tidings of great joy. Rejoice,
O king; for the taint is removed from your blood, and the stain from
your crown. Justice, long delayed, is at last triumphant.

C H A R L E S — What are you talking about? Who are you?

L A D V E N U — I am Brother Martin.

CHARLES—And who, saving your reverence, may Brother Martin be?

LADVENU—I held this cross when The Maid perished in the fire. Twenty-five years have passed since then: nearly ten thousand days. And on every one of those days I have prayed to God to justify His daughter on earth as she is justified in heaven.

CHARLES [*reassured, sitting down on the foot of the bed*] Oh, I remember now. I have heard of you. You have a bee in your bonnet about The Maid. Have you been at the inquiry?

LADVENU—I have given my testimony.

CHARLES—Is it over?

LADVENU—It is over.

CHARLES—Satisfactorily?

LADVENU—The ways of God are very strange.

CHARLES—How so?

LADVENU—At the trial which sent a saint to the stake as a heretic and a sorceress, the truth was told; the law was upheld; mercy was shewn beyond all custom; no wrong was done but the final and dreadful wrong of the lying sentence and the pitiless fire. At this inquiry from which I have just come, there was shameless perjury, courtly corruption, calumny of the dead who did their duty according to their lights, cowardly evasion of the issue, testimony made of idle tales that could not impose on a ploughboy. Yet out of this insult to justice, this defamation of the Church, this orgy of lying and foolishness, the truth is set in the noonday sun on the hilltop; the white robe of innocence is cleansed from the smirch of the burning faggots; the holy life is sanctified; the true heart that lived through the flame is consecrated; a great lie is silenced for ever; and a great wrong is set right before all men.

CHARLES—My friend: provided they can no longer say that I was crowned by a witch and a heretic, I shall not fuss about how the trick has been done. Joan would not have fussed about it if it came all right in the end: she was not that sort: I knew her. Is her rehabilitation complete? I made it pretty clear that there was to be no nonsense about it.

LADVENU—It is solemnly declared that her judges were full of corruption, cozenage, fraud, and malice. Four falsehoods.

CHARLES—Never mind the falsehoods: her judges are dead.

LADVENU—The sentence on her is broken, annulled, annihilated, set aside as non-existent, without value or effect.

CHARLES—Good. Nobody can challenge my consecration now, can they?

LADVENU—Not Charlemagne nor King David himself was more sacredly crowned.

CHARLES [*rising*] Excellent. Think of what that means to me!

LADVENU—I think of what it means to her!

CHARLES—You cannot. None of us ever knew what anything meant to her. She was like nobody else; and she must take care of herself wherever she is; for I cannot take care of her; and neither can you, whatever you may think: you are not big enough. But I will tell you this about her. If you could bring her back to life, they would burn her again within six months, for all their present adoration of her. And you would hold up the cross, too, just the same. So [*crossing himself*] let her rest; and let you and I mind our own business, and not meddle with hers.

LADVENU—God forbid that I should have no share in her, nor she in me! [*He turns and strides out as he came, saying.*] Henceforth my path will not lie through palaces, nor my conversation be with kings.

CHARLES [*following him towards the door, and shouting after him*] Much good may it do you, holy man! [*He returns to the middle of the chamber, where he halts, and says quizzically to himself.*] That was a funny chap. How did he get in? Where are my people? [*He goes impatiently to the bed, and swings the rattle. A rush of wind through the open door sets the walls swaying agitatedly. The candles go out. He calls in the darkness.*] Hallo! Someone come and shut the windows: everything is being blown all over the place. [*A flash of summer lightning shews up the lancet window. A figure is seen in silhouette against it.*] Who is there? Who is that? Help! Murder!

[*Thunder. He jumps into bed, and hides under the clothes.*]

JOAN'S VOICE—Easy, Charlie, easy. What art making all that noise for? No one can hear thee. Thourt asleep.

[*She is dimly seen in a pallid greenish light by the bedside.*]

CHARLES [*peeping out*] Joan! Are you a ghost, Joan?

JOAN—Hardly even that, lad. Can a poor burnt-up lass have a ghost? I am but a dream that thourt dreaming. [*The light increases: they become plainly visible as he sits up.*] Thou looks older, lad.

CHARLES—I am older. Am I really asleep?

JOAN—Fallen asleep over thy silly book.

CHARLES—That's funny.

JOAN—Not so funny as that I am dead, is it?

CHARLES—Are you really dead?

JOAN—As dead as anybody ever is, laddie. I am out of the body.

CHARLES—Just fancy! Did it hurt much?

JOAN—Did what hurt much?

CHARLES—Being burnt.

JOAN—Oh, that! I cannot remember very well. I think it did at first; but then it all got mixed up; and I was not in my right mind until

1827

I was free of the body. But do not thou go handling fire and thinking it will not hurt thee. How hast been ever since?

CHARLES – Oh, not so bad. Do you know, I actually lead my army out and win battles? Down into the moat up to my waist in mud and blood. Up the ladders with the stones and hot pitch raining down. Like you.

JOAN – No! Did I make a man of thee after all, Charlie?

CHARLES – I am Charles the Victorious now. I had to be brave because you were. Agnes put a little pluck into me too.

JOAN – Agnes! Who was Agnes?

CHARLES – Agnes Sorel. A woman I fell in love with. I dream of her often. I never dreamed of you before.

JOAN – Is she dead, like me?

CHARLES – Yes. But she was not like you. She was very beautiful.

JOAN [*laughing heartily*] Ha ha! I was no beauty: I was always a rough one: a regular soldier. I might almost as well have been a man. Pity I wasnt: I should not have bothered you all so much then. But my head was in the skies; and the glory of God was upon me; and, man or woman, I should have bothered you as long as your noses were in the mud. Now tell me what has happened since you wise men knew no better than to make a heap of cinders of me?

CHARLES – Your mother and brothers have sued the courts to have your case tried over again. And the courts have declared that your judges were full of corruption and cozenage, fraud and malice.

JOAN – Not they. They were as honest a lot of poor fools as ever burned their betters.

CHARLES – The sentence on you is broken, annihilated, annulled: null, non-existent, without value or effect.

JOAN – I was burned, all the same. Can they unburn me?

CHARLES – If they could, they would think twice before they did it. But they have decreed that a beautiful cross be placed where the stake stood, for your perpetual memory and for your salvation.

JOAN – It is the memory and the salvation that sanctify the cross, not the cross that sanctifies the memory and the salvation. [*She turns away, forgetting him.*] I shall outlast that cross. I shall be remembered when men will have forgotten where Rouen stood.

CHARLES – There you go with your self-conceit, the same as ever! I think you might say a word of thanks to me for having had justice done at last.

CAUCHON [*appearing at the window between them*] Liar!

CHARLES – Thank you.

JOAN – Why, if it isnt Peter Cauchon! How are you, Peter? What luck have you had since you burned me?

C A U C H O N – None. I arraign the justice of Man. It is not the justice of God.

J O A N – Still dreaming of justice, Peter? See what justice came to with me! But what has happened to thee? Art dead or alive?

C A U C H O N – Dead. Dishonored. They pursued me beyond the grave. They excommunicated my dead body: they dug it up and flung it into the common sewer.

J O A N – Your dead body did not feel the spade and the sewer as my live body felt the fire.

C A U C H O N – But this thing that they have done against me hurts justice; destroys faith; saps the foundation of the Church. The solid earth sways like the treacherous sea beneath the feet of men and spirits alike when the innocent are slain in the name of law, and their wrongs are undone by slandering the pure of heart.

J O A N – Well, well, Peter, I hope men will be the better for remembering me; and they would not remember me so well if you had not burned me.

C A U C H O N – They will be the worse for remembering me: they will see in me evil triumphing over good, falsehood over truth, cruelty over mercy, hell over heaven. Their courage will rise as they think of you, only to faint as they think of me. Yet God is my witness I was just: I was merciful: I was faithful to my light: I could do no other than I did.

C H A R L E S [*scrambling out of the sheets and enthroning himself on the side of the bed*] Yes: it is always you good men that do the big mischiefs. Look at me! I am not Charles the Good, nor Charles the Wise, nor Charles the Bold. Joan's worshippers may even call me Charles the Coward because I did not pull her out of the fire. But I have done less harm than any of you. You people with your heads in the sky spend all your time trying to turn the world upside down; but I take the world as it is, and say that top-side-up is right-side-up; and I keep my nose pretty close to the ground. And I ask you, what king of France has done better, or been a better fellow in his little way?

J O A N – Art really king of France, Charlie? Be the English gone?

D U N O I S [*coming through the tapestry on* JOAN's *left, the candles relighting themselves at the same moment, and illuminating his armor and surcoat cheerfully*] I have kept my word: the English are gone.

J O A N – Praised be God! now is fair France a province in heaven. Tell me all about the fighting, Jack. Was it thou that led them? Wert thou God's captain to thy death?

D U N O I S – I am not dead. My body is very comfortably asleep in my bed at Chateaudun; but my spirit is called here by yours.

J O A N – And you fought them my way, Jack: eh? Not the old way, chaffering for ransoms; but The Maid's way: staking life against death, with the heart high and humble and void of malice, and nothing counting under God but France free and French. Was it my way, Jack?

DUNOIS — Faith, it was any way that would win. But the way that won was always your way. I give you best, lassie. I wrote a fine letter to set you right at the new trial. Perhaps I should never have let the priests burn you; but I was busy fighting; and it was the Church's business, not mine. There was no use in both of us being burned, was there?

CAUCHON — Ay! put the blame on the priests. But I, who am beyond praise and blame, tell you that the world is saved neither by its priests nor its soldiers, but by God and His Saints. The Church Militant sent this woman to the fire; but even as she burned, the flames whitened into the radiance of the Church Triumphant.

[*The clock strikes the third quarter. A rough male voice is heard trolling an improvised tune.*]

alla marcia   *molto cantabile*

Rum tum trumpledum,
Bacon fat and rumpledum,
Old Saint mumpledum,
Pull his tail and stumpledum
  O my Ma—ry Ann!

[*A ruffianly* ENGLISH SOLDIER *comes through the curtains and marches between* DUNOIS *and* JOAN.]

DUNOIS — What villainous troubadour taught you that doggrel?

THE SOLDIER — No troubadour. We made it up ourselves as we marched. We were not gentlefolks and troubadours. Music straight out of the heart of the people, as you might say. Rum tum trumpledum, Bacon fat and rumpledum, Old Saint mumpledum, Pull his tail and stumpledum: that dont mean anything, you know; but it keeps you marching. Your servant, ladies and gentlemen. Who asked for a saint?

JOAN — Be you a saint?

THE SOLDIER — Yes, lady, straight from hell.

DUNOIS — A saint, and from hell!

THE SOLDIER — Yes, noble captain: I have a day off. Every year, you know. Thats my allowance for my one good action.

CAUCHON — Wretch! In all the years of your life did you do only one good action?

1830

THE SOLDIER—I never thought about it: it came natural like. But they scored it up for me.

CHARLES—What was it?

THE SOLDIER—Why, the silliest thing you ever heard of. I—

JOAN [*interrupting him by strolling across to the bed, where she sits beside* CHARLES] He tied two sticks together, and gave them to a poor lass that was going to be burned.

THE SOLDIER—Right. Who told you that?

JOAN—Never mind. Would you know her if you saw her again?

THE SOLDIER—Not I. There are so many girls! and they all expect you to remember them as if there was only one in the world. This one must have been a prime sort; for I have a day off every year for her; and so, until twelve o'clock punctually, I am a saint, at your service, noble lords and lovely ladies.

CHARLES—And after twelve?

THE SOLDIER—After twelve, back to the only place fit for the likes of me.

JOAN [*rising*] Back there! You! that gave the lass the cross!

THE SOLDIER [*excusing his unsoldierly conduct*] Well, she asked for it; and they were going to burn her. She had as good a right to a cross as they had; and they had dozens of them. It was her funeral, not theirs. Where was the harm in it?

JOAN—Man: I am not reproaching you. But I cannot bear to think of you in torment.

THE SOLDIER [*cheerfully*] No great torment, lady. You see I was used to worse.

CHARLES—What! worse than hell?

THE SOLDIER—Fifteen years' service in the French wars. Hell was a treat after that.

[JOAN *throws up her arms, and takes refuge from despair of humanity before the picture of the Virgin.*]

THE SOLDIER [*continuing*]—Suits me somehow. The day off was dull at first, like a wet Sunday. I dont mind it so much now. They tell me I can have as many as I like as soon as I want them.

CHARLES—What is hell like?

THE SOLDIER—You wont find it so bad, sir. Jolly. Like as if you were always drunk without the trouble and expense of drinking. Tip top company too: emperors and popes and kings and all sorts. They chip me about giving that young judy the cross; but I dont care: I stand up to them proper, and tell them that if she hadnt a better right to it than they, she'd be where they are. That dumbfounds them, that does. All they can do is gnash their teeth, hell fashion; and I just laugh, and go off singing the old chanty: Rum tum trumple—Hullo! Who's that knocking at the door?

> [*They listen. A long gentle knocking is heard.*]

C H A R L E S – Come in.

> [*The door opens; and an old priest, white-haired, bent, with a silly but benevolent smile, comes in and trots over to* JOAN.]

T H E   N E W C O M E R – Excuse me, gentle lords and ladies. Do not let me disturb you. Only a poor old harmless English rector. Formerly chaplain to the cardinal: to my lord of Winchester. John de Stogumber, at your service. [*He looks at them inquiringly.*] Did you say anything? I am a little deaf, unfortunately. Also a little—well, not always in my right mind, perhaps; but still, it is a small village with a few simple people. I suffice: I suffice: they love me there; and I am able to do a little good. I am well connected, you see; and they indulge me.

J O A N – Poor old John! What brought thee to this state?

D E   S T O G U M B E R – I tell my folks they must be very careful. I say to them, 'If you only saw what you think about you would think quite differently about it. It would give you a great shock. Oh, a great shock.' And they all say 'Yes, parson: we all know you are a kind man, and would not harm a fly.' That is a great comfort to me. For I am not cruel by nature, you know.

T H E   S O L D I E R – Who said you were?

D E   S T O G U M B E R – Well, you see, I did a very cruel thing once because I did not know what cruelty was like. I had not seen it, you know. That is the great thing: you must see it. And then you are redeemed and saved.

C A U C H O N – Were not the sufferings of our Lord Christ enough for you?

D E   S T O G U M B E R – No. Oh no: not at all. I had seen them in pictures, and read of them in books, and been greatly moved by them, as I thought. But it was no use: it was not our Lord that redeemed me, but a young woman whom I saw actually burned to death. It was dreadful: oh, most dreadful. But it saved me. I have been a different man ever since, though a little astray in my wits sometimes.

C A U C H O N – Must then a Christ perish in torment in every age to save those that have no imagination?

J O A N – Well, if I saved all those he would have been cruel to if he had not been cruel to me, I was not burnt for nothing, was I?

D E   S T O G U M B E R – Oh no; it was not you. My sight is bad: I cannot distinguish your features: but you are not she: oh no: she was burned to a cinder: dead and gone, dead and gone.

T H E   E X E C U T I O N E R [*stepping from behind the bed curtains on* CHARLES's *right, the bed being between them*] She is more alive than you, old man. Her heart would not burn; and it would not drown. I was a master at my craft: better than the master of Paris, better than the master of Toulouse; but I could not kill The Maid. She is up and alive everywhere.

THE EARL OF WARWICK [*sallying from the bed curtains on the other side, and coming to* JOAN'S *left hand*] Madam: my congratulations on your rehabilitation. I feel that I owe you an apology.

JOAN – Oh, please dont mention it.

WARWICK [*pleasantly*] The burning was purely political. There was no personal feeling against you, I assure you.

JOAN – I bear no malice, my lord.

WARWICK – Just so. Very kind of you to meet me in that way: a touch of true breeding. But I must insist on apologizing very amply. The truth is, these political necessities sometimes turn out to be political mistakes; and this one was a veritable howler; for your spirit conquered us, madam, in spite of our faggots. History will remember me for your sake, though the incidents of the connection were perhaps a little unfortunate.

JOAN – Ay, perhaps just a little, you funny man.

WARWICK – Still, when they make you a saint, you will owe your halo to me, just as this lucky monarch owes his crown to you.

JOAN [*turning from him*] I shall owe nothing to any man: I owe everything to the spirit of God that was within me. But fancy me a saint! What would St Catherine and St Margaret say if the farm girl was cocked up beside them!

A clerical-looking gentleman in black frockcoat and trousers, and tall hat, in the fashion of the year 1920, suddenly appears before them in the corner on their right. They all stare at him. Then they burst into uncontrollable laughter.

THE GENTLEMAN – Why this mirth, gentlemen?

WARWICK – I congratulate you on having invented a most extraordinarily comic dress.

THE GENTLEMAN – I do not understand. You are all in fancy dress: I am properly dressed.

DUNOIS – All dress is fancy dress, is it not, except our natural skins?

THE GENTLEMAN – Pardon me: I am here on serious business, and cannot engage in frivolous discussions. [*He takes out a paper, and assumes a dry official manner.*] I am sent to announce to you that Joan of Arc, formerly known as The Maid, having been the subject of an inquiry instituted by the Bishop of Orleans—

JOAN [*interrupting*] Ah! They remember me still in Orleans.

THE GENTLEMAN [*emphatically, to mark his indignation at the in-*

terruption]—by the Bishop of Orleans into the claim of the said Joan of Arc to be canonized as a saint—

J O A N [*again interrupting*] But I never made any such claim.

T H E G E N T L E M A N [*as before*]—the Church has examined the claim exhaustively in the usual course, and, having admitted the said Joan successively to the ranks of Venerable and Blessed,—

J O A N [*chuckling*] Me venerable!

T H E G E N T L E M A N——has finally declared her to have been endowed with heroic virtues and favored with private revelations, and calls the said Venerable and Blessed Joan to the communion of the Church Triumphant as Saint Joan.

J O A N [*rapt*] Saint Joan!

T H E G E N T L E M A N—On every thirtieth day of May, being the anniversary of the death of the said most blessed daughter of God, there shall in every Catholic church to the end of time be celebrated a special office in commemoration of her; and it shall be lawful to dedicate a special chapel to her, and to place her image on its altar in every such church. And it shall be lawful and laudable for the faithful to kneel and address their prayers through her to the Mercy Seat.

J O A N—Oh no. It is for the saint to kneel.

[*She falls on her knees, still rapt.*]

T H E G E N T L E M A N [*putting up his paper, and retiring beside the* EXECUTIONER] In Basilica Vaticana, the sixteenth day of May, nineteen hundred and twenty.

D U N O I S [*raising* JOAN] Half an hour to burn you, dear Saint, and four centuries to find out the truth about you!

D E S T O G U M B E R—Sir: I was chaplain to the Cardinal of Winchester once. They always would call him the Cardinal of England. It would be a great comfort to me and to my master to see a fair statue to The Maid in Winchester Cathedral. Will they put one there, do you think?

T H E G E N T L E M A N—As the building is temporarily in the hands of the Anglican heresy, I cannot answer for that.

[*A vision of the statue in Winchester Cathedral is seen through the window.*]

D E S T O G U M B E R—Oh look! look! that is Winchester.

J O A N—Is that meant to be me? I was stiffer on my feet.

[*The vision fades.*]

T H E G E N T L E M A N—I have been requested by the temporal authorities of France to mention that the multiplication of public statues to The Maid threatens to become an obstruction to traffic. I do so as a matter of courtesy to the said authorities, but must point out on behalf of the Church that The Maid's horse is no greater obstruction to traffic than any other horse.

JOAN – Eh! I am glad they have not forgotten my horse.

[A *vision of the statue before Rheims Cathedral appears.*]

JOAN – Is that funny little thing me too?

CHARLES – That is Rheims Cathedral where you had me crowned. It must be you.

JOAN – Who has broken my sword? My sword was never broken. It is the sword of France.

DUNOIS – Never mind. Swords can be mended. Your soul is unbroken; and you are the soul of France.

[*The vision fades. The* ARCHBISHOP *and the* INQUISITOR *are now seen on the right and left of* CAUCHON.]

JOAN – My sword shall conquer yet: the sword that never struck a blow. Though men destroyed my body, yet in my soul I have seen God.

CAUCHON [*kneeling to her*] The girls in the field praise thee; for thou hast raised their eyes; and they see that there is nothing between them and heaven.

DUNOIS [*kneeling to her*] The dying soldiers praise thee, because thou art a shield of glory between them and the judgment.

THE ARCHBISHOP [*kneeling to her*] The princes of the Church praise thee, because thou hast redeemed the faith their worldlinesses have dragged through the mire.

WARWICK [*kneeling to her*] The cunning counsellors praise thee, because thou hast cut the knots in which they have tied their own souls.

DE STOGUMBER [*kneeling to her*] The foolish old men on their deathbeds praise thee, because their sins against thee are turned into blessings.

THE INQUISITOR [*kneeling to her*] The judges in the blindness and bondage of the law praise thee, because thou hast vindicated the vision and the freedom of the living soul.

THE SOLDIER [*kneeling to her*] The wicked out of hell praise thee, because thou hast shewn them that the fire that is not quenched is a holy fire.

THE EXECUTIONER [*kneeling to her*] The tormentors and executioners praise thee, because thou hast shewn that their hands are guiltless of the death of the soul.

CHARLES [*kneeling to her*] The unpretending praise thee, because thou hast taken upon thyself the heroic burdens that are too heavy for them.

JOAN – Woe unto me when all men praise me! I bid you remember that I am a saint, and that saints can work miracles. And now tell me: shall I rise from the dead, and come back to you a living woman?

A sudden darkness blots out the walls of the room as they all spring to their feet in consternation. Only the figures and the bed remain visible.

J O A N – What! Must I burn again? Are none of you ready to receive me?

C A U C H O N – The heretic is always better dead. And mortal eyes cannot distinguish the saint from the heretic. Spare them.

[*He goes out as he came.*]

D U N O I S – Forgive us, Joan: we are not yet good enough for you. I shall go back to my bed.

[*He also goes.*]

W A R W I C K – We sincerely regret our little mistake; but political necessities, though occasionally erroneous, are still imperative; so if you will be good enough to excuse me—

[*He steals discreetly away.*]

T H E   A R C H B I S H O P – Your return would not make me the man you once thought me. The utmost I can say is that though I dare not bless you, I hope I may one day enter into your blessedness. Meanwhile, however—

[*He goes.*]

T H E   I N Q U I S I T O R – I who am of the dead, testified that day that you were innocent. But I do not see how The Inquisition could possibly be dispensed with under existing circumstances. Therefore—

[*He goes.*]

D E   S T O G U M B E R – Oh, do not come back: you must not come back. I must die in peace. Give us peace in our time, O Lord!

[*He goes.*]

T H E   G E N T L E M A N – The possibility of your resurrection was not contemplated in the recent proceedings for your canonization. I must return to Rome for fresh instructions.

[*He bows formally, and withdraws.*]

T H E   E X E C U T I O N E R – As a master in my profession I have to consider its interests. And, after all, my first duty is to my wife and children. I must have time to think over this.

[*He goes.*]

C H A R L E S – Poor old Joan! They have all run away from you except this blackguard who has to go back to hell at twelve o'clock. And what can I do but follow Jack Dunois' example, and go back to bed too?

[*He does so.*]

J O A N   [*sadly*] Goodnight, Charlie.

C H A R L E S   [*mumbling in his pillows*] Goo ni.

[*He sleeps. The darkness envelops the bed.*]

J O A N   [*to the soldier*] And you, my one faithful? What comfort have you for Saint Joan?

T H E   S O L D I E R – Well, what do they all amount to, these kings and captains and bishops and lawyers and such like? They just leave you in the ditch to bleed to death; and the next thing is, you meet them down there, for all the airs they give themselves. What I say is, you have as good a right to your notions as they have to theirs, and perhaps better. [*Settling himself for a lecture on the subject.*] You see, it's like this. If— [*The first stroke of midnight is heard softly from a distant bell.*] Excuse me: a pressing appointment—

[*He goes on tiptoe.*]
[*The last remaining rays of light gather into a white radiance descending on* JOAN. *The hour continues to strike.*]

JOAN—O God that madest this beautiful earth, when will it be ready to receive Thy saints? How long, O Lord, how long?

PIRANDELLO DISTILS SHAW

The Italian Playwright Discovers
the Puritan Poet Idealist Sublimated in "Saint Joan"

By Luigi Pirandello

THE AUDIENCE bewildered me.

At the première of *Saint Joan*, by George Bernard Shaw, I felt myself a real foreigner, suddenly brought face to face with this mysterious America of yours. Though it was not altogether bewilderment, I felt, as I went home from the play, that I had learned something interesting and unexpected about the psychology of the American.

During the first three acts of *Saint Joan*[1] I noted with great satisfaction the rapt attention, the shrewd and intelligent smiling, the hearty laughter and the sincere applause with which every shaft of wit or irony in this admirable and inimitable Shavian dialogue was welcomed by an audience keenly aware of the artistic treat that was spread before it. But then came the fourth act, which seemed to me the best in the whole play—the trial and condemnation of the Maid—where Shaw's dramatic power rises to its height, and where he really succeeds in awakening a deep and intense emotion. I had been expecting, in view of the preceding cordiality of the audience, to see people jump to their feet and break into unrestrained applause. Nothing of the kind! I looked around the theatre in surprise. It was as though I had been suddenly transported into a world wholly unknown and incomprehensible to me. The spectators sat for the most in silence.

From *The New York Times*, January 13, 1924. Copyright © 1924 by The New York Times Company. Reprinted by permission of the Pirandello Estate and The New York Times.

[1] It would seem that the production, unlike the published script, was divided into four acts. [E.B.]

1838

For a moment or two I was oppressed with a sudden sense of mortification at my own incompetence. But then my own feelings were so great that I could not help asking a question that was a question half of protest to the friends about me. Had that scene been a failure? Had no one been moved by that almost divine explosion of passion in the Maid just before she was dragged away to the stake? I received in reply a suggestion that few had applauded for the very reason that the emotion in the audience was so great. And then, indeed, I was more surprised than ever.

I am sure that, had an act as powerful as the fourth act of *Saint Joan* been produced on any one of the numerous Italian stages, all the people present would have jumped to their feet, even before the curtain fell, to start a frenzied applause that would have called the actors, and possibly the author, to the footlights, not once, but many times, to receive the gratitude of the audience for the anguish it had suffered, and its joy for having witnessed such a triumph of art. But here, on the other hand, a certain sense of modesty seemed to be uppermost. A certain sense of shame at being deeply moved, a need of hiding emotion, and of getting rid of it as soon as possible. To applaud would have meant confessing this emotion to one's self and then publicly to others; and few seemed willing thus to betray themselves.

But then, to tell the truth, I was not as well satisfied as I had been at the applause during the three preceding acts, though these, in a somewhat different way, were just as deserving. As an Italian, I could not think it fair that an author should be applauded when he makes us laugh, and rewarded with silence when he brings tears to our eyes. Perhaps the reason is that it is harder to make an Italian laugh than it is to make him weep.

At any rate, I have a strong impression that for some time past George Bernard Shaw has been growing more and more serious. He has always believed in himself, and with good reason. But in a number of plays, after his first successes, he did not seem to believe very much in what he was doing. This, at least, may properly be suspected; since it cannot be denied that in his eagerness to defend his own intellectual position against the so-called "bourgeois morality," he not infrequently abandoned all pretensions to seriousness as an artist. Now, however, he seems to be believing less in himself, and more in what he is doing. From the epilogue of this drama on Joan of Arc we may gather almost explicitly the reason for which Shaw wrote it. This world, he seems to say, is not made for saints to live in. We must take the people who live in it for what they are, since it is not vouchsafed them to be anything else.

In fact, as we look carefully and deeply at this work of Shaw, taken as a whole, we cannot help detecting in it that curious half-humorous melancholy which is peculiar to the disillusioned idealist. Shaw has always

1839

had too keen a sense of reality not to be aware of the conflict between it and his social and moral ideals. The various phases of reality, as they were yesterday, as they are today, as they will be tomorrow, come forward in the persons who represent them before the ideal phantom of Joan (now a Saint without her knowing it). Each of these type persons justifies his own manner of being, and confesses the sin of which he was guilty, but in such a way as to show that he is unable really to mend his ways—so true is it that each is today as he was yesterday, and will be tomorrow as he is today. Joan listens to them all, but she is not angry. She has for them just a tolerant pity. She can only pray that the world may some time be made beautiful enough to be a worthy abode for the saints!

This new tolerance and pity rise from the most secret depths of poetry that exist in Shaw. Whenever, instead of tolerating, instead of pitying, he loses his temper at the shock of reality against his ideals, and then, for fear of betraying his anger—which would be bad mannered—begins to harass himself and his hearers with the dazzling brilliancy of his paradoxes, Shaw, the artist properly speaking, suffers more or less seriously—he falls to the level of the *jeu d'esprit* which is amusing in itself, though it irremediably spoils the work of art. I may cite in point a passage in the second act of *Saint Joan*, where the Archbishop expatiates on the differences between fraud and miracles. "Frauds deceive," says he. "An event which creates faith does not deceive, therefore it is not a fraud but a miracle." Such word play is for amusement only. A work that would do something more than amuse must always respect the deeper demands of art, and so respecting these, the witticism is no longer a witticism but true art.

In none of Shaw's work that I can think of have considerations of art been so thoroughly respected as in *Saint Joan*. The four acts of this drama begin, as they must begin, with Joan's request for soldiers of Robert de Baudricourt to use in driving the English from "the sweet land of France." And they end, as they must end, with the trial and execution of Joan. Shaw calls this play a chronicle. In fact, the drama is built up episode by episode, moment by moment, some of them rigorously particular and free from generality—truly in the style of the chronicles—though usually they tend to be [have?—E.B.] what I call deliberate "constructiveness." The hens have not been laying, when suddenly they begin to lay. The wind has long been blowing from the east, and suddenly it begins blowing from the west. Two miracles! Then there are other simple, naive things, such as the recognition of the blood royal in the third act, which likewise seems to be a miracle.

But these moments are interspersed with other moments of irony and satire, of which either the Church or the English are the victims. However, this attempt to present the chronicle inside what is really history does not seem to me quite as happy as it was in *Caesar and Cleopatra*. In *Saint Joan*, history, or rather character historically conceived, weighs a bit too heavily on the living fluid objectivity of the chronicle, and the events in the play somehow lose that sense of the unexpected which is the breath of true life. We know in advance where we are going to come out. The characters, whether historical or typical, do not quite free themselves from the fixity that history had forced upon them and from the significant role they are to play in history.

Joan herself, who is presented to us as a fresh creature of the open fields, full of burning faith and self-confidence, remains that way from the beginning to the end of the play; and she makes a little too obvious her intention not to be reciting a historical role and to remain that dear, frank, innocent, inspired child that she is. Yes, Joan, as she really was in her own little individual history, must have been much as Shaw imagined her. But he seems to look on her once and for all, so to speak, quite without reward for the various situations in which she will meet life in the course of the story.

And she is kept thus simple and unilinear by the author just to bring her airy, refreshing ingenuousness into contrast with the artificial, sophisticated—or, as I say, "deliberate" or "constructed"—complexity of her accusers. There is, in other words, something mechanical, foreordained, fixed, about her character. Much more free and unobstructed in his natural impulses, much more independent of any deliberate restraints, and accordingly much more "living" (from my point of view) is the Chaplain, de Stogumber, the truly admirable creation in this drama, and a personage on which Shaw has surely expended a great deal of affectionate effort.

At a certain moment Joan's faith in her "voices" is shaken. And this charming little creature, hitherto steadfastly confident in the divine inspiration which has many times saved her from death in battle, is suddenly filled with terror at the torment awaiting her. She says she is ready to sign the recantation of all that she has said and done. And she does sign it. But then, on learning from her judges that the sentence of death is only to be changed into a sentence of life imprisonment, she seizes the document in a sudden burst of emotion and tears it to pieces. "Death is far better than this!" she cries.[2] She could never live without the free air of the fields, the beauty of the green meadows, the warm light of the sun. And she falls fainting into the arms of the executioners, who drag her off to the stake.

At this moment Shaw carries his protagonists to a summit of noble

[2] But not verbatim. And if in the 1923 production she "fell fainting . . . etc." that was the director's idea, not the author's. [E.B.]

poetry with which any other author would be content; and we may be sure that any other author would have lowered the curtain on this scene. But Shaw cannot resist the pressure and the inspiration of the life he well knows must be surging in such circumstances in his other character—the Chaplain. He rushes on toward a second climax of not less noble poetry, depicting with magnificent elan the mad remorse, the hopeless penitence of Stogumber, thus adding to our first crisis of exquisite anguish another not less potent and overwhelming.

Rarely has George Bernard Shaw attained higher altitudes of poetic emotion than here. There is a truly great poet in Shaw; but this combative Anglo-Irishman is often willing to forget that he is a poet, so interested is he in being a citizen of his country, or a man of the twentieth-century society, with a number of respectable ideas to defend, a number of sermons to preach, a number of antagonists to rout from the intellectual battlefield. But here, in *Saint Joan*, the poet comes into his own again, with only a subordinate role left, as a demanded compensation, to irony and satire. To be sure *Saint Joan* has all the savor and all the attractiveness of Shaw's witty polemical dialogue. But for all of these keen and cutting thrusts to left and right in Shaw's usual style of propaganda, *Saint Joan* is a work of poetry from beginning to end.

This play represents in marvelous fashion what, among so many elements of negation, is the positive element, indeed the fundamental underpinning, in the character, thought and art of this great writer—an outspoken Puritanism, which brooks no go-betweens and no mediations between man and God; a vigorous and independent vital energy, that frees itself restlessly and with joyous scorn from all the stupid and burdensome shackles of habit, routine and tradition, to conquer for itself a natural law more consonant with the poet's own being, and more rational and more sound. Joan, in fact, cries to her judges: "If you command me to declare that all that I have done and said, that all the visions and revelations I have had were not from God, then that is impossible. I will not declare it for anything in the world. What God made me do, I will never go back on; and what He has commanded, or shall command, I will not fail to do, in spite of any man alive. That is what I mean by impossible. And in case the Church should bid me do anything contrary to the command I have from God, I will not consent to it, no matter what it may be."

Joan, at bottom, quite without knowing it, and still declaring herself a faithful daughter of the Church, is a Puritan, like Shaw himself—affirming her own life impulse, her unshakable, her even tyrannical will to live, by accepting death itself. Joan, like Shaw, cannot exist without a life that is free and fruitful. When she tears up her recantation in the face of her deaf and blind accusers, she exemplifies the basic germ of Shaw's art, which is the germ also of his spiritual life.

THE SAINT AS TRAGIC HERO

By Louis L. Martz

SAINTS AND MARTYRS have frequently been regarded as impossible subjects for true tragedy. The reasons have been forcibly summed up by
Butcher in his standard commentary on Aristotle's *Poetics*. One trouble
is, he says, that Goodness "is apt to be immobile and uncombative. In
refusing to strike back it brings the action to a standstill." This is exactly the objection sometimes made to T. S. Eliot's presentation of
Becket, who, in *Murder in the Cathedral*, is certainly immobile and, in a
sense, uncombative:

> We are not here to triumph by fighting, by stratagem, or by re-
> sistance,
> Not to fight with beasts as men. We have fought the beast
> And have conquered. We have only to conquer
> Now, by suffering.

But even in the case of more combative saints, such as Joan of Arc,
Butcher would see a serious difficulty: "Impersonal ardour in the cause
of right," he says, does not have "the same dramatic fascination as the
spectacle of human weakness or passion doing battle with the fate it has
brought upon itself." And in short, the chief difficulty is that "the death
of the martyr presents to us not the defeat, but the victory of the individual; the issue of a conflict in which the individual is ranged on the

From *Tragic Themes in Western Literature*, ed. Cleanth Brooks. New Haven:
Yale University Press, 1955. Copyright © 1955 by the Yale University Press. Reprinted by permission of the author.

same side as the higher powers, and the sense of suffering consequently lost in that of moral triumph."[1] This, I suppose, is what I. A. Richards also means when he declares that "The least touch of any theology which has a compensating Heaven to offer the tragic hero is fatal"[2]—fatal, that is, to the tragic effect. But we remember:

> Good night, sweet prince,
> And flights of angels sing thee to thy rest.

And we remember the transfiguration of Oedipus at Colonus. Hamlet and Oedipus, we might argue, are in the end on the side of the higher powers. I do not know what we should call Oedipus at Colonus, if he is not a kind of saint, and there is something almost saintly in Hamlet's acute sensitivity to evil. Butcher concedes that Aristotle does not take account of this exceptional type of tragedy "which exhibits the antagonism between a pure will and a disjointed world."[3] We are drawn, then, into some discussion of the nature of tragedy, into some discussion of the plight of tragedy today, and into some discussion, also, of another excellent kind of writing, sometimes called tragic, in which the modern world has achieved a peculiar eminence.

Let us begin with this other kind, for it lacks the touch of any theology. I am thinking of the kind represented by Hemingway's A *Farewell to Arms*, particularly of the attitude represented by the dying words of Hemingway's heroine: " 'I'm going to die,' she said; then waited and said, 'I hate it' . . . Then a little later, 'I'm not afraid. I just hate it.' . . . 'Don't worry, darling, . . . I'm not a bit afraid. It's just a dirty trick.' " This scene is painful and pitiful as all that earlier misery in the same novel, during the rainy retreat from Caporetto, at the beginning of which Hemingway's hero sums up the central impact of the book, in words that are often quoted: "I was always embarrassed by the words sacred, glorious, and sacrifice and the expression in vain." And he proceeds to emphasize his embarrassment in words that echo a biblical cadence, faintly, and ironically: "We had heard them, sometimes standing in the rain almost out of earshot, so that only the shouted words came through, and had read them, on proclamations that were slapped up by billposters over other proclamations, now for a long time, and I had seen nothing sacred,

---

[1] S. H. Butcher, *Aristotle's Theory of Poetry and Fine Art, with a Critical Text and Translation of the Poetics* (4th ed., London: Macmillan & Co., Ltd., 1932), pp. 310–12.

[2] I. A. Richards, *Principles of Literary Criticism* (New York: Harcourt, Brace & World, Inc., 1948), p. 246.

[3] Butcher, p. 325.

and the things that were glorious had no glory and the sacrifices were like the stockyards at Chicago if nothing was done with the meat except to bury it."[4]

The tragedies of Oedipus, Phèdre, Samson, or Hamlet certainly include something like this sense of shattered illusions, this painful recognition of man's fragility, and this pitiful recognition of the inadequacy of human love—but along with, in the same moment with, equally powerful affirmations of the validity of these terms sacred, glorious, sacrifice, and the expression in vain. Tragedy seems simultaneously to doubt and to believe in such expressions: tragedy seems never to know what Wallace Stevens calls "an affirmation free from doubt"—and yet it always seems to contain at least the Ghost of an affirmation. Oedipus the King and Samson Agonistes, blind and erring, still sacrifice themselves "gloriously," as Milton puts it. Racine's drama of Phèdre affirms the validity of the Law of Reason, even as the heroine dissolves herself in passion. And Hamlet sees mankind, simultaneously, as the most angelical and the most vicious of earthly creatures; like the Chorus of *Murder in the Cathedral*, Hamlet "knows and does not know."

This sense of a double vision at work in tragedy is somewhat akin to I. A. Richards' famous variation on Aristotle, where Richards finds the essence of tragedy to reside in a "balanced poise." In the "full tragic experience," Richards declares, "there is no suppression. The mind does not shy away from anything." But Richards himself, like Hemingway's hero, then proceeds to shy away from transcendental matters, when he declares that the mind, in tragedy, "stands uncomforted, unintimidated, alone and self-reliant." This, it seems, will not quite square with Richards' ultimate account of tragedy as "perhaps the most general, all-accepting, all-ordering experience known."[5]

A clearer account, at least a more dogmatic account, of this double vision of tragedy has been set forth by Joyce in his *Portrait of the Artist*. "Aristotle has not defined pity and terror," says Stephen Dedalus, "I have." "Pity is the feeling which arrests the mind in the presence of whatsoever is grave and constant in human sufferings and unites it with the human sufferer. Terror is the feeling which arrests the mind in the presence of whatsoever is grave and constant in human sufferings and unites it with the secret cause."[6] Tragedy, then, seems to demand both the human sufferer and the secret cause: that is to say, the doubt, the pain, the pity of the human sufferer: and the affirmation, the awe, the

---

[4] Ernest Hemingway, *A Farewell to Arms* (New York: Charles Scribner's Sons, 1929), pp. 353–54, 196.

[5] Richards, pp. 246–48.

[6] James Joyce, *A Portrait of the Artist as a Young Man* (New York: B. W. Huebsch, 1916), p. 239.

terror of the secret cause. It is an affirmation even though the cause is destructive in its immediate effects: for this cause seems to affirm the existence of some universal order of things.

From this standpoint we can estimate the enormous problem that faces the modern writer in his quest for tragedy. With Ibsen, for example, this power of double vision is in some difficulty. In *Ghosts* or in *Rosmersholm* the element of affirmation is almost overwhelmed by the horror and the suffering that come from the operation of the secret cause —here represented by the family heritage—the dead husband, the dead wife. The affirmation is present, however, in the salvation of an individual's integrity. Ibsen's *Ghosts*, which has the rain pouring down outside for most of the play, nevertheless ends with a view of bright sunshine on the glaciers: symbolizing, perhaps, the clear self-realization which the heroine has achieved. But it is not a very long step before we exit—left—from these shattered drawing rooms into the rain of Ernest Hemingway, where we have the human sufferers, "alone and self-reliant," without a touch of any secret cause. We are in the world of pity which Santayana has beautifully described in a passage of his *Realms of Being*, where he speaks of the "unreasoning sentiment" he might feel in seeing a "blind old beggar" in a Spanish town: "pity simply, the pity of existence, suffusing, arresting, rendering visionary the spectacle of the moment and spreading blindly outwards, like a light in the dark, towards objects which it does not avail to render distinguishable."

It seems a perfect account of the central and powerful effect achieved in many of the best efforts of the modern stage, or movie, or novel, works of pity, where pity dissolves the scene, resolves it into the dew that Hamlet considers but transcends. Thus *A Farewell to Arms* is enveloped in symbolic rain; in *The Naked and the Dead* humanity is lost in the dim Pacific jungle; and the haze of madness gradually dissolves the realistic setting of *A Streetcar Named Desire* or *Death of a Salesman*. In the end, Willy Loman has to plant his garden in the dark. "The pity of existence . . . spreading blindly outwards . . . towards objects which it does not avail to render distinguishable."

The problem of the tragic writer in our day appears to be: how to control this threatened dissolution, how to combine this "unreasoning sentiment" with something like the different vision that Santayana goes on to suggest: "Suppose now that I turn through the town gates and suddenly see a broad valley spread out before me with the purple sierra in the distance beyond. This expanse, this vastness, fills my intuition; also, perhaps, some sense of the deeper breath which I draw as if my breast expanded in sympathy with the rounded heavens."[7] Thus we often find

[7] George Santayana, *Realms of Being* (New York: Charles Scribner's Sons, 1942), pp. 147-49.

that the modern writer who seeks a tragic effect will attempt, by some device, such as Ibsen's family heritage or his view of the glacier, to give us the experience of a secret cause underlying his work of pity—to give it broader dimensions, sharper form, to render the ultimate objects distinguishable, to prevent it from spreading blindly outwards. We can see this plainly in O'Neill's *Mourning Becomes Electra*, where O'Neill, by borrowing from Aeschylus the ancient idea of a family curse, is able to give his drama a firm, stark outline, and to endow his heroine with something like a tragic dignity. The only trouble is that this Freudian version of a family curse is not secret enough: it tends to announce itself hysterically, all over the place: "I'm the last Mannon. I've got to punish myself!" In the end we feel that this family curse has been shipped in from Greece and has never quite settled down in New England.

Eliot has described much the same difficulty which appears in his play *The Family Reunion*, where he too, even more boldly than O'Neill, has tried to borrow the Furies from Aeschylus. Eliot deploys his Furies, quite impolitely, in the middle of Ibsen's drawing room. As we might expect, they were not welcome: "We tried every possible manner of presenting them," says Eliot. "We put them on the stage, and they looked like uninvited guests who had strayed in from a fancy-dress ball. We concealed them behind gauze, and they suggested a still out of a Walt Disney film. We made them dimmer, and they looked like shrubbery just outside the window. I have seen other expedients tried"; Eliot adds, "I have seen them signalling from across the garden, or swarming onto the stage like a football team, and they are never right. They never succeed in being either Greek goddesses or modern spooks. But their failure," he concludes, "is merely a symptom of the failure to adjust the ancient with the modern."[8] Or, we might say, a failure to adjust the ancient Aeschylean symbol of a secret cause with the modern human sufferer.

How, then, can it be done? It is in their approach to this problem that *Saint Joan* and *Murder in the Cathedral* reveal their peculiar power, in an approach that seems to have been made possible by this fact: that both Shaw and Eliot feel they cannot depend upon their audience to accept their saintly heroes as divinely inspired. The dramaturgy of both plays is based upon a deliberate manipulation of the elements of religious skepticism or uncertainty in the audience.

As Eliot's play moves toward the somber conclusion of its first half, the Four Tempters cry out in the temptation of self-pity ("It's just a dirty trick"):

[8] T. S. Eliot, *Poetry and Drama* (Cambridge, Mass.: Harvard University Press, 1951), p. 37.

Man's life is a cheat and a disappointment . . .
All things become less real, man passes
From unreality to unreality.
This man [Becket] is obstinate, blind, intent
On self-destruction,
Passing from deception to deception,
From grandeur to grandeur to final illusion . . .

And a page later the Chorus too cries out from the world of Ernest Hemingway, with also, perhaps, a slight reminiscence of the millrace in
Rosmersholm:

We have seen the young man mutilated,
The torn girl trembling by the mill-stream.
And meanwhile we have gone on living,
Living and partly living,
Picking together the pieces,
Gathering faggots at nightfall,
Building a partial shelter,
For sleeping, and eating and drinking and laughter.

And then, at the very close of Part I, Becket sums up the whole attitude
when he turns sharply to address the audience:

I know
What yet remains to show you of my history
Will seem to most of you at best futility,
Senseless self-slaughter of a lunatic,
Arrogant passion of a fanatic.
I know that history at all times draws
The strangest consequence from remotest cause.

It is exactly the challenge that Shaw has thrown at his readers in the
Preface to *Saint Joan:* "For us to set up our condition as a standard of
sanity, and declare Joan mad because she never condescended to it, is to
prove that we are not only lost but irredeemable."

Eliot and Shaw, then, seem to be assuming that the least touch of
theology in their plays will serve—to raise a question. And so the saint
may become a figure well adapted to arouse something very close to a
tragic experience: for here the words sacred, glorious, sacrifice, and the expression in vain may become once again easily appropriate; while at the
same time the uncertainty of the audience's attitude—and to some extent
the dramatist's own—may enable him to deal also with the painful and

pitiful aspects of experience that form the other side of the tragic tension.

But this conflict, this double vision, is not, in these plays, primarily contained within the figure of the saint as tragic hero: Joan and Becket do not here represent humanity in the way of Hamlet, or King Oedipus— by focusing within themselves the full tragic tension. They are much more like Oedipus at Colonus, who, although a pitiful beggar in appearance, speaks now through the power of a superhuman insight. Most of his mind lies beyond suffering: he feels that he has found the secret cause, and under the impulse of that cause he moves onward magnificently to his death and transfiguration. The sense of human suffering in *Oedipus at Colonus* is conveyed chiefly in retrospect, or in the sympathetic outcries of the Chorus, the weeping of the rejected Polynices, and the anguish of the two daughters whom Oedipus must leave behind.

To see these plays as in any sense tragic it seems that we must abandon the concept of a play built upon an ideal Aristotelian hero, and look instead for a tragic experience that arises from the interaction between a hero who represents the secret cause, and the other characters, who represent the human sufferers. The point is brought out, ironically, by the Archbishop, near the end of Shaw's play, when he warns Joan against the sin of pride, saying, "The old Greek tragedy is rising among us. It is the chastisement of hubris." Joan replies with her usual bluntness, asking, "How can you say that I am disobedient when I always obey my voices, because they come from God." But when the Archbishop insists that "all the voices that come to you are the echoes of your own wilfulness," when he declares angrily, "You stand alone: absolutely alone, trusting to your own conceit, your own ignorance, your own headstrong presumption, your own impiety," we are reminded of Creon berating Oedipus at Colonus, and we are reminded too of Oedipus' long declaration of innocence when Joan turns away, "her eyes skyward," saying, "I have better friends and better counsel than yours."

There is nothing complex about the character of Shaw's Joan; it is the whole fabric of the play that creates something like a tragic tension. For whatever he may say in his preface, Shaw the dramatist, through his huge cast of varied human types, probes the whole range of belief and disbelief in Joan's voices. "They come from your imagination," says the feeble de Baudricourt in the opening scene. "Of course," says Joan, "That is how the messages of God come to us." Cauchon believes the girl to be "inspired, but diabolically inspired." "Many saints have said as much as Joan," Ladvenu suggests. Dunois, her only friend, senses some aura of divinity about her, but becomes extremely uneasy when she talks about her voices. "I should think," he says, "you were a bit cracked if I hadn't noticed that you give me very sensible reasons for what you do, though I hear you telling others you are only obeying Madame Saint Catherine."

Louis L. Martz

"Well," she replies, "I have to find reasons for you, because you do not believe in my voices. But the voices come first; and I find the reasons after: whatever you may choose to believe." *Whatever you may choose to believe*: there is the point, and as the figure of Joan flashes onward through the play, with only one lapse in confidence—her brief recantation —Shaw keeps his play hovering among choices in a highly modern state of uncertainty: we know and do not know: until at the close Shaw seems to send us over on the side of affirmation. We agree, at least, with the words of the French captain in the opening scene: "There is something about her. . . . Something. . . . I think the girl herself is a bit of a miracle."

She is, as Eliot would say, "a white light still and moving," the simple *cause* of every other word and action in the play; and her absolute simplicity of vision cuts raspingly through all the malign or well-intentioned errors of the world, until in its wrath the world rises up in the form of all its assembled institutions and declares by the voice of all its assembled doctors that this girl is—as Shaw says—*insufferable.*[9]

Thus Joan's apparent resemblance to the Aristotelian hero: her extreme self-confidence, her brashness, her appearance of rash impetuosity—all this becomes in the end a piece of Shavian irony, for her only real error in the play is the one point where her superb self-confidence breaks down in the panic of recantation. And so the hubris is not Joan's but Everyman's. The characters who accuse Joan of pride and error are in those accusations convicting themselves of the pride of self-righteousness and the errors of human certitude. It is true that the suffering that results from this pride and error remains in Shaw's play rather theoretical and remote: and yet we feel it in some degree: in the pallor and anguish of Joan as she resists the temptation to doubt her voices, in the rather unconvincing screams of Stogumber at the close, and, much more effectively, in the quiet, controlled sympathy of Ladvenu. It would seem, then, that some degree of tragedy resides in this failure of Everyman to recognize absolute Reality, the secret cause, when it appears in the flesh. Must then, cries Cauchon in the Epilogue, "Must then a Christ perish in torment in every age to save those that have no imagination?" It is the same symbolism that Eliot has evoked in the beginning of his play, where the Chorus asks: "Shall the Son of Man be born again in the litter of scorn?"

We need not be too greatly concerned with Shaw's bland assertions that he is letting us in on the truth about the Middle Ages, telling us in the play all we need to know about Joan. Books and articles have appeared —a whole cloudburst of them—devoted to proving that Shaw's methods of historical research in his play and in his preface are open to serious

[9] See the amusing anecdote recorded by Archibald Henderson, *Bernard Shaw, Playboy and Prophet* (New York: Appleton-Century-Crofts, 1932), pp. 693–95.

question. But Shaw gave that game away long ago when he announced: "I deal with all periods; but I never study any period but the present, which I have not yet mastered and never shall";[10] or when he said, with regard to Cleopatra's cure for Caesar's baldness, that his methods of scholarship, as compared with Gilbert Murray's, consisted in "pure divination."[11] The Preface to *Saint Joan* lays down a long barrage of historicity, which in the end is revealed as a remarkable piece of Shavio-Swiftian hoaxing: for in the last few pages of that long preface he adds, incidentally, that his use of the "available documentation" has been accompanied by "such powers of divination as I possess"; he concedes that for some figures in his play he has invented "appropriate characters" "in Shakespear's manner"; and that, fundamentally, his play is built upon what he calls "the inevitable flatteries of tragedy." That is, there is no historical basis for his highly favorable characterizations of Cauchon and the Inquisitor, upon which the power and point of the trial scene are founded.

I do not mean to say, however, that our sense of history is irrelevant to an appreciation of Shaw's play. There is a point to be made by considering such a book as J. M. Robertson's *Mr. Shaw and "The Maid,"* which complains bitterly, upon historical grounds, against Shaw's "instinct to put things both ways."[12] This is a book, incidentally, which Eliot has praised very highly because it points out that in this kind of subject "Facts matter," and that "to Mr. Shaw, truth and falsehood . . . do not seem to have the same meaning as to ordinary people."[13] But the point lies rather in the tribute that such remarks pay to the effectiveness of Shaw's realistic dramaturgy.

Shaw is writing, as he and Ibsen had to write, within the conventions of the modern realistic theater—conventions which Eliot escaped in *Murder in the Cathedral* because he was writing this play for performance at the Canterbury Festival. But in his later plays, composed for the theater proper, Eliot has also been forced to, at least he has chosen to, write within these stern conventions.

Now in the realistic theater, as Francis Fergusson has suggested, the artist seems to be under the obligation to pretend that he is not an artist at all, but is simply interested in pursuing the truth "in some pseudoscientific sense."[14] Thus we find the relation of art to life so often driven

---

[10] Shaw, Preface to *The Sanity of Art* (New York: B. R. Tucker, 1908), p. 5.
[11] See Shaw's notes appended to *Caesar and Cleopatra: Nine Plays*, p. 471.
[12] J. M. Robertson, *Mr. Shaw and "The Maid"* (London: Cobden-Sanderson, 1926), p. 85.
[13] T. S. Eliot, *Criterion*, 4 (April 1926), 390.
[14] Francis Fergusson, *The Idea of a Theater* (Princeton: Princeton University Press, 1949), p. 147.

home on the modern stage by such deep symbolic actions as removing the cubes from ice trays or cooking an omelette for dinner. Shaw knows that on this stage facts matter—or at least the appearance of facts—and in this need for a dramatic realism lies the basic justification for Shaw's elaborately argued presentation of Joan as a Protestant and Nationalist martyr killed by the combined institutional forces of feudalism and the Church. Through these historical theories, developed within the body of the play, Joan is presented as the agent of a transformation in the actual world; the theories have enough plausibility for dramatic purposes, and perhaps a bit more; this, together with Shaw's adaptation of the records of Joan's trial, gives him all the "facts" that he needs to make his point in the modern theater.

Some of Joan's most Shavian remarks are in fact her own words as set down in the long records of her trial: as, for example, where her questioner asks whether Michael does not appear to her as a naked man. "Do you think God cannot afford clothes for him?" answers Joan, in the play and in the records. Shaw has made a skillful selection of these answers, using, apparently, the English translation of the documents edited by Douglas Murray;[15] and he has set these answers together with speeches of his own modeled upon their tone and manner. In this way he has been able to bring within the limits of the realistic theater the very voice that rings throughout these trial records, the voice of the lone girl fencing with, stabbing at, baffling, and defeating the crowd of some sixty learned men: a voice that is not speaking within the range of the other voices that assail her. Thus we hear her in the following speech adapted from half-a-dozen places in the records:

> "I have said again and again that I will tell you all that concerns this trial. But I cannot tell you the whole truth: God does not allow the whole truth to be told. . . . It is an old saying that he who tells too much truth is sure to be hanged. . . . I have sworn as much as I will swear; and I will swear no more."[16]

Or, following the documents much more closely, her answers thus resound when the questioners attempt to force her to submit her case to the

[15] *Jeanne D'Arc, Maid of Orleans, Deliverer of France; Being the Story of her Life, her Achievements, and her Death, as attested on Oath and Set forth in the Original Documents,* ed. by T. Douglas Murray (New York: McClure, Phillips, 1902; published in England the same year). See p. 42: "Do you think God has not wherewithal to clothe him?" This contains a translation of the official Latin documents published by Jules Quicherat in 1841–49.

[16] Cf. Murray, pp. 5–6, 8–9, 14–15, 18, 22, 33. See p. 103 for next example.

Church on earth: "I will obey The Church," says Joan, "provided it does not command anything impossible."

> If you command me to declare that all that I have done and said, and all the visions and revelations I have had, were not from God, then that is impossible: I will not declare it for anything in the world. What God made me do I will never go back on; and what He has commanded or shall command I will not fail to do in spite of any man alive. That is what I mean by impossible. And in case The Church should bid me do anything contrary to the command I have from God, I will not consent to it, no matter what it may be.

In thus maintaining the tone of that—extraordinary—voice, Shaw has, I think, achieved an effect that is in some ways very close to the effect of the "intersection of the timeless with time" which Eliot has achieved in his play, and which he has described in "The Dry Salvages":

> Men's curiosity searches past and future
> And clings to that dimension. But to apprehend
> The point of intersection of the timeless
> With time, is an occupation for the saint—
> No occupation either, but something given
> And taken, in a lifetime's death in love,
> Ardour and selflessness and self-surrender.

An obvious similarity between the two plays may be seen in the tone of satirical wit that runs through both—notably in the ludicrous prose speeches that Eliot's murdering Knights deliver to the audience in self-defense. These have an essentially Shavian purpose: "to shock the audience out of their complacency," as Eliot has said, going on to admit, "I may, for aught I know, have been slightly under the influence of *St. Joan.*"[17] The atmosphere of wit is evident also in the first part of Eliot's play, in the cynical attitude of the Herald who announces Becket's return:

> The streets of the city will be packed to suffocation,
> And I think that his horse will be deprived of its tail,
> A single hair of which becomes a precious relic.

Or, more important, in the speeches of the Four Tempters, who match the Four Knights of Part II, and who tend to speak, as the Knights also

[17] Eliot, *Poetry and Drama*, p. 30.

do in places, in a carefully calculated doggerel that betrays their fundamental shallowness:

> I leave you to the pleasures of your higher vices,
> Which will have to be paid for at higher prices.
> Farewell, my Lord, I do not wait upon ceremony,
> I leave as I came, forgetting all acrimony,
> Hoping that your present gravity
> Will find excuse for my humble levity.
> If you will remember me, my Lord, at your prayers,
> I'll remember you at kissing-time below the stairs.

In all these ways Eliot, like Shaw, maintains his action in the "real"
world: and by other means as well. By keeping before us the central
question of our own time: "Is it war or peace?" asks Eliot's priest.
"Peace," replies the Herald, "but not the kiss of peace./ A patched up
affair, if you ask my opinion." By the frequently realistic imagery of the
Chorus, made up of "the scrubbers and sweepers of Canterbury." By the
frequent use in Part II of the recorded words that passed between Becket
and the Knights in the year 1170.[18] By throwing our minds back to the
literary forms of the Middle Ages: to *Everyman*, from which Eliot has
taken a good many hints for the tone and manner of Becket's encounter
with the Tempters, and which, as he says, he has kept in mind as a model
for the versification of his dialogue.[19] To this last we should also add a
special device of heavy alliteration (particularly notable in the Second
Temptation), which seems to work in two ways: it reminds us of the
English alliterative verse of the Middle Ages, and thus gives the play a
further historical focus, and it also suggests here a rhetoric of worldly
ambition in keeping with the temptation that Becket is undergoing:

> Think, my Lord,
> Power obtained grows to glory,
> Life lasting, a permanent possession,
> A templed tomb, monument of marble.
> Rule over men reckon no madness.

Both Eliot and Shaw, then, have in their own ways taken pains to place
their action simultaneously in the "real" past and the "real" present: an
action firmly fixed in time must underlie the shock of intersection.

[18] See William Holden Hutton, *S. Thomas of Canterbury. An account of his
Life and Fame from the Contemporary Biographers and other Chroniclers* (London, 1889), esp. pp. 234–45.
[19] Eliot, *Poetry and Drama*, pp. 27–28.

But of course, in Eliot's play the cause of intersection, the agent of transformation, the saint, is utterly different from Shaw's, and thus the plays become, so obviously, different. Shaw's Joan is the active saint, operating in the world; Eliot's Becket is a contemplative figure, ascetic, "withdrawn to contemplation," holding within his mind, and reconciling there alone, the stresses of the world. His immobility is his strength, he is the still point, the center of the world that moves about him, as his sermon is the center of the play.

One is struck here by the similarity between the total conception of Eliot's play and of *Oedipus at Colonus*. Both heroes, after a long period of wandering, have found, at their entrance, their place of rest and their place of death, in a sacred spot: Becket in his Cathedral, Oedipus in the sacred wood of the Furies or Eumenides. Both heroes maintain the attitude that Oedipus states at the outset: "nevermore will I depart from my rest in this land." Both reveal in their opening speeches the view that, as Oedipus says, "patience is the lesson of suffering."[20] Both are then subjected to various kinds of temptations to leave the spot; both are forced to recapitulate their past while enduring these trials; both remain immobile, unmovable; both win a glorious death and by that death benefit the land in which they die. Both are surrounded by a large cast of varied human sufferers, who do not understand the saint, who try to deflect him from his ways, and who in some cases mourn his loss bitterly: the cry of Eliot's priest at the end is like the cries of Antigone and Ismene:

> O father, father, gone from us, lost to us,
> How shall we find you, from what far place
> Do you look down on us?

I suspect that *Oedipus at Colonus* has in fact had a deep and early influence upon Eliot's whole career: "Sweeney among the Nightingales" alludes to this very wood, which Sophocles' Chorus describes as a place where

> The sweet, sojourning nightingale
> Murmurs all day long. . . .
> And here the choiring Muses come,
> And the divinity of love
> With the gold reins in her hand.[21]

[20] *The Tragedies of Sophocles*, trans. Sir Richard C. Jebb (Cambridge: Cambridge University Press, 1904), pp. 63, 61.
[21] Sophocles, *Oedipus at Colonus*, trans. Robert Fitzgerald (New York: Harcourt, Brace & World, Inc., 1941), pp. 55–56.

The fact that the Muses haunt this wood may throw some light too upon the title of Eliot's first book of essays, *The Sacred Wood*, the book in which he revealed his early interest in the possibility of a poetic drama.

But our main point here is the way in which this deeply religious tragedy of Sophocles, which had already provided a strong formative precedent for Milton's *Samson Agonistes*, now provides us with a precedent for regarding Eliot's saint's play as a tragedy. The precedent may also explain why a strong coloring of Greek-like fatalism runs throughout Eliot's Christian play: a coloring which some of Eliot's critics have found disturbing. But these classical reminiscences of Destiny and Fate and Fortune's wheel remind us only of the base upon which Eliot is building: they do not delimit his total meaning. We can see this amalgamation of Greek and Christian at work in Becket's opening speech—the most important speech of the play, which all the rest of the play explores and illustrates. It is the speech which Becket's Fourth Tempter, his inmost self, repeats in mockery, word for word, twenty pages later, and thus suggests that these Temptations—of pleasure, worldly power, and spiritual pride—are to be regarded as fundamentally a recapitulation of the stages by which Becket has reached the state of mind he displays at his entrance. He believes that he has found a secret cause, and he enters prepared to die in that belief: "Peace," he says to the worried priest, and then, referring to the Chorus of anxious women, continues:

> They speak better than they know, and beyond your understanding.
> They know and do not know, what it is to act or suffer.
> They know and do not know, that acting is suffering
> And suffering is action. Neither does the actor suffer
> Nor the patient act. But both are fixed
> In an eternal action, an eternal patience
> To which all must consent that it may be willed
> And which all must suffer that they may will it,
> That the pattern may subsist, for the pattern is the action
> And the suffering, that the wheel may turn and still
> Be forever still.

We can worry the ambiguities of those words "suffering" and "patient" as long as we wish: in the end Becket keeps his secret almost as stubbornly as Joan or Oedipus:

> I have had a tremor of bliss, a wink of heaven, a whisper,
> And I would no longer be denied; all things
> Proceed to a joyful consummation.

But halfway between these two passages lies Becket's Christmas sermon, presented as a four-page interlude between the play's two parts. It is one of the most surprisingly successful moments in the modern theater, for who would expect to find a sermon, and an interesting sermon, here? It owes its success to an atmosphere of restrained and controlled mystery, and to the fact that it is not really an interlude at all, but a deep expression of the play's central theme, binding the play's two parts into one. Becket is speaking of this word *Peace*, the word that dominates the play, for all the actors and sufferers in the play are seeking peace, on their own terms. But the meaning of the word for Becket is conveyed only obliquely, by Becket's tone, his poise, his humility, his acceptance, "Thus devoted, concentrated in purpose." He can display only by his own action and suffering what this word Peace means to him, for he is trying to explain the meaning of the unspoken Word that lies locked in the visible and verbal paradoxes of acting and suffering.

And only in this way, too, can Becket display that submission of the will by which he avoids the final temptation of spiritual pride. The Temptations make it clear that Becket has been a proud man—even an arrogant man: the first priest, the Tempters, and the Knights all accuse him, with some reason, of pride. And we hear him speaking at times, throughout the play, and even at the very end, in a harsh, acid tone, which here and there is uncomfortably close to condescension. Eliot's control of the character is not perhaps as firm as we could wish; though there is nothing that a skillful actor cannot handle, for the central conception is clear: like Oedipus, Becket is still a man, and retains the marks of his natural character: but in the sermon we grasp his saintliness.

At the same time Becket conveys to us the essence of the view of Tragedy that we are here considering. Becket's sermon ponders the fact that in the services of Christmas the Church celebrates birth and death simultaneously. Now, "as the World sees," Becket says, "this is to behave in a strange fashion. For who in the World will both mourn and rejoice at once and for the same reason?" And this is true on other occasions, he adds: "so also, in a smaller figure, we both rejoice and mourn in the death of martyrs. We mourn, for the sins of the world that has martyred them; we rejoice, that another soul is numbered among the Saints. . . ."

It is this tension, this double vision, that Eliot presents in his great choral odes. What Eliot has done is to allow everyone in his play except the Chorus and Becket to remain the simplest possible types—simpler even than Shaw's: ciphers who serve their functions: to provide an outline of the action and a setting for the problem. Into the cries of the Chorus he has poured the tragic experience of suffering humanity, caught in the grip of a secret cause: "We are forced to bear witness."

The Chorus opens the play with fear and reluctance and hopelessness, asking who it is who shall

> Stretch out his hand to the fire, and deny his master? who shall be warm
> By the fire, and deny his master?

They know and do not know who it is—themselves—bending to the earth like animals seeking their protective coloring:

> Now I fear disturbance of the quiet seasons:
> Winter shall come bringing death from the sea,
> Ruinous spring shall beat at our doors,
> Root and shoot shall eat our eyes and our ears,
> Disastrous summer burn up the beds of our streams
> And the poor shall wait for another decaying October.

These dead do not desire resurrection; and when their Lord Archbishop reappears to them, they can only cry out, "O Thomas, return, Archbishop; return, return to France. . . . Leave us to perish in quiet." They would like to go on "living and partly living," like Shaw's Dauphin, who irritably shies away from Joan, saying, "I want to sleep in a comfortable bed." Eliot's Chorus starts from this point—by the fireside and the bed— a point which Shaw's chorus of varied actors hardly goes beyond. But Eliot's Chorus moves far beyond this point, undergoing what Kenneth Burke or Francis Fergusson might call a ritual of transformation. They are not at all the "foolish, immodest and babbling women" which Eliot's priest calls them, but the heart of humanity moving under the impulse of a half-realized cause. Under this impulse they have moved, by the end of Part I, into the range of a "stifling scent of despair," which nevertheless is not spreading blindly outwards: for the Chorus

> The forms take shape in the dark air:
> Puss-purr of leopard, footfall of padding bear,
> Palm-pat of nodding ape, square hyaena waiting
> For laughter, laughter, laughter. The Lords of Hell are here.

But after Becket's sermon the Chorus has taken some heart: they no longer seem to fear the spring:

> When the leaf is out on the tree, when the elder and may
> Burst over the stream, and the air is clear and high,

And voices trill at windows, and children tumble in front of the door,
What work shall have been done, what wrong
Shall the bird's song cover, the green tree cover, what wrong
Shall the fresh earth cover?

From this oscillation between despair and a half-hope arises the play's greatest poetry, as the Chorus moves on far out of the range of ordinary fears and hopes into a nightmare vision that renews and extends the animal imagery, and the dense imagery of taste and smell and the other senses, by which the Chorus had expressed its horror at the close of Part I; but now there is more than horror: the Chorus is moving on here to a vision of humanity's living relation with all being, to a sense that all of creation from the worm to the Prince is involved in this sacrifice:

I have smelt them, the death-bringers, senses are quickened
By subtile forebodings . . .
        I have tasted
The savour of putrid flesh in the spoon. I have felt
The heaving of earth at nightfall, restless, absurd. I have heard
Laughter in the noises of beasts that make strange noises . . .
        I have eaten
Smooth creatures still living, with the strong salt taste of living
   things under sea . . .
        In the air
Flirted with the passage of the kite, I have plunged with the kite
   and cowered with the wren. . . .
        I have seen
Rings of light coiling downwards, leading
To the horror of the ape. . . .
I have consented, Lord Archbishop, have consented.

Beyond this recognition of responsibility for the action and the suffering, there lies a step into the vision of ultimate horror which they face just before the murder: a vision of utter spiritual death: the Dark Night of the Soul:

Emptiness, absence, separation from God;
The horror of the effortless journey, to the empty land
Which is no land, only emptiness, absence, the Void. . . .

This, paradoxically, is their moment of deepest vision, of greatest courage; the point at which they fully comprehend their need for the sacrifice about to be permitted, suffered, and which provides the answer to their cries during the very act of the murder:

> Clear the air! clean the sky! wash the wind! take the stone from the stone, take the skin from the arm, take the muscle from the bone, and wash them. Wash the stone, wash the bone, wash the brain, wash the soul, wash them wash them!

Like King Oedipus they are, without quite realizing it, being washed in this "rain of blood" that is blinding their eyes.

As these cries from the conscience of humanity fade away, the lights fade out—and then come on again in the foreground with a glaring brightness—as the four Murderers step forward, make their bows, and present their ridiculous speeches of defense—in the manner of an after-dinner speaker: "I knew Becket well, in various official relations; and I may say that I have never known a man so well qualified for the highest rank of the Civil Service." Or in the manner of the parliamentary orator: "I must repeat one point that the last speaker has made. While the late Archbishop was Chancellor, he wholeheartedly supported the King's designs: this is an important point, which, if necessary, I can substantiate." Or in the manner of the brisk attorney: "I think, with these facts before you, you will unhesitatingly render a verdict of Suicide while of Unsound Mind."

The lights fade out again, the Knights disappear, and then gradually the lights come on once more, to reveal the priests and the Chorus in their old positions. It is as if the Knights had never spoken: the conscience of humanity has been working deep within while the Knights were speaking on the surface, and now the Chorus sums up its discoveries, its transformation, in a psalm of praise, in which once again it affirms a union with the whole creation, but this time in a tone of joy and peace:

> We praise Thee, O God, for Thy glory displayed in all the creatures of the earth,
> In the snow, in the rain, in the wind, in the storm; in all of Thy creatures, both the hunters and the hunted. . . .
> They affirm Thee in living; all things affirm Thee in living; the bird in the air, both the hawk and the finch; the beast on the earth, both the wolf and the lamb; the worm in the soil and the worm in the belly. . . .
> Even in us the voices of seasons, the snuffle of winter, the song of spring, the drone of summer, the voices of beasts and of birds, praise Thee.

Those words from the final chorus may remind us again of the long ten-
tacles of correlated imagery that reach throughout these choral odes:
imagery of beasts and birds and worms; of seasons, of violent death, of
the daily hardships of the partly living life: with the result that these
choral odes grow together into a long poem, interwoven with verse and
prose pitched at a lower intensity; and by this interweaving of the odes,
even more than by Becket, the play is drawn into unity.

We can see now the effect that these different manifestations of a
secret cause have had upon the total construction of our two saint's plays.
Eliot's play, focused on a contemplative saint, displays what we might
call a semi-circular structure: with Becket as the still center, and the
Chorus sweeping out around him in a broad dramatic action, a poetical
ballet of transformation. Shaw's play, based on an active saint, develops
instead a linear structure, as of a spear driving straight for the mark. It is
marred, here and there, by irrelevant or maladjusted witticisms, and the
whole character of Stogumber is a misfortune. Yet Joan and her voices
seem to work like key symbols in a poem: appearing in a carefully designed sequence of different contexts: six scenes, with six differing moods,
moving from farce to high comedy, to a romantic glimpse of the warrior
Joan in shining armor, and from here into an area of deepening somber-
ness, until, by the fifth scene, the world of Shaw's play, too, has been
transformed—from the foolish to the tragic. Now we have in his play, too,
the dim silence of the Cathedral, with Joan praying symbolically before
the stations of the Cross: her white raiment revealing the saint whose
mission is now nearly complete. The king is crowned; she has shown
France how to win; and now, as her allies, one by one, and even Dunois,
fail to answer the unbearable demands of the superhuman, Joan goes
forth to meet the cheering crowd who will kiss her garments and line her
roadway with palms. The way is now prepared for the massive trial scene,
the tragic agon, which presents what Eliot calls "a symbol perfected in
death."

And then, the Epilogue. Many have found this a disconcerting, inar-
tistic mixture of farce, satire, and didactic explanation. I agree. But I do
not see why the Epilogue should spoil the play. An epilogue is no part of
the dramatic action: it is the author's chance to step forward, relaxed
and garrulous, and to talk the play over with the audience. Traditionally,
it is true, the epilogue is recited by only one performer—by Prospero, for
instance. There is a slight difference here: Shaw has had his entire cast
recite the Epilogue. But it is still appended commentary on the action,
not a part of the action. Moreover, this kind of thing is not without
precedent in performances of tragedy. The ancient Greeks appear to have
liked exactly this kind of release in their festivals of tragedy, since they
demanded that each dramatist, after presenting his three tragedies,

should provide them with their satyr-play, usually of an uproarious and ribald variety, sometimes burlesquing elements of the very story that had just been seen in tragic dignity. The Epilogue is Shaw's satyr-play: a bursting forth of that strong sense of the ridiculous which Shaw has, during the play proper, subjected to a remarkable control—remarkable, that is, for Shaw.

It seems possible, then, to find some place, within the spacious area of tragedy, for our two saint's plays. It seems possible, if we will not demand an Aristotelian hero, and if we may view the area of tragedy as a sort of scale or spectrum ranging between the two poles of doubt and affirmation: or, to put it more precisely, between the pole of fruitless suffering and the pole of universal cause. Not a scale of value, but a spectrum of various qualities, with *A Farewell to Arms* marking one extreme, outside the area of tragedy, and Shakespeare's *Tempest*, perhaps, marking the other extreme. In between, within the area of tragedy, would lie an enormous variety of works that would defy any rigorous attempt at definition, except that all would show in some degree a mingled atmosphere of doubt and affirmation, of human suffering and secret cause. Far over toward the side of fruitless suffering we might find the plays of Ibsen, or *Othello*; somewhere in the middle, *Hamlet*, or *Oedipus Rex*; and far over toward the other side we might find a triad of strongly affirmative tragedies: *Oedipus at Colonus*, *Samson Agonistes*, and *Murder in the Cathedral*; and still farther over, perhaps hanging on by his hands to the very rim of tragedy—we might even find a place for Bernard Shaw.

J. M. SYNGE

The Playboy of the Western World

A PLAY CAN BECOME an accepted classic without ever having been appreciated for the kind of thing it really was. Such a play is *The Playboy of the Western World* by J. M. Synge (1871–1909). It is probably the most famous of all Irish plays, but what is famous about it? At best the rich lingo its characters speak or miscellaneous drolleries of character and incident. Missing from the conception of the play that has come down to us is any contact with its substance: like *The Importance of Being Earnest,* and with less provocation, *The Playboy* has been taken to be about "nothing." But it is about Ireland, and, in Quentin Anderson's words,

> the idea that Ireland has been swept bare of courage by oppression and is obsessed by a desire to take violent action against its oppressors. (This demand for violence is visible in any crowd gathered about an accident, and was expressed by the Cape Codder who told me after seeing an airplane crash that it was the only thing he had ever "really witnessed" in his fifty years.) Among such people the fear-driven Christy appears, and his fantasy of killing his father becomes the community's myth. But Christy strikes his father a second time and destroys the myth by reducing it to the commonplace of brutality. The idea has been put to work, but it does not appear in the play—that is wholly given over to the characters who make and break the myth of heroism.[1]

[1] "Notes on the Theatre," *Kenyon Review,* Winter 1949.

1863

J. M. Synge

The Playboy of the Western World is also what today would be called "political theatre." Those who rioted at the first performance in 1907 had their reasons, for the play is continuous with its author's *Manchester Guardian* articles describing the poverty of the "Western World," and the passage in his book on the Aran Islands which bears on the plot of *Playboy* also explains what the theme of "protecting the criminal" meant to Synge and his countrymen:

> This impulse to protect the criminal is universal in the west. It seems partly due to the association between justice and the hated English jurisdiction, but more directly to the primitive feeling of these people, who are never criminals yet always capable of crime, that a man will not do wrong unless he is under the influence of a passion which is as irresponsible as a storm on the sea. If a man has killed his father, and is already sick and broken with remorse, they can see no reason why he should be dragged away and killed by the law.

On the background of the beautiful, evocative title of Synge's play (which earlier bore rather ordinary titles like *The Murderer* and *Murder Will Out* and *The Fool of Farnham*) Maurice Bourgeois provided an excellent note long ago (*John Millington Synge and the Irish Theatre*, 1913):

> The word "playboy" (Irish *búachaill barra*, literally "boy of the game,") a term used in the Irish game of "hurling" (*camánaidheacht*) is Hibernian slang. Its exact meaning (not to be found in Wright's *English Dialect Dictionary* (iv. 543, *s.v.* "play-boy"), which gives only the older acceptations of the word: 1. the devil; w. a playful woman) is "hoaxer, humbugger, mystificator (*not* impostor), one who does sham things." Mr. William Boyle, the well-known Abbey Theatre playwright, uses the word in this sense in his comedy, *The Eloquent Dempsey* (Dublin: O'Donoghue, Gill, 1907), p. 18. In Synge's use of it, it seems to have three implicit by-meanings: (a) one who is played with; (b) one who plays like a player (i.e. a comedian and also an athlete or champion: witness the sports in the play); (c) one who is full of the play-spirit: "a wild dare-devil is called a play-boy [as in Synge's well-known comedy]" ("The Irish Dialect of English," by Mary Hayden and Marcus Hartog, *Fortnightly Review*, April 1909, p. 779 & n. 1). The word, which is half-humorous and half-poetical, is a very rich one, and (like "philanderer," which, Mr. Bernard Shaw tells me, has its exact equivalent only in Swedish) is exceedingly difficult to translate.—"The West-

ern World" is the English equivalent of the Gaelic folk-phrase *an domhain shiar,* describing the Atlantic seaboard of Ireland as distinguished from the Dublin side, "The Eastern World" (*an domhain shoir*).—The whole title seems to echo that of W. H. Mazwell's well-known volume, *Wild Sports of the West* (London: Richard Bentley, 1838), which may have vaguely suggested it.

On the background of our play in Synge's life *J. M. Synge* by David H. Greene and Edward M. Stephens (1959) is recommended, while the first seventy-eight pages of T. R. Henn's edition of the *Plays and Poems* (1963) give an admirable account of Synge's dramatic art. A portion of this account is printed below.

THE PLAYBOY OF THE
WESTERN WORLD
[1907]

Annotated by
WILLIAM E. HART

CHARACTERS

CHRISTOPHER MAHON

OLD MAHON *his father, a squatter*

MICHAEL JAMES FLAHERTY (*called* MICHAEL JAMES) *a publican*

MARGARET FLAHERTY (*called* PEGEEN MIKE) *his daughter*

WIDOW QUIN *a woman of about thirty*

SHAWN KEOGH *her [second] cousin, a young farmer*

PHILLY CULLEN *and* JIMMY FARRELL *small farmers[1]*

SARA TANSEY *village girls*
SUSAN BRADY
HONOR BLAKE
NELLY

A BELLMAN

SOME PEASANTS

The action takes place near a village, on a wild coast of Mayo. The First Act passes on an evening of autumn, the other two Acts on the following day.

---

[1] SMALL FARMERS: poor farmers

ACT ONE

Scene: Country public house or shebeen, very rough and untidy. There is a sort of counter on the right with shelves, holding many bottles and jugs, just seen above it. Empty barrels stand near the counter. At back, a little to left of counter, there is a door into the open air, then, more to the left, there is a settle with shelves above it, with more jugs, and a table beneath a window. At the left there is a large open fireplace, with turf fire, and a small door into inner room. PEGEEN, *a wild-looking but fine girl, of about twenty, is writing at table. She is dressed in the usual peasant dress.*

P E G E E N [*slowly as she writes*] Six yards of stuff for to make a yellow gown. A pair of lace boots with lengthy heels on them and brassy eyes. A hat is suited for a wedding day. A fine tooth comb. To be sent with three barrels of porter in Jimmy Farrell's creel cart[1] on the evening of the coming Fair[2] to Mister Michael James Flaherty. With the best compliments of this season. Margaret Flaherty.

S H A W N   K E O G H [*a fat and fair young man comes in as she signs, looks round awkwardly, when he sees she is alone*] Where's himself?[3]

P E G E E N [*without looking at him*] He's coming. [*She directs letter.*] To Mister Sheamus Mulroy, Wine and Spirit Dealer, Castlebar.[4]

S H A W N [*uneasily*] I didn't see him on the road.

P E G E E N – How would you see him [*licks stamp and puts it on letter*] and it dark night this half hour gone by?

S H A W N [*turning towards door again*] I stood a while outside wondering would I have a right to pass on or to walk in and see you, Pegeen Mike [*comes to fire*], and I could hear the cows breathing, and sighing in the stillness of the air, and not a step moving any place from this gate to the bridge.

ACT I: [1] CREEL CART: cart with open, barred, or grated sides used to carry turf, sheep, pigs, etc. [2] FAIR: the high day for talk and commerce in livestock, held in the middle of the month. [3] HIMSELF: the master of the house, Michael James. [4] CASTLEBAR: a principal city of East Mayo.

P E G E E N [*putting letter in envelope*] It's above at the cross-roads he is meeting Philly Cullen; and a couple more are going along with him to Kate Cassidy's wake.[5]

S H A W N [*looking at her blankly*] And he's going that length in the dark night?

P E G E E N [*impatiently*] He is surely, and leaving me lonesome on the scruff of the hill. [*She gets up and puts envelope on dresser, then winds clock.*] Isn't it long the nights are now, Shawn Keogh, to be leaving a poor girl with her own self counting the hours to the dawn of day?

S H A W N [*with awkward humour*] If it is, when we're wedded in a short while you'll have no call[6] to complain, for I've little will to be walking off to wakes or weddings in the darkness of the night.

P E G E E N [*with rather scornful good humour*] You're making mighty certain, Shaneen,[7] that I'll wed you now.

S H A W N – Aren't we after making a good bargain,[8] the way we're only waiting these days on Father Reilly's dispensation[9] from the bishops, or the Court of Rome.

P E G E E N [*looking at him teasingly, washing up at dresser*] It's a wonder, Shaneen, the Holy Father'd be taking notice of the likes of you; for if I was him I wouldn't bother with this place where you'll meet none but Red Linahan, has a squint in his eye, and Patcheen is lame in his heel, or the mad Mulrannies were driven from California and they lost in their wits. We're a queer lot these times to go troubling the Holy Father on his sacred seat.

S H A W N [*scandalized*] If we are, we're as good this place as another, maybe, and as good these times as we were for ever.

P E G E E N [*with scorn*] As good, is it? Where now will you meet the like of Daneen Sullivan knocked the eye from a peeler,[10] or Marcus Quin, God rest him, got six months for maiming ewes, and he a great warrant[11] to tell stories of holy Ireland till he'd have the old women shedding down tears about their feet. Where will you find the like of them, I'm saying?

S H A W N [*timidly*] If you don't, it's a good job, maybe; for [*with peculiar emphasis on the words*] Father Reilly has small conceit[12] to have that kind walking around and talking to the girls.

P E G E E N [*impatiently, throwing water from basin out of the door*] Stop tormenting me with Father Reilly [*imitating his voice*] when

---

[5] WAKE: the watching of the dead, once an occasion for riot and drunkenness.
[6] NO CALL: no need. [7] SHANEEN: little Shawn. [8] BARGAIN: Shawn's fair day view of marriage. [9] DISPENSATION: to marry his *second* cousin. [10] PEELER: policeman, so-called after Sir Robert Peel. [11] A GREAT WARRANT: a great gift for, a great hand at. [12] CONCEIT: a liking, a fancy for.

I'm asking only what way[13] I'll pass these twelve hours of dark, and
not take my death with the fear.

[*Looking out of door.*]

SHAWN [*timidly*] Would I fetch you the Widow Quin, maybe?

PEGEEN – Is it the like of that murderer? You'll not, surely.

SHAWN [*going to her, soothingly*] Then I'm thinking himself will stop
along with you when he sees you taking on, for it'll be a long night-
time with great darkness, and I'm after feeling a kind of fellow above
in the furzy ditch, groaning wicked like a maddening dog, the way[14]
it's good cause you have, maybe, to be fearing now.

PEGEEN [*turning on him sharply*] What's that? Is it a man you seen?

SHAWN [*retreating*] I couldn't see him at all; but I heard him groaning out, and breaking his heart. It should have been a young man from
his words speaking.

PEGEEN [*going after him*] And you never went near to see was he
hurted or what ailed him at all?

SHAWN – I did not, Pegeen Mike. It was a dark lonesome place to be
hearing the like of him.

PEGEEN – Well, you're a daring fellow, and if they find his corpse
stretched above in the dews of dawn, what'll you say then to the peelers, or the Justice of the Peace?

SHAWN [*thunderstruck*] I wasn't thinking of that. For the love of
God, Pegeen Mike, don't let on[15] I was speaking of him. Don't tell
your father and the men is coming above; for if they heard that story,
they'd have great blabbing this night at the wake.

PEGEEN – I'll maybe tell them, and I'll maybe not.

SHAWN – They are coming at the door. Will you whisht,[16] I'm saying?

PEGEEN – Whisht yourself.

She goes behind counter. MICHAEL JAMES, *fat jovial publican, comes in
followed by* PHILLY CULLEN, *who is thin and mistrusting, and* JIMMY
FARRELL, *who is fat and amorous, about forty-five.*

MEN [*together*] God bless you. The blessing of God on this place.

PEGEEN – God bless you kindly.[17]

MICHAEL [*to men who go to the counter*] Sit down now, and take
your rest. [*Crosses to* SHAWN *at the fire.*] And how is it you are, Shawn
Keogh? Are you coming over the sands to Kate Cassidy's wake?

SHAWN – I am not, Michael James. I'm going home the short cut to
my bed.

PEGEEN [*speaking across the counter*] He's right too, and have you no

13 WHAT WAY: how. 14 THE WAY: so that. 15 LET ON: don't admit.
16 WHISHT: be quiet, shut up. 17 GOD BLESS YOU KINDLY: Irish ritual blessing on
entering a house.

shame, Michael James, to be quitting off for the whole night, and leaving myself lonesome in the shop?

M I C H A E L [*good-humouredly*] Isn't it the same whether I go for the whole night or a part only? and I'm thinking it's a queer daughter you are if you'd have me crossing backward through the Stooks[18] of the Dead Women, with a drop taken.[19]

P E G E E N – If I am a queer daughter, it's a queer father'd be leaving me lonesome these twelve hours of dark, and I piling the turf with the dogs barking, and the calves mooing, and my own teeth rattling with the fear.

J I M M Y [*flatteringly*] What is there to hurt you, and you a fine, hardy girl would knock the head of any two men in the place?

P E G E E N [*working herself up*] Isn't there the harvest boys[20] with their tongues red for drink, and the ten tinkers[21] is camped in the east glen, and the thousand militia[22]—bad cess[23] to them!—walking idle through the land. There's lots surely to hurt me, and I won't stop alone in it, let himself do what he will.

M I C H A E L – If you're that afeard,[24] let Shawn Keogh stop along with you. It's the will of God, I'm thinking, himself should be seeing to you now.

[*They all turn on* SHAWN.]

S H A W N [*in horrified confusion*] I would and welcome,[25] Michael James, but I'm afeard of Father Reilly; and what at all would the Holy Father and the Cardinals of Rome be saying if they heard I did the like of that?

M I C H A E L [*with contempt*] God help you! Can't you sit in by the hearth with the light lit and herself[26] beyond in the room? You'll do that surely, for I've heard tell there's a queer fellow above, going mad or getting his death, maybe, in the gripe[27] of the ditch, so she'd be safer this night with a person here.

S H A W N [*with plaintive despair*] I'm afeard of Father Reilly, I'm saying. Let you not be tempting me, and we near married itself.

P H I L L Y [*with cold contempt*] Lock him in the west room. He'll stay then and have no sin to be telling to the priest.

M I C H A E L [*to* SHAWN, *getting between him and the door*] Go up now.[28]

---

[18] STOOKS: rocks or low dunes along the sea-shore, shaped like *stooks*, shocks of corn generally containing 12 sheaves. [19] DROP TAKEN: drunk. [20] HARVEST BOYS: workers who migrated to Scotland and England to help with the harvest and who returned in late autumn with a few pounds to help survive the winter. [21] TINKERS: the gypsies of the Irish roads. [22] MILITIA: part of the military garrison that once numbered over 35,000 in Ireland and no friend to the people. [23] BAD CESS: bad luck. [24] AFEARD: afraid. [25] WOULD AND WELCOME: gladly. [26] AND HERSELF: while Pegeen is. [27] GRIPE: the hollow, the trench. [28] GO UP NOW: get back to the hearth.

SHAWN [*at the top of his voice*] Don't stop me, Michael James. Let me out of the door, I'm saying, for the love of the Almighty God. Let me out [*trying to dodge past him*]. Let me out of it, and may God grant you His indulgence in the hour of need.

MICHAEL [*loudly*] Stop your noising, and sit down by the hearth.

> [*Gives him a push and goes to counter laughing.*]

SHAWN [*turning back, wringing his hands*] Oh, Father Reilly and the saints of God, where will I hide myself today? Oh, St. Joseph and St. Patrick and St. Brigid, and St. James, have mercy on me now!

> [SHAWN *turns round, sees door clear, and makes a rush for it.*]

MICHAEL [*catching him by the coat-tail*] You'd be going, is it?

SHAWN [*screaming*] Leave me go, Michael James, leave me go, you old Pagan, leave me go, or I'll get the curse of the priests on you, and of the scarlet-coated bishops of the courts of Rome.

[*With a sudden movement he pulls himself out of his coat, and disappears out of the door, leaving his coat in* MICHAEL'*s hands.*]

MICHAEL [*turning round, and holding up coat*] Well, there's the coat of a Christian man. Oh, there's sainted glory this day in the lonesome west; and by the will of God I've got you a decent man, Pegeen, you'll have no call to be spying after if you've a score of young girls, maybe, weeding in your fields.

PEGEEN [*taking up the defence of her property*] What right have you to be making game of a poor fellow for minding the priest, when it's your own the fault is, not paying a penny pot-boy[29] to stand along with me and give me courage in the doing of my work?

> [*She snaps the coat away from him,*
> *and goes behind counter with it.*]

MICHAEL [*taken aback*] Where would I get a pot-boy? Would you have me send the bell-man screaming in the streets of Castlebar?

SHAWN [*opening the door a chink and putting in his head, in a small voice*] Michael James!

MICHAEL [*imitating him*] What ails you?

SHAWN – The queer dying fellow's beyond looking over the ditch. He's come up, I'm thinking, stealing your hens. [*Looks over his shoulder.*] God help me, he's following me now [*he runs into room*], and if he's heard what I said, he'll be having my life, and I going home lonesome in the darkness of the night.

For a perceptible moment they watch the door with curiosity. Someone coughs outside. Then CHRISTY MAHON, *a slight young man, comes in very tired and frightened and dirty.*

[29] POT-BOY: a menial in a public house.

CHRISTY [*in a small voice*] God save all here!

MEN – God save you kindly.

CHRISTY [*going to the counter*] I'd trouble you for a glass of porter, woman of the house.

[*He puts down coin.*]

PEGEEN [*serving him*] You're one of the tinkers, young fellow, is beyond camped in the glen?

CHRISTY – I am not; but I'm destroyed walking.

MICHAEL [*patronizingly*] Let you come up then to the fire. You're looking famished with the cold.

CHRISTY – God reward you. [*He takes up his glass and goes a little way across to the left, then stops and looks about him.*] Is it often the polis[30] do be coming into this place, master of the house?

MICHAEL – If you'd come in better hours, you'd have seen "Licensed for the sale of Beer and Spirits, to be consumed on the premises," written in white letters above the door, and what would the polis want spying on me, and not a decent house within four miles, the way every living Christian is a bona fide,[31] saving one widow alone?

CHRISTY [*with relief*] It's a safe house, so.

He goes over to the fire, sighing and moaning. Then he sits down putting his glass beside him and begins gnawing a turnip, too miserable to feel the others staring at him with curiosity.

MICHAEL [*going after him*] Is it yourself is fearing the polis? You're wanting,[32] maybe?

CHRISTY – There's many wanting.

MICHAEL – Many surely, with the broken harvest and the ended wars.[33] [*He picks up some stockings, etc., that are near the fire, and carries them away furtively.*] It should be larceny, I'm thinking?

CHRISTY [*dolefully*] I had it in my mind it was a different word and a bigger.

PEGEEN – There's a queer lad. Were you never slapped in school, young fellow, that you don't know the name of your deed?

CHRISTY [*bashfully*] I'm slow at learning, a middling scholar only.

MICHAEL – If you're a dunce itself, you'd have a right to know that larceny's robbing and stealing. Is it for the like of that you're wanting?

CHRISTY [*with a flash of family pride*] And I the son of a strong

30 POLIS: police. 31 BONA FIDE: a genuine traveler, i.e., one who having traveled four or more miles could be served after licensing hours. 32 WANTING: wanted by police. 33 ENDED WARS: perhaps both the Land Wars (1879–82) and the Boer War (1899–1902).

farmer[34] [*with a sudden qualm*], God rest his soul, could have bought up the whole of your old house a while since, from the butt of his tail-pocket,[35] and not have missed the weight of it gone.

MICHAEL [*impressed*] If it's not stealing, it's maybe something big.

CHRISTY [*flattered*] Aye; it's maybe something big.

JIMMY—He's a wicked-looking young fellow. Maybe he followed after a young woman on a lonesome night.

CHRISTY [*shocked*] Oh, the saints forbid, mister; I was all times a decent lad.

PHILLY [*turning on* JIMMY] You're a silly man, Jimmy Farrell. He said his father was a farmer a while since, and there's himself now in a poor state. Maybe the land was grabbed[36] from him, and he did what any decent man would do.

MICHAEL [*to* CHRISTY, *mysteriously*] Was it bailiffs?[37]

CHRISTY—The divil a one.[38]

MICHAEL—Agents?[39]

CHRISTY—The divil a one.

MICHAEL—Landlords?

CHRISTY [*peevishly*] Ah, not at all, I'm saying. You'd see the like of them stories on any little paper of a Munster[40] town. But I'm not calling to mind any person, gentle, simple, judge or jury, did the like of me.

[*They all draw nearer with delighted curiosity.*]

PHILLY—Well, that lad's a puzzle-the-world.

JIMMY—He'd beat Dan Davies' circus, or the holy missioners making sermons on the villainy of man. Try him again, Philly.

PHILLY—Did you strike golden guineas[41] out of solder, young fellow, or shilling coins itself?

CHRISTY—I did not mister, not sixpence nor a farthing[42] coin.

JIMMY—Did you marry three wives maybe? I'm told there's a sprinkling have done that among the holy Luthers[43] of the preaching north.

CHRISTY [*shyly*] I never married with one, let alone with a couple or three.

---

[34] STRONG FARMER: a well-to-do farmer with a large farm and much cattle. [35] TAIL-POCKET: of the old-fashioned swallow-tailed coat. [36] LAND WAS GRABBED: the common landlord practice of seizing tenant's land and evicting him for failing to pay the "rack-rent;" an action often attended with the most inhuman cruelty, rapine, and murder. [37] BAILIFFS: district officials charged with collecting the tax. [38] DIVIL A ONE: strong negative. [39] AGENTS: landlord representatives serving process on tenants failing to pay "the rent." The reference is to what Chesterfield called "the deputy of deputy of deputy system of land tenure." [40] MUNSTER: South-Western province of Ireland including Kerry. [41] GOLDEN GUINEAS: old English coin once worth 21 shillings. [42] FARTHING: coin worth one-quarter of English penny. [43] HOLY LUTHERS: Presbyterians.

1875

PHILLY–Maybe he went fighting for the Boers,[44] the like of the man beyond, was judged to be hanged, quartered and drawn. Were you off east, young fellow, fighting bloody wars for Kruger[45] and the freedom of the Boers?

CHRISTY–I never left my own parish till Tuesday was a week.[46]

PEGEEN [*coming from counter*] He's done nothing, so. [*To* CHRISTY.] If you didn't commit murder or a bad, nasty thing, or false coining, or robbery, or butchery, or the like of them, there isn't anything that would be worth your troubling for to run from now. You did nothing at all.

CHRISTY [*his feelings hurt*] That's an unkindly thing to be saying to a poor orphaned traveller, has a prison behind him, and hanging before, and hell's gap gaping below.

PEGEEN [*with a sign to the men to be quiet*] You're only saying it. You did nothing at all. A soft lad the like of you wouldn't slit the windpipe of a screeching sow.

CHRISTY [*offended*] You're not speaking the truth.

PEGEEN [*in mock rage*] Not speaking the truth, is it? Would you have me knock the head of you with the butt of the broom?

CHRISTY [*twisting round on her with a sharp cry of horror*] Don't strike me. I killed my poor father, Tuesday was a week, for doing the like of that.

PEGEEN [*with blank amazement*] Is it killed your father?

CHRISTY [*subsiding*] With the help of God I did surely, and that the Holy Immaculate Mother may intercede for his soul.

PHILLY [*retreating with* JIMMY] There's a daring fellow.

JIMMY–Oh, glory be to God!

MICHAEL [*with great respect*] That was a hanging crime, mister honey. You should have had good reason for doing the like of that.

CHRISTY [*in a very reasonable tone*] He was a dirty man, God forgive him, and he getting old and crusty, the way I couldn't put up with him at all.

PEGEEN–And you shot him dead?

CHRISTY [*shaking his head*] I never used weapons. I've no licence, and I'm a law-fearing man.

MICHAEL–It was with a hilted knife maybe? I'm told, in the big world, it's bloody knives they use.

CHRISTY [*loudly, scandalized*] Do you take me for a slaughter-boy?

[44] BOERS: South African War (1899–1902); the Boers had a number of Irish Brigades fighting the British. [45] KRUGER: Stephen, J. P. (1825–1904), South African statesman and leader of 1880 Boer Rebellion. [46] TILL TUESDAY WAS A WEEK: a week ago Tuesday.

PEGEEN—You never hanged him, the way Jimmy Farrell hanged his dog from the licence,[47] and had it screeching and wriggling three hours at the butt of a string, and himself swearing it was a dead dog, and the peelers swearing it had life?

CHRISTY—I did not then. I just riz[48] the loy[49] and let fall the edge of it on the ridge of his skull, and he went down at my feet like an empty sack, and never let a grunt or groan from him at all.

MICHAEL [*making a sign to* PEGEEN *to fill* CHRISTY's *glass*] And what way weren't you hanged, mister? Did you bury him then?

CHRISTY [*considering*] Aye. I buried him then. Wasn't I digging spuds in the field?

MICHAEL—And the peelers never followed after you the eleven days that you're out?

CHRISTY [*shaking his head*] Never a one of them, and I walking forward facing hog, dog, or divil on the highway of the road.

PHILLY [*nodding wisely*] It's only with a common week-day kind of a murderer them lads would be trusting their carcase, and that man should be a great terror when his temper's roused.

MICHAEL—He should then. [*To* CHRISTY.] And where was it, mister honey, that you did the deed?

CHRISTY [*looking at him with suspicion*] Oh, a distant place, master of the house, a windy corner of high distant hills.

PHILLY [*nodding with approval*] He's a close man,[50] and he's right surely.

PEGEEN—That'd be a lad with the sense of Solomon to have for a pot-boy, Michael James, if it's the truth you're seeking one at all.

PHILLY—The peelers is fearing him, and if you'd that lad in the house there isn't one of them would come smelling around if the dogs itself were lapping poteen[51] from the dung-pit of the yard.

JIMMY—Bravery's a treasure in a lonesome place, and a lad would kill his father, I'm thinking, would face a foxy divil with a pitchpike[52] on the flags of hell.

PEGEEN—It's the truth they're saying, and if I'd that lad in the house, I wouldn't be fearing the loosèd kharki cut-throats,[53] or the walking dead.

CHRISTY [*swelling with surprise and triumph*] Well, glory be to God!

MICHAEL [*with deference*] Would you think well to stop here and be

---

[47] FROM THE LICENCE: on account of the dog licence fee which he either would not or could not pay.   [48] RIZ: raised; an example of strong inflection preferred by the Irish.   [49] LOY: a long narrow spade.   [50] CLOSE MAN: a tight-lipped man.   [51] POTEEN: illicit whiskey.   [52] PITCHPIKE: pitchfork.   [53] LOOSÈD KHARKI CUT-THROATS: the English Garrison.

pot-boy, mister honey, if we gave you good wages, and didn't destroy you with the weight of work?

SHAWN [*coming forward uneasily*] That'd be a queer kind to bring into a decent quiet household with the like of Pegeen Mike.

PEGEEN [*very sharply*] Will you wisht? Who's speaking to you?

SHAWN [*retreating*] A bloody-handed murderer the like of . . .

PEGEEN [*snapping at him*] Whisht I am saying; we'll take no fooling from your like at all. [*To* CHRISTY *with a honeyed voice.*] And you, young fellow, you'd have a right to stop, I'm thinking, for we'd do our all and utmost to content your needs.

CHRISTY [*overcome with wonder*] And I'd be safe this place from the searching law?

MICHAEL – You would, surely. If they're not fearing you, itself, the peelers in this place is decent droughty[54] poor fellows, wouldn't touch a cur dog and not give warning in the dead of night.

PEGEEN [*very kindly and persuasively*] Let you stop a short while anyhow. Aren't you destroyed walking with your feet in bleeding blisters, and your whole skin needing washing like a Wicklow sheep.

CHRISTY [*looking round with satisfaction*] It's a nice room, and if it's not humbugging me you are, I'm thinking that I'll surely stay.

JIMMY [*jumps up*] Now, by the grace of God, herself[55] will be safe this night, with a man killed his father holding danger from the door, and let you come on, Michael James, or they'll have the best stuff drunk at the wake.

MICHAEL [*going to the door with men*] And begging your pardon, mister, what name will we call you, for we'd like to know?

CHRISTY – Christopher Mahon.

MICHAEL – Well, God bless you, Christy, and a good rest till we meet again when the sun'll be rising to the noon of day.

CHRISTY – God bless you all.

MEN – God bless you.

[*They go out except* SHAWN, *who lingers at door.*]

SHAWN [*to* PEGEEN] Are you wanting me to stop along with you and keep you from harm?

PEGEEN [*gruffly*] Didn't you say you were fearing Father Reilly?

SHAWN – There'd be no harm staying now, I'm thinking, and himself in it[56] too.

PEGEEN – You wouldn't stay when there was need for you, and let you step off nimble this time when there's none.

SHAWN – Didn't I say it was Father Reilly . . .

---

[54] DROUGHTY: thirsty. [55] HERSELF: Pegeen. [56] HIMSELF IN IT: Christy here.

PEGEEN – Go on, then, to Father Reilly [*in a jeering tone*], and let him put you in the holy brotherhoods,[57] and leave that lad to me.

SHAWN – If I meet the Widow Quin . . .

PEGEEN – Go on, I'm saying, and don't be waking this place with your noise. [*She hustles him out and bolts door.*] That lad would wear the spirits from the saints of peace. [*Bustles about, then takes off her apron and pins it up in the window as a blind.* CHRISTY *watching her timidly. Then she comes to him and speaks with bland good-humour.*] Let you stretch out now by the fire, young fellow. You should be destroyed travelling.

CHRISTY [*shyly again, drawing off his boots*] I'm tired surely, walking wild eleven days, and waking fearful in the night.

> [*He holds up one of his feet, feeling his blisters,*
> *and looking at them with compassion.*]

PEGEEN [*standing beside him, watching him with delight*] You should have had great people in your family, I'm thinking, with the little, small feet you have, and you with a kind of a quality name,[58] the like of what you'd find on the great powers and potentates of France and Spain.

CHRISTY [*with pride*] We were great surely, with wide and windy acres of rich Munster land.

PEGEEN – Wasn't I telling you, and you a fine, handsome young fellow with a noble brow?

CHRISTY [*with a flash of delighted surprise*] Is it me?

PEGEEN – Aye. Did you never hear that from the young girls where you come from in the west or south?

CHRISTY [*with venom*] I did not then. Oh, they're bloody[59] liars in the naked parish where I grew a man.

PEGEEN – If they are itself, you've heard it these days, I'm thinking, and you walking the world telling out your story to young girls or old.

CHRISTY – I've told my story no place till this night, Pegeen Mike, and it's foolish I was here, maybe, to be talking free, but you're decent people, I'm thinking, and yourself a kindly woman, the way I wasn't fearing you at all.

PEGEEN [*filling a sack with straw*] You've said the like of that, maybe, in every cot[60] and cabin where you've met a young girl on your way.

---

[57] HOLY BROTHERHOODS: religious groups of men with vows of poverty, chastity, and obedience. [58] QUALITY NAME: a gentry name, an aristocrat. [59] BLOODY: in the West a mild expletive like beastly or bloomin'. Recall the furor over Shaw's use of it in *Pygmalion*. [60] COT: a small cabin or cottage.

CHRISTY [*going over to her, gradually raising his voice*] I've said it nowhere till this night, I'm telling you, for I've seen none the like of you the eleven long days I am walking the world, looking over a low ditch or a high ditch on my north or south, into stony scattered fields, or scribes[61] of bog, where you'd see young, limber girls, and fine prancing women making laughter with the men.

PEGEEN – If you weren't destroyed travelling, you'd have as much talk and streeleen,[62] I'm thinking, as Owen Roe O'Sullivan[63] or the poets of the Dingle Bay,[64] and I've heard all times it's the poets are your like, fine fiery fellows with great rages when their temper's roused.

CHRISTY [*drawing a little nearer to her*] You've a power[65] of rings, God bless you, and would there be any offence if I was asking are you single now?

PEGEEN – What would I want wedding so young?

CHRISTY [*with relief*] We're alike, so.

PEGEEN [*she puts sack on settle and beats it up*] I never killed my father. I'd be afeard to do that, except I was the like of yourself with blind rages tearing me within, for I'm thinking you should have had great tussling when the end was come.

CHRISTY [*expanding with delight at the first confidential talk he has ever had with a woman*] We had not then. It was a hard woman[66] was come over the hill, and if he was always a crusty kind when he'd a hard woman setting him on, not the divil himself or his four fathers[67] could put up with him at all.

PEGEEN [*with curiosity*] And isn't it a great wonder that one wasn't fearing you?

CHRISTY [*very confidentially*] Up to the day I killed my father, there wasn't a person in Ireland knew the kind I was, and I there drinking, waking, eating, sleeping, a quiet, simple poor fellow with no man giving me heed.

PEGEEN [*getting a quilt out of cupboard and putting it on the sack*] It was the girls were giving you heed maybe, and I'm thinking it's most conceit you'd have to be gaming[68] with their like.

CHRISTY [*shaking his head, with simplicity*] Not the girls itself, and I won't tell you a lie. There wasn't anyone heeding me in that place saving only the dumb beasts of the field.

[*He sits down at fire.*]

---

61 SCRIBES: long and narrow strips of arable land. 62 STREELEEN: chatter. 63 OWEN ROE O'SULLIVAN: 18th century Kerry poet, something of a playboy himself. 64 DINGLE BAY: a large inlet of the Kerry coast. 65 A POWER: a large quantity. 66 HARD WOMAN: dreadful woman. 67 FOUR FATHERS: whole family. 68 GAMING: fooling.

PEGEEN [*with disappointment*] And I thinking you should have been living the like of a king of Norway or the eastern world.[69]

> [*She comes and sits beside him after placing bread*
> *and mug of milk on the table.*]

CHRISTY [*laughing piteously*] The like of a king, is it? And I after toiling, moiling,[70] digging, dodging[71] from the dawn till dusk with never a sight of joy or sport saving only when I'd be abroad in the dark night poaching rabbits on hills, for I was a divil to poach, God forgive me, [*very naively*] and I near got six months for going with a dung fork and stabbing a fish.

PEGEEN – And it's that you'd call sport, is it, to be abroad in the darkness with yourself alone?

CHRISTY – I did, God help me, and there I'd be as happy as the sunshine of St. Martin's Day,[72] watching the light passing the north or the patches of fog, till I'd hear a rabbit starting to screech and I'd go running in the furze. Then when I'd my full share I'd come walking down where you'd see the ducks and geese stretched sleeping on the highway of the road, and before I'd pass the dunghill, I'd hear himself snoring out, a loud lonesome snore he'd be making all times, the while he was sleeping, and he a man'd be raging all times, the while he was waking, like a gaudy officer you'd hear cursing and damning and swearing oaths.

PEGEEN – Providence and Mercy, spare us all!

CHRISTY – It's that you'd say surely if you seen him and he after drinking for weeks, rising up in the red dawn, or before it maybe, and going out into the yard as naked as an ash tree in the moon of May, and shying clods against the visage of the stars till he'd put the fear of death into the banbhs[73] and the screeching sows.

PEGEEN – I'd be well-nigh afeard of that lad myself, I'm thinking. And there was no one in it but the two of you alone?

CHRISTY – The divil a one, though he'd sons and daughters walking all great states and territories of the world, and not a one of them, to this day, but would say their seven curses on him, and they rousing up to let a cough or sneeze, maybe, in the deadness of the night.

PEGEEN [*nodding her head*] Well, you should have been a queer lot. I never cursed my father the like of that, though I'm twenty and more years of age.

CHRISTY – Then you'd have cursed mine, I'm telling you, and he a man never gave peace to any, saving when he'd get two months or

---

[69] EASTERN WORLD: a sort of wonderland in Irish folktales. [70] MOILING: working hard. [71] DODGING: going at a slow pace over a small job. [72] ST. MARTIN'S DAY: November 11th. [73] BANBHS: young pigs.

three, or be locked in the asylums for battering peelers or assaulting men, [*with depression*] the way it was a bitter life he led me till I did up a Tuesday and halve his skull.

PEGEEN [*putting her hand on his shoulder*] Well, you'll have peace in this place, Christy Mahon, and none to trouble you, and it's near time a fine lad like you should have your good share of the earth.

CHRISTY – It's time surely, and I a seemly fellow with great strength in me and bravery of . . .

[*Someone knocks.*]

CHRISTY [*clinging to* PEGEEN] Oh, glory! it's late for knocking, and this last while I'm in terror of the peelers, and the walking dead.

[*Knocking again.*]

PEGEEN – Who's there?

VOICE [*outside*] Me.

PEGEEN – Who's me?

VOICE – The Widow Quin.

PEGEEN [*jumping up and giving him the bread and milk*] Go on now with your supper, and let on[74] to be sleepy, for if she found you were such a warrant to talk, she'd be stringing gabble till the dawn of day.

[*He takes bread and sits shyly with his back to the door.*]

PEGEEN [*opening door, with temper*] What ails you, or what is it you're wanting at this hour of the night?

WIDOW QUIN [*coming in a step and peering at* CHRISTY] I'm after meeting Shawn Keogh and Father Reilly below, who told me of your curiosity man, and they fearing by this time he was maybe roaring, romping on your hands with drink.

PEGEEN [*pointing to* CHRISTY] Look now is he roaring, and he stretched out drowsy with his supper and his mug of milk. Walk down and tell that to Father Reilly and to Shaneen Keogh.

WIDOW QUIN [*coming forward*] I'll not see them again, for I've their word[75] to lead that lad forward for to lodge with me.

PEGEEN [*in blank amazement*] This night, is it?

WIDOW QUIN [*going over*] This night. "It isn't fitting," says the priesteen,[76] "to have his likeness lodging with an orphaned girl." [*To* CHRISTY.] God save you, mister!

CHRISTY [*shyly*] God save you kindly.

WIDOW QUIN [*looking at him with half-amused curiosity*] Well, aren't you a little smiling fellow? It should have been great and bitter torments did rouse your spirits to a deed of blood.

CHRISTY [*doubtfully*] It should, maybe.

[74] LET ON: pretend. [75] WORD: their orders. [76] PRIESTEEN: little priest, used contemptuously.

WIDOW QUIN – It's more than "maybe" I'm saying, and it'd soften
my heart to see you sitting so simple with your cup and cake, and you
fitter to be saying your catechism than slaying your da.[77]

PEGEEN [*at counter, washing glasses*] There's talking[78] when any'd
see he's fit to be holding his head high with the wonders of the world.
Walk on from this, for I'll not have him tormented and he destroyed
travelling since Tuesday was a week.

WIDOW QUIN [*peaceably*] We'll be walking surely when his supper's done, and you'll find we're great company, young fellow, when
it's of the like of you and me you'd hear the penny poets[79] singing
in an August Fair.

CHRISTY [*innocently*] Did you kill your father?

PEGEEN [*contemptuously*] She did not. She hit himself[80] with a
worn pick, and the rusted poison did corrode his blood the way he
never overed it,[81] and died after. That was a sneaky kind of murder
did win small glory with the boys itself.

[*She crosses to* CHRISTY'S *left.*]

WIDOW QUIN [*with good-humour*] If it didn't, maybe all knows a
widow woman has buried her children and destroyed her man is a
wiser comrade for a young lad than a girl, the like of you, who'd go
helter-skeltering after any man would let you a wink upon the road.

PEGEEN [*breaking out into wild rage*] And you'll say that, Widow
Quin, and you gasping with the rage you had racing the hill beyond
to look on his face.

WIDOW QUIN [*laughing derisively*] Me, is it? Well, Father Reilly
has cuteness[82] to divide you now. [*She pulls* CHRISTY *up.*] There's
great temptation in a man did slay his da, and we'd best be going,
young fellow; so rise up and come with me.

PEGEEN [*seizing his arm*] He'll not stir. He's pot-boy in this place,
and I'll not have him stolen off and kidnapped while himself's abroad.

WIDOW QUIN – It'd be a crazy pot-boy'd lodge him in the shebeen[83]
where he works by day, so you'd have a right to come on, young fellow,
till you see my little houseen,[84] a perch off on the rising hill.

PEGEEN – Wait till morning, Christy Mahon. Wait till you lay eyes
on her leaky thatch is growing more pasture[85] for her buck goat than
her square of fields, and she without a tramp itself to keep in order
her place at all.

---

[77] DA: father.   [78] THERE'S TALKING: ironically—grand talk, great talk.   [79] PENNY
POETS: ballad-singers.   [80] HIMSELF: her husband.   [81] OVERED IT: recovered.
[82] CUTENESS: sharpness or ingenuity.   [83] SHEBEEN: an unlicensed place where in-
toxicating liquors are sold.   [84] HOUSEEN: little house.   [85] PASTURE: her thatch
roof has been up so long that grass has taken root there.

WIDOW QUIN—When you see me contriving in my little gardens, Christy Mahon, you'll swear the Lord God formed me to be living lone, and that there isn't my match in Mayo for thatching, or mowing, or shearing a sheep.

PEGEEN [*with noisy scorn*] It's true the Lord God formed you to contrive indeed. Doesn't the world know you reared a black ram at your own breast, so that the Lord Bishop of Connaught felt the elements of a Christian, and he eating it after in a kidney stew? Doesn't the world know you've been shaving the foxy skipper from France[86] for a threepenny bit and a sop of grass tobacco would wring the liver from a mountain goat you'd meet leaping the hills?

WIDOW QUIN [*with amusement*] Do you hear her now, young fellow? Do you hear the way she'll be rating at your own self when a week is by?

PEGEEN [*to* CHRISTY] Don't heed her. Tell her to go on into her pigsty and not plague us here.

WIDOW QUIN—I'm going; but he'll come with me.

PEGEEN [*shaking him*] Are you dumb, young fellow?

CHRISTY [*timidly, to* WIDOW QUIN] God increase you;[87] but I'm pot-boy in this place, and it's here I'd liefer[88] stay.

PEGEEN [*triumphantly*] Now you have heard him, and go on from this.

WIDOW QUIN [*looking round the room*] It's lonesome this hour crossing the hill, and if he won't come along with me, I'd have a right maybe to stop this night with yourselves. Let me stretch out on the settle, Pegeen Mike; and himself can lie by the hearth.

PEGEEN [*short and fiercely*] Faith,[89] I won't. Quit off[90] or I will send you now.

WIDOW QUIN [*gathering her shawl up*] Well, it's a terror to be aged a score. [*To* CHRISTY.] God bless you now, young fellow, and let you be wary, or there's right torment will await you here if you go romancing with her like, and she waiting only, as they bade me say, on a sheepskin parchment[91] to be wed with Shawn Keogh of Killakeen.

CHRISTY [*going to* PEGEEN *as she bolts door*] What's that she's after saying?

PEGEEN—Lies and blather, you've no call to mind. Well, isn't Shawn Keogh an impudent fellow to send up spying on me? Wait till I lay hands on him. Let him wait, I'm saying.

CHRISTY—And you're not wedding him at all?

[86] SKIPPER FROM FRANCE: from French trawlers fishing off the coast. [87] GOD INCREASE YOU: meaning your substance, an Irish blessing. [88] LIEFER: rather. [89] FAITH: in faith, not to be used lightly. [90] QUIT OFF: get out. [91] SHEEPSKIN PARCHMENT: the dispensation.

PEGEEN – I wouldn't wed him if a bishop came walking for to join us here.

CHRISTY – That God in glory may be thanked for that.

PEGEEN – There's your bed now. I've put a quilt upon you I'm after quilting a while since[92] with my own two hands, and you'd best stretch out now for your sleep, and may God give you a good rest till I call you in the morning when the cocks will crow.

CHRISTY [*as she goes to inner room*] May God and Mary and St. Patrick bless you and reward you, for your kindly talk. [*She shuts the door behind her. He settles his bed slowly, feeling the quilt with immense satisfaction.*] Well, it's a clean bed and soft with it,[93] and it's great luck and company I've won me in the end of time—two fine women fighting for the likes of me—till I'm thinking this night wasn't I a foolish fellow not to kill my father in the years gone by.

[92] A WHILE SINCE: a while ago. [93] SOFT WITH IT: soft too.

ACT TWO

Scene: As before. Brilliant morning light. CHRISTY, *looking bright and cheerful, is cleaning a girl's boots.*

CHRISTY [*to himself, counting jugs on dresser*] Half a hundred beyond. Ten there. A score that's above. Eighty jugs. Six cups and a broken one. Two plates. A power of glasses. Bottles, a schoolmaster'd be hard set to count, and enough in them, I'm thinking, to drunken all the wealth and wisdom of the County Clare.[1] [*He puts down the boot carefully.*] There's her boots now, nice and decent for her evening use, and isn't it grand brushes she has? [*He puts them down and goes by degrees to the looking-glass.*] Well, this'd be a fine place to be my whole life talking out with swearing Christians, in place of my old dogs and cat, and I stalking around, smoking my pipe and drinking my fill, and never a day's work but drawing a cork an odd time, or wiping a glass, or rinsing out a shiny tumbler for a decent man. [*He takes the looking-glass from the wall and puts it on the back of a chair; then sits down in front of it and begins washing his face.*] Didn't I know rightly I was handsome, though it was the divil's own mirror we had beyond, would twist a squint across an angel's brow, and I'll be growing fine from this day, the way I'll have a soft lovely skin on me and won't be the like of the clumsy young fellows do be ploughing all times in the earth and dung. [*He starts.*] Is she coming again? [*He looks out.*] Stranger girls. God help me, where'll I hide myself away and my long neck naked to the world? [*He looks out.*] I'd best go to the room maybe till I'm dressed again.

He gathers up his coat and the looking-glass, and runs into the inner room. The door is pushed open, and SUSAN BRADY *looks in, and knocks on door.*

SUSAN—There's nobody in it.

[*Knocks again.*]

ACT II: [1] COUNTY CLARE: Western county bordering the Atlantic between Galway and Kerry.

1886

NELLY [*pushing her in and following her, with* HONOR BLAKE *and* SARA TANSEY] It'd be early for them both to be out walking the hill.

SUSAN – I'm thinking Shawn Keogh was making game of us and there's no such man in it at all.

HONOR [*pointing to straw and quilt*] Look at that. He's been sleeping there in the night. Well, it'll be a hard case[2] if he's gone off now, the way we'll never set our eyes on a man killed his father, and we after rising early and destroying ourselves running fast on the hill.

NELLY – Are you thinking them's his boots?

SARA [*taking them up*] If they are, there should be his father's track on them. Did you never read in the papers the way murdered men do bleed and drip?

SUSAN – Is that blood there, Sara Tansey?

SARA [*smelling it*] That's bog water, I'm thinking, but it's his own they are surely, for I never seen the like of them for whitey mud, and red mud, and turf on them, and the fine sands of the sea. That man's been walking, I'm telling you.

[*She goes down right, putting on one of his boots.*]

SUSAN [*going to window*] Maybe he's stolen off to Belmullet[3] with the boots of Michael James, and you'd have a right so to follow after him, Sara Tansey, and you the one yoked the ass cart and drove ten miles to set your eyes on the man bit the yellow lady's nostril on the northern shore.

[*She looks out.*]

SARA [*running to window, with one boot on*] Don't be talking, and we fooled to-day. [*Putting on the other boot.*] There's a pair do fit me well, and I'll be keeping them for walking to the priest, when you'd be ashamed this place, going up winter and summer with nothing worth while to confess at all.

HONOR [*who has been listening at door*] Whisht! there's some one inside the room. [*She pushes door a chink open.*] It's a man.

[SARA *kicks off boots and puts them where they were.* *They all stand in a line looking through chink.*]

SARA – I'll call him. Mister! Mister! [*He puts in his head.*] Is Pegeen within?

CHRISTY [*coming in as meek as a mouse, with the looking-glass held behind his back*] She's above on the cnuceen,[4] seeking the nanny goats, the way she'd have a sup of goat's milk for to colour my tea.

SARA – And asking your pardon, is it you's the man killed his father?

---

[2] A HARD CASE: a sad state of affairs. [3] BELMULLET: small seaport on Mullet peninsula. [4] CNUCEEN: Irish for little hill.

CHRISTY [*sidling toward the nail where the glass was hanging*] I am, God help me!

SARA [*taking eggs she has brought*] Then my thousand welcomes to you, and I've run up with a brace of duck's eggs for your food to-day. Pegeen's ducks is no use, but these are the real rich sort. Hold out your hand and you'll see it's no lie I'm telling you.

CHRISTY [*coming forward shyly, and holding out his left hand*] They're a great and weighty size.

SUSAN—And I run up with a pat of butter, for it'd be a poor thing to have you eating your spuds dry, and you after running a great way since you did destroy your da.

CHRISTY—Thank you kindly.

HONOR—And I brought you a little cut of a cake, for you should have a thin stomach on you, and you that length walking the world.

NELLY—And I brought you a little laying pullet—boiled and all she is —was crushed at the fall of night by the curate's car. Feel the fat of that breast, Mister.

CHRISTY—It's bursting, surely.

[*He feels it with the back of his hand, in which he holds the presents.*]

SARA—Will you pinch it? Is your right hand too sacred for to use at all? [*She slips round behind him.*] It's a glass he has. Well, I never seen to this day a man with a looking-glass held to his back. Them that kills their fathers is a vain lot surely.

[GIRLS *giggle.*]

CHRISTY [*smiling innocently and piling presents on glass*] I'm very thankful to you all to-day. . . .

WIDOW QUIN [*coming in quickly, at door*] Sara Tansey, Susan Brady, Honor Blake! What in glory has you here at this hour of day?

GIRLS [*giggling*] That's the man killed his father.

WIDOW QUIN [*coming to them*] I know well it's the man; and I'm after putting him down in the sports below for racing, leaping, pitching, and the Lord knows what.

SARA [*exuberantly*] That's right, Widow Quin. I'll bet my dowry that he'll lick the world.

WIDOW QUIN—If you will, you'd have a right to have him fresh and nourished in place of nursing a feast. [*Taking presents.*] Are you fasting or fed, young fellow?

CHRISTY—Fasting, if you please.

WIDOW QUIN [*loudly*] Well, you're the lot. Stir up now and give him his breakfast. [*To* CHRISTY.] Come here to me [*she puts him on bench beside her while the girls make tea and get his breakfast*] and let you tell us your story before Pegeen will come, in place of grinning your ears off like the moon of May.

1888

CHRISTY [*beginning to be pleased*] It's a long story; you'd be destroyed listening.

WIDOW QUIN—Don't be letting on to be shy, a fine, gamey,[5] treacherous lad the like of you. Was it in your house beyond you cracked his skull?

CHRISTY [*shy but flattered*] It was not. We were digging spuds in his cold, sloping, stony, divil's patch of a field.

WIDOW QUIN—And you went asking money of him, or making talk of getting a wife would drive him from his farm?

CHRISTY—I did not, then; but there I was, digging and digging, and "You squinting idiot," says he, "let you walk down now and tell the priest you'll wed the Widow Casey in a score of days."

WIDOW QUIN—And what kind was she?

CHRISTY [*with horror*] A walking terror from beyond the hills, and she two score and five years, and two hundredweights and five pounds in the weighing scales, with a limping leg on her, and a blinded eye, and she a woman of noted misbehaviour with the old and young.

GIRLS [*clustering round him, serving him*] Glory be.

WIDOW QUIN—And what did he want driving you to wed her?

[*She takes a bit of the chicken.*]

CHRISTY [*eating with growing satisfaction*] He was letting on I was wanting a protector from the harshness of the world, and he without a thought the whole while but how he'd have her hut to live in and her gold to drink.

WIDOW QUIN—There's maybe worse than a dry hearth and a widow woman and your glass at night. So you hit him then?

CHRISTY [*getting almost excited*] I did not. "I won't wed her," says I, "when all know she did suckle me for six weeks when I came into the world, and she a hag this day with a tongue on her has the crows and seabirds scattered, the way they wouldn't cast a shadow on her garden with the dread of her curse."

WIDOW QUIN [*teasingly*] That one should be right company.

SARA [*eagerly*] Don't mind her. Did you kill him then?

CHRISTY—"She's too good for the like of you," says he, "and go on now or I'll flatten you out like a crawling beast has passed under a dray."[6] "You will not if I can help it," says I. "Go on," says he, "or I'll have the divil making garters of your limbs to-night." "You will not if I can help it," says I.

[*He sits up, brandishing his mug.*]

SARA—You were right surely.

CHRISTY [*impressively*] With that the sun came out between the

[5] GAMEY: merry. [6] DRAY: a little cart with or without wheels.

cloud and the hill, and it shining green in my face. "God have mercy on your soul," says he, lifting a scythe; "or on your own," says I, raising the loy.

s u s a n – That's a grand story.

h o n o r – He tells it lovely.

c h r i s t y [*flattered and confident, waving bone*] He gave a drive with the scythe, and I gave a lep[7] to the east. Then I turned around with my back to the north, and I hit a blow on the ridge of his skull, laid him stretched out, and he split to the knob of his gullet.

[*He raises the chicken bone to his Adam's apple.*]

g i r l s [*together*] Well, you're a marvel! Oh, God bless you! You're the lad surely!

s u s a n – I'm thinking the Lord God sent him this road to make a second husband to the Widow Quin, and she with a great yearning to be wedded, though all dread her here. Lift him on her knee, Sara Tansey.

w i d o w q u i n – Don't tease him.

s a r a [*going over to dresser and counter very quickly, and getting two glasses and porter*] You're heroes surely, and let you drink a supeen[8] with your arms linked like the outlandish lovers in the sailor's song. [*She links their arms and gives them the glasses.*] There now. Drink a health to the wonders of the western world,[9] the pirates, preachers, poteen-makers, with the jobbing jockies;[10] parching peelers, and the juries fill their stomachs selling judgments of the English law.

[*Brandishing the bottle.*]

w i d o w q u i n – That's a right toast, Sara Tansey. Now Christy.

They drink with their arms linked, he drinking with his left hand, she with her right. As they are drinking, pegeen mike *comes in with a milk can and stands aghast. They all spring away from* christy. *He goes down left.* widow quin *remains seated.*

p e g e e n [*angrily to* sara] What is it you're wanting?

s a r a [*twisting her apron*] An ounce of tobacco.

p e g e e n – Have you tuppence?[11]

s a r a – I've forgotten my purse.

p e g e e n – Then you'd best be getting it and not be fooling us here. [*To the* widow quin, *with more elaborate scorn.*] And what is it you're wanting, Widow Quin?

w i d o w q u i n [*insolently*] A penn'orth[12] of starch.

---

[7] lep: a leap. [8] supeen: a little sup. [9] western world: western Ireland. [10] jobbing jockies: men who go round breaking in horses. [11] tuppence: two pence. [12] penn'orth: penny worth.

PEGEEN [*breaking out*] And you without a white shift[13] or a shirt in your whole family since the drying of the flood. I've no starch for the like of you, and let you walk on now to Killamuck.

WIDOW QUIN [*turning to* CHRISTY, *as she goes out with the girls*] Well, you're mighty huffy this day, Pegeen Mike, and, you young fellow, let you not forget the sports and racing when the noon is by.

[*They go out.*]

PEGEEN [*imperiously*] Fling out that rubbish and put them cups away. [CHRISTY *tidies away in great haste.*] Shove in the bench by the wall. [*He does so.*] And hang that glass[14] on the nail. What disturbed it at all?

CHRISTY [*very meekly*] I was making myself decent only, and this a fine country for young lovely girls.

PEGEEN [*sharply*] Whisht your talking of girls.

[*Goes to counter on right.*]

CHRISTY—Wouldn't any wish to be decent in a place . . .

PEGEEN—Whisht I'm saying.

CHRISTY [*looks at her face for a moment with great misgivings, then as a last effort, takes up a loy, and goes towards her, with feigned assurance*] It was with a loy the like of that I killed my father.

PEGEEN [*still sharply*] You've told me that story six times since the dawn of day.

CHRISTY [*reproachfully*] It's a queer thing you wouldn't care to be hearing it and them girls after walking four miles to be listening to me now.

PEGEEN [*turning round astonished*] Four miles?

CHRISTY [*apologetically*] Didn't himself say there were only bona fides[15] living in the place?

PEGEEN—It's bona fides by the road they are, but that lot came over the river lepping[16] the stones. It's not three perches when you go like that, and I was down this morning looking on the papers the post-boy does have in his bag. [*With meaning and emphasis.*] For there was great news this day, Christopher Mahon.

[*She goes into room on left.*]

CHRISTY [*suspiciously*] Is it news of my murder?

PEGEEN [*inside*] Murder, indeed.

CHRISTY [*loudly*] A murdered da?

PEGEEN [*coming in again and crossing right*] There was not, but a

---

[13] SHIFT: a woman's slip. [14] GLASS: the mirror. [15] BONA FIDES: earlier Michael James had reassured Christy that no one except a widow lived within four miles of his public house so that anyone coming at any hour could *bona fide* call for a drink and be served without prejudice to the licensing laws. [16] LEPPING: leaping.

story filled half a page of the hanging of a man. Ah, that should be a fearful end, young fellow, and it worst of all for a man destroyed his da, for the like of him would get small mercies, and when it's dead he is, they'd put him in a narrow grave, with cheap sacking wrapping him round, and pour down quicklime on his head, the way you'd see a woman pouring any frish-frash[17] from a cup.

CHRISTY [*very miserably*] Oh, God help me. Are you thinking I'm safe? You were saying at the fall of night, I was shut of[18] jeopardy and I here with yourselves.

PEGEEN [*severely*] You'll be shut of jeopardy no place if you go talking with a pack of wild girls the like of them do be walking abroad with the peelers, talking whispers at the fall of night.

CHRISTY [*with terror*] And you're thinking they'd tell?

PEGEEN [*with mock sympathy*] Who knows, God help you?

CHRISTY [*loudly*] What joy would they have to bring hanging to the likes of me?

PEGEEN—It's queer joys they have, and who knows the thing they'd do, if it'd make the green stones cry itself to think of you swaying and swiggling at the butt of a rope, and you with a fine, stout neck, God bless you! the way you'd be a half an hour, in great anguish, getting your death.

CHRISTY [*getting his boots and putting them on*] If there's that terror of them, it'd be best, maybe, I went on wandering like Esau[19] or Cain and Abel[20] on the sides of Neifin[21] or the Erris plain.[22]

PEGEEN [*beginning to play with him*] It would, maybe, for I've heard the Circuit Judges this place is a heartless crew.

CHRISTY [*bitterly*] It's more than Judges this place is a heartless crew. [*Looking up at her.*] And isn't it a poor thing to be starting again and I a lonesome fellow will be looking out on women and girls the way the needy fallen spirits do be looking on the Lord?

PEGEEN—What call[23] have you to be that lonesome when there's poor girls walking Mayo in their thousands now?

CHRISTY [*grimly*] It's well you know what call I have. It's well you know it's a lonesome thing to be passing small towns with the lights shining sideways when the night is down, or going in strange places

---

[17] FRISH-FRASH: a kind of Indian meal and raw cabbage boiled down as thin as gruel. [18] SHUT OF: to be rid of. [19] ESAU: elder son of Isaac and Rebekah and brother of Jacob. Christy, like Esau, has lost his birthright—the right to inherit Old Mahon's "divil's patch," and so must provide for himself. [20] CAIN AND ABEL: Christy like Cain is guilty of murder and now shares the curse of Cain to be a wanderer and a fugitive on the face of the earth. [21] NEIFIN: Mayo's Mount Nephin (Irish, *Néifin*) just west of Lough Conn. [22] ERRIS PLAIN: the plain of North Mayo. [23] WHAT CALL: what right.

with a dog noising before you and a dog noising behind, or drawn to the cities where you'd hear a voice kissing and talking deep love in every shadow of the ditch, and you passing on with an empty, hungry stomach failing from your heart.

PEGEEN – I'm thinking you're an odd man, Christy Mahon. The oddest walking fellow I ever set my eyes on to this hour to-day.

CHRISTY – What would any be but odd men and they living lonesome in the world?

PEGEEN – I'm not odd, and I'm my whole life with my father only.

CHRISTY [*with infinite admiration*] How would a lovely handsome woman the like of you be lonesome when all men should be thronging around to hear the sweetness of your voice, and the little infant children should be pestering your steps I'm thinking, and you walking the roads.

PEGEEN – I'm hard set to know what way a coaxing fellow the like of yourself should be lonesome either.

CHRISTY – Coaxing?

PEGEEN – Would you have me think a man never talked with the girls would have the words you've spoken to-day? It's only letting on you are to be lonesome, the way you'd get around me now.

CHRISTY – I wish to God I was letting on; but I was lonesome all times, and born lonesome, I'm thinking, as the moon of dawn.

[*Going to door.*]

PEGEEN [*puzzled by his talk*] Well, it's a story I'm not understanding at all why you'd be worse than another, Christy Mahon, and you a fine lad with the great savagery to destroy your da.

CHRISTY – It's little I'm understanding myself, saving only that my heart's scalded this day, and I going off stretching out the earth between us, the way I'll not be waking near you another dawn of the year till the two of us do arise to hope or judgment with the saints of God, and now I'd best be going with my wattle[24] in my hand, for hanging is a poor thing [*turning to go*], and it's little welcome only is left me in this house to-day.

PEGEEN [*sharply*] Christy! [*He turns round.*] Come here to me. [*He goes towards her.*] Lay down that switch and throw some sods on the fire. You're pot-boy in this place, and I'll not have you mitch off[25] from us now.

CHRISTY – You were saying I'd be hanged if I stay.

PEGEEN [*quite kindly at last*] I'm after going down and reading the fearful crimes of Ireland for two weeks or three, and there wasn't a

[24] WATTLE: a short thick stick. [25] MITCH OFF: to sneak away, to play truant.

word of your murder. [*Getting up and going over to the counter.*]
They've likely not found the body. You're safe so[26] with ourselves.

CHRISTY [*astonished, slowly*] It's making game of me you were [*following her with fearful joy*], and I can stay so, working at your side,
and I not lonesome from this mortal day.

PEGEEN – What's to hinder you staying, except the widow woman or
the young girls would inveigle[27] you off?

CHRISTY [*with rapture*] And I'll have your words from this day filling
my ears, and that look is come upon you meeting my two eyes, and I
watching you loafing around in the warm sun, or rinsing your ankles
when the night is come.

PEGEEN [*kindly, but a little embarrassed*] I'm thinking you'll be a
loyal young lad to have working around, and if you vexed me a while
since with your leaguing[28] with the girls, I wouldn't give a thraneen[29]
for a lad hadn't a mighty spirit in him and a gamey heart.

[SHAWN KEOGH *runs in carrying a cleeve*[30] *on his back,
followed by the* WIDOW QUIN.]

SHAWN [*to* PEGEEN] I was passing below, and I seen your mountainy
sheep eating cabbages in Jimmy's field. Run up or they'll be bursting
surely.

PEGEEN – Oh, God mend them![31]

[*She puts a shawl over her head and runs out.*]

CHRISTY [*looking from one to the other. Still in high spirits*] I'd best
go to her aid maybe. I'm handy with ewes.

WIDOW QUIN [*closing the door*] She can do that much, and there is
Shaneen has long speeches for to tell you now.

[*She sits down with an amused smile.*]

SHAWN [*taking something from his pocket and offering it to* CHRISTY]
Do you see that, mister?

CHRISTY [*looking at it*] The half of a ticket to the Western States![32]

SHAWN [*trembling with anxiety*] I'll give it to you and my new hat
[*pulling it out of hamper*]; and my breeches with the double seat
[*pulling it out*]; and my new coat is woven from the blackest shearings
for three miles around [*giving him the coat*]; I'll give you the whole of
them, and my blessing, and the blessing of Father Reilly itself, maybe,
if you'll quit from this and leave us in the peace we had till last night
at the fall of dark.

---

[26] SAFE SO: in that case. [27] INVEIGLE: lure. [28] LEAGUING: mixing with.
[29] THRANEEN: a straw, a withered stalk of meadow grass. [30] CLEEVE: a basket, a
creel. [31] GOD MEND THEM: serve them right. [32] HALF . . . STATES: one-way
ticket to America.

1894

CHRISTY [*with a new arrogance*] And for what is it you're wanting to get shut of me?

SHAWN [*looking to the* WIDOW *for help*] I'm a poor scholar with middling faculties to coin a lie, so I'll tell you the truth, Christy Mahon. I'm wedding with Pegeen beyond, and I don't think well of having a clever fearless man the like of you dwelling in her house.

CHRISTY [*almost pugnaciously*] And you'd be using bribery for to banish me?

SHAWN [*in an imploring voice*] Let you not take it badly, mister honey, isn't beyond the best place for you where you'll have golden chains and shiny coats and you riding upon hunters with the ladies of the land.

[*He makes an eager sign to the* WIDOW QUIN *to come to help him.*]

WIDOW QUIN [*coming over*] It's true for him, and you'd best quit off and not have that poor girl setting her mind on you, for there's Shaneen thinks she wouldn't suit you though all is saying that she'll wed you now.

[CHRISTY *beams with delight.*]

SHAWN [*in terrified earnest*] She wouldn't suit you, and she with the divil's own temper the way you'd be strangling one another in a score of days. [*He makes the movement of strangling with his hands.*] It's the like of me only that she's fit for, a quiet simple fellow wouldn't raise a hand upon her if she scratched itself.

WIDOW QUIN [*putting* SHAWN'S *hat on* CHRISTY] Fit them clothes on you anyhow, young fellow, and he'd maybe loan them to you for the sports. [*Pushing him towards inner door.*] Fit them on and you can give your answer when you have them tried.

CHRISTY [*beaming, delighted with the clothes*] I will then. I'd like herself to see me in them tweeds and hat.

[*He goes into room and shuts the door.*]

SHAWN [*in great anxiety*] He'd like herself to see them. He'll not leave us, Widow Quin. He's a score of divils in him the way it's well nigh certain he will wed Pegeen.

WIDOW QUIN [*jeeringly*] It's true all girls are fond of courage and do hate the like of you.

SHAWN [*walking about in desperation*] Oh, Widow Quin, what'll I be doing now? I'd inform again him,[33] but he'd burst from Kilmainham[34] and he'd be sure and certain to destroy me. If I wasn't so God-fearing, I'd near have courage to come behind him and run a pike[35] into his side. Oh, it's a hard case to be an orphan and not to have your

33 AGAIN HIM: against him. 34 KILMAINHAM: once notorious Dublin jail.
35 PIKE: pitchfork.

father that you're used to, and you'd easy kill and make yourself a hero in the sight of all. [*Coming up to her.*] Oh, Widow Quin, will you find me some contrivance when I've promised you a ewe?

WIDOW QUIN – A ewe's a small thing, but what would you give me if I did wed him and did save you so?

SHAWN [*with astonishment*] You?

WIDOW QUIN – Aye. Would you give me the red cow you have and the mountainy ram, and the right of way across your rye path, and a load of dung at Michaelmas,[36] and turbary[37] upon the western hill?

SHAWN [*radiant with hope*] I would surely, and I'd give you the wedding-ring I have, and the loan of a new suit, the way you'd have him decent on the wedding-day. I'd give you two kids for your dinner, and a gallon of poteen, and I'd call the piper on the long car[38] to your wedding from Crossmolina[39] or from Ballina.[40] I'd give you . . .

WIDOW QUIN That'll do, so, and let you whisht, for he's coming now again.

[CHRISTY *comes in very natty in the new clothes.*
WIDOW QUIN *goes to him admiringly.*]

WIDOW QUIN – If you seen yourself now, I'm thinking you'd be too proud to speak to us at all, and it'd be a pity surely to have your like sailing from Mayo to the Western World.[41]

CHRISTY [*as proud as a peacock*] I'm not going. If this is a poor place itself, I'll make myself contented to be lodging here.

[WIDOW QUIN *makes a sign to* SHAWN *to leave them.*]

SHAWN – Well, I'm going measuring the racecourse while the tide is low, so I'll leave you the garments and my blessing for the sports to-day. God bless you!

[*He wriggles out.*]

WIDOW QUIN [*admiring* CHRISTY] Well, you're mighty spruce, young fellow. Sit down now while you're quiet till you talk with me.

CHRISTY [*swaggering*] I'm going abroad on the hillside for to seek Pegeen.

WIDOW QUIN – You'll have time and plenty for to seek Pegeen, and you heard me saying at the fall of night the two of us should be great company.

CHRISTY – From this out I'll have no want of company when all sorts is bringing me their food and clothing [*he swaggers to the door, tightening his belt*], the way they'd set their eyes upon a gallant orphan

---

[36] MICHAELMAS: feast of St. Michael and All Angels, September 29th. [37] TURBARY: right to cut turf (peat). [38] LONG CAR: an enlarged, four-wheeled, jaunting car. [39] CROSSMOLINA: a small market town of North-East Mayo. [40] BALLINA: market town and small seaport of North Mayo. [41] WESTERN WORLD: America.

cleft his father with one blow to the breeches belt. [*He opens door, then staggers back.*] Saints of glory! Holy angels from the throne of light!

WIDOW QUIN [*going over*] What ails you?

CHRISTY – It's the walking spirit of my murdered da!

WIDOW QUIN [*looking out*] Is it that tramper?

CHRISTY [*wildly*] Where'll I hide my poor body from that ghost of hell?

> [*The door is pushed open, and* OLD MAHON *appears on threshold.* CHRISTY *darts in behind door.*]

WIDOW QUIN [*in great amusement*] God save you, my poor man.

MAHON [*gruffly*] Did you see a young lad passing this way in the early morning or the fall of night?

WIDOW QUIN – You're a queer kind to walk in not saluting at all.

MAHON – Did you see the young lad?

WIDOW QUIN [*stiffly*] What kind was he?

MAHON – An ugly young streeler[42] with a murderous gob[43] on him, and a little switch in his hand. I met a tramper seen him coming this way at the fall of night.

WIDOW QUIN – There's harvest hundreds do be passing these days for the Sligo[44] boat. For what is it you're wanting him, my poor man?

MAHON – I want to destroy him for breaking the head on me with the clout of a loy. [*He takes off a big hat, and shows his head in a mass of bandages and plaster, with some pride.*] It was he did that, and amn't I a great wonder to think I've traced him ten days with that rent in my crown?

WIDOW QUIN [*taking his head in both hands and examining it with extreme delight*] That was a great blow. And who hit you? A robber maybe?

MAHON – It was my own son hit me, and he the divil a robber, or anything else, but a dirty, stuttering lout.

WIDOW QUIN [*letting go his skull and wiping her hands in her apron*] You'd best be wary of a mortified scalp, I think they call it, lepping around with that wound in the splendour of the sun. It was a bad blow surely, and you should have vexed him fearful to make him strike that gash in his da.

MAHON – Is it me?

WIDOW QUIN [*amusing herself*] Aye. And isn't it a great shame when the old and hardened do torment the young?

[42] STREELER: an idle, slovenly person. [43] GOB: mouth. [44] SLIGO: large town and seaport north of Mayo. Seasonal migrants sailed from Sligo for Scotland and England to seek work as harvesters and, with their meagre earnings, to return to pay the rents on their tiny holdings.

M A H O N [*raging*] Torment him is it? And I after holding out with the patience of a martyred saint till there's nothing but destruction on, and I'm driven out in my old age with none to aid me.

W I D O W Q U I N [*greatly amused*] It's a sacred wonder the way that wickedness will spoil a man.

M A H O N – My wickedness, is it? Amn't I after saying it is himself has me destroyed, and he a liar on walls,[45] a talker of folly, a man you'd see stretched the half of the day in the brown ferns with his belly to the sun.

W I D O W Q U I N – Not working at all?

M A H O N – The divil a work, or if he did itself, you'd see him raising up a haystack like the stalk of a rush, or driving our last cow till he broke her leg at the hip, and when he wasn't at that he'd be fooling over little birds he had—finches and felts[46]—or making mugs at his own self in the bit of a glass we had hung on the wall.

W I D O W Q U I N [*looking at* CHRISTY] What way was he so foolish? It was running wild after the girls maybe?

M A H O N [*with a shout of derision*] Running wild, is it? If he seen a red petticoat coming swinging over the hill, he'd be off to hide in the sticks, and you'd see him shooting out his sheep's eyes between the little twigs and the leaves, and his two ears rising like a hare looking out through a gap. Girls, indeed!

W I D O W Q U I N – It was drink maybe?

M A H O N – And he a poor fellow would get drunk on the smell of a pint. He'd a queer rotten stomach, I'm telling you, and when I gave him three pulls from my pipe a while since, he was taken with contortions till I had to send him in the ass cart to the females' nurse.

W I D O W Q U I N [*clasping her hands*] Well, I never till this day heard tell of a man the like of that!

M A H O N – I'd take a mighty oath you didn't surely, and wasn't he the laughing joke of every female woman where four baronies meet, the way the girls would stop their weeding if they seen him coming the road to let a roar at him, and call him the looney[47] of Mahon's.

W I D O W Q U I N – I'd give the world and all to see the like of him. What kind was he?

M A H O N – A small low fellow.

W I D O W Q U I N – And dark?

M A H O N – Dark and dirty.

W I D O W Q U I N [*considering*] I'm thinking I seen him.

---

[45] LIAR ON WALLS: perhaps of the gossiping and boasting of men leaning against field walls. [46] FELTS: fieldfares. [47] LOONEY: idle, stupid fellow.

1898

M A H O N   [*eagerly*] An ugly young blackguard.[48]

W I D O W   Q U I N – A hideous, fearful villain, and the spit of you.

M A H O N – What way is he fled?

W I D O W   Q U I N – Gone over the hills to catch a coasting steamer to the north or south.

M A H O N – Could I pull up on him now?

W I D O W   Q U I N – If you'll cross the sands below where the tide is out, you'll be in it as soon as himself, for he had to go round ten miles by the top of the bay. [*She points to the door.*] Strike down by the head beyond and then follow on the roadway to the north and east.

[M A H O N *goes abruptly.*]

W I D O W   Q U I N   [*shouting after him*] Let you give him a good vengeance when you come up with him, but don't put yourself in the power of the law, for it'd be a poor thing to see a judge in his black cap reading out his sentence on a civil warrior the like of you.

[*She swings the door to and looks at* C H R I S T Y, *who is cowering in terror, for a moment, then she bursts into a laugh.*]

W I D O W   Q U I N – Well, you're the walking playboy of the western world, and that's the poor man you had divided to his breeches belt.

C H R I S T Y   [*looking out: then, to her*] What'll Pegeen say when she hears that story? What'll she be saying to me now?

W I D O W   Q U I N – She'll knock the head of you, I'm thinking, and drive you from the door. God help her to be taking you for a wonder, and you a little schemer making up a story you destroyed your da.

C H R I S T Y   [*turning to the door, nearly speechless with rage, half to himself*] To be letting on he was dead, and coming back to his life, and following after me like an old weasel tracing a rat, and coming in here laying desolation between my own self and the fine women of Ireland, and he a kind of carcase that you'd fling upon the sea.[49] . . .

W I D O W   Q U I N   [*more soberly*] There's talking[50] for a man's one only son.

C H R I S T Y   [*breaking out*] His one son, is it? May I meet him with one tooth and it aching, and one eye to be seeing seven and seventy divils in the twists of the road, and one old timber leg on him to limp into the scalding grave. [*Looking out.*] There he is now crossing the strands, and that the Lord God would send a high wave to wash him from the world.

W I D O W   Q U I N   [*scandalised*] Have you no shame? [*Putting her hand on his shoulder and turning him round.*] What ails you? Near crying, is it?

[48] BLACKGUARD: a scoundrel.   [49] CARCASE . . . SEA: dead sheep and cattle are pushed over the cliffs into the ocean.   [50] THERE'S TALKING: ironically, that's a fine thing to be saying.

CHRISTY [*in despair and grief*] Amn't I after seeing the love-light of the star of knowledge[51] shining from her brow, and hearing words would put you thinking on the holy Brigid[52] speaking to the infant saints, and now she'll be turning again, and speaking hard words to me, like an old woman with a spavindy ass[53] she'd have, urging on a hill.

WIDOW QUIN—There's poetry talk for a girl you'd see itching and scratching, and she with a stale stink of poteen on her from selling in the shop.

CHRISTY [*impatiently*] It's her like is fitted to be handling merchandise in the heavens above, and what'll I be doing now, I ask you, and I a kind of wonder was jilted by the heavens when a day was by.

  [*There is a distant noise of girls' voices.* WIDOW QUIN *looks from window and comes to him, hurriedly.*]

WIDOW QUIN—You'll be doing like myself, I'm thinking, when I did destroy my man, for I'm above many's the day, odd times in great spirits, abroad in the sunshine, darning a stocking or stitching a shift, and odd times again looking out on the schooners, hookers,[54] trawlers is sailing the sea, and I thinking on the gallant hairy fellows are drifting beyond, and myself long years living alone.

CHRISTY [*interested*] You're like me, so.

WIDOW QUIN—I am your like, and it's for that I'm taking a fancy to you, and I with my little houseen above where there'd be myself to tend you, and none to ask were you a murderer or what at all.

CHRISTY—And what would I be doing if I left Pegeen?

WIDOW QUIN—I've nice jobs you could be doing, gathering shells to make a whitewash for our hut within, building up a little goose-house, or stretching a new skin on an old curragh[55] I have, and if my hut is far from all sides, it's there you'll meet the wisest old men, I tell you, at the corner of my wheel,[56] and it's there yourself and me will have great times whispering and hugging. . . .

VOICES [*outside, calling far away*] Christy! Christy Mahon! Christy!

CHRISTY—Is it Pegeen Mike?

WIDOW QUIN—It's the young girls, I'm thinking, coming to bring you to the sports below, and what is it you'll have me to tell them now?

CHRISTY—Aid me for to win Pegeen. It's herself only that I'm seeking

---

[51] STAR OF KNOWLEDGE: conventional Irish love-image. [52] BRIGID: St. Brigid, or Bride (*ca.* 451–525), Abbess of Kildare, and, after St. Patrick greatest and most venerated of Irish saints. [53] SPAVINDY ASS: an ass lame with spavin, a disease of the hock. [54] HOOKERS: a one-masted fishing-smack. [55] CURRAGH: (or curagh) a light, open boat made of a frame-work of lath covered formerly with hide or leather but now with tarred canvas. [56] WHEEL: spinning wheel.

1900

now. [WIDOW QUIN *gets up and goes to window.*] Aid me for to win her, and I'll be asking God to stretch a hand to you in the hour of death, and lead you short cuts through the Meadows of Ease, and up the floor of Heaven to the Footstool of the Virgin's Son.

WIDOW QUIN – There's praying!

VOICES [*nearer*] Christy! Christy Mahon!

CHRISTY [*with agitation*] They're coming. Will you swear to aid and save me for the love of Christ?

WIDOW QUIN [*looks at him for a moment*] If I aid you, will you swear to give me a right of way I want, and a mountainy ram, and a load of dung at Michaelmas, the time that you'll be master here?

CHRISTY – I will, by the elements and stars of night.

WIDOW QUIN – Then we'll not say a word of the old fellow, the way Pegeen won't know your story till the end of time.

CHRISTY – And if he chances to return again?

WIDOW QUIN – We'll swear he's a maniac and not your da. I could take an oath I seen him raving on the sands to-day.

[GIRLS *run in.*]

SUSAN – Come on to the sports below. Pegeen says you're to come.

SARA TANSEY – The lepping's beginning, and we've a jockey's suit to fit upon you for the mule race on the sands below.

HONOR – Come on, will you?

CHRISTY – I will then if Pegeen's beyond.

SARA – She's in the boreen[57] making game of Shaneen Keogh.

CHRISTY – Then I'll be going to her now.

[*He runs out followed by the girls.*]

WIDOW QUIN – Well, if the worst comes in the end of all, it'll be great game to see there's none to pity him but a widow woman, the like of me, has buried her children and destroyed her man.

[*She goes out.*]

---

57 BOREEN: a narrow road, a lane.

ACT THREE

Scene: As before. Later in the day. JIMMY *comes in, slightly drunk*

JIMMY [*calls*] Pegeen! [*Crosses to inner door.*] Pegeen Mike! [*Comes back again into the room.*] Pegeen! [PHILLY *comes in in the same state.*] [*To* PHILLY.] Did you see herself?

PHILLY – I did not; but I sent Shawn Keogh with the ass cart for to bear him home. [*Trying cupboards which are locked.*] Well, isn't he a nasty man to get into such staggers at a morning wake? and isn't herself the divil's daughter for locking, and she so fussy after that young gaffer,[1] you might take your death with drought and none to heed you?

JIMMY – It's little wonder she'd be fussy, and he after bringing bankrupt ruin on the roulette man, and the trick-o'-the-loop[2] man, and breaking the nose of the cockshot-man,[3] and winning all in the sports below, racing, lepping, dancing, and the Lord knows what! He's right luck, I'm telling you.

PHILLY – If he has, he'll be rightly hobbled[4] yet, and he not able to say ten words without making a brag of the way he killed his father, and the great blow he hit with the loy.

JIMMY – A man can't hang by his own informing, and his father should be rotten by now.

[OLD MAHON *passes window slowly.*]

PHILLY – Supposing a man's digging spuds in that field with a long spade, and supposing he flings up the two halves of that skull, what'll be said then in the papers and the courts of law?

JIMMY – They'd say it was an old Dane,[5] maybe, was drowned in the flood. [OLD MAHON *comes in and sits down near door listening.*] Did you never hear tell of the skulls they have in the city of Dublin, ranged out like blue jugs in a cabin of Connaught?

PHILLY – And you believe that?

ACT III: [1] GAFFER: a young chap. [2] TRICK-O'-THE-LOOP: to guess the center loop in a little leather belt. [3] COCKSHOT-MAN: a man with his face blackened, except one cheek and eye, standing shots of a wooden ball behind a board with a large hole in the middle. [4] HOBBLED: legs tied together like an animal. [5] DANE: Vikings raided Irish coast from the 9th to the 12th centuries.

J I M M Y [*pugnaciously*] Didn't a lad see them and he after coming from harvesting in the Liverpool boat? "They have them there," says he, "making a show of the great people there was one time walking the world. White skulls and black skulls and yellow skulls, and some with full teeth, and some haven't only but one."

P H I L L Y – It was no lie, maybe, for when I was a young lad, there was a graveyard beyond the house with the remnants of a man who had thighs as long as your arm. He was a horrid man, I'm telling you, and there was many a fine Sunday I'd put him together for fun, and he with shiny bones, you wouldn't meet the like of these days in the cities of the world.

M A H O N [*getting up*] You wouldn't is it? Lay your eyes on that skull, and tell me where and when there was another the like of it, is splintered only from the blow of a loy.

P H I L L Y – Glory be to God! And who hit you at all?

M A H O N [*triumphantly*] It was my own son hit me. Would you believe that?

J I M M Y – Well, there's wonders hidden in the heart of man!

P H I L L Y [*suspiciously*] And what way was it done?

M A H O N [*wandering about the room*] I'm after walking hundreds and long scores of miles, winning clean beds and the fill of my belly four times in the day, and I doing nothing but telling stories of that naked truth. [*He comes to them a little aggressively.*] Give me a supeen and I'll tell you now.

> [WIDOW QUIN *comes in and stands aghast behind him.*
> *He is facing* JIMMY *and* PHILLY, *who are on the left.*]

J I M M Y – Ask herself beyond. She's the stuff hidden in her shawl.

W I D O W Q U I N [*coming to* MAHON *quickly*] You here, is it? You didn't go far at all?

M A H O N – I seen the coasting steamer passing, and I got a drought upon me and a cramping leg, so I said, "The divil go along with him," and turned again. [*Looking under her shawl.*] And let you give me a supeen, for I'm destroyed travelling since Tuesday was a week.

W I D O W Q U I N [*getting a glass, in a cajoling tone*] Sit down then by the fire and take your ease for a space. You've a right to be destroyed indeed, with your walking, and fighting, and facing the sun. [*Giving him poteen from a stone jar she has brought in.*] There now is a drink for you, and may it be to your happiness and length of life.

M A H O N [*taking glass greedily, and sitting down by fire*] God increase you!

W I D O W Q U I N [*taking men to the right stealthily*] Do you know what? That man's raving from his wound to-day, for I met him a while

1903

since telling a rambling tale of a tinker had him destroyed. Then he heard of Christy's deed, and he up and says it was his son had cracked his skull. O isn't madness a fright, for he'll go killing someone yet, and he thinking it's the man has struck him so?

JIMMY [*entirely convinced*] It's a fright surely. I knew a party was kicked in the head by a red mare, and he went killing horses a great while, till he eat the insides of a clock and died after.

PHILLY [*with suspicion*] Did he see Christy?

WIDOW QUIN – He didn't. [*With a warning gesture.*] Let you not be putting him in mind of him, or you'll be likely summoned if there's murder done. [*Looking round at* MAHON.] Whisht! He's listening. Wait now till you hear me taking him easy and unravelling all. [*She goes to* MAHON.] And what way are you feeling, mister? Are you in content-ment now?

MAHON [*slightly emotional from his drink*] I'm poorly only, for it's a hard story the way I'm left to-day, when it was I did tend him from his hour of birth, and he a dunce never reached his second book, the way he'd come from school, many's the day, with his legs lamed under him, and he blackened with his beatings like a tinker's ass. It's a hard story, I'm saying, the way some do have their next and nighest raising up a hand of murder on them, and some is lonesome getting their death with lamentation in the dead of night.

WIDOW QUIN [*not knowing what to say*] To hear you talking so quiet, who'd know you were the same fellow we seen pass to-day?

MAHON – I'm the same surely. The wrack and ruin of threescore years; and it's a terror to live that length, I tell you, and to have your sons going to the dogs against you, and you wore out scolding them, and skelping[6] them, and God knows what.

PHILLY [*to* JIMMY] He's not raving. [*To* WIDOW QUIN.] Will you ask him what kind was his son?

WIDOW QUIN [*to* MAHON, *with a peculiar look*] Was your son that hit you a lad of one year and a score maybe, a great hand at racing and lepping and licking the world?

MAHON [*turning on her with a roar of rage*] Didn't you hear me say he was the fool of men, the way from this out he'll know the orphan's lot with old and young making game of him and they swearing, raging, kicking at him like a mangy cur.

[*A great burst of cheering outside, some way off.*]

MAHON [*putting his hands to his ears*] What in the name of God do they want roaring below?

[6] SKELPING: hitting.

1904

WIDOW QUIN [*with the shade of a smile*] They're cheering a young lad, the champion playboy of the Western World.

[*More cheering.*]

MAHON [*going to window*] It'd split my heart to hear them, and I with pulses in my brain-pan[7] for a week gone by. Is it racing they are?

JIMMY [*looking from door*] It is then. They are mounting him for the mule race will be run upon the sands. That's the playboy on the winkered[8] mule.

MAHON [*puzzled*] That lad, is it? If you said it was a fool he was, I'd have laid a mighty oath he was the likeness of my wandering son. [*Uneasily, putting his hand to his head.*] Faith, I'm thinking I'll go walking for to view the race.

WIDOW QUIN [*stopping him, sharply*] You will not. You'd best take the road to Belmullet, and not be dilly-dallying in this place where there isn't a spot you could sleep.

PHILLY [*coming forward*] Don't mind her. Mount there on the bench and you'll have a view of the whole. They're hurrying before the tide will rise, and it'd be near over if you went down the pathway through the crags below.

MAHON [*mounts on bench,* WIDOW QUIN *beside him*] That's a right view again the edge of the sea. They're coming now from the point. He's leading. Who is he at all?

WIDOW QUIN – He's the champion of the world, I tell you, and there isn't a hap'orth[9] isn't falling lucky to his hands to-day.

PHILLY [*looking out, interested in the race*] Look at that. They're pressing him now.

JIMMY – He'll win it yet.

PHILLY – Take you time, Jimmy Farrell. It's too soon to say.

WIDOW QUIN [*shouting*] Watch him taking the gate. There's riding.

JIMMY [*cheering*] More power to the young lad!

MAHON – He's passing the third.

JIMMY – He'll lick them yet!

WIDOW QUIN – He'd lick them if he was running races with a score itself.

MAHON – Look at the mule he has, kicking the stars.

WIDOW QUIN – There was a lep! [*Catching hold of* MAHON *in her excitement.*] He's fallen! He's mounted again! Faith, he's passing them all!

JIMMY – Look at him skelping her!

[7] BRAIN-PAN: the skull. [8] WINKERED: wearing blinkers. [9] HAP'ORTH: a halfpenny worth.

1905

PHILLY—And the mountain girls hooshing[10] him on!

JIMMY—It's the last turn! The post's cleared for them now!

MAHON—Look at the narrow place. He'll be into the bogs! [*With a yell.*] Good rider! He's through it again!

JIMMY—He's neck and neck!

MAHON—Good boy[11] to him! Flames, but he's in!

[*Great cheering, in which all join.*]

MAHON [*with hesitation*] What's that? They're raising him up. They're coming this way. [*With a roar of rage and astonishment.*] It's Christy! by the stars of God! I'd know his way of spitting and he astride the moon.

[*He jumps down and makes a run for the door, but* WIDOW QUIN *catches him and pulls him back.*]

WIDOW QUIN—Stay quiet, will you? That's not your son. [*To* JIMMY.] Stop him, or you'll get a month for the abetting of manslaughter and be fined as well.

JIMMY—I'll hold him.

MAHON [*struggling*] Let me out! Let me out, the lot of you! till I have my vengeance on his head to-day.

WIDOW QUIN [*shaking him, vehemently*] That's not your son. That's a man is going to make a marriage with the daughter of this house, a place with fine trade, with a licence, and with poteen too.

MAHON [*amazed*] That man marrying a decent and a moneyed[12] girl! Is it mad yous are? Is it in a crazy-house for females that I'm landed now?

WIDOW QUIN—It's mad yourself is with the blow upon your head. That lad is the wonder of the Western World.

MAHON—I seen it's my son.

WIDOW QUIN—You seen that you're mad. [*Cheering outside.*] Do you hear them cheering him in the zig-zags of the road? Aren't you after saying that your son's a fool, and how would they be cheering a true idiot born?

MAHON [*getting distressed*] It's maybe out of reason[13] that that man's himself. [*Cheering again.*] There's none surely will go cheering him. Oh, I'm raving with a madness that would fright the world! [*He sits down with his hand to his head.*] There was one time I seen ten scarlet divils letting on they'd cork my spirit in a gallon can; and one time I seen rats as big as badgers sucking the lifeblood from the butt of my lug;[14] but I never till this day confused that dribbling idiot with a likely man. I'm destroyed surely.

---

10 HOOSHING: a cry used to scare or drive away fowls, pigs.   11 GOOD BOY: brave and tough.   12 MONEYED: publicans are usually wealthy.   13 OUT OF REASON: mad to think.   14 LUG: ear.

1906

WIDOW QUIN – And who'd wonder when it's your brain-pan that is gaping now?

MAHON – Then the blight of the sacred drought upon myself and him, for I never went mad to this day, and I not three weeks with the Limerick[15] girls drinking myself silly, and parlatic[16] from the dusk to dawn. [*To* WIDOW QUIN, *suddenly.*] Is my visage astray?

WIDOW QUIN – It is then. You're a sniggering maniac, a child could see.

MAHON [*getting up more cheerfully*] Then I'd best be going to the union[17] beyond, and there'll be a welcome before me, I tell you [*with great pride*], and I a terrible and fearful case, the way that there I was one time, screeching in a straightened waistcoat, with seven doctors writing out my sayings in a printed book. Would you believe that?

WIDOW QUIN – If you're a wonder itself, you'd best be hasty, for them lads caught a maniac one time and pelted the poor creature till he ran out, raving and foaming, and was drowned in the sea.

MAHON [*with philosophy*] It's true mankind is the divil when your head's astray. Let me out now and I'll slip down the boreen, and not see them so.

WIDOW QUIN [*showing him out*] That's it. Run to the right, and not a one will see.

[*He runs off.*]

PHILLY [*wisely*] You're at some gaming, Widow Quin; but I'll walk after him and give him his dinner and a time to rest, and I'll see then if he's raving or as sane as you.

WIDOW QUIN [*annoyed*] If you go near that lad, let you be wary of your head, I'm saying. Didn't you hear him telling he was crazed at times?

PHILLY – I heard him telling a power; and I'm thinking we'll have right sport, before night will fall.

[*He goes out.*]

JIMMY – Well, Philly's a conceited and foolish man. How could that madman have his senses and his brain-pan slit? I'll go after them and see him turn on Philly now.

[*He goes;* WIDOW QUIN *hides poteen behind counter. Then hubbub outside.*]

VOICES – There you are! Good jumper! Grand lepper! Darlint boy! He's the racer! Bear him on, will you!

---

[15] LIMERICK: one of the six counties of Munster whose capital city, Limerick, is situated at the head of the Shannon estuary. [16] PARLATIC: paralytic. [17] UNION: poorhouse, a concomitant of Irish landlordism, used to give shelter to tramps, the destitute and the imbecile.

1907

[CHRISTY *comes in, in jockey's dress, with*
PEGEEN MIKE, SARA, *and other girls, and men.*]

PEGEEN [*to crowd*] Go on now and don't destroy him and he drench-
ing with sweat. Go along, I'm saying, and have your tug-of-warring till
he's dried his skin.

CROWD—Here's his prizes! A bagpipes! A fiddle was played by a poet
in the years gone by! A flat and three-thorned blackthorn[18] would lick
the scholars out of Dublin town!

CHRISTY [*taking prizes from the men*] Thank you kindly, the lot of
you. But you'd say it was little only I did this day if you'd seen me a
while since striking my one single blow.

TOWN CRIER [*outside, ringing a bell*] Take notice, last event of this
day! Tug-of-warring on the green below! Come on, the lot of you!
Great achievements for all Mayo men!

PEGEEN—Go on, and leave him for to rest and dry. Go on, I tell you,
for he'll do no more.

[*She hustles crowd out;* WIDOW QUIN *following them.*]

MEN [*going*] Come on then. Good luck for the while!

PEGEEN [*radiantly, wiping his face with her shawl*] Well, you're the
lad, and you'll have great times from this out when you could win
that wealth of prizes, and you sweating in the heat of noon!

CHRISTY [*looking at her with delight*] I'll have great times if I win
the crowning prize I'm seeking now, and that's your promise that
you'll wed me in a fortnight, when our banns[19] is called.

PEGEEN [*backing away from him*] You've right daring to go ask me
that, when all knows you'll be starting to some girl in your own town-
land, when your father's rotten in four months, or five.

CHRISTY [*indignantly*] Starting from you, is it? [*He follows her.*] I
will not, then, and when the airs is warming in four months, or five,
it's then yourself and me should be pacing Neifin[20] in the dews of
night, the times sweet smells do be rising, and you'd see a little, shiny
new moon, maybe, sinking on the hills.

PEGEEN [*looking at him playfully*] And it's that kind of a poacher's
love you'd make, Christy Mahon, on the sides of Neifin, when the
night is down?

CHRISTY—It's little you'll think if my love's a poacher's, or an earl's
itself, when you'll feel my two hands stretched around you, and I
squeezing kisses on your puckered lips, till I'd feel a kind of pity for
the Lord God is all ages sitting lonesome in his golden chair.

[18] BLACKTHORN: a shillelagh.   [19] BANNS: public announcement in church of a
proposed marriage.   [20] NEIFIN: Mount Nephin. Its name belongs to the popular
Irish love song of Connaught "The Brow of Néfin".

1908

PEGEEN–That'll be right fun, Christy Mahon, and any girl would walk her heart out before she'd meet a young man was your like for eloquence, or talk, at all.

CHRISTY [*encouraged*] Let you wait, to hear me talking, till we're astray in Erris,[21] when Good Friday's[22] by, drinking a sup from a well, and making mighty kisses with our wetted mouths, or gaming in a gap of sunshine, with yourself stretched back unto your necklace, in the flowers of the earth.

PEGEEN [*in a lower voice, moved by his tone*] I'd be nice so, is it?

CHRISTY [*with rapture*] If the mitred bishops seen you that time, they'd be the like of the holy prophets, I'm thinking, do be straining the bars of Paradise to lay eyes on the Lady Helen of Troy, and she abroad, pacing back and forward, with a nosegay in her golden shawl.

PEGEEN [*with real tenderness*] And what is it I have, Christy Mahon, to make me fitting entertainment for the like of you, that has such poet's talking, and such bravery of heart?

CHRISTY [*in a low voice*] Isn't there the light of seven heavens in your heart alone, the way you'll be an angel's lamp to me from this out, and I abroad in the darkness, spearing salmons in the Owen, or the Carrowmore?[23]

PEGEEN–If I was your wife, I'd be along with you those nights, Christy Mahon, the way you'd see I was a great hand at coaxing bailiffs, or coining funny nicknames for the stars of night.

CHRISTY–You, is it? Taking your death in the hailstones, or in the fogs of dawn.

PEGEEN–Yourself and me would shelter easy in a narrow bush, [*with a qualm of dread*] but we're only talking, maybe, for this would be a poor, thatched place to hold a fine lad is the like of you.

CHRISTY [*putting his arm round her*] If I wasn't a good Christian, it's on my naked knees I'd be saying my prayers and paters[24] to every jackstraw you have roofing your head, and every stony pebble is paving the laneway to your door.

PEGEEN [*radiantly*] If that's the truth, I'll be burning candles[25] from this out to the miracles of God that have brought you from the south to-day, and I, with my gowns bought ready, the way that I can wed you, and not wait at all.

CHRISTY–It's miracles, and that's the truth. Me there toiling a long while, and walking a long while, not knowing at all I was drawing all times nearer to this holy day.

[21] ERRIS: a barony of North-West Mayo. [22] GOOD FRIDAY'S: when spring has come. [23] OWEN . . . CARROWMORE: Owen River and Lough Carrowmore of North-West Mayo. [24] PATERS: paternosters. [25] BURNING CANDLES: votive lights.

P E G E E N – And myself, a girl, was tempted often to go sailing the seas till I'd marry a Jew-man, with ten kegs of gold, and I not knowing at all there was the like of you drawing nearer, like the stars of God.

C H R I S T Y – And to think I'm long years hearing women talking that talk, to all bloody fools, and this the first time I've heard the like of your voice talking sweetly for my own delight.

P E G E E N – And to think it's me is talking sweetly, Christy Mahon, and I the fright of seven townlands for my biting tongue. Well, the heart's a wonder; and, I'm thinking, there won't be our like in Mayo, for gallant lovers, from this hour, to-day. [*Drunken singing is heard outside.*] There's my father coming from the wake, and when he's had his sleep we'll tell him, for he's peaceful then.

[*They separate.*]

M I C H A E L [*singing outside*]–
 The jailor and the turnkey
  They quickly ran us down,
 And brought us back as prisoners
  Once more to Cavan town.

[*He comes in supported by* SHAWN.]

 There we lay bewailing
  All in a prison bound. . . .

[*He sees* CHRISTY. *Goes and shakes him drunkenly by the hand, while* PEGEEN *and* SHAWN *talk on the left.*]

M I C H A E L [*to* CHRISTY] The blessing of God and the holy angels on your head, young fellow. I hear tell you're after winning all in the sports below; and wasn't it a shame I didn't bear you along with me to Kate Cassidy's wake, a fine, stout lad, the like of you, for you'd never see the match of it for flows of drink, the way when we sunk her bones at noonday in her narrow grave, there were five men, aye, and six men, stretched out retching speechless on the holy stones.

C H R I S T Y [*uneasily, watching* PEGEEN] Is that the truth?

M I C H A E L – It is then, and aren't you a louty[26] schemer to go burying your poor father unbeknownst[27] when you'd a right to throw him on the crupper[28] of a Kerry mule and drive him westwards, like holy Joseph[29] in the days gone by, the way we could have given him a decent burial, and not have him rotting beyond, and not a Christian drinking a smart drop to the glory of his soul?

C H R I S T Y [*gruffly*] It's well enough he's lying, for the likes of him.

M I C H A E L [*slapping him on the back*] Well, aren't you a hardened slayer? It'll be a poor thing for the household man where you go sniffing

---

[26] LOUTY: stupid. [27] UNBEKNOWNST: in secret. [28] CRUPPER: rump. [29] JOSEPH: reference to the great and elaborate funeral Joseph gave to his father Jacob. *Genesis* L. 1–14.

for a female wife; and [*pointing to* SHAWN] look beyond at that shy and decent Christian I have chosen for my daughter's hand, and I after getting the gilded dispensation this day for to wed them now.

CHRISTY—And you'll be wedding them this day, is it?

MICHAEL [*drawing himself up*] Aye. Are you thinking, if I'm drunk itself, I'd leave my daughter living single with a little frisky rascal is the like of you?

PEGEEN [*breaking away from* SHAWN] Is it the truth the dispensation's come?

MICHAEL [*triumphantly*] Father Reilly's after reading it in gallous[30] Latin, and "It's come in the nick of time," says he; "so I'll wed them in a hurry, dreading that young gaffer who'd capsize the stars."

PEGEEN [*fiercely*] He's missed his nick of time, for it's that lad, Christy Mahon, that I'm wedding now.

MICHAEL [*loudly with horror*] You'd be making him a son to me, and he wet and crusted with his father's blood?

PEGEEN—Aye. Wouldn't it be a bitter thing for a girl to go marrying the like of Shaneen, and he a middling kind of a scarecrow, with no savagery or fine words in him at all?

MICHAEL [*gasping and sinking on a chair*] Oh, aren't you a heathen daughter to go shaking the fat of my heart, and I swamped and drownded with the weight of drink? Would you have them turning on me the way that I'd be roaring to the dawn of day with the wind upon my heart? Have you not a word to aid me, Shaneen? Are you not jealous at all?

SHAWN [*in great misery*] I'd be afeard to be jealous of a man did slay his da.

PEGEEN—Well, it'd be a poor thing to go marrying your like. I'm seeing there's a world of peril for an orphan girl, and isn't it a great blessing I didn't wed you, before himself came walking from the west or south?

SHAWN—It's a queer story you'd go picking a dirty tramp up from the highways of the world.

PEGEEN [*playfully*] And you think you're a likely beau to go straying along with, the shiny Sundays of the opening year, when it's sooner on a bullock's liver you'd put a poor girl thinking than on the lily or the rose?

SHAWN—And have you no mind of my weight of passion, and the holy dispensation, and the drift[31] of heifers I am giving, and the golden ring?

PEGEEN—I'm thinking you're too fine for the like of me, Shawn Keogh

[30] GALLOUS: fine. [31] DRIFT: herd.

of Killakeen, and let you go off till you'd find a radiant lady with droves of bullocks on the plains of Meath,[32] and herself bedizened[33] in the diamond jewelleries of Pharaoh's ma. That'd be your match, Shaneen. So God save you now!

[*She retreats behind* CHRISTY.]

SHAWN – Won't you hear me telling you . . . ?

CHRISTY [*with ferocity*] Take yourself from this, young fellow, or I'll maybe add a murder to my deeds to-day.

MICHAEL [*springing up with a shriek*] Murder is it? Is it mad yous are? Would you go making murder in this place, and it piled with poteen for our drink to-night? Go on to the foreshore if it's fighting you want, where the rising tide will wash all traces from the memory of man.

[*Pushing* SHAWN *towards* CHRISTY.]

SHAWN [*shaking himself free, and getting behind* MICHAEL] I'll not fight him, Michael James. I'd liefer live a bachelor, simmering in passions to the end of time, than face a lepping savage the like of him has descended from the Lord knows where. Strike him yourself, Michael James, or you'll lose my drift of heifers and my blue bull from Sneem.

MICHAEL – Is it me fight him, when it's father-slaying he's bred to now? [*Pushing* SHAWN.] Go on you fool and fight him now.

SHAWN [*coming forward a little*] Will I strike him with my hand?

MICHAEL – Take the loy is on your western side.

SHAWN – I'd be afeard of the gallows if I struck with that.

CHRISTY [*taking up the loy*] Then I'll make you face the gallows or quit off[34] from this.

[SHAWN *flies out of the door.*]

CHRISTY – Well, fine weather be after him, [*going to* MICHAEL, *coaxingly*] and I'm thinking you wouldn't wish to have that quaking blackguard in your house at all. Let you give us your blessing and hear her swear her faith to me, for I'm mounted on the springtide of the stars of luck, the way it'll be good for any to have me in the house.

PEGEEN [*at the other side of* MICHAEL] Bless us now, for I swear to God I'll wed him, and I'll not renege.

MICHAEL [*standing up in the centre, holding on to both of them*] It's the will of God, I'm thinking, that all should win an easy or a cruel end, and it's the will of God that all should rear up lengthy families for the nurture of the earth. What's a single man, I ask you, eating a bit in one house and drinking a sup in another, and he with

[32] MEATH: County Meath in the midlands where the land is exceptionally fertile.
[33] BEDIZENED: dressed in vulgar finery. [34] QUIT OFF: get out.

1912

no place of his own, like an old braying jackass strayed upon the rocks? [*To* CHRISTY.] It's many would be in dread to bring your like into their house for to end them, maybe, with a sudden end; but I'm a decent man of Ireland, and I liefer face the grave untimely and I seeing a score of grandsons growing up little gallant swearers by the name of God, than go peopling my bedside with puny weeds the like of what you'd breed, I'm thinking, out of Shaneen Keogh. [*He joins their hands.*] A daring fellow is the jewel of the world, and a man did split his father's middle with a single clout, should have the bravery of ten, so may God and Mary and St. Patrick bless you, and increase you from this mortal day.

CHRISTY *and* PEGEEN — Amen, O Lord!

[*Hubbub outside.*]

[OLD MAHON *rushes in, followed by all the crowd, and* WIDOW QUIN. *He makes a rush at* CHRISTY, *knocks him down, and begins to beat him.*]

PEGEEN [*dragging back his arm*] Stop that, will you? Who are you at all?

MAHON — His father, God forgive me!

PEGEEN [*drawing back*] Is it rose from the dead?

MAHON — Do you think I look so easy quenched with the tap of a loy?

[*Beats* CHRISTY *again.*]

PEGEEN [*glaring at* CHRISTY] And it's lies you told, letting on you had him slitted, and you nothing at all.

CHRISTY [*catching* MAHON's *stick*] He's not my father. He's a raving maniac would scare the world. [*Pointing to* WIDOW QUIN.] Herself knows it is true.

CROWD — You're fooling Pegeen! The Widow Quin seen him this day, and you likely knew! You're a liar!

CHRISTY [*dumbfounded*] It's himself was a liar, lying stretched out with an open head on him, letting on he was dead.

MAHON — Weren't you off racing the hills before I got my breath with the start I had seeing you turn on me at all?

PEGEEN — And to think of the coaxing glory we had given him, and he after doing nothing but hitting a soft blow and chasing northward in a sweat of fear. Quit off from this.

CHRISTY [*piteously*] You've seen my doings this day, and let you save me from the old man; for why would you be in such a scorch of haste to spur me to destruction now?

PEGEEN — It's there your treachery is spurring me, till I'm hard set to think you're the one I'm after lacing in my heart-strings half an hour gone by. [*To* MAHON.] Take him on from this, for I think bad the world should see me raging for a Munster liar, and the fool of men.

MAHON — Rise up now to retribution, and come on with me.

1913

CROWD [*jeeringly*] There's the playboy! There's the lad thought he'd rule the roost in Mayo. Slate[35] him now, mister.

CHRISTY [*getting up in shy terror*] What is it drives you to torment me here, when I'd asked the thunders of the might of God to blast me if I ever did hurt to any saving only that one single blow.

MAHON [*loudly*] If you didn't, you're a poor good-for-nothing, and isn't it by the like of you the sins of the whole world are committed?

CHRISTY [*raising his hands*] In the name of the Almighty God. . . .

MAHON – Leave troubling the Lord God. Would you have Him sending down droughts, and fevers, and the old hen[36] and the cholera morbus?[37]

CHRISTY [*to* WIDOW QUIN] Will you come between us and protect me now?

WIDOW QUIN – I've tried a lot, God help me, and my share is done.

CHRISTY [*looking round in desperation*] And I must go back into my torment is it, or run off like a vagabond straying through the Unions with the dusts of August making mudstains in the gullet of my throat, or the winds of March blowing on me till I'd take an oath I felt them making whistles of my ribs within?

SARA – Ask Pegeen to aid you. Her like does often change.

CHRISTY – I will not then, for there's torment in the splendour of her like, and she a girl any moon of midnight would take pride to meet, facing southwards on the heaths of Keel.[38] But what did I want crawling forward to scorch my understanding at her flaming brow?

PEGEEN [*to* MAHON, *vehemently, fearing she will break into tears*] Take him on from this or I'll set the young lads to destroy him here.

MAHON [*going to him, shaking his stick*] Come on now if you wouldn't have the company to see you skelped.

PEGEEN [*half laughing, through her tears*] That's it, now the world will see him pandied,[39] and he an ugly liar was playing off the hero, and the fright of men.

CHRISTY [*to* MAHON, *very sharply*] Leave me go!

CROWD – That's it. Now Christy. If them two set fighting, it will lick the world.

MAHON [*making a grab at* CHRISTY] Come here to me.

CHRISTY [*more threateningly*] Leave me go, I'm saying.

MAHON – I will maybe, when your legs is limping, and your back is blue.

CROWD – Keep it up, the two of you. I'll back the old one. Now the playboy.

[35] SLATE: thrash. [36] OLD HEN: influenza. [37] CHOLERA MORBUS: cholera plague. [38] KEEL: village on Achill Island. [39] PANDIED: flogged on the extended palm with a cane or ruler, a punishment to schoolboys.

1914

CHRISTY [*in low and intense voice*] Shut your yelling, for if you're after making a mighty man of me this day by the power of a lie, you're setting me now to think if it's a poor thing to be lonesome, it's worse maybe go mixing with the fools of earth.

[MAHON *makes a movement towards him.*]

CHRISTY [*almost shouting*] Keep off . . . lest I do show a blow unto the lot of you would set the guardian angels winking in the clouds above.

[*He swings round with a sudden rapid movement and picks up a loy.*]

CROWD [*half frightened, half amused*] He's going mad! Mind yourselves! Run from the idiot!

CHRISTY — If I am an idiot, I'm after hearing my voice this day saying words would raise the topknot[40] on a poet in a merchant's town.[41] I've won your racing, and your lepping, and . . .

MAHON — Shut your gullet and come on with me.

CHRISTY — I'm going, but I'll stretch you first.

He runs at OLD MAHON *with the loy, chases him out of the door, followed by crowd and* WIDOW QUIN. *There is a great noise outside, then a yell, and dead silence for a moment.* CHRISTY *comes in, half dazed, and goes to fire.*

WIDOW QUIN [*coming in, hurriedly, and going to him*] They're turning again you. Come on, or you'll be hanged, indeed.

CHRISTY — I'm thinking, from this out, Pegeen'll be giving me praises, the same as in the hours gone by.

WIDOW QUIN [*impatiently*] Come by the back door. I'd think bad to have you stifled on the gallows tree.

CHRISTY [*indignantly*] I will not, then. What good'd be my lifetime, if I left Pegeen?

WIDOW QUIN — Come on, and you'll be no worse than you were last night; and you with a double murder this time to be telling to the girls.

CHRISTY — I'll not leave Pegeen Mike.

WIDOW QUIN [*impatiently*] Isn't there the match of her in every parish public,[42] from Binghamstown[43] unto the plain of Meath? Come on, I tell you, and I'll find you finer sweethearts at each waning moon.

CHRISTY — It's Pegeen I'm seeking only, and what'd I care if you brought me a drift of chosen females, standing in their shifts itself, maybe, from this place to the Eastern World?

SARA [*runs in, pulling off one of her petticoats*] They're going to hang

40 TOPKNOT: pompon. 41 MERCHANT'S TOWN: poets gathered at fairs in merchant towns. 42 PARISH PUBLIC: public-house. 43 BINGHAMSTOWN: a village on the Mullet.

1915

him. [*Holding out petticoat and shawl.*] Fit these upon him, and let him run off to the east.

WIDOW QUIN – He's raving now; but we'll fit them on him, and I'll take him, in the ferry, to the Achill[44] boat.

CHRISTY [*struggling feebly*] Leave me go, will you? when I'm thinking of my luck to-day, for she will wed me surely, and I a proven hero in the end of all.

[*They try to fasten petticoat round him.*]

WIDOW QUIN – Take his left hand, and we'll pull him now. Come on, young fellow.

CHRISTY [*suddenly starting up*] You'll be taking me from her? You're jealous, is it, of her wedding me? Go on from this.

[*He snatches up a stool, and threatens them with it.*]

WIDOW QUIN [*going*] It's in the madhouse they should put him, not in jail, at all. We'll go by the back door, to call the doctor, and we'll save him so.

[*She goes out, with* SARA, *through inner room. Men crowd in the doorway.* CHRISTY *sits down again by the fire.*]

MICHAEL [*in a terrified whisper*] Is the old lad killed surely?

PHILLY – I'm after feeling the last gasps quitting his heart.

[*They peer in at* CHRISTY.]

MICHAEL [*with a rope*] Look at the way he is. Twist a hangman's knot on it, and slip it over his head, while he's not minding at all.

PHILLY – Let you take it, Shaneen. You're the soberest of all that's here.

SHAWN – Is it me to go near him, and he the wickedest and worst with me? Let you take it, Pegeen Mike.

PEGEEN – Come on, so.

[*She goes forward with the others, and they drop the double hitch over his head.*]

CHRISTY – What ails you?

SHAWN [*triumphantly, as they pull the rope tight on his arms*] Come on to the peelers, till they stretch you now.

CHRISTY – Me!

MICHAEL – If we took pity on you, the Lord God would, maybe, bring us ruin from the law[45] to-day, so you'd best come easy, for hanging is an easy and a speedy end.

CHRISTY – I'll not stir. [*To* PEGEEN.] And what is it you'll say to me, and I after doing it this time in the face of all?

PEGEEN – I'll say, a strange man is a marvel, with his mighty talk; but

44 ACHILL: large island on the Mayo coast. 45 RUIN . . . LAW: because of the poteen.

1916

what's a squabble in your back yard, and the blow of a loy, have taught me that there's a great gap between a gallous story and a dirty deed. [*To men.*] Take him on from this, or the lot of us will be likely put on trial for his deed to-day.

CHRISTY [*with horror in his voice*] And it's yourself will send me off, to have a horny-fingered hangman hitching his bloody slip-knots at the butt of my ear.

MEN [*pulling rope*] Come on, will you?

[*He is pulled down on the floor.*]

CHRISTY [*twisting his legs round the table*] Cut the rope, Pegeen, and I'll quit the lot of you, and live from this out, like the madmen[46] of Keel, eating muck and green weeds, on the faces of the cliffs.

PEGEEN—And leave us to hang, is it, for a saucy liar, the like of you? [*To men.*] Take him on, out from this.

SHAWN—Pull a twist on his neck, and squeeze him so.

PHILLY—Twist yourself. Sure he cannot hurt you, if you keep your distance from his teeth alone.

SHAWN—I'm afeard of him. [*To* PEGEEN.] Lift a lighted sod, will you, and scorch his leg.

PEGEEN [*blowing the fire with a bellows*] Leave go now, young fellow, or I'll scorch your shins.

CHRISTY—You're blowing for to torture me? [*His voice rising and growing stronger.*] That's your kind, is it? Then let the lot of you be wary, for, if I've to face the gallows, I'll have a gay march down, I tell you, and shed the blood of some of you before I die.

SHAWN [*in terror*] Keep a good hold, Philly. Be wary, for the love of God. For I'm thinking he would liefest[47] wreak his pains on me.

CHRISTY [*almost gaily*] If I do lay my hands on you, it's the way you'll be at the fall of night, hanging as a scarecrow for the fowls of hell. Ah, you'll have a gallous jaunt I'm saying, coaching out through Limbo with my father's ghost.

SHAWN [*to* PEGEEN] Make haste, will you? Oh, isn't he a holy terror, and isn't it true for Father Reilly, that all drink's a curse that has the lot of you so shaky and uncertain now?

CHRISTY—If I can wring a neck among you, I'll have a royal judgment looking on the trembling jury in the courts of law. And won't there be crying out in Mayo the day I'm stretched upon the rope with ladies in their silks and satins snivelling in their lacy kerchiefs, and they rhyming songs and ballads on the terror of my fate?

[*He squirms round on the floor and bites* SHAWN's *leg.*]

[46] MADMEN: gone mad from hunger in the famine days.   [47] LIEFEST: most willingly.

SHAWN [*shrieking*] My leg's bit on me. He's the like of a mad dog, I'm thinking, the way that I will surely die.

CHRISTY [*delighted with himself*] You will then, the way you can shake out hell's flags of welcome for my coming in two weeks or three, for I'm thinking Satan hasn't many have killed their da in Kerry, and in Mayo too.

[OLD MAHON *comes in behind on all fours and looks on unnoticed.*]

MEN [*to* PEGEEN] Bring the sod, will you?

PEGEEN [*coming over*] God help him so.

[*Burns his leg.*]

CHRISTY [*kicking and screaming*] O, glory be to God!

[*He kicks loose from the table, and they all drag him towards the door.*]

JIMMY [*seeing* OLD MAHON] Will you look what's come in?

[*They all drop* CHRISTY *and run left.*]

CHRISTY [*scrambling on his knees face to face with* OLD MAHON] Are you coming to be killed a third time, or what ails you now?

MAHON—For what is it they have you tied?

CHRISTY—They're taking me to the peelers to have me hanged for slaying you.

MICHAEL [*apologetically*] It is the will of God that all should guard their little cabins from the treachery of law, and what would my daughter be doing if I was ruined or was hanged itself?

MAHON [*grimly, loosening* CHRISTY] It's little I care if you put a bag on her back, and went picking cockles till the hour of death; but my son and myself will be going our own way, and we'll have great times from this out telling stories of the villainy of Mayo, and the fools is here. [*To* CHRISTY, *who is freed.*] Come on now.

CHRISTY—Go with you, is it? I will then, like a gallant captain with his heathen slave. Go on now and I'll see you from this day stewing my oatmeal and washing my spuds, for I'm master of all fights from now. [*Pushing* MAHON.] Go on, I'm saying.

MAHON—Is it me?

CHRISTY—Not a word out of you. Go on from this.

MAHON [*walking out and looking back at* CHRISTY *over his shoulder*] Glory be to God! [*With a broad smile.*] I am crazy again!

[*Goes.*]

CHRISTY—Ten thousand blessings upon all that's here, for you've turned me a likely gaffer in the end of all, the way I'll go romancing through a romping lifetime from this hour to the dawning of the judgment day.

[*He goes out.*]

1918

MICHAEL—By the will of God, we'll have peace now for our drinks.
Will you draw the porter, Pegeen?

SHAWN [*going up to her*] It's a miracle Father Reilly can wed us in the
end of all, and we'll have none to trouble us when his vicious bite is
healed.

PEGEEN [*hitting him a box on the ear*] Quit my sight. [*Putting her
shawl over her head and breaking out into wild lamentations.*] Oh my
grief, I've lost him surely. I've lost the only playboy of the Western
World.

"THE PLAYBOY OF THE WESTERN WORLD," A PREFACE

By J. M. Synge

IN WRITING *The Playboy of the Western World,* as in my other plays, I have used one or two words only that I have not heard among the country people of Ireland, or spoken in my own nursery before I could read the newspapers. A certain number of the phrases I employ I have heard also from herds and fishermen along the coast from Kerry to Mayo, or from beggar-women and ballad-singers nearer Dublin; and I am glad to acknowledge how much I owe to the folk-imagination of these fine people. Anyone who has lived in real intimacy with the Irish peasantry will know that the wildest sayings and ideas in this play are tame indeed, compared with the fancies one may hear in any little hillside cabin in Geesala, or Carraroe, or Dingle Bay. All art is a collaboration; and there is little doubt that in the happy ages of literature, striking and beautiful phrases were as ready to the storyteller's or the playwright's hand, as the rich cloaks and dresses of his time. It is probable that when the Elizabethan dramatist took his ink-horn and sat down to his work he used many phrases that he had just heard, as he sat at dinner, from his mother or his children. In Ireland, those of us who know the people have the same privilege. When I was writing *The Shadow of the Glen,* some years ago, I got more aid than any learning could have given me from a chink in the floor of the old Wicklow house where I was staying, that let me hear what was being said

From *The Playboy of the Western World and Riders to the Sea* by John Millington Synge, edited by William E. Hart. New York: Appleton-Century-Crofts, 1966. Copyright © 1966 by The Meredith Corporation. Reprinted by permission of Appleton-Century-Crofts.

1920

by the servant girls in the kitchen. This matter, I think, is of importance, for in countries where the imagination of the people, and the language they use, is rich and living, it is possible for a writer to be rich and copious in his words, and at the same time to give the reality, which is the root of all poetry, in a comprehensive and natural form. In the modern literature of towns, however, richness is found only in sonnets, or prose poems, or in one or two elaborate books that are far away from the profound and common interests of life. One has, on one side, Mallarmé and Huysmans producing this literature; and on the other, Ibsen and Zola dealing with the reality of life in joyless and pallid words. On the stage one must have reality, and one must have joy; and that is why the intellectual modern drama has failed, and people have grown sick of the false joy of the musical comedy, that has been given them in place of the rich joy found only in what is superb and wild in reality. In a good play every speech should be as fully flavoured as a nut or apple, and such speeches cannot be written by anyone who works among people who have shut their lips on poetry. In Ireland, for a few years more, we have a popular imagination that is fiery and magnificent, and tender; so that those of us who wish to write start with a chance that is not given to writers in places where the springtime of the local life has been forgotten, and the harvest is a memory only, and the straw has been turned into bricks.

1921

"THE PLAYBOY
OF THE WESTERN WORLD"

By T. R. Henn

I

THE PLAYBOY does not lend itself readily to classification; as we revolve it in our hands many facets take light and fire. In one mood we may suggest that it is sheer extravagant comedy, with elements of strong farce in the "resurrection" of Christy Mahon's father, and in the deflation of the boastful man, the revelation of a massive and mock-heroic lie. As such, it embodies the classic elements of reversal and recognition. Yet it is comedy that might have ended (for we are prepared from the first for a possible wedding) with Pegeen winning her Playboy and Old Mahon marrying the Widow Quin; comedy which at the end is edged, skilfully and unexpectedly, into a semi-tragedy. From another point of view we may call it "free" comedy, in which moral issues are reversed, transcended or ignored in the desire for "energy", though this view will be only part of the truth. It is helpful to quote Yeats:[1]

From *The Plays and Poems of J. M. Synge* (London: Methuen & Co., Ltd., 1963), and specifically from the Introduction of the Editor, T. R. Henn. Reprinted by permission of Associated Book Publishers, Ltd., London.

[1] *Explorations* (1962), pp. 161–62. This was a frequent thought: cf. "The Stare's Nest by My Window"
> We had fed the heart on fantasies,
> The heart's grown brutal from the fare:
> *More substance in our enmities*
> *Than in our love . . .*

1922

In a country like Ireland, where personifications have taken the place of life, men have more hate than love, for the unhuman is nearly the same as the inhuman, but literature, which is a part of that charity that is the forgiveness of sins, will make us understand men however little they conform to our expectations. We will be more interested in heroic men than in heroic actions, and will have a little distrust for everything that can be called good or bad in itself with a very confident heart.

Again we may see *The Playboy* (carrying Yeats' thought a stage further) as a Dionysiac comedy, in which the instincts are, within Synge's conventions, given uninhibited play; this in keeping with his demand for what is "superb and wild in reality". So the Playboy himself becomes a country Don Juan, rejoicing in his new-found power to excite the admiration of women,[2] and the very growth of the language, "richly flavoured as a nut or an apple", reflects his desire for "an imagination that is fiery and magnificent and tender".

We turn the play on its axis, and satire seems to predominate. It is a satire (but with more than a hint of approval) on the proverbial willingness of the West to give shelter to the malefactor and murderer, which goes back to the Elizabethan wars of conquest, the shipwrecked sailors of the Armada, and beyond. Then the Playboy may become a comic Oedipus, "the man who killed his da"; the mutual descriptions of each other by father and son give some point to the classic situation.[3] There is satire in the pursuit of man by woman, the comic reversal of the conventional view; we may remember how Shakespeare and Shaw turned that theme to account, and the additional flavour lent to it by the romantically fostered idea of modest Irish womanhood. Indeed, we may carry the idea of the mock-heroic still further, and see in Christy Mahon an Odysseus, the wanderer cast up and seeking refuge; his triumph in the sports on the sea-shore a parody of the Greek games. We might then have a tragi-comic piece with the Widow Quin as Nausicaa, a chorus of girls, the village pub for a palace. But again we may see it, if we will, as tragedy. The Playboy finds his soul through a lie, the "gallous story" of his parricide. Under the stimulus of heady admiration from men and women he grows in stature and in poetry. Detail is elaborated, the fatal blow struck by the potato-spade (we may note the irony)[4] becomes more final, more

[2] We may remember Othello's reported wooing of Desdemona: "Mark with what violence she loved the Moor but for bragging and telling her fantastical lies . . ."

[3] See *The Comic Effect of the Playboy of the Western World*, by Susan Solomont (1962), Chapter I. [E.B.]

[4] There may even be an echo of a once-popular song, "The Kerry Recruit": "So I buttered me brogues, and shook hands with me spade."

heroic.[5] He is indeed of the company of poets, "fine fiery fellows with great rages when their temper's roused". Under the shock of his father's reappearance (and the old man's account of his son's character has prepared the audience for this) he staggers, weakens and is finally reconciled; though with a new certainty of himself. He is "master of all fights from now". His father accepts the situation: "Glory be to God!" (*with a broad smile*) "I am crazy again." The final "turn" reminds us of the end of *The Shadow:* "By the will of God, we'll have peace now for our drinks." But it is Pegeen who is the heroine-victim. She has found her man, made him, won him in the teeth of opposition from her own sex. The marriage has been approved, in a superb drunken half-parody of the traditional blessing, by her father. From that marriage would come, because of Christy's heroic and virile virtues which have grown, mushroom-like, out of the tale of parricide, a band of "little gallant swearers by the name of God". At the end Pegeen's loss is absolute, beyond comfort, for she has lost her illusion of greatness in her man, and his body too; the complacent Shawn has seen the obstacle to his marriage removed.

> Oh my grief, I've lost him surely. I've lost the only Playboy of the Western World.

II

Synge intended that the play should run its course between antinomies. It is, for all its apparent simplicity of plot, a delicately balanced system of ironies, ambivalences, both of words and situation. We may quote his letter to the press after the storm of abuse which its production aroused:

> The Playboy is not a play with a "purpose" in the modern sense of the word,

(he is thinking perhaps of Shaw, Brieux, and the then current misrepresentations of Ibsen as a didactic dramatist)

> —but, although parts of it are or are meant to be extravagant comedy, still a great deal that is in it and a great deal more that is behind it is perfectly serious when looked at in a certain light. This is often the case, I think, with comedy, and no one is quite sure today

---

[5] Compare as stages in the narration: "I just riz the loy and let fall the edge of it on the ridge of his skull". ". . . the way they'd set their eyes upon a gallant orphan cleft his father with one blow to the breeches belt."

whether Shylock or Alceste should be played seriously or not. There are, it may be hinted, several sides to *The Playboy*.[6]

We may examine first the direct consequences of these "several sides" of the play. Synge's conflict with outraged Irish morality had begun as early as 1903, when the portrait of Nora in *The Shadow* was felt to be a slur on Irish womanhood. But the week that followed the first production of *The Playboy* on 26 January 1907 was a continuous riot, with a hysteria that recalls the first production of Victor Hugo's *Hernani* (with its violation of the formal Alexandrine) or the reception of Ibsen's *Ghosts* in London. We may quote from Lady Gregory:

> There was a battle of a week. Every night protestors with their trumpets came and raised a din. Every night the police carried some of them off to the police courts. Every afternoon the paper gave reports of the trial before a magistrate who had not heard or read the play and who insisted on being given details of its incidents by the accused and by the police . . . There was a very large audience on the first night . . . Synge was there, but Mr Yeats was giving a lecture in Scotland. The first act got its applause, and the second, though one felt that the audience were a little puzzled, a little shocked at the wild language. Near the end of the third act there was some hissing. We had sent a telegram to Mr Yeats after the end of the first act "Play great success"; but at the end we sent another— "Audience broke up in disorder at the word shift".[7]

We may attempt first to set out the main causes of offence, however innocent they may appear to a modern audience. As a background it is well to remember the image of Romantic Ireland, sedulously fostered in the 90's: the Land of Saints, the country whose Literary Renaissance would save European culture. Ireland was the home of the most ancient Christian tradition; her women were models of chastity and purity. Against this are to be set the "heroic" aspects of homicide, countless jests on the subject during the agrarian troubles,[8] the Phoenix Park murders, the raw material of the play itself:

> An old man on the Aran Islands told me the very tale on which *The Playboy* is founded, beginning with the words: "If any gentleman

[6] Maurice Bourgeois, *J.M.S. and the Irish Theatre* (1913), p. 208.
[7] *Our Irish Theatre.*
[8] A shot fired in the dusk might provoke the hoary joke: "There goes another landlord"; and there were times when one did not sit between the window and a lamp. See, e.g., Lady Gregory's *Journals.*

has done a crime we'll hide him. There was a gentleman that killed his father, and I had him in my own house six months till he got away to America."[9]

As for the "wild language", Lady Gregory and the actors[10] had indeed protested against its coarseness before the play was produced. But it was, at least overtly, an indelicacy rather than a blasphemy that triggered off the riot:

> . . . a drift of chosen females, standing in their shifts itself, maybe, from this place to the eastern world.

The rancour of the mob centres on the fatal *shift*; in an access of outraged modesty, Victorian in character, but connected somehow with the idea that the very word was insulting to the womanhood of Ireland, whose chastity and purity had become a national myth, even as the saintliness of the island as a whole. It is probable that the audience, in their bewilderment at the more subtle ironies of the play, missed the full point of the phrase. The picture of Mayo maidens perceived in terms of a slave market, or a throng of Eastern houris, is made yet more fantastic in that the term *drift* is applied to a drove of heifers; and it is possible that they took the point of the *eastern* world (Leinster or Dublin) as opposed to the Western of Connemara or Mayo.

We may quote some of Yeats' account of the attacks on "this wild, laughing thing":

> Picturesque, poetical, fantastical, a masterpiece of style and of music, the supreme work of our dialect theatre, his *Playboy* roused the populace to fury. We played it under police protection, seventy police in the theatre the last night, and five hundred, some newspaper said, keeping order in the streets outside. It is never played before any Irish audience for the first time without something or other being flung at the players. In New York a currant cake and a watch were flung, the owner of the watch claiming it at the stage-

[9] Yeats, *Essays and Introductions*, pp. 337–38. Synge's own version is in *Aran Islands*, pp. 64–65, together with some interesting aspects of the morality of this action.

[10] "Synge has just had an operation on his throat and has come through it all right. . . . When he woke out of the ether sleep his first words, to the great delight of the doctor, who knows his plays, were: 'May God damn the English, they can't even swear without vulgarity.' This tale delights the Company, who shudder at the bad language they have to speak in his plays" (Yeats, *Letters*, ed. Wade, p. 496).

1926

door afterwards. The Dublin audience has, however, long since accepted the play.[11]

And again:

> The Irish nationalists in America mobilized every force they could touch to boycott the [Abbey] plays throughout the Eastern States. The fight took much the same form everywhere, though it was fiercer in some towns than in others. It started in a prejudice, not the less violent for its ignorance and generally among the members of the Gaelic League, against the picture of Irish life and morals which the plays of the new school were said to give. The general prejudice was entangled with and sometimes manipulated by political prejudices of a far-reaching and almost infinitely complex kind. And mingled again with both was the religious prejudice of some sections at least of the Church.[12]

It seems to me likely that the offensive word was no more than a catalyst for the general but indeterminate unease caused by a number of other factors in the play; and these factors in this are themselves complicated by Synge's technique of producing, deliberately, an ebb and flow in the audience's response to character and situation. The perception of ironies and ambivalences will, of course, vary with the type of audience, its age and its environment. It is worth noting, for example, that *The Playboy* was more popular in England, *The Shadow* in Ireland; and the Dublin audiences in 1907 might well have been particularly sensitive to anything provided by the "Anglo-Irish Ascendancy" group of writers. The more subtle, dispassionate and balanced the irony the less likely it is that the general pattern will be perceived, and the more probable that overt points of conventional distaste will be selected for attack. In *The Tinker's Wedding* Synge pleaded, unavailingly, for the recognition of a humour without malice. That of *The Playboy*, fantastic as it may be, was probably too close to observation to be taken lightly.

Synge's attitude to Ireland and to the Irish peasantry was highly ambivalent: insight combined with toleration, love without passion. We may think of broadly similar positions taken up by Swift, Shaw, Yeats. Love and understanding are not inseparable from a detached mockery. But the union of these may be so subtle, so fluctuating and yet so integral to the whole system of values in the play, that we may examine briefly some of the instances.

[11] *Autobiographies* (1955), p. 569. (This was written in 1925.)
[12] Una Ellis-Fermor, *The Irish Dramatic Movement* (1939), p. 54.

His irony is founded most often on incongruity, the perception of polar opposites;[13] and within the broad rhythm of the play's construction, the manipulation of character so that it rises and falls, retreats and advances in the sympathy of the audience, to form its characteristic patterns. The irony may go unperceived, or be furiously rejected, when one of the poles from which the current passes is felt by the audience to be unacceptable; whether as involving religion, womanhood, King Lear's "nature", drunkenness, or aesthetic delicacy. (Curiously enough, the morbid, particularly of the churchyard, seems to go unchallenged; the accessories or instruments of death have a perennial attraction for a peasantry.)

It was a lady novelist of the early nineteenth century who noted the proclivity of the Irish for swearing, and on those somewhat tenuous grounds asserted the Grecian origin of the Milesians. "It is certain that the habit of confirming every assertion with an oath is as prevalent among the Irish as it was among the ancient, and is among the modern Greeks."[14] In the Notes to these plays I have drawn attention to some instances of a pleasant and at best devotional practice in this respect. But rapid and violent verbal conjunction may give quite another aspect. Consider, for instance:

> . . . or Marcus Quin, God rest him, got six months for maiming ewes—

("God rest him" is the normal pious expletive concerning the dead, but here a little incongruous with his crime)

> —and he a great warrant to tell stories of holy Ireland . . .

—where the second clause links "holy Ireland" with "God rest him", and both combine ironically with the "six months for maiming ewes". But set against this triangle there are two background references: to the Moonlighters and the agrarian troubles with their horrible practice of maiming cattle, horses, sheep by hamstringing or cutting off their tails. The second is to the juxtaposition of "holy Ireland", the kind of reference embodied in Yeats' poem whose title is the first three words:

[13] These "metaphysical" juxtapositions are everywhere, particularly when he wishes to emphasize the humanity of his characters: e.g. "I've a grand story of the great queens of Ireland, with white necks on them the like of Sarah Casey, and fine arms would hit you a slap the way Sarah Casey would hit you." "At your age you should know there are nights when a king like Conchubor would spit upon his arm ring, and queens will stick their tongues out at the rising moon."

[14] Sydney Owenson, *The Wild Irish Girl.*

Beautiful lofty things: O'Leary's noble head;
My father upon the Abbey stage, before him a raging crowd:
"This Land of Saints," and then as the applause died out,
"Of plaster Saints;" his beautiful mischievous head thrown back.[15]

Something of the same metaphysical conjunction (which emerges only
when distanced) is in Shawn's agonized cry "Oh, Father Reilly and the
saints of God, where will I hide myself today?" Sometimes we have a
double counterpointing, when the romantic the religious and the realistic
meet in a vortex characteristic of Synge's technique:

> Amn't I after seeing the love-light of the star of knowledge shining
> from her brow, and hearing words would put you thinking on the
> holy Brigid speaking to the infant saints, and now she'll be turning
> again, and speaking hard words to me, like an old woman with a
> spavindy ass she'd have, urging on a hill.

or,

> There's poetry talk for a girl you'd see itching and scratching, and
> she with a stale stink of poteen on her from selling in the shop.

More subtle and less definable is Sara's speech as she tries on the boots:

> There's a pair do fit me well, and I'll be keeping them for walking
> to the priest, when you'd be ashamed this place, going up winter
> and summer with nothing worth while to confess at all.

—when the ideas of confession and barefoot penance have a kind of subtle
and uneasy association. It is the same with the convolutions of the plot.
The Playboy's epic blow grows steadily in narration; but it is counter-
pointed and parodied by Pegeen's account of how the Widow Quin
killed *her* man:

> She hit himself with a worn pick, and the rusted poison did corrode
> his blood the way he never overed it, and died after. That was a
> sneaky kind of murder did win small glory with the boys itself.

and yet again Pegeen's

[15] *Collected Poems,* p. 348.

1929

And to think of the coaxing glory we had given him, and he after doing nothing but hitting a soft blow and chasing northward in a sweat of fear.

There are the overt attacks on custom; the terrifying description of Kate Cassidy's wake is balanced against Michael's drunken blasphemy:

> . . . aren't you a louty schemer to go burying your poor father un-beknownst when you'd a right to throw him on the crupper of a Kerry mule and drive him westwards, *like holy Joseph in the days gone by*, the way we would have given him a decent burial, and not have him rotting beyond, *and not a Christian drinking a smart drop to the glory of his soul?*

Now the uneasiness set up in an audience is caused, not by the extravagance of these syntactical conjunctions, but because each one of them is, *in itself*, perfectly natural and in common use, and is therefore elusive. It is Synge's art, which has something in common with Pope's, of suggesting value or its depreciation in this manner. Much the same is true of the plot, with its fantastical propositions. Does murder become heroic just because the blow is a good one, or because it and its context are narrated poetically? Granted that the police, together with the "khaki cut-throats", are natural enemies of the community, embodying "the treachery of the law", is it a moral act to shelter wrong-doers? Is a murderer likely to be a proper protector for Pegeen while the others are out? Is his reported valour a sufficient counterweight to the impropriety of his being left alone with her? If women are so easily won by poetical speech combined with inferred virility, what is the position of the conventional timid man as represented by Shawn Keogh?

Old Mahon boasting of his drink and lechery, his treatment in hospital, is in some sense a counterpart to the boasting of his son. They go off together, united in an utter reversal of this relationship.

> Go with you, is it? I will then, like a gallant captain with his heathen slave.

and old Mahon's comment, that oblique and perhaps profound comment on metaphysics:

> Glory be to God! I am crazy again.

So Synge's art makes the characters and the themes advance and retreat

1930

from the audience. Outrageous statements become logical,[16] and the language of hyperbole makes them still more credible, in relation to the reality which is being questioned.

It is being questioned, of course, in the very title. A geographer could fix the scene of *The Playboy* with some accuracy. It is obviously in northwest Mayo, within sight of the sea-shore, and of the dominant mountain Nephin. It is not far from Belmullet and Castlebar. The Western World is the land lying westward of the Shannon; proverbial for its 'wildness' and poverty; isolated from the civilized East and South, and the dour virtues of the 'black North'. Perhaps there are connotations of the Holy Islands, the Country of the Sunset, St Brandon. Yet it is a *world*, fantastic, romantic, brutal and sentimental, all at once. In the play Synge's own ambivalent attitude is fully apparent:

> I once said to John Synge, "Do you write out of love or hate for Ireland?" and he replied, "I have often asked myself that question . . ."[17]

Let us be frank about it. Synge's satiric view is constantly focused, with more or less directness, towards certain aspects of the peculiar blend of paganism and Roman Catholicism that he saw in the West. The pious ejaculations can, by juxtaposition and contrast, become loaded with ironies that demand both distance and an Anglo-Irish viewpoint to imagine their full implications. The unseen Father Reilly hovers in the background of *The Playboy* as the guardian of peasant morality, the supporter of the cowardly and feeble Shawn; whose comments on each situation are yet those of the ordinary moral man. Against settled and dull convention and a religion which can be made to appear superficial there are set Synge's tinkers, tramps, fishermen, publicans, in their actual or potential vitality. Yeats recognized the potential conflicts in a letter to Ricketts:

> I notice that when anybody here writes a play it always works out, whatever the ideas of the writer, into a cry for a more abundant and intense life. Synge and "AE" the poet are staying here, and though they have come to their task from the opposite sides of the heavens they are both stirring the same pot—something of a witches' cauldron, I think.[18]

[16] Perhaps this is the reason for the inclusion of *The Playboy* in the Surrealist Manifesto (Owen Quinn in *Envoy*).
[17] Yeats, *Letters*, ed. Wade, p. 618.
[18] ibid., p. 436.

T. R. Henn

The Playboy exists as a work of art, and in a sense all comments on it are futile or irrelevant. The complexity that gives it life must be apprehended with all our senses. Its verbal harmonies and disharmonies are integral with its verbal rhythms and idiom, its characters with the waves and currents of the plot. We stand back from it, and we may remember Shaw:

> . . . the admirable comedies of Synge, who, having escaped from Ireland to France, drew mankind in the manner of Molière, and discreetly assured the public that this was merely the human nature of the Blasket Islands, and that, of course, civilized people never admired boastful criminals nor esteemed them according to the atrocities they pretended to commit. The Playboy's real name was Synge; and the famous libel on Ireland (and who is Ireland that she should not be libelled as other countries are by their great comedians?) was the truth about the world.[19]

[19] Bernard Shaw, *The Matter with Ireland*, p. 84.

1932

LUIGI PIRANDELLO

Right You Are
Six Characters in Search of an Author

ALL THE PLAYWRIGHTS of this volume are modern in a broad sense, but with Luigi Pirandello (1867–1936) we come to modernity in the narrow sense. This modernity begins around 1910—and is perceptible not only in writing, but in music and painting. "For Pirandello," Martin Esslin has said:

> more than any other playwright has been responsible for a revolution in man's attitude to the world, in its way as significant as the revolution caused by Einstein's discovery of the concept of relativity. Pirandello has transformed our whole concept of *reality* in human relations by showing that the human personality—character, in stage terms—is not a fixed and static entity but an infinitely fluid, blurred and *relative* concept . . . Pirandello's influence pervades the contemporary drama . . .[1]

That two Pirandello plays are printed here, to Chekhov's one, is not to imply that anybody rates one playwright twice as high as the other. If more ample space is being assigned to the Italian, it is because of his relevance here and now. He is ours. He is one of the best of ours and, as Mr. Esslin stresses, one of the most formative of ours. The Editor's further comments are reserved for essays following the two plays.

[1] "Author in Search of Pirandello," *The New York Times*, June 25, 1967.

RIGHT YOU ARE

[1917]

English Version by
ERIC BENTLEY

CHARACTERS

THE GOVERNOR	*of the Province*
CENTURI	*Police Commissioner*
COUNCILLOR AGAZZI	
DINA	*his daughter*
AMALIA	*his wife*
LAMBERTO LAUDISI	*her brother*
SIGNOR PONZA	*an executive secretary under Agazzi*
SIGNORA PONZA	*his wife*
SIGNORA FROLA	*his mother-in-law*
SIGNOR SIRELLI	*friends of the Agazzis'*
SIGNORA SIRELLI	
SIGNORA CINI	*a friend of Signora Sirelli's*
SIGNORA NENNI	*a friend of Signora Cini's*
BUTLER	
A MAN	
A SECOND MAN	
OTHER CITIZENS	

The Place: A province in central Italy
The Time: The present

ACT ONE

Scene 1: *The curtain rises on the home of* COUNCILLOR AGAZZI. *In the drawing room are* AMALIA, DINA, *and* LAUDISI. LAUDISI *is walking across the room, irritated. A man of about forty, quick and lithe, he dresses well without overdoing it; he has on a violet-colored smoking jacket with black lapels and braid.*

LAUDISI—Aha! So he's gone to take the matter up with the Governor?

AMALIA [*about forty-five, grey hair. Makes a great show of importance because of her husband's place in society, at the same time giving us to understand that she could play the part all by herself and on many occasions would take quite a different line from his*] Heavens, Lamberto, just for a member of his staff?

LAUDISI—Member of his staff? In the Government Building, yes. But not at home!

DINA [*nineteen years old. Has a certain air of understanding everything better than her mother or her father. But this air is softened by considerable youthful charm*] But he's come here and put his mother-in-law in an apartment right next to ours—on our floor!

LAUDISI—Wasn't he entitled to? There was an apartment for rent, so he rented it for his mother-in-law. [*Petulant, laying it on thick.*] Or do you think the old lady should have asked your permission? Just because your father is above her son-in-law at the office?

AMALIA—What do you mean? As a matter of fact, Dina and I took the initiative and went to visit her first. [*With emphasis.*] She didn't receive us.

LAUDISI—And now what's your husband gone running to the Governor for? Is he appealing to the authorities? To *force* them into an act of courtesy?

AMALIA—Into an act of just reparation anyway! You don't leave two ladies standing at the door like a couple of posts.

LAUDISI—What a pompous attitude! Aren't people allowed to stay home and enjoy a little privacy?

AMALIA – All right, if you don't wish to realize that we were the ones who tried to be courteous to a stranger. We went to her first.

DINA – Now really, Uncle, be sensible! If you like we'll be frank and admit it: we were courteous out of curiosity. But, come, isn't that natural?

LAUDISI – Natural, by all means: you've all got nothing to do.

DINA – Now, look, Uncle. There you stand minding your own business. Taking no notice what other people are doing. Good. I come into the room. And there—on the little table just in front of you—cool as a cucumber, or rather with a long face like that jailbird we were talking about—I set down—well, what?—let's say a pair of the cook's shoes.

LAUDISI [*impatiently*] What have the cook's shoes to do with it?

DINA [*quickly*] Ha, you see? You're amazed. You find it queer and at once ask the why and wherefore.

LAUDISI [*pauses, smiles coldly, speedily recovers*] What a girl! Pretty bright, aren't you? But you're talking with me, don't forget. You come and put the cook's shoes on the table just to awaken my curiosity. Obviously—since you did it with this in mind—you can't reproach me if I ask: "But *why* are the cook's shoes here on the table, my dear?" Just as you have to show me that this Signor Ponza—rascal and boor as your father calls him—*intentionally* found an apartment for his mother-in-law here in this house.

DINA – All right. Let's suppose it wasn't intentional. You can't deny that the strange way the man lives would be bound to arouse the curiosity of the whole town, it's only natural. Think. He arrives. He finds a place to live on the top floor of that murky tenement, the one on the edge of town, looking out on the orchards . . . Have you seen it? Inside, I mean?

LAUDISI – You've been to see it?

DINA – Yes, Uncle. With Mother. And we're not the only ones either. Everybody's been to see it. There's a courtyard, and is it dark! Like a well. Way up on the top floor there's a balcony with an iron railing. They let baskets down from it on ropes.

LAUDISI – What of it?

DINA [*with amazement and indignation*] That's where he's put his wife: up there.

AMALIA – While he puts his mother-in-law here—next door to us.

LAUDISI – In a nice apartment with a central location. Lucky mother-in-law!

AMALIA – Lucky? He's just compelling her to live apart from her daughter!

LAUDISI – Who told you? Couldn't it be her own idea? She may want more freedom.

D I N A – What nonsense, Uncle! Everyone knows it's his idea.

A M A L I A – Now look. Everyone understands a daughter leaving her mother's house when she gets married—and going to live with her husband—in another city, if necessary. But you don't mean to say you understand it if a mother—unable to bear being away from the daughter—follows her and then is compelled to live apart from her in a city where after all *she's* a stranger too?

L A U D I S I – Why not? Have you no imagination? Is it so hard to suppose that through her fault, or his, or nobody's, there might be some . . . incompatibility of character through which, even in those conditions . . .

D I N A [*interrupting, amazed*] What, Uncle? Between mother and daughter?

L A U D I S I – Why between mother and daughter?

A M A L I A – Because it couldn't be the other two, they're always together.

D I N A – It's true. To everyone's astonishment, husband and mother-in-law are always together.

A M A L I A – He comes here every evening—to keep her company.

D I N A – Even in the day he usually comes over a couple of times.

L A U D I S I – You suspect they make love maybe—husband and mother-in-law?

D I N A – Uncle! How can you speak so of a poor old lady?

A M A L I A – He never brings her daughter. Never, never, never does he bring his wife to her own mother!

L A U D I S I – She must be sick, poor girl, and can't go out of doors . . .

D I N A – Nonsense. The mother goes there . . .

A M A L I A – She goes, yes, just to look on from a distance! Everyone knows the poor mother isn't allowed to go up to the daughter's apartment.

D I N A – She can only talk to her from the courtyard below.

A M A L I A – From the courtyard, understand?

D I N A – While her daughter is up there on the balcony—in the sky practically! The poor old thing enters the courtyard, pulls the rope, the bell rings up above, the daughter comes out on the balcony, and the old lady talks to her, from the bottom of that well, stretching her neck back like this. Imagine! She doesn't even see her, she's blinded by the sunlight pouring down from above.

[*There is a knock at the door and the* BUTLER *appears.*]

1939

Luigi Pirandello

Scene 2: *The same, the* BUTLER, *then* SIGNORA SIRELLI, SIGNOR SIRELLI, SIGNORA CINI

BUTLER – Are you at home, Signora?

AMALIA – Who is it?

BUTLER – Signor Sirelli, Signora Sirelli, and another lady, Signora.

AMALIA – Very well, show them in.

[*The* BUTLER *bows and leaves.*]

AMALIA [*to* SIGNORA SIRELLI] How are you, my dear?

SIGNORA SIRELLI [*fattish, red-faced, still young, dressed with exaggerated provincial elegance, burning with restless curiosity*] [*harsh to her husband*] I've ventured to bring my good friend Signora Cini who *so* much wanted to meet you!

AMALIA – How are you, Signora? Do sit down, everybody. [*Making the introductions.*] This is my daughter, Dina. My brother, Lamberto Laudisi.

SIRELLI [*bald, around forty, fat, with oiled hair and much pretense of elegant dress, squeaking, shiny shoes*] [*bowing*] Signora! Signorina!

[*Shaking* LAUDISI'S *hand.*]

SIGNORA SIRELLI – Ah, dear Signora, we come here as to the fountain, two poor women *athirst* for news!

AMALIA – News of what, ladies?

SIGNORA SIRELLI – Why, of this blessed new secretary in the Government Building. No one in town talks of anything else!

SIGNORA CINI [*an old fool, full of greedy malice veiled beneath an air of naïveté*] We feel such curiosity about it, such curiosity!

AMALIA – But we don't know any more about it than you, believe me, Signora!

SIRELLI [*to his wife, as if scoring a triumph*] What did I tell you? They don't know any more than me, maybe less. [*Turning to the others.*] The reason why this poor mother can't go and visit her daughter, for example–do you know what it really is?

AMALIA – I was just speaking of it with my brother.

LAUDISI – In whose opinion you've all gone mad!

DINA [*quickly, so as to ignore* LAUDISI] Because the husband–so they say–forbids her to.

SIGNORA CINI [*in a tone of lamentation*] Not enough of a reason, Signorina.

1940

SIGNORA SIRELLI [*pressing the issue*] Not nearly enough, there's more to it!

SIRELLI [*with a gesture to attract attention*] A piece of news for you, hot off the griddle. [*Emphasizing every syllable.*] He keeps her under lock and key!

AMALIA—Whom? His mother-in-law?

SIRELLI—No, Signora. His wife!

SIGNORA SIRELLI—His wife, his wife!

SIGNORA CINI [*in a tone of lamentation*] Under lock and key!

DINA—You understand, Uncle? You who wish to excuse—

SIRELLI [*astonished*] What? You'd want to excuse this monster?

LAUDISI—But I don't wish to excuse him in the least! I say that your curiosity—begging all your pardons—is insufferable—if only because it is useless.

SIRELLI—Useless?

LAUDISI—Useless! Useless, good ladies!

SIGNORA CINI—Useless? To try and find out?

LAUDISI—Find out what, if I may ask? What can we really know of other people, who they are, what they are, what they are doing, why they are doing it—

SIGNORA SIRELLI—By demanding news, information—

LAUDISI—If anyone should be abreast of all the news, that person is you, Signora—with a husband like yours, always informed of everything!

SIRELLI [*trying to interrupt*] Excuse me—

SIGNORA SIRELLI—No, no, my dear: I admit it's the truth! [*Turning to* AMALIA.] The truth, my dear, is that, with a husband who always claims to know *everything*, I never manage to know *anything*!

SIRELLI—No wonder! She's never satisfied with what I tell her. Always suspects that a thing is not as I have said. Maintains, as a matter of fact, that it *can't* be as I have said. And in the end decides it must be exactly the opposite.

SIGNORA SIRELLI—Now just a minute, if you come and tell me—

LAUDISI [*laughs aloud*] May I say something, Signora? I will answer your husband. My dear man, how do you expect your wife to be satisfied with the things you tell her if you—as is natural—present them as they are to you?

SIGNORA SIRELLI—As they absolutely cannot be!

LAUDISI—Ah no, Signora, permit me to say that now *you* are in the wrong! To your husband, rest assured, things are as he tells you they are!

SIRELLI—They are what they *really* are, what they *really* are!

1941

SIGNORA SIRELLI—Not in the least. You are always wrong!

SIRELLI—*You* are wrong, I beg you to believe. *I* am right!

LAUDISI—No, no, my dear friends. Neither of you is wrong. May I explain? I'll prove it to you. [*He rises and goes to the middle of the room.*] Both of you see me? You do see me, don't you?

SIRELLI—Why, of course.

LAUDISI—No, no, don't speak too quickly, my friend. Come here!

SIRELLI [*looks at him, smiles, perplexed and a little disconcerted, not wishing to lend himself to a joke he doesn't understand*] What for?

SIGNORA SIRELLI [*pushing him. Her voice is irritable*] Go on.

LAUDISI [*to* SIRELLI *who has now approached, trembling*] You see me? Take a better look. Touch me.

SIGNORA SIRELLI [*to her husband, who still hesitates to touch him*] Touch him!

LAUDISI [*to* SIRELLI, *who has raised one hand with which he gingerly touches his shoulder*] That's it, well done. You're sure you touch me—just as you see me—isn't that so?

SIRELLI—I'd say so.

LAUDISI—You can't doubt it, of course. Go back to your seat.

SIGNORA SIRELLI [*to her husband who has remained in front of* LAUDISI, *stupefied*] It's no use standing there blinking, go and sit down!

LAUDISI [*to* SIGNORA SIRELLI, *now that her husband has gone back, still in a stupor, to his seat*] Now would *you* like to come, Signora? [*Quickly, before she can move.*] No, no, I'll come to you. [*He is now before her, down on one knee.*] You see me, don't you? Raise one little hand, touch me. [*And as* SIGNORA SIRELLI, *still seated, places one hand on his shoulder, bending down to kiss it.*] Dear little hand!

SIRELLI [*warningly*] Uh, uh.

LAUDISI—Take no notice of him. Are you, too, certain that you touch me just as you see me? You can't doubt it, can you? But I beg you, don't tell your husband, or my sister, or my niece, or this lady here, Signora—

SIGNORA CINI [*prompting*] Cini.

LAUDISI—Cini. Don't tell them *what* you see in me, because all four will tell you you are wrong, whereas you are not wrong in the least: I really am as you see me. But, dear lady, that doesn't stop me really being as your husband sees me, as my sister sees me, as my niece sees me, as this lady here, Signora—

SIGNORA CINI [*prompting*] Cini.

LAUDISI—Cini sees me—for they aren't wrong either.

SIGNORA SIRELLI—How's that? You're a different person for each one of us?

LAUDISI—Certainly I am, dear lady, aren't you?

1942

SIGNORA SIRELLI [*in a rush*] No, no, no, no, no! As I see it, I'm myself and that's that.

LAUDISI–As *I* see it, I'm *myself* and that's that. And if you people don't see me as I see myself, I say you're wrong–but this is all so much presumption–in me or in you, dear lady.

SIRELLI–May I ask what you hope to conclude with all this hocus-pocus?

LAUDISI–You think there's no conclusion to be drawn? Well, well. You're all so anxious to find out who other people are and what things are like, almost as if people and things were simply this way or that way.

SIGNORA SIRELLI–According to you, then, one can never know the truth?

SIGNORA CINI–Why, if seeing and touching aren't believing . . .

LAUDISI–But they are, dear lady, rest assured! All I'm saying is: respect what other people see and touch even if it's the opposite of what *you* see and touch!

SIGNORA SIRELLI–Listen to him! I turn my back on you, I won't talk with you any more. I don't want to go mad.

LAUDISI–Well, that's enough then. Go on talking of Signora Frola and Signor Ponza, her son-in-law. I won't interrupt again.

AMALIA–God be praised! You'd do even better, my dear Lamberto, if you would leave us.

DINA–Yes, leave us, Uncle, do, do!

LAUDISI–Why should I? It amuses me to hear you talk. I'll keep my mouth shut, don't worry. At the most I'll permit myself a quiet smile –and if I actually burst out laughing you'll just have to excuse me.

SIGNORA SIRELLI–And to think that we had come to find out . . . ! Now, Signora, isn't your husband above this Signor Ponza in the office?

AMALIA–The office is one thing, the home another, Signora.

SIGNORA SIRELLI–That's right, I understand! But haven't you even tried to see his mother-in-law who lives here?

DINA–Oh yes, Signora. Twice.

SIGNORA CINI [*with a start; then, with greedy, intent concentration*] Ah! So you *have* talked to her?

AMALIA–She didn't receive us, my dear.

SIRELLI, SIGNORA SIRELLI, SIGNORA CINI–Oh!!! How is that possible?

DINA–We went there this morning for the second time–

AMALIA–The first time we waited more than a quarter of an hour at the door. Nobody came to open it, we couldn't so much as leave a visiting card. Today we tried again–

1943

DINA [*with a gesture of horror*] And *he* came to the door!

SIGNORA SIRELLI—That face of his! There's something *bad* in it. It's a public menace, the whole town is affected. Then the way he dresses, always in black . . . All three of them wear black, his wife too —the old lady's daughter—isn't that so?

SIRELLI [*with annoyance*] You know that no one has even seen the old lady's daughter! I've told you a thousand times. One *supposes* she wears black . . . They're from a village in Marsica—

AMALIA—Yes, totally destroyed, it seems—

SIRELLI—Razed to the ground in the last earthquake.

DINA—I heard they lost all their relatives.

SIGNORA CINI [*anxious to take up the interrupted discussion*] Yes, yes—so, *he* came to the door?

AMALIA—The moment I saw him in front of me with that face of his I was struck dumb. I couldn't even find the words to say we'd come to call on his mother-in-law. He said nothing either! Didn't even thank me.

DINA—Oh, well, he did bow!

AMALIA—Only just: he nodded his head like this.

DINA—His eyes spoke, though, didn't they? They're a wild beast's eyes, not a man's.

SIGNORA CINI [*as above*] What next? What did he say next?

DINA—He was very embarrassed—

AMALIA—And very dishevelled. He told us his mother-in-law was not well, that he wanted to thank us for our courtesy, then he just stood there in the doorway waiting for us to go!

DINA—What a humiliation!

SIRELLI—He's a boor. Oho, you can be sure *he's* at the bottom of the whole thing. Maybe he has his mother-in-law under lock and key too!

SIGNORA SIRELLI—The nerve of the man! To behave like that to a lady—the wife of a superior!

AMALIA—This time my husband really got indignant. He said the fellow was gravely lacking in respect and off he's gone to make a strong protest to the Governor and demand satisfaction.

DINA—Oh good, here *is* Father!

Scene 3: The same, COUNCILLOR AGAZZI

AGAZZI [*fifty, red hair, untidy, with beard, gold-rimmed glasses; an air of authority and malevolence*] My dear Sirelli. [*He approaches, bows, and shakes hands with* SIGNORA SIRELLI.] Signora.

1944

AMALIA [*introducing him to* SIGNORA CINI] My husband—Signora Cini.

AGAZZI [*bows, shakes hands*] Delighted. [*He then turns, almost solemnly, to his wife and daughter.*] I have to report that Signora Frola will be here at any moment.

SIGNORA SIRELLI [*clapping her hands, exultant*] Really? She'll be here?

AGAZZI—It had to be done. Could I tolerate such a glaring misdemeanor towards my home, towards my women folk?

SIRELLI—Quite so. Just what we were saying.

SIGNORA SIRELLI—And it would be good to take this opportunity—

AGAZZI [*anticipating*] To notify the Governor of everything the town is saying in regard to this gentleman? Don't worry, I've done so!

SIRELLI—Oh, good, good!

SIGNORA CINI—Such *inexplicable* things! Absolutely *inconceivable!*

AMALIA—Positively *wild!* Do you know he keeps them under lock and key—both of them!

DINA—Well, Mother, we don't know about the mother-in-law yet.

SIGNORA SIRELLI—It's certain about his wife, though!

SIRELLI—What about the Governor?

AGAZZI—Yes, the Governor . . . well . . . it made a profound impression on him . . .

SIRELLI—That's good.

AGAZZI—Something had got through to him too, of course, and now, like the rest of us, he sees how advisable it is to clear up this mystery. To find out the truth.

[LAUDISI *laughs aloud.*]

AMALIA—The only thing missing in the picture: Lamberto laughing!

AGAZZI—What's he found to laugh at this time?

SIGNORA SIRELLI—He says it's not possible to discover the truth!

Scene 4: *The same, the* BUTLER, *then* SIGNORA FROLA

BUTLER [*comes to the doorway and announces*] A visitor, Signora. Signora Frola.

SIRELLI—Ah! Here she is.

AGAZZI—We'll soon see if it's possible to discover the truth, my dear Lamberto.

SIGNORA SIRELLI—Wonderful! Oh, I'm so glad!

AMALIA [*rising, to* AGAZZI] Shall we have her come in?

AGAZZI—Yes, yes, show her in. But let's set the stage. Move your chairs back a little, will you? That's it. Now sit down, I beg you. Wait till she arrives. We should all be seated. Seated.

The BUTLER *withdraws. After a brief pause* SIGNORA FROLA *enters and all rise.* SIGNORA FROLA *is an old lady, neat, unpretentious, very affable; with a great sadness in her eyes, softened by the sweet smile that is constantly on her lips.* AMALIA *goes forward and extends her hand.*

AMALIA—Come in, Signora. [*Holding her hand, she introduces her.*] Signora Cini. Signora Sirelli, my good friend. Signor Sirelli. My husband. My daughter, Dina. My brother, Lamberto Laudisi. Please sit down, Signora.

SIGNORA FROLA—I'm most distressed. I've come to beg pardon for having neglected my duty till today. It was so gracious of you, Signora, to honor me with a visit when it was for me to be the first to come.

AMALIA—Among neighbors, Signora, we take no notice whose turn comes first. Especially since you're alone here and strange to the neighborhood, we thought you might be in need . . .

SIGNORA FROLA—Thank you, thank you . . . you are too kind . . .

SIGNORA SIRELLI—You are alone in our town, Signora?

SIGNORA FROLA—No, I have a married daughter. She came here too not long ago.

SIRELLI—The Signora's son-in-law is a secretary in the Government Building—Signor Ponza—isn't that so?

SIGNORA FROLA—That's right, yes. And I do hope Councillor Agazzi will excuse me . . . and my son-in-law too . . .

AGAZZI—To tell you the truth, Signora, I did take it rather ill—

SIGNORA FROLA [*interrupting*] You were right, quite right! But you must excuse him! Believe me when I say we are still overwhelmed by . . . what happened.

AMALIA—Of course, you were in that terrible disaster!

SIGNORA SIRELLI—You lost relatives?

SIGNORA FROLA—All of them—all, Signora. There isn't a trace of our village left. Just a heap of ruins with fields all round. Deserted.

SIRELLI—Just what we heard.

SIGNORA FROLA—I only had a sister—and her daughter, unmarried luckily . . . But it was a much harder blow for my poor son-in-law: mother, two brothers, a sister, the brothers' wives, the sister's husband, two nephews . . .

SIRELLI—A massacre!

SIGNORA FROLA—Blows you can never recover from. It's like being —stunned.

1946

AMALIA—It certainly is.

SIGNORA SIRELLI—And all from one moment to the next. It's enough to drive people mad.

SIGNORA FROLA—Your mind doesn't work, you forget and overlook things without in the least meaning to, Councillor.

AGAZZI—Please, Signora, not a word of excuse!

AMALIA—This terrible . . . blow was one of the reasons my daughter and I came to see you . . . first.

SIGNORA SIRELLI [*writhing with curiosity*] That's right. They knew how alone you were! Though . . . excuse me, Signora, for wondering how it is . . . with your daughter here . . . after such a blow . . . that . . . [*After this enterprising start she is suddenly bashful.*] . . . it seems to me that survivors would feel the need to stand together—

SIGNORA FROLA [*continuing, to save her from embarrassment*] How it is that I am quite alone?

SIRELLI—Exactly! It does seem strange—to be frank with you.

SIGNORA FROLA [*distressed*] Yes, I understand. [*Then, trying a possible way out.*] But—when your son or your daughter gets married, it's my opinion they should be left to themselves—to make their own life, that's all.

LAUDISI—How right you are! And this life must be a new life, revealing itself in the new relationship with wife or husband.

SIGNORA SIRELLI—But not to the extent, my dear Laudisi, of excluding the mother's life from her own!

LAUDISI—Who talked of exclusion? We are talking now, if I understand the matter, of a mother who sees that her daughter neither can nor should stay tied to her as she was before—because now she has a life of her own.

SIGNORA FROLA [*with keen gratitude*] That's it, that's how it is, ladies! Thank you, that's exactly what I was trying to say.

SIGNORA CINI—But I'm sure your daughter *does* come—does come quite often—to keep you company?

SIGNORA FROLA [*uncomfortable*] Surely . . . of course . . . we see each other, naturally . . .

SIRELLI [*promptly*] Yet your daughter never goes out—at any rate no one has ever seen her!

SIGNORA CINI—Perhaps she has children to look after?

SIGNORA FROLA [*promptly*] No. There are no children yet. And maybe she will never have any—now. She's been married seven years. She has things to do in the house, of course. But that isn't it. [*She smiles in her distress, adding, as another possible way of escape.*] In small towns we're used to staying home all the time, we women are used to it.

AGAZZI—Even when there's a mother for us to go and see? A mother who doesn't live with us any more?

AMALIA—But the Signora does go to see her daughter, doesn't she?

SIGNORA FROLA [*promptly*] Certainly. Oh, yes! I go once or twice a day.

SIRELLI—You climb all those stairs twice a day—to the top floor of that tenement?

SIGNORA FROLA [*growing pale, still trying to turn the torture of this questioning into a smile*] No, it's true I don't go up, you're right, ladies, they'd be too many for me, the stairs. I don't go up. My daughter comes to the balcony in the courtyard and—we see each other, we talk.

SIGNORA SIRELLI—Only that way? You never see her close up?

DINA [*with her arm around her mother's neck*] As a daughter, I don't claim my mother would climb ninety or a hundred stairs for me, but I wouldn't be satisfied with seeing her, with talking to her from a distance, without embracing her, without feeling her near me.

SIGNORA FROLA [*keenly disturbed, embarrassed*] You are right. Oh, well, I see I have to speak out. I wouldn't like you to think something of my daughter that is not the case—that she isn't fond of me, isn't considerate toward me. As for myself—I'm her mother—ninety or a hundred stairs wouldn't keep a mother away, even if she *is* old and tired, when such a prize awaits her at the top, and she can press her daughter to her heart.

SIGNORA SIRELLI [*triumphant*] Aha! Just what we said, Signora! There must be a reason!!

AMALIA [*pointedly*] You see, Lamberto: there *is* a reason!

SIRELLI [*promptly*] Your son-in-law, eh?

SIGNORA FROLA—Oh dear, please, please, don't think ill of him! He's such a fine young fellow. You can't imagine how kind he is— what tender and delicate affection he shows me—how much attention he pays me! To say nothing of the loving care he lavishes on my daughter! Believe me, I couldn't have wished her a better husband!

SIGNORA SIRELLI—But . . . in that case . . .

SIGNORA CINI—He can't be the reason!

AGAZZI—Of course not. It doesn't seem to me *possible* he should forbid his wife to go and see her mother—or her mother to come and be with *her* a little!

SIGNORA FROLA—Forbid? But I never said he forbade it. It's our-selves, Councillor, my daughter and I: we do without each other's com-pany—of our own accord, believe me—for his sake.

1948

AGAZZI—But how, pray, could he take offense? I don't see it.

SIGNORA FROLA—It's not a matter of offense, Councillor. It's a feeling . . . a feeling, ladies, rather hard to understand. But when you do understand it, it's not hard—to sympathize—although it may mean we have to make a real sacrifice, my daughter and I.

AGAZZI—At least you must admit it's *strange*, what you have to tell us, Signora.

SIRELLI—It certainly is. It arouses, and justifies, curiosity.

AGAZZI—Curiosity—and suspicion.

SIGNORA FROLA—Against him? Please, please don't say that! *What* could anyone suspect, Councillor?

AGAZZI—Nothing at all. Don't be disturbed. I'm saying that suspicion *could* arise.

SIGNORA FROLA—Oh no, no! *What* can they suspect, if we are in perfect agreement? My daughter and I are satisfied, completely satisfied!

SIGNORA SIRELLI—He's jealous, perhaps?

SIGNORA FROLA—Jealous of her mother? I don't think you could call it that. Though, of course, I can't claim to know. Look, he wants his wife's heart all to himself. He admits my daughter loves me too, must love me, he fully and gladly admits it, but he wants her love to come to me through him, *he* wants to bring it to me.

AGAZZI—No, I don't see. If you'll forgive me, I consider it the purest cruelty, behavior like that.

SIGNORA FROLA—Cruelty!! No, NO!! Don't call it cruelty, Councillor, it's something else, believe me. I don't know how to put it into words. . . . His *nature*, that's it. Or—maybe—maybe it's a kind of—illness, call it that. It's—it's the fullness of his love, a love entire, exclusive. She must live shut up in it. With no doors: she mustn't go out and no one else must come in.

DINA—Not even her mother?

SIRELLI—Sheer selfishness I call that!

SIGNORA FROLA—Perhaps. But a selfishness that gives itself utterly and provides a world to live in—for his own wife. After all it would be selfishness on my part, were I to force my way into this closed world of love—when my daughter is happy within it. Happy and adored. To a mother, ladies, that should be enough, shouldn't it? For the rest, if I see her, if I talk to my daughter . . . [*With a graceful, confidential movement.*] The little basket in the courtyard carries a few words up to her, and a few words back to me . . . our letters give the day's news. I'm satisfied with that. And by this time I'm used to it—I'm resigned, you might say. It doesn't hurt me now.

1949

A M A L I A – Well, of course, if you're both satisfied, you and your daughter . . .

S I G N O R A F R O L A [*rising*] We are, we are! Because he's so kind, believe me! He couldn't be more so. We all have our weaknesses, don't we? and we need each other's sympathy. [*Taking her leave of* AMALIA.] Signora. [*Taking her leave first of* SIGNORA CINI, SIGNORA SIRELLI, SIRELLI, *then turning to* COUNCILLOR AGAZZI.] You *will* excuse me, won't you?

A G A Z Z I – Don't mention it, my dear Signora. We are most grateful for your visit.

S I G N O R A F R O L A [*nods to* DINA *and* LAUDISI, *then turns to* AMALIA] Please don't—just stay here—please don't come to the door.

A M A L I A – Why, of course I will, it's my duty, Signora.

> [SIGNORA FROLA *leaves the room with* AMALIA, *who returns a moment later.*]

S I R E L L I – Well, well, well! Are you satisfied with the explanation?

A G A Z Z I – What explanation? It seems to me everything is still shrouded in mystery.

S I G N O R A S I R E L L I – And who knows how much this poor soul of a mother must suffer!

D I N A – Her daughter too, poor thing.

> [*Pause.*]

S I G N O R A C I N I [*from the corner of the room whither she has retired to hide her tears, with a strident explosion*] She was nearly crying, the whole time!

A M A L I A – I noticed it when she said she'd climb far more than a hundred stairs just to press her daughter to her heart!

L A U D I S I – I thought she was trying to protect her son-in-law from suspicion. That seemed to be the whole aim of her visit.

S I G N O R A S I R E L L I – Not at all. Why, heavens, she had no idea how to excuse what he has done!

S I R E L L I – Excuse? Excuse violence? Excuse downright barbarism?

Scene 5: The same, the BUTLER, then PONZA

B U T L E R [*coming to the doorway*] Signor Agazzi, Signor Ponza is here. He wishes to be received.

S I G N O R A S I R E L L I – Ah! That man!!

> [*General surprise. A movement of anxious curiosity, almost of dismay.*]

A G A Z Z I – He wants *me* to receive him?

BUTLER—Yes, Signore, that's what he says.

SIGNORA SIRELLI—Oh please, Councillor, receive him, receive him *here!* I'm almost afraid, but I'm so curious to see him close up! The monster!!

AMALIA—What does he want?

AGAZZI—Let's find out. Show him in. Be seated, everybody. We must all be seated!

The BUTLER *bows and withdraws. A moment's pause. Enter* PONZA. *Thickset, dark, almost fierce-looking, clad all in black, thick black hair, low forehead, big black moustache. He keeps clenching his fists, speaks with an effort, with barely suppressed violence. From time to time he wipes his sweat off with a black-bordered handkerchief. When he speaks his eyes stay hard, fixed, dismal.*

Come in, come right in, Signor Ponza. [*Introducing him.*] The new executive secretary: Signor Ponza. My wife—Signora Sirelli—Signora Cini—my daughter—Signor Sirelli—my brother-in-law, Laudisi. Please sit down.

PONZA—Thank you. I'll only be troubling you for a moment.

AGAZZI—Would you like to speak with me in private?

PONZA—No, I can—I can speak in front of everybody. It's better that way. The declaration I have to make is a matter of duty—*my* duty—

AGAZZI—You mean about your mother-in-law's not visiting us? You really needn't bother, because—

PONZA—It's not that, Councillor. I feel I must tell you my mother-in-law, Signora Frola, would undoubtedly have come to visit you before your wife and daughter had the goodness to come to her, had I not done all I could to prevent her doing so. I couldn't permit her either to pay visits or to receive them.

AGAZZI [*with pride and resentment*] And why not, may I ask?

PONZA [*getting more excited all the time despite his efforts to control himself*] I suppose my mother-in-law has been talking to you all? Has told you I forbid her to enter my home and see her daughter?

AMALIA—No, no! She was full of consideration and kindness toward you.

DINA—She had nothing but good to say of you.

AGAZZI—She said she refrains from entering her daughter's home of her own accord, out of respect for a feeling of yours which we frankly admit we don't understand.

SIGNORA SIRELLI—In fact if we were to say what we really think of it . . .

AGAZZI—Yes. It seemed to us a piece of cruelty. Real cruelty.

1951

P O N Z A – I came here expressly to clear this up, Councillor. This lady's condition is a pitiful one, but my own is scarcely less pitiful. For I see I am obliged to beg pardon, I am obliged to tell you all about a misfortune which—which only such violence as this could compel me to reveal. [*He stops a moment to look at everyone. Then, in a slow and staccato voice.*] Signora Frola is mad.

E V E R Y O N E [*jumping out of his skin*] Mad?

P O N Z A – She's been mad for four years.

S I G N O R A S I R E L L I [*with a cry*] Heavens, she doesn't *seem* mad!

A G A Z Z I [*stunned*] What? Mad?

P O N Z A – She doesn't *seem* mad, but she *is* mad. And her madness consists precisely in believing that I don't wish her to see her daughter. [*With terrible excitement, almost ferocious perturbation.*] And what daughter, in heaven's name? Her daughter died four years ago.

E V E R Y O N E [*flabbergasted*] Died? Oh! What? Died?

P O N Z A – Four years ago. That's what drove her mad.

S I R E L L I – Then, the lady who is your wife today?

P O N Z A – I married again. Two years ago.

A M A L I A – And the old lady thinks your present wife is her daughter?

P O N Z A – Such has been her good fortune, one might almost say. She was under surveillance, not allowed to go out. But one day, through her window, she saw me in the street with my second wife. She thought it was her daughter, still alive. She started laughing, trembling all over. At a single blow she was free of the dark desperation she had fallen into—only to find herself in another insanity. At first she was exultant, ecstatic. Then, bit by bit, she grew calmer and, despite the anguish in her heart, managed to subside into an attitude of resignation. She is satisfied, as you could see. She persists in believing that her daughter is not dead but that I want to keep her all to myself and not let anyone see her. She seems quite cured. So much so that, to hear her talk, you wouldn't think she was mad in the least.

A M A L I A – Not in the least!

S I G N O R A S I R E L L I – It's true, she does say she's satisfied now.

P O N Z A – She tells everyone that. And is grateful and affectionate to me. Because I try to back her up in every possible way, even if it means heavy sacrifices. I have to maintain two households. I oblige my wife —who, luckily, complies in the spirit of charity—to confirm the illusion of being her daughter. She comes to the window, talks to her, writes to her. But—well, my friends, there are human limits to charity, to duty. I can't compel my wife to live with her. In the meanwhile she lives in a prison, poor woman, I have to lock her up—for fear *she* might one day climb those stairs and knock on our door. Yes, she is peaceful now, and of a gentle disposition in any case, but you will understand how my wife would feel were the old lady to shower motherly caresses on her. She'd shudder from head to foot.

AMALIA [*with a start: horror and pity mixed*] Oh, of course! Poor lady, just imagine!

SIGNORA SIRELLI [*to her husband and* SIGNORA CINI] Ah, so she *wishes* to be under lock and key, did you hear?

PONZA [*cutting her short*] Councillor Agazzi, you will understand that I couldn't have permitted this visit of my mother-in-law's—except that I had to.

AGAZZI—I understand perfectly. Yes, it's clear to me now.

PONZA—I know people should keep their misfortunes to themselves. But I was compelled to have my mother-in-law come here. And I was obliged to make this declaration of my own. With a position like mine to keep up. We can't have the people in town believing a public official would do such things. Believing he would keep a poor mother from seeing her daughter. Out of jealousy or anything else. [*Rises.*] Councillor Agazzi. [*He bows. Then passing* LAUDISI *and* SIRELLI, *he nods to them.*] Gentlemen.

[*He leaves.*]

AMALIA [*in astonishment*] Oh!! So she's mad!!!

SIGNORA SIRELLI—Poor lady: mad!

DINA—So that's it; she thinks herself still a mother, but that woman isn't her daughter! [*Horrified, she buries her face in her hands.*] Heavens!

SIGNORA CINI—Who could ever have guessed such a thing?

AGAZZI—Well, I don't know . . . from the way she talked—

LAUDISI—You knew all along?

AGAZZI—Not exactly . . . but it *is* true she—didn't quite know what to say.

SIGNORA SIRELLI—But that's only natural. She's lost her reason.

SIRELLI—I wonder, though. It's strange—for a mad woman. She wasn't very reasonable, certainly. But all this trying to explain why her son-in-law doesn't want to let her see her daughter. All this excusing of him and quickly adapting herself to her own improvisations of the moment . . .

AGAZZI—Gracious! That's precisely the proof that she's mad—the fact that she seeks excuses for her son-in-law without finding a single one that's halfway convincing.

AMALIA—Yes, yes. She was always saying things and then taking them back again.

AGAZZI [*to* SIRELLI] D'you think anyone who wasn't mad could accept such conditions? To see her daughter only at the window—with

1953

the excuse she gives about the morbid love of the husband who wants his wife all to himself?

SIRELLI—I don't know. *Would* a madwoman accept such conditions? And resign herself to them? I find it strange, very strange. [*To* LAUDISI.] What do you say?

LAUDISI—Me? Why, nothing.

Scene 6: The same, the BUTLER, then SIGNORA FROLA

BUTLER [*knocking, then appearing in the doorway, excited*] Excuse me, sir. Signora Frola is here again.

AMALIA [*upset*] Heavens, what now? Shall we never be rid of her?

SIGNORA SIRELLI—Never be rid of her? Oh, you mean because she's mad—I see.

SIGNORA CINI—Lord, Lord, who knows what she'll say this time? Still, I'd like to hear it.

SIRELLI—I'm curious about it too. I'm not at all convinced she *is* mad.

DINA—Look, Mother, there's nothing to be afraid of. She's so calm.

AGAZZI—We must receive her, of course. Let's hear what it is she wants. If there's trouble, we can take care of it. But let's set the stage. And be seated, everybody. We must all be seated. [*To the* BUTLER.] Show her in.

[*The* BUTLER *withdraws.*]

AMALIA—Help me, all of you, please! I don't know how to talk to her now.

[SIGNORA FROLA *re-enters.* AMALIA *rises and comes towards her, frightened. The others look on in dismay.*]

SIGNORA FROLA—Excuse me.

AMALIA—Come in, come right in, Signora. My friends are still here, as you see—

SIGNORA FROLA [*with very mournful affability, smiling*] The look you all give me . . . you too, dear Signora, you think I'm a poor madwoman, don't you?

AMALIA—Why, no, Signora, what are you saying?

SIGNORA FROLA [*with profound sorrow*] The first time you came I didn't even go to the door, it was better that way. I never thought you'd come again. My son-in-law opened the door without thinking. So you had called, and I had to return the visit. Alas, I knew what the consequences would be!

AMALIA—Not at all, believe me. We're very pleased to see you again.

SIRELLI—The Signora is troubled . . . we don't know why: let her speak.

SIGNORA FROLA—Wasn't it my son-in-law who just left?

AGAZZI—Well, yes. He came—he came, Signora, to talk with me about—office business, that's all.

SIGNORA FROLA [*wounded, with great consternation*] That's a little white lie—you're saying it just to soothe me down . . .

AGAZZI—No, no, Signora, be assured, I'm telling the truth.

SIGNORA FROLA [*as above*] At least he was calm? He talked calmly?

AGAZZI—Yes, yes, completely calm, wasn't he?

[*Everyone assents, confirms.*]

SIGNORA FROLA—Oh dear, you all think *you're* reassuring *me* whereas what I want is to reassure you about him!

SIGNORA SIRELLI—On what score, Signora? If we repeat that—

AGAZZI—He spoke with me about some office business—

SIGNORA FROLA—I see how you all look at me! But wait. It's not a matter of me at all. From the way you look at me I see that his coming here has proved what I should never have revealed for all the gold in the world. You can all bear witness that not long ago I didn't know what to reply to your questions. Believe me, they hurt, they hurt very much. And I gave you an explanation of this strange way of living—an explanation that could satisfy no one, I see that. But could I tell you the real reason? Could I tell you the story he tells—that my daughter died four years ago and that I'm a poor madwoman who believes she's still alive and that he doesn't want me to see her?

AGAZZI [*stunned by the profound note of sincerity in* SIGNORA FROLA] Ah! What's this? Your daughter?

SIGNORA FROLA [*quickly, anxiously*] You know it's true. Why try to hide it? That's what he told you . . .

SIRELLI [*hesitating, but scrutinizing her*] Yes . . . in fact . . . he did say . . .

SIGNORA FROLA—I know. And unhappily I know how it will stir him up to feel compelled to say it of me. Our situation, Councillor, is one we've been able to handle—by ceaseless effort, in the face of great suffering—but only this way: by living as we are living. I quite understand how it attracts attention, provokes scandal, arouses suspicion. On the other hand, he's a good worker, scrupulous, conscientious—you must have tried him out already.

AGAZZI—Well, actually, I haven't had the chance to discover.

SIGNORA FROLA—Please don't judge from the way it looks now! He's good—everyone he's ever worked for said so. So why should he be tormented with an investigation of his family life? I told you, Councillor: you're investigating a situation which is under control. To bring it out in the open is simply to hurt him in his career.

AGAZZI – Signora, please don't distress yourself in this way! No one wishes to torment him.

SIGNORA FROLA – Oh dear, how can I help being distressed when I see him compelled to give everybody an absurd explanation, a horrible explanation. Can you seriously believe that my daughter is dead? That I am mad? That his present wife is his second? But for him, it's a *necessity* to say it is so. Only in this way could he find peace and self-respect. Yet he himself admits the enormity of what he says. Whenever he's compelled to say it, he gets terribly excited, he's quite overcome—you must have noticed!

AGAZZI – Yes . . . in fact, he was . . . he was rather excited.

SIGNORA SIRELLI – Oh dear, what are we to make of it now? It's him?

SIRELLI – Of course. It must be. [*Triumphant.*] My friends, I told you so!

AGAZZI – My God, is it possible?

[*Much agitation all round.*]

SIGNORA FROLA [*quickly, joining her hands*] Please, please, good people! What are you thinking? It's only . . . he has one sore spot that mustn't be touched. Be reasonable: would I leave my daughter alone with him if he were really mad? No! You can test what I say at any time at the office, Councillor; you'll find he performs his duties to perfection!

AGAZZI – Well, Signora, you owe us an explanation—a clear explanation. Is it possible that your son-in-law came here and *invented* the whole story?

SIGNORA FROLA – Yes, Signore, it is. Let me explain it to you. But you must sympathize with him, Councillor.

AGAZZI – What? Then it isn't true that your daughter is dead?

SIGNORA FROLA [*horrified*] Why no, heaven forbid!

AGAZZI [*very annoyed, shouting*] Then it's he that's mad!

SIGNORA FROLA [*supplicating*] No, no . . . look . . .

SIRELLI [*triumphant*] But it must be, it must be!

SIGNORA FROLA – No, no, look! He's not mad. Let me speak. You've seen him: he has a strong constitution, he's violent. When he got married he was seized with a veritable frenzy of love. My daughter is so delicate, he came near to destroying her—with the force of his passion. On the advice of the doctors and all the relations—even his (dead now, poor things!)—my daughter was taken off in secret and shut up in a sanitarium. He was already quite—exalted by excess of love, so when he couldn't find her in the house, oh! my friends, he fell into such a desperate state of mind. He *really* believed she was dead. Would hear of nothing else. Wanted to wear black. Did all sorts of crazy things. And wouldn't budge from his idea. A year later, when my daughter was well again, and blooming, and was brought back to him, he said no, it wasn't she, no, no, he looked and looked: it wasn't she. What torture, my friends! He would go up to her, seem to recognize her, and then— no, no! To induce him to take her, I got together with his friends and we went through the pretense of a second wedding.

SIGNORA SIRELLI—Ah! So that's why he says . . .

SIGNORA FROLA—Yes, but for some time now he hasn't believed it himself. That's why he has to convince other people, he can't help it. To relieve his own insecurity, you understand? For maybe, from time to time, the fear flashes across his mind that his wife might be taken from him again. [*In a lower tone, taking them into her confidence with a smile.*] That's why he keeps her under lock and key, keeps her all to himself. But he adores her. I am sure of it. And my daughter is satisfied. [*Rising.*] Now I must be going. I mustn't be here if he comes back again in that excited state. [*She sighs sweetly, with a movement of her joined hands.*] We must be patient. That poor girl must pretend she's not herself but someone else, and I—I must pretend I'm mad, my friends! What of it? As long as *he's* at peace. Please don't come to the door. I know the way. Goodbye, goodbye!

[*Bowing and nodding to everyone, she hurriedly withdraws. They all remain standing, looking at each other, astounded, dumbfounded. Silence.*]

LAUDISI [*coming center*] You're looking each other over? The truth, hm?

[*He bursts out laughing.*]

1957

ACT TWO

Scene 1: When the curtain rises, AMALIA, DINA, *and* SIGNORA SIRELLI *are talking in the music room. In the drawing room are* AGAZZI, LAUDISI, *and* SIRELLI. AGAZZI *is on the phone, standing by his desk.* LAUDISI *and* SIRELLI, *seated, are looking in his direction, waiting.*

AGAZZI—Hello. Yes. Is that Police Commissioner Centuri? Well? Yes, fine. [*After listening for some time.*] But really, how is that possible? [*Another long wait.*] I quite understand, but if we could keep at it . . . [*Another wait.*] It's really very strange we can't . . . [*Pause.*] I see, yes, I see. [*Pause.*] That'll do for now then, we'll have to see . . . Goodbye.

[*He puts down the receiver and walks forward.*]

SIRELLI [*anxiously*] Well?

AGAZZI—Nothing.

SIRELLI—They can't find anything at all?

AGAZZI—Everything's either dispersed or destroyed: the city hall, the municipal archives, all records of births, deaths, and marriages.

SIRELLI—But aren't there survivors who could give testimony?

AGAZZI—We've no news of any. And if there *are* some, it's going to be damned hard to find them at this point.

SIRELLI—So there's nothing for it but believing one or other of the two of them? Just that: no proofs, nothing.

AGAZZI—Unfortunately.

LAUDISI [*rising and drawing the curtains between the two rooms*] Would you like to take *my* advice? Believe them both.

AGAZZI—Very well, and what if—

SIRELLI—What if one says black and the other says white?

LAUDISI—In that case, believe neither.

SIRELLI—You're trying to be funny. There may be no precise facts, the proofs may be missing, but the truth—the truth must be on one side or the other.

LAUDISI—Precise facts. Hm. What would you deduce from precise facts?

1958

AGAZZI—Now, really. Take the daughter's death certificate—I mean if it's Signora Frola that's mad. It's true we can't find it, but then we can't find anything—yet it must have existed—and it might turn up tomorrow—and if it did—why, it'd be clear that *he's* in the right—the husband.

SIRELLI—Would you deny the validity of the evidence if you were given this certificate?

LAUDISI—I? I'm not denying anything. I'm very careful not to. It's you who feel the need of precise facts, documents and so forth. So you can affirm or deny. I wouldn't know what to do with them. For me reality isn't in *them*—it's in the two people, in the hearts of the two people. And how could *I* get into *their* hearts? All I know is what they tell me.

SIRELLI—Exactly. And doesn't each of them tell you the other is mad? Either *she's* mad or *he's* mad, there's no getting away from it. Well, which?

AGAZZI—That is the question.

LAUDISI—In the first place, it's not true each says the other is mad. Signor Ponza says Signora Frola is mad. She not only denies this, she denies that *he* is mad too. At worst, she says, he was . . . "exalted with excess of love" but that now he's completely well.

SIRELLI—Then you incline, as I do, toward *her* version of the story?

AGAZZI—It's clear the whole thing can be satisfactorily explained on the basis of her statement.

LAUDISI—The whole thing can be satisfactorily explained on the basis of his statement too.

SIRELLI—Then—neither of them is mad? But, damn it, one of them *must* be!

LAUDISI—Then, which? You can't say. Nor can anyone else. And this isn't just because your precise facts have been wiped out—dispersed or destroyed—in some accident, a fire or an earthquake. No, it's because they have wiped them out in themselves, in their hearts. Do you see that? She has created for him, or he for her, a fantasy. This fantasy is as real as reality. And they're living inside it now, with perfect harmony. They have found peace there. They breathe and see and hear and touch there. It is their reality, and no document could conceivably destroy it. At best a document might do *you* some good, it could satisfy your foolish curiosity. But no document has turned up, so here you are faced by two things—fantasy and reality—and you can't tell the one from the other. That is your punishment. Marvellous, isn't it?

AGAZZI—That's just philosophy, my dear fellow. Wait. We'll see if we can't get to the bottom of this.

SIRELLI—We've listened to him and we've listened to her. We now

put both stories together—confront one version with the other—and figure out where fantasy begins, where reality leaves off. Don't you think
we'll succeed?

LAUDISI – All I ask is that you let me go on laughing when you've
finished.

AGAZZI – Well, well, we'll see who'll be laughing when we've finished.
Now let's lose no time. I have an idea! [*He goes towards the music
room and calls.*] Amalia, Signora Sirelli, will you come in here now?

Scene 2: *The same,* AMALIA, SIGNORA SIRELLI, DINA

SIGNORA SIRELLI [*to* LAUDISI, *threatening him with one finger*]
Still at it, you naughty man!

SIRELLI – He's incorrigible.

SIGNORA SIRELLI – Here we all are—in the grip of a mighty passion
—determined to get to the heart of the mystery if we go mad in the
process—I didn't sleep a wink last night, myself—and *you*, you are cold
and indifferent?

AGAZZI – Please, Signora, simply ignore him. Just sit down all of you
and pay attention to me.

LAUDISI – Yes, just pay attention to my brother-in-law. He's preparing you the best of sleeping pills for tonight.

AGAZZI – Well now, where were we? Oh, yes, my idea! You ladies
will go to Signora Frola's . . .

AMALIA – But will she receive us?

AGAZZI – Oh yes, I think so.

DINA – It's our duty to return the visit.

AMALIA – But if he doesn't want to allow her to pay visits or receive
them?

SIRELLI – That was before. When no one knew anything yet. But
now she's been forced to speak and in her own way she's explained
her reason for being so reserved . . .

SIGNORA SIRELLI – She may even enjoy speaking to us of her
daughter.

DINA – She's so good-natured! I haven't a doubt in the world—he's the
one that's mad.

AGAZZI – Let's not rush the verdict. Now, er, listen to me a moment.
[*He looks at the clock.*] Don't stay there long—a quarter of an hour,
not more.

SIRELLI [*to his wife*] Make a note of it.

1960

SIGNORA SIRELLI [*an angry outburst*] May I ask *why* you say that to *me?*

SIRELLI – Why, because once you start talking—

DINA [*preventing a quarrel*] A quarter of an hour: *I'll* make a note of it.

AGAZZI – I must go to the Government Building. I'll be back here at eleven. That's not more than twenty minutes or so from now.

SIRELLI [*fretting*] What about me?

AGAZZI – Wait. [*To the women.*] A little before eleven use some pretext to get Signora Frola to come here.

AMALIA – Pretext—what pretext?

AGAZZI – Any pretext. You'll find one in the normal course of conversation, won't you? Or are you women for nothing? You have Dina and Signora Sirelli to help you . . . You'll bring her into the music room, of course. [*He goes to the threshold of the music room.*] Now, let's set the stage! These doors must be left open—wide open like this —so we can hear you talking from in here. On my desk I leave these papers, which I should be taking with me. Office business—a brief specially prepared for Signor Ponza. I pretend to forget it and so find an excuse to bring Ponza here.

SIRELLI [*as above*] What about me? Where do I come in? And when?

AGAZZI – When? Several minutes past eleven. When the ladies are in the music room and I am here with him. You come for your wife. Through that door. [*Pointing stage left.*] I introduce you to Ponza as you're passing through this room. Then I ask you to invite the ladies to join us in here. When they all come in, Ponza will be sitting here. I then put Signora Frola here. [*He indicates the two ends of a little sofa.*] So they'll be side by side and—

LAUDISI – We discover the truth!

DINA – Now really, Uncle, when the two of them meet face to face—

AGAZZI – Take no notice of him, for heaven's sake! Go on, go on, there isn't a moment to lose!

SIGNORA SIRELLI – Yes, let's be going, let's be going. [*To* LAUDISI.] I won't shake hands with you!

LAUDISI – Then I'll do it for you, Signora. [*He shakes one hand with the other.*] Good luck!

[AMALIA, DINA *and* SIGNORA SIRELLI *leave.*]

AGAZZI [*to* SIRELLI] Shall we be going too, hm? Let's go.

SIRELLI – Yes, let's. Goodbye, Lamberto.

LAUDISI – Goodbye, goodbye.

[AGAZZI *and* SIRELLI *leave.*]

1961

Luigi Pirandello

Scene 3: LAUDISI, *then the* BUTLER

LAUDISI [*walks round the room a bit, grinning to himself, and nodding. Then he stops before the large mirror on the mantelpiece, looks
at his own reflection, and talks to it.*] Ah, so there you are! [*He waves
at it with two fingers, winks wickedly, and laughs sarcastically.*] Well,
old boy, which of us two is the madman? [*He raises one hand and levels the index finger at his reflection which in turn levels its index
finger at him. Again the sarcastic laugh.*] Yes, I know: I say *you* and
you point your finger at *me.* Come now, between ourselves, we know
each other pretty well, the two of us. The only trouble is, I see you one
way and other people see you another way. So what becomes of you,
my dear fellow? Here am I. I can touch myself. I can see myself. But
what can I make of you—the you that other people see, I mean—what
is it to me? I can't touch it. I can't see it. In short, you're a creature of
fantasy, a phantom, a ghost! Well, you see *these* madmen? They're
ghosts too. But do they know it? Not in the least. "Let's set the stage.
Signor Ponza will be sitting here. I'll put Signora Frola here . . ."
Driven by curiosity, they go running after other ghosts—the Ponza
they take him to be, the Frola *they* take her to be—*other* ghosts are
something else again—
                    [*The* BUTLER *enters but stops in his tracks, astounded,
                    to hear* LAUDISI's *last words. He then announces.*]
BUTLER—Signor Lamberto.
LAUDISI—Uh?
BUTLER—There are two ladies here. Signora Cini and another.
LAUDISI—Do they want me?
BUTLER—They asked for the mistress, Signore. I said she'd gone to
visit Signora Frola next door and so . . .
LAUDISI—And so?
BUTLER—They looked at each other. Then they slapped their little
hands with their gloves. "Really?" they said, "Really?" Then they
asked very anxiously if there was no one at all at home.
LAUDISI—And you said no one at all.
BUTLER—No, I said there was you, Signore.
LAUDISI—Me? Oh, no, only the fellow they take me for.
BUTLER [*more astonished than ever*] What do you say, Signore?
LAUDISI—You really think they're the same man?

1962

BUTLER [*as above, miserably attempting a smile, his mouth open*] I don't understand.

LAUDISI—Who are you talking to?

BUTLER [*dumbfounded*] What?! Who am I talking to? You, Signore!!!!

LAUDISI—And you're quite sure I'm the same man those ladies are asking for?

BUTLER—Well, Signore . . . I wouldn't know. . . . They said the mistress's brother . . .

LAUDISI—Oh, I see . . . in that case, it *is* me, isn't it? . . . show them in, show them in . . .

> [*The* BUTLER *withdraws but turns several times to look at* LAUDISI. *He hardly believes his own eyes.*]

Scene 4: The same, SIGNORA CINI, SIGNORA NENNI

SIGNORA CINI—May we come in?

LAUDISI—Please do, Signora.

SIGNORA CINI—They told me Signora Agazzi isn't here. I have brought my friend Signora Nenni with me. [*She introduces* SIGNORA NENNI, *an old woman even more foolish and affected than herself. She too is full of greedy curiosity but is wary, upset.*] She so much wished to meet the Signora—

LAUDISI—Signora Frola?

SIGNORA CINI—No, no, Signora Agazzi, your sister.

LAUDISI—Oh, she'll be coming, she'll be here soon. Signora Frola too. Please be seated. [*He invites them to sit on the little sofa. Then deftly inserting himself between them.*] May I? Three can sit on it quite comfortably. Signora Sirelli is with them.

SIGNORA CINI—Yes. The butler told us.

LAUDISI—It's all arranged, you know. Oh, it'll be such a scene, such a scene! Soon. At eleven o'clock. Here.

SIGNORA CINI [*dizzy*] Arranged? What's arranged?

LAUDISI [*mysteriously, first with a gesture—that of joining the tips of his forefingers—then with his voice*] The meeting. [*A gesture of admiration.*] A great idea!

SIGNORA CINI—What—what meeting?

LAUDISI—A meeting of those two. First, *he* will come in *here*.

> [*He points towards the door on the left.*]

SIGNORA CINI—Signor Ponza?

1963

LAUDISI—Yes. And *she* will be brought in *there*.

[*He points towards the music room.*]

SIGNORA CINI—Signora Frola?

LAUDISI—Precisely. [*Again, with an expressive gesture first, then with his voice.*] Can't you see it? Both of them here on this sofa, the one confronting the other, and the rest of us all around watching and listening? A great idea!

SIGNORA CINI—In order to find out—

LAUDISI—The truth! But we know it already. Nothing remains but to unmask it.

SIGNORA CINI [*with surprise and the keenest anxiety*] Ah! We know it already? Who is it then? Which of the two? Which is it?

LAUDISI—Let's see. Guess. Which would you say?

SIGNORA CINI [*hesitant*] Well . . . I . . . look . . .

LAUDISI—He or she? Let's see . . . Guess . . . Come on!

SIGNORA CINI—I . . . I guess . . . him!

LAUDISI [*looks at her for a moment*] He it is!

SIGNORA CINI [*tickled*] It is? Ah, so that's it. Of course! It *had* to be him!

SIGNORA NENNI [*tickled*] Him! We said so. We women said so.

SIGNORA CINI—And how did it come to light? Are there proofs? Documents?

SIGNORA NENNI—The police department found them, I suppose? We said so. With the Governor's authority behind us, we couldn't fail!

LAUDISI [*motions them to come closer, and then speaks quietly to them, mysteriously, weighing each syllable*] The license of the second marriage!

SIGNORA CINI [*taking it like a blow on the nose*] Second?

SIGNORA NENNI [*bewildered*] What's that? The *second* marriage?

SIGNORA CINI [*reviving, but put out*] Then . . . then *he* was right!

LAUDISI—Facts are facts, dear ladies. The license of the second marriage—so it seems—is pretty clear.

SIGNORA NENNI [*almost weeping*] Then *she* is the mad one!

LAUDISI—Yes, it does seem to be she.

SIGNORA CINI—What's this? Before, you said him, now you say her?

LAUDISI—Yes, dear lady, because the license—this license of the second marriage—could quite well have been gotten up with the help of friends to strengthen his delusion that his present wife is his second. A forged document, understand? In line with Signora Frola's explanation.

SIGNORA CINI—Ah! A document—without validity?

LAUDISI—That is, that is to say . . . with whatever validity, dear ladies, with whatever value anyone wants to give it. Remember, there are also the messages Signora Frola says she received every day from her daughter. Let down into the courtyard in a basket. There are those messages, aren't there?

SIGNORA CINI—What if there are?

LAUDISI—More documents, Signora! Even these written messages are documents, with whatever value you wish to give them. Signor Ponza comes along and says they're forged—just done to strengthen Signora Frola's delusion.

SIGNORA CINI—Oh dear, then we know nothing for certain?

LAUDISI—Nothing, how do you mean, nothing? Let's not exaggerate. Tell me, how many days are there in the week?

SIGNORA CINI—Why, seven.

LAUDISI—Monday, Tuesday, Wednesday . . .

SIGNORA CINI [*feeling invited to continue*] Thursday, Friday, Saturday—

LAUDISI—Sunday! [*Turning to the other woman.*] And months in the year?

SIGNORA NENNI—Twelve!

LAUDISI—January, February, March . . .

SIGNORA CINI [*struck with a bright idea*] We've got it: you want to make fun of us!!

Scene 5: *The same,* DINA

DINA [*suddenly comes running in*] Uncle, please . . . [*Seeing* SIGNORA CINI, *she stops.*] Oh, Signora, you here?

SIGNORA CINI—Yes, I came with Signora Nenni—

LAUDISI—Who so much wanted to meet Signora Frola.

SIGNORA NENNI—No, no, please . . .

SIGNORA CINI—Go on teasing us! Oh, Dina dear, he's been getting us all mixed up! I feel like a train entering a station: poum, poum, poum, poum, all the time switching from one track to another! We're dizzy!

DINA—Oh, he's being so naughty. With all of us. But wait. We have all the proof we need now— I'll just tell Mother you're here, and we'll drop the whole thing. Oh, Uncle, if you only heard her! What a wonderful old lady she is! How she talks! How good she is! Her apartment is so neat, so elegant, everything in order, white covers on the furniture . . . She showed us all her daughter's letters.

1965

SIGNORA CINI—Very well . . . but if . . . as Signor Laudisi was saying . . .

DINA—What does *he* know about it? He hasn't read them!

SIGNORA NENNI—Couldn't they be forged?

DINA—Forged, what *do* you mean? Could a mother mistake her daughter's way of saying things? The last letter, yesterday . . . [*She stops— hearing the sound of voices from the music room.*] Ah, there they are, they must be back already.

[*She goes to the curtains to look.*]

SIGNORA CINI [*following her at a run*] With her? With Signora Frola?

DINA—Yes, you two come with me. We all have to be in the music room. Is it eleven yet, Uncle?

Scene 6: *The same,* AMALIA

AMALIA [*suddenly coming in from the music room. She too is agitated*] We can do without now: there's no further need of proof!

DINA—Quite right. Just what I think.

AMALIA [*hastily acknowledging* SIGNORA CINI's *presence, sad and anxious*] How are you, Signora?

SIGNORA CINI [*introducing* SIGNORA NENNI] This is Signora Nenni. She came with me to—

AMALIA [*hurriedly greeting* SIGNORA NENNI *too*] A pleasure, I'm sure. [*Pause.*] There's no further doubt. It's *he!*

SIGNORA CINI—It's *he?* You're sure it's *he?*

DINA—Let's not go on deceiving the old lady this way, let's tell Father it's all off.

AMALIA—Oh, this bringing her over to our apartment, it's a betrayal!

LAUDISI—Oh, an outrage, an outrage, you're right! It's even becoming clear to me that she's the one. She must be, she *is!*

AMALIA—She's the one? What? What do you say?

LAUDISI—I say it's she, she, she!

AMALIA—Oh, stop it!

DINA—*We're* quite sure the opposite is the case!

SIGNORA CINI *and* SIGNORA NENNI [*overjoyed, to* LAUDISI] Really? You really mean it's she?

LAUDISI—Sure, I mean it. You're all very certain—and *I'm* all very certain!

DINA—Oh, come on, let's get out of here. Don't you see he's doing it on purpose?

1966

AMALIA—Yes. Let's get out, ladies. [*In the doorway.*] Please excuse us.

[*Exeunt* SIGNORA CINI, SIGNORA NENNI, AMALIA. DINA *starts to go.*]

LAUDISI [*calling her to him*] Dina!

DINA—I don't want to listen to you. Leave me alone.

LAUDISI—Let's close these doors—if there's no further need of proof.

DINA—What about Father? It's he that's left them open. He'll be here any moment with that man. If he found them closed . . . You know Father.

LAUDISI—But you'd all explain—*you* would, especially—that there was no need to keep them open. Aren't you convinced?

DINA—Utterly.

LAUDISI [*with a challenging smile*] Then close them.

DINA—You want the pleasure of seeing I still haven't decided. I won't close the doors—but only because of Father.

LAUDISI [*as above*] Shall *I* close them then?

DINA—That's entirely your affair.

LAUDISI—Unlike you, I can't claim to be sure it's he that's mad.

DINA—Just come into the music room and listen to the old lady for a minute as we have. You'll not have a doubt in the world. Will you come?

LAUDISI—Yes, I'll come. And I can close the doors? Since it's entirely my affair?

DINA—I see. Even before you hear her talk . . .

LAUDISI—No, my dear. It's because I'm sure that by this time your father agrees that there's no need of proof.

DINA—Father agrees?

LAUDISI—Of course. He's talking with *him*. There can, therefore, be no doubt: by this time he's certain it's *she* that's mad. [*He approaches the folding doors with decision.*] I'll close the doors.

DINA [*suddenly restraining him*] No. [*Then, correcting herself.*] I'm sorry . . . but if that's what you think . . . we'd better leave them open . . . [LAUDISI *bursts into his usual laugh.*] I mean because of Father.

LAUDISI—Your father will say because of the rest of you. But we can leave them open.

From the music room comes the sound of the piano. It is an old melody, full of sweet and mournful grace, "Il mio ben, quando verrà?" from the opera Nina Mad Through Love *by Paisiello.*

DINA—Ah! It's she, do you hear? It's *she*, playing!

LAUDISI—The old lady?

DINA – Yes. She told us her daughter was always playing that tune. In the old days. Do you hear how sweetly she plays? Let's go in.

Scene 7: AGAZZI, PONZA, *then* SIRELLI

After LAUDISI *and* DINA *have left, the stage is empty for a while. The sound of the piano from the next room continues. Then* PONZA *comes in by the door on the left with* AGAZZI. *Hearing the music, he is profoundly disturbed; he becomes more and more so, as the present scene progresses.*

AGAZZI [*in the doorway*] After you, after you, please. [*He has* PONZA *enter, then he himself enters, and goes towards the desk to take the papers that he has pretended to forget.*] Here's where I must have left them. Please be seated. [PONZA *remains standing. He looks agitatedly towards the music room whence the sound of the music is still pouring.*] And here they are, in fact! [*He takes the papers and approaches* PONZA, *leafing through them.*] It's a suit that's been dragging on for years, as I was telling you, a mess of complications! [*He too turns towards the music room, irritated by the piano.*] This music! At such a moment! [*Turning he makes a gesture of contempt, as if to say:* "These women!"] Who is playing? [*He goes to look into the music room through the open door, sees* SIGNORA FROLA *at the piano. Gesture of amazement.*] Ah! Look!!

PONZA [*coming over to him, convulsed*] In God's name, is it she? Is *she* playing?

AGAZZI – Yes. It's your mother-in-law! How well she plays!

PONZA – But what *is* this? They've brought her here—again? And they make her play?

AGAZZI – Well, I don't see any harm in that.

PONZA – But, please, not *that*, not *that* tune! It's the one her daughter used to play.

AGAZZI – Oh dear, it hurts you to hear her play it?

PONZA – It's not me. It hurts *her*. It does her incalculable harm. I told you, Councillor, I told the ladies what the condition of poor Signora Frola is—

AGAZZI [*endeavoring to calm him in his ever increasing agitation*] Yes, yes . . . but . . .

PONZA [*continuing*] And that she must be left in peace! That she can't receive visits—or pay them! I'm the only one—the only one—who knows how to look after her. You are ruining her, ruining her!

A G A Z Z I – Not at all. How so? Our women folk know perfectly well . . . [*The music suddenly stops, and so does* AGAZZI. *A chorus of approval is heard from the music room.*] You see? . . . Just listen . . .

    [*From the music room the two following speeches are heard:*]
D I N A – You still play wonderfully, Signora!
S I G N O R A F R O L A – *I* play wonderfully? What about Lina? You should hear my daughter Lina. How *she* plays!
P O N Z A [*fretting, digging his nails into his hands*] Do you hear?! She say, "my daughter Lina"?!
A G A Z Z I – Yes, of course, her daughter.

    [*Again from the music room:*]
S I G N O R A F R O L A – No, it's true, she's not been able to play. Since that time. That's maybe what gives her most pain, poor child!
A G A Z Z I – It seems natural enough . . . she thinks her still alive . . .
P O N Z A – But you mustn't make her say these things. She mustn't say them. Did you hear? "Since that time." She said "since that time." Because it's the old piano. You don't know. It's the piano my first wife played.

At this point SIRELLI *comes in by the door on the left. When he hears* PONZA'S *last words and notes his extreme exasperation, he stops in his tracks, dumbfounded.* AGAZZI *is also dismayed but signals to him to come over.*

A G A Z Z I – Ask the ladies to come in here, will you?
        [*Giving the two men a wide berth,*
    SIRELLI *goes to the music room and calls the ladies.*]
P O N Z A – The ladies? Here?! No, no! Better . . .

Scene 8: The same, SIGNORA FROLA, SIGNORA AMALIA, SIGNORA SIRELLI, DINA, SIGNORA CINI, SIGNORA NENNI, LAUDISI.

Having seen SIRELLI'S *dismay, the ladies and* LAUDISI *are quite upset as they come in.* SIGNORA FROLA, *seeing her son-in-law's extreme excitement —he is shaking all over, like an animal in pain—is panic-stricken. When he rails against her in the following scene with the utmost violence, from time to time she gives the company significant looks. The scene is swift and tense.*

1969

PONZA – You–here? Here–again? What have you come for?

SIGNORA FROLA – Well, I came . . . don't be impatient . . .

PONZA – You came here to repeat . . . What have you been saying, what have you been saying to these ladies?

SIGNORA FROLA – Nothing, I swear, nothing!

PONZA – Nothing? What do you mean, nothing? I heard! This gentleman heard too! [*He points at* AGAZZI.] You said "she plays." Who plays? Lina? You know perfectly well your daughter has been dead for four years.

SIGNORA FROLA – Of course she has, my dear. Please be calm!

PONZA – You said "she hasn't been able to play any more–since that time." How right you are: she hasn't been able to play since that time –because she's *dead!*

SIGNORA FROLA – Yes, yes, quite. Didn't I say so myself, ladies? Didn't I say she hasn't been able to play since that time? She's dead!

PONZA – Then why do you still think about the piano?

SIGNORA FROLA – I don't, I honestly don't, I never think of it!

PONZA – I smashed it. As you well know. I smashed it when your daughter died. So that this–other–wife couldn't touch it–and in any case she can't play! You know she doesn't play!

SIGNORA FROLA – Certainly she can't play, certainly!

PONZA – And what was her name? She was called Lina, wasn't she– your daughter? Now tell these people what my second wife is called. Just tell them. You know well enough: what's her name?

SIGNORA FROLA – Julia. Her name is Julia. But it *is*, I tell you: it's Julia!

PONZA – Julia, then. Not Lina. And this winking at people–when you tell them her name's Julia–don't do it!

SIGNORA FROLA – Winking? I wasn't winking!

PONZA – Yes, you were, I saw you, you were winking at them all, you want to ruin me, you want these people to believe I still wish to keep your daughter all to myself as if she weren't dead at all. [*He breaks down in terrible sobs.*] As if she weren't dead at all!

SIGNORA FROLA [*quickly, with infinite tenderness and humility, running to him*] I want that? No, no, NO, dearest! Please be calm now. I never said such things–did I, did I, ladies?

AMALIA *and* SIGNORA SIRELLI – No, no, she never said anything of the sort. She always said she was dead!

SIGNORA FROLA – Yes, didn't I? I said she's dead. Of course. And that you're so kind to me. [*To the ladies.*] I did, didn't I? Ruin you? Hurt you? I?

PONZA [*rising, terrible*] All the same you go around in other people's houses looking for a piano. Then you play the sonatinas she used to play—and tell them "Lina plays them like this, Lina plays them better!"

SIGNORA FROLA—No, it was . . . just . . . to show . . .

PONZA—But you can't! You mustn't! Playing the pieces your dead daughter used to play—how can you possibly think of such a thing?

SIGNORA FROLA—You're right, poor boy—poor boy! [*She is deeply touched and weeps.*] I'll never do it again, never, never again!

PONZA [*coming close to her, with terrible violence*] Go! Get out! Get out!

SIGNORA FROLA—Yes, yes . . . I'm going, I'm going . . . Oh, dear! [*Backing out, she sends beseeching looks to the company, as if asking that they be considerate to her son-in-law. Weeping, she withdraws.*]

Scene 9: The same, minus SIGNORA FROLA

Overcome with pity and terror, they look at PONZA. *But he, as soon as his mother-in-law has left, completely changes his mood. He is calm. He reassumes his normal manner, and says simply*

PONZA—I must ask you all to forgive me for the scene I had to make. It was a necessary remedy for the harm you had done her, with your compassion. Of course you didn't intend it. You didn't even know.

AGAZZI [*astounded, like all the others*] What? You were just pretending?

PONZA—I had to, I'm afraid. It's the only way, don't you see, to hold her to her illusion—my shouting out the truth like that—as if it were madness? You will forgive me, won't you? And I must beg to be excused; she needs me.

[*He leaves, hurriedly. Once more they are all astounded, silent, looking each other over.*]

LAUDISI [*coming center*] So this, my friends, is the truth!

[*He bursts out laughing.*]

1971

ACT THREE

Scene 1: LAUDISI *is lounging in an armchair, reading. Through the folding doors that lead to the music room comes the confused noise of many voices. The* BUTLER *brings in* POLICE COMMISSIONER CENTURI *through the door on the left.*

BUTLER – Will you come in here, please? I'll go and tell the Councillor.

LAUDISI [*turns and notices* CENTURI] Oh, Commissioner Centuri! [*He rises hurriedly and recalls the* BUTLER.] Wait a moment! [*To* CENTURI.] Any news?

CENTURI [*tall, stiff, frowning, about forty*] Well yes, we *have* heard something.

LAUDISI – Oh, good. [*To the* BUTLER.] You may go. I'll call my brother-in-law myself, when the time comes. [*He indicates the folding doors with a nod. The* BUTLER *bows and goes out.*] So you've performed the miracle. You're saving a city. You hear? You hear the noise they're making? Well, is the news definite?

CENTURI – We *have* managed to track down a few people—

LAUDISI – From Ponza's village? They know about him?

CENTURI – Yes—up to a point. The few facts we have seem certain.

LAUDISI – Oh, good, good. What, for example?

CENTURI – Well, here are the papers I've been sent.

[*He takes an open yellow envelope with a document in it out of the inside pocket of his coat and hands it to* LAUDISI.]

LAUDISI – Let's see, let's see. [*He takes the document out of the envelope and reads it to himself, from time to time interjecting an oh! or an ah!—his tone changing from satisfaction to doubt, then to something like commiseration, and finally to complete disenchantment.*] No, no, no! This amounts to absolutely nothing, there's nothing definite in this, Commissioner.

CENTURI – That's all we could find out.

LAUDISI – But not one of the doubtful points is cleared up. [*Looks at him, then with sudden resolution.*] Do you want to do a good deed,

1972

Commissioner? Perform a distinguished service to the community and earn the gratitude of God Almighty?

CENTURI [*looking at him, perplexed*] What service do you mean, exactly?

LAUDISI—Well, look. Sit down there. [*He points to the desk.*] Tear up this half-page of information, it doesn't get us any further. And on the other half of the page write something precise and certain.

CENTURI [*astonished*] Me? What do you mean? What sort of thing?

LAUDISI—Anything. Whatever you like. In the name of his two fellow townsmen, the ones you tracked down. For the general good! To restore peace and quiet to our town! They want something *true*—it doesn't matter *what*—so long as it's good and factual, categorical, specific. You give it to them!

CENTURI [*with emphasis, getting heated, and more or less offended*] How can I give it to them if I don't have it? Do you wish me to commit forgery? I'm amazed you dare propose such a thing to me. I'm more than amazed, in fact. Now that's enough: please present me to Councillor Agazzi at once!

LAUDISI [*opens his arms in a gesture of surrender*] At once.

He goes over to the folding doors and opens them. Immediately the noise of all the people in the music room is louder. But as soon as LAUDISI *steps through the doorway the shouting stops. From the music room one hears* LAUDISI'S *voice announcing:* "COMMISSIONER CENTURI *has arrived. He has definite news from people who know!"* *Applause and cries of hooray greet the announcement.* COMMISSIONER CENTURI *gets disturbed because he knows the information he brings will not suffice to satisfy so much expectation.*

Scene 2: *The same,* AGAZZI, SIRELLI, LAUDISI, AMALIA, DINA, SIGNORA SIRELLI, SIGNORA CINI, SIGNORA NENNI *and many other men and women*

[*They all rush in with* AGAZZI *at their head, inflamed, exultant, clapping their hands and shouting.*]

ALL—Good work, Centuri!

AGAZZI [*with arms outstretched*] My dear Centuri, I was sure of it: you couldn't miss!

ALL—Good work, good work! Let's see, let's see the proofs! Right now! Who is it? Which is the one?

CENTURI [*astonished, uncomprehending, lost*] There's some mistake . . . I er . . . well, Councillor . . .

1973

A G A Z Z I – Please, ladies and gentlemen, quiet, please!

C E N T U R I – It's true, I . . . er, left no stone unturned, but if Signor Laudisi says I also—

A G A Z Z I – That you also bring definite news!

S I R E L L I – Precise facts!

L A U D I S I [*loudly, decisively, warningly*] Not many facts but precise ones! From people he managed to track down. In Signor Ponza's own village. People who know.

A L L – At last! Oh, at last, at last!

C E N T U R I [*shrugging, presenting the document to* AGAZZI] Here you are, Councillor.

A G A Z Z I [*opening it up amid the press of all the people who are milling around*] Now let's see, let's see.

C E N T U R I [*resentful, approaching* LAUDISI] Now really, Signor Laudisi . . .

L A U D I S I [*quickly, loudly*] Let him read it, for heaven's sake, let him read it!

A G A Z Z I – Just be patient one moment longer, ladies and gentlemen. And don't press so close, I can't read! *That's* better.

> [*There is a moment's pause. Then, into the silence, is projected the precise, firm voice of* LAUDISI.]

L A U D I S I – I've already read it!

A L L [*leaving* AGAZZI *and rushing noisily over to* LAUDISI] You have? Well? What does it say? They know the answer?

L A U D I S I [*very formally*] It is certain, it is irrefutable, we have the testimony of a fellow townsman of Signor Ponza's—that Signora Frola has been in a sanitarium!

A L L [*disappointed, crestfallen*] Oh!

S I G N O R A S I R E L L I – Signora Frola?

D I N A – Was it definitely she?

A G A Z Z I [*who has read the document in the meantime, waves it, and shouts*] No, no, no! There's nothing of the sort here at all!

A L L [*leaving* LAUDISI, *they rush back to* AGAZZI, *shouting*] What's this? What do you say, what do you say?

L A U D I S I [*loudly, to* AGAZZI] But there is! It says "the lady." It specifically says "the lady"!

A G A Z Z I [*louder*] Not at all! This man only says he "thinks" so, he isn't even sure. In any event he doesn't profess to know if it was mother or daughter!

A L L [*satisfied*] Ah!

L A U D I S I [*insisting*] But it must be the mother, it must be!

S I R E L L I – Not in the least, it's the daughter, it's the daughter!

S I G N O R A S I R E L L I – Besides the old lady told us so herself!

1974

A M A L I A – Exactly–that's right–when they took the poor girl from her husband secretly–

D I N A – –and shut her up in a sanitarium!

A G A Z Z I – Besides, this informant isn't even from the same village. He says he "often went there," that he "doesn't quite recall," that "he thinks he heard it said" . . .

S I R E L L I – Oh, just hearsay!

L A U D I S I – Excuse me for saying so, but if you're all so convinced that Signora Frola is right, what more do you want? Have done with the whole thing once and for all! It's he that's mad, and that's all there is to say.

S I R E L L I – That's all very well, my dear man, if we could ignore the Governor's opinion. But he believes just the opposite. He makes a great show of the confidence he feels in Signor Ponza and *his* version of the story.

C E N T U R I – That's very true. The Governor believes in Signor Ponza, he told *me* so too!

A G A Z Z I – But this is because the Governor hasn't talked with the old lady next door.

S I G N O R A S I R E L L I – Exactly! He's only talked with *him!*

S I R E L L I – But there are others who agree with the Governor!

A M A N – I do, for instance! I do! Because I know a similar case: a mother who's gone mad at the death of her daughter and believes her son-in-law is refusing to let her see the girl. The same thing!

S E C O N D M A N – Oh no, because *that* son-in-law has remained a widower and lives alone, whereas Signor Ponza is not alone, he—

L A U D I S I [*as an idea dawns on him*] Good heavens, do you hear that? Now we have the answer. For heaven's sake—Columbus's egg! [*Clapping the* S E C O N D M A N *on the shoulder.*] Good work, my dear fellow! Did you all hear what he said?

A L L [*perplexed, not comprehending*] What's this? *What* did he say?

S E C O N D M A N [*amazed*] What did I say? I've no idea . . .

L A U D I S I – What did he say? But he's solved the whole question. Hold on a minute, everybody! [*To* A G A Z Z I.] The Governor is to come here?

A G A Z Z I – Yes, we're expecting him . . . But why? Explain.

L A U D I S I – It's no use his coming here to talk with Signora Frola. Up to now he believes in her son-in-law. When he's talked with the old lady he won't know himself which of the two to believe. No, that won't do. It's something else that the Governor must do here. One thing in particular.

A L L – And what's that?

L A U D I S I [*with an air of triumph*] What is it? Didn't you hear what

1975

our friend said? "Signor Ponza is not alone." In other words, he has a wife!

SIRELLI—You mean, we could get his *wife* to talk?! I see, I see.

DINA—But he keeps her locked up, doesn't he?

SIRELLI—The Governor would have to use his authority and *order* her to speak!

AMALIA—Certainly, she's the one to tell us the truth!

SIGNORA SIRELLI—How so? She'd say whatever her husband wants.

LAUDISI—Yes—*if* she had to talk with him present.

SIRELLI—Then she should talk with the Governor in private!

AGAZZI—Surely. The authority of the Governor will do the trick. When she's alone with him she'll undoubtedly explain just how things really are, of course she will, don't you agree, Centuri?

CENTURI—Not a doubt of it—if the Governor is interested!

AGAZZI—It's the only way. We must tell him about it and spare him the trouble of coming over. Would you mind looking after it, Centuri?

CENTURI—Not a bit. I'll go at once. Good day, everyone.

[*He bows and leaves.*]

SIGNORA SIRELLI [*clapping her hands*] At last! Good for Laudisi!

DINA—Good old uncle, what a clever idea!

ALL—Good work, good work! Yes, it's the only way, the only way!

AGAZZI—Of course. Why didn't we think of it before?

SIRELLI—Think of it. No one's ever seen her. It's as if the poor woman didn't exist!

LAUDISI [*struck with another bright idea*] Oh! By the way, you're all sure she exists?

AMALIA—Now really, Lamberto!

SIRELLI [*pretending to laugh*] You want us to doubt her very existence?

LAUDISI—Just a minute. You say yourselves no one has ever seen her!

DINA—Not at all. There's the old lady who sees her and talks to her every day.

SIGNORA SIRELLI—What's more, her husband admits it.

LAUDISI—Very good. But reflect a moment. To be strictly logical, all you'd expect to find in that apartment is a phantom. A ghost.

ALL—A ghost?

AGAZZI—Oh come on, drop it for once.

LAUDISI—Let me finish. The ghost of a second wife, if Signora Frola is right. The ghost of her daughter, if Signor Ponza is right. It remains to be seen, my friends, if what is a ghost to husband or mother, is also a real person—to herself. Having come so far, we can permit ourselves to doubt it.

A M A L I A – Run along with you. You just want everyone to be as mad as you.

SIGNORA NENNI – Good heavens, it gives me the creeps!

SIGNORA CINI – I don't know what pleasure it can give you to frighten us this way!

ALL – Nothing of the sort! He's joking!

SIRELLI – She's a woman of flesh and blood, there's no reason to doubt it. And we'll get her to talk, we'll get her to talk!

AGAZZI – It was you yourself that proposed to have her talk with the Governor—just a minute ago!

LAUDISI – Why, yes, if it's really a woman that's up in that apartment —a woman in the ordinary sense of the word. But think it over, ladies and gentlemen, how *can* it be a woman in the ordinary sense of the word? It can't. That's why I say I doubt her very existence.

SIGNORA SIRELLI – Heavens, he *is* trying to drive us mad!

LAUDISI – Well, we'll see, we'll see.

ALL [*confused voices*] But other people have seen her, haven't they? She comes out in the courtyard, doesn't she? She writes messages to her mother. He's doing this just to make fun of us!

Scene 3: The same, CENTURI

CENTURI [*entering amid the general hubbub, excited, and announcing*] The Governor is here! The Governor is here!

AGAZZI – The Governor here? What have you been up to?

CENTURI – I met him on his way over—with Signor Ponza—

SIRELLI – With Signor Ponza!

AGAZZI – Heavens, no! If he's with Ponza, they're probably going to visit the old lady next door. Please, Centuri, will you wait outside and ask the Governor to step in here for a moment as he promised me?

CENTURI – Certainly, sir.

[*He leaves in haste through the door on the left.*]

AGAZZI – My friends, I must ask you to retire to the music room for a while.

SIGNORA SIRELLI – You'll put it to him properly, won't you? It's the only way, the only way!

AMALIA – This way, ladies, please!

AGAZZI – You'll stay, won't you, Sirelli? You too, Lamberto. [*The others all go into the music room. To* LAUDISI.] But let me do the talking, won't you?

LAUDISI – I'll be glad to. In fact if you'd prefer me to leave too . . .

A G A Z Z I – Oh no, it's better if you stay. [*He closes the folding doors.*] Ah, here he comes.

Scene 4: LAUDISI, AGAZZI, SIRELLI, *the* GOVERNOR, CENTURI

G O V E R N O R [*about sixty, tall, fat, an air of complaisant good nature. Entering by door on left*] My dear Agazzi! Oh, you're here, are you, Sirelli? My dear Laudisi!

[*He shakes hands all round.*]

L A U D I S I – How are you, Governor?

A G A Z Z I – Come right in, Centuri, sit here, will you? Sirelli, you sit there. Will you sit here, Governor? I hope you don't mind my asking you to come here first?

G O V E R N O R – I was intending to come, just as I promised. I'd have come afterwards anyway. Well, Sirelli, I've been hearing about you. They tell me you're all inflamed and agitated over this matter of the new secretary—more agitated than anyone else!

S I R E L L I – *That's* not quite true, Governor. I don't think you can find anyone in town who's not just as agitated as I am.

A G A Z Z I – That is so. Everybody's terribly agitated.

G O V E R N O R – Well, I can't for the life of me understand why.

A G A Z Z I – Because it hasn't been your lot to see certain goings on. Now *we* have the old lady right next door, his mother-in-law, you know—

S I R E L L I – Forgive me, Governor, but you haven't heard what she has to say, have you?

G O V E R N O R – I was just going to see her. [*To* AGAZZI.] I'd promised you I'd listen to her here as you wished. But her son-in-law came to beg me to go to her place. He was desperate about it—it's all the gossip that bothers him. Now the point is, do you think he'd send me to her if he weren't quite sure the visit would confirm his own version of the story?

A G A Z Z I – Certainly he would. When *he's* present, the old lady—

S I R E L L I [*cutting in*] Would say whatever he wants her to say, Governor! And that's the proof that it's not she that's mad!

A G A Z Z I – We put it to the test, right here, only yesterday!

G O V E R N O R – Well, yes, but he deliberately makes her believe it's he that's mad. He forewarned me of that. How otherwise could the poor old thing keep her illusion? But think what torture it is for poor Ponza!

S I R E L L I – That is, if it's not *she* who permits *him* the illusion of believing her daughter dead—so he won't live in constant fear of her being taken away again! In that case, you must realize, Governor, it's the old lady who's being tortured now, not Ponza.

AGAZZI—Well, that's the point at issue. I'm sure *you*— [*to the* GOVERNOR] must be wondering—

SIRELLI—We're *all* wondering—

GOVERNOR—But are you? Not very seriously, I think. None of you seem to have any doubts about the matter. I'm on the other side, and I have no doubts either. What about you, Laudisi?

LAUDISI—Pardon me, Governor; I've promised my brother-in-law to hold my tongue.

AGAZZI [*with a start*] Now really, what are you saying? If you're asked a question, reply for heaven's sake! You know why I asked him to be quiet, don't you? Because for the past two days he's been amusing himself making the mystery more mysterious.

LAUDISI—Don't believe him, Governor. It's just the other way round: I've been doing my best to clear the mystery up.

SIRELLI—Oh yes, and d'you know how? By maintaining it's impossible to discover the truth. By creating the suspicion that there's no woman in Ponza's house at all—but a ghost!

GOVERNOR [*enjoying it all*] What, really? Not so bad!

AGAZZI—Oh, please! You know *him*; it's no use taking any notice of *him*.

LAUDISI—Though it was through me you were invited over, Governor.

GOVERNOR—Because you also think I'd do well to talk with the old lady next door?

LAUDISI—Nothing of the kind. You do best to stick by Signor Ponza's version of the story.

GOVERNOR—Oh, I see. So you agree that Signor Ponza—

LAUDISI [*quickly*] No! I want all the others to stick by Signora Frola's version and make an end of the matter.

AGAZZI—You see how it is? Would you call that logic?

GOVERNOR—One moment. [*To* LAUDISI.] In your opinion, then, what the old lady says is also trustworthy?

LAUDISI—Absolutely. From beginning to end. Like what *he* says.

GOVERNOR—What are we to make of it then—

SIRELLI—If what they say is contradictory?

AGAZZI [*irritated, with decision*] Would you listen to me for a moment? I haven't committed myself. I lean to neither one version nor the other—and I don't intend to till later. *He* may be right, *she* may be right. The point is we must find out. And there's but one way to do so.

SIRELLI—And— [*pointing at* LAUDISI] he has suggested what it is.

GOVERNOR—He has? Well, let's hear it.

AGAZZI – Since none of the other evidence amounts to proof, the only thing is for you to use your authority and extract a confession from the wife!

GOVERNOR – Signora Ponza?

SIRELLI – Not in the presence of her husband, naturally.

AGAZZI – In private. So she'll tell the truth.

SIRELLI – So she'll explain whether she's the old lady's daughter as we think she must be—

AGAZZI – Or whether she's a second wife who's agreed to play the part of the old lady's daughter as Signor Ponza would have us believe—

GOVERNOR – And as I certainly believe myself! Well, by all means. This seems the only way to me too. Poor Ponza himself desires nothing better than to convince everyone he is right. He's been utterly accommodating. He'll be happier than anybody about this. And it will certainly ease *your* minds, my friends. Will you do something for me, Centuri?

[CENTURI *rises.*]

Go and bring Signor Ponza from next door. Tell him I'd like to see him a moment.

CENTURI – Certainly.

[*Bows and leaves.*]

AGAZZI – If only he consents!

GOVERNOR – He'll consent at once, just watch! We'll make an end of the whole matter in the space of a few minutes. Right here before your eyes.

AGAZZI – What? In *my* place?

SIRELLI – You think he'll want to bring his wife *here*?

GOVERNOR – Leave me alone. I said: right here. Because otherwise you'll all be thinking I—

AGAZZI – No, no, no! What are you saying?

SIRELLI – That? Never!

GOVERNOR – Come off it. Since you know I felt sure all along that *he* was in the right, you'd think I was just hushing the matter up, protecting a public servant. No, I say! I want you all to hear. [*Then to* AGAZZI.] Is your wife at home?

AGAZZI – Yes, she's in the next room, with some other ladies . . .

GOVERNOR – Aha! Subversive activities in the back room! You can hardly object if I make the place serve a more useful purpose. Let's set the stage. We'll put Ponza here. Will you and Sirelli sit opposite with me, Agazzi? That's it!

Scene 5: *The same,* CENTURI, PONZA

CENTURI – Signor Ponza!

GOVERNOR – Thank you, Centuri. Please bring him in.

> [PONZA *appears in the doorway.*]

CENTURI – Come in, come right in, Signor Ponza.

> [PONZA *bows.*]

GOVERNOR – Please be seated, my dear Ponza.

> [PONZA *bows again and sits down.*]

GOVERNOR – You know these gentlemen . . . Sirelli . . .

> [PONZA *rises and bows.*]

AGAZZI – Yes, I already introduced them. That is Laudisi, my brother-in-law.

> [PONZA *bows.*]

GOVERNOR – I sent for you, my dear Ponza, to tell you that here, with my friends . . .

[*No sooner has he started speaking than* PONZA *is visibly very disturbed, deeply agitated. The* GOVERNOR, *aware of this, stops.*]
You wish to say something?

PONZA – Yes. I ask to be transferred to another town. As of today.

GOVERNOR – But why? You spoke so reasonably with me not long ago, so . . .

PONZA – Yes, but now I'm the target of insufferable persecution.

GOVERNOR – Now, come: let's not exaggerate!

AGAZZI [*to* PONZA] Persecution, did you say? Do you mean by me?

PONZA – Persecution by everybody. And that's why I'm going. I'm going, Governor. A relentless, ferocious investigation of my private life —that's what it is—and I won't stand for it. It will end in ruining the . . . labor of love that I'm devoting my life to—not counting the cost. I love and respect that poor old lady more than if she were my own mother; yet, yesterday, I was compelled to attack her with the most cruel violence. And now, in her apartment, I find her in such a state of degradation and over-excitement—

AGAZZI [*interrupting, calm*] It's strange—because, to us, the old lady always spoke with the utmost calm. The over-excitement was all yours, Signor Ponza. And is so now!

PONZA – Because none of you know what you are making me go through!

GOVERNOR – Come, come, calm yourself, my dear Ponza! What is the matter? I am here. And you know with how much trust and sympathy I've always listened to you, isn't that true?

P O N Z A – It's true—as far as you're concerned. And I'm grateful, Governor.

G O V E R N O R – Well then! Look, you love and respect your wife's mother as if she were your own. I'd like you to realize that my friends here are curious to find out the truth precisely because *they* are fond of the old lady too.

P O N Z A – But they are killing her, Governor. I warned them repeatedly.

G O V E R N O R – Really, my dear Ponza, once this thing is cleared up, you'll not be troubled by them again. And we'll clear it up right away, there's no problem. You yourself can remove the last doubt from the minds of these friends—not from mine, I'm already convinced—in the simplest, surest way.

P O N Z A – How so, if they don't believe a word I speak?

A G A Z Z I – That is not true. When you came here, after your mother-in-law's first visit, to tell us she was mad, we all believed you. We were amazed but we believed you. [*To the* GOVERNOR.] But immediately afterwards, you understand, the old lady returned—

G O V E R N O R – Yes, yes, I know, you told me . . . [*Continues, turning towards* PONZA.] She returned to give the version of the story which you yourself wish her to accept. It's surely not so hard to see that a painful doubt might arise in the mind of anyone who heard *her* after hearing *you*. What it boils down to is that our friends have had difficulty in completely believing you, my dear Ponza, since they heard what your mother-in-law had to say. There's only one thing to do. You and your mother-in-law must retire for a moment. *You* feel sure you are telling the truth, *I* feel sure you are too. So you can't have anything against having it *re*-told by the only person—besides the two of you—that's in a position to re-tell it.

P O N Z A – Who is that?

G O V E R N O R – Why—your wife?

P O N Z A – My wife? [*With force and indignation.*] Oh, no! Never!

G O V E R N O R – And why not, may I ask?

P O N Z A – I'm to bring my wife here for the satisfaction of people who won't believe me?

G O V E R N O R [*promptly*] I beg your pardon, it's for *my* satisfaction. Is it really so hard to arrange?

P O N Z A – But, Governor! Not my wife! Don't ask that! Leave my wife out of this! Just believe *me!*

G O V E R N O R – Now, really, if you talk this way, I too will start thinking you don't *want* us to believe you.

A G A Z Z I – He tried in every possible way to stop his mother-in-law coming here in the first place. Even at the cost of being rude to my wife and daughter.

PONZA   [*bursting out in sheer exasperation*] What do you all want of me, in God's name? You've had the old lady, wasn't that enough? Must you get your hands on my wife too? I cannot put up with this violence, Governor. My wife is not leaving our apartment! I won't hand her over. It's enough that *you* believe me. I'm filling out the blanks for my transfer. Then I go.

[*He rises.*]

GOVERNOR   [*bringing down his fist on the desk*] Wait! In the first place you will not speak in that tone before Councillor Agazzi and me. I won't stand for it. I have shown *you* courtesy and deference. In the second place you are refusing to supply a proof which I—and not the others—am asking for. I am asking for it in *your* interest, I can't see how it can possibly harm you. I repeat: your obstinacy makes *me* begin to doubt you too. My colleague and I can perfectly well receive a lady—or even, if you prefer, come to your home . . .

PONZA—You make it a matter of duty?

GOVERNOR—I repeat: I am *asking* this for your own good. My position entitles me to *demand* it.

PONZA—Very well, very well. If that's how it is. I will bring my wife here, and have done with it. But who can guarantee that the old lady won't see her?

GOVERNOR—Yes . . . it's true she's just next door . . .

AGAZZI   [*quickly*] We could go to the Signora's apartment.

PONZA—No, no, it was you I was thinking of. I meant I don't want you to prepare any more of these catastrophic surprises.

AGAZZI—You needn't worry, as far as we're concerned.

GOVERNOR—Or, look, if it suits you better, you could take the lady to the Government Building.

PONZA—No, no, I'll bring her here at once. Then I'll go next door and keep an eye on Signora Frola. I'm going, Governor. Then it will be over, over!

[*He leaves angrily.*]

Scene 6: The same, minus PONZA

GOVERNOR—I didn't expect this opposition on his part, I must confess.

AGAZZI—Now he'll go and make his wife say what *he* wants said, just watch.

1983

GOVERNOR – No, no. Don't worry about that. I shall question the lady myself.

SIRELLI – Really, the way he's always so worked up!

GOVERNOR – No, no, it's the first time—the very first—that I've seen him this way. Perhaps it's the idea of bringing his wife—

SIRELLI – The idea of setting her free, you mean!

GOVERNOR – Oh, his keeping her locked up—after all, that can be explained without assuming he's mad!

SIRELLI – Excuse me, Governor, you still haven't heard the old lady, poor creature!

AGAZZI – He says himself he keeps his wife locked up because of her mother.

GOVERNOR – Even if that isn't the case, he might still keep her locked up. He might be jealous. He might simply be a jealous husband.

SIRELLI – To the extent of not having a maid or a cleaning woman? He compels his wife to do all the housework herself.

AGAZZI – And *he* does the shopping. Every morning.

CENTURI – That's true, sir. I've seen him. He carries his parcels home with a little boy to help him—

SIRELLI – —and the little boy stays outside!

GOVERNOR – But good heavens, he told me about that and sincerely deplored it!

LAUDISI [*playfully*] Reliable sources of information report . . .

GOVERNOR – He does it to economize, Laudisi. Having to maintain two households . . .

SIRELLI – Well, we wouldn't criticize him from that viewpoint. But really, Governor, do you believe a second wife would take on the—

AGAZZI [*getting heated*] The lowest household chores!—

SIRELLI [*continuing*] For someone who was once her husband's mother-in-law and—to her—is a total stranger?

AGAZZI – Yes, yes, doesn't it seem a bit much?

GOVERNOR – It does, rather . . .

CENTURI – It certainly does . . .

LAUDISI [*interrupting*] Too much for "a second wife"—if that's all she is.

GOVERNOR [*quickly*] Let's admit—it *is* too much. Even this, however, can be explained—not, it's true, as generosity on her part—but definitely as jealousy on his. And, mad or not mad, he is jealous. That at least is established, it seems to me.

[*At this point the confused noise of many voices is heard from the music room.*]

AGAZZI – Heavens, what's going on in there?

Scene 7: *The same,* AMALIA

AMALIA [*rushes in through the folding doors in the utmost consternation, announcing*] Signora Frola! Signora Frola is here!

AGAZZI – No, by God! Who sent for her!

AMALIA – No one. She came of her own accord.

GOVERNOR – No, for heaven's sake! Not now!! Have her sent away, Signora!

AGAZZI – Yes, at once! Don't let her in! Stop her at all costs! If he found her here, he'd think it was an ambush!

Scene 8: *The same,* SIGNORA FROLA, *and all the others*

[SIGNORA FROLA *enters trembling, weeping, imploring, a handkerchief in her hand, in the midst of an excited crowd.*]

SIGNORA FROLA – For pity's sake, good people, for pity's sake! You tell them, tell them all, Councillor!

AGAZZI [*coming forward, highly annoyed*] I tell *you*, Signora, go away at once! You simply cannot stay here!

SIGNORA FROLA [*lost*] But why? Why? [*To* AMALIA.] I turn to you, you are kind . . .

AMALIA – But look, look, the Governor is here—

SIGNORA FROLA – You, Governor. For pity's sake! I wanted to come to you.

GOVERNOR – Please don't be impatient, Signora. At the moment I cannot take care of you. You really must leave at once.

SIGNORA FROLA – Yes, I *am* leaving. I'm leaving today. I'm going away, Governor, going away for good!

AGAZZI – No, no, Signora. Please be kind enough to withdraw to your apartment next door for just one moment. Do me this favor. You can talk with the Governor afterwards.

SIGNORA FROLA – But why? What's the matter? What's the matter?

AGAZZI [*losing his patience*] Your son-in-law is about to return. He will be here at any moment. You understand?

SIGNORA FROLA – Will he? In that case, yes . . . I'll be going . . . I'll be going at once. I only wanted to say this to you all: for pity's sake, stop! You believe you're doing good to me but you're doing me unspeakable harm! I shall be compelled to leave if you keep on acting

1985

like this. To be gone this very day and leave him in peace! What in the world do you want of him—here—now? What should he come here and do? Oh, Governor!

GOVERNOR—We want nothing of him, Signora, just don't worry. Be calm and leave us, I beg you.

AMALIA—Please leave, Signora, please oblige us!

SIGNORA FROLA—Oh dear, Signora, you people are depriving me of the only comfort I had left: to see my daughter, at least from a distance.

[*She starts crying.*]

GOVERNOR—Who says so? You have no need to go away. We are asking you to leave the room for one moment. Don't worry!

SIGNORA FROLA—But I'm thinking of *him*, Governor! I came here to intercede with you all for him, not for myself!

GOVERNOR—Very well. You needn't worry on his account either, I give you my word. Everything will be taken care of, just see.

SIGNORA FROLA—How? With all these people persecuting him?

GOVERNOR—No, Signora, that's not true. I am here, and I'm on his side. Don't worry!

SIGNORA FROLA—Thank you. You mean, you've understood . . . ?

GOVERNOR—Yes, Signora, yes. I have understood.

SIGNORA FROLA—We are satisfied to live in this way. My daughter is satisfied. So . . . Well, you attend to it . . . because if you don't, there's nothing for it but for me to go away. Just that: go away and never see her again, even from a distance as at present . . . I *beg* you to leave him in peace!

[*At this point there is a movement in the crowd. All start making signs. Some look back into the music room. Suppressed exclamations.*]

VOICES—Oh dear . . . here she is, here she is!

SIGNORA FROLA [*noting the dismay and disorder, groans in perplexity and trembles*] What's the matter? What's the matter?

Scene 9: *The same*, SIGNORA PONZA, *then* PONZA

The crowd divides up on either hand to let SIGNORA PONZA *pass. She comes forward, erect, in mourning, her face hidden under a thick veil, black, impenetrable.*

SIGNORA FROLA [*letting out a harrowing cry of frantic joy*] Ah!!! Lina! Lina! Lina!

She rushes forward and embraces the veiled lady with all the thirst of a mother who hasn't embraced her daughter for years. At the same time PONZA *is heard shouting outside. Immediately afterwards he rushes in.*

PONZA — Julia! Julia! Julia! [*Hearing his cries,* SIGNORA PONZA, *though still in the arms of* SIGNORA FROLA, *grows rigid.* PONZA, *coming in, at once sees his mother-in-law thus desperately embracing his wife. He is furious and shrieks.*] Ah!!! Just as I said! Is this how you repay my good faith? Cowards!

SIGNORA PONZA [*turning her veiled head, with almost austere solemnity*] Don't be afraid, don't be afraid. Go!

PONZA [*quietly, lovingly, to* SIGNORA FROLA] Yes, let's be going, let's be going.

SIGNORA FROLA [*who has withdrawn from the embrace, trembling all over, humble, echoes his words at once, urgent*] Yes, let's be going, let's be going . . .

PONZA *and* SIGNORA FROLA *embrace and exchange caresses. Their weeping makes a plaintive duet. Whispering affectionate words to each other, they withdraw. Silence. The company watches them until they have quite disappeared. Then everybody turns round, dismayed and moved, to look at the veiled lady.*

SIGNORA PONZA [*after having looked at them through her veil, says with dark solemnity*] After this, what more can you want of me, ladies and gentlemen? There has been a misfortune here, as you see, which should remain hidden. Only in this way can the remedy work— the remedy our compassion has provided.

GOVERNOR [*moved*] We should like to respect such compassion, Signora. We should wish you to tell us, however—

SIGNORA PONZA [*with slow, staccato speech*] What? The truth? It is simply this. I am Signora Frola's daughter—

ALL [*with a gasp of pleasure*] Ah!

SIGNORA PONZA [*without pausing, as above*] And I am Signor Ponza's second wife—

ALL [*astonished, disappointed, in low voices*] Oh! But . . . ?

SIGNORA PONZA [*without pausing, as above*] And to myself I am no one. No one.

GOVERNOR — No, no, Signora, at least to yourself you must be either one or the other!

SIGNORA PONZA — No! To myself—I am the one that each of you thinks I am.

Luigi Pirandello

[*She looks at them all through her veil just for
an instant; and then withdraws. Silence.*]
LAUDISI—That, my dear friends, was the voice of truth! [*He looks
round at them with derisive defiance.*] Are you satisfied?
[*He bursts out laughing.*]

AFTER "THE WILD DUCK"

By Eric Bentley

On the face of it, *Right You Are* is the purest instance of "drama of ideas" in the history of the theatre, a veritable exhibition of an idea, the statement of a proposition—namely, that truth is relative and subjective: what seems to me, or you, to be so *is* so. The statement is made in the (Italian) title, explained by a leading character (Laudisi), and embodied in what the author himself designates a parable. Pirandello seems as single-minded as Aesop, his parable a simple fable, apologue, or exemplum.

If it is rare to find a play so deliberately dedicated to a principle, it is rarer to find one dedicated to a principle that none of us will assent to. What would "assent" mean, anyway? That a certain principle which "seems so" to Pirandello also "seems so" to you or me? What if it did? How can we be sure that it is the same principle as the one he is talking about? Furthermore, if *Right You Are* is true only for Pirandello, why did he write it down? If a man holds the view that views are incommunicable, how can he hope to communicate *that* view? In short, we could not assent to the idea of *Right You Are* even if we would.

Was Pirandello a fool? Had he not taken that elementary lesson in philosophy in which the instructor triumphs over relativism and scepticism by observing that relativism must not become absolute and that the

sceptic should be sceptical of scepticism? There is evidence on the point
—for example, the following debate:

A – The world is my idea (*rappresentazione*), and the world is purely
ideal (*una idealità*) . . . The world—all that is external to the ego
—exists only according to the idea one has of it. I do not see what is;
what I see, is.

B – Or is not, my dear fellow. Because you may see badly. That exist-
ences outside ours should be little more than appearances without
reality outside the ego is supposed by the champions of an idealism
which the English call solipsism, and you know that it isn't a new
notion—English writers following the philosophy of Berkeley have
given it fantastic form. And you will know *Through the Looking
Glass*. Suppose, my dear fellow, that I, let us say, do not exist outside
your ego except as you see me? This means that your consciousness is
one-sided, that you are not conscious of me, that you have no *realization* of me within you (to use an expression of Josiah Royce), that
your idea does not live for me.

And it must be so. And here, to turn to art, is our true point of
difference. For me the world is not solely ideal, that is, it is not confined to the notion I can form of it: outside me the world exists of
itself and alongside me; and in my representation or idea of the
world I am to propose to *realize* it as much as I can, creating for
myself a consciousness in which it exists—in me as in itself, seeing
it as it sees itself, feeling it as it feels itself. And so, nothing symbolic and apparent for me, everything will be real and alive!

Since Pirandello[1] is not A but B we are forced, I think, to admit that
he knew what he was doing and are free to ask: if the relativism is a joke,
what is serious in the play? In the midst of an earnest discussion in a
Westport home,[2] someone appealed to the maid who was bringing in the
tea things, "What did *you* get out of *Right You Are?*" "I guess it just
says, keep your nose out of other folks' business," she replied, thus proving all over again how right Molière was to consult his cook. Such is indeed the simple message not only implicit in the action of the play but
explicitly stated by Laudisi at the outset as the serious moral conclusion
to the frivolous philosophical argument. "Respect what other people see
and touch even if it's the opposite of what you see and touch." The reader

[1] Writing in the weekly journal *Il Marzocco*, March 7, 1897, in reply to Ugo
Ojetti (A), *Il Marzocco*, February 28, 1897.
[2] The present essay was written shortly after its author had directed two productions of the play: one at the Brattle Theatre, Cambridge, the other at the
Westport Country Playhouse.

should go on to ask, as the actor must, not only what Laudisi says but what he does. For more than two acts, he tries to discourage people from interfering with the lives of others. In the third act, he decides that talk is useless, but his goal is unchanged: he hopes that a coup de théâtre may succeed where reason failed—succeed in demonstrating the wickedness and futility of interference.

Pirandello once said he wanted the play to indicate the triumph of the imagination over mere facts. But the imagination he shows us is not a philosophical or literary power of imagining what is not, it is insight into what is, insight by means of sympathy, it is compassion, it is love. While the ostensible principle of his play is an unacceptable metaphysic, the real principle is: love your neighbor. To realize how far truth is subjective is to realize that one must respect the subject. Pirandello is defending the person against the dehumanizing influence of society. His special care is for the sanctity of the intimate affections, the right to possess your soul in peace and privacy. These ideas are as old as *Antigone* but have become more relevant than ever with the rise of the police state. And it is not just fanatics—Communists or the persecutors of Communists—who are open to attack. "Many of our best friends" have for years been boosting the public interest and the objective fact above the private interest and the subjective fact. The inner life of man has been neglected and mocked, without any perceptible public gain.

The seemingly cryptic figure of the veiled lady in *Right You Are* is perhaps the simplest expression of indignation at this neglect in modern literature. She is the inner sanctum, the holy of holies. Her life being love, she has achieved complete self-sacrifice, she has no identity; she exists only in relationship, she is wife to the husband, daughter to the mother; she is what the husband thinks she is, she is what the mother thinks she is, she is what *you* think she is. On the literal plane, all this is absurd, of course, yet hardly more so than the rest of the play. It is all—to quote Pirandello's own perfect characterization—*una gran diavoleria*, a big joke, a piece of deviltry.

Now under what circumstances does a man champion a philosophy he knows to be fallacious? When he wants to enjoy himself and throw ideas about like colored balls. "You're simply being paradoxical," we say to a friend who champions an error with gusto. But the truth is *not* simple. Part of it is that he has been enjoying the comedy of intellect. Another part is that by stating an error he wants to make you more aware of the truth. Laudisi is not quite a devil's advocate. His method is more like the inverse of a reductio ad absurdum: he doesn't take plausible premises and prove that they lead to disastrous consequences, he takes implausible premises and derives very desirable consequences from them. We have seen how he derives from his "absolute relativism" the principle of the golden rule. It is also important to see the totality of Laudisi's speeches in the context of other characters' speeches. Laudisi constitutes a sort of frame for the picture or—more correctly perhaps—the spectacles we see the picture through.

Once the "deviltry" of the play is conceded, even its final leap into the realm of symbol seems fully justified. The audience may be cheated of the answer it is waiting for, but it accepts the *image* of the veiled lady unquestioningly. At that point, in performance, there is usually a gasp of astonishment signaling to the actors that the bullet has shot home. And nothing could better illustrate what this play is like than the fact that its climax is an image. If our first discovery is that the idea of the play is not "truth is relative" but "love your neighbor," our second is that *Right You Are* is not, in any narrow sense, a "drama of ideas" at all. To convince himself he had ideas, Pirandello had to redefine the term. "An artist's 'ideas,'" he wrote in his essay on humor, "are not abstract ideas but feelings, sentiments, which become the center of his inner life, take hold of his spirit, shake it, and, by shaking it, create a body of images." *Six Characters in Search of an Author* may have started in Pirandello's mind with an image of Madama Pace's establishment which he took a note of years before. He also tells us that *Right You Are* was born from "the frightening image" in a dream of "a deep courtyard with no exit."[3] It is with the imagination, not the ratiocinative faculty, that this court-yard is transformed into the home of the Ponzas (the idea of "no exit" being left to Jean Paul Sartre).

For Pirandello was an artist and, in the fullest professional sense, a playwright. He described one of his plays as "Pinero with a difference," and *Right You Are* is a thriller, almost a who-done-it—with a difference. The audience modestly identifies itself with the foolish busybodies, anx-iously asks: Is the girl *her* daughter or *his* second wife?—is led to the one answer and the other in rapid alternation, only to be authoritatively told at the end that the girl is *both* her daughter and his second wife. Luckily, there is another "difference" besides the famous ending—that this thriller contains two other dramas, a tragedy and a comedy.

The tragic action of *Right You Are*, bounded by the arrival and de-parture of the Ponza-Frola family, derives from an unknown "misfor-tune"; the exposure of three lives to the public gaze re-opens the wound; they decide to leave.

The comic action derives from the conflict between Laudisi and the townspeople (principally, of course, his own family). The three acts cor-respond to three stages in this conflict. In the first, the "crowd"—in effect a chorus—investigates the lives of the unhappy trio to the point where

[3] See *Almanacco Letterario Bompiani*, 1938.

two of them come forward in turn and make confessions. In the second, the crowd has the "great idea" of confronting Ponza and Frola. Up to this point, Laudisi has practiced dissuasion. But when, in the third act, the police commissioner refuses to write a fictitious explanation that will satisfy everyone's curiosity, Laudisi the peacemaker becomes Laudisi the mischief-maker. He caps the coups de théâtre of the first two acts with an even greater one by giving Sirelli the idea of bringing over Signora Ponza. At the end, his point is proved and he is victor.

This comic action is repetitious. Yet, if Acts One and Two of Pirandello's play present the same drama three times, the very fact that unfriendly critics are not bored but irritated suggests a positive process rather than merely the author's inability to think of something else to say. For one thing, it is repetition and *change*—change in speed and change in magnitude. Farce (and this is farce-comedy) is a mechanism very like many of the weird and whirling vehicles of a fairground. Its favorite trick is acceleration to a climax—which is reached, in Pirandello's play, just before the final meeting of the Ponzas and Signora Frola. In each act, the same drama takes place: the Ponza-Frolas are the actors, the townspeople the audience. But it is a bigger, "louder" drama every time. And the tempo is stepped up. Now, while the repetition that stems from sterility merely bores, positive repetition, especially when accompanied by a crescendo and an accelerando, is dangerously full of life and tends to act directly on the nervous system. In more Dionysian works— say in O'Neill's *Emperor Jones* or Ravel's *Bolero*—this is readily admitted. What we are less ready to see is the manic element in *comic* repetition. Perhaps the final subtlety of *Right You Are* is that the sad and sinister traits that are overt in the Ponza-Frola story lurk also in the farce that frames it; hysteria and madness are not far below the surface. However this may be, manic repetition is of the essence of farce—as any page of Molière's prose will testify. John Gay's Macheath is arrested, not once, but twice, the second arrest being superfluous by the standards of modern dramaturgy, but integral to the pattern of classic farce-comedy. A farce-comedy consists of concentric circles of repetition: around the inner ring of phrases, the outer ring of incidents.

In taking Laudisi to be a comic character, I do not mean that he should be continuously funny but that such a figure is closer to the tradition of clowning than to that of wise uncles, doctor friends, and ministering psychoanalysts. Tell the actor of this part that Laudisi is a *raisonneur*, and you will get spectacles, an avuncular manner, prosy explanatoriness; the philosophy will ride him, not he it. Laudisi is Harlequin in modern dress, a Harlequin who has invaded the realm of philosophy, and who behaves there as he had behaved elsewhere. All his scenes are gags—from the little episode in which he teaches the Sirellis philosophy, through the mirror scene, the butler scene, and the scene with Signora Cini and Signora Nenni on the couch, all the way to his inventing of a ghost story and actual raising up of a ghost. He is what the Italian theatre calls a *brillante*, and should sparkle. He needs the bounding energy, the diabolical rhythm, that we associate with the tradition of the commedia dell'arte. The challenge of the part today is that it needs these things much more than what we usually require of our serious actors: subtlety of characterization. The actor of the role of Laudisi does not have the task of helping the audience to understand a complex person with such and such a life history; he serves, rather, the more technical function of a link between the comic chorus and the tragic trio, and also between the action onstage and the audience. He needs a highly developed technique because he has to turn like lightning from one activity to another, from one interlocutor to another, to effect transitions from triviality to seriousness, from tears to laughter, and in the last act to take the play and lift it into the world of fantasy. He needs a personality of strength as well as charm because his presence has to be felt even when he is silent and still.

From the two groups into which the rest of the cast falls, the play demands two distinct ways of acting. One group must play tragedy with a tempestuousness forgotten on our Anglo-American stage and believed to be somewhat foreign to our temperament. The part of Ponza presents the Stanislavsky-trained actor with a teasing problem: what to do about the motivation of a character whose motivation is a mystery? I suppose such an actor can invent motives out of whole cloth, but a pre-Stanislavsky actor, for whom such questions did not arise, would be in a simpler position; he need not ask why Ponza is nearly fainting, he can just take Pirandello's word for it. Pirandello is pointedly uninterested in the final psychological explanation of Ponza's passion, he is presenting the passion itself. The actor's task is to do likewise—and to do it within the imposed frame of a social type (the white-collar worker). Fernand Ledoux at the Comédie Française has shown that it can be done. Yet, to be sure, the alarming Latin way in which emotion leaps from pianissimo to fortissimo in so few words presents the non-Latin actor with a problem. In all modern drama there is nothing harder to do—or even to decide *how* to do—than the final meeting and exit of the tragic trio.

No less forgotten and just as often considered foreign (usually French) is the style of comedy required from the second group of actors. Here again it is futile to hunt the motive. The actor's attention has to be transferred from individual psychology where nowadays it too often concentrates itself on to the task of cooperation with other actors in a matter of craftsmanship. He must suspend his belief that it is harder and better to act a Chekhov role than that of a Keystone cop. He must not resist

Pirandello's method by complaining that the characters are not sufficiently individualized. Who ever said the Keystone cops were not sufficiently individualized? One could praise them for not being *excessively* individualized; though any one of them could always step out of the group and have just as much individuality as he needed.

An author who insists on a character being six feet one and having an I.Q. of 120 may be said to be creating "closed" characters; an author who leaves the actor large leeway is creating open ones. Traditionally, the theatre deals in open characters; the author's points can be made in a dozen different ways—with actors of different physique using different "line-readings," and so forth. The members of Pirandello's chorus are open characters. Each actor can try his own way of making the main point (Agazzi's self-importance, for example), and it is for the director to decide if the attempt is in place. The nine actors concerned can be asked to make a quick study of their parts and come to rehearsal each with a creation—a Daumier portrait, as it were. In rehearsal it is discovered whether these creations work. If and when they begin to do so, they have to be coordinated. Comic characters most commonly run in pairs. Sirelli is a crony of Agazzi, Signora Cini of Signora Sirelli, Signora Nenni of Signora Cini: ideally all these pairs would become comic couples enjoying as easy and active a relationship as comedian and straight man in vaudeville. A part like that of Signora Sirelli, which barely catches the attention of the reader, in a production by a *maître* like Dullin, becomes a Dickensian gem. The richness of the part stems, technically speaking, from the fact that the actress can play three distinct relationships—to her husband (whom she bickers with), to Laudisi (whom she flirts with), to Cini (whom she patronizes).

No particular style should be imposed on the actors or even spoken of. A true style will come, if at all, as the bloom on a fruit that has ripened by natural growth and good gardening. You can no more tell an actor to perform with style than you can tell him to be funny. And stylization is the last refuge of the theatrical charlatan. Artificial speech and gesture that can be imposed by decree are not worth decreeing. Such "artificial" style as we have admired—say Gielgud in Wilde—is the product, not of a decree, but of practice.

The nine chorus members of *Right You Are* will bring with them (one hopes) a technique acquired in farce or vaudeville, but they will not at once be permitted to display their antics because this play needs (as what play does not?) a certain air of naturalness; only thus can the unnatural and macabre elements have their full effect. Hence the primary aim of the acting must be social satire: we are moving in middle-class circles in a provincial town.

Some caricaturists start with an exact likeness. When they later distort and exaggerate, they take their cue from the truth: only a long nose is made longer, only a small eye smaller, a fat man fatter. This principle applies to the chorus characters in *Right You Are*—and to the stage design.

I want my designer to give me an actual room belonging to the right time and place—not necessarily the room in every detail, but enough to suggest its solid, corporeal presence. He must not "stylize" the room with playful fancies of his own. (A common mistake of playful designers is to caricature the pictures on the wall. If the point is, for example, that a picture is sentimental, an actual picture, well chosen, would make the point more forcibly. Openly to make the picture ridiculous is to insult the spectator by instructing him how to respond. And of all instructions, "Now laugh!" is the most risky. The quantity of laughter out front is generally in inverse ratio to that on stage. "Chucklesome" productions are sepulchral.) The stage designer's legitimate distortion of actuality must take the form of omission of the unnecessary, and concentration on the necessary, elements.

"What do the characters *do* onstage?" I was asked by a famous actor who was worried at the absence in the script of all allusion to eating, drinking, and smoking, and the various activities which his naturalistic technique would be helpless without. I do not believe the answer is to insert them; they contribute nothing. "Necessary" means "necessary to the play as Pirandello conceived it," a classic comedy, an elemental tragedy, a slender thriller—anything but a piece of genre painting. What do these people do? They gossip. The furniture of gossip is—the chair. It therefore seemed to me in keeping with Pirandello's almost fanatic lean-mindedness to provide the actors with nothing but chairs. Lester Polakov wished to fill the stage with monstrous chairs, their backs five or six feet high, so that the actors would spend the evening threading their way through a forest of furniture. The high backs would mask so much of the stage that the "blocking" problem would be enormous. But some day the idea should be tried.

In both my productions I raised the curtain on an unpeopled stage with a ring of chairs in the center facing inwards to suggest that, the day before, perhaps, a circle of gossips had sat there with their heads together. During the first scene Amalia and Dina are rearranging the chairs in a semicircle, and from here on, the chief physical action was the grouping and re-grouping of the chairs; for not only is the whole crowd always gossiping, but the Agazzi family is forever receiving visitors, forever setting the stage for the latest drama and preparing an "auditorium" for the onlookers. It seems apt to give Agazzi and his wife a nervous passion for re-ordering their room. In addition to satirizing the lower-middle-class love of tidiness and symmetry, it is an external, theatrical equivalent of the inner tension and fever.

In Act One, the interviews with Ponza and Frola are presented with the chorus forming a semicircle and the object of their scrutiny occupying the only remaining seat, the piano stool, in the middle. In my mind I had the image of an operating room with watching students. In Act Two Pirandello has written a scene with Laudisi on a couch between two ladies. I decided to make the couch the cynosure of all eyes throughout the act by having Agazzi choose it as the projected meeting place for Ponza and Frola. The actual meeting takes place in the open space in front, the chorus standing behind the couch and semicircle of chairs. Here I had in mind a prize ring with a crowd around—or animals in a cage before a crowd of onlookers. The third act is essentially that old standby among theatrical scenes—a trial scene. The drawing room becomes a sort of court of appeals with the Governor as the chief justice. Accordingly, I brought the one large table of the set out of its corner and placed it at right angles to the audience near stage center. When the Governor sat behind it, flanked by Centuri, Agazzi, and Sirelli, a bench of judges was readily suggested.

I shall not detain the reader with the minor details of my scheme. They were not the same in the two productions I did, nor would they be the same in any future production. The scheme itself is but one possibility among many. I should be interested in trying, sometime, a more naturalistic treatment. Given a cast of trained clowns, I should also be interested in trying a *less* naturalistic treatment: I can imagine a chorus of comedians jumping up and sitting down like jack-in-the-boxes. Directors understandably stress the tragedy more or the comedy more, according to the special abilities of the actors on hand. The French production I saw was delightful light comedy; my own productions seemed to succeed better on the tragic side. The ideal production that one should aim at would be no compromise or half-way house between tragedy and comedy, drama and farce, but a synthesis of the two. I even think I know how the synthesis might be arrived at, and that is by casting English character actors as the chorus, and American realistic actors as Ponza and Frola. (I would then keep the whole cast on to do *Six Characters* with the same dual distribution. And so I find myself making the conventional plea for cooperation between the English-speaking peoples.)

I have dwelt on the practicalities of staging because no playwright of our time has had a mind more utterly theatrical. In the Appendix to the Columbia edition of the play I discuss the short story which *Right You Are* is based on and find the theatrical version better. An artist of course does not go from one medium to another out of a desire for something better but out of a need for something other. Almost until he wrote *Right*

You Are Pirandello said he would not write plays; he feared those misinterpretations at the hands of actors which he later depicted in *Six Characters*. Even after *Right You Are*, he spoke of the plays as a "parenthesis" within the writing of his fiction. If in the latter part of his career he was more a playwright than a story writer it was because the drama—much as he resisted it—corresponded to his vision of life. A poet, whose mind worked in images, he was obsessed, or inspired, by one master-image: that of the theatre. From it he ultimately elaborated his "trilogy of the theatre in the theatre." But already in *Right You Are*, when we see Ponza acting out his drama before his drawing room audience, we are witnessing "theatre in the theatre."

The notion that "all the world's a stage and all the men and women merely players" is one of the commonplaces of western civilization. A charming version of it in Italian runs:

> mondo è teatro e l'uomo è marionetta:
> se voi guardate bene nella vita
> ognun vi rappresenta una scenetta

> ["world is theatre, and man is marionette:
> if you take a good look at life,
> everyone in it is playing his little scene"]

At this late date a restatement of the commonplace would itself be commonplace; Pirandello's vision finds expression in a special application of it. To say that a man is an actor is normally to condemn him, and the normal procedure of criticism, satire, comedy, is to remove his mask. Pirandello's play *Vestire gli ignudi*, following Ibsen's *Wild Duck*, shows the calamitous consequences of so doing. The collective title of his plays is *Maschere nude* (*Naked Masks*). People mask the fact that they are masked; Pirandello strips this fact bare and excuses it. The "mask" of his title resembles the *fantasma* (fantasy, ghost) of Laudisi, the *pupo* (puppet) of Ciampa (who is the Laudisi of *Cap and Bells*), the *pagliacetto* (doll) of Diego Cinci (who is the Laudisi of *Each in His Own Way*). Laudisi's mirror speech makes it clear that error consists, not in having a ghost, wearing a mask, but in chasing *il fantasma altrui*, the ghosts of other people, the masks of others, in the belief that these are not ghosts and masks, but souls and faces. That there *is* a soul, a center of identity, is not questioned by Diego Cinci at least, for he denounces the false mask of one Prestino on the grounds that it does not correspond with what he "really is and can be."

The word *maschera* is also used to define the actors of the commedia dell'arte who each played one fixed role. The critic who said Pirandello was not interested in characters but in *maschere* probably meant pretty much what people mean when they damn an author for creating "types," not "individuals": types are assumed to be characters of contemptible cardboard, mere snap judgments on social groups. The roles of the commedia are a great deal more. They offer as fair a field to the psychologist as any of the modern typologies, and like the latter they represent a delving below both individual and social distinctions for the very elements of our humanity. Now, several of Pirandello's critics (first among them Massimo Bontempelli, I believe) have noticed the elemental quality in his Ponzas and Frolas and have recorded their impression that the maestro has rendered human nature in its raw and general state prior to individuation. This being so, one is tempted to take the *maschere* in the phrase *maschere nude* to mean the human archetypes, human beings stripped of the accretions of civilization. If this isn't what Pirandello meant, it is, so to say, what he ought to have meant. He had every right to claim that he dealt in such archetypes—if only, by the nature of the case, gropingly, by intuition. And the chief function of the theatre in Pirandello's life was that it helped him to do so.

SIX CHARACTERS
IN SEARCH OF AN AUTHOR
[1921]

English Version by
ERIC BENTLEY

TRANSLATOR'S NOTE

The theatre envisaged is of the type most usual where and when the play was written—Italy, 1921. Attempts to substitute a non-Italian type of theatre of a latter date break down because unless very drastic changes are made in the script, you are still left with items that don't properly fit. You cannot, for example, pretend this is an Off Broadway theatre in 1969 if you then proceed to call a character "Second Actress"—Actor's Equity Association hasn't a single member who would accept the title. With such things in mind, the translator decided simply to translate. And so the reader has the job of imagining a theatre he is probably not familiar with—a theatre in which, for example, there is a prompter in a prompter's box, center stage.

The second most important personage in the play is called, in the original, Direttore-Capocomico. A Direttore is a managing director or manager. Capocomico one would first be inclined to translate as Actor Manager, and the Actor Managers of the Victorian age did direct the plays. The only trouble here is that Pirandello's Capocomico obviously does not act. He is a Director-Manager, and I think there is, in American English, no alternative to calling him the Director, even though the present-day Italian word for that is Regista. It is a matter of the evolution of this particular profession. The Direttore-Capocomico is an intermediate figure between the old Actor Managers and the new Directors. Pirandello gets to the latter in a later play, *Tonight We Improvise.*

One note on the stage directions. In this play, there are few personal names, so that characters are generally referred to as just *him* or *her.* This forces the author to insert very many parentheses on the pattern of "Pointing to the Father." When possible, the translator has shortened these to just (to stick to the example) "the Father" in parentheses.

The Italian text followed is that of the *Maschere Nude* as reprinted by Monadori in 1948. This represents Pirandello's final revision of the play. The translation published in America by the E. P. Dutton Company was based on an earlier Italian text, namely, on the first edition of 1921. The three substantial passages in the first edition which Pirandello cut from his later revisions are included here in footnotes, so that, for the first time, the American reader gets a chance to see what Pirandello's changes amounted to.

CHARACTERS OF THE PLAY IN THE MAKING

THE FATHER
THE MOTHER
THE SON   *aged 22*
THE STEPDAUGHTER   *aged 18*
THE BOY   *aged 14* *(these two do*
THE LITTLE GIRL   *aged 4* *not speak)*
Then, called into being: MADAM PACE

ACTORS IN THE COMPANY

THE DIRECTOR (*Direttore-Capocomico*)

LEADING LADY

LEADING MAN

SECOND ACTRESS

INGENUE

JUVENILE LEAD

OTHER ACTORS AND ACTRESSES

STAGE MANAGER

PROMPTER

PROPERTY MAN

TECHNICIAN

DIRECTOR'S SECRETARY

STAGE DOOR MAN

STAGE CREW

Daytime. On the stage of a playhouse.

AUTHOR'S NOTE

The play has neither acts nor scenes. The performance should be interrupted twice: first—without any lowering of the curtain—when the Director and the chief among the Characters retire to put the scenario together and the Actors leave the stage; second when the Technician lets the curtain down by mistake.

When the audience arrives in the theater, the curtain is raised; and the stage, as normally in the daytime, is without wings or scenery and almost completely dark and empty. From the beginning we are to receive the impression of an unrehearsed performance.

Two stairways, left and right respectively, connect the stage with the auditorium.

On stage the dome of the prompter's box has been placed on one side of the box itself. On the other side, at the front of the stage, a small table and an armchair with its back to the audience, for the DIRETTORE-CAPOCOMICO (DIRECTOR).

Two other small tables of different sizes with several chairs around them have also been placed at the front of the stage, ready at need for the rehearsal. Other chairs here and there, left and right, for the actors, and at the back, a piano, on one side and almost hidden.

As soon as the houselights dim, the TECHNICIAN *is seen entering at the door on stage. He is wearing a blue shirt, and a tool bag hangs from his belt. From a corner at the back he takes several stage-braces, then arranges them on the floor downstage, and kneels down to hammer some nails in. At the sound of the hammering, the* STAGE MANAGER *comes running from the door to the dressing rooms.*

STAGE MANAGER—Oh! What are *you* doing?
TECHNICIAN—What am I doing? Hammering.
STAGE MANAGER—At this hour? [*He looks at the clock.*] It's tenthirty already. The Director will be here any moment for the rehearsal.
TECHNICIAN—But I gotta have time to work, too, see.
STAGE MANAGER—You will have, but not now.
TECHNICIAN—When?

2004

STAGE MANAGER – Not during rehearsal hours. Now move along, take all this stuff away, and let me set the stage for the second act of *The Game of Role Playing.*

Muttering, grumbling, the TECHNICIAN *picks up the stage-braces and goes away. Meanwhile, from the door on stage, the* ACTORS OF THE COMPANY *start coming in, both men and women, one at a time at first, then in twos, at random, nine or ten of them, the number one would expect as the cast in rehearsals of Pirandello's play,* The Game of Role Playing,[1] *which is the order of the day. They enter, greet the* STAGE MANAGER *and each other, all saying good-morning to all. Several go to their dressing rooms. Others, among them the* PROMPTER, *who has a copy of the script rolled up under his arm, stay on stage, waiting for the* DIRECTOR *to begin the rehearsal. Meanwhile, either seated in conversational groups, or standing, they exchange a few words among themselves. One lights a cigarette, one complains about the part he has been assigned, one reads aloud to his companions items of news from a theater journal. It would be well if both the* ACTRESSES *and the* ACTORS *wore rather gay and brightly colored clothes and if this first improvised scene* (scena a soggetto) *combined vivacity with naturalness. At a certain point, one of the actors can sit down at the piano and strike up a dance tune. The younger actors and actresses start dancing.*

STAGE MANAGER [*clapping his hands to call them to order*] All right, that's enough of that. The Director's here.

The noise and the dancing stop at once. The ACTORS *turn and look towards the auditorium from the door of which the* DIRECTOR *is now seen coming. A bowler hat on his head, a walking stick under his arm, and a big cigar in his mouth, he walks down the aisle and, greeted by the* ACTORS, *goes on stage by one of the two stairways. The* SECRETARY *hands him his mail: several newspapers and a script in a wrapper.*

DIRECTOR – Letters?
SECRETARY – None. That's all the mail there is.
DIRECTOR [*handing him the script*] Take this to my room. [*Then, looking around and addressing himself to the* STAGE MANAGER.] We can't see each other in here. Would you like to give us a little light?
STAGE MANAGER – Okay.

He goes to give the order, and shortly afterwards, the whole left side of the stage where the ACTORS *are is lit by a vivid white light. Meanwhile,*

[1] *Il giuoco delle parti,* published in English as *The Rules of the Game.*

the PROMPTER *has taken up his position in his box. He uses a small lamp and has the script open in front of him.*

DIRECTOR [*clapping his hands*] Very well, let's start. [*To the* STAGE MANAGER.] Someone missing?
STAGE MANAGER—The Leading Lady.
DIRECTOR—As usual! [*He looks at the clock.*] We're ten minutes late already. Fine her for that, would you, please? Then she'll learn to come on time.
> [*He has not completed his rebuke when the voice of the* LEADING LADY *is heard from the back of the auditorium.*]
LEADING LADY—No, no, for Heaven's sake! I'm here! I'm here!

She is dressed all in white with a big, impudent hat on her head and a cute little dog in her arms. She runs down the aisle and climbs one of the sets of stairs in great haste.

DIRECTOR—You've sworn an oath always to keep people waiting.
LEADING LADY—You must excuse me. I just couldn't find a taxi in time. But you haven't even begun, I see. And I'm not on right away. [*Then, calling the* STAGE MANAGER *by name, and handing the little dog over to him.*] Would you please shut him in my dressing room?
DIRECTOR [*grumbling*] And the little dog to boot! As if there weren't enough dogs around here. [*He claps his hands again and turns to the* PROMPTER.] Now then, the second act of *The Game of Role Playing*. [*As he sits down in his armchair.*] Quiet, gentlemen. Who's on stage?

The ACTRESSES *and* ACTORS *clear the front of the stage and go and sit on one side, except for the three who will start the rehearsal and the* LEADING LADY, *who, disregarding the* DIRECTOR's *request, sits herself down at one of the two small tables.*

DIRECTOR [*to the* LEADING LADY] You're in this scene, are you?
LEADING LADY—Me? No, no.
DIRECTOR [*irritated*] Then how about getting up, for Heaven's sake.
> [*The* LEADING LADY *rises and goes and sits beside the other* ACTORS *who have already gone to one side.*]
DIRECTOR [*to the* PROMPTER] Start, start.
PROMPTER [*reading from the script*] "In the house of Leone Gala. A strange room, a combined study and dining room."
DIRECTOR [*turning to the* STAGE MANAGER] We'll use the red room.
STAGE MANAGER [*making a note on a piece of paper*] Red room. Very good.

PROMPTER [*continuing to read from the script*] "The table is set and the desk has books and papers on it. Shelves with books on them, and cupboards with lavish tableware. Door in the rear through which one goes to Leone's bedroom. Side door on the left through which one goes to the kitchen. The main entrance is on the right."

DIRECTOR [*rising and pointing*] All right, now listen carefully. That's the main door. This is the way to the kitchen. [*Addressing himself to the* ACTOR *playing the part of Socrates.*] You will come on and go out on this side. [*To the* STAGE MANAGER.] The compass at the back. And curtains.

[*He sits down again.*]

STAGE MANAGER [*making a note*] Very good.

PROMPTER [*reading as before*] "Scene One. Leone Gala, Guido Venanzi, Filippo called Socrates." [*To the* DIRECTOR.] Am I supposed to read the stage directions too?

DIRECTOR—Yes, yes, yes! I've told you that a hundred times!

PROMPTER [*reading as before*] "At the rise of the curtain, Leone Gala, wearing a chef's hat and apron, is intent on beating an egg in a saucepan with a wooden spoon. Filippo, also dressed as a cook, is beating another egg. Guido Venanzi, seated, is listening."

LEADING ACTOR [*to the* DIRECTOR] Excuse me but do I really have to wear a chef's hat?

DIRECTOR [*annoyed by this observation*] I should say so! It's in the script.

[*And he points at it.*]

LEADING ACTOR—But it's ridiculous, if I may say so.

DIRECTOR [*leaping to his feet, furious*] "Ridiculous, ridiculous!" What do you expect me to do? We never get a good play from France any more, so we're reduced to producing plays by Pirandello, a fine man and all that, but neither the actors, the critics, nor the audience are ever happy with his plays, and if you ask me, he does it on purpose. [*The* ACTORS *laugh. And now he rises and coming over to the* LEADING ACTOR *shouts.*] A cook's hat, yes, my dear man! And you beat eggs. And you think you have nothing more in your hands than the beating of eggs? Guess again. You symbolize the shell of those eggs. [*The* ACTORS *resume their laughing, and start making ironical comments among themselves.*] Silence! And pay attention while I explain. [*Again addressing himself to the* LEADING ACTOR.] Yes, the shell: that is to say the empty *form* of reason without the *content* of instinct, which is blind. You are reason, and your wife is instinct in the game of role playing. You play the part assigned you, and you're your own puppet —of your own free will. Understand?

Luigi Pirandello

LEADING ACTOR [*extending his arms, palms upwards*] Me? No.

DIRECTOR [*returning to his place*] Nor do I. Let's go on. Wait and see what I do with the ending. [*In a confidential tone.*] I suggest you face three-quarters front. Otherwise, what with the abstruseness of the dialogue, and an audience that can't hear you, goodbye play! [*Again clapping.*] Now, again, order! Let's go.

PROMPTER – Excuse me, Sir, may I put the top back on the prompter's box? There's rather a draft.

DIRECTOR – Yes, yes, do that.

The STAGE DOOR MAN *has entered the auditorium in the meanwhile, his braided cap on his head. Proceeding down the aisle, he goes up on stage to announce to the* DIRECTOR *the arrival of the* SIX CHARACTERS, *who have also entered the auditorium, and have started following him at a certain distance, a little lost and perplexed, looking around them.*

Whoever is going to try and translate this play into scenic terms must take all possible measures not to let these SIX CHARACTERS *get confused with the* ACTORS OF THE COMPANY. *Placing both groups correctly, in accordance with the stage directions, once the* SIX *are on stage, will certainly help, as will lighting the two groups in contrasting colors. But the most suitable and effective means to be suggested here is the use of special masks for the* CHARACTERS: *masks specially made of material which doesn't go limp when sweaty and yet masks which are not too heavy for the* ACTORS *wearing them, cut out and worked over so they leave eyes, nostrils, and mouth free. This will also bring out the inner significance of the play. The* CHARACTERS *in fact should not be presented as ghosts but as created realities, unchanging constructs of the imagination, and therefore more solidly real than the* ACTORS *with their fluid naturalness. The masks will help to give the impression of figures constructed by art, each one unchangeably fixed in the expression of its own fundamental sentiment, thus:*

remorse *in the case of the* FATHER; revenge *in the case of the* STEP-DAUGHTER; disdain *in the case of the* SON; grief *in the case of the* MOTHER, *who should have wax tears fixed in the rings under her eyes and on her cheeks, as with the sculpted and painted images of the* mater dolorosa *in church. Their clothes should be of special material and design, without extravagance, with rigid, full folds like a statue, in short not suggesting a material you might buy at any store in town, cut out and tailored at any dressmaker's.*

The FATHER *is a man of about 50, hair thin at the temples, but not bald, thick moustache coiled round a still youthful mouth that is often open in an uncertain, pointless smile. Pale, most notably on his broad forehead: blue eyes, oval, very clear and piercing; dark jacket and light trousers: at times gentle and smooth, at times he has hard, harsh outbursts.*

The MOTHER *seems scared and crushed by an intolerable weight of shame and self-abasement. Wearing a thick black crepe widow's veil, she is modestly dressed in black, and when she lifts the veil, the face does not show signs of suffering, and yet seems made of wax. Her eyes are always on the ground.*

The STEPDAUGHTER, *18, is impudent, almost insolent. Very beautiful, and also in mourning, but mourning of a showy elegance. She shows contempt for the timid, afflicted, almost humiliated manner of her little brother, rather a mess of a* BOY, *14, also dressed in black, but a lively tenderness for her little sister, a* LITTLE GIRL *of around 4, dressed in white with black silk sash round her waist.*

The SON, *22, tall, almost rigid with contained disdain for the* FATHER *and supercilious indifference towards the* MOTHER, *wears a mauve topcoat and a long green scarf wound round his neck.*

STAGE DOOR MAN [*beret in hand*] Excuse me, your honor.

DIRECTOR [*rudely jumping on him*] What is it now?

STAGE DOOR MAN [*timidly*] There are some people here asking for you.

> [*The* DIRECTOR *and the* ACTORS *turn in astonishment to look down into the auditorium.*]

DIRECTOR [*furious again*] But I'm rehearsing here! And you know perfectly well no one can come in during rehearsal! [*Turning again toward the house.*] Who are these people? What do they want?

THE FATHER [*stepping forward, followed by the others, to one of the two little stairways to the stage*] We're here in search of an author.

DIRECTOR [*half angry, half astounded*] An author? What author?

FATHER – Any author, sir.

DIRECTOR – There's no author here at all. It's not a new play we're rehearsing.

STEPDAUGHTER [*very vivaciously as she rushes up the stairs*] Then so much the better, sir! We can be your new play!

ONE OF THE ACTORS [*among the racy comments and laughs of the others*] Did you hear that?

FATHER [*following the* STEPDAUGHTER *onstage*] Certainly, but if the author's not here . . . [*To the* DIRECTOR.] Unless *you'd* like to be the author?

The MOTHER, *holding the* LITTLE GIRL *by the hand, and the* BOY *climb the first steps of the stairway and remain there waiting. The* SON *stays morosely below.*

DIRECTOR—Is this your idea of a joke?

FATHER—Heavens, no! Oh, sir, on the contrary: we bring you a painful drama.

STEPDAUGHTER—We can make your fortune for you.

DIRECTOR—Do me a favor, and leave. We have no time to waste on madmen.

FATHER [*wounded, smoothly*] Oh, sir, you surely know that life is full of infinite absurdities which, brazenly enough, do not need to appear probable, because they're true.

DIRECTOR—What in God's name are you saying?

FATHER—I'm saying it can actually be considered madness, sir, to force oneself to do the opposite: that is, to give probability to things so they will seem true. But permit me to observe that, if this is madness, it is also the *raison d'être* of your profession.

[*The* ACTORS *become agitated and indignant.*]

DIRECTOR [*rising and looking him over*] It is, is it? It seems to you an affair for madmen, our profession?

FATHER—Well, to make something seem true which is not true . . . without any need, sir: just for fun . . . Isn't it your job to give life on stage to creatures of fantasy?

DIRECTOR [*immediately, making himself spokesman for the growing indignation of his* ACTORS] Let me tell you something, my good sir. The actor's profession is a very noble one. If, as things go nowadays, our new playwrights give us nothing but stupid plays, with puppets in them instead of men, it is our boast, I'd have you know, to have given life—on these very boards—to immortal works of art.

[*Satisfied, the* ACTORS *approve and applaud their* DIRECTOR.]

FATHER [*interrupting and bearing down hard*] Exactly! That's just it. You have created living beings—*more* alive than those that breathe and wear clothes! Less real, perhaps; but more true! We agree completely!

[*The* ACTORS *look at each other, astounded.*]

DIRECTOR—What? You were saying just now . . .

FATHER—No, no, don't misunderstand me. You shouted that you hadn't time to waste on madmen. So I wanted to tell you that no one knows better than you that Nature employs the human imagination to carry her work of creation on to a higher plane!

DIRECTOR—All right, all right. But what are you getting at, exactly?

FATHER—Nothing, sir. I only wanted to show that one may be born to this life in many modes, in many forms: as tree, as rock, water or butterfly . . . or woman. And that . . . characters are born too.

DIRECTOR [*his amazement ironically feigned*] And you—with these companions of yours—were born a character?

FATHER—Right, sir. And alive, as you see.

[*The* DIRECTOR *and the* ACTORS *burst out laughing as at a joke.*]
FATHER [*wounded*] I'm sorry to hear you laugh, because, I repeat, we carry a painful drama within us, as you all might deduce from the sight of that lady there, veiled in black.

As he says this, he gives his hand to the MOTHER *to help her up the last steps and, still holding her by the hand, he leads her with a certain tragic solemnity to the other side of the stage, which is suddenly bathed in fantastic light. The* LITTLE GIRL *and the* BOY *follow the* MOTHER; *then the* SON, *who stands on one side at the back; then the* STEPDAUGHTER *who also detaches herself from the others—downstage and leaning against the proscenium arch. At first astonished at this development, then overcome with admiration, the* ACTORS *now burst into applause as at a show performed for their benefit.*

DIRECTOR [*bowled over at first, then indignant*] Oh, stop this! Silence please! [*Then, turning to the* CHARACTERS.] And you, leave! Get out of here! [*To the* STAGE MANAGER.] For God's sake, get them out!
STAGE MANAGER [*stepping forward but then stopping, as if held back by a strange dismay*] Go! Go!
FATHER [*to the* DIRECTOR] No, look, we, um—
DIRECTOR [*shouting*] I tell you we've got to work!
LEADING MAN—It's not right to fool around like this . . .
FATHER [*resolute, stepping forward*] I'm amazed at your incredulity! You're accustomed to seeing the created characters of an author spring to life, aren't you, right here on this stage, the one confronting the other? Perhaps the trouble is there's no script *there* [*pointing to the* PROMPTER'S *box*] with us in it?
STEPDAUGHTER [*going right up to the* DIRECTOR, *smiling, coquettish*] Believe me, we really are six characters, sir. Very interesting ones at that. But lost. Adrift.
FATHER [*brushing her aside*] Very well: lost, adrift. [*Going right on.*] In the sense, that is, that the author who created us, made us live, did not wish, or simply and materially was not able, to place us in the world of art. And that was a real crime, sir, because whoever has the luck to be born a living character can also laugh at death. He will never die! The man will die, the writer, the instrument of creation; the creature will never die! And to have eternal life it doesn't even take extraordinary gifts, nor the performance of miracles. Who was Sancho Panza? Who was Don Abbondio?[2] But they live forever because, as live germs, they have the luck to find a fertile matrix, an imagination

[2] A humble priest in Manzoni's *The Betrothed.*

which knew how to raise and nourish them, make them live through all eternity!

DIRECTOR—That's all well and good. But what do you people want here?

FATHER—We want to live, sir.

DIRECTOR [*ironically*] Through all eternity?

FATHER—No, sir. But for a moment at least. In you.

AN ACTOR—Well, well, well!

LEADING LADY—They want to live in us.

JUVENILE LEAD [*pointing to the* STEPDAUGHTER] Well, I've no objection, so long as I get that one.

FATHER—Now look, look. The play is still in the making. [*To the* DIRECTOR.] But if you wish, and your actors wish, we can make it right away. Acting in concert.

LEADING MAN [*annoyed*] Concert? We don't put on concerts! We do plays, dramas, comedies!

FATHER—Very good. That's why we came.

DIRECTOR—Well, where's the script?

FATHER—Inside us, sir. [*The* ACTORS *laugh*.] The drama is inside us. It *is* us. And we're impatient to perform it. According to the dictates of the passion within us.

STEPDAUGHTER [*scornful, with treacherous grace, deliberate impudence*] My passion—if you only knew, sir! My passion—for him!

[*She points to the* FATHER *and makes as if to embrace him but then breaks into a strident laugh.*]

FATHER [*an angry interjection*] You keep out of this now. And please don't laugh that way!

STEPDAUGHTER—No? Then, ladies and gentlemen, permit me. A two months' orphan, I shall dance and sing for you all. Watch how!

She mischievously starts to sing "Beware of Chu Chin Chow" by Dave Stamper, reduced to fox trot or slow one step by Francis Salabert: the first verse, accompanied by a step or two of dancing.[3] While she sings

[3] Pirandello gives four lines of the song in French, and hitherto the English translators have followed him. However, the song is an American one, music by Dave Stamper, lyrics by Gene Buck, from the Ziegfeld Follies, 1917. Here are the words:

In a fairy book a Chinese crook
Has won such wondrous fame
But nowadays he appears in plays
And Chu Chin Chow's his name.
With his forty thieves he now achieves
A great success each night.

and dances, the ACTORS, *especially the young ones, as if drawn by some strange fascination, move towards her and half raise their hands as if to take hold of her. She runs away and when the* ACTORS *burst into applause she just stands there, remote, abstracted, while the* DIRECTOR *protests.*

ACTORS *and* ACTRESSES [*laughing and clapping*] Brava! Fine! Splendid!

DIRECTOR [*annoyed*] Silence! What do you think this is, a night spot? [*Taking the* FATHER *a step or two to one side, with a certain amount of consternation.*] Tell me something. Is she crazy?

FATHER — Crazy? Of course not. It's much worse than that.

STEPDAUGHTER [*running over at once to the* DIRECTOR] Worse! Worse! Not crazy but worse! Just listen: I'll play it for you right now, this drama, and at a certain point you'll see me—when this dear little thing—[*she takes the* LITTLE GIRL *who is beside the* MOTHER *by the hand and leads her to the* DIRECTOR]—isn't she darling? [*Takes her in her arms and kisses her.*] Sweetie! Sweetie! [*Puts her down again and adds with almost involuntary emotion.*] Well, when God suddenly takes this little sweetheart away from her poor mother, and that idiot there— [*thrusting the* BOY *forward, rudely seizing him by a sleeve*] does the stupidest of things, like the nitwit that he is [*with a shove she drives him back towards the* MOTHER], then you will see me take to my heels. Yes, ladies and gentlemen, take to my heels! I can hardly wait for that

---

Just lend an ear and listen here
And I will put you right:
 Beware of Chu Chin Chow!
 Take care, he's coming now!
 He's a robber from the Orient
 And he's filled with Chinese sentiment.
 At night when lights are low
 He wanders to and fro.
 He's the master of his art.
 He can steal a girlie's heart.
 Love he'll plunder, he's a wonder:
 Chu Chin Chow!

Mister Chu Chin Chow you must allow
Has a manner all his own
For he does not woo as others do
He's never quite alone.
With his forty jugs he carries hugs
And kisses to bestow.
'Tis in the sand he'll win your hand,
This Chinese Romeo.
 Beware of Chu Chin Chow, etc.

moment. For after what happened between him and me—[*she points to the* FATHER *with a horrible wink*] something very intimate, you understand—I can't stay in such company any longer, witnessing the anguish of our mother on account of that fool there—[*she points to the* SON] just look at him, look at him!—how indifferent, how frozen, because he is the legitimate son, that's what he is, full of contempt for me, for him [*the* BOY], and for that little creature [*the* LITTLE GIRL], because we three are bastards, d'you see? bastards. [*Goes to the* MOTHER *and embraces her.*] And this poor mother, the common mother of us all, he—well, he doesn't want to acknowledge her as *his* mother too, and he looks down on her, that's what he does, looks on her as only the mother of us three bastards, the wretch!

She says this rapidly in a state of extreme excitement. Her voice swells to the word: "bastards!" and descends again to the final "wretch," almost spitting it out.

MOTHER [*to the* DIRECTOR, *with infinite anguish*] In the name of these two small children, sir, I implore you . . . [*She grows faint and sways.*] Oh, heavens . . .

FATHER [*rushing over to support her with almost all the* ACTORS *who are astonished and scared*] Please! Please, a chair, a chair for this poor widow!

ACTORS [*rushing over*]—Is it true then?—She's *really* fainting?

DIRECTOR—A chair!

One of the ACTORS *proffers a chair. The others stand around, ready to help. The* MOTHER, *seated, tries to stop the* FATHER *from lifting the veil that hides her face.*

FATHER [*to the* DIRECTOR] Look at her, look at her . . .

MOTHER—Heavens, no, stop it!

FATHER—Let them see you.

[*He lifts her veil.*]

MOTHER [*rising and covering her face with her hands, desperate*] Oh, sir, please stop this man from carrying out his plan. It's horrible for me!

DIRECTOR [*surprised, stunned*] I don't know where we're at! What's this all about? [*To the* FATHER.] Is this your wife?

FATHER [*at once*] Yes, sir, my wife.

DIRECTOR—Then how is she a widow, if you're alive?

[*The* ACTORS *relieve their astonishment in a loud burst of laughter.*]

FATHER [*wounded, with bitter resentment*] Don't laugh! Don't laugh like that! Please! Just that is her drama, sir. She had another man. Another man who should be here!

MOTHER [*with a shout*] No! No!

STEPDAUGHTER – He had the good luck to die. Two months ago, as I told you. We're still in mourning, as you see.

FATHER – But he's absent, you see, not just because he's dead. He's absent—take a look at her, sir, and you will understand at once!—Her drama wasn't in the love of two men for whom she was incapable of feeling anything—except maybe a little gratitude (not to me, but to him)—She is not a woman, she is a mother!—And her drama—a powerful one, very powerful—is in fact all in those four children which she bore to her two men.

MOTHER – *My* men? Have you the gall to say I wanted two men? It was him, sir. He forced the other man on me. Compelled—yes, compelled—me to go off with him!

STEPDAUGHTER [*cutting in, roused*] It's not true!

MOTHER [*astounded*] How d'you mean, not true?

STEPDAUGHTER – It's not true! It's not true!

MOTHER – And what can you know about it?

STEPDAUGHTER – It's not true. [*To the* DIRECTOR.] Don't believe it. Know why she says it? For his sake. [*Pointing to the* SON.] His indifference tortures her, destroys her. She wants him to believe that, if she abandoned him when he was two, it was because he [*the* FATHER] compelled her to.

MOTHER [*with violence*] He did compel me, he did compel me, as God is my witness! [*To the* DIRECTOR.] Ask him if that isn't true. [*Her husband.*] Make him tell him. [*The* SON.] She couldn't know anything about it.

STEPDAUGHTER – With my father, while he lived, I know you were always happy and content. Deny it if you can.

MOTHER – I don't deny it, I don't . . .

STEPDAUGHTER – He loved you, he cared for you! [*To the* BOY, *with rage.*] Isn't that so? Say it! Why don't you speak, you dope?

MOTHER – Leave the poor boy alone. Why d'you want to make me out ungrateful, daughter? I have no wish to offend your father! I told him [*the* FATHER] I didn't abandon my son and my home for my own pleasure. It wasn't my fault.

FATHER – That's true, sir. It was mine.

[*Pause.*]

LEADING MAN [*to his companions*] What a show!

LEADING LADY – And *they* put it on—for us.

JUVENILE LEAD – Quite a change!

DIRECTOR [*who is now beginning to get very interested*] Let's listen to this, let's listen!

And saying this, he goes down one of the stairways into the auditorium, and stands in front of the stage, as if to receive a spectator's impression of the show.

SON [*without moving from his position, cold, quiet, ironic*] Oh yes, you can now listen to the philosophy lecture. He will tell you about the Demon of Experiment.

FATHER—You are a cynical idiot, as I've told you a hundred times. [*To the* DIRECTOR, *now in the auditorium.*] He mocks me, sir, on account of that phrase I found to excuse myself with.

SON [*contemptuously*] Phrases!

FATHER—Phrases! Phrases! As if they were not a comfort to everyone: in the face of some unexplained fact, in the face of an evil that eats into us, to find a word that says nothing but at least quiets us down!

STEPDAUGHTER—Quiets our guilt feelings too. That above all.

FATHER—Our guilt feelings? Not so. I have never quieted my guilt feelings with words alone.

STEPDAUGHTER—It took a little money as well, didn't it, it took a little dough! The hundred lire he was going to pay me, ladies and gentlemen!

[*Movement of horror among the* ACTORS.]

SON [*with contempt towards the* STEPDAUGHTER] That's filthy.

STEPDAUGHTER—Filthy? The dough was there. In a small pale blue envelope on the mahogany table in the room behind the shop. Madam Pace's [*pronounce: Pah-chay*] shop. One of those Madams who lure us poor girls from good families into their *ateliers* under the pretext of selling *Robes et Manteaux*.

SON—And with those hundred lire he was going to pay she has bought the right to tyrannize over us all. Only it so happens—I'd have you know—that he never actually incurred the debt.

STEPDAUGHTER—Oh, oh, but we were really going to it, I assure you!

[*She bursts out laughing.*]

MOTHER [*rising in protest*] Shame, daughter! Shame!

STEPDAUGHTER [*quickly*] Shame? It's my revenge! I am frantic, sir, frantic to live it, live that scene! The room . . . here's the shop-window with the coats in it; there's the bed-sofa; the mirror; a screen; and in front of the window the little mahogany table with the 100 lire in the pale blue envelope. I can see it. I could take it. But you men should turn away now: I'm almost naked. I don't blush any more. It's he that blushes now. [*Points to the* FATHER.] But I assure you he was very pale, very pale, at that moment. [*To the* DIRECTOR.] You must believe me, sir.

DIRECTOR – You lost me some time ago.

FATHER – Of course! Getting it thrown at you like that! Restore a little order, sir, and let *me* speak. And never mind this ferocious girl. She's trying to heap opprobrium on me by withholding the relevant explanations!

STEPDAUGHTER – This is no place for longwinded narratives!

FATHER – I said—explanations.

STEPDAUGHTER – Oh, certainly. Those that suit your turn.

[*At this point, the* DIRECTOR *returns to the stage to restore order.*]

FATHER – But that's the whole root of the evil. Words. Each of us has, inside him, a world of things—to everyone, his world of things. And how can we understand each other, sir, if, in the words I speak, I put the sense and value of things as they are inside me, whereas the man who hears them inevitably receives them in the sense and with the value they have for him, the sense and value of the world inside him? We think we understand each other but we never do. Consider: the compassion, all the compassion I feel for this woman [*the* MOTHER] has been received by her as the most ferocious of cruelties!

MOTHER – You ran me out of the house.

FATHER – Hear that? Ran her out. It *seemed to her* that I ran her out.

MOTHER – You can talk; I can't . . . But, look, sir, after he married me . . . and who knows why he did? I was poor, of humble birth . . .

FATHER – And that's why. I married you for your . . . humility. I loved you for it, believing . . . [*He breaks off, seeing her gestured denials; seeing the impossibility of making himself understood by her, he opens his arms wide in a gesture of despair, and turns to the* DIRECTOR.] See that? She says No. It's scarifying, isn't it, sir, scarifying, this deafness of hers, this mental deafness! She has a heart, oh yes, where her children are concerned! But she's deaf, deaf in the brain, deaf, sir, to the point of desperation!

STEPDAUGHTER [*to the* DIRECTOR] All right, but now make him tell you what his intelligence has ever done for us.

FATHER – If we could only foresee all the evil that can result from the good we believe we're doing!

At this point, the LEADING LADY, *who has been on hot coals seeing the* LEADING MAN *flirt with the* STEPDAUGHTER, *steps forward and asks of the* DIRECTOR.

2017

LEADING LADY – Excuse me, is the rehearsal continuing?

DIRECTOR – Yes, of course! But let me listen a moment.

JUVENILE LEAD – This is something quite new.

INGENUE – Very interesting!

LEADING LADY – If that sort of thing interests you.

[*And she darts a look at the* LEADING MAN.]

DIRECTOR [*to the* FATHER] But you must give us *clear* explanations.

[*He goes and sits down.*]

FATHER – Right. Yes. Listen. There was a man working for me. A poor man. As my secretary. Very devoted to me. Understood *her* [*the* MOTHER] very well. There was mutual understanding between them. Nothing wrong in it. They thought no harm at all. Nothing off color about it. No, no, he knew his place, as she did. They didn't do anything wrong. Didn't even think it.

STEPDAUGHTER – So he thought it *for* them. And did it.

FATHER – It's not true! I wanted to do them some good. And myself too, oh yes, I admit. I'd got to this point, sir: I couldn't say a word to either of them but they would exchange a significant look. The one would consult the eyes of the other, asking how what I had said should be taken, if they didn't want to put me in a rage. That sufficed, you will understand, to keep me continuously in a rage, in a stage of unbearable exasperation.

DIRECTOR – Excuse me, why didn't you fire him, this secretary?

FATHER – Good question! That's what I did do, sir. But then I had to see that poor woman remain in my house, a lost soul. Like an animal without a master that one takes pity on and carries home.

MOTHER – No, no, it's—

FATHER [*at once, turning to her to get it in first*] Your son? Right?

MOTHER – He'd already snatched my son from me.

FATHER – But not from cruelty. Just so he'd grow up strong and healthy. In touch with the soil.

STEPDAUGHTER [*pointing at the latter, ironic*] And just look at him!

FATHER [*at once*] Uh? Is it also my fault if he then grew up this way? I sent him to a wetnurse, sir, in the country, a peasant woman. I didn't find her [*the* MOTHER] strong enough, despite her humble origin. I'd married her for similar reasons, as I said. All nonsense maybe, but there we are. I always had these confounded aspirations towards a certain solidity, towards what is morally sound. [*Here the* STEPDAUGHTER *bursts out laughing.*] Make her stop that! It's unbearable!

DIRECTOR – Stop it. I can't hear, for Heaven's sake!

Suddenly, again, as the DIRECTOR *rebukes her, she is withdrawn and remote, her laughter cut off in the middle. The* DIRECTOR *goes down again from the stage to get an impression of the scene.*

FATHER – I couldn't bear to be with that woman any more. [*Points to the* MOTHER.] Not so much, believe me, because she irritated me, and even made me feel physically ill, as because of the pain—a veritable anguish—that I felt on her account.

MOTHER – And he sent me away!

FATHER – Well provided for. And to that man. Yes, sir. So she could be free of me.

MOTHER – And so *he* could be free.

FATHER – That, too. I admit it. And much evil resulted. But I intended good. And more for her than for me, I swear it! [*He folds his arms across his chest. Then, suddenly, turning to the* MOTHER.] I never lost sight of you, never lost sight of you till, from one day to the next, unbeknown to me, he carried you off to another town. He noticed I was interested in her, you see, but that was silly, because my interest was absolutely pure, absolutely without ulterior motive. The interest I took in her new family, as it grew up, had an unbelievable tenderness to it. Even she could bear witness to that!

[*He points to the* STEPDAUGHTER.]

STEPDAUGHTER – Oh, very much so! I was a little sweetie. Pigtails over my shoulders. Panties coming down a little bit below my skirt. A little sweetie. He would see me coming out of school, at the gate. He would come and see me as I grew up . . .

FATHER – This is outrageous. You're betraying me!

STEPDAUGHTER – I'm not! What do you mean?

FATHER – Outrageous. Outrageous. [*Immediately, still excited, he continues in a tone of explanation, to the* DIRECTOR.] My house, sir, when she had left it, at once seemed empty. [*Points to the* MOTHER.] She was an incubus. But she filled my house for me. Left alone, I wandered through these rooms like a fly without a head. This fellow here [*the* SON] was raised away from home. Somehow, when he got back, he didn't seem mine any more. Without a mother between me and him, he grew up on his own, apart, without any relationship to me, emotional or intellectual. And then—strange, sir, but true—first I grew curious, then I was gradually attracted toward *her* family, which I had brought into being. The thought of *this* family began to fill the void around me. I had to—really had to—believe she was at peace, absorbed in the simplest cares of life, lucky to be away and far removed from the complicated torments of my spirit. And to have proof of this, I would go and see that little girl at the school gate.

STEPDAUGHTER – Correct! He followed me home, smiled at me and, when I was home, waved to me, like this! I would open my eyes wide and look at him suspiciously. I didn't know who it was. I told mother. And she guessed right away it was him. [*The* MOTHER *nods.*] At first she didn't want to send me back to school for several days. When I did go, I saw him again at the gate—the clown!—with a brown paper bag in his hand. He came up to me, caressed me, and took from the bag a lovely big Florentine straw hat with a ring of little May roses round it—for me!

DIRECTOR – You're making too long a story of this.

SON [*contemptuously*] Story is right! Fiction! Literature!

FATHER – Literature? This is life, sir. Passion!

DIRECTOR – Maybe! But not actable!

FATHER – I agree. This is all preliminary. I wouldn't *want* you to act it. As you see, in fact, she [*the* STEPDAUGHTER] is no longer that little girl with pigtails—

STEPDAUGHTER – —and the panties showing below her skirt!

FATHER – The drama comes now, sir. Novel, complex—

STEPDAUGHTER [*gloomy, fierce, steps forward*] – What my father's death meant for us was—

FATHER [*not giving her time to continue*] – poverty, sir. They returned, unbeknown to me. She's so thick headed. [*Pointing to the* MOTHER.] It's true she can hardly write herself, but she could have had her daughter write, or her son, telling me they were in need!

MOTHER – But, sir, how could I have guessed he felt the way he did?

FATHER – Which is just where you always went wrong. You could never guess how I felt about anything!

MOTHER – After so many years of separation, with all that had happened . . .

FATHER – And is it my fault if that fellow carried you off as he did? [*Turning to the* DIRECTOR.] From one day to the next, as I say. He'd found some job someplace. I couldn't even trace them. Necessarily, then, my interest dwindled, with the years. The drama breaks out, sir, unforeseen and violent, at their return. When I, alas, was impelled by the misery of my still living flesh . . . Oh, and what misery that is for a man who is alone, who has not wanted to form debasing relationships, not yet old enough to do without a woman, and no longer young enough to go and look for one without shame! Misery? It's horror, horror, because no woman can give him love any more.—Knowing this, one should go without! Well, sir, on the outside, when other people are watching, each man is clothed in dignity: but, on the inside, he knows what unconfessable things are going on within him. One gives way, gives way to temptation, to rise again, right afterwards, of course, in a great hurry to put our dignity together again, complete, solid, a stone on a grave that hides and buries from our eyes every sign of our shame and even the very memory of it! It's like that with everybody. Only the courage to say it is lacking—to say certain things.

STEPDAUGHTER—The courage to do them, though—everybody's got that.

FATHER—Everybody. But in secret. That's why it takes more courage to say them. A man only has to say them and it's all over: he's labelled a cynic. But, sir, he isn't! He's just like everybody else. Better! He's better because he's not afraid to reveal, by the light of intelligence the red stain of shame, there, in the human beast, which closes its eyes to it. Woman—yes, woman—what is she like, actually? She looks at us, inviting, tantalizing. You take hold of her. She's no sooner in your arms than she shuts her eyes. It is the sign of her submission. The sign with which she tells the man: Blind yourself for I am blind.

STEPDAUGHTER—How about when she no longer keeps them shut? When she no longer feels the need to hide the red stain of shame from herself by closing her eyes, and instead, her eyes dry now and impassive, sees the shame of the man, who has blinded himself even without love? They make me vomit, all those intellectual elaborations, this philosophy that begins by revealing the beast and then goes on to excuse it and save its soul . . . I can't bear to hear about it! Because when a man feels obliged to *reduce* life this way, reduce it all to "the beast," throwing overboard every vestige of the truly human, every aspiration after chastity, all feelings of purity, of the ideal, of duties, of modesty, of shame, then nothing is more contemptible, more nauseating than his wretched guilt feelings! Crocodile tears!

DIRECTOR—Let's get to the facts, to the facts! This is just discussion.

FATHER—Very well. But a fact is like a sack. When it's empty, it won't stand up. To make it stand up you must first pour into it the reasons and feelings by which it exists. I couldn't know that—when that man died and they returned here in poverty—she went out to work as a dressmaker to support the children, nor that the person she went to work for was that . . . that Madam Pace!

STEPDAUGHTER—A highclass dressmaker, if you'd all like to know! To all appearances, she serves fine ladies, but then she arranges things so that the fine ladies serve *her* . . . without prejudice to ladies not so fine!

MOTHER—Believe me, sir, I never had the slightest suspicion that that old witch hired me because she had her eye on my daughter . . .

STEPDAUGHTER—Poor momma! Do you know, sir, what the woman did when I brought her my mother's work? She would point out to me the material she'd ruined by giving it to my mother to sew. And she deducted for that, she deducted. And so, you understand, I paid, while that poor creature thought she was making sacrifices for me and those two by sewing, even at night, Madam Pace's material!

[*Indignant movements and exclamations from the* ACTORS.]

DIRECTOR [*without pause*] And there, one day, you met—

STEPDAUGHTER [*pointing to the* FATHER]—him, him, yes sir! An old client! Now there's a scene for you to put on! Superb!

FATHER—Interrupted by her—the mother—

STEPDAUGHTER [*without pause, treacherously*]—almost in time!—

FATHER [*shouting*] No, no, *in* time! Because, luckily, I recognized the girl in time. And I took them all back, sir, into my home. Now try to visualize my situation and hers, the one confronting the other—she as you see her now, myself unable to look her in the face any more.

STEPDAUGHTER—It's too absurd! But—afterwards—was it possible for me to be a modest little miss, virtuous and wellbred, in accordance with those confounded aspirations towards a certain solidity, towards what is morally sound?

FATHER—And therein lies the drama, sir, as far as I'm concerned: in my awareness that each of us thinks of himself as *one* but that, well, it's not true, each of us is many, oh so many, sir, according to the possibilities of being that are in us. We are one thing for this person, another for that! Already *two* utterly different things! And with it all, the illusion of being always one thing for all men, and always this one thing in every single action. It's not true! Not true! We realize as much when, by some unfortunate chance, in one or another of our acts, we find ourselves suspended, hooked. We see, I mean, that we are not wholly in that act, and that therefore it would be abominably unjust to judge us by that act alone, to hold us suspended, hooked, in the pillory, our whole life long, as if our life were summed up in that act! Now do you understand this girl's treachery? She surprised me in a place, in an act, in which she should never have had to know me—I couldn't be that way for her. And she wants to give me a reality such as I could never had expected I would have to assume for her, the reality of a fleeting moment, a shameful one, in my life! This, sir, this is what I feel most strongly. And you will see that the drama will derive tremendous value from this. But now add the situation of the others! His . . .

[*He points to the* SON.]

SON [*shrugging contemptuously*] Leave me out of this! It's none of my business.

FATHER—What? None of your business?

SON—None. And I *want* to be left out. I wasn't made to be one of you, and you know it.

STEPDAUGHTER—We're common, aren't we?—And he's so refined.— But from time to time I give him a hard, contemptuous look, and he looks down at the ground. You may have noticed that, sir. He looks down at the ground. For he knows the wrong he's done me.

SON [*hardly looking at her*] Me?

STEPDAUGHTER—You! You! I'm on the streets because of you! [*A movement of horror from the* ACTORS.] Did you or did you not, by your attitude, deny us—I won't say the intimacy of home but even the hospitality which puts guests at their ease? We were the intruders, coming to invade the kingdom of your legitimacy! I'd like to have you see, sir, certain little scenes between just him and me! He says I tyrannized over them all. But it was entirely because of his attitude that I started to exploit the situation he calls filthy, a situation which had brought me into his home with my mother, who is also *his* mother, *as its mistress!*

SON [*coming slowly forward*] They can't lose, sir, three against one, an easy game. But figure to yourself a son, sitting quietly at home, who one fine day sees a young woman arrive, an impudent type with her nose in the air, asking for his father, with whom she has heaven knows what business; and then he sees her return, in the same style, accompanied by that little girl over there; and finally he sees her treat his father—who can say why?—in a very ambiguous and cool manner, demanding money, in a tone that takes for granted that he *has* to give it, has to, is obligated—

FATHER——but I *am* obligated: it's for your mother!

SON—How would I know? When, sir [*to the* DIRECTOR], have I ever seen her? When have I ever heard her spoken of. One day I see her arrive with her [*the* STEPDAUGHTER], with that boy, with that little girl. They say to me: "It's your mother too, know that?" I manage to figure out from her carryings-on [*pointing at the* STEPDAUGHTER] why they arrived in our home from one day to the next . . . What I'm feeling and experiencing I can't put into words, and wouldn't want to. I wouldn't want to confess it, even to myself. It cannot therefore result in any action on my part. You can see that. Believe me, sir, I'm a character that, dramatically speaking, remains unrealized. I'm out of place in their company. So please leave me out of it all!

FATHER—What? But it's just because you're so—

S O N [*in violent exasperation*]—I'm so what? How would *you* know?
When did you ever care about me?

F A T H E R—*Touché! Touché!* But isn't even that a dramatic situation?
This withdrawnness of yours, so cruel to me, and to your mother who,
on her return home is seeing you almost for the first time, a grown man
she doesn't recognize, though she knows you're her son . . . [*Pointing
out the* MOTHER *to the* DIRECTOR.] Just look at her, she's crying.

S T E P D A U G H T E R [*angrily, stamping her foot*] Like the fool she is!

F A T H E R [*pointing her out to the* DIRECTOR] And she can't abide him,
you know. [*Again referring to the* SON.]—He says it's none of his business. The truth is he's almost the pivot of the action. Look at that little boy, clinging to his mother all the time, scared, humiliated . . .
It's all because of *him*. [*The* SON.] Perhaps the most painful situation
of all is that little boy's: he feels alien, more than all the others, and
the poor little thing is so mortified, so anguished at being taken into
our home—out of charity, as it were . . . [*Confidentially.*] He's just
like his father: humble, doesn't say anything . . .

D I R E C T O R—He won't fit anyway. You've no idea what a nuisance children are on stage.

F A T H E R—But he wouldn't be a nuisance for long. Nor would the little
girl, no, she's the first to go . . .[4]

D I R E C T O R—Very good, yes! The whole thing interests me very much
indeed. I have a hunch, a definite hunch, that there's material here
for a fine play!

S T E P D A U G H T E R [*trying to inject herself*] With a character like me
in it!

F A T H E R [*pushing her to one side in his anxiety to know what*
DIRECTOR *will decide*] You be quiet!

D I R E C T O R [*going right on, ignoring the interruption*] Yes, it's new
stuff . . .

---

4 The first edition had the Father continue as follows:—"Because, finally, the
drama is all in this: when the mother re-enters my home, the family she had elsewhere, which was being, as it were, super-imposed on the first one, comes to an
end, it's alien, it can't grow in this soil. The little girl dies, the little boy comes to
a tragic end, the older girl flees. And so, after all the torment, there remain—we
three—myself, the mother, the son. And when the alien family is gone, we too find
ourselves alien—the one to the other. We find ourselves utterly desolated. As he
(pointing to the Son) scornfully said, it's the revenge of the Demon of Experiment which, alas, I carry inside me, a demon that makes me seek an impossible
good, which is what happens when absolute faith is lacking—the faith that enables us humbly to accept life as it is—instead, in our pride, we try to take it
over, creating for other persons a reality we consider to be in their line; but sir, it
isn't; each of us has his own reality within him, to be respected before God, even
when it harms us."

FATHER—Very new!

DIRECTOR—You had some gall, though, to come and throw it at me this way . . .

FATHER—Well, you see, sir, born as we are to the stage . . .

DIRECTOR—You're amateurs, are you?

FATHER—No. I say: "born to the stage" because . . .

DIRECTOR—Oh, come on, you must have done some acting!

FATHER—No, no, sir, only as every man acts the part assigned to him —by himself or others—in this life. In me you see passion itself, which —in almost all people, as it rises—invariably becomes a bit theatrical . . .

DIRECTOR—Well, never mind! Never mind about that!—You see, my dear sir, without the author . . . I could direct you to an author . . .

FATHER—No, no, look: you be the author!

DIRECTOR—Me? What are you talking about?

FATHER—Yes, you. You. Why not?

DIRECTOR—Because I've never been an author, that's why not!

FATHER—Couldn't you be one now, hm? There's nothing to it. Everyone's doing it. And your job is made all the easier by the fact that you have us—here—alive—right in front of your nose!

DIRECTOR—It wouldn't be enough.

FATHER—Not enough? Seeing us live our own drama . . .

DIRECTOR—I know, but you always need someone to write it!

FATHER—No. Just someone to take it down, maybe, since you have us here—in action—scene by scene. It'll be enough if we piece together a rough sketch for you, then you can rehearse it.

DIRECTOR [*tempted, goes up on stage again*] Well, I'm almost, almost tempted . . . Just for kicks . . . We could actually rehearse . . .

FATHER—Of course you could! What scenes you'll see emerge! I can list them for you right away.

DIRECTOR—I'm tempted . . . I'm tempted . . . Let's give it a try . . . Come to my office. [*Turns to the* ACTORS.] Take a break, will you? But don't go away. We'll be back in fifteen or twenty minutes. [*To the* FATHER.] Let's see what we can do . . . Maybe we can get something very extraordinary out of all this . . .

FATHER—We certainly can. Wouldn't it be better to take *them* along?
[*He points to the* CHARACTERS.]

DIRECTOR—Yes, let them all come. [*Starts going off, then comes back to address the* ACTORS.] Now don't forget. Everyone on time. Fifteen minutes.

[DIRECTOR *and* SIX CHARACTERS *cross the stage and disappear. The* ACTORS *stay there and look at one another in amazement.*]

LEADING MAN—Is he serious? What's he going to do?

JUVENILE – This is outright insanity.
A THIRD ACTOR – We have to improvise a drama right off the bat?
JUVENILE LEAD – That's right. Like *Commedia dell'Arte.*
LEADING LADY – Well, if he thinks *I'm* going to lend myself to that sort of thing . . .
INGENUE – Count me out.
A FOURTH ACTOR [*alluding to the* CHARACTERS] I'd like to know who those people are.
THE THIRD ACTOR – Who would they be? Madmen or crooks!
JUVENILE LEAD – And he's going to pay attention to them?
INGENUE – Carried away by vanity! Wants to be an author now . . .
LEADING MAN – It's out of this world. If this is what the theatre is coming to, my friends . . .
A FIFTH ACTOR – I think it's rather fun.
THE THIRD ACTOR – Well! We shall see. We shall see.

And chatting thus among themselves, the ACTORS *leave the stage, some using the little door at the back, others returning to their dressing rooms.*
  The curtain remains raised. The performance is interrupted by a twenty-minute intermission.

Bells ring. The performance is resumed.[5]

From dressing rooms, from the door, and also from the house, the ACTORS, *the* STAGE MANAGER, *the* TECHNICIAN, *the* PROMPTER, *the* PROPERTY MAN *return to the stage; at the same time the* DIRECTOR *and the* SIX CHARACTERS *emerge from the office.*

As soon as the house lights are out, the stage lighting is as before.

DIRECTOR – Let's go, everybody! Is everyone here? Quiet! We're beginning.

[*Calls the* TECHNICIAN *by name.*]

TECHNICIAN – Here!

DIRECTOR – Set the stage for the parlor scene. Two wings and a backdrop with a door in it will do, quickly please!

The TECHNICIAN *at once runs to do the job, and does it while the* DIRECTOR *works things out with the* STAGE MANAGER, *the* PROPERTY MAN, *the* PROMPTER, *and the* ACTORS. *This indication of a set consists of two wings, a drop with a door in it, all in pink and gold stripes.*

DIRECTOR [*to the* PROPERTY MAN] See if we have some sort of bedsofa in the prop room.

PROPERTY MAN – Yes, sir, there's the green one.

STEPDAUGHTER – No, no, not green! It was yellow, flowered, plush, and very big. Extremely comfortable.

PROPERTY MAN – Well, we have nothing like that.

DIRECTOR – But it doesn't matter. Bring the one you have.

[5] In the first edition, a passage follows most of which is found at a later point of the revised text. But this interesting speech of the Son was dropped: "Perform this! . . . As if there were any reason! But he (the Father) has found the meaning. As if everyone couldn't find the meaning of anything that happens in this life, *his* meaning, corresponding to *his* presuppositions! (Pause) He complains, this man, of having been discovered *where* he shouldn't have been and doing *what* he shouldn't have been doing—caught in an act which should have remained hidden, outside that reality which he should have sustained for other people. And I? Hasn't he acted in such a way as to force me to discover what no son should ever discover? That father and mother are alive and are man and woman, for each other, outside that reality of father and mother which we give them. For, as soon as this reality is uncovered, our life is no longer tied to that man and that woman except at a single point—one which will only shame them, should we see it!"

STEPDAUGHTER – Doesn't matter? Madam Pace's famous *chaise longue!*

DIRECTOR – This is just for rehearsal. Please don't meddle! [*To the* STAGE MANAGER.] See if we have a display case—long and rather narrow.

STEPDAUGHTER – The table, the little mahogany table for the pale blue envelope!

STAGE MANAGER [*to the* DIRECTOR] There's the small one. Gilded.

DIRECTOR – All right. Get that one.

FATHER – A large mirror.

STEPDAUGHTER – And the screen. A screen, please, or what'll I do?

STAGE MANAGER – Yes, ma'am, we have lots of screens, don't worry.

DIRECTOR [*to the* STEPDAUGHTER] A few coat hangers?

STEPDAUGHTER – A great many, yes.

DIRECTOR [*to the* STAGE MANAGER] See how many we've got, and have them brought on.

STAGE MANAGER – Right, sir, I'll see to it.

The STAGE MANAGER *also hurries to do his job and while the* DIRECTOR *goes on talking with the* PROMPTER *and then with the* CHARACTERS *and the* ACTORS, *has the furniture carried on by stagehands and arranges it as he thinks fit.*

DIRECTOR [*to the* PROMPTER] Meanwhile you can get into position. Look: this is the outline of the scenes, act by act. [*He gives him several sheets of paper.*] You'll have to be a bit of a virtuoso today.

PROMPTER – Shorthand?

DIRECTOR [*pleasantly surprised*] Oh, good! You know shorthand?

PROMPTER – I may not know prompting, but shorthand . . . [*Turning to a stage hand.*] Get me some paper from my room—quite a lot—all you can find!

[*The stagehand runs off and returns a little later with a wad of paper which he gives to the* PROMPTER.]

DIRECTOR [*going right on, to the* PROMPTER] Follow the scenes line by line as we play them, and try to pin down the speeches, at least the most important ones. [*Then, turning to the* ACTORS.] Clear the stage please, everyone! Yes, come over to this side and pay close attention.

[*He indicates the left.*]

LEADING LADY – Excuse me but—

DIRECTOR [*forestalling*] There'll be no improvising, don't fret.

LEADING MAN – Then what are we to do?

DIRECTOR – Nothing. For now, just stop, look, and listen. Afterwards you'll be given written parts. Right now we'll rehearse. As best we can. With them doing the rehearsing for us.

[*He points to the* CHARACTERS.]

FATHER [*amid all the confusion on stage, as if he'd fallen from the clouds*] We're rehearsing? How d'you mean?

DIRECTOR—Yes, for them. You rehearse for them.

[*Indicates the* ACTORS.]

FATHER—But if we are the characters . . .

DIRECTOR—All right, you're characters, but, my dear sir, characters don't perform here, actors perform here. The characters are there, in the script—[*he points to the* PROMPTER'S *box*] when there *is* a script!

FATHER—Exactly! Since there isn't, and you gentlemen have the luck to have them right here, alive in front of you, those characters . . .

DIRECTOR—Oh, great! Want to do it all yourselves? Appear before the public, do the acting yourselves?

FATHER—Of course. Just as we are.

DIRECTOR [*ironically*] I'll bet you'd put on a splendid show!

LEADING MAN—Then what's the use of staying?

DIRECTOR [*without irony, to the* CHARACTERS] Don't run away with the idea that you can act! That's laughable . . . [*And in fact the* ACTORS *laugh.*] Hear that? They're laughing. [*Coming back to the point.*] I was forgetting. I must cast the show. It's quite easy. It casts itself. [*To the* SECOND ACTRESS.] You, ma'am, will play the Mother. [*To the* FATHER.] You'll have to find her a name.

FATHER—Amalia, sir.

DIRECTOR—But that's this lady's real name. We wouldn't want to call her by her real name!

FATHER—Why not? If that is her name . . . But of course, if it's to be this lady . . . [*He indicates the* SECOND ACTRESS *with a vague gesture.*] To me she [*the* MOTHER] is Amalia. But suit yourself . . . [*He is getting more and more confused.*] I don't know what to tell you . . . I'm beginning to . . . oh, I don't know . . . to find my own words ringing false, they sound different somehow.

DIRECTOR—Don't bother about that, just don't bother about it. We can always find the right sound. As for the name, if you say Amalia, Amalia it shall be; or we'll find another. For now, we'll designate the characters thus: [*To the* JUVENILE LEAD.] You're the Son. [*To the* LEADING LADY.] You, ma'am, are of course the Stepdaughter.

STEPDAUGHTER [*excitedly*] What, what? That one there is me?

[*She bursts out laughing.*]

DIRECTOR [*mad*] What is there to laugh at?

LEADING LADY [*aroused*] No one has ever dared laugh at me! I insist on respect—or I quit!

STEPDAUGHTER—But, excuse me, I'm not laughing at you.

2029

DIRECTOR [*to the* STEPDAUGHTER] You should consider yourself honored to be played by . . .

LEADING LADY [*without pause, contemptuously*]—"That one there!"

STEPDAUGHTER—But I wasn't speaking of you, believe me. I was speaking of me. I don't see me in you, that's all. I don't know why . . . I guess you're just not like me!

FATHER—That's it, exactly, my dear sir! What is *expressed* in us . . .

DIRECTOR—Expression, expression! You think that's your business? Not at all!

FATHER—Well, but what *we* express . . .

DIRECTOR—But you don't. You don't express. You provide us with raw material. The actors give it body and face, voice and gesture. They've given expression to much loftier material, let me tell you. Yours is on such a small scale that, if it stands up on stage at all, the credit, believe me, should all go to my actors.

FATHER—I don't dare contradict you, sir, but it's terribly painful for us who are as you see us—with these bodies, these faces—

DIRECTOR [*cutting in, out of patience*]—that's where make-up comes in, my dear sir, for whatever concerns the face, the remedy is make-up!

FATHER—Yes. But the voice, gesture—

DIRECTOR—Oh, for Heaven's sake! You can't exist here! Here the actor acts you, and that's that!

FATHER—I understand, sir. But now perhaps I begin to guess also why our author who saw us, alive as we are, did not want to put us on stage. I don't want to offend your actors. God forbid! But I feel that seeing myself acted . . . I don't know by whom . . .

LEADING MAN [*rising with dignity and coming over, followed by the gay young* ACTRESSES *who laugh*] By me, if you've no objection.

FATHER [*humble, smooth*] I'm very honored, sir. [*He bows.*] But however much art and willpower the gentleman puts into absorbing me into himself . . .

[*He is bewildered now.*]

LEADING MAN—Finish. Finish.

[*The* ACTRESSES *laugh.*]

FATHER—Well, the performance he will give, even forcing himself with make-up to resemble me, well, with that figure [*all the* ACTORS *laugh*] he can hardly play me as I am. I shall rather be—even apart from the face—what he interprets me to be, as he feels I am—if he feels I am anything—and not as I feel to myself inside myself. And it seems to me that whoever is called upon to judge us should take this into account.

DIRECTOR—So now you're thinking of what the critics will say? And I was still listening! Let the critics say what they want. We will concentrate on putting on your play! [*He walks away a little, and looks around.*] Come on, come on. Is the set ready? [*To the* ACTORS *and the* CHARACTERS.] Don't clutter up the stage, I want to be able to see! [*He goes down from the stage.*] Let's not lose any more time! [*To the* STEPDAUGHTER.] Does the set seem pretty good to you?

STEPDAUGHTER—Oh! But I can't recognize it!

DIRECTOR—Oh my God, don't tell me we should reconstruct Madam Pace's back room for you! [*To the* FATHER.] Didn't you say a parlor with flowered wallpaper?

FATHER—Yes, sir. White.

DIRECTOR—It's not white. Stripes. But it doesn't matter. As for furniture we're in pretty good shape. That little table—bring it forward a bit! [*Stagehands do this. To the* PROPERTY MAN.] Meanwhile you get an envelope, possibly a light blue one, and give it to the gentleman.

[*Indicating the* FATHER.]

PROPERTY MAN—A letter envelope?

DIRECTOR *and* FATHER—Yes, a letter envelope.

PROPERTY MAN—I'll be right back.

[*He exits.*]

DIRECTOR—Come on, come on. It's the young lady's scene first. [*The* LEADING LADY *comes forward.*] No, no, wait. I said the young lady. [*Indicating the* STEPDAUGHTER.] You will just watch—

STEPDAUGHTER [*adding, without pause*]—watch me live it!

LEADING LADY [*resenting this*] I'll know how to live it too, don't worry, once I put myself in the role!

DIRECTOR [*raising his hands to his head*] Please! No more chatter! Now, scene one. The Young Lady with Madam Pace. Oh, and how about this Madam Pace?

[*Bewildered, looking around him, he climbs back on stage.*]

FATHER—She isn't with us, sir.

DIRECTOR—Then what do we do?

FATHER—But she's alive. She's alive too.

DIRECTOR—Fine. But where?

FATHER—I'll tell you. [*Turning to the* ACTRESSES.] If you ladies will do me the favor of giving me your hats for a moment.

THE ACTRESSES [*surprised a little, laughing a little, in chorus*]— What?—Our hats?—What does he say?—Why?—Oh, dear!

DIRECTOR—What are you going to do with the ladies' hats?

[*The* ACTORS *laugh.*]

FATHER—Oh, nothing. Just put them on these coathooks for a minute. And would some of you be so kind as to take your coats off too?

2031

Luigi Pirandello

ACTORS [*as before*] Their coats too?—And then?—He's nuts!
AN ACTRESS OR TWO [*as above*]—But why?—Just the coats?
FATHER—Just so they can be hung there for a moment. Do me this favor. Will you?
ACTRESSES [*taking their hats off, and one or two of them their coats, too, continuing to laugh, and going to hang the hats here and there on the coathooks*]—Well, why not?—There!—This is getting to be really funny!—Are we to put them on display?
FATHER—Exactly! That's just right, ma'am: on display!
DIRECTOR—May one enquire *why* you are doing this?
FATHER—Yes, sir. If we set the stage better, who knows but she may come to us, drawn by the objects of her trade . . . [*Inviting them to look toward the entrance at the back.*] Look! Look!

The entrance at the back opens, and MADAM PACE *walks a few paces downstage, a hag of enormous fatness with a pompous wig of carrot-colored wool and a fiery red rose on one side of it, a l'espagnole, heavily made up, dressed with gauche elegance in garish red silk, a feathered fan in one hand and the other hand raised to hold a lighted cigarette between two fingers. At the sight of this apparition, the* DIRECTOR *and the* ACTORS *at once dash off the stage with a yell of terror, rushing down the stairs and making as if to flee up the aisle. The* STEPDAUGHTER, *on the other hand, runs to* MADAM PACE—*deferentially, as to her boss.*

STEPDAUGHTER [*running to her*] Here she is, here she is!
FATHER [*beaming*] It's she! What did I tell you? Here she is!
DIRECTOR [*overcoming his first astonishment, and incensed now*] What tricks are these?
              [*The next four speeches are more or less simultaneous.*]
LEADING MAN—What goes on around here?
JUVENILE LEAD—Where on earth did she come from?
INGENUE—They must have been holding her in reserve.
LEADING LADY—Hocus pocus! Hocus pocus!
FATHER [*dominating these protests*] Excuse me, though! Why, actually, would you want to destroy this prodigy in the name of vulgar truth, this miracle of a reality that is born of the stage itself—called into being by the stage, drawn here by the stage, and shaped by the stage—and which has more right to live on the stage than you have because it is much truer? Which of you actresses will later re-create Madam Pace? This lady *is* Madam Pace. You must admit that the actress who re-creates her will be less true than this lady—who is Madam Pace. Look: my daughter recognized her, and went right over to her. Stand and watch the scene!

2032

Hesitantly, the DIRECTOR *and the* ACTORS *climb back on stage. But the scene between the* STEPDAUGHTER *and* MADAM PACE *has begun during the protest of the* ACTORS *and the* FATHER's *answer: sotto voce, very quietly, in short naturally—as would never be possible on a stage. When, called to order by the* FATHER, *the* ACTORS *turn again to watch, they hear* MADAM PACE, *who has just placed her hand under the* STEPDAUGHTER's *chin in order to raise her head, talk unintelligibly. After trying to hear for a moment, they just give up.*

D I R E C T O R – Well?

L E A D I N G M A N – What's she saying?

L E A D I N G L A D Y – One can't hear a thing.

J U V E N I L E L E A D – Louder!

S T E P D A U G H T E R [*leaving* MADAM PACE, *who smiles a priceless smile, and walking down towards the* ACTORS] Louder, huh? How d'you mean: louder? These aren't things that can be said louder. I was able to say them loudly—to shame him—[*indicating the* FATHER] that was my revenge. For Madam, it's different, my friends: it would mean—jail.

D I R E C T O R – Oh my God! It's like that, is it? But, my dear young lady, in the theater one must be heard. And even we couldn't hear you, right here on the stage. How about an audience out front? There's a scene to be done. And anyway you *can* speak loudly—it's just between yourselves, we won't be standing here listening like now. Pretend you're alone. In a room. The back room of the shop. No one can hear you. [*The* STEPDAUGHTER *charmingly and with a mischievous smile tells him No with a repeated movement of the finger.*] Why not?

S T E P D A U G H T E R [*sotto voce, mysteriously*] There's someone who'll hear if she [MADAM PACE] speaks loudly.

D I R E C T O R [*in consternation*] Is someone else going to pop up now?
[*The* ACTORS *make as if to quit the stage again.*]

F A T H E R – No, no, sir. She means me. I'm to be there—behind the door —waiting. And Madam knows. So if you'll excuse me. I must be ready for my entrance.
[*He starts to move.*]

D I R E C T O R [*stopping him*] No, wait. We must respect the exigencies of the theater. Before you get ready—

S T E P D A U G H T E R [*interrupting him*] Let's get on with it! I tell you I'm dying with desire to live it, to live that scene! If he's ready, I'm more than ready!

D I R E C T O R [*shouting*] But first we have to get that scene out of you and her! [*Indicating* MADAM PACE.] Do you follow me?

STEPDAUGHTER – Oh dear, oh dear, she was telling me things you already know—that my mother's work had been badly done once again, the material is ruined, and I'm going to have to bear with her if I want her to go on helping us in our misery.

MADAM PACE [*coming forward with a great air of importance*] Si, si, señor, porque yo no want profit. No advantage, no.

DIRECTOR [*almost scared*] What, what? She talks like *that?!*

[*All the* ACTORS *loudly burst out laughing.*]

STEPDAUGHTER [*also laughing*] Yes, sir, she talks like that—half way between Spanish and English—very funny, isn't it?

MADAM PACE – Now that is not good manners, no, that you laugh at me! Yo hablo the English as good I can, señor!

DIRECTOR – And it *is* good! Yes! Do talk that way, ma'am! It's a sure fire effect! There couldn't be anything better to, um, soften the crudity of the situation! Do talk that way! It's fine!

STEPDAUGHTER – Fine! Of course! To have certain propositions put to you in a lingo like that. Sure fire, isn't it? Because, sir, it seems almost a joke. When I hear there's "an old señor" who wants to "have good time con migo," I start to laugh—don't I, Madam Pace?

MADAM PACE – Old, viejo, no. Viejito—leetle beet old, si, darling? Better like that: if he no give you fun, he bring you prudencia.

MOTHER [*jumping up, to the stupefaction and consternation of all the* ACTORS, *who had been taking no notice of her, and who now respond to her shouts with a start and, smiling, try to restrain her, because she has grabbed* MADAM PACE's *wig and thrown it on the floor*] Witch! Witch! Murderess! My daughter!

STEPDAUGHTER [*running over to restrain her* MOTHER] No, no, momma, no, please!

FATHER [*running over too at the same time*] Calm down, calm down! Sit here.

MOTHER – Then send that woman away!

STEPDAUGHTER [*to the* DIRECTOR, *who also has run over*] It's not possible, not possible that my mother should be here!

FATHER [*also to the* DIRECTOR] They can't be together. That's why, you see, the woman wasn't with us when we came. Their being together would spoil it, you understand.

DIRECTOR – It doesn't matter, doesn't matter at all. This is just a preliminary sketch. Everything helps. However confusing the elements, I'll piece them together somehow. [*Turning to the* MOTHER *and sitting her down again in her place.*] Come along, come along, ma'am, calm down: sit down again.

STEPDAUGHTER [*who meanwhile has moved center stage again. Turning to* MADAM PACE] All right, let's go!

MADAM PACE—Ah, no! No thank you! Yo aqui no do nada with your mother present.

STEPDAUGHTER—Oh, come on! Bring in that old señor who wants to have good time con migo! [*Turning imperiously to all the others.*] Yes, we've got to have it, this scene!—Come on, let's go! [*To* MADAM PACE.] You may leave.

MADAM PACE—Ah si, I go, I go, go seguramente . . .

[*She makes her exit furiously, putting her wig back on, and looking haughtily at the* ACTORS *who applaud mockingly.*]

STEPDAUGHTER [*to the* FATHER] And you can make your entrance. No need to go out and come in again. Come here. Pretend you're already in. Right. Now I'm here with bowed head, modest, huh? Let's go! Speak up! With a different voice, the voice of someone just in off the street: "Hello, miss."

DIRECTOR [*by this time out front again*] Now look: are you directing this, or am I? [*To the* FATHER *who looks undecided and perplexed.*] Do it, yes. Go to the back. Don't leave the stage, though. And then come forward.

The FATHER *does it, almost dismayed. Very pale; but already clothed in the reality of his created life, he smiles as he approaches from the back, as if still alien to the drama which will break upon him. The* ACTORS *now pay attention to the scene which is beginning.*

DIRECTOR [*softly, in haste, to the* PROMPTER *in the box*] And you, be ready now, ready to write!

THE SCENE

FATHER [*coming forward, with a different voice*] Hello, miss.

STEPDAUGHTER [*with bowed head and contained disgust*] Hello.

FATHER [*scrutinizing her under her hat which almost hides her face and noting that she is very young, exclaims, almost to himself, a little out of complaisance and a little out of fear of compromising himself in a risky adventure*] Oh . . . —Well, I was thinking, it wouldn't be the first time, hm? The first time you came here.

STEPDAUGHTER [*as above*] No, sir.

FATHER—You've been here other times? [*And when the* STEPDAUGHTER *nods.*] More than one? [*He waits a moment for her to answer, then again scrutinizes her under her hat; smiles; then says*] Well then, hm . . . it shouldn't any longer be so . . . May I take this hat off for you?

STEPDAUGHTER [*without pause, to forestall him, not now containing her disgust*] No, sir, I will take it off!

[*And she does so in haste, convulsed.*]

The MOTHER, *watching the scene with the* SON *and with the two others, smaller and more her own, who are close to her all the time, forming a group at the opposite side of the stage from the* ACTORS, *is on tenterhooks as she follows the words and actions of* FATHER *and* STEPDAUGHTER *with varied expression: grief, disdain, anxiety, horror, now hiding her face, now emitting a moan.*

MOTHER – Oh God! My God!

FATHER [*is momentarily turned to stone by the moaning; then he reassumes the previous tone*] Now give it to me: I'll hang it up for you. [*He takes the hat from her hands.*] But I could wish for a little hat worthier of such a dear, lovely little head! Would you like to help me choose one? From the many Madam has?—You wouldn't?

INGENUE [*interrupting*] Oh now, come on, those are *our* hats!

DIRECTOR [*without pause, very angry*] Silence, for Heaven's sake, don't try to be funny!—This is the stage. [*Turning back to the* STEPDAUGHTER.] Would you begin again, please?

STEPDAUGHTER [*beginning again*] No, thank you, sir.

FATHER – Oh, come on now, don't say no. Accept one from me. To please me . . . There are some lovely ones you know. And we would make Madam happy. Why else does she put them on display?

STEPDAUGHTER – No, no, sir, look: I wouldn't even be able to wear it.

FATHER – You mean because of what the family would think when they saw you come home with a new hat on? Think nothing of it. Know how to handle that? What to tell them at home?

STEPDAUGHTER [*breaking out, at the end of her rope*] But that's not why, sir. I couldn't wear it because I'm . . . as you see me. You might surely have noticed!

[*Points to her black attire.*]

FATHER – In mourning, yes. Excuse me. It's true: I do see it. I beg your pardon. I'm absolutely mortified, believe me.

STEPDAUGHTER [*forcing herself and plucking up courage to conquer her contempt and nausea*] Enough! Enough! It's for me to thank you, it is not for you to be mortified or afflicted. Please pay no more attention to what I said. Even for me, you understand . . . [*She forces herself to smile and adds.*] I need to forget I am dressed like this.

DIRECTOR [*interrupting, addressing himself to the* PROMPTER *in his box, and going up on stage again*] Wait! Wait! Don't write. Leave that last sentence out, leave it out! [*Turning to the* FATHER *and* STEP-DAUGHTER.] It's going very well indeed. [*Then to the* FATHER *alone.*] This is where you go into the part we prepared. [*To the* ACTORS.] Enchanting, that little hat scene, don't you agree?

STEPDAUGHTER—Oh but the best is just coming. Why aren't we continuing?

DIRECTOR—Patience one moment. [*Again addressing himself to the* ACTORS.] Needs rather delicate handling, of course . . .

LEADING MAN——with a certain *ease*—

LEADING LADY—Obviously. But there's nothing to it. [*To the* LEADING MAN.] We can rehearse it at once, can't we?

LEADING MAN—As far as I'm . . . Very well, I'll go out and make my entrance.

       [*And he does go out by the back door, ready to re-enter.*]

DIRECTOR [*to the* LEADING LADY] And so, look, your scene with that Madam Pace is over. I'll write it up later. You are standing . . . Hey, where are you going?

LEADING LADY—Wait. I'm putting my hat back on . . .

       [*She does so, taking the hat from the hook.*]

DIRECTOR—Oh yes, good.—Now, you're standing here with your head bowed.

STEPDAUGHTER [*amused*] But she's not wearing black!

LEADING LADY—I *shall* wear black! And I'll carry it better than you!

DIRECTOR [*to the* STEPDAUGHTER] Keep quiet, please! Just watch. You can learn something. [*Claps his hands.*] Get going, get going! The entrance!

       [*And he goes back out front to get an impression of the stage.*]

The door at the back opens, and the LEADING MAN *comes forward, with the relaxed, waggish manner of an elderly Don Juan. From the first speeches, the performance of the scene by the* ACTORS *is quite a different thing, without, however, having any element of parody in it—rather, it seems corrected, set to rights. Naturally, the* STEPDAUGHTER *and the* FATHER, *being quite unable to recognize themselves in this* LEADING LADY *and* LEADING MAN *but hearing them speak their own words express in various ways, now with gestures, now with smiles, now with open protests, their surprise, their wonderment, their suffering, etc. as will be seen forthwith.*

The PROMPTOR'S *voice is clearly heard from the box.*[6]

[6] In Italian rehearsals, traditionally, the prompter reads all the lines a few seconds ahead of the actors until the latter have completely memorized their roles, if indeed they ever do.

LEADING MAN—Hello, miss.

FATHER [*without pause, unable to contain himself*] No, no!
[*The* STEPDAUGHTER *seeing how the* LEADING MAN
makes his entrance has burst out laughing.]

DIRECTOR [*coming from the proscenium, furious*] Silence here! And
stop that laughing at once! We can't go ahead till it stops.

STEPDAUGHTER [*coming from the proscenium*] How can I help
it? This lady [*the* LEADING LADY] just stands there. If she's supposed
to be me, let me tell you that if anyone said hello to me in that manner
and that tone of voice, I'd burst out laughing just as I actually did!

FATHER [*coming forward a little too*] That's right . . . the manner,
the tone . . .

DIRECTOR—Manner! Tone! Stand to one side now, and let me see
the rehearsal.

LEADING MAN [*coming forward*] If I'm to play an old man entering
a house of ill—

DIRECTOR—Oh, pay no attention, please. Just begin again. It was
going fine. [*Waiting for the* ACTOR *to resume.*] Now then . . .

LEADING MAN—Hello, miss.

LEADING LADY—Hello.

LEADING MAN [*re-creating the* FATHER's *gesture of scrutinizing her
under her hat, but then expressing very distinctly first the complaisance
and then the fear*] Oh . . . Well . . . I was thinking it wouldn't be
the first time, I hope . . .

FATHER [*unable to help correcting him*] Not "I hope." "Would it?"
"Would it?"

DIRECTOR—He says: "Would it?" A question.

LEADING MAN [*pointing to the* PROMPTER] I heard: "I hope."

DIRECTOR—Same thing! "Would it." Or: "I hope." Continue, continue.—Now, maybe a bit less affected . . . Look, I'll do it for you.
Watch me . . . [*Returns to the stage, then repeats the bit since the
entrance.*]—Hello, miss.

LEADING LADY—Hello.

DIRECTOR—Oh, well . . . I was thinking . . . [*Turning to the* LEAD-
ING MAN *to have him note how he has looked at the* LEADING LADY
under her hat.] Surprise . . . fear and complaisance. [*Then, going on,
and turning to the* LEADING LADY.] It wouldn't be the first time, would
it? The first time you came here. [*Again turning to the* LEADING MAN
with an enquiring look.] Clear? [*To the* LEADING LADY.] Then you say:
No, sir. [*Back to the* LEADING MAN.] How shall I put it? Plasticity!
[*Goes back out front.*]

LEADING LADY—No, sir.

LEADING MAN—You came here other times? More than one?

DIRECTOR—No, no, wait. [*Indicating the* LEADING LADY.] First let her nod. "You came here other times?"

[*The* LEADING LADY *raises her head a little, closes her eyes painfully as if in disgust, then nods twice at the word "Down" from the* DIRECTOR.]

STEPDAUGHTER [*involuntarily*] Oh, my God!

> [*And she at once puts her hand on her mouth to keep the laughter in.*]

DIRECTOR [*turning round*] What is it?

STEPDAUGHTER [*without pause*] Nothing, nothing.

DIRECTOR [*to the* LEADING MAN] That's your cue. Go straight on.

LEADING MAN—More than one? Well then, hm . . . it shouldn't any longer be so . . . May I take this little hat off for you?

The LEADING MAN *says this last speech in such a tone and accompanies it with such a gesture that the* STEPDAUGHTER, *her hands on her mouth, much as she wants to hold herself in, cannot contain her laughter, which comes bursting out through her fingers irresistibly and very loud.*

LEADING LADY [*returning to her place, enraged*] Now look, I'm not going to be made a clown of by that person!

LEADING MAN—Nor am I. Let's stop.

DIRECTOR [*to the* STEPDAUGHTER, *roaring*] Stop it! Stop it!

STEPDAUGHTER—Yes, yes. Forgive me, forgive me . . .

DIRECTOR—You have no manners! You're presumptuous! So there!

FATHER [*seeking to intervene*] That's true, yes, that's true, sir, but forgive . . .

DIRECTOR [*on stage again*] Forgive nothing! It's disgusting!

FATHER—Yes, sir. But believe me, it has such a strange effect—

DIRECTOR—Strange? Strange? What's strange about it?

FATHER—I admire your actors, sir, I really admire them, this gentleman [LEADING MAN] and that lady [LEADING LADY] but assuredly . . . well, they're not us . . .

DIRECTOR—So what? How *could* they be you, if they're the actors?

FATHER—Exactly, the actors! And they play our parts well, both of them. But of course, to us, they seem something else—that tries to be the same but simply isn't!

DIRECTOR—How d'you mean: isn't? What is it then?

FATHER—Something that . . . becomes theirs. And stops being ours.

DIRECTOR—Necessarily! I explained that to you!

FATHER—Yes. I understand, I do under—

DIRECTOR—Then that will be enough! [*Turning to the* ACTORS.] We'll be rehearsing by ourselves as we usually do. Rehearsing with authors present has always been hell, in my experience. There's no satisfying them. [*Turning to the* FATHER *and the* STEPDAUGHTER.] Come along then. Let's resume. And let's hope you find it possible not to laugh this time.

STEPDAUGHTER – Oh, no, I won't be laughing this time around. My big moment comes up now. Don't worry!

DIRECTOR – Very well, when she says: "Please pay no more attention to what I said . . . Even for me—you understand . . ." [*Turning to the* FATHER.] You'll have to cut right in with: "I understand, oh yes, I understand . . ." and ask her right away—

STEPDAUGHTER [*interrupting*] Oh? Ask me what?

DIRECTOR – —why she is in mourning.

STEPDAUGHTER – No, no, look: when I told him I needed to forget I was dressed like this, do you know what his answer was? "Oh, good! Then let's take that little dress right off, shall we?"

DIRECTOR – Great! Terrific! It'll knock 'em right out of their seats!

STEPDAUGHTER – But it's the truth.

DIRECTOR – Truth, is it? Well, well, well. This is the theatre! Our motto is: truth up to a certain point!

STEPDAUGHTER – Then what would you propose?

DIRECTOR – You'll see. You'll see it. Just leave me alone.

STEPDAUGHTER – Certainly not. From my nausea—from all the reasons one more cruel than another why I am what I am, why I am "that one there"—you'd like to cook up some romantic, sentimental concoction, wouldn't you? He asks me why I'm in mourning, and I tell him, through my tears, that Papa died two months ago! No, my dear sir! He has to say what he did say: "Then let's take that little dress right off, shall we?" And I, with my two-months mourning in my heart, went back there—you see? behind that screen—and—my fingers quivering with shame, with loathing—I took off my dress, took off my corset . . .

DIRECTOR [*running his hands through his hair*] Good God, what are you saying?

STEPDAUGHTER [*shouting frantically*] The truth, sir, the truth!

DIRECTOR – Well, yes, of course, that must be the truth . . . and I quite understand your horror, young lady. Would you try to understand that all that is impossible *on the stage?*

STEPDAUGHTER – Impossible? Then, thanks very much, I'm leaving.

DIRECTOR – No, no, look . . .

STEPDAUGHTER – I'm leaving, I'm leaving! You went in that room, you two, didn't you, and figured out "what is possible on the stage"? Thanks very much. I see it all. He wants to skip to the point where he can act out his [*exaggerating*] spiritual travail! But I want to play *my* drama. Mine!

DIRECTOR   [*annoyed, shrugging haughtily*] Oh well, *your* drama. This is not just your drama, if I may say so. How about the drama of the others? His drama [*the* FATHER], hers? [*The* MOTHER.] We can't let one character hog the limelight, just taking the whole stage over, and overshadowing all the others! Everything must be placed within the frame of one harmonious picture! We must perform only what is performable! I know as well as you do that each of us has a whole life of his own inside him and would like to bring it all out. But the difficult thing is this: to bring out only as much as is needed—in relation to the others—and in this to *imply* all the rest, *suggest* what remains inside! Oh, it would be nice if every character could come down to the footlights and tell the audience just what is brewing inside him—in a fine monologue or, if you will, a lecture! [*Good-natured, conciliatory.*] Miss, you will have to *contain yourself.* And it will be in your interest. It could make a bad impression—let me warn you—this tearing fury, this desperate disgust—since, if I may say so, you confessed having been with others at Madam Pace's—before him—more than once!

STEPDAUGHTER   [*lowering her head, pausing to recollect, a deeper note in her voice*] It's true. But to me the others are also *him*, all of them equally!

DIRECTOR   [*not getting it*] The others? How d'you mean?

STEPDAUGHTER—People "go wrong." And wrong follows on the heels of wrong. Who is responsible, if not whoever it was who first brought them down? Isn't that always the case? And for me that is him. Even before I was born. Look at him, and see if it isn't so.

DIRECTOR—Very good. And if he has so much to feel guilty about, can't you appreciate how it must weigh him down? So let's at least permit him to act it out.

STEPDAUGHTER—And how, may I ask, how could he act out all that "noble" guilt, all those so "moral" torments, if you propose to spare him the horror of one day finding in his arms—after having bade her take off the black clothes that marked her recent loss—a woman now, and already gone wrong—that little girl, sir, that little girl whom he used to go watch coming out of school? [*She says these last words in a voice trembling with emotion. The* MOTHER, *hearing her say this, is overcome with uncontrollable anguish, which comes out first in suffocated moans and subsequently bursts out in bitter weeping. The emotion takes hold of everyone. Long pause. As soon as the* MOTHER *gives signs of calming down, somber, determined.*] We're just among ourselves now. Still unknown to the public. Tomorrow you will make of us the show you have in mind. You will put it together in your way. But would you like to really see—our drama? Have it explode —the real thing?

DIRECTOR—Of course. Nothing I'd like better. And I'll use as much of it as I possibly can!

STEPDAUGHTER—Very well. Have this Mother here go out.

MOTHER [*ceasing to weep, with a loud cry*] No, no! Don't allow this, don't allow it!

DIRECTOR—I only want to take a look, ma'am.

MOTHER—I can't, I just can't!

DIRECTOR—But if it's already happened? Excuse me but I just don't get it.

MOTHER—No, no, it's happening now. It's always happening. My torment is not a pretence! I am alive and present—always, in every moment of my torment—it keeps renewing itself, it too is alive and always present. But those two little ones over there—have you heard them speak? They cannot speak, sir, not any more! They still keep clinging to me—to keep my torment alive and present. For themselves they don't exist, don't exist any longer. And she [*the* STEPDAUGHTER], she just fled, ran away from me, she's lost, lost . . . If I see her before me now, it's for the same reason: to renew the torment, keep it always alive and present forever—the torment I've suffered on her account too —forever!

FATHER [*solemn*] The eternal moment, sir, as I told you. She [*the* STEPDAUGHTER] is here to catch me, fix me, hold me there in the pillory, hanging there forever, hooked, in that single fleeting shameful moment of my life! She cannot give it up. And, actually, sir, *you* cannot spare me.

DIRECTOR—But I didn't say I wouldn't use that. On the contrary, it will be the nucleus of the whole first act. To the point where she [*the* MOTHER] surprises you.

FATHER—Yes, exactly. Because that is the sentence passed upon me: all our passion which has to culminate in her [*the* MOTHER's] final cry!

STEPDAUGHTER—It still rings in my ears. It's driven me out of my mind, that cry!—You can present me as you wish, sir, it doesn't matter. Even dressed. As long as at least my arms—just my arms—are bare. Because it was like this. [*She goes to the* FATHER *and rests her head on his chest.*] I was standing like this with my head on his chest and my arms round his neck like this. Then I saw something throbbing right here on my arm. A vein. Then, as if it was just this living vein that disgusted me, I jammed my eyes shut, like this, d'you see? and buried my head on his chest. [*Turning to the* MOTHER.] Scream, scream, mamma! [*Buries her head on the* FATHER's *chest and with her shoul-*

ders raised as if to avoid hearing the scream she adds in a voice stifled
with torment.] Scream as you screamed then!

MOTHER [*rushing forward to part them*] No! My daughter! My
daughter! [*Having pulled her from him.*] Brute! Brute! It's my daughter, don't you see—my daughter!

DIRECTOR [*the outburst having sent him reeling to the footlights,
while the* ACTORS *show dismay*] Fine! Splendid! And now: curtain,
curtain!

FATHER [*running to him, convulsed*] Right! Yes! Because that, sir,
is how it actually was!

DIRECTOR [*in admiration and conviction*] Yes, yes, of course! Curtain! Curtain!

Hearing this repeated cry of the DIRECTOR, *the* TECHNICIAN *lets down the
curtain, trapping the* DIRECTOR *and the* FATHER *between curtain and
footlights.*

DIRECTOR [*looking up, with raised arms*] What an idiot! I say Curtain, meaning that's how the act should end, and they let down the
actual curtain! [*He lifts a corner of the curtain so he can get back on
stage. To the* FATHER.] Yes, yes, fine, splendid! Absolutely sure fire!
Has to end that way. I can vouch for the first act.

[*Goes behind the curtain with the* FATHER.]

When the curtain rises we see that the stagehands have struck that first "indication of a set," and have put on stage in its stead a small garden fountain. On one side of the stage, the ACTORS *are sitting in a row, and on the other are the* CHARACTERS. *The* DIRECTOR *is standing in the middle of the stage, in the act of meditating with one hand, fist clenched, on his mouth.*

DIRECTOR [*shrugging after a short pause*] Yes, well then, let's get to the second act. Just leave it to me as we agreed beforehand and everything will be all right.

STEPDAUGHTER—Our entrance into his house [*the* FATHER] in spite of him. [*The* SON.]

DIRECTOR [*losing patience*] Very well. But leave it all to me, I say.

STEPDAUGHTER—In spite of him. Just let that be clear.

MOTHER [*shaking her head from her corner*] For all the good that's come out of it . . .

STEPDAUGHTER [*turning quickly on her*] It doesn't matter. The more damage to us, the more guilt feelings for him.

DIRECTOR [*still out of patience*] I understand, I understand. All this will be taken into account, especially at the beginning. Rest assured.

MOTHER [*supplicatingly*] Do make them understand, I beg you, sir, for my conscience sake, for I tried in every possible way—

STEPDAUGHTER [*continuing her* MOTHER's *speech, contemptuously*] To placate me, to advise me not to give him trouble. [*To the* DIRECTOR.] Do what she wants, do it because it's true. I enjoy the whole thing very much because, look: the more she plays the suppliant and tries to gain entrance into his heart, the more he holds himself aloof: he's an absentee! How I relish this!

DIRECTOR—We want to get going—on the second act, don't we?

STEPDAUGHTER—I won't say another word. But to play it all in the garden, as you want to, won't be possible.

DIRECTOR—Why won't it be possible?

STEPDAUGHTER—Because he [*the* SON] stays shut up in his room, on his own. Then again we need the house for the part about this poor bewildered little boy, as I told you.

DIRECTOR—Quite right. But on the other hand, we can't change the

2044

scenery in view of the audience three or four times in one act, nor can we stick up signs—

LEADING MAN—They used to at one time . . .

DIRECTOR—Yes, when the audiences were about as mature as that little girl.

LEADING LADY—They got the illusion more easily.

FATHER [*suddenly, rising*] The illusion, please don't say illusion! Don't use that word! It's especially cruel to us.

DIRECTOR [*astonished*] And why, if I may ask?

FATHER—Oh yes, cruel, cruel! You should understand that.

DIRECTOR—What word would you have us use anyway? The illusion of creating here for our spectators—

LEADING MAN——By our performance—

DIRECTOR——the illusion of a reality.

FATHER—I understand, sir, but perhaps you do not understand us. Because, you see, for you and for your actors all this—quite rightly—is a game—

LEADING LADY [*indignantly interrupting*] Game! We are not children, sir. We act in earnest.

FATHER—I don't deny it. I just mean the game of your art which, as this gentleman rightly says, must provide a perfect illusion of reality.

DIRECTOR—Yes, exactly.

FATHER—But consider this. We [*he quickly indicates himself and the other five* CHARACTERS], we have no reality outside this illusion.

DIRECTOR [*astonished, looking at his* ACTORS *who remain bewildered and lost*] And that means?

FATHER [*after observing them briefly, with a pale smile*] Just that, ladies and gentlemen. How should we have any other reality? What for you is an illusion, to be created, is for us our unique reality. [*Short pause. He takes several short steps toward the* DIRECTOR, *and adds.*] But not for us alone, of course. Think a moment. [*He looks into his eyes.*] Can you tell me who you are?

[*And he stands there pointing his first finger at him.*]

DIRECTOR [*upset, with a half-smile*] How do you mean, who I am? I am I.

FATHER—And if I told you that wasn't true because you are me?

DIRECTOR—I would reply that you are out of your mind.

[*The* ACTORS *laugh.*]

FATHER—You are right to laugh: because this is a game. [*To the* DIRECTOR.] And you can object that it's only in a game that that gentleman there [LEADING MAN], who is himself, must be me, who am myself. I've caught you in a trap, do you see that?

[ACTORS *start laughing again.*]

DIRECTOR [*annoyed*] You said all this before. Why repeat it?

FATHER—I won't—I didn't intend to say that. I'm inviting you to emerge from this game. [*He looks at the* LEADING LADY *as if to forestall what she might say.*] This game of art which you are accustomed to play here with your actors. Let me again ask quite seriously: Who are you?

DIRECTOR [*turning to the* ACTORS, *amazed and at the same time irritated*] The gall of this fellow! Calls himself a character and comes here to ask me who I am!

FATHER [*dignified, but not haughty*] A character, sir, can always ask a man who he is. Because a character really has his own life, marked with his own characteristics, by virtue of which he is always someone. Whereas, a man—I'm not speaking of you now—*a man* can be no one.

DIRECTOR—Oh sure. But you are asking me! And I am the manager, understand?

FATHER [*quite softly with mellifluous modesty*] Only in order to know, sir, if you as you now are see yourself . . . for example, at a distance in time. Do you see the man you once were, with all the illusions you had then, with everything, inside you and outside, as it seemed then—as it was then for you!—Well sir, thinking back to those illusions which you don't have any more, to all those things which no longer seem to be what at one time they were for you, don't you feel, not just the boards of this stage, but the very earth beneath slipping away from you? For will not all that you feel yourself to be now, your whole reality of today, as it is now, inevitably seem an illusion tomorrow?

DIRECTOR [*who has not followed exactly, but has been staggered by the plausibilities of the argument*] Well, well, what do you want to prove?

FATHER—Oh nothing sir. I just wanted to make you see that if *we* [*pointing again at himself and the other* CHARACTERS] have no reality outside of illusion, it would be well if you should distrust your reality because, though you breathe it and touch it today, it is destined like that of yesterday to stand revealed to you tomorrow as illusion.

DIRECTOR [*deciding to mock him*] Oh splendid! And you'll be telling me next that you and this play that you have come to perform for me are truer and more real than I am.

FATHER [*quite seriously*] There can be no doubt of that, sir.

DIRECTOR—Really?

FATHER—I thought you had understood that from the start.

DIRECTOR—More real than me?

FATHER—If your reality can change overnight . . .

DIRECTOR—Of course it can, it changes all the time, like everyone else's.

FATHER [*with a cry*] But ours does not, sir. You see, that is the difference. It does not change, it cannot ever change or be otherwise because it is already fixed, it is what is, just that, forever—a terrible thing, sir!—an immutable reality. You should shudder to come near us.[7]

DIRECTOR [*suddenly struck by a new idea, he steps in front of the* FATHER] I should like to know, however, when anyone ever saw a character get out of his part and set about expounding and explicating it, delivering lectures on it. Can you tell me? I have never seen anything like that.

FATHER—You have never seen it, sir, because authors generally hide

---

[7] In the first edition, the following passage occurs here:

FATHER—If you are truly conscious that your reality, on the other hand, your reality in time is an ephemeral and extremely fleeting illusion which you unconsciously invent, today in this way and tomorrow in some other way according to cases, according to conditions and will and feelings which you invent with the intellect which shows them to you today in one way and tomorrow . . . who knows how: illusions of reality as acted out in that fatuous comedy of life which does not end, which cannot ever end because, if tomorrow it should end, then goodbye, all is finished.

DIRECTOR—In the name of God, I wish you at least would stop your philosophizing and let's see if we might end this play which you people have brought me! Too much reasoning, too much reasoning, my dear sir.—You know you almost seem to me a . . . [*he interrupts and looks him over from top to toe*] . . . exactly, yes: You introduced yourself here as a—let's put it this way—as a character created by an author who decided not to make a play out of you. Correct?

FATHER—That's the simple truth, sir.

DIRECTOR—Cut it out. None of us believes you. Such things can't be seriously believed, you must know that. You know what I rather think is going on? I think that you are adopting the manner of a certain author whom I particularly detest—let me admit that—although, unfortunately, I've had to put on some of his works. I happen to have been rehearsing one of them when you all came. [*Turning to the* ACTORS.] Think what we gained by the exchange! From the frying pan into the fire!

FATHER—I don't know, sir, what author you may be alluding to, but believe me, I feel, I feel what I think. And only those who do not think about what they feel would say I am just reasoning: they are blind to their own feelings. I know, I know that many consider such self-blinding much more human, but the opposite is true, sir, for man never reasons so much—on or off the point—as when he suffers. He wants to see the cause of his sufferings, he wants to know who is giving them to him, if this is just or unjust. When, on the other hand, he is enjoying himself, he just accepts the enjoyment and stops reasoning—as if to enjoy oneself were a right. Only the animals suffer without reasoning, sir. Yet put on stage a man who reasons in the midst of his suffering, and everyone will object. But let him suffer like an animal and everyone will say: "Oh yes, he is human."

DIRECTOR—And in the meanwhile you go on reasoning, huh?

FATHER—Because I suffer, sir. I am not reasoning, I am crying aloud the why and wherefore of my suffering.

the travail of their creations. When characters are alive and turn up, living, before their author, all that author does is follow the words and gestures which they propose to him. He has to want them to be as they themselves want to be. Woe betide him if he doesn't! When a character is born, he at once acquires such an independence, even of his own author, that the whole world can imagine him in innumerable situations other than those the author thought to place him in. At times he acquires a meaning that the author never dreamt of giving him.

DIRECTOR – Certainly, I know that.

FATHER – Then why all this astonishment at us? Imagine what a misfortune it is for a character such as I described to you—given life in the imagination of an author who then wished to deny him life—and tell me frankly: isn't such a character, given life and left without life, isn't he right to set about doing just what we are doing now as we stand here before you, after having done just the same—for a very long time, believe me—before *him,* trying to persuade him, trying to push him . . . I would appear before him sometimes, sometimes she [*looks at* STEPDAUGHTER] would go to him, sometimes that poor mother . . .

STEPDAUGHTER [*coming forward as if in a trance*] It's true. I too went there, sir, to tempt him, many times, in the melancholy of that study of his, at the twilight hour, when he would sit stretched out in his armchair, unable to make up his mind to switch the light on, and letting the evening shadows invade the room, knowing that these shadows were alive with us and that we were coming to tempt him . . . [*As if she saw herself still in that study and felt only annoyance at the presence of all of these* ACTORS.] Oh, if only you would all go away! Leave us alone! My mother there with her son—I with this little girl— the boy there always alone—then I with him—[*the* FATHER] then I by myself, I by myself . . . in those shadows. [*Suddenly she jumps up as if she wished to take hold of herself in the vision she has of herself lighting up the shadows and alive.*] Ah my life! What scenes, what scenes we went there to propose to him: I, I tempted him more than the others.

FATHER – Right, but perhaps that was the trouble: you insisted too much. You thought you could seduce him.

STEPDAUGHTER – Nonsense. He wanted me that way. [*She comes up to the* DIRECTOR *to tell him as in confidence.*] If you ask me, sir, it was because he was so depressed, or because he despised the theater the public knows and wants . . .

DIRECTOR – Let's continue. Let's continue, for Heaven's sake. Enough theories, I'd like some facts. Give me some facts.

STEPDAUGHTER – It seems to me that we have already given you

more facts than you can handle—with our entry into his [*the* FA-
THER's] house! You said you couldn't change the scene every five minutes or start hanging signs.

DIRECTOR—Nor can we, of course not, we have to combine the scenes
and group them in one simultaneous close-knit action. Not your idea
at all. You'd like to see your brother come home from school and
wander through the house like a ghost, hiding behind the doors, and
brooding on a plan which—how did you put it—?

STEPDAUGHTER——shrivels him up, sir, completely shrivels him up,
sir.

DIRECTOR—"Shrivels him up!" What an expression! All right then:
his growth was stunted except for his eyes. Is that what you said?

STEPDAUGHTER—Yes, sir. Just look at him.

[*She points him out next to the* MOTHER.]

DIRECTOR—Good girl. And then at the same time you want this little
girl to be playing in the garden, dead to the world. Now, the boy in
the house, the girl in the garden, is that possible?

STEPDAUGHTER—Happy in the sunshine! Yes, that is my only reward, her pleasure, her joy in that garden! After the misery, the squalor
of a horrible room where we slept, all four of us, she with me: just
think of the horror of my contaminated body next to hers! She held
me tight, oh so tight with her loving innocent little arms! In the garden
she would run and take my hand as soon as she saw me. She did not
see the big flowers, she ran around looking for the teeny ones and
wanted to show them to me, oh the joy of it!

*Saying this and tortured by the memory she breaks into prolonged des-
perate sobbing, dropping her head onto her arms which are spread out on
the work table.*

Everyone is overcome by her emotion. The DIRECTOR *goes to her almost paternally and says to comfort her.*

DIRECTOR—We'll do the garden. We'll do the garden, don't worry,
and you'll be very happy about it. We'll bring all the scenes together
in the garden. [*Calling a stagehand by name.*] Hey, drop me a couple
of trees, will you, two small cypress trees, here in front of the fountain.

[*Two small cypress trees are seen descending from the flies. A stagehand
runs on to secure them with nails and a couple of braces.*]

DIRECTOR [*to the* STEPDAUGHTER] Something to go on with anyway.
Gives us an idea. [*Again calling the stagehand by name.*] Hey, give me
a bit of sky.

STAGEHAND [*from above*] What?

DIRECTOR—Bit of sky, a backcloth, to go behind that fountain. [*A white backdrop is seen descending from the flies.*] Not white, I said sky. It doesn't matter, leave it, I'll take care of it. [*Shouting.*] Hey, Electrician, put these lights out. Let's have a bit of atmosphere, lunar atmosphere, blue background, and give me a blue spot on that backcloth. That's right. That's enough. [*At his command a mysterious lunar scene is created which induces the* ACTORS *to talk and move as they would on an evening in the garden beneath the moon; to* STEPDAUGHTER.] You see? And now instead of hiding behind doors in the house the boy could move around here in the garden and hide behind trees. But it will be difficult, you know, to find a little girl to play the scene where she shows you the flowers. [*Turning to the* BOY.] Come down this way a bit. Let's see how this can be worked out. [*And when the* BOY *doesn't move.*] Come on, come on. [*Then dragging him forward he tries to make him hold his head up but it falls down again every time.*] Oh dear, another problem, this boy . . . What *is* it? . . . My God, he'll have to say something . . . [*He goes up to him, puts a hand on his shoulder and leads him behind one of the tree drops.*] Come on. Come on. Let me see. You can hide a bit here . . . Like this . . . You can stick your head out a bit to look . . . [*He goes to one side to see the effect. The* BOY *has scarcely run through the actions when the* ACTORS *are deeply affected; and they remain quite overwhelmed.*] Ah! Fine! Splendid! [*He turns again to the* STEPDAUGHTER.] If the little girl surprises him, looking out and runs over to him don't you think she might drag a few words out of him too?

STEPDAUGHTER [*jumping to her feet*] Don't expect him to speak while *he's* here. [*She points to the* SON.] You have to send *him* away first.

SON [*going resolutely toward one of the two stairways*] Suits me. Glad to go. Nothing I want more.

DIRECTOR [*immediately calling him*] No. Where are you going? Wait.

The MOTHER *rises, deeply moved, in anguish at the thought that he is really going. She instinctively raises her arms as if to halt him, yet without moving away from her position.*

SON [*arriving at the footlights, where the* DIRECTOR *stops him*] I have absolutely nothing to do here. So let me go please. Just let me go.

DIRECTOR—How do you mean, you have nothing to do?

STEPDAUGHTER [*placidly, with irony*] Don't hold him! He won't go.

FATHER – He has to play the terrible scene in the garden with his mother.

SON [*unhesitating, resolute, proud*] I play nothing. I said so from the start. [*To the* DIRECTOR.] Let me go.

STEPDAUGHTER [*running to the* DIRECTOR *to get him to lower his arms so that he is no longer holding the* SON *back*] Let him go. [*Then turning to the* SON *as soon as the* DIRECTOR *has let him go.*] Very well, go. [*The* SON *is all set to move toward the stairs but, as if held by some occult power, he cannot go down the steps. While the* ACTORS *are both astounded and deeply troubled, he moves slowly across the footlights straight to the other stairway. But having arrived there he remains poised for the descent but unable to descend. The* STEPDAUGHTER *who has followed him with her eyes in an attitude of defiance bursts out laughing.*] He can't, you see. He can't. He has to stay here, has to. Bound by a chain, indissolubly. But if I who do take flight, sir, when that happens which has to happen, and precisely because of the hatred I feel for him, precisely so as not to see him again—very well, if *I* am still here and can bear the sight of him and his company—you can imagine whether *he* can go away. He who really must, must remain here with that fine father of his and that mother there who no longer has any other children. [*Turning again to the* MOTHER.] Come on, Mother, come on. [*Turning again to the* DIRECTOR *and pointing to the* MOTHER.] Look, she got up to hold him back. [*To the* MOTHER, *as if exerting a magical power over her.*] Come. Come . . . [*Then to the* DIRECTOR.] You can imagine how little she wants to display her love in front of your actors. But so great is her desire to get at him that—look, you see— she is even prepared to live her scene.

[*In fact the* MOTHER *has approached and no sooner has the* STEPDAUGHTER *spoken her last words than she spreads her arms to signify consent.*]

SON [*without pause*] But I am not, I am not. If I cannot go I will stay here, but I repeat: I will play nothing.

FATHER [*to the* DIRECTOR, *enraged*] You can force him, sir.

SON – No one can force me.

FATHER – I will force you.

STEPDAUGHTER – Wait, wait. First the little girl must be at the fountain. [*She runs to take the* LITTLE GIRL, *drops on her knees in front of her, takes her little face in her hands.*] My poor little darling, you look bewildered with those lovely big eyes of yours. Who knows where you think you are? We are on a stage, my dear. What is a stage? It is a place where you play at being serious, a place for play-acting, where we will now play-act. But seriously! For real! You too . . . [*She embraces her, presses her to her bosom and rocks her a little.*] Oh, little darling, little darling, what an ugly play you will enact! What a

horrible thing has been planned for you, the garden, the fountain . . .
All pretence, of course, that's the trouble my sweet, everything is make-
believe here, but perhaps for you my child a make-believe fountain is
nicer than a real one for playing in, hmm? It will be a game for the
others, but not for you, alas, because you are real, my darling, and are
actually playing in a fountain that is real, beautiful, big, green with
many bamboo plants reflected in it and giving it shade. Many, many
ducklings can swim in it, breaking the shade to bits. You want to take
hold of one of these ducklings . . . [*With a shout that fills everyone
with dismay.*] No! No, my Rosetta! Your mother is not looking after
you because of that beast of a son. A thousand devils are loose in my
head . . . and he . . . [*She leaves the* LITTLE GIRL *and turns with her
usual hostility to the* BOY.] And what are you doing here, always looking
like a beggar child? It will be your fault too if this little girl drowns—
with all your standing around like that. As if I hadn't paid for everybody when I got you all into this house. [*Grabbing one of his arms
to force him to take a hand out of his pocket.*] What have you got
there? What are you hiding? Let's see this hand. [*Tears his hand out of
his pocket, and to the horror of everyone discovers that it holds a small
revolver. She looks at it for a moment as if satisfied and then says.*] Ah!
Where did you get that and how? [*And as the* BOY *in his confusion,
with his eyes staring and vacant all the time, does not answer her.*]
Idiot, if I were you I wouldn't have killed myself, I would have killed
one of those two—or both of them—the father and the son!

*She hides him behind the small cypress tree from which he had been
looking out, and she takes the* LITTLE GIRL *and hides her in the fountain,
having her lie down in it in such a way as to be quite hidden. Finally, the*
STEPDAUGHTER *goes down on her knees with her face in her hands which
are resting on the rim of the fountain.*

DIRECTOR—Splendid! [*Turning to the* SON.] And at the same
time . . .
SON [*with contempt*] And at the same time, nothing. It is not true,
sir. There was never any scene between me and her. [*He points to the*
MOTHER.] Let her tell you herself how it was.

Meanwhile the SECOND ACTRESS *and the* JUVENILE LEAD *have detached
themselves from the group of* ACTORS. *The former has started to observe
the* MOTHER, *who is opposite her, very closely. And the other has started
to observe the* SON. *Both are planning how they will recreate the roles.*

MOTHER—Yes, it is true, sir. I had gone to his room.

SON – My room, did you hear that? Not the garden.

DIRECTOR – That is of no importance. We have to rearrange the action, I told you that.

SON [*noticing that the* JUVENILE LEAD *is observing him*] What do *you* want?

JUVENILE LEAD – Nothing. I am observing you.

SON [*turning to the other side where the* SECOND ACTRESS *is*] Ah, and here we have you to re-create the role, eh?

[*He points to the* MOTHER.]

DIRECTOR – Exactly, exactly. You should be grateful, it seems to me, for the attention they are giving you.

SON – Oh yes, thank you. But you still haven't understood that you cannot do this drama. We are not inside you, not in the least, and your actors are looking at us from the outside. Do you think it's possible for us to live before a mirror which, not content to freeze us in the fixed image it provides of our expression also throws back at us an unrecognizable grimace purporting to be ourselves?

FATHER – That is true. That is true. You must see that.

DIRECTOR [*to the* JUVENILE LEAD *and the* SECOND ACTRESS] Very well, get away from here.

SON – No good. I won't cooperate.

DIRECTOR – Just be quiet a minute and let me hear your mother. [*To the* MOTHER.] Well? You went into his room?

MOTHER – Yes sir, into his room. I was at the end of my tether. I wanted to pour out all of the anguish which was oppressing me. But as soon as he saw me come in—

SON – —There was no scene. I went away. I went away so there would be no scene. Because I have never made scenes, never, understand?

MOTHER – That's true. That's how it was. Yes.

DIRECTOR – But now there's got to be a scene between you and him. It is indispensable.

MOTHER – As for me sir, I am ready. If only you could find some way to have me speak to him for one moment, to have me say what is in my heart.

FATHER [*going right up to the* SON, *very violent*] You will do it! For your mother! For your mother!

SON [*more decisively than ever*] I will do nothing!

FATHER [*grabbing him by the chest and shaking him*] By God, you will obey! Can't you hear how she is talking to you? Aren't you her son?

SON [*grabbing his* FATHER] No! No! Once and for all let's have done with it!

[*General agitation. The* MOTHER, *terrified, tries to get between them to separate them.*]

MOTHER   [*as before*] Please, please!

FATHER   [*without letting go of the* SON] You must obey, you must obey!

SON   [*wrestling with his* FATHER *and in the end throwing him to the ground beside the little stairway, to the horror of everyone*] What's this frenzy that's taken hold of you? To show your shame and ours to everyone? Have you no restraint? I won't cooperate, I won't cooperate! And that is how I interpret the wishes of the man who did not choose to put us on stage.

DIRECTOR – But you came here.

SON   [*pointing to his* FATHER] He came here—not me!

DIRECTOR – But aren't you here too?

SON – It was he who wanted to come, dragging the rest of us with him, and then getting together with you to plot not only what really happened, but also—as if that did not suffice—*what did not happen.*

DIRECTOR – Then tell me. Tell me what did happen. Just tell me. You came out of your room without saying a thing?

SON   [*after a moment of hesitation*] Without saying a thing. In order not to make a scene.

DIRECTOR   [*driving him on*] Very well, and then, what did you do then?

SON   [*while everyone looks on in anguished attention, he moves a few steps on the front part of the stage*] Nothing . . . crossing the garden . . .

[*He stops, gloomy, withdrawn.*]

DIRECTOR   [*always driving him on to speak, impressed by his reticence*] Very well, crossing the garden?

SON   [*desperate, hiding his face with one arm*] Why do you want to make me say it, sir? It is horrible.

[*The* MOTHER *trembles all over, and stifles groans, looking towards the fountain.*]

DIRECTOR   [*softly, noticing this look of hers, turning to the* SON, *with growing apprehension*] The little girl?

SON   [*looking out into the auditorium*] Over there—in the fountain . . .

FATHER   [*on the ground, pointing compassionately toward the* MOTHER] And she followed him, sir.

DIRECTOR   [*to the* SON, *anxiously*] And then you . . .

SON   [*Slowly, looking straight ahead all the time*] I ran out. I started to fish her out . . . but all of a sudden I stopped. Behind those trees I saw something that froze me: the boy, the boy was standing there, quite still. There was madness in his eyes. He was looking at his drowned sister in the fountain. [*The* STEPDAUGHTER, *who has been* bent over the fountain, hiding the LITTLE GIRL, *is sobbing desperately, like an echo from the bottom. Pause.*] I started to approach and then . . .

> [*From behind the trees where the* BOY *has been hiding, a revolver shot rings out.*]

M O T H E R [*running up with a tormented shout, accompanied by the* SON *and all the* ACTORS *in a general tumult*] Son! My son! [*And then amid the hubbub and the disconnected shouts of the others.*] Help! Help!

D I R E C T O R [*amid the shouting, trying to clear a space while the* BOY *is lifted by his head and feet and carried away behind the backcloth*] Is he wounded, is he wounded, really?

Everyone except the DIRECTOR *and the* FATHER, *who has remained on the ground beside the steps, has disappeared behind the backcloth which has served for a sky, where they can still be heard for a while whispering anxiously. Then from one side and the other of this curtain, the* ACTORS *come back on stage.*

L E A D I N G A C T R E S S [*re-entering from the right, very much upset*] He's dead! Poor boy! He's dead! What a terrible thing!

L E A D I N G A C T O R [*re-entering from the left, laughing*] How do you mean, dead? Fiction, fiction, one doesn't believe such things.

O T H E R A C T O R S [*on the right*] Fiction? Reality! Reality! He is dead!

O T H E R A C T O R S [*on the left*] No! Fiction! Fiction!

F A T H E R [*rising, and crying out to them*] Fiction indeed! Reality, reality, gentlemen, reality!

> [*Desperate, he too disappears at the back.*]

D I R E C T O R [*at the end of his rope*] Fiction! Reality! To hell with all of you! Lights, lights, lights! [*At a single stroke the whole stage and auditorium is flooded with very bright light. The* DIRECTOR *breathes again, as if freed from an incubus and they all look each other in the eyes, bewildered and lost.*] Things like this don't happen to me, they've made me lose a whole day. [*He looks at his watch.*] Go, you can all go. What could we do now anyway? It is too late to pick up the rehearsal where we left off. See you this evening. [*As soon as the* ACTORS *have gone he talks to the* ELECTRICIAN *by name.*] Hey, Electrician, lights out. [*He has hardly said the words when the theater is plunged for a moment into complete darkness.*] Hey, for God's sake, leave me at least one light! I like to see where I am going!

Immediately, from behind the backcloth, as if the wrong switch had been pulled, a green light comes on which projects the silhouettes, clear-cut and large, of the CHARACTERS, minus the BOY and the LITTLE GIRL. *See-ing the silhouettes, the* DIRECTOR, *terrified, rushes from the stage. At the same time the light behind the backcloth goes out and the stage is again lit in nocturnal blue as before.*

Slowly, from the right side of the curtain, the SON *comes forward first, followed by the* MOTHER *with her arms stretched out towards him; then from the left side, the* FATHER. *They stop in the middle of the stage and stay there as if in a trance. Last of all from the right, the* STEPDAUGHTER *comes out and runs towards the two stairways. She stops on the first step, to look for a moment at the other three, and then breaks into a harsh laugh before throwing herself down the steps; she runs down the aisle between the rows of seats; she stops one more time and again laughs, looking at the three who are still on stage; she disappears from the audi-torium, and from the lobby her laughter is still heard. Shortly thereafter the curtain falls.*

PREFACE TO "SIX CHARACTERS IN SEARCH OF AN AUTHOR"

By Luigi Pirandello
translated by Eric Bentley

IT SEEMS like yesterday but is actually many years ago that a nimble little maidservant entered the service of my art. However, she always comes fresh to the job.

She is called Fantasy.

A little puckish and malicious, if she likes to dress in black no one will wish to deny that she is often positively bizarre and no one will wish to believe that she always does everything in the same way and in earnest. She sticks her hand in her pocket, pulls out a cap and bells, sets it on her head, red as a cock's comb, and dashes away. Here today, there tomorrow. And she amuses herself by bringing to my house—since I derive stories and novels and plays from them—the most disgruntled tribe in the world, men, women, children, involved in strange adventures which they can find no way out of; thwarted in their plans; cheated in their hopes; with whom, in short, it is often torture to deal.

Well, this little maidservant of mine, Fantasy, several years ago, had the bad inspiration or ill-omened caprice to bring a family into my house. I wouldn't know where she fished them up or how, but, according to her, I could find in them the subject for a magnificent novel.

I found before me a man about fifty years old, in a dark jacket and light trousers, with a frowning air and ill-natured, mortified eyes; a poor woman in widow's weeds leading by one hand a little girl of four and by the other a boy of rather more than ten; a cheeky and "sexy" girl, also clad in black but with an equivocal and brazen pomp, all atremble with a lively, biting contempt for the mortified old man and for a young fellow of twenty who stood on one side closed in on himself as if he despised them all. In short, the six characters who are seen coming on stage at the beginning of the play. Now one of them and now another—often beating down one another—embarked on the sad story of their adventures, each shouting his own reasons, and projecting in my face his disordered passions, more or less as they do in the play to the unhappy Manager.

What author will be able to say how and why a character was born in his fantasy? The mystery of artistic creation is the same as that of birth. A woman who loves may desire to become a mother; but the desire by itself, however intense, cannot suffice. One fine day she will find herself a mother without having any precise intimation when it began. In the same way an artist imbibes very many germs of life and can never say how and why, at a certain moment, one of these vital germs inserts itself into his fantasy, there to become a living creature on a plane of life superior to the changeable existence of every day.

I can only say that, without having made any effort to seek them out, I found before me, alive—you could touch them and even hear them breathe—the six characters now seen on the stage. And they stayed there in my presence, each with his secret torment and all bound together by the one common origin and mutual entanglement of their affairs, while I had them enter the world of art, constructing from their persons, their passions, and their adventures a novel, a drama, or at least a story.

Born alive, they wished to live.

To me it was never enough to present a man or a woman and what is special and characteristic about them simply for the pleasure of presenting them; to narrate a particular affair, lively or sad, simply for the pleasure of narrating it; to describe a landscape simply for the pleasure of describing it.

There are some writers (and not a few) who do feel this pleasure and, satisfied, ask no more. They are, to speak more precisely, historical writers.

But there are others who, beyond such pleasure, feel a more profound spiritual need on whose account they admit only figures, affairs, landscapes which have been soaked, so to speak, in a particular sense of life and acquire from it a universal value. These are, more precisely, philosophical writers.

I have the misfortune to belong to these last.

I hate symbolic art in which the presentation loses all spontaneous movement in order to become a machine, an allegory—a vain and misconceived effort because the very fact of giving an allegorical sense to a presentation clearly shows that we have to do with a fable which by itself has no truth either fantastic or direct; it was made for the demonstration of some moral truth. The spiritual need I speak of cannot be satisfied—or seldom, and that to the end of a superior irony, as for example in Ariosto—by such allegorical symbolism. This latter starts from a concept, and from a concept which creates or tries to create for itself an image. The former on the other hand seeks in the image—which must remain alive and free throughout—a meaning to give it value.

Now, however much I sought, I did not succeed in uncovering this meaning in the six characters. And I concluded therefore that it was no use making them live.

I thought to myself: "I have already afflicted my readers with hundreds and hundreds of stories. Why should I afflict them now by narrating the sad entanglements of these six unfortunates?"

And, thinking thus, I put them away from me. Or rather I did all I could to put them away.

But one doesn't give life to a character for nothing.

Creatures of my spirit, these six were already living a life which was their own and not mine any more, a life which it was not in my power any more to deny them.

Thus it is that while I persisted in desiring to drive them out of my spirit, they, as if completely detached from every narrative support, characters from a novel miraculously emerging from the pages of the book that contained them, went on living on their own, choosing certain moments of the day to reappear before me in the solitude of my study and coming—now one, now the other, now two together—to tempt me, to propose that I present or describe this scene or that, to explain the effects that could be secured with them, the new interest which a certain unusual situation could provide, and so forth.

For a moment I let myself be won over. And this condescension of mine, thus letting myself go for a while, was enough, because they drew from it a new increment of life, a greater degree of clarity and addition, consequently a greater degree of persuasive power over me. And thus as it became gradually harder and harder for me to go back and free myself from them, it became easier and easier for them to come back and tempt me. At a certain point I actually became obsessed with them. Until, all of a sudden, a way out of the difficulty flashed upon me.

"Why not," I said to myself, "present this highly strange fact of an author who refuses to let some of his characters live though they have been born in his fantasy, and the fact that these characters, having by now life in their veins, do not resign themselves to remaining excluded from the world of art? They are detached from me; live on their own; have acquired voice and movement; have by themselves—in this struggle for existence that they have had to wage with me—become dramatic characters, characters that can move and talk on their own initiative; already see themselves as such; have learned to defend themselves against me; will even know how to defend themselves against others. And so let them go where dramatic characters do go to have life: on a stage. And let us see what will happen."

That's what I did. And, naturally, the result was what it had to be: a mixture of tragic and comic, fantastic and realistic, in a humorous situation that was quite new and infinitely complex, a drama which is conveyed by means of the characters, who carry it within them and suffer it, a drama, breathing, speaking, self-propelled, which seeks at all costs to find the means of its own presentation; and the comedy of the vain attempt at an improvised realization of the drama on stage. First, the surprise of the poor actors in a theatrical company rehearsing a play by day on a bare stage (no scenery, no flats). Surprise and incredulity at the sight of the six characters announcing themselves as such in search of an author. Then, immediately afterwards, through that sudden fainting fit of the Mother veiled in black, their instinctive interest in the drama of which they catch a glimpse in her and in the other members of the strange family, an obscure, ambiguous drama, coming about so unexpectedly on a stage that is empty and unprepared to receive it. And gradually the growth of this interest to the bursting forth of the contrasting passions of Father, of Step-Daughter, of Son, of that poor Mother, passions seeking, as I said, to overwhelm each other with a tragic, lacerating fury.

And here is the universal meaning at first vainly sought in the six characters, now that, going on stage of their own accord, they succeed in finding it within themselves in the excitement of the desperate struggle which each wages against the other and all wage against the Manager and the actors, who do not understand them.

Without wanting to, without knowing it, in the strife of their bedevilled souls, each of them, defending himself against the accusations of the others, expresses as his own living passion and torment the passion and torment which for so many years have been the pangs of my spirit: the deceit of mutual understanding irremediably founded on the empty abstraction of the words, the multiple personality of everyone corresponding to the possibilities of being to be found in each of us, and finally the inherent tragic conflict between life (which is always moving and changing) and form (which fixes it, immutable).

Two above all among the six characters, the Father and the Step-Daughter, speak of that outrageous unalterable fixity of their form in which he and she see their essential nature expressed permanently and immutably, a nature that for one means punishment and for the other revenge; and they defend it against the factitious affectations and unaware volatility of the actors, and they try to impose it on the vulgar Manager who would like to change it and adapt it to the so-called exigencies of the theatre.

If the six characters don't all seem to exist on the same plane, it is not because some are figures of first rank and others of the second, that is, some are main characters and others minor ones—the elementary perspective necessary to all scenic or narrative art—nor is it that any are not completely created—for their purpose. They are all six at the same point of artistic realization and on the same level of reality, which is the fantastic level of the whole play. Except that the Father, the Step-Daughter, and also the Son are realized as mind; the Mother as nature; the Boy as a presence watching and performing a gesture and the Baby unaware of it all. This fact creates among them a perspective of a new sort. Unconsciously I had had the impression that some of them needed to be fully realized (artistically speaking), others less so, and others merely sketched in as elements in a narrative or presentational sequence: the most alive, the most completely created, are the Father and the Step-Daughter who naturally stand out more and lead the way, dragging themselves along beside the almost dead weight of the others—first, the Son, holding back; second, the Mother, like a victim resigned to her fate, between the two children who have hardly any substance beyond their appearance and who need to be led by the hand.

And actually! actually they had each to appear in that stage of creation which they had attained in the author's fantasy at the moment when he wished to drive them away.

If I now think about these things, about having intuited that necessity, having unconsciously found the way to resolve it by means of a new perspective, and about the way in which I actually obtained it, they seem like miracles. The fact is that the play was really conceived in one of those spontaneous illuminations of the fantasy when by a miracle all the elements of the mind answer to each other's call and work in divine accord. No human brain, working "in the cold," however stirred up it might be, could ever have succeeded in penetrating far enough, could ever have been in a position to satisfy all the exigencies of the play's form. Therefore the reasons which I will give to clarify the values of the play must not be thought of as intentions that I conceived beforehand when I prepared myself for the job and which I now undertake to defend, but only as discoveries which I have been able to make afterwards in tranquillity.

I wanted to present six characters seeking an author. Their play does not manage to get presented—precisely because the author whom they seek is missing. Instead is presented the comedy of their vain attempt with all that it contains of tragedy by virtue of the fact that the six characters have been rejected.

But can one present a character while rejecting him? Obviously, to present him one needs, on the contrary, to receive him into one's fantasy before one can express him. And I have actually accepted and realized the six characters: I have, however, accepted and realized them as rejected: in search of *another* author.

What have I rejected of them? Not themselves, obviously, but their drama, which doubtless is what interests them above all but which did not interest me—for the reasons already indicated.

And what is it, for a character—his drama?

Every creature of fantasy and art, in order to exist, must have his drama, that is, a drama in which he may be a character and for which he *is* a character. This drama is the character's *raison d'être*, his vital function, necessary for his existence.

In these six, then, I have accepted the "being" without the reason for being. I have taken the organism and entrusted to it, not its own proper function, but another more complex function into which its own function entered, if at all, only as a datum. A terrible and desperate situation especially for the two—Father and Step-Daughter—who more than the others crave life and more than the others feel themselves to be characters, that is, absolutely need a drama and therefore their own drama— the only one which they can envisage for themselves yet which meantime they see rejected: an "impossible" situation from which they feel they must escape at whatever cost; it is a matter of life and death. True, I have given them another *raison d'être*, another function: precisely that "impossible" situation, the drama of being in search of an author and rejected. But that this should be a *raison d'être*, that it should have become their real function, that it should be necessary, that it should suffice, they can hardly suppose; for they have a life of their own. If someone were to tell them, they wouldn't believe him. It is not possible to believe that the sole reason for our living should lie in a torment that seems to us unjust and inexplicable.

I cannot imagine, therefore, why the charge was brought against me that the character of the Father was not what it should have been because it stepped out of its quality and position as a character and invaded at times the author's province and took it over. I who understand those who don't quite understand me see that the charge derives from the fact that the character expresses and makes his own a torment of spirit which is recognized as mine. Which is entirely natural and of absolutely no significance. Aside from the fact that this torment of spirit in the character of the Father derives from causes, and is suffered and lived for reasons, that have nothing to do with the drama of my personal experience, a fact which alone removes all substance from the criticism, I want to make it clear that the inherent torment of my spirit is one thing, a torment which

I can legitimately—provided that it be organic—reflect in a character, and that the activity of my spirit as revealed in the realized work, the activity that succeeds in forming a drama out of the six characters in search of an author is another thing. If the Father participated in this latter activity, if he competed in forming the drama of the six characters without an author, then and only then would it by all means be justified to say that he was at times the author himself and therefore not the man he should be. But the Father suffers and does not create his existence as a character in search of an author. He suffers it as an inexplicable fatality and as a situation which he tries with all his powers to rebel against, which he tries to remedy: hence it is that he is a character in search of an author and nothing more, even if he expresses as his own the torment of my spirit. If he, so to speak, assumed some of the author's responsibilities, the fatality would be completely explained. He would, that is to say, see himself accepted, if only as a rejected character, accepted in the poet's heart of hearts, and he would no longer have any reason to suffer the despair of not finding someone to construct and affirm his life as a character. I mean that he would quite willingly accept the *raison d'être* which the author gives him and without regrets would forego his own, throwing over the Manager and the actors to whom in fact he runs as his only recourse.

There is one character, that of the Mother, who on the other hand does not care about being alive (considering being alive as an end in itself). She hasn't the least suspicion that she is *not* alive. It has never occurred to her to ask how and why and in what manner she lives. In short, she is not aware of being a character, inasmuch as she is never, even for a moment, detached from her role. She doesn't know she has a role.

This makes her perfectly organic. Indeed, her role of Mother does not of itself, in its natural essence, embrace mental activity. And she does not exist as a mind. She lives in an endless continuum of feeling, and therefore she cannot acquire awareness of her life—that is, of her existence as a character. But with all this, even she, in her own way and for her own ends, seeks an author, and at a certain stage seems happy to have been brought before the Manager. Because she hopes to take life from him, perhaps? No: because she hopes the Manager will have her present a scene with the Son in which she would put so much of her own life. But it is a scene which does not exist, which never has and never could take place. So unaware is she of being a character, that is, of the life that is possible to her, all fixed and determined, moment by moment, in every action, every phrase.

She appears on stage with the other characters but without understanding what the others make her do. Obviously, she imagines that the itch for life with which the husband and the daughter are afflicted and for which she herself is to be found on stage is no more than one of the usual incomprehensible extravagances of this man who is both tortured and torturer and—horrible, most horrible—a new equivocal rebellion on the part of that poor erring girl. The Mother is completely passive. The events of her own life and the values they assume in her eyes, her very character, are all things which are "said" by the others and which she only once contradicts, and that because the maternal instinct rises up and rebels within her to make it clear that she didn't at all wish to abandon either the son or the husband: the Son was taken from her and the husband forced her to abandon him. She is only correcting data; she explains and knows nothing.

In short, she is nature. Nature fixed in the figure of a mother.

This character gave me a satisfaction of a new sort, not to be ignored. Nearly all my critics, instead of defining her, after their habit, as "unhuman"—which seems to be the peculiar and incorrigible characteristic of all my creatures without exception—had the goodness to note "with real pleasure" that at last a *very human* figure had emerged from my fantasy. I explain this praise to myself in the following way: since my poor Mother is entirely limited to the natural attitude of a Mother with no possibility of free mental activity, being, that is, little more than a lump of flesh completely alive in all its functions—procreation, lactation, caring for and loving its young—without any need therefore of exercising her brain, she realizes in her person the true and complete "human type." That must be how it is, since in a human organism nothing seems more superfluous than the mind.

But the critics have tried to get rid of the Mother with this praise without bothering to penetrate the nucleus of poetic values which the character in the play represents. A very human figure, certainly, because mindless, that is, unaware of being what she is or not caring to explain it to herself. But not knowing that she is a character doesn't prevent her from being one. That is her drama in my play. And the most living expression of it comes spurting out in her cry to the Manager who wants her to think all these things have happened already and therefore cannot now be a reason for renewed lamentations: "No, it's happening now, it's happening always! My torture is not a pretence, signore! I am alive and present, always, in every moment of my torture: it is renewed, alive and present, always!" This she *feels*, without being conscious of it, and feels it therefore as something inexplicable: but she feels it so terribly that she doesn't think it *can* be something to explain either to herself or to others. She feels it and that is that. She feels it as pain, and this pain is immediate; she cries it out. Thus she reflects the growing fixity of life in a form —the same thing, which in another way, tortures the Father and the Step-Daughter. In them, mind. In her, nature. The mind rebels and, as best it may, seeks an advantage; nature, if not aroused by sensory stimuli, weeps.

Conflict between life-in-movement and form is the inexorable condition not only of the mental but also of the physical order. The life which in order to exist has become fixed in our corporeal form little by little kills that form. The tears of a nature thus fixed lament the irreparable, continuous aging of our bodies. Hence the tears of the Mother are passive and perpetual. Revealed in three faces, made significant in three distinct and simultaneous dramas, this inherent conflict finds in the play its most complete expression. More: the Mother declares also the particular value of artistic form—a form which does not delimit or destroy its own life and which life does not consume—in her cry to the Manager. If the Father and Step-Daughter began their scene a hundred thousand times in succession, always, at the appointed moment, at the instant when the life of the work of art must be expressed with that cry, it would always be heard, unaltered and unalterable in its form, not as a mechanical repetition, not as a return determined by external necessities, but on the contrary, alive every time and as new, suddenly born *thus forever!* embalmed alive in its incorruptible form. Hence, always, as we open the book, we shall find Francesca alive and confessing to Dante her sweet sin, and if we turn to the passage a hundred thousand times in succession, a hundred thousand times in succession Francesca will speak her words, never repeating them mechanically, but saying them as though each time were the first time with such living and sudden passion that Dante every time will turn faint. All that lives, by the fact of living, has a form, and by the same token must die—except the work of art which lives forever in so far as it *is* form.

The birth of a creature of human fantasy, a birth which is a step across the threshold between nothing and eternity, can also happen suddenly, occasioned by some necessity. An imagined drama needs a character who does or says a certain necessary thing; accordingly this character is born and is precisely what he had to be. In this way Madame Pace is born among the six characters and seems a miracle, even a trick, realistically portrayed on the stage. It is no trick. The birth is real. The new character is alive not because she was alive already but because she is now happily born as is required by the fact of her being a character—she is obliged to be as she is. There is a break here, a sudden change in the level of reality of the scene, because a character can be born in this way only in the poet's fancy and not on the boards of a stage. Without anyone's noticing it, I have all of a sudden changed the scene: I have gathered it up again into my own fantasy without removing it from the spectator's eyes. That is, I have shown them, instead of the stage, my own fantasy in the act of creating—my own fantasy in the form of this same stage. The sudden and uncontrollable changing of a visual phenomenon from one level of reality to another is a miracle comparable to those of the saint who sets his own statue in motion: it is neither wood nor stone at such a moment. But the miracle is not arbitrary. The stage—a stage which accepts the fantastic reality of the six characters—is no fixed, immutable datum. Nothing in this play exists as given and preconceived. Everything is in the making, is in motion, is a sudden experiment: even the place in which this unformed life, reaching after its own form, changes and changes again contrives to shift position organically. The level of reality changes. When I had the idea of bringing Madame Pace to birth right there on the stage, I felt I could do it and I did it. Had I noticed that this birth was unhinging and silently, unnoticed, in a second, giving another shape, another reality to my scene, I certainly wouldn't have brought it about. I would have been afraid of the apparent lack of logic. And I would have committed an ill-omened assault on the beauty of my work. The fervor of my mind saved me from doing so. For, despite appearances, with their specious logic, this fantastic birth is sustained by a real necessity in mysterious, organic relation with the whole life of the work.

That someone now tells me it hasn't all the value it could have because its expression is not constructed but chaotic, because it smacks of romanticism, makes me smile.

I understand why this observation was made to me: because in this work of mine the presentation of the drama in which the six characters are involved appears tumultuous and never proceeds in an orderly manner. There is no logical development, no concatenation of the events. Very true. Had I hunted it with a lamp I couldn't have found a more disordered, crazy, arbitrary, complicated, in short, romantic way of presenting "the drama in which the six characters are involved." Very true. But I have not presented that drama. I have presented another—and I won't undertake to say again what!—in which, among the many fine things that everyone, according to his tastes, can find, there is a discreet satire on romantic procedures: in the six characters thus excited to the point where they stifle themselves in the roles which each of them plays in a certain drama while I present them as characters in another play which they don't know and don't suspect the existence of, so that this inflammation of their passions—which belongs to the realm of romantic procedures —is humorously "placed," located in the void. And the drama of the six characters presented not as it would have been organized by my fantasy had it been accepted but in this way, as a rejected drama, could not exist in the work except as a "situation," with some little development, and could not come out except in indications, stormily, disorderedly, in violent foreshortenings, in a chaotic manner: continually interrupted, sidetracked, contradicted (by one of its characters), denied, and (by two others) not even seen.

There is a character indeed—he who denies the drama which makes him a character, the Son—who draws all his importance and value from being a character not of the comedy in the making—which as such hardly appears—but from the presentation that I made of it. In short, he is the only one who lives solely as "a character in search of an author"—inasmuch as the author he seeks is not a dramatic author. Even this could not be otherwise. The character's attitude is an organic product of my conception, and it is logical that in the situation it should produce greater confusion and disorder and another element of romantic contrast.

But I had precisely to *present* this organic and natural chaos. And to present a chaos is not at all to present chaotically, that is, romantically. That my presentation is the reverse of confused, that it is quite simple, clear, and orderly, is proved by the clarity which the intrigue, the characters, the fantastic and realistic, dramatic and comic levels of the work have had for every public in the world and by the way in which, for those with more searching vision, the unusual values enclosed within it come out.

Great is the confusion of tongues among men if criticisms thus made find words for their expression. No less great than this confusion is the intimate law of order which, obeyed in all points, makes this work of mine classical and typical and at its catastrophic close forbids the use of words. Though the audience eventually understands that one does not create life by artifice and that the drama of the six characters cannot be presented without an author to give them value with his spirit, the Manager remains vulgarly anxious to know how the thing turned out, and the "ending" is remembered by the Son in its sequence of actual moments, but without any sense and therefore not needing a human voice for its expression. It happens stupidly, uselessly, with the going-off of a mechanical weapon on stage. It breaks up and disperses the sterile experiment of the characters and the actors, which has apparently been made without the assistance of the poet.

The poet, unknown to them, as if looking on at a distance during the whole period of the experiment, was at the same time busy creating—with it and of it—his own play.

FATHER'S DAY

By Eric Bentley

A MAN HAS A WIFE and a male child. He also has a male secretary. Between the wife and the secretary there arises what the husband considers an understanding of a harmless sort. He wants to help them in some way, but whenever he speaks to them they exchange a significant look that seems to ask how they should receive what he says if they are not to annoy him. But this itself annoys him. He ends up firing the secretary. Then he sends the wife after him. In the wife's view, he fairly throws her into the secretary's arms; and the pair set up house together. The husband, however, does not lose interest in the wife. His continued interest, indeed, though he considers it "pure" (that is: asexual) is a source of embarrassment to the former secretary. When a daughter is born to the lovers the husband is interested in her too—more, perhaps, even, than he had been in the wife. And when she becomes a schoolgirl, he waits for school coming out, then on at least one occasion seeks her out, and gives her a present. The girl does not know who the strange gentleman is. At a certain point the secretary can bear the whole situation no longer, and he takes his family—there are three children by this time—to live somewhere else, out of the stepfather's reach. Subsequently the secretary dies. His family of four is now destitute; they have to sleep all in the same room. And at some point they return to the place where the husband lived. Here the mother gets employment as a kind of seamstress. But her employer's real interest is in employing the daughter, now in her late teens, as a prostitute. The dressmaker's shop is a front for a brothel. One day, the husband, a client of the establishment, presents himself and would have taken the girl in his arms had not the mother suddenly turned up to cry: "But it's my daughter!" After this encounter, the husband takes his wife back into his home along with his three stepchildren. At the time, he is living with his own son, now in his early twenties. This legitimate son is offended by the presence of the three bastards, and wanders from room to room in his father's house, feeling displaced and desolate. The three bastards react to his hostility. The little girl, aged four, drowns herself in the fountain in the garden. The other child, a fourteen-year-old boy, witnesses the drowning, fails to offer any assistance, then shoots himself. The mother, who might have been keeping an eye on the young pair, was, instead, following her twenty-two-year-old son around the house, begging for forgiveness. He rushes out into the garden to escape her, and there comes upon his stepbrother just at the moment the latter watches his sister die and kills himself. After this debacle, the older girl runs away from home. Left behind are father, mother, and son . . .

I am trying to tell the story of *Sei personaggi in cerca d'autore*, or rather the story of the six characters *in* the play. This is quite hard, and an analysis of the work might well begin with the reasons *why* it is hard. The first reason is pretty much what it would be with an Ibsen play. It is hard to tell the story of, say, *Ghosts* because it comes out in fragments and the fragments have to be painstakingly fitted together. The Ibsenite has, above all, to be able to take a hint; he even has to have the detective's knack of snapping up bits of evidence and holding them in reserve till he can connect them with something else. However, while Ibsen's fragments come together into a complete and coherent picture, like the pieces of a jigsaw puzzle, Pirandello defies a number of the normal expectations and, by the usual criteria, his picture is incomplete. As to *location*, for instance, which in the drama, at least since Aristotle, has always been considered something to have a clear understanding about. In most plays one knows exactly where everything takes place, and in plays where the location is somewhat abstract, there is a convention to make this abstractness acceptable to its audience. In retelling Pirandello's story just now, however, I paused several times, hoping to insert a phrase indicating where someone had gone or returned to. The husband's house could be in Rome, I suppose, but couldn't it just as easily be anywhere else with a climate favorable to fountains? Could I even say: "returned to the city"? Not even that; because the only clues are a school, a house with a fountain in the garden, and a modiste's shop that is also a brothel; things that exist in small towns and villages as well. It is not, of course, that one insists on naturalism, but that one cannot react without a degree of bafflement to not knowing *under what circumstances* the secretary lived with the wife in city, town, or village; how far away he then took her; where the bedroom in which all four slept was to be found; and so on. But the queries as to *place* only lead to similar queries on other topics, and notably *time*. Here at least Pirandello has marked certain boundaries, notably the ages of the four children. Since the legitimate son is twenty-two, and the eldest bastard is eighteen, it follows that the transfer of the wife from husband to lover occurred about twenty years ago. Yet, in the Pirandellian context, how little this arithmetic means! In Ibsen, doing such arithmetic usually proves well worthwhile, but in *Six Characters* it would never be done at all, except by such an undiscourageable investigator as myself, willing to follow any trail. This trail has proved a false one. In the rare instances where exact notation of the passage of time is going to affect our sense of drama, Pirandello does the arithmetic for us. The reiterated statement that the secretary died "two months ago" tells us that the death marks the beginning of the Action that is this play, just as the father's death marks the beginning of the Hamlet action, and the aunt's death the beginning of the action of *Enrico IV*.

Generally, time and space, in the story of the *Six Characters*, are alike rather abstract and are tokens of a pervasive abstractness. *Who is the Father?* The question: what does he do? is no more answered than: where does he live? To place him, either literally or figuratively, all we can do is remark that his vocabulary marks him as something of an intellectual—a student of Pirandellian philosophy, even—and that his having a secretary and a sizable house (with rooms to wander through and a garden with a fountain in it) marks him as well-to-do. By contrast, wife and secretary are defined as *poor*, the Italian word *umile* leaving open whether they were just of humble birth or also humble by nature. Of the elder girl we know that poverty made her a prostitute; and we see that she resents her father. Of the two youngest children we learn little except that their birth was illegitimate. The young man is so withdrawn and silent that we can be told he is a character not fully created because not suited to a play at all: only part of him, as it were, is there. To say the least, then, these are people of no particular background. We can say they are Italians, but our evidence is only that the play is written in Italian. We can say they are bourgeois, yet even for this the evidence is largely negative: in our culture, the bourgeois is the norm, and the speech of this play is normal, except for Madama Pace who, like lower-class New York City today, has a Spanish accent. Incidentally, only Madama Pace has a name. Does that make her the only character portrayed with particularity? Hardly; her name is a symbolic one. It means peace, and is presumably used ironically: she brings, not peace, but a pair of scissors.

Plays without what are called individual characters, with characters labelled The Father and the like, are no new thing. They were the usual thing in the Expressionist plays of the second decade of this century, the decade during which the ideas for *Six Characters* came to Pirandello.[1] Is this an Expressionist play, then? One is certainly encouraged to believe so by the stage direction in which the six are introduced. All, says the author, are to wear masks which

> will help to give the impression of figures constructed by art, each one unchangeably fixed in the expression of its own fundamental sentiment, thus: REMORSE in the case of the Father; REVENGE in the case of the Stepdaughter; DISDAIN in the case of the Son; GRIEF in the case of the Mother, who should have wax tears fixed in the rings under her eyes and on her cheeks, as with the sculpted and painted images of the *mater dolorosa* in church.

Here we are being offered abstract qualities as characters, as in those medieval moralities which are the ancestors of Expressionist drama. But the fact is that the stage direction does little to prepare us for what is offered by way of character in the dialogue itself—not abstract qualities or general ideas but emotional conflict of very unusual vividness, vivacity, and fullness. The word Expressionism is not the clue we need.

What is? Perhaps the phrase: *dream play*. Some of the earliest critics of Pirandello's plays noticed that, in them, "life is a dream." Two features, more than anything else, contributed to this impression: first, the "dreamlike" comings and goings to and from nowhere of Pirandello's

[1] The evidence for this is in two short stories, "La tragedia d'un personaggio" (1911) and "Colloqui coi personaggi" (1915), in a letter to his son Stefano dated 1917, and in a passage (undated) from a projected novel-in-the-making cited in the sixth volume of the collected works (1960). This last-named passage is about Madama Pace's establishment, and suggests the possibility that it was with this image that *Six Characters* began—a tempting point in the light of the interpretation of the play offered above. The letter to Stefano is also cited to this extent in the sixth volume of the collected works:

> "... But I already have my head full of novelties! So many short stories . . . And a queer thing, so sad, so very sad: *Six Characters in Search of an Author:* novel-in-the-making. Maybe you understand. Six characters, caught in a terrible drama, who visit me to get themselves put into a novel. An obsession. And I dont want to know about it. I tell them it's no use. What do I care about *them?* What do I care about anything? And they show me all their sores. And I send them packing . . .—and in this way finally the novel-*in*-the-making turns out to be *made.*"

Incidentally, in the projected novel-in-the-making, Madama Pace's shop did have a precise location: Rome.

people; second, that the author seems haunted, "possessed," by these people. Now the first of these features, appearing by itself, need not signify very much. It is a formal device any author might choose to adopt. It would prove nothing more than that, perhaps, he had read Strindberg. The second feature, however, if further explored, will lead us deep into Pirandello's play, whereupon we shall also learn that, for him, the first feature was not lightly adopted or trivially used.

What is Pirandello possessed *by?* That drama should present the dynamics of relationship, and not separate individual portraits, is in the nature of the genre. But Pirandello is an extremist in this regard. No one has made do with so few individual traits and details of background while managing to make the contact between people so electric. This kind of drama, one is tempted to say, is ALL relationship and NO character. Six *Non*-Characters in Search of an Author! Or, translating this from negative to positive: In Search of an Author, these relationships—Man/Wife, Father/Daughter, Mother/Son. There can be little doubt what Pirandello is possessed by: elemental family relationships. Our next questions, then, should be: if he has not offered us a cold typicality but has brought relationships to passionate life, how has he done it? If he has not approached these relationships in the accepted, naturalistic way, how *has* he approached them? And now our queries are turning back on themselves, for Pirandello's method has already been touched on, and is that of dreams, not the dreams of the older literary tradition, either, but the actual fantasies of our actual day and night dreaming. And here it would be well to limit the word phantasy to the technical sense given it by Freud when he said: "Phantasies are psychical façades constructed to bar the way to . . . memories" of primal scenes.[2] (Like Freud's translator I will spell the word with "ph" when this sense is intended.) This may be only one kind of fantasy among many, but it is amazing how close to the principal images and thoughts of *Six Characters* Freud's definition brings us.

In this play we are never far away from primal scenes, and specifically three of them: incest of father with daughter; the child seeing the parents make love; and sibling murder. Each of these scenes is veiled by at least one layer of phantasy. Even the sibling murder, which comes closest to such a scene, is not actually a murder: the boy refrained from preventing a suicide. In the case of the incest, two layers of phantasy at once present themselves. The girl is not a daughter but a stepdaughter, and the lovemaking does not quite take place. The most thoroughly hidden of the

[2] See letter to Fliess dated May 2, 1897, and the accompanying note. Also *The Interpretation of Dreams*, translated by James Strachey, Basic Books edition, p. 491.

three primal scenes is that of the son seeing his father in the role of lover; and how strong was Pirandello's wish to hide this scene is shown in the fact that he deleted from later editions this passage from the first:

> Hasn't he (it is the Son, speaking of the Father) acted in such a way as to force me to discover what no son should ever discover? That father and mother are alive and are man and woman, for each other, outside the reality we give them. For as soon as this reality is uncovered, our life is no longer tied to that man and that woman except at a single point—one which will only shame them should we see it.

A single point. One touches one's parents at the moment one is conceived. There, for the one and only time, as the parental genitals touch, are all three of us touching. It is the only togetherness life affords. Such is the painfully vivid Pirandellian version of this primal scene. It links the Old Testament shame at the sight of parental nakedness with the Pascalian sense of hopeless isolation in an alien universe. The specific veils the scene wears are also of interest. First, this Son has not discovered *anyone* making love. What he has done is notice the erotic quality in a relationship he did not expect to be erotic. It was not that of his father and mother. It was that of his father and his stepsister. But the suspicion is—and it is not the suspicion of the son alone—that the stepsister is taking the mother's place in bed.

A psychoanalyst, Dr. Charles Kligerman, has made an observation that digs deeper into the plot of *Six Characters* than anything, so far as I know, that purely literary critics have said. It is that we have here, not an assortment, but a *sequence* of phantasies, each more primitive than the last—each belonging to an earlier phase of our lives than the last. "In other words, from adult father/daughter incest there is a retreat to the earlier Oedipal triangle, and then a sudden regression to the primitive sibling rivalry, with wishful phantasy of murder followed by guilty suicide."[3]

The dramatist cannot be content merely to present phantasies (or fantasies either), he must arrange them in significant progression. It is Dr. Kligerman's thesis, I take it, that the three main phantasies constitute a dramatic beginning, middle, and end. The question is: of what? That they make up the beginning, middle, and end of the six characters' own story is pretty clear. Does that make them the beginning, middle, and end of the whole work? Rather naturally, giving psychology priority

[3] "A psychoanalytic study of Pirandello's *Six Characters in Search of an Author*," by Charles Kligerman, *Journal of the American Psychoanalytic Association*, October 1962.

over dramatic art, our psycho-analytic interpreter seems to answer this in the affirmative, and backs up his answer with biographical rather than artistic evidence. "The Father, Son and Boy," says Dr. Kligerman, "all represent different levels of conflict within the author." This may well be a true statement on the *sources* of the matter presented. It does not follow that the three characters, once created, are best considered as three aspects of one character. All the characters a playwright "creates" come out of himself, just as his dreams do, and may similarly correspond to parts of himself. The important thing, artistically, is that they then become objectified, and demand to be seen, not as aspects of their author, but as his creations. If this is true, our protagonist in *Six Characters* has real others (not himself in other forms) to act upon and be acted upon by. This is a man and his son, not a man and himself, though, biologically and symbolically, a man and his son are overlapping categories.

And the end of the family story is not, as I think Dr. Kligerman assumes, the double suicide, but the situation that ensues thereon. It is described thus in the first edition:

> Because, finally, the drama is all in this: when the mother re-enters my home, the family she had elsewhere, which was now being, as it were, superimposed on the first one, comes to an end, it's alien, it can't grow in this soil. The little girl dies, the little boy comes to a tragic end, the older girl flees. And so, after all the torment, there remain we three—myself, the mother, the son. And when the alien family is gone, we too find ourselves alien, the one to the other. We find ourselves utterly desolated.

The Father is given these words toward the end of Act One.[4] Later Pirandello must have concluded both that the passage comes at the wrong place and that it is too explicit. He put it off to the very end of the play and did the job without words: the final version states in a stage direction that father, mother, and son are left on stage at the end when the daughter rushes out of their home. They form a tableau with the mother's arms outstretched towards the obdurate son. Which I take to mean that the double suicide is not the final phantasy. Rather, the dramatist insists on returning to the Oedipal image: the family story begins and ends with father, mother, and son. The daughter and two younger children came and went. Their father had gone forever just before we meet them. *The second family is killed off.* We see the effect upon the first family which lives on, bearing the brunt.

[4] I should perhaps say Section One, as the Italian editions have no act divisions. But many Americans know the play from a translation that names the sections Acts.

2074

So far I have been talking exclusively of the six characters' story, which is complete (as complete as it is going to be) before the show starts: it is all time past. Does nothing happen on stage except a re-enactment of this past? Does nothing happen before our eyes and now, for the first time, in the present? Certainly it does. The six characters enter a theatre and ask the director to make a play of them. He toys with the idea, finds himself, indeed, devoting the day to trying it out. A negative decision is reached, and that is the end. The first edition actually closes with the line, and it is a very good curtain line: "*E mi hanno fatto perdere una giornata!*"—"And they've made me lose a whole day."

I am describing now, of course, the conceit or *trovata* which gave the play fame, and even notoriety, the idea of an encounter between a company of actors and the roles they might be asked to play. Can it be disposed of lightly? "The plot of the play within a play," Dr. Kligerman says, "contains the essential drama, for the rest is comic badinage . . . and a great deal of discussion . . ." If valid, this would be a devastating criticism: no dramatic masterpiece would have so much dead wood in it. Conversely, if this is a great play, expressive in all its parts, then both the "badinage" and the "great deal of discussion" will be found to be necessary to its structure. Let us look further into the matter.

Drama is action. "An encounter between a company of actors and the roles they might play: "this is a formula for action, but as it stands it is too general. Action has to be more specific than that. Who exactly is doing what to whom? We have always to come to this question. Take the first bit of it first: *who is doing?* It needs hardly a moment's reflection on *Six Characters in Search of an Author* to produce an answer that comes from an overpowering impression. *The Father is doing.* If an Action is here being propelled forward by a character, then that propeller is the Father. He is indeed so maniacally insistent that he might seem at times to be lifting the play up bodily. His insistency is a huge motif, and a huge portion of the play. *What* is he doing? He is demanding that his drama be staged. Why? He is persuaded that he will be thereby justified. A hostile interpretation of his character will be rejected, a friendly one endorsed. Does he really believe this? It is hard to say. He is so intent on stressing what should be, it is hard to know if he is confident that it will be. If he gets nowhere, will he settle for less? It looks very much as if the less that he will settle for is the act of pleading itself. He evidently gets a release from just talking, from unburdening himself. He is, among other things, an Ancient Mariner, buttonholing people and inflicting his story on them. And one knows what satisfaction all Ancient Mariners get from this kind of thing, because every one of us is something of an Ancient Mariner. For this mariner, certainly, saying his piece is a matter of life and death. I am reminded of a patient cited in R. D. Laing's book

Eric Bentley

The Divided Self as saying that he talked as an act of self-preservation. That is, of course, to imply that his existence was threatened. And the sense of such a threat is felt in all the big talking in Pirandello—that of his Enrico, that of his Ponza and Frola, and that of the Father. The topic, here, is schizophrenia, and Pirandello's plays have become easier to comprehend in the light of studies of schizoid problems written in the past several decades.

It is interesting that in two generations a great dramatist has led the psychologists in providing a classic image of modern man. Ibsen, just before Freud, presented Modern Man as Neurotic. Pirandello, anticipating the study of schizophrenia by a whole school of psychiatrists from Minkowski to Laing, showed how integral to modern life is "the schizophrenic experience." His Henry IV is the schizophrenic as tragic hero.

> . . . the experience and behavior that gets labelled schizophrenic is a special strategy that a person invents in order to live in an unlivable situation.[5]

In *Così è (se vi pare)*, the Ponza/Frola narrative is an elaboration of such a special strategy, neither more nor less. Such strategies constitute the sanity of the insane, the rationality of the irrational. That is one paradox which Pirandello has in common with recent psychologists. Another is that the sane may not be any more rational. So one can regard the insane as sane, and the sane as insane. In 1967 the thought is no longer new, but new testimony to its truth is printed in each day's newspaper.

What is the Father doing? He is talking to live, that is, to avoid getting killed. He is fighting off the arrows of the Indian hordes of the soul. The world's *implosion* Dr. Laing calls that kind of threat. The Father is also trying to keep from drowning, from inundation. Dr. Laing speaks of *engulfment*. Like a witch doctor, the Father hopes to hold the devils and hobgoblins at arms' length. In short, he is what our grandparents called a lunatic. He is "mad as a hatter." Critics and actors who have resisted this conclusion have never got very far with *Six Characters in Search of an Author*.

Yet the father's manic behavior on stage is the least of it. In drama, as in life, character is found in concentrated form in men's decisions and actions which entail decisions. What have been this man's decisions? Since he is nothing if not a father and a husband, we must ask what he has done for his son and his wife. When the former was a baby he sent him into the

[5] *The Politics of Experience*, by R. D. Laing. New York: Pantheon Books, 1967.

2076

country to be nursed. It would be healthier. This is a rich man who prefers the ways of the poor. But when does he have his son brought back? We are not told, except that it was too late. The boy returned as an alien and an enemy. And the wife? He pushed her into the arms of his secretary. These, too, were good, simple people—also poor—who understood each other. In short, the father's actions have been such as to destroy his own family by driving them away. Obviously, he is what is usually called schizophrenic, and must isolate himself, even though isolation, in turn, becomes torture. If he can't stand company, equally he cannot stand himself. Desperate measures are taken against the outer world on behalf of the inner world, but to no avail. The inner world feels as insecure as ever, and the Father goes out in search of . . . well, in the first instance, company.

Two is company. That is: company is sex. The Father becomes a client of Madama Pace's, the Pacifying Madam. What, in external terms, goes wrong at her place we know. What does it all signify? Again, it suffices to look closely at the specific data. His wife he considered motherly but asexual. Madama Pace is a mother who sells sex. She is motherhood degraded, and she is sex degraded. As Dr. Kligerman has noticed, she is the "giantess of the nursery," the castrating nanny, and, according to the first version, carries scissors. Perhaps it was defensiveness that made Pirandello omit the scissors from the revised text; surely they are a vivid touch. And the Stepdaughter, whatever else she is, is the Mother when young, the Mother with sex-appeal, as in *Enrico IV*, where the Emperor embraces the daughter instead of the mother. What is the substance of the encounter at Madama Pace's? The evil mother offers our man a girl. The girl says: My father just died. The man says: take your dress off. The good mother rushes in, crying: stop, that's my daughter! A hideous little instrument of self-torture, this phantasy, though no more so than a thousand others in the chronicles of schizophrenia.

In nothing is the complexity of Pirandello's dramaturgy more evident than in this creation, Madama Pace. She is not one of the six characters. She is conjured up by the spirit of the theatre on the initiative of the Father. What does he mean by this initiative, and what does his author mean? *Six Characters in Search of an Author* can be conceived of as many concentric circles, in which case Madama Pace might well be the innermost circle: play within play within play within play . . . Now the most helpful insight into plays within plays—or rather dreams within dreams—has been Freud's. He remarked that we dream we are dreaming when we especially wish to disown a particular phantasy as "only a dream." And the phantasies we particularly wish to disown present what troubles us most in a rather blunt form. Madama Pace is not one of the actors, she is not one of the six, she is conjured up by one of the six, or by his "idea of a theatre." Most likely (as psychoanalysts will suggest) she is what troubles Pirandello. Certainly she is what troubles the Father: his mother as "giantess of the nursery," as castrator. Above all as procuress—provider and degrader of sexual pleasure. The Father is this play's Dr. Faustus, and she is his bad angel.

If she is a go-between, between whom does she go? Between the two families that the six characters consist of. And the story of the six can usefully be seen as a confrontation of these two groups, the legitimate and the illegitimate, pursuing licit and illicit love. Each of the three traumatic situations I have described brings the two groups into desperate conflict: father with his wife's illegitimate daughter, adulterous mother with the legitimate son, illegitimate younger children with the legitimate son. It is appropriate to this play that one finds oneself proposing different ways of looking at it. Each way is likely to have its peculiar advantage. And the schema just provided has the advantage of bringing out the special importance of the Son. He "dominates" two of the bad situations, and is not outside the third one (since he reacts strongly to the "incest"). When we speak of sibling murder, we can cite the Son as the murderer of both younger children.

If the confrontation of the legitimate and the illegitimate families is important to the structure of the play, what of the confrontation we began to look into a few minutes ago, that of the family with the theatrical troupe? Of all the concentric circles, this is perhaps the outermost one. Which in itself might tend to make a psychiatrist regard it as the least important, since the doctor's job is to look for hidden disease and penetrate disguises. Art, however, is not a disease, and in theatre art the disguise is in a clear sense the *ding an sich*. Nor—contrary to what many academic as well as clinical critics assume—does the artist harbor a general prejudice in favor of hidden meanings and against obvious ones. On the contrary, the weight to be given to the most external of the dramas in *Six Characters* must be decided without prejudice against externality. It is wholly a question of what weight, by his own artistic means, did Pirandello give to it.

Well, to begin with, he derived the title of the whole work from it, and considering how unerring his intuition was apt to be in such matters, this "small" item should not be overlooked. Granted that the substance of Action in the work is inner, neurotic, and even schizophrenic experience, what of the ever-present fact that the vehicle of Action is this conceit: characters in search of an author? It is a search with two aspects: the wish for a play to be *written* and the wish for it to be *enacted*. Let us take the second aspect first.

Enactment. If there is anything we are not in doubt about after we have seen this play it is that, for its author, all the world is a stage.

"Totus mundus facit histrionem," as the motto of the Globe Theatre read. But the idea receives a specific application here that is not so obvious. What happens when the actors try to enact the *scene* in Madama Pace's shop? They fail. But the point of the passage is lost when the actors are presented as inept. That kind of failure has too little content. A bad actor is a bad actor, period. What relationship does Pirandello define between the real thing and the re-enactment? Is it not that of a translation that cannot in the nature of things be a faithful one? The best analogy I can find is with the attempt to reconstruct a dream with the aid of notes jotted down upon waking. The notes are very definite, perhaps; but they are fragmentary. There are gaps, and above all the tone of feeling that characterized the whole world of the dream has gone. The Pirandellian re-enactment is incomplete and deeply unsatisfying in just this way.

But enactment is only an offshoot anyway, an offshoot of what is to be enacted: the author's work. IN CERCA D'AUTORE. And *who* is searching for him? Six characters? Not really. There is no evidence that the two children think themselves engaged in such a search. Like children generally, they are dragged along. The older boy definitely objects to the search, practices civil disobedience against it: that is what breaks up the experiment, and precipitates the end of the play. The mother is distressed by the experiment, and gets dragged in against her will. That leaves just two characters who do search for an author—the Father and the Stepdaughter. And only these two had previously pleaded with the author who created them to make them part of a complete work of art:

> . . . trying to persuade him, trying to push him . . . I would appear before him sometimes, sometimes she would go to him, sometimes that poor mother . . . (*The Father*)

> . . . I too went there, sir, to tempt him, many times, in the melancholy of that study of his, at the twilight hour when he would sit stretched out in his armchair, unable to make up his mind to switch the light on, and letting the evening shadows invade the room, knowing that these shadows were alive with us . . . (*The Stepdaughter*)

Even the Stepdaughter has only a conditional interest in finding an author, the condition being that the Father insists on finding him. Then she will meet the challenge. The Father is the challenger: it is his project. And the play *Six Characters in Search of an Author* is his play—not in the sense that other characters are aspects of him but in the sense that he is consistently the prime mover. The story of the six starts from his actions —in marrying, in becoming a father, but even more in driving wife and

2079

son out. It starts again from his actions on the death of his rival: meeting the daughter at Madama Pace's, taking the family back into his house. The various family catastrophes stem from him. He is the base of that Oedipal triangle on which the family story rests. Last—and, to a dramatic critic, not least—he takes the initiative in the new and present Action. Our play begins with the arrival of the Father at the theatre, and from then on what we are witnessing is the encounter of the Father with the *Capocomico.* The latter is a Director, not an Author—yet another of the play's special twists—but the question before us is whether he will take on a writer's chores and write, as well as direct, the play into which the six characters would properly fit. As soon as he has decided not to, "our play is done," and Father's day is over.

It is odd that anyone should speak of character conflicts in *Six Characters* without mentioning the one that stands in the foreground and works its way out in the primary Action. I suppose it could only happen because of that prejudice in favor of the secret and murky that I was speaking of. In itself the confrontation Father/Director is an archetypal affair: the confrontation of pathetic suffering humanity with the authorities. And these authorities are portrayed, in almost Shavian fashion, not as hostile and malicious, but as open-natured, well-meaning, and far more reasonable than suffering humanity. It is true they are also smug, a little stupid, and very much out of contact—theirs is the lifestyle of bureaucrats and organization men.

Which would just be a picture of normal experience except that Pirandello pushes it, in his usual manner, far beyond the normalities; and Father and Director come to embody two sides of a schizophrenic situation. Through the Father we glimpse the inner world of modern man, through the Director, the outer. Both these worlds are shown as spiritually impoverished. The inner world of the Father contains nothing much besides his two or three phantasies and the pain he feels in failing to justify himself. The Director's outer world is reduced to rituals that preserve the appearances and maintain the occasion, habits, routines, clichés. *All that either the Father or the Director do is repeat themselves,* a factor which is close to the central metaphor of the play: life as theatre. Which aspect of theatre is exhibited in this play? Not performance. Only rehearsal—*répétition.* The stage is bare. The auditorium is empty. The theatre, too, is impoverished and deprived. The bourgeois drama, which had become thrilling through a kind of claustrophobic tension, here dissolves in agoraphobia, its opposite.

What is the Father seeking in the Director? An author who will put him in a play and justify him. In what sense "justify"? First of all, defend him from the Stepdaughter's charge of bestiality by citing the sexual needs of middle aged men living apart from their wives, and so on. Is that all? Nothing in *Six Characters* is ever all. If the plot has an outer-most circle, the theme hasn't. It reaches out towards infinity, a place where there is either emptiness or God. It should not be too surprising that a great play of dead or agonized fatherhood reverberates with the sense of God the Father, or rather of his absence—the "death of God." A search for an author can easily suggest a search for the Author of our being, and the main metaphor of the play has reminded some people of Calderón's *El Gran Teatro del Mundo*. I only wonder they haven't com-mented on the opening words of that work: "Sale el Autor." "Enter the Author in a starry mantle with nine rays of light in groups of threes on his hat." This is, of course, God.

It is not necessary to assume that Pirandello had Calderón in mind, or that he thought directly of God at all. God is meaning, God is au-thority and authorship, God is fatherhood. A poignant sense of the absence of all these burns through every page of *Six Characters in Search of an Author*.

To me, the deepest—or perhaps I mean soundest—interpretation of the search for an author would stress neither God nor literary authorship but fatherhood and I like to think I derive this choice, not from personal predilection, but from the text. The concisest way of stating what the Father demands of the Director in human terms—and Pirandello is al-ways in search of the centrally human—is to say he is asking him to be his father. "Father me." "Rescue me from this maniacal female." "Tell me what is so, re-assure me, help me find my place in the story, in the scheme of things, take from me this burden which I cannot bear but which you can." And the Director is very much the daddy of his troupe: that is established at his first entrance. But being the daddy of these lightweight Thespians is one thing, taking on suffering, schizoid human-ity is another, particularly in the case of one who calls himself "Father" and should be able to fend for himself. In any event, the Director is another very inadequate Father. Something of a grotesque, he stands in the same relationship to fatherhood as Madama Pace does to mother-hood. (Father, Director, Secretary-Lover: three fathers. Mother, Pace, Stepdaughter: three mothers. Another of this play's many symmetries.) But while she castrates, he is castrated: he has the character of the traditional impotent old clown. Our intellectual author transposes this impotence to the literary plane where the Director can prove impotent to make art from the Father's life, life from the Father's art.

In one respect the word *author* is exactly right in suggesting just what a *father* might be expected to provide. When the Father finds the right playwright he will not be content to be given some dialogue in which he can rapidly discomfit his stepdaughter. His ambition goes far beyond that. He is not even saying: "Write a melodrama, and make me the hero."

2081

He is saying: "A person is an entity with no clear meaning—an entity close to nonentity—unless there is an author to make him part of (*a part in*) a play."

A severed hand, Aristotle has it, is not a hand at all, because it could only function as a hand by belonging to arm and body. A character severed from a play is not even a character. A person severed from his family is not even a person. But what is he? And what can he do about it? We need to watch the words and actions of the Father to find the answer to such questions. Is the Father's quest as hopeless as the effort to graft a hand back onto an arm? Or is success in the quest within the power of an Author—in one sense or another of the word "author"? This is not a play that provides answers. At any rate it is not a play that provides positive answers. But neither is it a play in which the objects of yearning have been eliminated. Nostalgia pervades it. Nostalgia for what? For some kind of "togetherness." Is this just a regressive fantasy, the longing for the union of embryo and mother? *Child* and mother? There is something here of the modern isolated individual's longing for a social community, but again it is a longing directed backwards towards some golden age, not forwards towards a new society. By consequence it is a fantasy, not of freedom, but of freely accepted bondage . . .

If only the Father could be part of a play, so he explains in the terms of Pirandello's literary conceit, he would have the permanence of Sancho Panza or Don Abbondio. Interpreting the play, we might translate this back into terms of life, thus: *to have a part in a play* means *to be a member of a family*, and the family is seen as an organism in which each cell lives in and by a happy interdependence. Before such a family could exist, the kind of life we find in Pirandello's play would need to be enormously enriched. It requires a texture far finer than phantasy and fear and guilt can provide. God is love; Father, too, would have to be love. That is the kind of Father this Father is in search of in a play which might just as well be called A *Father in Search of a Father*.

The crowning, and Pirandellian, irony comes when the Director's contribution to the proposed "drama," instead of enriching it, actually impoverishes it further. I am speaking of his work on the *scene* in Act Two. What he starts from is a piece of raw life, or rather a piece of raw erotic phantasy. Give this bit of life or phantasy to a Shakespeare, in the age of Shakespeare, and it becomes *Antony and Cleopatra* with noble enough roles in it for many. All our Director can do is convert it into what in America we would call Broadway drama, in which the already attenuated naturalism of the *scene* has to be further attenuated in the interests of middleclass entertainment.

Shakespeare proves in *Hamlet* that the schizophrenia of an Ophelia can be part of a grand design. Pirandello is interested in showing that in life she would encounter someone like the Director in *Six Characters* or the Doctor in *Enrico IV*. That is to say, she would be on her own. Which is what schizophrenia is. Art is sane. Life is schizoid; and offers only schizoid solutions, as in *Cosi è (si vi pare)*. In *Enrico IV*, the schizoid solution is a starting point, then the "sane" people break it to pieces, as it is always the itch of "sane" people to do. One must reckon with this itch in the Director and Actors in *Six Characters*. Yet the play exhibits neither a solution nor a cataclysm—only a constantly re-enacted phantasy, a father journeying endlessly onwards like the Flying Dutchman.

Now what the Dutchman was searching for was love. Is the Father's aim all that different?

This is the point at which that "great deal of discussion" which Dr. Kligerman complains of can perhaps be comprehended, for the bulk of it consists of long speeches made by the Father. If, as most critics have assumed, they are really there as exposition of a philosophy, then surely they will be an unwelcome intrusion. What is their content? I'd say that two main points are made, one directed at the Stepdaughter (particularly towards the end of Act One), one directed at the Director (particularly at the beginning of Act Three). The first point is that personality is not unitary but multiple. The second point is that illusion *is* reality. In the context it is not essential that these topics be regarded as interesting in themselves. They are dramatized. Which is to say, they become Action. Just as talking is something the Father has to do to live, so resorting to the particular "talking points" he makes is a matter of urgent necessity for him. If the theory of multiple personality did not exist he would have to invent it. It gets him off the hook on which the incident at Madama Pace's had hung him. He is not necessarily right, however, even though his view coincides with the author's philosophy. From the point of view of drama, I would hold that he is wrong. For the art of drama, as Aristotle explained, takes for granted that actions do define a character. A man *is* what he does at Madama Pace's, and all his talk about really being otherwise is so much . . . well, talk. Whatever Pirandello may have believed, his dramas are drama, and present people as their actions. True, talking is an action—the Father's principal action most of the time—but it is precisely his compulsive talking that inclines us not to accept the endless self-pity and self-justification at face value. The Father *feels* that he is many and not one. But that, as we blithely say, is *"his* problem." He is a very irresponsible man, if sane; and, if not responsible for his actions, then insane. On either assumption, he needs just the philosophy Pirandello gives him. Nothing diffuses responsibility more conveniently than the theory that one is a succession of different people. And if one is insane, one is surely entitled to complain a good deal of that radical disjunction which is one's fate. One may even project it on everyone else.

Freud compares paranoid fantasies to metaphysical systems. It is a comparison that makes some sense in reverse. The Pirandellian metaphysics provides apt fantasies for his mentally disturbed characters.

I gave as the Father's second philosophic idea that illusion is reality. Which is also "what everybody knows about Luigi Pirandello." To say that illusion is reality is, on the face of it, nonsense but can be construed as sense by taking it paradoxically. It is as a paradox that the notion has its primary use to Pirandello. For paradoxes, when expanded, become comedies. The expansion happens, in Pirandello, by doubling and re-doubling. Take, in our play, the opposites *life* and *art*. The actors are from *life*. The characters are from *art*. However, nothing begins to "pop" as comedy, as drama, until the author reverses the proposition. The characters are more *real*, are therefore portrayed more as what we regard as people from *life*: they have instincts, impulses, private lives. The actors are less real, and are therefore portrayed as artifacts, as "types," as creatures out of a play. In short the actors are from art. The characters from life. What one might call the intellectual comedy of *Six Characters in Search of an Author* is built upon this reversibility of the key terms. And what is the truth? Which is "really" life, and which is "really" art? There Pirandello-Laudisi lies in wait for us—laughing. Everything in his little system (or *game*, if we must be up-to-date) works both ways. Nothing is "really" so, because everything is "really" so.

Now a person making use of this system—a person playing this game—can have everything both ways. Which is a very nice way to have everything: it is what we all want, though in proportion as we cease to be childish or sick we learn to do without a good deal of what we all want. The Father, however, *is* childish and sick. The Pirandellian game is after his own heart. In Act Two, he is essentially telling the actors to subordinate their *art* to *life*. All that is wrong with their performance is that it isn't naturalistic, it isn't exactly what happened in Madama Pace's shop. But in his theoretical vein, he usually exalts art *above* life. Similarly, he can use the word illusion in a pejorative sense, as when he tells the Director that the actors' lives are more an illusion than the characters' lives, while in the same breath speaking of illusion with respect and a kind of nostalgic awe. All of this is word play, word *game*, inconclusive, and in principle endless—and therefore very depressing. Pirandello can call Laudisi-ism "devilment" and ask for a comedic tone, but it is black comedy at best: its underside is despair. Pursue any statement the Father may offer as consolation, and you will find it lets you down with a bump. For example: art as a solution to the bafflements of impermanence. As a statue you can live forever. The only thing is: you're dead. Petrifaction is no answer, but only corresponds to yet another schizoid wish. And anyone who knows this particular Father will quickly sense that his wish to be a work of art is his wish to escape from flesh and blood, that is, from life. As with other schizophrenics, the great fear of being killed does not prevent him from yearning for death. Indeed it is at this stage of the argument that we realize that the Father's two main points have, for him, the same point: he wants to get out of his own skin. He is "one." But he cites as an alibi that nobody is one, we are each of us a hundred thousand. He is real. But he cites as an alibi that nobody is real. He is trying to non-exist. His personality can, as it were, be diffused horizontally, losing itself in moments or states of mind, alleged other personalities. Or it can be diffused vertically in vapors of idea. But total non-existence is too terrifying to flatly accept. One has to try and coax it into acceptability. By paradox. By dialectic. All of which is evasion, though, for a schizophrenic, a necessary evasion.

"If the self is not true to itself, it is in despair," says Kierkegaard. Pirandello depicts a despair so deep that his schizophrenics cannot afford to admit they have selves to be untrue to. The theory of multiple personality is a byproduct of the despair, and, for the Father, a necessary fiction.

The very notion that illusion is reality stems from defeatism. Philosophically, it represents the breakdown of the Hegelian tradition in which there was always a reality to offset appearances. Once the reality starts to be eroded, there will eventually be nothing left but the appearances; and at this point in time philosophers start to advocate *accepting facts at face value*—face value is the only value they have or the world has. Hence, for example, a contemporary of Pirandello's who later became the house philosopher of Mussolini, Giovanni Gentile, wrote in 1916: "The true is what is in the making."[6]

In this respect, there are only two interpretations of *Six Characters in Search of an Author*. According to one, the play itself endorses Gentile, endorses the Father's philosophic utterances. According to the other, which I subscribe to, the play is larger than the Father, "places" him in a larger setting, makes his pathos unsympathetic. I am not going to argue that the play embodies a positive faith. A critic who recently did this had to rely upon a single sentence that is present only in the first edition.[7] I am arguing that it is not a philosophical play at all because the philosophy is harnessed to a non-philosophical chariot. The content is psychopathological from beginning to end.

Perhaps I've said overmuch about psychological motifs. This is an ex-

[6] *The Theory of Mind as Pure Act.* New York: Macmillan, 1922.
[7] *La giara e altre novelle*, a cura di Giuseppe Lanza. Milano: Mondadori, 1965, page 15.

uberant, excessive, Sicilian work, and from perhaps overmuch suggestiveness may easily come overmuch critical suggestion. Let my last comments be about the form of the work. The first thing a traditional critic—if such a person still exists—would notice about this search for an author is that it respects the unities of time, place, and action. In other words, it conspicuously possesses that compact and classic dramatic structure which the "play in the making" (with its story of the six) conspicuously lacks. The space of time covered is literally the time spent in the theatre plus enough extra hours or minutes to permit the Director to call the session a "whole day"—if we must take *him* literally. Place is given in an equally literal way. And there is something Pirandellian in the fact that such literalness could be a brainstorm. What earned the Maestro the highest compliments for originality was that in this work the boards of the theatre represent—the boards of the theatre. That is to say, they do not represent, they are. They are appearances which are the reality: the quintessential Pirandellian principle.

The final point of this handling of place is a dialectical one. The boards of the theatre are to be so definite, so "real" because the "real" streets of the town and country, the gardens, the houses and rooms are to be so shadowy, so "unreal." The interaction of these two elements gives Pirandello a goodly part of his play—and a good deal that is peculiar to his play.

Time also is handled dialectically. Over against this flatly undistorted present on the stage is the story of the six, all of which is already past. The six are trying to pull all this baggage of theirs, as the patient does on the doctor's couch, from the dim, anaesthetic past into the garish, stinging present. The past of the six and the present of the acting troupe are so clearly demarcated that some people see only the one, some only the other, whereas, to realize what Pirandello is up to, we not only have to see both but the constant reaction of one upon the other. There is a further complication. The past and present of the six are *not* clearly demarcated, but, on the contrary, are deliberately mingled, as in dreams. Hence, for example, though the Stepdaughter has already left her parents, here she is back with them, and the younger children, who have died, are alive again. They will die again, and the play will end with the Stepdaughter leaving her parents . . . But I am afraid that in turning from content to form, I have *been turned back*, by the work itself, from form to content.

One last notation. By an error which was to create a possibly permanent misunderstanding, *Six Characters in Search of an Author* in its first edition was subtitled: "a play in the making."[8] But the play in the mak-

---

[8] The Italian original reads: "una commedia da fare." In the translation most widely read in America, this has been rendered: "a comedy in the making." But in

ing is the projected play about the six characters that never gets made. The play that gets made is the play about the encounter of the six characters (seven, finally) with the Director and his acting troupe. This of course includes as much of the unwritten play as is needed. Finally, then, *Six Characters* became a play fully made. Bernard Shaw said he had never come across so original a play.[9] It is a supreme contribution that says something profound about the theatre and about life seen as theatre and seen by means of theatre. The originality should not blind us to the beauty of the form or to that existential anguish which is the content.

Italian, as in French, a "commedia" (comédie) is not necessarily comic, and the word should often be translated as a "play." (That the story of the six should turn out comic is out of the question.) Secondly, if the phrase "in the making" suggests, as I think it does, that there are the makings of a play in this material (which is the opposite of what Pirandello is saying), then it is a mistranslation of "da fare," which means, literally, "to make," and, less literally, "to be made," "yet to be made," "not yet made." Incidentally, "in the making" cited above from Giovanni Gentile does not translate "da fare." Gentile's original reads: "Vero è quel che si fa," which would be rendered literally: "True is that which is done."

[9] When Pirandello's preface to *Six Characters* was published in French translation (*Revue de Paris*, 15 July 1925), Pirandello added this paragraph to the text:

> Si ma modestie ne peut accepter l'affirmation de G.-B. Shaw, à savoir que les "Six personnages en quête d'auteur" constitue l'oeuvre la plus originale et la plus puissante de tous les théâtres, antiques et modernes, de toutes les nations, ma conscience sait bien que leur apparition dans l'histoire du théâtre italien marque une date qu'on ne pourra oublier.

When at a later date, this passage was brought to Shaw's attention, he commented:

> I have no recollection of the extravagant dictum you quote: but I rank P. as first rate among playwrights and have never come across a play so *original* as Six Chracters [sic].
> —*The Shavian*, February 1964.

BERTOLT BRECHT

Mother Courage
The Caucasian Chalk Circle

SINCE THE PLAYS OF PIRANDELLO first startled the theatre and the world
around 1920, the one great new presence in world theatre has been that
of Bertolt Brecht (1898–1956), who is still in process of being discovered. The reader who wishes to receive the full impact of Brecht, and
discover him for himself, will need to read far more than two plays, but
the two big plays printed here should serve both to arouse interest and
give a fair idea "what Brecht is about." As with Pirandello, the Editor
reserves extended comment until after the text of the plays.

MOTHER COURAGE
AND HER CHILDREN
A Chronicle of the Thirty Years' War
[1939]

English Version by
ERIC BENTLEY

CHARACTERS

MOTHER COURAGE

KATTRIN   *her dumb daughter*

EILIF   *her elder son*

SWISS CHEESE   *her younger son*

RECRUITING OFFICER

SERGEANT

COOK

SWEDISH COMMANDER

CHAPLAIN

ORDNANCE OFFICER

YVETTE POTTIER

MAN WITH THE BANDAGE

ANOTHER SERGEANT

OLD COLONEL

CLERK

YOUNG SOLDIER

OLDER SOLDIER

PEASANT

PEASANT WOMAN

YOUNG MAN

OLD WOMAN

ANOTHER PEASANT

ANOTHER PEASANT WOMAN

YOUNG PEASANT

LIEUTENANT

VOICE

ONE

Spring, 1624. In Dalarna, the Swedish Commander Oxenstierna is re-cruiting for the campaign in Poland. The canteen woman Anna Fierling, commonly known as Mother Courage, loses a son.

> [*Highway outside a town. A* SERGEANT *and a*
> RECRUITING OFFICER *stand shivering.*]

RECRUITING OFFICER – How the hell can you line up a squadron in a place like this? You know what I keep thinking about, Sergeant? Suicide. I'm supposed to knock four platoons together by the twelfth —four platoons the Chief's asking for! And they're so friendly around here, I'm scared to go to sleep at night. Suppose I do get my hands on some character and squint at him so I don't notice he's pigeon-chested and has varicose veins. I get him drunk and relaxed, he signs on the dotted line. I pay for the drinks, he steps outside for a minute. I have a hunch I should follow him to the door, and am I right? Off he's shot like a louse from a scratch. You can't take a man's word any more, Sergeant. There's no loyalty left in the world, no trust, no faith, no sense of honor. I'm losing my confidence in mankind, Sergeant.

SERGEANT – What they could use around here is a good war. What else can you expect with peace running wild all over the place? You know what the trouble with peace is? No organization. And when do you get organization? In a war. Peace is one big waste of equipment. Anything goes, no one gives a damn. See the way they eat? Cheese on pumpernickel, bacon on the cheese? Disgusting! How many horses have they got in this town? How many young men? Nobody knows! They haven't bothered to count 'em! That's peace for you! I've been in places where they haven't had a war for seventy years and you know what? The people haven't even been given names! They don't know who they are! It takes a war to fix that. In a war, everyone registers, everyone's name's on a list. Their shoes are stacked, their corn's in the bag, you count it all up—cattle, men, *et* cetera—and you take it away! That's the story: no organization, no war!

RECRUITING OFFICER – It's the God's truth.

SERGEANT – Of course, a war's like any good deal: hard to get going. But when it does get moving, it's a pisser, and they're all scared of peace, like a dice player who can't stop—'cause when peace comes they have to pay up. Of course, *until* it gets going, they're just as scared of war, it's such a novelty!

RECRUITING OFFICER – Hey, look, here's a canteen wagon. Two women and a couple of fellows. Stop the old lady, Sergeant. And if there's nothing doing this time, you won't catch me freezing my ass in the April wind any longer.

A harmonica is heard. A canteen wagon rolls on, drawn by two young fellows. MOTHER COURAGE *is sitting on it with her dumb daughter,* KATTRIN.

MOTHER COURAGE – A good day to you, Sergeant!

SERGEANT [*barring the way*] Good day to *you!* Who d'you think *you* are?

MOTHER COURAGE – Tradespeople.

[*She sings.*]

Stop all the troops: here's Mother Courage!
Hey, Captain, let them come and buy!
For they can get from Mother Courage
Boots they will march in till they die!
Your marching men do not adore you
(Packs on their backs, lice in their hair)
But it's to death they're marching for you
And so they need good boots to wear!
   Christians, awake! Winter is gone!
   The snows depart! Dead men sleep on!
   Let all of you who still survive
   Get out of bed and look alive!

Your men will walk till they are dead, sir,
But cannot fight unless they eat.
The blood they spill for you is red, sir,
What fires that blood is my red meat.
Cannon is rough on empty bellies:
First with my meat they should be crammed.
Then let them go and find where hell is
And give my greetings to the damned!
   Christians, awake! Winter is gone!
   The snows depart! Dead men sleep on!

Let all of you who still survive
Get out of bed and look alive!

SERGEANT – Halt! Where are you from, riffraff?

EILIF – Second Finnish Regiment!

SERGEANT – Where are your papers?

MOTHER COURAGE – Papers?

SWISS CHEESE – But this is Mother Courage!

SERGEANT – Never heard of her. Where'd she get a name like that?

MOTHER COURAGE – They call me Mother Courage 'cause I was afraid I'd be ruined, so I drove through the bombardment of Riga like a madwoman, with fifty loaves of bread in my cart. They were going moldy, what else could I do?

SERGEANT – No funny business! Where are your papers?

MOTHER COURAGE [*rummaging among papers in a tin box and clambering down from her wagon*] Here, Sergeant! Here's a missal–I got it in Altötting to wrap my cucumbers in. Here's a map of Moravia –God knows if I'll ever get there–the birds can have it if I don't. And here's a document saying my horse hasn't got hoof and mouth disease –pity he died on us, he cost fifteen guilders, thank God I didn't pay it. Is that enough paper?

SERGEANT – Are you pulling my leg? Well, you've got another guess coming. You need a license and you know it.

MOTHER COURAGE – Show a little respect for a lady and don't go telling these grown children of mine I'm pulling anything of yours. What would I want with you? My license in the Second Protestant Regiment is an honest face. If *you* wouldn't know how to read it, that's not my fault, I want no rubber stamp on it anyhow.

RECRUITING OFFICER – Sergeant, we have a case of insubordination on our hands. Do you know what we need in the army? Discipline!

MOTHER COURAGE – I was going to say sausages.

SERGEANT – Name?

MOTHER COURAGE – Anna Fierling.

SERGEANT – So you're all Fierlings.

MOTHER COURAGE – I was talking about me.

SERGEANT – And I was talking about your children.

MOTHER COURAGE – Must they all have the same name? [*Pointing to the elder son.*] This fellow, for instance, I call him Eilif Noyocki. Why? He got the name from his father who told me he was called Koyocki. Or was it Moyocki? Anyhow, the lad remembers him to this day. Only the man he remembers is someone else, a Frenchman with a pointed beard. But he certainly has his father's brains–that man could whip the breeches off a farmer's backside before he could turn around. So we all have our own names.

SERGEANT – You're all called something different?

MOTHER COURAGE – Are you pretending you don't understand?

SERGEANT [*pointing at the younger son*] He's Chinese, I suppose.

MOTHER COURAGE – Wrong again. Swiss.

SERGEANT – After the Frenchman?

MOTHER COURAGE – Frenchman? What Frenchman? Don't confuse the issue, Sergeant, or we'll be here all day. He's Swiss, but he happens to be called Feyos, a name that has nothing to do with his father, who was called something else—a military engineer, if you please, and a drunkard.

[SWISS CHEESE *nods, beaming; even* KATTRIN *smiles.*]

SERGEANT – Then how come his name's Feyos?

MOTHER COURAGE – Oh, Sergeant, you have no imagination. *Of course* he's called Feyos: when he came, I was with a Hungarian. He didn't mind. He had a floating kidney, though he never touched a drop. He was a very *honest* man. The boy takes after him.

SERGEANT – But that wasn't his father!

MOTHER COURAGE – I said: he took after him. I call him Swiss Cheese. Why? Because he's good at pulling wagons. [*Pointing to her daughter.*] And that is Kattrin Haupt, she's half German.

SERGEANT – A nice family, I must say!

MOTHER COURAGE – And we've seen the whole wide world together —this wagonload and me.

SERGEANT – We'll need all that in writing. [*He writes.*] You're from Bamberg in Bavaria. What are you doing *here*?

MOTHER COURAGE – I can't wait till the war is good enough to come to Bamberg.

RECRUITING OFFICER – And you two oxen pull the cart. Jacob Ox and Esau Ox! D'you ever get out of harness?

EILIF – Mother! May I smack him in the puss? I'd like to.

MOTHER COURAGE – I'd like *you* to stay where you are. And now, gentlemen, what about a brace of pistols? Or a belt? Sergeant? Yours is worn clean through.

SERGEANT – It's something else *I'm* looking for. These lads of yours are straight as birch trees, strong limbs, massive chests. . . . What are such fine specimens doing out of the army?

MOTHER COURAGE [*quickly*] A soldier's life is not for sons of mine!

RECRUITING OFFICER – Why not? It means money. It means fame. Peddling shoes is woman's work. [*To* EILIF.] Step this way and let's see if that's muscle or chicken fat.

MOTHER COURAGE – It's chicken fat. Give him a good hard look, and he'll fall right over.

RECRUITING OFFICER – Yes, and kill a calf in the falling!

[*He tries to hustle* EILIF *away.*]

MOTHER COURAGE—Let him alone! He's not for you!

RECRUITING OFFICER—He called my face a puss. That is an insult. The two of us will now go and settle the affair on the field of honor.

EILIF—Don't worry, Mother, I can handle him.

MOTHER COURAGE—Stay here. You're never happy till you're in a fight. He has a knife in his boot and he knows how to use it.

RECRUITING OFFICER—I'll draw it out of him like a milk tooth. Come on, young fellow!

MOTHER COURAGE—Officer, I'll report you to the Colonel, and he'll throw you in jail. His lieutenant is courting my daughter.

SERGEANT—Go easy. [*To* MOTHER COURAGE.] What have you got against the service, wasn't his own father a soldier? Didn't you say he died a soldier's death?

MOTHER COURAGE—This one's just a baby. You'll lead him like a lamb to the slaughter. I know you, you'll get five guilders for him.

RECRUITING OFFICER [*to* EILIF] First thing you know, you'll have a lovely cap and high boots, how about it?

EILIF—Not from you.

MOTHER COURAGE—"Let's you and me go fishing," said the angler to the worm. [*To* SWISS CHEESE.] Run and tell everybody they're trying to steal your brother! [*She draws a knife.*] Yes, just you try, and I'll cut you down like dogs! We sell cloth, we sell ham, we are peaceful people!

SERGEANT—You're peaceful all right: your knife proves that. Why, you should be ashamed of yourself. Give me that knife, you hag! You admit you live off the war, what else *could* you live off? Now tell me, how can we have a war without soldiers?

MOTHER COURAGE—Do they have to be mine?

SERGEANT—So that's the trouble. The war should swallow the peach stone and spit out the peach, hm? Your brood should get fat off the war, but the poor war must ask nothing in return, it can look after itself, can it? Call yourself Mother Courage and then get scared of the war, your breadwinner? Your sons aren't scared, I know that much.

EILIF—Takes more than a war to scare me.

SERGEANT—Correct! Take me. The soldier's life hasn't done *me* any harm, has it? I enlisted at seventeen.

MOTHER COURAGE—You haven't reached seventy.

SERGEANT—I will, though.

MOTHER COURAGE—Above ground?

SERGEANT—Are you trying to rile me, telling me I'll die?

MOTHER COURAGE—Suppose it's the truth? Suppose I see it's your fate? Suppose I *know* you're just a corpse on furlough?

SWISS CHEESE—She can look into the future. Everyone says so.

RECRUITING OFFICER—Then by all means look into the Sergeant's future. It might amuse him.

SERGEANT—I don't believe in that stuff.

MOTHER COURAGE—Helmet!

> [*The* SERGEANT *gives her his helmet.*]

SERGEANT—It means less than a crap in the grass. Anything for a laugh.

MOTHER COURAGE [*taking a sheet of parchment and tearing it in two*] Eilif, Swiss Cheese, Kattrin! So shall we all be torn in two if we let ourselves get too deep into this war! [*To the* SERGEANT.] I'll give you the bargain rate, and do it free. Watch! Death is black, so I draw a black cross.

SWISS CHEESE—And the other she leaves blank, see?

MOTHER COURAGE—I fold them, put them in the helmet, and mix 'em up together, the way we're all mixed up together from our mother's womb on. Now draw!

> [*The* SERGEANT *hesitates.*]

RECRUITING OFFICER [*to* EILIF] I don't take just anybody. I'm choosy. And you've got guts, I like that.

SERGEANT [*fishing around in the helmet*] It's silly. Means as much as blowing your nose.

SWISS CHEESE—The black cross! Oh, his number's up!

RECRUITING OFFICER—Don't let them get under your skin. There aren't enough bullets to go around.

SERGEANT [*hoarsely*] You cheated me!

MOTHER COURAGE—You cheated yourself the day you enlisted. And now we must drive on. There isn't a war every day in the week, we must get to work.

SERGEANT—Hell, you're not getting away with this! We're taking that bastard of yours with *us!*

EILIF—I'd like that, Mother.

MOTHER COURAGE—Quiet—you Finnish devil, you!

EILIF—And Swiss Cheese wants to be a soldier, too.

MOTHER COURAGE—That's news to me. I see I'll have to draw lots for all three of you.

> [*She goes to the back to draw the crosses on bits of paper.*]

RECRUITING OFFICER [*to* EILIF] People've been saying the Swedish soldier is religious. That kind of loose talk has hurt us a lot. One verse of a hymn every Sunday—and then only if you have a voice . . .

MOTHER COURAGE [*returning with the slips and putting them in the* SERGEANT'*s helmet*] So they'd desert their old mother, would they, the scoundrels? They take to war like a cat to cream. But I'll consult these slips, and they'll see the world's no promised land, with a "Join up, son, you're officer material!" Sergeant, I'm afraid for them, very afraid they won't get through this war. They have terrible qualities, all three. [*She holds the helmet out to* EILIF.] There. Draw your lot. [EILIF *fishes in the helmet, unfolds a slip. She snatches it from him.*] There you have it: a cross. Unhappy mother that I am, rich only in a mother's sorrows! He dies. In the springtime of his life, he must go. If he's a soldier, he must bite the dust, that's clear. He's too brave, like his father. And if he doesn't use his head, he'll go the way of all flesh, the slip proves it. [*Hectoring him.*] Will you use your head?

EILIF – Why not?

MOTHER COURAGE – It's using your head to stay with your mother. And when they make fun of you and call you a chicken, just laugh.

RECRUITING OFFICER – If you're going to wet your pants, I'll try your brother.

MOTHER COURAGE – I told you to laugh. Laugh! Now it's your turn, Swiss Cheese. You should be a better bet, you're honest. [*He fishes in the helmet.*] Why are you giving that slip such a funny look? You've drawn a blank for sure. It can't be there's a cross on it. It can't be I'm going to lose *you*. [*She takes the slip.*] A cross? Him too! Could it be 'cause he's so simple? Oh, Swiss Cheese, you'll be a goner too, if you aren't honest, honest, honest the whole time, the way I always brought you up to be, the way you always bring me all the change when you buy me a loaf. It's the only way you can save yourself. Look, Sergeant, if it isn't a black cross!

SERGEANT – It's a cross! I don't understand how *I* got one. I always stay well in the rear. [*To the* OFFICER.] But it can't be a trick: it gets *her* children too.

SWISS CHEESE – It gets me too. But I don't accept it!

MOTHER COURAGE [*to* KATTRIN] And now all I have left for certain is you, you're a cross in yourself, you have a good heart. [*She holds the helmet up high toward the wagon but takes the slip out herself.*] Oh, I could give up in despair! There must be some mistake, I didn't mix them right. Don't be too kind, Kattrin, just don't, there's a cross in your path too. Always be very quiet, it can't be hard, you can't speak. Well, so now you know, all of you: be careful, you'll need to be. Now let's climb on the wagon and move on.

[*She returns the helmet to the* SERGEANT *and climbs on the wagon.*]

RECRUITING OFFICER [*to the* SERGEANT] Do something!

SERGEANT – I don't feel very well.

RECRUITING OFFICER—Maybe you caught a chill when you handed over your helmet in this wind. Get her involved in a business transaction! [*Aloud.*] That belt, Sergeant, you could at least take a look at it. These good people live by trade, don't they? Hey, all of you, the Sergeant wants to buy the belt!

MOTHER COURAGE—Half a guilder. A belt like that is worth two guilders.

[*She clambers down again from the wagon.*]

SERGEANT—It isn't new. But there's too much wind here. I'll go and look at it behind the wagon.

[*He does so.*]

MOTHER COURAGE—I don't find it windy.

SERGEANT—Maybe it's worth half a guilder at that. There's silver on it.

MOTHER COURAGE [*following him behind the wagon*] A solid six ounces worth!

RECRUITING OFFICER [*to* EILIF] And we can have a drink, just us men. I'll advance you some money to cover it. Let's go.

[EILIF *stands undecided.*]

MOTHER COURAGE—Half a guilder, then.

SERGEANT—I don't understand it. I always stay in the rear. There's no safer spot for a sergeant to be. You can send the others on ahead in quest of fame. My appetite is ruined. I can tell you right now: I won't be able to get anything down.

MOTHER COURAGE—You shouldn't take on so, just because you can't eat. Just stay in the rear. Here, take a slug of brandy, man.

[*She gives him brandy.*]

RECRUITING OFFICER [*taking* EILIF *by the arm and making off toward the back*] Ten guilders in advance and you're a soldier of the king and a stout fellow and the women will be mad about you. And you can give me a smack in the puss for insulting you.

[*Both leave.*]

[*Dumb* KATTRIN *jumps down from the wagon and lets out harsh cries.*]

MOTHER COURAGE—Coming, Kattrin, coming! The Sergeant's just paying up. [*She bites the half guilder.*] I'm suspicious of all money, I've been badly burned, Sergeant. But this money's good. And now we'll be going. Where's Eilif?

SWISS CHEESE—Gone with the recruiting officer.

MOTHER COURAGE [*standing quite still, then*] Oh, you simpleton! [*To* KATTRIN.] You *can't* speak, I know. You are innocent.

SERGEANT—That's life. Take a slug yourself, Mother. Being a soldier isn't the worst that could happen. You want to live off war and keep you and yours out of it, do you?

MOTHER COURAGE—You must help your brother now, Kattrin.
[*Brother and sister get into harness together and pull the wagon.*
MOTHER COURAGE *walks at their side. The wagon gets under way.*]
SERGEANT [*looking after them*]
  When a war gives you all you earn
  One day it may claim something in return!

TWO

In the years 1625 and 1626 Mother Courage journeys through Poland in the baggage train of the Swedish army. She meets her son again before the fortified town of Wallhof.—Of the successful sale of a capon and great days for the brave son.

Tent of the SWEDISH COMMANDER. *Kitchen next to it. Thunder of cannon. The* COOK *is quarreling with* MOTHER COURAGE, *who is trying to sell him a capon.*

COOK – Sixty hellers for that miserable bird?

MOTHER COURAGE – Miserable bird? This fat fowl? Your Commander is a glutton. Woe betide you if you've nothing for him to eat. This capon is worth sixty hellers to you.

COOK – They're ten hellers a dozen on every corner.

MOTHER COURAGE – A capon like this on every corner! With a siege going on and people all skin and bones? Maybe you can get a field rat! I said maybe. Because we're all out of *them* too. Don't you see the soldiers running five deep after one hungry little field rat? All right then, in a siege, my price for a giant capon is fifty hellers.

COOK – But we're not "in a siege," we're doing the besieging, it's the other side that's "in a siege," when will you get this into your head?

MOTHER COURAGE – A fat lot of difference that makes, we haven't got a thing to eat either. They took everything into the town with them before all this started, and now they've nothing to do but eat and drink, I hear. It's us I'm worried about. Look at the farmers around here, they haven't a thing.

COOK – Certainly they have. They hide it.

MOTHER COURAGE [*triumphant*] They have not! They're ruined, that's what. They're so hungry I've seen 'em digging up roots to eat. I could boil your leather belt and make their mouths water with it. That's how things are around here. And I'm expected to let a capon go for forty hellers!

COOK – Thirty. Not forty. I said thirty hellers.

2102

MOTHER COURAGE—I say this is no ordinary capon. It was a talented animal, so I hear. It would only feed to music—one march in particular was its favorite. It was so intelligent it could count. Forty hellers is too much for all this? I know *your* problem: if you don't find something to eat and quick, the Chief will—cut—your—fat—head—off!

COOK—All right, just watch. [*He takes a piece of beef and lays his knife on it.*] Here's a piece of beef, I'm going to roast it. I give you one more chance.

MOTHER COURAGE—Roast it, go ahead, it's only one year old.

COOK—One *day* old! Yesterday it was a cow. I saw it running around.

MOTHER COURAGE—In that case it must have started stinking before it died.

COOK—I don't care if I have to cook it for five hours. We'll see if it's still hard after that.

[*He cuts into it.*]

MOTHER COURAGE—Put plenty of pepper in, so the Commander won't smell the smell.

[*The* SWEDISH COMMANDER, *a* CHAPLAIN, *and* EILIF *enter the tent.*]

COMMANDER [*clapping* EILIF *on the shoulder*] In the Commander's tent with you, my son! Sit at my right hand, you happy warrior! You've played a hero's part, you've served the Lord in his own Holy War, *that's* the thing! And you'll get a gold bracelet out of it when we take the town if *I* have any say in the matter! We come to save their souls and what do they do, the filthy, shameless peasant pigs? Drive their cattle away from *us*, while they stuff their priests with beef at both ends! But you showed 'em. So here's a can of red wine for you, we'll drink together! [*They do so.*] The Chaplain gets the dregs, he's pious. Now what would you like for dinner, my hearty?

EILIF—How about a slice of meat?

COMMANDER—Cook, meat!

COOK—Nothing to eat, so he brings company to eat it!

[MOTHER COURAGE *makes him stop talking; she wants to listen.*]

EILIF—Tires you out, skinning peasants. Gives you an appetite.

MOTHER COURAGE—Dear God, it's my Eilif!

COOK—Who?

MOTHER COURAGE—My eldest. It's two years since I saw him, he was stolen from me in the street. He must be in high favor if the Commander's invited him to dinner. And what do you have to eat? Nothing. You hear what the Commander's guest wants? Meat! Better take my advice, buy the capon. The price is one guilder.

[*The* COMMANDER *has sat down with* EILIF *and the* CHAPLAIN.]

COMMANDER [*roaring*] Cook! Dinner, you pig, or I'll have your head!

COOK – This is blackmail. Give me the damn thing!

MOTHER COURAGE – A miserable bird like this?

COOK – You were right. Give it here. It's highway robbery, fifty hellers.

MOTHER COURAGE – I said one guilder. Nothing's too high for my eldest, the Commander's guest of honor.

COOK [*giving her the money*] Well, you might at least pluck it till I have a fire going.

MOTHER COURAGE [*sitting down to pluck the capon*] I can't wait to see his face when he sees me. This is my brave and clever son. I have a stupid one as well but he's honest. The daughter is nothing. At least, she doesn't talk: we must be thankful for small mercies.

COMMANDER – Have another can, my son, it's my favorite Falernian. There's only one cask left—two at the most—but it's worth it to meet a soldier that still believes in God! The shepherd of our flock here just looks on, he only preaches, he hasn't a clue how anything gets done. So now, Eilif, my son, give us the details: tell us how you fixed the peasants and grabbed the twenty bullocks. And let's hope they'll soon be here.

EILIF – In one day's time. Two at the most.

MOTHER COURAGE – Now that's considerate of Eilif—to bring the oxen tomorrow—otherwise my capon wouldn't have been so welcome today.

EILIF – Well, it was like this. I found out that the peasants had hidden their oxen and—on the sly and chiefly at night—had driven them into a certain wood. The people from the town were to pick them up there. I let them get their oxen in peace—they ought to know better than me where they are, I said to myself. Meanwhile I made my men crazy for meat. Their rations were short and I made sure they got shorter. Their mouths'd water at the sound of any word beginning with MEA . . . , like measles.

COMMANDER – Smart fella.

EILIF – Not bad. The rest was a snap. Only the peasants had clubs and outnumbered us three to one and made a murderous attack on us. Four of them drove me into a clump of trees, knocked my good sword from my hand, and yelled, "Surrender!" What now, I said to myself, they'll make mincemeat of me.

COMMANDER – What did you do?

EILIF – I laughed.

COMMANDER – You what?

EILIF – I laughed. And so we got to talking. I came right down to business and said: "Twenty guilders an ox is too much, I bid fifteen." Like I wanted to buy. That foxed 'em. So while they were scratching their heads, I reached for my good sword and cut 'em to pieces. Necessity knows no law, huh?

COMMANDER – What do *you* say, shepherd of the flock?

CHAPLAIN – Strictly speaking, that saying is not in the Bible. Our Lord made five hundred loaves out of five so that no such necessity would arise. When he told men to love their neighbors, their bellies were full. Things have changed since his day.

COMMANDER [*laughing*] Things have changed! A swallow of wine for those wise words, you pharisee! [*To* EILIF.] You cut 'em to pieces in a good cause, our fellows were hungry and you gave 'em to eat. Doesn't it say in the Bible "Whatsoever thou doest for the least of these my children, thou doest for me?" And what *did* you do for 'em? You got 'em the best steak dinner they ever tasted. Moldy bread is not what they're used to. They always ate white bread, and drank wine in their helmets, before going out to fight for God.

EILIF – I reached for my good sword and cut 'em to pieces.

COMMANDER – You have the makings of a Julius Caesar, why, you should be presented to the King!

EILIF – I've seen him—from a distance of course. He seemed to shed a light all around. I must try to be like him!

COMMANDER – I think you're succeeding, my boy! Oh, Eilif, you don't know how I value a brave soldier like you! I treat such a chap as my very own son. [*He takes him to the map.*] Take a look at our position, Eilif, it isn't all it might be, is it?

> [MOTHER COURAGE *has been listening and is now plucking angrily at her capon.*]

MOTHER COURAGE – He must be a very bad Commander.

COOK – Just a gluttonous one. Why bad?

MOTHER COURAGE – Because he needs *brave* soldiers, that's why. If his plan of campaign was any good, why would he need *brave* soldiers, wouldn't plain, ordinary soldiers do? Whenever there are great virtues, it's a sure sign something's wrong.

COOK – You mean, it's a sure sign something's right.

MOTHER COURAGE – I mean what I say. Why? When a general or a king is stupid and leads his soldiers into a trap, they need this virtue of courage. When he's tightfisted and hasn't enough soldiers, the few he does have need the heroism of Hercules—another virtue. And if he's slovenly and doesn't give a damn about anything, they have to be as wise as serpents or they're finished. Loyalty's another virtue and you need plenty of it if the king's always asking too much of you. All virtues which a well-regulated country with a good king or a good general wouldn't need. In a good country virtues wouldn't be necessary. Everybody could be quite ordinary, middling, and, for all I care, cowards.

Bertolt Brecht

COMMANDER – I bet your father was a soldier.

EILIF – I've heard he was a great soldier. My mother warned me. I know a song about that.

COMMANDER – Sing it to us. [*Roaring.*] Bring that meat!

EILIF – It's called The Song of the Wise Woman and the Soldier.

[*He sings and at the same time does a war dance with his saber.*]
A shotgun will shoot and a jackknife will knife,
If you wade in the water, it will drown you,
Keep away from the ice, if you want my advice,
Said the wise woman to the soldier.

But that young soldier, he loaded his gun,
And he reached for his knife, and he started to run:
For marching never could hurt him!
From the north to the south he will march through the land
With his knife at his side and his gun in his hand:
That's what the soldiers told the wise woman.

Woe to him who defies the advice of the wise!
If you wade in the water, it will drown you!
Don't ignore what I say or you'll rue it one day,
Said the wise woman to the soldier.

But that young soldier, his knife at his side
And his gun in his hand, he steps into the tide:
For water never could hurt him!
When the new moon is shining on yonder church tower
We are all coming back, go and pray for that hour:
That's what the soldiers told the wise woman.

MOTHER COURAGE [*continues the song from her kitchen, beating on a pan with a spoon*]
Then the wise woman spoke: you will vanish like smoke
Leaving nothing but cold air behind you!
Just watch the smoke fly! Oh God, don't let him die!
Said the wise woman to the soldier.

EILIF – What's that?

MOTHER COURAGE [*singing on*]
And the lad who defied the wise woman's advice,
When the new moon shone, floated down with the ice:
He waded in the water and it drowned him.

The wise woman spoke, and they vanished like smoke,
And their glorious deeds did not warm us.
Your glorious deeds do not warm us!

2106

COMMANDER – What a kitchen I've got! There's no end to the liberties they take!

[EILIF *has entered the kitchen and embraced his mother.*]

EILIF – To see you again! Where are the others?

MOTHER COURAGE [*in his arms*] Happy as ducks in a pond. Swiss Cheese is paymaster with the Second Regiment, so at least he isn't in the fighting. I couldn't keep him out altogether.

EILIF – Are your feet holding up?

MOTHER COURAGE – I've a bit of trouble getting my shoes on in the morning.

[*The* COMMANDER *has come over.*]

COMMANDER – So you're his mother! I hope you have more sons for me like this fellow.

EILIF – If I'm not the lucky one: to be feasted by the Commander while you sit listening in the kitchen!

MOTHER COURAGE – Yes. I heard all right.

[*She gives him a box on the ear.*]

EILIF [*his hand on his cheek*] Because I took the oxen?

MOTHER COURAGE – No. Because you didn't surrender when the four peasants let fly at you and tried to make mincemeat of you! Didn't I teach you to take care of yourself? You Finnish devil, you!

[*The* COMMANDER *and the* CHAPLAIN *stand laughing in the doorway.*]

THREE

Three years pass and Mother Courage, with parts of a Finnish regiment, is taken prisoner. Her daughter is saved, her wagon likewise, but her honest son dies.

A camp. The regimental flag is flying from a pole. Afternoon. All sorts of wares hanging on the wagon. MOTHER COURAGE'S *clothesline is tied to the wagon at one end, to a cannon at the other. She and* KATTRIN *are folding the washing on the cannon. At the same time she is bargaining with an* ORDNANCE OFFICER *over a bag of bullets.* SWISS CHEESE, *in paymaster's uniform now, looks on.* YVETTE POTTIER, *a very good-looking young person, is sewing at a colored hat, a glass of brandy before her. She is in stocking feet. Her red boots are near by.*

OFFICER – I'm letting you have the bullets for two guilders. Dirt cheap. 'Cause I need the money. The Colonel's been drinking with the officers for three days and we're out of liquor.

MOTHER COURAGE – They're army property. If they find 'em on me, I'll be court-martialed. You sell your bullets, you bastards, and send your men out to fight with nothing to shoot with.

OFFICER – Oh, come on, you scratch my back, and I'll scratch yours.

MOTHER COURAGE – I won't take army stuff. Not at *that* price.

OFFICER – You can resell 'em for five guilders, maybe eight, to the Ordnance Officer of the Fourth Regiment. All you have to do is give him a receipt for twelve. He hasn't a bullet left.

MOTHER COURAGE – Why don't you do it yourself?

OFFICER – I don't trust him. We're friends.

MOTHER COURAGE [*taking the bag*] Give it here. [*To* KATTRIN.] Take it around to the back and pay him a guilder and a half. [*As the* OFFICER *protests.*] I said a guilder and a half! [KATTRIN *drags the bag away. The* OFFICER *follows.* MOTHER COURAGE *speaks to* SWISS CHEESE.] Here's your underwear back, take care of it; it's October now, autumn may come at any time; I purposely don't say it must come, I've learned from experience there's nothing that must come, not even the

2108

seasons. But your books *must* balance now you're the regimental pay-master. *Do* they balance?

SWISS CHEESE—Yes, Mother.

MOTHER COURAGE—Don't forget they made you paymaster because you're honest and so simple you'd never think of running off with the cash. Don't lose that underwear.

SWISS CHEESE—No, Mother. I'll put it under the mattress.

[*He starts to go.*]

OFFICER—I'll go with you, paymaster.

MOTHER COURAGE—Don't teach him any monkey business.

[*Without a good-by the* OFFICER *leaves with* SWISS CHEESE.]

YVETTE [*waving to him*] You might at least say good-by!

MOTHER COURAGE [*to* YVETTE] I don't like that. *He's* no sort of company for my Swiss Cheese. But the war's not making a bad start. Before all the different countries get into it, four or five years'll have gone by like nothing. If I look ahead and make no mistakes, business will be good. Don't you know you shouldn't drink in the morning with your illness?

YVETTE—Who says I'm ill? That's libel!

MOTHER COURAGE—They all say so.

YVETTE—They're all liars. I'm desperate, Mother Courage. They all avoid me like a stinking fish. Because of those lies. So what am I ar-ranging my hat for? [*She throws it down.*] That's why I drink in the morning. I never used to, it gives you crow's feet. But what's the dif-ference? Every man in the regiment knows me. I should have stayed at home when my first was unfaithful. But pride isn't for the likes of us, you eat dirt or down you go.

MOTHER COURAGE—Now don't you start again with your friend Peter and how it all happened—in front of my innocent daughter.

YVETTE—She's the one that should hear it. So she'll get hardened against love.

MOTHER COURAGE—That's something no one ever gets hardened against.

YVETTE—I'll tell you about it, and get it off my chest. I grew up in Flanders' fields, that's where it starts, or I'd never even have caught sight of him and I wouldn't be here in Poland today. He was an army cook, blond, a Dutchman, but thin. Kattrin, beware of thin men! I didn't. I didn't even know he'd had another girl before me and she called him Peter Piper because he never took his pipe out of his mouth the whole time, it meant so little to him.

[*She sings "The Fraternization Song."*]

When I was almost seventeen
The foe came to our land

And laying aside his saber
He took me gently by the hand.

> First came the May Day Rite
> Then came the May Day night.
> The pipes played and the drums did beat.
> The foe paraded down the street.
> And then with us they took their ease
> And fraternized behind the trees.

Our foes they came in plenty.
A cook was my own foe.
I hated him by daylight
But in the dark I loved him so.

> First comes the May Day Rite
> Then comes the May Day night.
> The pipes play and the drums do beat.
> The foe parades down every street.
> And then with us they take their ease
> And fraternize behind the trees.

The heavens seemed to open
Such passion did I feel.
But my people never understood
The love I felt was real.

> One day the sun rose slow
> On all my pain and woe.
> My loved one, with the other men,
> Presented arms and stood at ease
> Then marched away past all those trees
> And never did come back again.

I made the mistake of running after him, I never found him. It's five
years ago now.

[*With swaying gait she goes behind the wagon.*]

MOTHER COURAGE—You've left your hat.

YVETTE—For the birds.

MOTHER COURAGE—Let this be a lesson to you, Kattrin, never start
anything with a soldier. The heavens do seem to open, so watch out!
Even with men who're not in the army life's no honeypot. He tells you
he'd like to kiss the ground under your feet—did you wash 'em yesterday, while we're on the subject?—and then if you don't look out, your
number's up, you're his slave for life. Be glad you're dumb, Kattrin:

you'll never contradict yourself, you'll never want to bite your tongue off because you spoke out of turn. Dumbness is a gift from God. Here comes the Commander's cook, what's bothering *him?*

[*Enter the* COOK *and the* CHAPLAIN.]

CHAPLAIN – I bring a message from your son Eilif. The cook came with me. You've made, ahem, an impression on him.

COOK – I thought I'd get a little whiff of the balmy breeze.

MOTHER COURAGE – You're welcome to that if you behave yourself, and even if you don't I think I can handle you. But what does Eilif want? I don't have any money.

CHAPLAIN – Actually, I have something to tell his brother, the paymaster.

MOTHER COURAGE – He isn't here. And he isn't anywhere else either. He's not his brother's paymaster, and I won't have him led into temptation. Let Eilif try it on with someone else! [*She takes money from the purse at her belt.*] Give him this. It's a sin. He's speculating in mother love, he ought to be ashamed of himself.

COOK – Not for long. He has to go with his regiment now—to his death maybe. Send some more money, or you'll be sorry. You women are hard —and sorry afterward. A glass of brandy wouldn't cost very much, but you refuse to provide it, and six feet under goes your man and you can't dig him up again.

CHAPLAIN – All very touching, my dear cook, but to fall in this war is not a misfortune, it's a blessing. This is a war of religion. Not just any old war but a special one, a religious one, and therefore pleasing unto God.

COOK – Correct. In one sense it's a war because there's fleecing, bribing, plundering, not to mention a little raping, but it's different from all other wars because it's a war of religion. That's clear. All the same, it makes you thirsty.

CHAPLAIN [*to* MOTHER COURAGE, *pointing at the* COOK] I tried to hold him off but he said you'd bewitched him. He dreams about you.

COOK [*lighting a clay pipe*] Brandy from the fair hand of a lady, that's for me. And don't embarrass me any more: the stories the chaplain was telling me on the way over still have me blushing.

MOTHER COURAGE – A man of his cloth! I must get you both something to drink or you'll be making improper advances out of sheer boredom.

CHAPLAIN – That is indeed a temptation, said the court chaplain, and gave way to it. [*Turning toward* KATTRIN *as he walks.*] And who is this captivating young person?

MOTHER COURAGE – She's not a captivating young person, she's a respectable young person.

[*The* CHAPLAIN *and the* COOK *go with* MOTHER COURAGE
behind the cart, and one hears them talk politics.]

MOTHER COURAGE—The trouble here in Poland is that the Poles *would* keep meddling. It's true our King moved in on them with man, beast, and wagon, but instead of keeping the peace the Poles attacked the Swedish King when he was in the act of peacefully withdrawing. So they were guilty of a breach of the peace and their blood is on their own heads.

CHAPLAIN—Anyway, our King was thinking of nothing but freedom. The Kaiser enslaved them all, Poles and Germans alike, so our King *had* to liberate them.

COOK—Just what *I* think. Your health! Your brandy is first-rate, I'm never mistaken in a face. [KATTRIN *looks after them, leaves the washing, goes to the hat, picks it up, sits down, and takes up the red boots.*] And the war is a war of religion. [*Singing while* KATTRIN *puts the boots on.*] "A mighty fortress is our God . . ." [*He sings a verse or so of Luther's hymn.*] And talking of King Gustavus, this freedom he tried to bring to Germany cost him a pretty penny. Back in Sweden he had to levy a salt tax, the poorer folks didn't like it a bit. Then, too, he had to lock up the Germans and even cut their heads off, they clung so to slavery and their Kaiser. Of course, if no one had *wanted* to be free, the King would have got quite mad. First it was just Poland he tried to protect from bad men, especially the Kaiser, then his appetite grew with eating, and he ended up protecting Germany too. Now Germany put up a pretty decent fight. So the good King had nothing but worries in return for his outlay and his goodness, and of course he had to get his money back with taxes, which made bad blood, but he didn't shrink even from that. For he had one thing in his favor anyway, God's Holy Word, which was all to the good, because otherwise they could have said he did it for profit. That's how he kept his conscience clear. He always put conscience first.

MOTHER COURAGE—It's plain you're no Swede, or you'd speak differently of the Hero King.

CHAPLAIN—What's more, you eat his bread.

COOK—I don't eat his bread. I bake his bread.

MOTHER COURAGE—He's unbeatable. Why? His men believe in him. [*Earnestly.*] To hear the big fellows talk, they wage war from fear of God and for all things bright and beautiful, but just look into it, and you'll see they're not so silly: they want a good profit out of it, or else the little fellows like you and me wouldn't back 'em up.

COOK—That's right.

CHAPLAIN—And as a Dutchman you'd do well to see which flag's flying here before you express an opinion!

MOTHER COURAGE—All good Protestants forever!

COOK—A health!

KATTRIN *has begun to strut about with* YVETTE's *hat on, copying* YVETTE's *sexy walk. Suddenly cannon and shots. Drums.* MOTHER COURAGE, *the* COOK, *and the* CHAPLAIN *rush around to the front of the cart, the last two with glasses in their hands. The* ORDNANCE OFFICER *and a* SOLDIER *come running to the cannon and try to push it along.*

MOTHER COURAGE—What's the matter? Let me get my washing off that gun, you slobs!

[*She tries to do so.*]

OFFICER—The Catholics! Surprise attack! We don't know if we can get away! [*To the* SOLDIER.] Get that gun!

[*He runs off.*]

COOK—For heaven's sake! I must go to the Commander. Mother Courage, I'll be back in a day or two—for a short conversation.

[*He rushes off.*]

MOTHER COURAGE—Hey, you've left your pipe!

COOK [*off*] Keep it for me, I'll need it!

MOTHER COURAGE—This *would* happen just when we were making money.

CHAPLAIN—Well, I must be going too. Yes, if the enemy's so close, it can be dangerous. "Blessed are the peacemakers," a good slogan in war time! If only I had a cloak.

MOTHER COURAGE—I'm lending no cloaks. Not even to save a life, I'm not. I've had experience in that line.

CHAPLAIN—But I'm in special danger. Because of my religion.

MOTHER COURAGE [*bringing him a cloak*] It's against my better judgment. Now run!

CHAPLAIN—I thank you, you're very generous, but maybe I'd better stay and sit here. If I run, I might attract the enemy's attention, I might arouse suspicion.

MOTHER COURAGE [*to the* SOLDIER] Let it alone, you dolt, who's going to pay you for this? It'll cost you your life, let me hold it for you.

SOLDIER [*running away*] You're my witness: I tried!

MOTHER COURAGE—I'll swear to it! [*Seeing* KATTRIN *with the hat.*] What on earth are you up to—with a whore's hat! Take it off this minute! Are you mad? With the enemy coming? [*She tears the hat off her head.*] Do you want them to find you and make a whore of you? And she has the boots on too, straight from Babylon. I'll soon fix that. [*She*

2113

tries to get them off.] Oh, God, Chaplain, help me with these boots, I'll be right back.

[*She runs to the wagon.*]

YVETTE [*entering and powdering her face*] What's that you say: the Catholics are coming? Where's my hat? Who's been trampling on it? I can't run around in that, what will they think of me? And I don't even have a mirror. [*To the* CHAPLAIN.] How do I look—too much powder?

CHAPLAIN—Just, er, right.

YVETTE—And where are my red boots? [*She can't find them because* KATTRIN *is hiding her feet under her skirt.*] I left them here! Now I've got to go barefoot to my tent, it's a scandal!

[*Exit.*]

[SWISS CHEESE *comes running in carrying a cash box.*
MOTHER COURAGE *enters with her hands covered with ashes.*]

MOTHER COURAGE [*to* KATTRIN] Ashes! [*To* SWISS CHEESE.] What have you got there?

SWISS CHEESE—The regimental cash box.

MOTHER COURAGE—Throw it away! Your paymastering days are over!

SWISS CHEESE—It's a trust!

[*He goes to the back.*]

MOTHER COURAGE [*to the* CHAPLAIN] Off with your pastor's cloak, Chaplain, or they'll recognize you, cloak or no cloak. [*She is rubbing ashes into* KATTRIN'S *face.*] Keep still. A little dirt, and you're safe. A calamity! The sentries were drunk. Well, one must hide one's light under a bushel, as they say. When a soldier sees a clean face, there's one more whore in the world. Especially a Catholic soldier. For weeks on end, no grub. Then, when the plundering starts and they steal some, they jump on top of the womenfolk. That should do. Let me look at you. Not bad. Looks like you've been rolling in muck. Don't tremble. Nothing can happen to you now. [*To* SWISS CHEESE.] Where've you left the cash box?

SWISS CHEESE—I thought I'd just put it in the wagon.

MOTHER COURAGE [*horrified*] What! In my wagon? God punish you for a prize idiot! If I just look away for a moment! They'll hang all three of us!

SWISS CHEESE—Then I'll put it somewhere else. Or escape with it.

MOTHER COURAGE—You'll stay where you are. It's too late.

CHAPLAIN [*still changing his clothes*] For heaven's sake: the flag!

MOTHER COURAGE [*taking down the flag*] God in heaven! I don't notice it any more. I've had it twenty-five years.

[*The thunder of cannon grows.*]

[*Three days later. Morning. The cannon is gone.* MOTHER COURAGE, KATTRIN, *the* CHAPLAIN, *and* SWISS CHEESE *sit anxiously eating.*]

SWISS CHEESE – This is the third day I've been sitting here doing nothing, and the Sergeant, who's always been patient with me, may be slowly beginning to ask, "Where on earth is Swiss Cheese with that cash box?"

MOTHER COURAGE – Be glad they're not on the trail.

CHAPLAIN – What about me? I can't hold a service here or I'll be in hot water. It is written, "Out of the abundance of the heart, the tongue speaketh." But woe is me if *my* tongue speaketh!

MOTHER COURAGE – That's how it is. Here you sit—one with his religion, the other with his cash box, I don't know which is more dangerous.

CHAPLAIN – We're in God's hands now!

MOTHER COURAGE – I hope we're not *that* desperate, but it *is* hard to sleep nights. 'Course it'd be easier if *you* weren't here, Swiss Cheese, all the same I've not done badly. I told them I was against the Antichrist, who's a Swede with horns on his head. I told them I noticed his left horn's a bit threadbare. When they cross-examined me, I always asked where I could buy holy candles a bit cheaper. I know these things because Swiss Cheese's father was a Catholic and made jokes about it. They didn't quite believe me but they needed a canteen, so they turned a blind eye. Maybe it's all for the best. We're prisoners. But so are lice in fur.

CHAPLAIN – The milk is good. As far as quantity goes, we may have to reduce our Swedish appetites somewhat. We are defeated.

MOTHER COURAGE – Who's defeated? The defeats and victories of the fellows at the top aren't always defeats and victories for the fellows at the bottom. Not at all. There've been cases where a defeat is a victory for the fellows at the bottom, it's only their honor that's lost, nothing serious. In Livonia once, our Chief took such a knock from the enemy, in the confusion I got a fine gray mare out of the baggage train, it pulled my wagon seven months—till we won and there was an inventory. But in general both defeat and victory are a costly business for us that haven't got much. The best thing is for politics to get stuck in the mud. [*To* SWISS CHEESE.] Eat!

SWISS CHEESE – I don't like it. How will the sergeant pay his men?

MOTHER COURAGE – Soldiers in flight don't get paid.

SWISS CHEESE – Well, they could claim to be. No pay, no flight. They can refuse to budge.

MOTHER COURAGE – Swiss Cheese, your sense of duty worries me. I've brought you up to be honest because you're not very bright. But

2115

don't overdo it. And now I'm going with the Chaplain to buy a Catholic flag and some meat. There's no one can hunt out meat like him, sure as a sleepwalker. He can tell a good piece of meat from the way his mouth waters. A good thing they let me stay in the business. In business you ask what price, not what religion. And Protestant trousers keep you just as warm.

CHAPLAIN—As the mendicant monk said when there was talk of the Lutherans turning the whole world upside down: Beggars will *always* be needed. [MOTHER COURAGE *disappears into the wagon.*] She's worried about the cash box. Up to now they've ignored us—as if we were part of the wagon—but can it last?

SWISS CHEESE—I can get rid of it.

CHAPLAIN—That's almost *more* dangerous. Suppose you're seen. They have spies. Yesterday morning one jumped out of the very hole I was relieving myself in. I was so scared I almost broke out in prayer—*that* would have given me away all right! I believe their favorite way of finding a Protestant is smelling his excrement. The spy was a little brute with a bandage over one eye.

MOTHER COURAGE [*clambering out of the wagon with a basket*] I've found you out, you shameless hussy! [*She holds up* YVETTE's *red boots in triumph.*] Yvette's red boots! She just swiped them—because you went and told her she was a captivating person. [*She lays them in the basket.*] Stealing Yvette's boots! But *she* disgraces herself for money, *you* do it for nothing—for pleasure! I told you, you must wait for the peace. No soldiers! Save your proud peacock ways for peacetime!

CHAPLAIN—I don't find her proud.

MOTHER COURAGE—Prouder than she can afford to be. I like her when people say "I never noticed the poor thing." I like her when she's a stone in Dalarna, where there's nothing but stones. [*To* SWISS CHEESE.] Leave the cash box where it is, do you hear? And pay attention to your sister, she needs it. Between the two of you, you'll be the death of me yet. I'd rather take care of a bag of fleas.

[*She leaves with the* CHAPLAIN. KATTRIN *clears the dishes away.*]

SWISS CHEESE—Not many days more when you can sit in the sun in your shirtsleeves. [KATTRIN *points to a tree.*] Yes, the leaves are yellow already. [*With gestures,* KATTRIN *asks if he wants a drink.*] I'm not drinking, I'm thinking. [*Pause.*] She says she can't sleep. So I *should* take the cash box away. I've found a place for it. I'll keep it in the mole hole by the river till the time comes. I might get it tonight before sun rise and take it to the regiment. How far can they have fled in three days? The Sergeant's eyes'll pop out of his head. "I give you the cash box to take care of, and what do you do," he'll say, "but hand it right

back to me: you've disappointed me most pleasantly, Swiss Cheese."
Yes, Kattrin, I *will* have a glass now!

When KATTRIN *reappears behind the wagon two men confront her. One
of them is a* SERGEANT. *The other doffs his hat and flourishes it in a
showy greeting. He has a bandage over one eye.*

MAN WITH THE BANDAGE—Good morning, young lady. Have you
seen a man from the Second Protestant Regiment?
[*Terrified,* KATTRIN *runs away, spilling her brandy. The two men
look at each other and then withdraw after seeing* SWISS CHEESE.]
SWISS CHEESE [*starting up from his reflection*] You're spilling it!
What's the matter with you, have you hurt your eye? I don't understand. Yes, and I must be going, too. I've decided it's the thing to do.
[*He stands up. She does all she can to make him aware of the danger
he is in. He only pushes her away.*] I'd like to know what you mean. I
know you mean well, poor thing, you just can't get it out. And don't
trouble yourself about the brandy, I'll live to drink so much of it,
what's one glass? [*He takes the cash box out of the wagon and puts it
under his coat.*] I'll be back right away. But don't hold me up or I'll
have to scold you. Yes, I know you mean well. If you could only speak!

*When she tries to hold him back he kisses her and pulls himself free. Exit.
She is desperate and runs up and down, emitting little sounds.* MOTHER
COURAGE *and the* CHAPLAIN *return.* KATTRIN *rushes at her mother.*

MOTHER COURAGE—What *is* it, what *is* it, Kattrin? Control yourself! Has someone done something to you? Where is Swiss Cheese?
[*To the* CHAPLAIN.] Don't stand around, get that Catholic flag up!
[*She takes a Catholic flag out of her basket
and the* CHAPLAIN *runs it up the pole.*]
CHAPLAIN [*bitterly*] All good Catholics forever!
MOTHER COURAGE—Now, Kattrin, calm down and tell all about it,
your mother understands you. What, that little bastard of mine's taken
the cash box away? I'll box his ears for him, the rascal! Now take your
time and don't try to talk, use your hands. I don't like it when you
howl like a dog, what'll the Chaplain think of you? You're giving him
the creeps. A man with one eye was here?
CHAPLAIN—That fellow with one eye is an informer! Have they caught
Swiss Cheese? [KATTRIN *shakes her head, shrugs her shoulders.*] This
is the end.
[*Voices off. The two men bring in* SWISS CHEESE.]

2117

SWISS CHEESE – Let me go. I've nothing on me. You're breaking my shoulder! I am innocent.

SERGEANT – This is where he comes from. These are his friends.

MOTHER COURAGE – Us? Since when?

SWISS CHEESE – I don't even know 'em. I was just getting my lunch here. Ten hellers it cost me. Maybe you saw me sitting on that bench. It was too salty.

SERGEANT – Who *are* you people, anyway?

MOTHER COURAGE – Law-abiding citizens! It's true what he says. He bought his lunch here. And it was too salty.

SERGEANT – Are you pretending you don't know him?

MOTHER COURAGE – I can't know all of them, can I? I don't ask, "What's your name and are you a heathen?" If they pay up, they're not heathens to me. Are you a heathen?

SWISS CHEESE – Oh, no!

CHAPLAIN – He sat there like a law-abiding fellow and never once opened his mouth. Except to eat. Which is necessary.

SERGEANT – Who do you think *you* are?

MOTHER COURAGE – Oh, he's my barman. And you're thirsty, I'll bring you a glass of brandy. You must be footsore and weary!

SERGEANT – No brandy on duty. [*To* SWISS CHEESE.] You were carrying something. You must have hidden it by the river. We saw the bulge in your shirt.

MOTHER COURAGE – Sure it was him?

SWISS CHEESE – I think you mean another fellow. There *was* a fellow with something under his shirt, I saw him. I'm the wrong man.

MOTHER COURAGE – I think so too. It's a misunderstanding. Could happen to anyone. Oh, I know what people are like, I'm Mother Courage, you've heard of me, everyone knows about me, and I can tell you this: he looks honest.

SERGEANT – We're after the regimental cash box. And we know what the man looks like who's been keeping it. We've been looking for him two days. It's you.

SWISS CHEESE – No, it's not!

SERGEANT – And if you don't shell out, you're dead, see? Where is it?

MOTHER COURAGE [*urgently*] 'Course he'd give it to you to save his life. He'd up and say, *I've* got it, here it is, you're stronger than me. He's not *that* stupid. Speak, little stupid, the Sergeant's giving you a chance!

SWISS CHEESE – What if I haven't got it?

SERGEANT – Come with us. We'll get it out of you.

[*They take him off.*]

MOTHER COURAGE [*shouting after them*] He'd tell you! He's not *that* stupid! And don't you break his shoulder!

[*She runs after them.*]

[*The same evening. The* CHAPLAIN *and* KATTRIN *are rinsing glasses and polishing knives.*]

CHAPLAIN—Cases of people getting caught like this are by no means unknown in the history of religion. I am reminded of the Passion of Our Lord and Savior. There's an old song about it.

[*He sings "The Song of the Hours."*]

In the first hour of the day
Simple Jesus Christ was
Presented as a murderer
To the heathen Pilate.

Pilate found no fault in him
No cause to condemn him
So he sent the Lord away.
Let King Herod see him!

Hour the third: the Son of God
Was with scourges beaten
And they set a crown of thorns
On the head of Jesus.

And they dressed him as a king
Joked and jested at him
And the cross to die upon
He himself must carry.

Six: they stripped Lord Jesus bare.
To the cross they nailed him.
When the blood came gushing, he
Prayed and loud lamented.

Each upon his cross, two thieves
Mocked him like the others.
And the bright sun crept away
Not to see such doings.

Nine: Lord Jesus cried aloud
That he was forsaken!
In a sponge upon a pole
Vinegar was fed him.

Then the Lord gave up the ghost
And the earth did tremble.
Temple curtains split in twain.
Cliffs fell in the ocean.

Evening: they broke the bones
Of the malefactors.
Then they took a spear and pierced
The side of gentle Jesus.

And the blood and water ran
And they laughed at Jesus.
Of this simple son of man
Such and more they tell us.

MOTHER COURAGE [*entering, excited*] It's life and death. But the Sergeant will still listen to us. The only thing is, he mustn't know it's our Swiss Cheese, or they'll say we helped him. It's only a matter of money, but where can *we* get money? Isn't Yvette here yet? I talked to her on the way over. She's picked up a Colonel who may be willing to buy her a canteen business.

CHAPLAIN – You'd sell the wagon, everything?

MOTHER COURAGE – Where else would I get the money for the Sergeant?

CHAPLAIN – What are you to live off?

MOTHER COURAGE – That's just it.

[*Enter* YVETTE *with a hoary old* COLONEL.]

YVETTE [*embracing* MOTHER COURAGE] *Dear* Mistress Courage, we meet again. [*Whispering.*] He didn't say no. [*Aloud.*] This is my friend, my, um, business adviser. I happened to hear you might sell your wagon. Due to special circumstances, I'd like to think about it.

MOTHER COURAGE – I want to pawn it, not sell it. And nothing hasty. In war time you don't find another wagon like that so easy.

YVETTE [*disappointed*] Only pawn it? I thought you wanted to sell. I don't know if I'm interested. [*To the* COLONEL.] What do *you* think, my dear?

COLONEL – I quite agree with you, bunny.

MOTHER COURAGE – It's only for pawn.

YVETTE – I thought you *had* to have the money.

MOTHER COURAGE [*firmly*] I do have to have it. But I'd rather wear my feet off looking for an offer than just sell. Why? We live off the wagon. It's an opportunity for you, Yvette. Who knows when you'll have another such? Who knows when you'll find another business adviser?

COLONEL – Take it, take it!

YVETTE – My friend thinks I should go ahead, but I'm not sure, if it's only for pawn. You think we should buy it outright, don't you?

COLONEL – I do, bunny, I do!

MOTHER COURAGE – Then you must go and find something that's for sale. Maybe you'll find it—if you have the time, and your friend goes with you, let's say in about a week, or two weeks, you may find the right thing.

YVETTE – Yes, we can certainly look around for something. I love going around looking, I love going around with you, Poldy . . .

COLONEL – Really? Do you?

YVETTE – Oh, it's lovely! I could take two weeks of it!

COLONEL – Really, could you?

YVETTE – If you get the money, when are you thinking of paying it back?

MOTHER COURAGE – In two weeks. Maybe one.

YVETTE – I can't make up my mind. Poldy, advise me, *chéri!* [*She takes the* COLONEL *to one side.*] She'll *have* to sell, don't worry. That Lieutenant—the blond one, you know the one I mean—he'll lend me the money. He's *mad* about me, he says I remind him of someone. What do you advise?

COLONEL – Oh. I have to warn you against *him.* He's no good. He'll exploit the situation. I told you, bunny, I told you *I'd* buy you something, didn't I tell you that?

YVETTE – I simply can't let you!

COLONEL – Oh, please, please!

YVETTE – Well, if you think the Lieutenant might exploit the situation I *will* let you!

COLONEL – I do think so.

YVETTE – So you advise me to?

COLONEL – I do, bunny, I do!

YVETTE [*returning to* MOTHER COURAGE] My friend says all right. Write me out a receipt saying the wagon's mine when the two weeks are up—with everything in it. I'll just run through it all now, the two hundred guilders can wait. [*To the* COLONEL.] You go ahead to the camp, I'll follow, I must go over all this so nothing'll be missing later from *my* wagon!

COLONEL – Wait, I'll help you up! [*He does so.*] Come soon, honey bun!

[*Exit.*]

MOTHER COURAGE – Yvette, Yvette!

YVETTE – There aren't many boots left!

MOTHER COURAGE – Yvette, this is no time to go through the

wagon, yours or not yours. You promised you'd talk to the Sergeant about Swiss Cheese. There isn't a minute to lose. He's up before the court-martial one hour from now.

YVETTE—I just want to count these shirts again.

MOTHER COURAGE [*dragging her down the steps by the skirt*] You hyena, Swiss Cheese's life's at stake! And don't say who the money comes from. Pretend he's your sweetheart, for heaven's sake, or we'll all get it for helping him.

YVETTE—I've arranged to meet One Eye in the bushes. He must be there by now.

CHAPLAIN—And don't hand over all two hundred, a hundred and fifty's sure to be enough.

MOTHER COURAGE—Is it your money? I'll thank you to keep your nose out of this, I'm not doing *you* out of your porridge. Now run, and no haggling, remember his life's at stake.

[*She pushes* YVETTE *off.*]

CHAPLAIN—I didn't want to talk you into anything, but what are we going to live on? You have an unemployable daughter around your neck.

MOTHER COURAGE—I'm counting on that cash box, smart aleck. They'll pay his expenses out of it.

CHAPLAIN—You think she can work it?

MOTHER COURAGE—It's in her own interest: I pay the two hundred and she gets the wagon. She knows what she's doing, she won't have her Colonel on the string forever. Kattrin, go and clean the knives, use pumice stone. And don't *you* stand around like Jesus in Gethsemane. Get a move on, wash those glasses. There'll be over fifty cavalrymen here tonight, and you'll be saying you're not used to being on your feet. "Oh my poor feet, in church I never had to run around like this!" I think they'll let us have him. Thanks be to God they're corruptible. They're not wolves, they're human and after money. God is merciful, and men are bribable, that's how His will is done on earth as it is in Heaven. Corruption is our only hope. As long as there's corruption, there'll be merciful judges and even the innocent may get off.

[YVETTE *comes in panting.*]

YVETTE—They'll do it for two hundred if you make it snappy—these things change from one minute to the next. I'd better take One Eye to my Colonel at once. He confessed he had the cash box, they put the thumbscrews on him. But he threw it in the river when he noticed them coming up behind him. So it's gone. Shall I run and get the money from my Colonel?

MOTHER COURAGE—The cash box gone? How'll I ever get my two hundred back?

YVETTE – So you thought you could get it from the cash box? I *would* have been sunk. Not a hope, Mother Courage. If you want your Swiss Cheese, you'll have to pay. Or should I let the whole thing drop, so you can keep your wagon?

MOTHER COURAGE – I wasn't figuring on this. But you needn't hound me, you'll get the wagon, it's yours already, and it's been mine seventeen years. I need a minute to think it over, it's all so sudden. What can I do? I *can't* pay two hundred. You *should* have haggled with them. I must hold on to something, or any passer-by can kick me in the ditch. Go and say I'll pay a hundred and twenty or the deal's off. Even then I lose the wagon.

YVETTE – They won't do it. And anyway, One Eye's in a hurry. He keeps looking over his shoulder all the time, he's so worked up. Hadn't I better give them the whole two hundred?

MOTHER COURAGE [*desperate*] I can't pay it! I've been working thirty years. She's twenty-five and still no husband. I have her to think of. So leave me alone. I know what I'm doing. A hundred and twenty or no deal.

YVETTE – You know best.

[*She runs off.*]

MOTHER COURAGE *turns away and slowly walks a few paces to the rear. Then she turns around, looks neither at the* CHAPLAIN *nor her daughter, and sits down to help* KATTRIN *polish the knives.*

MOTHER COURAGE – Don't break the glasses, they're not ours. Watch what you're doing, you're cutting yourself. Swiss Cheese will be back, I'll give two hundred, if I have to. You'll get your brother back. With eighty guilders we could pack a hamper with goods and begin again. It wouldn't be the end of the world.

CHAPLAIN – The Bible says: the Lord will provide.

MOTHER COURAGE – Rub them dry, I said. [*They clean the knives in silence.*] They say the war will stop soon. How would it? I ask. And no one can answer me. [*Slowly.*] The King and the Pope are mortal enemies, their Faith is different. They must go for each other till one of them drops dead, neither of them can relax till then. Even so they can't get on with it. Why not? The Emperor is in the way, and they both have something against him. They're not going to fight each other to the death with the Emperor lurking about till they're half dead so he can fall on both of 'em! No, they're banding together against the Emperor so he'll drop dead first and they can go for each other. [*Suddenly* KATTRIN *runs sobbing behind the wagon.*] Someone once offered me five hundred guilders for the wagon. I didn't take it. My Eilif, wherever he may be, thought I'd taken it and cried all night.

[YVETTE *comes running in.*]

Y V E T T E – They won't do it. I warned you. One Eye was going to drop it then and there. There's no point, he said. He said the drums would roll any second now and that's the sign a verdict has been reached. I offered a hundred and fifty, he didn't even shrug. I could hardly get him to stay there while I came here.

M O T H E R   C O U R A G E – Tell him I'll pay two hundred. Run! [YVETTE *runs.* MOTHER COURAGE *sits, silent. The* CHAPLAIN *has stopped doing the glasses.*] I believe–I've haggled too long.

In the distance, a roll of drums. The CHAPLAIN *stands up and walks toward the rear.* MOTHER COURAGE *remains seated. It grows dark. It gets light again.* MOTHER COURAGE *has not moved.* YVETTE *appears, pale.*

Y V E T T E – Now you've done it–with your haggling. You can keep the wagon now. He got eleven bullets in him. I don't know why I still bother about you, you don't deserve it, but I just happened to learn they don't think the cash box is really in the river. They suspect it's here, they think you're connected with him. I think they're going to bring him here to see if you'll give yourself away when you see him. You'd better not know him or we're in for it. And I'd better tell you straight, they're just behind me. Shall I keep Kattrin away? [MOTHER COURAGE *shakes her head.*] Does she know? Maybe she never heard the drums or didn't understand.

M O T H E R   C O U R A G E – She knows. Bring her.

YVETTE *brings* KATTRIN, *who walks over to her mother and stands by her.* MOTHER COURAGE *takes her hand. Two men come on with a stretcher; there is a sheet on it and something underneath. Beside them, the* SERGEANT. *They put the stretcher down.*

S E R G E A N T – Here's a man we can't identify. But he has to be registered to keep the records straight. He bought a meal from you. Look at him, see if you know him. [*He pulls back the sheet.*] Do you know him? [MOTHER COURAGE *shakes her head.*] What? You never saw him before he took that meal? [MOTHER COURAGE *shakes her head.*] Lift him up. Throw him in the carrion pit. He has no one that knows him.

[*They carry him off.*]

FOUR

Mother Courage sings "The Song of the Great Capitulation."

[*Outside an officer's tent.* MOTHER COURAGE *waits.*
A CLERK *looks out of the tent.*]

CLERK—I know you. You had a Protestant paymaster with you, he was hiding out with you. Better make no complaint.

MOTHER COURAGE—But I'm innocent and if I give up it'll look as if I have a bad conscience. They cut everything in my wagon to ribbons with their sabers and then claimed a fine of five thalers for nothing and less than nothing.

CLERK—For your own good, keep your trap shut. We haven't many canteens, so we let you stay in business, especially if you've a bad conscience and have to pay a fine now and then.

MOTHER COURAGE—I'm going to file a complaint.

CLERK—As you wish. Wait here till the Captain has time.

[*He withdraws into the tent.*]

[*A* YOUNG SOLDIER *comes storming in.*]

YOUNG SOLDIER—Screw the Captain! Where *is* the son of a bitch? Swiping my reward, spending it on brandy for his whores, I'll rip his belly open!

AN OLDER SOLDIER [*coming after him*] Shut your hole, you'll wind up in the stocks.

YOUNG SOLDIER—Come out, you thief, I'll make lamb chops out of you! I was the only one in the squad who swam the river and *he* grabs my money, I can't even buy myself a beer. Come on out! And let me slice you up!

OLDER SOLDIER—Holy Christ, he'll destroy himself!

YOUNG SOLDIER—Let me go or I'll run *you* down too. This has got to be settled!

OLDER SOLDIER—Saved the Colonel's horse and didn't get the reward. He's young, he hasn't been at it long.

MOTHER COURAGE—Let him go. He doesn't have to be chained, he's not a dog. Very reasonable to want a reward. Why else should he want to shine?

YOUNG SOLDIER—He's in there pouring it down! You're all nice. I've done something special, I want the reward!

MOTHER COURAGE—Young man, don't scream at *me*, I have my own troubles. And go easy with your voice, you may need it when the Captain comes. The Captain'll come and you'll be hoarse and can't make a sound, so he'll have to deny himself the pleasure of sticking you in the stocks till you pass out. The screamers don't scream long, only half an hour, after which they have to be sung to sleep, they're all in.

YOUNG SOLDIER—I'm not all in, and sleep's out of the question. I'm hungry. They're making their bread out of acorns and hempseed, and not even much of that. He's whoring on my money, and I'm hungry. I'll murder him!

MOTHER COURAGE—I understand: you're hungry. Last year your Commander ordered you people out of the streets and into the fields. So the crops got trampled down. I could have got ten guilders for boots, if anyone'd had ten guilders, and if I'd had any boots. He didn't expect to be around this year, but he is, and there's famine. I understand: you're angry.

YOUNG SOLDIER—It's no use your talking. I won't stand for injustice!

MOTHER COURAGE—You're quite right. But how long? How long won't you stand for injustice? One hour? Or two? You haven't asked yourself that, have you? And yet it's the main thing. It's pure misery to sit in the stocks. Especially if you leave it till then to decide you do stand for injustice.

YOUNG SOLDIER—I don't know why I listen to you. Screw that Captain! Where is he?

MOTHER COURAGE—You listen because you know I'm right. Your rage has calmed down already. It was a short one and you'd need a long one. But where would you find it?

YOUNG SOLDIER—Are you trying to say it's not right to ask for the money?

MOTHER COURAGE—Just the opposite. I only say, your rage won't last. You'll get nowhere with it, it's a pity. If your rage was a long one, I'd urge you on. Slice him up, I'd advise you. But what's the use if you *don't* slice him up because you can feel your tail between your legs? You stand there and the Captain lets you have it.

OLDER SOLDIER—You're quite right, he's crazy.

YOUNG SOLDIER—All right, we'll see whether I slice him up or not. [*He draws his sword.*] When he comes out, I slice him up!

CLERK [*looking out*] The Captain will be out in a minute. [*In the tone of military command.*] Be seated!

[*The* YOUNG SOLDIER *sits.*]
MOTHER COURAGE—And he *is* seated. What did I tell you? You are
seated. They know us through and through. They know how they must
work it. Be seated! And we sit. And in sitting there's no revolt. Better
not stand up again—not the way you did before—don't stand up again.
And don't be embarrassed in front of me, I'm no better, not a scrap.
They've drawn our teeth, haven't they? If we say boo, it's bad for busi-
ness. Let me tell you about the great capitulation.
[*She sings "The Song of the Great Capitulation."*]
Long ago when I was a green beginner
I believed I was a special case.

(None of your ordinary run of the mill girls, with my looks and my
talent, and my love of the higher things in life!)

And if I picked a hair out of my dinner
I would put the cook right in his place.

(All or nothing. Anyhow, never the second best. I am the master of my
Fate. I'll take no orders from no one.)

Then a little bird whispered in my ear:
"That's all very well, but wait a year
And you will join the big brass band
And with your trumpet in your hand
You'll march in lockstep with the rest.
Then one day, look! The battalions wheel!
The whole thing swings from east to west!
And falling on your knees, you'll squeal:
The Lord God, He knows best!
(But don't give *me* that!)"

And a month or two before that year was over
I had learned to drink their cup of tea.

(Two children round your neck, and the price of bread and what all!)

And the day soon came when I was to discover
They had me just where they wanted me.

(You must get in good with people. If you scratch my back, I'll scratch
yours. Don't stick your neck out.)

And that little bird whispered in my ear:
"You didn't even take a year!
And you have joined the big brass band
And with your trumpet in your hand

2127

You marched in lockstep with the rest.
But one day, look! The battalions wheeled!
The whole thing swung from east to west!
And falling on your knees, you squealed:
The Lord God, He knows best!
(But don't give *me* that!)"

Yes, our hopes are high, our plans colossal!
And we hitch our wagon to a star!

(Where there's a will there's a way. One can't hold a good man down.)

We can move mountains, says St. Paul the great Apostle
And yet: how heavy one cigar!

(We must cut our coat according to our cloth.)

For that little bird whispers in your ear:
"That's all very well but wait a year
And we will join the big brass band
And with our trumpet in our hand
We march in lockstep with the rest.
But one day, look! The battalions wheel!
The whole thing swings from east to west!
And falling on our knees, we squeal:
The Lord God, He knows best!
(But don't give *me* that!)"

And so I think you should stay here with your sword drawn if you're set on it and your anger is big enough. You have good cause, I admit. But if your anger is a short one, you'd better go.

YOUNG SOLDIER—Kiss my ass.

[*He stumbles off, the other* SOLDIER *following him.*]

CLERK [*sticking his head out*] The Captain is ready now. You can file your complaint.

MOTHER COURAGE—I've thought better of it. I'm not complaining.

[*Exit.*]

[*The* CLERK *looks after her, shaking his head.*]

FIVE

Two years have passed. The war covers wider and wider territory. Forever on the move, the little wagon crosses Poland, Moravia, Bavaria, Italy, and again Bavaria. 1631. Tilly's victory at Magdeburg costs Mother Courage four officers' shirts.

The wagon stands in a war-ravaged village. Faint military music from the distance. Two SOLDIERS *are being served at a counter by* KATTRIN *and* MOTHER COURAGE. *One of them has a woman's fur coat about his shoulders.*

MOTHER COURAGE—What, you can't pay? No money, no brandy! They can play victory marches, they should pay their men.

FIRST SOLDIER—I want my brandy! I arrived too late for plunder. The Chief allowed one hour to plunder the town, it's a swindle. He's not inhuman, he says. So I suppose they bought him off.

CHAPLAIN [*staggering in*] There are more in the farmhouse. A family of peasants. Help me someone. I need linen!

[*The* SECOND SOLDIER *goes with him.* KATTRIN *is getting very excited. She tries to get her mother to bring linen out.*]

MOTHER COURAGE—I have none. I sold all my bandages to the regiment. I'm not tearing up my officers' shirts for these people.

CHAPLAIN [*calling over his shoulder*] I said I need linen!

MOTHER COURAGE [*stopping* KATTRIN *from entering the wagon*] Not a thing! They can't pay, and why? They have nothing and they pay nothing!

CHAPLAIN [*to a* WOMAN *he is carrying in*] Why did you stay out there in the line of fire?

WOMAN—Our farm—

MOTHER COURAGE—Think they'd ever let go of *anything*? And now I'm supposed to pay. Well, I won't!

FIRST SOLDIER—They're Protestants, why should they be Protestants?

MOTHER COURAGE—Protestant, Catholic, what do *they* care? Their farm's gone, that's what.

SECOND SOLDIER—They're not Protestants anyway, they're Catholics.

FIRST SOLDIER—In a bombardment we can't pick and choose.

A PEASANT [*brought on by the* CHAPLAIN] My arm's gone.

CHAPLAIN—Where's that linen?

[*All look at* MOTHER COURAGE, *who does not budge.*]

MOTHER COURAGE—I can't give you any. With all I have to pay out —taxes, duties, bribes. . . . [KATTRIN *takes up a board and threatens her mother with it, emitting gurgling sounds.*] Are you out of your mind? Put that board down or I'll let you have one, you lunatic! I'm giving nothing, I don't dare, I have myself to think of. [*The* CHAPLAIN *lifts her bodily off the steps of the wagon and sets her down on the ground. He takes out shirts from the wagon and tears them in strips.*] My shirts, my officers' shirts!

[*From the house comes the cry of a child in pain.*]

PEASANT—The child's still in there.

[KATTRIN *runs in.*]

CHAPLAIN [*to the* WOMAN] Stay where you are. She's getting it for you.

MOTHER COURAGE—Hold her back, the roof may fall in!

CHAPLAIN—I'm not going back in there!

MOTHER COURAGE [*pulled in both directions*] Go easy on my expensive linen.

[*The* SECOND SOLDIER *holds her back.* KATTRIN *brings a baby out of the ruins.*]

MOTHER COURAGE—Another baby to drag around, you must be pleased with yourself. Give it to its mother this minute! Or do I have to fight you again for hours till I get it from you? Are you deaf? [*To the* SECOND SOLDIER.] Don't stand about gawking, go back there and tell 'em to stop that music, I can see their victory without it. I have nothing but losses from your victory!

CHAPLAIN [*bandaging*] The blood's coming through.

[KATTRIN *is rocking the child and half humming a lullaby.*]

MOTHER COURAGE—There she sits, happy as a lark in all this misery. Give the baby back, the mother is coming to! [*She sees the* FIRST SOLDIER. *He had been handling the drinks, and is now trying to make off with the bottle.*] God's truth! You beast! You want another victory, do you? Then pay for it!

FIRST SOLDIER—I have nothing.

MOTHER COURAGE [*snatching the fur coat back*] Then leave this coat, it's stolen goods anyhow.

CHAPLAIN—There's still someone in there.

SIX

Before the city of Ingolstadt in Bavaria Mother Courage is present at the funeral of the fallen Commander, Tilly. Conversations take place about war heroes and the duration of the war. The Chaplain complains that his talents are lying fallow and Kattrin gets the red boots. The year is 1632.

The inside of a canteen tent. The inner side of a counter at the rear. Rain. In the distance, drums and funeral music. The CHAPLAIN *and the regimental* CLERK *are playing draughts.* MOTHER COURAGE *and her daughter are taking an inventory.*

CHAPLAIN – The funeral procession is just starting out.

MOTHER COURAGE – Pity about the Chief – twenty-two pairs of socks – getting killed that way. They say it was an accident. There was a fog over the fields that morning, and the fog was to blame. The Chief called up another regiment, told 'em to fight to the death, rode back again, missed his way in the fog, went forward instead of back, and ran smack into a bullet in the thick of battle – only four lanterns left. [*A whistle from the rear. She goes to the counter. To a* SOLDIER.] It's a disgrace the way you're all skipping your Commander's funeral!

[*She pours a drink.*]

CLERK – They shouldn't have handed the money out before the funeral. Now the men are all getting drunk instead of going to it.

CHAPLAIN [*to the* CLERK] Don't you have to be there?

CLERK – I stayed away because of the rain.

MOTHER COURAGE – It's different for you, the rain might spoil your uniform. I hear they wanted to ring the bells for his funeral, which is natural, but it came out that the churches had been shut up by his orders, so the poor Commander won't be hearing any bells when they lower him in his grave. Instead, they'll fire off three shots so the occasion won't be *too* sober – sixteen leather belts.

A VOICE FROM THE COUNTER – Service! One brandy!

MOTHER COURAGE – Your money first. No, you *can't* come inside the tent, not with those boots on. You can drink outside, rain or no rain. I only let officers in here. [*To the* CLERK.] The Chief had his troubles lately, I hear. There was unrest in the Second Regiment because he didn't pay 'em. He said it was a war of religion and they must fight it free of charge.

[*Funeral march. All look toward the rear.*]

CHAPLAIN – Now they're filing past the body.

MOTHER COURAGE – I feel sorry for a Commander or an Emperor like that—when he might have had something special in mind, something they'd talk about in times to come, something they'd raise a statue to him for. The conquest of the world now, *that's* a goal for a Commander, he wouldn't know any better. . . . Lord, worms have got into the biscuits. . . . In short, he works his hands to the bone and then it's all spoiled by the common riffraff that only wants a jug of beer or a bit of company, not the higher things in life. The finest plans have always been spoiled by the littleness of them that should carry them out. Even Emperors can't do it all by themselves. They count on support from their soldiers and the people round about. Am I right?

CHAPLAIN [*laughing*] You're right, Mother Courage, till you come to the soldiers. They do what they can. Those fellows outside, for example, drinking their brandy in the rain, I'd trust 'em to fight a hundred years, one war after another, two at a time if necessary. And I wasn't trained as a commander.

MOTHER COURAGE – . . . Seventeen leather belts. . . . Then you don't think the war might end?

CHAPLAIN – Because a Commander's dead? Don't be childish, they grow on trees. There are always heroes.

MOTHER COURAGE – Well, I wasn't asking for the sake of argument. I was wondering if I should buy up a lot of supplies. They happen to be cheap just now. But if the war ended, I might just as well throw them away.

CHAPLAIN – I realize you are serious, Mother Courage. Well, there've always been people going around saying some day the war will end. I say, you can't be sure the war will *ever* end. Of course it may have to pause occasionally—for breath, as it were—it can even meet with an accident—nothing on this earth is perfect—a war of which we could say it left nothing to be desired will probably never exist. A war can come to a sudden halt—from unforeseen causes—you can't think of everything—a little oversight, and the war's in the hole, and someone's got to pull it out again! The someone is the Emperor or the King or the Pope. They're such friends in need, the war has really nothing to worry about, it can look forward to a prosperous future.

A SOLDIER [*singing at the counter*]

> One schnapps, mine host, make haste!
> We have no time to waste:
> We must be shooting, shooting, shooting
> Our Emperor's foes uprooting!

Make it a double. This is a holiday.

MOTHER COURAGE—If I was sure you're right . . .

CHAPLAIN—Think it out for yourself: how *could* the war end?

SOLDIER [*off-stage*]

> Two breasts, mine host, make haste!
> For we have no time to waste:
> We must be hating, hating, hating
> We cannot keep our Emperor waiting!

CLERK [*suddenly*] What about peace? Yes, peace. I'm from Bohemia. I'd like to get home once in a while.

CHAPLAIN—Oh, you would, would you? Dear old peace! What happens to the hole when the cheese is gone?

SOLDIER [*off-stage*]

> Your blessing, priest, make haste!
> For we have no time to waste:
> We must be dying, dying, dying
> Our Emperor's greatness glorifying!

CLERK—In the long run you can't live without peace!

CHAPLAIN—Well, I'd say there's peace even in war, war has its islands of peace. For war satisfies *all* needs, even those of peace, yes, they're provided for, or the war couldn't keep going. In war—as in the very thick of peace—you can take a crap, and between one battle and the next there's always a beer, and even on the march you can snatch a nap —on your elbow maybe, in a gutter—something can always be managed. Of course you can't play cards during an attack, but neither can you while ploughing the fields in peace time: it's when the victory's won that there are possibilities. You have your leg shot off, and at first you raise quite an outcry as if it *was* something, but soon you calm down or take a swig of brandy, and you end up hopping about, and the war is none the worse for your little misadventure. And can't you be fruitful and multiply in the thick of slaughter—behind a barn or somewhere? Nothing can keep you from it very long in any event. And so the war has your offspring and can carry on. War is like love, it always finds a way. Why *should* it end?

[KATTRIN *has stopped working. She stares at the* CHAPLAIN.]

MOTHER COURAGE—Then I *will* buy those supplies, I'll rely on you.

[KATTRIN *suddenly bangs a basket of glasses down on the ground and runs out.* MOTHER COURAGE *laughs.*] Kattrin! Lord, Kattrin's still going to wait for peace. I promised her she'll get a husband—when it's peace.
[*She runs after her.*]

CLERK [*standing up*] I win. You were talking. You pay.

MOTHER COURAGE [*returning with* KATTRIN] Be sensible, the war'll go on a bit longer, and we'll make a bit more money, then peace'll be all the nicer. Now you go into the town, it's not ten minutes walk, and bring the things from the Golden Lion, just the more expensive ones, we can get the rest later in the wagon. It's all arranged, the clerk will go with you, most of the soldiers are at the Commander's funeral, nothing can happen to you. Do a good job, don't lose anything, Kattrin, think of your trousseau!

[KATTRIN *ties a cloth around her head and leaves with the* CLERK.]

CHAPLAIN—You don't mind her going with the Clerk?

MOTHER COURAGE—She's not so pretty anyone would want to ruin her.

CHAPLAIN—The way you run your business and always come through is highly commendable, Mother Courage—I see how you got your name.

MOTHER COURAGE—The poor need courage. Why? They're lost. That they even get up in the morning is something—in *their* plight. Or that they plough a field—in war time. Even their bringing children into the world shows they have courage, for they have no prospects. They have to hang each other one by one and slaughter each other in the lump, so if they want to look each other in the face once in a while, well, it takes courage. That they put up with an Emperor and a Pope, that takes an unnatural amount of courage, for *they* cost you your life. [*She sits, takes a small pipe from her pocket and smokes it.*] You might chop me a bit of firewood.

CHAPLAIN [*reluctantly taking his coat off and preparing to chop wood*] Properly speaking, I'm a pastor of souls, not a woodcutter.

MOTHER COURAGE—But I don't have a soul. And I do need wood.

CHAPLAIN—What's that little pipe you've got there?

MOTHER COURAGE—Just a pipe.

CHAPLAIN—I think it's a very particular pipe.

MOTHER COURAGE—Oh?

CHAPLAIN—The cook's pipe in fact. The cook from the Oxenstierna Regiment.

MOTHER COURAGE—If you know, why beat about the bush?

CHAPLAIN—Because I don't know if you've been *aware* that's what you've been smoking. It was possible you just rummaged among your belongings and your fingers just lit on a pipe and you just took it. In pure absent-mindedness.

MOTHER COURAGE—How do you know that's not it?

CHAPLAIN—It isn't. You *are* aware of it.

> [*He brings the ax down on the block with a crash.*]

MOTHER COURAGE—What if I was?

CHAPLAIN—I must give you a warning, Mother Courage, it's my duty. You are unlikely to see the gentleman again but that's no pity, you're in luck. Mother Courage, he did not impress me as trustworthy. On the contrary.

MOTHER COURAGE—Really? He was such a nice man.

CHAPLAIN—Well! So that's what you call a nice man. I do not. [*The ax falls again.*] Far be it from me to wish him ill, but I cannot—cannot —describe him as nice. No, no, he's a Don Juan, a cunning Don Juan. Just look at that pipe if you don't believe me. You must admit it tells all.

MOTHER COURAGE—I see nothing special in it. It's been used, of course.

CHAPLAIN—It's bitten halfway through! He's a man of great violence! It is the pipe of a man of great violence, you can see *that* if you've any judgment left!

> [*He deals the block a tremendous blow.*]

MOTHER COURAGE—Don't bite my chopping block halfway through!

CHAPLAIN—I told you I had no training as a woodcutter. The care of souls was my field. Around here my gifts and capabilities are grossly misused. In physical labor my God-given talents find no—um—adequate expression—which is a sin. You haven't heard me preach. Why, I can put such spirit into a regiment with a single sermon that the enemy's a mere flock of sheep to them and their own lives no more than smelly old shoes to be thrown away at the thought of final victory! God has given me the gift of tongues. I can preach you out of your senses!

MOTHER COURAGE—I need my senses. What would I do without them?

CHAPLAIN—Mother Courage, I have often thought that—under a veil of plain speech—you conceal a heart. You are human, you need warmth.

MOTHER COURAGE—The best way of warming this tent is to chop plenty of firewood.

CHAPLAIN—You're changing the subject. Seriously, my dear Courage, I sometimes ask myself how it would be if our relationship should be somewhat more firmly cemented. I mean, now the wild wind of war has whirled us so strangely together.

MOTHER COURAGE—The cement's pretty firm already. I cook your meals. And you lend a hand—at chopping firewood, for instance.

CHAPLAIN [*going over to her, gesturing with the ax*] You know what

I mean by a close relationship. It has nothing to do with eating and woodcutting and such base necessities. Let your heart speak!

MOTHER COURAGE—Don't come at me like that with your ax, that'd be *too* close a relationship!

CHAPLAIN—This is no laughing matter, I am in earnest. I've thought it all over.

MOTHER COURAGE—Dear Chaplain, be a sensible fellow. I like you, and I don't want to heap coals of fire on your head. All I want is to bring me and my children through in that wagon. It isn't just mine, the wagon, and anyway I've no mind to start any adventures. At the moment I'm taking quite a risk buying these things when the Commander's fallen and there's all this talk of peace. Where would you go, if I was ruined? See? You don't even know. Now chop some firewood and it'll be warm of an evening, which is quite a lot in times like these. What was that? [*She stands up.* KATTRIN *enters, breathless, with a wound across the eye and forehead. She is dragging all sorts of articles, parcels, leather goods, a drum, etc.*] What is it, were you attacked? On the way back? She was attacked on the way back! I'll bet it was that soldier who got drunk on my liquor. I should never have let you go. Dump all that stuff! It's not bad, the wound is only a flesh wound. I'll bandage it for you, it'll all be healed up in a week. They're worse than animals.

[*She bandages the wound.*]

CHAPLAIN—I reproach them with nothing. At home they never did these shameful things. The men who start the wars are responsible, they bring out the worst in people.

MOTHER COURAGE—Didn't the Clerk walk you back home? That's because you're a respectable girl, he thought they'd leave you alone. The wound's not at all deep, it will never show. There: all bandaged up. Now, I've got something for you, rest easy. I've been keeping them secret. [*She digs* YVETTE's *red boots out of a bag.*] Well, what do you see? You always wanted them. Now you have them. [*She helps her to put the boots on.*] Put them on quick, before I change my mind. It will never show, though it wouldn't bother *me* if it did. The ones they like fare worst. They drag them around till they're finished. Those they don't care for they leave alone. I've seen so many girls, pretty as they come in the beginning, then all of a sudden they're so ugly they'd scare a wolf. They can't even go behind a tree on the street without having something to fear from it. They lead a frightful life. Like with trees: the tall, straight ones are cut down for roof timber, and the crooked ones can enjoy life. So this wound here is really a piece of luck. The boots have kept well. I gave them a good cleaning before I put them away.

[KATTRIN *leaves the boots and creeps into the wagon.*]

CHAPLAIN [*when she's gone*] I hope she won't be disfigured?

MOTHER COURAGE—There'll be a scar. She needn't wait for peace now.

CHAPLAIN—She didn't let them get any of the stuff.

MOTHER COURAGE—Maybe I shouldn't have made such a point of it. If only I ever knew what went on inside her head. Once she stayed out all night, once in all the years. Afterward she seemed much the same, except that she worked harder. I could never get out of her what happened. I worried about it for quite a while. [*She picks up the things* KATTRIN *spilled and sorts them angrily.*] This is war. A nice source of income, I must say!

[*Cannon shots.*]

CHAPLAIN—Now they're lowering the Commander into his grave! A historic moment.

MOTHER COURAGE—It's a historic moment to me when they hit my daughter over the eye. She's all but finished now, she'll never get a husband, and she's so mad about children! Even her dumbness comes from the war. A soldier stuck something in her mouth when she was little. I'll never see Swiss Cheese again, and where my Eilif is the Good Lord knows. Curse the war!

SEVEN

Mother Courage at the height of her business career.

A highway. The CHAPLAIN, MOTHER COURAGE, *and her daughter* KATTRIN
pull the wagon, and new wares are hanging from it. MOTHER COURAGE
wears a necklace of silver coins.

MOTHER COURAGE—I won't let you spoil my war for me. Destroys
the weak, does it? Well, what does peace do for 'em, huh? War feeds
its people better.

[*She sings.*]

> If war don't suit your disposition
> When victory comes, you will be dead.
> War is a business proposition:
> But not with cheese, with steel instead!
> Christians, awake! Winter is gone!
> The snows depart! Dead men sleep on!
> Let all of you who still survive
> Get out of bed and look alive!

And staying in one place won't help either. Those who stay at home
are the first to go.

[*She sings.*]

> Too many seek a bed to sleep in:
> Each ditch is taken, and each cave
> And he who digs a hole to creep in
> Finds he has dug an early grave.
> And many a man spends many a minute
> In hurrying toward some resting place.
> You wonder, when at last he's in it
> Just why the fellow forced the pace.

[*The wagon proceeds.*]

EIGHT

1632. In this same year Gustavus Adolphus fell in the battle of Lützen. The peace threatens Mother Courage with ruin. Her brave son performs one heroic deed too many and comes to a shameful end.

[*A camp. A summer morning. In front of the wagon, an* OLD WOMAN *and her son. The son is dragging a large bag of bedding.*]

MOTHER COURAGE [*from inside the wagon*] Must you come at the crack of dawn?

YOUNG MAN – We've been walking all night, twenty miles it was, we have to be back today.

MOTHER COURAGE [*still inside*] What do I want with bed feathers? People don't even have houses.

YOUNG MAN – At least wait till you see 'em.

OLD WOMAN – Nothing doing here either, let's go.

YOUNG MAN – And let 'em sign away the roof over our heads for taxes? Maybe she'll pay three guilders if you throw in that bracelet. [*Bells start ringing.*] You hear, Mother?

VOICES [*from the rear*] It's peace! The King of Sweden's been killed!

[MOTHER COURAGE *sticks her head out of the wagon. She hasn't done her hair yet.*]

MOTHER COURAGE – Bells! What are the bells for, middle of the week?

CHAPLAIN [*crawling out from under the wagon*] What's that they're shouting?

YOUNG MAN – It's peace.

CHAPLAIN – Peace!

MOTHER COURAGE – Don't tell me peace has broken out—when I've just gone and bought all these supplies!

CHAPLAIN [*calling, toward the rear*] Is it peace?

VOICE [*from a distance*] They say the war stopped three weeks ago. I've only just heard.

CHAPLAIN [*to* MOTHER COURAGE] Or why would they ring the bells?

VOICE – A great crowd of Lutherans have just arrived with wagons— they brought the news.

Y O U N G   M A N — It's peace, Mother. [*The* OLD WOMAN *collapses.*] What's the matter?

M O T H E R   C O U R A G E   [*back in the wagon*] Kattrin, it's peace! Put on your black dress, we're going to church, we owe it to Swiss Cheese! Can it be true?

Y O U N G   M A N — The people here say so too, the war's over. Can you stand up? [*The* OLD WOMAN *stands up, dazed.*] I'll get the harness shop going again now, I promise you. Everything'll be all right, father will get his bed back. . . . Can you walk? [*To the* CHAPLAIN.] She felt ill, it was the news. She didn't believe there'd ever be peace again. Father always said there would. We're going home.

[*They leave.*]

M O T H E R   C O U R A G E   [*off*] Give her some brandy.

C H A P L A I N — They've left already.

M O T H E R   C O U R A G E   [*still off*] What's going on in the camp over there?

C H A P L A I N — They're all getting together. I think I'll go over. Shall I put my pastor's coat on again?

M O T H E R   C O U R A G E — Better get the exact news first, and not risk being taken for the Antichrist. I'm glad about the peace even though I'm ruined. At least I've got two of my children through the war. Now I'll see my Eilif again.

C H A P L A I N — And who may this be coming down from the camp? Well, if it isn't our Swedish Commander's cook!

C O O K   [*somewhat bedraggled, carrying a bundle*] Who's here? The Chaplain!

C H A P L A I N — Mother Courage, a visitor!

[MOTHER COURAGE *clambers out.*]

C O O K — Well, I promised I'd come over for a brief conversation as soon as I had time. I didn't forget your brandy, Mrs. Fierling.

M O T H E R   C O U R A G E — Jesus, the Commander's cook! After all these years! Where is Eilif, my eldest?

C O O K — Isn't he here yet? He went on ahead yesterday, he was on his way over.

C H A P L A I N — I *will* put my pastor's coat on. I'll be back.

[*He goes behind the wagon.*]

M O T H E R   C O U R A G E — He may be here any minute then. [*She calls toward the wagon.*] Kattrin, Eilif's coming! Bring a glass of brandy for the cook, Kattrin! [KATTRIN *doesn't come.*] Just pull your hair over it. Mr. Lamb is no stranger. [*She gets the brandy herself.*] She won't come out. Peace is nothing to her, it was too long coming. They hit her right over the eye. You can hardly see it now. But she thinks people stare at her.

COOK — Ah yes, war!

[*He and* MOTHER COURAGE *sit.*]

MOTHER COURAGE — Cook, you come at a bad time: I'm ruined.

COOK — What? That's terrible!

MOTHER COURAGE — The peace has broken my neck. On the Chaplain's advice I've gone and bought a lot of supplies. Now everybody's leaving and I'm holding the baby.

COOK — How could you listen to the Chaplain? If I'd had time—but the Catholics were too quick for me—I'd have warned you against him. He's a windbag. Well, so now he's the big man round here!

MOTHER COURAGE — He's been doing the dishes for me and helping with the wagon.

COOK — With the wagon—him! And I'll bet he's told you a few of his jokes. He has a most unhealthy attitude to women. I tried to influence him but it was no good. He isn't sound.

MOTHER COURAGE — Are you sound?

COOK — If I'm nothing else, I'm sound. Your health!

MOTHER COURAGE — Sound! Only one person around here was ever sound, and I never had to slave as I did then. He sold the blankets off the children's beds in the spring, and he called my harmonica unchristian. You aren't recommending yourself if you *admit* you're sound.

COOK — You fight tooth and nail, don't you? I like that.

MOTHER COURAGE — Don't tell me you've been dreaming of my teeth and nails.

COOK — Well, here we sit, while the bells of peace do ring, and you pouring your famous brandy as only you know how!

MOTHER COURAGE — I don't think much of the bells of peace at the moment. I don't see how they can hand out all this pay that's in arrears. And then where shall I be with my famous brandy? Have you all been paid?

COOK [*hesitating*] Not exactly. That's why we disbanded. In the circumstances, I thought, why stay? For the time being, I'll look up a couple of friends. So here I sit—with you.

MOTHER COURAGE — In other words, you're broke.

COOK [*annoyed by the bells*] It's about time they stopped that racket! I'd like to set myself up in some business. I'm fed up with being their cook. I'm supposed to make do with tree roots and shoe leather, and then they throw my hot soup in my face! Being a cook nowadays is a dog's life. I'd sooner be a soldier, but of course, it's peace now. [*As the* CHAPLAIN *turns up, wearing his old coat.*] We'll talk it over later.

CHAPLAIN — The coat's pretty good. Just a few moth holes.

COOK — I don't know why you take the trouble. You won't find another pulpit. Who could you incite now to earn an honest living or risk his life for a cause? Besides, I have a bone to pick with you.

2141

CHAPLAIN – Have you?

COOK – I have. You advised a lady to buy superfluous goods on the pretext that the war would never end.

CHAPLAIN [*hotly*] I'd like to know what business it is of yours?

COOK – It's unprincipled behavior! How can you give unwanted advice? And interfere with the conduct of other people's business?

CHAPLAIN – Who's interfering now, I'd like to know? [*To* MOTHER COURAGE.] I had no idea you were such a close friend of this gentleman and had to account to *him* for everything.

MOTHER COURAGE – Now don't get excited. The cook's giving his personal opinion. You can't deny your war was a flop.

CHAPLAIN – You have no respect for peace, Courage. You're a hyena of the battlefield!

MOTHER COURAGE – A what?

COOK – Who insults my girl friend insults me!

CHAPLAIN – I am *not* speaking to you, your intentions are only too transparent! [*To* MOTHER COURAGE.] But when I see *you* take peace between finger and thumb like a snotty old hanky, my humanity rebels! It shows that you want war, not peace, for what you get out of it. But don't forget the proverb: he who sups with the devil must use a long spoon!

MOTHER COURAGE – Remember what one fox said to another that was caught in a trap? "If you stay there, you're just asking for trouble!" There isn't much love lost between me and the war. And when it comes to calling me a hyena, you and I part company.

CHAPLAIN – Then why all this grumbling about the peace just as everyone's heaving a sigh of relief? Is it for the junk in your wagon?

MOTHER COURAGE – My goods are not junk. I live off them. You've been living off them.

CHAPLAIN – You live off war. Exactly.

COOK [*to the* CHAPLAIN] As a grown man, you should know better than to go around advising people. [*To* MOTHER COURAGE.] Now, in your situation you'd be smart to get rid of certain goods at once—before the prices sink to nothing. Get ready and get going, there isn't a moment to lose!

MOTHER COURAGE – That's sensible advice, I think I'll take it.

CHAPLAIN – Because the cook says so.

MOTHER COURAGE – Why didn't *you* say so? He's right, I must get to the market.

[*She climbs into the wagon.*]

COOK – One up for me, Chaplain. You have no presence of mind. You should have said, "I gave you advice? Why, I was just talking politics!"

2142

And you shouldn't take me on as a rival. Cockfights are not becoming to your cloth.

CHAPLAIN – If you don't shut your trap, I'll murder you, cloth or no cloth!

COOK [*taking his boots off and unwinding the wrappings on his feet*] If you hadn't degenerated into a godless tramp, you could easily get yourself a parsonage, now it's peace. Cooks won't be needed, there's nothing to cook, but there's still plenty to believe, and people will go right on believing it.

CHAPLAIN – Mr. Lamb, please don't drive me out! Since I became a tramp, I'm a somewhat better man. I couldn't preach to 'em any more.

[YVETTE POTTIER *enters, decked out in black, with a stick. She is much older, fatter, and heavily powdered. Behind her, a* SERVANT.]

YVETTE – Hullo, everybody! Is this Mother Courage's establishment?

CHAPLAIN – Quite right. And with whom have we the pleasure?

YVETTE – I am Madame Colonel Starhemberg, good people. Where's Mother Courage?

CHAPLAIN [*calling to the wagon*] Madame Colonel Starhemberg wants to speak to you!

MOTHER COURAGE [*from inside*] Coming!

YVETTE [*calling*] It's Yvette!

MOTHER COURAGE [*inside*] Yvette!

YVETTE – Just to see how you're getting on! [*As the* COOK *turns around in horror.*] Peter!

COOK – Yvette!

YVETTE – Of all things! How did *you* get here?

COOK – On a cart.

CHAPLAIN – Well! You know each other? Intimately?

YVETTE – I'll say. [*Scrutinizing the* COOK.] You're fat.

COOK – For that matter, *you're* no beanpole.

YVETTE – Anyway, it's lucky we've met, tramp. Now I can tell you what I think of you.

CHAPLAIN – Do so, tell him all, but wait till Mother Courage comes out.

COOK – Now don't make a scene . . .

MOTHER COURAGE [*coming out, laden with goods*] Yvette! [*They embrace.*] But why are you in mourning?

YVETTE – Doesn't it suit me? My husband, the Colonel, died several years ago.

MOTHER COURAGE – The old fellow that nearly bought my wagon?

YVETTE – His elder brother.

MOTHER COURAGE – So you're not doing badly. Good to see one person who got somewhere in the war.

YVETTE – I've had my ups and downs.

MOTHER COURAGE – Don't let's speak ill of colonels. They make money like hay.

CHAPLAIN [*to the* COOK] If I were you, I'd put my shoes on again. [*To* YVETTE.] You promised to give us your opinion of this gentleman.

COOK – Now, Yvette, don't make a stink!

MOTHER COURAGE – He's a friend of mine, Yvette.

YVETTE – He's—Peter Piper, that's who.

MOTHER COURAGE – What!

COOK – Cut the nicknames. My name's Lamb.

MOTHER COURAGE [*laughing*] Peter Piper? Who turned the women's heads? And I've been keeping your pipe for you.

CHAPLAIN – And smoking it.

YVETTE – Lucky I can warn you against him. He's a bad lot. You won't find worse on the whole coast of Flanders. He got more girls in trouble than . . .

COOK – That's a long time ago, it isn't true any more.

YVETTE – Stand up when you talk to a lady! Oh, how I loved that man; and all the time he was having a little bowlegged brunette. He got *her* into trouble too, of course.

COOK – I seem to have brought *you* luck!

YVETTE – Shut your trap, you hoary ruin! And you take care, Mother Courage, this type is still dangerous even in decay!

MOTHER COURAGE [*to* YVETTE] Come with me, I must get rid of this stuff before the prices fall.

YVETTE [*concentrating on the* COOK] Miserable cur!

MOTHER COURAGE – Maybe you can help me at army headquarters, you have contacts.

YVETTE – Seducer!

MOTHER COURAGE [*shouting into the wagon*] Kattrin, church is all off, I'm going to market!

YVETTE – Whore hunter!

MOTHER COURAGE [*still to* KATTRIN] When Eilif comes, give him something to drink!

YVETTE – That a man like him should have been able to turn me from the straight and narrow! I have my own star to thank that I rose none the less to the heights! But I've put an end to your tricks, Peter Piper, and one day—in a better life than this—the Lord God will reward me! Come, Mother Courage!

[*She leaves with* MOTHER COURAGE.]

CHAPLAIN – As our text this morning let us take the saying: the mills of God grind slowly. And you complain of my jokes!

COOK – I never have any luck. I'll be frank, I was hoping for a good hot dinner, I'm starving. And now they'll be talking about me, and she'll get a completely wrong picture. I think I should go before she comes back.

CHAPLAIN—I think so too.

COOK—Chaplain, peace makes me sick. Mankind must perish by fire and sword, we're born and bred in sin! Oh, how I wish I was roasting a great fat capon for the Commander—God knows where *he's* got to—with mustard sauce and those little yellow carrots . . .

CHAPLAIN—Red cabbage—with capon, red cabbage.

COOK—You're right. But he always wanted yellow carrots.

CHAPLAIN—He never understood a thing.

COOK—You always put plenty away.

CHAPLAIN—Under protest.

COOK—Anyway, you must admit, those were the days.

CHAPLAIN—Yes, that I might admit.

COOK—Now you've called her a hyena, there's not much future for you here either. What are you staring at?

CHAPLAIN—It's Eilif!

> [*Followed by two soldiers with halberds,* EILIF *enters. His hands are fettered. He is white as chalk.*]

CHAPLAIN—What's happened to you?

EILIF—Where's Mother?

CHAPLAIN—Gone to town.

EILIF—They said she was here. I was allowed a last visit.

COOK [*to the* SOLDIERS] Where are you taking him?

A SOLDIER—For a ride.

> [*The other* SOLDIER *makes the gesture of throat cutting.*]

CHAPLAIN—What has he done?

SOLDIER—He broke in on a peasant. The wife is dead.

CHAPLAIN—Eilif, how could you?

EILIF—It's no different. It's what I did before.

COOK—That was in war time.

EILIF—Shut your hole. Can I sit down till she comes?

SOLDIER—No.

CHAPLAIN—It's true. In war time they honored him for it. He sat at the Commander's right hand. It was bravery. Couldn't we speak with the military police?

SOLDIER—What's the use? Stealing cattle from a peasant, what's brave about that?

COOK—It was just stupid.

EILIF—If I'd been stupid, I'd have starved, smarty.

COOK—So you were bright and paid for it.

CHAPLAIN—At least we must bring Kattrin out.

EILIF – Let her alone. Just give me some brandy.

SOLDIER – No.

CHAPLAIN – What shall we tell your mother?

EILIF – Tell her it was no different. Tell her it was the same. Oh, tell her nothing.

[*The* SOLDIERS *take him away.*]

CHAPLAIN – I'll come with you, I'll . . .

EILIF – I don't need a priest!

CHAPLAIN – You don't know—yet.

[*He follows him.*]

COOK [*calling after him*] I'll have to tell her, she'll want to see him!

CHAPLAIN – Better tell her nothing. Or maybe just that he was here, and he'll return, maybe tomorrow. Meantime I'll be back and can break the news.

[*He leaves quickly.*]

[*The* COOK *looks after him, shakes his head, then walks about uneasily. Finally, he approaches the wagon.*]

COOK – Hello! Won't you come out? You want to sneak away from the peace, don't you? Well, so do I! I'm the Swedish Commander's cook, remember me? I was wondering if you've got anything to eat in there —while we're waiting for your mother. I wouldn't mind a bit of bacon —or even bread—just to pass the time. [*He looks in.*] She's got a blanket over her head.

[*The thunder of cannon.*]
[MOTHER COURAGE *runs in, out of breath,
still carrying the goods.*]

MOTHER COURAGE – Cook, the peace is over, the war's on again, has been for three days! I didn't get rid of this stuff after all, thank God! There's a shooting match in the town already—with the Lutherans. We must get away with the wagon. Pack, Kattrin! What's on *your* mind? Something the matter?

COOK – Nothing.

MOTHER COURAGE – But there is. I see it in your face.

COOK – Because the war's on again, most likely. May it last till tomorrow evening, so I can get something in my belly!

MOTHER COURAGE – You're not telling me.

COOK – Eilif was here. Only he had to go away again.

MOTHER COURAGE – He was here? Then we'll see him on the march. I'll be with our side this time. How'd he look?

COOK – The same.

MOTHER COURAGE – He'll *never* change. And the war couldn't get *him*, he's bright. Help me with the packing. [*She starts it.*] Did he tell you anything? Is he well in with the Provost? Did he tell you about his heroic deeds?

COOK [*darkly*] He's done one of them again.

MOTHER COURAGE—Tell me about it later. [KATTRIN *appears.*] Kattrin, the peace is over, we're on the move again. [*To the* COOK.] What *is* the matter with you?

COOK—I'll enlist.

MOTHER COURAGE—A good idea. Where's the Chaplain?

COOK—In the town. With Eilif.

MOTHER COURAGE—Stay with us a while, Lamb, I need a bit of help.

COOK—This matter of Yvette . . .

MOTHER COURAGE—Hasn't done you any harm at all in my eyes. Just the opposite. Where there's smoke, there's fire, they say. You'll come?

COOK—I may as well.

MOTHER COURAGE—The Twelfth Regiment's under way. Into harness with you! Maybe I'll see Eilif before the day is out, just think! That's what I like best. Well, it wasn't such a long peace, we can't grumble. Let's go!

[*The* COOK *and* KATTRIN *are in harness.*]

[MOTHER COURAGE *sings.*]

From Ulm to Metz, past dome and steeple
My wagon always moves ahead.
The war can care for all its people
So long as there is steel and lead.
Though steel and lead are stout supporters
A war needs human beings too.
Report today to your headquarters!
If it's to last, this war needs you!

NINE

The great war of religion has lasted sixteen years and Germany has lost half its inhabitants. Those who are spared in battle die by plague. Over once blooming countryside hunger rages. Towns are burned down. Wolves prowl the empty streets. In the autumn of 1634 we find Mother Courage in the Fichtelgebirge not far from the road the Swedish army is taking. Winter has come early and is hard. Business is bad. Only begging remains. The cook receives a letter from Utrecht and is sent packing.

[*In front of a half-ruined parsonage. Early winter. A gray morning. Gusts of wind.* MOTHER COURAGE *and the* COOK *at the wagon in shabby clothes.*]

COOK – There are no lights on. No one's up.

MOTHER COURAGE – But it's a parsonage. The parson'll have to leave his feather bed and ring the bells. Then he'll have some hot soup.

COOK – Where'll he get it from? The whole village is starving.

MOTHER COURAGE – The house is lived in. There was a dog barking.

COOK – If the parson has anything, he'll hang on to it.

MOTHER COURAGE – Maybe if we sang him something . . .

COOK – I've had enough. [*Suddenly.*] I didn't tell you, a letter came from Utrecht. My mother's died of cholera, the inn is mine. There's the letter, if you don't believe me. I'll show it to you, though my aunt's railing about me and my ups and downs is none of your business.

MOTHER COURAGE [*reading*] Lamb, I'm tired of wandering, too. I feel like a butcher's dog taking meat to my customers and getting none myself. I've nothing more to sell and people have nothing to pay with. In Saxony someone tried to force a chestful of books on me in return for two eggs. And in Württemberg they would have let me have their plough for a bag of salt. Nothing grows any more, only thorn bushes. In Pomerania I hear the villagers have been eating their younger children. Nuns have been caught committing robbery.

COOK – The world's dying out.

MOTHER COURAGE – Sometimes I see myself driving through hell with this wagon and selling brimstone. And sometimes I'm driving through heaven handing our provisions to wandering souls! If only we

2148

could find a place where there's no shooting, me and my children—what's left of 'em—we might rest a while.

COOK—We could open this inn together. Think about it, Courage. *My* mind's made up. With or without you, I'm leaving for Utrecht. And today too.

MOTHER COURAGE—I must talk to Kattrin, it's a bit sudden, and I don't like to make my decisions in the cold on an empty stomach. [KATTRIN *emerges from the wagon.*] Kattrin, I've something to tell you. The cook and I want to go to Utrecht, he's been left an inn. You'd be able to stay put and get to know some people. Many a man'd be prepared to take on a girl with a position. Looks aren't everything. I like the idea. I get on well with the cook. I'll say this for him: he has a head for business. We'd be sure of our dinner, that would be all right, wouldn't it? You'd have your own bed, what do you think of *that*? In the long run, this is no life, on the road. You might be killed any time. You're eaten up with lice as it is. And we must decide now, because otherwise we go north with the Swedes. They must be over there somewhere. [*She points left.*] I think we'll decide to go, Kattrin.

COOK—Anna, I must have a word with you alone.

MOTHER COURAGE—Go back inside, Kattrin.

[KATTRIN *does so.*]

COOK—I'm interrupting because there's a misunderstanding, Anna. I thought I wouldn't have to say it right out, but I see I must. If you're bringing *her*, it's all off. Do we understand each other?

[KATTRIN *has her head out of the back of the wagon and is listening.*]

MOTHER COURAGE—You mean I leave Kattrin behind?

COOK—What do you think? There's no room in the inn, it isn't one of those places with three counters. If the two of us look lively we can earn a living, but three's too many. Let Kattrin keep your wagon.

MOTHER COURAGE—I was thinking we might find her a husband in Utrecht.

COOK—Don't make me laugh. With that scar? And old as she is? And dumb?

MOTHER COURAGE—Not so loud!

COOK—Loud or soft, what is, is. That's another reason I can't have her in the inn. Customers don't like having something like that always before their eyes. You can't blame them.

MOTHER COURAGE—Shut up. I told you not to talk so loud.

COOK—There's a light in the parsonage, we can sing now!

MOTHER COURAGE—Cook, how could she pull the wagon by herself? The war frightens her. She can't bear it. She has terrible dreams. I hear her groan at night, especially after battles. What she sees in her dreams I don't know. She suffers from sheer pity. The other day I found her with a hedgehog that we'd run over.

COOK – The inn's too small. [*Calling.*] Worthy Sir, menials, and all within! We now present the song of Solomon, Julius Caesar, and other great souls who came to no good, so you can see we're law-abiding folk too, and have a hard time getting by, especially in winter.

[*He sings "The Song of the Great Souls of this Earth."*]

King Solomon was very wise,
So what's his history?
He came to view this life with scorn,
Yes, he came to regret he ever had been born
Declaring: all is vanity.
King Solomon was very wise,
But long before the day was out
The consequence was clear, alas:
His wisdom 'twas that brought him to this pass.
A man is better off without.

For the virtues are dangerous in this world, as our fine song tells. You're better off without, you have a nice life, breakfast included—some good hot soup maybe . . . I'm an example of a man who's not had any, and I'd like some, I'm a soldier, but what good did my bravery do me in all those battles? None at all. I might just as well have wet my pants like a poltroon and stayed at home. For why?

Old Julius Caesar, he was brave.
His fame shall never cease.
He sat like a god on an altar piece.
Yet they tore brave old Julius limb from valiant limb
And Brutus helped to slaughter him.
Old Julius was very brave
But long before the day was out
The consequence was clear, alas:
His bravery 'twas that brought him to this pass.
A man is better off without.

[*Under his breath.*] They don't even look out. [*Aloud.*] Worthy Sir, menials, and all within! You could say, no, courage isn't the thing to fill a man's belly, try honesty, that should be worth a dinner, at any rate it must have *some* effect. Let's see.

You all know honest Socrates
Who always spoke the truth.
They owed him thanks for that, you'd think,
But what happened? Why, they put hemlock in his drink

And swore that he misled the youth.
How honest was this Socrates!
Yet long before the day was out
The consequence was clear, alas:
His honesty had brought him to this pass.
A man is better off without.

Yes, we're told to be unselfish and share what we have, but what if we have nothing? And those who do share it don't have an easy time either, for what's left when you're through sharing? Unselfishness is a very rare virtue—it doesn't pay.

Unselfish Martin could not bear
His fellow creatures' woes.
He met a poor man in the snows
And he gave this poor fellow half his cloak to wear:
So both of them fell down and froze.
His brothers' woes he could not bear,
So long before the day was out
The consequence was clear, alas:
Unselfishness had brought him to this pass.
A man is better off without.

That's how it is with us. We're law-abiding folk, we keep to ourselves, don't steal, don't kill, don't burn the place down. And in this way we sink lower and lower and the song proves true and there's no soup going. And if we were different, if we were thieves and killers, maybe we could eat our fill! For virtues bring no reward, only vices. Such is the world, need it be so?

God's ten commandments we have kept
And acted as we should.
It has not done us any good.
All you people who sit beside a roaring fire
O help us in our need so dire!
The ten commandments we have kept
And long before the day was out
The consequence was clear, alas:
Our godliness has brought us to this pass.
A man is better off without.

VOICE [*from above*] You there! Come up! There's some soup here for you!

MOTHER COURAGE—Lamb, I couldn't swallow a thing. I don't say what you said is unreasonable, but was it your last word? We've always understood each other.

COOK – Yes, Anna. Think it over.

MOTHER COURAGE – There's nothing to think over. I'm not leaving her here.

COOK – You're going to be silly, but what can I do? I'm not inhuman, it's just that the inn's a small one. And now we must go up, or there'll be nothing doing here too, and we've been singing in the cold for nothing.

MOTHER COURAGE – I'll fetch Kattrin.

COOK – Better stick something in your pocket for her. If there are three of us, they'll get a shock.

[*Exeunt.*]

KATTRIN *clambers out of the wagon with a bundle. She makes sure they are both gone. Then, on a wagon wheel, she lays out a skirt of her mother's and a pair of the cook's trousers side by side and easy to see. She has just finished, and has picked up her bundle, when* MOTHER COURAGE *returns.*

MOTHER COURAGE [*with a plate of soup*] Kattrin! Stay where you are, Kattrin! Where do you think you're going with that bundle? [*She examines the bundle.*] She's packed her things. Were you listening? I told him there was nothing doing, he can *have* Utrecht and his lousy inn, what would we want with a lousy inn? [*She sees the skirt and trousers.*] Oh, you're a stupid girl, Kattrin, what if I'd seen that and you gone? [*She takes hold of* KATTRIN *who is trying to leave.*] And don't think I've sent him packing on your account. It was the wagon. You can't part us, I'm too used to it, it was the wagon. Now we're leaving and we'll put the cook's things here where he'll find 'em, the stupid man. [*She clambers up and throws a couple of things down to go with the trousers.*] There! He's fired. The last man I'll take into *this* business! Now let's be going, you and me. This winter'll pass, like all the others. Get into harness, it looks like snow.

[*They harness themselves to the wagon, turn it around, and start out. A gust of wind. Enter the* COOK, *still chewing. He sees his things.*]

TEN

During the whole of 1635 Mother Courage and Kattrin pull the wagon along the roads of central Germany in the wake of the ever more tattered armies.

[*On the highway.* MOTHER COURAGE *and* KATTRIN *are pulling the wagon. They come to a prosperous farmhouse. Someone inside is singing.*]

VOICE—

In March a bush we planted
To make the garden gay.
In June we were enchanted:
A lovely rose was blooming
The balmy air perfuming!
Blest are they
Who have gardens gay!
In June we were enchanted.

When snow falls helter-skelter
And loudly blows the storm
Our farmhouse gives us shelter.
The winter's in a hurry
But we've no cause to worry.
We are warm
In the midst of the storm!
Our farmhouse gives us shelter.

[MOTHER COURAGE *and* KATTRIN *have stopped to listen. Then they start out again.*]

ELEVEN

January, 1636. Catholic troops threaten the Protestant town of Halle. The stone begins to speak. Mother Courage loses her daughter and journeys onward alone. The war is not yet near its end.

The wagon, very far gone now, stands near a farmhouse with a straw roof. It is night. Out of the woods come a LIEUTENANT *and three* SOLDIERS *in full armor.*

LIEUTENANT—And there mustn't be a sound. If anyone yells, cut him down.

FIRST SOLDIER—But we'll have to knock—if we want a guide.

LIEUTENANT—Knocking's a natural noise, it's all right, could be a cow hitting the wall of the cowshed.

[*The* SOLDIERS *knock at the farmhouse door. An* OLD PEASANT WOMAN *opens. A hand is clapped over her mouth. Two* SOLDIERS *enter.*]

A MAN'S VOICE—What is it?

[*The* SOLDIERS *bring out an* OLD PEASANT *and his son.*]

LIEUTENANT [*pointing to the wagon on which* KATTRIN *has appeared*] There's one. [*A* SOLDIER *pulls her out.*] Is this everybody that lives here?

PEASANTS [*alternating*] That's our son. And that's a girl that can't talk. Her mother's in town buying up stocks because the shopkeepers are running away and selling cheap. They're canteen people.

LIEUTENANT—I'm warning you. Keep quiet. One sound and we'll crack you over the head with a pike. And I need someone to show us the path to the town. [*He points to the* YOUNG PEASANT.] You! Come here!

YOUNG PEASANT—I don't know any path!

SECOND SOLDIER [*grinning*] He don't know any path!

YOUNG PEASANT—I don't help Catholics.

LIEUTENANT [*to the* SECOND SOLDIER] Let him feel your pike in his side.

2154

YOUNG PEASANT [*forced to his knees, the pike at his throat*] I'd rather die!

SECOND SOLDIER [*again mimicking*] He'd rather die!

FIRST SOLDIER—I know how to change his mind. [*He walks over to the cowshed.*] Two cows and a bull. Listen, you. If you aren't going to be reasonable, I'll saber your cattle.

YOUNG PEASANT—Not the cattle!

PEASANT WOMAN [*weeping*] Spare the cattle, Captain, or we'll starve!

LIEUTENANT—If he must be pigheaded!

FIRST SOLDIER—I think I'll start with the bull.

YOUNG PEASANT [*to the old one*] Do I have to? [*The older one nods.*] I'll do it.

PEASANT WOMAN—Thank you, thank you, Captain, for sparing us, for ever and ever, Amen.

[*The* OLD MAN *stops her going on thanking him.*]

FIRST SOLDIER—I knew the bull came first all right!

[*Led by the* YOUNG PEASANT, *the* LIEUTENANT *and the* SOLDIERS *go on their way.*]

OLD PEASANT—I wish we knew what it was. Nothing good, I suppose.

PEASANT WOMAN—Maybe they're just scouts. What are you doing?

OLD PEASANT [*setting a ladder against the roof and climbing up*] I'm seeing if they're alone. [*On the roof.*] Things are moving—all over. I can see armor. And cannon. There must be more than a regiment. God have mercy on the town and all within!

PEASANT WOMAN—Are there lights in the town?

OLD PEASANT—No, they're all asleep. [*He climbs down.*] There'll be an attack, and they'll all be slaughtered in their beds.

PEASANT WOMAN—The watchman'll give warning.

OLD PEASANT—They must have killed the watchman in the tower on the hill or he'd have sounded his horn before this.

PEASANT WOMAN—If there were more of us . . .

OLD PEASANT—But being that we're alone with that cripple . . .

PEASANT WOMAN—There's nothing we can do, is there?

OLD PEASANT—Nothing.

PEASANT WOMAN—We can't get down there. In the dark.

OLD PEASANT—The whole hillside's swarming with 'em.

PEASANT WOMAN—We could give a sign?

OLD PEASANT—And be cut down for it?

PEASANT WOMAN—No, there's nothing we can do. [*To* KATTRIN.] Pray, poor thing, pray! There's nothing we can do to stop this bloodshed, so even if you can't talk, at least pray! He hears, if no one else does. I'll help you. [*All kneel,* KATTRIN *behind.*] Our Father, which art

2155

in Heaven, hear our prayer, let not the town perish with all that lie therein asleep and fearing nothing. Wake them, that they rise and go the walls and see the foe that comes with fire and sword in the night down the hill and across the fields. [*Back to* KATTRIN.] God protect our mother and make the watchman not sleep but wake ere it's too late. And save our son-in-law, too, O God, he's there with his four children, let them not perish, they're innocent, they know nothing— [*To* KATTRIN, *who groans.*]—one of them's not two years old, the eldest is seven. [KATTRIN *rises, troubled.*] Heavenly Father, hear us, only Thou canst help us or we die, for we are weak and have no sword nor nothing; we cannot trust our own strength but only Thine, O Lord; we are in Thy hands, our cattle, our farm, and the town too, we're all in Thy hands, and the foe is nigh unto the walls with all his power. [KATTRIN, *unperceived, has crept off to the wagon, has taken something out of it, put it under her apron, and has climbed up the ladder to the roof.*] Be mindful of the children in danger, especially the little ones, be mindful of the old folk who cannot move, and of all Christian souls, O Lord.

OLD PEASANT—And forgive us our trespasses as we forgive them that trespass against us. Amen.

> [*Sitting on the roof,* KATTRIN *takes a drum from under her apron and starts to beat it.*]

PEASANT WOMAN—Heavens, what's she doing?

OLD PEASANT—She's out of her mind!

PEASANT WOMAN—Get her down, quick. [*The* OLD PEASANT *runs to the ladder but* KATTRIN *pulls it up on the roof.*] She'll get us in trouble.

OLD PEASANT—Stop it this minute, you silly cripple!

PEASANT WOMAN—The soldiers'll come!

OLD PEASANT [*looking for stones*] I'll stone you!

PEASANT WOMAN—Have you no pity, have you no heart? We have relations there too, four grandchildren, but there's nothing we can do. If they find us now, it's the end, they'll stab us to death!

> [KATTRIN *is staring into the far distance, toward the town. She goes on drumming.*]

PEASANT WOMAN [*to the* PEASANT] I told you not to let that riffraff on your farm. What do *they* care if we lose our cattle?

LIEUTENANT [*running back with* SOLDIERS *and the* YOUNG PEASANT] I'll cut you all to bits!

PEASANT WOMAN—We're innocent, sir, there's nothing we can do. She did it, a stranger!

LIEUTENANT—Where's the ladder?

OLD PEASANT—On the roof.

2156

LIEUTENANT [*calling*] Throw down the drum. I order you! [KAT-TRIN *goes on drumming.*] You're all in this, but you won't live to tell the tale.

OLD PEASANT—They've been cutting down fir trees around here. If we bring a tall enough trunk we can knock her off the roof . . .

FIRST SOLDIER [*to the* LIEUTENANT] I beg leave to make a sug-gestion. [*He whispers something to the* LIEUTENANT, *who nods.*] Listen, you! We have an idea—for your own good. Come down and go with us to the town. Show us your mother and we'll spare her.

[KATTRIN *goes on drumming.*]

LIEUTENANT [*pushing him away*] She doesn't trust you, no wonder with your face. [*He calls up to* KATTRIN.] Hey, you! Suppose I give you my word? I'm an officer, my word's my bond! [KATTRIN *drums harder.*] Nothing is sacred to her.

Nothing is sacred to her.

YOUNG PEASANT—Sir, it's not just because of her mother!

FIRST SOLDIER—This can't go on, they'll hear it in the town as sure as hell.

LIEUTENANT—We must make another noise with something. Louder than that drum. What can we make a noise with?

FIRST SOLDIER—But we mustn't make a noise!

LIEUTENANT—A harmless noise, fool, a peacetime noise!

OLD PEASANT—I could start chopping wood.

LIEUTENANT—That's it! [*The* PEASANT *brings his ax and chops away.*] Chop! Chop harder! Chop for your life! [KATTRIN *has been listening, beating the drum less hard. Very upset, and peering around, she now goes on drumming.*] It's not enough. [*To the* FIRST SOLDIER.] You chop too!

OLD PEASANT—I've only one ax. [*He stops chopping.*]

LIEUTENANT—We must set fire to the farm. Smoke her out.

OLD PEASANT—That's no good, Captain. When they see fire from the town, they'll know everything.

[*During the drumming* KATTRIN *has been listening again. Now she laughs.*]

LIEUTENANT—She's laughing at us, that's too much, I'll have her guts if it's the last thing I do. Bring a musket!

[*Two* SOLDIERS *off.* KATTRIN *goes on drumming.*]

PEASANT WOMAN—I have it, Captain. That's their wagon over there, Captain. If we smash that, she'll stop. It's all they have, Captain.

LIEUTENANT [*to the* YOUNG PEASANT] Smash it! [*Calling.*] If you don't stop that noise, we'll smash your wagon!

[*The* YOUNG PEASANT *deals the wagon a couple of feeble blows with a board.*]

2157

P E A S A N T   W O M A N   [*to* KATTRIN] Stop, you little beast!
　　　　　　　　　　　[KATTRIN *stares at the wagon and pauses.*
　　　Noises of distress come out of her. But she goes on drumming.]
L I E U T E N A N T – Where are those sons of bitches with that gun?
F I R S T   S O L D I E R – They can't have heard anything in the town or
　we'd hear their cannon.
L I E U T E N A N T   [*calling*] They don't hear you. And now we're going to
　shoot you. I'll give you one more chance: throw down that drum!
Y O U N G   P E A S A N T   [*dropping the board, screaming to* KATTRIN]
　Don't stop now! Or they're all done for. Go on, go on, go on . . .
　　　　[*The* SOLDIER *knocks him down and beats him with his pike.*
　　　　　　　　KATTRIN *starts crying but goes on drumming.*]
P E A S A N T   W O M A N – Not in the back, you're killing him!
　　　　　　　　　　[*The* SOLDIERS *arrive with the musket.*]
S E C O N D   S O L D I E R – The Colonel's foaming at the mouth. We'll be
　court-martialed.
L I E U T E N A N T – Set it up! Set it up! [*Calling while the musket is
　set up on forks.*] Once and for all: stop that drumming! [*Still crying,*
　KATTRIN *is drumming as hard as she can.*] Fire!
　　　　　[*The* SOLDIERS *fire.* KATTRIN *is hit. She gives the drum
　　　　　　　another feeble beat or two, then slowly collapses.*]
L I E U T E N A N T – That's an end to the noise.

*But the last beats of the drum are lost in the din of cannon from the
town. Mingled with the thunder of cannon, alarm bells are heard in
the distance.*

F I R S T   S O L D I E R – She made it.

TWELVE

Toward morning. The drums and pipes of troops on the march, receding. In front of the wagon Mother Courage sits by Kattrin's body. The peasants of the last scene are standing near.

PEASANTS – You must leave, woman. There's only one regiment to go. You can never get away by yourself.
MOTHER COURAGE – Maybe she's fallen asleep.

[She sings.]

> Lullaby, baby, what's that in the hay?
> The neighbor's kids cry but mine are gay.
> The neighbor's kids are dressed in dirt:
> Your silks are cut from an angel's skirt.
> They are all starving: you have a pie.
> If it's too stale, you need only cry.
> Lullaby, baby, what's rustling there?
> One lad fell in Poland. The other is—where?

You shouldn't have told her about the children.
PEASANTS – If you hadn't gone off to the town to get your cut, maybe it wouldn't have happened.
MOTHER COURAGE – She's asleep now.
PEASANTS – She's not asleep, it's time you realized. She's gone. You must get away. There are wolves in these parts. And the bandits are worse.
MOTHER COURAGE – That's right.

[She goes and fetches a cloth from the wagon to cover up the body.]

PEASANT WOMAN – Have you no one now? Someone you can go to?
MOTHER COURAGE – There's one. My Eilif.
PEASANT *[while* MOTHER COURAGE *covers the body]* Find him then. Leave *her* to us. We'll give her a proper burial. You needn't worry.
MOTHER COURAGE – Here's money for the expenses.

[She pays the PEASANT. *The* PEASANT *and his son shake her hand and carry* KATTRIN *away.]*

Bertolt Brecht

PEASANT WOMAN [*also taking her hand, and bowing, as she goes away*] Hurry!

MOTHER COURAGE [*harnessing herself to the wagon*] I hope I can pull the wagon by myself. Yes, I'll manage, there's not much in it now. I must get back into business.

[*Another regiment passes at the rear with pipe and drum.*]
[MOTHER COURAGE *starts pulling the wagon.*]

MOTHER COURAGE—Hey! Take me with you!

[*Soldiers are heard singing.*]

Dangers, surprises, devastations!
The war moves on, but will not quit.
And though it last three generations,
We shall get nothing out of it.
Starvation, filth, and cold enslave us.
The army robs us of our pay.
But God may yet come down and save us:
His holy war won't end today.

Christians, awake! Winter is gone!
The snows depart! Dead men sleep on!
Let all of you who still survive
Get out of bed and look alive!

MASS SUFFERING
MUTE AND ABSURD

By Eric Bentley

As WE LOOK BACK today upon the career of Bertolt Brecht (1898–1956) two periods of maximum creativity define themselves. The first came with the onset of manhood: Brecht had written some of his finest poetry, dramatic and otherwise, before he was twenty-five. The second came when he had perforce to withdraw from the hectic political activity of the Depression Years and lead the life of an exile during the later Thirties and earlier Forties. This is the period of *The Good Woman of Setzuan, The Life of Galileo Galilei, The Caucasian Chalk Circle,* and of what many regard as his masterpiece, *Mother Courage and Her Children.*

In this play, and *Galileo,* Brecht withdrew, not only from Nazi Germany, but from the twentieth century, and it is not without interest that the century he took in exchange was, in both instances, the seventeenth. It is the century of greatness, a century that opens with William Shakespeare and closes with Isaac Newton. Brecht finds in that century the roots of his own philosophy of life, scientific humanism. "Of all the days," he writes of the day when Galileo had to decide whether to abjure Copernicus, "that was the one / An age of reason could have begun." This at any rate is the "thesis" in the dialectical process: the "antithesis" is symbolized by the Thirty Years' War (1618–48).

For Germans, this is not "just another war." In the way it bore down upon whole cities and populations, it remained unique in German history until 1944–45. Since Brecht's play was finished before World War II began, this "cross-reference" has a sadly prophetic character.

One wonders if some friend mailed Brecht a copy of an English book that came out the year before he wrote *Mother Courage*, namely, *The Thirty Years War* by C. V. Wedgwood. Here is Miss Wedgwood's summing-up:

> After the expenditure of so much human life to so little purpose, men might have grasped the essential futility of putting the beliefs of the mind to the judgement of the sword. Instead, they rejected religion as an object to fight for and found others.
>
> As there was no compulsion towards a conflict which, in despite of the apparent bitterness of the parties, took so long to engage and needed so much assiduous blowing to fan the flame, so no right was vindicated by its ragged end. The war solved no problem. Its effects, both immediate and indirect, were either negative or disastrous. Morally subversive, economically destructive, socially degrading, confused in its causes, devious in its course, futile in its result, it is the outstanding example in European history of meaningless conflict. The overwhelming majority in Europe, the overwhelming majority in Germany, wanted no war; powerless and voiceless, there was no need even to persuade them that they did. The decision was made without thought of them. Yet of those who, one by one, let themselves be drawn into the conflict, few were irresponsible and nearly all were genuinely anxious for an ultimate and better peace. Almost all—one excepts the King of Sweden—were actuated rather by fear than by lust of conquest or passion of faith. They wanted peace and they fought for thirty years to be sure of it. They did not learn then, and have not since, that war breeds only war.

Whether or not Brecht read Miss Wedgwood, there is an author we can be sure he did read: Hans Jakob Christoffel von Grimmelshausen (1620?–76), author of *The Life of the Arch-Impostor and Adventuress Courage*. Yet this work does not stand to *Mother Courage* as *The Beggar's Opera* stands to *The Threepenny Opera*. What Brecht took from Grimmelshausen was not a structure, nor yet a story, nor yet a protagonist. He took a name, and he took atmosphere. He entered Grimmelshausen's world and carried some of it away with him. He carried away, especially, Grimmelshausen's sense of death—death on a tremendous scale and all a result of man's inhumanity to man. A reader without German can check on this by dipping into the one Grimmelshausen work which has been translated into English, *The Adventurous Simplicissmus* (Bison Books, 1962).

Mother Courage and Her Children is coming to be accepted universally as one of the important plays of the past quarter century. Critics in the East wish it had an optimistic ending, and critics in the West wish it was a traditional tragedy; which is to say that it is a play that both parties worry over, and which neither can get around.

"Pessimistic" or "untragic" as he may be, Brecht has put his finger on what Sir Herbert Read has shrewdly called "the problem of our age":

> The problem of our age is not a problem of conscience or commitment—of why people choose to die in wars for or against communism or fascism. The problem is rather why people who have no personal convictions of any kind allow themselves to suffer for indefinite or undefined causes, drifting like shoals of fish into invisible nets. The problem is mass-suffering, mute and absurd . . .

Oddly enough, this quotation is taken from a passage in which Sir Herbert is complaining of the absence of tragic poetry in our day:

> We live in a tragic age, but we are unable to express ourselves in tragic poetry. We are inarticulate and our only art is mockery or self-pity. Our fatalism gives us a stoical appearance, but it is not a genuine stoicism. It is a dull animal endurance of misfortune, unfocussed and unexpressed . . . There seems to be a direct connection between our inarticulateness, which implies a lack of emotional purgation, and our readiness to respond to mass appeals. Modern war in all its destructiveness is a dumb acceptance of this anonymous fate. Our armies, as Matthew Arnold said, are ignorant and clash by night.

But supposing this dull animal endurance, this inarticulateness, this dumb acceptance of anonymous fate is precisely the subject? Suppose the writer is not lost in it but sees it? Suppose he himself is not "ignorant," but can show the "clash by night" in a flood of light? We might still conclude that Brecht has not achieved tragedy (that is a matter of semantics) but we shall begin to see the point of his whole approach. It is because he is not identified with Mother Courage as academicians, East or West, want him to be, that he does not fall into the trap Sir Herbert mentions, the trap of self-pity. "Our only art is mockery or self-pity." There is plenty of mockery in *Mother Courage*, but surely it is not such persiflage, or defensive irony, as Sir Herbert presumably had in mind? This mockery helps to *dispel* self-pity.

It also includes a robust humor through which the protagonist ceases to be "average" in the usual modern sense—a sort of lowest common

2163

factor, the human animal seen abstractly, as in public opinion surveys—
and becomes someone who, however lacking in the attributes of saint or
heroine, is every inch a person.

When *Death of a Salesman* came out, there were discussions as to
whether the story of such a "little man" as Willie Loman (low man)
could be regarded as tragic. If not, it was implied, then the poor chap
would be left all alone with his littleness in outer darkness. About
Mother Courage, one need have no such worries. Brecht need not rise
up, like Arthur Miller, to broaden the theory of tragedy lest his protagonist be left out of things. Not being the abstract "little man,"
Mother Courage can stand the outer darkness. She may even light it up.
She represents, one might say, an alternative to tragedy.

But she does not represent Marxist optimism except when a director—
as in Moscow, 1960, I believe—changes the ending and has her become a
pacifist. Of traditional tragedy, *Mother Courage and Her Children* retains the sense of overriding fate, the sheer inevitability. Is this pessimism? That, too, is a matter of semantics. I think it makes good sense to
say, No, and again to claim that Brecht's work comes as an answer to a
problem formulated by Sir Herbert Read. "Our fatalism gives us a stoical
appearance, but it is not a genuine stoicism." Mother Courage doesn't
present a stoical appearance, but I think she does embody a genuine
stoicism. Though her name is an irony, and she is, in the first instance,
a coward, she also, in the last analysis, needs courage—needs it merely to
continue, merely to exist, and this courage is there—inside her—when she
looks for it. A human being, she has human resources.

To clinch the point one need only ask oneself what a naturalistic playwright would do with Mother Courage at the end of his play. Would
he not kill her off, probably by her own hand? Yet how grotesque this
"solution" seems to anyone who has inhabited the world of Brecht's
drama. Cannot Mother Courage say, with the same good right as the
aristocratic Rilke: *Wer spricht von Siegen? Überstehn ist alles:* "Who
talks of victories? To see it through is everything"?

2164

WHO IS MOTHER COURAGE?

By Eric Bentley

THE ROLE is hard to play and is always being miscast. Why? "Because middle-aged actresses are such ladies and lack earthiness." But who has succeeded in the role? Outstandingly, Helene Weigel. Is she very earthy, is she notably proletarian? On the contrary—there is nothing proletarian about her except her opinions. Then what is it those other ladies lack that Helene Weigel has? Among other things, I would suggest: an appreciation of the role, an understanding of what is in it, and above all the ability to portray contradictions. For whenever anyone says, "Mother Courage is essentially X" it is equally reasonable for someone to retort: "Mother Courage is essentially the exact opposite of X."

Mother Courage is essentially courageous. That is well-known, isn't it? Mr. Tennessee Williams has written of the final moment of Brecht's play as one of the inspiring moments in all theatre—inspiring because of the woman's indomitability. On she marches with her wagon after all that has happened, a symbol of the way humanity itself goes on its way after all that has happened, *if* it can find the courage. And after all we don't have to wait for the final scene to learn that we have to deal with a woman of considerable toughness and resilience. This is not the first time she has shown that she can pick up the pieces and continue. One might even find courage in the very first scene where we learn that she has not been content to cower in some corner of Bamberg but has boldly come to meet

From the program of *The National Theatre*, London; reprinted as preface to the Grove Press edition to *Mother Courage*. Copyright © 1966 by Eric Bentley. Reprinted by permission of the author.

the war. A trouble-shooter, we might say on first meeting the lady, but the reverse of a coward.

Yet it is impossible to continue on this tack for long without requiring an: *On the other hand.* Beginning with the reason why she is nicknamed "Courage" in the first place.

> They call me Mother Courage because I was afraid I'd be ruined, so I drove through the bombardment of Riga like a madwoman with fifty loaves of bread in my cart. They were going moldy, what else could I do?

Did those who gave her the name intend a joke against an obvious coward? Or did they think she was driven by heroic valor when in fact she was impelled by sheer necessity? Either way her act is utterly devoid of the moral quality imputed. Whether in cowardice or in down-to-earth realism, her stance is Falstaffian. What is courage? A word.

Somewhere hovering over this play is the image of a pre-eminently courageous mother who courageously tries to hold on to her young. More than one actress, offering herself for the role, has seen this image and nothing else. Yet valor is conspicuously absent at those times when Mother Courage (however unwittingly) seals the fate of her children. At moments when, in heroic melodrama, the protagonist would be riding to the rescue, come hell or high water, Mother Courage is in the back room concluding a little deal. For her, it is emphatically not "a time for greatness." *She is essentially cowardly.*

A basic contradiction, then, which the actress in the role must play both sides of, or the play will become the flat and simple thing which not a few journalistic commentators have declared it to be. An actress may be said to be beginning to play Mother Courage when she is putting both courage and cowardice into the role with equal conviction and equal effect. She is still only beginning to play it, though; for, as she proceeds with her interpretation, she will find that, in this play, courage and cowardice are not inherent and invariable qualities but by-products.

Of what? We can hunt for the answer by looking further into particular sequences of action. It is not really from cowardice that Mother Courage is in the back room concluding a little deal when her children are claimed by the war. It is from preoccupation with "business." Although *Mother Courage* is spoken of as a war play, it is actually a business play, in the sense that the incidents in it, one and all, are business transactions—from the deal with the belt in Scene One, through the deal with the capon in Scene Two, the deal with the wagon in Scene Three, the deals with bullets and shirts in Scene Five, through to the economical funeral arrangements of the final scene. And since these transactions (except for the last) are what Courage supports her children by, they are "necessary." Those who condemn her have to face the question: what alternative had she? Of what use would it have been to save the life of Swiss Cheese if she lacked the wherewithal to *keep* him alive? The severe judge will answer that she could take a chance on this, provided she does save his life. But this is exactly Mother Courage's own position. She is fully prepared to take the chance if she has to. It is in determining whether she has to that her boy's life slips through her fingers: life or death is a matter of timing.

To say that Swiss Cheese is a victim of circumstances, not of Courage's character, will not, however, be of much use to the actress interpreting this character. If cowardice is *less* important here than at first appears, what is *more* important? Surely it is a failure in understanding, rather than in virtue. Let me elaborate.

Though only one of Brecht's completed plays is about anyone that a university would recognize as a philosopher, several of his plays present what one might call philosophers in disguise, such as Schweyk, the philosopher of a pub in Prague, and Azdak, the philosopher of a Georgian village. To my mind, *Mother Courage is above all a philosopher*, defining the philosopher along Socratic lines as a person who likes to talk all the time and explain everything to everybody. (A simple trait in itself, one would think, yet there have been actresses and directors who wish to have all Courage's speeches shortened into mere remarks. But your philosopher never makes remarks; he always speechifies; hence such abridgement enforces a radical misinterpretation of character.) I do not mean at all that Courage is an idle or armchair philosopher whose teachings make no contact with life. On the contrary, her ideas are nothing if not a scheme of life by which, she hopes, her family is to do pretty well in a world which is doing pretty badly.

Here one sees the danger of thinking of Mother Courage as the average person. Rather, she resembles the thoughtfully ambitious modern mother of the lower-middle or better-paid working class who wants her children to win scholarships and end up in the Labour Cabinet. (Minister of Education: Kattrin. Chancellor of the Exchequer: Swiss Cheese. Minister of War: Eilif.) Has it escaped attention that if one of her children turns out a cutthroat, this is blamed on circumstances ("Otherwise, I'd have starved, smarty"), while *the other two are outright heroes?* Anyone who considers this an average family takes a far higher view of the average than is implicit in the works of Bertolt Brecht.

What is the philosophy of this philosopher? Reduced to a single proposition, it is that if you concede defeat on the larger issue, you can achieve some nice victories in smaller ways. The larger issue is whether the world can be changed. It can't. But brandy is still drunk, and can be sold. One can survive, and one can help one's children to survive by teaching each to make appropriate use of the qualities God gave him. The proposition I have just mentioned will apply to this upbringing. A child endowed with a particular talent or virtue should not pursue it to its logical end: defeat on such projects should be conceded at the outset. The child should cunningly exploit his characteristic talent for its incidental uses along the way. In this fashion the unselfishness of a Swiss Cheese or a Kattrin can be harnessed to selfishness. The result, if the philosophy works, is that while the world may shoot itself to blazes, the little Courage family, one and all, will live out its days in moderate wealth and moderate happiness. The scheme is not utopian. Just the opposite: the hope is to make optimism rational by reducing human demands to size.

The main reason it doesn't work is that the little world which Mother Courage's wisdom tries to regulate is dependent upon the big world which she has given up as a bad job. Small business is part of the big war which is part of the big business of ownership of *all* the means of production and distribution. No more than the small businessman can live in a separate economic system from the big, can the small philosopher live in a separate philosophic system from the big. *Mother Courage*, one can conclude, exposes the perennial illusions of the petit bourgeois scheme of things. This has of course often been done before in modern literature. But usually only the idealism has been exposed. Mother Courage, on the other hand, could claim to be a cynic. She has the theatre audience laughing most of the time on the score of this cynicism—by which *she* deflates illusions. Cynicism is nothing, after all, if not "realistic." What a cynical remark lays bare *has* to be the truth. Brecht makes the truth of his play the more poignant through the fact that the cynicism in it ultimately favors illusion. Mother Courage had gone to all lengths to trim her sails to the wind but even then the ship wouldn't move. So there is irony within irony (as, in Brecht's work, there usually is). Courage's cynicism can cut down the windy moralizing of the Chaplain easily enough, but only to be itself cut down by a world that cannot be comprehended even by this drastically skeptical kind of thinking.

What alternative did Mother Courage have? The only alternatives shown in the play are, on the one hand, the total brutalization of men like the Swedish Commander (and, for that matter, her own son Eilif) and, on the other hand, the martyrdom achieved by Swiss Cheese and Kattrin. Presumably, to the degree that the playwright criticizes her, he is pushing her toward the second alternative. Yet, not only would such a destiny be completely out of character, within the terms of the play itself it is not shown to be really preferable. Rather, the fruitlessness of both deaths is underlined. Why add a third?

Given her character, Mother Courage had no alternative to what she thought—or, for that matter, to the various "bad" things she did. In this case, can she be condemned? Logically, obviously not; but was Brecht logical? The printed editions of the play indicate that he made changes in his script to render Mother Courage less sympathetic. In other words, after having made her thoroughly sympathetic in his first version, Brecht later wanted her less so. One can see the sense of the changes in polemical terms: he did not wish to seem to condone behavior which is to be deplored. But to make this point, is it necessary to make Mother Courage a less good person? Personally I would think not, and I should like to see *Courage* played sometime in the Urtext of 1940 and without the later "improvements." But one should not minimize the complexity of the problem. Like many other playwrights, Brecht wanted to show a kind of inevitability combined with a degree of free will, and if it doesn't matter whether Courage is less good or more, because she is trapped by circumstances, then the play is fatalistic. I tend to think it *is* fatalistic as far as the movement of history is concerned, and that the element of hope in it springs only from Brecht's rendering of human character. Brecht himself is not satisfied with this and made changes in the hope of suggesting that things might have been different had Mother Courage acted otherwise. (What would she have done? Established Socialism in seventeenth-century Germany? One must not ask.)

Brecht has stressed, in his Notes, that Mother Courage never sees the light, never realizes what has happened, is incapable of learning. As usual, Brecht's opinions, as stated in outside comments, are more doctrinaire than those to be found embodied in the plays. It may be true that Mother Courage never sees that "small business" is a hopeless case, though to prove even this Brecht had to manufacture the evidence by inserting, later, the line at the end: "I must get back into business." She does see through her own philosophy of education. The "Song of Solomon" in Scene Nine concedes that the program announced in Scene One has failed. The manipulation of the virtues has not worked: "a man is better off without." The song is perhaps more symbolic, as well as more schematic, than most Brechtians wish Brecht to be, for there is a verse about each of her children under the form of famous men (Eilif is Caesar, Swiss Cheese is Socrates, Kattrin is St. Martin) but more important is that this is the "Song of Solomon" (from *Threepenny Opera*) and that Solomon is Courage herself:

> King Solomon was very wise
> So what's his history?
> He came to view this world with scorn
> Yes, he came to regret he ever had been born
> Declaring: all is vanity.

King Solomon was very wise
But long before the day was out
The consequence was clear, alas:
It was his wisdom brought him to this pass.
A man is better off without.

I have heard the question asked whether this conclusion was not already reached in the "Song of the Great Capitulation" in Scene Four.
Both songs are songs of defeat (Brecht's great subject) but of two different defeats. The second is defeat total and final: Courage has staked
everything on wisdom, and wisdom has ruined her and her family. The
first is the setback of "capitulation," that is of disenchantment. When
Yvette was only seventeen she was in love, and love was heaven. Soon
afterward she had learned to "fraternize behind the trees"; she had capitulated. It is perhaps hard to imagine Courage as a younger and different person from the woman we meet in the play, but in the "Song of the
Great Capitulation" we are definitely invited to imagine her as a young
woman who thought she could storm the heavens, whose faith seemed
able to move mountains.

Scene Four is one of several in this play which one can regard as the
whole play in miniature. For Brecht is not finished when he has set forth
the character of Mother Courage as one who has passed from youthful
idealism to cynical realism. For many a playwright, that would no doubt
be that, but Courage's exchange with the angry young soldier leads to
other things. We discover that Mother Courage is not a happy Machiavel-
lian, boasting of her realism as an achievement. We find that she is
deeply ashamed. And in finding this, we discover in Courage the mother
of those two roaring idealists (not to say again: martyrs) Swiss Cheese
and Kattrin. "Kiss my arse," says the soldier, and why? His bad language
had not hitherto been directed at her. But she has been kind to him only
to be cruel. If she has not broken his spirit, she has done something
equally galling: she has made clear to him how easily his spirit can be
broken. When you convert a person to the philosophy of You Can't Win,
you can hardly expect to earn his gratitude at the same time.

In the way Courage puts matters to the soldier we see how close she
came to being a truly wise woman. We also discover in this scene that,
despite the confident tone of her cynical lingo, Courage is not really sure
of herself and her little philosophy. She teaches the soldier that it is futile
to protest, but she apparently does not know this herself until she reminds herself of it, for she has come here precisely to protest. Here we
learn to recognize in Courage not only contradiction but conflict. She
knows what she has thought. She is not sure what to think.

And this is communicated by Brecht in a very bold—or, if you prefer, just poetic—manner. For while Courage does not give herself to despair until the end (and not even then for those who can take at face value her: "I must get back into business"), she had correctly foreseen the end from the beginning: the despair she gives herself to had been there from the moment of capitulation. At times it would strike her between the eyes: she is very responsive and, for example, has worked out the Marxist interpretation of religion for herself. Scene Two contains a song she had taught Eilif as a boy: it accurately predicts the manner of his death. In Scene One she predicts doom for the whole family in her elaborate pantomime of fortunetelling. And it could be said that everything is there from the start, for the first thing Mother Courage does is to try and sell things by announcing an early death for her prospective customers. The famous "Song of Mother Courage" is the most extraordinary parody of the kind of song any real *vivandière* might try to attract customers with. Mother Courage's Come and buy! is nothing other than: Come and die! In that respect, her fortunetelling is on the level, and her wisdom is valid.

Scene Four, I have been saying, is one of several in this play which one can regard as the whole play in miniature. The main purpose of the play, for Brecht, was, I think, to generate anger over what it shows. Yet Brecht realizes how pointless angry plays have been—and angry speeches outside the drama. It is said that Clifford Odets' *Waiting for Lefty* made millionaires angry for as long as it took them to get from their seats to where their chauffeurs tactfully waited for them at the end of the block. Such is the anger of the social drama in general.

There is the anger of a sudden fit, which boils up and over and is gone. And there is the anger which informs the work of long years of change. *Why* can't the world be changed? For Mother Courage, it is not from any inherent unchangeability in the world. It is because our wish to change it is not strong enough. Nor is this weakness innate. It is simply that our objection to the present world isn't as strong as it once was. What is outrageous does not outrage us as it once did. Today, it only arouses the "short rage" of Brecht's soldier—and of Courage herself—not the long one that is required. Because we—they—have capitulated.

Capitulation is not just an idea but a feeling, an agony in fact, and is located not just in the scene of the Great Capitulation but in the whole play of *Mother Courage.* Everything that happens is related to it, above all the things that are furthest away from it: namely, the deaths of Swiss Cheese and Kattrin. And if these children are what their mother made them, then their refusal to capitulate stems from her, is her own youth, her own original nature.

The ultimate achievement of an actress playing this role would be that she made us sense to what an extent Courage's children are truly hers.

THE CAUCASIAN CHALK CIRCLE

[1944]

English Version by
ERIC BENTLEY

CHARACTERS

OLD MAN	*on the right*
PEASANT WOMAN	*on the right*
YOUNG PEASANT	
A VERY YOUNG WORKER	
OLD MAN	*on the left*
PEASANT WOMAN	*on the left*
AGRICULTURIST KATO	
GIRL TRACTORIST	
WOUNDED SOLDIER	
THE DELEGATE	*from the capital*
THE SINGER	
GEORGI ABASHWILI	*the Governor*
NATELLA	*the Governor's wife*
MICHAEL	*their son*
SHALVA	*an adjutant*
ARSEN KAZBEKI	*a fat prince*
MESSENGER	*from the capital*
NIKO MIKADZE	*doctors*
MIKA LOLADZE	
SIMON SHASHAVA	*a soldier*
GRUSHA VASHNADZE	*a kitchen maid*
OLD PEASANT	*with the milk*
CORPORAL	
PRIVATE	
PEASANT	*and his wife*
LAVRENTI VASHNADZE	*Grusha's brother*
ANIKO	*his wife*
PEASANT WOMAN	*for a while Grusha's mother-in-law*

JUSSUP	*her son*
MONK	
AZDAK	*village recorder*
SHAUWA	*a policeman*
GRAND DUKE	
DOCTOR	
INVALID	
LIMPING MAN	
BLACKMAILER	
LUDOVICA	
INNKEEPER	*her father-in-law*
STABLEBOY	
POOR OLD PEASANT WOMAN	
IRAKLI	*her brother-in-law, a bandit*
THREE WEALTHY FARMERS	
ILLO SHUBOLADZE	*lawyers*
SANDRO OBOLADZE	
OLD MARRIED COUPLE	

SOLDIERS, SERVANTS, PEASANTS, BEGGARS, MUSICIANS, MERCHANTS, NOBLES, ARCHITECTS

The time and the place: After a prologue, set in 1945, we move back perhaps 1000 years.

The action of *The Caucasian Chalk Circle* centers on Nuka (or Nukha), a town in Azerbaijan. However, the capital referred to in the prologue is not Baku (capital of Soviet Azerbaijan) but Tiflis (or Tbilisi), capital of Georgia. When Azdak, later, refers to "the capital" he means Nuka itself, though whether Nuka was ever capital of *Georgia* I do not know: in what reading I have done on the subject I have only found Nuka to be the capital of a Nuka Khanate.

The word "Georgia" has not been used in this English version because of its American associations; instead, the alternative name "Grusinia" (in Russian, Gruziya) has been used.

The reasons for resettling the old Chinese story in Transcaucasia are not far to seek. The play was written when the Soviet chief of state, Joseph Stalin, was a Georgian, as was his favorite poet, cited in the Prologue, Mayakovsky. And surely there is a point in having this story acted out at the place where Europe and Asia meet, a place incomparably rich

in legend and history. Here Jason found the Golden Fleece. Here Noah's
Ark touched ground. Here the armies of both Genghis Khan and Tamer-
lane wrought havoc.

E.B.

PROLOGUE

Summer, 1945.

*Among the ruins of a war-ravaged Caucasian village the members of two
Kolkhoz villages, mostly women and older men, are sitting in a circle,
smoking and drinking wine. With them is a* DELEGATE *of the State Reconstruction Commission from Nuka.*

PEASANT WOMAN [*left pointing*] In those hills over there we
stopped three Nazi tanks, but the apple orchard was already destroyed.

OLD MAN [*right*] Our beautiful dairy farm: a ruin.

GIRL TRACTORIST – I laid the fire, Comrade.

[*Pause.*]

DELEGATE – Nuka, Azerbaijan S.S.R. Delegation received from the
goat-breeding Kolkhoz "Rosa Luxemburg." This is a collective farm
which moved eastwards on orders from the authorities at the approach
of Hitler's armies. They are now planning to return. Their delegates
have looked at the village and the land and found a lot of destruction.
[*Delegates on the right nod.*] But the neighboring fruit farm—Kolkhoz
[*to the left*] "Galinsk"—proposes to use the former grazing land of
Kolkhoz "Rosa Luxemburg" for orchards and vineyards. This land lies
in a valley where grass doesn't grow very well. As a delegate of the
Reconstruction Commission in Nuka I request that the two Kolkhoz
villages decide between themselves whether Kolkhoz "Rosa Luxemburg" shall return or not.

OLD MAN [*right*] First of all, I want to protest against the time limit
on discussion. We of Kolkhoz "Rosa Luxemburg" have spent three days
and three nights getting here. And now discussion is limited to half a
day.

WOUNDED SOLDIER [*left*] Comrade, we haven't as many villages
as we used to have. We haven't as many hands. We haven't as much
time.

2176

GIRL TRACTORIST—All pleasures have to be rationed. Tobacco is rationed, and wine. Discussion should be rationed.

OLD MAN [*right, sighing*] Death to the fascists! But I will come to the point and explain why we want our valley back. There are a great many reasons, but I'll begin with one of the simplest. Makinä Abakidze, unpack the goat cheese. [*A peasant woman from right takes from a basket an enormous cheese wrapped in a cloth. Applause and laughter.*] Help yourselves, Comrades, start in!

OLD MAN [*left, suspiciously*] Is this a way of influencing us?

OLD MAN [*right, amid laughter*] How could it be a way of influencing you, Surab, you valley-thief? Everyone knows you'll take the cheese and the valley, too. [*Laughter.*] All I expect from you is an honest answer. Do you like the cheese?

OLD MAN [*left*] The answer is: yes.

OLD MAN [*right*] Really. [*Bitterly.*] I ought to have known you know nothing about cheese.

OLD MAN [*left*] Why not? When I tell you I like it?

OLD MAN [*right*] Because you can't like it. Because it's not what it was in the old days. And why not? Because our goats don't like the new grass as they did the old. Cheese is not cheese because grass is not grass, that's the thing. Please put that in your report.

OLD MAN [*left*] But your cheese is excellent.

OLD MAN [*right*] It isn't excellent. It's just passable. The new grazing land is no good, whatever the young people may say. One can't live there. It doesn't even smell of morning in the morning.

[*Several people laugh.*]

DELEGATE—Don't mind their laughing: they understand you. Comrades, why does one love one's country? Because the bread tastes better there, the air smells better, voices sound stronger, the sky is higher, the ground is easier to walk on. Isn't that so?

OLD MAN [*right*] The valley has belonged to us from all eternity.

SOLDIER [*left*] What does *that* mean—from all eternity? Nothing belongs to anyone from all eternity. When you were young you didn't even belong to yourself. You belonged to the Kazbeki princes.

OLD MAN [*right*] Doesn't it make a difference, though, what kind of trees stand next to the house you are born in? Or what kind of neighbors you have? Doesn't that make a difference? We want to go back just to have you as our neighbors, valley-thieves! Now you can all laugh again.

OLD MAN [*left, laughing*] Then why don't you listen to what your neighbor, Kato Wachtang, our agriculturist, has to say about the valley?

PEASANT WOMAN [*right*] We've not said all we have to say about our valley. By no means. Not all the houses are destroyed. As for the dairy farm, at least the foundation wall is still standing.

DELEGATE—You can claim State support—here and there—you know that. I have suggestions here in my pocket.

PEASANT WOMAN [*right*] Comrade Specialist, we haven't come here to haggle. I can't take your cap and hand you another, and say "This one's better." The other one might *be* better, but you *like* yours better.

GIRL TRACTORIST—A piece of land is not a cap—not in our country, Comrade.

DELEGATE—Don't get mad. It's true we have to consider a piece of land as a tool to produce something useful, but it's also true that we must recognize love for a particular piece of land. As far as I'm concerned, I'd like to find out more exactly what you [*to those on the left*] want to do with the valley.

OTHERS—Yes, let Kato speak.

KATO [*rising; she's in military uniform*] Comrades, last winter, while we were fighting in these hills here as Partisans, we discussed how, once the Germans were expelled, we could build up our fruit culture to ten times its original size. I've prepared a plan for an irrigation project. By means of a cofferdam on our mountain lake, 300 hectares of unfertile land can be irrigated. Our Kolkhoz could not only cultivate more fruit, but also have vineyards. The project, however, would pay only if the disputed valley of Kolkhoz "Rosa Luxemburg" were also included. Here are the calculations.

[*She hands* DELEGATE *a briefcase.*]

OLD MAN [*right*] Write into the report that our Kolkhoz plans to start a new stud farm.

GIRL TRACTORIST—Comrades, the project was conceived during days and nights when we had to take cover in the mountains. We were often without ammunition for our half-dozen rifles. Even finding a pencil was difficult.

[*Applause from both sides.*]

OLD MAN [*right*] Our thanks to the Comrades of Kolkhoz "Galinsk" and all those who've defended our country!

[*They shake hands and embrace.*]

PEASANT WOMAN [*left*] In doing this our thought was that our soldiers—both your men and our men—should return to a still more productive homeland.

GIRL TRACTORIST—As the poet Mayakovsky said: "The home of the Soviet people shall also be the home of Reason!"

The delegates excluding the OLD MAN *have got up, and with the* DELE-GATE *specified proceed to study the Agriculturist's drawings. Exclamations such as:* "Why is the altitude of fall 22 meters?"—"This rock will have to be blown up"—"Actually, all they need is cement and dynamite" —"They force the water to come down here, that's clever!"

A VERY YOUNG WORKER [*right, to* OLD MAN, *right*] They're going to irrigate all the fields between the hills, look at that, Aleko!

OLD MAN [*right*] I'm not going to look. I knew the project would be good. I won't have a pistol pointed at me!

DELEGATE – But they only want to point a pencil at you!

[*Laughter.*]

OLD MAN [*right, gets up gloomily, and walks over to look at the drawings*] These valley-thieves know only too well that we in this country are suckers for machines and projects.

PEASANT WOMAN [*right*] Aleko Bereshwili, you have a weakness for new projects. That's well known.

DELEGATE – What about my report? May I write that you will all support the cession of your old valley in the interests of this project when you get back to your Kolkhoz?

PEASANT WOMAN [*right*] I will. What about you, Aleko?

OLD MAN [*right, bent over drawings*] I suggest that you give us copies of the drawings to take along.

PEASANT WOMAN [*right*] Then we can sit down and eat. Once he has the drawings and he's ready to discuss them, the matter is settled. I know him. And it will be the same with the rest of us.

[*Delegates laughingly embrace again.*]

OLD MAN [*left*] Long live the Kolkhoz "Rosa Luxemburg" and much luck to your horse-breeding project!

PEASANT WOMAN [*left*] In honor of the visit of the delegates from Kolkhoz "Rosa Luxemburg" and of the Specialist, the plan is that we all hear a presentation of the Singer Arkadi Tscheidse.

[*Applause.* GIRL TRACTORIST *has gone off to bring the* SINGER.]

PEASANT WOMAN [*right*] Comrades, your entertainment had better be good. It's going to cost us a valley.

PEASANT WOMAN [*left*] Arkadi Tscheidse knows about our discussion. He's promised to perform something that has a bearing on the problem.

KATO – We wired Tiflis three times. The whole thing nearly fell through at the last minute because his driver had a cold.

PEASANT WOMAN [*left*] Arkadi Tscheidse knows 21,000 lines of verse.

OLD MAN [*left*] He's hard to get. You and the Planning Commission should persuade him to come north more often, Comrade.

DELEGATE—We are more interested in economics, I'm afraid.

OLD MAN [*left, smiling*] You arrange the redistribution of vines and tractors, why not songs?

Enter the SINGER *Arkadi Tscheidse, led by* GIRL TRACTORIST. *He is a well-built man of simple manners, accompanied by* FOUR MUSICIANS *with their instruments. The artists are greeted with applause.*

GIRL TRACTORIST—This is the Comrade Specialist, Arkadi.

[*The* SINGER *greets them all.*]

DELEGATE—Honored to make your acquaintance. I heard about your songs when I was a boy at school. Will it be one of the old legends?

SINGER—A very old one. It's called "The Chalk Circle" and comes from the Chinese. But we'll do it, of course, in a changed version. Comrades, it's an honor for me to entertain you after a difficult debate. We hope you will find that the voice of the old poet also sounds well in the shadow of Soviet tractors. It may be a mistake to mix different wines, but old and new wisdom mix admirably. Now I hope we'll get something to eat before the performance begins—it would certainly help.

VOICES—Surely. Everyone into the Club House!

[*While everyone begins to move,* DELEGATE *turns to* GIRL TRACTORIST.]

DELEGATE—I hope it won't take long. I've got to get back tonight.

GIRL TRACTORIST—How long will it last, Arkadi? The Comrade Specialist must get back to Tiflis tonight.

SINGER [*casually*] It's actually two stories. An hour or two.

GIRL TRACTORIST [*confidentially*] Couldn't you make it shorter?

SINGER—No.

VOICE—Arkadi Tscheidse's performance will take place here in the square after the meal.

[*And they all go happily to eat.*]

ONE: THE NOBLE CHILD

As the lights go up, the SINGER *is seen sitting on the floor, a black sheepskin cloak round his shoulders, and a little, well-thumbed notebook in his hand. A small group of listeners—the chorus—sits with him. The manner of his recitation makes it clear that he has told his story over and over again. He mechanically fingers the pages, seldom looking at them. With appropriate gestures, he gives the signal for each scene to begin.*

SINGER – In olden times, in a bloody time,
   There ruled in a Caucasian city—
   Men called it City of the Damned—
   A Governor.
   His name was Georgi Abashwili.
   He was rich as Croesus
   He had a beautiful wife
   He had a healthy baby.
   No other governor in Grusinia
   Had so many horses in his stable
   So many beggars on his doorstep
   So many soldiers in his service
   So many petitioners in his courtyard.
   Georgi Abashwili—how shall I describe him to you?
   He enjoyed his life.
   On the morning of Easter Sunday
   The Governor and his family went to church.

At the left a large doorway, at the right an even larger gateway. BEGGARS *and* PETITIONERS *pour from the gateway, holding up thin* CHILDREN, *crutches, and petitions. They are followed by* IRONSHIRTS, *and then, expensively dressed, the* GOVERNOR'S FAMILY.

BEGGARS *and* PETITIONERS – Mercy! Mercy, Your Grace! The
   taxes are too high.
   – I lost my leg in the Persian War, where can I get . . .

– My brother is innocent, Your Grace, a misunderstanding . . .

– The child is starving in my arms!

– Our petition is for our son's discharge from the army, our last remaining son!

– Please, Your Grace, the water inspector takes bribes.

[*One servant collects the petitions. Another distributes coins from a purse. Soldiers push the crowd back, lashing at them with thick leather whips.*]

S O L D I E R – Get back! Clear the church door!

[*Behind the* GOVERNOR, *his* WIFE, *and the* ADJUTANT, *the* GOVERNOR'S CHILD *is brought through the gateway in an ornate carriage.*]

C R O W D – The baby!

– I can't see it, don't shove so hard!

– God bless the child, Your Grace!

S I N G E R [*while the crowd is driven back with whips*] For the first time on that Easter Sunday, the people saw the Governor's heir.

Two doctors never moved from the noble child, apple of the Governor's eye.

Even the mighty Prince Kazbeki bows before him at the church door.

[*The* FAT PRINCE *steps forwards and greets the* FAMILY.]

F A T   P R I N C E – Happy Easter, Natella Abashwili! What a day! When it was raining last night, I thought to myself, gloomy holidays! But this morning the sky was gay. I love a gay sky, a simple heart, Natella Abashwili. And little Michael is a governor from head to foot! Tititi!

[*He tickles the* CHILD.]

G O V E R N O R ' S   W I F E – What do you think, Arsen, at last Georgi has decided to start building the east wing. All those wretched slums are to be torn down to make room for the garden.

F A T   P R I N C E – Good news after so much bad! What's the latest on the war, Brother Georgi? [*The* GOVERNOR *indicates a lack of interest.*] Strategical retreat, I hear. Well, minor reverses are to be expected. Sometimes things go well, sometimes not. Such is war. Doesn't mean a thing, does it?

G O V E R N O R ' S   W I F E – He's coughing. Georgi, did you hear? [*She speaks sharply to the* DOCTORS, *two dignified men standing close to the little carriage.*] He's coughing!

F I R S T   D O C T O R [*to the* SECOND] May I remind you, Niko Mikadze, that I was against the lukewarm bath? [*To the* GOVERNOR'S WIFE.] There's been a little error over warming the bath water, Your Grace.

S E C O N D   D O C T O R [*equally polite*] Mika Loladze, I'm afraid I can't agree with you. The temperature of the bath water was exactly what our great, beloved Mishiko Oboladze prescribed. More likely a slight draft during the night, Your Grace.

GOVERNOR'S WIFE – But do pay more attention to him. He looks feverish, Georgi.

FIRST DOCTOR [*bending over the* CHILD] No cause for alarm, Your Grace. The bath water will be warmer. It won't occur again.

SECOND DOCTOR [*with a venomous glance at the* FIRST] I won't forget that, my dear Mika Loladze. No cause for concern, Your Grace.

FAT PRINCE – Well, well, well! I always say: "A pain in my liver? Then the doctor gets fifty strokes on the soles of his feet." We live in a decadent age. In the old days one said: "Off with his head!"

GOVERNOR'S WIFE – Let's go into church. Very likely it's the draft here.

The procession of FAMILY *and* SERVANTS *turns into the doorway. The* FAT PRINCE *follows, but the* GOVERNOR *is kept back by the* ADJUTANT, *a handsome young man. When the crowd of* PETITIONERS *has been driven off, a young dust-stained* RIDER, *his arm in a sling, remains behind.*

ADJUTANT [*pointing at the* RIDER, *who steps forward*] Won't you hear the messenger from the capital, Your Excellency? He arrived this morning. With confidential papers.

GOVERNOR – Not before Service, Shalva. But did you hear Brother Kazbeki wish me a happy Easter? Which is all very well, but I don't believe it did rain last night.

ADJUTANT [*nodding*] We must investigate.

GOVERNOR – Yes, at once. Tomorrow.

They pass through the doorway. The RIDER, *who has waited in vain for an audience, turns sharply round and, muttering a curse, goes off. Only one of the palace guards—*SIMON SHASHAVA—*remains at the door.*

SINGER – The city is still.
Pigeons strut in the church square.
A soldier of the Palace Guard
Is joking with a kitchen maid
As she comes up from the river with a bundle.
[*A girl—*GRUSHA VASHNADZE—*comes through the gateway with a bundle
made of large green leaves under her arm.*]

SIMON – What, the young lady is not in church? Shirking?

GRUSHA – I was dressed to go. But they needed another goose for the banquet. And they asked me to get it. I know about geese.

SIMON – A goose? [*He feigns suspicion.*] I'd like to see that goose.

[GRUSHA *does not understand.*] One must be on one's guard with women. "I only went for a fish," they tell you, but it turns out to be something else.

GRUSHA [*walking resolutely toward him and showing him the goose*] There! If it isn't a fifteen-pound goose stuffed full of corn, I'll eat the feathers.

SIMON — A queen of a goose! The Governor himself will eat it. So the young lady has been down to the river again?

GRUSHA — Yes, at the poultry farm.

SIMON — Really? At the poultry farm, down by the river . . . not higher up maybe? Near those willows?

GRUSHA — I only go to the willows to wash the linen.

SIMON [*insinuatingly*] Exactly.

GRUSHA — Exactly what?

SIMON [*winking*] Exactly that.

GRUSHA — Why shouldn't I wash the linen by the willows?

SIMON [*with exaggerated laughter*] "Why shouldn't I wash the linen by the willows!" That's good, really good!

GRUSHA — I don't understand the soldier. What's so good about it?

SIMON [*slyly*] "If something I know someone learns, she'll grow hot and cold by turns!"

GRUSHA — I don't know what I could learn about those willows.

SIMON — Not even if there was a bush opposite? That one could see everything from? Everything that goes on there when a certain person is—"washing linen"?

GRUSHA — What does go on? Won't the soldier say what he means and have done?

SIMON — Something goes on. Something can be seen.

GRUSHA — Could the soldier mean I dip my toes in the water when it's hot? There's nothing else.

SIMON — There's more. Your toes. And more.

GRUSHA — More what? At most my foot?

SIMON — Your foot. And a little more.

[*He laughs heartily.*]

GRUSHA [*angrily*] Simon Shashava, you ought to be ashamed of yourself! To sit in a bush on a hot day and wait till a girl comes and dips her legs in the river! And I bet you bring a friend along too!

[*She runs off.*]

SIMON [*shouting after her*] I didn't bring any friend along!

[*As the* SINGER *resumes his tale, the* SOLDIER *steps into the doorway as though to listen to the service.*]

SINGER — The city lies still

But why are there armed men?
The Governor's palace is at peace
But why is it a fortress?
And the Governor returned to his palace
And the fortress was a trap
And the goose was plucked and roasted
But the goose was not eaten this time
And noon was no longer the hour to eat:
Noon was the hour to die.

From the doorway at the left the FAT PRINCE *quickly appears, stands still, looks around. Before the gateway at the right two* IRONSHIRTS *are squatting and playing dice. The* FAT PRINCE *sees them, walks slowly past, making a sign to them. They rise: one goes through the gateway, the other goes off at the right. Muffled voices are heard from various directions in the rear: "To your posts!" The palace is surrounded. The* FAT PRINCE *quickly goes off. Church bells in the distance. Enter, through the doorway, the Governor's family and procession, returning from church.*

GOVERNOR'S WIFE [*passing the* ADJUTANT] It's impossible to live in such a slum. But Georgi, of course, will only build for his little Michael. Never for me! Michael is all! All for Michael!

The procession turns into the gateway. Again the ADJUTANT *lingers behind. He waits. Enter the wounded* RIDER *from the doorway. Two* IRONSHIRTS *of the Palace Guard have taken up positions by the gateway.*

ADJUTANT [*to the* RIDER] The Governor does not wish to receive military news before dinner—especially if it's depressing, as I assume. In the afternoon His Excellency will confer with prominent architects. They're coming to dinner too. And here they are! [*Enter three gentlemen through the doorway.*] Go to the kitchen and eat, my friend. [*As the* RIDER *goes, the* ADJUTANT *greets the* ARCHITECTS.] Gentlemen, His Excellency expects you at dinner. He will devote all his time to you and your great new plans. Come!
ONE OF THE ARCHITECTS—We marvel that His Excellency intends to build. There are disquieting rumors that the war in Persia has taken a turn for the worse.
ADJUTANT—All the more reason to build! There's nothing to those rumors anyway. Persia is a long way off, and the garrison here would let itself be hacked to bits for its Governor. [*Noise from the palace.*

Bertolt Brecht

The shrill scream of a woman. Someone is shouting orders. Dumb-founded, the ADJUTANT *moves toward the gateway. An* IRONSHIRT *steps out, points his lance at him.*] What's this? Put down that lance, you dog.

ONE OF THE ARCHITECTS—It's the Princes! Don't you know the Princes met last night in the capital? And they're against the Grand Duke and his Governors? Gentlemen, we'd better make ourselves scarce.

[*They rush off. The* ADJUTANT *remains helplessly behind.*]

ADJUTANT [*furiously to the Palace Guard*] Down with those lances! Don't you see the Governor's life is threatened?

The IRONSHIRTS *of the Palace Guard refuse to obey. They stare coldly and indifferently at the* ADJUTANT *and follow the next events without interest.*

SINGER—O blindness of the great!
They go their way like gods,
Great over bent backs,
Sure of hired fists,
Trusting in the power
Which has lasted so long.
But long is not forever.
O change from age to age!
Thou hope of the people!

[*Enter the* GOVERNOR, *through the gateway, between two* SOLDIERS *armed to the teeth. He is in chains. His face is gray.*]

Up, great sir, deign to walk upright!
From your palace the eyes of many foes follow you!
And now you don't need an architect, a carpenter will do.
You won't be moving into a new palace
But into a little hole in the ground.
Look about you once more, blind man!

[*The arrested man looks round.*]

Does all you had please you?
Between the Easter Mass and the Easter meal
You are walking to a place whence no one returns.

[*The* GOVERNOR *is led off. A horn sounds an alarm. Noise behind the gateway.*]

When the house of a great one collapses
Many little ones are slain.

Those who had no share in the *good* fortunes of the mighty
Often have a share in their *misfortunes.*
The plunging wagon
Drags the sweating oxen down with it
Into the abyss.

[*The* SERVANTS *come rushing through the gateway in panic.*]

SERVANTS [*among themselves*] – The baskets!

– Take them all into the third courtyard! Food for five days!

– The mistress has fainted! Someone must carry her down.

– She must get away.

– What about us? We'll be slaughtered like chickens, as always.

– Goodness, what'll happen? There's bloodshed already in the city, they say.

– Nonsense, the Governor has just been asked to appear at a Princes' meeting. All very correct. Everything'll be ironed out. I heard this on the best authority . . .

[*The two* DOCTORS *rush into the courtyard.*]

FIRST DOCTOR [*trying to restrain the other*] Niko Mikadze, it is your duty as a doctor to attend Natella Abashwili.

SECOND DOCTOR – My duty! It's yours!

FIRST DOCTOR – Whose turn is it to look after the child today, Niko Mikadze, yours or mine?

SECOND DOCTOR – Do you really think, Mika Loladze, I'm going to stay a minute longer in this accursed house on that little brat's account? [*They start fighting. All one hears is:* "You neglect your duty!" *and* "Duty, my foot!" *Then the* SECOND DOCTOR *knocks the* FIRST *down.*] Go to hell!

[*Exit.*]

[*Enter the soldier,* SIMON SHASHAVA. *He searches in the crowd for* GRUSHA.]

SIMON – Grusha! There you are at last! What are you going to do?

GRUSHA – Nothing. If worst comes to worst, I've a brother in the mountains. How about you?

SIMON – Forget about me. [*Formally again.*] Grusha Vashnadze, your wish to know my plans fills me with satisfaction. I've been ordered to accompany Madam Abashwili as her guard.

GRUSHA – But hasn't the Palace Guard mutinied?

SIMON [*seriously*] That's a fact.

GRUSHA – Isn't it dangerous to go with her?

SIMON – In Tiflis, they say: Isn't the stabbing dangerous for the knife?

GRUSHA – You're not a knife, you're a man, Simon Shashava, what has that woman to do with you?

SIMON—That woman has nothing to do with me. I have my orders, and I go.

GRUSHA—The soldier is pigheaded: he is running into danger for nothing—nothing at all. I must get into the third courtyard, I'm in a hurry.

SIMON—Since we're both in a hurry we shouldn't quarrel. You need time for a good quarrel. May I ask if the young lady still has parents?

GRUSHA—No, just a brother.

SIMON—As time is short—my second question is this: Is the young lady as healthy as a fish in water?

GRUSHA—I may have a pain in the right shoulder once in a while. Otherwise I'm strong enough for my job. No one has complained. So far.

SIMON—That's well known. When it's Easter Sunday, and the question arises who'll run for the goose all the same, she'll be the one. My third question is this: Is the young lady impatient? Does she want apples in winter?

GRUSHA—Impatient? No. But if a man goes to war without any reason and then no message comes—that's bad.

SIMON—A message will come. And now my final question . . .

GRUSHA—Simon Shashava, I must get to the third courtyard at once. My answer is yes.

SIMON [*very embarrassed*] Haste, they say, is the wind that blows down the scaffolding. But they also say: The rich don't know what haste is. I'm from . . .

GRUSHA—Kutsk . . .

SIMON—The young lady has been inquiring about me? I'm healthy, I have no dependents, I make ten piasters a month, as paymaster twenty piasters, and I'm asking—very sincerely—for your hand.

GRUSHA—Simon Shashava, it suits me well.

SIMON [*taking from his neck a thin chain with a little cross on it*] My mother gave me this cross, Grusha Vashnadze. The chain is silver. Please wear it.

GRUSHA—Many thanks, Simon.

SIMON [*hangs it round her neck*] It would be better to go to the third courtyard now. Or there'll be difficulties. Anyway, I must harness the horses. The young lady will understand?

GRUSHA—Yes, Simon.

[*They stand undecided.*]

SIMON—I'll just take the mistress to the troops that have stayed loyal. When the war's over, I'll be back. In two weeks. Or three. I hope my intended won't get tired, awaiting my return.

GRUSHA—Simon Shashava, I shall wait for you.

Go calmly into battle, soldier
The bloody battle, the bitter battle
From which not everyone returns:
When you return I shall be there.
I shall be waiting for you under the green elm
I shall be waiting for you under the bare elm
I shall wait until the last soldier has returned
And longer
When you come back from the battle
No boots will stand at my door
The pillow beside mine will be empty
And my mouth will be unkissed.
When you return, when you return
You will be able to say: It is just as it was.

SIMON – I thank you, Grusha Vashnadze. And good-bye!

[*He bows low before her. She does the same before him. Then she runs quickly off without looking round. Enter the* ADJUTANT *from the gateway.*]

ADJUTANT [*harshly*] Harness the horses to the carriage! Don't stand there doing nothing, scum!

SIMON SHASHAVA *stands to attention and goes off. Two* SERVANTS *crowd from the gateway, bent low under huge trunks. Behind them, supported by her women, stumbles* NATELLA ABASHWILI. *She is followed by a* WOMAN *carrying the* CHILD.

GOVERNOR'S WIFE – I hardly know if my head's still on. Where's Michael? Don't hold him so clumsily. Pile the trunks onto the carriage. No news from the city, Shalva?

ADJUTANT – None. All's quiet so far, but there's not a minute to lose. No room for all those trunks in the carriage. Pick out what you need.
[*Exit quickly.*]

GOVERNOR'S WIFE – Only essentials! Quick, open the trunks! I'll tell you what I need. [*The trunks are lowered and opened. She points at some brocade dresses.*] The green one! And, of course, the one with the fur trimming. Where are Niko Mikadze and Mika Loladze? I've suddenly got the most terrible migraine again. It always starts in the temples. [*Enter* GRUSHA.] Taking your time, eh? Go and get the hot water bottles this minute! [GRUSHA *runs off, returns later with hot water bottles; the* GOVERNOR'S WIFE *orders her about by signs.*] Don't tear the sleeves.

A YOUNG WOMAN – Pardon, madam, no harm has come to the dress.

GOVERNOR'S WIFE – Because I stopped you. I've been watching you

for a long time. Nothing in your head but making eyes at Shalva
Tzereteli. I'll kill you, you bitch!

[*She beats the* YOUNG WOMAN.]

ADJUTANT [*appearing in the gateway*] Please make haste, Natella
Abashwili. Firing has broken out in the city.

[*Exit.*]

GOVERNOR'S WIFE [*letting go of the* YOUNG WOMAN] Oh dear, do
you think they'll lay hands on us? Why should they? Why? [*She herself
begins to rummage in the trunks.*] How's Michael? Asleep?

WOMAN WITH THE CHILD—Yes, madam.

GOVERNOR'S WIFE—Then put him down a moment and get my
little saffron-colored boots from the bedroom. I need them for the
green dress. [*The* WOMAN *puts down the* CHILD *and goes off.*] Just look
how these things have been packed! No love! No understanding! If
you don't give them every order yourself . . . At such moments you
realize what kind of servants you have! They gorge themselves at your
expense, and never a word of gratitude! I'll remember this.

ADJUTANT [*entering, very excited*] Natella, you must leave at once!

GOVERNOR'S WIFE—Why? I've got to take this silver dress—it cost
a thousand piasters. And that one there, and where's the wine-colored
one?

ADJUTANT [*trying to pull her away*] Riots have broken out! We
must leave at once. Where's the baby?

GOVERNOR'S WIFE [*calling to the* YOUNG WOMAN *who was holding
the baby*] Maro, get the baby ready! Where on earth are you?

ADJUTANT [*leaving*] We'll probably have to leave the carriage behind and go ahead on horseback.

The GOVERNOR'S WIFE *rummages again among her dresses, throws some
onto the heap of chosen clothes, then takes them off again. Noises, drums
are heard. The* YOUNG WOMAN *who was beaten creeps away. The sky begins to grow red.*

GOVERNOR'S WIFE [*rummaging desperately*] I simply cannot find
the wine-colored dress. Take the whole pile to the carriage. Where's
Asja? And why hasn't Maro come back? Have you all gone crazy?

ADJUTANT [*returning*] Quick! Quick!

GOVERNOR'S WIFE [*to the* FIRST WOMAN] Run! Just throw them
into the carriage!

ADJUTANT—We're not taking the carriage. And if you don't come
now, I'll ride off on my own.

GOVERNOR'S WIFE [*as the* FIRST WOMAN *can't carry everything*]
Where's that bitch Asja? [*The* ADJUTANT *pulls her away.*] Maro, bring

the baby! [*To the* FIRST WOMAN.] Go and look for Masha. No, first take the dresses to the carriage. Such nonsense! I wouldn't dream of going on horseback!

Turning round, she sees the red sky, and starts back rigid. The fire burns. She is pulled out by the ADJUTANT. *Shaking, the* FIRST WOMAN *follows with the dresses.*

MARO [*from the doorway with the boots*] Madam! [*She sees the trunks and dresses and runs toward the* CHILD, *picks it up, and holds it a moment.*] They left it behind, the beasts. [*She hands it to* GRUSHA.] Hold it a moment.

[*She runs off, following the* GOVERNOR'S WIFE.]

[*Enter* SERVANTS *from the gateway.*]

COOK – Well, so they've actually gone. Without the food wagons, and not a minute too early. It's time for us to clear out.

GROOM – This'll be an unhealthy neighborhood for quite a while. [*To one of the* WOMEN.] Suliko, take a few blankets and wait for me in the foal stables.

GRUSHA – What have they done with the Governor?

GROOM [*gesturing throat cutting*] Fffft.

A FAT WOMAN [*seeing the gesture and becoming hysterical*] Oh dear, oh dear, oh dear, oh dear! Our master Georgi Abashwili! A picture of health he was, at the morning Mass—and now! Oh, take me away, we're all lost, we must die in sin like our master, Georgi Abashwili!

OTHER WOMAN [*soothing her*] Calm down, Nina! You'll be taken to safety. You've never hurt a fly.

FAT WOMAN [*being led out*] Oh dear, oh dear, oh dear! Quick! Let's all get out before they come, before they come!

A YOUNG WOMAN – Nina takes it more to heart than the mistress, that's a fact. They even have to have their weeping done for them.

COOK – We'd better get out, all of us.

ANOTHER WOMAN [*glancing back*] That must be the East Gate burning.

YOUNG WOMAN [*seeing the* CHILD *in* GRUSHA's *arms*] The baby! What are you doing with it?

GRUSHA – It got left behind.

YOUNG WOMAN – She simply left it there. Michael, who was kept out of all the drafts!

[*The* SERVANTS *gather round the* CHILD.]

2191

GRUSHA – He's waking up.

GROOM – Better put him down, I tell you. I'd rather not think what'd happen to anybody who was found with that baby.

COOK – That's right. Once they get started, they'll kill each other off, whole families at a time. Let's go.

[*Exeunt all but* GRUSHA, *with the* CHILD *on her arm, and* TWO WOMEN.]

TWO WOMEN – Didn't you hear? Better put him down.

GRUSHA – The nurse asked me to hold him a moment.

OLDER WOMAN – She's not coming back, you simpleton.

YOUNGER WOMAN – Keep your hands off it.

OLDER WOMAN [*amiably*] Grusha, you're a good soul, but you're not very bright, and you know it. I tell you, if he had the plague he couldn't be more dangerous.

GRUSHA [*stubbornly*] He hasn't got the plague. He looks at me! He's human!

OLDER WOMAN – Don't look at *him*. You're a fool—the kind that always gets put upon. A person need only say, "Run for the salad, you have the longest legs," and you run. My husband has an ox cart—you can come with us if you hurry! Lord, by now the whole neighborhood must be in flames.

Both women leave, sighing. After some hesitation, GRUSHA *puts the sleeping* CHILD *down, looks at it for a moment, then takes a brocade blanket from the heap of clothes and covers it. Then both women return, dragging bundles.* GRUSHA *starts guiltily away from the* CHILD *and walks a few steps to one side.*

YOUNGER WOMAN – Haven't you packed anything yet? There isn't much time, you know. The Ironshirts will be here from the barracks.

GRUSHA – Coming!

She runs through the doorway. Both women go to the gateway and wait. The sound of horses is heard. They flee, screaming. Enter the FAT PRINCE *with drunken* IRONSHIRTS. *One of them carries the* GOVERNOR's *head on a lance.*

FAT PRINCE – Here! In the middle! [*One soldier climbs onto the other's back, takes the head, holds it tentatively over the door.*] That's not the middle. Farther to the right. That's it. What I do, my friends, I do well. [*While with hammer and nail, the soldier fastens the head to the wall by its hair.*] This morning at the church door I said to

Georgi Abashwili: "I love a gay sky." Actually, I prefer the lightning that comes out of a gay sky. Yes, indeed. It's a pity they took the brat along, though, I need him, urgently.

Exit with IRONSHIRTS *through the gateway. Trampling of horses again. Enter* GRUSHA *through the doorway looking cautiously about her. Clearly she has waited for the* IRONSHIRTS *to go. Carrying a bundle, she walks toward the gateway. At the last moment, she turns to see if the* CHILD *is still there. Catching sight of the head over the doorway, she screams. Horrified, she picks up her bundle again, and is about to leave when the* SINGER *starts to speak. She stands rooted to the spot.*

SINGER—As she was standing between courtyard and gate,
   She heard or she thought she heard a low voice calling.
   The child called to her,
   Not whining, but calling quite sensibly,
   Or so it seemed to her.
   "Woman," it said, "help me."
   And it went on, not whining, but saying quite sensibly:
   "Know, woman, he who hears not a cry for help
   But passes by with troubled ears will never hear
   The gentle call of a lover nor the blackbird at dawn
   Nor the happy sigh of the tired grape-picker as the Angelus rings."
           [*She walks a few steps toward the* CHILD *and bends over it.*]
   Hearing this she went back for one more look at the child:
   Only to sit with him for a moment or two,
   Only till someone should come,
   His mother, or anyone.
               [*Leaning on a trunk, she sits facing the* CHILD.]
   Only till she would have to leave, for the danger was too great,
   The city was full of flame and crying.
                   [*The light grows dimmer, as though
                   evening and night were coming on.*]
   Fearful is the seductive power of goodness!

GRUSHA *now settles down to watch over the* CHILD *through the night. Once, she lights a small lamp to look at it. Once, she tucks it in with a coat. From time to time she listens and looks to see whether someone is coming.*

And she sat with the child a long time,
Till evening came, till night came, till dawn came.
She sat too long, too long she saw

Bertolt Brecht

The soft breathing, the small clenched fists,
Till toward morning the seduction was complete
And she rose, and bent down and, sighing, took the child
And carried it away.
    [She does what the SINGER *says as he describes it.]*
As if it was stolen goods she picked it up.
As if she was a thief she crept away.

TWO: THE FLIGHT
INTO THE NORTHERN MOUNTAINS

SINGER – When Grusha Vashnadze left the city
  On the Grusinian highway
  On the way to the Northern Mountains
  She sang a song, she bought some milk.
CHORUS – How will this human child escape
  The bloodhounds, the trap-setters?
  Into the deserted mountains she journeyed
  Along the Grusinian highway she journeyed
  She sang a song, she bought some milk.
[GRUSHA VASHNADZE *walks on. On her back she carries the* CHILD *in a sack, in one hand is a large stick, in the other a bundle. She sings.*]

  The Song of the Four Generals

Four generals
Set out for Iran.
With the first one, war did not agree.
The second never won a victory.
For the third the weather never was right.
For the fourth the men would never fight.
Four generals
And not a single man!
Sosso Robakidse
Went marching to Iran
With him the war did so agree
He soon had won a victory.
For him the weather was always right.
For him the men would always fight.
Sosso Robakidse,
He is our man!

[A *peasant's cottage appears.*]

GRUSHA [*to the* CHILD] Noontime is meal time. Now we'll sit hopefully in the grass, while the good Grusha goes and buys a little pitcher

2195

of milk. [*She lays the* CHILD *down and knocks at the cottage door. An* OLD MAN *opens it.*] Grandfather, could I have a little pitcher of milk? And a corn cake, maybe?

OLD MAN – Milk? We have no milk. The soldiers from the city have our goats. Go to the soldiers if you want milk.

GRUSHA – But grandfather, you must have a little pitcher of milk for a baby?

OLD MAN – And for a God-bless-you, eh?

GRUSHA – Who said anything about a God-bless-you? [*She shows her purse.*] We'll pay like princes. "Head in the clouds, backside in the water." [*The peasant goes off, grumbling, for milk.*] How much for the milk?

OLD MAN – Three piasters. Milk has gone up.

GRUSHA – Three piasters for this little drop? [*Without a word the* OLD MAN *shuts the door in her face.*] Michael, did you hear that? Three piasters! We can't afford it! [*She goes back, sits down again, and gives the* CHILD *her breast.*] Suck. Think of the three piasters. There's nothing there, but you *think* you're drinking, and that's something. [*Shaking her head, she sees that the* CHILD *isn't sucking any more. She gets up, walks back to the door, and knocks again.*] Open, grandfather, we'll pay. [*Softly.*] May lightning strike you! [*When the* OLD MAN *appears.*] I thought it would be half a piaster. But the baby must be fed. How about one piaster for that little drop?

OLD MAN – Two.

GRUSHA – Don't shut the door again. [*She fishes a long time in her bag.*] Here are two piasters. The milk better be good. I still have two days' journey ahead of me. It's a murderous business you have here— and sinful, too!

OLD MAN – Kill the soldiers if you want milk.

GRUSHA [*giving the* CHILD *some milk*] This is an expensive joke. Take a sip, Michael, it's a week's pay. Around here they think we earned our money just sitting on our behinds. Oh, Michael, Michael, you're a nice little load for a girl to take on!

[*Uneasy, she gets up, puts the* CHILD *on her back, and walks on. The* OLD MAN, *grumbling, picks up the pitcher and looks after her unmoved.*]

SINGER – As Grusha Vashnadze went northward
   The Princes' Ironshirts went after her.

CHORUS – How will the barefoot girl escape the Ironshirts,
   The bloodhounds, the trap-setters?
   They hunt even by night.
   Pursuers never tire.
   Butchers sleep little.
       [*Two* IRONSHIRTS *are trudging along the highway.*]

CORPORAL – You'll never amount to anything, blockhead, your heart's not in it. Your senior officer sees this in little things. Yesterday, when I made the fat gal, yes, you grabbed her husband as I commanded, and you did kick him in the belly, at my request, but did you *enjoy* it, like a loyal Private, or were you just doing your duty? I've kept an eye on you blockhead, you're a hollow reed and a tinkling cymbal, you won't get promoted. [*They walk a while in silence.*] Don't think I've forgotten how insubordinate you are, either. Stop limping! I forbid you to limp! You limp because I sold the horses, and I sold the horses because I'd never have got that price again. You limp to show me you don't like marching. I know you. It won't help. You wait. Sing!

TWO IRONSHIRTS [*singing*] Sadly to war I went my way
Leaving my loved one at her door.
My friends will keep her honor safe
Till from the war I'm back once more.

CORPORAL – Louder!

TWO IRONSHIRTS [*singing*] When 'neath a headstone I shall be
My love a little earth will bring:
"Here rest the feet that oft would run to me
And here the arms that oft to me would cling."

[*They begin to walk again in silence.*]

CORPORAL – A good soldier has his heart and soul in it. When he receives an order, he gets a hard-on, and when he drives his lance into the enemy's guts, he comes. [*He shouts for joy.*] He lets himself be torn to bits for his superior officer, and as he lies dying he takes note that his corporal is nodding approval, and that is reward enough, it's his dearest wish. *You* won't get any nod of approval, but you'll croak all right. Christ, how'm I to get my hands on the Governor's bastard with the help of a fool like you!

[*They stay on stage behind.*]

SINGER – When Grusha Vashnadze came to the River Sirra
Flight grew too much for her, the helpless child too heavy.
In the cornfields the rosy dawn
Is cold to the sleepless one, only cold.
The gay clatter of the milk cans in the farmyard where the smoke rises
Is only a threat to the fugitive.
She who carries the child feels its weight and little more.

GRUSHA *stops in front of a farm. A fat* PEASANT WOMAN *is carrying a milk can through the door.* GRUSHA *waits until she has gone in, then approaches the house cautiously.*

GRUSHA [*to the* CHILD] Now you've wet yourself again, and you know

I've no linen. Michael, this is where we part company. It's far enough from the city. They wouldn't want you *so* much that they'd follow you all *this* way, little good-for-nothing. The peasant woman is kind, and can't you just smell the milk? So farewell, Michael, I'll forget how you kicked me in the back all night to make me walk faster. And you can forget the meager fare—it was meant well. I'd like to have kept you— your nose is so tiny—but it can't be. I'd have shown you your first rabbit, I'd have trained you to keep dry, but now I must turn around. My sweetheart the soldier might be back soon, and suppose he didn't find me? You can't ask that, can you?

She creeps up to the door and lays the CHILD *on the threshold. Then, hiding behind a tree, she waits until the* PEASANT WOMAN *opens the door and sees the bundle.*

PEASANT WOMAN—Good heavens, what's this? Husband!

PEASANT—What is it? Let me finish my soup.

PEASANT WOMAN [*to the* CHILD] Where's your mother then? Haven't you got one? It's a boy. Fine linen. He's from a good family, you can see that. And they just leave him on our doorstep. Oh, these are times!

PEASANT—If they think we're going to feed it, they're wrong. You can take it to the priest in the village. That's the best we can do.

PEASANT WOMAN—What'll the priest do with him? He needs a mother. There, he's waking up. Don't you think we could keep him, though?

PEASANT [*shouting*] No!

PEASANT WOMAN—I could lay him in the corner by the armchair. All I need is a crib. I can take him into the fields with me. See him laughing? Husband, we have a roof over our heads. We can do it. Not another word out of you!

She carries the CHILD *into the house. The* PEASANT *follows protesting.* GRUSHA *steps out from behind the tree, laughs, and hurries off in the opposite direction.*

SINGER—Why so cheerful, making for home?

CHORUS—Because the child has won new parents with a laugh,
   Because I'm rid of the little one, I'm cheerful.

SINGER—And why so sad?

CHORUS—Because I'm single and free, I'm sad
   Like someone who's been robbed

Someone who's newly poor.

> [*She walks for a short while, then meets the two* IRONSHIRTS *who point their lances at her.*]

CORPORAL—Lady, you are running straight into the arms of the Armed Forces. Where are you coming from? And when? Are you having illicit relations with the enemy? Where is he hiding? What movements is he making in your rear? How about the hills? How about the valleys? How are your stockings held in position? [GRUSHA *stands there frightened.*] Don't be scared, we always withdraw, if necessary . . . what, blockhead? I always withdraw. In that respect at least, I can be relied on. Why are you staring like that at my lance? In the field no soldier drops his lance, that's a rule. Learn it by heart, blockhead. Now, lady, where are you headed?

GRUSHA—To meet my intended, one Simon Shashava, of the Palace Guard in Nuka.

CORPORAL—Simon Shashava? Sure, I know him. He gave me the key so I could look you up once in a while. Blockhead, we are getting to be unpopular. We must make her realize we have honorable intentions. Lady, behind apparent frivolity I conceal a serious nature, so let me tell you officially: I want a child from you. [GRUSHA *utters a little scream.*] Blockhead, she understands me. Uh-huh, isn't it a sweet shock? "Then first I must take the noodles out of the oven, Officer. Then first I must change my torn shirt, Colonel." But away with jokes, away with my lance! We are looking for a baby. A baby from a good family. Have you heard of such a baby, from the city, dressed in fine linen, and suddenly turning up here?

GRUSHA—No, I haven't heard a thing.

[*Suddenly she turns round and runs back, panic-stricken. The* IRONSHIRTS *glance at each other, then follow her, cursing.*]

SINGER—Run, kind girl! The killers are coming!

Help the helpless babe, helpless girl!

And so she runs!

CHORUS—In the bloodiest times

There are kind people.

> [*As* GRUSHA *rushes into the cottage, the* PEASANT WOMAN *is bending over the* CHILD's *crib.*]

GRUSHA—Hide him. Quick! The Ironshirts are coming! I laid him on your doorstep. But he isn't mine. He's from a good family.

PEASANT WOMAN—Who's coming? What Ironshirts?

GRUSHA—Don't ask questions. The Ironshirts that are looking for it.

PEASANT WOMAN—They've no business in my house. But I must have a little talk with you, it seems.

GRUSHA—Take off the fine linen. It'll give us away.

PEASANT WOMAN—Linen, my foot! In this house I make the decisions! "*You* can't vomit in *my* room!" Why did you abandon it? It's a sin.

GRUSHA [*looking out of the window*] Look, they're coming out from behind those trees! I shouldn't have run away, it made them angry. Oh, what shall I do?

PEASANT WOMAN [*looking out of the window and suddenly starting with fear*] Gracious! Ironshirts!

GRUSHA—They're after the baby.

PEASANT WOMAN—Suppose they come in!

GRUSHA—You mustn't give him to them. Say he's yours.

PEASANT WOMAN—Yes.

GRUSHA—They'll run him through if you hand him over.

PEASANT WOMAN—But suppose they ask for it? The silver for the harvest is in the house.

GRUSHA—If you let them have him, they'll run him through, right here in this room! You've got to say he's yours!

PEASANT WOMAN—Yes. But what if they don't believe me?

GRUSHA—You must be firm.

PEASANT WOMAN—They'll burn the roof over our heads.

GRUSHA—That's why you must say he's yours. His name's Michael. But I shouldn't have told you. [*The* PEASANT WOMAN *nods.*] Don't nod like that. And don't tremble—they'll notice.

PEASANT WOMAN—Yes.

GRUSHA—And stop saying yes, I can't stand it. [*She shakes the* WOMAN.] Don't you have any children?

PEASANT WOMAN [*muttering*] He's in the war.

GRUSHA—Then maybe *he's* an Ironshirt? Do you want *him* to run children through with a lance? You'd bawl him out. "No fooling with lances in my house!" you'd shout, "is that what I've reared you for? Wash your neck before you speak to your mother!"

PEASANT WOMAN—That's true, he couldn't get away with anything around here!

GRUSHA—So you'll say he's yours?

PEASANT WOMAN—Yes.

GRUSHA—Look! They're coming!

[*There is a knocking at the door. The women don't answer. Enter* IRONSHIRTS. *The* PEASANT WOMAN *bows low.*]

CORPORAL—Well, here she is. What did I tell you? What a nose I have! I *smelt* her. Lady, I have a question for you. Why did you run away? What did you think I would do to you? I'll bet it was something unchaste. Confess!

GRUSHA [*while the* PEASANT WOMAN *bows again and again*] I'd left some milk on the stove, and I suddenly remembered it.

CORPORAL – Or maybe you imagined I looked at you unchastely? Like there could be something between us? A carnal glance, know what I mean?

GRUSHA – I didn't see it.

CORPORAL – But it's possible, huh? You admit that much. After all, I might be a pig. I'll be frank with you: I could think of all sorts of things if we were alone. [*To the* PEASANT WOMAN.] Shouldn't you be busy in the yard? Feeding the hens?

PEASANT WOMAN [*falling suddenly to her knees*] Soldier, I didn't know a thing about it. Please don't burn the roof over our heads.

CORPORAL – What are you talking about?

PEASANT WOMAN – I had nothing to do with it. She left it on my doorstep, I swear it!

CORPORAL [*suddenly seeing the* CHILD *and whistling*] Ah, so there's a little something in the crib! Blockhead, I smell a thousand piasters. Take the old girl outside and hold on to her. It looks like I have a little cross-examining to do. [*The* PEASANT WOMAN *lets herself be led out by the* PRIVATE, *without a word*.] So, you've *got* the child I wanted from you!

> [*He walks toward the crib.*]

GRUSHA – Officer, he's mine. He's not the one you're after.

CORPORAL – I'll just take a look.

> [*He bends over the crib.*]
> [GRUSHA *looks round in despair.*]

GRUSHA – He's mine! He's mine!

CORPORAL – Fine linen!

GRUSHA *dashes at him to pull him away. He throws her off and again bends over the crib. Again looking round in despair, she sees a log of wood, seizes it, and hits the* CORPORAL *over the head from behind. The* CORPORAL *collapses. She quickly picks up the* CHILD *and rushes off.*

SINGER – And in her flight from the Ironshirts
   After twenty-two days of journeying
   At the foot of the Janga-Tau Glacier
   Grusha Vashnadze decided to adopt the child.

CHORUS – The helpless girl adopted the helpless child.

> [GRUSHA *squats over a half-frozen stream to get
>   the* CHILD *water in the hollow of her hand.*]

GRUSHA – Since no one else will take you, son,
   I must take you.

Since no one else will take you, son,
You must take me.
O black day in a lean, lean year,
The trip was long, the milk was dear,
My legs are tired, my feet are sore:
But I wouldn't be without you any more.
I'll throw your silken shirt away
And wrap you in rags and tatters.
I'll wash you, son, and christen you in glacier water.
We'll see it through together.

    [*She has taken off the child's fine linen and wrapped it in a rag.*]

S I N G E R – When Grusha Vashnadze
Pursued by the Ironshirts
Came to the bridge on the glacier
Leading to the villages of the Eastern Slope
She sang the Song of the Rotten Bridge
And risked two lives.

A wind has risen. The bridge on the glacier is visible in the dark. One rope is broken and half the bridge is hanging down the abyss. MERCHANTS, *two men and a woman, stand undecided before the bridge as* GRUSHA *and the* CHILD *arrive. One man is trying to catch the hanging rope with a stick.*

F I R S T M A N – Take your time, young woman. You won't get across here anyway.

G R U S H A – But I *have* to get the baby to the east side. To my brother's place.

M E R C H A N T W O M A N – Have to? How d'you mean, "have to"? I have to get there, too—because I have to buy carpets in Atum—carpets a woman had to sell because her husband had to die. But can *I* do what I have to? Can she? Andrei's been fishing for that rope for hours. And I ask you, how are we going to fasten it, even if he gets it up?

F I R S T M A N [*listening*] Hush, I think I hear something.

G R U S H A – The bridge isn't quite rotted through. I think I'll try it.

M E R C H A N T W O M A N – I wouldn't—if the devil himself were after me. It's suicide.

F I R S T M A N [*shouting*] Hi!

G R U S H A – Don't shout! [*To the* MERCHANT WOMAN.] Tell him not to shout.

F I R S T M A N – But there's someone down there calling. Maybe they've lost their way.

MERCHANT WOMAN—Why shouldn't he shout? Is there something funny about you? Are they after you?

GRUSHA—All right, I'll tell. The Ironshirts are after me. I knocked one down.

SECOND MAN—Hide our merchandise!

[*The* WOMAN *hides a sack behind a rock.*]

FIRST MAN—Why didn't you say so right away? [*To the others.*] If they catch her they'll make mincemeat out of her!

GRUSHA—Get out of my way. I've got to cross that bridge.

SECOND MAN—You can't. The precipice is two thousand feet deep.

FIRST MAN—Even with the rope it'd be no use. We could hold it up with our hands. But then we'd have to do the same for the Ironshirts.

GRUSHA—Go away.

[*There are calls from the distance:* "Hi, up there!"]

MERCHANT WOMAN—They're getting near. But you can't take the child on that bridge. It's sure to break. And look!

[GRUSHA *looks down into the abyss. The* IRONSHIRTS *are heard calling again from below.*]

SECOND MAN—Two thousand feet!

GRUSHA—But those men are worse.

FIRST MAN—You can't do it. Think of the baby. Risk your life but not a child's.

SECOND MAN—With the child she's that much heavier!

MERCHANT WOMAN—Maybe she's *really* got to get across. Give *me* the baby. I'll hide it. Cross the bridge alone!

GRUSHA—I won't. We belong together. [*To the* CHILD.] "Live together, die together."

[*She sings.*]

The Song of the Rotten Bridge

Deep is the abyss, son,
I see the weak bridge sway
But it's not for us, son,
To choose the way.

The way I know
Is the one you must tread,
And all you will eat
Is my bit of bread.

Of every four pieces
You shall have three.
Would that I knew
How big they will be!

Bertolt Brecht

Get out of my way, I'll try it without the rope.
MERCHANT WOMAN–You are tempting God!
[*There are shouts from below.*]
GRUSHA–Please, throw that stick away, or they'll get the rope and
follow me.

Pressing the CHILD *to her, she steps onto the swaying bridge. The* MER-
CHANT WOMAN *screams when it looks as though the bridge is about to
collapse. But* GRUSHA *walks on and reaches the far side.*

FIRST MAN–She made it!
MERCHANT WOMAN [*who has fallen on her knees and begun to
pray, angrily*] I still think it was a sin.
[*The* IRONSHIRTS *appear; the* CORPORAL's *head is bandaged.*]
CORPORAL–Seen a woman with a child?
FIRST MAN [*while the* SECOND MAN *throws the stick into the abyss*]
Yes, there! But the bridge won't carry you!
CORPORAL–You'll pay for this, blockhead!
[GRUSHA, *from the far bank, laughs and shows the* CHILD
to the IRONSHIRTS. *She walks on. The wind blows.*]
GRUSHA [*turning to the* CHILD] You mustn't be afraid of the wind.
He's a poor thing too. He has to push the clouds along and he gets quite
cold doing it. [*Snow starts falling.*] And the snow isn't so bad, either,
Michael. It covers the little fir trees so they won't die in winter. Let
me sing you a little song.
[*She sings.*]

The Song of the Child

Your father is a bandit
A harlot the mother who bore you.
Yet honorable men
Shall kneel down before you.
Food to the baby horses
The tiger's son will take.
The mothers will get milk
From the son of the snake.

THREE: IN THE NORTHERN MOUNTAINS

SINGER – Seven days the sister, Grusha Vashnadze,
  Journeyed across the glacier
  And down the slopes she journeyed.
  "When I enter my brother's house," she thought,
  "He will rise and embrace me."
  "Is that you, sister?" he will say,
  "I have long expected you.
  This is my dear wife,
  And this is my farm, come to me by marriage,
  With eleven horses and thirty-one cows. Sit down.
  Sit down with your child at our table and eat."
  The brother's house was in a lovely valley.
  When the sister came to the brother,
  She was ill from walking.
  The brother rose from the table.

A fat peasant couple rise from the table. LAVRENTI VASHNADZE *still has a napkin round his neck, as* GRUSHA, *pale and supported by a* SERVANT, *enters with the* CHILD.

LAVRENTI – Where've you come from, Grusha?
GRUSHA [*feebly*] Across the Janga-Tu Pass, Lavrenti.
SERVANT – I found her in front of the hay barn. She has a baby with her.
SISTER-IN-LAW – Go and groom the mare.
                                    [*Exit the* SERVANT.]
LAVRENTI – This is my wife Aniko.
SISTER-IN-LAW – I thought you were in service in Nuka.
GRUSHA [*barely able to stand*] Yes, I was.
SISTER-IN-LAW – Wasn't it a good job? We were told it was.
GRUSHA – The Governor got killed.
LAVRENTI – Yes, we heard there were riots. Your aunt told us. Remember, Aniko?
SISTER-IN-LAW – Here with us, it's very quiet. City people always

2205

want something going on. [*She walks toward the door, calling.*] Sosso, Sosso, don't take the cake out of the oven yet, d'you hear? Where on earth are you?

[*Exit, calling.*]

LAVRENTI [*quietly, quickly*] Is there a father? [*As she shakes her head.*] I thought not. We must think up something. She's religious.

SISTER-IN-LAW [*returning*] Those servants! [*To* GRUSHA.] You have a child.

GRUSHA—It's mine.

[*She collapses.* LAVRENTI *rushes to her assistance.*]

SISTER-IN-LAW—Heavens, she's ill—what are we going to do?

LAVRENTI [*escorting her to a bench near the stove*] Sit down, sit. I think it's just weakness, Aniko.

SISTER-IN-LAW—As long as it's not scarlet fever!

LAVRENTI—She'd have spots if it was. It's only weakness. Don't worry, Aniko. [*To* GRUSHA.] Better, sitting down?

SISTER-IN-LAW—Is the child hers?

GRUSHA—Yes, mine.

LAVRENTI—She's on her way to her husband.

SISTER-IN-LAW—I see. Your meat's getting cold. [LAVRENTI *sits down and begins to eat.*] Cold food's not good for you, the fat mustn't get cold, you know your stomach's your weak spot. [*To* GRUSHA.] If your husband's not in the city, where is he?

LAVRENTI—She got married on the other side of the mountain, she says.

SISTER-IN-LAW—On the other side of the mountain. I see.

[*She also sits down to eat.*]

GRUSHA—I think I should lie down somewhere, Lavrenti.

SISTER-IN-LAW—If it's consumption we'll all get it. [*She goes on cross-examining her.*] Has your husband got a farm?

GRUSHA—He's a soldier.

LAVRENTI—But he's coming into a farm—a small one—from his father.

SISTER-IN-LAW—Isn't he in the war? Why not?

GRUSHA [*with effort*] Yes, he's in the war.

SISTER-IN-LAW—Then why d'you want to go to the farm?

LAVRENTI—When he comes back from the war, he'll return to his farm.

SISTER-IN-LAW—But you're going there now?

LAVRENTI—Yes, to wait for him.

SISTER-IN-LAW [*calling shrilly*] Sosso, the cake!

GRUSHA [*murmuring feverishly*] A farm—a soldier—waiting—sit down, eat.

SISTER-IN-LAW—It's scarlet fever.

GRUSHA [*starting up*] Yes, he's got a farm!

LAVRENTI—I think it's just weakness, Aniko. Would you look after the cake yourself, dear?

SISTER-IN-LAW—But when will he come back if war's broken out again as people say? [*She waddles off, shouting.*] Sosso! Where on earth are you? Sosso!

LAVRENTI [*getting up quickly and going to* GRUSHA] You'll get a bed in a minute. She has a good heart. But wait till after supper.

GRUSHA [*holding out the* CHILD *to him*] Take him.

LAVRENTI [*taking it and looking around*] But you can't stay here long with the child. She's religious, you see.

[GRUSHA *collapses.* LAVRENTI *catches her.*]

SINGER—The sister was so ill,
The cowardly brother had to give her shelter.
Summer departed, winter came.
The winter was long, the winter was short.
People mustn't know anything.
Rats mustn't bite.
Spring mustn't come.

[GRUSHA *sits over the weaving loom in a workroom. She and the* CHILD, *who is squatting on the floor, are wrapped in blankets. She sings.*]

The Song of the Center

And the lover started to leave
And his betrothed ran pleading after him
Pleading and weeping, weeping and teaching:
"Dearest mine, dearest mine
When you go to war as now you do
When you fight the foe as soon you will
Don't lead with the front line
And don't push with the rear line
At the front is red fire
In the rear is red smoke
Stay in the war's center
Stay near the standard bearer
The first always die
The last are also hit
Those in the center come home."

Michael, we must be clever. If we make ourselves as small as cockroaches, the sister-in-law will forget we're in the house, and then we can stay till the snow melts.

Bertolt Brecht

[*Enter* LAVRENTI. *He sits down beside his sister.*]

L A V R E N T I – Why are you sitting there muffled up like coachmen, you two? Is it too cold in the room?

G R U S H A [*hastily removing one shawl*] It's not too cold, Lavrenti.

L A V R E N T I – If it's too cold, you shouldn't be sitting here with the child. Aniko would never forgive herself! [*Pause.*] I hope our priest didn't question you about the child?

G R U S H A – He did, but I didn't tell him anything.

L A V R E N T I – That's good. I wanted to speak to you about Aniko. She has a good heart but she's very, very sensitive. People need only mention our farm and she's worried. She takes everything hard, you see. One time our milkmaid went to church with a hole in her stocking. Ever since, Aniko has worn two pairs of stockings in church. It's the old family in her. [*He listens.*] Are you sure there are no rats around? If there are rats, you couldn't live here. [*There are sounds as of dripping from the roof.*] What's that, dripping?

G R U S H A – It must be a barrel leaking.

L A V R E N T I – Yes, it must be a barrel. You've been here six months, haven't you? Was I talking about Aniko? [*They listen again to the snow melting.*] You can't imagine how worried she gets about your soldier-husband. "Suppose he comes back and can't find her!" she says and lies awake. "He can't come before the spring," I tell her. The dear woman! [*The drops begin to fall faster.*] When d'you think he'll come? What do *you* think? [GRUSHA *is silent.*] Not before the spring, you agree? [GRUSHA *is silent.*] You don't believe he'll come at all? [GRUSHA *is silent.*] But when the spring comes and the snow melts here and on the passes, you can't stay on. They may come and look for you. There's already talk of an illegitimate child. [*The "glockenspiel" of the falling drops has grown faster and steadier.*] Grusha, the snow is melting on the roof. Spring is here.

G R U S H A – Yes.

L A V R E N T I [*eagerly*] I'll tell you what we'll do. You need a place to go, and, because of the child [*he sighs*], you have to have a husband, so people won't talk. Now I've made cautious inquiries to see if we can find you a husband. Grusha, I *have* one. I talked to a peasant woman who has a son. Just the other side of the mountain. A small farm. And she's willing.

G R U S H A – But I *can't* marry! I must wait for Simon Shashava.

L A V R E N T I – Of course. That's all been taken care of. You don't need a man in bed—you need a man on paper. And I've found you one. The son of this peasant woman is going to die. Isn't that wonderful? He's at his last gasp. And all in line with our story—a husband from the other side of the mountain! And when you met him he was at the last gasp. So you're a widow. What do you say?

GRUSHA – It's true I could use a document with stamps on it for Michael.

LAVRENTI – Stamps make all the difference. Without something in writing the Shah couldn't prove he's a Shah. And you'll have a place to live.

GRUSHA – How much does the peasant woman want?

LAVRENTI – Four hundred piasters.

GRUSHA – Where will you find it?

LAVRENTI [*guiltily*] Aniko's milk money.

GRUSHA – No one would know us there. I'll do it.

LAVRENTI [*getting up*] I'll let the peasant woman know.

[*Quick exit.*]

GRUSHA – Michael, you make a lot of work. I came by you as the pear tree comes by sparrows. And because a Christian bends down and picks up a crust of bread so nothing will go to waste. Michael, it would have been better had I walked quickly away on that Easter Sunday in Nuka in the second courtyard. Now I *am* a fool.

SINGER – The bridegroom was on his deathbed when the bride arrived. The bridegroom's mother was waiting at the door, telling her to hurry. The bride brought a child along. The witness hid it during the wedding.

On one side the bed. Under the mosquito net lies a very sick man. GRUSHA *is pulled in at a run by her future mother-in-law. They are followed by* LAVRENTI *and the* CHILD.

MOTHER-IN-LAW – Quick! Quick! Or he'll die on us before the wedding. [*To* LAVRENTI.] I was never told she had a child already.

LAVRENTI – What difference does it make? [*Pointing toward the dying man.*] It can't matter to him—in his condition.

MOTHER-IN-LAW – To him? But I'll never survive the shame! We are honest people. [*She begins to weep.*] My Jussup doesn't have to marry a girl with a child!

LAVRENTI – All right, make it another two hundred piasters. You'll have it in writing that the farm will go to you: but she'll have the right to live here for two years.

MOTHER-IN-LAW [*drying her tears*] It'll hardly cover the funeral expenses. I hope she'll really lend a hand with the work. And what's happened to the monk? He must have slipped out through the kitchen window. We'll have the whole village on our necks when they hear

Jussup's end is come! Oh dear! I'll go get the monk. But he mustn't see the child!

L A V R E N T I – I'll take care he doesn't. But why only a monk? Why not a priest?

M O T H E R - I N - L A W – Oh, he's just as good. I only made one mistake: I paid half his fee in advance. Enough to send him to the tavern. I only hope . . .

> [*She runs off.*]

L A V R E N T I – She saved on the priest, the wretch! Hired a cheap monk.

G R U S H A – You *will* send Simon Shashava to see me if he turns up after all?

L A V R E N T I – Yes. [*Pointing at the* SICK PEASANT.] Won't you take a look at him? [GRUSHA, *taking* MICHAEL *to her, shakes her head.*] He's not moving an eyelid. I hope we aren't too late.

They listen. On the opposite side enter neighbors who look around and take up positions against the walls, thus forming another wall near the bed, yet leaving an opening so that the bed can be seen. They start murmuring prayers. Enter the MOTHER-IN-LAW *with a* MONK. *Showing some annoyance and surprise, she bows to the guests.*

M O T H E R - I N - L A W – I hope you won't mind waiting a few moments? My son's bride has just arrived from the city. An emergency wedding is about to be celebrated. [*To the* MONK *in the bedroom.*] I might have known you couldn't keep your trap shut. [*To* GRUSHA.] The wedding can take place at once. Here's the license. Me and the bride's brother [LAVRENTI *tries to hide in the background, after having quietly taken* MICHAEL *back from* GRUSHA. *The* MOTHER-IN-LAW *waves him away*] are the witnesses.

GRUSHA *has bowed to the* MONK. *They go to the bed. The* MOTHER-IN-LAW *lifts the mosquito net. The* MONK *starts reeling off the marriage ceremony in Latin. Meanwhile the* MOTHER-IN-LAW *beckons to* LAVRENTI *to get rid of the* CHILD, *but fearing that it will cry he draws its attention to the ceremony,* GRUSHA *glances once at the* CHILD, *and* LAVRENTI *waves the* CHILD's *hand in a greeting.*

M O N K – Are you prepared to be a faithful, obedient, and good wife to this man, and to cleave to him until death you do part?

G R U S H A [*looking at the* CHILD] I am.

M O N K [*to the* SICK PEASANT] Are you prepared to be a good and loving husband to your wife until death you do part?

[*As the* SICK PEASANT *does not answer,
the* MONK *looks inquiringly around.*]

MOTHER-IN-LAW—Of course he is! Didn't you hear him say yes?

MONK—All right. We declare the marriage contracted! How about extreme unction?

MOTHER-IN-LAW—Nothing doing! The wedding cost quite enough. Now I must take care of the mourners. [*To* LAVRENTI.] Did we say seven hundred?

LAVRENTI—Six hundred. [*He pays.*] Now I don't want to sit with the guests and get to know people. So farewell, Grusha, and if my widowed sister comes to visit me, she'll get a welcome from my wife, or I'll show my teeth.

[*Nods, gives the* CHILD *to* GRUSHA, *and leaves.
The mourners glance after him without interest.*]

MONK—May one ask where this child comes from?

MOTHER-IN-LAW—Is there a child? I don't see a child. And you don't see a child either—you understand? Or it may turn out I saw all sorts of things in the tavern! Now come on. [*After* GRUSHA *has put the* CHILD *down and told him to be quiet, they move over left,* GRUSHA *is introduced to the neighbors.*] This is my daughter-in-law. She arrived just in time to find dear Jussup still alive.

ONE WOMAN—He's been ill now a whole year, hasn't he? When our Vassili was drafted he was there to say good-bye.

ANOTHER WOMAN—Such things are terrible for a farm. The corn all ripe and the farmer in bed! It'll really be a blessing if he doesn't suffer too long, I say.

FIRST WOMAN [*confidentially*] You know why we thought he'd taken to his bed? Because of the draft! And now his end is come!

MOTHER-IN-LAW—Sit yourselves down, please! And have some cakes!

She beckons to GRUSHA *and both women go into the bedroom, where they pick up the cake pans off the floor. The guests, among them the* MONK, *sit on the floor and begin conversing in subdued voices.*

ONE PEASANT [*to whom the* MONK *has handed the bottle which he has taken from his soutane*] There's a child, you say! How can that have happened to Jussup?

A WOMAN—She was certainly lucky to get herself married, with him so sick!

MOTHER-IN-LAW—They're gossiping already. And wolfing down the funeral cakes at the same time! If he doesn't die today, I'll have to bake some more tomorrow!

GRUSHA—I'll bake them for you.

MOTHER-IN-LAW—Yesterday some horsemen rode by, and I went out to see who it was. When I came in again he was lying there like a corpse! So I sent for you. It can't take much longer.

[*She listens.*]

MONK—Dear wedding and funeral guests! Deeply touched, we stand before a bed of death and marriage. The bride gets a veil; the groom, a shroud: how varied, my children, are the fates of men! Alas! One man dies and has a roof over his head, and the other is married and the flesh turns to dust from which it was made. Amen.

MOTHER-IN-LAW—He's getting his own back. I shouldn't have hired such a cheap one. It's what you'd expect. A more expensive monk would behave himself. In Sura there's one with a real air of sanctity about him, but of course he charges a fortune. A fifty piaster monk like that has no dignity, and as for piety, just fifty piasters' worth and no more! When I came to get him in the tavern he'd just made a speech, and he was shouting: "The war is over, beware of the peace!" We must go in.

GRUSHA [*giving* MICHAEL *a cake*] Eat this cake, and keep nice and still, Michael.

The two women offer cakes to the guests. The dying man sits up in bed. He puts his head out from under the mosquito net, stares at the two women, then sinks back again. The MONK *takes two bottles from his soutane and offers them to the peasant beside him. Enter three* MUSI-CIANS *who are greeted with a sly wink by the* MONK.

MOTHER-IN-LAW [*to the* MUSICIANS] What are you doing here? With instruments?

ONE MUSICIAN—Brother Anastasius here [*pointing at the* MONK] told us there was a wedding on.

MOTHER-IN-LAW—What? You brought them? Three more on my neck! Don't you know there's a dying man in the next room?

MONK—A very tempting assignment for a musician: something that could be either a subdued Wedding March or a spirited Funeral Dance.

MOTHER-IN-LAW—Well, you might as well play. Nobody can stop you eating in any case.

[*The* MUSICIANS *play a potpourri. The women serve cakes.*]

MONK—The trumpet sounds like a whining baby. And you, little drum, what have you got to tell the world?

DRUNKEN PEASANT [*beside the* MONK, *sings*] There was a young
  woman who said:
I thought I'd be happier, wed.
But my husband is old
And remarkably cold
So I sleep with a candle instead.

> [*The* MOTHER-IN-LAW *throws the* DRUNKEN PEASANT *out.*
> *The music stops. The guests are embarrassed.*]

GUESTS [*loudly*] – Have you heard? The Grand Duke is back! But the
  Princes are against him.
  – They say the Shah of Persia has lent him a great army to restore
  order in Grusinia.
  – But how is that possible? The Shah of Persia is the enemy . . .
  – The enemy of Grusinia, you donkey, not the enemy of the Grand
  Duke!
  – In any case, the war's over, so our soldiers are coming back.

> [GRUSHA *drops a cake pan.* GUESTS *help her pick up the cake.*]

AN OLD WOMAN [*to* GRUSHA] Are you feeling bad? It's just excitement about dear Jussup. Sit down and rest a while, my dear.

> [GRUSHA *staggers.*]

GUESTS – Now everything'll be the way it was. Only the taxes'll go up
  because now we'll have to pay for the war.
GRUSHA [*weakly*] Did someone say the soldiers are back?
A MAN – I did.
GRUSHA – It can't be true.
FIRST MAN [*to a woman*] Show her the shawl. We bought it from
  a soldier. It's from Persia.
GRUSHA [*looking at the shawl*] They are here.

> [*She gets up, takes a step, kneels down in prayer, takes*
> *the silver cross and chain out of her blouse, and kisses it.*]

MOTHER-IN-LAW [*while the guests silently watch* GRUSHA] What's
  the matter with you? Aren't you going to look after our guests? What's
  all this city nonsense got to do with us?
GUESTS [*resuming conversation while* GRUSHA *remains in prayer*]
  – You can buy Persian saddles from the soldiers too. Though many
  want crutches in exchange for them.
  – The leaders on one side can win a war, the soldiers on both sides lose
  it.
  – Anyway, the war's over. It's something they can't draft you any more.

> [*The dying man sits bolt upright in bed. He listens.*]

  – What we need is two weeks of good weather.
  – Our pear trees are hardly bearing a thing this year.

2213

MOTHER-IN-LAW [*offering cakes*] Have some more cakes and welcome! There are more!

The MOTHER-IN-LAW *goes to the bedroom with the empty cake pans. Unaware of the dying man, she is bending down to pick up another tray when he begins to talk in a hoarse voice.*

PEASANT – How many more cakes are you going to stuff down their throats? D'you think I can shit money?
> [*The* MOTHER-IN-LAW *starts, stares at him aghast,*
> *while he climbs out from behind the mosquito net.*]

FIRST WOMAN [*talking kindly to* GRUSHA *in the next room*] Has the young wife got someone at the front?

A MAN – It's good news that they're on their way home, huh?

PEASANT – Don't stare at me like that! Where's this wife you've saddled me with?

[*Receiving no answer, he climbs out of bed and in his nightshirt staggers into the other room. Trembling, she follows him with the cake pan.*]

GUESTS [*seeing him and shrieking*] Good God! Jussup!

[*Everyone leaps up in alarm. The women rush to the door.* GRUSHA, *still on her knees, turns round and stares at the man.*]

PEASANT – A funeral supper! You'd enjoy that, wouldn't you? Get out before I throw you out! [*As the guests stampede from the house, gloomily to* GRUSHA.] I've upset the apple cart, huh?
> [*Receiving no answer, he turns round and takes a*
> *cake from the pan which his mother is holding.*]

SINGER – O confusion! The wife discovers she has a husband.
By day there's the child, by night there's the husband.
The lover is on his way both day and night.
Husband and wife look at each other.
The bedroom is small.

Near the bed the PEASANT *is sitting in a high wooden bathtub, naked, the* MOTHER-IN-LAW *is pouring water from a pitcher. Opposite* GRUSHA *cowers with* MICHAEL, *who is playing at mending straw mats.*

PEASANT [*to his mother*] That's her work, not yours. Where's she hiding out now?

MOTHER-IN-LAW [*calling*] Grusha! The peasant wants you!

GRUSHA [*to* MICHAEL] There are still two holes to mend.

PEASANT [*when* GRUSHA *approaches*] Scrub my back!

GRUSHA – Can't the peasant do it himself?

PEASANT – "Can't the peasant do it himself?" Get the brush! To hell

2214

with you! Are you the wife here? Or are you a visitor? [*To the* MOTHER-IN-LAW.] It's too cold!

MOTHER-IN-LAW—I'll run for hot water.

GRUSHA—Let me go.

PEASANT—You stay here. [*The* MOTHER-IN-LAW *exits.*] Rub harder. And no shirking. You've seen a naked fellow before. That child didn't come out of thin air.

GRUSHA—The child was not conceived in joy, if that's what the peasant means.

PEASANT [*turning and grinning*] You don't look the type.

[GRUSHA *stops scrubbing him, starts back. Enter the* MOTHER-IN-LAW.]

PEASANT—A nice thing you've saddled me with! A simpleton for a wife!

MOTHER-IN-LAW—She just isn't cooperative.

PEASANT—Pour—but go easy! Ow! Go easy, I said. [*To* GRUSHA.] Maybe you did something wrong in the city . . . I wouldn't be surprised. Why else should you be here? But I won't talk about that. I've not said a word about the illegitimate object you brought into my house either. But my patience has limits! It's against nature. [*To the* MOTHER-IN-LAW.] More! [*To* GRUSHA.] And even if your soldier does come back, you're married.

GRUSHA—Yes.

PEASANT—But your soldier won't come back. Don't you believe it.

GRUSHA—No.

PEASANT—You're cheating me. You're my wife and you're not my wife. Where you lie, nothing lies, and yet no other woman can lie there. When I go to work in the morning I'm tired—when I lie down at night I'm awake as the devil. God has given you sex—and what d'you do? I don't have ten piasters to buy myself a woman in the city. Besides, it's a long way. Woman weeds the fields and opens up her legs, that's what our calendar says. D'you hear?

GRUSHA [*quietly*] Yes. I didn't mean to cheat you out of it.

PEASANT—She didn't mean to cheat me out of it! Pour some more water! [*The* MOTHER-IN-LAW *pours.*] Ow!

SINGER—As she sat by the stream to wash the linen
  She saw his image in the water
  And his face grew dimmer with the passing moons.
  As she raised herself to wring the linen
  She heard his voice from the murmuring maple
  And his voice grew fainter with the passing moons.
  Evasions and sighs grew more numerous,
  Tears and sweat flowed.
  With the passing moons the child grew up.

2215

Bertolt Brecht

[GRUSHA *sits by a stream, dipping linen into the water.*
In the rear, a few children are standing.]

GRUSHA [*to* MICHAEL] You can play with them, Michael, but don't
let them boss you around just because you're the littlest.

[MICHAEL *nods and joins the children. They start playing.*]

BIGGEST BOY–Today it's the Heads-Off Game. [*To a* FAT BOY.]
You're the Prince and you laugh. [*To* MICHAEL.] You're the Governor.
[*To a* GIRL.] You're the Governor's wife and you cry when his head's
cut off. And I do the cutting. [*He shows his wooden sword.*] With this.
First, they lead the Governor into the yard. The Prince walks in front.
The Governor's wife comes last.

[*They form a procession. The* FAT BOY *is first and laughs. Then comes*
MICHAEL, *then the* BIGGEST BOY, *and then the* GIRL, *who weeps.*]

MICHAEL [*standing still*] Me cut off head!

BIGGEST BOY–That's my job. You're the littlest. The Governor's the
easy part. All you do is kneel down and get your head cut off–simple.

MICHAEL–Me want sword!

BIGGEST BOY–It's mine!

[*He gives* MICHAEL *a kick.*]

GIRL [*shouting to* GRUSHA] He won't play his part!

GRUSHA [*laughing*] Even the little duck is a swimmer, they say.

BIGGEST BOY–You can be the Prince if you can laugh.

[MICHAEL *shakes his head.*]

FAT BOY–I laugh best. Let him cut off the head just once. Then you
do it, then me.

Reluctantly, the BIGGEST BOY *hands* MICHAEL *the wooden sword and*
kneels down. The FAT BOY *sits down, slaps his thigh, and laughs with all*
his might. The GIRL *weeps loudly.* MICHAEL *swings the big sword and*
"cuts off" the head. In doing so, he topples over.

BIGGEST BOY–Hey! I'll show you how to cut heads off!

MICHAEL *runs away. The children run after him.* GRUSHA *laughs, follow-*
ing them with her eyes. On looking back, she sees SIMON SHASHAVA *stand-*
ing on the opposite bank. He wears a shabby uniform.

GRUSHA–Simon!

SIMON–Is that Grusha Vashnadze?

GRUSHA–Simon!

SIMON [*formally*] A good morning to the young lady. I hope she is
well.

2216

GRUSHA [*getting up gaily and bowing low*] A good morning to the soldier. God be thanked he has returned in good health.

SIMON – They found better fish, so they didn't eat me, said the haddock.

GRUSHA – Courage, said the kitchen boy. Good luck, said the hero.

SIMON – How are things here? Was the winter bearable? The neighbor considerate?

GRUSHA – The winter was a trifle rough, the neighbor as usual, Simon.

SIMON – May one ask if a certain person still dips her toes in the water when rinsing the linen?

GRUSHA – The answer is no. Because of the eyes in the bushes.

SIMON – The young lady is speaking of soldiers. Here stands a paymaster.

GRUSHA – A job worth twenty piasters?

SIMON – And lodgings.

GRUSHA [*with tears in her eyes*] Behind the barracks under the date trees.

SIMON – Yes, there. A certain person has kept her eyes open.

GRUSHA – She has, Simon.

SIMON – And has not forgotten? [GRUSHA *shakes her head.*] So the door is still on its hinges as they say? [GRUSHA *looks at him in silence and shakes her head again.*] What's this? Is anything not as it should be?

GRUSHA – Simon Shashava, I can never return to Nuka. Something has happened.

SIMON – What can have happened?

GRUSHA – For one thing, I knocked an Ironshirt down.

SIMON – Grusha Vashnadze must have had her reasons for that.

GRUSHA – Simon Shashava, I am no longer called what I used to be called.

SIMON [*after a pause*] I do not understand.

GRUSHA – When do women change their names, Simon? Let me explain. Nothing stands between us. Everything is just as it was. You must believe that.

SIMON – Nothing stands between us and yet there's something?

GRUSHA – How can I explain it so fast and with the stream between us? Couldn't you cross the bridge there?

SIMON – Maybe it's no longer necessary.

GRUSHA – It is very necessary. Come over on this side, Simon, quick!

SIMON – Does the young lady wish to say someone has come too late?

[GRUSHA *looks up at him in despair, her face streaming with tears.* SIMON *stares before him. He picks up a piece of wood and starts cutting it.*]

SINGER – So many words are said, so many left unsaid.

The soldier has come.

Where he comes from, he does not say.
Hear what he thought and did not say:
"The battle began, gray at dawn, grew bloody at noon.
The first man fell in front of me, the second behind me, the third at
   my side.
I trod on the first, left the second behind, the third was run through
   by the captain.
One of my brothers died by steel, the other by smoke.
My neck caught fire, my hands froze in my gloves, my toes in my socks.
I fed on aspen buds, I drank maple juice, I slept on stone, in water."

SIMON – I see a cap in the grass. Is there a little one already?

GRUSHA – There is, Simon. There's no keeping *that* from you. But
please don't worry, it is not mine.

SIMON – When the wind once starts to blow, they say, it blows through
every cranny. The wife need say no more.

                    [GRUSHA *looks into her lap and is silent.*]

SINGER – There was yearning but there was no waiting.
The oath is broken. Neither could say why.
Hear what she thought but did not say:
"While you fought in the battle, soldier,
The bloody battle, the bitter battle
I found a helpless infant
I had not the heart to destroy him
I had to care for a creature that was lost
I had to stoop for breadcrumbs on the floor
I had to break myself for that which was not mine
That which was other people's.
Someone must help!
For the little tree needs water
The lamb loses its way when the shepherd is asleep
And its cry is unheard!"

SIMON – Give me back the cross I gave you. Better still, throw it in the
stream.

                              [*He turns to go.*]

GRUSHA   [*getting up*] Simon Shashava, don't go away! He isn't mine!
He isn't mine! [*She hears the children calling.*] What's the matter,
children?

VOICES – Soldiers! And they're taking Michael away!

                    [GRUSHA *stands aghast as two* IRONSHIRTS, *with*
                    MICHAEL *between them, come toward her.*]

ONE OF THE IRONSHIRTS – Are you Grusha? [*She nods.*] Is this
your child?

GRUSHA – Yes. [SIMON *goes.*] Simon!

IRONSHIRT—We have orders, in the name of the law, to take this child, found in your custody, back to the city. It is suspected that the child is Michael Abashwili, son and heir of the late Governor Georgi Abashwili, and his wife, Natella Abashwili. Here is the document and the seal.

[*They lead the* CHILD *away.*]

GRUSHA [*running after them, shouting*] Leave him here. Please! He's mine!

SINGER—The Ironshirts took the child, the beloved child.
The unhappy girl followed them to the city, the dreaded city.
She who had borne him demanded the child.
She who had raised him faced trial.
Who will decide the case?
To whom will the child be assigned?
Who will the judge be? A good judge? A bad?
The city was in flames.
In the judge's seat sat Azdak.[1]

[1] The name Azdak should be accented on the second syllable. [E.B.]

FOUR: THE STORY OF THE JUDGE

SINGER – Hear the story of the judge
  How he turned judge, how he passed judgment, what kind of judge he was.
  On that Easter Sunday of the great revolt, when the Grand Duke was overthrown
  And his Governor Abashwili, father of our child, lost his head
  The Village Scrivener Azdak found a fugitive in the woods and hid him in his hut.

  [AZDAK, *in rags and slightly drunk,*
  is helping an old beggar into his cottage.]

AZDAK – Stop snorting, you're not a horse. And it won't do you any good with the police to run like a snotty nose in April. Stand still, I say. [*He catches the* OLD MAN, *who has marched into the cottage as if he'd like to go through the walls.*] Sit down. Feed. Here's a hunk of cheese. [*From under some rags, in a chest, he fishes out some cheese, and the* OLD MAN *greedily begins to eat.*] Haven't eaten in a long time, huh? [*The* OLD MAN *growls.*] Why were you running like that, asshole? The cop wouldn't even have seen you.

OLD MAN – Had to! Had to!

AZDAK – Blue funk? [*The* OLD MAN *stares, uncomprehending.*] Cold feet? Panic? Don't lick your chops like a Grand Duke. Or an old sow. I can't stand it. We have to accept respectable stinkers as God made them, but not you! I once heard of a senior judge who farted at a public dinner to show an independent spirit! Watching you eat like that gives me the most awful ideas. Why don't you say something? [*Sharply.*] Show me your hand. Can't you hear? [*The* OLD MAN *slowly puts out his hand.*] White! So you're not a beggar at all! A fraud, a walking swindle! And I'm hiding you from the cops like you were an honest man! Why were you running like that if you're a landowner? For that's what you are. Don't deny it! I see it in your guilty face! [*He gets up.*] Get out! [*The* OLD MAN *looks at him uncertainly.*] What are you waiting for, peasant-flogger?

OLD MAN – Pursued. Need undivided attention. Make proposition . . .

AZDAK – Make what? A proposition? Well, if that isn't the height of insolence. He's making me a proposition! The bitten man scratches his fingers bloody, and the leech that's biting him makes him a proposition! Get out, I tell you!

OLD MAN—Understand point of view! Persuasion! Pay hundred thousand piasters one night! Yes?

AZDAK—What, you think you can buy me? For a hundred thousand piasters? Let's say a hundred and fifty thousand. Where are they?

OLD MAN—Have not them here. Of course. Will be sent. Hope do not doubt.

AZDAK—Doubt very much. Get out!

> [*The* OLD MAN *gets up, waddles to the door.*
> *A* VOICE *is heard offstage.*]

VOICE—Azdak!

> [*The* OLD MAN *turns, waddles to the opposite corner, stands still.*]

AZDAK [*calling out*] I'm not in! [*He walks to door.*] So you're sniffing around here again, Shauwa?

SHAUWA [*reproachfully*] You caught another rabbit, Azdak. And you'd promised me it wouldn't happen again!

AZDAK [*severely*] Shauwa, don't talk about things you don't understand. The rabbit is a dangerous and destructive beast. It feeds on plants, especially on the species of plants known as weeds. It must therefore be exterminated.

SHAUWA—Azdak, don't be so hard on me. I'll lose my job if I don't arrest you. I know you have a good heart.

AZDAK—I do not have a good heart! How often must I tell you I'm a man of intellect?

SHAUWA [*slyly*] I know, Azdak. You're a superior person. You say so yourself. I'm just a Christian and an ignoramus. So I ask you: When one of the Prince's rabbits is stolen, and I'm a policeman, what should I do with the offending party?

AZDAK—Shauwa, Shauwa, shame on you. You stand and ask me a question, than which nothing could be more seductive. It's like you were a woman—let's say that bad girl Nunowna, and you showed me your thigh—Nunowna's thigh, that would be—and asked me: "What shall I do with my thigh, it itches?" Is she as innocent as she pretends? Of course not. I catch a rabbit, but you catch a man. Man is made in God's image. Not so a rabbit, you know that. I'm a rabbit-eater, but you're a man-eater, Shauwa. And God will pass judgment on you. Shauwa, go home and repent. No, stop, there's something . . . [*He looks at the* OLD MAN *who stands trembling in the corner.*] No, it's nothing. Go home and repent. [*He slams the door behind* SHAUWA.] Now you're surprised, huh? Surprised I didn't hand you over? I couldn't hand over a bedbug to that animal. It goes against the grain.

Now don't tremble because of a cop! So old and still so scared? Finish your cheese, but eat it like a poor man, or else they'll still catch you. Must I even explain how a poor man behaves? [*He pushes him down, and then gives him back the cheese.*] That box is the table. Lay your elbows on the table. Now, encircle the cheese on the plate like it might be snatched from you at any moment—what right have you to be safe, huh?—now, hold your knife like an undersized sickle, and give your cheese a troubled look because, like all beautiful things, it's already fading away. [AZDAK *watches him.*] They're after you, which speaks in your favor, but how can we be sure they're not mistaken about you? In Tiflis one time they hanged a landowner, a Turk, who could prove he quartered his peasants instead of merely cutting them in half, as is the custom, and he squeezed twice the usual amount of taxes out of them, his zeal was above suspicion. And yet they hanged him like a common criminal—because he was a Turk—a thing he couldn't do much about. What injustice! He got onto the gallows by a sheer fluke. In short, I don't trust you.

SINGER—Thus Azdak gave the old beggar a bed,
And learned that old beggar was the old butcher, the Grand Duke himself,
And was ashamed.
He denounced himself and ordered the policeman to take him to Nuka, to court, to be judged.

In the court of justice three IRONSHIRTS *sit drinking. From a beam hangs a man in judge's robes. Enter* AZDAK, *in chains, dragging* SHAUWA *behind him.*

AZDAK [*shouting*] I've helped the Grand Duke, the Grand Thief, the Grand Butcher, to escape! In the name of justice I ask to be severely judged in public trial!

FIRST IRONSHIRT—Who's this queer bird?

SHAUWA—That's our Village Scrivener, Azdak.

AZDAK—I am contemptible! I am a traitor! A branded criminal! Tell them, flatfoot, how I insisted on being tied up and brought to the capital. Because I sheltered the Grand Duke, the Grand Swindler, by mistake. And how I found out afterwards. See the marked man denounce himself! Tell them how I forced you to walk half the night with me to clear the whole thing up.

SHAUWA—And all by threats. That wasn't nice of you, Azdak.

AZDAK—Shut your mouth, Shauwa. You don't understand. A new age is upon us! It'll go thundering over you. You're finished. The police will be wiped out—poof! Everything will be gone into, everything will be brought into the open. The guilty will give themselves up. Why? They couldn't escape the people in any case. [*To* SHAUWA.] Tell them how I shouted all along Shoemaker Street [*with big gestures, looking at the* IRONSHIRTS] "In my ignorance I let the Grand Swindler escape! So tear me to pieces, brothers!" I wanted to get it in first.

FIRST IRONSHIRT – And what did your brothers answer?

SHAUWA – They comforted him in Butcher Street, and they laughed themselves sick in Shoemaker Street. That's all.

AZDAK – But with you it's different. I can see you're men of iron. Brothers, where's the judge? I must be tried.

FIRST IRONSHIRT [*pointing at the hanged man*] There's the judge. And please stop "brothering" us. It's rather a sore spot this evening.

AZDAK – "There's the judge." An answer never heard in Grusinia before. Townsman, where's His Excellency the Governor? [*Pointing to the ground.*] There's His Excellency, stranger. Where's the Chief Tax Collector? Where's the official Recruiting Officer? The Patriarch? The Chief of Police? There, there, there—all there. Brothers, I expected no less of you.

SECOND IRONSHIRT – What? *What* was it you expected, funny man?

AZDAK – What happened in Persia, brother, what happened in Persia?

SECOND IRONSHIRT – What did happen in Persia?

AZDAK – Everybody was hanged. Viziers, tax collectors. Everybody. Forty years ago now. My grandfather, a remarkable man by the way, saw it all. For three whole days. Everywhere.

SECOND IRONSHIRT – And who ruled when the Vizier was hanged?

AZDAK – A peasant ruled when the Vizier was hanged.

SECOND IRONSHIRT – And who commanded the army?

AZDAK – A soldier, a soldier.

SECOND IRONSHIRT – And who paid the wages?

AZDAK – A dyer. A dyer paid the wages.

SECOND IRONSHIRT – Wasn't it a weaver, maybe?

FIRST IRONSHIRT – And why did all this happen, Persian?

AZDAK – Why did all this happen? Must there be a special reason? Why do you scratch yourself, brother? War! Too long a war! And no justice! My grandfather brought back a song that tells how it was. I will sing it for you. With my friend the policeman. [*To* SHAUWA.] And hold the rope tight. It's very suitable.

[*He sings, with* SHAUWA *holding the rope tight around him.*]

The Song of Injustice in Persia

Why don't our sons bleed any more? Why don't our daughters weep? Why do only the slaughterhouse cattle have blood in their veins?

Why do only the willows shed tears on Lake Urmia?

The king must have a new province, the peasant must give up his
savings.

That the roof of the world might be conquered, the roof of the cottage
is torn down.

Our men are carried to the ends of the earth, so that great ones can
eat at home.

The soldiers kill each other, the marshals salute each other.

They bite the widow's tax money to see if it's good, their swords break.

The battle was lost, the helmets were paid for.

Refrain: Is it so? Is it so?

SHAUWA [*refrain*] Yes, yes, yes, yes, yes it's so.

AZDAK – Want to hear the rest of it?

[*The* FIRST IRONSHIRT *nods.*]

SECOND IRONSHIRT [*to* SHAUWA] Did he teach you that song?

SHAUWA – Yes, only my voice isn't very good.

SECOND IRONSHIRT – No. [*To* AZDAK.] Go on singing.

AZDAK – The second verse is about the peace.

[*He sings.*]

The offices are packed, the streets overflow with officials.

The rivers jump their banks and ravage the fields.

Those who cannot let down their own trousers rule countries.

They can't count up to four, but they devour eight courses.

The corn farmers, looking round for buyers, see only the starving.

The weavers go home from their looms in rags.

Refrain: Is it so? Is it so?

SHAUWA [*refrain*] Yes, yes, yes, yes, yes it's so.

AZDAK – That's why our sons don't bleed any more, that's why our
daughters don't weep.

That's why only the slaughterhouse cattle have blood in their veins,
And only the willows shed tears by Lake Urmia toward morning.

FIRST IRONSHIRT – Are you going to sing that song here in town?

AZDAK – Sure. What's wrong with it?

FIRST IRONSHIRT – Have you noticed that the sky's getting red?
[*Turning round,* AZDAK *sees the sky red with fire.*] It's the people's
quarters on the outskirts of town. The carpet weavers have caught the
"Persian Sickness," too. And they've been asking if Prince Kazbeki
isn't eating too many courses. This morning they strung up the city
judge. As for us we beat them to pulp. We were paid one hundred
piasters per man, you understand?

AZDAK [*after a pause*] I understand.

2224

[*He glances shyly round and, creeping away,
sits down in a corner, his head in his hands.*]

IRONSHIRTS [*to each other*] —If there ever was a troublemaker it's him.

—He must've come to the capital to fish in the troubled waters.

SHAUWA—Oh, I don't think he's a really bad character, gentlemen. Steals a few chickens here and there. And maybe a rabbit.

SECOND IRONSHIRT [*approaching* AZDAK] Came to fish in the troubled waters, huh?

AZDAK [*looking up*] I don't know why I came.

SECOND IRONSHIRT—Are you in with the carpet weavers maybe? [AZDAK *shakes his head.*] How about that song?

AZDAK—From my grandfather. A silly and ignorant man.

SECOND IRONSHIRT—Right. And how about the dyer who paid the wages?

AZDAK [*muttering*] That was in Persia.

FIRST IRONSHIRT—And this denouncing of yourself? Because you didn't hang the Grand Duke with your own hands?

AZDAK—Didn't I tell you I let him run?

[*He creeps farther away and sits on the floor.*]

SHAUWA—I can swear to that: he let him run.

The IRONSHIRTS *burst out laughing and slap* SHAUWA *on the back.* AZDAK *laughs loudest. They slap* AZDAK *too, and unchain him. They all start drinking as the* FAT PRINCE *enters with a young man.*

FIRST IRONSHIRT [*to* AZDAK, *pointing at the* FAT PRINCE] There's your "new age" for you!

[*More laughter.*]

FAT PRINCE—Well, my friends, what is there to laugh about? Permit me a serious word. Yesterday morning the Princes of Grusinia overthrew the warmongering government of the Grand Duke and did away with his Governors. Unfortunately the Grand Duke himself escaped. In this fateful hour our carpet weavers, those eternal troublemakers, had the effrontery to stir up a rebellion and hang the universally loved city judge, our dear Illo Orbeliani. Ts—ts—ts. My friends, we need peace, peace, peace in Grusinia! And justice! So I've brought along my dear nephew Bizergan Kazbeki. He'll be the new judge, hm? A very gifted fellow. What do you say? I want your opinion. Let the people decide!

SECOND IRONSHIRT—Does this mean *we* elect the judge?

FAT PRINCE—Precisely. Let the people propose some very gifted fellow! Confer among yourselves, my friends. [*The* IRONSHIRTS *confer.*] Don't worry, my little fox. The job's yours. And when we catch the Grand Duke we won't have to kiss this rabble's ass any longer.

IRONSHIRTS [*among themselves*] – Very funny: they're wetting their pants because they haven't caught the Grand Duke.

– When the outlook isn't so bright, they say: "My friends!" and "Let the people decide!"

– Now he even wants justice for Grusinia! But fun is fun as long as it lasts! [*Pointing at* AZDAK.] *He* knows all about justice. Hey, rascal, would you like this nephew fellow to be the judge?

AZDAK – Are you asking me? You're not asking *me?!*

FIRST IRONSHIRT – Why not? Anything for a laugh!

AZDAK – You'd like to test him to the marrow, correct? Have you a criminal on hand? An experienced one? So the candidate can show what he knows?

SECOND IRONSHIRT – Let's see. We do have a couple of doctors downstairs. Let's use them.

AZDAK – Oh, no, that's no good, we can't take real criminals till we're sure the judge will be appointed. He may be dumb, but he must be appointed, or the law is violated. And the law is a sensitive organ. It's like the spleen, you mustn't hit it—that would be fatal. Of course you can hang those two without violating the law, because there was no judge in the vicinity. But judgment, when pronounced, must be pronounced with absolute gravity—it's all such nonsense. Suppose, for instance, a judge jails a woman—let's say she's stolen a corn cake to feed her child—and this judge isn't wearing his robes—or maybe he's scratching himself while passing sentence and half his body is uncovered—a man's thigh *will* itch once in a while—the sentence this judge passes is a disgrace and the law is violated. In short it would be easier for a judge's robe and a judge's hat to pass judgment than for a man with no robe and no hat. If you don't treat it with respect, the law just disappears on you. Now you don't try out a bottle of wine by offering it to a dog; you'd only lose your wine.

FIRST IRONSHIRT – Then what do you suggest, hairsplitter?

AZDAK – I'll be the defendant.

FIRST IRONSHIRT – You?

[*He bursts out laughing.*]

FAT PRINCE – What have you decided?

FIRST IRONSHIRT – We've decided to stage a rehearsal. Our friend here will be the defendant. Let the candidate be the judge and sit there.

FAT PRINCE – It isn't customary, but why not? [*To the* NEPHEW.] A mere formality, my little fox. What have I taught you? Who got there first—the slow runner or the fast?

NEPHEW – The silent runner, Uncle Arsen.

[*The* NEPHEW *takes the chair. The* IRONSHIRTS *and the* FAT PRINCE *sit on the steps. Enter* AZDAK, *mimicking the gait of the Grand Duke.*]

AZDAK [*in the Grand Duke's accent*] Is any here knows me? Am Grand Duke.

IRONSHIRTS – *What* is he?

– The Grand Duke. He knows him, too.

– Fine. So get on with the trial.

AZDAK – Listen! Am accused instigating war? Ridiculous! Am saying ridiculous! That enough? If not, have brought lawyers. Believe five hundred. [*He points behind him, pretending to be surrounded by lawyers.*] Requisition all available seats for lawyers!

[*The* IRONSHIRTS *laugh; the* FAT PRINCE *joins in.*]

NEPHEW [*to the* IRONSHIRTS] You really wish me to try this case? I find it rather unusual. From the taste angle, I mean.

FIRST IRONSHIRT – Let's go!

FAT PRINCE [*smiling*] Let him have it, my little fox!

NEPHEW – All right. People of Grusinia versus Grand Duke. Defendant, what have you got to say for yourself?

AZDAK – Plenty. Naturally, have read war lost. Only started on the advice of patriots. Like Uncle Arsen Kazbeki. Call Uncle Arsen as witness.

FAT PRINCE [*to the* IRONSHIRTS, *delightedly*] What a madcap!

NEPHEW – Motion rejected. One cannot be arraigned for declaring a war, which every ruler has to do once in a while, but only for running a war badly.

AZDAK – Rubbish! Did not run it at all! Had it run! Had it run by Princes! Naturally, they messed it up.

NEPHEW – Do you by any chance deny having been commander-in-chief?

AZDAK – Not at all! Always *was* commander-in-chief. At birth shouted at wet nurse. Was trained drop turds in toilet, grew accustomed to command. Always commanded officials rob my cash box. Officers flog soldiers only on command. Landowners sleep with peasants' wives only on strictest command. Uncle Arsen here grew his belly at *my* command!

IRONSHIRTS [*clapping*] He's good! Long live the Grand Duke!

FAT PRINCE – Answer him, my little fox: I'm with you.

NEPHEW – I shall answer him according to the dignity of the law. Defendant, preserve the dignity of the law!

AZDAK – Agreed. Command you proceed with trial!

NEPHEW – It is not your place to command me. You claim that the Princes forced you to declare war. How can you claim, then, that they —er—"messed it up"?

AZDAK – Did not send enough people. Embezzled funds. Sent sick horses. During attack, drinking in whorehouse. Call Uncle Arsen as witness.

NEPHEW – Are you making the outrageous suggestion that the Princes of this country did not fight?

AZDAK – No. Princes fought. Fought for war contracts.

FAT PRINCE *[jumping up]* That's too much! This man talks like a carpet weaver!

AZDAK – Really? Told nothing but truth.

FAT PRINCE – Hang him! Hang him!

FIRST IRONSHIRT *[pulling the* PRINCE *down]* Keep quiet! Go on, Excellency!

NEPHEW – Quiet! I now render a verdict: You must be hanged! By the neck! Having lost war!

AZDAK – Young man, seriously advise not fall publicly into jerky clipped speech. Cannot be watchdog if howl like wolf. Got it? If people realize Princes speak same language as Grand Duke, may hang Grand Duke *and Princes*, huh? By the way, must overrule verdict. Reason? War lost, but not for Princes. Princes won their war. Got 3,863,000 piasters for horses not delivered, 8,240,000 piasters for food supplies not produced. Are therefore victors. War lost only for Grusinia, which is not present in this court.

FAT PRINCE – I think that will do, my friends. [*To* AZDAK.] You can withdraw, funny man. [*To the* IRONSHIRTS.] You may now ratify the new judge's appointment, my friends.

FIRST IRONSHIRT – Yes, we can. Take down the judge's gown. [*One* IRONSHIRT *climbs on the back of the other, pulls the gown off the hanged man.*] [*To the* NEPHEW.] Now you run away so the right ass can get on the right chair. [*To* AZDAK.] Step forward! Go to the judge's seat! Now sit in it! [AZDAK *steps up, bows, and sits down.*] The judge was always a rascal! Now the rascal shall be a judge! [*The judge's gown is placed round his shoulders, the hat on his head.*] And what a judge!

SINGER – And there was civil war in the land.
The mighty were not safe.
And Azdak was made a judge by the Ironshirts.
And Azdak remained a judge for two years.

SINGER *and* CHORUS – When the towns were set afire
And rivers of blood rose higher and higher,
Cockroaches crawled out of every crack.
And the court was full of schemers

And the church of foul blasphemers.
In the judge's cassock sat Azdak.

AZDAK *sits in the judge's chair, peeling an apple.* SHAUWA *is sweeping out the hall. On one side an* INVALID *in a wheelchair. Opposite, a young man accused of blackmail. An* IRONSHIRT *stands guard, holding the Ironshirts' banner.*

AZDAK—In consideration of the large number of cases, the Court to-day will hear two cases at a time. Before I open the proceedings, a short announcement—I accept. [*He stretches out his hand. The* BLACK-MAILER *is the only one to produce any money. He hands it to* AZDAK.] I reserve the right to punish one of the parties for contempt of court. [*He glances at the* INVALID.] You [*to the* DOCTOR] are a doctor, and you [*to the* INVALID] are bringing a complaint against him. Is the doctor responsible for your condition?

INVALID—Yes. I had a stroke on his account.

AZDAK—That would be professional negligence.

INVALID—Worse than negligence. I gave this man money for his stud-ies. So far, he hasn't paid me back a cent. It was when I heard he was treating a patient free that I had my stroke.

AZDAK—Rightly. [*To a* LIMPING MAN.] And what are *you* doing here?

LIMPING MAN—I'm the patient, Your Honor.

AZDAK—He treated your leg for nothing?

LIMPING MAN—The wrong leg! My rheumatism was in the left leg, he operated on the right. That's why I limp.

AZDAK—And you were treated free?

INVALID—A five-hundred-piaster operation free! For nothing! For a God-bless-you! And I paid for this man's studies! [*To the* DOCTOR.] Did they teach you to operate free?

DOCTOR—Your Honor, it is the custom to demand the fee before the operation, as the patient is more willing to pay before an operation than after. Which is only human. In the case in question I was con-vinced, when I started the operation, that my servant had already re-ceived the fee. In this I was mistaken.

INVALID—He was mistaken! A good doctor doesn't make mistakes! He examines before he operates!

AZDAK—That's right: [*to* SHAUWA] Public Prosecutor, what's the other case about?

SHAUWA [*busily sweeping*] Blackmail.

BLACKMAILER—High Court of Justice, I'm innocent. I only wanted to find out from the landowner concerned if he really *had* raped his

2229

niece. He informed me very politely that this was not the case, and gave me the money only so I could pay for my uncle's studies.

A Z D A K – Hm. [*To the* DOCTOR.] You, on the other hand, can cite no extenuating circumstances for your offense, huh?

D O C T O R – Except that to err is human.

A Z D A K – And you are aware that in money matters a good doctor is a highly responsible person? I once heard of a doctor who got a thousand piasters for a sprained finger by remarking that sprains have something to do with blood circulation, which after all a less good doctor might have overlooked, and who, on another occasion made a real gold mine out of a somewhat disordered gall bladder, he treated it with such loving care. You have no excuse, Doctor. The corn merchant Uxu had his son study medicine to get some knowledge of trade, our medical schools are so good. [*To the* BLACKMAILER.] What's the landowner's name?

S H A U W A – He doesn't want it mentioned.

A Z D A K – In that case I will pass judgment. The Court considers the blackmail proved. And you [*to the* INVALID] are sentenced to a fine of one thousand piasters. If you have a second stroke, the doctor will have to treat you free. Even if he has to amputate. [*To the* LIMPING MAN.] As compensation, you will receive a bottle of rubbing alcohol. [*To the* BLACKMAILER.] You are sentenced to hand over half the proceeds of your deal to the Public Prosecutor to keep the landowner's name secret. You are advised, moreover, to study medicine—you seem well suited to that calling. [*To the* DOCTOR.] You have perpetrated an unpardonable error in the practice of your profession: you are acquitted. Next cases!

S I N G E R *and* C H O R U S – Men won't do much for a shilling.
For a pound they may be willing.
For twenty pounds the verdict's in the sack.
As for the many, all too many,
Those who've only got a penny—
They've one single, sole recourse: Azdak.

Enter AZDAK *from the caravansary on the highroad, followed by an old bearded* INNKEEPER. *The judge's chair is carried by a stableman and* SHAUWA. *An* IRONSHIRT, *with a banner, takes up his position.*

A Z D A K – Put me down. Then we'll get some air, maybe even a good stiff breeze from the lemon grove there. It does justice good to be done in the open: the wind blows her skirts up and you can see what she's got. Shauwa, we've been eating too much. These official journeys are exhausting. [*To the* INNKEEPER.] It's a question of your daughter-in-law?

INNKEEPER – Your Worship, it's a question of the family honor. I wish to bring an action on behalf of my son, who's away on business on the other side the mountain. This is the offending stableman, and here's my daughter-in-law.

[*Enter the* DAUGHTER-IN-LAW, *a voluptuous wench. She is veiled.*]

AZDAK [*sitting down*] I accept. [*Sighing, the* INNKEEPER *hands him some money.*] Good. Now the formalities are disposed of. This is a case of rape?

INNKEEPER – Your Honor, I caught the fellow in the act. Ludovica was in the straw on the stable floor.

AZDAK – Quite right, the stable. Lovely horses! I specially liked the little roan.

INNKEEPER – The first thing I did, of course, was to question Ludovica. On my son's behalf.

AZDAK [*seriously*] I said I specially liked the little roan.

INNKEEPER [*coldly*] Really? Ludovica confessed the stableman took her against her will.

AZDAK – Take your veil off, Ludovica. [*She does so.*] Ludovica, you please the Court. Tell us how it happened.

LUDOVICA [*well schooled*] When I entered the stable to see the new foal the stableman said to me on his own accord: "It's hot today!" and laid his hand on my left breast. I said to him: "Don't do that!" But he continued to handle me indecently, which provoked my anger. Before I realized his sinful intentions, he got much closer. It was all over when my father-in-law entered and accidentally trod on me.

INNKEEPER [*explaining*] On my son's behalf.

AZDAK [*to the* STABLEMAN] You admit you started it?

STABLEMAN – Yes.

AZDAK – Ludovica, you like to eat sweet things?

LUDOVICA – Yes, sunflower seeds!

AZDAK – You like to lie a long time in the bathtub?

LUDOVICA – Half an hour or so.

AZDAK – Public Prosecutor, drop your knife—there on the ground. [SHAUWA *does so.*] Ludovica, pick up that knife. [LUDOVICA, *swaying her hips, does so.*] See that? [*He points at her.*] The way it moves? The rape is now proven. By eating too much—sweet things, especially—by lying too long in warm water, by laziness and too soft a skin, you have raped that unfortunate man. Think you can run around with a behind like that and get away with it in court? This is a case of intentional assault with a dangerous weapon! You are sentenced to hand over to the Court the little roan which your father liked to ride "on his son's

2231

behalf." And now, come with me to the stables, so the Court can inspect the scene of the crime, Ludovica.

SINGER *and* CHORUS—When the sharks the sharks devour
Little fishes have their hour.
For a while the load is off their back.
On Grusinia's highways faring
Fixed-up scales of justice bearing
Strode the poor man's magistrate: Azdak.

And he gave to the forsaken
All that from the rich he'd taken
And a bodyguard of roughnecks was Azdak's.
And our good and evil man, he
Smiled upon Grusinia's Granny.
His emblem was a tear in sealing wax.

All mankind should love each other
But when visiting your brother
Take an ax along and hold it fast.
Not in theory but in practice
Miracles are wrought with axes
And the age of miracles is not past.

AZDAK'S *judge's chair is in a tavern. Three rich* FARMERS *stand before* AZDAK. SHAUWA *brings him wine. In a corner stands an* OLD PEASANT WOMAN. *In the open doorway, and outside, stand villagers looking on. An* IRONSHIRT *stands guard with a banner.*

AZDAK—The Public Prosecutor has the floor.
SHAUWA—It concerns a cow. For five weeks, the defendant has had a cow in her stable, the property of the farmer Suru. She was also found to be in possession of a stolen ham, and a number of cows belonging to Shutoff were killed after he asked the defendant to pay the rent on a piece of land.
FARMERS—It's a matter of my ham, Your Honor.
—It's a matter of my cow, Your Honor.
—It's a matter of my land, Your Honor.
AZDAK—Well, Granny, what have *you* got to say to all this?
OLD WOMAN—Your Honor, one night toward morning, five weeks ago, there was a knock at my door, and outside stood a bearded man with a cow. "My dear woman," he said, "I am the miracle-working Saint Banditus and because your son has been killed in the war, I bring you this cow as a souvenir. Take good care of it."
FARMERS—The robber, Irakli, Your Honor!

– Her brother-in-law, Your Honor!
– The cow-thief!
– The incendiary!
– He must be beheaded!

> [*Outside, a woman screams. The crowd grows restless,
> retreats. Enter the* BANDIT *Irakli with a huge ax.*]

BANDIT – A very good evening, dear friends! A glass of vodka!

FARMERS [*crossing themselves*] Irakli!

AZDAK – Public Prosecutor, a glass of vodka for our guest. And who are you?

BANDIT – I'm a wandering hermit, Your Honor. Thanks for the gracious gift. [*He empties the glass which* SHAUWA *has brought.*] Another!

AZDAK – I am Azdak. [*He gets up and bows. The* BANDIT *also bows.*] The Court welcomes the foreign hermit. Go on with your story, Granny.

OLD WOMAN – Your Honor, that first night I didn't yet know Saint Banditus could work miracles, it was only the cow. But one night, a few days later, the farmer's servants came to take the cow away again. Then they turned round in front of my door and went off without the cow. And bumps as big as a fist sprouted on their heads. So I knew that Saint Banditus had changed their hearts and turned them into friendly people.

> The BANDIT *roars with laughter.*]

FIRST FARMER – I know what changed them.

AZDAK – That's fine. You can tell us later. Continue.

OLD WOMAN – Your Honor, the next one to become a good man was the farmer Shutoff–a devil, as everyone knows. But Saint Banditus arranged it so he let me off the rent on the little piece of land.

SECOND FARMER – Because my cows were killed in the field.

> [*The* BANDIT *laughs.*]

OLD WOMAN [*answering* AZDAK'S *sign to continue*] Then one morning the ham came flying in at my window. It hit me in the small of the back. I'm still lame, Your Honor, look. [*She limps a few steps. The* BANDIT *laughs.*] Your Honor, was there ever a time when a poor old woman could get a ham *without* a miracle?

> [*The* BANDIT *starts sobbing.*]

AZDAK [*rising from his chair*] Granny, that's a question that strikes straight at the Court's heart. Be so kind as to sit here.

> [*The* OLD WOMAN, *hesitating, sits in the judge's chair.*]

AZDAK [*sits on the floor, glass in hand, reciting*] Granny
We could almost call you Granny Grusinia
The Woebegone
The Bereaved Mother

Whose sons have gone to war.
Receiving the present of a cow
She bursts out crying.
When she is beaten
She remains hopeful.
When she's not beaten
She's surprised.
On us
Who are already damned
May you render a merciful verdict
Granny Grusinia!

[*Bellowing at the* FARMERS.] Admit you don't believe in miracles, you atheists! Each of you is sentenced to pay five hundred piasters! For godlessness! Get out! [*The* FARMERS *slink out.*] And you Granny, and you [*to the* BANDIT] pious man, empty a pitcher of wine with the Public Prosecutor and Azdak!
SINGER *and* CHORUS—And he broke the rules to save them.
Broken law like bread he gave them,
Brought them to shore upon his crooked back.
At long last the poor and lowly
Had someone who was not too holy
To be bribed by empty hands: Azdak.

For two years it was his pleasure
To give the beasts of prey short measure:
He became a wolf to fight the pack.
From All Hallows to All Hallows
On his chair beside the gallows
Dispensing justice in his fashion sat Azdak.
SINGER—But the era of disorder came to an end.
The Grand Duke returned.
The Governor's wife returned.
A trial was held.
Many died.
The people's quarters burned anew.
And fear seized Azdak.

AZDAK's *judge's chair stands again in the court of justice.* AZDAK *sits on the floor, shaving and talking to* SHAUWA. *Noises outside. In the rear the* FAT PRINCE's *head is carried by on a lance.*

AZDAK—Shauwa, the days of your slavery are numbered, maybe even the minutes. For a long time now I have held you in the iron curb of reason, and it has torn your mouth till it bleeds. I have lashed you with reasonable arguments, I have manhandled you with logic. You are by nature a weak man, and if one slyly throws an argument in your path, you *have* to snap it up, you can't resist. It is your nature to lick the hand of some superior being. But superior beings can be of very different kinds. And now, with your liberation, you will soon be able to follow your natural inclinations, which are low. You will be able to follow your infallible instinct, which teaches you to plant your fat heel on the faces of men. Gone is the era of confusion and disorder, which I find described in the Song of Chaos. Let us now sing that song together in memory of those terrible days. Sit down and don't do violence to the music. Don't be afraid. It sounds all right. And it has a fine refrain.

[*He sings.*]

The Song of Chaos

Sister, hide your face! Brother, take your knife!
The times are out of joint!
Big men are full of complaint
And small men full of joy.
The city says:
"Let us drive the mighty from our midst!"
Offices are raided. Lists of serfs are destroyed.
They have set Master's nose to the grindstone.
They who lived in the dark have seen the light.
The ebony poor box is broken.
Sesnem[2] wood is sawed up for beds.
Who had no bread have full barns.
Who begged for alms of corn now mete it out.
SHAUWA [*refrain*] Oh, oh, oh, oh.
AZDAK [*refrain*] Where are you, General, where are you?
Please, please, please, restore order!

The nobleman's son can no longer be recognized;
The lady's child becomes the son of her slave-girl
The councilors meet in a shed.
Once, this man was barely allowed to sleep on the wall;

2 I do not know what kind of wood this is, so I have left the word exactly as it stands in the German original. The song is based on an Egyptian papyrus which Brecht cites as such in his essay, "Five Difficulties in the Writing of the Truth." I should think he must have come across it in Adolf Erman's *Die Literatur der Aegypter*, 1923, p. 130 ff. Erman too gives the word as Sesnem. The same papyrus is quoted in Karl Jaspers' *Man in the Modern Age* (Anchor edition, pp. 18–19) but without the sentence about the Sesnem wood. [E.B.]

Now, he stretches his limbs in a bed.
Once, this man rowed a boat; now, he owns ships.
Their owner looks for them, but they're his no longer.
Five men are sent on a journey by their master.
"Go yourself," they say, "we have arrived."
SHAUWA [*refrain*] Oh, oh, oh, oh.
AZDAK [*refrain*] Where are you, General, where are you?
Please, please, please, restore order!

Yes, so it might have been, had order been neglected much longer. But now the Grand Duke has returned to the capital, and the Persians have lent him an army to restore order with. The people's quarters are already aflame. Go and get me the big book I always sit on. [SHAUWA *brings the big book from the judge's chair.* AZDAK *opens it.*] This is the Statute Book and I've always used it, as you can testify. Now I'd better look in this book and see what they can do to me. I've let the down-and-outs get away with murder, and I'll have to pay for it. I helped poverty onto its skinny legs, so they'll hang me for drunkenness. I peeped into the rich man's pocket, which is bad taste. And I can't hide anywhere—everybody knows me because I've helped everybody.
SHAUWA—Someone's coming!
AZDAK [*in panic, he walks trembling to the chair*] It's the end. And now they'd enjoy seeing what a Great Man I am. I'll deprive them of that pleasure. I'll beg on my knees for mercy. Spittle will slobber down my chin. The fear of death is in me.

> [*Enter* NATELLA ABASHWILI, *the* GOVERNOR'S WIFE,
> *followed by the* ADJUTANT *and an* IRONSHIRT.]

GOVERNOR'S WIFE—What sort of a creature is that, Shalva?
AZDAK—A willing one, Your Highness, a man ready to oblige.
ADJUTANT—Natella Abashwili, wife of the late Governor, has just returned. She is looking for her two-year-old son, Michael. She has been informed that the child was carried off to the mountains by a former servant.
AZDAK—The child will be brought back, Your Highness, at your service.
ADJUTANT—They say that the person in question is passing it off as her own.
AZDAK—She will be beheaded, Your Highness, at your service.
ADJUTANT—That is all.
GOVERNOR'S WIFE [*leaving*] I don't like that man.
AZDAK [*following her to door, bowing*] At your service, Your Highness, it will all be arranged.

FIVE: THE CHALK CIRCLE

SINGER – Hear now the story of the trial
  Concerning Governor Abashwili's child
  And the determination of the true mother
  By the famous test of the Chalk Circle.

Law court in Nuka. IRONSHIRTS *lead* MICHAEL *across stage and out at the back.* IRONSHIRTS *hold* GRUSHA *back with their lances under the gateway until the child has been led through. Then she is admitted. She is accompanied by the former Governor's* COOK. *Distant noises and a fire-red sky.*

GRUSHA [*trying to hide*] He's brave, he can wash himself now.

COOK – You're lucky. It's not a real judge. It's Azdak, a drunk who doesn't know what he's doing. The biggest thieves have got by through him. Because he gets everything mixed up and the rich never offer him big enough bribes, the like of us sometimes do pretty well.

GRUSHA – I *need* luck right now.

COOK – Touch wood. [*She crosses herself.*] I'd better offer up another prayer that the judge may be drunk. [*She prays with motionless lips, while* GRUSHA *looks around, in vain, for the child.*] Why must you hold on to it at any price if it isn't yours? In days like these?

GRUSHA – He's mine. I brought him up.

COOK – Have you never thought what'd happen when she came back?

GRUSHA – At first I thought I'd give him to her. Then I thought she wouldn't come back.

COOK – And even a borrowed coat keeps a man warm, hm? [GRUSHA *nods.*] I'll swear to anything for you. You're a decent girl. [*She sees the soldier* SIMON SHASHAVA *approaching.*] You've done wrong by Simon, though. I've been talking with him. He just can't understand.

GRUSHA [*unaware of* SIMON's *presence*] Right now I can't be bothered whether he understands or not!

COOK – He knows the child isn't yours, but you married and not free "till death you do part"–he can't understand *that*.

2237

[GRUSHA *sees* SIMON *and greets him.*]

SIMON [*gloomily*] I wish the lady to know I will swear I am the father of the child.

GRUSHA [*low*] Thank you, Simon.

SIMON–At the same time I wish the lady to know my hands are not tied–nor are hers.

COOK–You needn't have said that. You know she's married.

SIMON–And it needs no rubbing in.

[*Enter an* IRONSHIRT.]

IRONSHIRT–Where's the judge? Has anyone seen the judge?

ANOTHER IRONSHIRT [*stepping forward*] The judge isn't here yet. Nothing but a bed and a pitcher in the whole house!

[*Exeunt* IRONSHIRTS.]

COOK–I hope nothing has happened to him. With any other judge you'd have as much chance as a chicken has teeth.

GRUSHA [*who has turned away and covered her face*] Stand in front of me. I shouldn't have come to Nuka. If I run into the Ironshirt, the one I hit over the head . . .

She screams. An IRONSHIRT *had stopped and, turning his back, had been listening to her. He now wheels around. It is the* CORPORAL, *and he has a huge scar across his face.*

IRONSHIRT [*in the gateway*] What's the matter, Shotta? Do you know her?

CORPORAL [*after staring for some time*] No.

IRONSHIRT–She's the one who stole the Abashwili child, or so they say. If you know anything about it you can make some money, Shotta.

[*Exit the* CORPORAL, *cursing.*]

COOK–Was it him? [GRUSHA *nods.*] I think he'll keep his mouth shut, or he'd be admitting he was after the child.

GRUSHA–I'd almost forgotten him.

[*Enter the* GOVERNOR'S WIFE, *followed by the* ADJUTANT *and two* LAWYERS.]

GOVERNOR'S WIFE–At least there are no common people here, thank God. I can't stand their smell. It always gives me migraine.

FIRST LAWYER–Madam, I must ask you to be careful what you say until we have another judge.

GOVERNOR'S WIFE–But I didn't say anything, Illo Shuboladze. I love the people with their simple straightforward minds. It's only that their smell brings on my migraine.

SECOND LAWYER–There won't be many spectators. The whole

population is sitting at home behind locked doors because of the riots in the people's quarters.

GOVERNOR'S WIFE [*looking at* GRUSHA] Is that the creature?

FIRST LAWYER–Please, most gracious Natella Abashwili, abstain from invective until it is certain the Grand Duke has appointed a new judge and we're rid of the present one, who's about the lowest fellow ever seen in judge's gown. Things are all set to move, you see.

[*Enter* IRONSHIRTS *from the courtyard.*]

COOK–Her Grace would pull your hair out on the spot if she didn't know Azdak is for the poor. He goes by the face.

IRONSHIRTS *begin fastening a rope to a beam.* AZDAK, *in chains, is led in, followed by* SHAUWA, *also in chains. The three* FARMERS *bring up the rear.*

AN IRONSHIRT–Trying to run away, were you?

[*He strikes* AZDAK.]

ONE FARMER–Off with his judge's gown before we string him up!

[IRONSHIRTS *and* FARMERS *tear off* AZDAK's *gown. His torn underwear is visible. Then someone kicks him.*]

AN IRONSHIRT [*pushing him into someone else*] Want a load of justice? Here it is!

Accompanied by shouts of "You take it!" *and* "Let me have him, Brother!" *they throw* AZDAK *back and forth until he collapses. Then he is lifted up and dragged under the noose.*

GOVERNOR'S WIFE [*who, during this* "ballgame," *has clapped her hands hysterically*] I disliked that man from the moment I first saw him.

AZDAK [*covered with blood, panting*] I can't see. Give me a rag.

AN IRONSHIRT–What is it you want to see?

AZDAK–You, you dogs! [*He wipes the blood out of his eyes with his shirt.*] Good morning, dogs! How goes it, dogs! How's the dog world? Does it smell good? Got another boot for me to lick? Are you back at each other's throats, dogs?

[*Accompanied by a* CORPORAL, *a dust-covered* RIDER *enters. He takes some documents from a leather case, looks at them, then interrupts.*]

RIDER–Stop! I bring a dispatch from the Grand Duke, containing the latest appointments.

CORPORAL [*bellowing*] Atten–shun!

RIDER–Of the new judge it says: "We appoint a man whom we have to thank for saving a life indispensable to the country's welfare–a certain Azdak of Nuka." Which is he?

SHAUWA [*pointing*] That's him, Your Excellency.

CORPORAL [*bellowing*] What's going on here?

AN IRONSHIRT—I beg to report that His Honor Azdak was already His Honor Azdak, but on these farmers' denunciation was pronounced the Grand Duke's enemy.

CORPORAL [*pointing at the* FARMERS] March them off! [*They are marched off. They bow all the time.*] See to it that His Honor Azdak is exposed to no more violence.

[*Exeunt* RIDER *and* CORPORAL.]

COOK [*to* SHAUWA] She clapped her hands! I hope he saw it!

FIRST LAWYER—It's a catastrophe.

[AZDAK *has fainted. Coming to, he is dressed again in judge's robes. He walks, swaying, toward the* IRONSHIRTS.]

AN IRONSHIRT—What does Your Honor desire?

AZDAK—Nothing, fellow dogs, or just an occasional boot to lick. [*To* SHAUWA.] I pardon you. [*He is unchained.*] Get me some red wine, the sweet kind. [SHAUWA *stumbles off.*] Get out of here, I've got to judge a case. [*Exeunt* IRONSHIRTS. SHAUWA *returns with a pitcher of wine.* AZDAK *gulps it down.*] Something for my backside. [SHAUWA *brings the Statute Book, puts it on the judge's chair.* AZDAK *sits on it.*] I accept.

[*The Prosecutors, among whom a worried council has been held, smile with relief. They whisper.*]

COOK—Oh dear!

SIMON—A well can't be filled with dew, they say.

LAWYERS [*approaching* AZDAK, *who stands up, expectantly*] A quite ridiculous case, Your Honor. The accused has abducted a child and refuses to hand it over.

AZDAK [*stretching out his hand, glancing at* GRUSHA] A most attractive person. [*He fingers the money, then sits down, satisfied.*] I declare the proceedings open and demand the whole truth. [*To* GRUSHA.] Especially from you.

FIRST LAWYER—High Court of Justice! Blood, as the popular saying goes, is thicker than water. This old adage . . .

AZDAK [*interrupting*] The Court wants to know the lawyers' fee.

FIRST LAWYER [*surprised*] I beg your pardon? [AZDAK, *smiling, rubs his thumb and index finger.*] Oh, I see. Five hundred piasters, Your Honor, to answer the Court's somewhat unusual question.

AZDAK—Did you hear? The question is unusual. I ask it because I listen in quite a different way when I know you're good.

FIRST LAWYER [*bowing*] Thank you, Your Honor. High Court of Justice, of all ties the ties of blood are strongest. Mother and child—is there a more intimate relationship? Can one tear a child from its mother? High Court of Justice, she has conceived it in the holy ecstasies of love. She has carried it in her womb. She has fed it with her blood. She has borne it with pain. High Court of Justice, it has been observed that the wild tigress, robbed of her young, roams restless through the mountains, shrunk to a shadow. Nature herself . . .

AZDAK [*interrupting, to* GRUSHA] What's your answer to all this and anything else that lawyer might have to say?

GRUSHA—He's mine.

AZDAK—Is that all? I hope you can prove it. Why should I assign the child to you in any case?

GRUSHA—I brought him up like the priest says "according to my best knowledge and conscience." I always found him something to eat. Most of the time he had a roof over his head. And I went to such trouble for him. I had expenses too. I didn't look out for my own comfort. I brought the child up to be friendly with everyone, and from the beginning taught him to work. As well as he could, that is. He's still very little.

FIRST LAWYER—Your Honor, it is significant that the girl herself doesn't claim any tie of blood between her and the child.

AZDAK—The Court takes note of that.

FIRST LAWYER—Thank you, Your Honor. And now permit a woman bowed in sorrow—who has already lost her husband and now has also to fear the loss of her child—to address a few words to you. The gracious Natella Abashwili is . . .

GOVERNOR'S WIFE [*quietly*] A most cruel fate, sir, forces me to describe to you the tortures of a bereaved mother's soul, the anxiety, the sleepless nights, the . . .

SECOND LAWYER [*bursting out*] It's outrageous the way this woman is being treated! Her husband's palace is closed to her! The revenue of her estates is blocked, and she is cold-bloodedly told that it's tied to the heir. She can't do a thing without that child. She can't even pay her lawyers!! [*To the* FIRST LAWYER, *who, desperate about this outburst, makes frantic gestures to keep him from speaking.*] Dear Illo Shuboladze, surely it can be divulged now that the Abashwili estates are at stake?

FIRST LAWYER—Please, Honored Sandro Oboladze! We agreed . . . [*To* AZDAK.] Of course it is correct that the trial will also decide if our noble client can take over the Abashwili estates, which are rather extensive. I say "also" advisedly, for in the foreground stands the human tragedy of a mother, as Natella Abashwili very properly explained in the first words of her moving statement. Even if Michael Abashwili were not heir to the estates, he would still be the dearly beloved child of my client.

2241

AZDAK – Stop! The Court is touched by the mention of estates. It's a proof of human feeling.

SECOND LAWYER – Thanks, Your Honor. Dear Illo Shuboladze, we can prove in any case that the woman who took the child is not the child's mother. Permit me to lay before the Court the bare facts. High Court of Justice, by an unfortunate chain of circumstances, Michael Abashwili was left behind on that Easter Sunday while his mother was making her escape. Grusha, a palace kitchen maid, was seen with the baby . . .

COOK – All her mistress was thinking of was what dresses she'd take along!

SECOND LAWYER [*unmoved*] Nearly a year later Grusha turned up in a mountain village with a baby and there entered into the state of matrimony with . . .

AZDAK – How'd you get to that mountain village?

GRUSHA – On foot, Your Honor. And he was mine.

SIMON – I'm the father, Your Honor.

COOK – I used to look after it for them, Your Honor. For five piasters.

SECOND LAWYER – This man is engaged to Grusha, High Court of Justice: his testimony is suspect.

AZDAK – Are you the man she married in the mountain village?

AZDAK [*to* GRUSHA] Why? [*Pointing at* SIMON.] Is he no good in bed? Tell the truth.

GRUSHA – We didn't get that far. I married because of the baby. So he'd have a roof over his head. [*Pointing at* SIMON.] He was in the war, Your Honor.

AZDAK – And now he wants you back again, huh?

SIMON – I wish to state in evidence . . .

GRUSHA [*angrily*] I am no longer free, Your Honor.

AZDAK – And the child, you claim, comes from whoring? [GRUSHA *doesn't answer.*] I'm going to ask you a question: What kind of child is he? A ragged little bastard? Or from a good family?

GRUSHA [*angrily*] He's an ordinary child.

AZDAK – I mean – did he have refined features from the beginning?

GRUSHA – He had a nose on his face.

AZDAK – A very significant comment! It has been said of me that I went out one time and sniffed at a rosebush before rendering a verdict – tricks like that are needed nowadays. Well, I'll make it short, and not listen to any more lies. [*To* GRUSHA.] Especially not yours. [*To all the accused.*] I can imagine what you've cooked up to cheat me! I know you people. You're swindlers.

GRUSHA [*suddenly*] I can understand your wanting to cut it short, now I've seen what you accepted!

AZDAK – Shut up! Did I accept anything from you?

GRUSHA   [*while the* COOK *tries to restrain her*] I haven't got anything.

AZDAK – True. Quite true. From starvelings I never get a thing. I might just as well starve, myself. You want justice, but do you want to pay for it, hm? When you go to a butcher you know you have to pay, but you people go to a judge as if you were off to a funeral supper.

SIMON   [*loudly*] When the horse was shod, the horsefly held out its leg, as the saying is.

AZDAK   [*eagerly accepting the challenge*] Better a treasure in manure than a stone in a mountain stream.

SIMON – A fine day. Let's go fishing, said the angler to the worm.

AZDAK – I'm my own master, said the servant, and cut off his foot.

SIMON – I love you as a father, said the Czar to the peasants, and had the Czarevitch's head chopped off.

AZDAK – A fool's worst enemy is himself.

SIMON – However, a fart has no nose.

AZDAK – Fined ten piasters for indecent language in court! That'll teach you what justice is.

GRUSHA   [*furiously*] A fine kind of justice! You play fast and loose with us because we don't talk as refined as that crowd with their lawyers.

AZDAK – That's true. You people are too dumb. It's only right you should get it in the neck.

GRUSHA – You want to hand the child over to her, and she wouldn't even know how to keep it dry, she's so "refined"! You know about as much about justice as I do!

AZDAK – There's something in that. I'm an ignorant man. Haven't even a decent pair of pants on under this gown. Look! With me, everything goes on food and drink—I was educated in a convent. Incidentally, I'll fine you ten piasters for contempt of court. And you're a very silly girl, to turn me against you, instead of making eyes at me and wiggling your backside a little to keep me in a good temper. Twenty piasters!

GRUSHA – Even if it was thirty, I'd tell you what I think of your justice, you drunken onion! [*Incoherently.*] How dare you talk to me like the cracked Isaiah on the church window? As if you were somebody? For you weren't born to this. You weren't born to rap your own mother on the knuckles if she swipes a little bowl of salt someplace. Aren't you ashamed of yourself when you see how I tremble before you? You've made yourself their servant so no one will take their houses from them —houses they had stolen! Since when have houses belonged to the bedbugs? But you're on the watch, or they couldn't drag our men into their wars! You bribetaker! [AZDAK *half gets up, starts beaming. With his little hammer he half-heartedly knocks on the table as if to get silence.*

2243

As GRUSHA's *scolding continues, he only beats time with his hammer.*]
I've no respect for you. No more than for a thief or a bandit with a
knife! You can do what you want. You can take the child away from
me, a hundred against one, but I tell you one thing: only extortioners
should be chosen for a profession like yours, and men who rape children! As punishment! Yes, let *them* sit in judgment on their fellow
creatures. It is worse than to hang from the gallows.

AZDAK [*sitting down*] Now it'll be thirty! And I won't go on squab-
bling with you—we're not in a tavern. What'd happen to my dignity as a
judge? Anyway, I've lost interest in your case. Where's the couple who
wanted a divorce? [*To* SHAUWA.] Bring 'em in. This case is adjourned
for fifteen minutes.

FIRST LAWYER [*to the* GOVERNOR's WIFE] Even without using
the rest of the evidence, Madam, we have the verdict in the bag.

COOK [*to* GRUSHA] You've gone and spoiled your chances with him.
You won't get the child now.

GOVERNOR'S WIFE—Shalva, my smelling salts!

[*Enter a very old couple.*]

AZDAK—I accept. [*The old couple don't understand.*] I hear you want
to be divorced. How long have you been together?

OLD WOMAN—Forty years, Your Honor.

AZDAK—And why do you want a divorce?

OLD MAN—We don't like each other, Your Honor.

AZDAK—Since when?

OLD WOMAN—Oh, from the very beginning, Your Honor.

AZDAK—I'll think about your request and render my verdict when
I'm through with the other case. [SHAUWA *leads them back.*] I need the
child. [*He beckons* GRUSHA *to him and bends not unkindly toward
her.*] I've noticed you have a soft spot for justice. I don't believe he's
your child, but if he *were* yours, woman, wouldn't you want him to be
rich? You'd only have to say he wasn't yours, and he'd have a palace
and many horses in his stable and many beggars on his doorstep and
many soldiers in his service and many petitioners in his courtyard,
wouldn't he? What do you say—don't you want him to be rich?

[GRUSHA *is silent.*]

SINGER—Hear now what the angry girl thought but did not say:

Had he golden shoes to wear
He'd be cruel as a bear
Evil would his life disgrace.
He'd laugh in my face.

Carrying a heart of flint
Is too troublesome a stint.
Being powerful and bad
Is hard on a lad.

Then let hunger be his foe!
Hungry men and women, no.
Let him fear the darksome night
But not daylight!

AZDAK—I think I understand you, woman.

GRUSHA [*suddenly and loudly*] I won't give him up. I've raised him, and he knows me.

[*Enter* SHAUWA *with the* CHILD.]

GOVERNOR'S WIFE—He's in rags!

GRUSHA—That's not true. But I wasn't given time to put his good shirt on.

GOVERNOR'S WIFE—He must have been in a pigsty.

GRUSHA [*furiously*] I'm not a pig, but there are some who are! Where did you leave your baby?

GOVERNOR'S WIFE—I'll show you, you vulgar creature! [*She is about to throw herself on* GRUSHA, *but is restrained by her lawyers.*] She's a criminal, she must be whipped. Immediately!

SECOND LAWYER [*holding his hand over her mouth*] Natella Abashwili, you promised . . . Your Honor, the plaintiff's nerves . . .

AZDAK—Plaintiff and defendant! The Court has listened to your case, and has come to no decision as to who the real mother is; therefore, I, the judge, am obliged to *choose* a mother for the child. I'll make a test. Shauwa, get a piece of chalk and draw a circle on the floor. [SHAUWA *does so.*] Now place the child in the center. [SHAUWA *puts* MICHAEL, *who smiles at* GRUSHA, *in the center of the circle.*] Stand near the circle, both of you. [*The* GOVERNOR'S WIFE *and* GRUSHA *step up to the circle.*] Now each of you take the child by one hand. [*They do so.*] The true mother is she who can pull the child out of the circle.

SECOND LAWYER [*quickly*] High Court of Justice, I object! The fate of the great Abashwili estates, which are tied to the child, as the heir, should not be made dependent on such a doubtful duel. In addition, my client does not command the strength of this person, who is accustomed to physical work.

AZDAK—She looks pretty well fed to me. Pull! [*The* GOVERNOR'S WIFE *pulls the* CHILD *out of the circle on her side;* GRUSHA *has let go and stands aghast.*] What's the matter with you? You didn't pull.

GRUSHA—I didn't hold on to him.

FIRST LAWYER [*congratulating the* GOVERNOR'S WIFE] What did I say! The ties of blood!

GRUSHA [*running to* AZDAK] Your Honor, I take back everything I said against you. I ask your forgiveness. But could I keep him till he can speak all the words? He knows a few.

AZDAK – Don't influence the Court. I bet you only know about twenty words yourself. All right, I'll make the test once more, just to be certain. [*The two women take up their positions again.*] Pull!

[*Again* GRUSHA *lets go of the* CHILD.]

GRUSHA [*in despair*] I brought him up! Shall I also tear him to bits? I can't!

AZDAK [*rising*] And in this manner the Court has determined the true mother. [*To* GRUSHA.] Take your child and be off. I advise you not to stay in the city with him. [*To the* GOVERNOR'S WIFE.] And you disappear before I fine you for fraud. Your estates fall to the city. They'll be converted into a playground for the children. They need one, and I've decided it'll be called after me: Azdak's Garden. [*The* GOVERNOR'S WIFE *has fainted and is carried out by the* LAWYERS *and the* ADJUTANT. GRUSHA *stands motionless.* SHAUWA *leads the* CHILD *toward her.*] Now I'll take off this judge's gown—it's got too hot for me. I'm not cut out for a hero. In token of farewell I invite you all to a little dance in the meadow outside. Oh, I'd almost forgotten something in my excitement . . . to sign the divorce decree.

[*Using the judge's chair as a table, he writes something on a piece of paper, and prepares to leave. Dance music has started.*]

SHAUWA [*having read what is on the paper*] But that's not right. You've not divorced the old people. You've divorced Grusha!

AZDAK – Divorced the wrong couple? What a pity! And I never retract! If I did, how could we keep order in the land? [*To the old couple.*] I'll invite you to my party instead. You don't mind dancing with each other, do you? [*To* GRUSHA *and* SIMON.] I've got forty piasters coming from you.

SIMON [*pulling out his purse*] Cheap at the price, Your Honor. And many thanks.

AZDAK [*pocketing the cash*] I'll be needing this.

GRUSHA [*to* MICHAEL] So we'd better leave the city tonight, Michael? [*To* SIMON.] You like him?

SIMON – With my respects, I like him.

GRUSHA – Now I can tell you: I took him because on that Easter Sunday I got engaged to you. So he's a child of love. Michael, let's dance.

She dances with MICHAEL, SIMON dances with the COOK, the old couple with each other. AZDAK stands lost in thought. The dancers soon hide *him from view. Occasionally he is seen, but less and less as more couples join the dance.*

s i n g e r – And after that evening Azdak vanished and was never seen
    again.
The people of Grusinia did not forget him but long remembered
The period of his judging as a brief golden age,
Almost an age of justice.

                [*All the couples dance off.* azdak *has disappeared.*]
But you, you who have listened to the Story of the Chalk Circle,
Take note what men of old concluded:
That what there is shall go to those who are good for it,
Children to the motherly, that they prosper,
Carts to good drivers, that they be driven well,
The valley to the waterers, that it yield fruit.

AN UN-AMERICAN CHALK CIRCLE?

By Eric Bentley

IN THE PROLOGUE TO *The Caucasian Chalk Circle*, the people of two collective farms in Georgia, U.S.S.R., debate their respective titles to the ownership of a piece of land. Up to now it has belonged to one farm, but now the other claims it could make better use of it. Who should own *anything?* Should possession be nine-tenths of the law? Or should law and possession be open to reconsideration? That is the question Brecht raises. In the first draft of the play, the date of this bit of action was the 1930's. Later, Brecht shifted it to 1945 for two reasons: first, so that the land can be approached as a new problem, in that the farmers on it had all been ordered East at the approach of Hitler's armies; second, so that the farmers newly claiming it can have partially earned it by having fought as Partisans against the invader.

The Prologue is a stumbling block for American audiences. Here are all these Communists—Russians at that—addressing each other as Comrades and so on. That is why, until very recently, the Prologue was always omitted from American productions. In 1965, however, it was included in the Minnesota Theatre Company's production without untoward incidents, and in 1966 it was included in the production of the Lincoln Center Repertory Company in New York. With the years the Prologue had not changed, but the world had. The existence of the U.S.S.R. (if not of the Republic of China) is now generally conceded in the U.S.A.

That Communists do use the word Comrades is taken in stride. There is even understanding for the fact that the playwright Bertolt Brecht sympathized with Communism in those days, even more consistently than Sartre and Peter Weiss do today.

However, disapproval of the Prologue is not caused merely by the labels. A deeper worry is provided by the *mode* of the dispute over the land. Land has always been fought over, often with guns. The expectation that some individual should pull a gun, or threaten to, is part of our stock response to the situation. But in this Prologue, this expectation receives a calculated disappointment. The conflict is, or has been, real, but a new way of resolving it has been found, a new attitude to antagonists has been found. Not to mention the new solution: the land goes to the "interlopers," the impostors, because they offer convincing evidence that they will be able to make better use of it. Both the conclusion and the road by which it is reached imply a complete reversal of the values by which our civilization has been living.

And Soviet civilization? Were we to visit Georgia, should we actually witness such decisions being made, and being arrived at in Brecht's way? It is certainly open to doubt even in 1966, while in 1945 nothing could have been more misleading than Brecht's Prologue if it was intended to give an accurate picture of Stalin's Russia. And we hear that Soviet citizens have themselves complained that, quite apart from the political point, they find nothing recognizably Russian in this German scene.

Is it thereby invalidated? "The home of the Soviet people shall also be the home of Reason!" That is certainly a key line in the Prologue, but the verb is *shall be*, not *is*. That Brecht aligned himself with Socialism, and saw the Soviet Union as the chief champion of Socialism, is clear, but it is only to say that he saw Russia as on the right path, not by any means as having arrived at the goal. Let the worried reader of the Prologue to *The Caucasian Chalk Circle* also read a poem which embodies some of Brecht's thoughts about the purges of 1936–37–38:

> My teacher
> Who was great and kind
> Has been shot, sentenced by a People's Court.
> As a spy. His name has been condemned.
> . . . .
> Suppose he is innocent?
> The sons of the people have found him guilty.
> . . . .
> The people have many enemies.
> In the highest positions
> Sit enemies. . . . .

On the supposition that he is innocent
What will he be thinking as he goes to his death?[1]

In any case, to prove Brecht wrong about Russia would not necessarily be to prove him wrong about Socialism.

A Socialist play—is this a play for Socialists only? That, ultimately, is for non-Socialists to decide for themselves. From Brecht's viewpoint a lot of people are potential Socialists who might—at this time, in this place—be very surprised to hear it. In principle it is a play for all who are not identified with those it shows to be the common enemy. And in actuality it may turn out to be a play even for some of those who *are* identified with the enemy, since they may not recognize the identification, preferring a life-illusion. French aristocrats applauded *Figaro*. *The Threepenny Opera* must have been enjoyed by many who, very shortly afterwards, voted for Hitler.

At any rate, the Prologue shows a country (forget it is Russia, if that offends you) where Reason has made inroads upon Unreason. Unreason, in *The Caucasian Chalk Circle*, takes the form of private property, and the laws that guarantee it. "Property is theft," and, by paradox, a private person who steals another private person's property, infringing the law, only re-enacts the original rape of the earth, and confirms the law—of private property. The characters in *Chalk Circle* who most firmly believe in private property are most actively engaged in fighting over private property—whether to cling to it or to grab it.

Where is private property's most sensitive spot? One learns the answer whenever a businessman announces that his son will be taking over the business. Or whenever a spokesman for all things holy comes to his favorite theme of mother and child.

> . . . of all ties, the ties of blood are strongest. Mother and child, is there a more intimate relationship? Can one tear a child from its mother? High Court of Justice, she has conceived it in the holy ecstasies of love, she has carried it in her womb, she has fed it with her blood, she has borne it with pain . . .

This is the voice of one of the spokesmen for all things holy in *The Caucasian Chalk Circle*. And so, when the possession of a child has been in dispute, whether at the court of Solomon in Israel, or before a Chinese magistrate in the year one thousand A.D., the question asked has only

[1] From *Are the People Infallible?*, tr. Eric Bentley. For the complete text, see *Tulane Drama Review*, X, No. 4 (Summer, 1966).

been: which womb did it come out of? Which loins begat it? It would seem that the ultimate locus of private property is in the private parts.

Plato had other plans. He knew that a given parent may in fact be the worst person to bring up his or her child. Our concern, he assumes, should be to produce the best human beings, the best society, not to sacrifice these ends to an after all arbitrary notion of "natural" right. The point about an umbilical cord is that it has to be cut. Children should be assigned to those best qualified to bring them up. . . . Plato's Republic *is* "the home of Reason"—the Georgia of *The Caucasian Chalk Circle* is not.

After a Prologue which provides a hint of what it would mean to begin to create a home for Reason on this earth, the play transports us to a world which, for all its exotic externals, is nothing other than the world we live in, *our* world, the world of Unreason, of Disorder, of Injustice. And so those who are upset by the idealizations of the Prologue, by its "Utopianism," need not fret. The play itself provides an image of life in its customary mode, soiled, stinking, cruel, and outrageous.

But even in a jungle, lovely flowers will spring up here and there, such being the fecundity of nature. And however badly our pastors and masters run our society, however much they pull to pieces that which they claim to be keeping intact, nature remains fecund, and human beings are born with human traits, and sometimes human strength outweighs human weakness, and human grace shows itself amid human ugliness. "In the bloodiest times," as our play has it, "there are kind people." Their kindness is arbitrary. No sociologist could deduce it from the historical process. Just the contrary. It represents the brute refusal of nature to be submerged in history and therefore, arguably (and this *is* Brecht's argument), the possibility that the creature should, at some future point, subdue history.

For the present, though—a present that has spread itself out through the whole course of historical time—the sociologists win, and man is not the master but the slave of society. History is the history of power struggles conducted (behind the moralistic rhetoric familiar to us all from the daily press) with minimum scrupulousness and maximum violence. To give way to the promptings of nature, to natural sympathy, to the natural love of the Good, is to be a Sucker. America invented that expressive word, and America's most articulate comedian, W. C. Fields, called one of his films: *Never Give a Sucker an Even Break*, which is the credo of Western Civilization as depicted in the works of Bertolt Brecht.

In *The Caucasian Chalk Circle*, however, a sucker gets an even break. That seems contradictory, does it not? And in the contradiction—or contradictiousness—lies the whole interest of the story. Or rather of its second part. In the first part, we see the inevitable working itself out. The sucker—the good girl who gives way to her goodness—is not given any breaks at all. She is punished for her non-sin, her anti-sin. She loses everything, both the child she has saved and adopted, and the soldier-fiancé whom she has loyally loved and waited for. She is abandoned, isolated, stripped, torn apart, like other people in Brecht's plays and our world who persist in the practice of active goodness.

> The Ironshirts took the child, the beloved child.
> The unhappy girl followed them to the city, the dreaded city.
> She who had borne him demanded the child.
> She who had raised him faced trial.

So ends part one: a complete Brecht play in itself. In part two Brecht was determined to put the question: suppose the inevitable did not continue to work itself out? Now how could he do this? By having a Socialist revolution destroy private property and establish the rule of Reason? That is what he would have done, had he been as narrow and doctrinaire as some readers of his Prologue assume. But what is in the Prologue is not in the play itself. For the second half of his play, Brecht invented a new version of the Chalk Circle legend, which is also a new version of another idea from literary tradition, the idea that the powers that be can sometimes be temporarily overthrown and a brief Golden Age ensue.

> Who will decide the case?
> To whom will the child be assigned?
> Who will the judge be? A good judge? A bad?
> The city was in flames.
> In the judge's seat sat—Azdak.

Inevitably, necessarily, a judge in the society depicted in *The Caucasian Chalk Circle* must assign a child to its actual mother. In that proposition, the law of private property seems to receive the sanction of Mother Nature herself, that is to say: the owners of private property are able to appeal to nature without conscious irony. Such an event, however, would give Brecht at best a brief epilogue to part one. What gives him a second part to his play, and one which enables him in the end to pick up the loose ends left by the Prologue, is that the judge is Azdak, and that Azdak is a mock king, an Abbot of Unreason, a Lord of Misrule, who introduces "a brief Golden Age, almost an age of justice."

> The reign of Zeus [says F. M. Cornford] stood in the Greek mind
> for the existing moral and social order; its overthrow, which is the
> theme of so many of the comedies, might be taken to symbolise . . .

the breaking up of all ordinary restraints, or again . . . the restoration of the Golden Age of Justice and Lovingkindness, that Age of Kronos which lingered in the imagination of poets, like the afterglow of a sun that had set below the horizon of the Age of Iron. The seasonal festivals of a Saturnalian character celebrated the return, for a brief interregnum, of a primitive innocence that knew not shame, and a liberty that at any other time would have been licentious. Social ranks were inverted, the slave exercising authority over the master. At Rome each household became a miniature republic, the slaves being invested with the dignities of office. A mock king was chosen to bear rule during the festival, like the mediaeval Abbot of Unreason or Lord of Misrule.[2]

But in this case how is the play any different from the Prologue, except in the temporariness of Azdak's project? Actually, its temporariness is of a piece with its precariousness, its freakishness, its skittishness, its semi-accidental quality. Only with a touch of irony can one say that Azdak establishes a Golden Age or even that he is a good judge. The age remains far from Golden, and his judging is often outrageous enough. But his *extra*ordinary outrages call our attention to the ordinary outrages of ordinary times—to the fact that outrage *is* ordinary, is the usual thing, and that we are shocked, not by injustice per se, but only by injustice that favors the poor and the weak. Azdak did not rebuild a society, nor even start a movement that had such an end in view. He only gave Georgia something to think about, provided a legend, a memory, an image.

So much for the ideological schema. But the play would be too rigidly schematic if Brecht had just brought together the Good Girl with the Appropriate Judge, using both characters simply as mouthpieces for a position. There is more to both of them than that. Azdak is indeed one of the most complex figures in modern drama.

Discussing the role of the Ironical Man in ancient comedy, F. M. Cornford remarks that "the special kind of irony" he practices is "feigned stupidity."

The word Ironist itself in the fifth century appears to mean "cunning" or (more exactly) "sly." Especially it meant the man who masks his batteries of deceit behind a show of ordinary good nature or indulges a secret pride and conceit of wisdom, while he affects ignorance and self-depreciation, but lets you see all the while that he could enlighten you if he chose, and so makes a mock of you. It was

[2] F. M. Cornford, *The Origin of Attic Comedy* (New York: Anchor Books, 1961).

2253

for putting on these airs that Socrates was accused of "irony" by his enemies.[3]

This passage lays out what I take to be the preliminary design of Azdak's character. But then Brecht complicates the design. Azdak is not simply an embodiment of an ironical viewpoint, he is a person with a particular history, who needs irony for a particular reason—and not all the time. Indeed it is through the chinks in the ironical armor that we descry the man. *Azdak is not being ironical when he tells us he wanted to denounce himself for letting the Grand Duke escape.* He supposed, it seems, that while the Grand Duke and his Governors were busy fighting the Princes, the carpet weavers had brought off a popular revolution, and, as a revolutionary, he wished to denounce himself for a counter-revolutionary act.

What kind of revolutionary? A very modern kind: a disenchanted one. Those who like to compare Azdak the Judge to Robin Hood should not omit to compare Azdak the Politician to Arthur Koestler. Before the present revolt of the carpet weavers, decades earlier, there had been another popular uprising. Azdak maintains, or pretends, that this was in his grandfather's time, forty years ago, and not in Georgia, but in Persia. His two songs—which lie at the very heart of the play—tell both of the conditions that produced the uprising and of the uprising itself.[4] The pretense

---

[3] *Ibid.*

[4] *The Song of Chaos:* Azdak's *Song of Chaos* is adapted from a translation of an ancient Egyptian lament, brought to notice in 1903, but dating back to about 2500 B.C. The document describes a state of social disintegration and revolt, and appeals to the King and other authorities to take action. Brecht reverses the point of view, as is his custom, but since he does so ironically, he is able to stay close to such words of the original as the following:

Nay, but the highborn are full of lamentations, and the poor are full of joy. Every town saith: "Let us drive out the powerful from our midst."

Nay, but the son of the highborn man is no longer to be recognized. The child of his lady is become [no more than] the son of his handmaid.

Nay, but the boxes of ebony are broken up. Precious sesnem wood is cut in pieces for beds.

Nay, but the public offices are opened and their lists are taken away. Serfs become lords of serfs.

Behold, ladies lie on cushions [in lieu of beds] and magistrates in the storehouse. He that could not sleep upon walls now possesseth a bed.

Behold, he that never built for himself a boat now possesseth ships. He that possessed the same looketh at them, but they are no longer his.

Translated from the Egyptian by A. M. Blackman, and published in *The Literature of the Ancient Egyptians* by Adolf Erman (London: Methuen & Co., 1927).

is that revolution represents disorder, and the suppression of revolutions, order, and that Azdak is appealing to the Generals to restore order. This last item is not a hollow pretense—or a single irony. For Azdak has not championed revolt. He has withdrawn into his shell. His job as a "village scrivener" is the outward token of the fact. In a note, Brecht advises the actor of the role not to imagine that Azdak's rags directly indicate his character. He wears them, Brecht says, as a Shakespearean sage wears the motley of a fool. Azdak is not lacking in wisdom. Only it is the bitter wisdom of the disillusioned intellectual, and, in Brecht's view, partly a false wisdom, prompted not alone by objective facts but quite as much by the "wise" man's own limitations.

Azdak has the characteristic limitation of the Brechtian rogue: cowardice. Or at any rate: courage insufficient to the occasion. He is Brecht's Herr Keuner saying "No" to tyranny only after the tyrant is safely dead. At least, this is how Azdak is if left to himself. Yet, like other human beings, he is not a fixed quantity, but influenceable by the flow of things, and especially by the people he meets. A passive sort of fellow, he acts less than he *reacts*. Our play describes his reaction to a new and unforeseen situation, and especially, in the end, to a single person: Grusha. Which gives the last section of the play its essential and organic movement.

Azdak needs drawing out, and what Brecht does is expose him to a series of persons and situations that do draw him out. (That he also brings with him into the Golden Age his unregenerate self creates the comic contradictions. It is hard, through all the little trial scenes, to tell where selfishness leaves off and generosity begins: this is a source of amusement, and also enables Brecht to question accepted assumptions on the relation of social and antisocial impulses.) The Test of the Chalk Circle with which the action culminates does not follow automatically from the philosophy of Azdak but is a product of dramatic development. At the outset he is in no mood to be so good or so wise. He has just been mercilessly beaten. But then he reacts in his especially sensitive way to all that ensues, and above all to the big speech in which Grusha denounces him. She could hardly know how she got under his skin. But her denunciation, quite guileless and spontaneous, happens to be couched in just the terms that come home to him. For she is representing him as a traitor to his class. Who does he think he is, that is setting himself up as a Lord over his own people? Well, in his own view, Azdak *was* something of a traitor to his class, but he has been busy for a year or two trying to make it up to them, and now Grusha is providing him with the happiest of all occasions to prove this. His decision to give her the child grows out of his sense of guilt and out of his delight in opportunities to make good.

One could say, too, that his earlier confrontation with Granny Grusinia prepares the way for the later one with Grusha. Here too, he has to be drawn out, partly by threats, but even more by finding again his original identification with the cause of the people. Between them, Granny Grusinia and Grusha are the Marxian, Brechtian version of the "eternal feminine" whom our blundering, uncourageous Faust needs, if he is to move "onwards and upwards." Hence, although the Chalk Circle incident occupies only a minute or two at the end of a long play, it is rightly used for the title of the whole.

The incident not only clarifies the meaning of Azdak, it brings together the various thematic threads of the play. In the first instance, there is the stated conclusion:

> Take note what men of old concluded:
> That what there is shall go to those who are good for it, thus:
> Children to the motherly, that they prosper,
> Carts to good drivers, that they be driven well,
> The valley to the waterers, that it yield fruit.

But this was never in doubt. Any spectator who has spent the evening hoping for a surprise at the end courted disappointment. He should have been warned by the Prologue. In an early draft, Brecht planned, I believe, to let the decision on the collective farms wait till the Chalk Circle story has been told. That, however, is politically ludicrous, if it means, as it would have to, that Soviet planners depend on folksingers, in the way that some other leaders depend upon astrologers. And an infringement of a main principle of Brechtian drama would have occurred: in this type of play, there should be no doubt as to what is going to happen, only as to how and why.

The valley is assigned to the waterers already in the Prologue, and already in the first scenes that follow we see that Michael has a bad mother but has been befriended by a better one. What remains to be said? On what grounds can we be asked to stay another couple of hours in the theatre? On a number of grounds, of course, but one sufficient reason would be: to see Grusha *become* the mother. This is not Plato's Republic, and Grusha a trained educator in a Platonic crèche. In the first phase of the action, her purpose is only to rescue the child, not keep it: she is going to leave it on a peasant's doorstep and return home. We see the child becoming hers by stages, so that, when Azdak gives his verdict in the final scene, he is not having a brilliant idea ("Grusha would be a splendid mother for this child") but recognizing an accomplished fact ("She *is* the mother of this child"). Another paradox: in this play that says possession is not nine-tenths of the law we learn that (in another sense) possession is ten-tenths of the law.

It should not escape notice that, in the end, the child becomes Simon Shashava's too:

GRUSHA – You like him?

SIMON – With my respects, I like him.

GRUSHA – Now I can tell you: I took him because on that Easter Sunday I got engaged to you. So he's a child of love.

Michael had been a child of the lovelessness of his actual mother and the lifelessness of his actual father, but now it turns out that he will have a father who has been spared death in war and is very much alive and a mother who did not experience love at his conception, nor yet at his delivery, but who loves him *now*. The phrase love-child is applied to bastards, and Michael, who was legitimate in the legal sense, however illegitimate humanly and morally, will now become a bastard in a sense which the story . . . legitimizes.

Your father is a bandit
A harlot the mother who bore you
Yet honorable men
Shall kneel down before you.

Food to the baby horses
The tiger's son will take.
The mothers will get milk
From the son of the snake.

Brecht's play broadens out into myth, and we hear many echoes—from the Bible, from Pirandello. But it is more relevant to see the phenomenon the other way around: not that Brecht lets his story spread outwards toward other stories, but that he uses other stories, and mythical patterns, and pulls them in, brings them, as we say, "down to earth," in concrete, modern meanings. Most important, in this regard, is Brecht's use of what a recent scholar has called festive comedy. *The Caucasian Chalk Circle* is not an *inquiry* into the dispute over ownership presented in the Prologue but a *celebration* of the assignment of the land to "those who are good for it."

A main preoccupation of this oldest form of comedy in Western tradition was with Impostors. The point of comedy was, and has remained, to expose the imposture. *The Caucasian Chalk Circle* does this, for what could be a more gross imposture than the claims to either rulership or parenthood of the Abashwili couple? But Brecht does not leave the ancient patterns alone. Even as he turns around the old tale of the Chalk

Circle, so also he plays his ironic, dialectical game with the Aristophanic patterns. *For Azdak and Grusha are impostors too.* That is what makes them brother and sister under the skin. In the impostor-mother, the impostor-judge recognizes his own.

> As if it was stolen goods she picked it up.
> As if she was a thief she sneaked away.

Thus the Singer, describing how Grusha got the baby. He is too generous. Legally, she *is* a thief; the child *is* stolen goods. And Azdak has "stolen" the judgeship, though, characteristically, not on his own initiative: he is, if you will, a receiver of stolen goods. The special pleasure for Azdak in his Chalk Circle verdict is that, at the moment when he will return his own "stolen" goods to their "rightful" owners, he is able to give Grusha and Simon "their" child in (what they can hope is) perpetuity.

I have called the irony a game, for art is a game, but this is not to say that Brecht's playfulness is capricious. In the inversion lies the meaning, and it is simply our good fortune that there is fun in such things, that, potentially at least, there is fun in *all* human contradictions and oppositions. The old patterns have, indeed, no meaning for Brecht *until* they are inverted. For instance, this important pattern: the return to the Age of Gold. We, the modern audience, Russian or American, *return* to the Age of Gold when we see Azdak inverting our rules and laws. Azdak *returns* to an Age of Gold when he nostalgically recalls the popular revolt of a former generation. On the other hand, the Age of Azdak is not, flatly, an Age of Gold at all, for it is an age of war and internecine strife in which just a little justice can, by a fluke, be done. Nor is the traditional image of a Golden Age anything like a revolutionary's happy memories of days on the barricades: just the reverse. Finally, Brecht repudiates our hankering after past Ages of Gold altogether. That revolutions, for Azdak, are identified with the past is precisely what is wrong with him. In *The Caucasian Chalk Circle*, we move back in order to move forward. The era of Azdak has the transitory character of the Saturnalia and so is properly identified with it. After the interregnum is over, the Mock King goes back into anonymity, like Azdak. But the Prologue suggests a *regnum* that is not accidental and shortlived, but deliberate and not *inter*. And then there is the ultimate inversion: that the Golden Age should be envisaged, not in the past, but in the future, and not in any fairyland or Heaven, but in Georgia.

The Russian Georgia, that is. But ours is included, at least in the sense that the play is about our twentieth-century world in general. As Brecht saw things, this century came in on a wave of democratic hope. A new age was dawning, or seemed to be. So universally was this felt that the most powerful of counter-revolutionary movements, the Hitler movement, had to represent itself as Socialist and announce, in its turn, the dawn of a new age. It could bring in no dawn of its own, of course, but in Germany it certainly prevented the arrival of the dawn that had seemed imminent.

And this grouping of forces is what we have in *The Caucasian Chalk Circle*. A true dawn is promised by the rebellious carpet weavers. It never arrives, because the Ironshirts are paid to cut the weavers to pieces. At this point, when a triumphant Fat Prince enters, very much in the likeness of Marshal Goering, Azdak points at him with the comment: There's your new age, all right! The thought of the new age, the longing for a new age, hovers over *The Caucasian Chalk Circle* from beginning to end, and any good production would seem haunted by it.

The Prologue will say different things to different people as to what has already been achieved and where. But to all it conveys Brecht's belief that the new age is possible. What his audience is to be haunted by is not a memory, a fantasy, or a dream, but a possibility.

BOOKS TO READ

IT SHOULD be easy enough for any interested reader to find other plays by our eighteen dramatists without bibliographical assistance. Libraries and bookstores abound in such items. The same goes for famous playwrights whose work did not find its way into this book. As for choosing among the different translations of foreign plays, there is something to be said for each reader making a choice himself—to begin with, purely on a basis of personal preference. It is in any case not difficult to find out that a certain set of translations has relatively high standing among the experts: a current example would be the complete Greek drama as published by the University of Chicago Press. In some instances, a translation published in this book is one of a whole group that could be read later: from our *Don Juan*, the reader can proceed to all of Donald Frame's Molière translations (New American Library); and so on. Finally, the present anthology can be seen as part of its Editor's own oeuvre, and it stands particularly close to his collections in the Doubleday Anchor Series, namely, *The Modern Theatre*, six volumes, and *The Classic Theatre*, four volumes. In short, it is not among plays that the general reader may be in danger of getting lost: it is among the commentaries. For this reason, a little help may be in order.

The following list of books has deliberately been kept short because very long bibliographies are merely discouraging: there is not world enough or time. On the other hand, anyone who needs further help will find it in the very books listed here, if not from formal bibliographies,

2261

then from the many literary references with which scholarly books necessarily abound.

The classics of dramatic theory (Aristotle, Hegel, Schopenhauer, Nietzsche . . .) are not listed here, nor is periodical literature, or foreign commentary. The list is limited to English language material available in book form. Available where? It would be a happy situation indeed if all good books remained in print. They do not; nor is it possible for bibliographies to keep pace with the in-again out-again of many titles. Some titles unavailable in bookstores at the time this list was compiled will doubtless be available there by the time the list is published; and vice versa. The word "available" can therefore only mean available *either* in bookstores *or* in such libraries as stock the more important drama titles.

In no sense is the following list offered as a list of "the best books on . . ." But it is based on experience of what students in the field have found stimulating and useful in an introductory way. To the specialist, some of the listings will look faintly simplistic. How can one represent Shakespeare scholarship in five titles, or Sophocles in one? But then the aim was not to "represent" any body of scholarship as such. The book was not addressed to specialists in the first place.

Each book listed here is linked to at least one of our eighteen playwrights. Books that treat more than one of the eighteen are listed under the first-named playwright only.

AESCHYLUS

Havelock, E. A.: THE CRUCIFIXION OF INTELLECTUAL MAN, 1950.
(Reissued as PROMETHEUS: WITH A TRANSLATION OF AESCHYLUS' PROMETHEUS BOUND, 1968)
Kaufmann, Walter: TRAGEDY AND PHILOSOPHY, 1968.
Kitto, H. D. F.: GREEK TRAGEDY, 1939.
————: FORM AND MEANING IN DRAMA, 1956.
Moulton, Richard G.: THE ANCIENT CLASSICAL DRAMA, 1890.
Thomson, George: AESCHYLUS AND ATHENS, 1941.

SOPHOCLES

Fergusson, Francis: THE IDEA OF A THEATER, 1949.

EURIPIDES

Dodds, E. R.: THE GREEKS AND THE IRRATIONAL, 1951.

Norwood, Gilbert: THE RIDDLE OF THE BACCHAE, 1908.
————: EURIPIDES AND SHAW, 1921.
Verrall, A. W.: THE BACCHANTS OF EURIPIDES, 1910.

WILLIAM SHAKESPEARE

Kettle, Arnold, ed.: SHAKESPEARE IN A CHANGING WORLD, 1964.
Knight, G. Wilson: THE WHEEL OF FIRE, 1930.
Kott, Jan: SHAKESPEARE, OUR CONTEMPORARY, 1964.
Price, Hereward T.: CONSTRUCTION IN SHAKESPEARE, 1951.
Spencer, Theodore: SHAKESPEARE AND THE NATURE OF MAN, 1942.

BEN JONSON

The richest source of lore on and around Ben Jonson is to be found in the collected works as published by Oxford University Press and edited by C. H. Herford and Percy Simpson (the first two volumes).

Partridge, Edward B.: THE BROKEN COMPASS, 1958.

LOPE DE VEGA

There is no book-length study of Lope's plays in English. As to essays, the two that will probably give the most help are printed above (Parker and Casalduero). A third is the introduction, by R. F. D. Pring-Mill, to the Hill and Wang Dramabook edition of FIVE PLAYS BY LOPE, *1960. There is useful background information in H. A. Rennert,* THE SPANISH STAGE IN THE TIME OF LOPE, *1909.*

CALDERÓN DE LA BARCA

An outstanding introduction to Calderón is to be found as the introduction to the Hill and Wang Dramabook edition of his FOUR PLAYS, *1961; it is by the translator, Edwin Honig.*

Sloman, A. E.: THE DRAMATIC CRAFTSMANSHIP OF CALDERÓN, 1958.
Wardropper, Bruce W., ed.: CRITICAL ESSAYS ON THE THEATRE OF CALDERÓN, 1965.

MOLIÈRE

Fernandez, Ramon: MOLIÈRE, THE MAN SEEN THROUGH THE PLAYS, 1958.
Moore, W. G.: MOLIÈRE, A NEW CRITICISM, 1949.

JEAN RACINE

Barthes, Roland: ON RACINE, 1964.
Goldmann, Lucien: THE HIDDEN GOD, 1964.
Vinaver, Eugène: RACINE AND POETIC TRAGEDY, 1955.

HEINRICH VON KLEIST

Stahl, E. L.: THE DRAMAS OF HEINRICH VON KLEIST, 1948.

HENRIK IBSEN

Fjelde, Rolf, ed.: IBSEN, A COLLECTION OF CRITICAL ESSAYS, 1965.
Valency, Maurice: THE FLOWER AND THE CASTLE, 1963.
Weigand, Hermann J.: THE MODERN IBSEN, 1925.

AUGUST STRINDBERG

Mortensen, B. M. E., and Downs, Brian W.: STRINDBERG, AN INTRODUCTION TO HIS LIFE AND WORK, 1949.

OSCAR WILDE

Ellmann, Richard, ed.: OSCAR WILDE, A COLLECTION OF CRITICAL ESSAYS, 1969.

ANTON CHEKHOV

Magarshack, David: CHEKHOV, THE DRAMATIST, 1953.
Valency, Maurice: THE BREAKING STRING, 1966.

BERNARD SHAW

Bentley, Eric: BERNARD SHAW, 1947.
Wilson, Colin: BERNARD SHAW, A RE-ASSESSMENT, 1969.

JOHN M. SYNGE

The most searching study of Synge's dramaturgy is to be found in the editor's introduction of the Methuen edition of Synge's PLAYS AND POEMS, 1963, *part of which is printed above.*

Greene, David H., and Stephens, Edward M.: J. M. SYNGE, 1871–1909, 1959.

LUIGI PIRANDELLO

Unhappily there are no books on Pirandello in English that compare with the best studies in Italian or German, but the following items are worth reading.

Büdel, Oskar: PIRANDELLO, 1966.
Cambon, Glauco, ed.: PIRANDELLO, A COLLECTION OF CRITICAL ESSAYS, 1967.
Starkie, Walter: LUIGI PIRANDELLO, 1927.
Vittorini, Domenico: THE DRAMA OF LUIGI PIRANDELLO, 1935.

BERTOLT BRECHT

The Grove Press edition of Brecht's works contains a number of studies by the present Editor.

Esslin, Martin: BRECHT: THE MAN AND HIS WORK, 1960.
Ewen, Frederic: BERTOLT BRECHT: HIS LIFE, HIS ART, AND HIS TIMES, 1967.
Willett, John: THE THEATRE OF BERTOLT BRECHT, 1959.